The Challenge of Democracy

Kennesaw State University Edition

Kenneth Janda | Jeffrey M. Berry |
Jerry Goldman | Deborah Schildkraut

CENGAGE
Learning

Australia • Brazil • Japan • Korea • Mexico • Singapore • Spain • United Kingdom • United States

The Challenge of Democracy: Kennesaw State University Edition

The Challenge of Democracy, 12th Edition
Includes Aplia Printed Access Card.
Kenneth Janda | Jeffrey M. Berry | Jerry Goldman | Deborah Schildkraut

© 2014, 2012, 2009 Cengage Learning. All rights reserved.

Senior Project Development Manager:
 Linda deStefano

Market Development Manager:
 Heather Kramer

Senior Production/Manufacturing Manager:
 Donna M. Brown

Production Editorial Manager:
 Kim Fry

Sr. Rights Acquisition Account Manager:
 Todd Osborne

For product information and technology assistance, contact us at
Cengage Learning Customer & Sales Support, 1-800-354-9706

For permission to use material from this text or product,
submit all requests online at **cengage.com/permissions**
Further permissions questions can be emailed to
permissionrequest@cengage.com

This book contains select works from existing Cengage Learning resources and was produced by Cengage Learning Custom Solutions for collegiate use. As such, those adopting and/or contributing to this work are responsible for editorial content accuracy, continuity and completeness.

Compilation © 2013 Cengage Learning
ISBN-13: 978-1-285-92109-9

ISBN-10: 1-285-92109-7
Cengage Learning
5191 Natorp Boulevard
Mason, Ohio 45040
USA

Cengage Learning is a leading provider of customized learning solutions with office locations around the globe, including Singapore, the United Kingdom, Australia, Mexico, Brazil, and Japan. Locate your local office at:

international.cengage.com/region.
Cengage Learning products are represented in Canada by Nelson Education, Ltd.
For your lifelong learning solutions, visit **www.cengage.com/custom.**
Visit our corporate website at **www.cengage.com.**

Printed in the United States of America

Brief Contents

Contents

PART II   **FOUNDATIONS OF AMERICAN GOVERNMENT**

3   The Constitution   48

Boxed Features

Compared with What?

Politics of Global Change

What Do You Know About …

Preface

The last revision of *The Challenge of Democracy* was sent to the printer just two years ago. Yet so much has happened since then it seems as though the Eleventh Edition was published a decade or so earlier. As we prepared the Twelfth Edition we had a chance to reflect on these past two turbulent years and, as we always do, have tried to put recent events and trends of this period into the larger framework of the book.

More than anything else, politics in the United States during these past two years has focused on the economy. After the United States fell precipitously into a recession during the last year of George W. Bush's presidency, our government has been consumed with trying to pull the economy out of its lethargy. During the recent presidential election, Republican challenger Mitt Romney built his whole campaign around trying to convince the American people that Barack Obama had been a failure and didn't really understand how market economies work. Over the course of Obama's first term, the economy improved slowly and unemployment fell below 8 percent a few months before the election in November of 2012. Although economic conditions were still far from full health, a majority of American voters believed that Obama deserved a second term and put the economy back in his hands by re-electing him.

Another issue that has been hotly and bitterly debated concerns President Obama's Affordable Care Act, which provides subsidized health insurance for those who cannot afford to purchase it on their own. On party-line votes Democrats in Congress enacted the law in 2010; Republicans, however, have continued to fight to keep the law from being implemented, believing that the program will damage the nation's health-care system. A challenge to the constitutionality of the law was adjudicated by the Supreme Court in June 2012, and in a divided decision, the Court upheld most provisions of the new law.

It's unlikely that the presidential election in 2012 will reduce the hyper-partisanship of the past two years. There are many divisions in the United States, not unusual in any country, but some measures (such as voting in Congress) show that polarization here is increasing. More broadly, some divisions are enduring as they involve basic values and not transitory issues.

Change has been the watchword in world politics. Of all the developments of the past two years across the globe, perhaps the most significant is the Arab Spring. Revolutions broke out across the Middle East, and some notorious dictators, such as Hosni Mubarak in Egypt and Muammar Gaddafi in Libya, were overthrown. In other countries revolutions have not yet succeeded, and the governments there remain in flux. Another story of enormous consequence is the debt crisis in the European Union (EU). Over the years a number of countries, notably Ireland, Greece, Spain, and Portugal, borrowed too much money and, when the world fell into recession, could not pay their bondholders back. This has been a difficult issue for the EU as it has had to bail out these countries to keep them from defaulting on their debt. The EU's stumbling economy directly affects the United States as the EU is the largest trading partner of the United States. If Europeans can't afford to buy as much in the way of American goods, then jobs are lost here as American companies don't need to produce as much.

Our emphasis on the importance of these recent events in the United States and throughout the world does not change the fundamental purpose of this text. *The Challenge of Democracy* is not a book centered on current events. Rather, we use the recent past to illustrate enduring features of American government. As with the previous eleven editions of this book, we build our text around two primary themes that remain as relevant today as when we first conceived of this project. The first is the clash among the values of freedom, order, and equality; the second focuses on the tensions between pluralist and majoritarian visions of democracy. Knowledge of these conflicts enables citizens to recognize and analyze the difficult choices they face in politics.

Over time we also recognized the growing impact of world politics on our governmental process. Our seventh edition (summer, 2001) added a third theme, globalization. The subsequent events of September 11, 2001, the war in Iraq, and the ongoing struggle in Afghanistan made the importance of globalization evident to all Americans. But globalization involves much more than the problems of conflict and terrorism. More than ever before, Americans are becoming citizens of the world. We cannot escape the deepening interrelationships with the rest of the world, even if it were desirable to do so. Each day, trade, travel, immigration, and the Internet make the world a more interdependent place. Despite all the forces that should bring different countries and cultures to a better understanding of one another, the world is far from a peaceful place. Thus, *The Challenge of Democracy* examines some of the ramifications of a smaller world on the large landscape of American politics.

Underlying both the updating of world events and the enduring relevance of our themes is our continuing effort to bring the best recent political science research into *The Challenge of Democracy*. We continually look for recent books and journal articles by our colleagues in the discipline that tell us something new, something important, and something that the readers of *The Challenge of Democracy* should know about. One of the tasks of authors of introductory texts is to synthesize original research, interpret sophisticated scholarly work, and convey what we know as political scientists to students just starting out in their exploration of the discipline. We invite our readers to look closely at our footnotes, the evidence that supports what we say in the text. If you feel that we missed a source that is particularly important, please let us know.

Thematic Framework

Through all twelve editions, we have striven to write a book that students will actually read, so we have sought to discuss politics—a complex subject—in a captivating and understandable way. American politics isn't dull, and its textbooks needn't be either. Equally important, we have sought to produce a book that students would credit for stimulating their thinking about politics. While offering all of the essential information about American government and politics, we feel that it is important to give students a framework for analyzing politics that they can use long after their studies have ended.

To accomplish these goals, we built *The Challenge of Democracy* around three dynamic themes that are relevant to today's world: the clash among the values of freedom, order, and equality; the tensions between pluralist and majoritarian visions of democracy; and the fundamental ways that globalization is changing American politics.

Freedom, Order, and Equality

The first theme is introduced in Chapter 1 ("Freedom, Order, or Equality?"), where we suggest that American politics often reflects conflicts between the values of freedom and order and between the values of freedom and equality. These value conflicts are prominent in contemporary American society, and they help to explain political controversy and consensus in earlier eras. For instance, in Chapter 3 ("The Constitution") we argue that the Constitution was designed to promote order and that it virtually ignored issues of political and social equality. Equality was later served, however, by several amendments to the Constitution. In Chapter 15 ("Order and Civil Liberties") and Chapter 16 ("Equality and Civil Rights"), we demonstrate that many of this nation's most controversial issues represent conflicts among individuals or groups who hold differing views on the values of freedom, order, and equality. Views on issues such as abortion are not just isolated opinions; they also reflect choices about the philosophy citizens want government to follow. Yet choosing among these values is difficult, sometimes excruciatingly so.

Pluralist and Majoritarian Visions of Democracy

The second theme, introduced in Chapter 2 ("Majoritarian or Pluralist Democracy?"), asks students to consider two competing models of democratic government. One way that government can make decisions is by means of *majoritarian* principles—that is, by taking the actions desired by a majority of citizens. A contrasting model of government, *pluralism,* is built around the interaction of decision makers in government with groups concerned about issues that affect them.

These models are not mere abstractions; we use them to illustrate the dynamics of the American political system. In Chapter 11 ("Congress"), we discuss rising partisanship in Congress. As parties have become more ideologically homogeneous, they have been demonstrating greater unity in their votes on the floor. Yet majoritarian tensions with pluralism remain in Congress. In Chapter 10 ("Interest Groups"), we also see the forces of pluralism at work. Interest groups of all types populate Washington, and these organizations represent the diverse array of interests that define our society. At the same time, the chapter explores ways in which pluralism favors wealthier, better organized interests.

Globalization's Impact on American Politics

The third theme, the impact of globalization on American politics, is introduced in Chapter 1 and then discussed throughout the text. The traditional notion of national sovereignty holds that each government is free to govern in the manner it feels best. As the world becomes a smaller place, however, national sovereignty is tested in many ways. When a country is committing human rights violations—putting people in jail for merely disagreeing with the government in power—should other countries try to pressure it to comply with common norms of justice? Do the democracies of the world have a responsibility to use their influence to try to limit the abuses of the powerless in societies where they are abused?

Another facet of globalization is the growth of international trade. In many ways the world has become a single marketplace, and industries in one country often face competitors from many other countries around the world. Must a country just stand by and let jobs "emigrate" from within its borders to other countries where companies can produce the same quality goods at cheaper prices? How will the United

States cope with the rising demand for oil worldwide as economies like those of China and India expand? These are just some of the issues that the Twelfth Edition explores.

Throughout the book we stress that students must make their own choices among the competing values and models of government. Although the four of us hold diverse and strong opinions about which choices are best, we do not believe it is our role to tell students our own answers to the broad questions we pose. Instead, we want our readers to learn firsthand that a democracy requires thoughtful choices. That is why we titled our book *The Challenge of Democracy*.

Our framework travels well over time. The civil rights struggles of the 1960s exemplified the utility of our theme emphasizing equality, as do more contemporary controversies surrounding gay rights, the rights of persons with disabilities, and affirmative action. We're just beginning to understand the privacy and personal freedom issues involving the Internet. Our theme of pluralism versus majoritarianism remains compelling as well. Pluralist images of America predate the adoption of the Constitution. In his defense of the proposed Constitution, James Madison defended the pursuit of self-interested goals by various groups in society, each looking out for its own good. A contrary view of democracy—majoritarian government—emphasizes control of government by majorities of voters through our party system. But the party system sometimes has a hard time channeling a majority of voters into majority rule. Prior to the Civil War, fissures in the party system made it difficult to understand exactly where the majority stood. More recently, in the 2000 election, Democrat Al Gore won more popular votes than Republican George Bush, but Bush won a majority of the electoral college, and—because a presidential election is a federal election—that's the majority that counts. Since the mid-1950s, more often than not, we've had divided government where one party controls the White House but the other controls at least one of the two houses of Congress. Which majority should be followed in such instances?

Our framework also travels well over space—to other countries with very different political heritages. One of the most important aspects of globalization is the number of countries that have recently made a transition to democracy or are currently trying to make that change. The challenge of democratization, however, is illustrated by ongoing developments in Iraq. Elections have been held, but democracy has been hindered by the lack of order. Bombings by one faction or another are common. The relevance of our other major theme is illustrated as well. One of the most difficult problems faced by those who wrote the country's new constitution was the dispute between the majority Shiites, who, not surprisingly, wanted a government that facilitates majority rule, and the minority Sunnis and Kurds, who wanted a more pluralistic system with firm protections against majority dominance.

One of our greatest satisfactions as authors of a book on American democracy is that it has been used in a number of countries where democracy has at least a foothold, if it hasn't yet fully flowered. Our publisher has donated copies of earlier editions of our book to English-speaking faculty and students in Bulgaria, Croatia, the Czech Republic, Georgia, Ghana, Hungary, Kenya, Poland, Romania, Russia, Slovakia, and South Africa. Moreover, the brief edition of our text has been translated into Russian, Hungarian, Georgian, Czech, and Korean. We are pleased that *The Challenge of Democracy* is now available to many more students in these countries—students who have been confronting the challenge of democracy in times of political transition.

Substantive Features of the Twelfth Edition

Chapter-Opening Vignettes

As in previous editions, each chapter begins with a vignette to draw students into the chapter's substance while exploring the book's themes. Chapter 2 ("Majoritarian or Pluralist Democracy?") opens with a new vignette on the Occupy Wall Street movement. In Chapter 6 ("The Media"), we examine political candidates' use of new media and the impact of new technology on journalism. Journalism, as we know, is changing fast and, some believe, not for the better. The opener for Chapter 9 ("Nominations, Elections, and Campaigns") offers a comparison between the 2010 British election and the 2012 election in the United States. A new vignette in Chapter 15 ("Order and Civil Liberties") discusses the controversy over whether the posting of a Christian prayer on the wall of a public high school violates the separation of church and state in our Constitution.

"Politics of Global Change"

In light of the growing emphasis in our book on globalization, each chapter includes a feature on global change. In these "Politics of Global Change" boxes, we examine various elements of political change—some troubling, some hopeful. In the feature "The U.S. Constitution Loses Some of Its Charm" in Chapter 3 ("The Constitution"), students will see how the influence of our Constitution on the constitutions of new nations has waned in recent years. In Chapter 11 ("Congress") we examine the process of "Creating a Legislature," looking at how the revolutionary movements in Egypt and Tunisia subsequently led to parliamentary elections in each nation. In Chapter 19 ("Global Policy"), the feature on "Foreign Oil: A Bit Less Dependent," discusses some very important trends: the United States is consuming less oil, its domestic production of oil is on the increase, and its net oil imports are down.

"Compared with What?"

We firmly believe that students can better evaluate how our political system works when they compare it with politics in other countries. Thus, each chapter has at least one boxed feature called "Compared with What?" that treats its topic in a comparative perspective. In Chapter 5 ("Public Opinion and Political Socialization") we look at "Capital Punishment across the World." Our comparative perspective in Chapter 7 ("Participation and Voting") reports on "Voter Turnout in European and American Elections." The "Compared with What?" feature in Chapter 12 ("The Presidency") focuses on Italy's former Prime Minister, Silvio Berlusconi, and his leadership during a time of economic decline for his country. In Chapter 17 ("Economic Policy") our feature offers recent figures on "Tax Burdens in Thirty-Four Countries." It's interesting to see which countries have relatively high taxes and which have relatively low taxes.

New to the Twelfth Edition

New and Refined Pedagogy for Student Learning

The Twelfth Edition of *The Challenge of Democracy* has undergone its most substantial physical transformation since 1989. Enlarging the trim size of our book allows ample space for the addition of new pedagogical aids intended to enhance student learning and comprehension of the material. New pedagogical aids included in every chapter are:

- Learning Outcomes and Aplia. **Learning Outcomes** for each topic begin each chapter. The Learning Outcomes are repeated with the relevant section head throughout the chapter text and in the corresponding **Aplia** questions. Students will be able to further their comprehension of the Learning Outcomes with the critical thinking questions in Aplia, and instructors will be able to assess student progress.
- The **bulleted chapter summary** is organized according to the section headings of the chapter.
- **"Assessing Your Understanding with Aplia … Your Virtual Tutor!"** at the end of each chapter is a self-test organized according to the Learning Outcomes of the chapter and presents engaging and thought-provoking questions designed to help students test their mastery and understanding of the chapter content.
- **Critical thinking questions** have been added to most feature boxes—"Compared with What?," "Politics of Global Change," and "What Do You Know About…"—helping students see how the boxed materials relate to and enhance the chapter text material.

New and Updated Content

In addition to these overall changes, we have made numerous changes through the chapters to keep our book fresh and up-to-date with contemporary politics. As teachers of the American government course as well as authors of the textbook, we understand and appreciate the intellectual investment that instructors have in the textbook that they have adopted. We hope the following chapter-by-chapter summary of substantial changes and revisions will facilitate the transition to the new edition.

Chapter 1: Freedom, Order, or Equality?
- New opening vignette on the Patient Protection and Affordable Care Act and the mandate to buy health insurance.
- Discussion of NATO strikes in Libya that toppled Qaddafi replaces one on U.N. action in Darfur.
- Elaborated the discussion of "police power" to mesh with opening vignette.
- New "Politics of Global Change" feature box "Globalization in the Classroom" plots the increase over time of foreign students studying in the United States and U.S. students studying abroad and concludes with critical thinking questions.

Chapter 2: Majoritarian or Pluralist Democracy?
- New opening vignette on Occupy Wall Street protestors and the Occupy movement.
- Added new Figure 2.3, "Americans Divided over Whether America Is Divided" (public perception of "haves" and "have nots" in the United States).
- Added example of Arab Spring revolutions in discussion of global trend toward democracy.
- Added discussion of Sunni-Shiite religious conflict in Iraq following overthrow of Saddam Hussein.
- New "Compared with What?" feature box "The Arab Spring." Includes a color-coded map to highlight countries where revolutions have been successful and those countries where control is contested.

- New "Politics of Global Change" feature box "Breaking Up Was the Easy Part" (on movements toward democracy in Russia, Ukraine, and Lithuania).

Chapter 3: The Constitution

- Revised and updated opening vignette on the path toward designing a constitution for the European Union.
- New "Politics of Global Change" feature box "The U.S. Constitution Loses Some of Its Charm" (on the declining influence of the U.S. Constitution on the constitutions of new nations).

Chapter 4: Federalism

- Updated opening vignette on the U.S. Supreme Court decision on Arizona's immigration law.
- New material added about the question of "coercive federalism," particularly as it relates to the Supreme Court's decision on the Affordable Care Act.

Chapter 5: Public Opinion and Political Socialization

- Revised opening vignette on public opinion regarding the death penalty.
- Revised and updated "Political Knowledge" section includes new examples and studies on the public's perception of crime rates and spending for foreign aid.
- New "Politics of Global Change" feature box "Worrying Less about Climate Change."
- New "Compared with What?" feature box "Capital Punishment across the World."

Chapter 6: The Media

- New opening vignette on political candidates' use of new media and the question of the effect of new technology on journalism.
- Merged section "People, Government, and Communications" with section "The Development of the Mass Media in the United States."
- Added discussion of online newspapers and experiments with paywall systems.
- Added discussion of decline of news magazines.
- Added discussion of wireless technology and mobile devices.
- Noted example of government response to provision of classified information to Wikileaks.
- New material on online-only news ventures discusses aggregators and original reporting.
- Added discussion of FCC and regulation of the Internet, Internet Service Providers (ISPs), and emerging technologies.
- Added discussion of soft news and added term *soft news* to glossary.
- Added new Figure 6.5, "Declining Trust in Accuracy and Objectivity of the Press."
- New "Compared with What?" feature box "Top Ten Countries for Penetration of 3G Mobile Devices."
- New "Politics of Global Change" feature box "The Global Rise of Citizen Journalists."

Chapter 7: Participation and Voting

- New opening vignette on "The Protester" as *TIME* magazine's 2011 Person of the Year; noted Egyptian women's demonstration in revolution in Egypt during Arab Spring.
- Added discussion of attempt to recall Wisconsin governor Scott Walker.

- Updated discussion of citizens' direct participation in government through referenda and initiatives.
- Added discussion of use of Internet and social media to improve citizen participation in government.
- Added discussion of Rock the Vote with illustration of Rock the Vote voter registration page.

Chapter 8: Political Parties

- New opening vignette on the tea party as a nationwide movement but not a national organization.
- New reference to Americans Elect, the aborted online effort to nominate a 2012 presidential ticket to be put on the ballot of all fifty states.
- Updated discussion of the Russian ballot using data from the 2011 parliamentary election.
- Elaborated explanation of the dynamics of our electoral system.
- Updated discussion of how the two parties reflect the values of freedom, order, and equality in their party platforms.
- Added text that critiques responsible party government in the context of divided government.

Chapter 9: Nominations, Elections, and Campaigns

- Updated opening vignette comparing the 2010 British general election with the 2012 general election in the United States.
- Incorporated discussion of changes in the presidential nomination process into the text.
- Streamlined discussion of the Bipartisan Campaign Reform Act (BCRA), deleting the material on "hard" and "soft" money in campaign finance.
- Expanded the discussion of *Citizens United* court case, introduced *SpeechNow.org v. FEC*, and defined Super PACs.
- Updated and streamlined discussion of public funding of presidential campaigns, including data on Super PACs and super bundlers.
- Added new information on microtargeting voters.
- Added new discussion of the outcome of the 2012 election.
- Updated Figure 9.1, "From Many to Two: Presidential Hopefuls Starting and Dropping Out," with information on Republican presidential hopefuls' announcements and withdrawals.
- Added new Figure 9.5, "Drifting Apart: Party Voting in the House of Representatives over Four Decades," and explained how divided government is incompatible with responsible party government.

Chapter 10: Interest Groups

- New opening vignette on Facebook and its Washington lobbyists.
- Updated discussion of former members of Congress as lobbyists, using example of former Connecticut Senator Christopher Dodd.
- Updated discussion of information campaigns using example of the AT&T attempted takeover of T-Mobile.
- Added discussion of Supreme Court decision in *Citizens United* case and resultant formation of Super PACs.
- Added new Figure 10.3, "The Lobbying Agenda Versus the Public's Agenda."
- New "Politics of Global Change" feature box "New Meaning to the Term 'China Lobby.'"

Chapter 11: Congress
- New opening vignette on results of 2010 Congressional elections and debate over government spending bill.
- Updated discussion of redistricting.
- Updated discussion of members' use of social media.
- Added discussion of cyberstalking and introduction of STALKERS Act in Congress.
- Combined sections "The Dance of Legislation: An Overview" and "Committees: The Workhorses of Congress" to create new section "The Lawmaking Process and the Importance of Committees."
- Added discussion of the "supercommittee" the Joint Select Committee on Deficit Reduction.
- Added discussion of increasing polarization and the difficulty in reaching compromises, even within parties.
- Revised discussion of filibustering to include explanation of "hold" and added term *hold* as a key term.
- Added discussion of ban on earmarks.
- New "Politics of Global Change" feature box "Creating a Legislature," focusing on democratic movements and parliamentary elections in Egypt and Tunisia.

Chapter 12: The Presidency
- New opening vignette on election day November 6, 2012, and reflections on Obama's presidency.
- Revised section on presidential efforts to influence public opinion, now including example of former Italian Prime Minister Silvio Berlusconi.
- Added new Figure 12.2, "It All Goes Back to the Economy," tracking approval ratings of Bush and Obama and index of economic conditions, illustrating correlation between popularity and economic performance.
- New "Politics of Global Change" feature box "Frequent Flyer," tracking number of days presidents (from Eisenhower through Obama) spent abroad.
- New "Compared with What?" feature box "From Berlusconi to Bankruptcy: The Costs of Failed Leadership," discussing how Berlusconi's performance affected Italy's economy and its relation with the EU.

Chapter 13: The Bureaucracy
- New opening vignette on government regulation of Plan B, the "morning-after" contraceptive pill.
- Added discussion of party effect on the level and type of regulation.
- Added new Figure 13.3, "It Makes a Difference," illustrating the correlation between political party control of government and the performance of regulatory agencies.
- Revised and updated "Compared with What?" feature box "Not So Big by Comparison," comparing the size of the U.S. government with that of other industrialized democracies.
- New "Politics of Global Change" feature box "For Whom the Debt Tolls," on the crisis within the EU.

Chapter 14: The Courts
- Condensed discussion of judicial review of state and local government and merged with section "Judicial Review of the Other Branches."

- Added discussion of Supreme Court release of oral argument transcripts on the Court's website and on audio recordings.
- New evidence on the declining market for newly minted lawyers and the decline in compensation for legal services.

Chapter 15: Order and Civil Liberties

- New opening vignette on controversy over whether the posting of a Christian prayer on the wall of a public high school violated the constitutional prohibition against establishment of religion.
- Converted Feature Story on Positive and Negative Rights to Table 15.1, "Examples of Positive and Negative Rights: Constitutional Rights and Human Rights."
- Added new section, "Order Versus Free Speech: When Words Hurt," with example of Supreme Court's decision in *Snyder* v. *Phelps* upholding free expression rights of members of Westboro Baptist Church picketing funerals of military personnel.
- Added new section, "Equality and Free Speech," using example of the *Citizens United* case.

Chapter 16: Equality and Civil Rights

- New opening vignette on affirmative action case and the debate over using race in admissions decisions, focusing on student Abigail Fisher and the University of Texas decision to deny her admission.
- Added information on 2012 Supreme Court decision on the Obama administration's health-care law.
- Deleted section "Racial Violence and Black Nationalism."
- Added discussion of Supreme Court's 2012 ruling on Arizona's immigration law.
- Added discussion of revisions to the Americans with Disabilities Act.
- Noted Obama's voiced opinion on same-sex marriage.
- Updated discussion of various states' decisions with regard to same-sex marriage.
- Observed the new "inactivity" principle limiting the use of the commerce power, the basis of modern civil rights legislation.

Chapter 17: Economic Policy

- New opening vignette discussing the growth of the national debt since 1936 and costs of paying it down.
- Added discussion of the "Austrian school" of economics and Friedrich Hayek, its leading theorist for contemporary politics.
- Added material describing how theories of Keynes and Hayek surfaced in the 2012 presidential campaign and enhanced discussion with an image from a ten-minute 2012 YouTube rap video presenting their clashing views from a libertarian perspective.
- Greatly condensed the section, "Three Decades of Budgetary Reform," reducing the discussion to one paragraph.
- Deleted references to "pay-go" restrictions on spending.
- Added discussion on calls for a balanced budget amendment.
- Added new paragraph on the politics of a national debt ceiling.
- Updated section on Warren Buffett's tax rate.
- Updated section comparing income inequality in the United States with that throughout the world.

Chapter 18: Policymaking and Domestic Policy This chapter combines the discussion of public policies and the policymaking process with the revised and updated discussion of domestic policies (from Eleventh Edition Chapter 19, "Domestic Policy").

- New opening vignette on designing and implementing public policies to meet people's basic needs without infringing on their personal freedom, using the example of the new health-care law.
- Revised discussion of differing approaches to states' use of tax policies to address budgetary problems.
- New example of FDA and USDA regulatory actions on the production and marketing of food.
- Revised discussion of incremental policy formulation, using the example of Corporate Fuel Economy Standards.
- Revised discussion of policy implementation, using the example of the Oil Pollution Act of 1990 in the case of the 2010 oil spill in the Gulf of Mexico.
- Revised discussion of policy evaluation, using the example of the lap band used in weight loss surgery.
- Revised discussion of welfare reform, including a new paragraph on reauthorization of TANF.
- Revised discussion of health-care reform, focusing on the debate over the Patient Protection and Affordable Care Act and the individual mandate to purchase health insurance.
- New material on the Obama administration's policies on education reform, including Obama's "Blueprint for Reform" and the "Race to the Top" program.
- Added new discussion of the DREAM Act.
- Deleted section on the nonprofit sector.
- Added new Figure 18.7, "Absent Federal Action, States Take on Immigration Reform," illustrating state actions addressing illegal immigration.

Chapter 19: Global Policy

- New opening vignette on interdependence of American markets and overseas manufacturing, using example of Apple's iPhone manufactured in China.
- Revised and updated discussion of war in Afghanistan.
- Added discussion of Western allies' cooperation on support for Libyan rebellion against Muammar Gaddafi.
- Added discussion of rising government debt in the world's market-oriented economies.
- New Figure 19.2, "An Unpopular War," illustrating declining public support of war in Afghanistan.
- New "Compared with What?" feature box "Young and Unemployed," discussing youth unemployment in Greece, Spain, Portugal, and across the Euro-zone.
- New "Politics of Global Change" feature box "Foreign Oil: A Bit Less Dependent," discussing and illustrating decline in U.S. oil consumption and import of oil from the Middle East and elsewhere.

About the Authors

Welcoming Our New Author

We are especially pleased and excited to welcome our fourth author, **Deborah Schildkraut**, to *The Challenge of Democracy* team. Wadsworth Publishers asked Jeff Berry to offer a profile of his Tufts colleague:

Debbie was an undergraduate at Tufts University—not surprisingly, she majored in political science! The next stop was Princeton University where she received her Ph.D. in 2000. Her first teaching job was at Oberlin College in Ohio, where she worked until 2004. She then accepted a position in the political science department at Tufts, coming back home as it were. Debbie's scholarship is impeccable, and she's become a leader in the political science profession in areas of public opinion, immigration, and political psychology. Her first book, *Press One for English* (Princeton University Press, 2005), was a study of public opinion about language and minorities in the United States. In 2011 she published *Americanism in the Twenty-First Century* (Cambridge University Press), which demonstrates that ethnic minorities embrace "American" values just as deeply as the rest of the population. This landmark study was recently awarded the prestigious Robert Lane Prize for the best book published during the previous year in the field of political psychology. At Tufts she teaches courses on political psychology, introductory American government, political science research methods, political representation, and the politics of ethnicity and American identity. She is also a mother to two young boys. When not working or chasing her sons around, Debbie likes to "take a hike," especially in New Hampshire's White Mountains.

Kenneth Janda is the Payson S. Wild Professor Emeritus of Political Science at Northwestern University. Dr. Janda has published extensively in comparative party politics, research methodology, and early use of computer technology in political science, for which he received awards from EDUCOM and support from Apple

Computer. His APSA awards include the Samuel Eldersveld Lifetime Achievement Award (2000) and the Frank J. Goodnow Award for distinguished service to the profession and the association (2009). Dr. Janda and fellow author Jerry Goldman shared APSA technology awards in 1992 for IDEAlog, the computer program, and in 2005 for IDEAlog, the website.

Jeffrey M. Berry is the John Richard Skuse Professor of Political Science at Tufts University. Dr. Berry is a recipient of the APSA's Samuel Eldersveld Lifetime Achievement Award (2009) and numerous "best book" awards from the APSA for *The Rebirth of Urban Democracy* (1994), from the Policy Studies Organization for *The New Liberalism* (1999), from the APSA for *A Voice for Nonprofits* (2004), and from the APSA for *Lobbying and Political Change* (2009).

Jerry Goldman is Professor Emeritus of Political Science at Northwestern University and Research Professor of Law at IIT Chicago-Kent College of Law where he is Director of the Oyez Project. Dr. Goldman is the 2010 recipient of the first APSA/CQ Press Award for Teaching Innovation in Political Science. He has received many other awards, including the American Bar Association's Silver Gavel for increasing the public's understanding of the law, the EDUCOM Medal, and the Roman & Littlefield Prize for Teaching Innovation. In 2012, Dr. Goldman made the Fastcase 50: "the fifty most interesting, provocative, and courageous leaders in the world of law, scholarship, and legal technology." Through the OYEZ Project, which uses images, audio, and video to bring the Supreme Court alive, he has brought the U.S. Supreme Court closer to everyone. Collaborating with experts in linguistics, psychology, computer science, and political science and with contributions by the National Science Foundation, Professor Goldman created a complete archive of fifty years of Supreme Court audio, which is now accessible on mobile devices through mobile apps Oyez Today and Pocket Justice.

For the Instructor: Innovative Teaching Tools

Aplia™ for *The Challenge of Democracy, 12e*

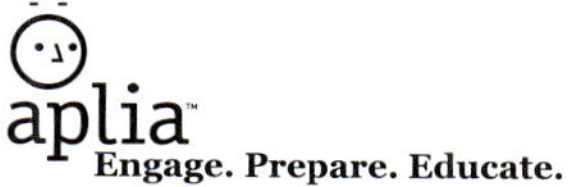

- Instant Access Code ISBN-13: 9781133953562
- Printed Access Card ISBN-13: 9781133955771
- Book with Printed Access Card ISBN-13: 9781133602330
- Easy to use, affordable, and effective, Aplia helps students learn and saves you time. It's like a virtual teaching assistant! Aplia helps you have more productive classes by providing assignments that get students thinking critically, reading assigned material, and reinforcing basic concepts—all before coming to class. The interactive questions also help students better understand the relevance of what they're learning and how to apply those concepts to the world around them.

Visually engaging videos, graphs, and political cartoons help capture students' attention and imagination, and an automatically included eBook provides convenient access. Aplia is instantly accessible via CengageBrain, www.cengage-brain.com, or through the bookstore via printed access code. Please contact your local Cengage sales representative for more information, and go to www.aplia.com/politicalscience to view a demo.

Free Companion Website for *The Challenge of Democracy*, 12e

- ISBN-13: 9781133940401
- This password-protected website for instructors features all of the free student assets plus an instructor's manual, book-specific PowerPoint® presentations, JoinIn™ "clicker" questions, Resource Integration Guide, and a test bank. Access your resources by logging into your account at www.cengage.com/login.

CourseReader: American Government 0-30 Selections

- Instant Access Code ISBN-13: 9781111479978
- Printed Access Card ISBN-13: 9781111479954
- CourseReader: American Government allows you to create your reader, your way, in just minutes. This affordable, fully customizable online reader provides access to thousands of permissions-cleared readings, articles, primary sources, and audio and video selections from the regularly updated Gale research library database. This easy-to-use solution allows you to search for and select just the material you want for your courses.

  Each selection opens with a descriptive introduction to provide context, and concludes with critical-thinking and multiple-choice questions to reinforce key points. CourseReader is loaded with convenient tools like highlighting, printing, note-taking, and downloadable MP3 audio files for each reading.

  CourseReader is the perfect complement to any Political Science course. It can be bundled with your current textbook, sold alone, or integrated into your learning management system. CourseReader 0-30 allows access to up to 30 selections in the reader.

  Please contact your Cengage sales representative for details or, for a demo please visit us at www.cengage.com/coursereader. To access CourseReader materials go to **www.cengage.com/sso**, click on "Create a New Faculty Account," and fill out the registration page. Once you are in your new SSO account, search for "CourseReader" from your dashboard and select "CourseReader: American Government." Then click "CourseReader 0-30: American Government Instant Access Code" and click "Add to my bookshelf." To access the live CourseReader, click on "CourseReader 0-30: American Government" under "Additional resources" on the right side of your dashboard.

Custom Enrichment Module: Latino-American Politics Supplement

- ISBN-13: 9781285184296
- Latino-American Politics is a 32-page custom supplement that uses real examples to detail politics related to Latino Americans. This can be added to your book via our custom publishing program.

Election 2012: An American Government Supplement

- Instant Access Code ISBN-13: 9781285420080
- Printed Access Card ISBN-13: 9781285090931
- Written by John Clark and Brian Schaffner, this booklet addresses the 2012 congressional and presidential races, with real-time analysis and references.

Political Science CourseMate for *The Challenge of Democracy, 12e*

- Instant Access Code ISBN-13: 9781133955818
- Printed Access Card ISBN-13: 9781133955825
- Cengage Learning's Political Science CourseMate brings course concepts to life with interactive learning, study tools, and exam preparation tools that support the printed textbook. Use **Engagement Tracker** to assess student preparation and engagement in the course, and watch student comprehension soar as your class works with the textbook-specific website. An **interactive eBook** allows students to take notes, highlight, search, and interact with embedded media. Other resources include video activities, animated learning modules, simulations, case studies, interactive quizzes, and timelines.

  The American Government NewsWatch is a real-time news and information resource, updated daily, that includes interactive maps, videos, podcasts, and hundreds of articles from leading journals, magazines, and newspapers from the United States and the world. Also included is the **KnowNow! American Government Blog**, which highlights three current events stories per week and consists of a succinct analysis of the story, multimedia, and discussion-starter questions. Access your course via www.cengage.com/login.

PowerLecture DVD with ExamView® for *The Challenge of Democracy, 12e*

- ISBN-13: 9781133944492
- An all-in-one multimedia resource for class preparation, presentation and testing, this DVD includes Microsoft® PowerPoint® slides, a test bank in both Microsoft® Word and ExamView® formats, online polling and JoinIn™ clicker questions, an Instructor's Manual, and a Resource Integration Guide.

  The book-specific **PowerPoint® slides** of lecture outlines, as well as photos, figures, and tables from the text, make it easy for you to assemble lectures for your course, while **the media-enhanced** slides help bring your lecture to life with audio and video clips, animated learning modules illustrating key concepts, tables, statistical charts, graphs, and photos from the book as well as outside sources.

  The **test bank**, revised by James Goss of Tarrant County College, offered in Microsoft Word® and ExamView® formats, includes 60+ multiple-choice questions with answers and page references along with 10 essay questions for each chapter. ExamView® features a user-friendly testing environment that allows you to not only publish traditional paper and computer based tests, but also Web-deliverable exams. **JoinIn**™ offers "clicker" questions covering key concepts, enabling instructors to incorporate student response systems into their classroom lectures.

  The **Instructor's Manual**, revised by Sharon Manna of North Lake College, includes learning objectives, chapter outlines, summaries, discussion questions, class activities and projects suggestions, tips on integrating media into your class, and suggested readings and Web resources. JoinIn™ offers "clicker" questions covering key concepts, enabling instructors to incorporate student response systems into their classroom lectures. A **Resource Integration Guide** provides a chapter-by-chapter outline of all available resources to supplement and optimize learning. Contact your Cengage representative to receive a copy upon adoption.

The Wadsworth News DVD for American Government 2014

- ISBN: 9781285053455
- This collection of two- to five-minute video clips on relevant political issues serves as a great lecture or discussion launcher.

IDEAlog

IDEAlog, two-time winner of Instructional Software awards from the American Political Science Association, is closely tied to the text's "value conflicts" theme. After a brief Tutorial about ideology, IDEAlog asks students to rate themselves on the two-dimensional tradeoff of freedom versus order and freedom versus equality. It then presents them with twenty recent poll questions—ten dealing with the conflict of freedom versus order and ten pertaining to freedom versus equality. Students' responses are classified according to libertarian, conservative, liberal, or communitarian ideological tendencies. IDEAlog is directly accessible to anyone at http://IDEAlog.org, but instructors who choose to register their classes receive a special login link for each class. Instructors then can obtain summary statistics about their students' scores on the ideology quiz.

USPolitics.org

The Twelfth Edition continues to be supported by uspolitics.org, Kenneth Janda's personal website for *The Challenge of Democracy*. This site offers a variety of teaching aids to instructors who adopt any version of *The Challenge of Democracy* for courses in American politics. It is divided into two sides: the student side is open to all users, but the instructor side is limited to teachers who register online at uspolitics.org as textbook adopters. The site offers some material not contained on Cengage Learning's own website, yet it also provides convenient links to the publisher's site.

For more information on the teaching tools that accompany *The Challenge of Democracy*, please contact your Cengage Learning sales representative.

For the Student: Effective Learning Aids

Aplia for *The Challenge of Democracy*, 12e

Easy to use, affordable, and convenient, Aplia helps you learn more and improve your grade in the course. Through interactive assignments, including videos, graphs, and political cartoons, you can better understand the essential concepts of American government and how they apply to real life.

Aplia helps prepare you to be more involved in class by strengthening your critical-thinking skills, reinforcing what you need to know, and helping you understand why it all matters. For your studying convenience, Aplia includes an eBook, accessible right next to your assignments.

Get instant access via CengageBrain or via a printed access card in your bookstore. Visit www.cengagebrain.com for more information. Aplia should be purchased only when assigned by your instructor as part of your course.

Political Science CourseMate for *The Challenge of Democracy*, 12e

Cengage Learning's Political Science CourseMate brings course concepts to life with interactive learning, study tools, and exam preparation tools that support the printed textbook. The more you study, the better the results. Make the most of your study time by accessing everything you need to succeed in one place. Read your textbook, take notes, watch videos, read case studies, take practice quizzes, and more—online with CourseMate. CourseMate also gives you access to the American Government **NewsWatch website**—a real-time news and information resource updated daily, and **KnowNow!**—the go-to blog about current events in American Government. Additionally, CourseMate for The Enduring Democracy includes "**The Connections App**," an interactive Web app that helps you better understand the relationship between historical and current events and their connection with basic concepts.

Purchase instant access via CengageBrain or via a printed access card in your bookstore. Visit www.cengagebrain.com for more information. CourseMate should be purchased only when assigned by your instructor as part of your course.

Free Companion Website for *The Challenge of Democracy, 12e*

Access chapter-specific interactive learning tools, including flashcards, quizzes, and more in your companion website, accessed through CengageBrain.com.

Acknowledgments

All authors are indebted to others for inspiration and assistance in various forms; textbook authors are notoriously so we again want to single out Professor Paul Manna of the College of William and Mary, who has assisted us in many different ways. Patti Conley contributed to some earlier editions of *The Challenge of Democracy*, and her work continues to be of value. Farhad Aspy Fatakia provided invaluable assistance optimizing IDEAlog to work on mobile devices; Leah Melani Christian at the Pew Research Center supplied us with 2012 survey data; and Simon Winchester helped us understand the history of the 1883 Krakatoa volcanic eruption. Timely information technology suggestions and assistance came from Jeff Parsons of The Oyez Project, Professor James Ferolo of Bradley University, and Dr. Francesco Stagno d'Alcontres of Centro Linguistico d'Ateneo Messinese. We also wish to express our gratitude to Professor Julieta Suárez Cao of the Instituto de Ciencia Politica of Pontificia Universidad Catolica de Chile, Hope Lozano-Bielat of Boston University, Farah Bushashia of Boston College, Professor Jennifer Cyr in the School of Government and Public Policy at the University of Arizona, Andrew Gruen of Cambridge University, and Tom Gaylord, Reference Librarian, and Matt Gruhn, Applications Specialist, at IIT Chicago-Kent College of Law for their helpful research assistance. We extend thanks as well to Joseph B. Maher, Esq., Deputy General Counsel, DHS; Brad Kieserman, Esq., Chief Counsel, FEMA; and Professor Timothy R. Johnson, University of Minnesota.

We have been fortunate to obtain the help of many outstanding political scientists across the country who provided us with critical reviews of our work as it has progressed through twelve separate editions. We found their comments enormously helpful, and we thank them for taking valuable time away from their own teaching and research to write their detailed reports. More specifically, our thanks go to the following instructors who reviewed the Twelfth Edition:

Ruth Ann Alsobrook, *Paris Junior College*	Sara Parker, *Chabot College*
Thomas Bowen, *Gloucester County College*	Beatrice Talpos, *Wayne County Community College District*
Van Davis, *National Park Community College*	Katrina Taylor, *Northern Arizona University*
Monte Freidig, *Santa Rosa Junior College*	Ronnie Tucker, *Shippensburg University*
Marilyn Gaar, *Johnson County Community College*	James Sheffield, *University of Oklahoma*
Kema Irogbe, *Claflin College*	Christine Sixta, *Francis Marion University*
Richard Kiefer, *Waubonsee Community College*	Sondra Venable, *University of New Orleans*
Melinda Kovacs, *Sam Houston State University*	Graham Wilson, *Boston University*
Farzeen Nasri, *Ventura College*	

We would also like to thank the following instructors who reviewed prior editions:

David Ahern, *University of Dayton*	Linda L. M. Bennett, *Wittenberg University*
Philip C. Aka, *Chicago State University*	Stephen Earl Bennett, *University of Cincinnati*
James Anderson, *Texas A&M University*	Elizabeth Bergman, *California State Polytechnic University, Pomona*
Greg Andranovich, *California State University, Los Angeles*	
Theodore Arrington, *University of North Carolina, Charlotte*	Thad Beyle, *University of North Carolina, Chapel Hill*
Denise Baer, *Northeastern University*	Bruce Bimber, *University of California, Santa Barbara*
Richard Barke, *Georgia Institute of Technology*	Michael Binford, *Georgia State University*
Brian Bearry, *University of Texas at Dallas*	Bonnie Browne, *Texas A&M University*

Jeffrey L. Brudney, *Cleveland State University*

Jane Bryant, *John A. Logan College*

J. Vincent Buck, *California State University, Fullerton*

Gregory A. Caldeira, *Ohio State University*

David E. Camacho, *Northern Arizona University*

Robert Casier, *Santa Barbara City College*

James Chalmers, *Wayne State University*

John Chubb, *Stanford University*

Allan Cigler, *University of Kansas*

Stanley Clark, *California State University, Bakersfield*

Ronald Claunch, *Stephen F. Austin State University*

Guy C. Clifford, *Bridgewater State College*

Gary Copeland, *University of Oklahoma*

Ruth A. Corbett, *Chabot College*

W. Douglas Costain, *University of Colorado at Boulder*

Cornelius P. Cotter, *University of Wisconsin, Milwaukee*

James L. Danielson, *Minnesota State University, Moorhead*

Christine L. Day, *University of New Orleans*

David A. Deese, *Boston College*

Victor D'Lugin, *University of Florida*

Douglas C. Dow, *University of Texas at Dallas*

Art English, *University of Arkansas*

Matthew EshbaughSoha, *University of North Texas*

Tim Fackler, *University of Texas, Austin*

Dennis Falcon, *Cerritos Community College*

Henry Fearnley, *College of Marin*

Elizabeth Flores, *Del Mar College*

David Madlock, *University of Memphis*

Michael Maggiotto, *University of South Carolina*

Edward S. Malecki, *California State University, Los Angeles*

Michael Margolis, *University of Cincinnati–McMicken College of Arts and Sciences*

Thomas R. Marshall, *University of Texas at Arlington*

Janet Martin, *Bowdoin College*

Steve J. Mazurana, *University of Northern Colorado*

Michael McConachie, *Collin College*

Wayne McIntosh, *University of Maryland*

David McLaughlin, *Northwest Missouri State University*

Don Melton, *Arapahoe Community College*

Melissa Michelson, *California State University, East Bay*

Dana Morales, *Montgomery College*

Jim Morrow, *Tulsa Junior College*

David Moskowitz, *The University of North Carolina, Charlotte*

William Mugleston, *Mountain View College*

William Murin, *University of Wisconsin–Parkside*

David Nice, *Washington State University*

David A. Nordquest, *Pennsylvania State University, Erie*

Bruce Odom, *Trinity Valley Community College*

Laura Katz Olson, *Lehigh University*

Bruce Oppenheimer, *Vanderbilt University*

Richard Pacelle, *Indiana University*

William J. Parente, *University of Scranton*

Tony Payan, *University of Texas, El Paso*

Robert Pecorella, *St. John's University*

James Perkins, *San Antonio College*

Denny E. Pilant, *Southwest Missouri State University*

Marc Pufong, *Valdosta State University*

Curtis Reithel, *University of Wisconsin–La Crosse*

Russell Renka, *Southeast Missouri State University*

Chester D. Rhoan, *Chabot College*

Michael J. Rich, *Emory University*

Richard S. Rich, *Virginia Tech*

Patricia S. Florestano, *University of Maryland*

Richard Foglesong, *Rollins College*

Steve Frank, *St. Cloud State University*

Mitchel Gerber, *Hofstra University*

Dana K. Glencross, *Oklahoma City Community College*

Dorith Grant-Wisdom, *Howard University*

Paul Gronke, *Duke University*

Sara A. Grove, *Shippensburg University*

David J. Hadley, *Wabash College*

Willie Hamilton, *Mt. San Jacinto College*

Kenneth Hayes, *University of Maine*

Ronald Hedlund, *University of Wisconsin–Milwaukee*

Richard Heil, *Fort Hays State University*

Beth Henschen, *The Institute for Community and Regional Development, Eastern Michigan University*

Marjorie Randon Hershey, *Indiana University*

Roberta Herzberg, *Indiana University*

Jack E. Holmes, *Hope College*

Peter Howse, *American River College*

Ronald J. Hrebenar, *University of Utah*

James B. Johnson, *University of Nebraska at Omaha*

William R. Keech, *Carnegie Mellon University*

Scott Keeter, *Pew Center*

Sarah W. Keidan, *Oakland Community College (Michigan)*

Linda Camp Keith, *Collin County Community College*

Beat Kernen, *Southwest Missouri State University*

Haroon Khan, *Henderson State University*

Dwight Kiel, *Central Florida University*

Nancy Pearson Kinney, *Washtenaw Community College*

Vance Krites, *Indiana University of Pennsylvania*

Clyde Kuhn, *California State University, Sacramento*

Jack Lampe, *Southwest Texas Junior College*

William Lester, *Jacksonville State University*

Brad Lockerbie, *University of Georgia*

Joseph Losco, *Ball State University*

Philip Loy, *Taylor University*

Stan Luger, *University of Northern Colorado*

Ronald I. Rubin, *Borough of Manhattan Community College, CUNY*

Gilbert K. St. Clair, *University of New Mexico*

Barbara Salmore, *Drew University*

Todd M. Schaefer, *Central Washington University*

Denise Scheberle, *University of Wisconsin–Green Bay*

Paul R. Schulman, *Mills College*

William A. Schultze, *San Diego State University*

Thomas Sevener, *Santa Rosa Junior College*

Kenneth S. Sherrill, *Hunter College*

Sanford R. Silverburg, *Catawba College*

Mark Silverstein, *Boston University*

Charles Sohner, *El Camino College*

Robert J. Spitzer, *SUNY Cortland*

Terry Spurlock, *Trinity Valley Community College*

Candy Stevens Smith, *Texarkana College*

Dale Story, *University of Texas at Arlington*

Nicholas Strinkowski, *Clark College*

Neal Tate, *University of North Texas*

James A. Thurber, *The American University*

Ronnie Tucker, *Shippensburg University*

John Tuman, *University of Nevada, Las Vegas*

Bedford Umez, *Lee College*

David Uranga, *Pasadena City College*

Eric M. Uslaner, *University of Maryland*

Lawson Veasey, *Jacksonville State University*

Charles E. Walcott, *Virginia Tech*

Richard J. Waldman, *University of Maryland*

Thomas G. Walker, *Emory University*

Benjamin Walter, *Vanderbilt University*

Shirley Ann Warshaw, *Gettysburg College*

Gary D. Wekkin, *University of Central Arkansas*

Jonathan West, *University of Miami*

Zaphon Wilson, *Armstrong Atlantic State University*

John Winkle, *University of Mississippi*

Clifford Wirth, *University of New Hampshire*

Wayne Wolf, *South Suburban College*

Mikel Wyckoff, *Northern Illinois University*

Ann Wynia, *North Hennepin Community College*

Jerry L. Yeric, *University of North Texas*

Finally, we want to thank the many people at Wadsworth/Cengage Learning who helped make this edition a reality. There's not enough room here to list all the individuals who helped us with the previous editions, so we say a collective thank-you for the superb work you did on *The Challenge of Democracy*. Political Science Acquisitions Editor Anita Devine could not have been more supportive, and we especially appreciate how tolerant she is of the constant stream of kvetching and moaning e-mails that we send her way. Betty Slack, our developmental editor, was a delight to work with. She had a light touch editing and shaping the changes we made in the manuscript. Our direct production contacts were extraordinarily efficient and helpful. A million thanks to Alison Eigel Zade, Andrea Clemente, and Alexa Orr, all of whom seemed to create order out of the chaos we created. Finally, thanks, too, to the sales representatives who do such a terrific job of bringing each new edition of *The Challenge of Democracy* to the attention of those who might use it.

K. J., J. B., J. G., D.S.

Dedication

This dedication is bit different than most as we want to recognize institutions rather than individuals. As we started talking about the Twelfth Edition, we began reflecting on our own introductions to political science. We were once undergraduates, taking classes in political science and learning from great professors who motivated and inspired us. More broadly, we studied at wonderful schools that provided us with intellectual and stimulating environments. We thank those institutions with humility and immense gratitude:

> *To Illinois State University, which steered me from Industrial Arts to Political Science*, K. J.

> *To the University of California at Berkeley, which took a young boy and opened the world to him*, J. B.

> *To Brooklyn College, with great role models in Professors Samuel J. Konefsky and Robert Hoffman*, J. G.

> *To Tufts University, where I discovered how one could use research to pursue political passions*, D. S.

APLIA QUICK START GUIDE

1. To get started, navigate to: login.cengagebrain.com

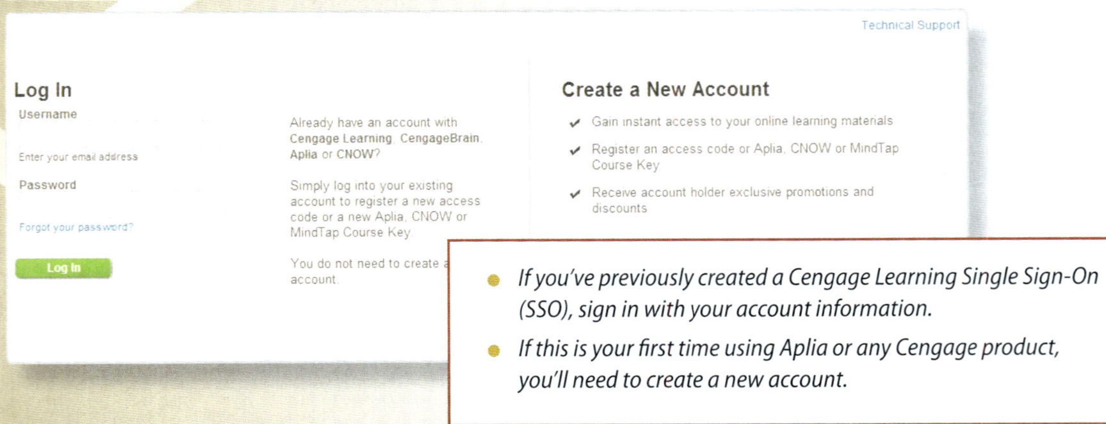

- *If you've previously created a Cengage Learning Single Sign-On (SSO), sign in with your account information.*
- *If this is your first time using Aplia or any Cengage product, you'll need to create a new account.*

2. Now you'll need to enter your
Aplia Course Key, which is provided by your instructor.

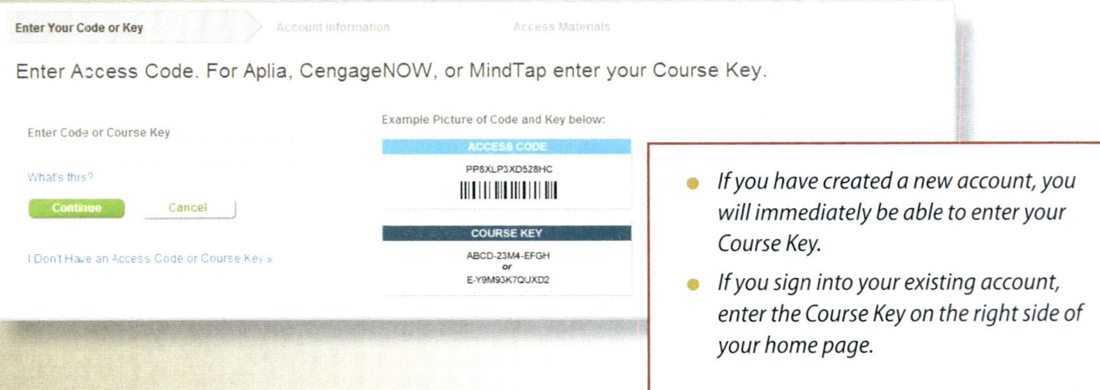

- *If you have created a new account, you will immediately be able to enter your Course Key.*
- *If you sign into your existing account, enter the Course Key on the right side of your home page.*

3. Confirm your course information,
and click "Continue" to continue to your registration.

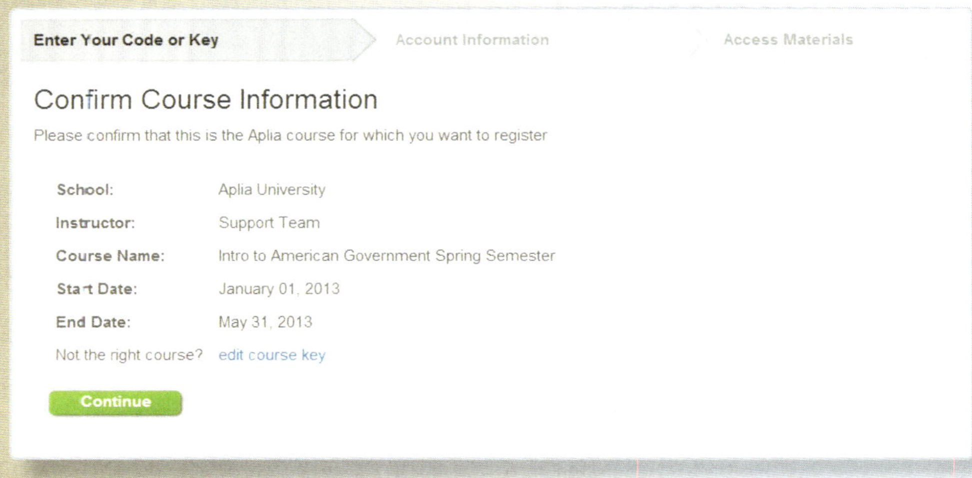

4. You can now access your Aplia course by clicking on the "Open" button next to the course. To pay for your Aplia course, click on the "See Payment Options" link under your course.

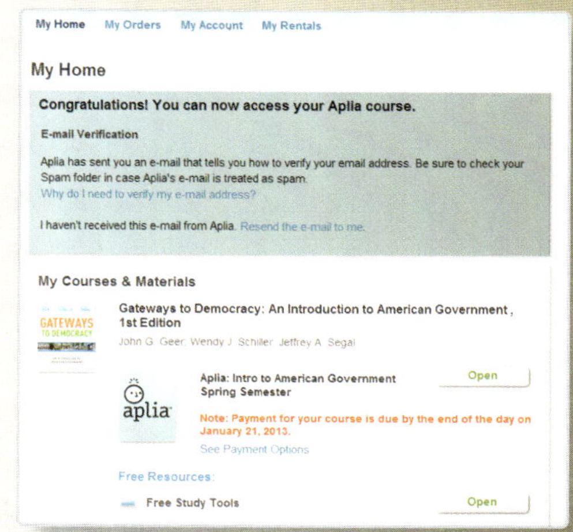

5. After clicking on the "Open" button, you will be directed to your Aplia course as shown below.

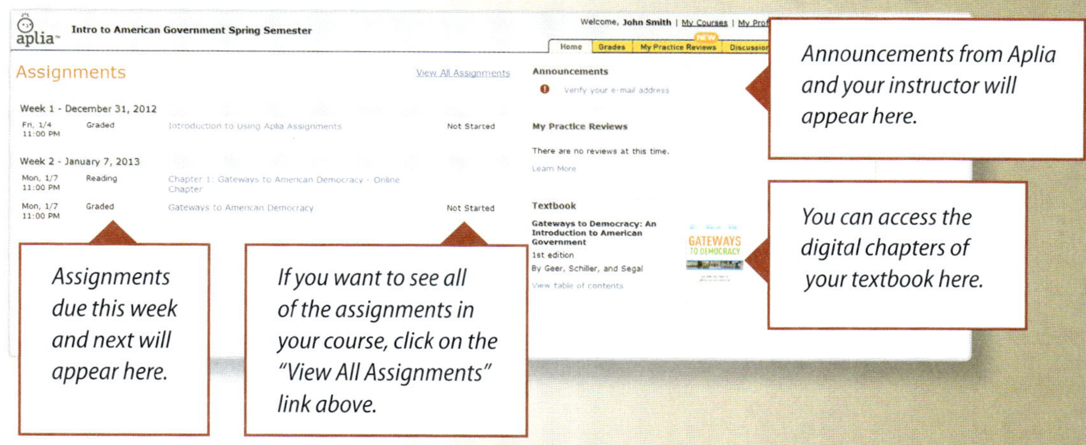

Announcements from Aplia and your instructor will appear here.

You can access the digital chapters of your textbook here.

Assignments due this week and next will appear here.

If you want to see all of the assignments in your course, click on the "View All Assignments" link above.

NEED HELP?

WITH YOUR APLIA COURSE?

- Click on the Support link in your Aplia course, and submit a case. Once your case is submitted, you can engage in a live chat to address your support issue.

WITH YOUR CENGAGEBRAIN ACCOUNT?

- Check the FAQs in the Support area of your CengageBrain home.
- Login to support.cengage.com using your CengageBrain account to get connected to an expert.
- Call 866-994-2427 Monday through Friday from 8 AM to 6 PM EST.

Freedom, Order, or Equality?

Are there limits to what government can require of its citizens? We know that governments can require automobile drivers and passengers to wear seat belts. Thinking that seat belts save lives and reduce injuries, every state but New Hampshire has such a law. We also know that governments can require the purchase of automobile insurance. Believing that mandatory coverage reduces insurance costs for everyone, every state but New Hampshire has such a law.

These laws were upheld under state constitutions, which typically empower state legislatures to care broadly for their residents' safety and welfare. The U.S. Constitution, however, grants very specific powers to Congress, and it does not grant a specific power that embraces requiring the use of seat belts and the purchase of automobile insurance. True, under its power to regulate interstate commerce, Congress passed a law that required manufacturers to install seat belts in all cars produced by 1968. But Congress did not require that drivers and passengers actually *use* the newly mandated seat belts. No national laws require the use of seat belts or the purchase of automobile insurance.

Can state governments require citizens to buy health insurance? Contending that mandatory coverage reduces health insurance costs for everyone, the Commonwealth of Massachusetts did just that in 2006. Under Republican governor Mitt Romney, Massachusetts required a minimum level of coverage for nearly all residents, provided free insurance to the poor, and penalized residents who failed to buy required insurance. It stands as the only state with such a law.

Can the national government require citizens to buy health insurance? Congress did just that in 2010. Under Democratic president Barack Obama, it passed the Patient Protection and Affordable Health Care Act, with the controversial "mandate" requiring nearly all Americans to buy coverage or pay a penalty. As in Massachusetts, the congressional mandate reflects the rationale that bringing both sick and healthy people into the pool of those insured is essential, because premiums paid by the healthy offset the cost of covering the sick.

From the beginning, controversy swirled over the national law to purchase health insurance. Massachusetts could require the purchase under its state constitution, but could Congress do the same under the U.S. Constitution? Could the law be justified under the Constitution's grant of congressional power "to regulate commerce"? Arguing not, legal challenges were filed in the courts. By November 2011, rulings were issued in five U.S. District Courts and five U.S. Courts of Appeals.[1] Seven of the rulings upheld the mandate, but three struck it down.

In arguments before the Court of Appeals for the District of Columbia Circuit, Judge Laurence Silberman asked a

Justice Department lawyer, who was defending the law, where she would draw the line in deciding what people could be forced to buy. For example, could the government force people to buy broccoli? "It depends," she said. Nevertheless, the Court upheld the mandate, and Judge Silberman wrote the opinion, saying, "It certainly is an encroachment on individual liberty, but it is no more so than a command that restaurants or hotels are obliged to serve all customers regardless of race."[2] Accordingly, a law to buy broccoli would presumably be a political judgment (and probably a fatal one), not a constitutional limitation.

The issue was eventually decided by the Supreme Court in June 2012. The Court ruled that the mandate to purchase health insurance could not be upheld under Congress's power to "regulate commerce," but it was constitutional under Congress's power to tax. That is, Congress could penalize (tax) people who did not purchase health insurance.

What the U.S. government can do constitutionally, politically, and practically to serve its citizens is the focus of our textbook. People will differ—as those in New Hampshire do from people in other states—in supporting laws about wearing seat belts and buying automobile insurance. (New Hampshire's state motto, "Live Free or Die," is more than a slogan.) People in other states seem more willing to surrender some degree of freedom to achieve a more orderly society with more equitable distribution of citizen benefits. This trade-off among the values of freedom, order, and equality lies at the heart of our discussion.

We probe the relationship between individual freedoms and personal security in the United States. We also examine the relationship between individual freedom and social equality as reflected in government policies, which often confront underlying dilemmas such as these:

Which is better: to live under a government that fiercely protects individual freedom or under one that infringes on freedom while fiercely guarding against threats to physical and economic security? *Which is better:* to let all citizens keep the same share of their income or to tax wealthier people at a higher rate to fund programs for poorer people? These questions pose dilemmas tied to opposing political philosophies that place different values on freedom, order, and equality.

This book explains American government and politics in the light of these dilemmas. It does more than explain the workings of our government; it encourages you to think about what government should—and should not—do. And it judges the American government against democratic ideals, encouraging you to think about how government should make its decisions. As the title of this book implies, *The Challenge of Democracy* argues that good government often poses difficult choices.

College students often say that American government and politics are hard to understand. In fact, many other people voice the same complaint. About 70 percent of people interviewed in 2008 agreed with the statement "Politics and government seem so complicated that a person like me can't understand what's going on."[3] We hope to improve your understanding of "what's going on" by analyzing the norms, or values, that people use to judge political events. Our purpose is not to preach what people ought to favor in making policy decisions; it is to teach what values are at stake.

Teaching without preaching is not easy; no one can completely exclude personal values from political analysis. But our approach minimizes the problem by concentrating on the dilemmas that confront governments when they are forced to choose between important policies that threaten equally cherished values, such as freedom of speech and personal security.

A prominent scholar defined *politics* as "the authoritative allocation of values for a society."[4] Every government policy reflects a choice between conflicting values. All government policies reinforce certain values (norms) at the expense of others. We want you to interpret policy issues (for example, should assisted suicide go unpunished?) with an understanding of the fundamental values in question (freedom of action versus order and protection of life) and the broader political context (liberal or conservative politics).

By looking beyond the specifics to the underlying normative principles, you should be able to make more sense out of politics. Our framework for analysis does not encompass all the complexities of American government, but it should help your knowledge grow by improving your comprehension of political information. We begin by considering the basic purposes of government. In short, why do we need it? Our main interest in this text is the purpose, value, and function of government as practiced in the United States. However, we live in an era of **globalization**—a term for the increasing interdependence of citizens and nations across the world.[5] So we must consider how politics at home and abroad interrelate, which is increasingly important to understanding our government.[6]

globalization
The increasing interdependence of citizens and nations across the world.

1.1 The Globalization of American Government

★ Define globalization and explain how globalization affects American politics and government.

Most people do not like being told what to do. Fewer still like being coerced into acting a certain way. Yet billions of people in countries across the world willingly submit to the coercive power of government. They accept laws that state on which side of the road to drive, how many wives (or husbands) they can have, what constitutes a contract, how to dispose of human waste—and how much they must pay to support the government that makes these coercive laws. In the first half of the twentieth century, people thought of government mainly in territorial terms. Indeed, a standard definition of **government** is the legitimate use of force—including firearms, imprisonment, and execution—within specified geographical boundaries to control human behavior. International relations and diplomacy have been based on the principle of national sovereignty, defined as "a political entity's externally recognized right to exercise final authority over its affairs."[7] Simply put, **national sovereignty** means that each national government has the right to govern its people as it wishes, without interference from other nations.

government
The legitimate use of force to control human behavior; also, the organization or agency authorized to exercise that force.

national sovereignty
A political entity's externally recognized right to exercise final authority over its affairs.

Some scholars argued strongly early in the twentieth century that a body of international law controlled the actions of supposedly sovereign nations, but their argument was essentially theoretical.[8] In the practice of international relations, there was no sovereign power over nations. Each enjoyed complete independence to govern its territory without interference from other nations. Although the League of Nations and later the United Nations were supposed to introduce supranational order into the world, even these international organizations explicitly respected national sovereignty as the guiding principle of international relations. The U.N. Charter, Article 2.1, states, "The Organization is based on the principle of the sovereign equality of all its Members."

National sovereignty, however, is threatened under globalization.[9] Consider the international community's concern with former Libyan dictator Moammar Gadhafi's military repression of political protests in 2011. His actions prompted the North Atlantic Treaty Organization (NATO) to establish a no-fly zone over Libya, shooting down Libyan planes and destroying Gadhafi's armor units. Ignoring Gadhafi's claims that NATO blatantly violated Libya's sovereignty, the International Criminal Court issued warrants for the arrest of Gadhafi, his son, and his intelligence chief for crimes against humanity. After a few weeks, Gadhafi was captured and killed, and the rebels took over the government.

Global forces also generate pressures for international law. Our government, you might be surprised to learn, is worried about this trend of holding nations accountable to international law. In fact, in 2002, the United States "annulled" its

Politics of Global Change

Globalization in the Classroom

Chances are, you can see the effects of globalization at your institution in the United States. As shown in the graph, in the mid-1970s only about 1.5 percent of higher education students came from foreign countries. By 2010, that percentage had more than doubled, with over 700,000 foreign students in American college classrooms. The total number of American students studying abroad is much lower, because the supply of U.S. students is much smaller than the supply of foreign students. However, the percentage of U.S. citizens studying abroad more than tripled since the late 1980s, underscoring the effects of globalization.

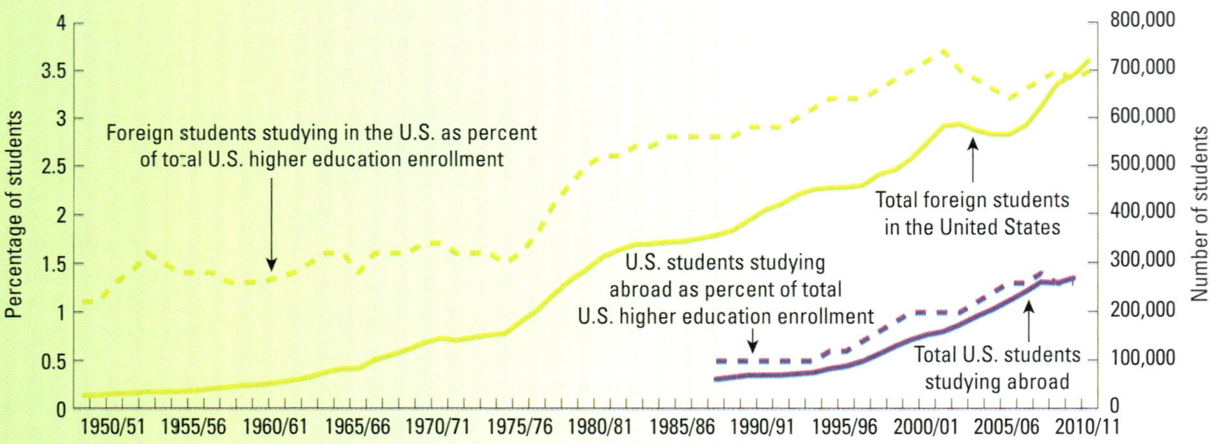

Source: Institute of International Education, "International Student Enrollment Trends, 1949/50–2010/11," Institute of International Education, 2011. Retrieved from http://www.iie.org/opendoors. Copyright © 2011 by the Institute of International Education. Reproduced by permission.

Critical Thinking

What do you suppose foreign students think about American government and politics? What might they find most appealing? What might they find most disturbing? If you know any foreign students, why not ask them?

signature to the 1998 treaty (no country had ever unsigned a treaty) to create an International Criminal Court that would define and try crimes against humanity.[10] Why would the United States oppose such an international court? One reason is its concern that U.S. soldiers stationed abroad might be arrested and tried in that court.[11] Another reason is the death penalty, practiced in the United States but abolished by more than half the countries in the world and all countries in the European Union. Indeed, in 1996, the International Commission of Jurists condemned the U.S. death penalty as "arbitrarily and racially discriminatory," and there is a concerted campaign across Europe to force the sovereign United States to terminate capital punishment.[12]

The United States is the world's most powerful nation, but as proved by the events of September 11, 2001, it is not invulnerable to foreign attack. Moreover, it is vulnerable to erosion of its sovereignty. As the world's superpower, should the United States be above international law if its sovereignty is compromised?

Although this text is about American national government, it recognizes the growing impact of international politics and world opinion on U.S. politics. (See "Politics of Global Change: Globalization in the Classroom.") The Cold War era of conflict with the Soviet Union, of course, had a profound effect on domestic politics because the nation spent heavily on the military and restricted trading with communist countries. Now we are closely tied through trade to former enemies (we import more goods from China—still communist—than from France and Britain combined), and we are thoroughly embedded in a worldwide economic, social, and political network. (See Chapter 19, "Global Policy," for an extended treatment of the economic and social dimensions of globalization.) More than ever before, we must discuss American politics while casting an eye abroad to see how foreign affairs affect our government and how American politics affects government in other nations.

★ 1.2 The Purposes of Government

★ Identify the purposes that government serves and trace their historical roots.

Governments at any level require citizens to surrender some freedom as part of being governed. Although some governments minimize their infringements on personal freedom, no government has as a goal the maximization of personal freedom. Governments exist to control; *to govern* means "to control." Why do people surrender their freedom to this control? To obtain the benefits of government. Throughout history, government has served two major purposes: maintaining order (preserving life and protecting property) and providing public goods. More recently, some governments have pursued a third purpose, promoting equality, which is more controversial.

Maintaining Order

Maintaining order is the oldest objective of government. **Order** in this context is rich with meaning. Let's start with "law and order." Maintaining order in this sense means establishing the rule of law to preserve life and protect property. To the seventeenth-century English philosopher Thomas Hobbes (1588–1679), preserving life was the most important function of government. In his classic philosophical treatise, *Leviathan* (1651), Hobbes described life without government as life in a "state of nature."

order
Established ways of social behavior. Maintaining order is the oldest purpose of government.

Leviathan, Hobbes's All-Powerful Sovereign

This engraving is from the 1651 edition of *Leviathan* by Thomas Hobbes. It shows Hobbes's sovereign brandishing a sword in one hand and the scepter of justice in the other. He watches over an orderly town, made peaceful by his absolute authority. But note that the sovereign's body is composed of tiny images of his subjects. He exists only through them. Hobbes explains that such government power can be created only if people "confer all their power and strength upon one man, or upon one assembly of men, that may reduce all their wills, by plurality of voices, unto one will."

Without rules, people would live as predators do, stealing and killing for their personal benefit. In Hobbes's classic phrase, life in a state of nature would be "solitary, poor, nasty, brutish, and short." He believed that a single ruler, or sovereign, must possess unquestioned authority to guarantee the safety of the weak and protect them from the attacks of the strong. Hobbes named his all-powerful government "Leviathan," after a biblical sea monster. He believed that complete obedience to Leviathan's strict laws was a small price to pay for the security of living in a civil society.

Most of us can only imagine what a state of nature would be like. But in some parts of the world, whole nations have experienced lawlessness. That has been the situation in Somalia since 1991, when the government was toppled and warlords feuded over territory. Until 2011, the government controlled only a portion of the capital, Mogadishu. Somali pirates still seize ships off its shore with impunity.[13] Throughout history, authoritarian rulers have used people's fear of civil disorder to justify taking power. Ironically, the ruling group itself—whether monarchy, aristocracy, or political party—then became known as the *established order*.

Hobbes's conception of life in the cruel state of nature led him to view government primarily as a means of guaranteeing people's survival. Other theorists, taking survival for granted, believed that government protects order by preserving private property (goods and land owned by individuals). Foremost among them was John Locke (1632–1704), an English philosopher. In *Two Treatises on Government* (1690), he wrote that the protection of life, liberty, and property was the basic objective of government. His thinking strongly influenced the Declaration of Independence; it is reflected in the Declaration's famous phrase identifying "Life, Liberty, and the Pursuit of Happiness" as "unalienable Rights" of citizens under government. Locke's defense of property rights became linked with safeguards for individual liberties in the doctrine of **liberalism**, which holds that the state should leave citizens free to further their individual pursuits.[14]

Not everyone believes that the protection of private property is a valid objective of government. The German philosopher Karl Marx (1818–1883) rejected the private ownership of property used in the production of goods or services. Marx's ideas form the basis of **communism**, a philosophy that gives ownership of all land and productive facilities to the people—in effect, to the government. In line with communist theory, the 1977 constitution of the former Soviet Union declared that the nation's land, minerals, waters, and forests "are the exclusive property of the state." Years after the Soviet Union collapsed, Russia remains deeply split over abandoning the old communist-era policies to permit the private ownership of land. Even today's

liberalism
The belief that states should leave individuals free to follow their individual pursuits. Note that this differs from the definition of *liberal* later in this chapter.

communism
A political system in which, in theory, ownership of all land and productive facilities is in the hands of the people, and all goods are equally shared. The production and distribution of goods are controlled by an authoritarian government.

market-oriented China still clings to the principle that all land belongs to the state, and not until 2007 did it pass a law that protected private homes and businesses.[15]

Providing Public Goods

After governments have established basic order, they can pursue other ends. Using their coercive powers, governments can tax citizens to raise money to spend on **public goods**, which are benefits and services available to everyone, such as education, sanitation, and parks. Public goods benefit all citizens but are not likely to be produced by the voluntary acts of individuals. The government of ancient Rome, for example, built aqueducts to carry fresh water from the mountains to the city. Road building was another public good provided by the Roman government, which also used the roads to move its legions and protect the established order.

    Government action to provide public goods can be controversial. During President James Monroe's administration (1817–1825), many people thought that building the Cumberland Road (between Cumberland, Maryland, and Wheeling, West Virginia) was not a proper function of the national government, the Romans notwithstanding. Over time, the scope of government functions in the United States has expanded. During President Dwight Eisenhower's administration in the 1950s, the federal government outdid the Romans' noble road building. Although a Republican opposed to big government, Eisenhower launched the massive interstate highway system at a cost of $27 billion (in 1950s dollars). Yet some government enterprises that have been common in other countries—running railroads, operating coal mines, and generating electric power—are politically controversial or even unacceptable in the United States. Hence, many people objected when the Bush administration took over General Motors and Chrysler in 2008 to facilitate an orderly bankruptcy. People disagree about how far the government ought to go in using its power to tax to provide public goods and services and how much of that realm should be handled by private business for profit.

Promoting Equality

The promotion of equality has not always been a major objective of government. It gained prominence only in the twentieth century, in the aftermath of industrialization and urbanization. Confronted by the paradox of poverty amid plenty, some political leaders in European nations pioneered extensive government programs to improve life for the poor. Under the emerging concept of the welfare state, government's role expanded to provide individuals with medical care, education, and a guaranteed income "from cradle to grave." Sweden, Britain, and other nations adopted welfare programs aimed at reducing social inequalities. This relatively new purpose of government has been by far the most controversial. People often oppose taxation for public goods (building roads and schools, for example) because of cost alone. They oppose more strongly taxation for government programs to promote economic and social equality on principle.

    The key issue here is government's role in redistributing income, that is, taking from the wealthy to give to the poor. Charity (voluntary giving to the poor) has a strong basis in Western religious traditions; using the power of the state to support the poor does not. (In his 1838 novel, *Oliver Twist,* Charles Dickens dramatized how government power was used to imprison the poor, not to support them.) Using the state to redistribute income was originally a radical idea, set forth by Karl Marx as the ultimate principle of developed communism: "from each according to his ability, to each according to his needs."[16] This extreme has never been realized in any

public goods
Benefits and services, such as parks and sanitation, that benefit all citizens but are not likely to be produced voluntarily by individuals.

Gene Herrick / AP Photo

Rosa Parks: She Sat for Equality

Rosa Parks had just finished a day's work as a seamstress and was sitting in the front of a bus in Montgomery, Alabama, going home. A white man claimed her seat, which he could do according to the law in December 1955. When she refused to move and was arrested, outraged blacks, led by Dr. Martin Luther King, Jr., began a boycott of the Montgomery bus company. Rosa Parks died in 2005 at age ninety-two and was accorded the honor of lying in state in the Capitol rotunda, the first woman to receive that tribute.

government, not even in communist states. But over time, taking from the rich to help the needy has become a legitimate function of most governments.

That function is not without controversy. Especially since the Great Depression of the 1930s, the government's role in redistributing income to promote economic equality has been a major source of policy debate in the United States. Despite inflation, the minimum wage had been frozen at $5.15 per hour from 1997 to 2007, when it was increased to $5.85. In 2009, Congress increased the minimum wage to $7.25 only because Democrats included the increase in a deal on funding the Iraq war.

Government can also promote social equality through policies that do not redistribute income. For example, in 2000, Vermont passed a law allowing persons of the same sex to enter a "civil union" granting access to similar benefits enjoyed by persons of different sexes through marriage. By 2010, the legislatures or courts in Connecticut, Iowa, Massachusetts, and New Hampshire put similar laws into effect. In this instance, laws advancing social equality may clash with different social values held by other citizens. Indeed, 31 states blocked same-sex marriages through public referenda.[17]

★ 1.3 A Conceptual Framework for Analyzing Government

★ Describe how political scientists use concepts to structure events and promote understanding.

Citizens have very different views of how vigorously they want government to maintain order, provide public goods, and promote equality. Of the three objectives, providing for public goods usually is less controversial than maintaining order or promoting equality. After all, government spending for highways, schools, and parks carries benefits for nearly every citizen. Moreover, services merely cost money. The cost of maintaining order and promoting equality is greater than money; it usually means a trade-off in basic values.

To understand government and the political process, you must be able to recognize these trade-offs and identify the basic values they entail. Just as people sit back from a wide-screen motion picture to gain perspective, to understand American government you need to take a broad view—a view much broader than that offered by examining specific political events. You need to use political concepts.

A concept is a generalized idea of a set of items or thoughts. It groups various events, objects, or qualities under a common classification or label. The framework that guides this book consists of five concepts that figure prominently in political analysis. We regard the five concepts as especially important to a broad understanding of American politics, and we use them repeatedly throughout this book. This framework will help you evaluate political events long after you have read this text.

The five concepts that we emphasize deal with the fundamental issues of what government tries to do and how it decides to do it. The concepts that relate to what government tries to do are *order, freedom,* and *equality.* All governments by definition value order; maintaining order is part of the meaning of government. Most governments at least claim to preserve individual freedom while they maintain order, although they vary widely in the extent to which they succeed. Few governments even profess to guarantee equality, and governments differ greatly in policies that pit equality against freedom. Our conceptual framework should help you evaluate the extent to which the United States pursues all three values through its government.

How government chooses the proper mix of order, freedom, and equality in its policymaking has to do with the process of choice. We evaluate the American governmental process using two models of democratic government: *majoritarian* and *pluralist.* Many governments profess to be democracies. Whether they are or are not depends on their (and our) meaning of the term. Even countries that Americans agree are democracies—for example, the United States and Britain—differ substantially in the type of democracy they practice. We can use our conceptual models of democratic government both to classify the type of democracy practiced in the United States and to evaluate the government's success in fulfilling that model.

The five concepts can be organized into two groups:

- Concepts that identify the values pursued by government:
    Freedom
    Order
    Equality
- Concepts that describe models of democratic government:
    Majoritarian democracy
    Pluralist democracy

The rest of this chapter examines freedom, order, and equality as conflicting values pursued by government. Chapter 2 discusses majoritarian democracy and pluralist democracy as alternative institutional models for implementing democratic government.

1.4 The Concepts of Freedom, Order, and Equality

★ Define freedom, order, and equality and discuss the various interpretations of each value.

These three terms—*freedom, order,* and *equality*—have a range of connotations in American politics. Both *freedom* and *equality* are positive terms that politicians have learned to use to their own advantage. Consequently, freedom and equality mean different things to different people at different times, depending on the political context in which they are used. *Order,* in contrast, has negative connotations for many people because it symbolizes government intrusion into private lives. Except during periods of social strife or external threat (for example, after September 11), few politicians in Western democracies openly call for more order. Because all governments infringe on freedom, we examine that concept first.

Freedom

Freedom can be used in two major senses: freedom of and freedom from. President Franklin Delano Roosevelt used the word in both senses in a speech he made shortly before the United States entered World War II. He described four freedoms: freedom

WHAT DO YOU KNOW ABOUT...

THE FOUR FREEDOMS?

Norman Rockwell became famous in the 1940s for the humorous, homespun covers he painted for the *Saturday Evening Post*, a weekly magazine. Inspired by an address to Congress in which President Roosevelt outlined his goals for world civilization, Rockwell painted *The Four Freedoms*, which were reproduced in the *Post* during February and March 1943. Their immense popularity led the government to print posters of the illustrations for the Treasury Department's war bond drive.

The Office of War Information also reproduced *The Four Freedoms* and circulated the posters in schools, clubhouses, railroad stations, post offices, and other public

© The Protected Art Archive/Alamy

Nawrocki Stock Photo/Custom Medical Stock Photo "CMSP Education"/Newscom

of religion, freedom of speech, freedom from fear, and freedom from want. The noted illustrator Norman Rockwell gave Americans a vision of these freedoms in a classic set of paintings published in the *Saturday Evening Post* and subsequently issued as posters to sell war bonds (see "What Do You Know about the Four Freedoms?" on page 12).

Freedom of is the absence of constraints on behavior; it means freedom *to* do something. In this sense, *freedom* is synonymous with *liberty*.[18] Two of Rockwell's paintings, *Freedom of Worship* and *Freedom of Speech,* exemplify this type of freedom. Freedom of religion, speech, press, and assembly (collectively called "civil liberties") are discussed in Chapter 15.

freedom of
An absence of constraints on behavior, as in *freedom of speech or freedom of religion.*

buildings. Officials even had copies circulated on the European front to remind soldiers of the liberties for which they were fighting. It is said that no other paintings in the world have ever been reproduced or circulated in such vast numbers as *The Four Freedoms.*

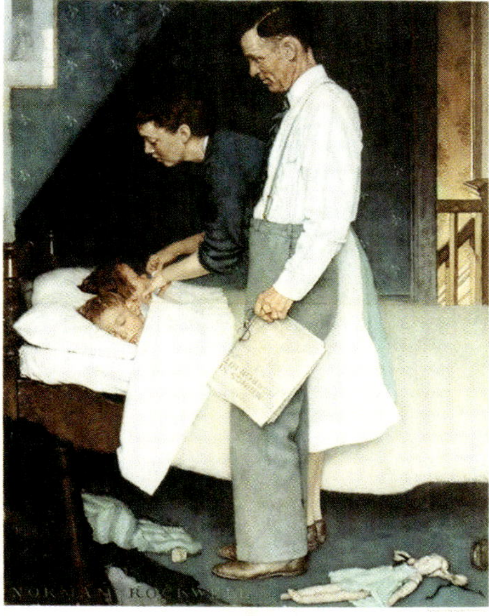

Critical Thinking

Times have changed since the 1940s. Which of these four freedoms would resonate best today with the American public? Which the least? Why? What has changed over the decades?

Compared with What?

The Importance of Order and Freedom in Other Nations

Compared with citizens in twenty-nine other nations, Americans do not value order very much. The World Values Survey asked respondents to select which of four national goals was "very important":

- Maintaining order in the nation
- Giving people more say in important government decisions
- Fighting rising prices
- Protecting freedom of speech

The United States ranked twenty-eighth in the list of those selecting "maintaining order" as very important. While American citizens do not value government control of social behavior as much as others, they do value freedom of speech more highly. Citizens in only three countries favor protecting freedom of speech more than citizens in the United States.

---

freedom from

Immunity, as in *freedom from want.*

Freedom from is the message of the other paintings, *Freedom from Fear* and *Freedom from Want.*[19] Here freedom suggests immunity from fear and want. In the modern political context, *freedom from* often symbolizes the fight against exploitation and oppression. The cry of the civil rights movement in the 1960s—"Freedom Now!"—conveyed this meaning. This sense of freedom corresponds to the "civil rights" discussed in Chapter 16. If you recognize that freedom in this sense means immunity from discrimination, you can see that it comes close to the concept of equality.[20] In this book, we avoid using *freedom* to mean "freedom from"; for this sense, we simply use *equality*. When we use *freedom,* we mean "freedom of."

Order

When *order* is viewed in the narrow sense of preserving life and protecting property, most citizens concede the importance of maintaining order and thereby grant the need for government. For example, "domestic Tranquility" (order) is cited in the preamble to the Constitution. However, when *order* is viewed in the broader sense of preserving the social order, some people argue that maintaining order is not a legitimate function of government (see "Compared with What? The Importance of Order and Freedom in Other Nations"). *Social order* refers to established patterns of authority in society and traditional modes of behavior. It is the accepted way of doing things. The prevailing social order prescribes behavior in many different areas: how students should dress in school (neatly, no purple hair) and behave toward their teachers (respectfully), who is allowed to marry (single adults of opposite sexes), what the press should not publish (sexually explicit photographs), and what the proper attitude toward religion and country should be (reverential). It is important to remember that the social order can change. Today, perfectly respectable men and women wear bathing suits that would have caused a scandal a century ago.

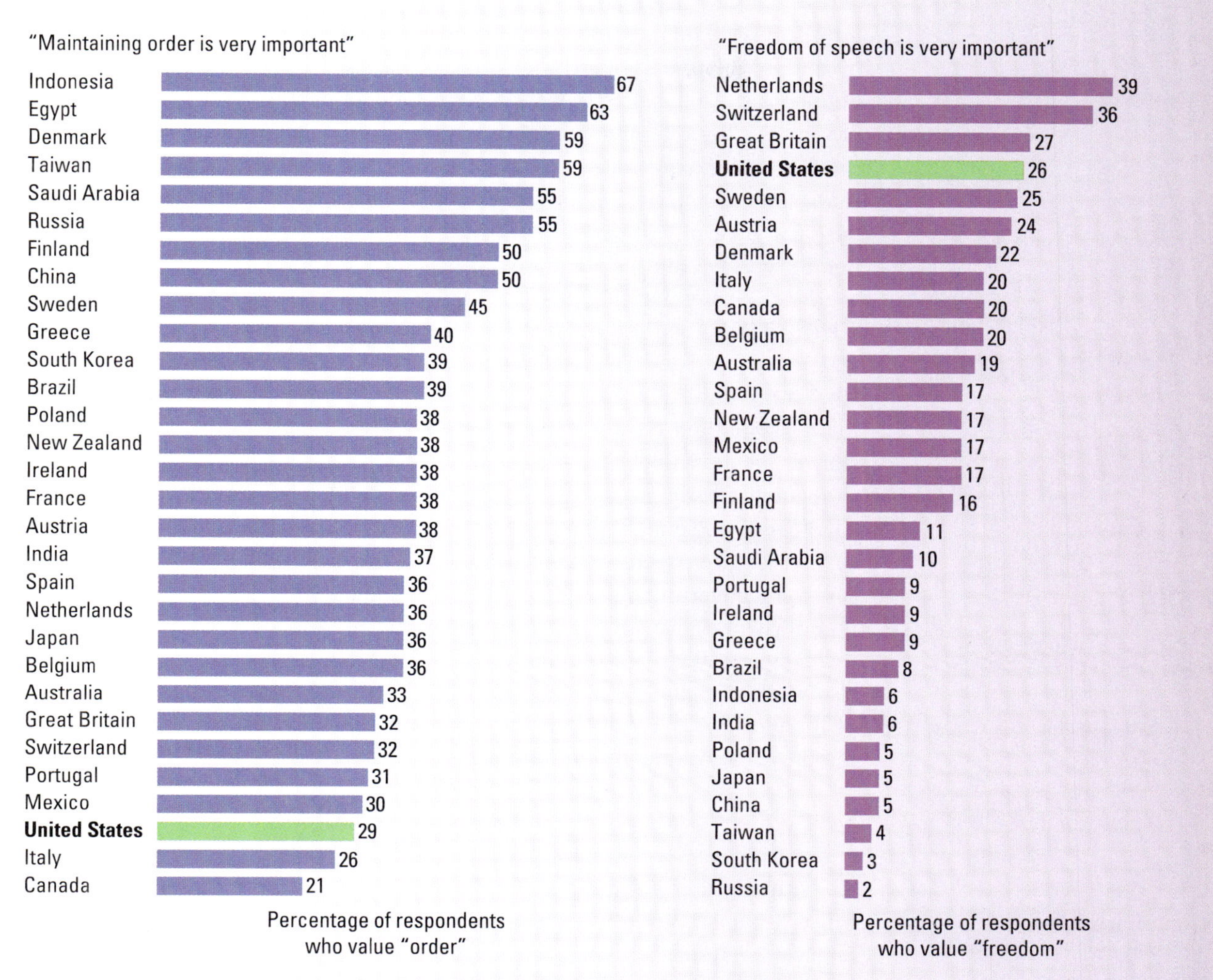

Source: These are combined data from the 1999–2001 and 2005–2007 waves of the World Values Survey. See Ronald Inglehart, "Materialist/Postmaterialist Priorities among Publics around the World" (discussion paper presented at the Institute of Social Research (ISR), University of Michigan, 14 February 2008).

Critical Thinking

What types of nations favor freedom of speech more than maintaining order? How about the reverse: Which nations favor maintaining order more than freedom of speech? In which group would you rather live—and why?

A state government can protect the established order by using its **police power**—its authority to safeguard residents' safety, health, welfare, and morals. Under legal tradition and constitutional provisions, state governments can act directly on residents under their police power. The national government only has powers granted by the Constitution and lacks a general police power. That explains why states can require automobile drivers and passengers to wear seat belts and the national government cannot. However, the national government can act on individuals if the action can be traced to a constitutionally delegated power. For example, in 1932, Congress passed the Federal Kidnapping Act, allowing the Federal Bureau of

police power
The authority of a government to maintain order and safeguard citizens' health, morals, safety, and welfare.

Investigation (FBI) to apprehend kidnappers. The law was based on the constitutional power to regulate interstate commerce, given that kidnappers usually demand ransom by mail or telephone (instrumentalities of interstate commerce) and might cross state boundaries. The extent to which governments at any level should use their police powers is a topic of ongoing debate in the United States and is constantly being redefined by the courts. In the 1980s, many states used their authority to pass legislation that banned smoking in public places. In the 1990s, a hot issue was whether the national government should control the dissemination of pornography on the Internet. Excepting child pornography, courts have tended to strike down such bans.

After September 11, 2001, Congress passed new laws increasing government's power to investigate suspicious activities by foreign nationals in order to deter terrorism. After the underwear bomber was thwarted from blowing up an airliner on Christmas Day 2009, airports began using full-body scanners to probe through clothing. Despite their desire to be safe from further attacks, some citizens feared the erosion of their civil liberties. Living in a police state—a government that uses its power to regulate nearly all aspects of behavior—might maximize safety, but at a considerable loss of personal freedom.

Most governments are inherently conservative; they tend to resist social change. But some governments aim to restructure the social order. Social change is most dramatic when a government is overthrown through force and replaced. This can occur through an internal revolution or a "regime change" effected externally. Societies can also work to change social patterns more gradually through the legal process. Our use of the term *order* in this book encompasses all three aspects: preserving life, protecting property, and maintaining traditional patterns of social relationships.

Equality

As with *freedom* and *order, equality* is used in different senses to support different causes. **Political equality** in elections is easy to define: each citizen has one and only one vote. This basic concept is central to democratic theory, a subject explored at length in Chapter 2. But when some people advocate political equality, they mean more than one person, one vote. These people contend that an urban ghetto dweller and the chairman of the board of Microsoft are not politically equal despite the fact that each has one vote. Through occupation or wealth, some citizens are more able than others to influence political decisions. For example, wealthy citizens can exert influence by advertising in the mass media or by contacting friends in high places. Lacking great wealth and political connections, most citizens do not have such influence. Thus, some analysts argue that equality in wealth, education, and status—that is, **social equality**—is necessary for true political equality.

There are two routes to promoting social equality: providing equal opportunities and ensuring equal outcomes. **Equality of opportunity** means that each person has the same chance to succeed in life. This idea is deeply ingrained in American culture. The U.S. Constitution prohibits titles of nobility and does not make owning property a requirement for holding public office. Public schools and libraries are open to all. For many people, the concept of social equality is satisfied by offering equal opportunities for advancement; it is not essential that people actually end up being equal. For others, true social equality means nothing less than **equality of outcome**.[21] President Lyndon B. Johnson expressed this view in 1965: "It is not enough just to open the gates of opportunity…. We seek … not just equality as a right and a theory but equality as a fact and equality as a result."[22] According to this outlook, it is not enough that governments provide people with equal opportunities;

political equality
Equality in political decision making: one vote per person, with all votes counted equally.

social equality
Equality in wealth, education, and status.

equality of opportunity
The idea that each person is guaranteed the same chance to succeed in life.

equality of outcome
The concept that society must ensure that people are equal, and governments must design policies to redistribute wealth and status so that economic and social equality is actually achieved.

they must also design policies that redistribute wealth and status so that economic and social equality are actually achieved. In education, equality of outcome has led to federal laws that require comparable funding for men's and women's college sports. In business, equality of outcome has led to certain affirmative action programs to increase minority hiring and to the active recruitment of women, blacks, and Latinos to fill jobs. Equality of outcome has also produced federal laws that require employers to pay men and women equally for equal work. In recent years, the very concept of affirmative action has come under scrutiny. In 2003, however, the U.S. Supreme Court supported affirmative action in the form of preferential treatment to minorities in college admissions.

Some link equality of outcome with the concept of government-supported **rights**— the idea that every citizen is entitled to certain benefits of government—that government should guarantee its citizens adequate (if not equal) housing, employment, medical care, and income as a matter of right. If citizens are entitled to government benefits as a matter of right, government efforts to promote equality of outcome become legitimized.

Clearly, the concept of equality of outcome is quite different from that of equality of opportunity, and it requires a much greater degree of government activity. It also clashes more directly with the concept of freedom. By taking from one to give to another, which is necessary for the redistribution of income and status, the government clearly creates winners and losers. The winners may believe that justice has been served by the redistribution. The losers often feel strongly that their freedom to enjoy their income and status has suffered.

Scott Olson/Getty Images News/Getty Images

Equality in the Military

While they still have a long way to go, women are being treated more equally in the military. Although they are not allowed in units engaged in direct combat, women nevertheless often find themselves in other combat situations and consequently risk being killed. As of August 2010, 124 women in the U.S. military had been killed by hostile fire in Iraq. That's more than twice as many women killed in the military from the end of World War II to the start of the Iraq war.

Source: Memorial website at http://nooniefortin.com/iraq.htm.

rights
The benefits of government to which every citizen is entitled.

★ 1.5 Two Dilemmas of Government

★ Analyze the inherent conflicts between freedom versus order and freedom versus equality.

The two major dilemmas facing American government early in the twenty-first century stem from the oldest and the newest objectives of government: maintaining order and promoting equality. Both order and equality are important social values, but government cannot pursue either without sacrificing a third important value: individual freedom. The clash between freedom and order forms the original dilemma of government; the clash between freedom and equality forms the modern dilemma of government. Although the dilemmas are different, each involves trading some amount of freedom for another value.

The Original Dilemma: Freedom versus Order

The conflict between freedom and order originates in the very meaning of government as the legitimate use of force to control human behavior. How much freedom must a citizen surrender to government? The dilemma has occupied philosophers for hundreds of years. In the eighteenth century, the French philosopher Jean-Jacques Rousseau (1712–1778) wrote that the problem of devising a proper government "is to find a form of association which will defend and protect with the whole common force the person and goods of each associate, and in which each, while uniting himself with all, may still obey himself alone, and remain free as before."[23]

The original purpose of government was to protect life and property and to make citizens safe from violence. How well is the American government doing today in providing law and order to its citizens? Almost 40 percent of the respondents in a 2011 national survey said that they were "afraid to walk alone at night" in areas within a mile of their home.[24] Simply put, Americans view violent crime (which actually has decreased in recent years[25]) as a critical issue and do not believe that their government adequately protects them.

Contrast the fear of crime in urban America with the sense of personal safety while walking in Moscow, Warsaw, or Prague when the old communist governments still ruled in Eastern Europe. It was common to see old and young strolling late at night along the streets and in the parks of these cities. The old communist regimes gave their police great powers to control guns, monitor citizens' movements, and arrest and imprison suspicious people, which enabled them to do a better job of maintaining order. Police and party agents routinely kept their citizens under surveillance—eavesdropping on phone conversations and opening mail from abroad—to ensure that they were not communicating privately with the capitalist world outside official channels. Communist governments deliberately chose order over freedom. With the collapse of communism came the end of strict social order. Respondents in a 2009 survey in nine former communist countries in Eastern Europe said that crime and illegal drugs were among their top national problems.[26]

The crisis over acquired immune deficiency syndrome (AIDS) adds a new twist to the dilemma of freedom versus order. Some health officials believe that AIDS, for which there is no known cure, is the greatest medical threat in the history of the United States. By 2009, more than 1.2 million cases of AIDS had been reported to the Centers for Disease Control and Prevention, and almost 600,000 of these people died.[27]

To combat the spread of the disease in the military, the Department of Defense began testing all applicants for the AIDS virus in the mid-1980s. Other government agencies have begun testing current employees, and some officials are calling for widespread mandatory testing within the private sector as well. Such programs are strongly opposed by those who believe they violate individual freedom. But those who are more afraid of the spread of AIDS than of an infringement on individual rights support aggressive government action to combat the disease.

The conflict between the values of freedom and order represents the original dilemma of government. In the abstract, people value both freedom and order; in real life, the two values inherently conflict. By definition, any policy that strengthens one value takes away from the other. The balance of freedom and order is an issue in enduring debates (whether to allow capital punishment) and contemporary challenges (whether to prohibit controversial YouTube videos). And in a democracy, policy choices hinge on how much citizens value freedom and how much they value order.

The Modern Dilemma: Freedom versus Equality

Popular opinion has it that freedom and equality go hand in hand. In reality, the two values usually clash when governments enact policies to promote social equality. Because social equality is a relatively recent government objective, deciding between policies that promote equality at the expense of freedom, and vice versa, is the modern dilemma of politics. Consider these examples:

During the 1960s, Congress (through the Equal Pay Act) required employers to pay women and men the same rate for equal work. This legislation means that some employers are forced to pay women more than they would if their compensation policies were based on their free choice.

During the 1970s, the courts ordered the busing of schoolchildren to achieve a fair distribution of blacks and whites in public schools. This action was motivated by concern for educational equality, but it also impaired freedom of choice.

During the 1980s, some states passed legislation that went beyond the idea of equal pay for equal work to the more radical notion of pay equity—that is, equal pay for comparable work. Women had to be paid at a rate equal to men's even if they had different jobs, providing the women's jobs were of "comparable worth." For example, if the skills and responsibilities of a female nurse were found to be comparable to those of a male laboratory technician in the same hospital, the woman's salary and the man's salary would have to be the same.

During the 1990s, Congress prohibited discrimination in employment, public services, and public accommodations on the basis of physical or mental disabilities. Under the 1990 Americans with Disabilities Act, businesses with twenty-five or more employees cannot pass over an otherwise qualified disabled person in employment or promotion, and new buses and trains have to be made accessible to them.

During the first decade of the 2000s, Congress passed the Genetic Information Nondiscrimination Act (GINA). Signed by President Bush in 2008, it prohibited companies from discriminating in hiring based on an individual's genetic tests, genetic tests of a family member, or family medical history.

These examples illustrate the challenge of using government power to promote equality. The clash between freedom and order is obvious, but the clash between freedom and equality is more subtle. Americans, who think of freedom and equality as complementary rather than conflicting values, often do not notice the clash. When forced to choose between the two, however, Americans are far more likely to choose freedom over equality than are people in other countries.

The conflicts among freedom, order, and equality explain a great deal of the political conflict in the United States. These conflicts also underlie the ideologies that people use to structure their understanding of politics.

1.6 Ideology and the Scope of Government

★ Distinguish among these terms: totalitarianism, socialism, capitalism, libertarianism, and anarchism.

People hold different opinions about the merits of government policies. Sometimes their views are based on self-interest. For example, older citizens are more likely than younger taxpayers to support senior discounts when riding public transportation. Policies also are judged according to individual values and beliefs. Some people hold

political ideology
A consistent set of values and beliefs about the proper purpose and scope of government.

assorted values and beliefs that produce contradictory opinions on government policies. Others organize their opinions into a **political ideology**—a consistent set of values and beliefs about the proper purpose and scope of government.

How far should government go to maintain order, provide public goods, and promote equality? In the United States (as in every other nation), citizens, scholars, and politicians have different answers. We can analyze their positions by referring to philosophies about the proper scope of government—that is, the range of its permissible activities. Imagine a continuum. At one end is the belief that government should do everything; at the other is the belief that government should not exist. These extreme ideologies, from the most government to the least government, and those that fall in between are shown in Figure 1.1.

Totalitarianism

totalitarianism
A political philosophy that advocates unlimited power for the government to enable it to control all sectors of society.

Totalitarianism is the belief that government should have unlimited power. A totalitarian government controls all sectors of society: business, labor, education, religion, sports, and the arts. A true totalitarian favors a network of laws, rules, and regulations that guides every aspect of individual behavior. The object is to produce a perfect society serving some master plan for "the common good." Totalitarianism has reached its terrifying full potential only in literature and films (for example, in George Orwell's *1984,* a novel about "Big Brother" watching everyone), but several societies have come perilously close to "perfection." Think of Germany under Hitler and the Soviet Union under Stalin. Not many people openly profess totalitarianism today, but the concept is useful because it anchors one side of our continuum.

Socialism

socialism
A form of rule in which the central government plays a strong role in regulating existing private industry and directing the economy, although it does allow some private ownership of productive capacity.

Whereas totalitarianism refers to government in general, **socialism** pertains to government's role in the economy. Like communism, socialism is an economic system

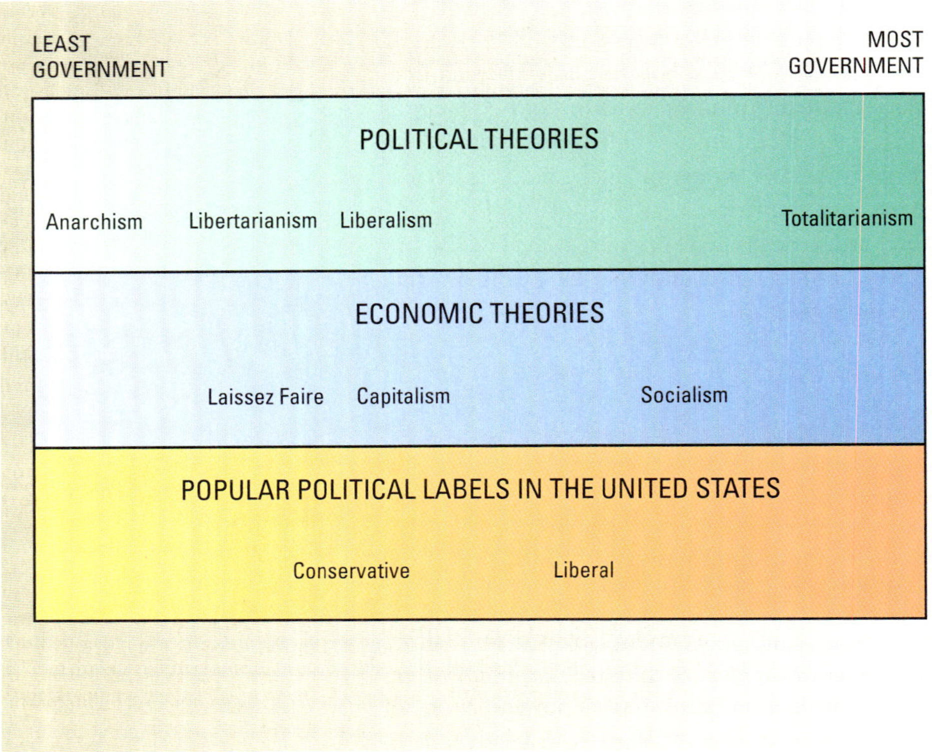

LEAST GOVERNMENT — MOST GOVERNMENT

POLITICAL THEORIES

Anarchism   Libertarianism   Liberalism   Totalitarianism

ECONOMIC THEORIES

Laissez Faire   Capitalism   Socialism

POPULAR POLITICAL LABELS IN THE UNITED STATES

Conservative   Liberal

FIGURE 1.1 Ideology and the Scope of Government

We can classify political ideologies according to the scope of action that people are willing to allow government in dealing with social and economic problems. In this chart, the three rows map out various philosophical positions along an underlying continuum ranging from least to most government. Notice that conventional politics in the United States spans only a narrow portion of the theoretical possibilities for government action. In popular usage, liberals favor a greater scope of government, and conservatives want a narrower scope. But over time, the traditional distinction has eroded and now oversimplifies the differences between liberals and conservatives. Figure 1.2 (p. 24) offers a more discriminating classification of liberals and conservatives.
Source: © Cengage Learning.

based on Marxist theory. Under socialism (and communism), the scope of government extends to ownership or control of the basic industries that produce goods and services. These include communications, mining, heavy industry, transportation, and energy. Although socialism favors a strong role for government in regulating private industry and directing the economy, it allows more room than communism does for private ownership of productive capacity. Many Americans equate socialism with the communism practiced in the old closed societies of the Soviet Union and Eastern Europe. But there is a difference. Although communism in theory was supposed to result in what Marx referred to as a "withering away" of the state, communist governments in practice tended toward totalitarianism, controlling not just economic life but also both political and social life through a dominant party organization. Some socialist governments, however, practice **democratic socialism**. They guarantee civil liberties (such as freedom of speech and freedom of religion) and allow their citizens to determine the extent of the government's activity through free elections and competitive political parties. Outside the United States, socialism is not universally viewed as inherently bad. In fact, the governments of Britain, Sweden, Germany, and France, among other democracies, have at times since World War II been avowedly socialist. More recently, the formerly communist regimes of Eastern Europe have abandoned the controlling role of government in their economies for strong doses of capitalism.

democratic socialism
A socialist form of government that guarantees civil liberties such as freedom of speech and religion. Citizens determine the extent of government activity through free elections and competitive political parties.

Capitalism

Capitalism also relates to the government's role in the economy. In contrast to both socialism and communism, **capitalism** supports free enterprise—private businesses operating without government regulation. Some theorists, most notably the late Nobel Prize–winning economist Milton Friedman, argue that free enterprise is necessary for free politics.[28] This argument, that the economic system of capitalism is essential to democracy, contradicts the tenets of democratic socialism. Whether it is valid depends in part on our understanding of democracy, a subject discussed in Chapter 2. The United States is decidedly a capitalist country, more so than Britain or most other Western nations. Despite the U.S. government's enormous budget, it owns or operates relatively few public enterprises. For example, railroads, airlines, and television stations, which are frequently owned by the government in other countries, are privately owned in the United States. But our government does extend its authority into the economic sphere, regulating private businesses and directing the overall economy. Both American liberals and conservatives embrace capitalism, but they differ on the nature and amount of government intervention in the economy they deem necessary or desirable.

capitalism
The system of government that favors free enterprise (privately owned businesses operating without government regulation).

Libertarianism

Libertarianism opposes all government action except what is necessary to protect life and property. **Libertarians** grudgingly recognize the necessity of government but believe that it should be as limited as possible and should not promote either order or equality. For example, libertarians grant the need for traffic laws to ensure safe and efficient automobile travel. But they oppose laws requiring motorcycle riders to wear helmets, and the libertarian ethos in New Hampshire keeps it the only state not requiring seat belts. Libertarians believe that social programs that provide food, clothing, and shelter are outside the proper scope of government. Helping the needy, they insist, should be a matter of individual choice. Libertarians also oppose government ownership of basic industries; in fact, they oppose any government intervention in

libertarianism
A political ideology that is opposed to all government action except as necessary to protect life and property.

libertarians
Those who are opposed to using government to promote either order or equality.

laissez faire
An economic doctrine that opposes any form of government intervention in business.

the economy. This kind of economic policy is called **laissez faire**, a French phrase that means "let (people) do (as they please)." Such an extreme policy extends beyond the free enterprise that most capitalists advocate.

Libertarians are vocal advocates of hands-off government in both the social and the economic spheres. Whereas Americans who favor a broad scope of government action shun the description *socialist,* libertarians make no secret of their identity. The Libertarian Party ran candidates in every presidential election from 1972 through 2012. However, not one of these candidates won more than 1 million votes.

Do not confuse libertarians with liberals—or with liberalism, the John Locke–inspired doctrine mentioned earlier. The words are similar, but their meanings are quite different. *Libertarianism* draws on *liberty* as its root (following Locke) and means "absence of governmental constraint." While both liberalism and libertarianism leave citizens free to pursue their private goals, libertarianism treats freedom as a pure goal; it's liberalism on steroids. In American political usage, *liberalism* evolved from the root word *liberal* in the sense of "freely," like a liberal serving of butter. Liberals see a positive role for government in helping the disadvantaged. Over time, *liberal* has come to mean something closer to *generous,* in the sense that liberals (but not libertarians) support government spending on social programs. Libertarians find little benefit in any government social program.

Anarchism

anarchism
A political philosophy that opposes government in any form.

Anarchism stands opposite totalitarianism on the political continuum. Anarchists oppose all government in any form. As a political philosophy, anarchism values absolute freedom. Because all government involves some restriction on personal freedom (for example, forcing people to drive on one side of the road), a pure anarchist would object even to traffic laws. Like totalitarianism, anarchism is not a popular philosophy, but it does have adherents on the political fringes.

Anarchists sparked street fights that disrupted meetings of the World Trade Organization (WTO) from Seattle (1999) to Geneva (2009). Labor unions had also protested meetings of the WTO, which writes rules that govern international trade, for failing to include labor rights on its agenda; environmental groups protested its promotion of economic development at the expense of the environment. But anarchists were against the WTO on *principle*—for concentrating the power of multinational corporations in a shadowy "world government." Discussing old and new forms of anarchy, journalist Joseph Kahn said, "Nothing has revived anarchism like globalization."[29] Although anarchism is not a popular philosophy, it is not merely a theoretical category, as anarchists in 2009 protested Obama's inauguration.

© Kevin Downs/Demotix/Corbis

Anarchists at the Inauguration

Anarchism as a philosophy views government as an unnecessary evil. Anarchists operate several websites that oppose capitalism and government in general. Their symbol is a circle and bar surrounding the letter "A." Here is their view of NATO and the world's eight leading economies, called G-8.

Liberals and Conservatives: The Narrow Middle

As shown in Figure 1.1, practical politics in the United States ranges over only the central portion of the continuum. The extreme positions—totalitarianism and anarchism—are rarely argued in public debates. And in this era of distrust of "big government," few American politicians would openly advocate socialism. However, more than 150 people ran for Congress in 2012 as candidates of the Libertarian Party. Although none won, American libertarians are sufficiently vocal to be heard in the debate over the role of government.

Still, most of that debate is limited to a narrow range of political thought. On one side are people commonly called *liberals;* on the other are *conservatives.* In popular usage, liberals favor more government, conservatives less. This distinction is clear when the issue is government spending to provide public goods. Liberals favor generous government support for education, wildlife protection, public transportation, and a whole range of social programs. Conservatives want smaller government budgets and fewer government programs. They support free enterprise and argue against government job programs, regulation of business, and legislation of working conditions and wage rates.

But on other topics, liberals and conservatives reverse their positions. In theory, liberals favor government activism, yet they oppose government regulation of abortion. In theory, conservatives oppose government activism, yet they support government surveillance of telephone conversations to fight terrorism. What's going on? Are American political attitudes hopelessly contradictory, or is something missing in our analysis of these ideologies today? Actually something *is* missing. To understand the liberal and conservative stances on political issues, we must look not only at the scope of government action but also at the purpose of government action. That is, to understand a political ideology, it is necessary to understand how it incorporates the values of freedom, order, and equality.

1.7 American Political Ideologies and the Purpose of Government

★ Explain how liberals, conservatives, libertarians, and communitarians view the role of government.

Much of American politics revolves around the two dilemmas just described: freedom versus order and freedom versus equality. The two dilemmas do not account for all political conflict, but they help us gain insight into the workings of politics and organize the seemingly chaotic world of political events, actors, and issues.

Liberals versus Conservatives: The New Differences

Liberals and conservatives *are* different, but their differences no longer hinge on the narrow question of the government's role in providing public goods. Liberals do favor more spending for public goods and conservatives less, but this is no longer the critical difference between them. Today that difference stems from their attitudes toward the purpose of government. **Conservatives** support the original purpose of government: maintaining social order. They are willing to use the coercive power of the state to force citizens to be orderly. They favor firm police action, swift and severe punishment for criminals, and more laws regulating behavior. Conservatives would not stop with defining, preventing, and punishing crime, however. They tend to want to preserve traditional patterns of social relations—the domestic role of women and business owners' authority to hire whom they wish, for example. For this reason, they do not think government should impose equality.

Liberals are less likely than conservatives to want to use government power to maintain order. In general, liberals are more tolerant of alternative lifestyles—for

conservatives
Those who are willing to use government to promote order but not equality.

liberals
Those who are willing to use government to promote equality but not order.

example, homosexual behavior. Liberals do not shy away from using government coercion, but they use it for a different purpose: to promote equality. They support laws that ensure equal treatment of homosexuals in employment, housing, and education; laws that force private businesses to hire and promote women and members of minority groups; laws that require public transportation to provide equal access to people with disabilities; and laws that order cities and states to reapportion election districts so that minority voters can elect minority candidates to public office. Conservatives do not oppose equality, but they do not value it to the extent of using the government's power to enforce equality. For liberals, the use of that power to promote equality is both valid and necessary.

A Two-Dimensional Classification of Ideologies

To classify liberal and conservative ideologies more accurately, we have to incorporate the values of freedom, order, and equality into the classification.[30] We can do this using the model in Figure 1.2. It depicts the conflicting values along two separate dimensions, each anchored in maximum freedom at the lower left. One dimension extends horizontally from maximum freedom on the left to maximum order on the right. The other extends vertically from maximum freedom at the bottom to maximum equality at the top. Each box represents a different ideological type: libertarians, liberals, conservatives, and communitarians.[31]

Libertarians value freedom more than order or equality. (We will use *libertarians* for people who have libertarian tendencies but may not accept the whole philosophy.)

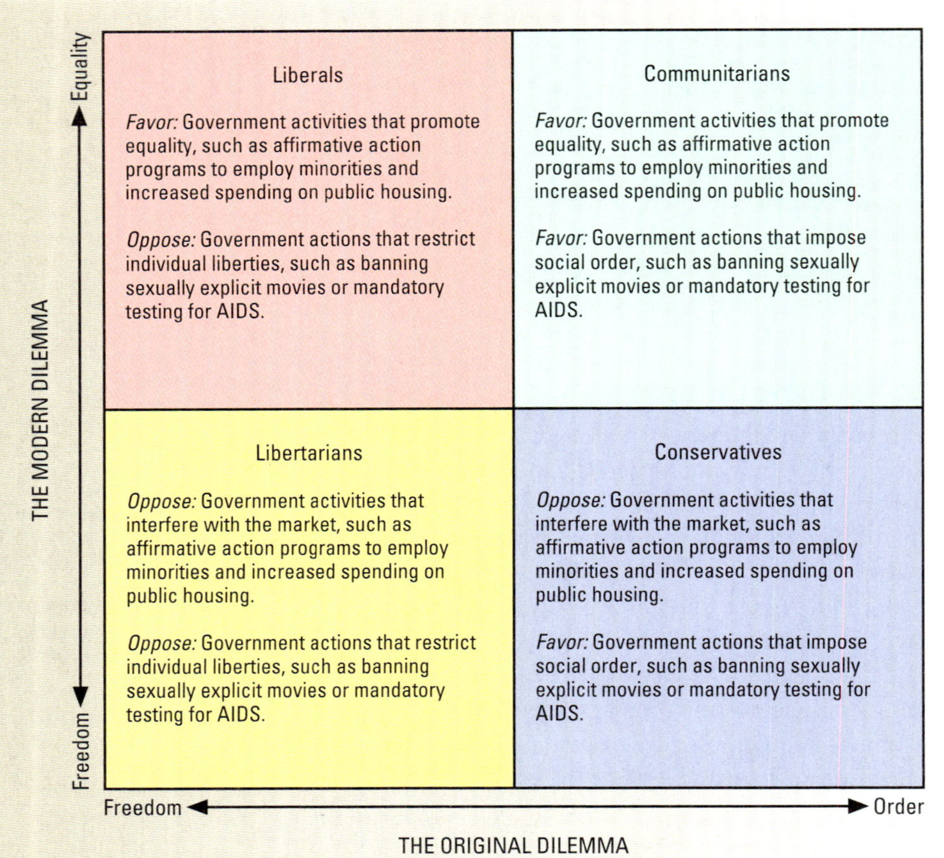

FIGURE 1.2 Ideologies: A Two-Dimensional Framework

The four ideological types are defined by the values they favor in resolving the two major dilemmas of government: how much freedom should be sacrificed in pursuit of order and equality, respectively. Test yourself by thinking about the values that are most important to you. Which box in the figure best represents your combination of values?
Source: © Cengage Learning.

In practical terms, libertarians want minimal government intervention in both the economic and the social spheres. For example, they oppose affirmative action and laws that restrict transmission of sexually explicit material.

Liberals value freedom more than order but not more than equality. They oppose laws that ban sexually explicit publications but support affirmative action. Conservatives value freedom more than equality but would restrict freedom to preserve social order. Conservatives oppose affirmative action but favor laws that restrict pornography.

Finally, we arrive at the ideological type positioned at the upper right in Figure 1.2. This group values both equality and order more than freedom. Its members support both affirmative action and laws that restrict pornography. We will call this new group **communitarians**.[32] The term is used narrowly in contemporary politics to reflect the philosophy of the Communitarian Network, a political movement founded by sociologist Amitai Etzioni.[33] This movement rejects both the liberal–conservative classification and the libertarian argument that "individuals should be left on their own to pursue their choices, rights, and self-interests."[34] Like liberals, Etzioni's communitarians believe that there is a role for government in helping the disadvantaged. Like conservatives, they believe that government should be used to promote moral values—preserving the family through more stringent divorce laws, protecting against AIDS through testing programs, and limiting the dissemination of pornography, for example.[35]

The Communitarian Network is not dedicated to big government, however. According to its platform, "The government should step in only to the extent that other social subsystems fail rather than seek to replace them."[36] Nevertheless, in recognizing the collective nature of society, the network's platform clearly distinguishes its philosophy from that of libertarianism:

> It has been argued by libertarians that responsibilities are a personal matter, that individuals are to judge which responsibilities they accept as theirs. As we see it, responsibilities are anchored in community. Reflecting the diverse moral voices of their citizens, responsive communities define what is expected of people; they educate their members to accept these values; and they praise them when they do and frown upon them when they do not.[37]

Although it clearly embraces the Communitarian Network's philosophy, our definition of communitarian (small *c*) is broader and more in keeping with the dictionary definition. Thus, communitarians favor government programs that promote both order and equality, somewhat in keeping with socialist theory.[38]

By analyzing political ideologies on two dimensions rather than one, we can explain why people can seem to be liberal on one issue (favoring a broader scope of government action) and conservative on another (favoring less government action). The answer hinges on the purpose of a given government action: Which value does it promote: order or equality?[39] According to our typology, only libertarians and communitarians are consistent in their attitude toward the scope of government activity, whatever its purpose. Libertarians value freedom so highly that they oppose most government efforts to enforce either order or equality. Communitarians (in our usage) are inclined to trade freedom for both order and equality. Liberals and conservatives, on the other hand, favor or oppose government activity depending on its purpose. As you will learn in Chapter 5, large groups of Americans fall into each of the four ideological categories. Because Americans increasingly choose four different resolutions to the original and modern dilemmas of government, the simple labels of *liberal* and *conservative* no longer describe contemporary political ideologies as well as they did in the 1930s, 1940s, and 1950s.

communitarians
Those who are willing to use government to promote both order and equality.

SUMMARY

The challenge of democracy lies in making difficult choices—choices that inevitably bring important values into conflict. This chapter has outlined a normative framework for analyzing the policy choices that arise in the pursuit of the purposes of government in an era of globalization.

1.1 The Globalization of American Government

- We live in an era of globalization—a term for the increasing interdependence of citizens and nations across the world. Globalization infringes on national sovereignty, the right of governments to govern their people as they wish. Global forces generate pressures for economic trade, observance of human rights, and governance by international law.
- More than ever before, foreign affairs affect American government, and American politics affects government in other nations.

1.2 The Purposes of Government

- Government requires citizens to surrender some freedom as part of being governed. People do so to obtain the benefits of government: maintaining order, providing public goods, and—more controversially—promoting equality.

1.3 A Conceptual Framework for Analyzing Government

- Political concepts are generalized ideas about government and politics. They provide broader views than those offered by examining specific political events.
- Our conceptual framework consists of five concepts organized into two groups: concepts that identify values pursued by government: freedom, order, and equality; and concepts that describe models of democratic government: majoritarian and pluralist democracy.

1.4 The Concepts of Freedom, Order, and Equality

- The terms *freedom, order,* and *equality* have varied connotations in American politics. *Freedom* and *equality* are positive terms that mean different things to different people at different times. *Order* has negative connotations for many because it symbolizes government intrusion into private lives.
- *Freedom* can be used in two major senses: freedom of and freedom from. We use it in the "freedom of" sense. Freedom of speech means freedom to speak.
- *Order* in politics means more than preserving life and property; it also means established patterns of authority in society and traditional modes of behavior.
- *Equality* in politics can be viewed narrowly as political equality (each person having one vote) or as social equality (equality in wealth, education, and status). It can also be viewed as equality of opportunity or of outcome.

1.5 Two Dilemmas of Government

- The conflict between the values of freedom and order represents the original dilemma of government.
- The modern dilemma of politics is the conflict between the values of freedom and equality.

1.6 Ideology and the Scope of Government

- Political ideology is defined as a consistent set of values and beliefs about the proper purpose and scope of government. Ideologies differ about the proper range of permissible activities.
- Totalitarianism is the belief that government should have unlimited power. Socialism extends the scope of government to ownership or control of the basic industries that produce goods and services. Capitalism is committed to free enterprise—private businesses operating without government regulation. Libertarianism opposes all government action except what is necessary to protect life and property. Anarchists oppose all government in any form.
- In the United States, most political debate is limited to a narrow range of political thought. On one side are *liberals;* on the other are *conservatives.*

1.7 **American Political Ideologies and the Purpose of Government**

- In popular usage, liberals favor more government, and conservatives less. That is, liberals support a broader role for government than do conservatives.
- Liberals and conservatives mainly quarrel over the purpose of government action. Conservatives may want less government, but they are willing to use the government's coercive power to impose social order. Liberals too are willing to use the coercive power of government, but for the purpose of promoting equality.
- Liberals value freedom more than order and equality more than freedom. Conservatives value order more than freedom and freedom more than equality. Libertarians choose freedom over both order and equality. Communitarians are willing to sacrifice freedom for both order and equality.

ASSESSING YOUR UNDERSTANDING WITH APLIA...YOUR VIRTUAL TUTOR!

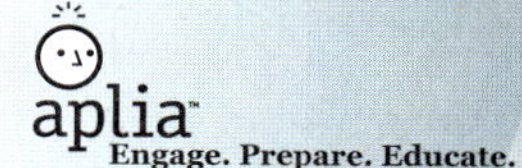

1.1 **Define globalization and explain how globalization affects American politics and government.**

1. What is globalization? Give an example.
2. Give an example of globalization's effect on American politics.
3. Give an example of the American government's effects on foreign politics.

1.2 **Identify the purposes that government serves and trace their historical roots.**

1. What are the major purposes of government, and which is most controversial?

1.3 **Describe how political scientists use concepts to structure events and promote understanding.**

1. What is a concept, and how does the use of concepts promote understanding?

1.4 **Define freedom, order, and equality and discuss the various interpretations of each value.**

1. Which of these concepts is linked most closely to the police power of a state?
2. Which is most closely linked to the concept of rights, and why?

1.5 **Analyze the inherent conflicts between freedom versus order and freedom versus equality.**

1. What are the two dilemmas of government, and which came first?
2. Which dilemma underlies the 1960 law requiring paying men and women the same rate for equal work? Why is it a dilemma?

1.6 **Distinguish among these terms: totalitarianism, socialism, capitalism, libertarianism, and anarchism.**

1. How do the terms *libertarianism*, *liberalism*, and *liberals* differ? In what ways are these terms similar?
2. Give an example of anarchism in contemporary American politics.

1.7 **Compare and contrast how liberals, conservatives, libertarians, and communitarians view the role of government.**

1. How can both liberals and conservatives favor greater scope of government?
2. What contemporary politicians exemplify the typological categories of liberal, conservative, libertarian, and communitarian?

2 Majoritarian or Pluralist Democracy?

 and Learning Outcomes

aplia
Engage. Prepare. Educate.

2.1 The Theory of Democratic Government
★ Distinguish between the two theories of democratic government used in political science: procedural and substantive.

2.2 Institutional Models of Democracy
★ Compare and contrast the majoritarian and pluralist models of democracy.

2.3 The Global Trend Toward Democracy
★ Evaluate the challenges facing countries trying to move toward a democratic form of government.

"We are the 99%!"

Their slogan was evocative and their method of protesting unusual. The Occupy Wall Street demonstrators brought tents and sleeping bags to Zuccotti Park, near Wall Street in New York City, and in September of 2011 they created a small encampment. The protestors claimed to represent the 99 percent of Americans who possess no special advantages in American society. The other 1 percent were defined as greedy financiers who have profited immensely during the recent economic downturn.

Occupy Wall Street protestors believed that the political and economic system is rigged in favor of the very rich. Amanda Clarke, a college student, said she was angry "because I don't have millions of dollars to give to my representative, so my voice is invalidated. And the fact that I'm graduating with tens of thousands of dollars in loans and there's no job market."[1]

The small encampment was composed of those who were unemployed, college students, retirees, leftist ideologues, and some who could only be described as just plain fed up. Occupy Wall Street caught the nation's attention—no small feat—and across the country, from Boston to Los Angeles, many other Occupy camps sprouted up.[2] The primary issue the protestors pushed forward, income inequality, is very real. Aggregate figures indicate that the gap between the wealthiest and the rest

of the population has grown. Yet the movement's political message didn't go much beyond its simple slogan about the 99 percent.

The Occupy movement stalled quickly as it made little effort to build organizations outside of the encampments. Occupy Wall Street's website boasted that the organization was "leaderless" and freely acknowledged that protestors had varying priorities in terms of what the American government ought to be addressing.[3]

Within a few months, most of the Occupy encampments were cleared out by local police. Given its leaderless structure, it's not surprising that the movement had difficulty establishing a second act. Even though the Occupy movement has drifted away, it can be credited with stimulating increased debate about income inequality in America. At the same time, it's not at all clear as to how equal income ought to be. In a free market economy, what constitutes a fair distribution of income? Occupy Wall Street didn't answer that question.

Since there's no clear answer as to what level of income inequality is acceptable, it's easy to dismiss the protestors' claim that they represented 99 percent of Americans. Yet the protestors were raising a broader criticism: that the political system doesn't really represent the majority of Americans. Polls do show that a majority of Americans want the wealthier taxed more, which would reduce income inequality.[4] Congress refuses to enact such a change, primarily because Republican legislators stand steadfastly against increasing taxes. Can we conclude that the Republicans are acting against the majority? Not quite so fast. In November of the previous year, less than a year before the Occupy movement took hold, Republicans won a landslide in the congressional elections.

Determining who is in the majority and what that majority wants are not simple tasks. Does this country really operate as a majoritarian democracy? Or is there an alternative way of understanding American democracy?

2.1 The Theory of Democratic Government

★ Distinguish between the two theories of democratic government used in political science: procedural and substantive.

The origins of democratic theory lie in ancient Greek political thought. Greek philosophers classified governments according to the number of citizens involved in the process. Imagine a continuum running from rule by one person, through rule by a few, to rule by many.

At one extreme is an **autocracy**, in which one individual has the power to make all important decisions. The concentration of power in the hands of one person (usually a monarch) was a more common form of government in earlier historical periods, although some countries are still ruled autocratically.

Oligarchy puts government power in the hands of an elite. At one time, the nobility or the major landowners commonly ruled as an aristocracy. Today, military leaders are often the rulers in countries governed by an oligarchy.

At the other extreme of the continuum is **democracy**, which means "rule by the people." Most scholars believe that the United States, Britain, France, and other countries in Western Europe are genuine democracies. Critics contend that these countries only appear to be democracies: although they hold free elections, they are actually run by wealthy business elites, out for their own benefit.

The Meaning and Symbolism of Democracy

Americans have a simple answer to the question "Who should govern?" It is "The people." Unfortunately, this answer is too simple. It fails to define who *the people* are. Should we include young children? Recent immigrants? Illegal aliens? This answer also fails to tell us how the people should do the governing. Should they be assembled in a stadium? Vote by mail? Choose others to govern for them? We need to take a closer look at what "government by the people" really means.

The word *democracy* originated in Greek writings around the fifth century B.C. *Demos* referred to the common people, the masses; *kratos* meant "power." The ancient Greeks were afraid of democracy—rule by rank-and-file citizens. That fear is evident in the term *demagogue*. We use that term today to refer to a politician who appeals to and often deceives the masses by manipulating their emotions and prejudices.

Many centuries after the Greeks defined democracy, the idea still carried the connotation of mob rule. When George Washington was president, opponents of a new political

autocracy
A system of government in which the power to govern is concentrated in the hands of one individual.

oligarchy
A system of government in which power is concentrated in the hands of a few people.

democracy
A system of government in which, in theory, the people rule, either directly or indirectly.

party disparagingly called it a *democratic* party. No one would do that in politics today. In fact, the term has become so popular that the names of more than 20 percent of the world's political parties contain some variation of the word *democracy*.[5] Americans reflexively support democracy as the best form of government but are less certain of what democracy entails or of alternative models of democracy.

There are two major schools of thought about what constitutes democracy. The first believes democracy is a form of government. It emphasizes the procedures that enable the people to govern: meeting to discuss issues, voting in elections, running for public office. The second sees democracy in the substance of government policies, in freedom of religion and the provision for human needs.[6] The procedural approach focuses on how decisions are made; the substantive approach is concerned with what government does.

Dennis Brack/Newscom

Time to Vote

However majorities may be formed, they must be expressed in our legislative system through the roll call of members. In the House of Representatives the scoreboard lists who has or has not participated during the open period for casting votes. The act of voting is done electronically and must be done on the floor of the House.

The Procedural View of Democracy

Procedural democratic theory sets forth principles that describe how government should make decisions. The principles address three distinct questions:

1. *Who* should participate in decision making?
2. *How much* should each participant's vote count?
3. *How many* votes are needed to reach a decision?

According to procedural democratic theory, all adults should participate in government decision making; everyone within the boundaries of the political community should be allowed to vote. If some people, such as recent immigrants, are prohibited from participating, they are excluded only for practical or political reasons. The theory of democracy itself does not exclude any adults from participation. We refer to this principle as **universal participation**.

How much should each participant's vote count? According to procedural theory, all votes should be counted *equally*. This is the principle of **political equality**.

Note that universal participation and political equality are two distinct principles. It is not enough for everyone to participate in a decision; all votes must carry equal weight. President Abraham Lincoln reportedly once took a vote among his cabinet members and found that they all opposed his position on an issue. He summarized the vote and the decision this way: "Seven noes, one aye—the ayes have it."[7] Everyone participated, but Lincoln's vote counted more than all the others combined. (No one ever said that presidents have to run their cabinets democratically.)

Finally, how many votes are needed to reach a decision? Procedural theory prescribes that a group should decide to do what the majority of its participants (a minimum of 50 percent plus one person) wants to do. This principle is called **majority rule**. (If participants divide over more than two alternatives and none receives a simple majority, the principle usually defaults to *plurality rule*, under which the group does what most participants want.)

procedural democratic theory
A view of democracy as being embodied in a decision-making process that involves universal participation, political equality, majority rule, and responsiveness.

universal participation
The concept that everyone in a democracy should participate in governmental decision making.

political equality
Equality in political decision making: one vote per person, with all votes counted equally.

majority rule
The principle—basic to procedural democratic theory— that the decision of a group must reflect the preference of more than half of those participating; a simple majority.

J.D. Pooley/Getty Images

Let the People Decide

After the Ohio state legislature passed a law restricting labor union organizing rights, union backers succeeded in putting an initiative on the statewide ballot. The union demonstration depicted reflected a broader animosity toward the law and when citizens subsequently got to vote, they decisively overturned the new statute.

A Complication: Direct Versus Indirect Democracy

The three principles of universal participation, political equality, and majority rule are widely recognized as necessary for democratic decision making. Small, simple societies can meet these principles with a direct or **participatory democracy**, in which all members of the group, rather than representatives they elect to govern on their behalf, meet to make decisions, observing political equality and majority rule.[8] The origins of participatory democracy go back to the Greek city-state, where the important decisions of government were made by the adult citizens meeting in an assembly. The people ruled themselves rather than having a small number of notables rule on their behalf. (In Athens, the people who were permitted to attend the assemblies did not include women, slaves, and those whose families had not lived there for generations. Thus, participation was not universal. Still, the Greek city-state represented a dramatic transformation in the theory of government.)[9]

participatory democracy
A system of government where rank-and-file citizens rule themselves rather than electing representatives to govern on their behalf.

Something close to participatory democracy is practiced in some New England towns, where rank-and-file citizens gather in a town meeting, often just once a year, to make key community decisions together. A town meeting is impractical in large cities, although some cities have incorporated participatory democracy in their decision-making processes by instituting forms of neighborhood government. For example, in Birmingham, Alabama; Dayton, Ohio; Portland, Oregon; and St. Paul, Minnesota, each area of the city is governed by a neighborhood council. The neighborhood councils have authority over zoning and land use questions, and they usually control some funds for the development of projects within their boundaries. All adult residents of a neighborhood may participate in the neighborhood council meetings, and the larger city government respects their decisions.[10]

Citizens warmly embrace the concept of participatory democracy.[11] Yet in the United States and virtually all other democracies, participatory democracy is rare. Few cities have decentralized their governments and turned power over to their neighborhoods. Participatory democracy is commonly rejected on the grounds that in large, complex societies, we need professional, full-time government officials to study problems, formulate solutions, and administer programs. Also, the assumption is that relatively few people will take part in participatory government. This, in fact, turns out to be the case. In a study of neighborhood councils in the cities mentioned above, only 16.6 percent of residents took part in at least one meeting during a two-year period.[12] In other respects, participatory democracy works rather well on the neighborhood level. Yet even if participatory democracy is appropriate for neighborhoods or small towns, how could it work for the national government? We cannot all gather at the Capitol in Washington to decide defense policy.

e-government
Online communication channels that enable citizens to easily obtain information from government and facilitate the expression of opinions to government officials.

New technologies have raised hopes that e-government might facilitate greater public involvement. **E-government** refers to the online communications channels that enable rank-and-file citizens to acquire information and documents as well as to register opinions and complaints to government officials.[13] E-government has made it much easier for citizens to find out about various government programs and services. For example, documents explaining government services in languages other than English can sometimes be found at a city hall website. Some states even permit a person to file a criminal complaint online. In Missouri, for example, the website for the state attorney general includes a form residents can fill out to inform the attorney general that some land site or property owner is violating environmental laws.[14]

E-government is a long way from e-democracy. So far it has not facilitated greater public deliberation and has expanded public involvement in only marginal ways. Still, it does make it easier to write your congressman (or state representative, or mayor, or whomever), so it does offer people a quick and convenient way to voice their opinions. Governments at all levels are experimenting with new forms of e-government in the hope that, over time, it will engage citizens more directly in the governmental process.

The framers of the U.S. Constitution had their own conception of democracy. They instituted **representative democracy**, a system in which citizens participate in government by electing public officials to make decisions on their behalf. Elected officials are expected to represent the voters' views and interests—that is, to serve as the agents of the citizenry and act for them.

Within the context of representative democracy, we adhere to the principles of universal participation, political equality, and majority rule to guarantee that elections are democratic. But what happens after the election? The elected representatives might not make the decisions the people would have made had they gathered for the same purpose. To account for this possibility in representative government, procedural theory provides a fourth decision-making principle: **responsiveness**. Elected representatives should respond to public opinion—what the majority of people wants. This does not mean that legislators simply cast their ballots on the basis of whether the people back home want alternative A or alternative B. Issues are not usually so straightforward. Rather, responsiveness means following the general contours of public opinion in formulating complex pieces of legislation.[15] By adding responsiveness to deal with the case of indirect democracy, we have four principles of procedural democracy:

- Universal participation
- Political equality
- Majority rule
- Government responsiveness to public opinion

The Substantive View of Democracy

According to procedural theory, the principle of responsiveness is absolute. The government should do what the majority wants, regardless of what that is. At first, this seems to be a reasonable way to protect the rights of citizens in a representative democracy. But think for a minute. Christians are the vast majority of the U.S. population. Suppose that the Christian majority backs a constitutional amendment to require Bible reading in public schools, that the amendment is passed by Congress, and that it is ratified by the states. From a strictly procedural view, the action would be democratic. But what about freedom of religion? What about the rights of minorities? To limit the government's responsiveness to public opinion, we must look outside procedural democratic theory to substantive democratic theory.

representative democracy
A system of government where citizens elect public officials to govern on their behalf.

responsiveness
A decision-making principle, necessitated by representative government, that implies that elected representatives should do what the majority of people wants.

substantive democratic theory
The view that democracy is embodied in the substance of government policies rather than in the policymaking procedure.

Substantive democratic theory focuses on the *substance* of government policies, not on the procedures followed in making those policies. It argues that in a democratic government, certain principles must be incorporated into government policies. Substantive theorists would reject a law that requires Bible reading in schools because it would violate a substantive principle, freedom of religion. The core of our substantive principles of democracy is embedded in the Bill of Rights and other amendments to the Constitution.

In defining the principles that underlie democratic government—and the policies of that government—most substantive theorists agree on a basic criterion: government policies should guarantee civil liberties (freedom of behavior, such as freedom of religion and freedom of expression) and civil rights (powers or privileges that government may not arbitrarily deny to individuals, such as protection against discrimination in employment and housing). According to this standard, the claim that the United States is a democracy rests on its record of ensuring its citizens these liberties and rights. (We look at how good this record is in Chapters 15 and 16.)

Agreement among substantive theorists breaks down when the discussion moves from civil rights to social rights (adequate health care, quality education, decent housing) and economic rights (private property, steady employment). Ordinary citizens divide on these matters too (see Figure 2.1). Theorists disagree most sharply on whether a government must promote social equality to qualify as a democracy. For example, must a state guarantee unemployment benefits and adequate public housing to be called democratic? Some insist that policies that promote social equality are essential to democratic government. Others restrict the requirements of substantive democracy to policies that safeguard civil liberties and civil rights. Americans differ considerably from the citizens of most other Western democracies in their view of the government's responsibility to provide social policies. In most other Western democracies, there is much more support for the view that jobs and incomes for the unemployed are a right.[16]

A theorist's political ideology tends to explain his or her position on what democracy really requires in substantive policies. Conservative theorists have a narrow view of the scope of democratic government and a narrow view of the social and economic

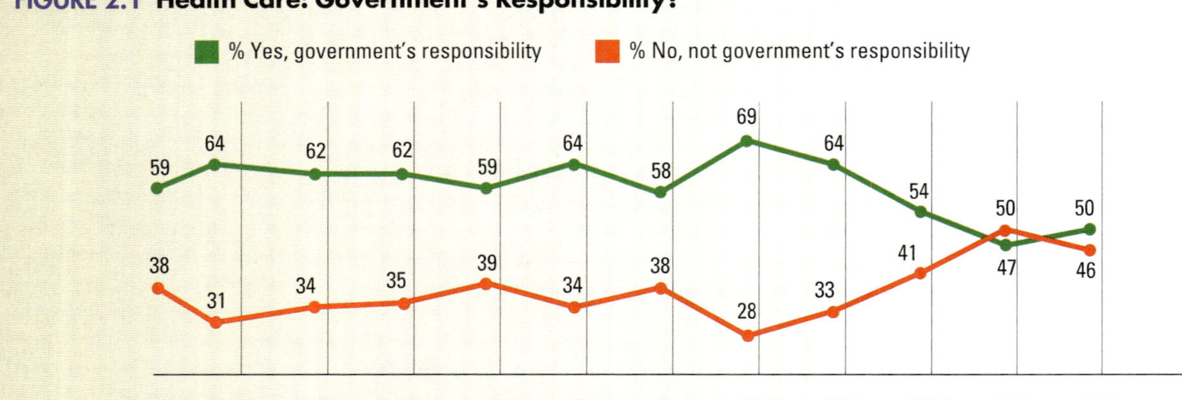

FIGURE 2.1 Health Care: Government's Responsibility?

Is health care a right in a democracy like ours? Opinions change over time and, interestingly, support for the position that health care is government's responsibility began to drop before Barack Obama took office. There's a sharp partisan split, with Republicans more antagonistic toward a government role in health care and Democrats more supportive.

Source: Gallup Poll, "More in U.S. Say Health Coverage Is Not Gov't. Responsibility," 13 November 2009. Copyright © 2009 Gallup, Inc. All rights reserved. The content is used with permission; however, Gallup retains all right of republication.

rights guaranteed by that government. Liberal theorists believe that a democratic government should guarantee its citizens a much broader spectrum of social and economic rights.

Procedural Democracy Versus Substantive Democracy

The problem with the substantive view of democracy is that it does not provide clear, precise criteria that allow us to determine whether a government is democratic. It is, in fact, open to unending arguments over which government policies are truly democratic. Substantive theorists are free to promote their pet values—separation of church and state, guaranteed employment, equal rights for women—under the guise of substantive democracy. When Americans are asked to define democracy in their own terms, roughly two-thirds mention freedoms, rights, or liberties. Relatively few describe democracy in terms of the political process or social benefits.[17]

The procedural viewpoint also has a problem. Although it presents specific criteria for democratic government, those criteria can produce undesirable social policies, such as those that harm minorities. This clashes with **minority rights**, the idea that all citizens are entitled to certain things that cannot be denied by the majority. Opinions proliferate on what those "certain things" are, but nearly everyone in the United States would agree, for example, on freedom of religion. One way to protect minority rights is to limit the principle of majority rule—by requiring a two-thirds majority or some other extraordinary majority for decisions on certain subjects, for example. Another way is to put the issue in the Constitution, beyond the reach of majority rule.

minority rights
The benefits of government that cannot be denied to any citizen by majority decisions.

The issue of prayer in school is a good example of the limits on majority rule. No matter how large, majorities in Congress cannot pass a law to permit organized prayer in public schools because the U.S. Supreme Court has determined that the Constitution forbids such a law. The Constitution could be changed so that it would no longer protect religious minorities, but amending the Constitution is a cumbersome process that involves extraordinary majorities. When limits such as these are put on the principle of majority rule, the minority often rules instead.

Clearly, then, procedural democracy and substantive democracy are not always compatible. In choosing one instead of the other, we are also choosing to focus on either procedures or policies. As authors of this text, we favor a compromise. On the whole, we favor the procedural conception of democracy because it more closely approaches the classical definition of democracy: "government by the people." And procedural democracy is founded on clear, well-established rules for decision making. But the theory has a serious drawback: it allows a democratic government to enact policies that can violate the substantive principles of democracy. Thus, pure procedural democracy should be diluted so that minority rights and civil liberties are guaranteed as part of the structure of government. If the compromise seems familiar, it is: the approach has been used in the course of American history to balance legitimate minority and majority interests.

★ 2.2 Institutional Models of Democracy

★ Compare and contrast the majoritarian and pluralist models of democracy.

A small group can agree to make democratic decisions directly by using the principles of universal participation, political equality, and majority rule. But even the smallest nations have too many citizens to permit participatory democracy at the national level. If nations want democracy, they must achieve it through some form of representative government, electing officials to make decisions. Even then, democratic government is not guaranteed. Governments must have a way to determine what the people want, as well as some way to translate those wants into decisions. In other words, democratic government requires institutional mechanisms—established procedures and organizations—to translate public opinion into government policy (and thus be responsive). Elections, political parties, legislatures, and interest groups (which we discuss in later chapters) are all examples of institutional mechanisms in politics.

Some democratic theorists favor institutions that closely tie government decisions to the desires of the majority of citizens. If most citizens want laws banning the sale of pornography, the government should outlaw pornography. If citizens want more money spent on defense and less on social welfare (or vice versa), the government should act accordingly. For these theorists, the essence of democratic government is majority rule and responsiveness.

Other theorists place less importance on the principles of majority rule and responsiveness. They do not believe in relying heavily on mass opinion; instead, they favor institutions that allow groups of citizens to defend their interests in the public policymaking process. Global warming is a good example. Everyone cares about it, but it is a complex problem with many competing issues at stake. What is critical here is to allow differing interests to participate so that all sides have the opportunity to influence policies as they are developed.

Both schools hold a procedural view of democracy, but they differ in how they interpret "government by the people." We can summarize the theoretical positions by using two alternative models of democracy. As a model, each is a hypothetical plan, a blueprint for achieving democratic government through institutional mechanisms. The majoritarian model values participation by the people in general; the pluralist model values participation by the people in groups.

majoritarian model of democracy
The classical theory of democracy in which government by the people is interpreted as government by the majority of the people.

The Majoritarian Model of Democracy

The **majoritarian model of democracy** relies on our intuitive, elemental notion of what is fair. It interprets "government by the people" to mean government by the *majority* of the people. The majoritarian model tries to approximate the people's role in a direct democracy within the limitations of representative government. To force the government to respond to public opinion, the majoritarian model depends on several mechanisms that allow the people to participate directly.

The popular election of government officials is the primary mechanism for democratic government in the majoritarian model. Citizens are expected to control their representatives' behavior by choosing wisely in the

Now *That's a* Town Meeting

For almost 700 years, citizens of Appenzell Inner-Rhodes, the smallest canton (like a township) in Switzerland, have gathered in the town square on the last Sunday in April to make political decisions by raised hands. At a recent meeting, Appenzellers adopted a leash law for dogs, approved updating property files on a computer, chose a new building commissioner, and acted on other public business before adjourning until the next year.

REUTERS / Arnd Wiegmann

first place and by reelecting or voting out public officials according to their perform-ance. Elections fulfill the first three principles of procedural democratic theory: uni-versal participation, political equality, and majority rule. The prospect of reelection and the threat of defeat at the polls are expected to motivate public officials to meet the fourth criterion: responsiveness.

Usually we think of elections only as mechanisms for choosing among candi-dates for public office. Majoritarian theorists also see them as a means for deciding government policies. An election on a policy issue is called a *referendum*. When citi-zens circulate petitions and gather a required minimum number of signatures to put a policy question on a ballot, it is called an *initiative*. Twenty-one states allow their legislatures to put referenda before the voters and give their citizens the right to place initiatives on the ballot. Five other states provide for one mechanism or the other. Eighteen states also allow the *recall* of state officials, a means of forcing a spe-cial election for an up-or-down vote on a sitting governor or state judge. Like initia-tives, a specified percentage of registered voters must sign a petition asking that a vote be held.[18]

Statewide initiatives and referenda have been used to decide a wide variety of im-portant questions, many with national implications. Although they are instruments of majoritarian democracy, initiatives are often sponsored by interest groups trying to mobilize broad-based support for a particular policy. In the spring of 2011, the Republican-controlled legislature in Ohio passed a law designed to restrict unions representing municipal workers like police or school teachers. This angered many there, and an initiative placed the issue on the ballot for a statewide election in November of the same year. A clear majority (61 percent) voted to overturn the law.[19]

In the United States, no provisions exist for referenda at the federal level. Some other countries do allow policy questions to be put before the public. In a national referendum in 2009, a clear majority of voters in Switzerland voted to ban construc-tion of minarets on any of the country's mosques. (Minarets are the thin spires atop a mosque.) This vote was clearly hostile to the country's small (5 percent) Muslim population. One of the dangers of referenda is the power of the majority to treat a minority in a harsh or intimidating way.[20]

The majoritarian model contends that citizens can control their government if they have adequate mechanisms for popular participation. It also assumes that citi-zens are knowledgeable about government and politics, that they want to participate in the political process, and that they make rational decisions in voting for their elected representatives.

Critics contend that Americans are not knowledgeable enough for majoritarian democracy to work. They point to research that shows that only 36 percent of a national sample of voters said that they follow news about politics "very closely."[21] Two scholars who have studied citizens' interest in politics conclude that most Amer-icans favor "stealth" democracy, noting, "The kind of government people want is one in which ordinary people do not have to get involved."[22] If most citizens feel that way, then majoritarian democracy is not viable, even with the wonders of modern in-formation technology.

Defenders of majoritarian democracy respond that although individual Ameri-cans may have only limited knowledge of or interest in government, the American public as a whole still has coherent and stable opinions on major policy questions. Public opinion does not fluctuate sharply or erratically, and change in the nation's views usually emerges incrementally. People can hold broad if imprecise values that are manifested in the way they vote and in the opinions they express on particular issues.

My Moms Got Married!

After the California Supreme Court ruled that gay marriage was to be allowed in that state, 18,000 same sex couples wed. This included Tori (left) and Kate Kendall, who brought their five-month-old, Zadie, to the ceremony. Five months after the court decision, however, voters passed an initiative (Proposition 8) that banned gay marriage in California. Same sex marriage supporters then took the case to federal court, and in August of 2010, a judge overturned the initiative because he believed that it instituted a discriminatory framework that had no "rational basis." Opponents of gay marriage were incensed and argued that the will of the people should be paramount. The case is now on appeal.

David McNew/Getty Images

An Alternative Model: Pluralist Democracy

For years, political scientists struggled valiantly to reconcile the majoritarian model of democracy with polls that showed widespread ignorance of politics among the American people. When 40 percent of the adult population doesn't even bother to vote in presidential elections, our form of democracy seems to be "government by *some* of the people."

The 1950s saw the evolution of an alternative interpretation of democracy, one tailored to the limited knowledge and participation of the real electorate, not an ideal one. It was based on the concept of *pluralism*—that modern society consists of innumerable groups that share economic, religious, ethnic, or cultural interests. Often people with similar interests organize formal groups—the Future Farmers of America, chambers of commerce, and animal protection groups are examples. Many social groups have little contact with government, but occasionally they find themselves backing or opposing government policies. An organized group that seeks to influence government policy is called an **interest group**. Many interest groups regularly spend much time and money trying to influence government policy (see Chapter 10). Among them are the International Brotherhood of Electrical Workers, the American Hospital Association, the National Association of Manufacturers, and the National Organization for Women.

The **pluralist model of democracy** interprets "government by the people" to mean government by people operating through competing interest groups. According to this model, democracy exists when many (plural) organizations operate separately from the government, press their interests on the government, and even challenge the government. Compared with majoritarian thinking, pluralist theory shifts the focus of democratic government from the mass electorate to organized groups. The criterion for democratic government changes from responsiveness to mass public opinion to responsiveness to organized groups of citizens.

The two major mechanisms in a pluralist democracy are interest groups and a decentralized structure of government that provides ready access to public officials and is open to hearing the groups' arguments for or against government policies. In a centralized structure, decisions are made at one point: the top of the hierarchy. The few decision makers at the top are too busy to hear the claims of competing interest groups or consider those claims in making their decisions. But a decentralized, complex government structure offers the access and openness necessary for pluralist democracy. For pluralists, the ideal system is one that divides government authority among numerous institutions with overlapping authority. Under such a system, competing interest groups have alternative points of access for presenting and arguing their claims.

interest group
An organized group of individuals that seeks to influence public policy; also called a *lobby*.

pluralist model of democracy
An interpretation of democracy in which government by the people is taken to mean government by people operating through competing interest groups.

Although many scholars have contributed to the model, pluralist democracy is most closely identified with political scientist Robert Dahl. According to Dahl, the fundamental axiom of pluralist democracy is that "instead of a single center of sovereign power there must be multiple centers of power, none of which is or can be wholly sovereign."[23] Some watchwords of pluralist democracy, therefore, are *divided authority, decentralization*, and *open access*.

On one level, pluralism is alive and well. As will be demonstrated in Chapter 10, interest groups in Washington are thriving, and the rise of many citizen groups has broadened representation beyond traditional business, labor, and professional groups. At the same time, the interest group system is not one that provides equal representation for all. Not surprisingly, the best represented sectors are those representing those who are in business or the professions. Those whose representation is relatively poor are low-income Americans and those who are most marginal in American society.[24]

The Majoritarian Model Versus the Pluralist Model

In majoritarian democracy, the mass public—not interest groups—controls government actions. The citizenry must therefore have some understanding of government and be willing to participate in the electoral process. Majoritarian democracy relies on electoral mechanisms that harness the power of the majority to make decisions. Conclusive elections and a centralized structure of government are mechanisms that aid majority rule. Cohesive political parties with well-defined programs also contribute to majoritarian democracy because they offer voters a clear way to distinguish alternative sets of policies. In terms of Congress, American parties are becoming more majoritarian as there is more unity among both Republicans and Democrats (see Figure 2.2).

Pluralism does not demand much knowledge from citizens in general. It requires specialized knowledge only from groups of citizens, in particular their leaders. In contrast to majoritarian democracy, pluralist democracy seeks to limit majority

FIGURE 2.2 Rising Majoritarianism

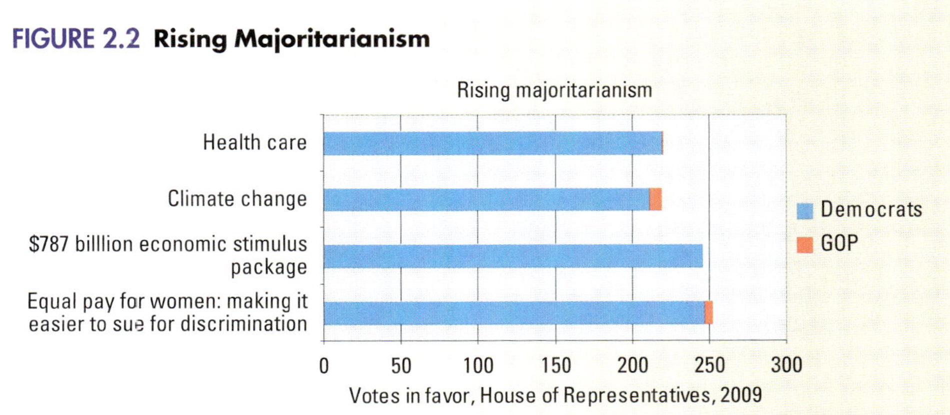

For some years now, our two congressional parties have been increasingly polarized. There is less in the way of bipartisanship—parties working together to fashion compromise legislation. Some people believe that this trend is a good thing as voters have a clear choice. Others believe that we do better as a country when our two parties moderate their ideologies and come together to fashion solutions that can bridge the gap between left and right.

Source: Susan Milligan, "Obama Domestic Agenda Largely a One-Party Effort," *Boston Globe,* 17 November 2009.

Politics of Global Change

Breaking Up Was the Easy Part

The momentous breakup of the Soviet Union, a Communist dictatorship, in 1991 led to independence for all of its fifteen republics. The largest and most powerful of these new countries, Russia, has not yet become a real democracy. A recent parliamentary election there was widely viewed as rigged. Similar accusations of fraud arose in the subsequent presidential election won by Vladimir Putin. The Ukraine moved toward democratic rule but recently moved backward as a former prime minister (and leader of the opposition to those now in power) was thrown in jail on trumped-up charges. In contrast, Lithuania quickly established itself as a democracy and later became a member of the European Union. Its economy has performed strongly since it fully implemented a market economy.

These three different countries with three different paths since 1991 reflect a marked similarity in one important respect: citizens in each believe ordinary citizens have gained little since 1991, while politicians and business owners have benefited greatly.

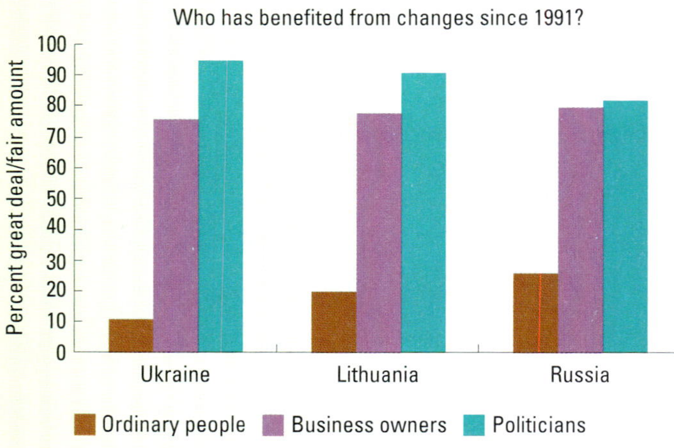

From "82% to 95%–Confidence in Democracy and Capitalism Wanes in Former Soviet Union," Pew Global Attitudes Project. Copyright © Pew Research Center. Reproduced by permission.

action so that interest groups can be heard. It relies on strong interest groups and a decentralized government structure—mechanisms that interfere with majority rule, thereby protecting minority interests. We could even say that pluralism allows minorities to rule.

An Undemocratic Model: Elite Theory

If pluralist democracy allows minorities to rule, how does it differ from **elite theory**—the view that a small group (a minority) makes most important government decisions? According to elite theory, important government decisions are made by an identifiable and stable minority that shares certain characteristics, particularly vast wealth and business connections.[25]

Elite theory argues that these few individuals wield power in America because they control its key financial, communications, industrial, and government institutions. Their power derives from the vast wealth of America's largest corporations and the perceived importance of the continuing success of those corporations to the growth of the economy. An inner circle of top corporate leaders not only provides effective advocates for individual companies and for the interests of capitalism in general but also supplies people for top government jobs, from which they can continue to promote their interests. Elitists might point, for example, to former vice president Dick Cheney. He went from previous work as secretary of defense for President George H. W. Bush to becoming head of Halliburton, a large oil services company, and then back to government, where, as George W. Bush's vice president, he acted as an outspoken proponent of more energy exploration.

According to elite theory, the United States is not a democracy but an oligarchy.[26] Although the voters appear to control the government through elections, elite theorists argue that the powerful few in society manage to define the issues and constrain the outcomes of government decision making to suit their own interests. Clearly, elite theory describes a government that operates in an undemocratic fashion.

Elite theory appeals to many people, especially those who believe that wealth dominates politics. The theory also provides plausible explanations for specific political decisions. Why, over the years, has the tax code included so many loopholes that favor the wealthy? The answer, claim adherents of elite theory, is that the policymakers never really change; they are all cut from the same cloth. Even when a liberal Democrat like Barack Obama is in the White House, many of the president's top economic policymakers are typically drawn from Wall Street or other financial institutions.

Political scientists have conducted numerous studies designed to test the validity of elite theory, but it has proven to be an exceptionally difficult idea to prove in any conclusive manner. Our government and society are enormous and enormously complex. If there were an elite that controlled American politics, it would have to be rather large as there are many wealthy and well-connected notables. What would be the coordinating mechanism that facilitated control by such an elite? And if such an elite exerted such influence, why wouldn't it be clearly evident?[27] Although not all studies come to the same conclusion, the preponderance of available evidence documenting concrete government decisions on many different issues does not generally support elite theory—at least in the sense that an identifiable ruling elite usually gets its way. Not surprisingly, elite theorists reject this view. They argue that studies of decisions made on individual issues do not adequately test the influence of the power elite. Rather, they contend that much of the elite's power comes from its ability to keep issues off the political agenda. That is, its power derives from its ability to keep people from questioning fundamental assumptions about American capitalism.[28]

Consequently, elite theory remains part of the debate about the nature of American government and is forcefully argued by some severe critics of our political system, such as the Occupy Wall Street protestors. Although we do not believe that the scholarly evidence supports elite theory, we do recognize that contemporary American pluralism favors some segments of society over others. On one hand, the poor

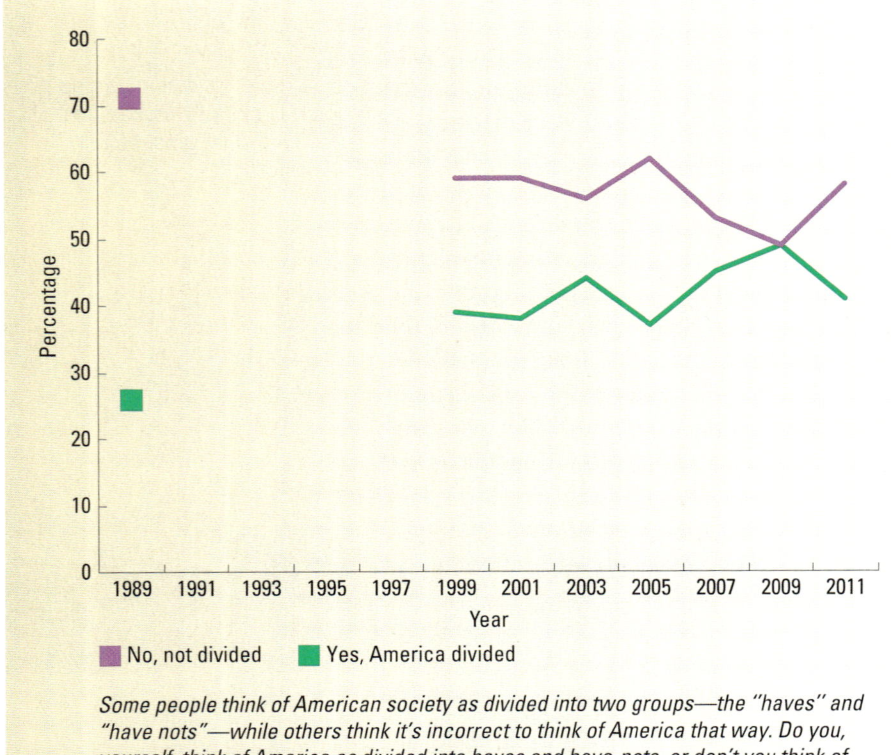

FIGURE 2.3 Americans Divided over Whether America Is Divided

Are we a nation of "haves" and "have nots"? In 1989, most Americans believed that the country was not divided. Over time the proportion of those indicating that the country is divided into haves and have nots increased. The most recent poll (2011) to ask this question found a modest majority believing we are not divided into two camps. Source: Lymari Morales, "Fewer Americans See U.S. Divided into 'Haves,' 'Have Nots,'" *Gallup Poll*, December 15, 2011. Copyright © 2011 Gallup, Inc. All rights reserved. The content is used with permission; however, Gallup retains all right of republication.

Some people think of American society as divided into two groups—the "haves" and "have nots"—while others think it's incorrect to think of America that way. Do you, yourself, think of America as divided into haves and have-nots, or don't you think of America that way? Note that the Gallup Poll did not ask this question between 1990 and 1998.

are chronically unorganized and are not well represented by interest groups. On the other hand, business is very well represented in the political system. Americans themselves are divided over whether American society is dominated by those who are wealthy (see Figure 2.3).

Elite Theory Versus Pluralist Theory

The key difference between elite and pluralist theory lies in the durability of the ruling minority. In contrast to elite theory, pluralist theory does not define government conflict in terms of a minority versus the majority; instead, it sees many different interests vying with one another in each policy area. In the management of national forests, for example, many interest groups—logging companies, recreational campers, and environmentalists, for example—have joined the political competition. They press their various viewpoints on government through representatives who are well informed about how relevant issues affect group members. According to elite theory, the financial resources of big logging companies ought to win out over the arguments of campers and environmentalists, but this does not always happen.

Pluralist democracy makes a virtue of the struggle between competing interests. It argues for government that accommodates the struggle and channels the result into government action. According to pluralist democracy, the public is best served if the government structure provides access for different groups to press their claims in competition with one another. Note that pluralist democracy does not insist that all groups have equal influence on government decisions. In the political struggle, wealthy, well-organized groups have an inherent advantage over poorer, inadequately organized groups. In fact, unorganized segments of the population may not even get their concerns placed on the agenda for government consideration, which means that what government does not discuss (its "nondecisions") may be as significant as what it does discuss and decide. Indeed, studies of the congressional agenda demonstrate that it is characterized by little in the way of legislation concerned with poor or low-income Americans, while business-related bills are plentiful.[29] This is a critical weakness of pluralism, and critics relentlessly attack the theory because it appears to justify great disparities in levels of political organization and resources among different segments of society.[30]

★ 2.3 The Global Trend Toward Democracy

★ Evaluate the challenges facing countries trying to move toward a democratic form of government.

We have proposed two models of democratic government. The majoritarian model conforms with classical democratic theory for a representative government. According to this model, democracy should be a form of government that features responsiveness to majority opinion. According to the pluralist model, a government is democratic if it allows minority interests to organize and press their claims on government freely.

No government actually achieves the high degree of responsiveness demanded by the majoritarian model. No government offers complete and equal access to the claims of all competing groups, as is required by an optimally democratic pluralist model. Still, some nations approach these ideals closely enough to be considered practicing democracies.

© Rob Crandall/The Image Works

On Tonight's Menu, Lots of Green

Elitist critics of American government point to the advantages that the wealthy have in our political system. The campaign finance system contributes to this belief. This Washington fundraiser gives lobbyists and wealthy donors a chance to mingle with policymakers and remind them who supports them financially.

Establishing Democracies

Whether a political system is "democratic" is not a simple yes-or-no question.[31] Governments can meet some criteria for a procedural democracy (universal participation, political equality, majority rule, and government responsiveness to public opinion) and fail to meet others. They can also differ in the extent to which they support freedom of speech and freedom of association, which create the necessary conditions for the practice of democracy. Various scholars and organizations have developed complicated databases that rate countries on a long list of indicators, providing a means of comparing countries along all criteria.[32] One research institution has found a global trend toward freedom every decade since 1975, though in the past few years there has been a slight drop in the number of democracies.[33] **Democratization** is a difficult process, and many countries fail completely or succeed only in the short run and lapse into a form of authoritarianism. The "Arab Spring"—revolutions in Egypt, Tunisia, and Libya, and protest movements in other Arab countries—has raised the hope that democracy will spread across the Middle East (see "Compared with What? The Arab Spring" on p. 44). It is too early to know if the overthrow of these dictatorships will lead to enduring democracies.

democratization

A process of transition as a country attempts to move from an authoritarian form of government to a democratic one.

Compared with What?

The Arab Spring

History may record the Arab Spring as the most important political story of the past few years. The chains of authoritarianism have been broken by rebellions in Egypt, Tunisia, and Libya. In other countries, notably Syria and Yemen, rebellions have not yet been successful. The bloody conflict in Syria has brought worldwide condemnation down on the regime of Bashar al-Assad. In countries where revolutions have been successful, democratic rule has yet to emerge. Transitions to democracy are challenging, and there is no assurance that democracy will replace totalitarianism.

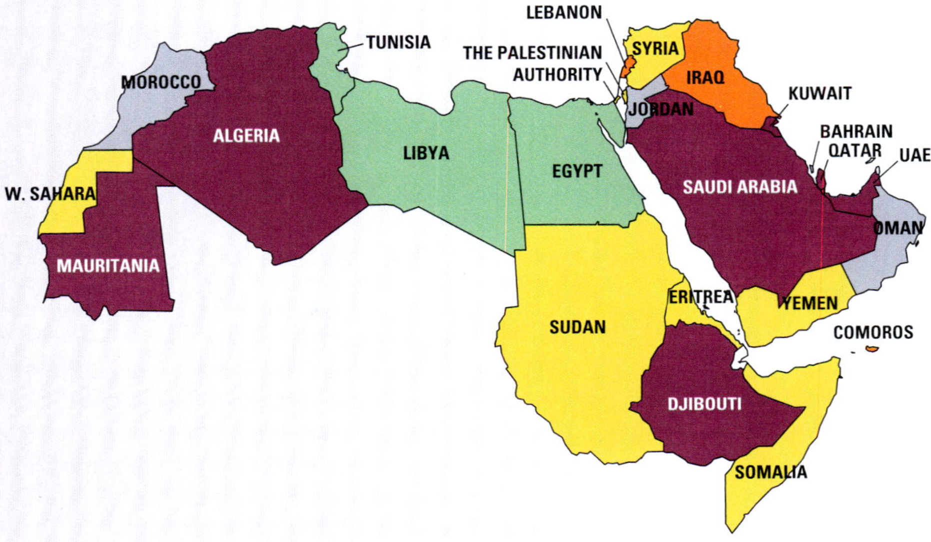

One reason that democratization can be so difficult is that ethnic and religious conflict is epidemic. Such conflict complicates efforts to democratize because antagonisms can run so deep that opposing groups do not want to grant political legitimacy to each other. A bitter irony of the United States' 2003 military overthrow of dictator Saddam Hussein's regime in Iraq is that religious conflict between Sunni and Shiites immediately came to the fore. These two branches of Islam reflect theological differences that have manifested themselves in the form of ethnic hatred. Iraq's steps toward democracy allowed enough freedom for open protest, and religious violence has continued to plague the country. Recently, the nation's Sunni vice president was accused by the Shiite prime minister of plotting to kill Shiite leaders.[34]

The political and economic instability that typically accompanies transitions to democracy makes new democratic governments vulnerable to attack by their opponents. The military will often revolt and take over the government on the ground that progress cannot occur until order is restored. As we noted in Chapter 1, all societies wrestle with the dilemma of choosing between freedom and order. The open political conflict that emerges in a new democracy may not be easily harnessed into a well-functioning government that tolerates opposition.[35] Despite such difficulties, strong forces are pushing authoritarian governments toward democratization. Nations find it difficult to succeed economically in today's world without establishing a market economy, and market economies (that is, capitalism) give people substantial freedoms. There is a strong relationship between economic prosperity and democracy; countries that have free markets tend to protect political freedoms as well.[36] Thus, authoritarian rulers may see economic reforms as a threat to their regime.

The United States has always faced a difficult foreign policy problem determining the degree to which it wants to invest in promoting democracy abroad. It is a noble goal, to be sure, but it may be difficult to impose democracy on a population that cannot accept the tolerance and freedoms allowed to all groups in society that democracy requires. Even as he wound down America's involvement in Iraq, President Obama found limited support for U.S. military intervention in Afghanistan. Close to two-thirds of Americans oppose the war there.[37]

Established democracies are also not free of the destabilizing effects of religious and ethnic conflict. Such countries usually try to cope with such pressures with some form of pluralism so that different groups feel they are being treated fairly by their government. Indeed, majoritarian democracy can be risky where ethnic and religious rivalries endure because a majority faction can use its votes to suppress minorities. Even in stable democracies where ethnic conflict is muted, disillusionment can grow and undermine confidence in the actions of government.[38] India, the world's largest democracy and a burgeoning economic power, is still plagued by periodic religious violence. In 2008 there was a terrible spate of violence directed at the tiny Christian minority in the state of Orissa. Mobs destroyed 1,400 homes, leaving thousands homeless, and 80 churches and prayer houses were set on fire.[39] More broadly, the tension between the Hindu majority and the significant Muslim minority in India is always palpable and violence occasionally erupts.[40]

American Democracy: More Pluralist Than Majoritarian

It is not idle speculation to ask what kind of democracy is practiced in the United States. The answer can help us understand why our government can be called democratic despite a low level of citizen participation in politics and despite government actions that sometimes run contrary to public opinion.

Throughout this book, we probe to determine how well the United States fits the two alternative models of democracy: majoritarian and pluralist. If our answer is not already apparent, it soon will be. We argue that the political system in the United States rates relatively low according to the majoritarian model of democracy but that it fulfills the pluralist model quite well. Yet the pluralist model is far from a perfect representation of democracy. Its principal drawback is that it favors the well organized, and the poor are the least likely to be members of interest groups. As one advocate of majoritarian democracy once wrote, "The flaw in the pluralist heaven is that the heavenly chorus sings with a strong upper-class accent."[41]

In recent years the parties have become more sharply divided along conservative and liberal dimensions, thus making our system a bit more majoritarian than has traditionally been the case. In particular, the two parties in Congress have become more ideologically homogeneous, thus giving voters a clearer opportunity to select a party more cohesive in its programmatic intent.[42] Yet this step toward majoritarianism has led to widespread criticism that our system of government is becoming too bitterly partisan. That is, as the members of Congress have become more ideological, they seem to have become less inclined to work together to achieve moderate, compromise solutions to the nation's problems. Some critics have also charged that ideological activists, who have mobilized more than moderates, have hijacked the parties and pulled them more sharply toward conservative and liberal extremes.[43] For those uncomfortable with more ideological parties, the continuing strong counterbalance of pluralism is welcome.

Given the survey data that show that the people's trust in American government has fallen over the years, it may seem that pluralist democracy is not serving us very well. Indeed, many Americans describe government and politicians in the harshest terms. Radio talk show hosts like Rush Limbaugh and politicians themselves pile invective on top of insult when they talk about what's wrong with Washington.[44] Compared with citizens in other developed nations, Americans fall in the middle concerning their satisfaction with democracy in the United States. But it's not at all clear that Americans would be more satisfied with another type of democracy.

This evaluation of the pluralist nature of American democracy may not mean much to you now. But you will learn that the pluralist model makes the United States look far more democratic than the majoritarian model would. Eventually, you will have to decide the answers to three questions:

1. Is the pluralist model truly an adequate expression of democracy, or is it a perversion of classical ideals, designed to portray America as democratic when it is not?
2. Does the majoritarian model result in a "better" type of democracy?
3. If it does, could new mechanisms of government be devised to produce a desirable mix of majority rule and minority rights?

Let these questions play in the back of your mind as you read more about the workings of American government in meeting the challenge of democracy.

SUMMARY

There are different forms of government around the world, one of which is democracy. But there is no one conception of democracy, and this chapter explores these differing beliefs about how a democracy ought to be constituted.

2.1 The Theory of Democratic Government

- The procedural view of democracy emphasizes democratic processes. Four procedural elements seem paramount: universal participation, political equality, majority rule, and government responsiveness to public opinion.
- Substantive democratic theory focuses on the substance of policies rather than procedures. It holds that there are some rights that are so important that they should not be subject to being overturned by majority decision.
- Not surprisingly, procedural democracy can come into conflict with substantive democracy. What substantive policies should be beyond the control of popular opinion?

2.2   Institutional Models of Democracy

- The majoritarian model of democracy is built around majority rule as evidenced by elections.
- Pluralist democracy conceives of democracy as a competition between opposing groups in society.
- Elite theorists believe that American government is dominated by a small set of wealthy individuals and large businesses.

2.3   The Global Trend Toward Democracy

- An increasing number of countries around the world have moved toward democratic governance. The process of democratization is difficult, though, and many democratizing countries fail and return to some form of authoritarianism.
- We compare the validity of majoritarian and pluralist models of democracy and conclude that the United States is a mix of both, but closer to pluralism.

ASSESSING YOUR UNDERSTANDING WITH APLIA…YOUR VIRTUAL TUTOR!

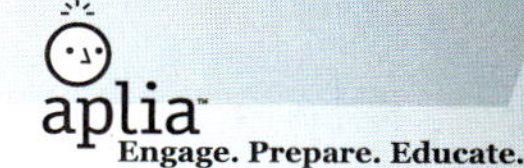

2.1   Distinguish between the two theories of democratic government used in political science: procedural and substantive.

1. How do procedural democracy and substantive democracy differ?
2. What is direct democracy? What is indirect democracy?

2.2   Compare and contrast the majoritarian and pluralist models of democracy.

1. What is the basic concept of majoritarian democracy?

2. What is the basic concept of pluralist democracy?
3. What are the criticisms at the heart of elite theory?

2.3   Evaluate the challenges facing countries trying to move toward a democratic form of government.

1. Offer an example of why democratization is difficult.

3 The Constitution

CHAPTER TOPICS and Learning Outcomes

aplia
Engage. Prepare. Educate.

3.1 The Revolutionary Roots of the Constitution
★ Explain the reasons for the colonies' declaration of independence from British rule.

3.2 From Revolution to Confederation
★ Identify the factors that led to the failure of the Confederation.

3.3 From Confederation to Constitution
★ Explain the major points of contention in the writing of the Constitution.

3.4 The Final Product
★ Explain the contribution of the Constitution to the American political tradition and the principles it establishes.

3.5 Selling the Constitution
★ Describe the actions taken to ensure the ratification of the Constitution.

3.6 Constitutional Change
★ Explain the procedures required to amend the Constitution.

3.7 An Evaluation of the Constitution
★ Evaluate the extent to which the Constitution reflects and embodies the principles of majoritarian or pluralist democracy.

"**Y**ou are the 'conventionists' of Europe. You therefore have the power vested in any political body: to succeed or to fail," claimed Chairman Valéry Giscard d'Estaing in his introductory speech on February 26, 2002, to the members of the Convention on the Future of Europe. The purpose of the convention, according to Giscard d'Estaing, was for the members to "agree to propose a concept of the European Union which matches our continental dimension and the requirements of the twenty-first century, a concept which can bring unity to our continent and respect for its diversity." If the members succeeded, he reassured them, no doubt they would in essence write "a new chapter in the history of Europe."[1] Integrating and governing twenty-seven nation-states with a total population of 500 million are, to say the least, daunting tasks, especially considering that many of those nation-states at one time or another were bitter enemies.

Over two centuries earlier, on March 31, 1787, from his home at Mount Vernon, George Washington penned a letter to James Madison. "I am glad to find," Washington wrote, "that Congress have recommended to the States to appear in the Convention proposed to be holden in Philadelphia in May. I think the reasons in favor, have the preponderancy of those against the measure."[2] Roughly two months later, in May, Washington would be selected by a unanimous vote to preside over the Constitutional Convention, known then as the Federal Convention, which was charged with revising the Articles of Confederation. Acting beyond its mandate, the body produced instead a new document altogether, which remains the oldest operating constitution in the world.

The path to a European constitution was strewn with pitfalls. Ratification required unanimity, which failed when presented to voters in several countries. Although the process in 1787 on one side of the Atlantic may have differed from that on the other side in 2002, the political passions that these efforts spawned were equally intense and highlight the fragility inherent in designing a constitution. And no wonder. The questions that challenged America's founders and that confronted the women and men charged with setting a future course for Europe do not have easy or obvious answers. A thoughtful European observer asked the same kinds of questions that confronted the delegates at Philadelphia: "How can a balance be achieved in the representation of large and small states? How much power should be conferred upon the federal level and what should be the jurisdiction of the EU today? What fundamental set of values underpins political unity? Is there a European equivalent to 'life, liberty and the pursuit of happiness'?"[3]

Taking a new tack, European Union (EU) advocates proposed a new form of agreement known as the "Treaty of Lisbon," also referred to as the Reform Treaty, which

SAUL LOEB/AFP/Getty Images

Leader of the Pack

In 2012, newly elected French President François Hollande (l) deferred to German Chancellor Angela Merkel (r) at a meeting in Chicago. Germany remains the EU's economic powerhouse and Merkel continues to call the shots in addressing the festering economic issues that have roiled the EU economy with ramifications worldwide. Operating with a single currency (the euro), member states have largely bowed to Germany's economic might.

was signed on December 13, 2007, during a European summit. Except for Ireland, all member nations submitted the treaty to their respective legislatures. The treaty's approval still required unanimity. Since voters were notoriously uneasy about EU policies, it seemed prudent to keep them at bay while the elected representatives debated the treaty's advantages and disadvantages. The Reform Treaty presented a still-longer version of the previous constitutional text but dropped nearly all the state-like symbols and terminology (the European flag and anthem, among others). It planned for an EU president, created a diplomatic service under a single foreign-affairs head, and smoothed the ability to make decisions by reducing the number of areas that called for unanimity among member nations.

Approval was uneasy. Ireland rejected the treaty in 2008, halting once more the effort toward European integration. But the sobering effects of economic toil soon gave Ireland a chance to reconsider. In October 2009, Irish voters agreed to the treaty by a substantial margin, hoping that the new EU would stave off economic catastrophe caused by the worldwide collapse in the financial sector.[4] Finally, on December 1, 2009, the treaty went into effect, bringing the EU one step closer to unity.

Economic forces continued to pound the EU through 2012 as creditors questioned whether the debt-ridden nations of Greece, Ireland, Italy, Portugal, and Spain would be able to pay or refinance their bonds. These economic tremors continue to generate shock waves in the American economy as they continue to rattle the EU economy. To stave off collapse of the monetary union, EU leaders (with the exception of Great Britain) have agreed in principle to greater central authority over their respective economies. The EU's political union now hinges on the willingness of individual states to cede more political and economic control to a central government and to relax the unanimity rule that gives any of the twenty-seven member nations a veto.[5] This parallels the same choice Americans faced as their initial attempt at government proved unworkable.

The American experience is sure to shed light on the future of a single Europe. In fact, the American experience parallels the European story, since Americans' first step toward unity resulted in failure and then an effort at redesign that ultimately proved successful. This chapter poses questions about the U.S. Constitution. How did it evolve? What form did it take? What values does it reflect? How can it be altered? Which model of democracy—majoritarian or pluralist—does it fit better? In these answers may lie hints of the formidable tasks facing the EU as it moves toward greater political and economic unity.

3.1 The Revolutionary Roots of the Constitution

★ Explain the reasons for the colonies' declaration of independence from British rule.

The U.S. Constitution contains just 4,300 words. But those 4,300 words define the basic structure of our national government. (In contrast, the failed European constitution was more than 60,000 words long. The Reform Treaty is still longer at 68,500 words.) A comprehensive document, the Constitution divides the national government into three branches, describes the powers of those branches and their connections, outlines the interaction between the government and the governed, and describes the relationship between the national government and the states. The Constitution makes itself the supreme law of the land and binds every government official to support it.

Most Americans revere the Constitution as political scripture. To charge that a political action is unconstitutional is akin to claiming that it is unholy. So the Constitution has taken on symbolic value that strengthens its authority as the basis of American government.

The U.S. Constitution, written in 1787 for an agricultural society huddled along the coast of a wild new land, now guides the political life of a massive urban society in the postnuclear age. The stability of the Constitution—and of the political system it created—is all the more remarkable because the Constitution itself was rooted in revolution. What is the evidence regarding the life expectancy of constitutions generally? (See "Compared with What? The Longevity of Constitutions," pp. 52–53.)

The U.S. Constitution was designed to prevent anarchy by forging a union of states. To understand the values embedded in the Constitution, we must understand its historical roots. They lie in colonial America, the revolt against British rule, and the failure of the Articles of Confederation that governed the new nation after the Revolution.

Freedom in Colonial America

Although they were British subjects, American colonists in the eighteenth century enjoyed a degree of freedom denied most other people in the world. In Europe, ancient customs and the relics of feudalism restricted private property, compelled support for established religions, and limited access to trades and professions. In America, landowners could control and transfer their property at will. In America, there were no compulsory payments to support an established church. In America, there was no ceiling on wages, as there was in most European countries, and no guilds of exclusive professional associations. In America, colonists enjoyed almost complete freedom of speech, press, and assembly.[6]

By 1763, Britain and the colonies had reached a compromise between imperial control and colonial self-government. America's foreign affairs and overseas trade were controlled by the king and Parliament, the British legislature; the rest was left to colonial rule. But the cost of administering the colonies was substantial. The colonists needed protection from the French and their American Indian allies during the Seven Years' War (1756–1763), an expensive undertaking. Because Americans benefited the most from that protection, their English countrymen argued, Americans should bear the cost.

The Road to Revolution

The British believed that taxing the colonies was the obvious way to meet the costs of administering the colonies. The colonists did not agree. They especially did not want to be taxed by a distant government in which they had no representation. Nevertheless, a series of taxes (including a tax on all printed matter) was imposed on the colonies by the Crown. In each instance, public opposition was widespread and immediate.

A group of citizens—merchants, lawyers, and prosperous traders—created an intercolonial association called the Sons of Liberty. This group destroyed taxed items (identified by special stamps) and forced the official stamp distributors to resign. In

Compared with What?

The Longevity of Constitutions

Compared with other constitutions across the world, the U.S. Constitution is an antique. Ratified in 1788, it is the world's second oldest constitution. (The tiny land-locked microstate of San Marino boasts the oldest constitution, dating to 1600.) But few 220-year-old antiques still work more or less as their designers intended. Other countries have constitutions, but they tend to come and go.

A national constitution is the fundamental law of a land. It must give voice to a set of inviolable principles that limit the powers of government by setting up governmental institutions and defining their relationships and patterns of authority. Even dictatorships require institutions through which to govern.

Some stable democracies lack a single document as a written constitution. Perhaps the most notable example is Britain, whose fundamental law inheres in other documents, such as the Magna Carta. Other democracies, like Brazil, have gone in the opposite direction by adopting "hyperconstitutions." Brazil tries to pack into its 1988 charter just about every facet of public life, making it one of the longest constitutions ever drafted, nearly six times the length of the U.S. Constitution.

How long do constitutions last? Constitutions have lasted only about seventeen years on average worldwide since 1789. The figure here illustrates many short life spans compared to long life spans, which vary by region and time. African constitutions survive on average ten years. Latin American constitutions last little more than twelve years. For example, the Dominican Republic and Haiti have changed their constitutions every three years. Constitutions in Western Europe last thirty-two years, while constitutions in Asia survive about nineteen years. From 1789 through World War I, the average life span of a constitution was twenty-one years. It has dropped to twelve years since the end of World War I. And whereas the life expectancy of individuals worldwide is increasing, the life expectancy of constitutions is not.

Three reasons may explain constitutional durability: (1) they tend to derive from an open, participatory process; (2) they tend to be specific; and (3) they tend to be flexible through amendment and interpretation.

October 1765, residents of Charleston, South Carolina, celebrated the forced resignation of the colony's stamp distributor by displaying a British flag with the word *Liberty* sewn across it. (They were horrified when a few months later local slaves paraded through the streets calling for "Liberty!")[7]

Women resisted the hated taxes by joining together in symbolic and practical displays of patriotism. A group of young women calling themselves the Daughters of Liberty met in public to spin homespun cloth and encourage the elimination of British cloth from colonial markets. They consumed American food and drank local herbal tea as symbols of their opposition.[8]

On the night of December 16, 1773, a group of colonists in Massachusetts reacted to a British duty on tea by organizing the Boston Tea Party. A mob boarded three ships and emptied 342 chests of that valuable substance into Boston Harbor. The act of defiance and destruction could not be ignored. "The die is now cast," wrote George III. "The Colonies must either submit or triumph."[9] In an attempt to reassert British control over its recalcitrant colonists, Parliament in 1774 passed the Coercive (or "Intolerable") Acts. One act imposed a blockade on Boston until the tea was paid for;

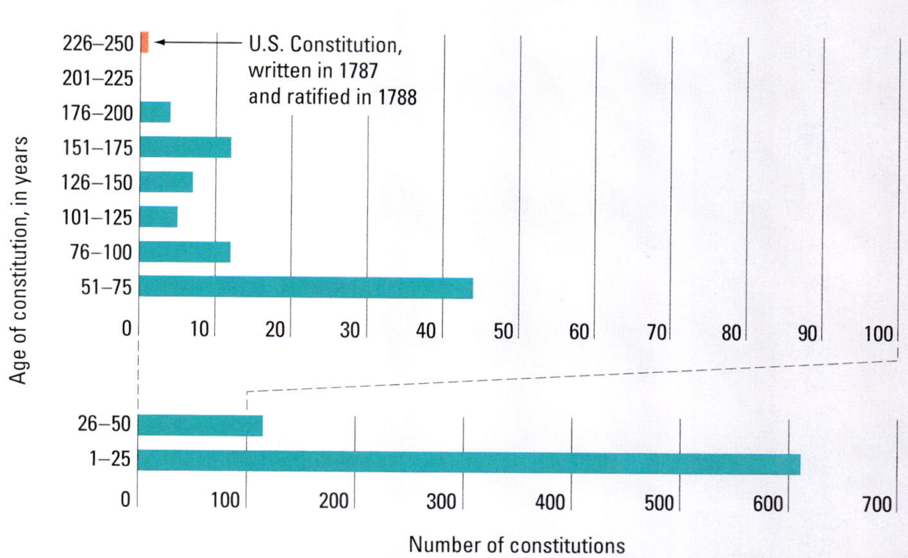

Source: Tom Ginsburg, Zack Elkins, and James Melton, "The Lifespan of Written Constitutions" (Paper No. 3, Law and Economics Workshop, University of California at Berkeley, 21 January 2008, available at http://repositories.cdlib.org/cgi/viewcontent.cgi?article=1212&context=berkeley_law_econ and http://www.loc.gov/aw/help/guide/nations/sanmarino.html, accessed 12 February 2008). Thanks to Prof. Tom Ginsburg who graciously shared his data for the figure.

Critical Thinking 

What might be some of the advantages and disadvantages of having a durable constitution?

another gave royal governors the power to quarter British soldiers in private American homes. The taxation issue became secondary; more important was the conflict between British demands for order and American demands for liberty. The Virginia and Massachusetts assemblies summoned a continental congress, an assembly that would speak and act for the people of all the colonies.

All the colonies except Georgia sent representatives to the First Continental Congress, which met in Philadelphia in September 1774. The objective was to restore harmony between Great Britain and the American colonies. In an effort at unity, all colonies were given the same voting power—one vote each. A leader, called the president, was elected. (The terms *president* and *congress* in American government trace their origins to the First Continental Congress.) In October, the delegates adopted a statement of rights and principles; many of these later found their way into the Declaration of Independence and the Constitution. For example, the congress claimed a right "to life, liberty, and property" and a right "peaceably to assemble, consider of their grievances, and petition the king." Then the congress adjourned, planning to reconvene in May 1775.

Courtesy of the John Carter Brown Library at Brown University

Uniquely American Protest

Americans protested the Tea Act (1773) by holding the Boston Tea Party (*background, left*) and by using a unique form of painful punishment, tarring and feathering, on the tax collector (see "STAMP ACT" upside-down on the Liberty Tree). An early treatise on the subject offered the following instructions: "First, strip a person naked, then heat the tar until it is thin, and pour upon the naked flesh, or rub it over with a tar brush. After which, sprinkle decently upon the tar, whilst it is yet warm, as many feathers as will stick to it."

Declaration of Independence
Drafted by Thomas Jefferson, the document that proclaimed the right of the colonies to separate from Great Britain.

social contract theory
The belief that the people agree to set up rulers for certain purposes and thus have the right to resist or remove rulers who act against those purposes.

Revolutionary Action

By early 1775, however, a movement that the colonists themselves were calling a revolution had already begun. Colonists in Massachusetts were fighting the British at Concord and Lexington. Delegates to the Second Continental Congress, meeting in May, faced a dilemma: Should they prepare for war, or should they try to reconcile with Britain? As conditions deteriorated, the Second Continental Congress remained in session to serve as the government of the colony-states.

On June 7, 1776, owing in large part to the powerful advocacy of John Adams of Massachusetts, a strong supporter of independence, the Virginia delegation called on the Continental Congress to resolve "that these United Colonies are, and of right ought to be, free and Independent States, that they are absolved from all allegiance to the British Crown, and that all political connection between them and the State of Great Britain is, and ought to be, totally dissolved." This was a difficult decision. Independence meant disloyalty to Britain and war, death, and devastation. The congress debated but did not immediately adopt the resolution. A committee of five men was appointed to prepare a proclamation expressing the colonies' reasons for declaring independence.

The Declaration of Independence

Thomas Jefferson, a young farmer and lawyer from Virginia who was a member of the committee, became the "pen" to John Adams's "voice."[10] Because Jefferson was erudite, a Virginian, and an extremely skilled writer, he drafted the proclamation. Jefferson's document, the **Declaration of Independence**, was modestly revised by the committee and then further edited by the congress. It remains a cherished statement of our heritage, expressing simply, clearly, and rationally the many arguments for separation from Great Britain.

The principles underlying the Declaration were rooted in the writings of the English philosopher John Locke and had been expressed many times by speakers in the congress and the colonial assemblies. Locke argued that people have God-given, or natural, rights that are inalienable—that is, they cannot be taken away by any government. According to Locke, all legitimate political authority exists to preserve these natural rights and is based on the consent of those who are governed. The idea of consent is derived from **social contract theory**, which states that the people agree to establish rulers for certain purposes, but they have the right to resist or remove rulers who violate those purposes.[11]

Jefferson used similar arguments in the Declaration of Independence. (See the appendix.) Taking his cue from a draft of the Virginia Declaration of Rights,[12] Jefferson wrote,

We hold these truths to be self-evident, that all men are created equal, that they are endowed by their Creator with certain unalienable rights, that among these are life, liberty, and the pursuit of happiness. That to secure these rights, governments are instituted among men, deriving their just powers from the consent of the governed. That whenever any form of government becomes destructive of these ends, it is the right of the people to alter or to abolish it, and to institute new government, laying its foundation on such principles, and organizing its power in such form, as to them shall seem most likely to effect their safety and happiness.

Historian Jack Rakove maintains that Jefferson was not proposing equality for individuals. Rather, he was asserting the equality of peoples to enjoy the same rights of self-government that other peoples enjoyed. "It was the collective right of revolution and self-government that the Declaration was written to justify—not a visionary or even utopian notion of equality within American society itself."[13]

He went on to list the many deliberate acts of the king that had exceeded the legitimate role of government. The last and lengthiest item on Jefferson's original draft of the Declaration was the king's support of the slave trade. Although Jefferson did not condemn slavery, he denounced the king for enslaving a people, engaging in the slave trade, and proposing that if the slaves were freed, they would attack their masters. When South Carolina and Georgia, two states with an interest in continuing the wretched practice, objected, Jefferson and the committee dropped the offending paragraph. Finally, Jefferson declared that the colonies were "Free and Independent States," with no political connection to Great Britain.

The major premise of the Declaration of Independence is that the people have a right to revolt if they determine that their government is denying them their legitimate rights. The long list of the king's actions was evidence of such denial. So the people had the right to rebel, to form a new government.

On July 2, 1776, the Second Continental Congress finally voted for independence. The vote was by state, and the motion carried 11–0. (Rhode Island was not present, and the New York delegation, lacking instructions, did not cast its yea vote until July 15.) Two days later, on July 4, the Declaration of Independence was approved, with

Toppling Tyrants: Then and Now

A gilded equestrian statue of George III once stood at the tip of Manhattan. On July 9, 1776, citizens responded to the news of the Declaration of Independence by toppling the statue. It was melted down and converted into musket balls. In 2011, rebels in Libya—with covert U.S. and overt NATO assistance—reenacted deposing their long-time dictator, Muammar Gaddafi.

few changes. Several representatives insisted on removing language they thought would incite the colonists. In the end, even though Jefferson's compelling words were left almost exactly as he had written them, the adjustments tugged at the Virginian's personal insecurities. According to historian Joseph Ellis, while the congress debated various changes to the document, "Jefferson sat silently and sullenly, regarding each proposed revision as another defacement."[14]

By August, fifty-five revolutionaries had signed the Declaration of Independence, pledging "our lives, our fortunes and our sacred honor" in support of their rebellion against the world's most powerful nation. This was no empty pledge: an act of rebellion was treason. Had they lost the Revolutionary War, the signers would have faced a gruesome fate. The punishment for treason was hanging and drawing and quartering—the victim was hanged until half-dead from strangulation, then disemboweled, and finally cut into four pieces while still alive. We celebrate the Fourth of July with fireworks and flag waving, parades, and picnics. We sometimes forget that the Revolution was a matter of life and death. The term *revolution* belies a fundamental feature of this conflict: it was a civil war "polarizing communities, destroying friendships, [and] dividing families."[15] As one noteworthy example, Benjamin Franklin's only son William was a loyalist.

The war imposed an agonizing choice on colonial Catholics, who were treated with intolerance by the overwhelmingly Protestant population. No other religious group found the choice so difficult. Catholics could either join the revolutionaries, who were opposed to Catholicism, or remain loyal to England and risk new hostility and persecution. But Catholics were few in number, perhaps twenty-five thousand at the time of independence (or 1 percent of the population). Anti-Catholic revolutionaries recognized that if Catholics opposed independence in Maryland and Pennsylvania, where their numbers were greatest, victory might be jeopardized. Furthermore, enlisting the support of Catholic France for the cause of independence would be difficult in the face of strong opposition from colonial Catholics. So the revolutionaries wooed Catholics to their cause.[16]

The War of Independence lasted far longer than anyone expected. It began in a moment of confusion, when a shot rang out as British soldiers approached the town of Lexington, Massachusetts, on April 19, 1775. The end came six and a half years later with Lord Cornwallis's surrender of his army of six thousand at Yorktown, Virginia, on October 19, 1781. It was a costly war: a greater percentage of the population died or was wounded during the Revolution than in any other U.S. conflict except the Civil War. And, until the Vietnam War, it was the longest conflict.[17]

Still, one in five colonists remained loyal to the British Crown. In New York, several hundred signed their own declaration of dependence. Prominent family names were easy to spot. But most signers were ordinary people: carpenters and blacksmiths, farmers, bakers, and perfumers. The document lacked Jefferson's rhetorical force, however. After the war, the loyalists were stripped of their rights, property, and dignity. As many as 80,000 abandoned the new United States for other parts of the British Empire. About half headed north to Canada, including 3,000 blacks, former slaves who secured their freedom by fighting for the British. In another migration, 1,200 of these former slaves relocated in 1792 to Sierra Leone, where they formed an experimental free black colony.[18]

With hindsight, of course, we can see that the British were engaged in an arduous and perhaps hopeless conflict. America was simply too vast to subdue without imposing total military rule. Britain also had to transport men and supplies over the enormous distance of the Atlantic Ocean. Also, the Americans' courtship of Britain's rivals, owing in large part to the indefatigable advocacy and diplomacy of John Adams,[19] resulted in support from the French navy and several million dollars in

Dutch loans that helped to bolster General Washington's revolutionary forces. Finally, although the Americans had neither paid troops nor professional soldiers, they were fighting for a cause: the defense of their liberty. The British never understood the power of this fighting faith or, given the international support for the American cause, the totality of the forces arrayed against them.

3.2 From Revolution to Confederation

★ Identify the factors that led to the failure of the Confederation.

By declaring their independence from England, the colonists left themselves without any real central government. So the revolutionaries proclaimed the creation of a **republic**. Strictly speaking, a republic is a government without a monarch, but the term had come to mean a government based on the consent of the governed, whose power is exercised by representatives who are responsible to them. A republic need not be a democracy, and this was fine with the founders; at that time, democracy was associated with mob rule and instability (see Chapter 2). The revolutionaries were less concerned with determining who would control their new government than with limiting its powers. They had revolted in the name of liberty, and now they wanted a government with strictly defined powers. To make sure they got one, they meant to define its structure and powers in writing.

republic
A government without a monarch; a government rooted in the consent of the governed, whose power is exercised by elected representatives responsible to the governed.

The Articles of Confederation

Barely a week after the Declaration of Independence was signed, the Second Continental Congress received a committee report entitled "Articles of Confederation and Perpetual Union." A **confederation** is a loose association of independent states that agree to cooperate on specified matters. In a confederation, the states retain their sovereignty, which means that each has supreme power within its borders. The central government is weak; it can only coordinate, not control, the actions of its sovereign states. Consequently, the individual states are strong.

confederation
A loose association of independent states that agree to cooperate on specified matters.

The congress debated the **Articles of Confederation**, the compact among the thirteen original colonies that established the first government of the United States, for more than a year. The Articles were adopted by the Continental Congress on November 15, 1777, and finally took effect on March 1, 1781, following approval by all thirteen states. For more than three years, then, Americans had fought a revolution without an effective government. Raising money, troops, and supplies for the war had daunted and exhausted the leadership.

Articles of Confederation
The compact among the thirteen original states that established the first government of the United States.

The Articles jealously guarded state sovereignty; their provisions clearly reflected the delegates' fears that a strong central government would resemble British rule. Article II, for example, stated, "Each state retains its sovereignty, freedom, and independence, and every power, jurisdiction, and right, which is not by this Confederation expressly delegated to the United States, in Congress assembled."

Under the Articles, each state, regardless of its size, had one vote in the congress. Votes on financing the war and other important issues required the consent of at least nine of the thirteen states. The common danger, Britain, had forced the young republic to function under the Articles, but this first effort at government was inadequate to the task. The delegates had succeeded in crafting a national government that was largely powerless.

The Articles failed for at least four reasons. First, they did not give the national government the power to tax. As a result, the congress had to plead for money from the states to pay for the war and carry on the affairs of the new nation. A government that cannot reliably raise revenue cannot expect to govern effectively. Second, the Articles made no provision for an independent leadership position to direct the government (the president was merely the presiding officer of the congress). The omission was deliberate—the colonists feared the reestablishment of a monarchy—but it left the nation without a leader. Third, the Articles did not allow the national government to regulate interstate and foreign commerce. (When John Adams proposed that the confederation enter into a commercial treaty with Britain after the war, he was asked, "Would you like one treaty or thirteen, Mr. Adams?")[20]

Finally, the Articles could not be amended without the unanimous agreement of the congress and the assent of all the state legislatures; thus, each state had the power to veto any changes to the confederation.

The goal of the delegates who drew up the Articles of Confederation was to retain power in the states. This was consistent with republicanism, which viewed the remote power of a national government as a danger to liberty. In this sense alone, the Articles were a grand success. They completely hobbled the infant government.

Disorder Under the Confederation

Once the Revolution had ended and independence was a reality, it became clear that the national government had neither the economic nor the military power to function effectively. Freed from wartime austerity, Americans rushed to purchase goods from abroad. The national government's efforts to restrict foreign imports were blocked by exporting states, which feared retaliation from their foreign customers. Debt mounted and, for many, bankruptcy followed.

The problem was particularly severe in Massachusetts, where high interest rates and high state taxes were forcing farmers into bankruptcy. In 1786, Daniel Shays, a Revolutionary War veteran, marched on a western Massachusetts courthouse with fifteen hundred supporters armed with barrel staves and pitchforks: they were protesting against high taxes levied by the state to retire its wartime debt.[21] Later, they attacked an arsenal. Called Shays's Rebellion, the revolt against the established order continued into 1787. Massachusetts appealed to the confederation for help. Horrified by the threat of domestic upheaval, the congress approved a $530,000 requisition for the

© ClassicStock / Alamy

Voting for Independence

The Second Continental Congress voted for independence on July 2, 1776. John Adams of Massachusetts viewed the day "as the most memorable epocha [significant event] in the history of America." In this painting by John Trumbull, the drafting committee presents the Declaration of Independence to the patriots who would later sign it. The committee, grouped in front of the desk, consisted of (*from left to right*) Adams, Roger Sherman (Connecticut), Robert Livingston (New York), Thomas Jefferson (Virginia), and Benjamin Franklin (Pennsylvania).

Trumbull painted the scene years after the event. Relying on Jefferson's faulty memory and his own artistic license, Trumbull created a scene that bears little resemblance to reality. First, there was no ceremonial moment when the committee presented its draft to the congress. Second, the room's elegance belied its actual appearance. Third, the doors are in the wrong place. Fourth, the heavy drapes substitute for actual venetian blinds. And, fifth, the mahogany armchairs replaced the plain Windsor design used by the delegates. Nevertheless, the painting remains an icon of American political history.

establishment of a national army. But the plan failed: every state except Virginia rejected the request for money. Finally, the governor of Massachusetts called out the militia and restored order.[22]

The rebellion demonstrated the impotence of the confederation and the urgent need to suppress insurrections and maintain domestic order. Proof to skeptics that Americans could not govern themselves, the rebellion alarmed all American leaders, with the exception of Jefferson. From Paris, where he was serving as American ambassador, he remarked, "A little rebellion now and then is a good thing; the tree of liberty must be refreshed from time to time with the blood of patriots and tyrants."[23]

3.3 From Confederation to Constitution

★ Explain the major points of contention in the writing of the Constitution.

Order, the original purpose of government, was breaking down under the Articles of Confederation. The "league of friendship" envisioned in the Articles was not enough to hold the nation together in peacetime.

Some states had taken halting steps toward encouraging a change in the national government. In 1785, Massachusetts asked the congress to revise the Articles of Confederation, but the congress took no action. In 1786, Virginia invited the states to attend a convention at Annapolis, Maryland, to explore revisions aimed at improving commercial regulation. The meeting was both a failure and a success. Only five states sent delegates, but they seized the opportunity to call for another meeting—with a far broader mission—in Philadelphia the next year. That convention would be charged with devising "such further provisions as shall appear ... necessary to render the constitution of the Federal Government adequate to the exigencies of the Union." The congress later agreed to the convention but limited its mission to "the sole and express purpose of revising the Articles of Confederation."[24]

Shays's Rebellion lent a sense of urgency to the task before the Philadelphia convention. The congress's inability to confront the rebellion was evidence that a stronger national government was necessary to preserve order and property—to protect the states from internal as well as external dangers. "While the Declaration was directed against an excess of authority," observed Supreme Court Justice Robert H. Jackson some one hundred fifty years later, "the Constitution [that followed the Articles of Confederation] was directed against anarchy."[25]

Twelve of the thirteen states named seventy-four delegates to convene in Philadelphia, the most important city in America, in May 1787. (Rhode Island, derisively renamed "Rogue Island" by a Boston newspaper, was the one exception. The state legislature sulkily rejected participating because it feared a strong national government.) Fifty-five delegates eventually showed up at the statehouse in Philadelphia, but no more than thirty were present at any one time during that sweltering spring and summer. The framers were not demigods, but many historians believe that such an assembly will not be seen again. Highly educated, they typically were fluent in Latin and Greek. Products of the Enlightenment, they relied on classical liberalism for the Constitution's philosophical underpinnings.

They were also veterans of the political intrigues of their states, and so were highly practical politicians who knew how to maneuver. Although well versed in ideas, they subscribed to the view expressed by one delegate that "experience must be

James Madison, Father of the Constitution

Although he dismissed the accolade "Father of the Constitution," Madison deserved it more than anyone else. As do most fathers, he exercised a powerful influence in debates (and was on the losing side of more than half of them).

© World History Archive/Alamy

Virginia Plan

A set of proposals for a new government, submitted to the Constitutional Convention of 1787; it included separation of the government into three branches, division of the legislature into two houses, and proportional representation in the legislature.

legislative branch

The lawmaking branch of government.

executive branch

The law-enforcing branch of government.

judicial branch

The law-interpreting branch of government.

our only guide, reason may mislead us."[26] Fearing for their fragile union, the delegates resolved to keep their proceedings secret.

The Constitutional Convention, at the time called the Federal Convention, officially opened on May 25. Within the first week, Edmund Randolph of Virginia had presented a long list of changes, suggested by fellow Virginian James Madison, that would replace the weak confederation of states with a powerful national government rather than revise it within its original framework. The delegates unanimously agreed to debate Randolph's proposal, called the **Virginia Plan**. Almost immediately, then, they rejected the idea of amending the Articles of Confederation, working instead to create an entirely new constitution.

The Virginia Plan

The Virginia Plan dominated the convention's deliberations for the rest of the summer, making several important proposals for a strong central government:

- That the powers of the government be divided among three separate branches: a **legislative branch**, for making laws; an **executive branch**, for enforcing laws; and a **judicial branch**, for interpreting laws.
- That the legislature consist of two houses. The first would be chosen by the people, the second by the members of the first house from among candidates nominated by the state legislatures.
- That each state's representation in the legislature be in proportion to the taxes it paid to the national government or in proportion to its free population.
- That an executive, consisting of an unspecified number of people, be selected by the legislature and serve for a single term.
- That the national judiciary include one or more supreme courts and other, lower courts, with judges appointed for life by the legislature.
- That the executive and a number of national judges serve as a council of revision, to approve or veto (disapprove) legislative acts. Their veto could be overridden by a vote of both houses of the legislature.
- That the scope of powers of all three branches be far greater than that assigned the national government by the Articles of Confederation and that the legislature be empowered to override state laws.

By proposing a powerful national legislature that could override state laws, the Virginia Plan clearly advocated a new form of government. It was to have a mixed structure, with more authority over the states and new authority over the people.

Madison was a monumental force in the ensuing debate on the proposals. He kept records of the proceedings that reveal his frequent and brilliant participation and give us insight into his thinking about freedom, order, and equality.

For example, his proposal that senators serve a nine-year term reveals his thinking about equality. Madison foresaw an increase "of those who will labor under all the hardships of life, and secretly sigh for a more equal distribution of its blessings. These may in time outnumber those who are placed above the feelings of indigence."[27] Power, then, could flow into the hands of the numerous poor. The stability of the senate, however, with its nine-year terms and election by the state legislatures, would provide a barrier against the "sighs of the poor" for more equality. Although most delegates shared Madison's apprehension about equality, the nine-year term was voted down.

The Constitution that emerged from the convention bore only a partial resemblance to the document Madison wanted to create. He endorsed seventy-one specific proposals, but he ended up on the losing side on forty of them.[28] And the parts of the Virginia Plan that were ultimately included in the Constitution were not adopted without challenge. Conflicts revolved primarily around the basis for representation in the legislature, the method of choosing legislators, and the structure of the executive branch.

The New Jersey Plan

When in 1787 it appeared that much of the Virginia Plan would be approved by the big states, the small states united in opposition. They feared that if each state's representation in the new legislature was based only on the size of its population, the states with large populations would be able to dominate the new government and the needs and wishes of the small states would be ignored. William Paterson of New Jersey introduced an alternative set of resolutions, written to preserve the spirit of the Articles of Confederation by amending rather than replacing them. The **New Jersey Plan** included the following proposals:

- That a single-chamber legislature have the power to raise revenue and regulate commerce.
- That the states have equal representation in the legislature and choose its members.
- That a multiperson executive be elected by the legislature, with powers similar to those proposed under the Virginia Plan but without the right to veto legislation.
- That a supreme tribunal be created, with a limited jurisdiction. (There was no provision for a system of national courts.)
- That the acts of the legislature be binding on the states—that is, that they be regarded as "the supreme law of the respective states," with the option of force to compel obedience.

After only three days of deliberation, the New Jersey Plan was defeated in the first major convention vote, 7–3. However, the small states had enough support to force a compromise on the issue of representation in the legislature. Table 3.1 compares the New Jersey Plan with the Virginia Plan.

New Jersey Plan
Submitted by the head of the New Jersey delegation to the Constitutional Convention of 1787, a set of nine resolutions that would have, in effect, preserved the Articles of Confederation by amending rather than replacing them.

TABLE 3.1	**Major Differences Between the Virginia Plan and the New Jersey Plan**	
Characteristic	**Virginia Plan**	**New Jersey Plan**
Legislature	Two chambers	One chamber
Legislative power	Derived from the people	Derived from the states
Executive	Unspecified size	More than one person
Decision rule	Majority	Extraordinary majority
State laws	Legislature can override	National law is supreme
Executive removal	By Congress	By a majority of the states
Courts	National judiciary	No provision for national judiciary
Ratification	By the people	By the states

The Great Compromise

The Virginia Plan provided for a two-chamber legislature, with representation in both chambers based on population. The idea of two chambers was never seriously challenged, but the idea of representation according to population stirred up heated and prolonged debate. The small states demanded equal representation for all states, but another vote rejected that concept for the House of Representatives. The debate continued. Finally, the Connecticut delegation moved that each state have an equal vote in the Senate. Still another poll showed that the delegations were equally divided on this proposal.

A committee was created to resolve the deadlock. It consisted of one delegate from each state, chosen by secret ballot. After working straight through the Independence Day recess, the committee reported reaching the **Great Compromise** (sometimes called the Connecticut Compromise). Representation in the House of Representatives would be apportioned according to the population of each state. Initially, there would be fifty-six members. Revenue-raising acts would originate in the House. Most important, the states would be represented equally in the Senate, with two senators each. Senators would be selected by their state legislatures, not directly by the people.

The deadlock broke when the Massachusetts delegation divided evenly, allowing the equal state vote to pass by the narrowest of margins, 5 states to 4.[29] The small states got their equal representation, the big states their proportional representation. The small states might dominate the Senate and the big states might control the House, but because all legislation had to be approved by both chambers, neither group would be able to dominate the other. To be perpetually assured of state equality, no amendment to the Constitution could violate the equal state representation principle.[30]

Compromise on the Presidency

Conflict replaced compromise when the delegates turned to the executive branch. They did agree on a one-person executive, a president, but they disagreed on how the executive would be selected and what the term of office would be. The delegates distrusted the people's judgment; some feared that popular election of the president would arouse public passions. Consequently, the delegates rejected the idea. At the same time, representatives of the small states feared that election by the legislature would allow the big states to control the executive.

Once again, a committee composed of one member from each participating state was chosen to find a compromise. That committee fashioned the cumbersome presidential election system we still use today, the **electoral college**. (The Constitution does not use the expression *electoral college*.) Under this system, a group of electors would be chosen for the sole purpose of selecting the president and vice president. Each state legislature would choose a number of electors equal to the number of its representatives in Congress. Each elector would then vote for two people. The candidate with the most votes would become president, provided that the number of votes constituted a majority; the person with the next-greatest number of votes would become vice president. (The procedure was changed in 1804 by the Twelfth Amendment, which mandates separate votes for each office.) If no candidate won a majority, the House of Representatives would choose a president, with each state casting one vote.

The electoral college compromise eliminated the fear of a popular vote for president. At the same time, it satisfied the small states. If the electoral college failed to elect a president, which the delegates expected would happen, election by the House would give every state the same voice in the selection process. Finally, the delegates

---

Great Compromise
Submitted by the Connecticut delegation to the Constitutional Convention of 1787, and thus also known as the Connecticut Compromise, a plan calling for a bicameral legislature in which the House of Representatives would be apportioned according to population and the states would be represented equally in the Senate.

electoral college
A body of electors chosen by voters to cast ballots for president and vice president.

agreed that the president's term of office should be four years and that presidents should be eligible for reelection with no limit on the number of terms any individual president could serve. (The Twenty-Second Amendment, ratified in 1951, now limits the presidency to two terms.)

The delegates also realized that removing a president from office would be a serious political matter. For that reason, they involved both of the other two branches of government in the process. The House alone was empowered to charge a president with "Treason, Bribery, or other high Crimes and Misdemeanors" (Article II, Section 4), by a majority vote. The Senate was given the sole power to try the president on the House's charges. It could convict, and thus remove, a president only by a two-thirds vote (an **extraordinary majority**, a majority greater than the minimum of 50 percent plus one). And the chief justice of the Supreme Court was required to preside over the Senate trial. Only two presidents have been impeached by the House: Andrew Johnson and Bill Clinton; neither was convicted.

extraordinary majority
A majority greater than the minimum of 50 percent plus one.

3.4 The Final Product

★ Explain the contribution of the Constitution to the American political tradition and the principles it establishes.

Once the delegates had resolved their major disagreements, they dispatched the remaining issues relatively quickly. A committee was then appointed to organize and write up the results of the proceedings. Twenty-three resolutions had been debated and approved by the convention; these were reorganized under seven articles in the draft constitution. The preamble, which was the last section to be drafted, begins with a phrase that would have been impossible to write when the convention opened. This single sentence contains four elements that form the foundation of the American political tradition:[31]

- *It creates a people:* "We the people of the United States" was a dramatic departure from a loose confederation of states.
- *It explains the reason for the Constitution:* "in order to form a more perfect Union" was an indirect way of saying that the first effort, the Articles of Confederation, had been inadequate.
- *It articulates goals:* "[to] establish Justice, insure domestic Tranquility, provide for the common defence, promote the general Welfare, and secure the Blessings of Liberty to ourselves and our Posterity"—in other words, the government exists to promote order and freedom.
- *It fashions a government:* "do ordain and establish this Constitution for the United States of America."

The Basic Principles

In creating the Constitution, the founders relied on four political principles—republicanism, federalism, separation of powers, and checks and balances—that together established a revolutionary new political order.

Republicanism is a form of government in which power resides in the people and is exercised by their elected representatives. The idea of republicanism may be traced to the Greek philosopher Aristotle (384–322 B.C.), who advocated a constitution that combined principles of both democratic and oligarchic government. The

republicanism
A form of government in which power resides in the people and is exercised by their elected representatives.

framers were determined to avoid aristocracy (rule by a hereditary class), monarchy (rule by one person), and direct democracy (rule by the people). A republic was both new and daring: no people had ever been governed by a republic on so vast a scale.

The framers themselves were far from sure that their government could be sustained. They had no model of republican government to follow; moreover, republican government was thought to be suitable only for small territories, where the interests of the public would be obvious and the government would be within the reach of every citizen. After the convention ended, Benjamin Franklin was asked what sort of government the new nation would have. "A republic," the old man replied, "if you can keep it."

federalism
The division of power between a central government and regional governments.

Federalism is the division of power between a central government and regional governments. Citizens are thus subject to two different bodies of law. Federalism can be seen as standing between two competing government schemes. On the one side is unitary government, in which all power is vested in a central authority. On the other side stands confederation, a loose union of powerful states. In a confederation, the states surrender some power to a central government but retain the rest. The Articles of Confederation, as we have seen, divided power between loosely knit states and a weak central government. The Constitution also divides power between the states and a central government, but it confers substantial powers on a national government at the expense of the states.

According to the Constitution, the powers vested in the national and state governments are derived from the people, who remain the ultimate sovereigns. National and state governments can exercise their power over people and property within their spheres of authority. But at the same time, by participating in the electoral process or by amending their governing charters, the people can restrain both the national and the state governments if necessary to preserve liberty.

The Constitution lists the powers of the national government and the powers denied to the states. All other powers remain with the states. Generally, the states are required to give up only the powers necessary to create an effective national government; the national government is limited in turn to the powers specified in the Constitution. Despite the specific lists, the Constitution does not clearly describe the spheres of authority within which the powers can be exercised. As we will discuss in Chapter 4, limits on the exercise of power by the national government and the states have evolved as a result of political and military conflicts; moreover, the limits have proved changeable.

Separation of powers and checks and balances are two distinct principles, but both are necessary to ensure that one branch does not dominate the government.

separation of powers
The assignment of lawmaking, law-enforcing, and law-interpreting functions to separate branches of government.

Separation of powers is the assignment of the lawmaking, law-enforcing, and law-interpreting functions of government to independent legislative, executive, and judicial branches, respectively. Separation of powers safeguards liberty by ensuring that all government power does not fall into the hands of a single person or group of people. However, the Constitution constrained majority rule by limiting the people's direct influence on the electoral process (see Figure 3.1). In theory, separation of powers means that one branch cannot exercise the powers of the other branches. In practice, however, the separation is far from complete. One scholar has suggested that what we have instead is "separate institutions sharing powers."[32]

checks and balances
A government structure that gives each branch some scrutiny of and control over the other branches.

Checks and balances is a means of giving each branch of government some scrutiny of and control over the other branches. The aim is to prevent the exclusive exercise of certain powers by any one of the three branches. For example, only Congress can enact laws. But the president (through the veto power) can cancel them,

FIGURE 3.1 The Constitution and the Electoral Process

The framers were afraid of majority rule, and that fear is reflected in the electoral process for national office described in the Constitution. The people, speaking through the voters, participated directly only in the choice of their representatives in the House. The president and senators were elected indirectly, through the electoral college and state legislatures. (Direct election of senators did not become law until 1913, when the Seventeenth Amendment was ratified.) Judicial appointments are, and always have been, far removed from representative links to the people. Judges are nominated by the president and approved by the Senate.
Source: © Cengage Learning.

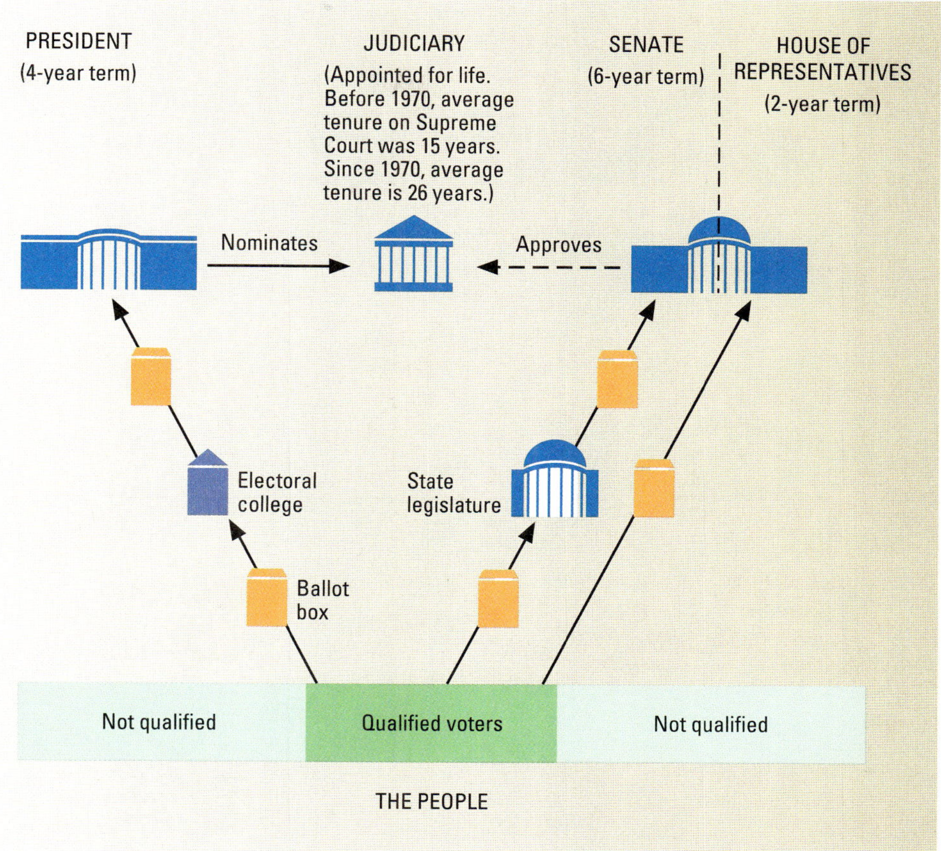

and the courts (by finding that a law violates the Constitution) can strike them down. The process goes on as Congress and the president sometimes begin the legislative process anew, attempting to reformulate laws to address the flaws identified by the Supreme Court in its decisions. In a "check on a check," Congress can override a president's veto by an extraordinary (two-thirds) majority in each chamber. Congress is also empowered to propose amendments to the Constitution, counteracting the courts' power to invalidate. Figure 3.2 (p. 66) depicts the relationship between separation of powers and checks and balances.

The Articles of the Constitution

In addition to the preamble, the Constitution contains seven articles. The first three establish the separate branches of government and specify their internal operations and powers. The remaining four define the relationships among the states, explain the process of amendment, declare the supremacy of national law, and explain the procedure for ratifying the Constitution.

Article I: The Legislative Article. In structuring their new government, the framers began with the legislative branch because they considered lawmaking the most important function of a republican government. Article I is the most detailed, and therefore the longest, of the articles. It grants substantial but limited legislative power to Congress (Article I begins: "All legislative Power herein granted...."). It defines the bicameral (two-chamber) character of Congress and describes the internal operating

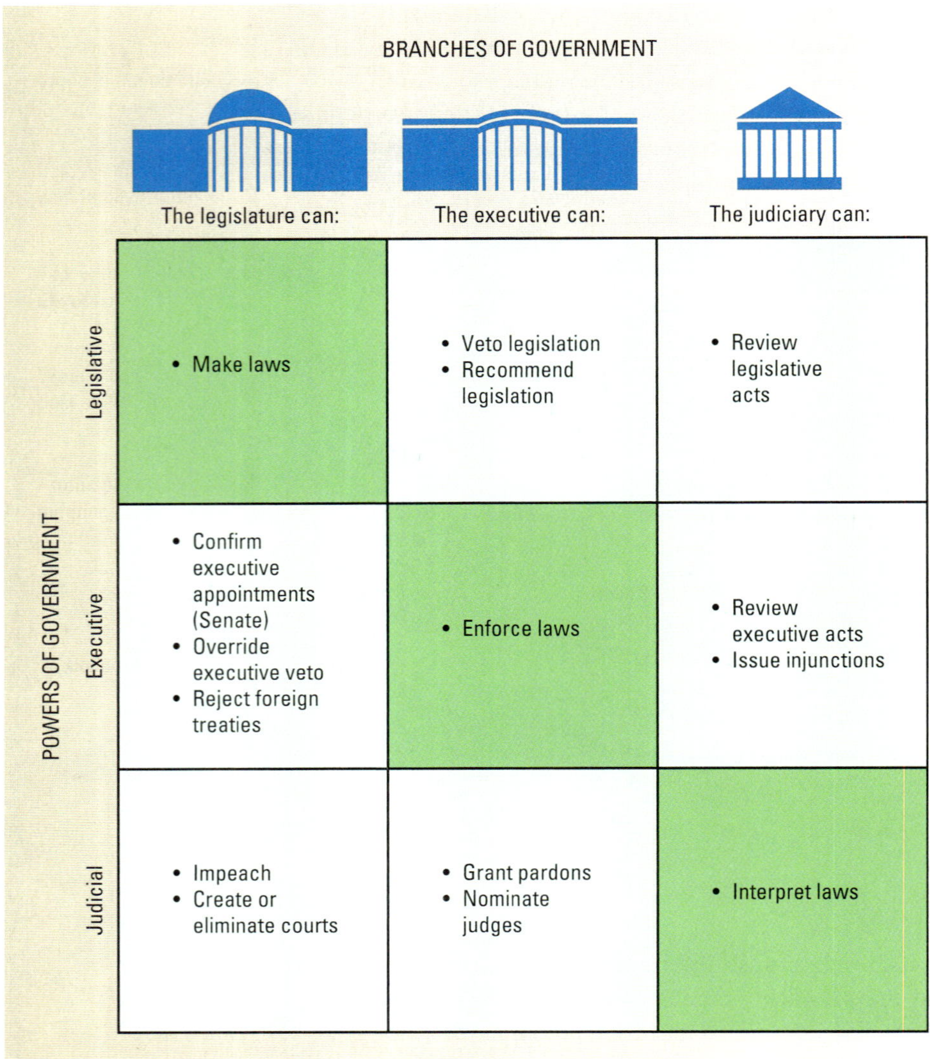

FIGURE 3.2 Separation of Powers and Checks and Balances

Separation of powers is the assignment of lawmaking, law-enforcing, and law-interpreting functions to the legislative, executive, and judicial branches, respectively. The phenomenon is illustrated by the diagonal from upper left to lower right in the figure. Checks and balances give each branch some power over the other branches. For example, the executive branch possesses some legislative power, and the legislative branch possesses some executive power. These checks and balances are listed outside the diagonal. Source: © Cengage Learning.

enumerated powers
The powers explicitly granted to Congress by the Constitution.

necessary and proper clause
The last clause in Section 8 of Article I of the Constitution, which gives Congress the means to execute its enumerated powers. This clause is the basis for Congress's implied powers. Also called the *elastic clause*.

implied powers
Those powers that Congress needs to execute its enumerated powers.

procedures of the House of Representatives and the Senate. Section 8 of Article I articulates the principle of **enumerated powers**, which means that Congress can exercise only the powers that the Constitution assigns to it. Eighteen powers are enumerated; the first seventeen are specific powers. For example, the third clause of Section 8 gives Congress the power to regulate interstate commerce. (One of the chief shortcomings of the Articles of Confederation was the lack of a means to cope with trade wars between the states. The solution was to vest control of interstate commerce in the national government.)

The last clause in Section 8, known as the **necessary and proper clause** (or the elastic clause), gives Congress the means to execute the enumerated powers (see the appendix). This clause is the basis of Congress's **implied powers**—those powers that Congress needs to execute its enumerated powers. For example, the power to levy and collect taxes (clause 1) and the power to coin money and regulate its value (clause 5), when joined with the necessary and proper clause (clause 18), imply that Congress has the power to charter a bank. Otherwise, the national government would have no means of managing the money it collects through its power to tax. Implied powers clearly expand the enumerated powers conferred on Congress by the Constitution.

Article II: The Executive Article. Article II grants executive power to a president. The article establishes the president's term of office, the procedure for electing the president by means of electors, the qualifications for becoming president, and the president's duties and powers. The last include acting as commander in chief of the military; making treaties (which must be ratified by a two-thirds vote in the Senate); and appointing government officers, diplomats, and judges (again, with the advice and consent of the Senate).

The president also has legislative powers—part of the constitutional system of checks and balances. For example, the Constitution requires that the president periodically inform Congress of "the State of the Union" and of the policies and programs that the executive branch intends to advocate in the coming year. Today, this is done annually in the president's State of the Union address. Under special circumstances, the president can also convene or adjourn Congress.

The duty to "take Care that the Laws be faithfully executed" in Section 3 has provided presidents with a reservoir of power. President Richard Nixon tried to use this power when he refused to turn over the Watergate tapes despite a judicial subpoena in a criminal trial. He claimed broad executive privilege, an extension of the executive power implied in Article II. But the Supreme Court rejected his claim, arguing that it violated the separation of powers, because the decision to release or withhold information in a criminal trial is a judicial, not an executive, function.

Article III: The Judicial Article. The third article was left purposely vague. The Constitution established the Supreme Court as the highest court in the land. But beyond that, the framers were unable to agree on the need for a national judiciary or on its

How Many Pens Does It Take to Sign a Bill into Law?

Answer: It depends on the number of people a president wants to thank. The president gives his approval to legislation by signing it into law. Beginning in the 1960s, the bill-signing ceremony became an art form, garnering much press attention. The president would typically employ many pens in small strokes for his signature and then distribute the pens as souvenirs to the people instrumental in the bill's passage. Here President Barack Obama picks up the first pen (*left*), signs a portion of his signature (*middle*), then jokes about the multiple pens he will use to complete his signature on the American Recovery and Reinvestment Act, Tuesday, February 17, 2009, during a ceremony at the Denver Museum of Nature and Science (*right*). We wonder whether the pens were manufactured in the United States.

size, its composition, or the procedures it should follow. They left these issues to Congress, which resolved them by creating a system of federal (that is, national) courts, separate from the state courts.

Unless they are impeached, federal judges serve for life. They are appointed to indefinite terms "during good Behaviour," and their salaries cannot be reduced while they hold office. These stipulations reinforce the separation of powers; they see to it that judges are independent of the other branches and that they do not have to fear retribution for their exercise of judicial power.

Congress exercises a potential check on the judicial branch through its power to create (and eliminate) lower federal courts. Congress can also restrict the power of the federal courts to decide cases. And, as we have noted, the president appoints, with the advice and consent of the Senate, the justices of the Supreme Court and the judges of the lower federal courts. Since the 1980s, especially, the judicial appointment process has become highly politicized, with both Democrats and Republicans accusing each other of obstructionism or extremism in several high-profile confirmation debates.

judicial review
The power to declare congressional (and presidential) acts invalid because they violate the Constitution.

Article III does not explicitly give the courts the power of **judicial review**, that is, the authority to invalidate congressional or presidential actions because they violate the Constitution. That power has been inferred from the logic, structure, and theory of the Constitution and from important court rulings, some of which we discuss in subsequent chapters.

The Remaining Articles. The remaining four articles of the Constitution cover a lot of ground. Article IV requires that the judicial acts and criminal warrants of each state be honored in all other states, and it forbids discrimination against citizens of one state by another state. This provision promotes equality; it keeps the states from treating outsiders differently from their own citizens. For example, suppose Smith and Jones both reside in Illinois, and an Illinois court awards Smith a judgment of $100,000 against Jones. Jones moves to Alaska, hoping to avoid payment. Rather than force Smith to bring a new lawsuit against Jones in Alaska, the Alaska courts give full faith and credit to the Illinois judgment, enforcing it as their own. The origin of Article IV can be traced to the Articles of Confederation.

Article IV also allows the addition of new states and stipulates that the national government will protect the states against foreign invasion and domestic violence.

Article V specifies the methods for amending (changing) the Constitution and guarantees equal state representation in the Senate. We will have more to say about this amendment process shortly.

supremacy clause
The clause in Article VI of the Constitution that asserts that national laws take precedence over state and local laws when they conflict.

An important component of Article VI is the **supremacy clause**, which asserts that when the Constitution, national laws, and treaties conflict with state or local laws, the first three take precedence over the last two. The stipulation is vital to the operation of federalism. In keeping with the supremacy clause, Article VI requires that all national and state officials, elected or appointed, take an oath to support the Constitution. The article also mandates that religious affiliation or belief cannot be a prerequisite for holding government office.

Finally, Article VII describes the ratification process, stipulating that approval by conventions in nine states would be necessary for the Constitution to take effect.

The Framers' Motives

Some argue that the Constitution is essentially a conservative document written by wealthy men to advance their own interests. One distinguished historian who wrote in the early 1900s, Charles A. Beard, maintained that the delegates had much to gain from a strong national government.[33] Many held government securities dating from the Revolutionary War that had become practically worthless under the Articles of Confederation. A strong national government would protect their property and pay off the nation's debts.

Beard's argument, that the Constitution was crafted to protect the economic interests of this small group of creditors, provoked a generation of historians to examine the existing financial records of the convention delegates. Their scholarship has largely discredited his once-popular view.[34] For example, it turns out that seven of the delegates who left the convention or refused to sign the Constitution held public securities worth more than twice the total of the holdings of the thirty-nine delegates who did sign. Moreover, the most influential delegates owned no securities. And only a few delegates appear to have directly benefited economically from the new government.[35] Still, there is little doubt about the general homogeneity of the delegates or about their concern for producing a stable economic order that would preserve and promote the interests of some more than others.

What did motivate the framers? Surely economic considerations were important, but they were not the major issues. The single most important factor leading to the Constitutional Convention was the inability of the national or state governments to maintain order under the loose structure of the Articles of Confederation. Certainly, order involved the protection of property, but the framers had a broader view of property than their portfolios of government securities. They wanted to protect their homes, their families, and their means of livelihood from impending anarchy.

Although they disagreed bitterly on the structure and mechanics of the national government, the framers agreed on the most vital issues. For example, three of the most crucial features of the Constitution—the power to tax, the necessary and proper clause, and the supremacy clause—were approved unanimously without debate; experience had taught the delegates that a strong national government was essential if the United States were to survive. The motivation to create order was so strong, in fact, that the framers were willing to draft clauses that protected the most undemocratic of all institutions: slavery.

The Slavery Issue

The institution of slavery was well ingrained in American life at the time of the Constitutional Convention, and slavery helped shape the Constitution, although it is mentioned nowhere by name in it. (According to the first national census in 1790, nearly 18 percent of the population—697,000 people—lived in slavery.) It is doubtful, in fact, that there would have been a Constitution if the delegates had had to resolve the slavery issue, for the southern states would have opposed a constitution that prohibited slavery. Opponents of slavery were in the minority, and they were willing to tolerate its continuation in the interest of forging a union, perhaps believing that the issue could be resolved another day.

The question of representation in the House of Representatives brought the slavery issue close to the surface of the debate at the Constitutional Convention, and it led to the Great Compromise. Representation in the House was to be based on population. But who counted in the population? States with large slave populations wanted all their inhabitants, slave and free, counted equally; states with few slaves wanted only the free population counted. The delegates agreed unanimously that in apportioning representation in the House and in assessing direct taxes, the population of each state was to be determined by adding "the whole Number of free Persons" and "three fifths of all other Persons" (Article I, Section 2). The phrase "all other Persons" is, of course, a substitute for "slaves."

The three-fifths formula had been used by the 1783 congress under the Articles of Confederation to allocate government costs among the states. The rule reflected the view that slaves were less efficient producers of wealth than free people, not that slaves were three-fifths human and two-fifths personal property.[36]

The three-fifths clause gave states with large slave populations (the South) greater representation in Congress than states with small slave populations (the North). If all slaves had been included in the count, the slave states would have had 50 percent of the seats in the House, an outcome that would have been unacceptable to the North. Had none of the slaves been counted, the slave states would have had 41 percent of House seats, which would have been unacceptable to the South. The three-fifths compromise left the South with 47 percent of the House seats, a sizable minority, but in all likelihood a losing one on slavery issues.[37] The overrepresentation resulting from the South's large slave populations translated into greater influence in selecting the president as well, because the electoral college was based on the size of the states' congressional delegations. The three-fifths clause also undertaxed states with large slave populations.

Another issue centered on the slave trade. Several southern delegates were uncompromising in their defense of the slave trade; other delegates favored prohibition. The delegates compromised, agreeing that the slave trade would not be ended before twenty years had elapsed (Article I, Section 9). Finally, the delegates agreed, without serious challenge, that fugitive slaves would be returned to their masters (Article IV, Section 2).

In addressing these points, the framers in essence condoned slavery. Tens of thousands of Africans were forcibly taken from their homes and sold into bondage. Many died on the journey to this distant land, and those who survived were brutalized and treated as less than human. Clearly, slavery existed in stark opposition to the idea that all men are created equal. Although many slaveholders, including Jefferson and Madison, agonized over it, few made serious efforts to free their own slaves. Most Americans seemed indifferent to slavery and felt no embarrassment at the apparent contradiction between the Declaration of Independence and slavery. Do the framers deserve contempt for their toleration and perpetuation of slavery? The most prominent founders—George Washington, John Adams, and Thomas Jefferson—expected slavery to wither away. A leading scholar of colonial history has offered a defense of their inaction: the framers were simply unable to transcend the limitations of the age in which they lived.[38]

Nonetheless, the eradication of slavery proceeded gradually in certain states. Opposition to slavery on moral or religious grounds was one reason. Economic forces, such as a shift in the North to agricultural production that was less labor intensive, were a contributing factor too. By 1787, Connecticut, Massachusetts, Pennsylvania, Rhode Island, and Vermont had abolished slavery or provided for gradual emancipation. No southern states followed suit, although several enacted laws making it easier for masters to free their slaves. The slow but perceptible shift on the slavery issue in many states masked a volcanic force capable of destroying the Constitutional Convention and the Union.

⭐ 3.5 Selling the Constitution

★ Describe the actions taken to ensure the ratification of the
Constitution.

Nearly four months after the Constitutional Convention opened, the delegates convened for the last time, on September 17, 1787, to sign the final version of their handiwork. Because several delegates were unwilling to sign the document, the last paragraph was craftily worded to give the impression of unanimity: "Done in Convention by the Unanimous Consent of the States present." Before it could take effect, the Constitution had to be ratified by a minimum of nine state conventions. The support of key states was crucial. In Pennsylvania, however, the legislature was slow to convene a ratifying convention. Pro-Constitution forces became so frustrated at this dawdling that they broke into a local boardinghouse and hauled two errant legislators through the streets to the statehouse so the assembly could schedule the convention.

The proponents of the new charter, who wanted a strong national government, called themselves Federalists. The opponents of the Constitution were quickly dubbed Antifederalists. They claimed, however, to be the true federalists because they wanted to protect the states from the tyranny of a strong national government. Elbridge Gerry, a vocal Antifederalist, called his opponents "rats" (because they favored ratification) and maintained that he was an "antirat."[39] Such is the Alice-in-Wonderland character of political discourse. Whatever they were called, the viewpoints of these two groups formed the bases of the first American political parties, as well as several enduring debates that politicians have wrestled with as they have attempted to balance the tradeoffs between freedom, order, and equality.

The *Federalist* Papers

The press was the mass medium of the eighteenth century. Newspapers and commentaries became a battlefield of words, filled with extravagant praise or vituperative condemnation of the proposed constitution. Beginning in October 1787, an exceptional series of eighty-five New York newspaper articles defending the Constitution appeared under the title *The Federalist: A Commentary on the Constitution of the United States.* These partisan essays bore the pen name Publius (for a Roman consul and defender of the Republic, Publius Valerius, who was later known as Publicola); they were written primarily by James Madison and Alexander Hamilton, with some assistance from John Jay. Reprinted extensively during the ratification battle, the *Federalist* papers have far greater influence today when read as dispassionate analyses on the meaning of the Constitution and the political theory it embodies.[40]

Not to be outdone, the Antifederalists offered their own intellectual basis for rejecting the Constitution. In several essays, the most influential published under the pseudonyms Brutus and Federal Farmer, the Antifederalists attacked the centralization of power in a strong national government, claiming it would obliterate the states, violate the social contract of the Declaration of Independence, and destroy liberty in the process. They defended the status quo, maintaining that the Articles of Confederation established true federal principles.[41]

Of all the *Federalist* papers, the most magnificent and most frequently cited is *Federalist* No. 10, written by James Madison. He argued that the proposed constitution was designed "to break and control the violence of faction." "By a faction,"

Madison wrote, "I understand a number of citizens, whether amounting to a majority or minority of the whole, who are united and actuated by some common impulse of passion, or of interest, adverse to the rights of other citizens, or to the permanent and aggregate interests of the community." No one has improved upon Madison's lucid and compelling argument, and it remains the touchstone on the problem of factions to this day.

Federalist No. 10 is available at www.cengagebrain.com/shop/ ISBN/0495906182.

What Madison called factions are today called interest groups or even political parties. According to Madison, "The most common and durable source of factions has been the various and unequal distribution of property." Madison was concerned not with reducing inequalities of wealth (which he took for granted) but with controlling the seemingly inevitable conflict that stems from them. The Constitution, he argued, was well constructed for this purpose.

Through the mechanism of representation, wrote Madison, the Constitution would prevent a "tyranny of the majority" (mob rule). The people would control the government not directly but indirectly through their elected representatives. And those representatives would have the intelligence and the understanding to serve the larger interests of the nation. Moreover, the federal system would require that majorities form first within each state and then organize for effective action at the national level. This and the vastness of the country would make it unlikely that a majority would form that would "invade the rights of other citizens."

The purpose of *Federalist* No. 10 was to demonstrate that the proposed government was not likely to be dominated by any faction. Contrary to conventional wisdom, Madison argued, the key to mending the evils of factions is to have a large republic—the larger, the better. The more diverse the society, the less likely it is that an unjust majority can form. Madison certainly had no intention of creating a majoritarian democracy; his view of popular government was much more consistent with the model of pluralist democracy discussed in Chapter 2.

Madison pressed his argument from a different angle in *Federalist* No. 51. Asserting that "ambition must be made to counteract ambition," he argued that the separation of powers and checks and balances would control efforts at tyranny from any source. If power is distributed equally among the three branches, he argued, each branch will have the capacity to counteract the others. In Madison's words, "usurpations are guarded against by a division of the government into distinct and separate departments." Because legislative power tends to predominate in republican governments, legislative authority is divided between the Senate and the House of Representatives, which have different methods of election and terms of office. Additional protection arises from federalism, which divides power "between two distinct governments"—national and state—and subdivides "the portion allotted to each … among distinct and separate departments." Madison called this arrangement of power, divided as it was across and within levels of government, a "compound republic."

Federalist No. 51 is available at www.cengagebrain.com/shop/ ISBN/0495906182.

The Antifederalists wanted additional separation of powers and additional checks and balances, which they maintained would eliminate the threat of tyranny entirely. The Federalists believed that such protections would make decisive national action virtually impossible. But to ensure ratification, they agreed to a compromise.

A Concession: The Bill of Rights

Despite the eloquence of the *Federalist* papers, many prominent citizens, including Thomas Jefferson, were unhappy that the Constitution did not list basic civil liberties—the individual freedoms guaranteed to citizens. The omission of a bill of rights was the chief obstacle to the adoption of the Constitution by the states. (Seven of the eleven state constitutions that were written in the first five years of independence included such a list.) The colonists had just rebelled against the British government to preserve their basic freedoms. Why did the proposed Constitution not spell out those freedoms?

The answer was rooted in logic, not politics. Because the national government was limited to those powers that were granted to it and because no power was granted to abridge the people's liberties, a list of guaranteed freedoms was not necessary. In *Federalist* No. 84, Hamilton went even further, arguing that the addition of a bill of rights would be dangerous. To deny the exercise of a nonexistent power might lead to the exercise of a power that is not specifically denied. For example, to declare that the national government shall make no law abridging free speech might suggest that the national government could prohibit activities in unspecified areas (such as divorce), which are the states' domain. Because it is not possible to list all prohibited powers, wrote Hamilton, any attempt to provide a partial list would make the unlisted areas vulnerable to government abuse.

But logic was no match for fear. Many states agreed to ratify the Constitution only after George Washington suggested adding a list of guarantees through the amendment process. Well in excess of one hundred amendments were proposed by the states. These were eventually narrowed to twelve, which were approved by Congress and sent to the states. Ten became part of the Constitution in 1791, after securing the approval of the required three-fourths of the states. Collectively, the ten amendments are known as the **Bill of Rights**. They restrain the national government from tampering with fundamental rights and civil liberties, and emphasize the limited character of the national government's power (see Table 3.2 on p. 74).

Bill of Rights
The first ten amendments to the Constitution. They prevent the national government from tampering with fundamental rights and civil liberties, and emphasize the limited character of national power.

Ratification

The Constitution officially took effect upon its ratification by the ninth state, New Hampshire, on June 21, 1788. However, the success of the new government was not ensured until July 1788, by which time the Constitution had been ratified by the key states of Virginia and New York after lengthy debate.

The reflection and deliberation that attended the creation and ratification of the Constitution signaled to the world that a new government could be launched peacefully. The French observer Alexis de Tocqueville (1805–1859) later wrote:

> That which is new in the history of societies is to see a great people, warned by its lawgivers that the wheels of government are stopping, turn its attention on itself without haste or fear, sound the depth of the ill, and then wait for two years to find the remedy at leisure, and then finally, when the remedy has been indicated, submit to it voluntarily without its costing humanity a single tear or drop of blood.[42]

★ 3.6 Constitutional Change

★ Explain the procedures required to amend the Constitution.

The founders realized that the Constitution would have to be changed from time to time. To this end, they specified a formal amendment process, and one that was used almost immediately to add the Bill of Rights. With the passage of time, the Constitution has also been altered through judicial interpretation and changes in political practice.

TABLE 3.2	The Bill of Rights

The first ten amendments to the Constitution are known as the Bill of Rights. The following is a list of those amendments, grouped conceptually. For the actual order and wording of the Bill of Rights, see the Appendix.

Guarantees	Amendment
Guarantees for Participation in the Political Process	
No government abridgment of speech or press; no government abridgment of peaceable assembly; no government abridgment of petitioning government for redress.	1
Guarantees Respecting Personal Beliefs	
No government establishment of religion; no government prohibition of free religious exercise.	1
Guarantees of Personal Privacy	
Owner's consent necessary to quarter troops in private homes in peacetime; quartering during war must be lawful.	3
Government cannot engage in unreasonable searches and seizures; warrants to search and seize require probable cause.	4
No compulsion to testify against oneself in criminal cases.	5
Guarantees Against Government's Overreaching	
Serious crimes require a grand jury indictment; no repeated prosecution for the same offense; no loss of life, liberty, or property without due process; no taking of property for public use without just compensation.	5
Criminal defendants will have a speedy public trial by impartial local jury; defendants are informed of accusation; defendants may confront witnesses against them; defendants may use judicial process to obtain favorable witnesses; defendants may have legal assistance for their defense.	6
Civil lawsuits can be tried by juries if controversy exceeds $20; in jury trials, fact finding is a jury function.	7
No excessive bail; no excessive fines; no cruel and unusual punishment.	8
Other Guarantees	
The people have the right to bear arms.	2
No government trespass on unspecified fundamental rights.	9
The states or the people retain all powers not delegated to the national government or denied to the states.	10

The Formal Amendment Process

The amendment process has two stages, proposal and ratification; both are necessary for an amendment to become part of the Constitution. The Constitution provides two alternatives for completing each stage (see Figure 3.3). Amendments can be proposed by a two-thirds vote in both the House of Representatives and the Senate or by a national convention, summoned by Congress at the request of two-thirds of the state legislatures. All constitutional amendments to date have been proposed by the first method; the second has never been used.

A proposed amendment can be ratified by a vote of the legislatures of three-fourths of the states or by a vote of constitutional conventions held in three-fourths of the states. Congress chooses the method of ratification. It has used the state

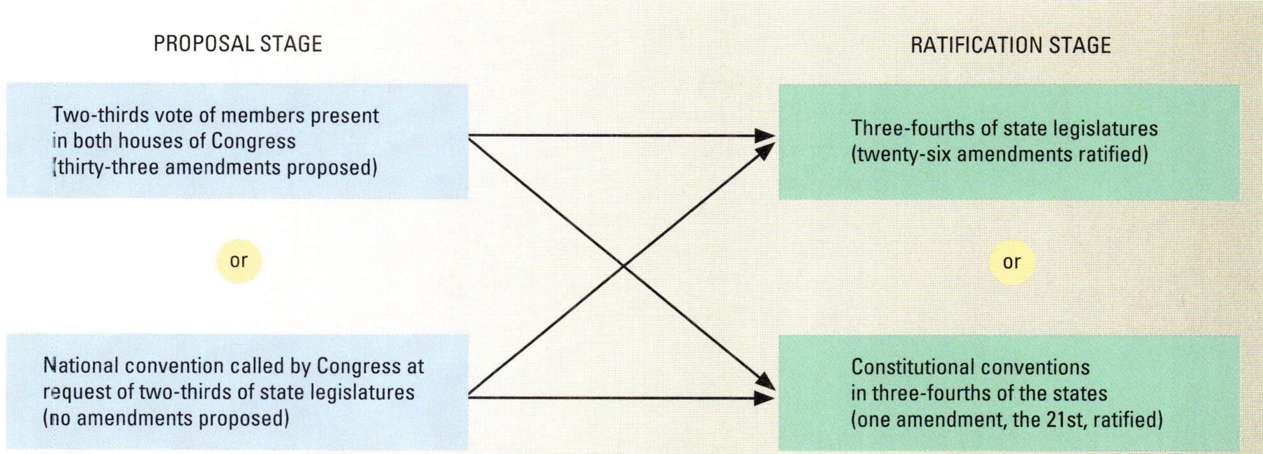

FIGURE 3.3 Amending the Constitution

Amending the Constitution requires two stages: proposal and ratification. Both Congress and the states can play a role in the proposal stage, but ratification is a process that must be fought in the states themselves. Once a state has ratified an amendment, it cannot retract its action. However, a state may reject an amendment and then reconsider its decision.
Source: © Cengage Learning.

convention method only once, for the Twenty-first Amendment, which repealed the Eighteenth Amendment (prohibition of intoxicating liquors). Congress may, in proposing an amendment, set a time limit for its ratification. Beginning with the Eighteenth Amendment, but skipping the Nineteenth, Congress has set seven years as the limit for ratification.

Note that the amendment process requires the exercise of extraordinary majorities (two-thirds and three-fourths). The framers purposely made it difficult to propose and ratify amendments (although nowhere near as difficult as under the Articles of Confederation). They wanted only the most significant issues to lead to constitutional change. Note, too, that the president plays no formal role in the process. Presidential approval is not required to amend the Constitution, although the president's political influence affects the success or failure of any amendment effort.

Calling a national convention to propose an amendment has never been tried, and the method raises several thorny questions. For example, the Constitution does not specify the number of delegates who should attend, the method by which they should be chosen, or the rules for debating and voting on a proposed amendment. Confusion surrounding the convention process has precluded its use, leaving the amendment process in congressional hands.[43] The major issue is the limits, if any, on the business of the convention. Remember that the convention in Philadelphia in 1787, charged with revising the Articles of Confederation, drafted an entirely new charter. Would a national convention called to consider a particular amendment be within its bounds to rewrite the Constitution? No one really knows.

Most of the Constitution's twenty-seven amendments were adopted to reflect changes in political thinking. The first ten amendments (the Bill of Rights) were the price of ratification, but they have been fundamental to our system of government. The last seventeen amendments fall into three main categories: they make public policy, they correct deficiencies in the government's structure, or they promote equality (see Table 3.3 on p. 76). One attempt to make public policy through a constitutional amendment was disastrous. The Eighteenth Amendment (1919) prohibited the manufacture or sale of intoxicating beverages, extinguishing the fifth largest industry in the nation. This amendment and the Thirteenth, barring the ownership of slaves, were the only provisions to limit the activities of citizens.[44] Prohibition lasted fourteen years and was an utter failure. Gangsters began bootlegging liquor, people died from drinking homemade spirits, and millions regularly broke the law by drinking anyway. Congress had to propose another amendment in 1933 to repeal the Eighteenth. The states ratified this amendment, the Twenty-first, in less than ten months, less time than it took to ratify the Fourteenth Amendment, guaranteeing citizenship, due process, and equal protection of the laws.

TABLE 3.3	Constitutional Amendments: 11 Through 27			
No.	**Proposed**	**Ratified**	**Intent***	**Subject**
11	1794	1795	G	Prohibits an individual from suing a state in federal court without the state's consent.
12	1803	1804	G	Requires the electoral college to vote separately for president and vice president.
13	1865	1865	E	Prohibits slavery.
14	1866	1868	E	Gives citizenship to all persons born or naturalized in the United States (including former slaves); prevents states from depriving any person of "life, liberty, or property, without due process of law," and declares that no state shall deprive any person of "the equal protection of the laws."
15	1869	1870	E	Guarantees that citizens' right to vote cannot be denied "on account of race, color, or previous condition of servitude."
16	1909	1913	E	Gives Congress the power to collect an income tax.
17	1912	1913	E	Provides for popular election of senators, who were formerly elected by state legislatures.
18	1917	1919	P	Prohibits the making and selling of intoxicating liquors.
19	1919	1920	E	Guarantees that citizens' right to vote cannot be denied "on account of sex."
20	1932	1933	G	Changes the presidential inauguration from March 4 to January 20 and sets January 3 for the opening date of Congress.
21	1933	1933	P	Repeals the Eighteenth Amendment.
22	1947	1951	G	Limits a president to two terms.
23	1960	1961	E	Gives citizens of Washington, D.C., the right to vote for president.
24	1962	1964	E	Prohibits charging citizens a poll tax to vote in presidential or congressional elections.
25	1965	1967	G	Provides for succession in event of death, removal from office, incapacity, or resignation of the president or vice president.
26	1971	1971	E	Lowers the voting age to eighteen.
27	1789	1992	G	Bars immediate pay increases to members of Congress.

*P: amendments legislating public policy; G: amendments correcting perceived deficiencies in government structure; E: amendments advancing equality.

Since 1787, about ten thousand constitutional amendments have been introduced; only a fraction has survived the proposal stage. Once Congress has approved an amendment, its chances for ratification are high. The Twenty-seventh Amendment, which prevents members of Congress from voting themselves immediate pay increases, was ratified in 1992. It had been submitted to the states in 1789 without a time limit for ratification, but it languished in a political netherworld until 1982, when a University of Texas student, Gregory D. Watson, stumbled upon the proposed amendment while researching a paper. At that time, only eight states had ratified the amendment. Watson earned a C for the paper; his professor remained unconvinced that the amendment was still pending.[45] Watson took up the cause, prompting renewed interest in the amendment. In May 1992, ratification by the Michigan legislature provided the decisive vote, 203 years after congressional approval of the proposed amendment.[46] Only six amendments submitted to the states have failed to be ratified.

Interpretation by the Courts

In *Marbury* v. *Madison* (1803), the Supreme Court declared that the courts have the power to nullify government acts that conflict with the Constitution. This is the power

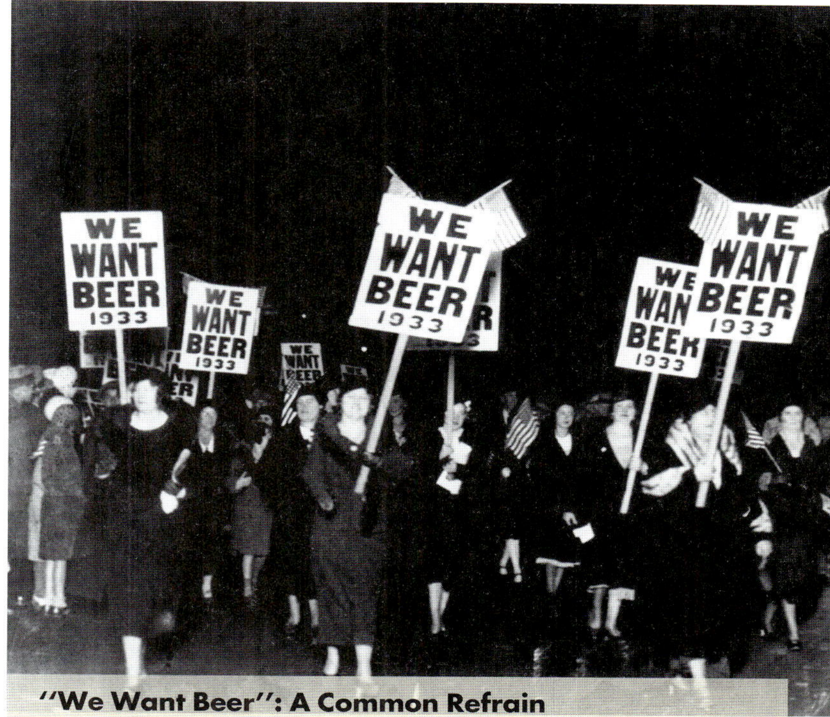

AP Photo

"We Want Beer": A Common Refrain

"We want beer" may be a popular refrain at tailgating parties and on certain college campuses today, but it was the basis of political protest in October 1932 when more than 20,000 protesters, many of them women, demanded repeal of the Eighteenth Amendment. The amendment, which was ratified in 1919, banned the manufacture, sale, and transportation of alcoholic beverages. The amendment was spurred by moral and social reform groups, such as the Women's Christian Temperance Union, founded by Evanston, Illinois, resident Frances Willard in 1874. The amendment proved to be an utter failure. People continued to drink, but their alcohol came from illegal sources.

of judicial review. (We will elaborate on judicial review in Chapter 14.) The exercise of judicial review forces the courts to interpret the Constitution. In a way, this makes a lot of sense. The judiciary is the law-interpreting branch of the government; as the supreme law of the land, the Constitution is fair game for judicial interpretation. It is problematic, in theory at least, that the Constitution does not expressly authorize courts to exercise this power. Judicial review is the courts' main check on the other branches of government. But in interpreting the Constitution, the courts cannot help but give new meaning to its provisions. This is why judicial interpretation is a principal form of constitutional change.

What guidelines should judges use in interpreting the Constitution? For one thing, they must realize that the usage and meaning of many words have changed during the past two hundred years. Judges must be careful to think about what the words meant at the time the Constitution was written. Some insist that they must also consider the original intent of the framers—not an easy task. Of course, there are records of the Constitutional Convention and of the debates surrounding ratification. But there are also many questions about the completeness and accuracy of those records, even Madison's detailed notes. And at times, the framers were deliberately vague in writing the document. This may reflect lack of agreement on, or universal understanding of, certain provisions in the Constitution. Some scholars and judges maintain that the search for original meaning is hopeless and that contemporary notions of constitutional provisions must hold sway. Critics say that this approach comes perilously close to amending the Constitution as judges see fit, transforming law interpreters into lawmakers. Still other scholars and judges maintain that judges face the unavoidable challenge of balancing two-hundred-year-old constitutional principles against the demands of modern society.[47] Whatever the approach, unelected judges with effective life tenure run the risk of usurping policies established by the people's representatives.

Political Practice

The Constitution is silent on many issues. It says nothing about political parties or the president's cabinet, for example, yet both have exercised considerable influence in American politics. Some constitutional provisions have fallen out of use. The electors in the electoral college, for example, were supposed to exercise their own judgment in voting for the president and vice president. Today, the electors function simply as a rubber stamp, validating the outcome of election contests in their states.

Meanwhile, political practice has altered the distribution of power without changes in the Constitution. The framers intended Congress to be the strongest branch of government. But the president has come to overshadow Congress. Presidents such as Abraham Lincoln and Franklin Roosevelt used their formal and informal powers imaginatively to respond to national crises. And their actions paved the way for future presidents, most recently George W. Bush, to enlarge further the powers of the office.

The framers could scarcely have imagined an urbanized nation of 314 million people stretching across a landmass some three thousand miles wide, reaching halfway over the Pacific Ocean, and stretching past the Arctic Circle. Never in their wildest nightmares could they have foreseen the destructiveness of nuclear weaponry or envisioned its effect on the power to declare war. The Constitution empowers Congress to consider and debate this momentous step. But with nuclear annihilation perhaps only minutes away and terrorist threats a real if unpredictable prospect since September 11, 2001, the legislative power to declare war is likely to give way to the president's power to wage war as the nation's commander in chief. Strict adherence to the Constitution in such circumstances could destroy the nation's ability to protect itself.

3.7 An Evaluation of the Constitution

★ Evaluate the extent to which the Constitution reflects and embodies the principles of majoritarian or pluralist democracy.

The U.S. Constitution is one of the world's most praised political documents. It is the oldest written national constitution and one of the most widely copied, sometimes word for word. It is also one of the shortest, consisting of about 4,300 words (not counting the amendments, which add 3,100 words). The brevity of the Constitution may be one of its greatest strengths. As we noted earlier, the framers simply laid out a structural framework for government; they did not describe relationships and powers in detail. For example, the Constitution gives Congress the power to regulate "Commerce … among the several States" but does not define interstate commerce. Such general wording allows interpretation in keeping with contemporary political, social, and technological developments. Air travel, for instance, unknown in 1787, now falls easily within Congress's power to regulate interstate commerce.

The generality of the U.S. Constitution stands in stark contrast to the specificity of most state constitutions and the constitutions of many emerging democracies. The California Constitution, for example, provides that "fruit and nut-bearing trees under the age of four years from the time of planting in orchard form and grapevines under the age of three years from the time of planting in vineyard form … shall be exempt from taxation" (Article XIII, Section 12). Because they are so specific, most state constitutions are much longer than the U.S. Constitution. The longest by far is the Alabama constitution, which is more than 300,000 words. That's longer than *Moby-Dick* or the *Bible.*

The constitution of the Republic of Slovenia, adopted in December 1991, prevents citizens from being "compelled to undergo medical treatment except in such cases as are determined by statute." In the Republic of Lithuania, the national constitution, adopted in October 1992, spells out in significant detail some of the free-speech rights of its citizens, including the protection that "citizens who belong to ethnic communities shall have the right to foster their language, culture, and customs."[48] But evidence reveals that the U.S. Constitution has become a dimming beacon for others to follow (see "Politics of Global Change: The U.S. Constitution Loses Some of Its Charm," pp. 80–81).

Freedom, Order, and Equality in the Constitution

The revolutionaries' first try at government was embodied in the Articles of Confederation. The result was a weak national government that leaned too much toward freedom at the expense of order. Deciding that the confederation was beyond correcting, the revolutionaries chose a new form of government—a compound or *federal* government—that was strong enough to maintain order but not so strong that it could dominate the states or infringe on individual freedoms. In short, the Constitution provided a judicious balance between order and freedom. It paid virtually no attention to equality. (Recall that the equality premise in the Declaration of Independence was meant for the colonists as a people, not as individuals.)

Consider social equality. The Constitution never mentioned the word *slavery,* a controversial issue even then. In fact, as we have seen, the Constitution implicitly condones slavery in the wording of several articles. Not until the ratification of the Thirteenth Amendment in 1865 was slavery prohibited.

The Constitution was designed long before social equality was ever even thought of as an objective of government. In fact, in *Federalist* No. 10, Madison held that protection of the "diversities in the faculties of men from which the rights of property originate" is "the first object of government." More than a century later, the Constitution was changed to incorporate a key device for the promotion of social equality—a national income tax. The Sixteenth Amendment (1913) gave Congress the power to collect an income tax; it was proposed and ratified to replace a law that had been declared unconstitutional in an 1895 Supreme Court case. The income tax had long been seen as a means of putting into effect the concept of progressive taxation, in which the tax rate increases with income. The Sixteenth Amendment gave progressive taxation a constitutional basis.[49] Progressive taxation later helped promote social equality through the redistribution of income; that is, higher-income people are taxed at higher rates to help fund social programs that benefit low-income people.

Social equality itself has never been, and is not now, a prime constitutional value. The Constitution has been much more effective in securing order and freedom. Nor did the Constitution take a stand on political equality. It left voting qualifications to the states, specifying only that people who could vote for "the most numerous Branch of the State Legislature" could also vote for representatives to Congress (Article I, Section 2). Most states at that time allowed only taxpaying or property-owning white males to vote. With few exceptions, blacks and women were universally excluded from voting. These inequalities have been rectified by several amendments (see Table 3.3).

Political equality expanded after the Civil War. The Fourteenth Amendment (adopted in 1868) guaranteed all persons, including blacks, citizenship. The Fifteenth Amendment (ratified in 1870) declared that "race, color, or previous condition of servitude" could not be used to deny citizens the right to vote. This did not automatically give blacks the vote; some states used other mechanisms to limit black enfranchisement. The Nineteenth Amendment (adopted in 1920) opened the way for women to vote by declaring that sex could not be used to deny citizens the right to vote. The Twenty-fourth Amendment (adopted in 1964) prohibited the poll tax (a tax that people had to pay to vote and that tended to disenfranchise poor blacks) in presidential and congressional elections. The Twenty-sixth Amendment (adopted in 1971) declared that age could not be used to deny citizens eighteen years or older the right to vote. One other amendment expanded the Constitution's grant of political equality. The Twenty-third Amendment (adopted in 1961) allowed residents of Washington, D.C., who are not citizens of any state, to vote for president.

Politics of Global Change

The U.S. Constitution Loses Some of Its Charm

Back in 1987, on the occasion of the 200th birthday of the U.S. Constitution, *Time* magazine observed that "of the 170 countries that exist today, more than 160 have written charters modeled directly or indirectly on the U.S. version." But today, that same constitution has lost some of its mojo. A detailed empirical study of 729 constitutions adopted by 188 countries from 1946 to 2006 reveals a different picture. In the 1960s and 1970s, democratic constitutions became similar to the U.S. Constitution, but then reversed course in the 1980s and 1990s. And by the first few years of the twenty-first century, the departures became more pronounced such that for the most recent period for which there is evidence, "the constitutions of the world's democracies are, on average, less familiar to the U.S. Constitution now than they were at the end of World War II."

Reasons for this shift abound. The U.S. Constitution is concise and old; it also guarantees few rights; and, as some Supreme Court justices have advocated, the document should be interpreted according to its meaning when it was crafted in 1787. These possible explanations may suggest that the U.S. Constitution has little appeal to a new nation. And the Constitution's declining influence may simply be an extension of a general decline in American power and prestige.

One of the study authors pithily summarized a central reason for the declining trend: "Nobody wants a copy of Windows 3.1." Supreme Court justice Ruth Bader Ginsburg echoed this sentiment in a 2012 interview on Egyptian television: "I would not look to the United States Constitution if I were drafting a constitution in the year 2012."

Of course, we should remember that constitutions offer only paper guarantees, so despite their high purpose and grand promises, what matters most is whether the guarantees they enshrined will be observed in practice.

The table on the facing page details the most common provisions in the constitutions of 188 countries in 1946 and 2006. The provisions in the U.S. Constitution appear in **bold**.

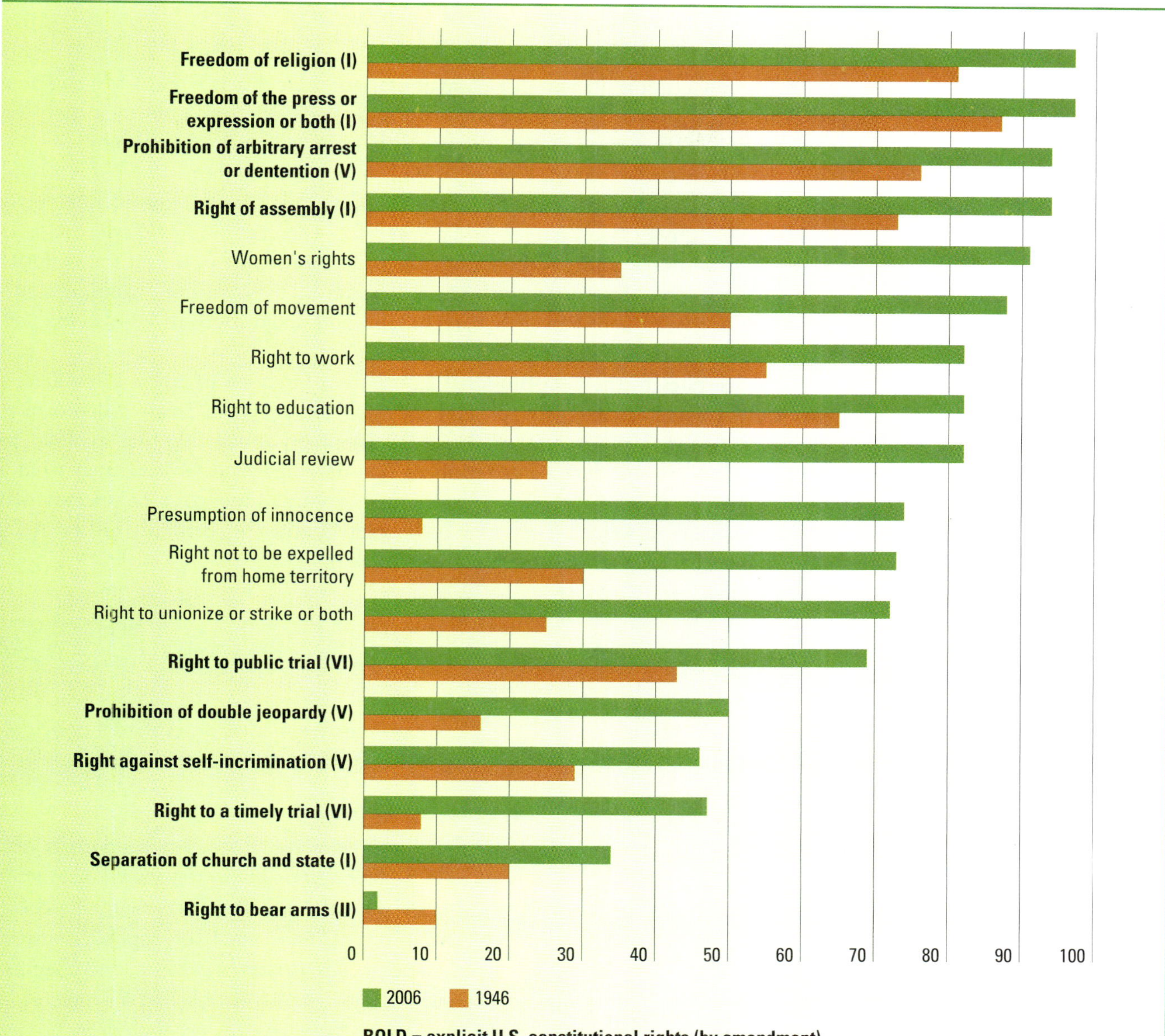

BOLD = explicit U.S. constitutional rights (by amendment).

Percentage of 188 constitutions containing selected provisions.

SOURCE: Adam Liptak, "Sidebar: 'We the People' Loses Appeal With People Around the World," *New York Times*, Feb. 7, 2012, p. A1; David S. Law and Mila Versteeg, "The Declining Influence of the United States Constitution" *New York University Law Review*, Vol. 87, No. 3, pp. 762–858 (June 2012); John Greenwald, Alastair Matheson, and Bing W. Wong, "A Gift to All Nations," *Time*, July 6, 1987, Vol. 130, pp. 92–95.

Critical Thinking

Which provisions of the U.S. Constitution have the most appeal in other countries? Which ones have the least appeal? What popular provisions lie outside the U.S. Constitution? Which provision has grown most in appeal in the period from 1946 to 2006? Only one provision has lost appeal. Which one? Speculate on the reasons for the growth and decline in these provisions.

The Constitution and Models of Democracy

Think back to our discussion of the models of democracy in Chapter 2. Which model does the Constitution fit: pluralist or majoritarian? Actually, it is hard to imagine a government framework better suited to the pluralist model of democracy than the Constitution of the United States. It is also hard to imagine a document more at odds with the majoritarian model. Consider Madison's claim, in *Federalist* No. 10, that government inevitably involves conflicting factions. This concept coincides perfectly with pluralist theory (see Chapter 2). Then recall his description in *Federalist* No. 51 of the Constitution's ability to guard against concentration of power in the majority through separation of powers and checks and balances. This concept—avoiding a single center of government power that might fall under majority control—also fits perfectly with pluralist democracy.

The delegates to the Constitutional Convention intended to create a republic, a government based on majority consent; they did not intend to create a democracy, which rests on majority rule. They succeeded admirably in creating that republic. In doing so, they also produced a government that developed into a democracy—but a particular type of democracy. The framers neither wanted nor got a democracy that fit the majoritarian model. They may have wanted, and they certainly did create, a government that conforms to the pluralist model.

SUMMARY

3.1 The Revolutionary Roots of the Constitution

- The Constitution was the end product of a revolutionary movement aimed at preserving existing liberties. The movement began with the Declaration of Independence, which proclaimed that everyone is entitled to certain rights and invoked the principle of equality of peoples. The conflict was also a civil war that divided communities and families.

3.2 From Revolution to Confederation

- After independence, a government was needed to replace the British monarchy. The Americans chose a republic and defined the structure of that republic in the Articles of Confederation. Although the Articles guaranteed the states the independence they coveted, they were a failure: they left the central government too weak to deal with disorder and insurrection.

3.3 From Confederation to Constitution

- The Constitutional Convention was fraught with debate over the strength of government at the state versus the national level and the nature of the presidency. To resolve these conflicts, compromises were carefully crafted that all delegates could support, even if only reluctantly.

3.4 The Final Product

- The Constitution that finally emerged replaced a loose union of powerful states with a strong but still limited national government, incorporating four political principles: republicanism, federalism, separation of powers, and checks and balances. It also established a system of checks and balances, giving each branch some scrutiny of and control over the others.

3.5 Selling the Constitution

- A major stumbling block to ratification of the Constitution proved to be its failure to list the individual liberties the Americans had fought to protect against the potential tyranny of a stronger central government. With the promise to add a bill of rights, the Constitution was ratified.

3.6 Constitutional Change

- The founders recognized that the Constitution would need to be amended to serve the changing needs of the citizenry. They therefore enumerated different formal methods for amending the document. In practice, the Constitution has also been modified through the Courts and through changes in political practice.

3.7 An Evaluation of the Constitution

- The Constitution was designed to strike a balance between order and freedom. While the framers did not set out to create a democracy, they nevertheless produced a democratic form of government. The framers also wanted a balance between the powers of the national government and those of the states, the exact nature of which would be contested for many years to come.

ASSESSING YOUR UNDERSTANDING WITH APLIA...YOUR VIRTUAL TUTOR!

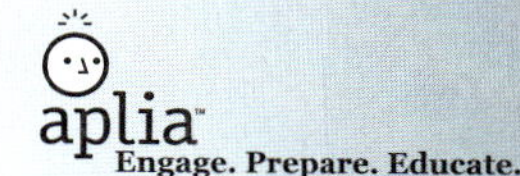

3.1 Explain the reasons for the colonies' declaration of independence from British rule.

1. Why did the colonies begin to protest against the British government, and what forms did this protest take?
2. What were the goals of the First and the Second Continental Congress?
3. What principles underpin the Declaration of Independence?

3.2 Identify the factors that led to the failure of the Confederation.

1. Why did the delegates to the Second Continental Congress seek to retain power in the states versus creating a strong central government?
2. Provide four reasons that help explain why the Articles of Confederation failed.

3.3 Explain the major points of contention in the writing of the Constitution.

1. What were the primary differences between the Virginia and New Jersey Plans?
2. What major compromises did the drafting of the Constitution entail?

3.4 Explain the contribution of the Constitution to the American political tradition and the principles it establishes.

1. Which powers are provided to Congress through the necessary and proper clause, and why are these important?

2. What was the primary motivation of the Constitutional Convention?
3. How did the Constitution originally address the institution of slavery?

3.5 Describe the actions taken to ensure the ratification of the Constitution.

1. Who were the Federalists and Antifederalists, and what were their main points of disagreement?
2. What is the Bill of Rights, and whose rights is it guaranteed to protect?

3.6 Explain the procedures required to amend the Constitution.

1. What are the two methods through which constitutional changes can be proposed, and what are the two methods for ratifying those changes?
2. What are the guidelines used by judges for interpreting the Constitution?

3.7 Evaluate the extent to which the Constitution reflects and embodies the principles of majoritarian or pluralist democracy.

1. What values does the Constitution secure? What values were not priorities at the time the Constitution was drafted?
2. Does the government created by the Constitution reflect the pluralist or majoritarian model of democracy?

4 Federalism

"The problem is all these illegals," said Luis, a legal Mexican immigrant who has lived and worked in Arizona for 16 years. "They come here expecting to find paradise, and it isn't. You have to work hard for everything. But at least there is work."[1] These are difficult times, especially in Arizona. The recession beginning in 2008; the ensuing trail of high, long-term unemployment; and the housing market collapse wreaked devastation on the state. Illegal immigration surged along with increased drug smuggling, human trafficking, and associated gang violence across Arizona's 362-mile border with Mexico.

For years, Arizonans—including Luis and his fellow legal immigrants—have borne the burden of illegals who have sought work and opportunity in the United States. President George W. Bush was determined to reform immigration laws, staunching the illegal tide, but he failed. Immigration reform was political kryptonite, weakening even the most powerful politicians who tried to address the issue. The public seethed at the prospect of illegals taking jobs from American citizens; of illegals using the social safety net to secure heath care, education, and housing; and of pregnant illegals crossing the border for the sole purpose of delivering their babies on American soil, thus qualifying their children immediately for American citizenship.[2] All of this and more proved too much for conservative Arizonans and their politicians.

In 2010, under Governor Jan Brewer, the state legislature adopted a law—SB1070—taking immigration matters into its own hands. The law is both broad and strict; it goes far beyond efforts in other states to address the problem of illegal immigration. More significantly, it goes further than the U.S. government has chosen to go.

U.S. law requires foreigners who are not citizens living in the United States—called aliens—to register with the government and carry their registration papers.[3] SB1070 took this requirement a step further by criminalizing the failure to carry the necessary papers. The new law obligates the police to determine a person's immigration status, when practicable during a "lawful stop, detention or arrest," if there is reasonable suspicion that the person is an illegal alien. The law also cracked down on those who hire, transport, or shelter illegal aliens.[4]

The national government sued Arizona in federal court, sending one of its highest-ranking officials from the Justice Department to argue its position. The United States rested its case on federalism grounds: the Constitution and laws of the United States place the matter of immigration solely in the hands of the national government, and the states remain duty-bound under the Constitution's supremacy clause (Article VI) to bow to national authority.

On July 28, just one day before the law was to go into effect, federal judge Susan Bolton blocked the main provisions of the law, including the requirement that police check the immigration status of those arrested or stopped. Her reasoning adopted the position of the United States: principles of federalism give exclusive power over immigration matters to the national government, trumping state efforts at regulating or enforcing national immigration laws as in Arizona.[5] Arizona appealed, but Bolton's decision withstood the challenge.[6] Undeterred by its two losses, Arizona appealed to the Supreme Court of the United States, which accepted the case for review and heard arguments from the parties in April 2012. Less than three months later, the court handed down its ruling.

In a 5–3 decision, the justices invalidated all but one of the provisions because they interfered with the national government's role in setting immigration policy. But the court upheld, at least for now, the part of the law that instructs law enforcement officials to check a person's immigration status if there is a reasonable suspicion that a person is in the country illegally. The justices left open further review should actual practice under this "show-me-your-papers" provision raise new constitutional challenges.[7]

Two elements of federalism are at work here. The first element is the respective **sovereignty**, or quality of being supreme in power or authority, of national and state governments. In the case of Arizona's efforts to confront illegal immigration, this distinction between different sovereignties was clear to Judge Bolton: authority rests principally with the national government. She did not invalidate the entire law, but only those portions that intrude on the national government's delegated or implied powers. The states cannot simply act on their own when the Constitution (Article I, Section 8, Clause 4) and laws of the United States assign responsibility for immigration and naturalization to the national government. A second element of federalism is the power of national (i.e., federal) courts to assure the supremacy of the U.S. Constitution and national laws. Such power was necessary, though not sufficient, to yoke separate states into one nation, or as the motto goes, "E pluribus unum."

Sovereignty also affects political leadership. A governor may not be a president's political equal, but governors have their own sovereignty apart from the national government. In this chapter, we examine American federalism in theory and in practice. Is the division of power between the nation and states a matter of constitutional principle or practical politics? How does the balance of power between the nation and states relate to the conflicts between freedom and order and between freedom and equality? Does the growth of federalism abroad affect us here at home? Does federalism reflect the pluralist or the majoritarian model of democracy?

sovereignty
The quality of being supreme in power or authority.

★ 4.1 Theories and Metaphors

★ Compare and contrast the two theories of federalism used to describe the American system of government.

The delegates who met in Philadelphia in 1787 were supposed to repair weaknesses in the Articles of Confederation. Instead, they tackled the problem of making one nation out of thirteen independent states by doing something much more radical: they wrote a new constitution and invented a new political form—federal government—that combined features of a confederacy with features of unitary government (see Chapter 3). Under the principle of **federalism**, two or more governments exercise power and authority over the same people and the same territory.

Still, this new national government did not intrude explicitly into the states' domain. The new constitution granted Congress express authority for only one service within the states, the creation of a postal system. Powers were meant to be exclusive

federalism
The division of power between a central government and regional governments.

or shared. For example, the governments of the United States and Pennsylvania share certain powers (the power to tax, for instance), but other powers belong exclusively to one or the other. As James Madison wrote in *Federalist* No. 10, "The federal Constitution forms a happy combination … [of] the great and aggregate interests being referred to the national, and the local and particular to state governments." So the power to coin money belongs to the national government, but the power to grant divorces remains a state prerogative. By contrast, authority over state militias may sometimes belong to the national government and sometimes to the states. The history of American federalism reveals that it has not always been easy to draw a line between what is "great and aggregate" and what is "local and particular."*

Nevertheless, federalism offered a solution to the problem of diversity in America. Citizens feared that without a federal system of government, majorities with different interests and values from different regions would rule them. Federalism also provided a new political model.

The history of American federalism is full of attempts to capture its true meaning in an adjective or metaphor. By one reckoning, scholars have generated nearly five hundred ways to describe federalism.[8] Perhaps this is not surprising given one scholar's view that the American federal system "is a highly protean form, subject to constant reinterpretation. It is long on change and confusion and very low on fixed, generally accepted principles."[9] Still, before complicating the picture too much, it will be useful to focus on two common representations of the system: dual federalism and cooperative federalism.

Dual Federalism

The term **dual federalism** sums up a theory about the proper relationship between the national government and the states. The theory has four essential parts. First, the national government rules by enumerated powers only. Second, the national government has a limited set of constitutional purposes. Third, each government unit—nation and state—is sovereign within its sphere. And, fourth, the relationship between nation and states is best characterized by tension rather than cooperation.[10]

Dual federalism portrays the states as powerful components of the federal system—in some ways, the equals of the national government. Under dual federalism, the functions and responsibilities of the national and state governments are theoretically different and practically separate from each other. Of primary importance in dual federalism are **states' rights**, which reserve to the states or to the people all rights not specifically conferred on the national government by the Constitution. According to the theory of dual federalism, a rigid wall separates the nation and the states. After all, if the states created the nation, by implication they can set limits on the activities of the national government. Proponents of states' rights believe that the powers of the national government should be interpreted narrowly.

Debates over states' rights often emerge over differing interpretations of a given national government policy or proposed policy. Whether the Constitution has delegated to the national government the power to make such policy or whether it remains with the states or the people is often an open and difficult question to answer. States' rights supporters insist that the activities of Congress should be confined to the enumerated powers. They support their view by quoting the Tenth Amendment: "The

dual federalism
A view holding that the Constitution is a compact among sovereign states, so that the powers of the national government and the states are clearly differentiated.

states' rights
The idea that all rights not specifically conferred on the national government by the U.S. Constitution are reserved to the states.

---

*The phrase Americans commonly use to refer to their central government—*federal government*—muddies the waters even more. Technically, we have a federal system of government, which encompasses both the national and state governments. To avoid confusion from here on, we use the term *national government* rather than *federal government* when we are talking about the central government.

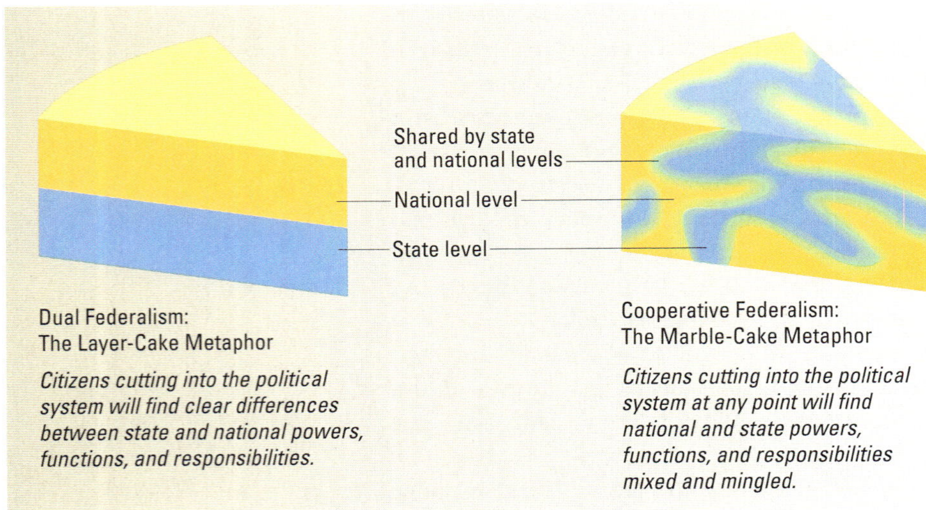

FIGURE 4.1 Metaphors for Federalism

The two views of federalism can be represented graphically.
Source: © Cengage Learning.

Dual Federalism: The Layer-Cake Metaphor

Citizens cutting into the political system will find clear differences between state and national powers, functions, and responsibilities.

Cooperative Federalism: The Marble-Cake Metaphor

Citizens cutting into the political system at any point will find national and state powers, functions, and responsibilities mixed and mingled.

implied powers
Those powers that Congress needs to execute its enumerated powers.

powers not delegated to the United States by the Constitution, nor prohibited by it to the States, are reserved to the States respectively, or to the people." Conversely, those people favoring national action frequently point to the Constitution's elastic clause, which gives Congress the **implied powers** needed to execute its enumerated powers.

Regardless of whether one favors national action or states' rights, political scientists use a metaphor to describe the idea of dual federalism. They call it *layer-cake federalism* (see Figure 4.1), in which the powers and functions of the national and state governments are as separate as the layers of a cake. Each government is supreme in its own layer, its own sphere of action. The two layers are distinct, and the dimensions of each layer are fixed by the Constitution.

Cooperative Federalism

cooperative federalism
A view holding that the Constitution is an agreement among people who are citizens of both state and nation, so there is much overlap between state powers and national powers.

Cooperative federalism, a phrase coined in the 1930s, is a different theory of the relationship between the national and state governments. It acknowledges the increasing overlap between state and national functions and rejects the idea of separate spheres, or layers, for the states and the national government. Cooperative federalism has three elements. First, national and state agencies typically undertake government functions jointly rather than exclusively. Second, the nation and states routinely share power. And third, power is not concentrated at any government level or in any agency; the fragmentation of responsibilities gives people and groups access to many venues of influence.

The bakery metaphor used to describe this type of federalism is a *marble cake* (see Figure 4.1).* The national and state governments do not act in separate spheres; they are intermingled in vertical and diagonal strands and swirls. In short, their functions are mixed in the American federal system. Critical to this theory is an expansive view of the Constitution's supremacy clause (Article VI), which specifically subordinates state law to national law and charges every government official with disregarding state laws that are inconsistent with the Constitution, national laws, or treaties.

Some scholars argue that the layer-cake metaphor has never accurately described the American political structure.[11] In practice, the national and state governments

---

*A marble cake is a rough mixture of yellow and chocolate cake batter resembling marble stone. If you've never seen or eaten a slice of marble cake, imagine mixing a swirl of vanilla and chocolate soft-freeze ice cream.

have many common objectives and have often cooperated to achieve them. In the nineteenth century, for example, cooperation, not separation, made it possible to develop transportation systems, such as canals, and to establish state land-grant colleges.

A critical difference between the theories of dual and cooperative federalism is the way they interpret two sections of the Constitution that define the relationship between the national and state governments. Article I, Section 8, lists the enumerated powers of Congress and then concludes with the **elastic clause**, which gives Congress the power to "make all Laws which shall be necessary and proper for carrying into Execution the foregoing Powers" (see Chapter 3). The Tenth Amendment reserves for the states or the people powers not assigned to the national government or denied to the states by the Constitution. Dual federalism postulates an inflexible elastic clause and a spacious Tenth Amendment. Cooperative federalism postulates a flexible elastic clause and confines the Tenth Amendment to a self-evident, obvious truth.

elastic clause
The last clause in Article I, Section 8, of the Constitution, which gives Congress the means to execute its enumerated powers. This clause is the basis for Congress's implied powers. Also called the *necessary and proper clause*.

⭐ 4.2 Federalism's Dynamics

★ Identify and explain each of the four forces that stimulate changes in the relationship between the national and state governments.

Although the Constitution establishes a kind of federalism, the actual and proper balance of power between the nation and states has always been more a matter of debate than of formal theory. Three broad principles help to underscore why. First, rather than operating in a mechanical fashion, American federalism is a flexible and dynamic system. The Constitution's inherent ambiguities about federalism, some of which we have discussed already, generate constraints but also opportunities for politicians, citizens, and interest groups to push ideas that they care about. Second, because of this flexibility, both elected and appointed officials across levels of government often make policy decisions based on pragmatic considerations without regard to theories of what American federalism should look like. In sum, politics and policy goals rather than pure theoretical or ideological commitments about federalism tend to dominate decision making. Third, there is a growing recognition among public officials and citizens that public problems (such as questions involving tradeoffs of freedom, order, and equality) cut across governmental boundaries. This section develops the first claim, and we explore the other two in later sections of this chapter.

The overall point these three claims illustrate is that to understand American federalism, one must know more than simply the powers that the Constitution assigns the different levels of government. Real understanding stems from recognizing the forces that can prompt changes in relationships between the national government and the states. In this section, we focus on four specific forces: national crises and demands, judicial interpretations, the expansion of grants-in-aid, and the professionalization of state governments.

National Crises and Demands

The elastic clause of the Constitution gives Congress the power to make all laws that are "necessary and proper" to carry out its responsibilities. By using this power in combination with its enumerated powers, Congress has been able to increase the scope of the national government tremendously during the previous two centuries. The greatest change has come about in times of crisis and national emergencies, such as the Civil War; the world wars; the Great Depression; the aftermath of

September 11, 2001; and the recession beginning in 2008. As an example, consider the Great Depression.

The Great Depression placed dual federalism in repose. The problems of the Depression proved too extensive for either state governments or private businesses to handle, so the national government assumed a heavy share of responsibility for providing relief and pursuing economic recovery. Under the New Deal, President Franklin D. Roosevelt's response to the Depression, Congress enacted various emergency relief programs designed to stimulate economic activity and help the unemployed. Many measures required the cooperation of the national and state governments. For example, the national government offered money to support state relief efforts; however, to receive these funds, states were usually required to provide administrative supervision or contribute some money of their own. Relief efforts were thus wrested from the hands of local bodies and centralized. Through the regulations it attached to funds, the national government extended its power and control over the states.[12]

Some call the New Deal era revolutionary. There is no doubt that the period was critical in reshaping federalism in the United States. The national and state governments had cooperated before, but the extent of their interactions during President Franklin Roosevelt's administration was unprecedented. In addition, the size of the national government and its budget increased tremendously. But perhaps the most significant change was in the way Americans thought about their problems and the role of the national government in solving them. Difficulties that at one time had been considered personal or local were now viewed as national problems requiring national solutions. The general welfare, broadly defined, became a legitimate concern of the national government.

In other respects, however, the New Deal was not so revolutionary. For example, Congress did not claim any new powers to address the nation's economic problems. Rather, the national legislature simply used its constitutional powers to suit the circumstances. Arguably those actions were consistent with the overall purpose of the U.S. Constitution, which, as the preamble states, was designed in part to "insure domestic Tranquility … [and] promote the general welfare."

Concerns over terrorist attacks on U.S. soil have expanded national power. In the month after the events of September 11, 2001, Congress swiftly passed and the president signed into law the USA-PATRIOT Act. (USA-PATRIOT is an acronym for **U**niting and **S**trengthening **A**merica by **P**roviding **A**ppropriate **T**ools **R**equired to **I**ntercept and **O**bstruct **T**errorism.) Among other provisions, the law expanded significantly the surveillance and investigative powers of the Department of Justice. After some disagreement about its structure and organization, federal policymakers created the Department of Homeland Security in 2002, a new department that united over twenty previously separate federal agencies under a common administrative structure. In a move to further expand domestic surveillance activities, President George W. Bush gave approval to wiretaps without warrants of American citizens suspected of terrorist ties. In 2011, President Barack Obama signed a four-year extension of the Act's key provisions.[13]

The role of the national government has also grown as it has responded to needs and demands that state and local governments were unwilling or unable to meet. To address the severe economic downturn saddling the nation, President Obama proposed and Congress quickly passed a $787 billion economic stimulus package in February 2009. No Republicans in the House of Representatives and only three Republicans in the Senate voted for the legislation, a clear signal of the charged partisan atmosphere in Washington. The American Recovery and Reinvestment Act offered substantial direct aid to states beleaguered by the recession in the form of Medicaid payments, extended unemployment benefits, school and infra-structure spending, and other grants. Several Republican governors rejected the money, arguing that the strings attached would mandate the states to more spending in the future. But the bluster receded as furious state legislators in both parties demanded the much-needed funds. When the deadline arrived, all governors signed on.[14]

Judicial Interpretation

How federal courts have interpreted the Constitution and federal law is another factor that has influenced the relationship between the national government and the states. The U.S. Supreme Court, the umpire of the federal system, settles disagreements over the powers of the national and state governments by deciding whether the actions of either are unconstitutional (see Chapter 14). In the nineteenth and early twentieth centuries, the Supreme Court often decided in favor of the states. Then, for nearly sixty years, from 1937 to 1995, the Court almost always supported the national government in contests involving the balance of power between nation and states. After 1995, a conservative U.S. Supreme Court tended to favor states' rights, but not without some notable and important exceptions. Exploring the Court's federalism jurisprudence provides a useful window on changes to the system that have transpired since the nation's founding.

AP Photo/Evan Vucci

An Environmental Catastrophe

On April 20, 2010, an oil rig explosion in the Gulf of Mexico, 41 miles from the coast of Louisiana, caused a sea floor oil gusher of unprecedented proportions. Nearly 5 million barrels of oil leaked into the Gulf before the well was capped on July 15. The well owner, British Petroleum, bore full responsibility for the damage and will pay billions of dollars in claims for the cleanup and loss of jobs throughout the Gulf states. The disaster occurred in waters under the jurisdiction of the national government. State and local officials played a subordinate role. President Barack Obama (*left*), LaFourche Parish (Louisiana) president Charlotte Randolph (*center*), and U.S. Coast Guard Admiral Thad Allen (*right*) look at booms set out to collect oil during a tour of areas affected by the oil spill.

Ends and Means. Early in the nineteenth century, the nationalist interpretation of federalism prevailed over states' rights. In 1819, under Chief Justice John Marshall (1801–1835), the Supreme Court expanded the role of the national government in the landmark case of *McCulloch* v. *Maryland*. The Court was asked to decide whether Congress had the power to establish a national bank and, if so, whether states had the power to tax that bank. In a unanimous opinion that Marshall authored, the Court conceded that Congress had only the powers conferred on it by the Constitution, which nowhere mentioned banks. However, Article I granted Congress the authority to enact all laws "necessary and proper" to the execution of Congress's enumerated powers. Marshall adopted a broad interpretation of this elastic clause: "Let the end be legitimate, let it be within the scope of the constitution, and all means which are appropriate, which are plainly adapted to that end, which are not prohibited, but consist with the letter and spirit of the constitution, are constitutional."

The Court clearly agreed that Congress had the power to charter a bank. But did the states (in this case, Maryland) have the power to tax the bank? Arguing that "the power to tax involves the power to destroy," Marshall insisted that a state could not tax the national government because the bank represents the interests of the whole

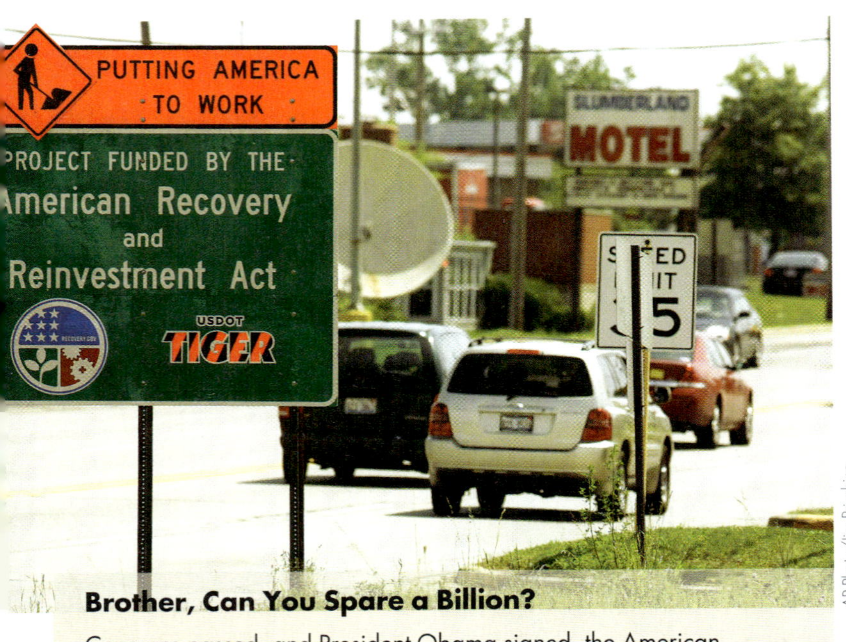

Brother, Can You Spare a Billion?

Congress passed, and President Obama signed, the American Recovery and Reinvestment Act in February 2009. This $787 billion package of federal spending includes direct aid to the states battered by the collapse of the economy in 2008. The aim is to create jobs and spur investment. Road repair and infrastructure projects are key components. You can track spending by zip code and much more at www.recovery.gov.

commerce clause
The third clause of Article I, Section 8, of the Constitution, which gives Congress the power to regulate commerce among the states.

nation; a state may not tax those it does not represent. Therefore, a state tax that interferes with the power of Congress to make law is void.[15] Marshall was embracing cooperative federalism, which sees a direct relationship between the people and the national government, with no need for the states to act as intermediaries. The framers of the Constitution did not intend to create a meaningless document, he reasoned. Therefore, they must have meant to give the national government all the powers necessary to carry out its assigned functions, even if those powers are only implied.

Especially from the late 1930s to the mid-1990s, the Supreme Court's interpretation of the Constitution's **commerce clause** was a major factor that increased the national government's power. The third clause of Article I, Section 8, states that "Congress shall have Power … To regulate Commerce … among the several States." In early Court decisions, beginning with *Gibbons* v. *Ogden* in 1824, Chief Justice Marshall interpreted the word *commerce* broadly to include virtually every form of commercial activity. But later courts would take a narrower view of that power.

Roger B. Taney became chief justice in 1836, and during his tenure (1836–1864), the Court's federalism decisions began to favor the states. The Taney Court took a more restrictive view of commerce and imposed firm limits on the powers of the national government. As Taney saw it, the Constitution spoke "not only in the same words, but with the same meaning and intent with which it spoke when it came from the hands of its framers and was voted on and adopted by the people of the United States."[16] In the infamous *Dred Scott* decision (1857), for example, the Court decided that Congress had no power to prohibit slavery in the territories.

The judicial winds shifted again during the Great Depression. After originally disagreeing with FDR's and the Congress's position that the economic crisis was a national problem that demanded national action, the Court, with no change in personnel, began to alter its course in 1937 and upheld several major New Deal measures. Perhaps the Court was responding to the 1936 election returns (Roosevelt had been reelected in a landslide, and the Democrats commanded a substantial majority in Congress), which signified the voters' endorsement of the use of national policies to address national problems. Or perhaps the Court sought to defuse the president's threat to enlarge the Court with justices sympathetic to his views ("The switch in time that saved nine," rhymed one observer). In any event, the Court abandoned its effort to maintain a rigid boundary between national and state power.[17]

The Umpire Strikes Back. In the 1990s, a series of important U.S. Supreme Court rulings involving the commerce clause suggested that the states' rights position was gaining ground once more. The Court's 5–4 ruling in *United States* v. *Lopez* (1995) held that Congress exceeded its authority under the commerce clause when it enacted a law in 1990 banning the possession of a gun in or near a school. A conservative majority, headed by Chief Justice William H. Rehnquist, concluded that having a gun in a school zone "has nothing to do with 'commerce' or any sort of economic enterprise, however broadly one might define those terms." Justices Sandra Day O'Connor, Antonin Scalia, Anthony Kennedy, and Clarence Thomas—all appointed by Republicans—joined in Rehnquist's opinion, putting the brakes on congressional power.[18]

Another piece of gun-control legislation, known as the Brady bill, produced similar eventual results. Congress enacted this law in 1993. It mandated the creation by November 1998 of a national system to check the background of prospective gun buyers in order to weed out, among others, convicted felons and those with mental illness. In the meantime, the law created a temporary system that called for local law enforcement officials to perform background checks and report their findings to gun dealers in their community. Several sheriffs challenged the law.

The Supreme Court agreed with the sheriffs, delivering a double-barreled blow to the local-enforcement provision in June 1997. In *Printz* v. *United States* (1997), the Court concluded that Congress could not require local officials to implement a regulatory scheme imposed by the national government. In language that seemingly invoked dual federalism, Justice Antonin Scalia, writing for the five-member conservative majority, argued that locally enforced background checks violated the principle of dual sovereignty by allowing the national government "to impress into its service—and at no cost to itself—the police officers of the 50 States." In addition, he wrote, the scheme violated the principle of separation of powers by congressional transfer of the president's responsibility to faithfully execute national laws to local law enforcement officials.[19]

A new and potentially limiting principal to the exercise of national power arose in the legal challenges to the Affordable Care Act. A 2012 blockbuster showdown in the Supreme Court produced a slim victory for the Act's proponents on the basis of the national government's taxing power, but five justices declared a limit to the use of national power under the commerce clause should it be used to regulate "inactivity." Moreover, by a 7–2 vote, the justices held that the national government could not threaten states with the complete loss of federal funding for Medicaid should states refuse to comply with the Act's health-care expansion.[20]

Federalism's Shifting Scales. In what appeared to signal the continuation of a pro–states' rights trajectory, in 2000 the justices struck down congressional legislation that had allowed federal court lawsuits for money damages for victims of crimes "motivated by gender." The Court held that the Violence Against Women Act violated both the commerce clause and Section 5 of the Fourteenth Amendment. Chief Justice Rehnquist, speaking for the five-person majority, declared that "the Constitution requires a distinction between what is truly national and what is truly local."[21]

But just as an umpire's strike zone can be ambiguous—is it knees to belt or knees to letters?—the Court more recently has veered from its states' rights direction on federalism. Perhaps the best-known decision in this vein is *Bush* v. *Gore*, the controversial Supreme Court decision resolving the 2000 presidential election. That tight election did not result in an immediate winner because the race in Florida was too close to call. Florida courts, interpreting Florida election law, had ordered ballot recounts, but a divided Supreme Court ordered a halt to the process and gave George W. Bush the victory.

In three recent death penalty cases, the Court reflected the ambiguity and dynamic nature that frequently characterize the American federal system. In 2002, the Court denied state power to execute a defendant who was mentally disabled, reasoning that because many states had deemed such a practice inappropriate, "evolving standards of decency" in the nation suggested it was time to halt the practice.[22] In 2005, the Court again relied on evolving standards of decency to strike down a state death penalty for seventeen-year-olds.[23] In both cases, the Court acted against the policy of individual states by asserting national power to declare that the death penalty in such circumstances amounted to cruel and unusual punishment and thus violated the Constitution.

Grants-in-Aid

Since the 1960s, the national government's use of financial incentives has rivaled its use of legislation and court decisions as a means of influencing its relationship with state governments. Simultaneously, state and local governments have increasingly looked to Washington for money. Leaders at these lower levels of government have attempted to push their own initiatives by getting leverage from new national interest in a variety of policy areas. Thus, if governors can somehow convince national policy-makers to adopt laws that buttress state priorities, then these state officials can advance their own priorities even as Washington's power appears to grow. Through a sort of back-and-forth process of negotiation and debate, the dynamics of the American federal system are revealed yet again. The principal arena where many of these interactions take place is in debates over federal grants-in-aid.

A **grant-in-aid** is money paid by one level of government to another level of government to be spent for a given purpose. Most grants-in-aid come with standards or requirements prescribed by Congress. Many are awarded on a matching basis; that is, a recipient government must make some contribution of its own, which the national government then matches. For example, the nation's primary health-care program for low-income people, Medicaid, works on this sort of matching basis. Grants-in-aid take two general forms: categorical grants and block grants.

Categorical grants target specific purposes, and restrictions on their use typically leave the recipient government relatively little formal discretion. Recipients today include state governments, local governments, and public and private nonprofit organizations. There are two kinds of categorical grants: formula grants and project grants. As their name implies, **formula grants** are distributed according to specific rules that define who is eligible for the grant and how much each eligible applicant will receive. The formulas may weigh factors such as state per capita income, number of school-age children, urban population, and number of families below the poverty line. Most grants, however, are **project grants**, which are awarded through a competitive application process. Such project grants have focused on health (substance abuse and HIV-AIDS programs); natural resources and the environment (radon, asbestos, and toxic pollution); and education, training, and employment (for disabled, homeless, and elderly persons).

In contrast to categorical grants, Congress awards **block grants** for broad, general purposes. They allow recipient governments considerable freedom to decide how to spend the money. Whereas a categorical grant promotes a specific activity—say, developing an ethnic heritage studies curriculum in public schools—a block grant might be earmarked only for elementary, secondary, and vocational education more generally. The state or local government receiving the block grant then chooses the specific educational programs to fund with it. The recipient might use some money to support ethnic heritage studies and some to fund consumer education programs. Or the recipient might choose to put all the money into consumer education programs and spend nothing on ethnic heritage studies.

grant-in-aid
Money provided by one level of government to another to be spent for a given purpose.

categorical grants
Grants-in-aid targeted for a specific purpose by either formula or project.

formula grants
Categorical grants distributed according to a particular set of rules, called a formula, that specify who is eligible for the grants and how much each eligible applicant will receive.

project grants
Categorical grants awarded on the basis of competitive applications submitted by prospective recipients to perform a specific task or function.

block grants
Grants-in-aid awarded for general purposes, allowing the recipient great discretion in spending the grant money.

Grants-in-aid are a method of redistributing income. Money is collected by the national government from the taxpayers of all fifty states. The money is then funneled back to state and local governments. Many grants have worked to reduce gross inequalities among states and their residents. But the formulas used to redistribute income are not impartial; they are highly political, established through a process of congressional horse-trading.

Although grants-in-aid have been part of the national government arsenal since the early twentieth century, they grew at an astonishing pace in the 1960s, when grant spending doubled every five years. Presidents Nixon and Reagan were strong advocates for redistributing money back to the states, and political support for such redistribution has remained strong. Controlling for inflation, in 1990 the national government returned $198 billion to the states. By 2010, the amount had increased to $527 billion.[24] The main trend, as illustrated in Figure 4.2, is an enormous growth in health-care spending, which now approaches 50 percent of all national grant funds to the states.

Whatever its form or purpose, grant money comes with strings attached. Some strings are there to ensure that recipients spend the money as the law specifies; other regulations are designed to evaluate how well the grant is working. To these ends, the national government may stipulate that recipients follow certain procedures. The

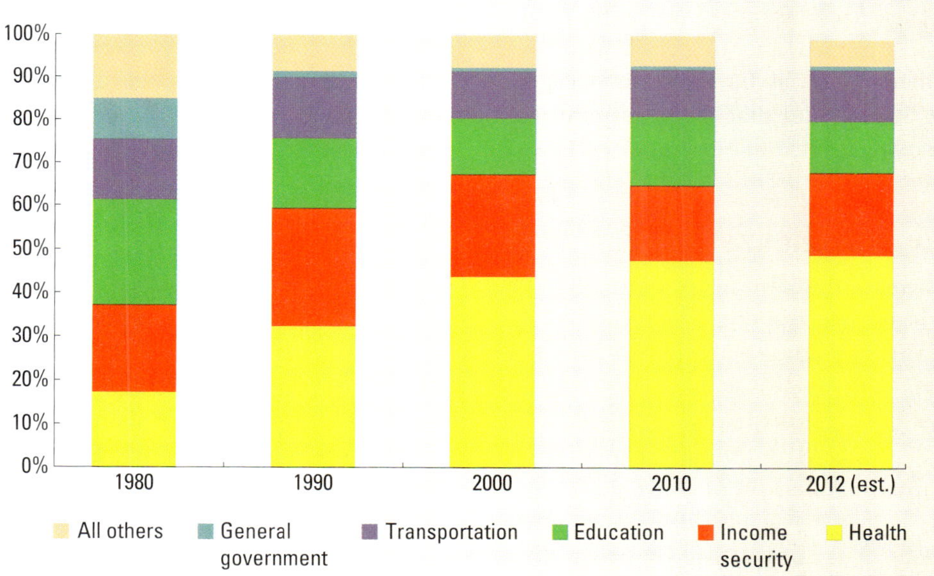

FIGURE 4.2 Trends in National Government Grants to States and Localities, Fiscal Year (FY) 1980 to 2012

National government grants to states and localities vary substantially. In 1980, education programs accounted for the biggest slice of the national government pie. In 1990, grants for health programs, reflecting the expanding costs of Medicaid, took the biggest slice, reaching more than 30 percent of all national government grants to state and local governments. In 2000, health grants exceeded 43 percent of all such national government spending. By 2012, despite a downturn in the overall budget, health grants consumed nearly 50 percent of national government grants to the states, yet another indicator of the nation's health-care crisis.

Source: Historical Tables, *Budget of the United States Government*, FY2012, Table 12.3, http://www.gpo.gov/fdsys/pkg/BUDGET-2012-TAB/pdf/BUDGET-2012-TAB.pdf.

national government may also attach restrictions designed to achieve some broad national goal not always closely related to the specific purpose of the grant. Consider the issue of drunk driving, for example.

The use of highway construction funds has proved an effective means to induce states to accept national standards. Congress threatened to reduce millions of dollars in these funds if states did not agree to prohibit the purchase or consumption of alcoholic beverages by persons under the age of twenty-one. Some states objected, claiming that the Tenth and Twenty-first amendments assigned them responsibility for matters such as alcoholic beverage consumption. In *South Dakota v. Dole* (1987), the Supreme Court conceded that direct congressional control of the drinking age in the states would be unconstitutional. Nevertheless, the Constitution does not bar the indirect achievement of such objectives. The seven-member majority argued that, far from being an infringement on states' rights, the law was a "relatively mild encouragement to the States to enact higher minimum drinking ages than they would otherwise choose." After all, Chief Justice William H. Rehnquist wrote, the goal of reducing drunk driving was "directly related to one of the main purposes for which highway funds are expended—safe interstate travel."[25] By 1988, every state in the nation had approved legislation setting twenty-one as the minimum drinking age.

In October 2000, following a three-year battle in Congress, President Bill Clinton signed new legislation establishing a tough national standard of .08 percent blood-alcohol level for drunk driving. All states now comply with this standard. Driver's license suspension or revocation traditionally follows conviction for alcohol-impaired driving.[26] The lure of financial aid has proved a powerful incentive for states to accept standards set by the national government, especially when those standards are aligned with priorities that the states and their citizens generally accept (here, reducing the incidence of drunk driving).

Professionalization of State Governments

A final important factor that has produced dynamic changes in the American federal system has been the emergence of state governments as more capable policy actors than they were in the past. While political scientists generally agree that the rise of competitive party politics in the South (see Chapter 8), the expansion of the interest group system (Chapter 10), and the growth of money in elections (Chapter 9) have all produced significant changes in American politics, nevertheless, many scholars and students rarely consider the expanded capabilities of state governments in the same light. That oversight is important, especially when one considers how far the states have come during the past four decades and how their progress has influenced the shape of American federalism.

It was not long ago that states were described as the weak links in the American policy system. Despite the crucial role that they played in the nation's founding and the legacy of dual federalism, observers both inside and outside the government were skeptical of their ability to contribute actively and effectively to national progress in the post–World War II era. In an oft-quoted book, former North Carolina governor Terry Sanford leveled heavy criticisms at the states, calling them ineffective, indecisive, and inattentive organizations that may have lost their relevance in an increasingly complicated nation and world.[27] Writing nearly twenty years earlier, in 1949, journalist Robert Allen was even less kind; he called the states "the tawdriest, most incompetent, most stultifying unit in the nation's political structure."[28]

But since the 1960s especially, states have become more capable and forceful policy actors. These changes have created better policy outcomes that have benefited citizens across the United States while simultaneously contributing to dynamic changes in the American federal system. If the situation was so bleak less than five decades ago, what happened to bring about the change? Several factors account for the change in perspective.[29]

First, the states have made many internal changes that have fostered their capabilities. Both governors and state legislators now employ more capably trained and experienced policy staff rather than part-time assistants with responsibilities across a wide range of policy areas. Second, legislatures now meet more days during the year, and elected officials in states receive higher salaries. Third, the appeal of higher salaries, in particular, has helped to attract more highly qualified people to run for state office. Fourth, the increasing ability of states to raise revenue, as a result of state tax and budgetary reforms that have transpired since the 1960s, has also given states greater leverage in designing and directing policy, rather than previous generations, where local property taxes played a more significant role in relation to state budget and tax policy. And, fifth, the unelected officials who work in state departments and administer state programs in areas such as transportation, social services, and law enforcement have become better educated. For instance, professional and service occupations account for more than half of all jobs at the state and local levels. In 2010, professional workers represented one-fifth of all state and local government employees. Most of these professional jobs require a college degree.[30]

As evidence of the dynamic relationships between the national government and the states, changes in national policy have also helped the states develop. Many federal grants-in-aid include components designed explicitly to foster capacity-building measures in state governments. Because the national government recognizes—often for political or practical reasons—that several of its domestic initiatives depend on capable implementation from state actors, members of Congress and presidents often design national laws with these capacity-building elements in mind.

One example is the Elementary and Secondary Education Act (ESEA), which became law in 1965. This act, passed as part of President Lyndon Johnson's Great Society effort, was designed to provide federal assistance to the nation's disadvantaged students. Though it is often overlooked, Title V of the law contained several provisions designed to strengthen state departments of education, the agencies that would be responsible for administering the bulk of other programs contained in the ESEA. Thus, although the law was often portrayed as an assertion of national power (which it was), it also helped set in motion changes that would allow state governments to improve their capabilities to make and administer K–12 education policy. Those new capabilities, which subsequent federal laws and internal state efforts have fostered, continued to influence the shape of both federal and state education policy, especially during the most recent revision of the ESEA as the No Child Left Behind Act of 2001.[31]

All of this is not to say that the states are without problems of their own. In some ways, they have been victims of their own success. Now that state capitals have become more viable venues where citizens and interest groups can agitate for their causes, the states have begun to face ever-increasing demands. Those requests can strain state administrators and legislative or gubernatorial staffs, who, while better educated and equipped than their predecessors, still struggle to set priorities and please their constituents.

Compared with What?

Working for the Public

The national government in the United States employs about 2 million people. But if we factor in individuals employed through federal grants and contracts, the number of national government employees balloons to around 15 million. When we factor in all public employees at the national, state, and local levels, we get a greater sense of the presence of government in our lives.

Figure A compares the number of public sector workers at all levels controlling for population across several countries. In this comparison, public sector employment is about 71 workers for every 1,000 Americans. This is about average across all the countries compared. Public sector employment in the United States is about half of that in Norway and Sweden, much smaller countries with substantial public welfare programs. Public sector employment in the United States is greater than that in the economically powerful countries of Germany and Japan.

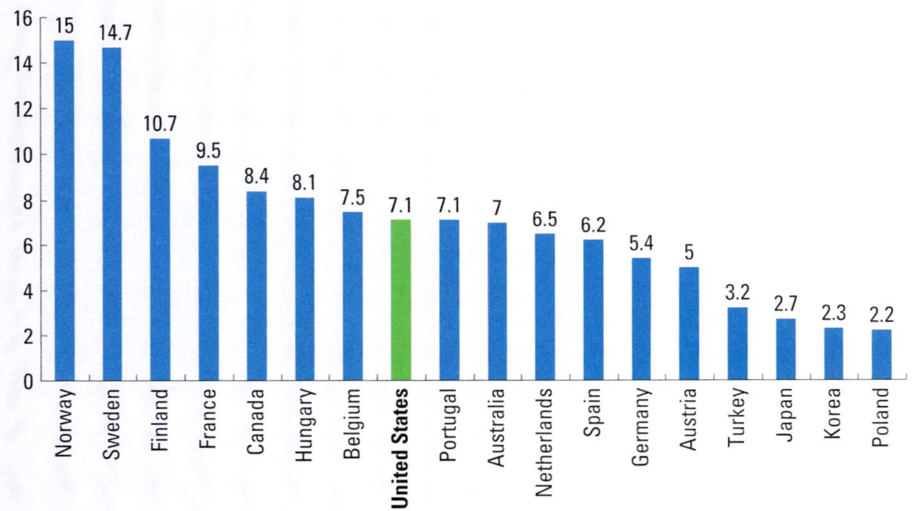

Figure A: Public Sector Employment as a Percentage of Total Population (2005)

The distribution of public sector employment between the national level on the one hand and the state and local levels on the other produces a different picture (see Figure B). By far, most public sector workers in the United States are found at the

4.3 Ideology, Policymaking, and American Federalism

★ Describe the role of ideology in shaping federalism.

As the previous section illustrated, American federalism appears to be in constant motion. This is due in large part to what some political scientists call state and local levels. Higher state and local employment is also characteristic of other federal systems, such as those of Australia, Germany, and Canada.

So if you ponder the question "Where is my government?" a postal worker would satisfy the federal part of the answer. Local government employees are far more numerous, working at the firehouse, the police station, or your local public school.

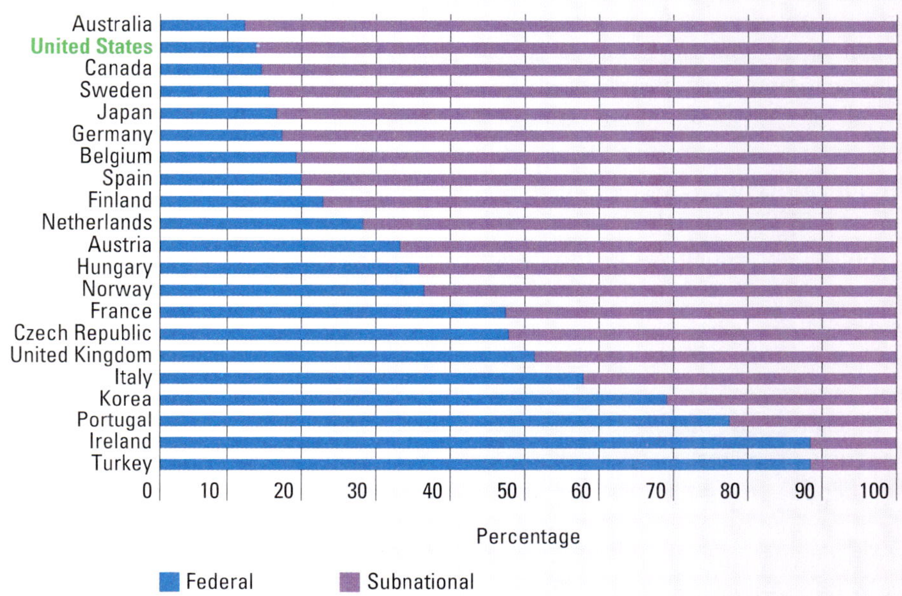

Figure B: Distribution of Employment Between the Federal and Subnational Levels of Government (2005)

Source: Adam Sheingate, "Why Can't Americans See the State?" *The Forum 7*, no. 4 (2010): 1–14; Paul C. Light, "The New True Size of Government," *Organizational Performance Initiative: Research Brief, Number 2* (Robert F. Wagner Graduate School of Public Service, New York University, August 2006), p. 11.

Critical Thinking

The size of the public sector and its distribution across national, state, and local governments vary considerably across countries. How might this smaller or larger "presence of government" affect your daily life?

policy entrepreneurs: citizens, interest groups, and officials inside government who attempt to persuade others to accept a particular view of the proper balance of freedom, order, and equality. The American federal system provides myriad opportunities for interested parties to push their ideas.

In essence, the existence of national and state governments—specifically, their executive, legislative, and judicial branches and their bureaucratic agencies—offers these entrepreneurs venues where they can attempt to influence policy and politics. Sometimes when doors are closed in one place, opportunities may be available elsewhere. The most creative of these entrepreneurs can work at multiple levels of government

policy entrepreneurs
Citizens, members of interest groups, or public officials who champion particular policy ideas.

Nutrition Facts

Serving Size ¾ cup (31g)
Servings Per Container about 11

Amount Per Serving	Cinnamon Toast Crunch	with ½ cup skim milk
Calories	130	170
Calories from Fat	30	30
	% Daily Value**	
Total Fat 3g*	**5%**	**5%**
Saturated Fat 0.5g	**2%**	**2%**
Trans Fat 0g		
Polyunsaturated Fat 0.5g		
Monounsaturated Fat 2g		
Cholesterol 0mg	**0%**	**1%**
Sodium 220mg	**9%**	**12%**
Potassium 45mg	**1%**	**7%**
Total Carbohydrate 25g	**8%**	**10%**
Dietary Fiber 1g	**4%**	**4%**
Sugars 10g		
Other Carbohydrate 14g		
Protein 1g		
Vitamin A	10%	15%
Vitamin C	10%	10%
Calcium	10%	25%
Iron	25%	25%
Vitamin D	10%	25%
Thiamin	25%	30%
Riboflavin	25%	35%
Niacin	25%	25%
Vitamin B_6	25%	25%
Folic Acid	25%	25%
Vitamin B_{12}	25%	35%
Phosphorus	4%	15%
Magnesium	2%	6%
Zinc	25%	30%
Copper	2%	2%

* Amount in cereal. A serving of cereal plus skim milk provides 3g total fat, less than 5mg cholesterol, 280mg sodium, 250mg potassium, 30g total carbohydrate (16g sugars) and 5g protein.

** Percent Daily Values are based on a 2,000 calorie diet. Your daily values may be higher or lower depending on your calorie needs:

	Calories	2,000	2,500
Total Fat	Less than	65g	80g
Sat Fat	Less than	20g	25g
Cholesterol	Less than	300mg	300mg
Sodium	Less than	2,400mg	2,400mg
Potassium		3,500mg	3,500mg
Total Carbohydrate		300g	375g
Dietary Fiber		25g	30g

Label Me

Food labeling follows a single national standard today as a result of the Nutrition Labeling and Education Act of 1990. The act preempted states from imposing different labeling requirements.

preemption
The power of Congress to enact laws by which the national government assumes total or partial responsibility for a state government function.

simultaneously, sometimes coordinating with one another to score political and policy victories.

In this section, we explore how views about American federalism can influence the shape of the nation's politics and policy. We also relate these issues to our ongoing discussion of political ideology, which we introduced in Chapter 1 (see Figure 1.2).

Ideology, Policymaking, and Federalism in Theory

To begin our discussion in this section, it will be helpful to return to the theories of dual and cooperative federalism mentioned earlier. Looking at those models of the nation's federal system helps capture some of what could be considered conventional wisdom about political ideology and federalism—in particular, the views of conservatives and liberals. In their efforts to limit the scope of the national government, conservatives are often associated with dual federalism. In contrast, it is often said that liberals, believing that one function of the national government is to bring about equality, are more likely to support the cooperative approach and more activism from Washington. Let's explore each of these general claims in a bit more detail.

Conservatives are frequently portrayed as believing that different states have different problems and resources and that returning control to state governments would promote diversity. States would be free to experiment with alternative ways to confront their problems. States would compete with one another. And people would be free to choose the state government they preferred by simply voting with their feet and moving to another state. An additional claim frequently attributed to the conservative approach to federalism is that the national government is too remote, too tied to special interests, and not responsive to the public at large. The national government overregulates and tries to promote too much uniformity. States are closer to the people and better able to respond to specific local needs.

In contrast, pundits and scholars often argue that what conservatives hope for, liberals fear. Liberals remember, so the argument goes, that the states' rights model allowed extreme political and social inequalities and that it supported racism. Blacks and city dwellers were often left virtually unrepresented by white state legislators who disproportionately served rural interests. The conclusion is that liberals believe the states remain unwilling or unable to protect the rights or provide for the needs of their citizens, whether those citizens are consumers seeking protection from business interests, defendants requiring guarantees of due process of law, or poor people seeking a minimum standard of living.

Ideology, Policymaking, and Federalism in Practice

Despite refrains such as "liberals love the national government" and "conservatives favor states' rights," these simplifications are only sometimes correct and, in fact, are often misleading. Recall our admonition from Chapter 1 that to grasp the differences between conservatives and liberals, one needs to understand not only these general labels but also the purposes of government under discussion. One illustration emerges from debates over the federal preemption of state power.

National Intervention in State Functions. Preemption is the power of Congress to enact laws by which the national government assumes complete or partial responsibility for a state government function. When the national government shoulders a new government function, it restricts the discretionary power of the states.

Congressional prohibition of state or local taxation of the Internet is an example of complete preemption.[32] It represents a loss of billions of dollars to state and local governments. Partial preemption occurs with the enactment of minimum national standards that states must meet if they wish to regulate the field. The Do Not Call Implementation Act of 2003 is an example of partial preemption. States retained authority to regulate telemarketing provided they met the minimum standards spelled out by the act.[33]

Preemption is a modern power. Congress passed only twenty-nine preemptive acts before 1900. In the ensuing sixty years, Congress preempted the power of states to legislate in certain areas an additional 153 times. The pace of preemption has accelerated. By 2000, or in just forty years, Congress enacted an additional 329 preemption statutes.[34] From 2001 to 2005, sixty-four new laws preempted state authority.[35] The vast majority of these recent preemption efforts were partial preemptions dealing with terrorism or environmental protection. For example, states are now forbidden to issue licenses to carriers of hazardous materials without a determination by the secretary of transportation that the person is not a security risk. This is a provision in the USA-PATRIOT Act.

Congressional preemption statutes infringe on state powers in two ways: through mandates and restraints. A **mandate** is a requirement that a state undertake an activity or provide a service, in keeping with minimum national standards. A mandate might require that states remove specified pollutants from public drinking water supplies, for example.

In contrast, a **restraint** forbids state governments from exercising a certain power. A restraint might prohibit states from dumping sewage into the ocean.

The increased use of preemption has given birth to a new theory of federalism. The pressure to expand national power inherent in cooperative federalism has reduced the national government's reliance on fiscal tools such as grants-in-aid. Instead, the national government has come to rely on regulatory tools such as mandates and restraints to ensure the supremacy of federal policy. According to this view, cooperative federalism has morphed into **coercive federalism**.[36]

Constraining Unfunded Mandates. State and local government officials have long objected to the national government's practice of imposing requirements without providing the financial support needed to satisfy them. For example, the provisions in the Americans with Disabilities Act require nearly all American business owners to make their business premises available to disabled customers, without providing any funds for the cost of reconstruction or additional interior space. By 1992, more than 170 congressional acts had established partially or wholly unfunded mandates.[37]

One of the early results of the Republican-led 104th Congress (1995–1997) was the Unfunded Mandates Relief Act of 1995. The legislation requires the Congressional Budget Office to prepare cost estimates of any newly proposed national legislation that would impose more than $50 million a year in costs on state and local governments or more than $100 million a year in costs on private business. It also requires a cost analysis of the impact of new agency regulations on governments and private businesses. Congress can still pass along to the states the costs of the programs it mandates, but only after holding a separate vote specifically imposing a requirement on other governments without providing the money to carry it out. Some observers expected that a Republican-controlled Congress and a Republican president would turn back the tide of unfunded mandates. However, that was not to be. Many mandates have fallen outside the precise contours of the Relief Act. While

mandate
A requirement that a state undertake an activity or provide a service, in keeping with minimum national standards.

restraint
A requirement laid down by act of Congress, prohibiting a state or local government from exercising a certain power.

coercive federalism
A view holding that the national government may impose its policy preferences on the states through regulations in the form of mandates and restraints.

it is likely that the cost estimates have served to temper or withdraw some mandates, the Relief Act has acted merely as a speed bump, slowing down others rather than deterring new efforts at regulation.[38] (It is important to note that the law does not apply to legislation protecting constitutional rights and civil rights or to antidiscrimination laws.)

The act's critics argue that large proportions of state appropriation budgets still must cover the costs of programs imposed by the national government. The National Conference of State Legislatures estimated, for example, that Real ID, a federally mandated program that imposes security, authentication, and issuance standards for states to issue driver's licenses and identification cards, will cost $11 billion through 2012.[39] To pay for the program, states may be forced to raise fees or taxes. In tough economic times, state legislators are loath to ask constituents to pay higher taxes. Since 2001, the national government has passed along more than $100 billion worth of unfunded mandates to the states.[40]

If Republicans were expecting a return of powers to the states during the presidency of George W. Bush, then they were likely disappointed. On his watch, the national government increased its power over the states. Through coercive federalism, the national government now calls the tune for still more activities that were once the sole province of individual states (see discussion under "Federalism's Shifting Scales" earlier in the chapter). But coercion has limits, as the Supreme Court recognized in its 2012 review of the Affordable Care Act.

4.4 Federalism and Electoral Politics

★ Describe the influence of federalism on elections at the state and national levels.

In addition to affecting the shape of American public policy, federalism plays a significant role in electoral politics. We have much more to say about elections in Chapter 9. For now, we focus on the ways that federalism is related to the outcome of both state and national elections.

National Capital–State Capital Links

State capitals often serve as proving grounds for politicians who aspire to national office. After gaining experience in a state legislature or serving in a statewide elected position (governor or attorney general, for example), elected officials frequently draw on that experience in making a pitch for service in the U.S. House, the Senate, or even the White House. The role that state political experience can play in making a run for the presidency seems to have become increasingly important in recent decades. Consider that four of the previous six candidates to be elected to the highest office in the land, a period dating back to 1976, had formerly served as governors: Jimmy Carter (Georgia), Ronald Reagan (California), Bill Clinton (Arkansas), and George W. Bush (Texas). George H. W. Bush and Barack Obama are the exceptions. Today, several prominent members of Congress also have past experience in statewide offices. Examples are Senator Lamar Alexander (Rep.), former governor of Tennessee; Senator Mark Warner (Dem.), former governor of Virginia; and Senator Ben Nelson (Dem.), former governor of Nebraska.

It is hard to underestimate the value of previous political experience in attempting to mount a campaign for national office. In addition to learning the craft of being a politician, experience in state politics can be critically important for helping a candidate to build up a network of contacts, die-hard constituents, and potential fundraisers. Past governors also have the benefit of being plugged into organizations such as the National Governors' Association and the Republican and Democratic governors' groups, which can help to cultivate national name recognition, friendships, and a reputation in Washington. Finally, considering that presidential elections are really a series of fifty different state-level contests, given the structure of the electoral college, a candidate for the White House can benefit tremendously from a friendly governor who can call into action his or her own political network on the candidate's behalf.

If state-level experience and friends can sometimes catapult an individual to national office, once secure in the Congress or the White House, national-level politicians frequently return to the states to stump for local favorites. In the 2010 election cycle, President Barack Obama sought unsuccessfully to maintain his party's control in Congress. Battered by an ailing economy, Democrats gave up a stunning sixty-three seats in the House, giving Republicans a clear majority. Republicans also gained six Senate seats, reducing the slender Democratic majority. And Republicans added to gains in the states where they held majorities in twenty-five state legislatures and governorships in twenty-nine. Presidential popularity (and unpopularity) cuts both ways.[41]

Matthew J. Lee/The Boston Globe via Getty Images

Joined at the Hip

Presidents routinely come to the aid of fellow office seekers, hoping to increase their party's fortunes in local and statewide races. In 2012, President Obama joined U.S. Senate candidate Elizabeth Warren at a June fundraiser. Warren is running against Scott Brown, the Republican Massachusetts incumbent. Brown surprised heavily Democratic Massachusetts voters in 2010 when he won the vacancy following the death of long-serving liberal senator, Edward Kennedy.

Congressional Redistricting

Perhaps even more important than activities on the campaign trail is the decennial process of congressional redistricting, which reveals crucial connections between federalism and the nation's electoral politics. Most generally, **redistricting** refers to the process of redrawing boundaries for electoral jurisdictions. This process, which occurs at all levels of government, becomes an extremely high-stakes game in the two years after each decennial national census in the United States. During that window of time, the U.S. Census Bureau produces and releases updated population counts for the nation. Those numbers are used to determine the number of seats that each state will have in the U.S. House, which are apportioned based on population.

redistricting
The process of redrawing political boundaries to reflect changes in population.

While it is relatively straightforward to determine how many seats each state will have, where the new district lines will be drawn is a hugely complicated and political process. Even in states that may not have lost or gained seats but have had population shifts—some areas grow at a rapid rate while others lose population, for example—the task of redistricting carries huge stakes. In large part, this is because state legislatures typically have the task of drawing the lines that define the congressional districts in their states. Given that this process happens only once every ten years and that the careers of U.S. House members and their party's relatively long-term fortunes in Congress can turn on decisions made in these state-level political debates, it is no wonder that the redistricting process commands significant national attention.

A final way that federalism can influence redistricting is through a process called *preclearance*. Under Section 5 of the Voting Rights Act, several states are required to submit their redistricting plans to the U.S. Department of Justice for approval. The process is quite complicated, but in essence it requires that states show how their proposed plans will not be "retrogressive in purpose or effect," meaning they will not dilute minority voting strength. Passing the test of preclearance, however, does not mean that a state's redistricting plans cannot be challenged for civil rights purposes or other grounds as defined in federal law and court decisions, such as rulings affirming the one person–one vote principle.

In short, both the politics of drawing congressional boundaries and the interactions between Justice Department officials and state legislators responsible for preclearance reveal the intimate connections between federalism and the redistricting process.[42]

4.5 Federalism and the American Intergovernmental System

★ Describe the role of local government in a federal system and illustrate how national, state, and local governments sometimes interact.

We have concentrated in this chapter on the links between the national and state governments in the federal system. Although the Constitution explicitly recognizes only national and state governments, the American federal system has spawned a multitude of local governments as well. It is worth considering these units because they help to illustrate the third main principle that we outlined near the beginning of this chapter: a growing recognition among public officials and citizens that public problems cut across governmental boundaries. Finding the right mix of national, state, and local involvement is a perennial challenge that dogs even the most savvy and experienced public officials.

Thousands of Governments

Based on data from 2007, the most recent year available, the U.S. Census Bureau estimates that in addition to the one national government and fifty state governments, the United States is home to over 89,000 local governments of different sorts.[43] These governments are mainly the product of the previous century of American history, with nearly all coming into existence during the 1900s.

Americans are citizens of both a nation and a state, and they also come under the jurisdiction of these various local government units. These units include **municipal governments**, the governments of cities and towns. Municipalities, in turn, are located in (or may contain or share boundaries with) counties, which are administered by **county governments**. (Sixteen states further subdivide counties into *townships* as units of government.) Most Americans also live in a **school district**, which is responsible for administering local elementary and secondary educational programs. They may also be served by one or more **special districts**, government units created to perform particular functions, typically when those functions, such as fire protection and water purification and distribution, spill across ordinary jurisdictional boundaries. Examples of special districts are the Port Authority of New York and New Jersey, the Chicago Sanitation District, and the Southeast Pennsylvania Transit Authority. Together, school districts and special districts add more than 50,000 units of government to the mix.

Local governments are created by state governments, either in their constitutions or through legislation. This means that their organization, powers, responsibilities, and effectiveness vary considerably from state to state. About forty states endow their cities with various forms of **home rule**—the right to enact and enforce legislation in certain administrative areas. Home rule gives cities a measure of self-government and freedom of action. In contrast, county governments, which are the main units of local government in rural areas, tend to have little or no legislative power. Instead, they ordinarily serve as administrative units, performing the specific duties assigned to them under state law, such as maintaining roads and administering health programs.

How can the ordinary citizen be expected to make sense of this maze of governments? And do these governments really benefit ordinary citizens?

In theory at least, one advantage of localizing government is that it brings government closer to the people; it gives them an opportunity to participate in the political process, to have a direct influence on policy. Localized government conjures visions of informed citizens deciding their own political fate—the traditional New England town meeting, repeated across the nation. From this perspective, overlapping governments appear compatible with a majoritarian view of democracy.

The reality is somewhat different, however. Studies have shown that people are much less likely to vote in local elections than in national elections.[44] In fact, voter turnout in local contests tends to be quite low (although the influence of individual votes is thus much greater). Furthermore, the fragmentation of powers, functions, and responsibilities among national, state, and local governments makes government as a whole seem complicated, and hence incomprehensible and inaccessible, to ordinary people. In addition, most people have little time to devote to public affairs, which can be very time-consuming. These factors tend to discourage individual citizens from pursuing politics and augment the influence of organized groups, which have the resources—time, money, and know-how—to sway policymaking (see Chapter 10). Instead of bringing government closer to the people and reinforcing majoritarian democracy, the system's enormous complexity tends to encourage pluralism.

Still, the large number of governments makes it possible for government to respond to the diversity of conditions in different parts of the country. States and cities differ enormously in population, size, economic resources, climate, and other characteristics—the diverse elements that French political philosopher Montesquieu

municipal governments
The government units that administer a city or town.

county governments
The government units that administer a county.

school district
The government unit that administers elementary and secondary school programs.

special districts
Government units created to perform particular functions, especially when those functions are best performed across jurisdictional boundaries.

home rule
The right to enact and enforce legislation locally.

argued should be taken into account in formulating laws for a society. Smaller political units are better able to respond to particular local conditions and can generally do so more quickly than larger units. Nevertheless, smaller units may not be able to muster the economic resources to meet some challenges. And in a growing number of policy areas, from education to environmental protection to welfare provision, citizens have come to see the advantages of coordinating efforts and sharing burdens across levels of government.

Crosscutting Responsibilities

The national government continues to support state and local governments. Yet spending pressures on state and local governments are enormous. The public demands better schools, harsher sentences for criminals (and more prisons to hold them), more and better day care for children, and nursing home assistance for the elderly. Bolstered by a strong national economy, many states cut income and business taxes in 2006. Other states provided local property tax relief. However, the deep and lengthy recession that began in 2008 has added extra strains on state finances. A majority of states reported their revenues have been hurt by the housing sector slump. Most, if not all, are seeing declines in their real estate transfer or recording taxes. Higher oil prices have given Alaska a budget surplus, but that's the exception. With high unemployment, lower property values, fewer property sales, and general economic sluggishness, tax revenues have not matched state expenditures. And since state budgets must balance each year (only the national government can print money), states must either cut services, raise taxes, or borrow money. Needless to say, these are not popular options.

In addition to ongoing policy development and financing the activities of government, sometimes crises press different levels of government into duty together. A tragic turn of events in October 2002 provides a case in point. During that month, the Washington, D.C., metropolitan area found itself under siege from what appeared to be random, yet chillingly precise, attacks from a rifle-wielding sniper. Before the assailants had been captured, ten people were killed and four others injured. Law enforcement agents also suggested that the Washington killings may have been related to similar murders in Alabama and Louisiana.

Officials at all levels of government in several states participated in what became a massive hunt for the killers. As the investigation unfolded, the local face that Americans became familiar with was Montgomery County (Maryland) Police Chief Charles Moose. His office exchanged a handful of messages with the assailants, and the chief

Kevin Moloney/The New York Times/Redux

Whose Rules?

Grand Staircase–Escalante National Monument in southern Utah was established by presidential decree in 1996. It sits on 1.7 million acres of austere and rugged land. The decree irked local residents, who had hoped for greater industrial development, which is now barred. They have fought back by claiming ownership of hundreds of miles of dirt roads, dry washes, and riverbeds in the monument. The conflicting signs illustrate the controversy. On the left, the local government, Kane County, approves use of all-terrain vehicles. On the right, the national government signals just the opposite.

became a regular figure on nightly news programs. Because some of the attacks also took place in Virginia, members of the Old Dominion State's local law enforcement and state police contributed their efforts. Finally, because the sniper killings came roughly one year after the attacks of 9/11, which raised the specter that they were connected to terrorism, and owing to the interstate nature of the crimes, federal law enforcement officials, including then Attorney General John Ashcroft, also participated in the hunt. Over the course of the investigation, apprehension, and trial phase of the case, the overlapping responsibilities and jurisdictions involved in the case revealed some of the strengths and weaknesses of the American federal system in action. Although many citizens were pleased to see such a comprehensive effort to halt the shootings, inevitably turf battles emerged among the various jurisdictions involved, as officials in national, state, and local government jockeyed with one another, sometimes to push for their own theories of how the case was unfolding, and, inevitably given the bright spotlight on the whole affair, to score political points with their constituents and the public at large.[45]

© John Munson/Star Ledger/Corbis

Cooperating Cops

Police forces at the national, state, and local level have separate and overlapping spheres of responsibility. Here members of the New York Police Department and the Joint Terrorism Task Force of the Federal Bureau of Investigation raided a New Jersey apartment in 2010 whose occupants were suspected to have ties to terrorism suspect Mohamed Hamoud Alessa who was arrested before getting on a plane at New York's JFK Airport. In 2011, Alessa and another suspect pleaded guilty in federal court to conspiracy to murder individuals on behalf of a foreign terrorist group.

4.6 Federalism and the International System

★ Analyze the role of federalism in American foreign policy.

In today's increasingly interconnected world, it is perhaps not surprising that federalism is more than simply a local curiosity for citizens of the United States. The dynamics of American federalism, in addition to helping shape the nation's politics, have begun to have more noticeable impacts in the international arena as well. And federalism as a system of government and governance is becoming increasingly important across the globe. In this section, we relate federalism to several evolving international issues and events.

American Federalism and World Politics

American federalism can have important impacts on how the United States deals with other nations, even in areas that clearly seem to be the prerogative of the national government. Trade policy is one good example.

Article I, Section 8, of the U.S. Constitution declares that the legislative branch shall have the power "to regulate Commerce with foreign Nations," and Section 10 prohibits individual states from entering "into any Treaty, Alliance, or Confederation," or, without Congress's consent, from laying "any Imposts or Duties on Imports or Exports, except what may be absolutely necessary for executing its inspection Laws." And even those imposts and duties "shall be for the Use of the Treasury of the United States." Article II, Section 2, reserves to the president the power to make treaties with other nations with the advice and consent of the Senate. These constitutional provisions provide the national government, but not the states, with significant justification and formal authority to develop foreign trade agreements and regulate imports and exports.

The national government also commands significant capacity to act in trade policy. The U.S. Department of Commerce, the Office of the U.S. Trade Representative, and the formal roles that the United States plays in international bodies such as the World Trade Organization provide federal officials with significant access to data and even formal decision-making power over trade-related issues on the domestic and global stages.

Despite what appears to be a clear mismatch between national and state officials on trade, state leaders do develop and advance their own trade agendas. It may come as a surprise to some readers, but trade policy has a noticeable intergovernmental component. In summarizing developments in state politics, two scholars have noted that states have become more aggressive in establishing their own outposts, so to speak, in other countries.[46] Today, all 50 states have international trade directors, and these officials coordinate several activities through an umbrella group called the State International Development Organizations (SIDO), an affiliate of the Council of State Governments. SIDO is like many other state-level groups that lobby Washington policymakers. However, the group also plays a more formal role by participating on a joint advisory panel with the U.S. Department of Commerce to help coordinate national and state export activities. Certainly, when national government officials advance agendas that would expand or restrict trade, states may see their own agendas to promote exports bolstered or challenged. Members of SIDO and other state leaders can advance their own state trade agendas by using and helping shape federal agendas in this area.[47]

Federalism Across the Globe

Supreme Court Justice Anthony Kennedy once observed that "federalism was our Nation's own discovery. The Framers split the atom of sovereignty. It was the genius of their idea that our citizens would have two political capacities, one state and one federal, each protected from incursion by the other."[48] Federalism is not an obsolete nineteenth-century form of government inappropriate in the contemporary world. In fact, the concept of the nation-state, developed in the seventeenth century, may be heading for the dustbin. (A *nation-state* is a country with defined and recognized boundaries whose citizens have common characteristics, such as race, religion, customs, and language.)

Some scholars have noted that we may be moving from a world of sovereign nation-states to a world of diminished state sovereignty and increased interstate linkages of a constitutionally federal character. Among the nearly 200 politically sovereign states in the world today, 24 are federations that together embrace about 2.5 billion people, or 40 percent of the world population. Almost 500 constituent or federated states serve as the building blocks of these 24 federations.[49] New versions of the federal idea continue to arise. Countries like Iraq and Sudan are transitioning to federalism, and others such as Sri Lanka and South Sudan are considering adoption of a federal system[50] (see "Politics of Global Change: Federalism, Iraqi Style" on pages 110–111).

The bumpy road toward the creation of a European superstate—in either a loose confederation or a binding federation—demonstrates the potential for as well as the limits of federalism to overcome long-held religious, ethnic, linguistic, and cultural divisions. The economic integration of such a superstate has created an alternative to the dominant currency, the U.S. dollar. And the creation of a single and expanding European market would serve as a magnet for buyers and sellers. The political unification of Europe seems to be more difficult to attain due to the resistance of some national populations and the lack of overall budgetary control, but European governments have not been dissuaded from their goal. They have found a new path—through the treaty—to circumvent the requirement of popular ratification and step closer to the goal of a unified Europe with its own unique federal structure.

4.7 Federalism and Pluralism

★ Discuss the changing relationship between federalism and pluralism.

At the nation's founding, the federal system of government in the United States was designed to allay citizens' fears that they might be ruled by a majority in a distant region with whom they did not necessarily agree or share interests. By recognizing the legitimacy of the states as political divisions, the federal system also recognizes the importance of diversity. The existence and cultivation of diverse interests are the hallmarks of pluralism.

Both of the main competing theories of federalism that we have explored support pluralism, but in somewhat different ways. Dual federalism aims to maintain important powers in the states and to protect those powers from an aggressive or assertive national government. The theory recognizes the importance of local and national standards, but it maintains that not all policy areas should be considered the same; some are more amenable to decision making and standards closer to home, while others are more appropriately national. Preserving this possible variety at the state level allows the people, if not a direct vote in policymaking, at least a choice of policies under which to live.

In contrast, cooperative federalism sees relations between levels of government in more fluid terms and is perfectly willing to override state standards for national ones depending on the issues at stake. Yet this view of federalism, while more amenable to national prerogatives, is highly responsive (at least in theory) to all manner of pressures from groups and policy entrepreneurs, including pressure at one level of government from those that might be unsuccessful at others. By blurring the lines of national and state responsibility, this type of federalism encourages petitioners to try their luck at whichever level of government offers them the best chance of success, or simultaneously to mount diverse sets of strategies across levels of government.

The national government has come to rely increasingly on its regulatory power to shape state policies. Through mandates and restraints, the national government has exercised a coercive form of federalism. This direction with policies flowing from Washington to the state and local levels signals a shift from a pluralist to a majoritarian model.

Politics of Global Change

Federalism, Iraqi Style

The United States and its coalition of willing partners deposed the Baathist regime of Saddam Hussein in Iraq. What form of government has replaced unitary dictatorial rule? In October 2005 the Iraqi people approved a new constitution that established a federal system with separate legislative, executive, and judicial functions. Whereas the United States made its transition from a highly dispersed system under the Articles of Confederation to a more centralized federal arrangement, Iraq has now moved from a highly centralized and unitary system under dictator Saddam Hussein to a more dispersed federal system under its new constitution.

The situation in Iraq is very complicated. Ethnic, tribal, and religious groups demand resources, territory, and autonomy. Arabs, Kurds, and Turkmen are the main ethnic groups. Although the population is almost entirely Muslim, the people divide into majority Shiite and minority Sunni sects. The Sunnis held sway under Saddam Hussein. Now the Shiites dominate.

Too little acknowledgment of group demands risks violent disruption. But giving too much authority to the various groups and the regions where they concentrate will fuel the very nationalisms that will divide Iraq. The fine line between too little and too much requires compromises in reallocating economic resources, dividing power between regional and central authority, and introducing a version of democracy that rules out extremists rooted in ethnic or religious intolerance.

Former U.S. Ambassador to Croatia Peter Galbraith, a critic of the Bush administration's Iraq policy but a strong defender of the new constitution, argues that "the constitution reflects the reality of the nation it is meant to serve." "There is," he says, "no meaningful Iraqi identity. In the north, you've got a pro-Western Kurdish population. In the south, you've got a Shiite majority that wants a 'pale version of an Iranian state.' And in the center you've got a Sunni population that is nervous about being trapped in a system in which it would be overrun."

These divisions over ethnic and religious lines were expressed in parliamentary elections and constitutional craftsmanship. The Kurds chose pro-autonomy leaders and opted for a constitution with strong regional control. The Shiites voted for religious parties and supported a decentralized republic along the lines of the early U.S. confederation. Many Sunnis who initially opted out of elections supported strong central government, fearing that the Kurds and Shiites might marginalize them. In such a context, federalism is the best political tool to accommodate conflicting interests. Indeed, the Iraqi constitution provides the foundation for a loose federal system in which only fiscal and foreign affairs issues will be handled by the national government.

Seven years after approving the Iraqi constitution, the country is at a stalemate. The three-way divide among Shiites, Sunni Arabs, and Kurds has turned a pluralistic democracy into an unsuitable device for reaching consensus. According to the former Iraqi national security adviser, Mowaffak al-Rubaie, "resolution can be achieved only through a system that incorporates regional federalism, with clear, mutually acceptable distributions of power between the regions and the central government. Such a system is in the interest of all Iraqis and is necessary if Iraq is to avoid partition or further civil strife." Critics, on the other hand, underline that the majority of Iraqis sees federalism as an imported and unwanted political solution. Scholars reunited in a symposium about Iraq's future agreed that the potential "partition of Iraq into three autonomous regions likely will lead to increased tensions between the factions'' and noted ''that many Iraqis associate the term partition with a western imposed division of the country.'' They also pointed out the challenge of incorporating Islamic beliefs into the constitution while maintaining a secular, democratic state. Nevertheless, there are reasons to be moderately optimistic about the future of democracy in the country: a poll conducted by the Brookings Institution in February 2009 shows that 64 percent of Iraqis considered that the country should be a democracy, versus the 19 percent who opted for an Islamic state. Only 14 percent claimed to prefer a government ruled by a strong leader.

The challenge of democracy is to find that delicate balance ensuring enough regional autonomy to satisfy ethnic or religious solidarity but not so much autonomy as to splinter the entire enterprise. American views of democracy may complicate the situation. An Iraq that emulates America's free-style democracy may promote the seeds of its own destruction by giving every zealot a forum. But constraining Iraqi democracy by ruling some extreme viewpoints out of bounds may call into question one of the reasons America intervened in Iraq in the first place: to plant a viable democracy in the Middle East.

SOURCES: Edward Wong, ''The World: New Wars in Iraq; Making Compromises to Keep a Country Whole,'' *New York Times*, 4 January 2004, Sec. 4, p. 4; David Brooks, ''Divided They Stand,'' *New York Times*, 25 August 2005; ''Iraq's Constitution,'' *Wall Street Journal*, 15 October 2005, p. A5; Mowaffak al-Rubaie, ''Federalism, Not Partition; A System Devolving Power to the Regions Is the Route to a Viable Iraq,'' *Washington Post*, 18 January 2008, p. A19; Matthew T. Simpson and Christina J. Sheetz, ''Rethinking the Future: The Next Five Years in Iraq,'' *American University International Law Review* 24, no. 2 (2008), available at http://ssrn.com/abstract=1319926; Thomas Sommer-Houdeville, ''Six Years Later: The Political Landscape in Iraq'' (Iraqi Civil Society Solidarity initiative, 25–31 March 2009); ''Iraq Index: Tracking Reconstruction and Security in Post-Saddam Iraq'' (Brookings Institution, 26 February 2010), available at http://www.brookings.edu/saban/iraq-index.aspx#archives.

Critical Thinking

Use the case of Iraqi federalism to relate how federalism can either unite or divide a country. Can you identify certain mechanisms, rules, or policies that might encourage unity and prevent division?

SUMMARY

4.1 Theories and Metaphors

- The government framework outlined in the Constitution reflects the original thirteen states' fear of a powerful central government and frustrations that the Articles of Federation produced. The division of powers sketched in the Constitution turns over ''great and aggregate'' matters to the national government, leaving ''local and particular'' concerns to the states. The product—federalism—was a new form of government that acknowledged the diversity of interests and values in America.

- Although it comes in many varieties, two types of federalism stand out because they capture valuable differences between the original and modern visions of a national government. Dual, or layer-cake, federalism wants to retain a strong separation between state and national powers, which, in essence, provides the states with a protective buffer against national encroachments.

- Cooperative, or marble-cake, federalism sees national and state government working together to solve national problems. In its own way, each view supports the pluralist model of democracy.

4.2 Federalism's Dynamics

- The ambiguities about federalism in the Constitution generate both constraints and opportunities for politicians, citizens, and interest groups to push issues that they care about.
- American federalism is both flexible and dynamic and subject to change from many different sources.
- National crises and demands from citizens frustrated with the responsiveness of state governments, judicial interpretations of the proper balance between states and the national government, changes in the system of grants-in-aid, and the professionalism of state governments have all contributed to changes in American federalism.

4.3 Ideology, Policymaking, and American Federalism

- Although it is common to associate conservative views with dual federalism and liberal views with the cooperative model, the ambiguity with which federalism is treated in the Constitution makes it difficult to pin clear ideological labels on particular theories of federalism.
- In practice, the combination of ideology and the specific policy context—that is, how one prioritizes freedom, order, and equality—rather than ideology alone drives conceptions of the proper nation–state balance across several policy areas.

4.4 Federalism and Electoral Politics

- Federalism plays a significant role in electoral politics, at both the state and national levels. Many national-level politicians have prior political experience in state government, and they often return to the states to stump for local favorites.
- Federalism also shapes the politics of drawing congressional boundaries. The interactions between Justice Department officials and the state legislators responsible for preclearance underscore the strong connections between federalism and the redistricting process.

4.5 Federalism and the American Intergovernmental System

- The American federal system has spawned thousands of local governments that also affect the balance between different levels of government in the country.
- While in principle these governments bring politics closer to individuals, the reality is that most citizens are less engaged in local than in national politics. Organized groups, with the time and resources to understand the minutiae of government at each level, are the most successful at influencing policy at the local level.
- Despite having specific jurisdictions, national, state, and local governments often must coordinate and work together. This is true for ongoing policy developments and public financing, but it is also the case when crisis brings the different levels of government into duty together.

4.6 Federalism and the International System

- The influence of American federalism extends outside the country's borders. In the area of international trade policy, for example, states have many channels through which they can advance particular agendas, despite the more prominent role that national government has in foreign policy.
- The United States is not the sole federal country in the world. Of the 195 politically sovereign states in the world today, 24 are federations, which are made up of 480 constituent or federated states. As a framework for government, federalism is becoming increasingly important in the world.

4.7 Federalism and Pluralism

- Because federalism recognizes the importance of diversity and the existence of multiple sources of authority, this type of government most clearly reflects the pluralist model.
- Still, the national government's regulatory power casts a coercive shadow over all state governments. This model of coercive federalism reflects the continuing ebb and flow of power moving from states to nation to states to nation.

ASSESSING YOUR UNDERSTANDING WITH APLIA...YOUR VIRTUAL TUTOR!

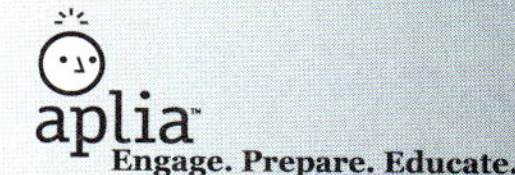

4.1 Compare and contrast the two theories of federalism used to describe the American system of government.

1. What is federalism, and what were the difficulties that it sought to overcome?
2. Define dual and cooperative federalism, and explain the metaphors used to describe them.
3. What are the primary differences between dual and cooperative federalism?

4.2 Identify and explain each of the four forces that stimulate changes in the relationship between the national and state governments.

1. How did the New Deal reshape federalism in the United States?
2. Explain how the Supreme Court's interpretation of the commerce clause expanded the national government's power.
3. What are the different kinds of grants that the national government can provide to the states?
4. What factors account for the growing professionalization of the states?

4.3 Describe the role of ideology in shaping federalism.

1. Define congressional preemption, and describe the two ways it can be exercised in practice.
2. What are unfunded mandates, and why do state and local governments object to them?
3. Explain why some analysts equate cooperative federalism with coercive federalism.

4.4 Describe the influence of federalism on elections at the state and national levels.

1. What skills can a prior experience in state politics provide for aspiring national-level politicians?
2. What is redistricting, and in what ways can federalism influence the redistricting process?

4.5 Describe the role of local government in a federal system and illustrate how national, state, and local governments sometimes interact.

1. Define and explain the relationship between municipal government and county government.
2. What are the advantages of localized government in theory, and how do these materialize in practice?
3. Why does crisis often lead to cooperation among the different levels of government?

4.6 Analyze the role of federalism in American foreign policy.

1. Describe two mechanisms through which states can influence trade policy.
2. What are some of the challenges to forming a European superstate?

4.7 Discuss the changing relationship between federalism and pluralism.

1. How do dual and cooperative forms of federalism support pluralism?
2. Why is American federalism becoming increasingly supportive of the majoritarian model?

5

Public Opinion and Political Socialization

CHAPTER TOPICS and Learning Outcomes

W hat does the United States have in common with China, Iran, Saudi Arabia, and Iraq? Give up? Those four countries led the world in number of executions from 2007 to 2010.[1] Although the death penalty is outlawed in most of the world—including every Western democracy (see "Compared with What? Capital Punishment across the World," p. 118)—it is very popular in the United States, and regularly backed two to one in national surveys over several decades.[2] Since the 1990s, however, death sentences have declined in the United States, and in 2009 New Mexico became the fifteenth state to repeal the death penalty—in part due to high costs of litigation.[3]

We can learn much about public opinion in America by reviewing how our government has administered the death penalty. During most of American history, government execution of those who threatened the social order was legal. In colonial times, capital punishment was imposed not just for murder but also for antisocial behavior—denying the "true" God, cursing one's parents, committing adultery, practicing witchcraft, even being a rebellious child.[4] Over the years, writers, editors, and clergy argued for abolishing the death sentence, and a few states responded by eliminating capital punishment. But the outbreak of World War I fed the public's fear of foreigners and radicals, leading to renewed support for the death penalty. The security needs of World War II and the postwar fears of Soviet communism fueled continued support for capital punishment.

After anticommunist hysteria subsided in the late 1950s, public opposition to the death penalty increased. But public opinion was neither strong enough nor stable enough to force state legislatures to outlaw it. In keeping with the pluralist model of democracy, efforts to abolish the death penalty shifted from the legislative arena to the courts. The opponents argued that the death penalty is cruel and unusual punishment and is therefore unconstitutional. Their argument apparently had some effect on public opinion: in 1966, a plurality of respondents opposed the death penalty for the first (and only) time since the Gallup Organization began polling the public on the question of capital punishment.

The states responded to this shift in public opinion by reducing the number of executions, until they stopped completely in 1968 in anticipation of a Supreme Court decision. By then, however, public opinion had again reversed in favor of capital punishment. Nevertheless, in 1972, the Court ruled in a 5–4 decision that the death penalty as imposed by existing state laws was unconstitutional.[5] The decision was not well received in many states, and thirty-five state legislatures passed new laws to get around the ruling. Meanwhile, as the nation's homicide rate increased, public approval of the death penalty jumped almost ten points and continued climbing.

In 1976, the Supreme Court changed its position and upheld three new state laws that let judges consider the defendant's record and the nature of the crime in deciding whether to impose a sentence of death.[6] The Court also rejected the argument that punishment by death in itself violates the Constitution, and it noted that public opinion favors the death penalty. Through the end of the 1970s, however, only three criminals were executed. Eventually, the states began to heed public concern about the crime rate. Over 1,100 executions have taken place since the 1976 Supreme Court ruling.[7]

Although public support for the death penalty remains high, Americans are divided on the issue. A majority of white Americans favors the death penalty for a person convicted of murder, while a majority of nonwhites opposes it.[8] Conservatives are more likely than liberals to support the death penalty. In a 2011 poll, 73 percent of all Republicans favored the death penalty, versus only 46 percent of all Democrats.[9] Many Americans are concerned that innocent persons have been executed. Indeed, since 1973, over 130 death row inmates have been exonerated of their crimes with the help of DNA testing.[10]

public opinion
The collective attitudes of citizens concerning a given issue or question.

Does the death penalty deter people from killing? Scholars are divided on the question.[11] So is the public, with large majorities saying that it does not lower the murder rate but that it does provide "an eye for an eye" justice.[12] **Public opinion** is simply the collective attitude of the citizens on a given issue or question. The history of public thinking on the death penalty reveals several characteristics of public opinion:

1. *The public's attitudes toward a given government policy can vary over time, often dramatically.* Opinions about capital punishment tend to fluctuate with threats to the social order. The public is more likely to favor capital punishment in times of war and when fear of foreign subversion and crime rates are high.

2. *Public opinion places boundaries on allowable types of public policy.* Stoning or beheading criminals is not acceptable to the modern American public (and surely not to courts interpreting the Constitution). Utah banned firing squads beginning in 2009, and only Oklahoma still offers that form of execution—if electrocution and lethal injection are declared unconstitutional.[13] Recent reports about pain suffered during both of those types of executions have made them also controversial.[14]

3. *If asked by pollsters, citizens are willing to register opinions on matters outside their experience.* People pronounce execution by lethal injection as more humane than electrocution, asphyxiation in a gas chamber, or hanging.[15]

4. *Governments tend to respond to public opinion.* State laws for and against capital punishment have reflected swings in the

EPA/Trent Nelson/Pool/Newscom

A Fatal Choice

Utah prisoner Ronnie Lee Gardner was executed by firing squad on June 18, 2010. Some bullet holes can be seen in the wood panel behind the chair. It was the first execution by firing squad in the United States in 14 years. Gardner had been condemned to death for murder in 2004 before Utah eliminated the choice between death by firing squad or lethal injection, so Gardner was allowed to choose. According to tradition, one of the officers' rifles was loaded with blanks. The execution attracted attention across the world, and this photo was in the British newspaper, *The Guardian*.

Source: http://www.guardian.co.uk/news/datablog/2011/sep/21/death-penalty-statistics-us.

public mood. The Supreme Court's 1972 decision against capital punishment came when public opinion on the death penalty was sharply divided; the Court's approval of capital punishment in 1976 coincided with a rise in public approval of the death penalty. Public opinion in Texas is strongly in favor of capital punishment; public opinion in states like New Jersey that have banned capital punishment is much less favorable.

5. *The government sometimes does not do what the people want.* Although public opinion overwhelmingly favors the death penalty for murder, there were only forty-six executions in 2010 (but over fourteen thousand murders that year).

The last two conclusions bear on our understanding of the majoritarian and pluralist models of democracy discussed in Chapter 2. Here, we probe more deeply into the nature, shape, depth, and formation of public opinion in a democratic government. What is the place of public opinion in a democracy? How do people acquire their opinions? What are the major lines of division in public opinion? How do individuals' ideology and knowledge affect their opinions?

★ 5.1 Public Opinion and the Models of Democracy

★ Identify the various roles played by public opinion in majoritarian and pluralist democracy.

Opinion polling, which involves interviewing a sample of citizens to estimate public opinion as a whole (see the feature "What Do You Know about Polling?" on p. 120), is such a common feature of contemporary life that we often forget it is a modern invention, dating only from the 1930s (see Figure 5.1, p. 119). In fact, survey methodology did not become a powerful research tool until the advent of computers in the 1950s. Before polling became a common part of the American scene, politicians, journalists, and everyone else could argue about what the people wanted, but no one really knew. Before the 1930s, observers of America had to guess at national opinion by analyzing newspaper stories, politicians' speeches, voting returns, and travelers' diaries. What if pollsters had been around when the colonists declared their independence from Britain in July 1776? We might have learned (as some historians estimate) that "40 percent of Americans supported the Revolution, 20 percent opposed it, and 40 percent tried to remain neutral."[16]

When no one really knows what the people want, how can the national government be responsive to public opinion? As we discussed in Chapter 3, the founders wanted to build public opinion into our government structure by allowing the direct election of representatives to the House and apportioning representation there according to population. The attitudes and actions of the House of Representatives, the framers thought, would reflect public opinion, especially on the crucial issues of taxes and government spending.

Bills passed by a majority of elected representatives do not necessarily reflect the opinion of a majority of citizens. This would not have bothered the framers because they never intended to create a full democracy, a government completely responsive to majority opinion. Although they wanted to provide for some consideration of public opinion, they had little faith in the ability of the masses to make public policy.

Compared with What?

Capital Punishment across the World

Compared with other advanced democracies, the United States follows an archaic code of justice. Every single Western European country plus Australia, Canada, and New Zealand have banned capital punishment. The United States' continued use of the death penalty puts it in company with authoritarian countries in Africa, Asia, and the Middle East that often disregard human rights.

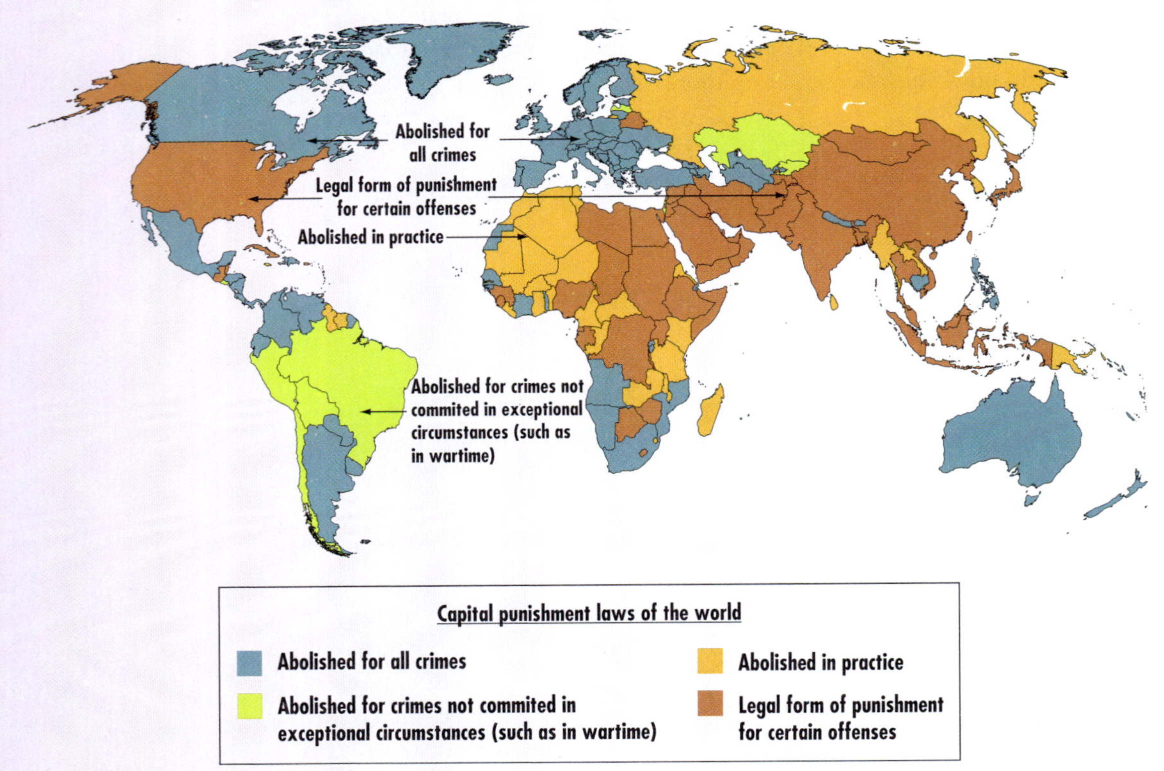

Source: http://en.wikipedia.org/wiki/File:Death_Penalty_World_Map.png.

Critical Thinking

Should the United States be concerned about the company it keeps concerning capital punishment? What American values underlie public support for the death penalty in the United States?

FIGURE 5.1 Gallup Poll Accuracy

One of the nation's oldest polls was started by George Gallup in the 1930s. The accuracy of the Gallup Poll in predicting presidential elections over sixty years is charted here. Although not always on the mark, its predictions have been fairly close. Gallup's final prediction for the 2000 election declared the race "too close to call." Indeed, the race in the electoral college remained too close to call for weeks after the election. The poll was most notably wrong in 1948, when it predicted that Thomas Dewey, the Republican candidate, would defeat the Democratic incumbent, Harry Truman, underestimating Truman's vote by 5.4 percentage points. In 1992, the Gallup Poll was off by a larger margin, but this time it identified the winner: Bill Clinton. Although third-party candidate Ross Perot was included in the presidential debates and spent vast sums on his campaign, Gallup kept with historical precedent and allocated none of the undecided vote to Perot. As a result, it overestimated Clinton's share. Just prior to the 2012 election, Gallup predicted that the popular vote would split 50 to 49 in favor of Mitt Romney. The vote did split 50 to 48, but in favor of Barack Obama. Still, Gallup was close. Source: Gallup Editors, "Romney 49%, Obama 48% in Gallup's Final Election Survey," November 5, 2012. Copyright © 2012 Gallup, Inc. All rights reserved. Reproduced by permission.

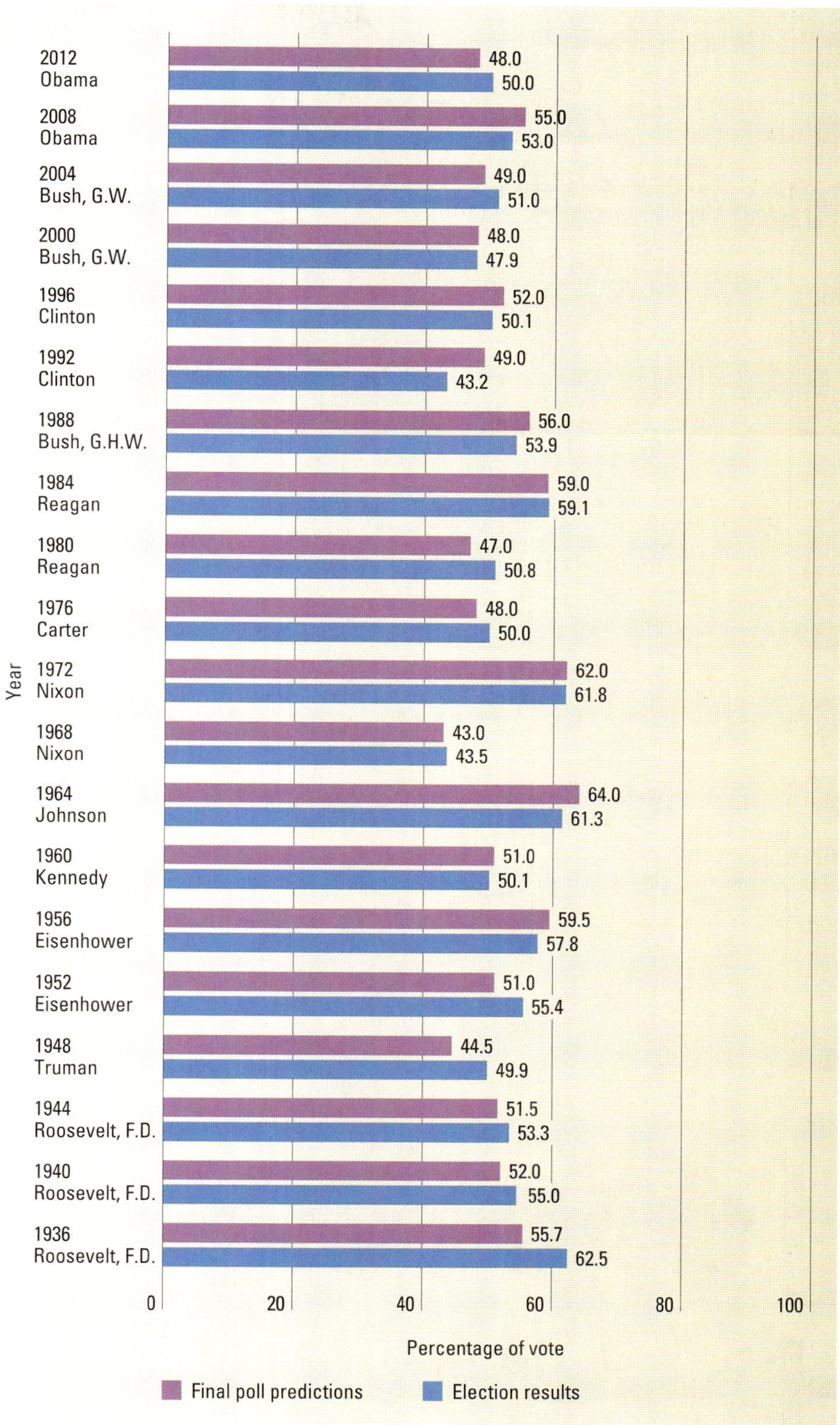

The majoritarian and pluralist models of democracy differ greatly in their assumptions about the role of public opinion in democratic government. According to the classic majoritarian model, the government should do what a majority of the public wants. Indeed, polls show that 70 percent of Americans think that the views of the majority should have "a great deal" of influence on the decisions of politicians.[17]

WHAT DO YOU KNOW ABOUT...

POLLING?

How can a pollster tell what the nation thinks by talking to only a few hundred people? The answer lies in the statistical theory of sampling. Briefly, the theory holds that a sample of individuals selected by chance from any population is representative of that population. This means that the traits of the individuals in the sample—their attitudes, beliefs, sociological characteristics, and physical features—reflect the traits of the whole population. Sampling theory does not claim that a sample exactly matches the population, only that it reflects the population with some predictable degree of accuracy.

Three factors determine the accuracy of a sample. The most important is how the sample is selected. For maximum accuracy, the individuals in the sample must be chosen randomly. Randomly does not mean "at whim," however; it means that every individual in the population has the same chance of being selected.

For a population as large and widespread as that of the United States, pollsters typically divide the country into geographical regions. Then they randomly choose areas and sample individuals who live within those areas. This departure from strict random sampling does decrease the accuracy of polls, but by only a relatively small amount. Today, most polls conducted by the mass media are done by telephone, with computers randomly dialing numbers within predetermined calling areas. (Random dialing ensures that even people with unlisted numbers are called.)

The second factor that affects accuracy is the size of the sample. The larger the sample is, the more accurately it represents the population. For example, a sample of four hundred randomly selected individuals is accurate to within (plus or minus) six percentage points 95 percent of the time. A sample of six hundred is accurate to within five percentage points. (Surprisingly, the proportion of the sample to the overall population has essentially no effect on the accuracy of most samples. A sample of, say, six hundred individuals will reflect the traits of a city, a state, or even an entire nation with equal accuracy. Why this statement is true is better discussed in a course on statistics.)

The final factor that affects the accuracy of sampling is the amount of variation in the population. If there were no variation, every sample would reflect the population's characteristics with perfect accuracy. The greater the variation is within the population, the greater is the chance that one random sample will be different from another.

The Gallup Poll and most other national opinion polls usually survey about fifteen hundred individuals and are accurate to within three percentage points 95 percent of the time. As shown in Figure 5.1, the predictions of the Gallup Poll for nineteen presidential elections since 1936 have deviated from the voting results by less than 1.0 percentage point. Even this small margin of error can mean an incorrect prediction in a close election. But for the purpose of estimating public opinion on political issues, a sampling error of three percentage points is acceptable.

Poll results can be wrong because of problems that have nothing to do with sampling theory. For example, question wording can bias the results. A CBS News poll in August 2009 found that including the words "similar to Medicare" in asking about a government-run health-care plan boosted support by 7 percent among persons aged 65 and older. * Survey questions are also prone to random error because interviewers are likely to obtain superficial responses from busy respondents who say anything, quickly, to get rid of them. Recently, some newspaper columnists have even urged readers to lie to pollsters outside voting booths, to confound election night television predictions. But despite the potential for abuses or distortions, modern polling has told us a great deal about public opinion in America.

*Katharine Q. Seelye, "Prescriptions Making Sense of the Health Care Debate; Does Public Care about Public Option?" *New York Times*, 29 November 2009, p. A27.

Critical Thinking 

Do polls help or hinder democratic government? Do they help or hinder effective government?

In contrast, pluralists argue that the public as a whole seldom demonstrates clear, consistent opinions on the day-to-day issues of government. At the same time, pluralists recognize that subgroups within the public do express opinions on specific matters—often and vigorously. The pluralist model requires that government institutions allow the free expression of opinions by these "minority publics." Democracy is at work when the opinions of many different publics clash openly and fairly over government policy.

Sampling methods and opinion polling have altered the debate about the majoritarian and pluralist models of democracy. One expert said, "Surveys produce just what democracy is supposed to produce—equal representation of all citizens."[18] Now that we know how often government policy runs against majority opinion, it becomes harder to defend the U.S. government as democratic under the majoritarian model. Even at a time when Americans overwhelmingly favored the death penalty for murderers, the Supreme Court decided that existing state laws applying capital punishment were unconstitutional.[19] Even after the Court approved new state laws as constitutional, relatively few murderers were actually executed. Consider, too, the case of prayer in public schools. In 1992 and again in 2000, the Supreme Court ruled against clergy-led prayers at public school graduations. Yet a survey showed that a clear majority of Americans (75 percent) did not agree with that ruling.[20] Because government policy sometimes runs against settled majority opinion, the majoritarian model is easily attacked as an inaccurate description of reality.

The two models of democracy make different assumptions about public opinion. The majoritarian model assumes that a majority of the people holds clear, consistent opinions on government policy. The pluralist model assumes that the public is often uninformed and ambivalent about specific issues, and opinion polls frequently support that claim. For example, Gallup polls on Obama's health-care legislation showed public support fluctuating narrowly around a 50–50 split, and the public divided 46–46 in agreeing and disagreeing with the 2012 Supreme Court decision upholding the legislation.[21]

What are the bases of public opinion? What principles, if any, do people use to organize their beliefs and attitudes about politics? Exactly how do individuals form their political opinions? We will look for answers to these questions in this chapter. In later chapters, we assess the effect of public opinion on government policies. The results should help you make up your own mind about the viability of the majoritarian and pluralist models in a functioning democracy.

Bettmann/Corbis

Stop the Presses! Oops, Too Late...

As the 1948 election drew near, few people gave President Harry Truman a chance to defeat his Republican opponent, Thomas E. Dewey. Polling was still new, and almost all the early polls showed Dewey far ahead. Most organizations simply stopped polling weeks before the election. The *Chicago Daily Tribune* believed the polls and proclaimed Dewey's victory before the votes were counted. Here, the victorious Truman triumphantly displays the most embarrassing headline in American politics. Later, it was revealed that the few polls taken closer to election day showed Truman catching up to Dewey. Clearly, polls estimate the vote only at the time they are taken.

 **5.2 The Distribution of Public Opinion**

★ Analyze the effects of skewed, bimodal, and normal distributions of opinion on public policy.

A government that tries to respond to public opinion soon learns that people seldom think alike. To understand and then act on the public's many attitudes and beliefs, government must pay attention to the way public opinion is distributed among the choices on a given issue. In particular, government must analyze the shape and the stability of that distribution.

Shape of the Distribution

The results of public opinion polls are often displayed in graphs such as those in Figure 5.2. The height of the columns indicates the percentage of those polled who gave each response, identified along the baseline. The shape of the opinion distribution depicts the pattern of all the responses when counted and plotted. The figure depicts three patterns of distribution: skewed, bimodal, and normal.

FIGURE 5.2 Three Distributions of Opinion

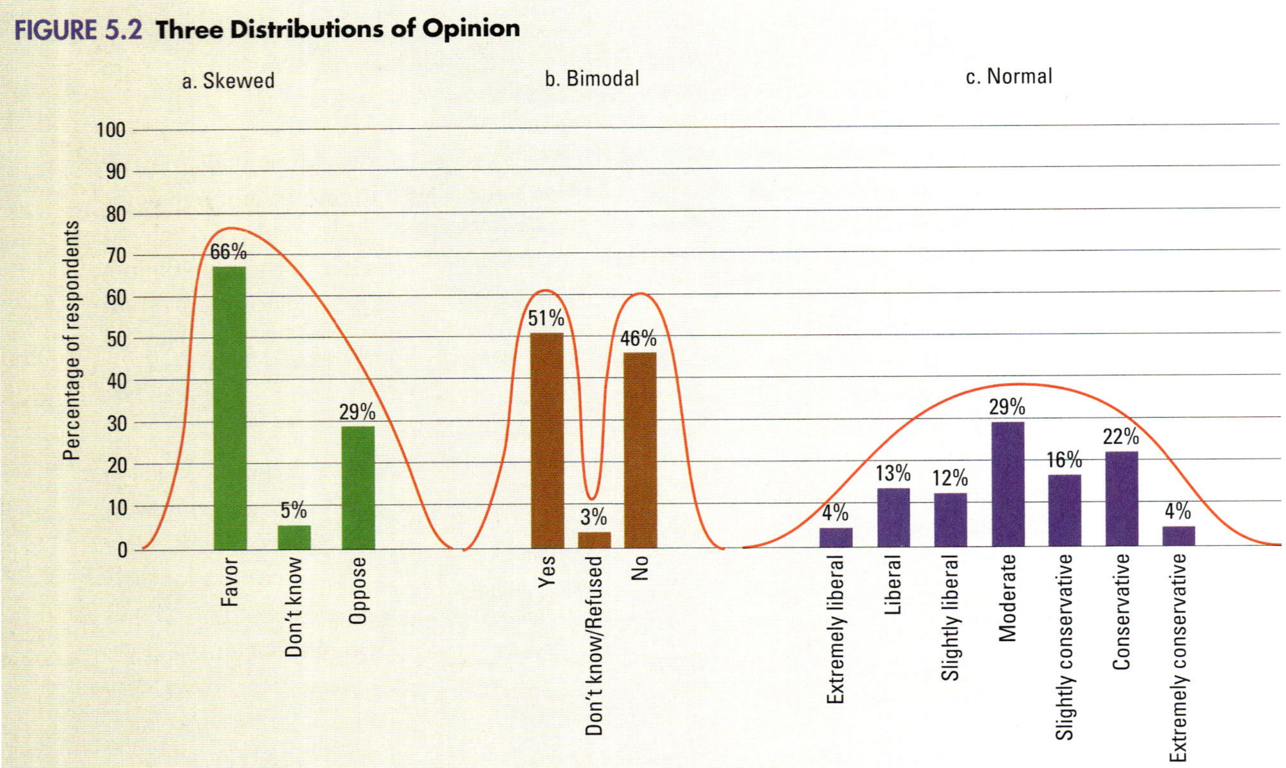

Here we superimpose three idealized patterns of distribution—skewed, bimodal, and normal—on three actual distributions of responses to survey questions. Although the actual responses do not match the ideal shapes exactly, the match is close enough that we can describe the distribution of (a) thoughts on the death penalty as skewed, (b) opinions on whether gays should adopt children as bimodal, and (c) ideological attitudes as approximately normal.
Source: 2008 American National Election Study, undertaken in collaboration by Stanford University and the University of Michigan.

Figure 5.2a plots the percentages of respondents surveyed in 2008 who favored or opposed imposing the death penalty for a person convicted of murder. The most frequent response ("favor") is called the *mode*. The mode produces a prominent "hump" in this distribution. The relatively few respondents who didn't know or were opposed to the death penalty lie to one side, in its "tail." Such an asymmetrical distribution is called a **skewed distribution**.

Figure 5.2b plots responses when participants were asked whether they believed gays should be allowed to adopt children. These responses fall into a **bimodal distribution**: respondents chose two categories with equal frequency, dividing almost evenly over whether gays can be adequate parents.

Figure 5.2c shows how respondents to a national survey in 2008 were distributed along a liberal–conservative continuum. Its shape resembles what statisticians call a **normal distribution**—a symmetrical, bell-shaped spread around a single mode, or most frequent response. Here, the mode ("moderate") lies in the center. Fewer people tended to classify themselves in each category toward the liberal and conservative extremes.

When public opinion is normally distributed on an issue, the public tends to support a moderate government policy on that issue. It will also tolerate policies that fall slightly to the left or to the right as long as they do not stray too far from the moderate center. In contrast, when opinion is sharply divided in a bimodal distribution, as it is over same-sex partners adopting a child (or Obama's health-care plan), there is great potential for political conflict. A skewed distribution, on the other hand, indicates that most respondents share the same opinion. When consensus on an issue is overwhelming, those with the minority opinion risk social ostracism and even persecution if they persist in voicing their view. If the public does not feel intensely about the issue, however, politicians can sometimes discount a skewed distribution of opinion. This is what has happened with the death penalty. Although most people favor capital punishment, it is not a burning issue for them. Thus, politicians can skirt the issue without serious consequences.

Stability of the Distribution

A **stable distribution** shows little change over time. Public opinion on important issues can change, but it is sometimes difficult to distinguish a true change in opinion from a difference in the way a question is worded. When different questions on the same issue produce similar distributions of opinion, the underlying attitudes are stable. When the same question (or virtually the same question) produces significantly different responses over time, an actual shift in public opinion probably has occurred.

We already discussed Americans' long-standing support of the death penalty. People's descriptions of themselves in ideological terms are another distribution that has remained stable. Chapter 1 argued for using a two-dimensional ideological typology based on the trade-offs of freedom for equality and freedom for order. However, most opinion polls ask respondents to place themselves along only a single liberal–conservative dimension, which tends to force libertarians and communitarians into the middle category. Historically, the ideological distribution of the public has been skewed toward conservatism in every presidential election since 1964.[22] In surveys since 1992, the public has become marginally more conservative, with the number of those classifying themselves as such rising from 36 to 41 percent at the end

skewed distribution
An asymmetrical but generally bell-shaped distribution (of opinions); its mode, or most frequent response, lies off to one side.

bimodal distribution
A distribution (of opinions) that shows two responses being chosen about as frequently as each other.

normal distribution
A symmetrical bell-shaped distribution (of opinions) centered on a single mode, or most frequent response.

stable distribution
A distribution (of opinions) that shows little change over time.

of 2011. Over the same period, people have also become somewhat more liberal, with the number of those classifying themselves as such rising from 17 to 21 percent. These opposite changes occurred at the cost of moderates, who declined from 43 to 36 percent.[23]

Sometimes changes occur within subgroups that are not reflected in overall public opinion. College students, for example, were far more liberal in the 1970s than in the 1980s (see Figure 5.3), but they have since turned more liberal and today are much more liberal than the general public. Moreover, public opinion in America is capable of massive change over time, even on issues that were once highly controversial. A good example is tolerance toward interracial marriage. In 1958, only 4 percent of Americans approved of it. By 2011, 88 percent approved, including 84 percent of whites.[24]

In trying to explain how political opinions are formed and how they change, political scientists cite the process of political socialization, the influence of cultural factors, and the interplay of ideology and knowledge. In the next several sections, we examine how these elements combine to create and influence public opinion.

FIGURE 5.3 Are Students More Conservative Than Their Parents?

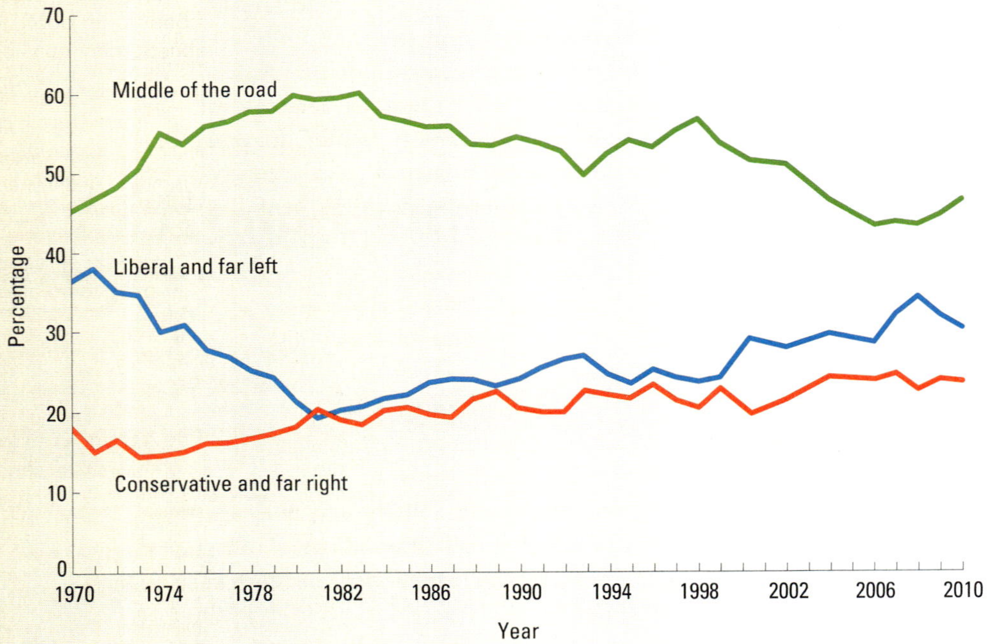

Do you remember filling out a questionnaire when you enrolled in college? If it asked about your political orientation, you may be represented in this graph. For almost four decades, researchers at the University of California, Los Angeles, have collected various data on entering freshmen, including asking them to characterize their political views as far left, liberal, middle of the road, conservative, or far right. In contrast to Americans in general, who have classified themselves as more conservative over time, college students now describe themselves as markedly more liberal than they did in the mid-1980s.

The proportion of students who characterize themselves as liberal reached its highest level in 35 years in 2008, at 31.0 percent. The percentage of incoming students who characterize themselves as politically middle-of-the-road, however, has seen a steady decline and in 2008 reached an all-time low of 43.3 percent, roughly the same percentage as in 1970. One in five students (20.7 percent) identified themselves as conservative in 2008, down from 23.1 percent in 2007.

Source: Higher Education Research Institute, University of California, Los Angeles, "The American Freshman: National Norms for Fall 2010," http://www.gseis.ucla.edu/heri/index.php. © 2011 The Regents of the University of California. All Rights Reserved. Used by permission.

★ 5.3 Political Socialization

★ Explain the influence of the agents of early socialization—family, school, community, and peers—on political learning.

Public opinion is grounded in political values. People acquire their values through **political socialization**, a complex process through which individuals become aware of politics, learn political facts, and form political values. Think for a moment about your political socialization. What is your earliest memory of a president? When did you first learn about political parties? If you identify with a party, how did you decide to do so? If you do not, why don't you? Who was the first liberal you ever met? The first conservative?

Obviously, the paths to political awareness, knowledge, and values vary among individuals, but most people are exposed to the same sources of influence, or agents of socialization, especially from childhood through young adulthood: family, school, community, peers, and, of course, the media.

The Agents of Early Socialization

Like psychologists, scholars of political socialization place great emphasis on early learning. Both groups point to two fundamental principles that characterize early learning:[25]

- *The primacy principle.* What is learned first is learned best.
- *The structuring principle.* What is learned first structures later learning.

The extent of the influence of any socializing agent depends on the extent of our exposure to it, our communication with it, and our receptivity to it. Because most people learn first from their family, the family tends to be an important agent of early socialization.

Family. In most cases, exposure, communication, and receptivity are highest in parent–child relationships. From their parents, children learn a wide range of values—social, moral, religious, economic, and political—that help shape their opinions. It is not surprising, then, that most people link their earliest memories of politics with their family. Moreover, when parents are interested in politics and maintain a favorable home environment for studying public affairs, they influence their children to become politically interested and informed.

One of the most politically important things that many children learn from their parents is party identification. They learn party identification in much the same way as they do religion. Children (very young children, anyway) imitate their parents. When parents share the same religion, children are almost always raised in that faith. When parents are of different religions, their children are more likely to follow one or the other than to choose an entirely different religion. Similarly, parental influence on party identification is greater when both parents strongly identify with the same party.[26] Overall, more than half of young American voters identify with the political party of their parents.[27] Moreover, those who change their partisanship are more likely to shift from being partisan to independent or from independent to partisan than to convert from one party to the other.[28]

Two crucial differences between party identification and religion may explain why youngsters are socialized into a religion much more reliably than into a political party. The first is that most parents care a great deal more about their religion than about their

political socialization
The complex process by which people acquire their political values.

politics, so they are more deliberate about exposing their children to religion. The second is that religious institutions recognize the value of socialization; they offer Sunday schools and other activities that reinforce parental guidance. American political parties, in contrast, sponsor few activities to win the hearts of little Democrats and Republicans, which leaves children open to counterinfluences in their school and community.

School. According to some researchers, schools have an influence on political learning that is equal to or greater than that of parents. Here, however, we have to distinguish between elementary and secondary schools, on the one hand, and institutions of higher education, on the other. Elementary schools prepare children in a number of ways to accept the social order. They introduce authority figures outside the family: the teacher, principal, police officer. They also teach the nation's slogans and symbols: the Pledge of Allegiance, the national anthem, national heroes, and holidays. And they stress the norms of group behavior and democratic decision making: respecting the opinions of others, voting for class officers. In the process, they teach youngsters about the value of political equality.

Children do not always understand the meaning of the patriotic rituals and behaviors they learn in elementary school. In fact, much of this early learning—in the United States and elsewhere—is more indoctrination than education. By the end of the eighth grade, however, children begin to distinguish between political leaders and government institutions. They become more aware of collective institutions, such as Congress and elections, than do younger children, who tend to focus on the president and other single figures of government authority. In sum, most children emerge from elementary school with a sense of national pride and an idealized notion of American government.

Although newer curricula in many secondary schools emphasize citizens' rights in addition to their responsibilities, high schools also attempt to build "good citizens." Field trips to the state legislature or the city council impress students with the majesty and power of government institutions. But secondary schools also offer more explicit political content in their curricula, including courses in recent U.S. history, civics, and American government. Better teachers challenge students to think critically about American government and politics; others focus on teaching civic responsibilities. The end product is a greater awareness of the political process and of the most prominent participants in that process. Students who have been taught skills such as letter writing and debating are more likely to participate in politics.[29]

Political learning at the college level can be much like that in high school, or it can be quite different. The degree of difference is greater if professors (or the texts they use) encourage their students to question authority. Questioning dominant political values does not necessarily mean rejecting them. For example, this text encourages you to recognize that freedom and equality, two values idealized in our culture, often conflict. It also invites you to think of democracy in terms of competing institutional models, one of which challenges the idealized notion of democracy. These alternative perspectives are meant to teach you about American political values, not to subvert those values. College courses that are intended to stimulate critical thinking have the potential to introduce students to political ideas that are radically different from those they bring to class. Most high school courses do not. Still, specialists in socialization contend that taking particular courses in college has little effect on attitude change, which is more likely to come from sustained interactions with classmates who hold different views.[30]

Community and Peers. Your community and your peers are different but usually overlapping groups. Your community is the people of all ages with whom you come in contact because they live or work near you. Peers are your friends, classmates, and coworkers. Usually they are your age and live or work within your community.

The makeup of a community has a lot to do with how the political opinions of its members are formed. Homogeneous communities—those whose members are similar in ethnicity, race, religion, or occupation—can exert strong pressures on both children and adults to conform to the dominant attitude. For example, if all your neighbors praise the candidates of one party and criticize the candidates of the other, it is difficult to voice or even hold a dissenting opinion. Communities made up of one ethnic group or religion may also voice negative attitudes about other groups. Although community socialization is usually reinforced in the schools, schools sometimes introduce students to ideas that run counter to community values. (One example is sex education.)

For both children and adults, peer groups sometimes provide a defense against community pressures. Adolescent peer groups are particularly effective protection against parental pressures. In adolescence, children rely on their peers to defend their dress and their lifestyle, not their politics. At the college level, however, peer group influence on political attitudes often grows substantially, sometimes fed by new information that clashes with parental beliefs.

Continuing Socialization

Political socialization continues throughout life. As parental and school influences wane in adulthood, peer groups (neighbors, coworkers, club members) assume a greater importance in promoting political awareness and developing political opinions. Because adults usually learn about political events from the mass media— newspapers, magazines, television, radio, and the Web—the media emerge as socialization agents.[31] Older Americans are more likely to rely on newspaper and television news for political information, while younger Americans are more likely to turn to the Internet. The mass media are so important in the political socialization of both children and adults that we devote a whole chapter—Chapter 6—to a discussion of their role.

Regardless of how people learn about politics, they gain perspective on government as they grow older. They are likely to measure new candidates (and new ideas) against those they remember. Their values also change, increasingly reflecting their own self-interest. As voters age, for example, they begin to see more merit in government spending for Social Security than they did when they were younger. Generational differences in values and historical experience translate into different public policy preferences. Finally, political education comes simply through exposure and familiarity. One example is voting, which people do with increasing regularity as they grow older: it becomes a habit.

Stephen Morton/Getty Images

Word of God?

A person's religiosity may be as important as his or her denominational identification in predicting political opinions. One measure of people's religiosity in a Christian-Judaic society is their opinion about the Bible. When asked about the nature of the Bible in 2011, about 30 percent of respondents said it was the actual word of God. About 49 percent regarded it as inspired by God but believed it should not be taken literally, and 17 percent viewed it as an ancient book of history, legends, fables, and moral precepts recorded by humans. Those who believed that the Bible is the literal word of God strongly favored government action to limit abortion. They were also much more likely to think that "creationism," a theory of the origin and development of life on Earth based on a strict reading of the Bible, should be taught in public schools alongside the theory of evolution.

Source: Data from Jeffrey M. Jones, "In U.S., 3 in 10 Say They Take the Bible Literally," Gallup Poll Report, 8 July 2011. Photo: Stephen Morton/Stringer/Getty Images.

5.4 Social Groups and Political Values

★ Compare and contrast the effects of education, income, region, race, ethnicity, religion, and gender on public opinion.

No two people are influenced by precisely the same socialization agents or in precisely the same way. Each individual experiences a unique process of political socialization and forms a unique set of political values. Still, people with similar backgrounds do share similar experiences, which means they tend to develop similar political opinions. In this section, we examine the ties between people's social background and their political values. In the process, we examine the ties between background and values by looking at responses to two questions posed by the 2008 American National Election Study (ANES).[32] Many questions in the survey tap the freedom-versus-order or freedom-versus-equality dimensions. The two we chose serve to illustrate the analysis of ideological types. These specific questions do not define or exhaust the typology; they merely illustrate it.

The first question dealt with abortion. The interviewer said, "There has been some discussion about abortion during recent years. Which opinion on this page best agrees with your view? You can just tell me the number of the opinion you choose":

1. "By law, abortion should never be permitted" [15 percent agreed].
2. "The law should permit abortion only in cases of rape, incest, or when the woman's life is in danger" [27 percent agreed].
3. "The law should permit abortion for reasons other than rape, incest, or danger to the woman's life, but only after the need for the abortion has been clearly established" [18 percent agreed].
4. "By law, a woman should be able to obtain an abortion as a matter of personal choice" [40 percent agreed].[33]

Those who chose the last category most clearly valued individual freedom over order imposed by government. Evidence shows that pro-choice respondents also tend to have concerns about broader issues of social order, such as the role of women and the legitimacy of alternative lifestyles.[34]

The second question posed by the 2008 ANES pertained to the role of government in guaranteeing employment:

Some people feel the government in Washington should see to it that every person has a job and a good standard of living. Suppose that these people are at one end of the scale.... Others think the government should just let each person get ahead on his own. Suppose these people were at the other end.... Where would you put yourself on this scale, or haven't you thought much about this?

Excluding respondents who "hadn't thought much" about this question, 31 percent wanted the government to provide every person with a living, and 20 percent were undecided. That left 49 percent who wanted the government to let people "get ahead" on their own. These respondents, who opposed government efforts to promote equality, apparently valued freedom over equality.

Overall, the responses to each of these questions were divided approximately equally. Somewhat under half the respondents (42 percent) felt that government should forbid or severely restrict abortions, and a slight majority (52 percent with rounding) considered or favored guaranteeing people a job and a good standard of living. However, sharp differences in attitudes emerged for both issues when the respondents were grouped by socioeconomic factors: education, income, region, race, religion, and sex. The differences are shown in Figure 5.4 as positive and negative deviations from the national average for each question. Bars that extend to the right identify groups that are more likely than most other Americans to sacrifice freedom for order (on the left-hand side of the figure) or equality (on the right-hand side). Next, we examine the opinion patterns more closely for each socioeconomic group.

Education

Education increases people's awareness and understanding of political issues. Higher education also promotes tolerance of unpopular opinions and behavior and invites citizens to see issues in terms of civil rights and liberties.[35] This result is clearly shown in the left-hand column of Figure 5.4, which shows that people with less education are more likely to outlaw abortions, while those with more education view abortion as a matter of a woman's choice.[36] When confronted with a choice between personal freedom and social order, college-educated individuals tend to choose freedom.

FIGURE 5.4 How Groups Differ on Two Questions of Order and Equality

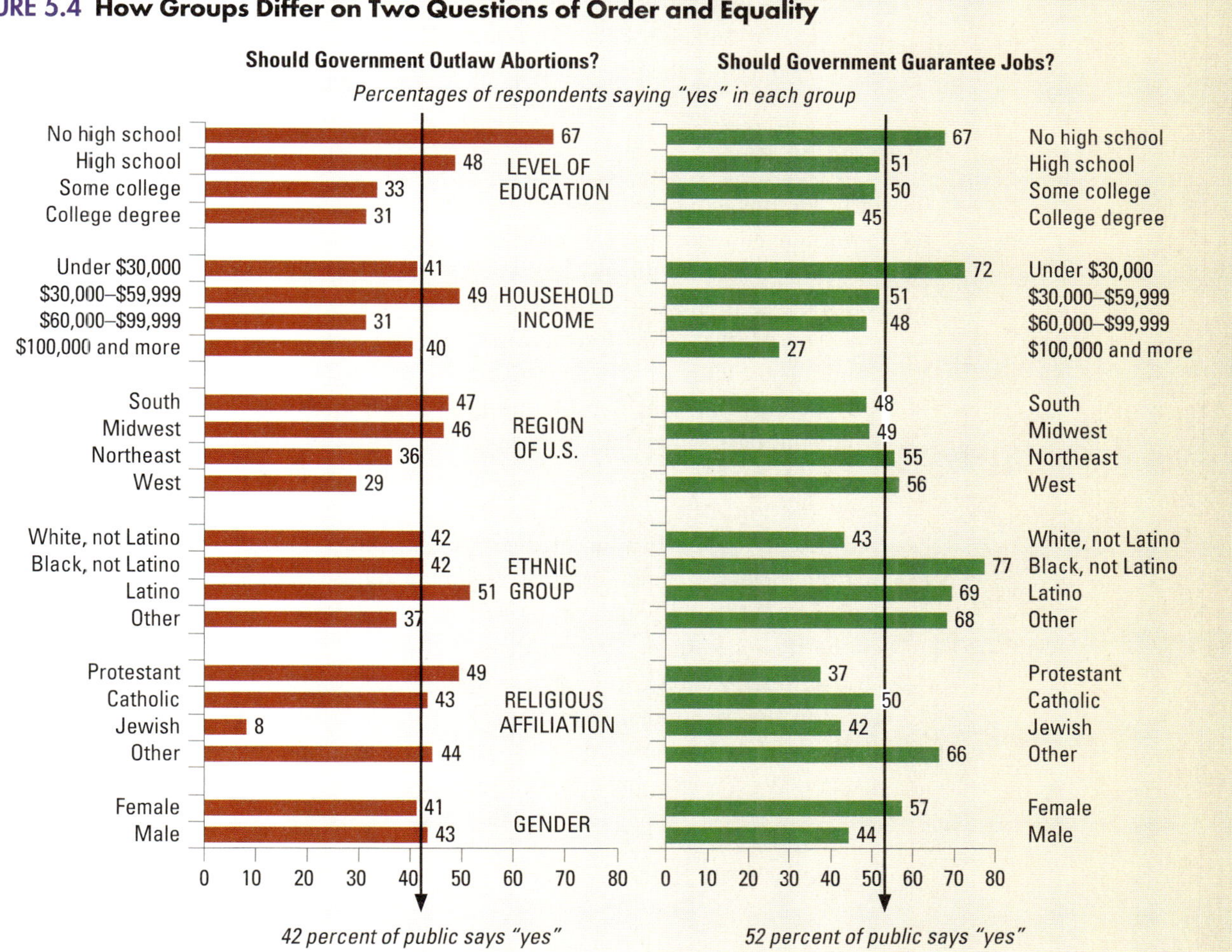

Two questions—one posing the dilemma of freedom versus order (regarding government limits on abortion) and the other the dilemma of freedom versus equality (regarding government guarantees of employment)—were asked of a national sample in 2008. Public opinion across the nation as a whole was sharply divided on each question. These two graphs show how respondents in several social groups deviated from the national mean for each question.

Source: Data from the 2008 American National Election Study, undertaken in collaboration by Stanford University and the University of Michigan.

With regard to the role of government in reducing income inequality, the right-hand column in Figure 5.4 shows that people with less education favor government action to guarantee jobs and a good standard of living. Those with more education oppose government action, favoring freedom over equality. You might expect better-educated people to be humanitarian and to support government programs to help the needy. However, because educated people tend to be wealthier, they would be taxed more heavily for such government programs. Moreover, they may believe that it is unrealistic to expect government to make such economic guarantees.

Income

In many countries, differences in social class, based on social background and occupation, divide people in their politics.[37] In the United States, the vast majority of citizens regard themselves as "middle class." Yet, as Figure 5.4 shows, wealth is consistently linked to opinions favoring a limited government role in promoting equality, less consistently to opinions about order. Those with lower incomes are more likely to favor government guarantees of employment and living conditions. Those with incomes under $60,000 also favor outlawing abortions more than those earning over $60,000. For both issues, wealth and education tend to have a similar effect on opinion: the groups with more education and higher income favor freedom.

Region

Early in our country's history, regional differences were politically important—important enough to spark a civil war between the North and South. For nearly a hundred years after the Civil War, regional differences continued to affect American politics. The moneyed Northeast was thought to control the purse strings of capitalism. The Midwest was long regarded as the stronghold of isolationism in foreign affairs. The South was virtually a one-party region, almost completely Democratic. And the individualistic West pioneered its own mixture of progressive politics.

In the past, differences in wealth fed cultural differences between these regions. In recent decades, however, the movement of people and wealth away from the Northeast and Midwest to the Sunbelt states in the South and Southwest has equalized the per capita income of the various regions. One result of this equalization is that the formerly "solid South" is no longer solidly Democratic. In fact, the South has tended to vote for Republican presidential candidates since 1968, and the majority of southern congressmen are now Republicans.

Figure 5.4 shows differences in public opinion on both economic and social issues in the four major regions of the United States. Respondents in the South and Midwest were more likely to favor restricting abortion. However, those in the Northeast and West were more supportive of government efforts to equalize income.

Ethnicity and Race

Over the course of American history, individuals of diverse ethnic and racial backgrounds have differed with respect to political values and opportunities. In the early twentieth century, the major ethnic minorities in America were composed of immigrants from Ireland, Italy, Germany, Poland, and other European countries who came to the United States in waves during the late 1800s and early 1900s. These immigrants entered a nation that had been founded by British settlers more than a hundred years earlier. They found themselves in a strange land, usually without money and unable to speak the language. Moreover, their religious backgrounds—mainly Catholic and Jewish—differed from that of the predominantly Protestant earlier settlers. These urban ethnics and their descendants became part of the great coalition of Democratic voters that President Franklin Roosevelt forged in the 1930s. And for years after, the European ethnics supported liberal candidates and causes more strongly than the original Anglo-Saxon immigrants did.[38]

From the Civil War through the civil rights movement of the 1950s and 1960s, African Americans fought to secure basic political rights such as the right to vote. Initially mobilized by the Republican Party—the party of Lincoln—following the Civil War, African Americans also forged strong ties with the Democratic Party during the New Deal era. Today, African Americans are still more likely to support liberal candidates and identify with the Democratic Party. African Americans constitute 12 percent of the population, with sizable voting blocs in northern cities and in southern states like Mississippi, Georgia, and Louisiana. In 2008, large majorities of African American voters supported Barack Obama over Senator Hillary Clinton (D-N.Y.) during the Democratic primaries. In the general election, over 95 percent of African Americans voted for Obama.

According to the U.S. Census Bureau, whites comprised 79 percent of the population in 2010 and will fall to 76 percent by 2030.[39] Those figures include Latinos, people of Latin American origin. They consist of both whites and nonwhites and are commonly but inaccurately regarded as a racial group. Excluding Latinos, whites comprised 65 percent of the population in 2010 and will fall to 58 percent by 2030. Although Latinos made up only 15 percent of the nation's population in 2010, they are projected to be 20 percent in 2030. Blacks will grow slightly to 14 percent by 2030. Asians and people of other races (including Native Americans) accounted for about 8 percent in 2010 and will increase to 10 percent by 2030.

Latinos who speak Spanish (Haitians and Brazilians usually do not) are also known as Hispanics. At the national level, Latinos (consisting of groups as different as Cubans, Mexicans, Haitians, and Puerto Ricans) have lagged behind African Americans in mobilizing and gaining political office. However, they constitute over 45 percent of the population in New Mexico and 37 percent in California and Texas—where they have fared better in politics.[40] Both Asians and Native Americans account for another 5 percent of the population. Like other minority groups, their political impact is greatest in cities or regions where they are concentrated and greater in number. For instance, Asian Americans constitute 39 percent of the population in Hawaii and 12 percent in California; Native Americans make up 13 percent of the population of Alaska and 9 percent of New Mexico.[41]

Members of minority groups display somewhat similar political attitudes on questions pertaining to equality.[42] The reasons are twofold.[43] First, racial minorities (excepting second-generation Asians) tend to have low **socioeconomic status**, a measure of social condition that includes education, occupational status, and income. Second, minorities have been targets of prejudice and discrimination and have benefited from government actions in support of equality. The right-hand column in Figure 5.4 clearly shows the effects of race on the freedom–equality issue. All minority groups, particularly African Americans, are much more likely than whites to favor government action to improve economic opportunity. Minority groups are also more likely to express dissatisfaction with the way immigrants are treated. For instance, 71 percent of Hispanics are dissatisfied with the treatment of immigrants, while only 44 percent of non-Hispanic whites are dissatisfied.[44] The abortion issue produces less difference, although Latinos favor government restrictions on abortion more than other groups.

socioeconomic status
Position in society, based on a combination of education, occupational status, and income.

Religion

Since the last major wave of European immigration in the 1930s and 1940s, the religious makeup of the United States has remained fairly stable. Today, 56 percent of the population are Protestant or non-Catholic Christian, 22 percent are Catholic, 13 percent profess no religion, and fewer than 2 percent are Jewish among the 9 percent other.[45] For many years, analysts found strong and consistent differences in the political opinions of Protestants, Catholics, and Jews.[46] Protestants were more conservative than Catholics, and Catholics tended to be more conservative than Jews.

As Figure 5.4 indicates, such broad religious groupings have little effect on attitudes about economic equality but more influence on attitudes about social order. Protestants favor government action to limit abortion even more than Catholics. Jews overwhelmingly favor a woman's right to choose. Differences among religious subgroups have emerged across many contemporary social and political issues. Evangelical Protestants are also more likely than members of other religious groups to oppose gay marriage and support the death penalty while favoring the right to life over abortion. Evangelicals and Jews are more likely to express support for Israel in Middle Eastern politics. Religious beliefs have been at the center of national and local debates over issues such as stem cell research, human cloning, and the teaching of evolution or creationism as the appropriate explanation for the development of life on Earth.[47]

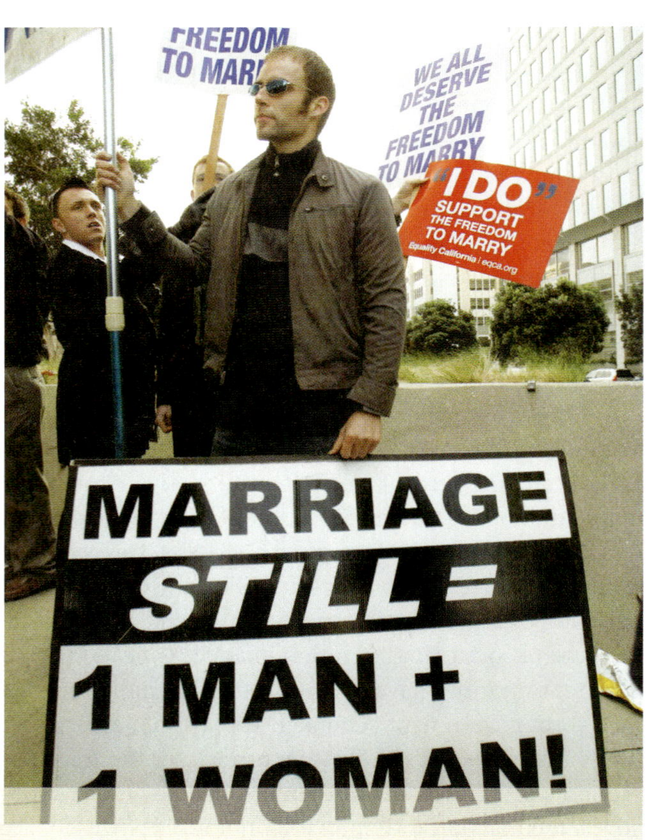

Clashing Opinions on Same-Sex Marriage

In May 2008 a ruling by the Supreme Court of California allowed gays to marry. In November 2008 California voters passed Proposition 8, which amended the state constitution to invalidate the court ruling. These protesters with opposite opinions on the issue appeared outside a federal court hearing a challenge to Proposition 8. In August 2010 a federal judge declared Proposition 8 to be unconstitutional under the Due Process and Equal Protection Clauses of the Fourteenth Amendment, setting the stage for appeal to the Supreme Court.

Gender

Men and women differ with respect to their political opinions on a broad array of social and political issues. As shown in the right-hand column of Figure 5.4, women are more likely than men to favor government actions to promote equality. Men and women differ less on the abortion issue (see the left-hand column in Figure 5.4). Surveys show that women are consistently more supportive than men are of both affirmative action and government spending for social programs. They are consistently less supportive of the death penalty and of going to war.[48]

Since gaining the right to vote with the passage of the Nineteenth Amendment in 1919, women have been mobilized by the major political parties. Contemporary politics is marked by a "gender gap": women tend to identify with the Democratic Party more than men do (see Figure 8.5 on p. 227), and they are much more likely than men to vote for Democratic presidential candidates. In the 2008 general election, Democrat Barack Obama won the support of 56 percent of female voters, while only 43 percent of female voters supported Republican John McCain, despite having Sarah Palin as his vice-presidential running mate.

5.5 From Values to Ideology

★ Define the concept of ideology, describe the liberal–conservative continuum, and assess the influence of ideology on public opinion.

We have just seen that differences in groups' responses to two survey questions reflect those groups' value choices between freedom and order and between freedom and equality. But to what degree do people's opinions on specific issues reflect their explicit political ideology (the set of values and beliefs they hold about the purpose and scope of government)? Political scientists generally agree that ideology influences public opinion on specific issues; they have much less consensus on the extent to which people think explicitly in ideological terms. They also agree that the public's ideological thinking cannot be categorized adequately in conventional liberal–conservative terms.

The Degree of Ideological Thinking in Public Opinion

Although today's media frequently use the terms *liberal* and *conservative,* some people think these terms are no longer relevant to American politics. Indeed, most voters tend not to use ideological concepts when discussing politics.[49] In one poll, voters were asked what they thought when someone was described as "liberal" or "conservative."[50] Few responded in explicitly political terms. Rather, most people gave dictionary definitions: "'liberals' are generous (a *liberal* portion). And 'conservatives' are moderate or cautious (a *conservative* estimate)." The two most frequent responses for *conservative* were "fiscally responsible or tight" (17 percent) and "closed-minded" (10 percent). For *liberal* the top two were "open-minded" (14 percent) and "free-spending" (8 percent). Only about 6 percent of the sample mentioned "degree of government involvement" in describing liberals and conservatives.

Ideological labels are technical terms used in analyzing politics, and most citizens don't play that sport. But if you want to play, you need suitable equipment. Scales and typologies, despite their faults, are essential for classification. No analysis, including the study of politics, can occur without classifying the objects being studied. The tendency to use ideological terms in discussing politics grows with increased education, which helps people understand political issues and relate them to one another.

People's personal political socialization experiences can also lead them to think ideologically. For example, children raised in strong union households may be taught to distrust private enterprise and value collective action through government.

True ideologues hold a consistent set of values and beliefs about the purpose and scope of government, and they tend to evaluate candidates in ideological terms. Some people respond to questions in ways that seem ideological but are not because they do not understand the underlying principles. For example, most respondents dutifully comply when asked to place themselves somewhere on a liberal–conservative continuum. The result, as shown earlier in Figure 5.2c, is an approximately normal distribution centering on "moderate," the modal category, which contains 29 percent of all respondents. But many people settle on moderate (a safe choice) when they do not clearly understand the alternatives. When allowed to say, "I haven't thought much about it"—24 percent of respondents in the survey acknowledged that they had not thought much about ideology and were excluded from the distribution.[51] The extent of ideological thinking in America, then, is even less than it might seem from responses to questions asking people to describe themselves as liberals or conservatives.[52] What conclusion should we draw from Figure 5.2c, which shows 28 percent of respondents placing themselves on the liberal side of a left–right scale, 29 percent in the middle, and 42 percent on the conservative side?

The Quality of Ideological Thinking in Public Opinion

What people's ideological self-placement means in the twenty-first century is not clear. At one time, the liberal–conservative continuum represented a single dimension: attitudes toward the scope of government activity. Liberals were in favor of more government action to provide public goods, and conservatives were in favor of less. This simple distinction is not as useful today. Many people who call themselves liberal no longer favor government activism in general, and many self-styled conservatives no longer oppose it in principle. Attitudes toward government also depend on which party controls the government. As a result, many people have difficulty deciding whether they are liberal or conservative, whereas others confidently choose identical points on the continuum for entirely different reasons. People describe themselves as liberal or conservative because of the symbolic value of the terms as much as for reasons of ideology.

Studies of the public's ideological thinking find that two themes run through people's minds when they are asked to describe liberals and conservatives. One theme associates liberals with change and conservatives with tradition. It corresponds to the distinction between liberals and conservatives on the exercise of freedom and the maintenance of order.[53]

The other theme has to do with equality. The conflict between freedom and equality was at the heart of President Roosevelt's New Deal economic policies (Social Security, minimum wage legislation, farm price supports) in the 1930s. The policies expanded the interventionist role of the national government to promote greater economic equality, and attitudes toward government intervention in the economy served to distinguish liberals from conservatives for decades afterward.[54] Attitudes toward government interventionism still underlie opinions about domestic *economic* policies. Liberals support intervention to promote economic equality; conservatives favor less government intervention and more individual freedom in economic activities. Conservatives, however, think differently about government action on *social* policies.

Chapter 1 proposed an alternative system of ideological classification based on people's relative evaluations of freedom, order, and equality. It described liberals as people who believe that government should promote equality, even if some freedom is lost in the process, but who oppose surrendering freedom to government-imposed order. Conservatives do not necessarily oppose equality but put a higher value on freedom than on equality when the two conflict. Yet conservatives are not above restricting freedom when threatened with the loss of order. So both groups value freedom, but one is more willing to trade freedom for equality, and the other is more inclined to trade freedom for order. If you have trouble thinking about these trade-offs on a single dimension, you are in good company. The liberal–conservative continuum presented to survey respondents takes a two-dimensional concept and squeezes it into a one-dimensional format.[55]

Ideological Types in the United States

Our ideological typology in Chapter 1 (see Figure 1.2, p. 24) classifies people as Liberals if they favor freedom over order and equality over freedom. (Here, capital letters signify our ideological classification; lowercase signifies ideological self-placement.) Conversely, Conservatives favor freedom over equality and order over freedom. Libertarians favor freedom over both equality and order—the opposite of Communitarians.[56] By cross-tabulating people's answers to the two questions from the 2008 ANES about freedom versus order (abortion) and freedom versus equality (government job guarantees), we can classify respondents according to their ideological tendencies. As shown in Figure 5.5 (p. 136), a substantial portion of respondents falls within each of the quadrants.* This finding indicates that people do not make decisions about government activity according to a one-dimensional ideological continuum. If they did, responses to the two questions would correlate and cluster diagonally in the Liberal and Conservative boxes. In fact, the correlation is virtually zero ($r = .07$). People's preferences for government action depend on what the action targets.

The Liberal pattern occurred most frequently (32 percent), with the Libertarians next (27 percent), and Conservatives (21 percent) barely outscoring Communitarians (19 percent). The size of the groups, which was determined by the particular questions, is not as important as the fact that the population divided into four significant groups in answering the questions. Indeed, the results resemble earlier findings by other researchers who conducted more exhaustive analyses involving more survey questions.[57] Of more interest are the pie charts in each quadrant. They represent the proportion of respondents in the same survey who self-described themselves as liberal, moderate, or conservative (see Figure 5.4b).

In Figure 5.5, three-quarters of *our* Conservatives (answering the questions on order and equality) also described *themselves* as conservatives, while more than half of our Liberals were also self-described liberals. In contrast, those we classified as Communitarian or Libertarian according to the order and equality questions showed less consistency in classifying themselves as liberal, moderate, or conservative.

Respondents who readily locate themselves on a single dimension running from liberal to conservative often go on to contradict their self-placement when answering questions that trade freedom for either order or equality.[58] A two-dimensional typology such as that in Figure 5.5 allows us to analyze responses more meaningfully.[59] A single dimension does not fit their preferences for government action concerning both economic and social issues. One reason so many Americans classify themselves as conservative on a one-dimensional scale is that they have no option to classify themselves as libertarian.

---

*Remember, however, that these categories—like the letter grades A, B, C, and D for courses—are rigid. The respondents' answers to both questions varied in intensity but were reduced to a simple yes or no to simplify this analysis. Many respondents would cluster toward the center of Figure 5.5 if their attitudes were represented more sensitively.

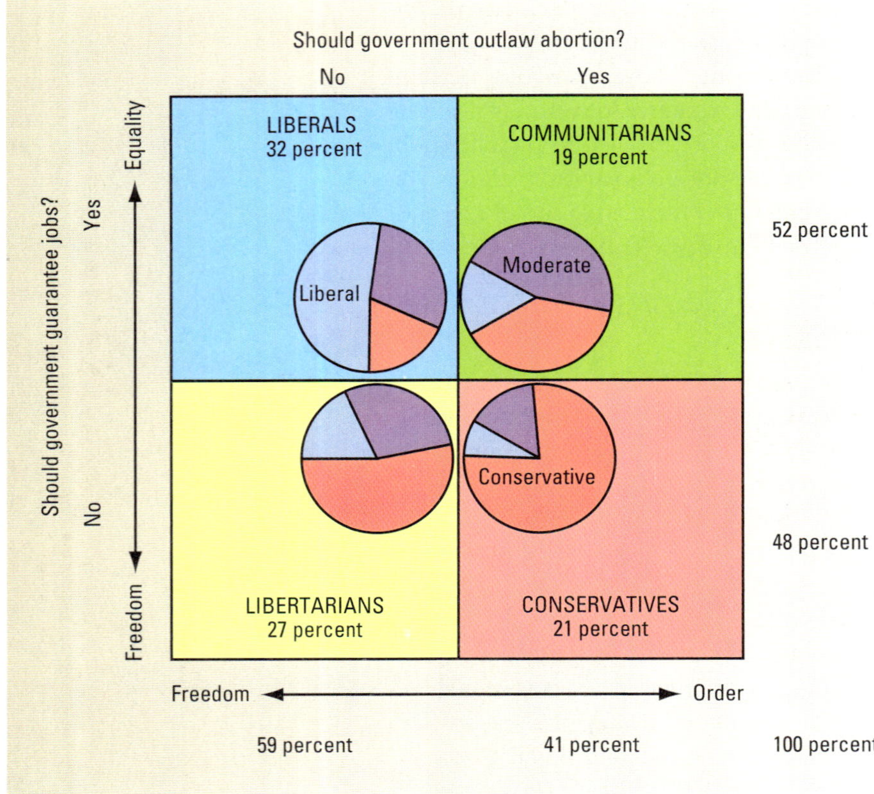

FIGURE 5.5 Respondents Classified by Ideological Tendencies

In the 2008 election survey, respondents were asked whether abortion should be outlawed by government or a matter of personal choice, and whether government should guarantee people a job and a good standard of living or people should get ahead on their own. (The questions are given verbatim on p. 130.) These two questions presented choices between freedom and order and between freedom and equality. People's responses to the two questions showed no correlation, demonstrating that these value choices cannot be explained by a one-dimensional liberal–conservative continuum. Instead, their responses can be analyzed more usefully according to four different ideological types. The pie charts in the center show the proportion of each group self-describing themselves as liberal, moderate, or conservative on the traditional one-dimensional scale.

Source: 2008 American National Election Study, undertaken in collaboration by Stanford University and the University of Michigan.

The ideological typology reflects important differences between diverse social groups. Communitarians are prominent among blacks and Latinos (33 percent) and among people with no high school degree (42 percent), groups that tend to look favorably on the benefits of government. Regional differences are small among the types, except that 44 percent of respondents in the West score as Liberal. Women tend to be Liberal (38 percent) and men Libertarian (33 percent). Indeed, Libertarians account for 51 percent of men making more than $100,000, who may believe that they have no need of government.

This more refined analysis of political ideology explains why even Americans who pay close attention to politics find it difficult to locate themselves on the liberal–conservative continuum. Their problem is that they are liberal on some issues and conservative on others. Forced to choose along just one dimension, they opt for the middle category, moderate. However, our analysis indicates that many people who classify themselves as liberal or conservative do fit these two categories in our typology. There is value, then, in the liberal–conservative distinction as long as we understand its limitations.

5.6 Forming Political Opinions

★ Assess the impact of knowledge, self-interest, and leadership on political opinions.

We have seen that people acquire their political values through socialization and that different social groups develop different sets of political values. We have also learned that some people, but only a minority, think about politics ideologically, holding a consistent set of political attitudes and beliefs. But how do those who are not ideologues—in other words, most citizens—form political opinions? As noted at the start of the chapter, the majoritarian and pluralist models of democracy make different assumptions about public opinion. Are most people well informed about politics? What can we say about the quality of public opinion in America?

Political Knowledge

In the United States today, education is compulsory (usually to age sixteen), and the literacy rate is relatively high. The country boasts an unparalleled network of colleges and universities, entered by two-thirds of all high school graduates. American citizens can obtain information from a variety of printed news sources and the Internet. They can keep abreast of national and international affairs through cable and television news programs, which bring live coverage of world events via satellite from virtually everywhere in the world. But how much do they know about politics?

In a comprehensive study of political knowledge two decades ago, political scientists Delli Carpini and Keeter collected 3,700 individual survey items that measured some type of factual knowledge about public affairs.[60] They focused on over two thousand items that clearly dealt with political facts, such as knowledge of political institutions and processes, contemporary public figures, political groups, and policy issues. The authors found that "many of the basic institutions and procedures of government are known to half or more of the public, as are the relative positions of the parties on many major issues."[61]

Current surveys of political knowledge report similar findings. Consider Pew Research Center's News IQ Survey, administered two or three times a year.[62] In November 2011, Pew researchers found that majorities answered most of nineteen items correctly. For example, "large majorities of the public know that Afghanistan and Pakistan share a border and can identify Hillary Clinton in a photograph as the nation's secretary of state." However, only about 40 percent correctly knew that Republicans only had a majority in the House. Republicans tended to outperform Democrats on the quiz, which may be due to the strong effects of education on knowledge and Republicans' greater education.

As much as people know about some political facts, the public shows less knowledge on some matters that are critical to public policy. According to a Gallup poll in late 2011, "the majority of Americans believe the nation's crime problem is getting worse, as they have believed for most of the past decade. Currently, 68% say there is more crime in the U.S. than there was a year ago."[63] Perhaps you too think that crime is getting worse, but the facts show otherwise. According to the Federal Bureau of Investigation, crime nationwide decreased: "Overall, the estimated volume of violent crimes in 2010 dropped 6 percent compared to the 2009 figure, the fourth consecutive year it has declined. For the eighth consecutive year, the volume of property crimes went down as well—2.7 percent."[64] Why then do people think that crime has increased? As explained in Chapter 6, the media tend to play up crime to gain audience.[65] In fact, the levels of homicide have dropped to levels last seen in the 1960s.[66] That people wrongly believe that crime has increased may contribute to distrust of government.

Another example concerning spending for foreign aid illustrates how little the public knows about government expenditures. A 2010 national survey asked respondents to indicate "what percentage of the federal budget goes to foreign aid."[67] The mean response was 21 percent, whereas the actual amount is about 1 percent. Asked what would be the "appropriate" expenditure for foreign aid, respondents on average suggested 11 percent. Given those results, the public might seem to favor a tenfold increase in foreign aid! Although some studies have shown that the *collective* opinion of the public can be interpreted as stable and meaningful—because random ignorance balances off both sides of an issue[68]—the public is simply misinformed on some important issues.

Moreover, individuals who strongly believe in certain causes may ignore information that questions their beliefs; they may even create false memories that support their beliefs. For instance, researchers found that individuals who thought the war in Iraq was fought to eliminate that country's weapons of mass destruction were more

Politics of Global Change

Worrying Less about Climate Change

Asked in three successive years whether climate change was a "serious problem," respondents in major countries showed declining concerns—except in China, where people became increasingly worried. Public opinion in the United States was not alarmed by climate change in 2008, and it was the least concerned among the eight countries in 2010.

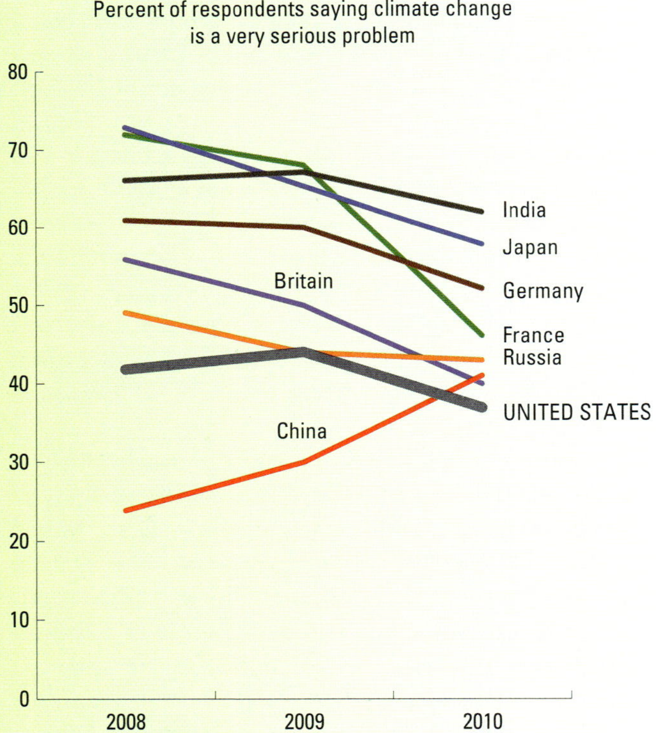

Source: Pew Research Center, "Obama More Popular Abroad Than at Home, Global Image of U.S. Continues to Benefit," Global Attitudes Project, 17 June 2010, p. 71. Copyright © 2010 by Pew Global Attitudes Project, a division of Pew Research Center For the People & the Press. Reproduced by permission. Prior to 2010, the question asked about "global warming" instead of "climate change."

Critical Thinking

Why do Americans seem less concerned about climate change than citizens in other major countries? Why might the Chinese public buck the trend in opinion about climate change?

likely to think that these weapons had been found after the start of the war.[69] They were less sensitive to news information that contradicted their initial beliefs. Finally, people in various countries differ in their understanding of the facts and their political consequences. As shown in the box, "Politics of Global Change: Worrying Less about Climate Change" (see p. 138), people in some countries were less worried in 2010 than in 2008—while some in a very large country worried much more.

Costs, Benefits, and Cues

Perhaps people do not think in ideological terms or know a wide variety of political facts, but they can tell whether a policy is likely to directly help or hurt them. The **self-interest principle** states that people choose what benefits them personally.[70] Self-interest plays an obvious role in how people form opinions on government policies with clear costs and benefits.[71] Tax payers tend to prefer low taxes to high taxes. Smokers tend to oppose bans on smoking in public places. Gun owners are less likely to support handgun control. Some people evaluate incumbent presidents according to whether they are better or worse off financially than they were four years ago. Group leaders often cue group members, telling them what policies they should support or oppose. (In the context of pluralist democracy, this often appears as grassroots support for or opposition to policies that affect only particular groups.)[72]

In some cases, individuals are unable to determine personal costs or benefits. This tends to be true of foreign policy, which few people interpret in terms of personal benefits. Here, many people have no opinion, or their opinions are not firmly held and are likely to change quite easily given almost any new information. For example, public approval of the war in Iraq and of former president Bush's handling of the war varied with positive news such as Iraqi elections and negative news such as the number of military casualties.

Public opinion that is not based on a complicated ideology may also emerge from the skillful use of cues. Individuals may use heuristics—mental shortcuts that require hardly any information—to make fairly reliable political judgments.[73] For instance, citizens can use political party labels to compensate for low information about the policy positions of candidates. Voters may have well-developed expectations or stereotypes about political parties that structure the way they evaluate candidates and process new information.[74] They assume that Democrats and Republicans differ from each other in predictable ways. Similarly, citizens take cues from trusted government officials and interest groups regarding the wisdom of bills pending in Congress or the ideology of Supreme Court nominees.

Political Leadership

Public opinion on specific issues is molded by political leaders, journalists, and policy experts. Politicians serve as cue givers to members of the public. Citizens with favorable views of a politician may be more likely to support his or her values and policy agenda. In one study, 49 percent of respondents were uncomfortable with the statement, "I have never believed the Constitution required our schools to be religion free zones," when it was presented anonymously; only 34 percent claimed to be uncomfortable when the statement was attributed to former president Bill Clinton.[75] In a different study, African Americans were presented with a statement about the need for blacks to rely more on themselves to get ahead in society; respondents agreed with the statement when it was attributed to black politicians (Jesse Jackson Sr. and Clarence Thomas) and disagreed when the statement was attributed to white politicians (George H. W. Bush and Ted Kennedy).[76]

self-interest principle
The implication that people choose what benefits them personally.

issue framing
The way that politicians or interest group leaders define an issue when presenting it to others.

Politicians routinely make appeals to the public on the basis of shared political ideology and self-interest. They collect and share information about social trends, policy options, and policy implementation. Competition and controversy among political elites provide the public with a great deal of information. But politicians are well aware that citizen understanding and support for an issue depend on its framing. In **issue framing**, politicians define the way that issues are presented, selectively invoking values or recalling history in the presentation. For example, opinion leaders might frame a reduction in taxes as "returning money to the people" or, quite differently, as "reducing government services." Politicians and other leaders can frame issues to change or reinforce public opinion. Such framing is sometimes referred to as "spin," and "spin doctors" are those who stand ready to reinforce or elaborate on the spin inherent in the framing.[77]

The ability of political leaders to influence public opinion has been enhanced enormously by the growth of the broadcast media, especially television.[78] The majoritarian model of democracy assumes that government officials respond to public opinion, but the evidence is substantial that this causal sequence is reversed—that public opinion responds to the actions of government officials.[79] If this is true, how much potential is there for public opinion to be manipulated by political leaders through the mass media? We examine the manipulative potential of the mass media in the next chapter.

SUMMARY

5.1 Public Opinion and the Models of Democracy

- Public opinion is more important to the majoritarian model of democracy than the pluralist model.

5.2 The Distribution of Public Opinion

- The shape of the distribution of opinion (skewed, bimodal, or normal) indicates how sharply the public is divided. Bimodal distributions harbor the greatest potential for political conflict.
- Because most Americans' ideological opinions are normally distributed around the moderate category on the familiar ideological continuum (and have been for decades), government policies can vary from left to right over time without provoking severe political conflict.
- The stability of a distribution over time indicates how settled people are in their opinions.

5.3 Political Socialization

- People form their values through the process of political socialization.
- The most important socialization agents in childhood and young adulthood are family, school, community, and peers.

5.4 Social Groups and Political Values

- Members of the same social group tend to experience similar socialization processes and thus to adopt similar values. People in different social groups that hold different values often express vastly different opinions.
- Differences in education, race, and religion tend to produce sharper divisions of opinion today on questions of order and equality than do differences in income or region.

5.5 From Values to Ideology

- Most people do not think about politics in ideological terms but readily classify themselves along a liberal–conservative continuum, many choosing the safe middle category, moderate.
- Others choose the moderate category because they have liberal views on some issues and conservative views on others. Their political orientation is better captured by a two-dimensional framework that analyzes ideology according to the values of freedom, order, and equality, which classifies people as Liberals, Conservatives, Libertarians, and Communitarians.

5.6 Forming Political Opinions

- Surveys show that the public does relatively well on quizzes of political facts, but people sometimes completely misunderstand critical issues in public policy. Citizens use party labels to compensate for their lack of detailed information about pending legislation or political candidates. Uninformed respondents are susceptible to cues of support or opposition from political leaders, communicated through the mass media.

- Sometimes the public shows clear and settled opinions on government policy, conforming to the majoritarian model. However, public opinion is often not firmly grounded in knowledge and may be unstable on given issues.

- Powerful groups are often divided over what they want government to do, which leaves politicians with a great deal of latitude in enacting specific policies in line with the pluralist model.

ASSESSING YOUR UNDERSTANDING WITH APLIA...YOUR VIRTUAL TUTOR!

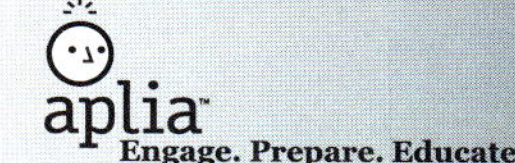

5.1 Identify the various roles played by public opinion in majoritarian and pluralist democracy.

1. What does the majoritarian model assume about the nature of public opinion?
2. What does the pluralist model assume about public opinion?

5.2 Analyze the effect of skewed, bimodal, and normal distributions of opinion on public policy.

1. Which distribution of opinion—skewed, bimodal, or normal—on a sensitive political issue provokes the greatest political challenge?
2. Cite a political issue on which American public opinion has been relatively stable since World War II. Cite an issue on which opinion has changed a great deal over the same period.

5.3 Explain the influence of the agents of early socialization—family, school, community, and peers—on political learning.

1. How do the primary principle and the structuring principle affect political learning?
2. How is acquiring a party identification similar to acquiring religion? How do the two processes differ?
3. When does political socialization stop?

5.4 Compare and contrast the effects of education, income, region, race, ethnicity, religion, and gender on public opinion.

1. Which social grouping—education, income, region, race, ethnicity, religion, or gender— has the strongest systematic effect on attitudes toward government's role in maintain order, such as outlawing abortions?
2. Which social grouping has the strongest systematic effect on attitudes toward government's role in promoting equality, such as guaranteeing jobs?
3. How do African Americans and Latinos differ from each other on outlawing abortions and guaranteeing jobs?

5.5 Define the concept of ideology, describe the liberal–conservative continuum, and assess the influence of ideology on public opinion.

1. Based on national responses to questions about abortion and government jobs, is the country fundamentally conservative, liberal, or divided in its ideological classification?

5.6 Assess the impact of knowledge, self-interest, and leadership on political opinions.

1. What evidence shows that people know little about politics—or, conversely, that they know a lot about government and political affairs?
2. How does the self-interest principle help explain by people vote according to party labels?
3. Using the concept of issue framing, pick a political issue and illustrate how Democratic and Republican candidates present it differently to voters.

6 The Media

CHAPTER TOPICS and Learning Outcomes

aplia
Engage. Prepare. Educate.

© Johner Images/Alamy

When Barack Obama announced he was running for president in 2007, he did it the way candidates traditionally did: He picked a symbolic location, ensured the attendance of an enthusiastic crowd, and invited journalists to cover the event. Speaking to thousands of supporters in Springfield, Illinois, Obama said, "In the shadow of the Old State Capitol, where Lincoln once called on a divided house to stand together, where common hopes and common dreams still live, I stand before you today to announce my candidacy for president of the United States of America." The crowd went crazy.[1]

In 2011, Obama announced his candidacy for reelection in a two-minute YouTube video posted on his campaign's website, which was accompanied by an e-mail sent out to supporters.[2] Forgoing the traditional scripted media event, he went directly to his base and into homes and offices around the globe. As in 2007, mainstream media outlets reported the announcement, but they were reporting about a Web posting that anyone with Internet access could view directly instead of having to rely on a truncated account of an actual event.

On the Republican side, Newt Gingrich also skipped the public appearance and announced his entrance to the 2012 campaign on Twitter. His tweet simply stated, "Today I am announcing my candidacy for President of the United States." The tweet was followed by a video on YouTube and Facebook. Mitt Romney likewise announced the creation of his campaign's exploratory committee on YouTube.[3]

While these social networking messages may lack the drama and energy of live events, they connect to citizens without being filtered, trimmed, and analyzed by journalists first. In our new technological era when politicians can communicate directly with the public, we are forced to wonder, what is to become of journalism? How do we even determine who is and is not a journalist? Throughout the twentieth century, a journalist was a trained professional who reported the news to the public after an editor had determined that the story met standards of accuracy and objectivity. Today, that understanding of journalistic behavior is in the throes of change. One recent study found that one-third of Internet users in the United States claim to have "actively contributed to the creation, commentary, or dissemination of news."[4]

Will the ways in which technology changes the practice of journalism make it harder for citizens to find objective and unbiased reporting? Is the notion of democratic accountability itself threatened? Or does the universality and interconnectivity of new media produce deeper and more widespread engagement with the political system?

Some observers argue that the challenges faced by traditional news reporting are a threat to democracy.

Traditional journalism invests heavily in investigative reporting, following up on stories once they are no longer on the front page and sending journalists both to faraway places to report on foreign events and to local statehouses to report on state and city politics.[5] Journalistic norms of objectivity and accountability provide readers with accurate information that allows them to draw their own conclusions about current affairs. When citizens turn instead to opinion blogs and Twitter feeds, the market for traditional journalism is threatened, and the important services it contributes to the public good could disappear, rendering citizens uninformed—or misinformed—and without an important check on public officials.

On the other side are people who find the new frontier in journalism exciting and democratizing. They argue that readers will still want investigative, local, and international reporting and that Web-based models able to fulfill that desire are emerging. ProPublica.org, for example, is a nonprofit online-only news site that focuses entirely on investigative journalism. In 2011, ProPublica won a Pulitzer Prize for its coverage of the role of Wall Street in the recession beginning in 2008. Champions of new media also say that the spread of mobile technology and social networking sites allow political information to reach ever broader audiences.[6]

People on both sides agree on three things. First, the challenges facing traditional journalism are here to stay; we cannot put the Internet genie back in the bottle. Second, the media continue to play a critical role in the democratic process. Third, this critical role demands that we carefully and continually study the impact of the rapidly changing media environment.

In this chapter, we describe the origin, growth, and change of the media; assess their objectivity; and examine their influence on politics. How have the various media promoted or frustrated democratic ideals over time? What consequences, if any, flow from liberal or conservative biases in the media? Who uses which media, and what do they learn? Do the media advance or retard equality in society? Does the concept of freedom of the press inhibit the government's effort to secure order? What new problems flow from globalization of the news media?

6.1 The Development of the Mass Media in the United States

★ Trace the evolution of the mass media in the United States and evaluate the impact of new technologies on journalism.

Communication is essential in a representative democracy. Elected officials need to inform the citizenry of their actions such that the people can effectively give their consent to be governed by the politicians of their choice. Likewise, citizens need to be able to communicate their wants and needs to elected officials such that those officials are able to provide adequate representation to their constituents.

Communication is simply the process of transmitting information from one individual or group to another. *Mass communication* is the process by which information is transmitted to large, heterogeneous, widely dispersed audiences. The term **mass media** refers to the means for communicating to these audiences. Traditionally, the mass media has been divided into two types: print and broadcast. *Print media*, such as newspapers, communicate information through the publication of words and pictures on paper. *Broadcast media*, such as radio and television, communicate

mass media
The means employed in mass communication; traditionally divided into print media and broadcast media.

The News Fairy?

While the Internet may be gaining in popularity as a source of news, many Internet news sites rely on traditional media sources for their information. These sites, such as Google News, are known as news aggregators. If newspapers fail, news aggregators will too.

information electronically, through sounds and images. The Internet has begun to render the distinction between print and broadcast media problematic, as most newspapers and magazines now have an online presence that provides video clips to accompany news articles, and most television and radio news programs have websites that provide text. And most of these sites provide opportunities for the public to comment and thus disseminate their own perspective. We are in what has been termed a "post-broadcast" age.[7]

More so now than at any other time in history, the opportunities for genuine two-way flows of information between citizens and government have been made possible by the interactivity of the Internet. It is now a central component of an ever-evolving mass media, which is a collection of technologies with the dual capability of reflecting and shaping our political views.

The media are not the only means of communication between citizens and government. As we discussed in Chapter 5, various agents of socialization (especially schools) function as "linkage mechanisms" that promote such communication. In later chapters, we discuss other mechanisms for communication: voting, political parties, campaigning, and interest groups. The media, however, are the only linkage mechanisms that specialize in communication.

Although this chapter concentrates on political uses of five prominent mass media—newspapers, magazines, radio, television, and the Internet—political content can also be transmitted through other mass media, such as recordings and motion pictures. Popular musicians often express political ideas in their music. In 2011, for example, Lady Gaga released the single "Born This Way," and created the Born This Way Foundation as a vehicle for combating bullying, an effort that garnered her a meeting with top aides at the White House regarding anti-bullying initiatives.[8]

Motion pictures often convey intense—and consequential—political messages. Michael Moore's *Sicko,* a 2007 Oscar-nominated documentary, was a blistering attack on the health-care system in the United States. One poll found that nearly half of Americans had either seen or heard of the movie one month after its release, and of those, nearly half said that the film made them more likely to think that health-care reform was needed.[9]

Although the record and film industries sometimes convey political messages, they are primarily in the business of entertainment. Our focus here is on mass media in the news industry. Figure 6.1 plots the increase in the number of Americans with access to radios, televisions, and the Internet from 1920 to the present. The growth of the country, technological inventions, and shifting political attitudes about the scope of government, as well as trends in entertainment, have shaped the development of the news media in the United States.[10]

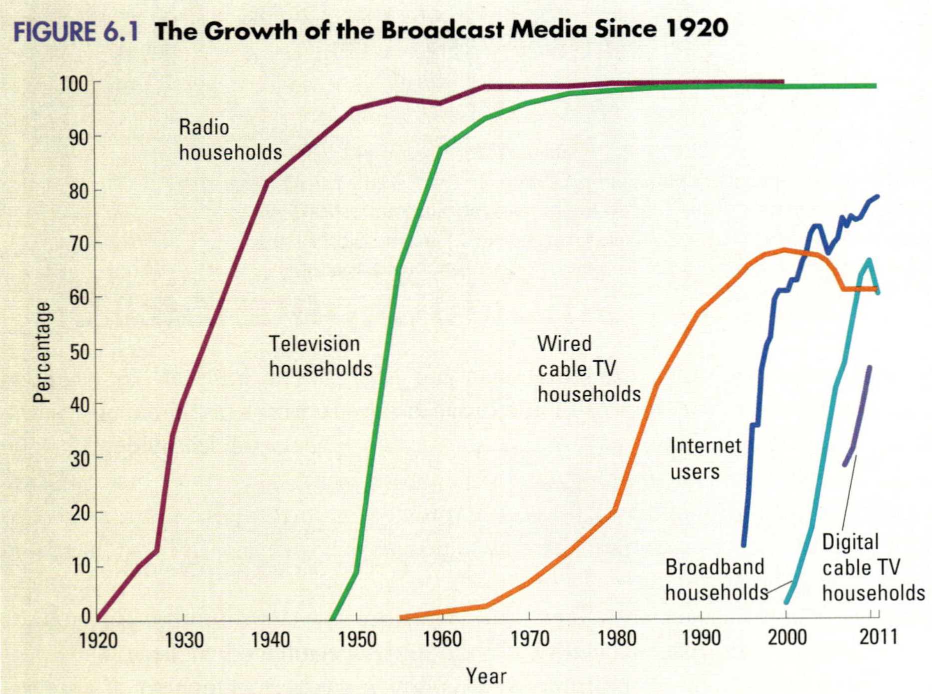

FIGURE 6.1 The Growth of the Broadcast Media Since 1920

The media environment in the United States has changed dramatically over time. This graph shows the percentage of all households or adults using a particular media technology: radio, television, cable TV, Internet, or broadband. In 1950, for instance, only 9 percent of all households had a television set. Within five years, almost two-thirds of all American households owned a television set. In 1995, only 14 percent of all adults reported using the Internet. Today over 80 percent of adults report using the Internet at home or work.

Sources: For data on radio, television, and cable TV, see Northwestern University's Media Information Center website: http://www.mediainfocenter.org. Additional data on radio households in the 1920s and 1930s are reported by Steve Craig, "How America Adopted Radio," *Journal of Broadcasting and Electronic Media* 48 (June 2004): 179–195. For television and cable TV, see also http://blog.nielsen.com/nielsenwire/wp-content/uploads/2009/07/tva_2008_071709.pdf and Stanley and Niemi, *Vital Statistics on American Politics, 2011-2012* (Washington, D.C.: CQ Press, 2012). For broadband and Internet statistics, see Pew Internet & American Life Project trend data available at http://www.pewinternet.org/.

Newspapers

When the Revolutionary War broke out in 1775, thirty-seven newspapers (all week-lies) were publishing in the colonies.[11] They had small circulations, so they were not really mass media but group media read by elites. The first newspapers were mainly political organs, financed by parties and advocating party causes. Newspapers did not move toward independent ownership and large circulations until the 1830s, once publishers discovered they could raise revenue through advertising instead of relying on parties.

By 1880, 971 daily newspapers and 8,633 weekly newspapers and periodicals were published in the United States. Most larger cities had many newspapers: New York had twenty-nine; Philadelphia, twenty-four; and San Francisco, twenty-one. Competition for readers grew fierce among the big-city dailies. Toward the end of the nineteenth century, imaginative publishers courted readers by entertaining them with photographs, comic strips, sports sections, advice columns, and stories of sex and crime.

By the 1960s, under pressure from both radio and television, intense competition among big-city dailies had nearly disappeared. New York had only three papers left by 1969, a pattern repeated in every large city in the country. By 2009, only twenty-six U.S. towns or cities had two or more competing dailies under separate ownership.[12] The net result is that newspaper circulation as a percentage of the U.S. population has dropped by 59 percent since 1947.[13] Some argue that the lack of competition mid-century is part of what allowed the journalistic norms of objectivity and accuracy to emerge; without having to pander to readers through sensationalism, reporters could focus on quality and depth.[14]

The daily paper with the largest circulation in 2010 (about 2 million copies) was the *Wall Street Journal,* followed closely by *USA Today* (1.8 million). The *New York Times,* which many journalists consider the best newspaper in the country, sold a little under 1 million daily copies, placing it third in circulation (see Figure 6.2). In comparison, *Us Weekly,* which carries stories about celebrities, had an average circulation of just under 2 million.[15] Neither the *Times* nor the *Wall Street Journal* carries comic strips, which no doubt limits their mass appeal. They also print more political news and analyses than most readers want.

While circulation of printed papers has declined, news readership is actually up, with many readers accessing newspapers online. But Web-based audiences generally access the news for free; most newspapers do not require paid subscriptions for their online content. As circulations decline, newspapers need to find ways to keep revenues up in order to continue offering a printed product and sustain bureaus across the country and around the world. So far, the *Wall Street Journal* is the only major newspaper with a long-standing successful practice of charging its online readers. In 2011, the *New York Times* instituted a system that allows users to see a limited number of articles for free but charges for unlimited access. Early assessments indicate that the paywall is a success, but only time will tell if the paper is able to raise enough revenue through subscriptions or whether readers will simply opt for free alternatives.[16] Many other newspapers are also experimenting with different types of online subscriptions.

Magazines

Magazines differ from newspapers not only in the frequency of their publication but also in the nature of their coverage. News-oriented magazines cover the news in a

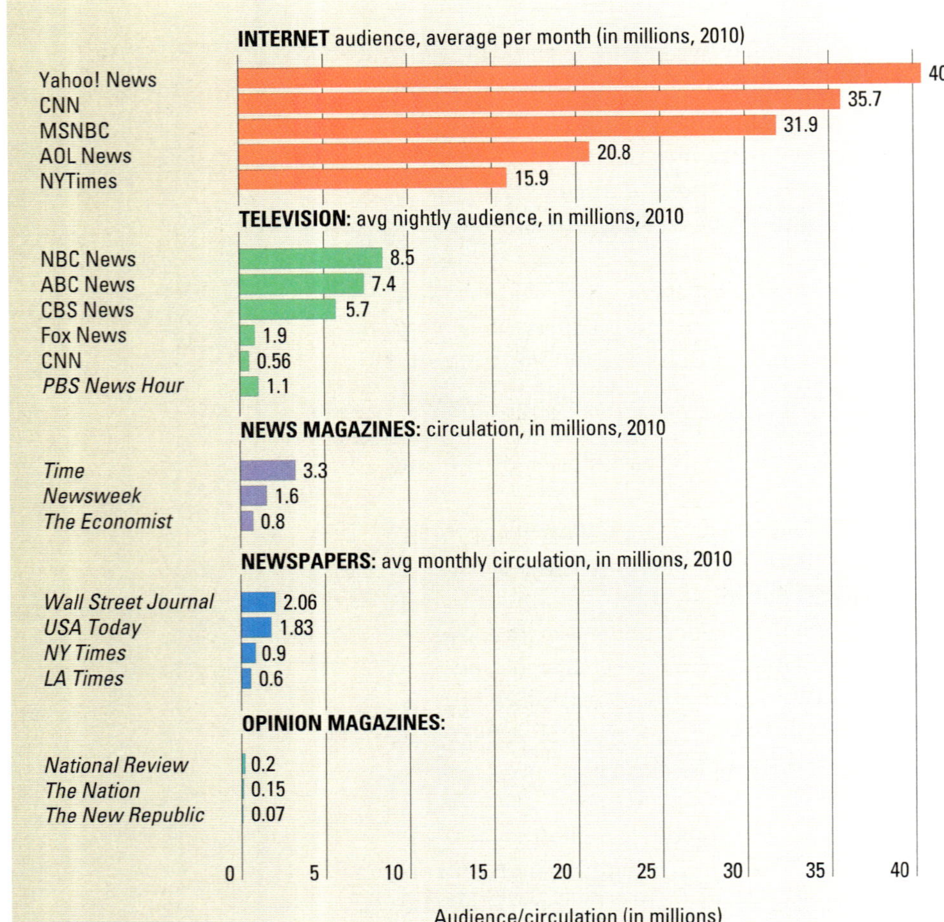

FIGURE 6.2 Audiences of Selected Media Sources

The big story in recent years is the enormous growth in the Internet news audience. The print version of the *New York Times*, for instance, has a circulation of under 1 million people. Yet nearly 16 million people visit the paper's website for news every month. Some major news magazines (published weekly) have more readers than newspapers do, but newspapers are published daily and there are more of them. Opinion magazines reach only a small fraction of the usual television news audience.

Sources: Newspaper circulation comes from Richard Perez-Pena, "More Readers Trading Newspapers for Web Sites," *New York Times*, 6 November 2007, p. C9. Data on the Internet, news and opinion magazines, and television are reported in "*The State of the News Media 2007–2009*," http://www.stateofthemedia.org.

more specialized manner than do daily newspapers and are often forums for opinions, not strictly news. The earliest public affairs magazines were founded in the mid-1800s, and two—*The Nation* and *Harper's*—are still publishing today. Such magazines were often politically influential, especially in framing arguments against slavery and later in publishing exposés of political corruption.

Even magazines with limited readerships can wield political power. Magazines may influence **attentive policy elites**—group leaders who follow news in specific areas—and thus influence mass opinion indirectly through a **two-step flow of communication**.

As scholars originally viewed the two-step flow, it conformed to the pluralist model of democracy. Once group leaders (for instance, union or industry leaders) became informed of political developments, they informed their more numerous followers, mobilizing them to apply pressure on government. Today, according to a revised interpretation of the two-step flow concept, policy elites are more likely to influence public opinion and other leaders by airing their views in the media. In this view, public deliberation on issues is mediated by these professional communicators who frame the issues in the media for popular consumption—that is, they define the way that issues will be viewed, heard, or read (see Chapter 5, page 139).[17]

Only one weekly news magazine—*Time* (founded in 1923)—enjoys big circulation numbers in the United States (3.3 million copies in 2010). Overall, news magazine circulation has declined in recent years much as newspaper circulation

attentive policy elites
Leaders who follow news in specific policy areas.

two-step flow of communication
The process in which a few policy elites gather information and then inform their more numerous followers, mobilizing them to apply pressure to government.

has. Such declines prompted *U.S. News & World Report,* a prominent weekly magazine since 1933, to become a monthly magazine in 2009. It stopped publishing as a regular magazine altogether in 2010, focusing instead on its more popular efforts, such as college rankings. Another once popular news weekly, *Newsweek* (also founded in 1933), saw a 32 percent decline in circulation from 2009 to 2010. Its parent company, the *Washington Post*, sold it for $1 in 2010 in order to be free from the magazine's debt. The new owner quickly re-sold the magazine to *The Daily Beast*, an online-only general interest magazine, where it continues to struggle in its effort to be both popular and profitable in the new media environment. Despite these troubles, the magazine continues to operate ten domestic and international bureaus.[18]

In contrast to these mainstream publications, there are also explicitly political magazines such as *The National Review* and *The Weekly Standard* that are aimed at the audience of policy elites more than the general public.

Radio

Regularly scheduled, continuous radio broadcasting began in 1920 on stations KDKA in Pittsburgh and WWJ in Detroit. Both stations claim to be the first commercial station, and both broadcast returns of the 1920 election of President Warren G. Harding. The first radio network, the National Broadcasting Company (NBC), was formed in 1926. Soon four networks were on the air, transforming radio into a national medium by linking thousands of local stations. Americans were quick to purchase and use this new technology (see Figure 6.1). Millions of Americans heard President Franklin D. Roosevelt deliver his first "fireside chat" in 1933.

Because the public could sense reporters' personalities over radio in a way they could not in print, broadcast journalists quickly became household names. Edward R. Murrow, one of the most famous radio news personalities, broadcast news of the merger of Germany and Austria by short-wave radio from Vienna in 1938 and during World War II gave stirring reports of German air raids on London.

Today there are nearly fifteen thousand licensed broadcast radio stations.[19] Despite the advent of iPods, Internet radio, and podcasts, nine out of ten Americans listen to a traditional AM/FM radio every week.[20] Radio listeners often tune into stations that have news and talk radio formats, and the audience for talk radio continues to grow. Surveys show that the audience of talk radio is more Republican, most likely because the majority of talk radio hosts, like Rush Limbaugh, are conservative.[21] Talk radio shows have been criticized for polarizing politics by publicizing extreme views.[22]

Television

Experiments with television began in France in the early 1900s. By 1940, twenty-three television stations were operating in the United States. Two stations broadcast the returns of Roosevelt's 1940 reelection.[23] By 1950, ninety-eight stations covered the major population centers of the country, although only 9 percent of households had televisions (see Figure 6.1).

The first coast-to-coast broadcast came in 1951: President Harry Truman's address to delegates at the Japanese peace treaty conference in San Francisco. That same year, Democratic senator Estes Kefauver of Tennessee called for television coverage of his committee's investigation into organized crime. For weeks, people with televisions invited their neighbors to watch underworld crime figures answering questions before the camera. And Kefauver became one of the first politicians to benefit from television coverage. Previously unknown and representing a small state, he won many of the 1952 Democratic presidential primaries and became the Democrats' vice-presidential candidate in 1956.

Many early anchors of television network news programs came to the medium already famous through their experience on radio. Now that the news audience could see the broadcasters as well as hear them, networks built their evening news around an "anchorman" chosen to inspire trust in viewers.

By 2012, the United States had more than thirteen hundred commercial and three hundred public television stations, and virtually every household (97 percent) had a television (and 84 percent of households had two or more sets).[24] Today, television claims the biggest news audience of all media outside the Internet. The three broadcast networks still have large audiences, but millions of viewers have drifted to more opinionated cable networks, especially MSNBC on the left and Fox News on the right. In fact, cable news is becoming a bit of a throwback; more and more it seems analogous to the early newspapers, which were blatantly political organizations. Research suggests that with viewers today having unprecedented choices, people who are more interested in politics increasingly desire partisan shows, while people who are less interested in politics simply avoid news programming altogether. Still, some researchers have disputed citizens' "mass migration" from traditional media, concluding instead that alternative news sources, particularly the Internet, supplement rather than displace print and broadcast sources.[25]

The Internet

What we today call the Internet began in 1969 when, with support from the U.S. Defense Department's Advanced Research Projects Agency, computers at four universities were linked to form ARPANET, which connected thirty-seven universities by 1972. New communications standards developed in 1983 allowed these networks to be linked, creating the Internet. At first, the Internet was used mainly to transmit e-mail among researchers. In 1991, European physicists devised a standardized system for encoding and transmitting a wide range of materials, including graphics and photographs, over the Internet. The World Wide Web (WWW) was born, and both personal and mass communication would never be the same. Now anyone with a computer and Internet access can read text, view images, and download data from websites worldwide. In January 1993 there were only fifty websites in existence. Today there are over 500 million sites and over 2 billion Web users worldwide.[26]

The development of wireless technology and mobile devices such as iPhones and

MPI/Stringer/Archive Photos/Getty Images

Watching the President on Television

Television revolutionized presidential politics by allowing millions of voters to look closely at the candidates' faces and judge their personalities in the process. This close-up of John Kennedy during a debate with Richard Nixon in the 1960 campaign showed Kennedy to good advantage. In contrast, close-ups of Nixon made him look as though he needed a shave. Kennedy won one of the closest elections in history; his good looks on television may have made the difference.

tablets has further extended the reach of electronic information. According to a recent report, 42 percent of American adults had smartphones in 2011 (including 52 percent of people age 18 to 29); 87 percent of them used their phone to access the Internet. Only 8 percent of Americans had tablet computers, but that was double the amount from just a year earlier. All media outlets with a presence on the Web are increasingly challenged to determine the best ways in which to make their information available on such devices.[27] (See "Compared with What? Top Ten Countries for Penetration of 3G Mobile Devices.")

It did not take long for the Internet to be incorporated into politics, and today virtually every government agency and political organization has its own website. Over 80 percent of Americans use the Internet, mostly people under the age of sixty-five and with at least a high school diploma. Internet users tend to live in large cities and suburbs. Whites are also more likely to be Internet users than blacks and Latinos (84 percent, 77 percent and 75 percent).[28] In 2011, 43 percent of Americans got most of their news online, making it second only to television.[29]

Many private citizens operate their own websites on politics and public affairs, daily posting their thoughts. An estimated 12 percent of Internet users have a so-called **blog** (for *weblog*); according to a survey of bloggers, about 35 percent of them discuss politics on their blogs.[30] Political blogs now regularly influence news reporting and politics. In 2011, P. J. Crowley, a spokesman for the State Department, gave a talk at a seminar in which he offered his personal view that he opposed the Pentagon's arrest and solitary confinement of an Army private who provided classified information to Wikileaks (an organization that posts classified government documents on the Web). Crowley called the Pentagon's actions "ridiculous and counterproductive and stupid." Two members of the audience posted Crowley's remarks on their blogs. Two days later, President Obama was asked during a traditional news conference whether he agreed with Crowley. He replied that he had asked the Pentagon to clarify whether its approach had been appropriate and that he had been assured that it was. For creating such a distraction for the President, the State Department, and the Pentagon, Crowley offered his resignation a mere three days after the comments were made. As this incident illustrates, the influence of political blogs on the course of American politics is largely indirect, influencing the types of stories that get picked up by the "mainstream media"; the actual percentage of Americans who read political blogs directly is only around 11 percent.[31]

Are bloggers journalists? Many political bloggers say they are. They have even formed the Media Bloggers Association, which seeks to establish formal recognition of journalist-bloggers as "real" journalists with the same credentials, access to sources, and protections against divulging sources that traditional journalists enjoy. In 2006, a state appeals court decided that bloggers do possess those protections, though other courts have issued contradictory rulings. Some fear that these trends will lead to a "wild west atmosphere" in which untrained private individuals can broadcast what they wish online to millions of readers without professional, organizational, or legal concerns about its source.[32] Research, however, shows the most prominent political bloggers are professional journalists from traditional news organizations and that the most popular news sites generally provide the same news in their offline and online formats.[33] In 2009, President Obama made history by calling on a reporter from the *Huffington Post,* then primarily a political blog, at his first press conference.[34] He made history again in 2011 by holding a town hall meeting on Twitter.[35]

Laugh and Learn

Many people learn about politics by watching comedians like Jon Stewart, the host of *The Daily Show.* Almost 30 percent of adults surveyed said that they learned about the 2008 political campaign from comedy shows like *The Daily Show, The Colbert Report,* or *Saturday Night Live.* Studies show that watching *The Daily Show* can improve people's ability to learn real facts about politics and current affairs.

Source: Michael A. Xenos and Amy B. Becker, "Moments of Zen: Effects of *The Daily Show* on Information Seeking and Political Learning," *Political Communication* 26 (2009): 317–332. Photo: AP Photo/ Jason DeCrow.

blog

A form of newsletter, journal, or "log" of thoughts for public reading, usually devoted to social or political issues and often updated daily. The term derives from *weblog.*

Compared with What?

Top Ten Countries for Penetration of 3G Mobile Devices

Compared with other major countries in the world, the United States lags in using mobile devices to access the Internet. By the end of 2011, only 18 percent of the world's population was estimated to have 3G mobile devices. The United States comes in sixth in terms of 3G penetration, with 64 percent of the population having mobile access to the Internet. Japan's rate of 3G adoption far exceeds that of all other countries.

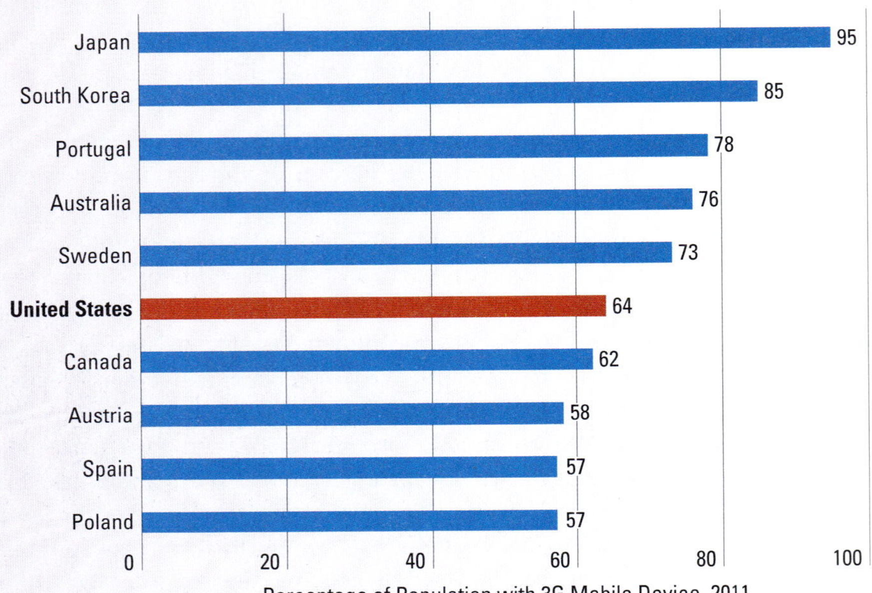

Source: KPCB Internet Trends 2012, http://www.kpcb.com/insights/2012-internet-trends.

Critical Thinking

How might the content and quality of news accessed on a mobile device differ from that of news accessed in a newspaper or on television? Do you think the democratic process will suffer or be enhanced as more and more people begin to get their news on mobile devices?

The most common sources for news online are primarily aggregators, which collect and post stories from other news sources, such as Yahoo! News or Google News, or websites associated with print or television news organizations, such as the *New York Times* or CNN. Online-only news ventures that do their own original reporting command a much smaller audience, but their presence continues to grow. Such sites include the *Huffington Post* (which recently merged with AOL), Global Post (which focuses on international news), and ProPublica (which specializes in investigative reporting).[36]

★ 6.2 Private Ownership of the Media

★ Evaluate the effect of privately owned mass media on the quality of political communication in the United States.

In the United States, people take private ownership of the media for granted. Indeed, most Americans would regard government ownership of the media as an unacceptable threat to freedom that would interfere with the marketplace of ideas and result in one-way communication: from government to citizens. When the government controls the news flow, the people may have little chance to learn what the government is doing or to pressure it to behave differently. Certainly that is true in China. The Chinese government employs thousands of Internet police to prevent "subversive content" from being disseminated to its nearly 500 million Web users. If an Internet user in China searches for "democracy movements," she is met with a screen that reads, "Page cannot be displayed." In 2010, censors blocked out information relating to the news that a jailed Chinese dissident Liu Xiaobo won the Nobel Peace Prize. Even text messages containing his name were intercepted. In 2011, when users of a Twitter-like site in China searched for information about popular uprisings in Egypt, they were met with "In accordance with the relevant laws, regulations, and policies, the search results could not be displayed."[37]

In other Western democracies, the print media are privately owned, but the broadcast media often are not. In the United States, except for about three hundred public television stations (out of about sixteen hundred total) and nine hundred public radio stations (out of over fifteen thousand), the broadcast media are privately owned.[38]

The Consequences of Private Ownership

Private ownership of the media gives the news industry in America more political freedom than any other in the world, but it also makes the media more dependent on advertising revenues to cover costs and make a profit. Because advertising rates are tied to audience size, news operations in America must appeal to the audiences they serve.

Much of the content of newspapers is advertising. After fashion reports, sports, comics, and so on, only a relatively small portion of any newspaper is devoted to news of any sort and only a fraction of that

ARTHUR TSANG/Reuters/Landov

Tank Man's Fans

This iconic image of a lone pro-democracy protestor in China's Tiananmen Square in 1989 is still unknown to many people in China since the image is officially censored. On the twentieth anniversary of the protests in 2009, however, some in China were able to see the image through a Tank Man fan site on Facebook.com. Tank Man's identity—and what happened to him after he was whisked away by two men—remain worldwide mysteries.

news—excluding stories about fires, murder trials, and the like—can be considered political. In terms of volume, the entertainment content offered by the mass media in the United States can vastly overshadow the news content. In other words, the media function more to entertain than provide news. Entertainment increases the audience, which increases advertising revenues. The profit motive creates constant pressure to increase the ratio of entertainment to news or to make the news itself more entertaining.

You might think that a story's political significance, educational value, or social importance determines whether the media cover it. The truth is that most potential news stories are not judged by such grand criteria. The primary criterion of a story's **newsworthiness** is usually its audience appeal, which is judged according to its potential impact on readers or listeners, its degree of sensationalism (exemplified by violence, conflict, disaster, or scandal), its treatment of familiar people or life situations, its close-to-home character, and its timeliness.[39] As Figure 6.3 shows, the content of news coverage often consists of topics that have little to do with elections, foreign affairs, government, or the economy.

The importance of audience appeal has led the news industry to calculate its audience carefully. The print media can easily determine the size of their circulations through sales figures, but the broadcast media must estimate their audience through various sampling techniques. A separate industry has developed to rate audience size impartially, and its ratings reports have resulted in a "ratings game," in which the media try to increase ratings by adjusting the delivery or content of their news.

newsworthiness
The degree to which a news story is important enough to be covered in the mass media.

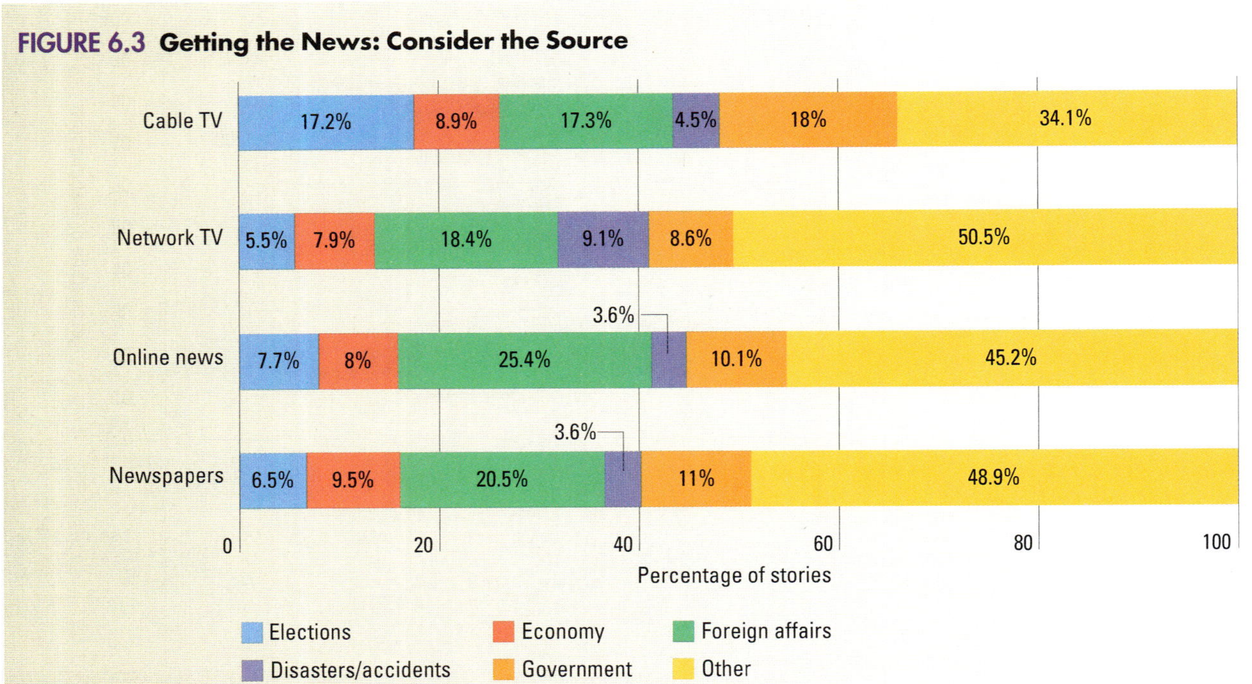

An analysis of over 50,000 news stories in 2011 (from the front pages of newspapers, major news programs, and Internet sites) shows that just a few categories dominated the news: elections, the economy, government, and foreign affairs. Cable TV was particularly devoted to election coverage, while online news sites and newspapers provided the most extensive coverage of foreign affairs. In all of these media, however, the category "other" predominates, reflecting the market-driven character of news media content.
Source: "A Year in the News Interactive, 2011," Pew Project for Excellence in Journalism, http://stateofthemedia.org/2012/year-in-the-news-3/.

Within the news industry, the process has been termed **market-driven journalism**—both reporting news and running commercials geared to a target audience.[40] For example, over 40 percent of network evening news viewers are over sixty-five years old, which is why these shows nearly always feature a health-related story and run one or more commercials related to prescription drugs.[41]

More citizens report watching local news than national news, and local news epitomizes market-driven journalism by matching audience demographics to advertising revenue while slighting news about government, policy, and public affairs.[42] Local television newscasts across the nation practice a "hook-and-hold" approach. They hook viewers at the start by airing alarming stories about crime, accidents, fires, and disasters. The middle of the broadcast has informative news about business, science, and politics that are not considered good viewing. To hold viewers to the end, stations tease them by promising soft topics on pop culture, human interest, or health. As a result, local news broadcasts across the country look much the same.[43]

At the national level, the nightly news broadcasts were once the crown jewels of independent broadcasting companies—ABC, CBS, and NBC—and valued for their public service. Now these broadcasts are cogs in huge corporate conglomerates. The Walt Disney Company, for example, owns ABC. NBC was owned by General Electric for years, but merged with the cable company Comcast in 2011, which has created a conglomerate that holds "the most significant collection of cable television assets in the world."[44] The merger has prompted concerns about whether viewer access to certain television content will be limited to Comcast customers and about whether cable bills will rise. More broadly, the merger highlights the fact that television nightly news is no longer a public service, but a profit center. Nonetheless, the financial reports from network news broadcasts are not good.

From 1980 to 2010, ABC, CBS, and NBC suffered severe losses in their prime-time programming audience, dropping from 52 million viewers to 21.6 million—despite an increase in population.[45] Increasingly, viewers turned to watching cable stations instead of network programs, or they turned away from television and toward the Internet. Audience declines brought declining profits and cutbacks in news budgets. As their parent corporations demanded that news programs "pay their way," the networks succumbed to **infotainment**—a mix of information and diversion oriented to personalities or celebrities, not linked to the day's events, and usually unrelated to public affairs or policy.[46] Over 12 million people tune in for morning shows such as NBC's *Today Show* that have long mixed news and celebrity interviews.

The Concentration of Private Ownership

Media owners can make more money by increasing their audience or by acquiring additional publications or stations. As illustrated by the NBC-Comcast merger discussed earlier, there is a decided trend toward concentrated ownership of the media, increasing the risk that a few owners could control the news flow to promote their own interests—much as political parties influenced the content of the earliest American newspapers. In fact, the number of independent newspapers has declined as newspaper chains (owners of two or more newspapers in different cities) have acquired more newspapers. The Gannett chain, which owns *USA Today,* now also owns nearly one hundred other daily newspapers throughout the United States.[47] Some observers argue that since newspapers are under relentless financial stress, they should consider rejecting the for-profit model and

market-driven journalism
Both reporting news and running commercials geared to a target audience defined by demographic characteristics.

infotainment
A mix of information and diversion oriented to personalities or celebrities, not linked to the day's events, and usually unrelated to public affairs or policy; often called "soft news."

instead operate as nonprofits. As nonprofits, newspapers would be financed through endowments, charitable donations, dues-paying members, and even the government, similar to how PBS and NPR operate on television and radio today. To date, a number of nonprofit news organizations have emerged; some focus on local issues, others on national issues, and others track policy-specific issues, such as health care. But no major newspaper has switched to the nonprofit model yet.[48]

At first glance, concentration of ownership does not seem to be a problem in the television industry. Although there are only three major networks, the networks usually do not own their affiliates. Most communities in the United States have a choice of multiple stations, which suggests that the electronic media offer diverse viewpoints. As with newspapers, however, chains sometimes own television stations in different cities, and ownership sometimes extends across different media. Rupert Murdoch's News Corporation is one of the world's largest media companies. Even after creating a separate company for its newpapers in 2012, the company still owns the Fox network, twenty-seven local Fox stations, several film companies and cable channels, and more.[49]

# 6.3 Government Regulation of the Media

★ Follow the evolution of government regulation of the media and identify the challenges that new media technologies present to existing regulations.

Although most of the mass media in the United States are privately owned, they do not operate free of government regulation. Broadcast media operate under more stringent regulations than print media, initially because of technical aspects of broadcasting. Lately, debates about government regulation of the Internet have become common. In general, government regulation of the mass media addresses three aspects of their operation: technical considerations, ownership, and content.

Technical and Ownership Regulations

In the early days of radio, stations that operated on similar frequencies in the same area often jammed each other's signals, and no one could broadcast clearly. At the broadcasters' insistence, Congress passed the Federal Radio Act (1927), which declared that the public owned the airwaves and private broadcasters could use them only by obtaining a license from the Federal Radio Commission. Thus, government regulation of broadcasting was not forced on the industry by socialist politicians; capitalist owners sought it to impose order on the use of the airwaves (thereby restricting others' freedom to enter broadcasting).

Seven years later, Congress passed the Federal Communications Act of 1934, a more sweeping law that created the **Federal Communications Commission (FCC)**, which has five members (no more than three from the same political party) nominated by the president for terms of five years. The commissioners can be removed from office only through impeachment and conviction. The FCC is thus an independent regulatory commission insulated from political control by either the president or Congress. (We discuss independent regulatory commissions in Chapter 13.) By law, its vague mandate is to "serve the public interest,

Federal Communications Commission (FCC)
An independent federal agency that regulates interstate and international communication by radio, television, telephone, telegraph, cable, and satellite.

convenience, and necessity." The FCC sets social, economic, and technical goals for the communications industry and deals with philosophical issues of regulation versus deregulation.[50] Today, the FCC's charge includes regulating interstate and international communications by radio, television, telephone, telegraph, cable, and satellite.

For six decades, the communications industry was regulated under the basic framework of the 1934 law that created the FCC. Pressured by businesses that wanted to exploit new electronic technologies, such as computers and satellite transmissions, Congress overhauled existing regulations in the Telecommunications Act of 1996.

The new law relaxed limitations on media ownership. For example, broadcasters were previously limited to owning only twelve television stations and forty radio stations. The 1996 law eliminated limits on the number of television stations one company may own, just as long as their coverage didn't extend beyond 35 percent of the market nationwide. As a result, CBS, Fox, and NBC doubled or tripled the number of stations that they owned.[51] The 1996 law also set no national limits for radio ownership and relaxed local limits. In its wake, Clear Channel Communications corporation, which owned thirty-six stations, gobbled up over eleven hundred, including all six stations serving Minot, North Dakota.[52] In addition, the FCC allowed local and long-distance telephone companies to compete with one another and to sell television services.[53]

Recently, the FCC has begun to regulate the Internet. Since Congress has not passed any laws that outline the role of the FCC with respect to the Internet, the FCC does not have jurisdiction to regulate content, although Internet service providers (ISPs) are subject to standing antimonopoly laws.[54] Nonetheless, the FCC has become involved in the regulation of emerging technologies, as issues of ownership, access, and cross-platform content have arisen. For instance, should regulations that apply to broadcast news also apply to the news program's website? What about when information from that website is transmitted through wireless communications to a mobile device instead of to a desktop computer via broadband? As one scholar recently put it, "The new communications technologies require a far more complete rethinking of the scope and purpose of federal regulation than has happened thus far."[55] In the absence of Congressional action clarifying the role of the FCC with respect to the Internet, policies and rules will evolve and be challenged bit by bit.

One such example is the current debate about "net neutrality," which refers to whether ISPs should be allowed to charge people more if they consume a large amount of bandwidth and whether ISPs can limit content options available to consumers. People who support net neutrality argue that data-intensive Internet activity should not be available only to those with greater ability to pay and that providers should not be allowed to determine which sites consumers can access. In 2010, the FCC adopted rules that would prevent ISPs from blocking or restricting consumer access to any legal Internet site. In 2011, House Republicans voted to block the FCC rules. They claim that the FCC overstepped its authority since Congress has not authorized it to regulate the Internet and that providers should be allowed to charge more to people who use their services more. The Senate, however, voted to allow the regulations. Verizon Communications, Inc., and other opponents of the FCC's action have filed suit in federal court.[56]

Such debates involve clashes between the freedom of ISPs to develop their own business plans (and their desire for order in the face of Internet congestion) and equality of access to information among the public. With the Internet being an essential medium for the transmission of news, it is arguably in the public interest to ensure that citizens are able to find information about politics in the most efficient and equitable way possible. Whether that requires more—or less—government regulation is still a matter of debate.

Regulation of Content

The First Amendment to the Constitution prohibits Congress from abridging the freedom of the press. Over time, *the press* has come to mean all media, and the courts have decided many cases that define how far freedom of the press extends under the law. Chapter 15 discusses the most important of these cases, which are often quite complex. Although the courts have had difficulty defining obscenity, they have not permitted obscene expression under freedom of the press. In 1996, however, a federal court overturned an attempt to limit transmission of "indecent" (not obscene) material on the Internet, calling the attempt "profoundly repugnant to First Amendment principles."[57]

Usually the courts strike down government attempts to restrain the press from disseminating the information, reports, or opinions it finds newsworthy. One notable exception concerns strategic information during wartime: the courts have supported censorship of information such as the sailing schedules of troop ships or the planned movements of troops in battle. Otherwise, they have recognized a strong constitutional case against press censorship. This stand has given the United States some of the freest, most vigorous news media in the world.

Because the broadcast media are licensed to use the public airwaves, they have been subject to some additional regulation, beyond what is applied to other media, of the content of their news coverage. The basis for the FCC's regulation of content lies in its charge to ensure that radio (and, later, television) stations would "serve the public interest, convenience, and necessity." For years, the FCC operated under three rules to promote the public interest concerning political matters. The *fairness doctrine* obligated broadcasters to provide fair coverage of all views on public issues. The *equal opportunities rule* (also known as the equal time rule) required any broadcast station that gave or sold time to a candidate for a public office to make an equal amount of time available under the same conditions to all other candidates for that office. The *reasonable access rule* required that stations make their facilities available for the expression of conflicting views on issues by all responsible elements in the community.

In 1987, the FCC repealed the *fairness doctrine*. Prior to its repeal, the news media tended to avoid controversial and partisan issues for fear of being in violation. Once broadcasters were no longer required to cover all views, they could express ideological viewpoints.[58] The National Association of Broadcasters says that the elimination of the fairness doctrine has played a large role in the proliferation of news and opinion alternatives now available to media consumers.[59] Indeed, some observers suggest that there might be too much diversity among news sources today and that the variation in content and quality is contributing to a population that is less informed and more polarized.[60]

Note that these content regulations were never imposed on the print media. And as noted earlier, news on the Internet has thus far been free from content regulations as well. In fact, one aspect of a free press is its ability to champion causes that it favors without having to argue the case for the other side. The broadcast media have traditionally been treated differently because they were licensed by the FCC to operate as semimonopolies. With the rise of one-newspaper cities and towns, however, competition among television stations is greater than among newspapers in virtually every market area. Advocates of dropping all FCC content regulations argue that the broadcast media should be just as free as other media to decide which candidates they endorse and which issues they support.

6.4 Functions of the Mass Media for the Political System

★ Analyze the role of the media in political socialization and the acquisition of political knowledge.

Most journalists consider "news" (at least *hard* news) to be an important event that happened within the past twenty-four hours. A presidential news conference or a suicide bombing qualifies as news. Who decides what is important? The media, of course. In this section, we discuss how the media cover political affairs, what they choose to report (what becomes "news"), who follows the news, and what they remember and learn from it. We are interested in four specific functions the mass media serve for the political system: *reporting* the news, *interpreting* the news, *setting the agenda* for government action, and *socializing* citizens about politics. Each one has important implications for the connections citizens forge with the political process.[61]

Reporting the News

All major news media seek to cover political events with firsthand reports from journalists on the scene. Because so many significant political events occur in the nation's capital, Washington has an immense press presence, with over 5,000 journalists in the congressional press corps alone.[62] Roughly fifty additional reporters are admitted to the White House press briefing room.[63] Since 1902, when President Theodore Roosevelt first provided space in the White House for reporters, the press has had special access to the president (though as Figure 6.4 shows, the number of presidential news conferences with reporters has declined in recent administrations). The media's relationship with the president is mediated primarily through the Office of the Press Secretary.

FIGURE 6.4 More News = Less Talk?

As press conferences have become more formal and scripted, they have also become less frequent. When journalists and the president had more of a collegial relationship, press conferences were common. Except for Bill Clinton, modern presidents are clustered at the bottom of this graph, which shows the number of presidential press conferences in the first year in office since 1922.

Sources: "The Frequency of the Message Is Medium," *CQ Weekly Online* 27 (July 2009): 1755. Copyright © 2009 by CQ-ROLL CALL GROUP. Reproduced with permission of CQ-ROLL CALL GROUP via Copyright Clearance Center.

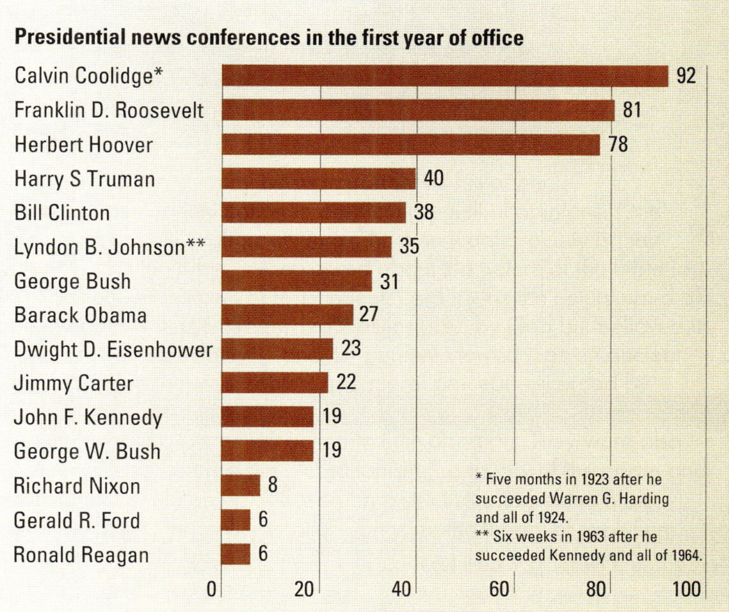

To meet daily deadlines, White House correspondents rely heavily on information they receive from the president's staff, each piece carefully crafted in an attempt to control the story. The most frequent form is the news release—a prepared text distributed to reporters in the hope that they will use it verbatim. A daily news briefing enables reporters to question the press secretary about news releases and allows television correspondents time to prepare their stories and film for the evening newscast. A news conference involves questioning high-level officials in the executive branch—including the president, on occasion. News conferences can appear to be freewheeling, but officials often carefully rehearse precise answers to anticipated questions.[64]

Occasionally, information is given "on background," meaning the information can be quoted, but reporters cannot identify the source. A vague reference—"a senior official says"—is all right. Information disclosed "off the record" cannot even be printed. Journalists who violate these well-known rules risk losing their welcome. In a sense, the press corps is captive to the White House, which feeds reporters the information they need to meet their deadlines and frames how it wants events covered on the evening news.

Most news about Congress comes from innumerable press releases issued by its 535 members and from an unending supply of congressional reports. Coverage of policy debates typically mirrors the intensity with which congressional actors seek to promote them.[65] A journalist can therefore report on Congress without inhabiting its press galleries. In an effort to save money in the face of tough times, many newspapers have cut the size of their Washington staff or eliminated it entirely. According to one report, "more than half the states do not have a single newspaper reporter dedicated to covering federal government."[66]

Congress banned microphones and cameras from its chambers until 1979, when the House permitted live coverage. Televised broadcasts of the House were surprisingly successful, thanks to C-SPAN (the Cable-Satellite Public Affairs Network), which feeds to most cable systems across the country and has a cultlike following among hundreds of thousands of regular viewers.[67] To share in the exposure, the Senate began television coverage in 1986. Occasionally, an event captured on C-SPAN becomes a major news story. In 2009, for example, Representative Alan Grayson (D-Fla.) argued on the floor of the House that the Republican health-care plan had two options: stay healthy or die quickly. The C-SPAN coverage was picked up on YouTube, which then led to days of commentary by pundits. It also led to a fundraising boon: in the two weeks following the broadcast, Grayson's reelection campaign raised over $150,000 from one website alone.[68] But the national attention helped his opponent too, and Grayson lost his 2010 reelection bid. This phenomenon of having a fiery quote picked up by the media, which then generates a spike in fundraising for the speaker (and often for his or her opponent was well), has been termed a "money blurt."[69]

In addition to these recognized sources of news, reporters occasionally benefit from leaks of information released by officials who are guaranteed anonymity. Officials may leak news to interfere with others' political plans or to float ideas ("trial balloons") past the public and other political leaders to gauge their reactions. At times, one carefully placed leak can turn into a gusher of media coverage through "pack journalism"—the tendency of journalists to adopt similar viewpoints toward the news simply because they hang around together, exchanging information and defining the day's news with one another.

Interpreting and Presenting the News

Media executives, news editors, and prominent reporters function as **gatekeepers** in directing the news flow: they decide which events to report and how to handle the elements in those stories.[70] They not only select what topics go through the gate but also are expected to uphold standards of careful reporting and principled journalism. The rise of the Internet has made more information and points of view available to the public, but the Internet also can spread factual errors and rumors. The Internet has no gatekeepers, and thus no constraints on its content.[71] Most journalists think the Internet has made journalism better, mostly because it is a powerful research tool and its ability to deliver information quickly promotes competition.[72]

A parade of unconnected one-minute news stories, flashing across the television screen every night, would boggle the eyes and minds of viewers. To make televised news understandable and to hold viewers' attention, editors and producers concentrate on individuals because individuals have personalities (political institutions do not—except for the presidency). A study of network news coverage of the president, Congress, and the Supreme Court in 2008–2009 found that 66 percent of the stories were about the presidency, compared with 28 percent on Congress and just 6 percent on the Supreme Court.[73]

During elections, the focus on personalities encourages **horse race journalism**, in which media coverage becomes primarily a matter of which candidate is leading in the polls and who has raised the most money. Over three-quarters of Americans say that they want more coverage of candidates' positions on the issues; almost half would also like less coverage of who is leading in the polls.[74] Yet study after study of news coverage of presidential elections find that horse race coverage dominates and that horse race content increases as election day approaches. Journalists cover the horse race because it offers new material daily, whereas the candidates' programs remain the same.[75]

Political campaigns lend themselves particularly well to media coverage, especially if the candidates create a **media event**—a situation that is too "newsworthy" to pass up. One tried-and-true method is to conduct a statewide walking campaign. Newspapers and television can take pictures of the candidate on the highway and conduct interviews with local folks who just spoke with the political hiker. (See Chapter 9 for further discussion of the media in political campaigns.) Television is particularly partial to events that have visual impact. Organized protests and fires, for example, "show well" on television, so television covers them. As Figure 6.3 shows, network news was much more likely to include stories of disasters and accidents in 2011 than other media.

Where the Public Gets Its News. Until the early 1960s, most people reported getting more of their news from newspapers than from any other source. Television nudged out newspapers as the public's major source of news in the early 1960s and has since remained dominant. According to one recent report, 66 percent of Americans name network or cable television as their primary source for news.[76] Thirty-one percent cite newspapers as their primary news source, while 43 percent say they turn to the Internet most. People in this survey were allowed to mention two sources, making it clear that the public consults multiple sources of news during the day—perhaps reading the paper at breakfast, checking the Internet at work, and ending the day watching television news. People under 30 get most of their news on the Internet and are the only age group to do so. Women are more likely than men to get their news from television, while men are more likely than women to get their news from radio and online sources. Blacks are more likely than whites and Latinos to rely on television, and whites are more likely than other ethnic groups to get news on the radio.[77]

Media Influence on Knowledge and Opinions. If, as surveys indicate, about 80 percent of the public read or hear the news each day, how much political information

horse race journalism
Election coverage by the mass media that focuses on which candidate is ahead rather than on national issues.

media event
A situation that is so "newsworthy" that the mass media are compelled to cover it. Candidates in elections often create such situations to garner media attention.

do they absorb? By all accounts, not much. A national survey in the fall of 2011 asked respondents nineteen questions about current events, including the name of the Speaker of the House (John Boehner) and the current unemployment rate (around 9 percent). On average, respondents got eleven questions out of nineteen correct.[78] When pollsters asked Americans to name the heads of state for Cuba, Great Britain, Russia, Mexico, and Germany, as well as the U.S. secretary of state, only 2 percent of respondents could name all six leaders; 18 percent of Americans could not name any.[79]

television hypothesis
The belief that television is to blame for the low level of citizens' knowledge about public affairs.

Numerous studies have found that those who rely on television for their news score lower on tests of knowledge about public affairs than those who rely on print media. Among media researchers, this finding has led to the **television hypothesis**— the belief that television is to blame for the low level of citizens' knowledge about public affairs.[80] This belief has a reasonable basis. We know that television tends to squeeze issues into short fragments, which makes it difficult to explain candidates' positions. Television also tends to cast abstract issues in personal terms to generate the visual content that the medium needs. Thus, viewers may become more adept at visually identifying the candidates and describing their personal habits than at outlining their positions on complex issues. Finally, because they are regulated by the FCC, television networks may be more concerned than newspapers about being fair and equal in covering the candidates. Recent research, however, suggests that newspapers differ from television less in content of coverage than in the amount; newspapers simply cover campaigns more extensively and intensively than television.[81] Whatever the explanation, the technological wonders of television may have contributed little to citizens' knowledge of public affairs. It may even discourage respect for different opinions since it tends to emphasize drama and conflict between political opponents.[82] It can also lead people to be less trusting of government.[83]

Additional ways in which the media cover the news can either exacerbate or diminish socioeconomic differences in levels of political knowledge. When the news is presented with lots of expert commentary—which tends to involve jargon and complex explanations—those who are more affluent and educated learn more from news coverage than those Americans who are less well off. But when the news is presented in a more contextual fashion—which tends to focus on the historical and factual background of an issue—socioeconomic differences in political knowledge diminish. Contextual information "gives meaning to what otherwise might seem like disconnected events and helps people understand why issues and problems deserve their attention."[84] Contextual information reduces knowledge gaps among users of both print and television news. In our age of the 24/7 news cycle, however, there is a tendency to provide contextual information when an event is new but to rely on expert commentary in subsequent coverage. As a result, people who do not pay attention to an issue right from the start might lose a valuable chance to learn about it, since journalists quickly move on to covering experts' views on the latest developments.

soft news
General entertainment programming that often includes discussions of political affairs.

News is also often communicated to the public via entertainment instead of journalism. So-called **soft news** refers to general entertainment programming that often includes discussions of political affairs. Programs such as *The Daily Show*, *The Late Show with David Letterman*, *The Today Show*, and *The View* all provide citizens with soft news. Research on the impact of soft news on the citizenry is mixed. Attention to soft news outlets has been shown to improve people's levels of political knowledge and even help them identify which politicians best match their own political preferences. But it can also lead people to be more cynical about politicians and the political process. In addition, it seems that candidate appearances on these shows tend to be beneficial to attitudes and engagement while commentary *about* politicians (which often involves sarcasm and satire) is more likely to be detrimental.[85]

Americans overwhelmingly believe that the media exert a strong influence on their political institutions, and nearly nine out of ten Americans believe that the media strongly influence public opinion.[86] However, measuring the extent of media influence on public opinion is difficult.[87] Because few of us learn about political events except through the media, it could be argued that the media create public opinion simply by reporting events. Consider the killing of Osama bin Laden and the subsequent seven-point rise in President Obama's approval rating.[88] Determining how much of that change was due to the actual event and how much was due to the way in which it was covered by the media is extremely difficult.

Setting the Political Agenda

Despite the media's potential for influencing public opinion, most scholars believe that the media's greatest influence on politics is found in their power to set the **political agenda**—a list of issues that people identify as needing government attention. Those who set the political agenda define which issues government decision makers should discuss and debate. Like a tree that falls in the forest without anyone around to hear it, an issue that does not get on the political agenda will not get any political attention. Sometimes the media force the government to confront issues once buried in the scientific community, such as global warming. Other times the media move the government to deal with unpleasant social issues, such as wrongful execution of the death penalty. However, the media can also keep high on the agenda issues that perhaps should attract fewer public resources.[89]

Crime is a good example. Local television news covers crime twice as much as any other topic.[90] Given that fear of crime today is about the same as it was in the mid-1960s, are the media simply reflecting a constantly high crime rate? Actually, crime rates have fallen in every major category (rape, burglary, robbery, assault, murder) since the 1980s.[91] As one journalist said, "Crime coverage is not editorially driven; it's economically driven. It's the easiest, cheapest, laziest news to cover."[92] Moreover, crime provides good visuals. ("If it bleeds, it leads.") So despite the falling crime rate, the public encounters a continuing gusher of crime news and believes that crime has increased over time.

However, the public's enduring concern with nonsensational issues, such as energy and the environment, can actually influence the amount of media coverage those types of issues receive. In other words, while the media often shape which issues the public thinks are important, sometimes the issues that the public thinks are important shape media coverage.[93]

The media's ability to influence public opinion by defining "the news" makes politicians eager to influence media coverage. Politicians attempt to affect not only public opinion but also the opinions of other political leaders. The president receives a daily digest of news and opinion from many sources, and top government leaders closely monitor the major national news sources. The mass media have become a network for communicating among attentive elites, all trying to influence one another. If the White House is under pressure on some policy matter, for example, it might supply a cabinet member or other high official to appear on one of the Sunday morning talk shows, such as *Face the Nation* (CBS). These programs draw less than half the audience of the network news shows, but all engage the guest in lengthy discussions. The White House's goal is to influence the thinking of other insiders, who faithfully watch the program, as much as to influence the opinions of the relatively small number of ordinary citizens who watch as well.[94] Of course, other political leaders appear on these programs, and criticism of

political agenda
A list of issues that need government attention.

Obama Messes with Texas

With comprehensive immigration reform stalled in Washington, President Obama went public in May 2011 by giving a speech in El Paso, Texas, on his administration's immigration record. Latinos make up an increasing share of the electorate, so reaching out to them on this issue was a strategy the administration hoped would put pressure on Republicans to start making progress on immigration reform.

JEWEL SAMAD/AFP/Getty Images

going public
A strategy whereby a president seeks to influence policy elites and media coverage by appealing directly to the American people.

the administration's policies, especially if from members of the president's own party, emboldens others to be critical too.

Presidents use other indirect means to try to influence political elites. In the strategy known as **going public**, the president travels around the country speaking to Americans directly about his policy agenda (see Chapter 12 for more on going public). The goal is twofold: first, to generate media coverage of the speaking event; and, second, to motivate citizens to pressure their representatives to support the president's agenda. The strategy of going public has become more common over time. Barack Obama attempted this strategy in July 2011, when he gave a televised address to the nation regarding the inability of members of Congress to reach a deal on lowering the deficit and raising amount of debt that the country is allowed to assume. He blatantly acknowledged his strategy, saying, "I'm asking you all to make your voice heard. If you want a balanced approach to reducing the deficit, let your member of Congress know. If you believe we can solve this problem through compromise, send that message." Americans immediately bombarded their representatives with phone calls and e-mails, resulting in many crashed websites.[95]

Socializing the Citizenry

The mass media act as important agents of political socialization, at least as influential as those described in Chapter 5.[96] Young people who rarely follow the news by choice nevertheless acquire political values through the entertainment function of the media. From the 1930s to the early 1950s, children learned from dramas and comedies on the radio; now they learn from television and other electronic media. The average eight to eighteen year old in America consumes over seven hours of media per day—and sees a lot of sex and hears countless swear words in prime time.[97] What children learned from radio was quite different from what they are learning now, however. In the golden days of radio, youngsters listening to the popular radio drama *The Shadow* heard repeatedly that "crime does not pay … the *Shadow* knows!" In program after program—*Dragnet, Junior G-Men, Gangbusters*—the message never varied: criminals are bad; the police are good; criminals get caught and are severely punished for their crimes.

Television today does not portray the criminal justice system in the same way, even in police dramas. Consider programs such as *Blue Blood*s, *Justified*, and *Dexter*, which are among the recent crop of shows that portray law enforcement officers and government agents as lawbreakers. Certainly, one cannot easily argue that years of television messages conveying distrust of law enforcement, disrespect for the criminal justice system, and violence help prepare law-abiding citizens.

Some scholars argue that the most important effect of the mass media, particularly television, is to reinforce the hegemony, or dominance, of the existing culture and order. According to this argument, social control functions not through institutions of force (police, military, and prisons) but through social institutions, such as the media, that cause people to accept "the way things are."[98] By displaying the lifestyles of the rich and famous, for example, the media induce the public to accept the unlimited accumulation of private wealth. Similarly, the media socialize citizens to value "the American way," to be patriotic, to back their country, "right or wrong."

So the media play contradictory roles in the process of political socialization. On the one hand, they promote popular support for government by joining in the celebration of national holidays, heroes' birthdays, political anniversaries, and civic accomplishments. On the other hand, the media erode public confidence by detailing politicians' extramarital affairs, airing investigative reports of possible malfeasance in office, and even showing television dramas about crooked cops.[99] Some critics contend that the media also give too much coverage to government opponents, especially to those who engage in unconventional opposition (see Chapter 7). However, strikes and violent confrontations draw large audiences and thus are "newsworthy" by the mass media standards.[100] In the aftermath of September 11, nearly half the respondents to a national survey thought that news organizations were "weakening the nation's defenses" by criticizing the military while the country was involved in a global war on terror.[101]

★ 6.5 Evaluating the Media in Government

★ Assess the impact of the media on democratic values and politics in the United States.

Are the media fair or biased in reporting the news? What contributions do the media make to democratic government? What effects do they have on the pursuit of freedom, order, and equality?

Is Reporting Biased?

News reports are presented as objective reality, yet critics of modern journalism contend that the news is filtered through the ideological biases of the media owners and editors (the gatekeepers) and the reporters themselves. Even citizens tend to be skeptical of the news and have become even more so over time (see Figure 6.5). Research suggests that as the parties have become more polarized (see Chapter 11) and as the presence of opinionated journalism has proliferated, political leaders increasingly go to ideologically friendly media outlets in order to criticize the rest of the media as an institution (former vice presidential candidate Sarah Palin took to calling the mainstream media the "lame stream" media). This elite criticism of the media in turn leads to greater skepticism of the press among the public. Their skepticism is consequential because people who distrust the media have been shown to be more resistant to learning new information about objective national events, such as changing economic conditions.[102]

The argument that news reports are politically biased has two sides. On the one hand, news reporters are often criticized for tilting their stories in a liberal direction, promoting social equality and undercutting social order.[103] On the other hand, wealthy and conservative media owners are suspected of preserving inequalities and

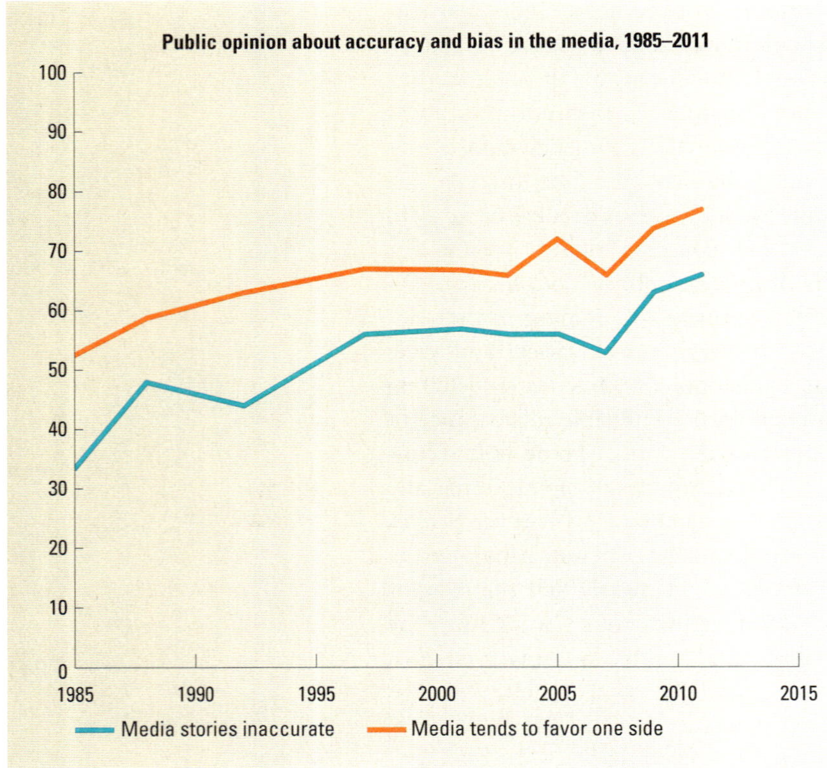

FIGURE 6.5 Rising Distrust in Accuracy and Objectivity of the Press

Over time, people have been asked whether news organizations generally get the facts straight or whether their stories and reports are often inaccurate. They have also been asked if they think that news organizations deal fairly with all sides or whether they tend to favor one side. The graph here shows that the public increasingly sees the news media as inaccurate and biased, especially in the past few years.

Source: "Press Widely Criticized but Trusted More than Other Information Sources: Views of the News Media: 1985–2011," Report by Pew Research Center for People and the Press, September 22, 2011. Copyright © 2011 by Pew Research Center. Reproduced by permission.

reinforcing the existing order by serving a relentless round of entertainment that numbs the public's capacity for critical analysis.[104] Let's evaluate these arguments, looking first at reporters.

Although the picture is far from clear, available evidence seems to confirm the charge of liberal leanings among reporters in the major news media. In a 2007 survey of journalists, 32 percent of the national press considered themselves "liberal," compared with only 8 percent who said they were "conservative."[105] Content analysis of the tone of ABC, CBS, and NBC network coverage of presidential campaigns from 1988 to 2004 concluded that Democratic candidates received more "good press" than Republicans in every election but 1988, when the Republican candidate, George H. W. Bush, benefited from better press.[106] However, one news medium—talk radio—is dominated by conservative views. Rush Limbaugh alone broadcasts to more than 15 million listeners. Other prominent conservative radio hosts—such as Sean Hannity—reach millions more.[107] The top independent and liberal talk show hosts, in contrast, have audiences of fewer than 3 million listeners.

The counterargument is that working journalists in the national and local media often conflict with their own editors, who tend to be more conservative.[108] Editors, in their function as gatekeepers, tend to tone down reporters' liberal leanings by editing their stories or not placing them well in the medium. Newspaper publishers are also free to endorse candidates. In sixteen of eighteen elections from 1932 to 2000, newspaper editorials favored the Republican candidate. In 2004, however, more editorials backed challenger John Kerry (208) than Bush (189). In 2008, the number of endorsements for Barack Obama far surpassed the number for John McCain: 287 versus 159. That year, the *Chicago Tribune* endorsed a Democrat for the first time in its 162-year history.[109]

Without question, incumbents—as opposed to challengers—enjoy much more news coverage simply from holding office and issuing official statements. Noncampaign news coverage leads to greater incumbent name recognition at election time, particularly for members of Congress (see Chapter 11). This coverage effect is independent of any bias in reporting on campaigns. For more prominent offices such as the presidency, however, a different news dynamic may come into play. When a powerful incumbent runs for reelection, journalists may feel a special responsibility to counteract his or her advantage by putting the opposite partisan spin on the news.[110] Thus, whether the media coverage of campaigns is seen as pro-Democratic (and therefore liberal) or pro-Republican (and therefore conservative) can depend on which party is in office at the time. A report of network news stories broadcast during the general election in 2008, when there was no incumbent, found that Obama received overwhelmingly positive coverage: 68 percent of stories about Obama were deemed positive. In stark contrast, only 33 percent of stories about McCain were considered positive.[111] Of course, bias in reporting is not limited to election campaigns, and different media may reflect different understandings of political issues. An important series of surveys about perceptions of the Iraq war were taken over the summer of 2003, after Bush had announced the end of combat. Substantial portions of the public held erroneous understandings of the war. For example, 27 percent in the September survey thought that world opinion supported the U.S. war against Iraq (when world opinion opposed the war), 21 percent thought that Iraq had been directly involved in the 9/11 attack (which our government never claimed and President Bush denied at a news conference),[112] and 24 percent thought that the United States had already found Iraqi weapons of mass destruction (when it had not). The researchers then analyzed which respondents held all three misperceptions by their primary source of news. Respondents who relied on the commercial television networks (Fox, CBS, ABC, CNN, or NBC) held the most misperceptions, with 45 percent of Fox viewers making all three mistakes compared with only about 15 percent for the other networks. Just 9 percent of those who relied on print media erred on all three facts. Broadcast media per se were not to blame, for a scant 4 percent of PBS viewers or listeners to National Public Radio were wrong on all items.[113]

Even the nation's outstanding newspapers can display biases. Scholars analyzed the content of coverage of the Palestinian–Israeli conflict in 2000 and 2001 printed in the *New York Times, Washington Post,* and *Chicago Tribune.* The *Post* and the *Tribune* were more similar to each other than to the *Times,* which was "the most slanted in a pro-Israeli direction, in accordance with long-standing criticisms of a pro-Israeli bias leveled against the American media by observers around the world."[114]

The mere act of choosing to cover some stories while not covering others can also be seen as bias, and in that sense, some degree of bias is inevitable. Those with an optimistic perspective on today's fractured and voluminous media environment maintain that now more than ever, it is possible to find some type of coverage on nearly any topic from nearly any political viewpoint. Such availability puts more pressure on citizens to act as their own editors and learn how to judge whether the information they find is complete and backed up with sufficient evidence.[115] That, however, is a tall order.

Contributions to Democracy

As noted earlier, in a democracy, communication must move in two directions: from government to citizens and from citizens to government. In fact, political communication in the United States mostly goes from government to citizens by passing through the media. The point is important because news reporters tend to be highly critical of politicians; they consider it their job to search for inaccuracies in fact and weaknesses in argument—practicing **watchdog journalism**.[116] Some observers have characterized the news media and the government as adversaries—each mistrusting

watchdog journalism
Journalism that scrutinizes public and business institutions and publicizes perceived misconduct.

the other, locked in competition for popular favor while trying to get the record straight. To the extent that this is true, the media serve both the majoritarian and the pluralist models of democracy well by improving the quality of information transmitted to the people about their government.[117]

The mass media transmit information in the opposite direction by reporting citizens' reactions to political events and government actions. The press has traditionally reflected public opinion (and often created it) in the process of defining the news and suggesting courses of government action. But the media's role in reflecting public opinion has become more refined in the information age. Since the 1820s, newspapers conducted straw polls of dubious quality that matched their own partisan inclinations.[118] After commercial polls (such as the Gallup polls) were established in the

Politics of Global Change

The Global Rise of Citizen Journalists

Traditionally, if authoritarian regimes wanted to prohibit information from reaching its citizens, all it had to do was control the press. Today, social networking makes it increasingly challenging for governments to do that. In 2011, for instance, citizens of Tunisia overthrew their longtime ruler, President Ben Ali. Information about events as they were unfolding spread throughout the country via social networks, like Facebook.

Jim Rankin/GetStock.com

Source: http://photogallery.thestar.com/941454; Jim Rankin/Toronto Star

Critical Thinking

When information about an event that someone witnesses is disseminated over a social network, should we consider that news? Is the person posting the information a journalist?

1930s, newspapers began to report more reliable readings of public opinion. By the 1960s, the media began to conduct their own surveys. The *New York Times,* for example, has conducted its own polls at a rate of roughly one poll per month since 2003.[119] Regularly reporting about public opinion is one of the most obvious ways in which the media can tell a story to their consumers—elites and ordinary Americans alike—about what the public believes at any point in time.

Citizens and journalists both complain that heavy reliance on polls during election campaigns causes the media to emphasize the horse race and slights the discussion of issues. But the media also use their polling expertise for other purposes, such as gauging support for going to war and for balancing the budget. Their net effect has been to generate more accurate knowledge of public opinion and to report that knowledge to public officials as well as to the public. Decades of public opinion research confirm that public opinion often influences policy, a clear indication of government functioning according to the majoritarian model of democracy.[120]

Effects on Freedom, Order, and Equality

The media in the United States have played an important role in advancing equality. Throughout the civil rights movement of the 1950s and 1960s, the media gave national coverage to conflict in the South as black children tried to attend white schools or civil rights workers were beaten and even killed in the effort to register black voters. Partly because of this media coverage, civil rights moved up on the political agenda, and coalitions formed in Congress to pass new laws promoting racial equality.

In general, the mass media offer spokespersons for any disadvantaged group an opportunity to state their case before a national audience and to work for a place on the political agenda. In 2011, Pulitzer Prize–winning journalist Jose Antonio Vargas wrote a moving story for the *New York Times Magazine* in which he "came out" as an undocumented immigrant who had been brought to the United States by his mother when he was child. He had previously worked for the *Washington Post* and many other news outlets, getting by for years with false documentation. Coming forward threatened his ability to continue working in the United States and raised the possibility of deportation, but it also put a dramatic national spotlight on debates about the DREAM Act, which would allow people who came to the country illegally as children to naturalize (see Chapter 18 for more on the DREAM Act).[121]

Although the media are willing to encourage government action to promote equality at the cost of some personal freedom, journalists resist government attempts to infringe on freedom of the press to promote order.[122] While the public tends to support a free press in theory, public support is not universal and wavers in practice. For example, when asked whether it is more important "that the government be able to censor news stories it feels threaten national security OR that the news media be able to report stories they feel are in the national interest," about one-third in a 2006 national survey favored government censorship.[123]

The media's ability to report whatever they wish and whenever they wish certainly erodes efforts to maintain order. For example, sensational media coverage of terrorist acts gives terrorists the publicity they seek, and portrayals of violence on television can encourage copycat crimes. The chaos that erupted among Muslims in 2006 over Islamic cartoons published in Danish newspapers to test freedom of expression resulted in deaths and destruction across the world. Freedom of the press is a noble value and one that has been important to democratic government. But we should not ignore the fact that democracies sometimes pay a price for pursuing it without qualification. At the same time, the disruption of order is not always a bad thing. As we saw in 2011 when revolutionary struggles to overthrow authoritarian regimes spread across the Middle East, new media technologies allow for information to be communicated freely in ways can enable citizens to make their preferences known in dramatic fashion (see "Politics of Global Change: The Global Rise of Citizen Journalists").

SUMMARY

6.1 The Development of the Mass Media in the United States

- The mass media transmit information to large, heterogeneous, and widely dispersed audiences through print, broadcasts, and the Internet.
- The mass media have traditionally been divided into print and broadcast formats, but the rise of digital communications has created a more complicated landscape and is rendering this traditional distinction problematic.
- The rise of digital communications has made it harder for printed newspapers, magazines, and broadcast news shows to retain audiences and raise revenue.

6.2 Private Ownership of the Media

- The mass media in the United States are privately owned and in business to make money, which they do mainly by selling space or airtime to advertisers.
- Both print and electronic media determine which events are newsworthy largely on the basis of audience appeal.
- The rise of mass-circulation newspapers in the 1830s produced a politically independent press in the United States. In their aggressive competition for readers, those newspapers often engaged in sensational reporting, a charge sometimes leveled at today's media.

6.3 Government Regulation of the Media

- The broadcast media operate under technical, ownership, and content regulations imposed by the government. Over the past two decades, the FCC has relaxed its rules limiting media ownership and ensuring fair and balanced representation of competing views.
- Comprehensive policy regarding regulation of Internet news has yet to be developed, resulting in clashes between the FCC, Congress, and media corporations.
- The regulation of media content is minimal and has largely been confined to broadcast media.

6.4 Functions of the Mass Media for the Political System

- The main function of the mass media is entertainment, but the media also perform the political functions of reporting news, interpreting news, setting the political agenda, and socializing citizens about politics.
- Thousands of journalists are assigned to report news out of Washington, D.C. Because Congress is a more decentralized institution, it is covered in a more decentralized manner than the president.
- What actually gets reported in the established media depends on media gatekeepers—the publishers and editors—yet we are entering an era in which the gatekeepers have less control over what poses as news, in terms of both what subjects are reported on and the veracity of the reports.
- Americans today get more news from television than from newspapers, and an increasing number of citizens turn to the Internet.
- Compared with television, newspapers usually do a more thorough job of informing the public about politics. Newspapers, however, have been facing unprecedented financial burdens in recent years and have been cutting back on their operations.
- Despite heavy exposure to news in the print and electronic media, the ability of most people to retain much political information is shockingly low.
- The media's most important effect on public opinion is in setting the country's political agenda. The role of the news media may be more important for affecting interactions

among attentive policy elites than in influencing public opinion.

- The media play more subtle, contradictory roles in political socialization, both promoting and undermining certain political and cultural values.

6.5   Evaluating the Media in Government

- Reporters from the national media tend to be more liberal than the public. Journalists' liberal leanings are checked somewhat by the conservative inclinations of their editors and publishers. If journalists systematically demonstrate any pronounced bias in their news reporting, it may be against incumbents and frontrunners, regardless of their party, rather than a bias that favors liberal Democrats.

- The media can promote equality, drawing national attention to disadvantaged groups that lack other political resources.

- From the standpoint of majoritarian democracy, one of the most important roles of the media is to facilitate communication from the people to the government through the reporting of public opinion polls.

- The media zealously defend the freedom of the press, even to the point of encouraging disorder by granting extensive publicity to violent protests, terrorist acts, and other threats to order.

ASSESSING YOUR UNDERSTANDING WITH APLIA...YOUR VIRTUAL TUTOR!

6.1   Trace the evolution of the mass media in the United States and evaluate the impact of new technologies on journalism.

1. How has the development the Internet challenged the traditional division between print and broadcast media?
2. Discuss arguments for and against the notion that bloggers are journalists.

6.2   Evaluate the effect of privately owned mass media on the quality of political communication in the United States.

1. How does the concept of newsworthiness affect the content of the news?
2. List concerns associated with the concentration of media ownership.

6.3   Follow the evolution of government regulation of the media and identify the challenges that new media technologies present to existing regulations.

1. Define the FCC and explain the role it plays in regulating the mass media.
2. What impact has the repeal of the fairness doctrine had on the content of the news?

3. Identify the ways in which the government regulates the Internet.

6.4   Analyze the role of the media in political socialization and the acquisition of political knowledge.

1. What media format do most Americans currently use to get the news?
2. Which media format is associated with higher levels of political knowledge?
3. What do most scholars believe is the media's greatest influence on politics?
4. Describe the phenomenon known as "going public."

6.5   Assess the impact of the media on democratic values and politics in the United States.

1. Identify the charges behind the claims that the media are liberal and/or that the media are conservative.
2. Discuss whether the media tend to advance order versus equality. What about order versus freedom?

Participation and Voting

CHAPTER TOPICS and Learning Outcomes

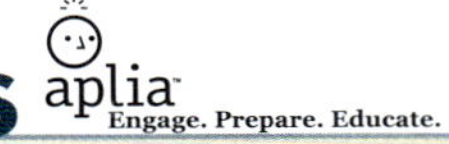

7.1 Democracy and Political Participation
★ Define political participation and distinguish among types of participation.

7.2 Unconventional Participation
★ Identify examples of unconventional participation in American history and evaluate their effectiveness.

7.3 Conventional Participation
★ Distinguish between supportive acts and influencing acts of political participation.

7.4 Participating Through Voting
★ Trace the expansion of suffrage in the United States and assess the impact of expanded suffrage on voting turnout.

7.5 Explaining Political Participation
★ Identify the factors that affect political participation, especially voting.

7.6 Participation and Freedom, Equality, and Order
★ Evaluate the relationship between the values of freedom, equality, and order and political participation in American democracy.

7.7 Participation and the Models of Democracy
★ Identify the purposes elections serve and explain the relationship between elections and majoritarian and pluralist models of democracy.

Scott Olson/Getty Images

I n 1927, *TIME* magazine began its tradition of choosing a "Man of the Year"—the person who did the most (for better or worse) to influence the year's events. Occasionally, *TIME* picked a "Woman of the Year," and sometimes it honored a group or class of people. For 2011, *TIME* chose "The Protester," saying:

> For capturing and highlighting a global sense of restless promise, for upending governments and conventional wisdom, for combining the oldest of techniques with the newest of technologies to shine a light on human dignity and, finally, for steering the planet on a more democratic though sometimes more dangerous path for the 21st century, the Protester is *TIME's* 2011 Person of the Year.[1]

Just days before the issue naming "The Protestor" as *TIME*'s "Person of the Year" was published on December 26, 2011, thousands of Egyptian women marched in Cairo to protest their sisters' treatment by soldiers, who beat, kicked, and stripped female demonstrators in Tahrir Square days earlier. Observers called it "the biggest women's demonstration in modern Egyptian history" and a rarity in the Arab world.[2] The demonstration was a fitting climax to a year of protest launched during the "Arab Spring" that toppled dictators in Tunisia, Egypt, and Libya and rattled regimes in Syria, Yemen, and Bahrain.

It is too early to tell what lasting effect the women's demonstration might have on Egyptian society and politics, but a week later, a Cairo court ordered an end to forced virginity tests on female prisoners who had been arrested in prior demonstrations.[3] Students who read this today may be shocked that Egyptian women had to mobilize and demonstrate to stop public beatings and secret virginity tests. However, only decades ago, American blacks had to mobilize and demonstrate to gain equal access to restaurants, schools, and voting.

Like the colonists in 1773, blacks in the 1950s employed unconventional but constitutionally protected forms of political protest. Like blacks decades ago, young people in 2011 (see Chapter 2) formed "occupy" camps to protest income inequality. Do Americans protest more or less than citizens in other countries? What other options do people have to participate in politics? How well does political protest fit with either the pluralist or majoritarian models of democracy?

In this chapter, we try to answer these and other important questions about popular participation in government. We begin by studying participation in democratic government, distinguishing between conventional forms of political participation and unconventional forms that still comply with democratic government. Then we evaluate the nature and extent of both types of participation in American politics. Next, we study the expansion of voting rights and voting as the major mechanism for mass participation in politics. Finally, we examine the extent to which the various forms of political participation serve the values of freedom, equality, and order and the majoritarian and pluralist models of democracy.

7.1 Democracy and Political Participation

★ Define political participation and distinguish among types of participation.

Government ought to be run by the people. That is the democratic ideal in a nutshell. But how much and what kind of citizen participation are necessary for democratic government? Neither political theorists nor politicians, neither idealists nor realists, can agree on an answer. Champions of direct democracy believe that if citizens do not participate directly in government affairs, making government decisions themselves, they should give up all pretense of living in a democracy. More practical observers contend that people can govern indirectly, through their elected representatives. And they maintain that choosing leaders through elections—formal procedures for voting—is the only workable approach to democracy in a large, complex nation.

Elections are a necessary condition of democracy, but they do not guarantee democratic government. Before the collapse of communism, the former Soviet Union regularly held elections in which more than 90 percent of the electorate turned out to vote, but the Soviet Union certainly did not function as a democracy because there was only one political party. Both the majoritarian and pluralist models of democracy rely on voting to varying degrees, but both models expect citizens to participate in politics in other ways. For example, they expect citizens to discuss politics, form interest groups, contact public officials, campaign for political parties, run for office, and even protest government decisions.

We define **political participation** as "those activities of citizens that attempt to influence the structure of government, the selection of government officials, or the policies of government."[4] This definition embraces both conventional and unconventional forms of political participation. In plain language, *conventional behavior* is behavior that is acceptable to the dominant culture in a given situation. Wearing a swimsuit at the beach in the United States is conventional; wearing one at a formal dance is not. Displaying campaign posters in front yards is conventional; spray-painting political slogans on buildings is not.

Figuring out whether a particular political act is conventional or unconventional can be difficult. We find the following distinction useful:

- **Conventional participation** is a relatively routine behavior that uses the established institutions of representative government, especially campaigning for candidates and voting in elections.
- **Unconventional participation** is a relatively uncommon behavior that challenges or defies established institutions or the dominant culture (and thus is personally stressful to participants and their opponents).

Voting and writing letters to public officials illustrate conventional political participation; staging sit-down strikes in public buildings and chanting slogans outside

political participation
Actions of private citizens by which they seek to influence or support government and politics.

conventional participation
Relatively routine political behavior that uses institutional channels and is acceptable to the dominant culture.

unconventional participation
Relatively uncommon political behavior that challenges or defies established institutions and dominant norms.

officials' windows are examples of unconventional participation. Other democratic forms of participation, such as political demonstrations, can be conventional (carrying signs outside an abortion clinic) or unconventional (linking arms to prevent entrance). Various forms of unconventional participation are often used by powerless groups to gain political benefits while working within the system.[5]

Terrorism is an extreme and problematic case of unconventional political behavior. Indeed, the U.S. legal code defines **terrorism** as "premeditated, politically motivated violence perpetrated against noncombatant targets by sub-national groups or clandestine agents, usually intended to influence an audience."[6] Timothy McVeigh, a decorated veteran of the 1991 Gulf War, bombed the federal building in Oklahoma City in 1995, taking 168 lives. McVeigh said he bombed the building because the federal government had become a police state hostile to gun owners, religious sects, and patriotic militia groups.[7] In 2001, al Qaeda carried out the infamous 9/11 attack on New York and Washington, D.C., killing almost 3,000 Americans and foreign nationals. In November 2009, U.S. Army Major Nidal Malik Hasan shot to death thirteen people at Fort Hood, Texas. Political goals motivated all three acts of terrorism. McVeigh acted because of domestic politics, al Qaeda and Hasan because of international politics. Although terrorist acts are political acts by definition, they do not qualify as political *participation* because terrorists do not seek to influence government but to destroy it.

Methods of unconventional political behavior, in contrast, are used by disadvantaged groups that resort to them in lieu of more conventional forms of participation used by most citizens. These groups accept government while seeking to influence it. Let us look at both unconventional and conventional political participation in the United States.

terrorism
Premeditated, politically motivated violence perpetrated against noncombatant targets by subnational groups or clandestine agents.

★ 7.2 Unconventional Participation

★ Identify examples of unconventional participation in American history and evaluate their effectiveness.

On Sunday, March 7, 1965, a group of about six hundred people attempted to march fifty miles from Selma, Alabama, to the state capitol at Montgomery to show their support for voting rights for blacks. (At the time, Selma had fewer than five hundred registered black voters, out of fifteen thousand eligible.)[8] Alabama governor George Wallace declared the march illegal and sent state troopers to stop it. The two groups met at the Edmund Pettus Bridge over the Alabama River at the edge of Selma. The peaceful marchers were disrupted and beaten by state troopers and deputy sheriffs—some on horseback—using clubs, bullwhips, and tear gas. The day became known as Bloody Sunday.

The march from Selma was a form of unconventional political participation. Marching fifty miles in a political protest is certainly not common; moreover, the march challenged the existing institutions that prevented blacks from voting. But they had been prevented from participating conventionally—voting in elections—for many decades, and they chose this unconventional method to dramatize their cause.

The march ended in violence because Governor Wallace would not allow even this peaceful mode of unconventional expression. The brutal response to the marchers helped the rest of the nation understand the seriousness of the civil rights problem in the South. Unconventional participation is stressful and occasionally violent, but sometimes it is worth the risk. In 2010, thousands of blacks and whites solemnly but triumphantly reenacted the march on its forty-fifth anniversary.

Support for Unconventional Participation

Unconventional political participation has a long history in the United States.[9] The Boston Tea Party of 1773, in which American colonists dumped three cargoes of British tea into Boston Harbor, was only the first in a long line of violent protests against British rule that eventually led to revolution. Yet we know less about unconventional than conventional participation. The reasons are twofold. First, since it is easier to collect data on conventional practices, they are studied more frequently. Second, political scientists are simply biased toward institutionalized, or conventional, politics. In fact, some basic works on political participation explicitly exclude any behavior that is "outside the system."[10] One major study of unconventional political action asked people whether they had engaged in or approved of three types of political participation other than voting: signing petitions, joining boycotts, and attending demonstrations.[11] As shown in Figure 7.1, only signing petitions was clearly regarded as conventional, in the sense that the behavior was widely practiced.

The marchers in Selma, although peaceful, were demonstrating against the established order. If we measure conventional participation according to the proportion of

March for Freedom, Forty-Five Years Later

On Sunday, March 7, 2010, thousands marched across the Edmund Pettus Bridge outside Selma, Alabama, to commemorate the "Bloody Sunday" forty-five years earlier when people were beaten during a voting rights protest.

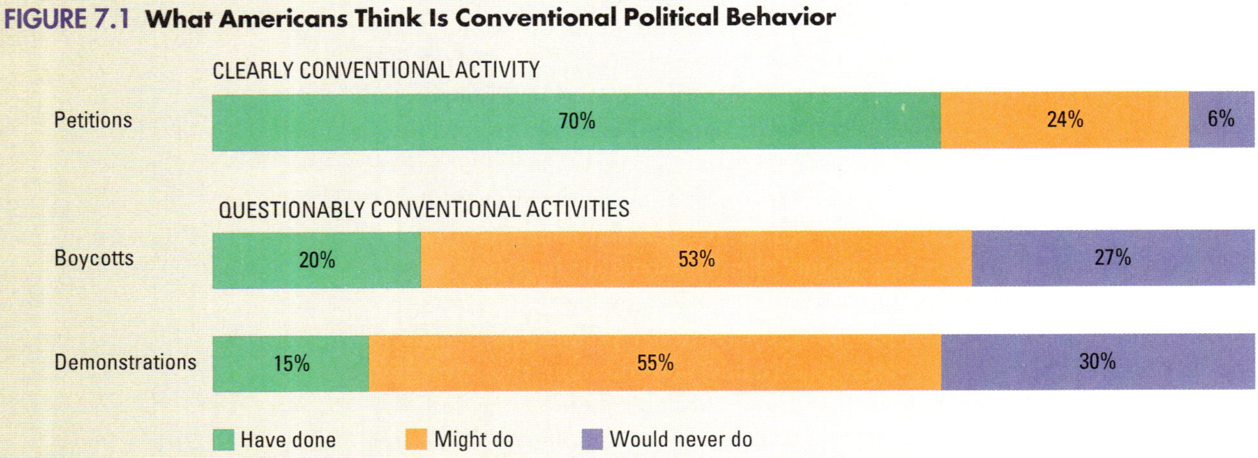

FIGURE 7.1 What Americans Think Is Conventional Political Behavior

A survey presented Americans with three forms of political participation outside the electoral process and asked whether they "have done," "might do," or "would never do" any of them. The respondents approved overwhelmingly of signing petitions, which was widely done and rarely ruled out. Even attending demonstrations (a right guaranteed in the Constitution) would "never" be done by 30 percent of the respondents. Boycotting products was less objectionable and more widely practiced. According to this test, attending demonstrations and boycotting products are only marginally conventional forms of political participation in the United States.

Source: 2005–2008 World Values Survey. The World Values Survey Association, based in Stockholm, conducts representative surveys in nations across the world. See http://www.worldvaluessurvey.org.

people who disapprove of the act, most demonstrations border on the unconventional, involving relatively few people. The same goes for boycotting products—for example, refusing to buy lettuce or grapes picked by nonunion farm workers. Demonstrations and boycotts are problem cases in deciding what is and is not conventional political participation.

The Effectiveness of Unconventional Participation

Vociferous antiabortion protests have discouraged many doctors from performing abortions, but they have not led to outlawing abortions. Does unconventional participation ever work (even when it provokes violence)? Yes. The unconventional activities of civil rights workers produced notable successes. Dr. Martin Luther King, Jr., led the 1955 Montgomery bus boycott (prompted by Rosa Parks's refusal to surrender her seat to a white man), which sparked the civil rights movement. He used **direct action** to challenge specific cases of discrimination, assembling crowds to confront businesses and local governments and demanding equal treatment in public accommodations and government. The civil rights movement organized more than 1,000 such newsworthy demonstrations nationwide—387 in 1965 alone.[12] And like the march in Selma, many of these protests provoked violent confrontations between whites and blacks.

Denied the usual opportunities for conventional political participation, minorities used unconventional politics to pressure Congress to pass a series of civil rights laws in 1957, 1960, 1964, and 1968—each one in some way extending national protection against discrimination by reason of race, color, religion, or national origin. (The 1964 act also prohibited discrimination in employment on the basis of sex.)

In addition, the Voting Rights Act of 1965 placed some state electoral procedures under federal supervision, protecting the registration of black voters and increasing their voting rate, especially in the South, where much of the violence occurred. Black protest activity—both violent and nonviolent—has also been credited with increased welfare support for blacks in the South.[13] The civil rights movement showed that social change can occur even when it faces violent opposition at first. In 1970, fewer than fifteen hundred blacks served as elected officials in the United States. In 2006, the number was more than nine thousand, and over five thousand Hispanics held elected office.[14] In 2008, Barack Obama became the first African American to be elected president of the United States.

Although direct political action and the politics of confrontation can work, using them requires a special kind of commitment. Studies show that direct action appeals most to those who both distrust the political system and have a strong sense of political efficacy—the feeling that they can do something to affect political decisions.[15] Whether this combination of attitudes produces behavior that challenges the system depends on the extent of organized group activity. The civil rights movement of the 1960s was backed by numerous organizations across the nation.

STOP NATO

NATO: TooMuchArmor TooLittleBrain EXTINCTION WELCOME!

Alex Garcia/Chicago Tribune/Landov

Antiwar Protest, 2012

In May 2012, representatives of 28 member nations of the North Atlantic Treaty Organization (NATO) met in Chicago. In turn, they were met by thousands of protesters opposed to war in general and to NATO in particular.

direct action
Unconventional participation that involves assembling crowds to confront businesses and local governments to demand a hearing.

The decision to use unconventional behavior also depends on the extent to which individuals develop a group consciousness—identification with their group and awareness of its position in society, its objectives, and its intended course of action.[16] These characteristics were present among blacks and young people in the mid-1960s and are strongly present today among blacks and, to a lesser degree, among Latinos. Indeed, some researchers contend that black consciousness has heightened both African Americans' distrust of the political system and their sense of individual efficacy, generating more political participation by poor blacks than by poor whites.[17]

Compared with What?

Popular Participation in Politics

Compared with citizens in eight other nations, Americans are not noticeably apathetic when it comes to politics. Over half of American respondents report that they voted in the last election (voting overestimates are common in most countries), signed a petition, or were interested in politics. Americans are notably less likely than respondents in other countries to join demonstrations. Survey researchers have only recently begun to ask whether respondents have ever joined an Internet political forum. In the United States, a little over 7 percent of respondents claim to have discussed politics on the Internet, which makes it a relatively infrequent act of political participation compared to these other activities.

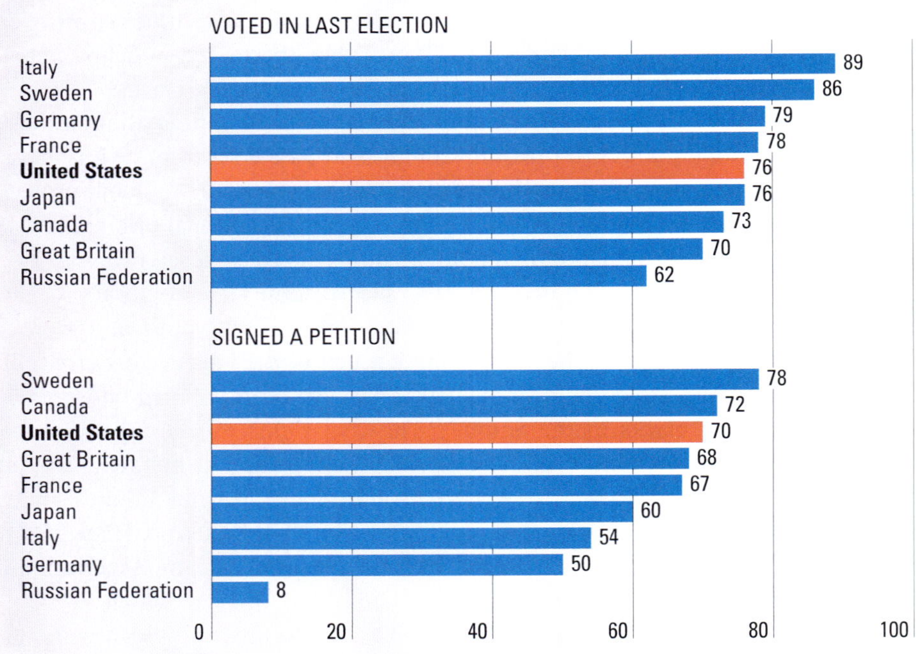

Unconventional Participation Around the World

Although most Americans disapprove of using certain forms of participation to protest government policies, U.S. citizens are about as likely to take direct action in politics as citizens of European democracies. Consider "Compared with What? Popular Participation in Politics," which shows how respondents in the United States compare with those in eight other countries on various modes of participation. Americans are just as likely as citizens of other countries to vote, sign a petition, be interested in politics, or boycott products—but they are less likely to join demonstrations. So compared with citizens in other nations, Americans are not markedly apathetic.

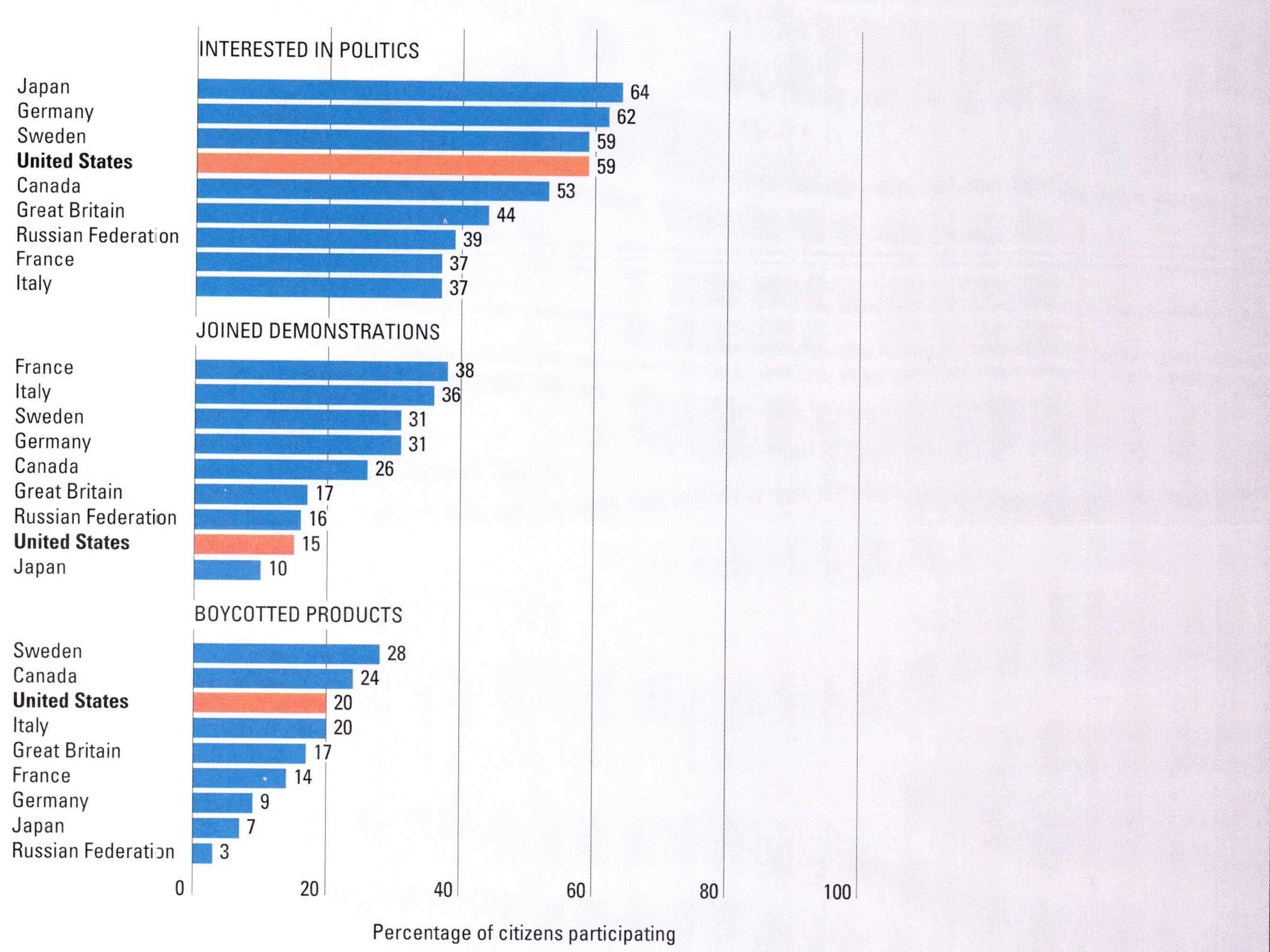

Source: International Social Survey Programme (ISSP) 2004: Citizenship Survey, http://zacat.gesis.org.

Critical Thinking

Are you surprised by these comparative findings? Did you think that Americans participated more than others in politics, or less?

Is something wrong with a political system if citizens resort to unconventional, and often disapproved-of, methods of political participation? To answer this question, we must first learn how much citizens use conventional methods of participation.

★ 7.3 Conventional Participation

★ Distinguish between supportive acts and influencing acts of political participation.

A practical test of the democratic nature of any government is whether citizens can affect its policies by acting through its institutions—meeting with public officials, supporting candidates, and voting in elections. (See "Compared with What? Popular Participation in Politics.") If people must operate outside government institutions to influence policymaking, as civil rights workers had to do in the South, the system is not democratic. Citizens should not have to risk their life and property to participate in politics, and they should not have to take direct action to force the government to hear their views. The objective of democratic institutions is to make political participation conventional—to allow ordinary citizens to engage in relatively routine, non-threatening behavior to get the government to heed their opinions, interests, and needs.

In a democracy, for a group to gather at a statehouse or city hall to dramatize its position on an issue—say, a tax increase—is not unusual. Such a demonstration is a form of conventional participation. The group is not powerless, and its members are not risking their personal safety by demonstrating. But violence can erupt between opposing groups demonstrating in a political setting, such as between pro-life and pro-choice groups. Circumstances, then, often determine whether organized protest is or is not conventional. In general, the less that the participants anticipate a threat, the more likely it is that the protest will be conventional.

Conventional political behaviors fall into two major categories: actions that show support for government policies and those that try to change or influence policies.

Supportive Behavior

supportive behavior
Action that expresses allegiance to government and country.

Supportive behavior is action that expresses allegiance to country and government. Reciting the Pledge of Allegiance and flying the American flag on holidays show support for both the country and, by implication, its political system. Such ceremonial activities usually require little effort, knowledge, or personal courage; that is, they demand little initiative on the part of the citizen. The simple act of turning out to vote is in itself a show of support for the political system. Other supportive behaviors, such as serving as an election judge in a nonpartisan election or organizing a holiday parade, demand greater initiative.

At times, people's perception of patriotism moves them to cross the line between conventional and unconventional behavior. In their eagerness to support the American system, they break up a meeting or disrupt a rally of a group they believe is radical or somehow "un-American." Radical groups may threaten the political system with wrenching change, but superpatriots pose their own threat by denying to others the nonviolent means of dissent.[18]

Influencing Behavior

Citizens use **influencing behavior** to modify or even reverse government policy to serve political interests. Some forms of influencing behavior seek particular benefits from government; other forms have broad policy objectives.

influencing behavior
Behavior that seeks to modify or reverse government policy to serve political interests.

Particular Benefits. Some citizens try to influence government to obtain benefits for themselves, their immediate families, or close friends. For example, citizens might pressure their alderman to rebuild the curbs on their street or vote against an increase in school taxes, especially if they have no children. Serving one's self-interest through the voting process is certainly acceptable to democratic theory. Each individual has only one vote, and no single voter can wrest particular benefits from government through voting unless a majority of the voters agrees.

Political actions that require considerable knowledge and initiative are another story. Individuals or small groups who influence government officials to advance their self-interest—for instance, to obtain a lucrative government contract—may secretly benefit without others knowing. Those who quietly obtain particular benefits from government pose a serious challenge to a democracy. Pluralist theory holds that groups ought to be able to make government respond to their special problems and needs. In contrast, majoritarian theory holds that government should not do what a majority does not want it to do. A majority of citizens might very well not want the government to do what any particular person or group seeks if it is costly to other citizens.

Citizens often ask for special services from local government. Such requests may range from contacting the city forestry department to remove a dead tree in front of a house to calling the county animal control center to deal with a vicious dog in the neighborhood. Studies of such "contacting behavior" find that it tends not to be empirically related to other forms of political activity. In other words, people who complain to city hall do not necessarily vote. Contacting behavior is related to socioeconomic status: people of higher socioeconomic status are more likely to contact public officials.[19]

Americans demand much more of their local government than of the national government. Although many people value self-reliance and individualism in national politics, most people expect local government to solve a wide range of social problems. A study of residents of Kansas City, Missouri, found that more than 90 percent thought the city had a responsibility to provide services in thirteen areas, including maintaining parks, setting standards for new home construction, demolishing vacant and unsafe buildings, ensuring that property owners clean up trash and weeds, and providing bus service. The researcher noted that "it is difficult to imagine a set of federal government activities about which there would [be] more consensus."[20] Citizens can also mobilize against a project. Dubbed the "not in my back yard," or NIMBY, phenomenon, such a mobilization occurs when citizens pressure local officials to stop undesired projects from being located near their homes.

Finally, contributing money to a candidate's campaign is another form of influencing behavior. Here, too, the objective can be particular or broad benefits, although determining which is which can sometimes be difficult. Several points emerge from this review of "particularized" forms of political participation. First, approaching government to serve one's particular interests is consistent with democratic theory because it encourages participation from an active citizenry. Second, particularized contact may be a unique form of participation, not necessarily related to other forms of participation such as voting. Third, such participation tends to be used more by

© Chris Madden

Toppling a Pyramid

In Egypt, a popular revolution ended thirty years of autocratic rule by President Hosni Mubarak, but the masses that led the revolution did not settle on a plan to govern after he was ousted. The military still dictated terms for new elections, and voting elected parties to parliament that comprised a religious majority. Parties representing liberal democratic values did not do well.

class action suit
A legal action brought by a person or group on behalf of a number of people in similar circumstances.

citizens who are advantaged in terms of knowledge and resources. Fourth, particularized participation may serve private interests to the detriment of the majority.

Broad Policy Objectives. We come now to what many scholars have in mind when they talk about political participation: activities that influence the selection of government personnel and policies. Here, too, we find behaviors that require little initiative (such as voting) and others that require high initiative (attending political meetings, persuading others how to vote).

Even voting intended to influence government policies is a low-initiative activity. Such "policy voting" differs from voting to show support or to gain special benefits in its broader influence on the community or society. Obviously, this distinction is not sharp: citizens vote for several reasons—a mix of allegiance, particularized benefits, and policy concerns. In addition to policy voting, many other low-initiative forms of conventional participation—wearing a candidate's T-shirt, visiting a candidate's website, posting a bumper sticker—are also connected with elections. In the next section, we focus on elections as a mechanism for participation. For now, we simply note that voting to influence policy is usually a low-initiative activity. As we discuss later, it actually requires more initiative to *register* to vote in the United States than to vote on election day. It is even easier to e-mail members of Congress than to vote.

Other types of participation designed to affect broad policies require high initiative. Running for office requires the most (see Chapter 9). Some high-initiative activities, such as attending party meetings and working on campaigns, are associated with the electoral process; others, such as attending legislative hearings and sending e-mails to Congress, are not. Although many nonelectoral activities involve making personal contact, their objective is often to obtain government benefits for some group of people—farmers, the unemployed, children, oil producers. In fact, studies of citizen contacts in the United States show that about two-thirds deal with broad social issues and only one-third are for private gain.[21] Few people realize that using the court system is a form of political participation, a way for citizens to press for their rights in a democratic society. Although most people use the courts to serve their particular interests, some also use them, as we discuss shortly, to meet broad objectives. Going to court demands high personal initiative.[22] It also requires knowledge of the law or the financial resources to afford a lawyer.

People use the courts for both personal benefit and broad policy objectives. A person or group can bring a **class action suit** on behalf of other people in similar circumstances. Lawyers for the National Association for the Advancement of Colored People pioneered this form of litigation in the famous school desegregation case *Brown* v. *Board of Education* (1954).[23] They succeeded in getting the Supreme Court to outlaw segregation in public schools, not just for Linda Brown, who brought the suit in Topeka, Kansas, but also for all others "similarly situated"—that is, for all other black students who wanted to attend desegregated schools. Participation through the courts is usually beyond the means of individual citizens, but it has proved effective for organized groups, especially those that have been unable to gain their objectives through Congress or the executive branch. Sometimes such court challenges help citizens without their knowing it. In 2009, Capital One (whose TV slogan is "What's in *your* wallet?") settled a class action suit over its credit cards, agreeing to drop contract language requiring customer disputes to be handled through binding arbitration instead of the legal system.[24]

Individual citizens can also try to influence policies at the national level by participating directly in the legislative process. One way is to attend congressional hearings, which are open to the public and are occasionally held outside Washington, D.C. Especially after World War II, the national government sought to increase citizen involvement in creating regulations and laws by making information on government activities available to interested parties. For example, government agencies were required to publish all proposed and approved regulations in the daily *Federal Register* and to make government documents available to citizens on request.

More recently, the Internet has allowed electronic access to information, allowing citizens to participate in government from their own homes. A comprehensive survey of national government websites reported 1,489 domains and 1,013 websites from 56 agencies.[25] Today, citizens can search the *Federal Register* online.[26] The government website USA.gov helps people find information online and offers video tutorials on standard topics. However, the private site GovTrack.us provides easier access to congressional voting records than the government site Thomas.gov.[27] Private sites also monitor more contentious issues. The Center for Responsible Politics covers campaign finance, lobbyists' spending, and other forms of political influence.[28] The National Institute on Money in State Politics covers similar ground for the states.[29] OMB Watch focuses on government spending and the budget deficit, while the Institute for Truth in Accounting lobbies to reduce the national debt.[30]

MAHMUD HAMS/AFP/Getty Images

Voting in Egypt

An Egyptian woman in Cairo casts her ballot in the 2011 election held after the revolution overthrew President Hosni Mubarak, who ruled for almost thirty years. It was widely regarded as the freest election in decades, and many women voted for the first time.

Conventional Participation in America

You may know someone who has testified at a congressional or administrative hearing or closely monitors governmental actions on the Internet, but the odds are that you do not. Such participation is high-initiative behavior. Relatively few people—only those with high stakes in the outcome of a decision—are willing to participate in this way. How often do Americans contact government officials and engage in other forms of conventional political participation compared with citizens in other countries?

The most common form of political behavior in most industrial democracies is voting for candidates. The rate of voting is known as **voter turnout**, the percentage of eligible voters who actually vote in a given election. Voting eligibility is hard to determine across American states, and there are different ways to estimate voter turnout.[31] However measured, voting for candidates in the United States is less common than it is in other countries, as demonstrated in "Compared with What? Voter Turnout in European and American Elections" on page 192. When voter turnout in the United States is compared with voting in sixteen other countries, the United States ranks at the *bottom* of the pack. This is a political paradox. On one hand, Americans are as likely as citizens in other democracies to engage in various forms of political participation. But when it comes to voting, the hand that casts the ballot, Americans rank dead last.

voter turnout
The percentage of eligible citizens who actually vote in a given election.

Other researchers noted this paradox and wrote, "If, for example, we concentrate our attention on national elections we will find that the United States is the least participatory of almost all other nations." But looking at the other indicators, they found that "political apathy, by a wide margin, is lowest in the United States. Interestingly, the high levels of overall involvement reflect a rather balanced contribution of both … conventional and unconventional politics."[32] Clearly, low voter turnout in the United States constitutes a puzzle, to which we will return.

★ 7.4 Participating Through Voting

★ Trace the expansion of suffrage in the United States and assess the impact of expanded suffrage on voting turnout.

The heart of democratic government lies in the electoral process. Whether a country holds elections—and if so, what kind—constitutes the critical difference between democratic and nondemocratic governments. Elections institutionalize mass participation in democratic government according to the three normative principles of procedural democracy discussed in Chapter 2: electoral rules specify *who* is allowed to vote, *how much* each person's vote counts, and *how many* votes are needed to win.

Again, elections are formal procedures for making group decisions. *Voting* is the act individuals engage in when they choose among alternatives in an election. **Suffrage** and **franchise** both mean the right to vote. By formalizing political participation through rules for suffrage and for counting ballots, electoral systems allow large numbers of people, who individually have little political power, to wield great power. Electoral systems decide collectively who governs and, in some instances, what government should do.

The simple act of holding elections is less important than the specific rules and circumstances that govern voting. According to democratic theory, everyone should be able to vote. In practice, however, no nation grants universal suffrage. All countries have age requirements for voting, and all disqualify some inhabitants on various grounds: lack of citizenship, criminal record, mental incompetence, and others. What is the record of enfranchisement in the United States?

suffrage
The right to vote. Also called the *franchise*.

franchise
The right to vote. Also called *suffrage*.

Expansion of Suffrage

The United States was the first country to provide for general elections of representatives through "mass" suffrage, but the franchise was far from universal. When the Constitution was framed, the idea of full adult suffrage was too radical to consider seriously. Instead, the framers left the issue of enfranchisement to the states, stipulating only that individuals who could vote for "the most numerous Branch of the State Legislature" could also vote for their representatives to the U.S. Congress (Article I, Section 2).

Initially, most states established taxpaying or property-holding requirements for voting. Virginia, for example, required ownership of twenty-five acres of settled land or five hundred acres of unsettled land. The original thirteen states began to lift such requirements after 1800. Expansion of the franchise accelerated after 1815, with the admission of new "western" states (Indiana, Illinois, Alabama), where land was more plentiful and widely owned. By the 1850s, the states had eliminated almost all taxpaying and property-holding requirements, thus allowing the working class—at least its white male members—to vote. Extending the vote to blacks and women took longer.

The Enfranchisement of Blacks. The Fifteenth Amendment, adopted shortly after the Civil War, prohibited the states from denying the right to vote "on account of race, color, or previous condition of servitude." However, the states of the old Confederacy worked around the amendment by reestablishing old voting requirements (poll taxes, literacy tests) that worked primarily against blacks. Some southern states also cut blacks out of politics through a cunning circumvention of the amendment. Because the amendment said nothing about voting rights in private organizations, these states denied blacks the right to vote in the "private" Democratic *primary* elections held to choose the party's candidates for the general election. Because the Democratic Party came to dominate politics in the South, the "white primary" effectively disenfranchised blacks, despite the Fifteenth Amendment. Finally, in many areas of the South, the threat of violence kept blacks from the polls.

The extension of full voting rights to blacks came in two phases, separated by twenty years. In 1944, the Supreme Court decided in *Smith* v. *Allwright* that laws preventing blacks from voting in primary elections were unconstitutional, holding that party primaries are part of the continuous process of electing public officials.[33] The Voting Rights Act of 1965, which followed Selma's Bloody Sunday by less than five months, suspended discriminatory voting tests. It also authorized federal registrars to register voters in seven southern states, where less than half of the voting-age population had registered to vote in the 1964 election. For good measure, the Supreme Court ruled in 1966 in *Harper* v. *Virginia State Board of Elections* that state poll taxes are unconstitutional.[34] Although long in coming, these actions by the national government to enforce political equality in the states dramatically increased the registration of southern blacks (see Figure 7.2).

The Enfranchisement of Women. The enfranchisement of women in the United States is a less sordid story than enfranchisement of blacks but still nothing to be proud of. Women had to fight long and hard to win the right to vote. Until 1869, women could not vote anywhere in the world.[35] American women began to organize to obtain suffrage in the mid-1800s. Known then as *suffragettes,* the early feminists

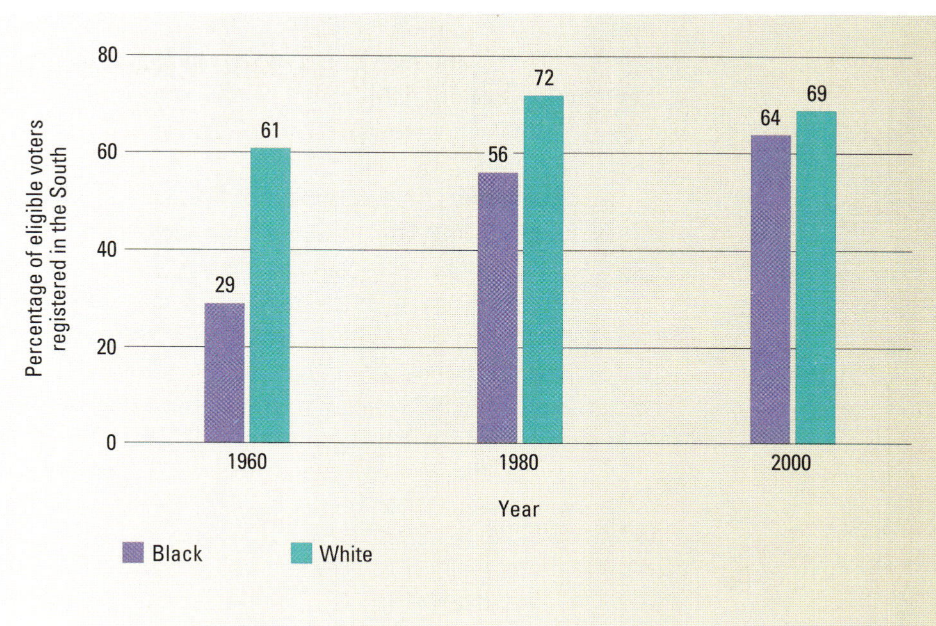

FIGURE 7.2 Voter Registration in the South, 1960, 1980, and 2000

As a result of the Voting Rights Act of 1965 and other national actions, black voter registration in the eleven states of the old Confederacy nearly doubled between 1960 and 1980. In 2000, there was very little difference between the voting registration rates of white and black voters in the Deep South.
Sources: Data for 1960 and 1980 are from U.S. Bureau of the Census, *Statistical Abstract of the United States*, 1982–1983 (Washington, D.C.: U.S. Government Printing Office, 1983), p. 488; data for 2000 come from the U.S. Census Bureau, *Current Population Report*, P20–542, Table 3, Internet release, 27 February 2002.

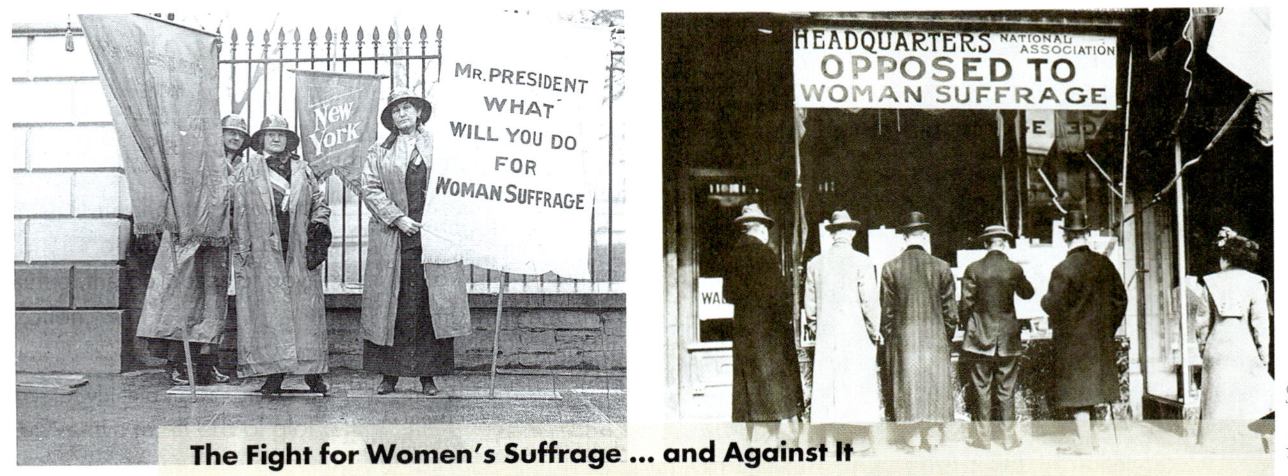

The Fight for Women's Suffrage ... and Against It

Militant suffragettes demonstrated outside the White House prior to ratification of the Nineteenth Amendment to the Constitution, which gave women the right to vote. Congress passed the proposed amendment in 1919, and it was ratified by the required number of states in time for the 1920 presidential election. Suffragettes' demonstrations were occasionally disrupted by men—and other women—who opposed extending the right to vote to women.

initially had a limited effect on politics.* Their first major victory did not come until 1869, when Wyoming, still a territory, granted women the right to vote. No state followed suit until 1893, when Colorado enfranchised women.

In the meantime, the suffragettes became more active. In 1884, they formed the Equal Rights Party and nominated Belva A. Lockwood, a lawyer (who could not herself vote), as the first woman candidate for president.[36] Between 1896 and 1918, twelve other states gave women the vote. Most of these states were in the West, where pioneer women often departed from traditional women's roles. Nationally, the women's suffrage movement intensified, often resorting to unconventional political behaviors (marches, demonstrations), which occasionally led to violent attacks from men and even other women. In 1919, Congress finally passed the Nineteenth Amendment, which prohibits states from denying the right to vote "on account of sex." The amendment was ratified in 1920, in time for the November election. A survey of Chicago voters in 1923 found that 75 percent of the men voted in the presidential election but only 46 percent of the women. Among women nonvoters, 11 percent cited "disbelief in woman's voting"; less than 2 percent cited "objection from husband."[37]

Evaluating the Expansion of Suffrage in America. The last major expansion of suffrage in the United States took place in 1971, when the Twenty-sixth Amendment lowered the voting age to eighteen. For most of its history, the United States has been far from the democratic ideal of universal suffrage. The United States initially restricted voting rights to white male taxpayers or property owners, and wealth requirements lasted until the 1850s. Through demonstrations and a constitutional amendment, women won the franchise only two decades before World War II. Through civil war, constitutional amendments, court actions, massive demonstrations, and congressional action, blacks finally achieved full voting rights only two decades after World War II. Our record has more than a few blemishes.

---

*The term *suffragist* applied to a person of either sex who advocated extending the vote to women, while *suffragette* was reserved for women who did so militantly.

But compared with other countries, the United States looks pretty democratic.[38] Women did not gain the vote on equal terms with men until 1921 in Norway; 1922 in the Netherlands; 1944 in France; 1946 in Italy, Japan, and Venezuela; 1948 in Belgium; and 1971 in Switzerland. Women are still not universally enfranchised. Among the Arab monarchies, Kuwait granted full voting rights to women in 2005. In 2011, Saudi Arabia finally announced that women could vote in municipal elections—beginning in 2015. Of course, no one at all can vote in the United Arab Emirates. In South Africa, blacks, who outnumber whites by more than four to one, were not allowed to vote freely in elections until 1994. With regard to voting age, about 85 percent of the world's countries allow eighteen-year-olds to vote. About fifteen countries set the minimum age at twenty or twenty-one. Fewer than ten allow persons under age eighteen to vote—including Austria, which allows voting at sixteen.[39]

When judged against the rest of the world, the United States, which originated mass participation in government through elections, has as good a record of providing for political equality in voting rights as other democracies and a better record than many others.

Voting on Policies

Disenfranchised groups have struggled to gain voting rights because of the political power that comes with suffrage. Belief in the ability of ordinary citizens to make political decisions and to control government through the power of the ballot box was strongest in the United States during the Progressive era, which began around 1900 and lasted until about 1925. **Progressivism** was a philosophy of political reform that trusted the goodness and wisdom of individual citizens and distrusted "special interests" (railroads, corporations) and political institutions (traditional political parties, legislatures).

The leaders of the Progressive movement were prominent politicians (former president Theodore Roosevelt, Senator Robert La Follette of Wisconsin) and eminent scholars (historian Frederick Jackson Turner, philosopher John Dewey). Not content to vote for candidates chosen by party leaders, the Progressives championed the **direct primary**—a preliminary election, run by the state governments, in which the voters choose the party's candidates for the general election. Wanting a mechanism to remove elected candidates from office, the Progressives backed the **recall**, a special election initiated by a petition signed by a specified number of voters. Although about twenty states provide for recall elections, this device is rarely used. Only a few state-wide elected officials have actually been unseated through recall.[40] Indeed, only one state governor had ever been unseated until 2003, when California voters threw out Governor Gray Davis in a bizarre recall election that placed movie actor Arnold Schwarzenegger in the governor's mansion. In 2012, Wisconsin voters also sought to recall Republican governor Scott Walker but failed.

The Progressives also championed the power of the masses to propose and pass laws, approximating citizen participation in policymaking that is the hallmark of direct democracy.[41] They developed two voting mechanisms for policymaking that are still in use:

- A **referendum** is a direct vote by the people on either a proposed law or an amendment to a state constitution. The measures subject to popular vote are known as *propositions.* Twenty-four states permit popular referenda on laws, and all but Delaware require a referendum for a constitutional amendment. Most referenda are placed on the ballot by legislatures, not voters.

progressivism
A philosophy of political reform based on the goodness and wisdom of the individual citizen as opposed to special interests and political institutions.

direct primary
A preliminary election, run by the state government, in which the voters choose each party's candidates for the general election.

recall
The process for removing an elected official from office.

referendum
An election on a policy issue.

initiative

A procedure by which voters can propose an issue to be decided by the legislature or by the people in a referendum. It requires gathering a specified number of signatures and submitting a petition to a designated agency.

- The **initiative** is a procedure by which voters can propose a measure to be decided by the legislature or by the people in a referendum. The procedure involves gathering a specified number of signatures from registered voters (usually 5 to 10 percent of the total in the state) and then submitting the petition to a designated state agency. Twenty-four states provide for some form of voter initiative.

Figure 7.3 shows the West's affinity for these democratic mechanisms. In 2010, voters in thirty-six states decided on 159 ballot propositions, most placed there by state legislatures, not citizen initiatives.[42] Voters approved most propositions, including ones in Arizona and Oklahoma against mandatory participation in a government health system. In the off-year election of 2011, only nine states voted on thirty-four propositions.[43] Most were approved, including (again) one in Ohio against

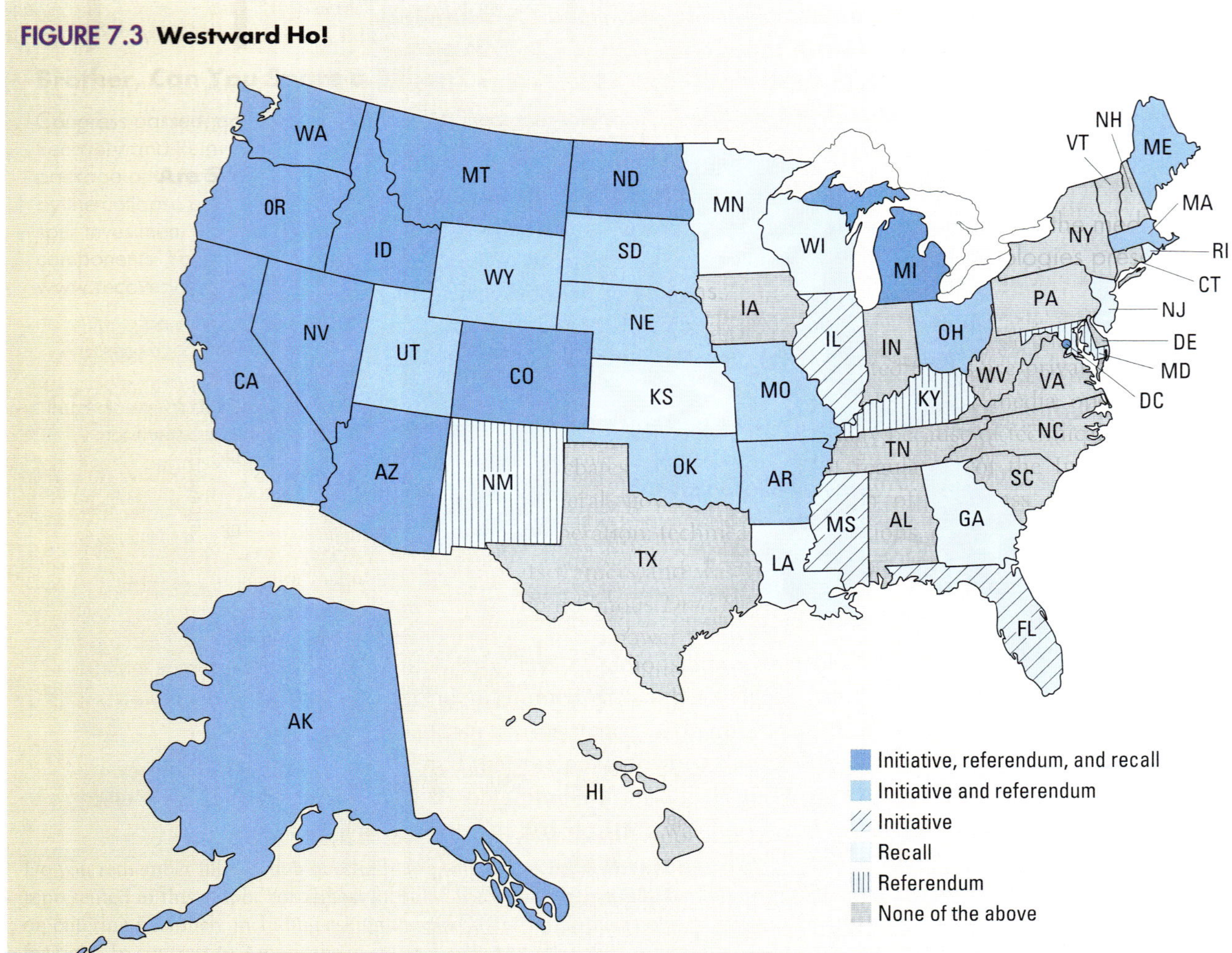

FIGURE 7.3 Westward Ho!

This map shows quite clearly the western basis of the initiative, referendum, and recall mechanisms intended to place government power directly in the hands of the people. Advocates of "direct legislation" sought to bypass entrenched powers in state legislatures. Established groups and parties in the East dismissed them as radicals and cranks, but they gained the support of farmers and miners in the Midwest and West. The Progressive forces usually aligned with Democrats in western state legislatures to enact their proposals, often against Republican opposition.

Source: National Conference on State Legislatures, http://www.ncsl.org/programs/legismgt/elect/irstates.htm.

mandatory participation in a government health system. But voters in Mississippi defeated one that defined a "person" to be a human being from the moment of fertilization.

What conclusion can we draw about the Progressives' legacy of mechanisms for direct participation in government? One seasoned journalist paints an unimpressive picture. He notes that an expensive "industry" developed in the 1980s that makes money circulating petitions and then managing the large sums of money needed to run a campaign to approve (or defeat) a referendum. In 1998, opponents of a measure to allow casino gambling on Native American land in California spent $25.8 million. This huge sum, however, paled in comparison to the $66.2 million spent during the campaign by the tribes that supported the measure. The initiative passed.[44]

Clearly, citizens can exercise great power over government policy through the mechanisms of the initiative and the referendum. What is not clear is whether these forms of direct democracy improve on the policies made by elected representatives.[45] However, recent research has shown that—especially in midterm elections, which are characterized by low turnout—ballot measures tend to increase voting turnout, knowledge of issues, and campaign contributions to interest groups.[46]

If the Internet had been around during their era, Progressives certainly would have endorsed it as a mechanism of direct democracy. At an elementary level, the Internet allows ordinary citizens who seek to initiate legislation to collect on petitions the thousands of signatures needed to place the proposal on the ballot. Pioneering websites, such as iSolon.org, aim at "exploring and advancing opportunities for democratic reform brought about by new information technologies," and the Brookings Institution proposes ways that social media can improve citizen engagement in political campaigns and invigorate American democracy.[47] Finally, there have been attempts to implement "deliberative democracy," which involves thorough deliberation of policy options (often involving the Internet) by a random sample of citizens who then propose legislation for adoption in a referendum.[48]

Voting for Candidates

We have saved for last the most visible form of political participation: voting to choose candidates for public office. Voting for candidates serves democratic government in two ways. First, citizens can choose the candidates they think will best serve their interests. If citizens choose candidates who are "like themselves" in personal traits or party affiliation, elected officials should tend to think as their constituents do on political issues and automatically reflect the majority's views when making public policy.

Second, voting allows the people to reelect the officials they guessed right about and to kick out those they guessed wrong about. This function is very different from the first. It makes public officials accountable for their behavior through the reward-and-punishment mechanism of elections. It assumes that officeholders are motivated to respond to public opinion by the threat of electoral defeat. It also assumes that the voters know what politicians are doing while they are in office and participate actively in the electoral process. We look at the factors that underlie voting choice in Chapter 9. Here, we examine Americans' reliance on the electoral process.

In national politics, voters seem content to elect just two executive officers—the president and vice president—and to trust the president to appoint a cabinet to round out his administration. But at the state and local levels, voters insist on selecting all kinds of officials. Every state elects a governor (and forty-five elect a lieutenant governor). Forty-two elect an attorney general; thirty-nine, a treasurer; and thirty-seven, a secretary of state. The list goes on, down through superintendents of schools, secretaries of agriculture, comptrollers, boards of education, and public utilities commissioners. Elected county officials commonly include commissioners, a sheriff, a treasurer, a clerk, a superintendent of schools, and a judge (often several). At the local level, voters elect all but about 600 of 15,300 school boards across the nation.[49] Instead of trusting state and local chief executives to appoint lesser administrators (as we do for more important offices at the national level), we expect voters to choose intelligently among scores of candidates they meet for the first time on a complex ballot in the polling booth.

Around the world, the number of countries holding regular, free, and fair elections has been rising (see "Politics of Global Change: The Growth of Electoral Democracy"). In the American version of democracy, our laws recognize no limit to voters' ability to make informed choices among candidates and thus to control government through voting. The reasoning seems to be that elections are good; therefore, more elections are better, and the most elections are best. By this thinking, the United States clearly has the best and most democratic government in the world because it is the undisputed champion at holding elections. The author of a study that compared elections in the United States with elections in twenty-six other democracies concluded:

> No country can approach the United States in the frequency and variety of elections, and thus in the amount of electoral participation to which its citizens have a right. No other country elects its lower house as often as every two years, or its president as frequently as every four years. No other country popularly elects its state governors and town mayors; no other has as wide a variety of nonrepresentative offices (judges, sheriffs, attorneys general, city treasurers, and so on) subject to election.… The average American is entitled to do far more electing—probably by a factor of three or four—than the citizen of any other democracy.[50]

However, we learn from "Compared with What? Voter Turnout in European and American Elections" that the United States ranks at the bottom of sixteen European countries in voter turnout in national elections. How do we square low voter turnout with Americans' devotion to elections as an instrument of democratic government? To complicate matters further, how do we square low voter turnout with the fact that Americans seem to participate in politics in various other ways?

★ 7.5 Explaining Political Participation

★ Identify the factors that affect political participation, especially voting.

As explained, political participation can be unconventional or conventional, can require little or much initiative, and can serve to support the government or influence its decisions. Researchers have found that people who take part in some form of political behavior often do not take part in others. For example, citizens who contact public officials to obtain special benefits may not vote regularly, participate in campaigns, or even contact officials about broader social issues. In fact, because particularized contacting serves individual rather than public interests, it is not even considered political behavior by some people.

This section examines some factors that affect the more obvious forms of political participation, with particular emphasis on voting. The first task is to determine how much patterns of participation vary within the United States over time.

Politics of Global Change

The Growth of Electoral Democracy

Nations are "electoral democracies" if they have (1) a competitive, multiparty system; (2) universal adult suffrage; (3) regularly contested free elections; and (4) free election campaigns—according to Freedom House. The Washington-based organization has scored nations over the last four decades, during which the spread of electoral democracies can be analyzed in three stages: (1) the period from 1974 to 1989 depicts a "third wave" of democratization (the others were in 1828–1926 and 1943–1962) caused by social modernization and international influences, (2) the boom from 1989 to 1994 was sparked by the collapse of communism, and (3) a plateau was reached after 1995.

Growth in countries and electoral democracies, 1973–2010

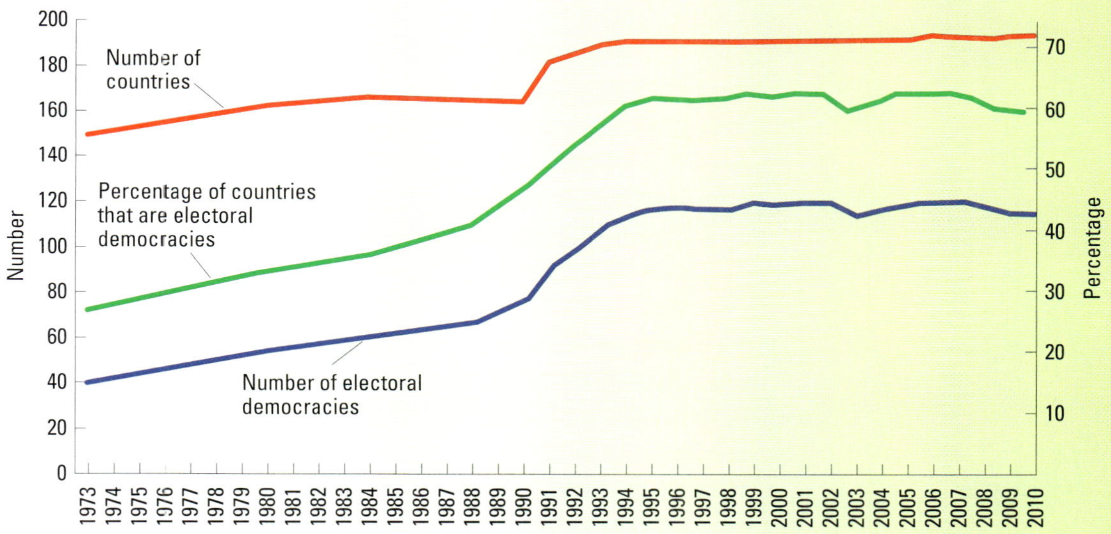

SOURCE: Freedom House elaborates their criteria at http://www.freedomhouse.org/template.cfm?page=351&ana_page=363&year=2010. The analysis comes from Larry Diamond, *The Spirit of Democracy* (New York: Times Books, 2008), p. 22; data up to 2004 come from Table 2. Freedom House supplied the data for 2007–2010.

Critical Thinking

Fewer than half of the world's countries are electoral democracies; why so few?

Patterns of Participation over Time

Did Americans become more politically apathetic in the 2000s than they were in the 1960s? Generally not, as plots of several measures of participation from 1952 through 2008 show little variation over time in the percentage of citizens who were interested

Compared with What?

Voter Turnout in European and American Elections

Compared with turnout rates in sixteen established European nations, voter turnout for American presidential elections ranks below all but three countries, and turnout for American congressional elections ranks below all sixteen. The European data show the percentage of the voting-age population voting in the most recent parliamentary election prior to 2012. The American data show voters as percentages of the eligible voting-age population that voted in the 2008 presidential election and the 2010 congressional election. Turnout in U.S. elections tends to average about fifteen points higher in presidential years than in congressional years.

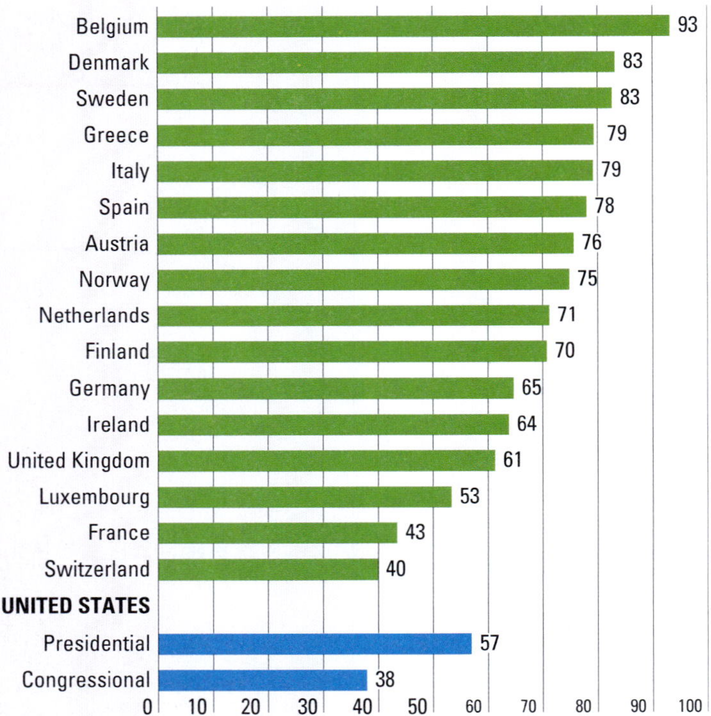

Sources: International IDEA, "Voter Turnout," http://www.idea.int/vt/viewdata.cfm#; and United States Election Project, http://elections.gmu.edu/voter_turnout.htm. The turnout rates are for the most recent elections prior to 2012 and are calculated for voting-age population.

Critical Thinking

Are Americans more politically apathetic than Europeans, or is our lower voting turnout due to some structural factors in U.S. politics?

in election campaigns, talked to others about voting, worked for candidates, or attended party meetings. The only substantial dip in participation occurred in voter turnout during the 1970s and 1980s. Turnout did increase to 1960s levels in 2004 and 2008, but even then voter turnout was much lower than in most European countries. Not only is voter turnout in the United States relatively low, but also turnout over two decades has decreased while other forms of participation have remained stable or even increased. What is going on? Who votes? Who does not? Why? And does it really matter?

The Standard Socioeconomic Explanation

Researchers have found that socioeconomic status is a good indicator of most types of conventional political participation. People with more education, higher incomes, and white-collar or professional occupations tend to be more aware of the effect of politics on their lives, to know what can be done to influence government actions, and to have the necessary resources (time and money) to take action. So they are more likely to participate in politics than are people of lower socioeconomic status. This relationship between socioeconomic status and conventional political involvement is called the **standard socioeconomic model** of participation.[51]

Unconventional political behavior is related to socioeconomic status, and in much the same way. Those who protest against U.S. government policies tend to be better educated. Moreover, this relationship holds in other countries too. One scholar notes: "Protest in advanced industrial democracies is not simply an outlet for the alienated and deprived; just the opposite often occurs."[52] In one major way, however, those who engage in unconventional political behavior differ from those who participate more conventionally: protesters tend to be younger.

Obviously, socioeconomic status does not account for all the differences in the ways people choose to participate in politics, even for conventional participation. Another important variable is age. Younger people are more likely to take part in demonstrations or boycotts and less likely to participate in conventional politics.[53] Younger people engage in more voluntary and charitable activities, but older Americans are more likely to vote, identify with the major political parties, and contact public officials.[54] Voting rates tend to increase as people grow older, until about age sixty-five, when physical infirmities begin to lower rates again.[55]

Two other variables—race and gender—have been related to participation in the past, but as times have changed, so have those relationships. Blacks, who had very low participation rates in the 1950s, now participate at rates comparable to whites when differences in socioeconomic status are taken into account.[56] Women also exhibited low participation rates in the past, but gender differences in political participation have virtually disappeared.[57] (The one exception is in attempting to persuade others how to vote, which women are less likely to do than men.)[58] Recent research on the social context of voting behavior has shown that married men and women are more likely to vote than those of either sex living without a spouse.[59]

Of all the social and economic variables, education is the strongest single factor in explaining most types of conventional political participation. A major study on civic participation details the impact of education:

> It affects the acquisition of skills; it channels opportunities for high levels of income and occupation; it places individuals in institutional settings where they can be recruited to political activity; and it fosters psychological and cognitive engagement with politics.[60]

standard socioeconomic model
A relationship between socioeconomic status and conventional political involvement: people with higher status and more education are more likely to participate than those with lower status.

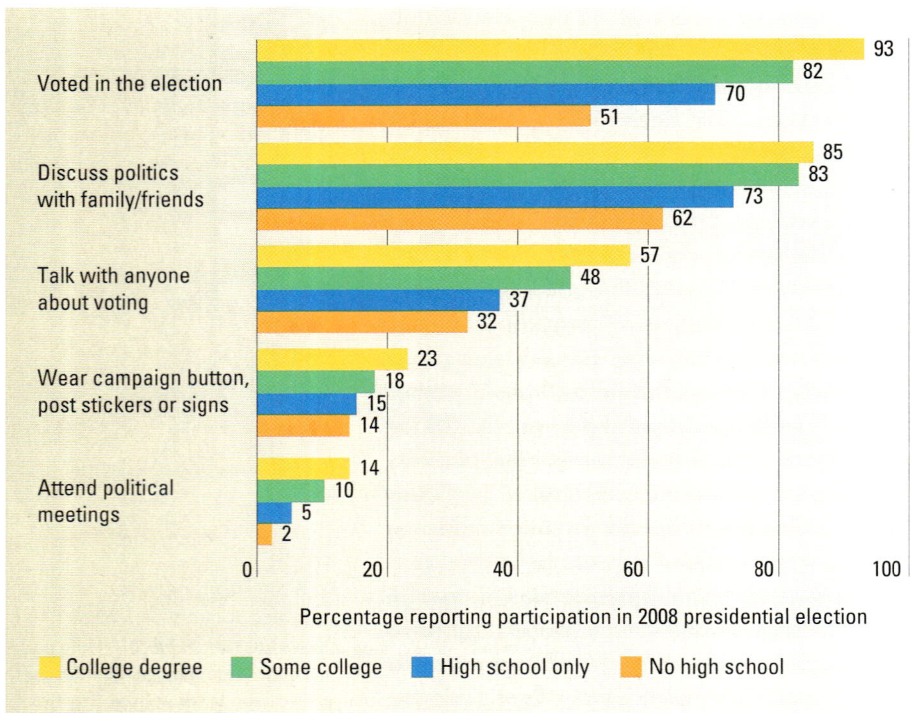

FIGURE 7.4 Effects of Education on Political Participation

Education has a powerful effect on political participation in the United States. These data from a 2008 sample show that level of education is directly related to five different forms of conventional political participation. (Respondents tend to overstate whether they voted.)

Source: This analysis was based on the 2008 American National Election Time Series Study (Ann Arbor, Mich., and Palo Alto, Calif.: University of Michigan and Stanford University).

Figure 7.4 shows the striking relationship between level of formal education and various types of conventional political behavior. The strong link between education and electoral participation raises questions about low voter turnout in the United States, both over time and relative to other democracies. The fact is that the proportion of individuals with college degrees is greater in the United States than in other countries. Moreover, that proportion has been increasing steadily. Why, then, is voter turnout in elections so low? And why has it been dropping over time?

Low Voter Turnout in America

Economists wonder why people vote at all. In economic models of rational behavior, individuals avoid actions that have no payoff, and elections are rarely so close that an individual voter decides an outcome.[61] Unlike economists, political scientists wonder why citizens fail to vote. Voting is a low-initiative form of participation that can satisfy all three motives for political participation: showing allegiance to the nation, obtaining particularized benefits, and influencing broad policy. How then do we explain the decline in voter turnout in the United States?

The Decline in Voting over Time. The graph of voter turnout in Figure 7.5 shows that turnout in presidential elections was higher in the 1950s and 1960s than in the 1970s, 1980s, and 1990s, but it increased somewhat in 2004 and 2008.[62] The downward trend began with a sizable drop between the 1968 and 1972 elections. During this period (in 1971, actually) Congress proposed and the states ratified the Twenty-sixth Amendment, which expanded the electorate by lowering the voting age from

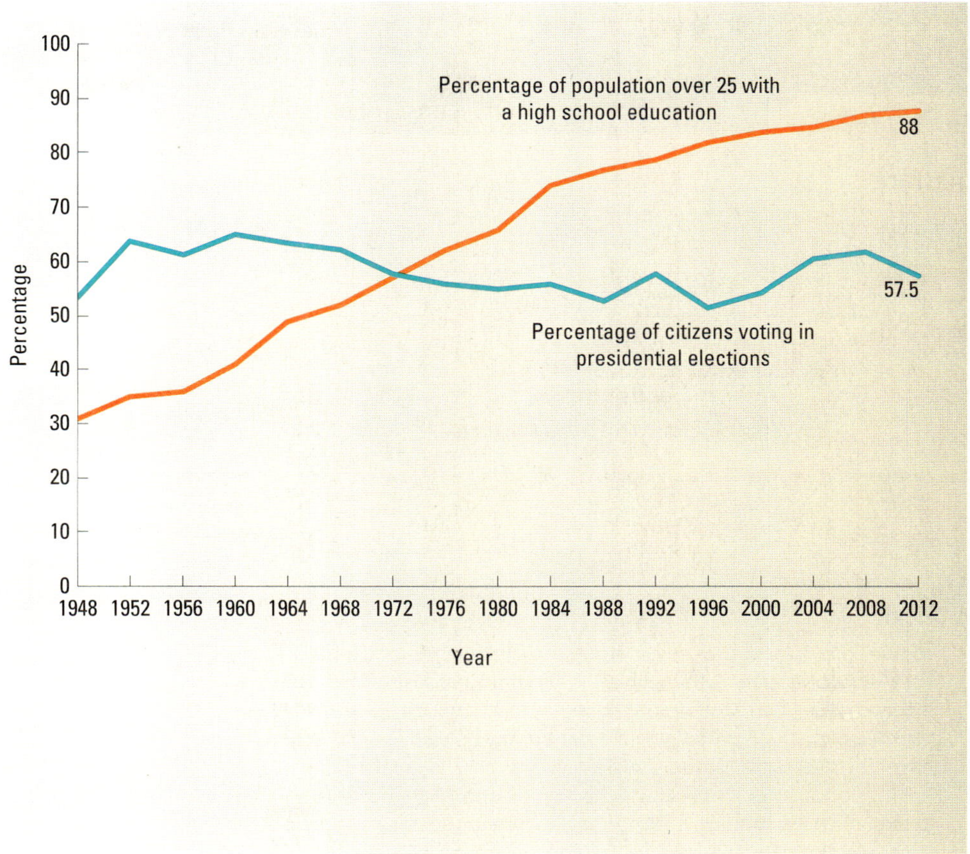

FIGURE 7.5 The Decline of Voter Turnout: An Unsolved Puzzle

Education strongly predicts the likelihood of voting in the United States. The percentage of adult citizens with a high school education or more has grown steadily since the end of World War II, but the overall rate of voter turnout trended downward from 1960 to 1996 and is still below the levels two decades after the war. Why turnout decreased as education increased is an unsolved puzzle in American voting behavior.

Sources: U.S. Census Bureau, Statistical Abstract 1962 and Statistical Abstract 2010, "Table A-1. Years of School Completed by People 25 Years and Over, by Age and Sex: Selected Years 1940 to 2008," Kevin Liptak, "Report Shows Turnout Lower than 2008 and 2004," CNN Blog, November 8, 2012; and Harold W. Stanley and Richard G. Niemi, *Vital Statistics on American Politics, 2009–2010* (Washington, D.C.: CQ Press, 2009), Table 1.1. The percentage voting in elections is based on the eligible voter population, not the voting-age population.

twenty-one to eighteen. Because people younger than twenty-one are much less likely to vote, their eligibility actually reduced the overall national turnout rate (the percentage of those eligible to vote who actually vote). Although young nonvoters inevitably vote more often as they grow up, observers estimate that the enfranchisement of eighteen-year-olds accounts for about one or two percentage points in the total decline in turnout since 1952. Nevertheless, that still leaves more than ten percentage points to be explained in the lower rates since 1972.[63]

Voter turnout has declined in most established democracies since the 1980s, but not as much as in the United States. Given that educational levels are increasing virtually everywhere, the puzzle is why turnout has decreased instead of increased. Many researchers have tried to solve this puzzle.[64] Some attribute most of the decline to changes in voters' attitudes toward politics: beliefs that government is no longer responsive to citizens, that politicians are too packaged, that campaigns are too long.[65] Another is a change in attitude toward political parties, along with a decline in the extent to which citizens identify with a political party (a topic we discuss in Chapter 8).[66] According to these psychological explanations, voter turnout in the United States is not likely to increase until the government does something to restore people's faith in the effectiveness of voting—with or without political parties.

According to the age explanation, turnout in the United States is destined to remain a percentage point or two below its highs of the 1960s because of the lower voting rate of citizens younger than twenty-one. Turnout rates do increase as young

VOTER REGISTRATION

powered by: ROCK THE VOTE

2 3 4 5

Registrant

En español

Email Address [ ] [?]

ZIP Code [ ] [?]

Date of Birth [ ] [?] MM-DD-YYYY

☐ I am a U.S. citizen.

☐ I am registering to vote for the first time.

you are an American citizen living abroad or a uniformed military voter, **click here** to register to vote.

NEXT STEP >

Register—and Rock the Vote

To increase turnout of young people, an organization called Rock the Vote was formed in 1990 within the recording industry (later incorporating the entertainment and sports communities) to mobilize young people to increase youth voter turnout. Rock the Vote claims to have registered more than 5 million young people to vote since, using "music, popular culture, new technologies and grassroots organizing to motivate and mobilize young people in our country to participate in every election, with the goal of seizing the power of the youth vote to create political and social change." (If you are eligible to vote but not registered, why not go try its website? Go to http://www.rockthevote.com/.)

Courtesy Rock the Vote

people age, which suggests that voting is habit forming.[67] In 2004, almost 49 percent of those eighteen to twenty-nine years old turned out to vote.[68] In 2008, the Obama campaign made a special appeal to young voters, and youth voter turnout increased to 52 percent.[69] Young people actually voted about one point more in 2012 although the overall turnout declined.

U.S. Turnout Versus Turnout in Other Countries. Scholars cite two factors to explain the low voter turnout in the United States compared with that in other countries. First are the differences in voting laws and administrative machinery. In a few countries, voting is compulsory, and obviously turnout is extremely high. But other methods can encourage voting: declaring election days to be public holidays or providing a two-day voting period. In 1845, Congress set election day for the first Tuesday after the first Monday in November, but a reform group—called "Why Tuesday?"—wants Congress to change election day to a weekend.[70]

Furthermore, nearly every other democratic country places the burden of registration on the government rather than on the individual voter. This is important. Voting in the United States is a two-stage process, and the first stage (going to the proper officials to register) has required more initiative than the second stage (going to the polling booth to cast a ballot). In most American states, the registration process has been separate from the voting process in terms of both time (usually voters had to register weeks in advance of an election) and geography (often voters had to register at the county courthouse, not their polling place).[71] The nine states that do allow citizens to register and vote on the same day have consistently higher voter participation rates.[72] Turnout is higher in Oregon, where everyone votes by mail.[73] No state votes by Internet, yet. In 2009, the city of Honolulu claimed to hold the first all-digital election—voting online or by phone—but it involved only about 115,000 voters.[74]

Regardless of voting ease, registration procedures for eligibility often are obscure, requiring potential voters to call around to find out what to do. People who move (and younger people move more frequently) have to reregister. In short, although voting requires little initiative, registration usually has required high initiative. If we compute voter turnout on the basis of those who are registered to vote, about 80 percent of Americans vote, a figure that moves the United States to the middle (but not the top) of all democratic nations.[75]

To increase turnout, Congress in 1993 passed the so-called motor-voter law, which aimed to increase voter registration by requiring states to permit registration by mail and when obtaining or renewing a driver's license and by encouraging registration at other facilities, such as public assistance agencies. By the 1997–1998 election cycle, over half of all voter registration took place through motor vehicle agencies and other agencies specified in the motor-voter law. Nevertheless, a 2009 study showed that half of all voters were unaware that they could register at motor vehicle offices.[76]

Besides burdensome registration procedures, another factor usually cited to explain low turnout in American elections is the lack of political parties that mobilize the vote of particular social groups, especially lower-income and less educated people.[77] American parties do make an effort to get out the vote, but neither party is as closely linked to specific groups as are parties in many other countries, where certain parties work hand in hand with specific ethnic, occupational, or religious groups. Research shows that strong party–group links can significantly increase turnout.[78] One important study claims that "changing mobilization patterns by parties, campaigns, and social movements accounts for at least half of the decline in electoral participation since the 1960s."[79]

Other research suggests that although well-funded, vigorous campaigns mobilize citizens to vote, the effect depends on the type of citizens, the nature of the election, and (yes) the weather.[80] Highly educated, low-income citizens are more likely to be stimulated to vote than are less educated, high-income citizens, but lower-class citizens can be more easily mobilized to vote in presidential elections than in nonpresidential elections.[81] Some thought that the Internet would invite new classes of people to participate in politics, but well-educated and high-income people are even more apt to participate online.[82] Citizens are more likely to turn out to vote when the elections are competitive or close.[83] One study observed that college students' decision to register and vote in their home state or in their college state depended in part on which had the more competitive races.[84]

To these explanations for low voter turnout in the United States—the traditional burden of registration and the lack of strong party–group links—we add another. Although the act of voting requires low initiative, the process of learning about the scores of candidates on the ballot in American elections requires a great deal of initiative. Some people undoubtedly fail to vote simply because they feel inadequate to the task of deciding among candidates for the many offices on the ballot in U.S. elections.

Teachers, newspaper columnists, and public affairs groups tend to worry a great deal about low voter turnout in the United States, suggesting that it signifies some sort of political sickness—or at least that it gives us a bad mark for democracy. Some others who study elections closely seem less concerned.[85] One scholar argues:

> Turnout rates do not indicate the amount of electing—the frequency … the range of offices and decisions, the "value" of the vote—to which a country's citizens are entitled…. Thus, although the turnout rate in the United States is below that of most other democracies, American citizens do not necessarily do less voting than other citizens; most probably, they do more.[86]

Despite such words of assurance, the nagging thought remains that turnout ought to be higher, so various organizations mount get-out-the-vote campaigns before elections. Civic leaders often back the campaigns because they value voting for its contribution to political order.

★ 7.6 Participation and Freedom, Equality, and Order

★ Evaluate the relationship between the values of freedom, equality, and order and political participation in American democracy.

As we have seen, Americans do participate in government in various ways and to a reasonable extent, compared with citizens of other countries. What is the relationship of political participation to the values of freedom, equality, and order?

Participation and Freedom

From the standpoint of normative theory, the relationship between participation and freedom is clear. Individuals should be free to participate in government and politics in the way they want and as much as they want. And they should be free not to participate as well. Ideally, all barriers to participation (such as restrictive voting registration and limitations on campaign expenditures) should be abolished, as should any schemes for compulsory voting. According to the normative perspective, we should not worry about low voter turnout because citizens should have the freedom not to vote as well as to vote.

In theory, freedom to participate also means that individuals should be able to use their wealth, connections, knowledge, organizational power (including sheer numbers in organized protests), or any other resource to influence government decisions, provided they do so legally. Of all these resources, the individual vote may be the weakest—and the least important—means of exerting political influence. Obviously, then, freedom as a value in political participation favors those with the resources to advance their own political self-interest.

Participation and Equality

The relationship between participation and equality is also clear. Each citizen's ability to influence government should be equal to that of every other citizen, so that differences in personal resources do not work against the poor or the otherwise disadvantaged.[87] Elections, then, serve the ideal of equality better than any other means of political participation. Formal rules for counting ballots—in particular, one person, one vote—cancel differences in resources among individuals.

At the same time, groups of people who have few resources individually can combine their votes to wield political power. Various European ethnic groups exercised this type of power in the late nineteenth and early twentieth centuries, when their votes won them entry to the sociopolitical system and allowed them to share in its benefits. More recently, blacks, Hispanics, homosexuals, and those with disabilities have used their voting power to gain political recognition. However, minorities often have had to use unconventional forms of participation to win the right to vote. As two major scholars of political participation put it, "Protest is the great equalizer, the political action that weights intensity as well as sheer numbers."[88]

Participation and Order

The relationship between participation and order is complicated. Some types of participation (pledging allegiance, voting) promote order and so are encouraged by those who value order; other types promote disorder and so are discouraged. Many citizens—men and women alike—even resisted giving women the right to vote for fear of upsetting the social order by altering the traditional roles of men and women.

Both conventional and unconventional participation can lead to the ouster of government officials, but the regime—the political system itself—is threatened more by unconventional participation. To maintain order, the government has a stake in converting unconventional participation to conventional participation whenever possible. We can easily imagine this tactic being used by authoritarian governments, but democratic governments also use it. According to documents obtained after September 11, 2001, the FBI not only increased surveillance of groups with suspected ties to foreign terrorists but also began monitoring other groups that protested public policies.[89]

Popular protests can spread beyond original targets. Think about student unrest on college campuses during the Vietnam War. In private and public colleges alike, thousands of students stopped traffic, occupied buildings, destroyed property, boycotted classes, disrupted lectures, staged guerrilla theater, and behaved in other unconventional ways to protest the war, racism, capitalism, the behavior of their college presidents, the president of the United States, the military establishment, and all other institutions. (We are not exaggerating here. Students did such things at our home universities after members of the National Guard shot and killed four students at a demonstration at Kent State University in Ohio on May 4, 1970.)

Confronted by civil strife and disorder in the nation's institutions of higher learning, Congress took action. On March 23, 1971, it enacted and sent to the states the proposed Twenty-sixth Amendment, lowering the voting age to eighteen. Three-quarters of the state legislatures had to ratify the amendment before it became part of the Constitution. Astonishingly, thirty-eight states (the required number) complied by July 1, establishing a new speed record for ratification and cutting the old record nearly in half.[90] (Ironically, voting rights were not high on the list of students' demands.)

Testimony by members of Congress before the Judiciary Committee stated that the eighteen-year-old vote would "harness the energy of young people and direct it into useful and constructive channels," to keep students from becoming "more militant" and engaging "in destructive activities of a dangerous nature."[91] As one observer argued, the right to vote was extended to eighteen-year-olds not because young people demanded it but because "public officials believed suffrage expansion to be a means of institutionalizing youths' participation in politics, which would, in turn, curb disorder."[92]

7.7 Participation and the Models of Democracy

★ Identify the purposes elections serve and explain the relationship between elections and majoritarian and pluralist models of democracy.

Ostensibly, elections are institutional mechanisms that implement democracy by allowing citizens to choose among candidates or issues. But elections also serve several other important purposes:[93]

- Elections socialize political activity. They transform what might otherwise consist of sporadic, citizen-initiated acts into a routine public function. That is, the opportunity to vote for change encourages citizens to refrain from demonstrating in the streets. This helps preserve government stability by containing and channeling away potentially disruptive or dangerous forms of mass political activity.
- Elections institutionalize access to political power. They allow ordinary citizens to run for political office or to play an important role in selecting political leaders. Working to elect a candidate encourages the campaign worker to identify problems or propose solutions to the newly elected official.
- Elections bolster the state's power and authority. The opportunity to participate in elections helps convince citizens that the government is responsive to their needs and wants, which reinforces its legitimacy.

Participation and Majoritarianism

Although the majoritarian model assumes that government responsiveness to popular demands comes through mass participation in politics, majoritarianism views participation rather narrowly. It favors conventional, institutionalized behavior—primarily voting in elections. Because majoritarianism relies on counting votes to determine what the majority wants, its bias toward equality in political participation is strong. Clearly, a class bias in voting exists because of the strong influence of socioeconomic status on turnout. Simply put, better-educated, wealthier citizens are more likely to participate in elections, and get-out-the-vote campaigns cannot counter this distinct bias.[94] Because it favors collective decisions formalized through elections, majoritarianism has little place for motivated, resourceful individuals to exercise private influence over government actions.

Majoritarianism also limits individual freedom in another way: its focus on voting as the major means of mass participation narrows the scope of conventional political behavior by defining which political actions are "orderly" and acceptable. By favoring equality and order in political participation, majoritarianism goes hand in hand with the ideological orientation of communitarianism (see Chapter 1).

Participation and Pluralism

Resourceful citizens who want the government's help with problems find a haven in the pluralist model of democracy. A decentralized and organizationally complex form of government allows many points of access and accommodates various forms of conventional participation in addition to voting. For example, wealthy people and well-funded groups can afford to hire lobbyists to press their interests in Congress. In one view of pluralist democracy, citizens are free to ply and wheedle public officials to further their own selfish visions of the public good. From another viewpoint, pluralism offers citizens the opportunity to be treated as individuals when dealing with the government, to influence policymaking in special circumstances, and to fulfill (insofar as possible in representative government) their social potential through participation in community affairs.

SUMMARY

7.1 Democracy and Political Participation

- Most people participate in politics in conventional ways—voting and using established institutions of representative government.
- Some participate in unconventional ways that challenge established institutions.
- Protesters who toppled dictators during the Arab Spring certainly behaved unconventionally.

7.2 Unconventional Participation

- The Boston Tea Party of 1773 that protested British rule was an early instance of unconventional participation in America.
- Citizens who marched for civil rights in the late 1950s and early 1960s succeeded in changing laws through unconventional political participation.

7.3 Conventional Participation

- Citizens often unconsciously participate in politics, for example by reciting the Pledge of Allegiance and flying the flag on holidays, which constitute supportive behavior.
- More consciously, citizens engage in high-initiative influencing behavior when they seek to modify or reverse government policy.
- American citizens engage in conventional and unconventional participation about as much as European citizens.

7.4 Participating Through Voting

- Although the United States was the first country to hold elections with mass suffrage, only white male property holders could vote initially.

- Although constitutional amendments after the Civil War gave blacks the right to vote, they were systematically blocked from voting until the Voting Rights Act of 1965 and subsequent court decisions.
- Women did not get the right to vote nationwide until the Nineteenth Amendment passed in 1920.
- Progressive reforms—the initiative and referendum—facilitated voting on state policies, but citizens cannot vote on national policies in a referendum.
- During the last four decades, a worldwide trend shows more nations qualifying as electoral democracies.
- Compared to Western European nations, voting turnout in the United States is very low.

7.5 Explaining Political Participation

- According to the standard socioeconomic model, increasing political participation is linked to increases in education, wealth, and occupational status.
- Voting turnout in the United States presents a puzzle, because voting turnout has remained flat or even declined while education has increased.
- Cited causes of low voting turnout are registration requirements, lack of strong parties to mobilize votes, and too frequent elections.

7.6 Participation and Freedom, Equality, and Order

- Freedom holds that people should be able to participate in politics as much (or as little) as they want and should be able to use all their resources in the process.

- Equality holds that each citizen's ability to influence government should be no greater than any other's, which is formally true in voting but not in influencing how others vote.
- Order is generally promoted by conventional participation but undercut by unconventional participation.

7.7 Participation and the Models of Democracy

- The majoritarian model assumes that government responds to popular demands expressed through conventional participation, primarily elections.
- The pluralist model encourages other forms of participation to influence government, including well-financed efforts to persuade both voters and officials.

ASSESSING YOUR UNDERSTANDING WITH APLIA...YOUR VIRTUAL TUTOR!

aplia Engage. Prepare. Educate.

7.1 Define political participation and distinguish among types of participation.

1. What distinguishes conventional from unconventional political participation?
2. Is terrorism a form of political participation?

7.2 Identify examples of unconventional participation in American history and evaluate their effectiveness.

1. Does unconventional political participation produce results? Give an historical example both ways.
2. Are Americans more or less likely than Europeans to engage in unconventional participation?

7.3 Distinguish between supportive acts and influencing acts of political participation.

1. Cite an example of supportive political behavior.
2. Cite an example of influencing political behavior.

3. How can suing in court constitute a form of political behavior?

7.4 Trace the expansion of suffrage in the United States and assess the impact of expanded suffrage on voting turnout.

1. Does expansion of suffrage in the United States compare well or poorly with most other countries?
2. Does voter turnout in the United States compare well or poorly with other countries?

7.5 Identify the factors that affect political participation, especially voting.

1. What is meant by the "standard socioeconomic model" for explaining political participation?
2. Compared with the level of education in the United States, has voting turnout fulfilled the standard socioeconomic model?
3. Which requires more citizen initiative, to register to vote or to vote itself? Why, and why does it matter?

7.6 **Evaluate the relationship between the values of freedom, equality, and order and political participation in American democracy.**

1. Which value—freedom, equality, or order—is best served by voting as a form of participation and why?
2. How can political participation both serve and undermine order?

7.7 **Identify the purposes elections serve and explain the relationship between elections and majoritarian and pluralist models of democracy.**

1. What purposes are served by elections other than selecting candidates or deciding issues?
2. Which model of democracy—majoritarian or pluralist—is better served by elections and why?

8 Political Parties

"Tea Party" or "tea party"? The nation's two premier newspapers differ on how to write it. The *New York Times* uses capital letters, treating the Tea Party as a distinct organization like the Republican Party or the Democratic Party. The *Wall Street Journal* writes tea party in lowercase, regarding it as a disorganized movement. Lowercase seems more appropriate, for the tea party—although a nationwide movement—lacks a national organization.

Research in 2011 identified about 800 local tea party organizations with perhaps 200,000 members.[1] More prominent in the media are regional organizations that seek to embrace local groups under their umbrella. Some adopt the tea party label; some do not. Among those that do are the Tea Party Express, National Tea Party Federation, Tea Party Patriots, Nationwide Tea Party Coalition, and Tea Party Nation. Among those that do not are Freedom Works, Americans for Prosperity, Independence Caucus, and Patriot Action Network. An Internet search also turns up scores of state and local tea party groups—often ten or more in a single state.

Tea party groups agree in advocating smaller government. They demand reduced government spending to lower the national debt while also favoring lower taxes. In the summer of 2009, for example, tea partiers protested against Democratic members of Congress for supporting President Obama's economic stimulus program and healthcare legislation. The tea party certainly affected the subsequent congressional election, framing it as a referendum on Obama's policies. In the 2010 primary elections, tea party groups endorsed and elected scores of Republican candidates committed to their positions; they endorsed no Democrats. In the 2010 general election, about half of all Republican congressional candidates were endorsed by one or more tea party groups.

In the congressional elections, voters favored Republican over Democratic candidates by 52 to 45 percent, reversing the 52–45 split enjoyed by Democrats in 2008. That swing of fourteen points favored Republican congressional candidates in general, as sixty-six Republicans won House seats in 2010 previously won by Democrats in 2008. Comparing the percentages of votes cast in both elections for seats contested by both parties shows that Republicans endorsed by the tea party won by similar percentage margins as those not endorsed.[2] Tea party endorsements did not increase the winning margins for their candidates; virtually all Republicans enjoyed comparable surges in votes in 2010. Tea party endorsements counted more for nominating Republican candidates in primary elections than in electing them in the general election.

As a movement, however, the tea party had a definite impact on the 2010 congressional elections by defining and sharpening Republican opposition to Obama and thus to Democrats running for reelection. Given that 435 congressional elections are scattered among fifty states, the tea party's decentralized nature posed no problem and perhaps constituted an advantage in 2010. The 2012 presidential election, however, involved a few candidates seeking one national office, for which a decentralized structure hurts, not helps.

Various tea party groups endorsed different Republican presidential hopefuls, and within groups, tea partiers were divided in 2012 among the leading candidates: Mitt Romney, Newt Gingrich, Rick Santorum, and Ron Paul. Simply put, the tea party was not a party to the 2012 presidential election.

U.S. politics is characterized by a two-party system. The Democratic and Republican parties have dominated national and state politics for more than 125 years. Their domination is more complete than that of any pair of parties in any other democratic government. Although all democracies have some form of multiparty politics, very few have a stable two-party system, Britain being the most notable exception (see "Compared with What? Only Two to Tangle"). Most people take our two-party system for granted, not realizing that it is arguably the most distinctive feature of American politics.

Why do we have any political parties? What functions do they perform? How did we become a nation of Democrats and Republicans? Do these parties truly differ in their platforms and behavior? Are parties really necessary for democratic government, or do they just get in the way of citizens and their government? In this chapter, we answer these questions by examining political parties, perhaps the most misunderstood element of American politics.

Compared with What?

Only Two to Tangle

Compared with party systems in other countries, the U.S. two-party system is unusual indeed. Most democracies have multiparty systems in which four or five parties win enough seats in the legislature to contest for government power. Even the few countries classified as having two-party systems have minor parties that regularly contest

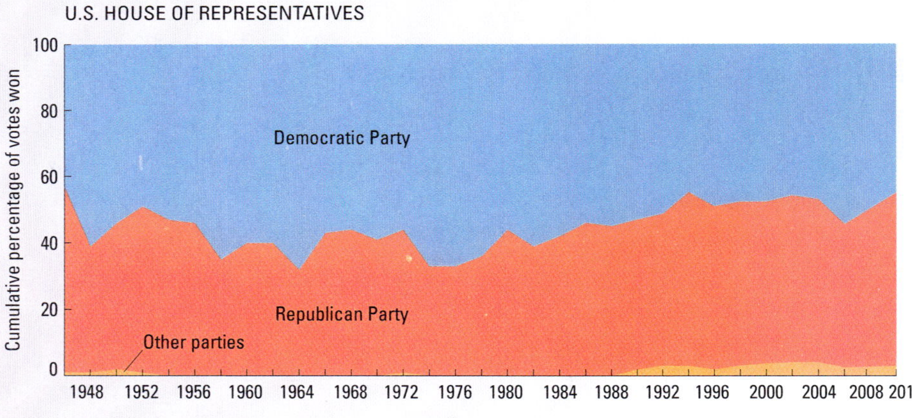

8.1 Political Parties and Their Functions

★ Define political party and list the functions performed by parties in democratic government.

According to democratic theory, the primary means by which citizens control their government is voting in free elections. Most Americans agree that voting is important. Of those surveyed after the 2008 presidential campaign, 89 percent felt that elections make the government "pay attention to what the people think."[3] Americans are not nearly as supportive of the role played by political parties in elections, however. Indeed, thousands of donors backed an organization, Americans Elect, that launched a nonpartisan online site (americanselect.org) to nominate a 2012 presidential ticket composed of candidates from different parties and that succeeded in getting on the ballot in scores of states. Apparently, many Americans think that politics would function better without political parties.

Nevertheless, Americans are quick to condemn as "undemocratic" countries that do not regularly hold elections contested by political parties. In truth, Americans have a love–hate relationship with political parties. They believe that parties are necessary for democratic government; at the same time, they think parties are somehow

seats and win enough votes to complicate national politics. The United Kingdom is the most notable example of a country reputed to have a two-party system. The purer U.S. pattern of two-party politics shows clearly in these graphs of votes cast for party candidates running for the U.S. House compared with votes cast for party candidates running for the British House of Commons.

Only 40 percent of Americans surveyed in 2011 "believed that the Republican and Democratic parties do an 'adequate job' of representing the people versus 52 percent who thought that they do 'such a poor job' that a third party was needed."*

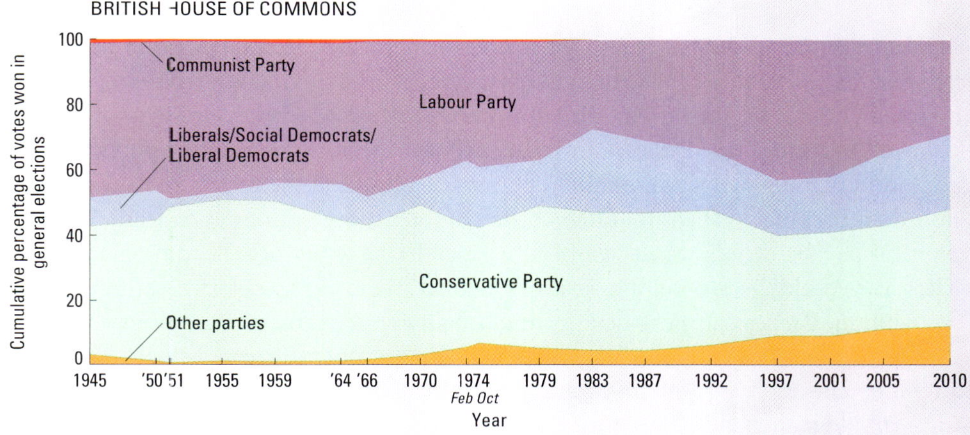

Sources: Thomas T Mackie and Richard Rose, *The International Almanac of Electoral History*, 3rd ed. (Washington, D.C.: CQ Press, 1991); http://www.electionguide.org, http://www.thegreenpapers.com/G06/HouseVoteByParty.phtml, and http://news.bbc.co.uk/2/shared/election2010/results/.

*Jeffrey M. Jones, "Support for Third U.S. Party Dips, but Is Still Majority View," Gallup Poll Report, 2 May 2011.

obstructionist and not to be trusted. This distrust is particularly strong among younger voters. To better appreciate the role of political parties in democratic government, we must understand exactly what parties are and what they do.

What Is a Political Party?

political party
An organization that sponsors candidates for political office under the organization's name.

nomination
Designation as an official candidate of a political party.

A **political party** is an organization that sponsors candidates for political office *under the organization's name.* The italicized part of this definition is important. True political parties select individuals to run for public office through a formal **nomination** process, which designates them as the parties' official candidates. This activity distinguishes the Democratic and Republican parties from interest groups. The AFL-CIO and the National Association of Manufacturers are interest groups. They often support candidates, but they do not nominate them to run as their avowed representatives. If they did, they would be transformed into political parties. Because the so-called "tea party" does not nominate its own candidates, it is not a political party. True, five political entrepreneurs ran as congressional candidates on the Tea Party label in 2010, but none were endorsed by significant tea party groups and all lost. In short, the sponsoring of candidates, designated as representatives of the organization, is what defines an organization as a party.

Most democratic theorists agree that a modern nation-state cannot practice democracy without at least two political parties that regularly contest elections. In fact, the link between democracy and political parties is so firm that many people define *democratic government* in terms of competitive party politics.[4] A former president of the American Political Science Association held that even for a small nation, "democracy is impossible save in terms of parties."[5]

Party Functions

political system
A set of interrelated institutions that links people with government.

Parties contribute to democratic government through the functions they perform for the **political system**—the set of interrelated institutions that link people with government. Four of the most important party functions are nominating candidates for election to public office, structuring the voting choice in elections, proposing alternative government programs, and coordinating the actions of government officials.

Nominating Candidates. Question: Is *every* American citizen qualified to hold public office? A few scholars have thought they were, proposing that government positions be filled "randomly"—that is, through lotteries.[6] Most observers, however, hold that political leadership requires certain abilities (if not special knowledge or public experience) and that not just anyone should be entrusted to head the government. The question then becomes, Who should be chosen among those who offer to lead? Without political parties, voters would confront a bewildering array of self-nominated candidates, each seeking votes on the basis of personal friendships, celebrity status, or name recognition. Parties can provide a form of quality control for their nominees through the process of peer review. Party insiders, the nominees' peers, usually know the strengths and faults of potential candidates much better than average voters do and thus can judge their suitability for representing the party. Founders of the Internet site, americanselect.org, thought that average voters would do better.

In nominating candidates, parties often do more than pass judgment on potential office seekers; sometimes they recruit talented individuals to become candidates. In this way, parties help not only to ensure a minimum level of quality among candidates who run for office but also to raise the quality of those candidates.

Structuring the Voting Choice. Political parties help democratic government by structuring the voting choice—reducing the number of candidates on the ballot to those who have a realistic chance of winning. Established parties—those with experience in contesting elections—acquire a following of loyal voters who guarantee the party's candidates a predictable base of votes. The ability of established parties to mobilize their supporters discourages nonparty candidates from running for office and new parties from forming. Consequently, the realistic choice is between candidates offered by the major parties, reducing the amount of new information that voters need to choose their leaders.

Contrast the voting decision in our stable competitive two-party system (and the outcome) with Russian voters' choices in their December 2011 parliamentary election to the State Duma, the lower house of the Russian Federation. The Russian ballot listed seven parties. Three parties failed to receive at least 7 percent of the parliamentary vote and thus won no seats. The four that did were seated in the previous parliament. United Russia, Prime Minister Vladimir Putin's party, lost seventy-seven seats but still emerged as the majority party. Election observers (and many Russian citizens) viewed the elections as fraudulent, but even in honest elections, the presence of multiple parties tends to split opposition to a dominant regime and prevent alternation in power. Two-party systems tend to promote citizens' ability to replace government leaders.

Proposing Alternative Government Programs. Parties help voters choose among candidates by proposing alternative programs of government action—the general policies their candidates will pursue if they gain office. In a stable party system, even if voters know nothing about the qualities of the parties' candidates, they can vote rationally for the candidates of the party that has policies they favor. The specific policies advocated vary from candidate to candidate and from election to election. However, the types of policies advocated by candidates of one party tend to differ from those proposed by candidates of other parties. Although there are exceptions, candidates of the same party tend to favor policies that fit their party's underlying political philosophy, or ideology.

In many countries, parties' names, such as *Conservative* and *Socialist,* reflect their political stance. The Democrats and Republicans have ideologically neutral names, but many minor parties in the United States have used their names to advertise their policies—for example, the Libertarian Party, the Socialist Party, and the Green Party.[7] The neutrality of the two major parties' names suggests that their policies are similar. This is not true. As we shall see, they regularly adopt very different policies in their platforms.

Coordinating the Actions of Government Officials. Finally, party organizations help coordinate the actions of public officials. A government based on the separation of powers, such as that of the United States, divides responsibilities for making public policy. The president and the leaders of the House and Senate are not required to cooperate with one another. Political party organizations are the major means for bridging the separate powers to produce coordinated policies that can govern the country effectively. Parties do this in two ways. First, candidates' and officeholders' political fortunes are linked to their party organization, which can bestow and withhold favors. Second, and perhaps more important in the United States, members of the same party in the presidency, the House, and the Senate tend to share political principles and thus often voluntarily cooperate in making policy.

So why do we have parties? One expert notes that successful politicians in the United States need electoral and governing majorities and that "no collection of ambitious politicians has long been able to think of a way to achieve their goals in this democracy save in terms of political parties."[8]

★ 8.2 A History of U.S. Party Politics

★ Outline the history of the U.S. political party system.

The two major U.S. parties are among the oldest in the world. In fact, the Democratic Party, founded in 1828 but with roots reaching back to the late 1700s, has a strong claim to being the oldest party in existence. Its closest rival is the British Conservative Party, formed in 1832, two decades before the Republican Party was organized in 1854. Several generations of citizens have supported the Democratic and Republican parties, and they are part of American history. They have become institutionalized in our political process.

The Preparty Period

Today we think of party activities as normal, even essential, to American politics. It was not always so. The Constitution makes no mention of political parties, and none existed when the Constitution was written in 1787. It was common then to refer to groups pursuing some common political interest as *factions*. Although factions were seen as inevitable in politics, they were also considered dangerous.[9] One argument for adopting the Constitution—proposed in *Federalist* No. 10 (see Chapter 3)—was that its federal system would prevent factional influences from controlling the government.

Factions existed even under British rule. In colonial assemblies, supporters of the governor (and thus of the Crown) were known as *Tories* or *Loyalists,* and their opponents were called *Whigs* or *Patriots.* After independence, the arguments over whether to adopt the Constitution produced a different alignment of factions. Those who backed the Constitution were loosely known as *Federalists,* their opponents as *Antifederalists.* At this stage, the groups could not be called parties because they did not sponsor candidates for election.

Elections then were vastly different from elections today. The Constitution provided for the president and vice president to be chosen by an **electoral college**—a body of electors who met in the capitals of their respective states to cast their ballots. Initially, in most states, the legislatures, not the voters, chose the electors (one for each senator and representative in Congress). Presidential elections in the early years of the nation, then, actually were decided by a handful of political leaders. (See Chapter 9 for a discussion of the electoral college in modern presidential politics.) Often they met in small, secret groups, called **caucuses**, to propose candidates for public office. Typically, they were composed of like-minded members of state legislatures and Congress. This was the setting for George Washington's election as the first president in 1789.

We can classify Washington as a Federalist because he supported the Constitution, but he was not a factional leader and actually opposed factional politics. His immense prestige, coupled with his political neutrality, left Washington unopposed for the office of president, and he was elected unanimously by the electoral college. During Washington's administration, however, the political cleavage sharpened between those who favored a stronger national government and those who wanted a less powerful, more decentralized national government.

The first group, led by Alexander Hamilton, proclaimed themselves *Federalists.* The second group, led by Thomas Jefferson, called themselves *Republicans.* (Although

---

electoral college
A body of electors chosen by voters to cast ballots for president and vice president.

caucus
A closed meeting of the members of a political party to decide questions of policy and the selection of candidates for office.

they used the same name, they were *not* the Republicans we know today.) The Jeffersonians chose the name *Republicans* to distinguish themselves from the "aristocratic" tendencies of Hamilton's Federalists. The Federalists countered by calling the Republicans the *Democratic Republicans,* attempting to link Jefferson's party to the disorder (and beheadings) in the French Revolution, led by "radical democrats."

The First Party System: Federalists and Democratic Republicans

Washington was reelected president unanimously in 1792, but his vice president, John Adams, was opposed by a candidate backed by the Democratic Republicans. This brief skirmish foreshadowed the nation's first party struggle over the presidency. Disheartened by the political split in his administration, Washington spoke out against "the baneful effects" of parties in his farewell address in 1796. Nonetheless, parties already existed in the political system, as Figure 8.1 (p. 212) shows. In the election of 1796, the Federalists supported Vice President John Adams to succeed Washington as president. The Democratic Republicans backed Thomas Jefferson for president but could not agree on a vice-presidential candidate. In the electoral college, Adams won seventy-one votes to Jefferson's sixty-eight, and both ran ahead of other candidates. At that time, the Constitution provided that the presidency would go to the candidate who won the most votes in the electoral college, with the vice presidency going to the runner-up (like a school election). So Adams, a Federalist, had to accept Jefferson, a Democratic Republican, as his vice president. Obviously, the Constitution did not anticipate a presidential contest between candidates from opposing political parties.

The party function of nominating candidates emerged more clearly in the election of 1800. Both parties caucused in Congress to nominate candidates for president and vice president. The result was the first true party contest for the presidency. The Federalists nominated John Adams and Charles Pinckney; the Democratic Republicans nominated Thomas Jefferson and Aaron Burr. This time, both Democratic Republican candidates won. However, the new party organization worked too well. According to the Constitution, each elector had to vote by ballot for two persons. The Democratic Republican electors unanimously cast their two votes for Jefferson and Burr. The presidency was to go to the candidate with the most votes, but due to party discipline the top two candidates were tied! Although Jefferson was the party's presidential candidate and Burr its vice-presidential candidate, the Constitution empowered the House of Representatives to choose either one of them as president. After seven days and thirty-six ballots, the House decided in favor of Jefferson.

The Twelfth Amendment, ratified in 1804, prevented a repeat of the troublesome election outcomes of 1796 and 1800. It required the electoral college to vote separately for president and vice president, implicitly recognizing that parties would nominate different candidates for the two offices.

The election of 1800 marked the beginning of the end for the Federalists, who lost the next four elections. By 1820, the Federalists were no more. The Democratic Republican candidate, James Monroe, was reelected in the first presidential contest without party competition since Washington's time. (Monroe received all but one electoral vote, reportedly cast against him so that Washington would remain the only president ever elected unanimously.) Ironically, the lack of partisan competition under Monroe, in what was dubbed the "Era of Good Feelings," also fatally weakened his party, the Democratic Republicans. Lacking competition, the Democratic Republicans neglected their function of nominating candidates. In the 1824 election, the party caucus's nominee was challenged by three other Democratic Republicans,

FIGURE 8.1 The Two-Party System in American History

1789	*Washington unanimously elected president*				**PREPARTY PERIOD**	
1792	*Washington unanimously reelected*					
1796	**Federalist** *Adams*	**Democratic Republican**				
1800	—	*Jefferson*			**FIRST PARTY SYSTEM**	
1804	—	*Jefferson*				
1808	—	*Madison*				
1812	—	*Madison*				
1816	—	*Monroe*				
1820		*Monroe*			**"ERA OF GOOD FEELINGS"**	
1824		*J. Q. Adams*				
1828		**Democratic** *Jackson*			**National Republican**	
1832		*Jackson*			**Whig**	
1836		*Van Buren*			—	
1840	**SECOND PARTY SYSTEM**	—			*Harrison*	
1844		*Polk*			—	
1848		—			*Taylor*	
1852		*Pierce*			—	
1856		*Buchanan*			**Republican**	
1860	**Constitutional Union** **Southern Democrat**	—			*Lincoln*	
1864		—			*Lincoln*	
1868		—			*Grant*	
1872		—			*Grant*	
1876	**THIRD PARTY SYSTEM**	—			*Hayes*	
1880		—			*Garfield*	
1884		*Cleveland*			—	
1888	**Rough Balance**	—			*Harrison*	
1892		*Cleveland*			—	
1896		—		**Populist**	*McKinley*	
1900		—			*McKinley*	
1904		—			*Roosevelt, T.*	
1908		—			*Taft*	
1912	**Republican Dominance**	*Wilson*		**Progressive**	—	
1916		*Wilson*			—	
1920		—			*Harding*	
1924		—			*Coolidge*	
1928		—			*Hoover*	
1932		*Roosevelt, F. D.*			—	
1936		*Roosevelt, F. D.*			—	
1940		*Roosevelt, F. D.*			—	
1944		*Roosevelt, F. D.*			—	
1948	**Democratic Dominance**	*Truman*		**States' Rights**	—	
1952		—			*Eisenhower*	
1956		—			*Eisenhower*	
1960		*Kennedy*			—	
1964		*Johnson*			—	
1968		—		**American Independent**	*Nixon*	
1972		—			*Nixon*	
1976		*Carter*			—	
1980		—		**Independent**	*Reagan*	
1984	**Rough Balance**	—			*Reagan*	
1988		—			*Bush, G. H. W.*	
1992		*Clinton*		**Independent**	—	
1996		*Clinton*		**Reform**	—	
2000		—		**Green**	*Bush, G. W.*	
2004		—			*Bush, G. W.*	
2008		*Obama*			—	
2012		*Obama*			—	

Over time, the American party system has undergone a series of wrenching transformations. Since 1856, the Democrats and the Republicans have alternated irregularly in power, each party enjoying a long period of dominance.

Source: © Cengage Learning.

including John Quincy Adams and Andrew Jackson, who together won 70 percent of the popular and electoral vote.

Although Jackson won more of the popular vote and electoral vote than Adams, he did not win the necessary majority in the electoral college. The House of Representatives again had to decide the winner. It chose the second-place John Quincy Adams (from the established state of Massachusetts) over the voters' choice, Jackson (from the frontier state of Tennessee). The factionalism among the leaders of the Democratic Republican Party became so intense that the party split in two.

The Second Party System: Democrats and Whigs

The Jacksonian faction of the Democratic Republican Party represented the common people in the expanding South and West, and its members took pride in calling themselves simply Democrats. Jackson ran again for the presidency as a Democrat in 1828, a milestone that marked the beginning of today's Democratic Party. That election was also the first mass election in U.S. history. In earlier elections, few people were entitled to vote. States began to drop restrictive requirements for voting after 1800, and voting rights for white males expanded even faster after 1815 (see Chapter 7). With the expansion of suffrage, more states began to allow voters, rather than state legislatures, to choose the presidential electors. Although voters had directly chosen many presidential electors in 1824, the total votes cast in that election numbered fewer than 370,000. By 1828, relaxed requirements for voting (and the use of popular elections to select presidential electors in more states) had increased the vote by more than 300 percent, to more than 1.1 million.

As the electorate expanded, the parties changed. No longer could a party rely on a few political leaders in the state legislatures to control votes in the electoral college. Parties now needed to campaign for votes cast by hundreds of thousands of citizens. Recognizing this new dimension of the nation's politics, the parties responded with a new method for nominating presidential candidates. Instead of selecting candidates in a closed caucus of party representatives in Congress, the parties devised the **national convention**. At these gatherings, delegates from state parties across the nation would choose candidates for president and vice president and adopt a statement of policies called a **party platform**. The Anti-Masonic Party, which was the first "third" party in American history to challenge the two major parties for the presidency, called the first national convention in 1831. The Democrats adopted the convention idea in 1832 to nominate Jackson for a second term, as did their new opponents that year, the National Republicans.

The label *National Republicans* applied to John Quincy Adams's faction of the former Democratic Republican Party. However, the National Republicans did not become today's Republican Party. Adams's followers called themselves National Republicans to signify their old Federalist preference for a strong national government, but the symbolism did not appeal to the voters, and the National Republicans lost to Jackson in 1832.

Elected to another term, Jackson began to assert the power of the nation over the states (acting more like a National Republican than a Democrat). His policies drew new opponents, who started calling him "King Andrew." A coalition made up of former National Republicans, Anti-Masons, and Jackson haters formed the Whig Party in 1834. The name referred to the English Whigs, who opposed the powers of the British throne; the implication was that Jackson was governing like a king. For the next thirty years, Democrats and Whigs alternated in the presidency. However, the issues of slavery and sectionalism eventually destroyed the Whigs from within. Although the party

national convention
A gathering of delegates of a single political party from across the country to choose candidates for president and vice president and to adopt a party platform.

party platform
The statement of policies of a national political party.

had won the White House in 1848 and had taken 44 percent of the vote in 1852, the Whigs were unable to field a presidential candidate in the 1856 election.

The Current Party System: Democrats and Republicans

In the early 1850s, antislavery forces (including some Whigs and antislavery Democrats) began to organize. At meetings in Jackson, Michigan, and Ripon, Wisconsin, they recommended the formation of a new party, the Republican Party, to oppose the extension of slavery into the Kansas and Nebraska territories. This party, founded in 1854, continues as today's Republican Party.

The Republican Party entered its first presidential election in 1856. It took 33 percent of the vote, and its candidate, John Frémont, carried eleven states—all in the North. Then, in 1860, the Republicans nominated Abraham Lincoln. The Democrats were deeply divided over the slavery issue and split into two parties. The Northern Democrats nominated Stephen Douglas. The Southern Democrats ran John Breckinridge. A fourth party, the Constitutional Union Party, nominated John Bell. Breckinridge won every southern state. Lincoln took 40 percent of the popular vote and carried every northern state.

critical election
An election that produces a sharp change in the existing pattern of party loyalties among groups of voters.

The election of 1860 is considered the first of four critical elections under the current party system.[10] A **critical election** is marked by a sharp change in the existing patterns of party loyalty among groups of voters. Moreover, this change in voting patterns, which is called an **electoral realignment**, does not end with the election but persists through several subsequent elections.[11] The election of 1860 divided the country politically between the northern states, whose voters mainly voted Republican, and the southern states, which were overwhelmingly Democratic. The victory of the North over the South in the Civil War cemented Democratic loyalties in the South.

electoral realignment
The change in voting patterns that occurs after a critical election.

For forty years, from 1880 to 1920, no Republican presidential candidate won even one of the eleven states of the former Confederacy. The South's solid Democratic record earned it the nickname the "Solid South." (Today's students may be puzzled, for the South has been "solid" for Republicans throughout their lifetimes.[12] That was not true prior to 1950, and the change is addressed below.) The Republicans did not puncture the Solid South until 1920, when Warren G. Harding carried Tennessee. The Republicans won five southern states in 1928, when the Democrats ran the first Catholic candidate, Al Smith. Republican presidential candidates won no more southern states until 1952, when Dwight Eisenhower broke the pattern of Democratic dominance in the South—ninety years after that pattern had been set by the Civil War.

Eras of Party Dominance Since the Civil War

The critical election of 1860 established the Democratic and Republican parties as the dominant parties in our **two-party system**. In a two-party system, most voters are so loyal to one or the other of the major parties that independent candidates or candidates from a third party (which means any minor party) have little chance of winning office. Third-party candidates tend to be more successful at the local or state level. Since the current two-party system was established, relatively few minor-party candidates have won election to the U.S. House, even fewer have won election to the Senate, and none has won the presidency.

two-party system
A political system in which two major political parties compete for control of the government. Candidates from a third party have little chance of winning office.

The voters in a given state, county, or community are not always equally divided in their loyalties between the Republicans and the Democrats. In some areas, voters typically favor the Republicans, whereas voters in other areas prefer the Democrats.

When one party in a two-party system regularly enjoys support from most voters in an area, it is called the *majority party* in that area; the other is called the *minority party*. Since the inception of the current two-party system, four periods (1860–1894, 1896–1930, 1932–1964, and 1968 to the present) have characterized the balance between the two major parties at the national level.

A Rough Balance: 1860–1894. From 1860 through 1894, the Grand Old Party (or GOP, as the Republican Party is sometimes called) won eight of ten presidential elections, which would seem to qualify it as the majority party. However, some of its success in presidential elections came from its practice of running Civil War heroes and from the North's domination of southern politics. Seats in the House of Representatives are a better guide to the breadth of national support. An analysis shows that the Republicans and Democrats won an equal number of congressional elections, each controlling the chamber for nine sessions between 1860 and 1894.

A Republican Majority: 1896–1930

A second critical election, in 1896, transformed the Republican Party into a true majority party. Grover Cleveland, a Democrat, occupied the White House, and the country was in a severe depression. The Republicans nominated William McKinley, governor of Ohio and a conservative, who stood for a high tariff against foreign goods and sound money tied to the value of gold. Rather than tour the country seeking votes, McKinley ran a dignified campaign from his Ohio home.

The Democrats, already in trouble because of the depression, nominated the fiery William Jennings Bryan. In stark contrast to McKinley, Bryan advocated the free and unlimited coinage of silver, which would mean cheap money and easy payment of debts through inflation. Bryan was also the nominee of the young Populist Party, an agrarian protest party that had proposed the free-silver platform Bryan adopted. "What Do You Know About ... The Wizard of Oz?" (pp. 216–17) explains that the book *The Wonderful Wizard of Oz*, which you probably know as a movie, was reportedly a Populist political fable.[13] Conservatives, especially businesspeople, were aghast at the Democrats' radical turn, and voters in the heavily populated Northeast and Midwest surged toward the Republican Party, many of them permanently. McKinley carried every northern state east of the Mississippi. The Republicans also won the House, and they retained their control of it in the next six elections.

The election of 1896 helped solidify a Republican majority in industrial America and forged a link between the Republican Party and business. In the subsequent electoral realignment, the Republicans emerged as a true majority party. The GOP dominated national politics—controlling the presidency,

Library of Congress

William Jennings Bryan: When Candidates Were Orators

Today, televised images of a candidate waving his hands and shouting to an audience would look silly. But candidates once had to resort to such tactics to be effective with large crowds. One of the most commanding orators around the turn of the twentieth century was William Jennings Bryan (1860–1925), whose stirring speeches extolling the virtues of the free coinage of silver were music to the ears of thousands of westerners and southern farmers.

WHAT DO YOU KNOW ABOUT...

THE WIZARD OF OZ?

Most Americans are familiar with *The Wizard of Oz* through the children's series or the 1939 motion picture. Some historians contend that the story was written as a political fable to promote the Populist movement around the turn of the twentieth century. Next time you see or read it, try interpreting the Tin Woodsman as the industrial worker, the Scarecrow as the struggling farmer, and the Wizard as the president, who is powerful only as long as he succeeds in deceiving the people. (Sorry, but in the book, Dorothy's ruby slippers were only silver shoes.)

The Wonderful Wizard of Oz was written by Lyman Frank Baum in 1900, during the collapse of the Populist movement. Through the Populist Party, midwestern farmers, in alliance with some urban workers, had challenged the banks, railroads, and other economic interests that squeezed farmers through low prices, high freight rates, and continued indebtedness.

The Populists advocated government ownership of railroad, telephone, and telegraph industries. They also wanted silver coinage. Their power grew during the 1893 depression, the worst in U.S. history until then, as farm prices sank to new lows, and unemployment was widespread.

In the 1894 congressional elections, the Populist Party got almost 40 percent of the vote. It looked forward to winning the presidency, and imposing the silver standard, in 1896. But in that election, which revolved around the issue of gold versus silver, Populist Democrat William Jennings Bryan lost to Republican William McKinley by ninety-five electoral votes. Bryan, a congressman from Nebraska and a gifted orator, ran again in 1900, but the Populist strength was gone.

Baum viewed these events in both rural South Dakota, where he edited a local weekly, and urban Chicago, where he wrote *Oz*. He mourned the destruction of the fragile alliance between the midwestern farmers (the Scarecrow) and the urban industrial workers (the Tin Woodsman). Along with Bryan (the Cowardly Lion, with a roar

the Senate, and the House—almost continuously from 1896 until the Wall Street crash of 1929, which burst big business's bubble and launched the Great Depression.*

A Democratic Majority: 1932–1964. The Republicans' majority status ended in the critical election of 1932 between incumbent president Herbert Hoover and the Democratic challenger, Franklin Delano Roosevelt. Roosevelt promised new solutions to unemployment and the economic crisis of the Great Depression. His campaign appealed to labor, middle-class liberals, and new European ethnic voters. Along with Democratic voters in the Solid South, urban workers in the North, Catholics, Jews, and white ethnic minorities formed "the Roosevelt coalition." The relatively few blacks who voted at that time tended to remain loyal to the Republicans—"the party of Lincoln."

Roosevelt was swept into office in a landslide, carrying huge Democratic majorities with him into the House and Senate to enact his liberal activist programs. The electoral realignment reflected by the election of 1932 made the Democrats the majority party. Not only was Roosevelt reelected in 1936, 1940, and 1944, but also Democrats held control of both houses of Congress in most sessions from 1933 through

---

*The only break in the GOP domination was in 1912, when Teddy Roosevelt's Progressive Conservative Party split from the Republicans, allowing Democrat Woodrow Wilson to win the presidency and giving the Democrats control of Congress, and again in 1916 when Wilson was reelected.

but little else), they had been taken down the yellow brick road (the gold standard) that led nowhere. Each journeyed to Emerald City seeking favors from the Wizard of Oz (the president). Dorothy, the symbol of Everyman, went along with them, innocent enough to see the truth before the others.

Along the way, they met the Wicked Witch of the East, who, Baum tells us, had kept the little Munchkin people "in bondage for many years, making them slave for her night and day." She also had put a spell on the Tin Woodsman, once an independent and hard-working man, so that each time he swung his axe, it chopped off a different part of his body. Lacking another trade, he "worked harder than ever," becoming like a machine, incapable of love, yearning for a heart. Another witch, the Wicked Witch of the West, clearly symbolizes the large industrial corporations.

The small group heads toward Emerald City, where the Wizard rules from behind a papier-mâché façade. Oz, by the way, is the abbreviation for ounce, the standard measure for gold.

Like all good politicians, the Wizard can be all things to all people. Dorothy sees him as an enormous head. The Scarecrow sees a gossamer fairy. The Woodsman sees an awful beast, the Cowardly Lion "a ball of fire so fierce and glowing he could scarcely bear to gaze upon it." Later, however, when they confront the Wizard directly, they see he is nothing more than "a little man, with a bald head and a wrinkled face." "I have been making believe," the Wizard confesses. "I'm just a common man." But the Scarecrow adds, "You're more than that … you're a humbug." "It was a great mistake my ever letting you into the Throne Room," admits the Wizard, a former ventriloquist and circus balloonist from Omaha.

This was Baum's ultimate Populist message. The powers-that-be survive by deception. Only people's ignorance allows the powerful to manipulate and control them. Dorothy returns to Kansas with the magical help of her silver shoes (the silver issue), but when she gets to Kansas she realizes her shoes "had fallen off in her flight through the air, and were lost forever in the desert." Still, she is safe at home with Aunt Em and Uncle Henry, simple farmers.

Source: Peter Dreier, "The Wizard of Oz: A Political Fable," *Today Journal*, 14 February 1986. Reprinted by permission of Pacific News Service, http://www.pacificnews.org.

1964. The only exceptions were Republican control of the House and Senate in 1947 and 1948 (under President Truman) and in 1953 and 1954 (under President Eisenhower). The Democrats also won the presidency in seven of nine elections. Moreover, national surveys from 1952 through 1964 show that Americans of voting age consistently and decidedly favored the Democratic Party.

A Rough Balance: 1968 to the Present. Scholars agree that an electoral realignment occurred after 1964, and some attribute the realignment to the turbulent election of 1968, sometimes called the fourth critical election.[14] The Republican Richard Nixon won in a very close race by winning five of the eleven southern states in the old Confederacy, while Democrat Hubert Humphrey won only one. The other five states were won by George Wallace, the candidate of the American Independent Party, made up primarily of southerners who defected from the Democratic Party. Wallace won no states outside the South.

Since 1968, Republican candidates for president have run very well in southern states and tended to win election—Nixon (twice), Reagan (twice), G. H. W. Bush, and G. W. Bush (twice). The record of party control of Congress has been more mixed since 1968. Democrats have controlled the House for most of the sessions, while the parties have split control of the Senate almost evenly.

Therefore, the period since 1968 rates as a "rough balance" between the parties, much like the period from 1860 to 1894. Today, both parties nationally are fairly close in electoral strength. However, the North–South coalition of Democratic voters forged by Roosevelt in the 1930s has completely crumbled. Two southern scholars wrote:

> It is easy to forget just how thoroughly the Democratic party once dominated southern congressional elections. In 1950 there were no Republican senators from the South and only 2 Republican representatives out of 105 in the southern House delegation.... A half-century later Republicans constituted *majorities* of the South's congressional delegations—13 of 22 southern senators and 71 of 125 representatives.[15]

Although party loyalty within regions has shifted inexorably, the Democratic coalition of urban workers and ethnic minorities still seems intact, if weakened. Indeed, rural voters have become decidedly more Republican.[16] Some scholars say that in the 1970s and 1980s, we were in a period of **electoral dealignment**, in which party loyalties became less important to voters as they cast their ballots. Others counter that partisanship increased in the 1990s in a gradual process of realignment not marked by a single critical election.[17] We examine the influence of party loyalty on voting in the next chapter, after we look at the operation of our two-party system.

electoral dealignment
A lessening of the importance of party loyalties in voting decisions.

★ 8.3 The American Two-Party System

★ Explain why two parties dominate the history of American politics.

Our review of party history in the United States has focused on the two dominant parties. But we should not ignore the special contributions of certain minor parties, among them the Anti-Masonic Party, the Populists, and the Progressives of 1912. In this section, we study the fortunes of minor, or third, parties in American politics. We also look at why we have only two major parties, explain how federalism helps the parties survive, and describe voters' loyalty to the two major parties today.

Minor Parties in America

Minor parties have always figured in party politics in America. Most minor parties in our political history have been one of four types:[18]

- *Bolter parties* are formed by factions that have split off from one of the major parties. Six times in the thirty-eight presidential elections from the Civil War to 2008, disgruntled leaders have "bolted the ticket" and challenged their former parties by forming new parties.[19] Bolter parties have occasionally won significant proportions of the vote. However, with the exception of Teddy Roosevelt's Progressive Party in 1912 and the possible exception of George Wallace's American Independent Party in 1968, bolter parties have not affected the outcome of presidential elections.
- *Farmer-labor parties* represented farmers and urban workers who believed that they, the working class, were not getting their share of society's wealth. The People's Party, founded in 1892 and nicknamed the "Populist Party," was a prime example of a farmer-labor party. The Populists won 8.5 percent of the vote in 1892 and also became the first third party since 1860 to win any electoral votes. Flushed by success, it endorsed William Jennings Bryan, the Democratic candidate, in 1896. When he lost, the party quickly faded. Farm and labor groups

revived many Populist ideas in the Progressive Party in 1924, which nominated Robert La Follette for the presidency. Although the party won 16.6 percent of the popular vote, it carried only La Follette's home state of Wisconsin and died in 1925. In 1944, however, the Minnesota Farmer-Labor Party merged with the Democrats to form the Democratic Farmer-Labor (DFL) Party. The DFL is Minnesota's Democratic Party today.

- *Parties of ideological protest* go further than farmer-labor parties in criticizing the established system. These parties reject prevailing doctrines and propose radically different principles, often favoring more government activism. The Socialist Party has been the most successful party of ideological protest. Even at its high point in 1912, however, it garnered only 6 percent of the vote, and Socialist candidates for president have never won a single state. Nevertheless, the Socialist Party persists, fielding a presidential ticket again in 2012. In recent years, protest parties have tended to come from the right, arguing against government action in society. Such is the program of the Libertarian Party, which stresses freedom over order and equality (see page 222). In contrast, the Green Party protests from the left, favoring government action to preserve the environment. Together, the Libertarian and Green Parties polled just over 1 percent of the total vote for their presidential candidates in 2012. Although both parties together ran nearly two hundred congressional candidates, they won relatively few votes (see Figure 8.2) and no seats.

- *Single-issue parties* are formed to promote one principle, not a general philosophy of government. The Anti-Masonic parties of the 1820s and 1830s, for example, opposed Masonic lodges and other secret societies. The Free Soil Party of the 1840s and 1850s worked to abolish slavery. The Prohibition Party, the most durable example of a single-issue party, was founded to oppose the consumption of alcoholic beverages, but recently its platform has taken conservative positions: favoring right-to-life, limiting immigration, and urging withdrawal from the World Bank. Prohibition candidates consistently won from 1 to 2 percent of the vote in nine presidential elections between 1884 and 1916, and the party has run candidates in every presidential election since, usually winning only a trickle of votes.

FIGURE 8.2 Party Candidates for the U.S. House in the 2012 Election

In 2012, as in other recent elections, the Democratic and Republican parties each ran candidates for the House of Representatives in about 90 percent of the 435 congressional districts. Of minor parties, only the Libertarian Party, the best-organized minor party in the nation, ran candidates in more than one hundred districts. In most of those districts, however, the Libertarian candidates usually got about 1 percent of the vote. All other minor parties ran fewer candidates than the Libertarians. Source: http://www.politico.com/2012-election/map/#/President/2012/. Not all precincts reported.

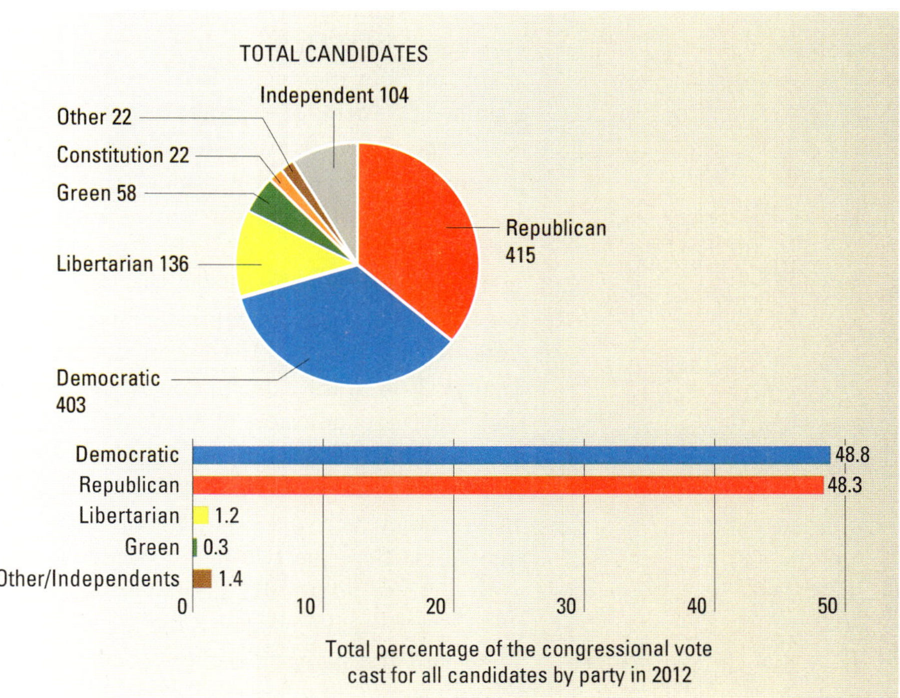

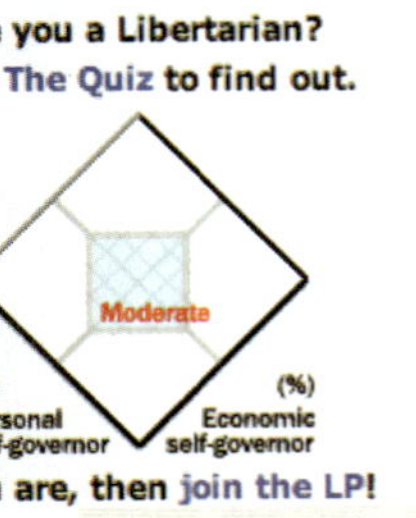

The Third-Party Theme

The Libertarian Party, founded in 1971, has run presidential candidates in every election since 1972, but no Libertarian candidate has ever won a million votes. In 2012, it ran more than 130 candidates for the 435 seats in the House of Representatives but elected none. It is true that Ron Paul, the 1988 Libertarian presidential candidate, was elected to Congress in 1996, but as a Republican. Nevertheless, the Libertarian Party's website justifiably describes itself as "America's third largest and fastest growing political party." That says something about the state of third parties in the United States.

America has a long history of third parties that operate on the periphery of our two-party system. Minor parties form primarily to express some voters' discontent with choices offered by the major parties and to work for their own objectives within the electoral system.[20]

How have minor parties fared historically? As vote getters, they have not performed well. However, bolter parties have twice won more than 10 percent of the vote. (Although Ross Perot won 19 percent of the vote in 1992, he ran as an independent. When he created the Reform Party and ran as its candidate in 1996, he won only 8 percent.)[21] More significantly, the Republican Party originated in 1854 as a single-issue third party opposed to slavery in the nation's new territories. In its first election, in 1856, the party came in second, displacing the Whigs. (Undoubtedly, the Republican exception to the rule has inspired the formation of other hopeful third parties.) Although surveys repeatedly show over half the public saying they want a third major party, voters tend not to support them at the polls.[22]

As policy advocates, minor parties have a slightly better record. At times, they have had a real effect on the policies adopted by the major parties. Women's suffrage, the graduated income tax, and the direct election of senators all originated with third parties.[23] Of course, third parties may fail to win more votes simply because their policies lack popular support. The Democrats learned this lesson in 1896, when they adopted the Populists' free-silver plank in their own platform. Both their candidate and their platform went down to defeat, hobbling the Democratic Party for decades. Beginning around the 1930s, third-party voting began to decline. Research attributes the decline to the Democratic Party's leftward shift to encompass issues raised by minor parties.[24]

Most important, minor parties function as safety valves. They allow those who are unhappy with the status quo to express their discontent within the system, to contribute to the political dialogue. Surely this was the function of Ralph Nader as the Green Party candidate in 2000, when it won 2.7 percent of the vote. (By drawing votes from Democrat Al Gore in key states, Nader also denied Gore a victory over George Bush in the closest popular vote in history.) If minor parties and independent candidates are indicators of discontent, what should we make of the numerous minor parties, detailed in Figure 8.3, which took part in the 2012 election? Not much. The number of third parties that contest elections is less important than the total number of votes they receive. Despite the presence of numerous minor parties in every presidential election, the two major parties usually collect more than 95 percent of the vote, as they did in 2012 despite challenges from candidates of other parties. In the 2010 congressional elections, the tea party movement blew off steam within the Republican Party by backing more conservative candidates. In that sense, it acted like a minor party, as a safety valve.

FIGURE 8.3 Candidates and Parties in the 2012 Presidential Election

CANDIDATE AND PARTY*	TOTAL POPULAR VOTE	PERCENTAGE OF POPULAR VOTE
Barack Obama (Democratic)	60,260,126	50.37
Mitt Romney (Republican)	57,504,560	48.07
Gary Johnson (Libertarian)	1,156,493	.97
Jill Stein (Green)	404,615	.34
Virgil Goode (Constitution)	114,200	.1
Roseanne Barr (Peace and freedom)	49,397	.04
Rocky Anderson (Justice)	35,589	.03
Thomas Hoefling (America's)	28,590	.02
Randall Terry (Independent)	12,928	.01
Richard Duncan (Independent)	12,097	.01
Peta Lindsay (Socialism and liberation)	7,050	.01
Chuck Baldwin (Kansas reform)	4,700	.00
Tom Stevens (Objectivist)	4,013	.00
Stewart Alexander (Socialist)	3,920	.00
Will Christensen (Oregon constitution)	3,800	.00
James Harris (Socialist workers)	3,436	.00
Jim Carlson (Grassroots)	3,168	.00
Merlin Miller (American third position)	2,598	.00
Samm Tittle (We the people)	2,497	.00
Jill Reed (Twelve visions)	2,377	.00
Gloria La Riva (Socialism and liberation)	1,524	.00
Jerry Litzel (Independent)	1,196	.00
Jerry White (Socialist equality)	1, 132	.00
Dean Morstad (Constitutional government)	1, 107	.00
Barbara Washer (Mississippi reform)	955	.00
Jeff Boss (NSA Did 911)	887	.00
Andre Barnett (Reform)	795	.00
Jack Fellure (Prohibition)	519	.00
Total	119,624,269	100%

*Party designations varied in some states. Not all precincts had reported in every state.

In addition to the candidates of the two major parties, 23 other candidates ran in various states under banners of more than a dozen parties. All of them together, however, captured less than 2 percent of the total vote.
Source: http://www.politico.com/2012-election/map/#/President/2012/.

Why a Two-Party System?

The history of party politics in the United States is essentially the story of two parties that have alternating control of the government. With relatively few exceptions, Americans conduct elections at all levels within the two-party system. Nevertheless, surveys show that about half of the population today think that the United States needs a third party. Why does the United States have only two major parties? Other democratic countries usually have multiparty systems, but they typically involve more than three parties. In truth, a political system with three relatively equal parties has never existed over a length of time in any country, for it is inherently unstable.[25]

The two most convincing explanations for the two-party system in the United States lie (1) in its electoral system and (2) in our historical pattern of political socialization. Consider first the electoral system, which sets the "rules of the game" under

majority representation
The system by which one office, contested by two or more candidates, is won by the single candidate who collects the most votes.

proportional representation
The system by which legislative seats are awarded to a party in proportion to the vote that party wins in an election.

which the parties play. Think of a U.S. election as a prizefight between two boxers. If a third boxer enters the ring, two gang up on one. In the typical U.S. election, two or more candidates contest each office, and the winner is the single candidate who collects the most votes, whether those votes constitute a majority or not. That rule tends to put only two candidates in the ring in the first place, resulting in the inherent instability of three-party systems. The two principles of *single winners* chosen by a *simple plurality* of votes produce an electoral system known as **majority representation** (despite its reliance on pluralities rather than majorities). Think about how American states choose representatives to Congress. A state entitled to ten representatives is divided into ten congressional districts, and each district elects one representative. Almost always, the ten representatives are Democrats and Republicans. Majority representation of voters through single-member districts is also a feature of most state legislatures.

Alternatively, a legislature might be chosen through a system of **proportional representation**, which awards legislative seats to each party in proportion to the total number of votes it wins in an election. Under this system, the state might hold a single statewide election for all ten seats, with multiple parties presenting their rank-ordered lists of ten candidates. Voters could vote for the party list they preferred, and the party's candidates would be elected from the top of each list, according to the proportion of votes won by the party. Thus, if a party got 30 percent of the vote in this example, its first three candidates would be elected.[26]

Although this form of election may seem strange, more democratic countries use it than use our system of majority representation. Proportional representation tends to produce (or perpetuate) several parties because each can win enough seats nationwide to wield some influence in the legislature. In contrast, our system of elections forces interest groups of all sorts to work within the two major parties, for only one candidate in each race stands a chance of being elected under plurality voting. Therefore, the system tends to produce only two parties. Moreover, the two major parties benefit from state laws that automatically list candidates on the ballot if their party won a sizable percentage of the vote in the previous election. These laws discourage minor parties, which usually have to collect thousands of signatures to get on a state ballot.[27]

The rules of our electoral system may explain why only two parties tend to form in specific election districts, but why do the same two parties (Democratic and Republican) operate within every state? The contest for the presidency is the key to this question. A candidate can win a presidential election only by amassing a majority of electoral votes from across the entire nation. Presidential candidates try to win votes under the same party label in each state in order to pool their electoral votes in the electoral college. The presidency is a big enough political prize to induce parties to harbor uncomfortable coalitions of voters (southern white Protestants allied with northern Jews and blacks in the Democratic Party, for example) just to win the electoral vote and the presidential election.

The American electoral system may force U.S. politics into a two-party mold, but why must the same two parties reappear from election to election? In fact, they do not. The earliest two-party system pitted the Federalists against the Democratic Republicans. A later two-party system involved the Democrats and the Whigs. More than 135 years ago, the Republicans replaced the Whigs in what is our two-party system today. But with modern issues so different from the issues then, why do the Democrats and Republicans persist? This is where the second explanation, political socialization, comes into play. The two parties persist simply because they have persisted. After more than one hundred years of political socialization, the two parties today have such a head start in structuring the vote that they discourage challenges from new parties. Third parties still try to crack the two-party system from time to time, but most have had little success. In truth, the two parties in power also write laws that make it hard for minor parties to get on the ballot, such as requiring petitions with thousands of signatures.[28]

The Federal Basis of the Party System

Focusing on contests for the presidency is a convenient and informative way to study the history of American parties, but it also oversimplifies party politics to the point of distortion. By concentrating only on presidential elections, we tend to ignore electoral patterns in the states, where elections often buck national trends. Even during its darkest defeats for the presidency, a party can still claim many victories for state offices. Victories outside the arena of presidential politics give each party a base of support that keeps its machinery oiled and ready for the next contest.[29]

Party Identification in America

The concept of **party identification** is one of the most important in political science. It signifies a voter's sense of psychological attachment to a party (which is not the same thing as voting for the party in any given election). Scholars measure party identification simply by asking, "Do you usually think of yourself as a Republican, a Democrat, an independent, or what?"[30] Voting is a behavior; identification is a state of mind. For example, millions of southerners voted for Eisenhower for president in 1952 and 1956 but continued to consider themselves Democrats. Again in the 1980s, millions of voters temporarily became "Reagan Democrats." Across the nation, more people identify with one of the two major parties than reject a party attachment. The proportions of self-identified Republicans, Democrats, and independents (no party attachment) in the electorate since 1952 are shown in Figure 8.4 (p. 224). Three significant points stand out:

party identification
A voter's sense of psychological attachment to a party.

- The proportion of Republicans and Democrats combined has exceeded that of independents in every year.
- The proportion of Democrats has consistently exceeded that of Republicans but has shrunk over time.
- The proportion of independents has nearly doubled over the period.

Although party identification predisposes citizens to vote for their favorite party, other factors may convince them to choose the opposition candidate. If they vote against their party often enough, they may rethink their party identification and eventually switch. Apparently, this rethinking has gone on in the minds of many southern Democrats over time. In 1952, about 70 percent of white southerners thought of themselves as Democrats, and fewer than 20 percent thought of themselves as Republicans. In 2012, white southerners were only 24 percent Democratic, whereas 35 percent were Republican and 41 percent were independent.[31] Much of the nationwide growth in the proportion of Republicans and independents (and the parallel drop in the number of Democrats) stems from changes in party preferences among white southerners and from migration of northerners, which translated into substantial gains in the proportion of Republicans.[32]

Who are the self-identified Democrats and Republicans in the electorate? Figure 8.5 (p. 225) shows party identification by various social groups in 2012. The effects of

FIGURE 8.4 Distribution of Party Identification, 1952–2012

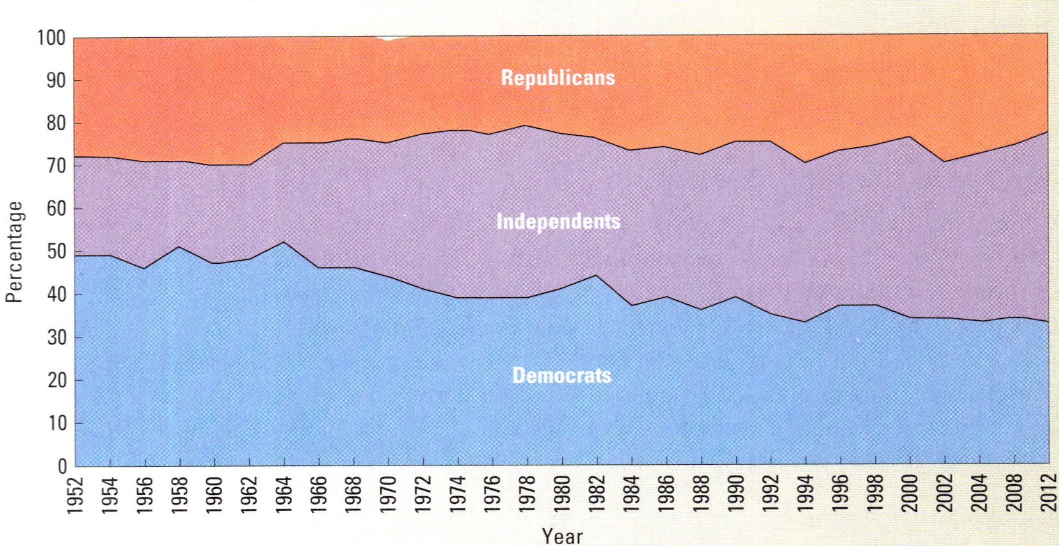

In every presidential election since 1952, voters across the nation have been asked, "Generally speaking, do you usually think of yourself as a Republican, a Democrat, an independent, or what?" Most voters think of themselves as either Republicans or Democrats, but the proportion of those who think of themselves as independents has increased over time. The size of the Democratic Party's majority has also shrunk. Nevertheless, most Americans today still identify with one of the two major parties, and Democrats still outnumber Republicans.

Source: Data for 1952 to 2008 come from the National Election Studies Guide to Public Opinion and Electoral Behavior, http://www.electionstudies. org/nesguide/nesguide.htm. The 2012 figure is based on the January 11–16, 2012 survey by the Pew Research Center for the People & the Press, kindly supplied by Senior Researcher, Dr. Leah Melani Christian. The few respondents (typically under 5 percent) who gave other answers were excluded from the graph.

socioeconomic factors are clear. People who have lower incomes and less education are more likely to think of themselves as Democrats rather than as Republicans. However, citizens with advanced degrees (such as college faculty) are more Democratic. The cultural factors of religion and ethnicity produce even sharper differences between the parties. Those who are unaffiliated with a religious group are strongly Democratic compared with those affiliated with religious groups but are mainly independent. Non-Hispanic whites are markedly more Republican than those in other ethnic groups. Finally, American politics has a gender gap: more women tend to be Democrats than men, and (although not shown here) this gap seems to widen with women's greater education.[33] The youngest citizens are more apt to be Democrats than Republicans, but most are independents. People tend to acquire party identification as they age.

The influence of region on party identification has changed over time, and strong regional differences no longer exist. Because of the high proportion of blacks in the South, it is still predominantly Democratic (in party identity, but not in voting because of lower turnout among low-income blacks). Despite the erosion of Democratic strength in the South, we still see elements of Roosevelt's old Democratic coalition of different socioeconomic groups. Perhaps the major change in that coalition has been the replacement of white European ethnic groups by blacks, attracted by the Democrats' backing of civil rights legislation in the 1960s leading to the critical election of 1968.

Nonwhites in general have become more Democratic than Republican today, as the ethnic composition of the United States is inexorably becoming less white.

FIGURE 8.5 Party Identification by Social Groups

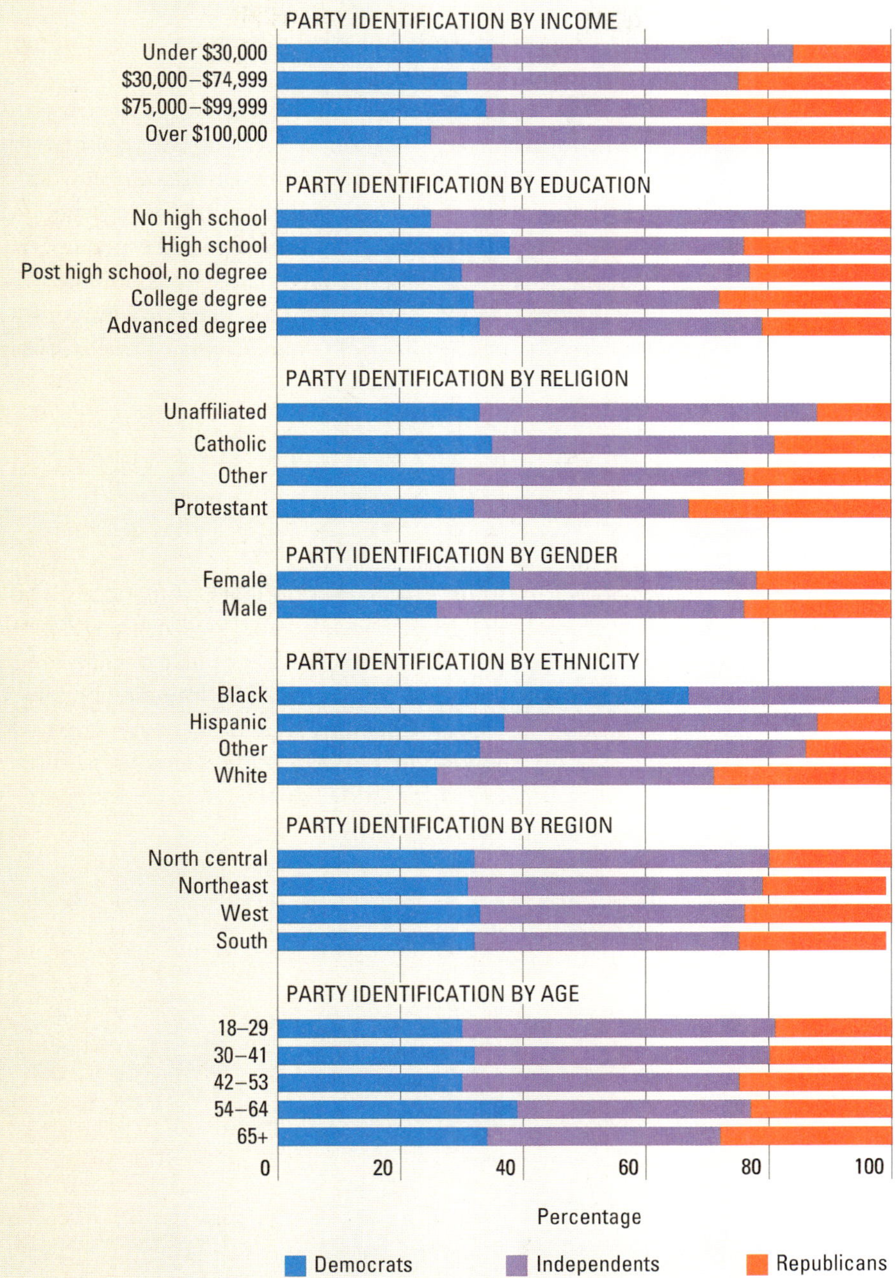

Respondents to a 2012 survey were grouped by seven socioeconomic criteria—income, education, religion, gender, ethnicity, region, and age—and analyzed according to their self-descriptions as Democrats, independents, or Republicans. As income increases, people are more likely to vote Republican. The same is true for education, except for those with advanced degrees. Protestants are far more likely to be Republican than those without religious affiliation, while women, Hispanics, and all nonwhite groups are more likely to be Democrats. Party identification varies relatively little by region. The main effect of age was to reduce the proportion of independents as respondents grew older. Younger citizens who tend to think of themselves as independents are likely to develop an identification with one party or the other as they mature.

Source: Data come from the January 11–16, 2012 survey by the Pew Research Center for the People & the Press, kindly supplied by Senior Researcher, Dr. Leah Melani Christian. Rounding errors were adjusted to total to 100 percent for each group.

Estimated at 65 percent in 2010, the non-Latino white population is projected to be only 58 percent in 2030. The Latino and nonwhite share of the population, estimated at 36 percent in 2010, is projected to be 44 percent by 2030.[34] Given that blacks, Asians, and Latinos are strongly Democratic, the Republican Party faces problems in the partisan implications of demographic change.

Studies show that about half of all Americans adopt their parents' party. But it often takes time for party identification to develop. The youngest group of voters is most likely to be independent, but people in their thirties and forties, who were socialized during the Reagan and first Bush presidencies, are more Republican. The oldest group not only is strongly Democratic but also shows the greatest partisan commitment (fewest independents), reflecting the fact that citizens become more interested in politics as they mature.[35] While partisanship has been declining in the United States, that is true elsewhere too (see "Politics of Global Change: Fewer Citizens Are Partying").

Politics of Global Change

Fewer Citizens Are Partying

As shown earlier in Figure 8.4, the proportion of Americans who identify with the Republican or Democratic parties has declined over time while the proportion of independents has increased. This chart shows a similar decline in formal party members for most European countries where citizens formally belong to political parties. Among nineteen European countries that provide available data over time, only Greece and Spain show an increase in party members as a percentage of the electorate. (Similar data exist for party identification in European countries.) Citizens everywhere seem less likely to party.

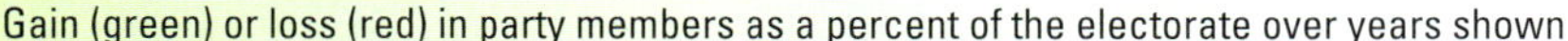

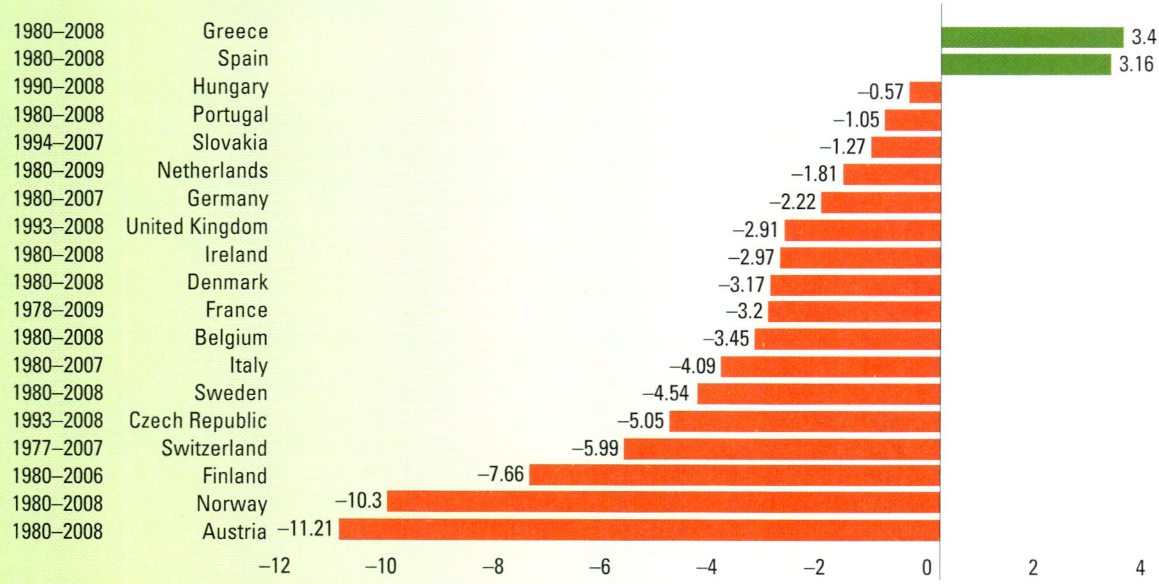

Source: Ingrid van Biezen, Peter Mair, and Thomas Poguntke, "Going, Going, … Gone? The Decline of Party Membership in Contemporary Europe," *European Journal of Political Research*, 51 (January 2012): 24–56. © 2011 Ingrid van Biezen, Peter Mair, and Thomas Poguntke, *European Journal of Political Research*. © 2011 European Consortium for Political Research. Reproduced by permission.

Americans tend to find their political niche and stay there.[36] The enduring party loyalty of American voters tends to structure the vote even before an election is held, and even before the candidates are chosen. In Chapter 9, we will examine the extent to which party identification determines voting choice. But first we will explore whether the Democratic and Republican parties have any significant differences between them.

8.4 Party Ideology and Organization

★ Compare and contrast the Democratic and Republican parties on the basis of ideology and organization.

George Wallace, a disgruntled Democrat who ran for president in 1968 on the American Independent Party ticket, complained that "there isn't a dime's worth of difference" between the Democrats and Republicans. Decades earlier, humorist Will Rogers said, "I am not a member of any organized political party—I am a Democrat." Wallace's comment was made in disgust, Rogers's in jest. Wallace was wrong; Rogers was close to being right. Here we will dispel the myth that the parties do not differ significantly on issues and explain how they are organized to coordinate the activities of party candidates and officials in government.

Differences in Party Ideology

George Wallace notwithstanding, there is more than a dime's worth of difference between the two parties. In fact, the difference amounts to many billions of dollars— the cost of the different government programs each party supports. Democrats are more disposed to government spending to advance social welfare (and hence to promote equality) than are Republicans. And social welfare programs cost money, a lot of money. Republicans decry massive social spending, but they are not averse to spending billions of dollars for the projects they consider important, among them national defense. Ronald Reagan portrayed the Democrats as big spenders, but his administration spent more than $1 trillion for defense. His Strategic Defense Initiative (the missile defense program labeled "Star Wars") cost billions before it was curtailed under the Democrats.[37] Although President George W. Bush introduced a massive tax cut, he also revived spending on missile defense, backed a $400 billion increase in Medicare, and proposed building a space platform on the moon for travel to Mars. One result was a huge increase in the budget deficit and a rare *Wall Street Journal* editorial against the 2003 GOP "spending spree."[38] Reflecting the influence of the tea party, however, the Republican Party in 2012 fervently opposed government spending, whereas Democrats still supported spending for social programs and to stimulate the economy.

Involved and Uninvolved Voters. As discussed in Chapter 5, relatively few ordinary voters think about politics in ideological terms. Party activists often do, however. Figure 8.6 compares all voters with party identifiers classified by their political involvement. "Involved" identifiers said that they cared "a lot" about the 2012 presidential candidates; the "uninvolved" cared less. The middle of the graph shows 42 percent of all voters describing themselves as conservative versus 31 percent liberal. Uninvolved

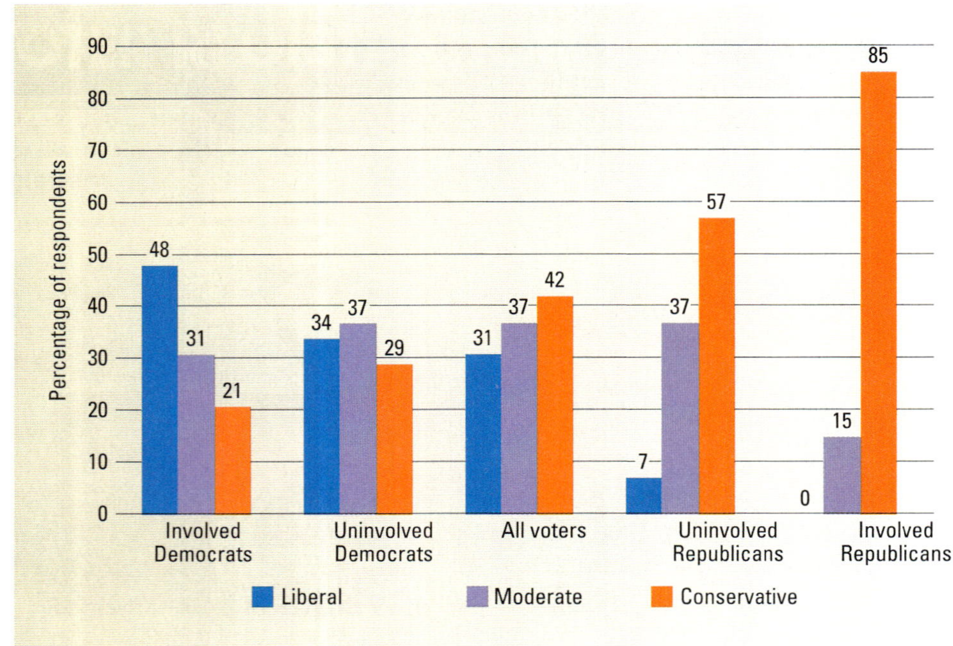

FIGURE 8.6 Ideologies of Involved and Uninvolved Party Voters in 2012

The Democratic and Republican parties differ substantially in their ideological centers of gravity, especially when party identifiers are classified according to their political involvement. Involved Democrats and Republicans were those who cared "a lot" about the 2012 presidential candidates. Uninvolved Democrats and Republicans cared less. Virtually none of the involved Republican identifiers described themselves as liberal, while almost all said they were conservative. Nearly half of involved Democrats described themselves as liberal.

Source: January 12, 2012 Pew Survey.

Democrats and Republicans differ somewhat more, with uninvolved Republicans being far more conservative. The ideological gap, however, becomes a yawning chasm between involved Democrats, 48 percent liberal, and involved Republicans, 85 percent conservative.

Platforms: Freedom, Order, and Equality. Surveys of voters' ideological orientation may merely reflect differences in their personal self-image rather than actual differences in party ideology. For another test of party philosophy, we can look to the platforms adopted at party conventions. Although many people feel that party platforms don't matter very much, several scholars have demonstrated, using different approaches, that winning parties tend to carry out much of their platforms when in office.[39] One study matched the parties' platform statements from 1948 to 1985 against subsequent allocations of program funds in the federal budget. Spending priorities turned out to be quite closely linked to the platform emphases of the party that won control of Congress, especially if the party also controlled the presidency.[40]

Party platforms also matter a great deal to the parties' convention delegates—and to the interest groups that support the parties.[41] The wording of a platform plank often means the difference between victory and defeat for factions within a party. Delegates fight not only over ideas but also over words.

The platforms adopted at both parties' conventions in 2012 were similar in length (about 26,000 words for the Democrats and 31,000 for the Republicans) but strikingly different in content. The Republicans mentioned "free" or "freedom" more than three times as often (73 to 19), while the Democrats referred to "equal" or "equality" or "inequality" more than four times as much (23 to 4). Republicans talked more about order than Democrats, mentioning "crime" or "criminals" more often (33 to 26) and swamping the Democrats with talk about "marriage" (21 to 4) and "abortion" (20 to 4). Republicans also drummed on "spending" almost five times as frequently (29 to 6), while Democrats talked more about "discrimination" (18 to 9 mentions).

Different but Similar. The Democrats and the Republicans have very different ideological orientations. Yet many observers claim that the parties are really quite similar in ideology compared to the different parties of other countries. Although both Republicans and Democrats favor a market economy over a planned economy more than parties elsewhere, Republicans do so more strongly than Democrats. A major cross-national study of party positions in Western countries since 1945 concludes that the United States experiences "a form of party competition that is as ideologically (or non-ideologically) driven as the other countries we have studied."[42]

National Party Organization

Most casual observers would agree with Will Rogers's description of the Democrats as an unorganized political party. It used to apply to the Republicans too, but this has changed since the 1970s, at least at the national level. Bear in mind the distinction between levels of party structure. American parties parallel our federal system: they have separate national and state organizations (and functionally separate local organizations, in many cases).

At the national level, each major party has four main organizational components:

- *National convention.* Every four years, each party assembles thousands of delegates from the states and U.S. territories (such as Puerto Rico and Guam) in a national convention for the purpose of nominating a candidate for president. This presidential nominating convention is also the supreme governing body of the party. It determines party policy through the platform, formulates rules to govern party operations, and designates a national committee, which is empowered to govern the party until the next convention.

- *National committee.* The **national committee**, which governs each party between conventions, is composed of party officials representing the states and territories, including the chairpersons of their party organizations. The Republican National Committee (RNC) has about 150 members, consisting of the national committeeman, national committeewoman, and a chairperson from each state and from the District of Columbia, Guam, Puerto Rico, and the Virgin Islands. The Democratic National Committee (DNC) has approximately 450 elected and appointed members, including, in addition to the national committee members and party chairs, members representing auxiliary organizations. The chairperson of each national committee is usually chosen by the party's presidential nominee and then duly elected by the committee. If the nominee loses the election, the national committee usually replaces the nominee's chairperson.

- *Congressional party conferences.* At the beginning of each session of Congress, the Republicans and Democrats in each chamber hold separate **party conferences** (the House Democrats call theirs a caucus) to select their party leaders and decide committee assignments. The party conferences deal only with congressional matters and have no structural relationship to each other and none with their national committees.

- *Congressional campaign committees.* Democrats and Republicans in the House and Senate also maintain separate **congressional campaign committees**, each of which raises its own funds to support its candidates in congressional elections. The separation of these organizations from the national committee tells us that the national party structure is loose; the national committee seldom gets involved with the election of any individual member of Congress. Moreover, even the congressional campaign organizations merely supplement the funds that senators and representatives raise on their own to win reelection.

national committee
A committee of a political party composed of party chairpersons and party officials from every state.

party conferences
A meeting to select party leaders and decide committee assignments, held at the beginning of a session of Congress by Republicans or Democrats in each chamber.

congressional campaign committee
An organization maintained by a political party to raise funds to support its own candidates in congressional elections.

It is tempting to think of the national party chairperson as sitting at the top of a hierarchical party organization that not only controls its members in Congress but also issues orders to the state committees and on down to the local level. Few ideas could be more wrong.[43] In fact, the RNC and DNC do not even really direct or control the crucial presidential campaigns. Prospective nominees hire their own campaign staffs during the party primaries to win delegates who will support them for nomination at the party conventions. Successful nominees then keep their winning staffs to contest the general election. The main role of a national committee is to support its candidate's personal campaign staff in the effort to win.

In this light, the national committees appear to be relatively useless organizations—as reflected in the 1964 book about them, *Politics Without Power*.[44] For many years, their role was essentially limited to planning for the next party convention. The committee would select the site, invite the state parties to attend, plan the program, and so on. Beginning in the 1970s, however, the roles of the DNC and RNC began to expand—but in different ways.

The Democratic story was dramatic. During the Vietnam War in 1968, an unpopular President Lyndon Johnson was challenged for renomination by prominent Democrats, including Senators Robert F. Kennedy and Eugene McCarthy. On March 31, after primary elections had begun, Johnson chose not to run for reelection. His vice president, Hubert Humphrey, then announced his candidacy. A month later Senator Kennedy was assassinated. Although Humphrey did not enter a single primary, he won the nomination over McCarthy at a riotous convention angry at the war and the role of party bosses in picking Humphrey. In an attempt to open the party to broader participation, a party commission formulated new guidelines for selecting delegates to the next convention in 1972. These guidelines promised party members a "full, meaningful and timely opportunity" to participate in the process. To comply with the new guidelines, many states used more open procedures, electing convention delegates in party primaries.

While the Democrats were busy in the 1970s with *procedural* reforms, the Republicans were making *organizational* reforms.[45] The RNC did little to open up its delegate selection process; Republicans were not inclined to impose quotas on state parties through their national committee. Instead, the RNC strengthened its fundraising, research, and service roles. Republicans acquired their own building and their own computer system, and in 1976 they hired the first full-time chairperson in the history of either national party. (Until then, the chairperson had worked part-time.) The new RNC chairman, William Brock, expanded the party's staff, launched new publications, held seminars, conducted election analyses, and advised candidates for state and legislative offices—things that national party committees in other countries had been doing for years. By the 2000 election, campaign finance analysts noted, American parties had become "an important source of funding in the race for the White House."[46]

The vast difference between the Democratic and Republican approaches to reforming the national committees shows in the funds raised by the DNC and RNC during election campaigns. Even though Republicans traditionally raised more campaign money than Democrats, they no longer relied on a relatively few wealthy contributors. As a matter of fact, the Republicans received more of their funds in small contributions (less than $100), mainly through direct-mail solicitation, than the Democrats. Until the 2008 election, the RNC raised far more money than the DNC, from many more citizens, as part of its long-term commitment to improving its organizational services. Beginning in 2002, however, significant changes occurred in how political parties could collect money to finance their activities. These campaign finance reforms are discussed in Chapter 9.

According to a major study of presidential party building, all Republican presidents, from Eisenhower through G. W. Bush, supported their national committee's organization efforts in order to build a Republican majority in the electorate. In contrast, Democratic presidents from Kennedy through Clinton "were not out to build a new majority but to make use of the one they had."[47] They tended to exploit, not build, the party organization. Obama fell back into the traditional pattern during his first term. By using his party to generate publicity for his administration's policy agenda while neglecting its organizational capacities at the state and local levels, Obama's behavior tended to parallel that of his Democratic predecessors.

State and Local Party Organizations

At one time, both major parties were firmly anchored by powerful state and local party organizations. Big-city party organizations, such as the Democrats' Tammany Hall in New York City and the Cook County Central Committee in Chicago, were called *party machines.*

A **party machine** was a centralized organization that dominated local politics by controlling elections—sometimes by illegal means, often by providing jobs and social services to urban workers in return for their votes. The patronage and social service functions of party machines were undercut when the government expanded unemployment compensation, aid to families with dependent children, and other social services. As a result, most local party organizations lost their ability to deliver votes and thus to determine the outcome of elections. However, machines remained strong in certain areas. In Nassau County, New York, for example, suburban Republicans showed that they could run a machine as well as urban Democrats.[48]

party machine
A centralized party organization that dominates local politics by controlling elections.

The individual state and local organizations of both parties vary widely in strength, but recent research has found that "neither the Republican nor Democratic party has a distinct advantage with regard to direct campaign activities."[49] Whereas once both the RNC and the DNC were dependent for their funding on "quotas" paid by state parties, now the funds flow the other way. In the 2007–2008 election cycle, the national party campaign committees transferred over $150 million to state and local parties.[50] In addition to money, state parties also received candidate training, poll data and research, and campaigning instruction.[51] The national committees have also taken a more active role in congressional campaigns.[52]

Decentralized but Growing Stronger

Although the national committees have gained strength over the past three decades, American political parties are still among the most decentralized parties in the world.[53] Not even the president can count on loyalty from the legislative members of his party. Consider the 2009 congressional vote on reforming health care, President Obama's most important policy initiative. Although the Democrats held 258 seats in the House, the bill passed only 220–215, as 39 Democrats (15 percent) voted against it. Although all Democrats voted for the bill to reach the 60 votes needed for passage in the Senate (all 39 Republicans opposed it), some Democratic Senators demanded and got changes before backing the President's plan.

Decentralization of power has always been the most distinguishing characteristic of American political parties. Moreover, the rise in the proportion of citizens who style themselves as independents suggests that our already weak parties are in further decline.[54] But there is evidence that our political parties *as organizations* are enjoying a period of resurgence. Indeed, both national parties have "globalized" their organizations, maintaining branches in over a dozen nations.[55] Both parties' national committees have never been better funded or more active in grassroots campaign activities.[56] And more votes in Congress are being decided along party lines. (See Chapter 11 for a discussion of the rise of party voting in Congress since the 1970s.) In fact, a specialist in congressional politics has concluded, "When compared to its predecessors of the past half-century, the current majority party leadership is more involved and more decisive in organizing the party and the chamber, setting the policy agenda, shaping legislation, and determining legislative outcomes."[57] However, the American parties have traditionally been so weak that these positive trends have not altered their basic character.[58] American political parties are still so organizationally diffuse and decentralized that they raise questions about how well they link voters to the government.

8.5 The Model of Responsible Party Government

★ Identify the principles of responsible party government and evaluate their role in majoritarian democracy.

According to the majoritarian model of democracy, parties are essential to making the government responsive to public opinion. In fact, the ideal role of parties in majoritarian democracy has been formalized in the four principles of **responsible party government**:[59]

responsible party government
A set of principles formalizing the ideal role of parties in a majoritarian democracy.

1. Parties should present clear and coherent programs to voters.
2. Voters should choose candidates on the basis of party programs.
3. The winning party should carry out its program once in office.
4. Voters should hold the governing party responsible at the next election for executing its program.

How well do these principles describe American politics? You've learned that the Democratic and Republican platforms are different and that they are much more ideologically consistent than many people believe. So the first principle is being met fairly well.[60] To a lesser extent, so is the third principle: once parties gain power, they usually try to do what they said they would do. As Obama's attempt to reform health care showed, however, not every party member will necessarily support the party's position. Moreover, the Republicans, who won control of the House of Representatives in the 2010 congressional election, failed to carry out their pledge to repeal Obama's health-care legislation, blocked by a Democratic Senate.

One can ask whether the model of responsible party government is suited to the American political system. Because governmental power is divided among the House, Senate, and president, a party must control all three components to carry out its program. In national surveys, people only favor one-party control of the presidency *and* congress if *their* party is in control. Otherwise, a majority favors divided government or thinks it makes no difference.[61]

From the standpoint of democratic theory and responsible parties, the real question involves principles 2 and 4: Do voters really pay attention to party platforms and policies when they cast their ballots?[62] And if so, do voters hold the governing party responsible at the next election for delivering, or failing to deliver, on its pledges? To answer these questions, we must consider in greater detail the parties' role in nominating candidates and structuring the voters' choices in elections. At the conclusion of Chapter 9, we will return to evaluating the role of political parties in democratic government.

SUMMARY

8.1 Political Parties and Their Functions

- Political parties perform four important functions: nominating candidates, structuring the voting choice, proposing alternative government programs, and coordinating the activities of government officials.
- Political parties have been performing these functions longer in the United States than in any other country.

8.2 A History of U.S. Party Politics

- The Democratic Party, founded in 1828, is the world's oldest political party.
- The Republican Party emerged as a major party after the 1856 election.
- Our two-party system has been marked by four critical elections.
- The election of 1860 established the Republicans as the major party in the North and the Democrats as the dominant party in the South.
- The election of 1896 strengthened the link between the Republican Party and business interests in the Northeast and Midwest, making it the majority party nationally for more than three decades.
- The election of 1932 during the Great Depression transformed the Democrats into the majority party for more than three decades.

- The election of 1968 ended the Democrats' domination of national politics, as Republican presidential candidates ran well in the South.
- Today, the two parties are roughly equal in electoral strength.

8.3 The American Two-Party System

- Minor parties have contributed ideas to the Democratic and Republican platforms but have not enjoyed much electoral success in America.
- Our two-party system is perpetuated by two principles of our electoral system: single-member districts and plurality rule.
- Also, the political socialization process causes most Americans to identify with either the Democratic or the Republican Party.
- Over the last sixty years, voters have been leaving the Democratic Party and becoming independents.
- Still, Democrats nationally outnumber Republicans, and together they outnumber independents.

8.4 Party Ideology and Organization

- Democratic identifiers and activists are more likely to describe themselves as liberal;

Republican identifiers and activists tend to be conservative.

- Democratic Party platforms stress equality over freedom; Republican platforms stress freedom but also emphasize the importance of restoring social order.
- Organizationally, the Republicans have recently become the stronger party at both the national and state levels, and both parties are showing signs of resurgence.

- Nevertheless, both parties are still very decentralized compared with parties in other countries.

8.5 The Model of Responsible Party Government

- American parties do tend to translate their platform positions into government policy if elected to power.
- Ironically, citizens do not pay much attention to platforms when voting.

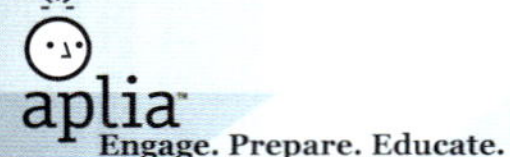

ASSESSING YOUR UNDERSTANDING WITH APLIA...YOUR VIRTUAL TUTOR!

8.1 Define political party and list the functions performed by parties in democratic government.

1. How does a political party differ from an interest group?
2. What are the major functions of political parties?

8.2 Outline the history of the U.S. political party system.

1. To which political party did President Washington belong?
2. How did the Twelfth Amendment to the Constitution affect how parties nominated presidential candidates?
3. How long have we had our current party system, with Democrats competing against Republicans?

8.3 Explain why two parties dominate the history of American politics.

1. What minor parties have won the most votes in presidential elections?
2. How does an electoral system based on majority representation favor two parties compared with one based on proportional representation?
3. What does ''party identification'' mean, how is it measured, and how stable has it been in America since the 1950s?

8.4 Compare and contrast the Democratic and Republican parties on the basis of ideology and organization.

1. In both parties, who tend to be more ideologically extreme, party voters or party activists?

2. How do the Democratic and Republican parties' platforms differ in invoking the concepts of freedom, order, and equality?

3. To what extent do the national committees of the Democratic and Republican parties control their parties' presidential campaigns?

8.5 **Identify the principles of responsible party government and evaluate their role in majoritarian democracy.**

1. Is there any evidence that the two major American political parties fulfill the first principle of responsible party government?

Nominations, Elections, and Campaigns

CHAPTER TOPICS and Learning Outcomes

9.1 The Evolution of Campaigning
★ Describe how election campaigns have changed over time.

9.2 Nominations
★ Explain the procedures followed in the nomination of both congressional and presidential candidates.

9.3 Elections
★ Describe the function of the electoral college and formulate arguments for and against the electoral vote system.

9.4 Campaigns
★ Analyze the American election campaign process in terms of political context, financial resources, and strategies and tactics for reaching the voters.

9.5 Explaining Voting Choice
★ Assess the effects of party identification, political issues, and candidate attributes on voter choice.

9.6 Campaigns, Elections, and Parties
★ Explain the significance of candidate-centered as opposed to party-centered election campaigns for both majoritarian and pluralist democracy.

American voters carry a heavy burden. They are asked to choose among *more* candidates for *more* offices *more* frequently than voters in any other country. Having the opportunity to choose government officials is a blessing of democracy, but learning enough about so many candidates to make informed choices is the curse of our unique and demanding electoral system.

As explained in Chapter 7, when Americans go to the polls in a general election, they are asked to choose among scores of candidates running for many different public offices at the local, state, and national levels. In the United States, an election is "general" in the sense that it includes various levels of government. In most other countries, a general election is very different and citizens have a much lighter burden in the polling booth.

Let's consider the difference between the 2012 general election in the United States and the 2010 general election in the United Kingdom, commonly called Britain. Like the United States, Britain is a democracy. Unlike the United States—but like most other democracies and nearly all European nations—Britain has a parliamentary, not a presidential, form of government.[1] Outlining how the British government operates illustrates how most established democracies operate.

The United Kingdom is led by a prime minister chosen by members in the elected house of parliament—the House of Commons. The party controlling the House selects the prime minister. Because a parliamentary system joins the executive and legislative powers, the prime minister becomes the head of government.[2] British governments are limited to five-year terms in office, but a general election is called if the prime minister loses support of parliament. A prime minister can also hold a general election earlier if the timing looks promising for his or her party. By British law, the parliament elected in 2005 had to expire on May 10, 2010, but the prime minister could have requested the Queen to dissolve parliament earlier.

In Britain, general elections are not held according to a fixed calendar, so no party can prepare for them far in advance. Because elections are timed to political needs (such as a vote of no confidence in the government), the campaign period is fixed and short. On April 5, 2010, Prime Minister Gordon Brown of the governing Labour Party called the election for May 6, leaving just 31 days for campaigning—about average for British parliamentary elections.[3] Punished for Britain's economic downturn, Brown's Labour Party was voted out of office and replaced by the Conservative Party, led by David Cameron. The Conservatives failed to win a majority of seats, but Cameron became prime minister with support from the smaller Social Democratic Party, led by Nick Gregg.

If the United Kingdom bases its elections on political needs, the United States bases its on planetary movements. In early November, after the Earth has traveled four times around the sun, the United States holds a presidential election. The timing is entirely predictable but has little to do with politics.[4] Predictability does carry some advantages for political stability, but it also has some negative consequences. A major negative is the multiyear length of our presidential election campaigns. Presidential hopefuls in the Republican Party began planning for the 2012 election soon after the 2008 election.

In the short campaigns preceding British general elections, voters are asked only to choose among one small set of candidates running for a single seat in parliament. The election is general only in the sense that all members of the House are up for election; there are *no other offices or issues on the ballot.*

This difference leaps out when comparing the ballots for the United States and Britain (see "Compared with What? The Voter's Burden in the United States and United Kingdom" on pp. 240–241). This difference dramatically translates into enormous differences in the total votes that are cast by voters in the two countries. The burden of being an informed voter is much greater here than there.

In this chapter, we probe more deeply into elections in the United States. We study how candidates are nominated in the United States and the factors that are important in causing voters to favor one nominee over another. We consider the role of election campaigns and how they have changed over time. We also address these important questions: How well do election campaigns inform voters? How important is money in conducting a winning campaign? What are the roles of party identification, issues, and candidate attributes in influencing voters' choices and thus election outcomes? How do campaigns, elections, and parties fit into the majoritarian and pluralist models of democracy?

9.1 The Evolution of Campaigning

★ Describe how election campaigns have changed over time.

Voting in free elections to choose leaders is the main way that citizens control government. As discussed in Chapter 8, political parties help structure the voting choice by reducing the number of candidates on the ballot to those who have a realistic chance of winning or who offer distinctive policies. An **election campaign** is an organized effort to persuade voters to choose one candidate over others competing for the same office. An effective campaign requires sufficient resources to acquire and analyze information about voters' interests, develop a strategy and matching tactics for appealing to these interests, deliver the candidate's message to the voters, and get them to cast their ballots.[5]

election campaign
An organized effort to persuade voters to choose one candidate over others competing for the same office.

In the past, political parties conducted all phases of the election campaign. As recently as the 1950s, state and local party organizations "felt the pulse" of their rank-and-file members to learn what was important to the voters. They chose the candidates and then lined up leading officials to support them and to ensure big crowds at campaign rallies. They also prepared buttons, banners, and newspaper advertisements that touted their candidates, proudly named under the prominent label of the party. Finally, candidates relied heavily on the local precinct and county party organizations to contact voters before elections, to mention their names, to extol their virtues, and—most importantly—to make sure their supporters voted, and voted correctly.

Today, candidates seldom rely much on political parties to conduct their campaigns. How do candidates learn about voters' interests today? By contracting for public opinion polls, not by asking the party. How do candidates plan their campaign strategy and tactics now? By hiring political consultants to devise clever sound bites (brief, catchy phrases) that will capture voters' attention on television, not by consulting party headquarters. How do candidates deliver their messages to voters? By conducting media campaigns, not by counting on party regulars to canvass the neighborhoods. Beginning with the 2004 election, presidential and congressional candidates have also relied heavily on the Internet to raise campaign funds and mobilize supporters.[6]

Increasingly, election campaigns have evolved from being party centered to being candidate centered.[7] This is not to say that political parties no longer have a role to play in campaigns, for they do. As noted in Chapter 8, the Democratic National Committee now exercises more control over the delegate selection process than it did before 1972. Since 1976, the Republicans have greatly expanded their national organization and fundraising capacity. But whereas the parties virtually ran election campaigns prior to the 1960s, now they exist mainly to support candidate-centered campaigns by providing services or funds to their candidates. Nevertheless, we will see that the party label is usually a candidate's prime attribute at election time.

Perhaps the most important change in American elections is that candidates don't campaign just to get elected anymore. Due to the Progressive movement in the 1920s that championed use of the direct primary to select party candidates (see page 189), candidates must campaign for *nomination* as well. As we said in Chapter 8, nominating candidates to run for office under the party label is one of the main functions of political parties. Party organizations once controlled that function. Even Abraham Lincoln served only one term in the House of Representatives before the party transferred the nomination for his House seat to someone else.[8] For most important offices today, however, candidates are no longer nominated *by* the party organization but *within* the party. Except when recruiting prominent individuals to challenge entrenched incumbents, party leaders seldom choose candidates; they merely organize and supervise the election process by which party *voters* choose the candidates. Because almost all aspiring candidates must first win a primary election to gain their party's nomination, those who would campaign for election must first campaign for nomination.[9]

9.2 Nominations

★ Explain the procedures followed in the nomination of both congressional and presidential candidates.

The distinguishing feature of the nomination process in American party politics is that it usually involves an election by party voters. National party leaders do not choose their party's nominee for president or even its candidates for House and Senate seats. Virtually no other political parties in the world nominate candidates to the national legislature through party elections.[10] In more than half the world's parties, local party leaders choose legislative candidates, and their national party organization must usually approve these choices.

Compared with What?

The Voter's Burden in the United States and United Kingdom

Compared with other countries, the United States puts a very heavy burden on its voters. Compare these two facsimiles of official specimen ballots for the 2010 general election in Britain and the 2012 general election in the United States. This long U.S. ballot, which asked voters to choose among 46 candidates for 29 different offices, is just a portion of the one that confronted voters in the city of Evanston, Illinois. They also were asked to retain or terminate 57 judges also on the ballot. In addition, they voted on a referendum to amend the U.S. Constitution to regulate political contributions from corporations. By contrast, the straightforward British ballot for the Oxford East constituency (which includes most of Oxford University) required citizens simply to choose one from seven party candidates for the House of Commons, shown with their addresses and party affiliations. As shown by the X, the Labour candidate won, getting 43 percent of the vote compared with 34 percent for the Liberal Democrat and 19 percent for the Conservative. All four of the remaining candidates won about 5 percent. Despite the presence of seven candidates, British voters' decision was simple. Compared with Britain (and virtually all other countries), voting is very complicated in the United States.

Voter Ballot for the 2010 Election in Britain's East Oxford Constituency

Vote for One Candidate Only

1	**ARGAR** Edward (address in the Cities of London and Westminster constituency) The Conservative Party Candidate	
2	**CRAWFORD** Roger Martin The Pigling, Woodview Nurseries, Shefford Road, Meppershall, Beds, SG17 5LL Equal Parenting Alliance	
3	**DHALL** Sushila (address in the Oxford West and Abingdon constituency) Green Party	
4	**GASPER** Julia Margaret 22 Trinity Road, Oxford, OX3 8LQ UK Independence Party	
5	**GODDARD** Steve 60 Rosamund Road, Oxford, OX2 8NX Liberal Democrats	
6	**O'SULLIVAN** David Andrew (address in the Brent East constituency) Socialist Equality Party	
7	**SMITH** Andrew 4 Flaxfield Road, Oxford, OX4 6QD The Labour Party Candidate	X

Voter Ballot for the 2012 United States General Election

City of Evanston, Cook County, Illinois, November 6

President and Vice President, U.S. (Vote For 1)

☐ Barack Obama — *Democratic*
☐ Mitt Romney — *Republican*
☐ Gary Johnson — *Libertarian*
☐ Jill Steir — *Green Party*

Representative, 9th District (Vote For 1)

☐ Janice Schakowsky — *Democratic*
☐ Timothy Wolfe — *Republican*

State Senator, 9th District (Vote For 1)

☐ Daniel Biss — *Democratic*
☐ Glenn Farkas — *Republican*

State Representative, 17th District (Vote For 1)

☐ Laura Fine — *Democratic*
☐ Kyle Frenk — *Republican*

Commissioner, Metro Water Reclamation Dist. (Vote For 1)

☐ Debra Shore — *Democratic*
☐ Kari Steele — *Democratic*
☐ Patrick Daley Thompson — *Democratic*
☐ Harold Ward — *Republican*
☐ Carl Segvich — *Republican*
☐ Dave Ehrlich — *Green Party*
☐ Karen Roothaan — *Green Party*
☐ Nasrin Khalili — *Green Party*

State's Attorney, Cook County (Vote For 1)

☐ Anita Alvarez — *Democratic*
☐ Lori Yokoyama — *Republican*

Clerk of the Circuit Court, Cook County (Vote For 1)

☐ Dorothy Brown — *Democratic*
☐ Diane Shapiro — *Republican*

Recorder, Cook County (Vote For 1)

☐ Karen Yarbrough — *Democratic*
☐ Sherri Griffith — *Republican*

Commissioner, 2nd District (Vote For 1)

☐ Michael Cabonargi — *Democratic*

Judge, Illinois Supreme Court (Vote For 1)

☐ Mary Theis — *Democratic*
☐ James Riley — *Republican*

Judge, Illinois Appellate Court, 1st District (Vote For 1)

☐ Mathias Delort — *Democratic*

Judge, Illinois Appellate Court, 1st District (Vote For 1)

☐ Nathaniel Howse — *Democratic*

Judge, Illinois Appellate Court, 1st District (Vote For 1)

☐ P. Neville — *Democratic*

Judge, Illinois Appellate Court, 1st District (Vote For 1)

☐ Jesse Reyes — *Democratic*

Judge, Illinois Appellate Court, 1st District (Vote For 1)

☐ Maureen Connors — *Democratic*

Judge, Illinois Appellate Court, 1st District (Vote For 1)

☐ Terrence Lavin — *Democratic*

Judge, Cook County Judicial Circuit (Vote For 1)

☐ Karen O'Malley — *Democratic*

Judge, Cook County Judicial Circuit (Vote For 1)

☐ Jean Prendergast Rooney — *Democratic*

Judge, Cook County Judicial Circuit (Vote For 1)

☐ Erica Reddick — *Democratic*

Judge, Cook County Judicial Circuit (Vote For 1)

☐ Russell Hartigan — *Democratic*

Judge, Cook County Judicial Circuit (Vote For 1)

☐ Cynthia Ramirez — *Democratic*

Judge, Cook County Judicial Circuit (Vote For 1)

☐ Diann Marsalek — *Democratic*

Judge, Cook County Judicial Circuit (Vote For 1)

☐ Lorna Propes — *Democratic*

Judge, Cook County Judicial Circuit (Vote For 1)

☐ Jessica O'Brien — *Democratic*

Judge, Cook County Judicial Circuit (Vote For 1)

☐ Pamela Leeming — *Democratic*

Judge, Cook County Judicial Circuit (Vote For 1)

☐ Michael Tully Mullen — *Democratic*

Judge, Cook County Judicial Circuit (Vote For 1)

☐ Elizabeth Hayes — *Democratic*

Judge, 9th Subcircuit (Vote For 1)

☐ Lionel Jean-Baptiste — *Democratic*

Judge, 9th Subcircuit (Vote For 1)

☐ Larry Axelrood — *Democratic*

Democrats and Republicans nominate their candidates for national and state offices in varying ways across the country, because each state is entitled to make its own laws governing the nomination process. (This is significant in itself, for political parties in most other countries are largely free of laws stating how they must select their candidates.)[11] We can classify nomination practices by the types of party elections held and the level of office sought.

Nomination for Congress and State Offices

In the United States, almost all aspiring candidates for major offices are nominated through a **primary election**, a preliminary election conducted within the party to select its candidates. Some forty states use primary elections alone to nominate candidates for all state and national offices, and primaries figure in the nomination processes of all the other states. The rules governing primary elections vary greatly by state, and they can change between elections. Hence, it is difficult to summarize the types of primaries and their incidence. Every state uses primary elections to nominate candidates for statewide office, but about ten states also use party conventions to place names on the primary ballots.[12] The nomination process, then, is highly decentralized, resting on the decisions of thousands, perhaps millions, of the party rank and file who participate in primary elections.

In both parties, only about half of the regular party voters (about one-quarter of the voting-age population) bother to vote in a given primary, although the proportion varies greatly by state and contest.[13] Early research on primary elections concluded that Republicans who voted in their primaries were more conservative than those who did not, whereas Democratic primary voters were more liberal than other Democrats. Some research disputed this finding, but recent studies suggest that primary voters are unrepresentative of the ideological orientation of other party voters.[14]

Some studies support another interpretation: although party activists who turn out for primaries and caucuses are not representative of the average party member, they subordinate their own views to select candidates "who will fare well in the general election."[15] Within the Republican Party in the 2010 election, however, the tea party movement worked to nominate strongly conservative House and Senate candidates over more moderate and arguably more electable candidates. Tea party choices fared better in House elections than in Senate elections, which some notable tea party candidates lost. Perhaps the most significant fact about primary elections in American politics today is the decline in competition for party nominations. One major study found that only "about 25 percent of statewide candidates face serious primary competition."[16]

There are four major types of primary elections, and variants of each type have been used frequently across all states to nominate candidates for state and congressional offices.[17] At one end of the spectrum are **closed primaries**, in which voters must register their party affiliation to vote on that party's potential nominees. At the other end are **open primaries**, in which any voter, regardless of party registration or affiliation, can choose either party's ballot. In between are **modified closed primaries**, in which individual state parties decide whether to allow those not registered with either party to vote with their party registrants, and **modified open primaries**, in which all those not already registered with a party can choose any party ballot and vote with party registrants. Voters in the states of Washington (in 2004) and California (in 2010) approved a single primary open to all candidates and in which the top two vote-getters stand for the general election. Brief experience with this "top two" primary system shows that winning candidates virtually always come from the two major parties.[18]

Most scholars believe that the type of primary held in a state affects the strength of its party organizations. Open primaries weaken parties more than closed primaries, for they allow voters to float between parties rather than require them to work within one. But the differences among types of primaries are much less important

---

primary election
A preliminary election conducted within a political party to select candidates who will run for public office in a subsequent election.

closed primaries
Primary elections in which voters must declare their party affiliation before they are given the primary ballot containing that party's potential nominees.

open primaries
Primary elections in which voters need not declare their party affiliation and can choose one party's primary ballot to take into the voting booth.

modified closed primaries
Primary elections that allow individual state parties to decide whether they permit independents to vote in their primaries and for which offices.

modified open primaries
Primary elections that entitle independent voters to vote in a party's primary.

than the fact that our parties have primaries at all—that parties choose candidates through elections. This practice originated in the United States and largely remains peculiar to us. Placing the nomination of party candidates in the hands of voters rather than party leaders is a key factor in the decentralization of power in American parties, which contributes more to pluralist than to majoritarian democracy.[19]

Nomination for President

The decentralized nature of American parties is readily apparent in how presidential hopefuls must campaign for their party's nomination for president. Each party formally chooses its presidential and vice-presidential candidates at a national convention held every four years in the summer prior to the November election. Until the 1960s, party delegates chose their party's nominee right at the convention, sometimes after repeated balloting over several candidates who divided the vote and kept anyone from getting the majority needed to win the nomination. In 1920, for example, the Republican National Convention deadlocked over two leading candidates after nine ballots. Party leaders then met in the storied "smoke-filled room" and compromised on Warren G. Harding, who won on the tenth ballot. Harding was not among the leading candidates and had won only a single primary (in his native Ohio). The last time that either party needed more than one ballot to nominate its presidential candidate was in 1952, when the Democrats took three ballots to nominate Adlai E. Stevenson. The Republicans that year nominated Dwight Eisenhower on only one ballot, but he won in a genuine contest with Senator Robert Taft. So Eisenhower also won his nomination on the convention floor.

Although 1952 was the last year a nominating majority was engineered by delegates inside the hall, delegates at the Democratic convention in 1960 and the Republican convention in 1964 also resolved uncertain outcomes. So did the 1968 Democratic convention, which critics charged was rigged. After President Lyndon Johnson unexpectedly announced on March 31, 1968, that he would not seek reelection, Democratic party leaders at the summer's Chicago convention anointed his Vice President Hubert Humphrey, who had not run in a single primary, as the party's nominee. (See page 232.) The ensuing riots at the convention and in the streets led to fundamental reforms in the delegate selection process in both parties beginning with the 1972 presidential election.

Prior to 1972, major party organizations dominated the presidential nominating process; there were few primaries, short campaigns, limited media coverage, and open conventions—during which the assembled delegates actually chose the nominee. The reverse has been true in every convention since. Both parties' nominating conventions now simply ratify

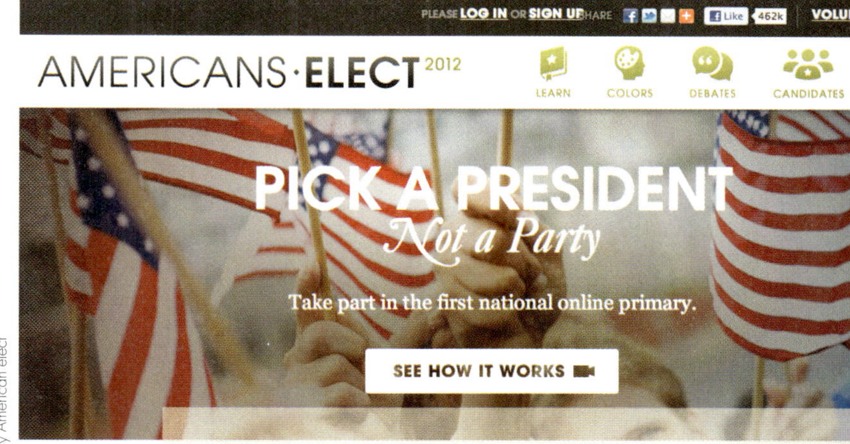

Courtesy American elect

Suppose You Held a Primary and Nobody Voted

In 2012, Americans Elect launched a website (americanselect.org) that invited citizens to choose a presidential ticket outside the major parties by voting on the Internet. Candidates needed 10,000 "clicks" by May 2012 to be listed on the party's online presidential primary ballot in June. Not enough citizens participated, so nobody was nominated. The leading candidate, Buddy Roemer (former Governor of Louisiana who switched from Democrat to Republican) had only 6,293 clicks. Next was Rocky Anderson (former Mayor of Salt Lake City) with 3,390. Even if you knew these headliners, you would be unlikely to know the two other candidates with more than 1,000 clicks. No one else even had 600. The experiment ended for lack of citizen interest.

the results of a complex process for selecting the convention delegates.[20] Most minor parties still choose their presidential candidates in national conventions. In 2012, a nonpartisan organization, Americans Elect, experimented with nominating presidential candidates online—and failed.

Selecting Convention Delegates. No national legislation specifies how the state parties must select delegates to their national conventions. Instead, state legislatures have enacted a bewildering variety of procedures, which often differ for Democrats and Republicans in the same state. The most important distinction in delegate selection is between the presidential primary and the local caucus. In 2012, both major parties in more than thirty states used primaries to select delegates to their presidential nominating conventions, and both parties in fewer than twenty states selected delegates through a combination of local caucuses and state conventions.[21]

presidential primary

A special primary election used to select delegates to attend the party's national convention, which in turn nominates the presidential candidate.

A **presidential primary** is a special primary held to select delegates to attend a party's national nominating convention. Party supporters typically vote for the candidate they favor as their party's nominee for president, and candidates win delegates according to various formulas. Democratic presidential primaries are *proportional,* meaning that candidates win delegates in rough proportion to the votes they win. Specifically, candidates who win at least 15 percent of the vote divide the state's delegates in proportion to the percentage of their primary votes. Prior to 2012, most Republican primaries followed the *winner-take-all* principle, which gives all the state's delegates to the candidate who wins a plurality of its vote. For 2012, however, some states adopted proportional rules for Republican primaries. Analyses expected that the rule changes would prolong the race for the party's nomination, because the leading candidate could not gobble up a majority of the delegates from states that held early primaries.

caucus/convention

A method used to select delegates to attend a party's national convention. Generally, a local meeting selects delegates for a county-level meeting, which in turn selects delegates for a higher-level meeting; the process culminates in a state convention that actually selects the national convention delegates.

The **caucus/convention** method of delegate selection has several stages. It begins with local meetings, or caucuses, of party supporters to choose delegates to attend a larger subsequent meeting, usually at the county level. Most delegates selected in the local caucuses openly back one of the presidential candidates. The county meetings select delegates to a higher level. The process culminates in a state convention, which selects the delegates to the national convention.

Primary elections were first used to select delegates to nominating conventions in 1912. Heralded as a party "reform," primaries spread like wildfire.[22] By 1916, a majority of delegates to both conventions were chosen through party elections, but presidential primaries soon dropped in popularity. From 1924 through 1960, rarely were more than 40 percent of the delegates to the national conventions chosen through primaries. Protests at the 1968 Democratic National Convention (see Chapter 8) sparked rule changes in the national party that required more "open" procedures for selecting delegates. Voting in primaries seemed the most open procedure. By 1972, this method of selection accounted for about 60 percent of the delegates at both party conventions. Now the parties in almost forty states rely on presidential primaries of some form, which generate about 80 percent of the delegates.[23]

Because most delegates selected in primaries are publicly committed to specific candidates, one usually can tell before a party's summer nominating convention who is going to be its nominee. Starting in 1972, we began learning the nominee's identity earlier and earlier, thanks to **front-loading** of delegate selection. This term describes the tendency during the past two decades for states to move their primaries earlier in the calendar year to gain attention from the media and the candidates. Some states moved their primaries back for the 2012 primary season. Whereas half the Republican delegates had been chosen by February 5 in 2008, half were not selected until April 24 in 2012.

Campaigning for the Nomination. The process of nominating party candidates for president is a complex, drawn-out affair that has no parallel in any other nation.[24] Would-be presidents announce their candidacy and begin campaigning many months before the first convention delegates are selected. Soon after one election ends, prospective candidates quietly begin lining up political and financial support for their likely race nearly four years later. This early, silent campaign has been dubbed the *invisible primary.*[25] (See Figure 9.1, p. 248, for dates when presidential hopefuls announced their candidacies—and their withdrawals.)

By historical accident, two small states, Iowa and New Hampshire, have become the testing ground of candidates' popularity with party voters. Accordingly, each basks in the media spotlight once every four years. The legislatures of both states are committed to leading the delegate selection process in their own way—Iowa using party caucuses and New Hampshire a direct primary—ensuring their states' share of national publicity and their bids for political history. The Iowa caucuses and the New Hampshire primary have served different functions in the presidential nominating process.[26] The contest in Iowa, attended by party activists, has traditionally tended to winnow out candidates, narrowing the field. The New Hampshire primary, typically held a week later, tests the Iowa front-runners' appeal to ordinary party voters, which foreshadows their likely strength in the general election. Because voting takes little effort by itself, more citizens are likely to vote in primaries than to attend caucuses, which can last for hours. In 2012, about 6.5 percent of the voting-age population participated in both parties' Iowa caucuses, whereas about 31 percent voted in both New Hampshire primaries.[27] These turnout rates were about half of those in 2008, when both parties had hot contests for the presidential nomination. In 2012, only the Republican Party featured caucus and primary contests.

From 1920 to 1972, New Hampshire's primary election led the nation in selecting delegates to the parties' summer conventions. But in 1972 Iowa chose its convention delegates in caucuses held even earlier. Since then, Iowa and New Hampshire agreed to be first in their methods of delegate selection.[28] As usual, the two states in 2012 fulfilled their role in winnowing down the field of presidential hopefuls.

Seven notables stood for the Iowa Republican caucuses on January 3, 2012. In alphabetical order, they were Michele Bachmann, Newt Gingrich, Jon Huntsman, Ron Paul, Rick Perry, Mitt Romney, and Rick Santorum. (See Figure 9.1 for candidates' background.) Romney (with 24.5 percent of the vote) was initially declared the winner, only to lose to Santorum (24.5 percent) by a handful of votes after the recount. Bachmann (who had depended on Iowa) won less than 5 percent of the vote and dropped out the next day. A week later in the New Hampshire primary, Romney won decisively, taking almost 40 percent of the vote, with Paul second at 23 percent. Huntsman (who had counted on New Hampshire) won only 17 percent and dropped out two days later. Perry (who had less than 1 percent of

front-loading
States' practice of moving delegate selection primaries and caucuses earlier in the calendar year to gain media and candidate attention.

FIGURE 9.1 From Many to Two: Presidential Hopefuls Starting and Dropping Out

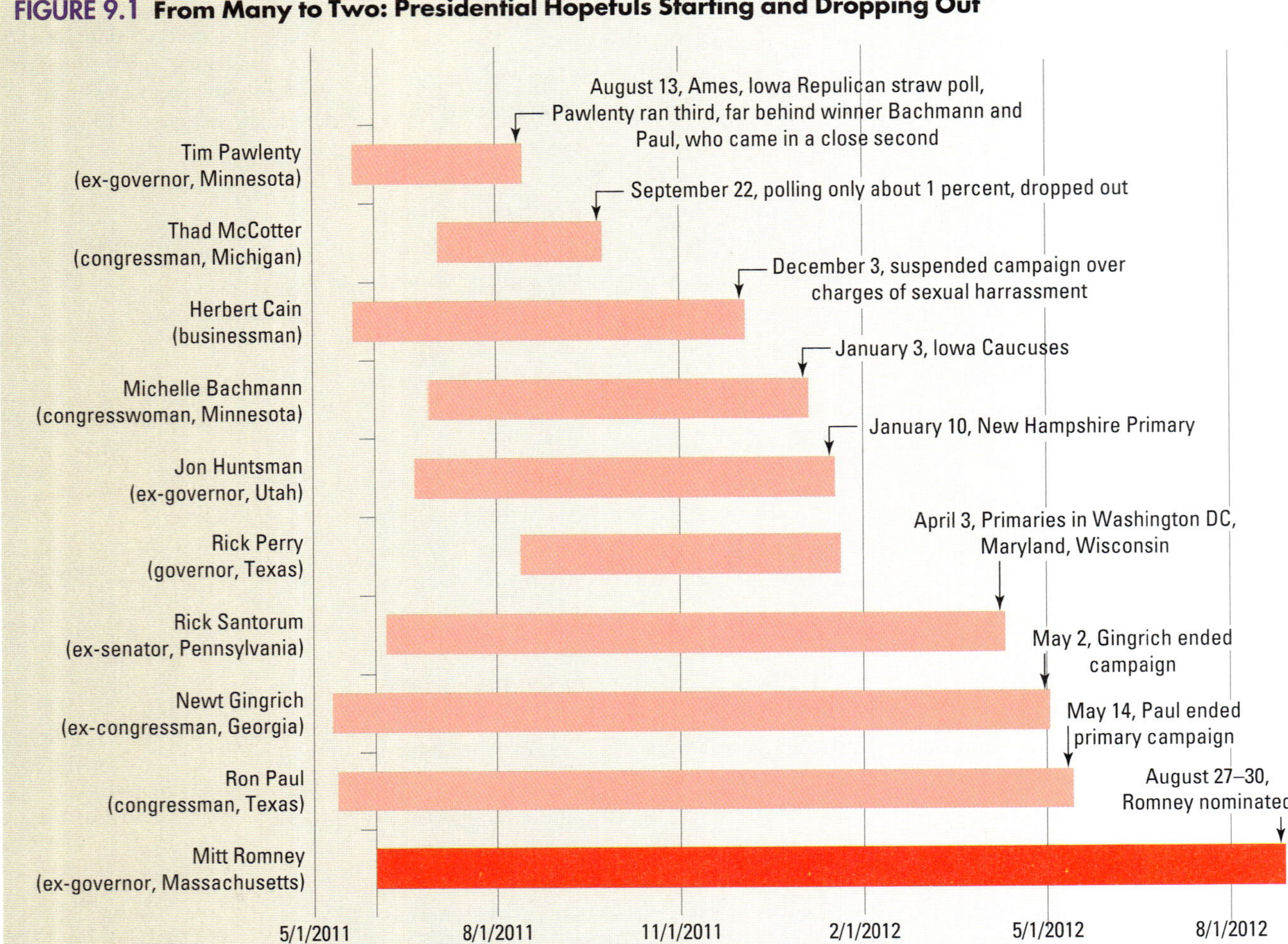

Over three hundred candidates filed with the Federal Election Commission (FEC) to run for president in 2012. The graph lists the ten Republicans who filed with the FEC as presidential candidates and who received significant early attention. As usual, some candidates withdrew before the delegate selection process began and others dropped out afterward for lack of support. By late January, only four hopefuls were competing in the numerous televised debates.
Source: © Cengage Learning.

the vote in New Hampshire after getting only 10 percent in Iowa) dropped out a few days later.

Thus, the Republican field was reduced to four for the third delegate selection contest in South Carolina on January 31. A third winner emerged as Gingrich took 40 percent of the vote, but his star faded ten days later when Romney decisively defeated Gingrich in the Florida primary. In ensuing contests, Romney and Santorum alternated as winners, setting up a protracted contest for convention delegates chosen in forty primaries over 168 days—the longest presidential primary season in history.[29] When Santorum dropped out on April 10, after the Maryland and Wisconsin primaries, Romney's nomination was guaranteed, Gingrich and Paul lingered a little before bowing to Romney's inevitable convention nomination.

Requiring prospective presidential candidates to campaign before many millions of party voters in scores of primaries and hundreds of thousands of party activists in caucus states has several consequences:

- *When no incumbent in the White House is seeking reelection, the presidential nominating process becomes contested in both parties.* This is what occurred in 2008, when twelve Republicans and ten Democrats met the Federal Election Commission (FEC) requirements for electronic filing of their presidential campaigns. In the complex mix of caucus and primary methods that states use to select convention delegates, timing and luck can affect who wins, and even an outside chance of success ordinarily attracts a half-dozen or so plausible contestants in either party lacking an incumbent president.

- *An incumbent president usually encounters little or no opposition for renomination within the party.* Thus, Obama was routinely renominated in 2012, but challenges can occur. In 1992, President George Herbert Walker Bush faced fierce opposition for the Republican nomination from Pat Buchanan. In 1968, President Lyndon Johnson faced such hostility within the Democratic Party that he declined to seek renomination.

- *Many hopefuls seek the presidential nomination of the opposition party.* In 2012, twelve notable Republicans filed with the FEC as presidential candidates along with hundreds (yes) of others not so notable.

- *The Iowa caucuses and New Hampshire primaries do matter.* Since the first Iowa caucus in 1972, eleven candidates in each party have won presidential nominations. All of the eleven Republican nominees were first in either Iowa or New Hampshire, as were nine of the Democrats.[30]

- *Candidates eventually favored by most party identifiers usually win their party's nomination.*[31] There have been only two exceptions to this rule since 1936, when poll data first became available: Adlai E. Stevenson in 1952 and George McGovern in 1972.[32] Both were Democrats; both lost impressively in the general election.

- *Candidates who win the nomination do so largely on their own and owe little or nothing to the national party organization, which usually does not promote a candidate.* In fact, Jimmy Carter won the nomination in 1976 against a field of nationally prominent Democrats, although he was a party outsider with few strong connections to the national party leadership. Barack Obama won in 2008 against Hillary Clinton, who had strong ties to Democratic Party leaders.

★ 9.3 Elections

> ★ Describe the function of the electoral college and formulate arguments for and against the electoral vote system.

By national law, all seats in the House of Representatives and one-third of the seats in the Senate are filled in a **general election** held in early November in even-numbered years. Every state takes advantage of the national election to fill some of the nearly 500,000 state and local offices across the country, which makes the election even more "general." When the president is chosen every fourth year, the election is identified as a *presidential election.* The intervening elections are known as *congressional, midterm,* or *off-year elections.*

general election
A national election held by law in November of every even-numbered year.

Presidential Elections and the Electoral College

In contrast to almost all other offices in the United States, the presidency does not go automatically to the candidate who wins the most votes. In fact, George W. Bush won the presidency in 2000 despite receiving fewer popular votes than Al Gore. Instead, a two-stage procedure specified in the Constitution decides elections for the president; it requires selection of the president by a group (college) of electors representing the states. Technically, we elect a president not in a national election but in a *federal* election.

The Electoral College: Structure. Surprising as it might seem, the term *electoral college* is not mentioned in the Constitution and is not readily found in books on American politics prior to World War II. One major dictionary defines a *college* as "a body of persons having a common purpose or shared duties."[33] The electors who choose the president of the United States became known as the electoral college largely during the twentieth century. Eventually, this term became incorporated into statutes relating to presidential elections, so it has assumed a legal basis.[34]

The Constitution (Article II, Section 1) says, "Each State shall appoint, in such Manner as the Legislature thereof may direct, a Number of Electors, equal to the whole Number of Senators and Representatives to which the State may be entitled in the Congress." Thus, each of the fifty states is entitled to one elector for each of its senators (100 total) and one for each of its representatives (435 votes total), totaling 535 electoral votes. In addition, the Twenty-third Amendment to the Constitution awarded three electoral votes (the minimum for any state) to the District of Columbia, although it elects no voting members of Congress. The total number of electoral votes therefore is 538. The Constitution specifies that a candidate needs a majority of electoral votes, or 270 today, to win the presidency. If no candidate receives a majority, the election is thrown into the House of Representatives. The House votes by state, with each state casting one vote. The candidates in the House election are the top three finishers in the general election. A presidential election has gone to the House only twice in American history, in 1800 and 1824, before a stable two-party system had developed.

Electoral votes are apportioned among the states according to their representation in Congress, which depends largely on their population. Because of population changes recorded by the 2010 census, the distribution of electoral votes among the states changed between the 2008 and 2012 presidential elections. Figure 9.2 shows the distribution of electoral votes for the 2012 election, indicating which states have lost and gained electoral votes. The clear pattern is the systemic loss of people and electoral votes in the north-central and eastern states and the gain in the western and southern states.

The Electoral College: Politics. In 1789, the first set of presidential electors was chosen under the new Constitution. Only three states chose their electors by direct popular vote; state legislatures selected electors in the others. Selection by state legislature remained the norm until 1792. Afterward, direct election by popular vote became more common, and by 1824 voters chose electors in eighteen of twenty-four states. Since 1860, all states have selected their electors through popular vote once they had entered the Union.[35] In the disputed 2000 presidential election, the Republican Florida state legislature threatened to resolve the dispute in favor of Bush by

FIGURE 9.2 Population Shifts and Political Gains and Losses Since 1960

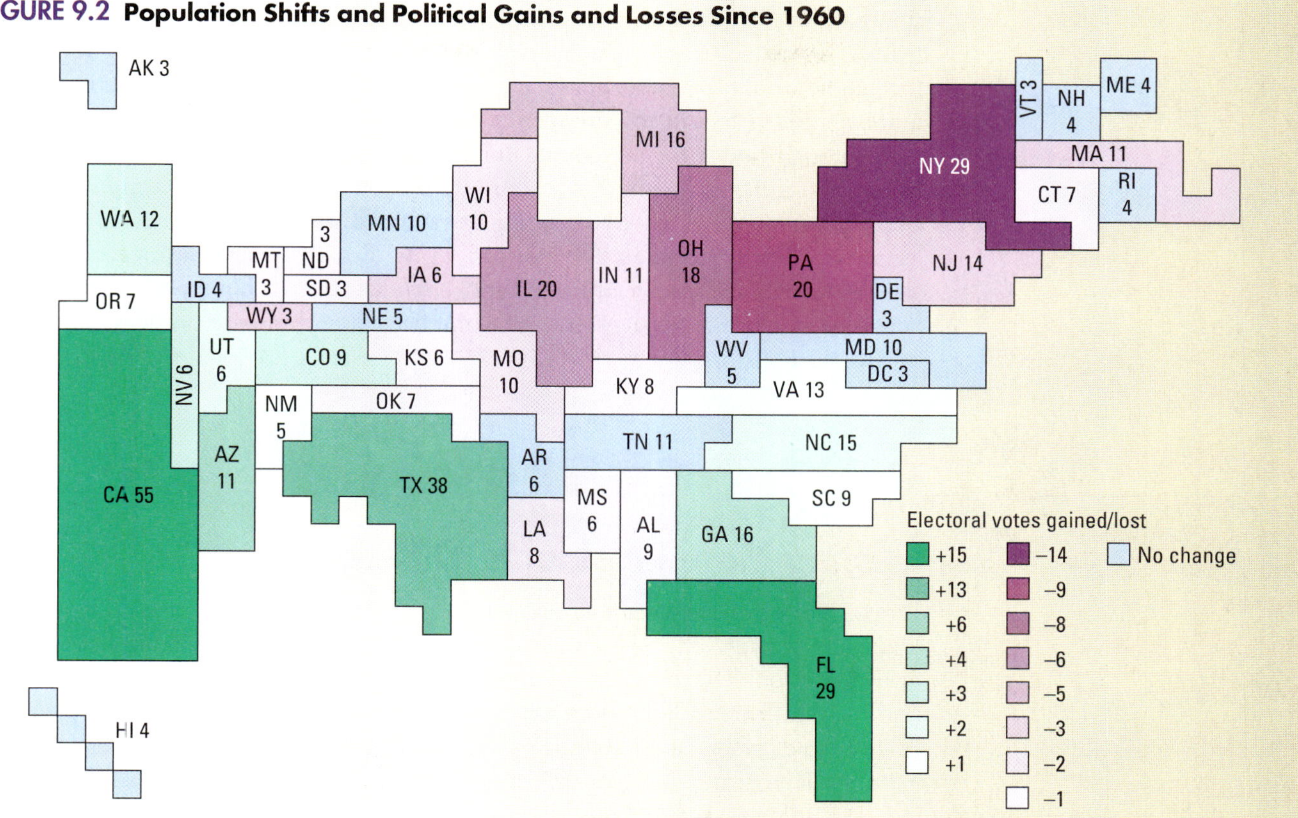

If the states were sized according to their electoral votes for the 2012 presidential election, the nation might resemble this map, on which states are drawn according to their population, based on the 2010 census. Each state has as many electoral votes as its combined representation in the Senate (always two) and the House (which depends on population). Although New Jersey is much smaller in area than Montana, New Jersey has far more people and is thus bigger in terms of "electoral geography." The coloring on this map shows the states that have gained electoral votes since 1960 (in shades of green) and those that have lost electoral votes (in shades of purple). States that have not had the number of their electoral votes changed since 1960 are blue. This map clearly reflects the drain of population (and seats in Congress) from the north-central and eastern states to the western and southern states. California, with two senators and fifty-three representatives in the 2012 election, will have fifty-five electoral votes for presidential elections until 2024, when reapportionment follows the 2020 census.

selecting its electors itself. There was precedent to do so, but it was a pre–Civil War precedent.

Of course, the situation in Florida was itself unprecedented due to the extremely close election in 2000. Voters nationwide favored the Democratic candidate, Al Gore, by a plurality of approximately 500,000 votes out of 105 million cast. But the presidential election is a *federal* election. A candidate is not chosen president by national popular vote but by a majority of the states' electoral votes. In every state but Maine and Nebraska, the candidate who wins a plurality of its popular vote—whether by 20 votes or 20,000 votes—wins *all* of the state's electoral votes. Gore and his Republican opponent, George W. Bush, ran close races in many states across the nation. Not counting Florida, Gore had won 267 electoral votes, just three short of the 270 he needed to claim the presidency.

But in Florida, which had twenty-five electoral votes in 2000, the initial vote count showed an extremely close race, with Bush ahead by the slimmest of margins. If Bush outpolled Gore by just a single vote, Bush could add its 25 electoral votes to the 246 he won in the other states, for a total of 271. That was just one more than the number needed to win the presidency. Gore trailed Bush by only about 2,000 votes, close enough to ask for a recount. But the recount proved difficult due to different ballots and different methods for counting them. After more than a month of ballot counting, recounting, more recounting, lawsuits, court decisions—and the Republican legislature's threat to select the electors on its own to ensure Bush's victory—Bush was certified as the winner of Florida's 25 *electoral* votes by a mere 537 *popular* votes. So ended one of the most protracted, complicated, and intense presidential elections in American history.[36]

Politics of Global Change

Electing More Presidents, Differently

Today, many nations elect their presidents, and do so differently from how presidents had been chosen. This chart shows how nations chose presidents in 428 elections from 1946 to 2010. Only 11 presidential elections were held in the postwar 1940s and most presidents then were elected by simple plurality vote. Argentina and the United States were the only countries to use an electoral college. As more countries became Democratic over the decades, more presidential elections occurred—135 in the 2000s. In that recent decade, only 31 elections decided the presidency by a simple plurality vote. In 87 elections, the winning candidate had to win a majority of the vote cast, not a simple plurality. Usually, this meant holding a second ballot some days later. In 12 elections, a qualified majority (more than a simple majority) was needed. The three elections that chose a president by an electoral college in the 2000s were all in the United States (2000, 2004, and 2008). Ireland held two elections by alternative vote, in which voters ranked candidates by their preferences.

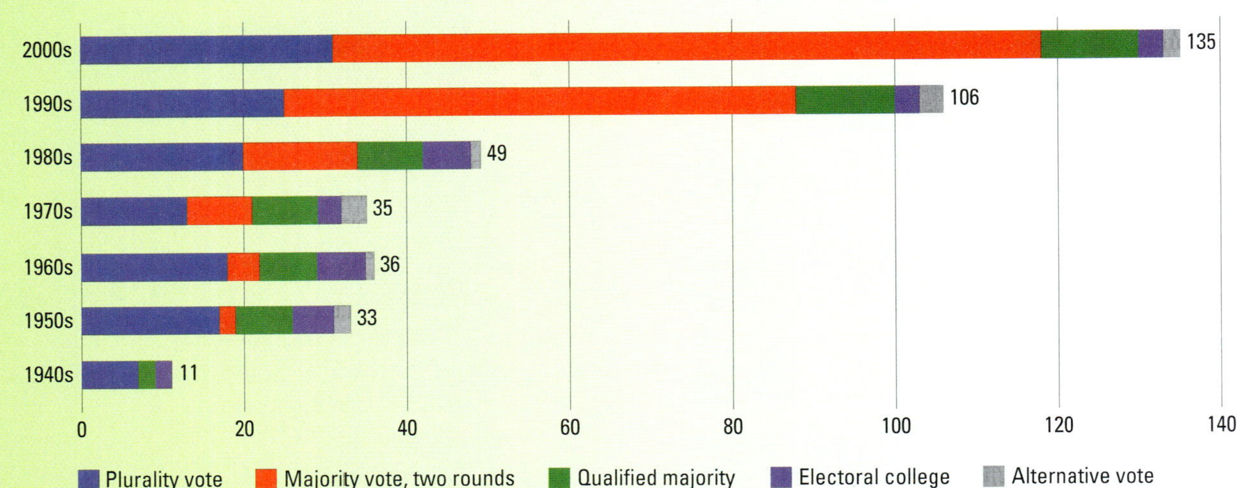

Source: Data were kindly provided in personal communication by Matt Golder from the forthcoming paper, Nils-Christian Bormann and Matt Golder, 2012, "Democratic Electoral Systems Around the World, 1946–2011."

The Electoral College: Abolish It? As shown in "Politics of Global Change: Electing More Presidents, Differently," more presidential elections are being held by more nations across the world, but very few elect presidents using a electoral college. Between 1789 and 2000, about seven hundred proposals to change the electoral college scheme were introduced in Congress.[37] Historically, polls have shown public opinion opposed to the electoral college.[38] Following the 2000 election, letters flooded into newspapers, urging anew that the system be changed.[39]

To evaluate the criticisms, one must first distinguish between the electoral "college" and the "system" of electoral votes. Strictly speaking, the electoral college is merely the set of individuals empowered to cast a state's electoral votes. In a presidential election, voters don't actually vote for a candidate; they vote for a slate of little-known electors (their names are often not on the ballot) pledged to one of the candidates. Most critics hold that the founding fathers argued for a body of electors because they did not trust people to vote directly for candidates. But one scholar contends that the device of independent electors was adopted by the Constitutional Convention as a compromise between those who favored having legislatures cast the states' electoral votes for president and those who favored direct popular election.[40] The electoral college allowed states to choose, and—as described in Chapter 8—all states gravitated to direct election of electors by 1860. Occasionally (but rarely), electors break their pledges when they assemble to cast their written ballots at their state capitol in December (electors who do so are called "faithless electors"). Indeed, this happened in 2004, when one of the ten Minnesota electors voted not for Democrat John Kerry, who won the state, but for his running mate, John Edwards. Electors vote by secret ballot, so no one knew which one voted for Edwards instead of Kerry.[41] Such aberrations make for historical footnotes but do not affect outcomes. Today, voters have good reason to oppose a body of electors to translate their decision, and few observers defend the electoral college itself.

The more troubling criticism centers on the electoral vote *system,* which makes for a federal rather than a national election. Many reformers favor a majoritarian method for choosing the president—by nationwide direct popular vote. They argue that it is simply wrong to have a system that allows a candidate who wins the most popular votes nationally to lose the election. Until 2000, that situation had not occurred since 1888, when Grover Cleveland won the popular vote but lost the presidency to Benjamin Harrison in the electoral college. During all intervening elections, the candidate winning a plurality of the popular vote also won a majority of the electoral vote. In fact, the electoral vote generally operated to magnify the margin of victory, as Figure 9.3 (p. 254) shows. Some scholars argued that this magnifying effect increased the legitimacy of presidents-elect who failed to win a majority of the popular vote, which happened in the elections of Kennedy, Nixon (first time), Clinton (both times), and certainly George W. Bush (first time).

The 2000 election proved that defenders of the electoral vote system can no longer claim that a federal election based on electoral votes yields the same outcome as a national election based on the popular vote. However, three lines of argument support selecting a president by electoral votes rather than by popular vote. First, if one supports a federal form of government as embodied within the Constitution, then one may defend the electoral vote system because it gives small states more weight in the vote: they have two senators, the same as large states. Second, if one favors presidential candidates campaigning on foot and in rural areas (needed to win most states) rather than campaigning via television to the one hundred most populous market areas to win the popular vote, then one might favor the electoral vote system.[42] Third,

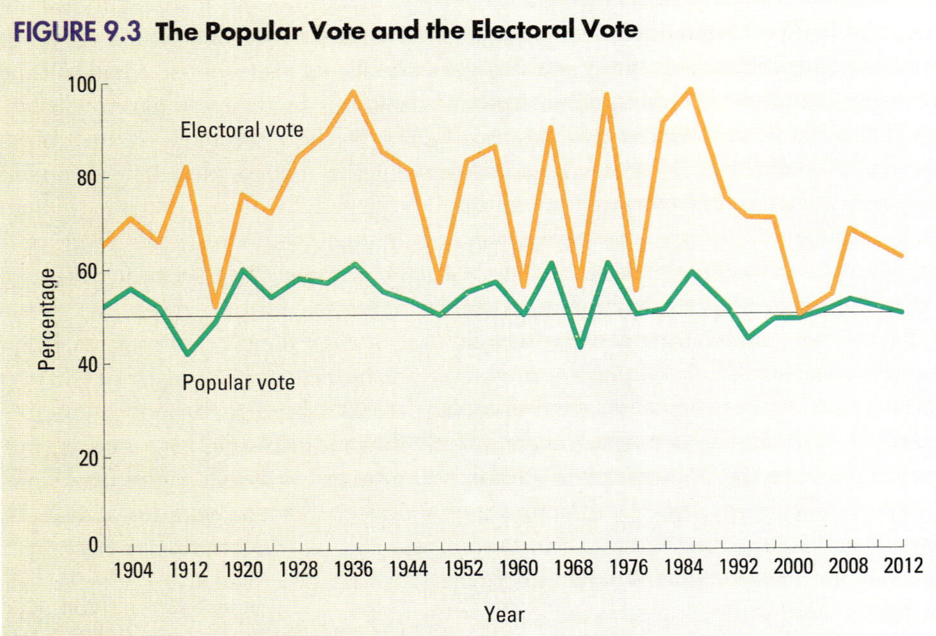

Strictly speaking, a presidential election is a federal election, not a national election. A candidate must win a majority (270) of the nation's total electoral vote (538). A candidate can win a plurality of the popular vote and still not win the presidency. Until 2000, the last time a candidate won most of the popular votes but did not win the presidency was in 1888. In every election between these two, the candidate who won a plurality of the popular vote won an even larger proportion of the electoral vote. So the electoral vote system magnified the winner's victory and thus increased the legitimacy of the president-elect. As we learned from the 2000 election, that result is not guaranteed.

Source: Harold W. Stanley and Richard G. Niemi, *Vital Statistics on American Politics, 2007–2008* (Washington, D.C.: CQ Press, 2008).

if you do not want to risk a *nationwide* recount in a close election (multiplying by fifty the counting problems in Florida in 2000), then you might want to keep the current system. So switching to selecting the president by popular vote has serious implications, which explains why Congress has not moved quickly to amend the Constitution.

Congressional Elections

In a presidential election, the candidates for the presidency are listed at the top of the ballot, followed by the candidates for other national offices and those for state and local offices. A voter is said to vote a **straight ticket** when she or he chooses the same party's candidates for all the offices. A voter who chooses candidates from different parties is said to vote a **split ticket**. About half of all voters say they split their tickets, and the proportion of voters who chose a presidential candidate from one party and a congressional candidate from the other has varied between 15 and 30 percent since 1952.[43] In the 1970s and 1980s, the common pattern was to elect a Republican as president while electing mostly Democrats to Congress. This produced a divided government, with the executive and legislative branches controlled by different parties (see Chapter 12). In the mid-1990s, the electorate flipped the pattern, electing a Democratic president but a Republican Congress.

straight ticket
In voting, a single party's candidates for all the offices.

split ticket
In voting, candidates from different parties for different offices.

Until the 1994 election, Democrats had maintained a lock on congressional elections for decades, winning a majority of House seats since 1954 and controlling the Senate for all but six years during that period. Republicans regularly complained that inequitable districts drawn by Democrat-dominated state legislatures had denied them their fair share of seats. For example, the Republicans won 46 percent of the congressional vote in 1992 but gained only 40 percent of the seats.[44] Despite the Republicans' complaint, election specialists note that sizable discrepancies between votes won and seats won are the inevitable consequence of **first-past-the-post elections**—a British term for elections conducted in single-member districts that award victory to the candidate with the most votes. In all such elections worldwide, the party that wins the most votes tends to win more seats than projected by its percentage of the vote.* Democrats won 53 percent of the aggregated vote for congressional candidates in 2008 and won 59 percent of the seats. In 2010, however, Republicans won 51 percent of the congressional vote and took 56 percent of the seats. These recent election results reveal no evidence of Democratic malapportionment of congressional districts. Both parties have enjoyed, and suffered, the mathematics of first-past-the-post elections.

Heading into the 2012 congressional elections, Republicans hoped to keep control of the House and perhaps win control of the Senate by campaigning against the economic policies of Democratic President Obama. The Republicans did retain firm control of the House of Representatives, losing only a couple of seats while holding a majority of about 35. However, Republicans not only failed to regain the Senate but lost a couple of seats that observers predicted they would win. As before the election, the two houses of Congress were controlled by different parties.

first-past-the-post elections
A British term for elections conducted in single-member districts that award victory to the candidate with the most votes.

★ 9.4 Campaigns

★ Analyze the American election campaign process in terms of political context, financial resources, and strategies and tactics for reaching the voters.

As political scientists Barbara Salmore and Stephen Salmore have observed, election campaigns have been studied more through anecdotes than through systematic analysis.[45] They developed an analytical framework that emphasizes the political context of the campaign, the financial resources available for conducting the campaign, and the strategies and tactics that underlie the dissemination of information about the candidate.

The Political Context

The two most important structural factors that face each candidate planning a campaign are the office the candidate is seeking and whether he or she is the *incumbent* (the current officeholder running for reelection) or the *challenger* (who seeks to replace

---

*If you have trouble understanding this phenomenon, think of a basketball team that scores, on average, 51 percent of the total points in all the games it plays. Such a team usually wins more than just 51 percent of its games because it tends to win the close ones.

the incumbent). Incumbents usually enjoy great advantages over challengers, especially in elections to Congress. Most congressional elections today are not very competitive. Of 2,175 congressional elections in the 2000s, only 41 (1.9 percent) were decided by 2 percentage points or fewer.[46] As explained in Chapter 11, incumbents in the House of Representatives are almost impossible to defeat, historically winning more than 95 percent of the time.[47] Incumbent senators are somewhat more vulnerable. An incumbent president is also difficult to defeat—but not impossible. Democrat Jimmy Carter was defeated for reelection in 1980, as was Republican George H. W. Bush in 1992. Of course, a nonincumbent will always triumph in an **open election**, one lacking an incumbent because of a resignation, death, or constitutional requirement.

open election
An election that lacks an incumbent.

Every candidate for Congress must also examine the characteristics of the state or district, including its physical size and the sociological makeup of its electorate. In general, the bigger and more populous the district or state and the more diverse the electorate, the more complicated and costly is the campaign. Obviously, running for president means conducting a huge, complicated, and expensive campaign. After losing the 2008 Republican presidential nomination to John McCain and after McCain lost the general election to Obama, Romney used funds remaining in his 2008 campaign chest to plan a billion-dollar campaign in 2012.[48] By 2010, Romney had a network of state organizations to supply funds for his presidential run.[49]

Despite talk about the decreased influence of party affiliation on voting behavior, the party preference of the electorate is an important factor in the context of a campaign. It is easier for a candidate to get elected when her or his party matches the electorate's preference, in part because raising the money needed to conduct a winning campaign is easier. Challengers for congressional seats, for example, get far less money from organized groups than do incumbents and must rely more on their personal funds and raising money from individual donors.[50] So where candidates represent the minority party, they have to overcome not only a voting bias but also a funding bias. Finally, significant political issues—such as economic recession, personal scandals, and war—not only affect a campaign but also can dominate it and even negate such positive factors as incumbency and the advantages of a strong economy. In 2012, Republicans attacked Obama for presiding over a weak economy and for passing the health-care legislation they derided as "Obamacare."

Financing

Regarding election campaigns, former House Speaker Thomas ("Tip") O'Neill said, "There are four parts to any campaign. The candidate, the issues of the candidate, the campaign organization, and the money to run the campaign with. Without money you can forget the other three."[51] Money pays for office space, staff salaries, cell phones, computers, travel expenses, campaign literature, and, of course, advertising in the mass media. A successful campaign requires a good campaign organization and a good candidate, but enough money will buy the best campaign managers, equipment, transportation, research, and consultants—making the quality of the organization largely a function of money.[52] That may be true, but money alone does not ensure a successful campaign. Initially in the campaign season, President Obama raised more campaign funds than all the candidates seeking the Republican nomination, but by the summer months, Mitt Romney's fundraising had caught up with and exceeded Obama's.

No one can run a successful presidential campaign without raising a great deal of money. Regulations of campaign financing for state elections vary according to the state. Campaign financing for federal elections is regulated by national legislation.

Regulating Campaign Financing. Early campaign financing laws had various flaws, and none provided for adequate enforcement. In 1971, during a period of party reform, Congress passed the Federal Election Campaign Act (FECA), which limited media spending and imposed stringent new rules for full reporting of campaign contributions and expenditures. The need for strict legislation soon became clear. In 1968, before FECA was enacted, House and Senate candidates reported spending $8.5 million on their campaigns. In 1972, with FECA in force, the same number of candidates admitted spending $88.9 million.[53]

Financial misdeeds during Nixon's 1972 reelection campaign forced major amendments to the original FECA in 1974. The new legislation created the **Federal Election Commission (FEC)**, an independent agency of six members appointed by the president with approval of the Senate. No more than three members may come from the same party, and their six-year appointments are staggered over time so that no one president appoints the entire commission. The FEC is charged with enforcing limits on financial contributions to national campaigns, requiring full disclosure of campaign spending, and administering the public financing of presidential campaigns, which began with the 1976 election.

The law also condoned the creation of **political action committees (PACs)** by corporations, labor unions, or "nonconnected" groups that could, under limits, collect money and contribute it to campaigns for federal office—that is, Congress and the presidency. (The role of PACs in congressional elections is discussed at length in Chapter 10.)

Some people opposed any limits on campaign contributions, viewing money as "free speech" and challenging the 1974 limits under the First Amendment. Although the Supreme Court upheld limits on contributions in 1976, it struck down limits on *spending* by individuals or organizations made independently on behalf of a national candidate—holding that such spending constituted free speech, protected under the First Amendment. It also limited the FEC to regulate only advertisements advocating a candidate's election or defeat with such words as "vote for" or "vote against."[54] The 1974 FECA (with minor amendments) governed national elections for almost three decades.

As campaign spending increased, some members of Congress spoke piously about strengthening campaign finance laws but feared altering the process that elected them. In 2002 a bill introduced by Republican senator John McCain (Arizona) and Democratic senator Russell Feingold (Wisconsin) finally passed as the Bipartisan Campaign Reform Act (BCRA; pronounced "bikra"). BCRA was fiercely challenged from several sources, including Republican conservatives who attacked McCain for limiting contributions and weakening the party. Nevertheless, the law was upheld by the Supreme Court in 2003 and took effect for the 2004 election.

In general, BCRA raised the old limits on individual spending and indexed them for inflation in future years. Here are the major BCRA limitations for 2011–2012 contributions by individuals, adjusted for inflation:

- $2,500 to a specific candidate in a separate election during a two-year cycle (primaries, general, and runoff elections count as separate elections);
- $10,000 per year to each state party or political committee;
- $30,800 per year to any national party committee;
- $5,000 per year to any PAC.

Note that the 2002 law did not raise the $5,000 contribution limit for PACs, which many thought already had too much influence in elections, and did not index PAC contributions for inflation.

Federal Election Commission (FEC)
A bipartisan federal agency of six members that oversees the financing of national election campaigns.

political action committee (PAC)
An organization that collects campaign contributions from group members and donates them to candidates for political office.

527 committees
Committees named after Section 527 of the Internal Revenue Code; they enjoy tax-exempt status in election campaigns if they are unaffiliated with political parties and take positions on issues, not specific candidates.

501(c)4 social welfare organizations
Groups named after Section 501 of the Internal Revenue Code that operate for promotion of social welfare; they are exempt from reporting donors if they spend most of their funds on issues, not candidates.

BCRA also banned large so-called soft-money contributions to national political parties. Ostensibly given for capital improvements and operating expenses, these funds were often channeled to state parties for electoral campaigns. It also banned organizations from running issue ads that named candidates in the weeks before an election. However, BCRA allowed issue-advocacy groups, called **527 committees** (after Section 527 of the Internal Revenue Code, which makes them tax-exempt organizations), to spend unlimited amounts for media advertising, as long as they did not expressly advocate a candidate's election or defeat. Spending by 527 committees increased from $151 million in 2002 to $489 million in 2008.[55]

In 2007, a more conservative Supreme Court struck down BCRA's ban of issue ads run before elections, which opened the door to massive independent campaign spending by nonparty groups. Many no longer organized as 527 committees, which were required to report their donors to the FEC, but as **501(c)4 social welfare organizations**, exploiting a legal loophole excusing them from disclosing donors.[56] According to the Center for Responsive Politics, these two types of groups spent about $525 million—split into $241 million by conservative groups and $286 million by liberal groups—in the 2010 election cycle.[57]

In January 2010 a bitterly divided Supreme Court departed from its precedents and ruled against BCRA's ban on spending by corporations in candidate elections.[58] Conservatives viewed its decision in *Citizens United* v. *Federal Election Commission* as defending freedom of speech,[59] while liberals saw it as opening the door to the corrupting influence of corporate money.[60] Beginning with the 2010 election, corporations, unions, and trade associations were free to run ads directly advocating a candidate's election for the first time since 1907, when Congress first banned using general corporate funds in federal election campaigns.[61] In the 2010 elections, for example, the Service Employees International Union spent over $15 million and the National Rifle Association spent over $7 million.

In March 2010, an Appeals court applied the *Citizens United* ruling in *SpeechNow.org* v. *FEC,* a decision that expanded the influence of private money in elections. It legalized a new category of funding organizations: "independent expenditures only political committees" or "Super PACs." If political committees make only independent expenditures and do not give money to candidates, they can accept funds in unlimited amounts to spend independently on election campaigns.[62] Unlike the $5,000 limit on contributions to PACs, there is no limit on contributions to *Super* PACs. While Super PACs must periodically disclose donations from individuals and for-profit groups, they need not disclose donations from nonprofit groups.[63]

By early 2012, Super PACs aligned with each of the Republican presidential candidates had spent more than $40 million dollars. "Restore Our future," the main Super PAC supporting Romney, raised $20 million and outspent the Romney campaign itself 2 to 1.[64] Ostensibly, Super PAC expenditures were supposed to have "no connection" with the official campaigns of candidates they were backing—despite the fact that Super PACs were often run by candidates' former campaign officials and political cronies. For example, the director of the Romney-oriented "Restore Our Future" Super PAC was Carl Forti, who ran Romney's 2008 presidential campaign. To parody what the law allowed, Stephen Colbert of Comedy Central's cable show, *The Colbert Report*, legally named Jon Stewart, his business partner at Comedy Central's *The Daily Show*, to run Colbert's own Super PAC, "Americans for a Better Tomorrow, Tomorrow."[65]

Super PACs quickly raised unprecedented amounts of money. By February, FEC filings identified fourteen individuals or corporations who had each given at least $1 million to "Restore Our Future," which backed Romney, while a Nevada casino owner and his wife gave $10 million to "Winning Our Future," which supported Gingrich.[66] "American Crossroads," a Super PAC dedicated to the defeat of Obama, got $12 million from billionaire Harold C. Simmons. Realizing that Republican Super PACs would raise huge sums, President Obama reversed his opposition to Super PACs in February and endorsed "Priorities USA Action," founded by two former White House aides. Comedian Bill Maher quickly gave it $1 million. And the number of Super PACs exploded as the campaign proceeded. By July 12, 2012, 548 Super PACs had registered with the Federal Election Commission.[67]

Public Financing of Presidential Campaigns.

The 1974 FECA provided for public funding of campaigns for presidential elections but not congressional elections. During the primary season, a presidential candidate could qualify for public funds by raising at least $5,000 in each of twenty states from private donations of no more than $250 each. The FEC matched these donations up to one-half of a preset spending limit—indexed for inflation—for each qualifying candidate. Candidates who raised up to $22.8 million in private funds would have that amount matched by up to $22.8 million in public funds, subject to the limitation that they could not spend more than the combined amount of $45.6 million in their primary campaigns.

From 1976 through 1992, all major candidates seeking their party's presidential nomination accepted public matching funds for their primary election campaigns and thus adhered to the spending limits. But candidates found that they could raise more money privately to spend in their primary campaigns. Wealthy publisher Steve Forbes declined public funds in 1996 and again in 2000, when George W. Bush also raised his own primary funds. In 2004, Bush and Democratic hopefuls Howard Dean and John Kerry all declined public money for their primary campaigns. In 2008, only six of the nineteen candidates who participated in both parties' primary debates relied on public funds.[68] By August 2012, only Libertarian presidential candidate Gary Johnson, Green Party candidate Jill Stein, and Buddy Roemer—who sought the nomination of the online organization, Americans Elect—had applied for and qualified for public matching funds.[69]

The public funding program for presidential elections in November operated somewhat differently. First, the campaign spending limit was double that for primary elections. Second, candidates who accepted public funds had no need to raise matching funds privately. They were simply reimbursed by the government up to the spending limit (indexed to inflation), which was $91.2 million in 2012. Candidates who accepted public funds could spend no more than that.

From 1976 to 2004, every major party nominee for president had accepted public funds (and spending limits) for the general election. In 2008, Republican candidate John McCain agreed to accept public funds, thus limiting his campaign spending to $84.1 million for the general election. Compare that with the $220 million McCain

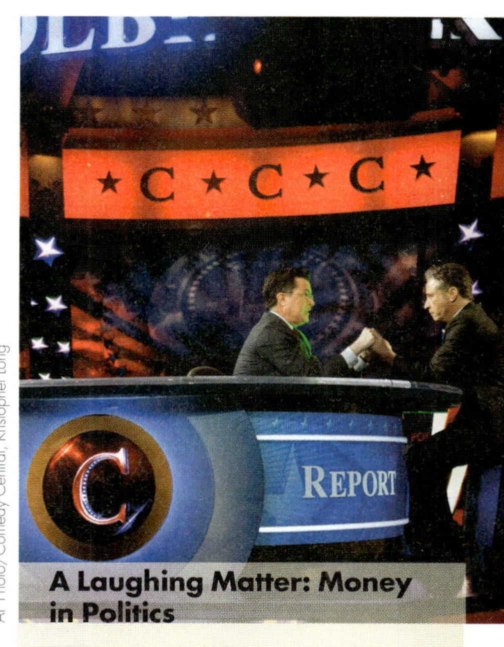

AP Photo/Comedy Central, Kristopher Long

A Laughing Matter: Money in Politics

In the summer of 2011, Stephen Colbert, host of the Comedy Central's *The Colbert Report*, created a Super PAC, "Americans for a Better Tomorrow, Tomorrow." When Colbert decided to run in the South Carolina primary to be president of South Carolina, his Super PAC spending would not be "independent" of his candidacy. So on January 12, 2012, he surrendered its control to his business partner, Jon Stewart, host of Comedy Central's *The Daily Show*. On January 30, after the primary, Colbert wrestled control back. View the videos for those dates at www.colbertnation.com—especially that for January 12, which laughingly explains the letter of the law.

raised just to win the nomination. Democratic candidate Obama refused public funds for both and raised $750 million to McCain's total of $304 million.[70] In 2012, neither party's candidate accepted public funds.

Private Financing of Congressional Campaigns. One might think that a party's presidential campaign would be closely coordinated with its congressional campaigns. However, campaign funds go to the presidential candidate, not to the party, and the national committee does not run the presidential campaign. Presidential candidates may join congressional candidates in public appearances for mutual benefit, but presidential campaigns are usually isolated—financially and otherwise—from congressional campaigns.

Candidates for national office raised more than $3 billion during the primary and general election campaigns in the 2007–2008 election cycle.[71] Obama and McCain together raised over $1.5 billion, while 1,544 candidates in primary and general election campaigns for the U.S. Congress in 2007–2008 raised almost $1.4 billion more.[72] Most were competing for the 435 seats in the House; only 34 Senate seats were up for election. Nevertheless, individual Senate candidates raised relatively more money because they had to compete in larger districts (states) rather than individual House districts, which average about 675,000 people.

Future Trends in Campaign Finance. Public funding of presidential campaigns was intended to equalize candidate spending as well as to limit it. After successfully equalizing and limiting spending for decades, public funding faces an uncertain future.[73] Today, prominent presidential candidates find that they can raise far more money for their campaigns than provided by public funding. Two major fundraising methods have made a huge difference. The first is the rise of contribution *bundlers* who collect legal campaign donations from individuals ($2,500 for the primary and $2,500 for the general elections in 2012) and then deliver the bundled donations to the candidate. Just as the 2010 *Citizens United* decision gave rise to Super PACs, it also gave rise to "super bundlers." Now fundraising professionals could collect from individual citizens $5,000 contributions to candidates, $5,000 contributions to PACs, and *unlimited* amounts for Super PACs simultaneously. For the first time, they could also collect *unlimited* contributions to PACs from corporations, which previously could not contribute to campaigns.[74] The second method of fundraising is through the Internet, and it is even more lucrative. Among all Republican presidential hopefuls in February 2012, only Mitt Romney had raised more money ($56 million) than Ron Paul ($26 million).[75] However, most of Romney's contributions ranged between $1,000 and $2,500. Most of Paul's contributions were under $200 and collected over the Internet.[76]

Although BCRA did ban national party committees from raising huge sums of soft money, it did not reduce the amount of money raised (and spent) for presidential campaigns. At least raising money on the Internet has a grassroots basis, in contrast to using money bundlers. But trying to prevent people from spending money to influence elections and politics is like trying to stop water flooding into a basement. Like water, money seeps around barriers. If people could no longer give massively to political parties, they gave to independent groups that campaigned for candidates separate from the parties. Due to the Supreme Court's 5–4 decision in *Citizens United*, citizens—especially wealthy ones—can contribute as much as they want to Super PACs to influence elections. The money genie has escaped from the public funding bottle, and future candidates for president are unlikely to accept the public funding limits imposed by the 1974 Federal Election Campaign Act.

Strategies and Tactics

In a military campaign, *strategy* is the overall scheme for winning the war, whereas *tactics* involve the conduct of localized hostilities. In an election campaign, strategy is the broad approach used to persuade citizens to vote for the candidate, and tactics determine the content of the messages and the way they are delivered.[77] Three basic strategies, which campaigns may blend in different mixes, are as follows:

- *A party-centered strategy,* which relies heavily on voters' partisan identification as well as on the party's organization to provide the resources necessary to wage the campaign;
- *An issue-oriented strategy,* which seeks support from groups that feel strongly about various policies;
- *A candidate-oriented strategy,* which depends on the candidate's perceived personal qualities, such as experience, leadership ability, integrity, independence, and trustworthiness.[78]

The campaign strategy must be tailored to the political context of the election. Clearly, a party-centered strategy is inappropriate in a primary because all contenders have the same party affiliation. Research suggests that a party-centered strategy is best suited to voters with little political knowledge.[79] How do candidates learn what the electorate knows and thinks about politics, and how can they use this information? Candidates today usually turn to pollsters and political consultants, of whom there are hundreds.[80] Well-funded candidates can purchase a "polling package" that includes:

- A benchmark poll, which provides "campaign information about the voting preferences and issue concerns of various groups in the electorate and a detailed reading of the image voters have of the candidates in the race";
- Focus groups, consisting of ten to twenty people "chosen to represent particular target groups (e.g., Latinos)[81] the campaign wants to reinforce or persuade ... led in their discussion by persons trained in small-group dynamics," giving texture and depth to poll results;
- A trend poll "to determine the success of the campaigns in altering candidate images and voting preferences";
- Tracking polls that begin in early October, "conducting short nightly interviews with a small number of respondents, keyed to the variables that have assumed importance."[82]

Professional campaign managers can use information from such sources to settle on a strategy that mixes party affiliation, issues, and images in its messages.[83] In major campaigns, the mass media disseminate these messages to voters through news coverage, advertising, and Internet services—around which a new industry has grown.[84]

Making the News. Campaigns value news coverage by the media for two reasons: the coverage is free, and it seems objective to the audience. If news stories do nothing more than report the candidate's name, that is important, for name recognition by itself often wins elections. To get favorable coverage, campaign managers cater to reporters' deadlines and needs.[85] Getting free news coverage is yet another advantage that incumbents enjoy over challengers, for incumbents can command attention simply by announcing political decisions—even if they had little to do with them. Members of Congress are so good at this, says one observer, that House members have made news organizations their "unwitting adjuncts."[86]

Campaigns vary in the effectiveness with which they transmit their messages through the news media. Effective tactics recognize the limitations of both the audience and the media. The typical voter is not deeply interested in politics and has trouble keeping track of multiple themes supported with details. By the same token, television is not willing to air lengthy statements from candidates. As a result, news coverage is often condensed to sound bites only a few seconds long.

The media often use the metaphor of a horse race in covering politics in the United States. In 2008, more than half the national news stories on television, in print, and online dealt with the horse race.[87] Ironically, evidence suggests that the national media focus more on campaign tactics and positioning than the state or local media do.[88] One longtime student of the media contends that reporters both enliven and simplify campaigns by describing them in terms of four basic scenarios: *bandwagons, losing ground, the front-runner,* and *the likely loser.*[89] Once the opinion polls show weakness or strength in a candidate, reporters dust off the appropriate story line.

The more time the press spends on the horse race, the less attention it gives to campaign issues. In fact, recent studies have found that in some campaigns, voters get more information from television ads than they do from television news.[90] Ads are more likely to be effective in low-visibility campaigns below the presidential level because the voters know less about the candidates at the outset and there is little "free" news coverage of the campaigns.[91]

Advertising the Candidate. In all elections, the first objective of paid advertising is name recognition. The next is to promote candidates by extolling their virtues. Finally, campaign advertising can have a negative objective: to attack one's opponent or play on emotions.[92] But name recognition is usually the most important. Studies show that many voters cannot recall the names of their U.S. senators or representatives, but they can recognize their names on a list—as on a ballot. Researchers attribute the high reelection rate for members of Congress mainly to high name recognition (see Chapter 11). Name recognition is the key objective during the primary season even in presidential campaigns, but other objectives become salient in advertising for the general election.

At one time, candidates for national office relied heavily on newspaper advertising; today, they overwhelmingly use the electronic media—primarily television. Political ads convey more substantive information than many people believe, but the amount varies by campaign. In his comprehensive study of campaign advertising in the last seven presidential elections, Darrell West found that political ads tended to mention candidates' policy preferences more in 1984, 1988, 1992, and 2000 and candidates' personal qualities more in 1996, 2004, and 2008.[93] In 1996, Bill Clinton drew fire for lack of "honesty and integrity"; in 2004, John Kerry was attacked for "flip-flopping" on issues and for false "heroism" in Vietnam; and in 2008 Obama was criticized for inexperience.

Other scholars have cautioned that the policy positions put forward in campaign ads may be misleading, if not downright deceptive.[94] West found that the 2008 presidential campaign was more positive than most recent ones, especially compared with 2004—the most negative since 1988.[95] Not all negatively toned ads qualify as *attack ads,* which advocate nothing positive. In 2012, television attack ads predominated in states prior to Republican caucuses or primary elections. Most were run by Super PACs, which spent 72 percent of their money on negative ads, compared with 27 percent spent by candidates' own campaigns.[96]

The term *contrast ads* describes those that both criticize an opponent and advocate policies of the sponsoring candidate.[97] A review of recent studies found that, ironically, both attack and contrast ads "actually carry more policy information than pure advocacy ads."[98] Regardless of whether people learn from political ads, scholars found, advertising does "a great deal to persuade potential voters" who viewed ads compared with those not seeing the ads.[99]

The media often inflate the effect of prominent ads by reporting them as news, which means that citizens are about as likely to see controversial ads during the news as in the ads' paid time slots. Although negative ads do convey information, some studies suggest that negative ads produce low voter turnout.[100] However, recent research shows that the existing level of political mistrust is more important than the negativity of the ads.[101] Moreover, negative ads seem to work differently for challengers (who show a tendency to benefit from them) than for incumbents (who tend to do better with more positive campaigns).[102] If these findings seem confusing, that's essentially the state of research on negative ads.[103] Researchers reviewing studies say that the connection between reality and perceptions is complex. Campaigns seen as negative by scholars are not necessarily viewed that way by voters.[104]

Using the Internet. The Internet debuted in presidential campaigns in 1992, when Democratic candidate Jerry Brown, former (and current) governor of California, sent e-mail messages to supporters.[105] Two decades later in 2012, campaigns used the Internet to "microtarget" voters, sending specific messages to computer screens of selected viewers.[106] As in online marketing, visits to campaign websites generate information for providers who slip digital markers or "cookies" into the users' computers. That information is matched with other user information (e.g., make of car) stored in a huge database. Campaign consultants then match those data with voting records, turnout, and party registration (but not voting choice, which is protected). Then they can frame ads targeted at visitors to conservative (or liberal) websites who shop for Lexus (or Ford) cars, who are registered Republicans (or Democrats), and who are frequent voters. Consultants can produce targeted Internet ads cheaply, transmit them with little expense, and—very importantly—send them quickly in reaction to breaking news.

Candidates like the Internet because it is fast, easy to use, and cheap—saving mailing costs and phone calls. Nevertheless, relatively few people get campaign news via the Internet. A national survey in January 2012 asked respondents whether they "learned something" about the presidential campaign or candidates from various news sources. Most people named some form of television (cable news, 36 percent; local TV news, 32 percent; network news, 26 percent), and only 25 percent named the Internet.[107] Although the survey was early in the primary season, 72 percent of respondents reported hearing or seeing campaign commercials, whereas only 16 percent received e-mails, 15 percent visited a candidate's website, and only 6 percent followed the candidate on Twitter or Facebook. Political "insiders," however, burn up the airwaves tweeting about their campaign prowess.

Despite the increased reliance on the Internet by candidates for campaigning and fundraising, Internet advertising got only a "small slice of campaign spending in 2008," according to a company that tracks advertising. Because Internet users seek out what they want to view, the best way to reach average voters is still through local broadcast television.[108]

9.5 Explaining Voting Choice

★ Assess the effects of party identification, political issues, and candidate attributes on voter choice.

Why do people choose one candidate over another? That is not easy to determine, but there are ways to approach the question. Individual voting choices can be analyzed as products of both long-term and short-term forces. Long-term forces operate throughout a series of elections, predisposing voters to choose certain types of candidates. Short-term forces are associated with particular elections; they arise from a combination of the candidates and issues of the time. Party identification is by far the most important long-term force affecting U.S. elections. The most important short-term forces are candidates' attributes and their policy positions.

Party Identification

Ever since the presidential election of 1952, when the University of Michigan's National Election Studies began, we have known that more than half the electorate decides how to vote before the party conventions end in the summer.[109] And voters who make an early voting decision generally vote according to their party identification. Despite frequent comments in the media about the decline of partisanship in voting behavior, party identification again had a substantial effect on the presidential vote in 2012, as Figure 9.4 shows. Each party's candidates, Barack Obama and Mitt Romney, won around 90 percent of self-described partisans of their party, with independents splitting their votes slightly in favor of Romney.

This is a common pattern in presidential elections. The winner holds nearly all the voters who identify with his party. The loser holds most of his fellow Democrats or Republicans, but some percentage defects to the winner, a consequence of short-term forces—the candidates' attributes and the issues—surrounding the election. The winner usually gets most of the independents, who split disproportionately for him, also because of short-term forces.

In 2012, the electorate favored the Democratic candidate. But as shown in Figure 8.4 on page 226, Democrats have consistently outnumbered Republicans over the past fifty years. Why, then, have Republican candidates won more presidential

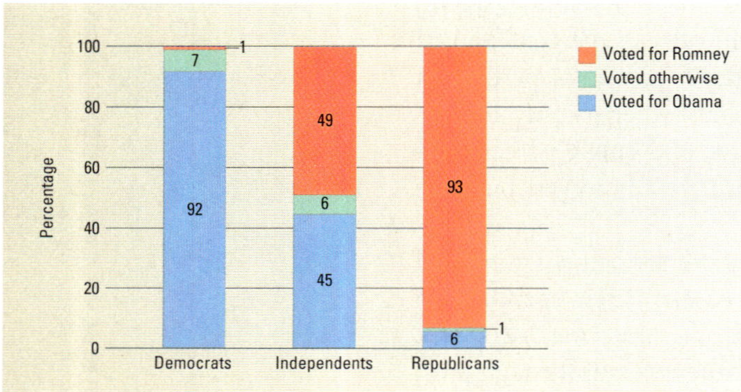

FIGURE 9.4 Effect of Party Identification on the Vote, 2012

The 2012 election showed that party identification still plays a key role in voting behavior. The chart shows the results of exit polls of thousands of voters as they left hundreds of polling places across the nation on election day. Voters were asked what party they identified with and how they voted for president. Those who identified with one of the two parties voted strongly for their party's candidate. Source: Data from *Wall Street Journal*, online report, November 7, 2012, "Exit Polls: Casting Ballots in 2012."

elections since 1952 than Democrats? For one thing, Democrats do not turn out to vote as consistently as Republicans do. For another, Democrats tend to defect more readily from their party. Defections are sparked by the candidates' attributes and the issues, which have usually favored Republican presidential candidates since 1952.

Prior to the 2012 election, polls showed strong relationships between ethnicity and party identification. By a margin of about ten percentage points, non-Hispanic whites described themselves more as Republicans than Democrats. In contrast, Blacks were more likely to identify as Democrats by about eight points. Hispanics were Democratic more than three to one, but Hispanics were less likely than whites or blacks to be registered and to vote.

Issues and Policies

Candidates exploit issues that they think are important to voters. Challengers usually campaign by pointing out problems—unemployment, inflation, war, civil disorders, corruption—and promising to solve them. Incumbents compile a record in office (for better or worse) and thus try to campaign on their accomplishments.

In 2012, the overriding campaign issue was the economy. With about 20 million Americans unemployed, the unemployment rate stuck at about eight percentages points, and the government facing a trillion dollar budget deficit and more than ten trillion dollars in national debt, Republican challenger Romney faulted President Obama for his handling of the economy. President Obama could justifiably claim that economic conditions were better than when he took office, but Romney contended that he could do better because of his business background.

Candidates' Attributes

Candidates' attributes are especially important to voters who lack good information about a candidate's past performance and policy stands—which means most of us. Without such information, voters search for clues about the candidates to try to predict their behavior in office.[110] Some fall back on their personal beliefs about religion, gender, and race in making political judgments.[111] Such stereotypic thinking accounts for the patterns of opposition and support met by, among others, a Catholic candidate for president (John Kennedy), a woman candidate for vice president (Geraldine Ferraro in 1984), a black contender for a presidential nomination (Jesse Jackson in 1984 and 1988), the first Jewish vice-presidential candidate of a major party (Joe Lieberman in 2000), the first African American presidential candidate (Barack Obama in 2008), and the first Mormon candidate (Mitt Romney).

National surveys taken a week before the 2012 election showed that voters had more favorable opinions of President Barack Obama than his Republican opponent, Mitt Romney. However, only about half the electorate approved of the job that Obama was doing as president.

Evaluating the Voting Choice

Choosing among candidates according to their personal attributes might be an understandable approach, but it is not rational voting, according to democratic theory. According to that theory, citizens should vote according to the candidates' past performance and proposed policies. Voters who choose between candidates on the basis of their policies are voting on the issues, a behavior that fits the

Hope Renewed

President Barack Obama and Vice-President Joe Biden were re-elected to another term in 2012, despite the nation's high unemployment rate and its huge national debt.

SHAWN THEW/EPA/Landov

Hope Denied

Republican presidential candidate, Mitt Romney, and his running mate, Representative Paul Ryan, won only 48 percent of the popular vote to 50 percent for Obama and Biden. According to exit polls, Romney and Ryan took almost 60 percent of the vote from whites, but the Democrats won over 70 percent from blacks, Hispanics, and Asians and 60 percent of voters from 18 to 29 years of age.

Jamie Sabau

idealized conception of democratic theory. However, issues, candidates' attributes, and party identification all figure in the voting decision, and scholars have incorporated these factors in statistical models to explain voting.[112]

Unfortunately for democratic theory, many studies of presidential elections show that issues are less important to voters than either party identification or the candidates' attributes. One exception occurred in 1972, when voters perceived George McGovern as too liberal for their tastes and issue voting exceeded party identification.[113] Recent research has found an increase in policy-based voting.[114] Although party voting has declined somewhat since the 1950s, the relationship between voters' positions on the issues and their party identification is clearer and more consistent today. For example, Democratic Party identifiers are now more likely than Republican identifiers to describe themselves as liberal, and they are more likely than Republican identifiers to favor government spending for Social Security and health care. The more closely party identification is aligned with ideological orientation, the more sense it makes to vote by party. Over the last four decades, as shown in Figure 9.5, the alignment of party and ideology has increased in congressional voting such that the fit is almost perfect. Virtually all Democrats in the House of Representatives have more liberal voting records than virtually all Republicans, who have more conservative records.

Campaign Effects

If party identification is the most important factor in the voting decision and is also resistant to short-term changes, there are definite limits to the capacity of a campaign to influence the outcome of elections.[115] In a close election, however, changing just a few votes means the difference between victory and defeat, so a campaign can be decisive even if its effects cannot be disentangled.

The Television Campaign. Because of the propensity of television news shows to offer only sound bites, candidates cannot rely on television news to get their message

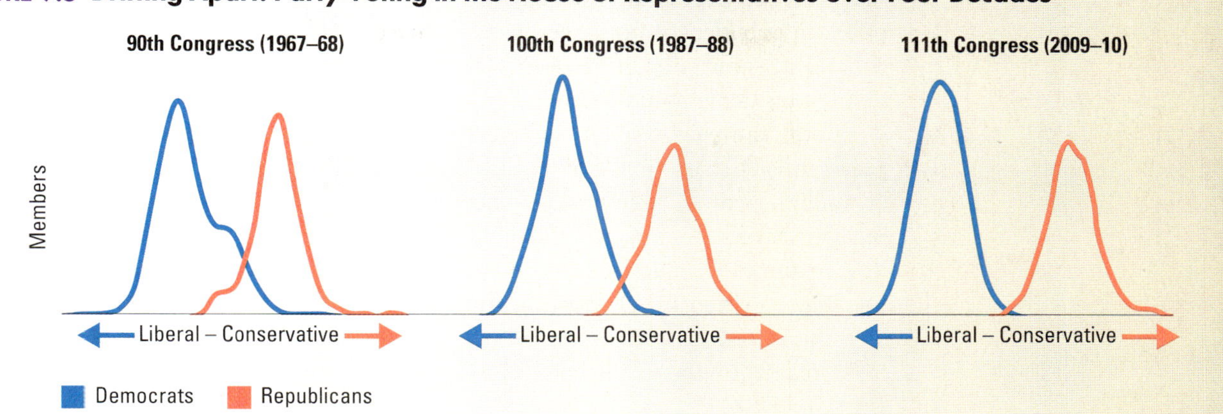

The three graphs illustrate how members of the House of Representatives have grown further apart ideologically over the past four decades. The base line estimates the representatives' liberal-conservative ideology as computed from hundreds of roll call votes in each congress. In the mid-1960s, some Republicans had more liberal voting records than Democrats, and some Democrats voted more as conservatives—a few being very conservative. By the late 1980s, the overlap had shrunk considerably. By 2009–2010, almost all Democrats were liberals and all Republicans were conservative.

Source: The graphs were kindly provided by Royce Carroll, Rice University. For the methodology, see http://voteview.com/dwnomin.htm. Reproduced by permission.

out. In 2008, remarks from the two major presidential candidates on network news programs averaged only 8.9 seconds, about a second less than in the 1988 election, when sound bite timing began.[116] In truth, the networks devoted about as much airtime to the presidential campaign as in the past, but they did not give the candidates themselves much time to speak. In the average presidential campaign story, reporters spoke about 74 percent of the time compared with the candidates' 11 percent. No wonder that presidential candidates volunteer to appear on entertainment television shows: they get the chance to talk to the public![117]

Although candidates seek free coverage on news and entertainment programs, they fight their election campaigns principally through television advertisements. Both candidates in 2012 hired professional consultants to plan their ad campaigns. Both sides also understood that a presidential election was not truly a national election to be fought across the nation but a *federal* election whose outcome would be decided in certain "battleground" or "swing" states.[118]

Entering the 2012 election, Obama's strategists knew that even if he won all of the same states as in 2008, he would lose six electoral votes because of reapportionment. But he would still have more than the 270 votes needed for reelection. Obama could count on 246 electoral votes from the twenty states that voted Democratic in 2004 and 2008, but Republicans could count on only 180 votes from twenty-two states that favored them both years. A total of 112 electoral votes rested with nine states that voted for Bush in 2004 but for Obama in 2008. Given that many white working-class voters had soured on Obama, Republicans hoped to pick up many of the nine: Colorado, Florida, Indiana, Iowa, Ohio, Nevada, New Mexico, North Carolina, and Virginia. Both campaigns focused on those states. On election night, Obama's campaign proved to be more successful, winning seven of the nine states, losing to Romney only in Indiana and narrowly in North Carolina. Obama outpolled Romney only 50 to 48 percent in the popular vote but his 332 electoral votes were 62 percent of the total of 538.

The Presidential Debates. In 1960, John F. Kennedy and Richard Nixon held the first televised presidential debate, but debates between the two Democratic and Republican presidential nominees were not used again until 1976. Since then, candidate debates in some form have been a regular feature of presidential elections, although sitting presidents have been reluctant to debate except on their own terms.

Both campaign staffs agreed to three presidential debates and one vice-presidential debate in October. Surveyed after the first debate (watched by almost 70 million people), viewers overwhelmingly thought a confident, articulate Romney out-performed a distracted Obama. Afterwards, Romney began to erode Obama's lead in the polls. The vice-presidential debate between Paul Ryan and an animated Joe Biden perked up Democratic enthusiasm somewhat. Although Obama marginally outperformed Romney in most polls after the last two debates, Romney clearly benefited from them, virtually erasing Obama's lead heading into the November election.

★ 9.6 Campaigns, Elections, and Parties

★ Explain the significance of candidate-centered as opposed to party-centered election campaigns for both majoritarian and pluralist democracy.

Election campaigns today tend to be highly personalized, candidate centered, and conducted outside the control of party organizations. The increased use of electronic media, especially television, has encouraged candidates to personalize their campaign messages; at the same time, the decline of party identification has decreased the power of party-related appeals. Although the party affiliations of the candidates and the party identifications of the voters jointly explain a good deal of electoral behavior, party organizations are not central to elections in America, and this situation has implications for democratic government.

Parties and the Majoritarian Model

According to the majoritarian model of democracy, parties link people with their government by making government responsive to public opinion. Chapter 8 outlined the model of responsible party government in a majoritarian democracy. This model holds that parties should present clear and coherent programs to voters, that voters should choose candidates according to the party programs, that the winning party should carry out its programs once in office, and that voters should hold the governing party responsible at the next election for executing its program. As noted in Chapter 8, the Republican and Democratic parties do follow the model because they formulate different platforms and tend to pursue their announced policies when in office. The weak links in this model of responsible party government are those that connect candidates to voters through campaigns and elections.

You have not read much in this book about the role of the party platform in nominating candidates, conducting campaigns, or explaining voters' choices. In nominating presidential candidates, basic party principles (as captured in the party platform) do interact with the presidential primary process, and the candidate who wins enough convention delegates through the primaries will surely be comfortable with any platform that her or his delegates adopt. But House and Senate nominations are rarely fought over the party platform. And thoughts about party platforms usually are virtually absent from campaigning and from voters' minds when they cast their ballots. Although voters care little about party platforms, platforms reflect party ideology, and Democrats and Republicans in Congress today are divided sharply over ideology. As shown in Figure 9.5, there was almost no overlap between House Democrats and Republicans concerning ideology in their voting records in 2009–2010. The pattern was similar among Senators, but not as sharply defined. Members of Congress may be behaving "responsibly" when voting cohesively according to their ideology, but they are probably not responding to the majority of the voters, who are ideologically more moderate.

Parties and the Pluralist Model

The way parties in the United States operate is more in keeping with the pluralist model of democracy than the majoritarian model. Our parties are not the basic mechanism through which citizens control their government; instead, they function as two giant interest groups. The parties' interests lie in electing and reelecting their candidates and in enjoying the benefits of public office. In past elections, the parties cared little about the positions or ideologies favored by their candidates for Congress or state offices. Within today's Republican Party, tea party groups work actively to nominate candidates that are suitably conservative. Perhaps to a lesser extent, liberal groups like MoveOn.org push to nominate and elect suitably progressive candidates.

Some scholars believe that stronger parties would strengthen democratic government, even if they could not meet all the requirements of the responsible party model.[119] Our parties already perform valuable functions in structuring the vote along partisan lines and in proposing alternative government policies, but stronger parties might also be able to play a more important role in coordinating government policies after elections. Fulfilling that role, however, presumes that the same party controls the House, the Senate, and the presidency. Under the common situation of divided government—when different parties control different branches—strong parties may simply block coordinated policies. At present, the decentralized nature of the nominating process and campaigning for office offer many opportunities for organized groups outside the parties to identify and back candidates who favor their interests.[120] Although this is in keeping with pluralist theory, it is certain to frustrate majority interests on occasion.

SUMMARY

9.1 The Evolution of Campaigning
- Campaigning has evolved from a party-centered to a candidate-centered process.

9.2 Nominations
- The successful candidate for public office must campaign first to win the party nomination, then to win the general election.

- Using primary elections to nominate candidates tends to decentralize power in American political parties.
- Democratic and Republican nominations for president are not decided at the parties' national conventions but determined in advance through the complex process of selecting delegates pledged to particular

candidates. However, candidates cannot win the nomination unless they have broad support within the party.
- Party nominees can legitimately say that they won through their own efforts and owe little to the party organization.

9.3 Elections

- The need to win a majority of votes in the electoral college structures presidential elections.
- Only twice in more than 100 years has a candidate won a majority of the popular vote and lost in the electoral college; the last time was in 2000.
- In fact, the electoral college usually magnifies the victory margin of the winning candidate.
- Since World War II, one party has often won the presidency while the other party controlled one or more chambers of Congress.
- Such divided government has interfered with party control of government.

9.4 Campaigns

- Money is essential in running a modern campaign for major office.
- Serious attempts to control campaign finance began in 1974 with passage of the Federal Election Campaign Act, which established the Federal Election Commission (FEC).
- The law restricted campaign contributions by corporations and labor unions and set limits on contributions by individuals.
- Court decisions in 2010 allowed unlimited contributions by corporations, labor unions, and individuals to influence elections as long as the expenditures were "uncoordinated" with candidates or parties.
- These decisions gave rise to Super PACs that raised and spent millions of dollars in the 2012 general election.
- The government does not provide funding for congressional campaigns, so candidates must raise contributions from individuals or PACs.

- Public funding for presidential elections began with the 1976 election, but by 1996 some candidates learned that they could raise more money privately than provided through public funds.
- In 2012, no major candidate seeking the presidency sought public funding.

9.5 Explaining Voting Choice

- Voting choice can be analyzed in terms of party identification, candidates' attributes, and policy positions.
- Party identification is still the most important long-term factor in shaping the voting decision, but few candidates rely on it in their campaigns—relying instead on personalized campaigns that stress their attributes and policies.
- Short-term factors stemming from a combination of the candidates and issues in the election can solidify support from one candidate's partisans nationally, encourage defections from the other's partisans, and capture a majority of the independents.
- Overall, however, presidential campaigns are not national but federal elections, and the winning candidate assembles an electoral vote majority by winning traditionally loyal states plus enough swing states.

9.6 Campaigns, Elections, and Parties

- The way that nominations, campaigns, and elections are conducted in America is out of keeping with the ideals of responsible party government that fit the majoritarian model of democracy.
- In particular, campaigns and elections do not function to link parties strongly to voters, as the model posits.
- American parties are better suited to the pluralist model of democracy, which sees them as major interest groups competing with lesser groups to further their own interests.

ASSESSING YOUR UNDERSTANDING WITH APLIA…YOUR VIRTUAL TUTOR!

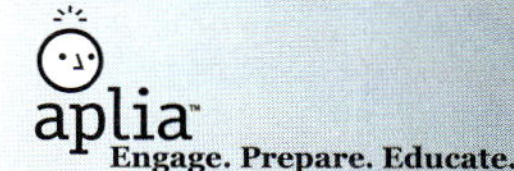

9.1 Describe how election campaigns have changed over time.

1. Candidates once relied on their parties to run election campaigns; on whom do they rely today?

9.2 Explain the procedures followed in the nomination of both congressional and presidential candidates.

1. What is the difference between an "open" and "closed" party primary? Which weakens political parties?
2. Since 1972, has the presidential nominating process become more or less open to control of party leaders?
3. Since 1972, have the national nominating conventions become more or less rubber-stamp institutions?

9.3 Describe the function of the electoral college and formulate arguments for and against the electoral vote system.

1. What is the difference between the electoral college and the electoral vote system?
2. Explain why a presidential election is a federal election, not a national election.
3. Like most citizens, you probably favor direct popular election of the president. Give some arguments for electing presidents by states casting electoral votes.

9.4 Analyze the American election campaign process in terms of political context, financial resources, and strategies and tactics for reaching the voters.

1. By what reasoning has the Supreme Court struck down attempts to regulate campaign finance?
2. Explain how the Court's 2010 decision in the *Citizens United* case has led to increased spending in federal election campaigns.
3. Do presidential candidates today rely more or less on public funding of campaigns? Why?

9.5 Assess the effects of party identification, political issues, and candidate attributes on voter choice.

1. Historically, which has the greater effect on voting for president, party identification or the candidates' issue positions?
2. What are "battleground states" in presidential elections and why are they important?

9.6 Explain the significance of candidate-centered as opposed to party-centered election campaigns for both majoritarian and pluralist democracy.

1. How well do political parties fulfill the expectations of the responsible model of party government set forth at the end of the preceding chapter on political parties?
2. Do American political parties operate more in keeping with the majoritarian or pluralist models of democracy?

10 Interest Groups

F

acebook needed a friend.

The target to be befriended was the federal government. The California-based social-networking company wanted to be on good terms with Congress and relevant administrative agencies because government policy can fundamentally affect Facebook's profitability.

Policymakers in Washington have raised many concerns about privacy on the Internet. When you go to a website, it is common for tracking services running on the site to monitor your subsequent movements around the Internet and then use or sell that information for advertising or market research purposes. Think of how much information Facebook has about its individual users (all 800 million of them, each of whom has an average of 130 "friends" and tracks in and out of Facebook each day).

Facebook's stated policy is that it does not share any personal information about its users with companies that advertise on the site. Nor does it sell such information to any outside parties. Nevertheless, Facebook's potential income from marketing members' personal preferences and their interactions with their friends is enormous. The general advertising it already sells generates revenues of close to $4 billion a year.

To provide it with better access to those in government, Facebook has recently expanded its Washington presence, adding staffers and moving to larger office space. It has made it a priority to hire staffers with important Washington experience, some from working for Democrats and some from working for Republicans. Recent hire Robert Gibbs was President Obama's press secretary. Joel Klein was a deputy chief of staff in the George W. Bush White House, and Micah Jordan also worked for President Bush.

Microsoft and Google, two other high-tech behemoths, ran into trouble by paying little attention to Washington. Those companies had to play catch-up when they found that the government was enacting policies that the companies found objectionable. Both companies now have substantial Washington offices. Facebook hopes that its Washington lobbyists can gain the respect of policymakers and have a seat at the bargaining table when relevant issues arise. The company is not going to be able to stop all policies it stands against, but it can hope to influence laws and regulations as they're being formulated. The general objective is to have an ongoing dialog with legislators and administrators.

Facebook is counting on its lobbyists to build relationships with policymakers so that government's door is always open to them. When it comes to access in Washington, it's good to have a lot of friends.[1]

In this chapter, we look at the central dynamic of pluralist democracy: the interaction of interest groups and government. In analyzing the process by which interest groups and lobbyists come to speak on behalf of different groups, we focus on several questions. How do interest groups form? Whom do they represent? What tactics do they use to convince policymakers that their views are best for the nation? Is the interest group system biased in favor of certain types of people? If so, what are the consequences?

★ 10.1 Interest Groups and the American Political Tradition

★ Identify the different roles that interest groups play in our political system.

interest group
An organized group of individuals that seeks to influence public policy. Also called a *lobby*.

lobby
See *interest group*.

lobbyist
A representative of an interest group.

An **interest group** is an organized body of individuals who share some political goals and try to influence public policy decisions. Among the most prominent interest groups in the United States are the AFL-CIO (representing labor union members), the American Farm Bureau Federation (representing farmers), the Business Roundtable (representing big business), and Common Cause (representing citizens concerned with reforming government). Interest groups are also called **lobbies**, and their representatives are referred to as **lobbyists**.

Interest Groups: Good or Evil?

A recurring debate in American politics concerns the role of interest groups in a democratic society. Are interest groups a threat to the well-being of the political system, or do they contribute to its proper functioning? A favorable early evaluation of interest groups can be found in the writings of Alexis de Tocqueville, a French visitor to the United States in the early nineteenth century. During his travels, Tocqueville marveled at the array of organizations he found, and he later wrote that "Americans of all ages, all conditions, and all dispositions, constantly form associations."[2] Tocqueville was suggesting that the ease with which we form organizations reflects a strong democratic culture.

Yet other early observers were concerned about the consequences of interest group politics. Writing in the *Federalist* papers, James Madison warned of the dangers of "factions," the major divisions in American society. In *Federalist* No. 10, written in 1787, Madison said it was inevitable that substantial differences would develop between factions. It was only natural for farmers to oppose merchants, tenants to oppose landlords, and so on. Madison further reasoned that each faction would do what it could to prevail over other factions, that each basic interest in society would try to persuade the government to adopt policies that favored it at the expense of others. He noted that the fundamental causes of faction were "sown in the nature of man."[3]

But Madison argued against trying to suppress factions. He concluded that factions can be eliminated only by removing our freedoms because "Liberty is to faction what air is to fire."[4] Instead, Madison suggested that relief from the self-interested advocacy of factions should come only through controlling the effects of that advocacy. The relief would be provided by a democratic republic in which government would mediate among opposing factions. The size and diversity of the nation as well as the structure of government would ensure that even a majority faction could never come to suppress the rights of others.[5]

How we judge interest groups—as "good" or "evil"—may depend on how strongly we are committed to freedom or equality (see Chapter 1). People dislike interest groups in general because they do not offer equal representation to all; some sectors of society are better represented than others. In a poll, four out of five respondents indicated that they believe it is common for lobbyists to bribe members of Congress.[6] Recent filings with Congress listed $3.5 billion in annual spending on lobbying, and as Figure 10.1 shows, individual lobbies spend vast sums as they try to influence legislation.[7] Interest groups have recently enjoyed unparalleled growth; many new groups have formed, and old ones have expanded. Apparently we distrust interest groups as a whole, but we like those that represent our views. Stated more bluntly, we hate lobbies—except those that speak on our behalf.

The Roles of Interest Groups

The "evil" side of interest group politics is all too apparent. Each group pushes its own selfish interests, which, despite the group's claims to the contrary, are not always in the best interest of other Americans. The "good" side of interest group advocacy may not be so clear. How do the actions of interest groups benefit our political system?[8]

Representation. Interest groups represent people before their government. Just as a member of Congress represents a particular constituency, so does a lobbyist. A

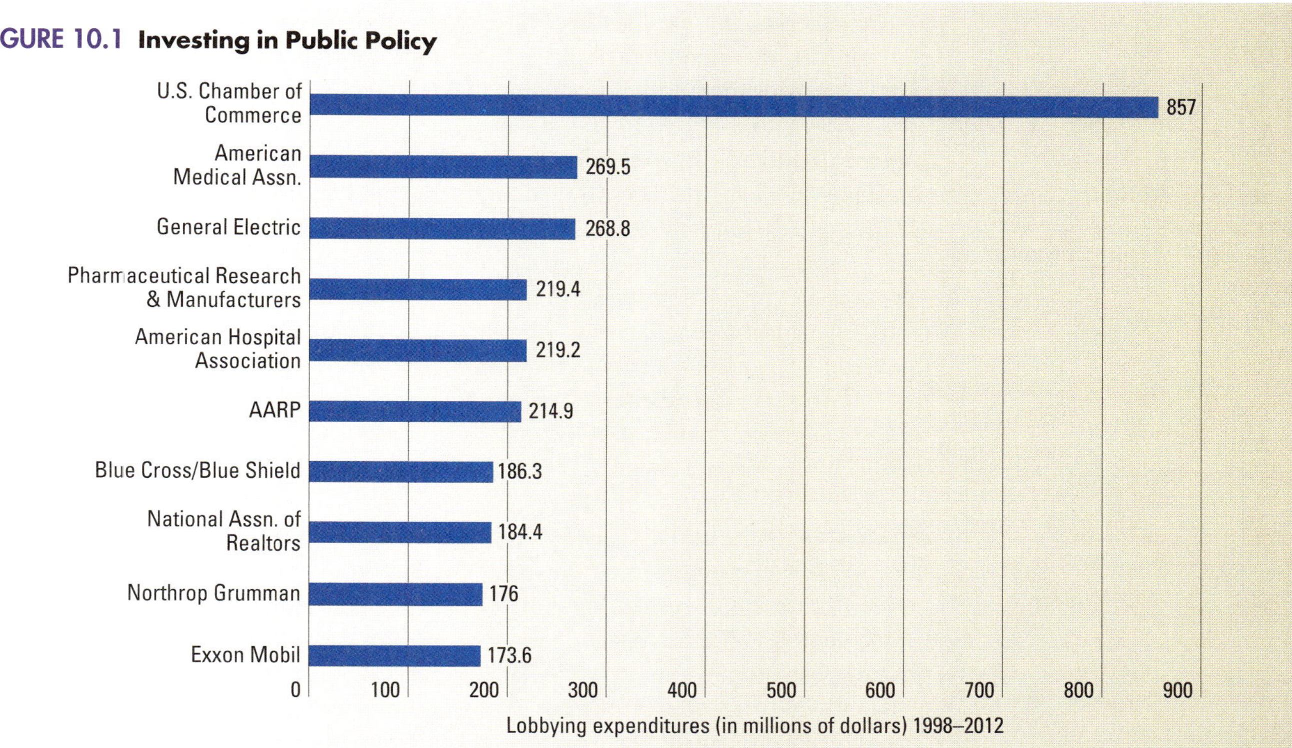

FIGURE 10.1 Investing in Public Policy

This list of the top ten spenders on lobbying for the period between 1998–2012 demonstrates the vast sum of money spent to influence public policy. The top spenders are, not surprisingly, predominantly business-related interest groups as a change in public policy can result in a business making or losing hundreds of millions of dollars.
Source: Center for Responsive Politics, "Top Spenders." Figures for 2012 through July 1 of that year.

lobbyist for the National Association of Broadcasters, for example, speaks for the interests of radio and television broadcasters when Congress or a government agency is considering a relevant policy decision.

Whatever the political interest—the cement industry, Social Security, endangered species—it helps to have an active lobby operating in Washington. Members of Congress represent a multitude of interests, some of them conflicting, from their own districts and states. Government administrators, too, are pulled in different directions and have their own policy preferences. Interest groups articulate their members' concerns, presenting them directly and forcefully in the political process.

Participation. Interest groups are vehicles for political participation. They provide a means by which like-minded citizens can pool their resources and channel their energies into collective political action. People band together because they know it is much easier to get government to listen to a group than to an individual. One farmer fighting against a new pesticide proposal in Congress probably will not get very far, but thousands of farmers united in an organization stand a much better chance of getting policymakers to consider their needs. Interest groups not only facilitate participation; they stimulate it as well. By asking people to write to their member of Congress or take other action, lobbies get people more involved in the political process than they otherwise would be.

Education. As part of their efforts to lobby government and increase their membership, interest groups help educate their members, the public at large, and government officials. As we noted in the opening of this chapter, some high-tech companies were slow to set up lobbying offices in Washington. As more and more issues affecting the industry received attention from government, high-tech executives began to realize that policymakers didn't have a sufficient understanding of the rapidly changing industry. To gain the attention of the policymakers they are trying to educate, interest groups need to provide them with information that is not easily obtained from other sources.

agenda building
The process by which new issues are brought into the political limelight.

Agenda Building. In a related role, interest groups bring new issues into the political limelight through a process called **agenda building**. American society has many problem areas, but public officials are not addressing all of them. Through their advocacy, interest groups make the government aware of problems and then try to see to it that something is done to solve them.[9] Labor unions, for example, have historically played a critical role in gaining attention for problems that were being systematically ignored. As Figure 10.2 shows, however, union membership has declined significantly over the years. As private sector employment in unionized industries has fallen, union membership among municipal government employees has become the largest sector of unionized workers.[10]

program monitoring
Keeping track of government programs; usually done by interest groups.

Program Monitoring. Finally, interest groups engage in **program monitoring**. Lobbies follow government programs that are important to their constituents, keeping abreast of developments in Washington and the communities where the policies are implemented. When a program is not operating as it should, concerned interest groups push administrators to change it in ways that promote the groups' goals. They draw attention to agency officials' transgressions and even file suit to stop actions they consider unlawful. The National Federation of Independent Business, a major trade association representing small businesses, uses a computer program to estimate the cost of federal regulations. Its policy analysts monitor new regulatory proposals and are prepared to initiate action directed at trying to force government to suspend those they feel are poorly supported by available scientific data.[11]

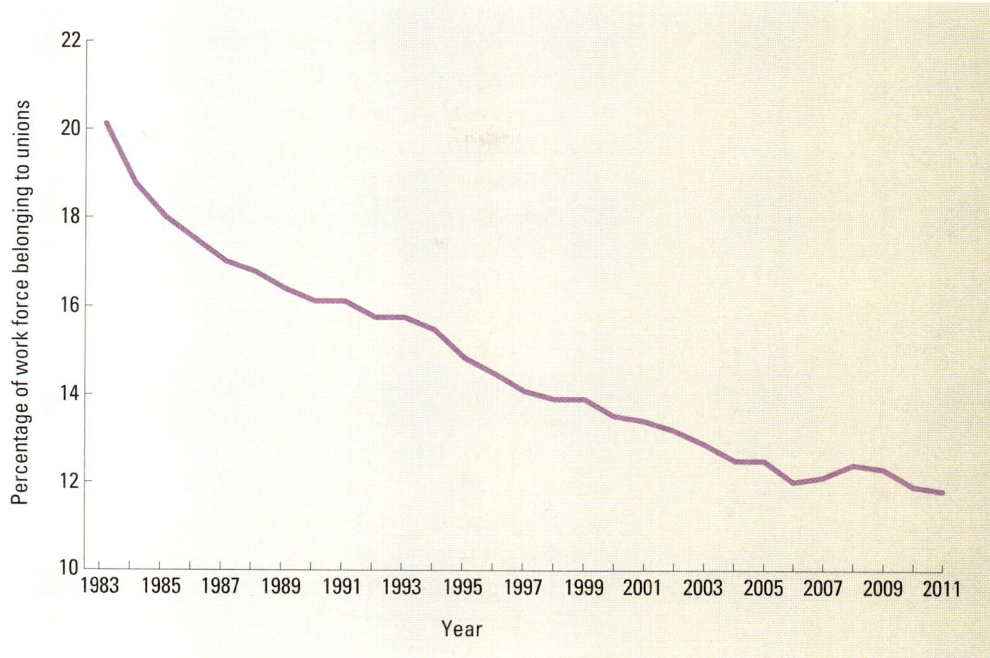

FIGURE 10.2 Labor Pains

Over the years, many manufacturing jobs in the United States have migrated overseas to developing countries with lower wages. That may be good for consumers (cheaper wages mean lower-cost products), but it has been bad for labor unions because workers in heavy industry have traditionally been the most likely to be unionized. Service sector workers like restaurant employees have been much harder for unions to organize.
Source: Bureau of Labor Statistics.

Interest groups do, then, play some positive roles in their pursuit of self-interest. But we should not assume that the positive side of interest groups neatly balances the negative. Questions remain about the overall influence of interest groups on public policy making. Most important, are the effects of interest group advocacy being controlled, as Madison believed they should be?

10.2 How Interest Groups Form

★ Analyze interest group success in terms of "entrepreneurial" behavior.

Do some people form interest groups more easily than others? Are some factions represented while others are not? Pluralists assume that when a political issue arises, interest groups with relevant policy concerns begin to lobby. Policy conflicts are ultimately resolved through bargaining and negotiation between the involved organizations and the government. Unlike Madison, who dwelled on the potential for harm by factions, pluralists believe interest groups are a good thing—that they contribute to democracy by broadening representation within the system.

An important part of pluralism is the belief that new interest groups form as a matter of course when the need arises. David Truman outlines this idea in his classic work *The Governmental Process*.[12] He says that when individuals are threatened by change, they band together in an interest group. For example, if government threatens to regulate a particular industry, the firms that compose that industry will start a trade association to protect their financial well-being. Truman sees a direct cause-and-effect relationship in all of this: existing groups stand in equilibrium until some type of disturbance (such as falling wages or declining farm prices) forces new groups to form.

Truman's thinking on the way interest groups form is like the "invisible hand" notion of laissez-faire economics: self-correcting market forces will remedy imbalances in the marketplace. But in politics, no invisible hand, no force, automatically causes interest groups to develop. Truman's disturbance theory paints an idealized portrait of interest group politics in America. In real life, people do not automatically organize when they are adversely affected by some disturbance. A good example of "nonorganization" can be found in Herbert Gans's book *The Urban Villagers*.[13] Gans, a sociologist, moved into the West End, a low-income neighborhood in Boston, during the late 1950s. The neighborhood had been targeted for urban redevelopment; the city was planning to replace old buildings with modern ones. This meant that the people living there—primarily poor Italian Americans who very much liked their neighborhood—would have to move.

Being evicted is a highly traumatic experience, so the situation in the West End certainly qualified as a bona fide disturbance according to Truman's scheme of interest group formation. Yet the people of the West End barely put up a fight to save their neighborhood. Residents remained largely unorganized; soon they were moved, and the buildings in the neighborhood were demolished.

Disturbance theory clearly fails to explain what happened (or didn't happen) in Boston's West End. An adverse condition or change does not automatically mean that an interest group will form. What, then, is the missing ingredient? Political scientist Robert Salisbury says that the quality of interest group leadership may be the crucial factor.[14]

Interest Group Entrepreneurs

Salisbury likens the role of an interest group leader to that of an entrepreneur in the business world. An entrepreneur is someone who starts new enterprises, usually at considerable personal financial risk. Salisbury says that an **interest group entrepreneur**, or organizer, succeeds or fails for many of the same reasons a business entrepreneur succeeds or fails. The interest group entrepreneur must have something attractive to "market" in order to convince people to join.[15] Potential members must be persuaded that the benefits of joining outweigh the costs. Someone starting a new union, for example, must convince workers that the union can win them wages high enough to more than offset membership dues. The organizer of an ideological group must convince potential members that the group can effectively lobby the government to achieve their particular goals.

The development of the United Farm Workers union shows the importance of leadership in the formation of an interest group. The union is made up of men and women who pick crops in California and other parts of the country. These pickers—predominantly poor, uneducated Mexican Americans—perform backbreaking work in the hot growing season.

Their chronically low wages and deplorable living conditions made the farm workers prime candidates for organization into a labor union. And throughout the twentieth century, various unions tried to organize them. Yet for many reasons, including distrust of union organizers, intimidation by employers, and lack of money to pay union dues, all failed. Then, in 1962, the late Cesar Chavez, a poor Mexican American, began to crisscross the Central Valley of California, talking to workers and planting the idea of a union. Chavez had been a farm worker himself (he first worked as a picker at the age of ten), and he was well aware of the difficulties that lay ahead for his newly organized union.

interest group entrepreneur
An interest group organizer or leader.

After a strike against grape growers failed in 1965, Chavez changed his tactic of trying to build a stronger union merely by recruiting a larger membership. Copying the civil rights movement, Chavez and his followers marched 250 miles to the state capitol in Sacramento to demand help from the governor. The march and other non-violent tactics began to draw sympathy from people who had no direct involvement in farming. Seeing the movement as a way to help poor members of the church, Catholic clergy were a major source of support. This support gave the charismatic Chavez greater credibility, and his followers cast him in the role of spiritual as well as political leader.[16]

Chavez subsequently called for a boycott, and a small but significant number of Americans stopped buying grapes. The growers, who had bitterly fought the union, were finally hurt economically. Under this and other economic pressures, they eventually agreed to recognize and bargain with the United Farm Workers. The union then helped its members with the wage and benefit agreements it was able to negotiate.

Who Is Being Organized?

Cesar Chavez is a good example of the importance of leadership in the formation of a new interest group. Despite many years of adverse conditions, efforts to organize farm workers had failed. The dynamic leadership of Cesar Chavez is what seems to have made the difference.

But another important element is at work in the formation of interest groups. The residents of Boston's West End and the farm workers in California were poor, uneducated or undereducated, and politically inexperienced—factors that made it extremely difficult to organize them into interest groups. If they had been well-to-do, educated, and politically experienced, they probably would have banded together immediately. People who have money, are educated, and know how the system operates are more confident that their actions can make a difference.[17] Together, these attributes give people more incentive to devote their time and ample resources to organizing and supporting interest groups.

Every existing interest group has its own history, but the three variables just discussed can help explain why groups may or may not become fully organized. First, an adverse change or disturbance can contribute to people's awareness that they need political representation. However, this alone does not ensure that an organization will form, and organizations have formed in the absence of a disturbance. Second, the quality of leadership is critical in the organization of interest groups. Some interest group entrepreneurs are more skilled than others at convincing people to join their organizations. Third, the higher the socioeconomic level of potential members is, the more likely they are to know the value of interest groups and to participate in politics by joining them.

Finally, not all interest groups have real memberships. In this sense "group" is a misnomer; some lobbying organizations are institutions that lack members but are affected by public policy and establish lobbying offices or hire lobbyists to represent them before government. Universities and hospitals, for example, don't have members but are well represented before government. Harvard University and the University of California typically spend upward of $600,000 a year on lobbying.[18] Sizeable corporations, large nonprofits, and business trade associations are usually quite astute at understanding just how valuable it is to have lobbyists in Washington.

Because wealthy and better-educated Americans are more likely to form and join lobbies, they seem to have an important advantage in the political process.

Nevertheless, as the United Farm Workers' case shows, poor and uneducated people are also capable of forming interest groups. The question that remains, then, is not *whether* various opposing interests are represented but *how well* they are represented. In terms of Madison's premise in *Federalist* No. 10, are the effects of faction—in this case, the advantages of the wealthy and well educated—being controlled? Before we can answer this question about how interest groups affect the level of political equality in our society, we need to turn our attention to the resources available to interest groups.

★ 10.3 Interest Group Resources

★ Identify the various resources available to interest groups and evaluate their role in interest group performance.

The strengths, capabilities, and influence of an interest group depend in large part on its resources. A group's most significant resources are its members, lobbyists, and money, including funds that can be contributed to political candidates. The sheer quantity of a group's resources is important, and so is the wisdom with which its resources are used.

Members

One of the most valuable resources an interest group can have is a large, politically active membership. If a lobbyist is trying to convince a legislator to support a particular bill, having a large group of members who live in the legislator's home district or state is tremendously helpful. A legislator who has not already taken a firm position on a bill might be swayed by the knowledge that voters back home are kept informed by interest groups of his or her votes on key issues. The American Association of Retired Persons (AARP) has a membership of 40 million, making it a feared interest group in Washington.[19]

Members give an organization not only the political muscle to influence policy but also financial resources. The more money an organization can collect through dues and contributions, the more people it can hire to lobby government officials and monitor the policy-making process. Greater resources also allow an organization to communicate with its members more and to inform them better. And funding helps a group maintain its membership and attract new members.

Maintaining Membership. To keep the members it already has, an organization must persuade them that it is doing a good job in its advocacy. Most lobbies use a newsletter and e-mails to keep members apprised of developments in government that relate to issues of concern to them. Interest groups use these communications as public relations tools to try to keep members believing that their lobby is playing a critical role in protecting their interests.

Business, professional, and labor associations generally have an easier time holding on to members than do citizen groups, whose basis of organization is a concern for issues not directly related to their members' jobs. In many companies, corporate membership in a trade group constitutes only a minor business expense. Big individual corporations have no memberships as such, but they often open their own lobbying offices in Washington. They have the advantage of being able to use institutional financial resources to support their lobbying; they do not have to rely on voluntary contributions. Labor unions are helped in states that require workers to affiliate with the union that is the bargaining agent with their employer. In contrast, citizen groups base their appeal on members' ideological sentiments. These groups face a difficult challenge: issues can blow hot and cold, and a particularly hot issue one year may not hold the same interest to citizens the next.

Attracting New Members. All membership groups are constantly looking for new adherents to expand their resources and clout. Groups that rely on ideological appeals have a special problem because the competition in most policy areas is intense. People concerned about the environment, for example, can join a seemingly infinite number of local, state, and national groups. The National Wildlife Federation, Environmental Defense, the Natural Resources Defense Council, Friends of the Earth, the National Audubon Society, the Wilderness Society, and the Sierra Club are just some of the national organizations that lobby on environmental issues. Groups try to distinguish themselves from competitors by concentrating on a few key issues and developing a reputation as the most involved and knowledgeable about them. The Sierra Club, one of the oldest and largest environmental groups, has long had a focus on protecting national parks. Some smaller organizations, such as Defenders of Wildlife and the Rainforest Action Network, have found a sufficient number of members to support their advocacy. Organizations in a crowded policy area must differentiate themselves from the competition and then aggressively market what they have to offer to potential contributors.

The Internet has become an increasingly important means of soliciting new members. Compared to direct mail—an interest group sending a letter and supporting material via old-fashioned "snail mail"—e-mail is much cheaper. E-mail directed to prospects may entice them to go the organization's website to learn more and, possibly, make a contribution. Ideological citizen groups depend heavily on Internet traffic to gain new supporters. Citizen groups working to put strict conservatives on the federal courts, such as the Judicial Crisis Network, the Committee for Justice, and the Judicial Action Network, have small offices and do not spend great sums on fundraising.[20] Use of the Internet helps these groups keep their costs down as they compete with one another for financial support, while they also cooperate with one another to try to keep liberal jurists off the federal courts.

Interest groups also use social-networking sites like Facebook for fundraising. There's no shortage of "Friends of [fill in the blank]"—postings that ask visitors to that page to make a generous contribution. These are typically ideological groups, and many try to tap the idealism of the generally youthful clientele of networking sites. The effectiveness of using social-networking sites to build interest group membership is not yet clear.

The Free-Rider Problem. Interest groups' use of aggressive marketing suggests that getting people who sympathize with a group's goals to join and support it with their contributions is difficult. Economists call this difficulty the **free-rider problem**, but we might call it, more colloquially, the "Let-George-do-it problem."[21] Funding for public television stations illustrates the dilemma. Almost all agree that public television, which survives in large part through viewers' contributions, is of great value. But only a fraction of those who watch public television contribute on a regular basis. Why? Because people can watch the programs whether they contribute or not. The free rider has the same access to public television as the contributor.

free-rider problem
The situation in which people benefit from the activities of an organization (such as an interest group) but do not contribute to those activities.

The same problem crops up for interest groups. When a lobbying group wins benefits, those benefits are not restricted to the members of the organization. For instance, if the U.S. Chamber of Commerce convinces Congress to enact a policy benefiting business, all businesses will benefit, not just those that actually pay the membership dues of the lobbying group. Thus, some executives may feel that their corporation doesn't need to spend the money to join the U.S. Chamber of Commerce, even though they might benefit from the group's efforts; they prefer instead to let others shoulder the financial burden.

The free-rider problem increases the difficulty of attracting paying members, but it certainly does not make the task impossible.[22] Many people realize that if everyone decides to let someone else do it, the job simply will not get done.[23] Millions of Americans contribute to interest groups because they are concerned about an issue or feel a responsibility to help organizations that work on their behalf. Also, many organizations offer membership benefits that have nothing to do with politics or lobbying. Business **trade associations**, for example, are a source of information about industry trends and effective management practices; they organize conventions at which members can learn, socialize, and occasionally find new customers or suppliers. An individual firm in the electronics industry may not care that much about the lobbying done by the Electronics Industries Alliance, but it may have a vital interest in the information about marketing and manufacturing that the organization provides. Successful interest groups are adept at supplying the right mix of benefits to their target constituency.

trade association
An organization that represents firms within a particular industry.

Lobbyists

Some of the money that interest groups raise is used to pay lobbyists who represent the organizations before the government. Lobbyists make sure that people in government know what their members want and that their organizations know what the government is doing. For example, when an administrative agency issues new regulations, lobbyists are right there to interpret the content and implications of the regulations for rank-and-file members. As one lobbyist put it, "The [clients who hire me] want to know what's going down the pipe. They want to be plugged into the system."[24]

Lobbyists can be full-time employees of their organization or employees of public relations or law firms who are hired on retainer. As noted earlier, when hiring a lobbyist, an interest group looks for someone who knows her or his way around Washington. Lobbyists are valued for their experience and their knowledge of how government operates. Karen Ignagni, the chief lobbyist for America's Health Insurance Plans, an industry trade group, was at the center of the negotiations over the Obama administration's health reform proposal. Ignagni's experience, vast knowledge of health care, and skills as a bargainer made her a formidable presence as Congress struggled to formulate a bill that could pass. The stakes for the insurance companies were enormous as industry executives worried that a government-run insurance plan could cost them customers. Her stature is such that she is paid $1.6 million annually.[25]

So lucrative is lobbying that many representatives and senators are drawn to it when they leave the Congress. After one recent session, seventy-seven former members of Congress who were defeated for re-election or left voluntarily were subsequently tracked as to their new occupation. Of the seventy-seven, thirty-two (42 percent) had taken jobs with a firm that lobbies.[26] One of those was Christopher Dodd, a former Democratic senator from Connecticut. Dobb was hired by the

Motion Picture Association of America, which represents six major Hollywood studios. His major task was to lead the fight against "digital theft" and improve access to China. His thirty-six-year career in Congress gave him innumerable contacts around Washington; he's someone who gets his phone calls returned.[27]

Many lobbyists have a law degree and find their legal backgrounds useful in bargaining and negotiating over laws and regulations. Because of their location, many Washington law firms are drawn into lobbying. Expanding interest group advocacy has created a boon for Washington law firms. Corporations without their own Washington office rely heavily on law firms to lobby for them before the national government.

The stereotype of lobbyists portrays them as people of dubious ethics because they trade on their connections and may hand out campaign donations to candidates for office as well as raise money for legislators. Lobbying is a much maligned profession, but the lobbyist's primary job is not to trade on favors or campaign contributions. It is rather to pass information on to both their employers and to policymakers. Investment firms, for example, need immediate knowledge of what government is contemplating in terms of policy changes because they can affect the value of their holdings. As one lobbyist noted, "[My] information has value on Wall Street so I sell it."[28] Likewise, lobbyists provide government officials and their staffs with a constant flow of data that support their organizations' policy goals. Lobbyist Elizabeth Moeller said of her job, "Finally, my nerdiness can pay off."[29] Lobbyists also try to build a compelling case for their goals, showing that the "facts" dictate that a particular change be made or avoided. What lobbyists are really trying to do, of course, is to convince policymakers that their data deserve more attention and are more accurate than those presented by opposing lobbyists. (See "Politics of Global Change: New Meaning to the Term 'China Lobby,'" pp. 284–285.)

Scott J. Ferrell/Congressional Quarterly/Getty Images

You Got Problems? Call Us

If your organization or cause needs representation in Washington, there's no shortage of free-standing lobbying shops and law firms ready to help. These partners in the lobbying firm the c2 Group advertise themselves as offering a "broad range of bipartisan government affairs consulting services." The firm's clients include Home Depot, PepsiCo, Porsche Cars North America, and the National Council of Coal Lessors.

Political Action Committees

One of the organizational resources that can make a lobbyist's job easier is a **political action committee (PAC)**. PACs pool campaign contributions from group members and donate the money to candidates for political office. As noted in Chapter 9, under federal law, a PAC can give as much as $5,000 to a candidate for Congress for each separate election. There are well over 4,000 PACs contributing to congressional candidates, and in the 2009–2010 campaign cycle, they gave close to $400 million to candidates for the House and Senate.[30]

A PAC can be the campaign-wing affiliate of an existing interest group or a wholly independent or nonconnected group. Super PACs tend to be strictly campaign instruments and are discussed in Chapter 9. The majority of PACs are small and donate only

political action committee (PAC)

An organization that pools campaign contributions from group members and donates those funds to candidates for political office.

Politics of Global Change

New Meaning to the Term "China Lobby"

When the Communist revolutionaries led by Mao Zedung finally succeeded in taking over the mainland in 1949, 2 million Chinese loyal to the defeated regime of Chiang Kai-Shek fled to the island of Taiwan. The United States had backed Chiang Kai-Shek and his government and continued to support him in Taiwan, which was renamed the Republic of China. The Communist People's Republic of China on the mainland was infuriated with America's backing of Taiwan, which they regarded as a renegade province.

In the United States, some stridently anti-Communist groups formed to support Taiwan and to keep the pressure on the United States to not establish friendly relations with Communist China. These pro-Taiwan groups became known as the "China Lobby." Given the United States' virulent anti-Communist attitude, the China Lobby had little trouble building support for the idea that Taiwan was an important bulwark against the Chinese Communists.

Given Communist China's immense size (now around 1.3 billion people), the U.S. refusal to engage the People's Republic was self-defeating for the United States. A breakthrough came in 1972 when President Richard Nixon visited Communist China and began the process of normalizing relations with the country. Nixon's initiative was a complete and utter defeat for the China Lobby, which, already in decline, quickly disappeared.

Today the United States and the People's Republic (which we now just call "China") are intertwined in many different ways. China remains an authoritarian state, but its economy has moved in significant ways toward free-market practices. It's not a true capitalist economy as the government is the owner of the businesses in many crucial industries, workers have few rights, and wages are suppressed by the government. Still, there are now strong elements of a market economy there.

Foreign trade has boomed between the two countries. American consumers benefit from low-cost imports, while many American manufacturers such as Boeing, Ford, and Caterpillar have substantial sales in China. There is a constant stream of disputes over trade practices and ongoing negotiations to address them. One recurring issue is that the United States accuses the Chinese government of undervaluing its currency, the *yuan*, which makes American goods more expensive in the Chinese market and Chinese goods less expensive in the United States.

Chinese firms have found that they need guidance on how to navigate the complexities of the American political process. When the Chinese company CNOOC

modest amounts, but approximately 1,300 PACs contributed at least $100,000 in the 2008 and 2010 elections.[31] Many PACs are large enough to gain recognition for the issues they care about. The National Association of Realtors had the largest PAC, with contributions of $3.8 million during the most recent two-year election cycle for which figures are available. Other leading contributors include AT&T ($3.3 million), the National Beer Wholesalers ($2.9 million), the International Brotherhood of Electrical Workers ($3.0 million), and the American Bankers Association ($2.8 million).[32]

tried to buy U.S. oil company Unocal in 2005, political opposition within the United States killed the $18.5 billion deal. Huawei Technologies also failed in its attempt to buy the Silicon Valley–based 3 Leaf Technologies because security concerns were raised in the United States.

T.J. Kirkpatrick/Getty Images

When the Chinese firm Alibaba began strategizing about purchasing Yahoo, it hired the Duberstein Group to help it avoid the problems that CNOOC and Huawei encountered. The Duberstein Group, whose principal is Kenneth Duberstein, former chief of staff to President Ronald Reagan, is well connected in Washington. Other Chinese firms have hired venerable law and lobbying firms such as Patton Boggs and Hogan & Hartson. As a basis of comparison, China did not have a single lobbyist in Washington in 1970. Today at least nineteen law and consulting firms work on behalf of Chinese companies. The new China Lobby looks a lot like all the other lobbies in Washington.

Source: Marja Pclmer, "Alibaba Hires Lobbyist Amid Yahoo Bid Talk," *Financial Times*, 29 December 2011; Ronald J. Hrebenar and Clive S. Thomas, "The Rise of the New Asian Lobbies in Washington, D.C." (paper presented at the annual meeting of the American Political Science Association, Seattle, WA, September 2011); John Newhouse, "Diplomacy, Inc.," *Foreign Affairs* (May/June 2009), http://www.foreignaffairs.com/print/64951; and Paul Eckert and Stella Dawson, "Insight: Ten Years On, American Business Rethinks China Dreams," Reuters. 9 December 2011, http://www.reuters.com/article/2011/12/09/us-usa-trade-wto-idUSTRE7B80EB20111209.

Lobbyists believe that campaign contributions help significantly when they are trying to gain an audience with a member of Congress. Members of Congress and their staffers generally are eager to meet with representatives of their constituencies, but their time is limited. However, a member of Congress or staffer would find it difficult to turn down a lobbyist's request for a meeting if the PAC of the lobbyist's organization had made a significant campaign contribution in the previous election. Lobbyists also regard contributions as a form of insurance in case of issues that might arise unexpectedly. As one scholar put it, the donations are given to protect "against unforeseen future dangers as the policymaking process develops."[33]

Typically, PACs, like most other interest groups, are highly pragmatic and adaptable organizations; pushing a particular political philosophy takes second place to achieving immediate policy goals.[34] Although many corporate executives strongly believe in a free-market economy, for example, their company PACs tend to hold congressional candidates to a much more practical standard and will donate to legislators of various ideological and partisan stripes. The goal of bipartisan contributions is to enhance access, no matter who is in power. Labor unions are an exception to this, donating almost exclusively to Democrats. Nonconnected PACs are highly ideological and tend to give to either conservatives or liberals.

Critics charge that PAC contributions influence public policy, yet political scientists have not been able to document any consistent link between campaign donations and the way members of Congress vote on the floor of the House and Senate.[35] The problem is this: Do PAC contributions influence votes in Congress, or are they just rewards for legislators who would vote for the group's interests anyway because of their long-standing ideology? How do we determine the answer to this question? Simply looking for the influence of PACs in the voting patterns of members of Congress may be shortsighted; influence can also be felt before bills get to the floor of the full House or Senate for a vote. Some sophisticated research shows that PAC donations do seem to influence what goes on in congressional committees.[36] Despite the advantages that organizations with ample resources have through PACs, there are those who defend the current system, emphasizing that interest groups and their members should have the freedom to participate in the political system through campaign donations.

★ 10.4 Lobbying Tactics

★ Compare and contrast different types of lobbying.

When an interest group decides to try to influence the government on an issue, its staff and officers must develop a strategy, which may include several tactics aimed at various officials or offices. Some tactics are utilized far more frequently than others, but all together, the tactics should use the group's resources as effectively as possible.

We turn here to the different types of lobbying tactics. Keep in mind that lobbying extends beyond the legislative branch. Groups can seek help from the courts and administrative agencies as well as from Congress. Moreover, interest groups may have to shift their focus from one branch of government to another. After a bill becomes a law, for example, a group that lobbied for the legislation will probably try to influence the administrative agency responsible for implementing the new law. Some policy decisions are left unresolved by legislation and are settled through regulations. Interest groups try to influence policy through court suits as well, though litigation can be expensive, and opportunities to go to court may be narrowly structured. Lobbying Congress and agencies is more common.

direct lobbying
Attempts to influence a legislator's vote through personal contact with the legislator.

Direct Lobbying

Direct lobbying relies on personal contact with policymakers. This interaction occurs when a lobbyist meets with a member of Congress, an agency official, or a staff member.

In their meetings, lobbyists usually convey their arguments by providing data about a specific issue. If a lobbyist from a chamber of commerce, for example, meets with a member of Congress about a bill the chamber backs, the lobbyist does not say (or even suggest), "Vote for this bill, or our people in the district will vote against you in the next election." Instead, the lobbyist might say, "If this bill is passed, we're going to see hundreds of new jobs created back home." The representative has no trouble at all figuring out that a vote for the bill can help in the next election.

Personal lobbying is a day-in, day-out process. It is not enough simply to meet with policymakers just before a vote or a regulatory decision. Lobbyists must maintain contact with congressional and agency staffers, constantly providing them with pertinent data. In their meetings with policymakers and through other tactics, lobbyists are trying to frame the issue at hand in terms most beneficial to their point of view. Is a gun-control bill before Congress a policy that would make our streets and schools safer from deranged, violent individuals who should not have access to guns—or is it a bill aimed at depriving law-abiding citizens of their constitutional right to bear arms?[37] Research has shown that once an issue emerges, it is very difficult for lobbyists to reframe it—that is, to influence journalists and policymakers alike to view the issue in a new light.[38] Testifying at committee hearings is a tactic that allows the interest group to put its views on record and make them widely known. Although testifying is one of the most visible parts of lobbying, it is generally considered window dressing as it does little by itself to persuade members of Congress.

Another direct but somewhat different approach is legal advocacy. Using this tactic, a group tries to achieve its policy goals through litigation. Claiming some violation of law, a group will file a lawsuit and ask that a judge make a ruling that will benefit the organization. When the Army Corps of Engineers announced plans to permit coal companies to blast off the top of mountains to facilitate their mining, environmental groups went to court alleging a violation of the Clean Water Act. The judge agreed, since the coal companies' actions would leave waste and rock deposits in adjoining streams.[39]

© Ted Soqui/Corbis

Sanchez Reaches Out

Usually we think of lobbying as a process where groups approach a government official. But sometimes the reverse is true: a policymaker might approach an interest group to try to gain its support for a specific proposal or just to promote a good working relationship. Here, Representative Loretta Sanchez (D-Calif.) works the room at a meeting of the Hispanic Leadership Summit.

Grassroots Lobbying

Grassroots lobbying involves an interest group's rank-and-file members and may include people outside the organization who sympathize with its goals. Grassroots tactics, such as letter-writing campaigns and protests, are often used in conjunction with direct lobbying by Washington representatives. Letters, e-mails, faxes, and telephone calls from a group's members to their representatives in Congress or to agency administrators add to a lobbyist's credibility in talks with these officials. Policymakers are more concerned about what a lobbyist says when they know that constituents are really watching their decisions.

grassroots lobbying
Lobbying activities performed by rank-and-file interest group members and would-be members.

Jahi Chikwendiu/The Washington Post via Getty Images

New Starring Role for Clooney: Getting Arrested

Groups protesting the Sudanese government's blockade of humanitarian aid to those starving in the country were after media coverage when they asked a number of celebrities to participate in civil disobedience outside Sudan's embassy in Washington. Popular film actor George Clooney had traveled to Sudan and witnessed the crisis there firsthand. He made a short speech to the assembled crowd and was arrested shortly thereafter. He did not serve any significant time in jail, but his participation led to a great deal of press coverage on the Sudanese crisis.

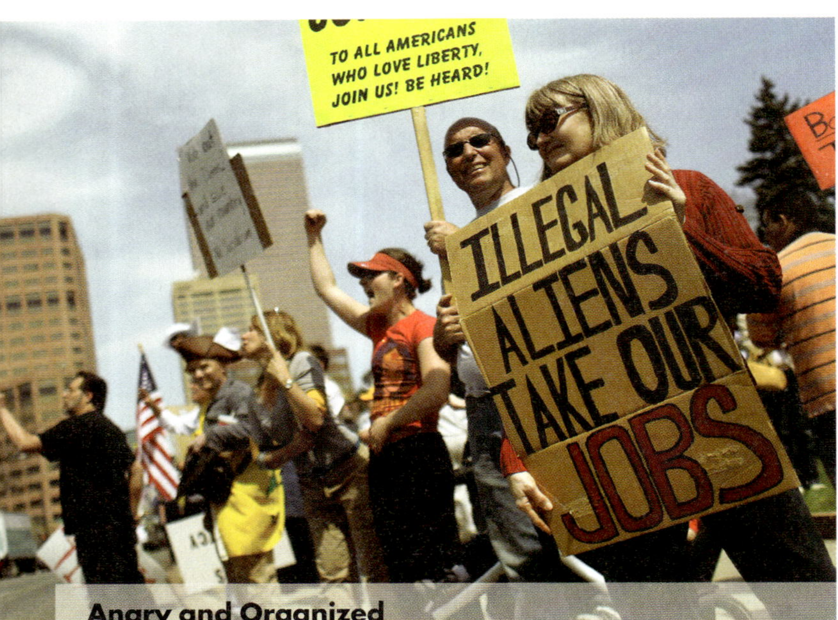

John Moore/Getty Images

Angry and Organized

Over the past few years, conservatives have become increasingly concerned about illegal immigration. Many conservative citizen groups have been highly vocal in trying to attract attention to the problem, such as these demonstrators in Denver. This group went out onto the streets on April 15, the day taxes are due, to add emphasis to their argument that illegal immigration has economic consequences.

Group members—especially influential members (such as corporation presidents or local civic leaders)—occasionally go to Washington to lobby. More ordinary citizens can have an impact too. Research shows that grassroots activity by women's groups is related to passage of legislation aimed at gender equality.[40]

The most common grassroots tactic is letter writing. "Write your member of Congress" is not just a slogan for a civics test. Legislators are highly sensitive to the content of their mail. Interest groups often launch letter-writing campaigns through their regular publications or special alerts. They may even provide sample letters and the names and addresses of specific policymakers. The Internet facilitates mobilization as an interest group office can communicate instantaneously with its members and followers and at virtually no cost through e-mail.

If people in government seem unresponsive to conventional lobbying tactics, a group might resort to some form of political protest. A protest or demonstration, such as picketing or marching, is designed to attract media attention to an issue. Protesters hope that television and newspaper coverage will help change public opinion and make policymakers more receptive to their group's demands. When Republicans in the Ohio State Legislature brought up a bill in 2011 restricting the collective bargaining rights of municipal unions there, it was greeted with widespread demonstrations by union members and sympathizers. The legislation was still passed, but angry union members succeeded in getting an initiative put on a statewide ballot and the law was overturned by the voters.

The main drawback to protesting is that policymaking is a long-term, incremental process, and a demonstration is short-lived. It is difficult to sustain anger and activism among group supporters—to keep large numbers of people involved in protest after protest. A notable exception was the civil rights demonstrations of the 1960s, which were sustained over a long period. National attention focused not only on the widespread demonstrations but also on the sometimes violent confrontations between protesters and white law enforcement officers. For example, the use of police dogs and high-power fire hoses against blacks marching in Alabama in the early 1960s angered millions of Americans who saw footage of the confrontations on television. By stirring public opinion, the protests hastened the passage of the Civil Rights Act of 1964 and the Voting Rights Act of 1965.

Information Campaigns

As the strategy of the civil rights movement shows, interest groups generally feel that public backing adds strength to their lobbying efforts. And because all interest groups believe they are absolutely right in their policy orientation, they think that they will get that backing if they can only make the public aware of their position and the evidence supporting it. To this end, interest groups launch **information campaigns,** which are organized efforts to gain public backing by bringing their views to the public's attention. The underlying assumption is that public ignorance and apathy are as much a problem as the views of competing interest groups. Various means are used to combat apathy. Some are directed at the larger public; others are directed at smaller audiences with long-standing interest in an issue.

    Public relations is one information campaign tactic. A public relations campaign might involve sending speakers to meetings in various parts of the country, producing pamphlets and handouts, taking out newspaper and magazine advertising, or establishing websites. When cell phone service provider AT&T took steps to take over T-Mobile, another provider, it found that the Department of Justice was resistant on antitrust grounds. If the AT&T and T-Mobile merger went through, 75 percent of the cell phone market would be controlled by just two companies, Verizon and the newly expanded AT&T. AT&T launched a public relations campaign with ads in the *Washington Post* and Washington-based political publications. Despite spending $40 million in advertising related to the merger, it failed to change the government's mind and abandoned its effort to absorb T-Mobile.[41]

    Sponsoring research is another way interest groups press their cases. When a group believes that evidence has not been fully developed in a certain area, it may commission research on the subject. In the controversy over illegal immigration, studies have proliferated as interest groups push their position forward. Lobbies on opposing sides of the issue have publicized research on matters such as the impact of illegal immigration on the overall economy, whether immigrants drive down wages, and whether undocumented aliens take jobs away from citizens who would otherwise fill them.

    Information campaigns may affect public opinion, which, presumably, will influence policymakers. However, research has shown that the public's priorities are not systematically reflected in the lobbying priorities of interest groups. Figure 10.3 (p. 290) shows the responses of citizens when the Gallup Poll asked them what they thought was the most important problem facing the United States. Those responses show little relationship to the issues that lobbyists were working on at the same time.

Coalition Building

A final aspect of lobbying strategy is **coalition building**, in which several organizations band together for the purpose of lobbying. Such joint efforts conserve or make more effective use of the resources of groups with similar views. Most coalitions are informal arrangements that exist only for the purpose of lobbying on a single issue. Coalitions most often form among groups that work in the same policy area and have similar constituencies, such as environmental groups or feminist groups. When an issue arises that several such groups agree on, they are likely to develop a coalition.

    Yet coalitions often extend beyond organizations with similar constituencies and similar outlooks. Environmental groups and business groups are often thought of as

information campaign
An organized effort to gain public backing by bringing a group's views to public attention.

coalition building
The banding together of several interest groups for the purpose of lobbying.

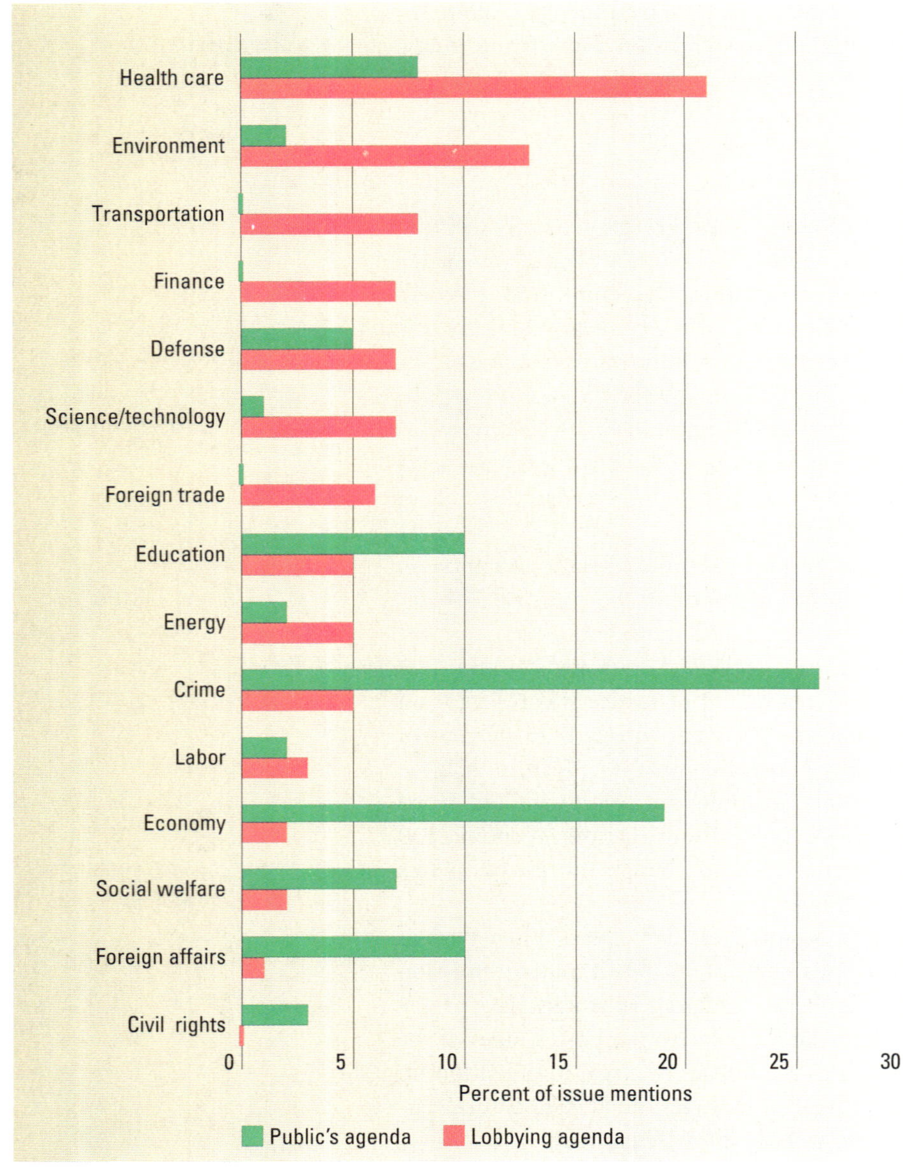

FIGURE 10.3 The Lobbying Agenda Versus the Public's Agenda

The figures for the lobbying agenda come from research by the authors listed at the end of this note. They interviewed a random sample of lobbyists and asked them what issue they were working at that time. Corresponding data for the public for the same year come from the Gallup Poll. Its question was "What is the most important problem facing the country today?"
Source: Adapted from David C. Kimball, Frank R. Baumgartner, Jeffrey M. Berry, Marie Hojnacki, and Beth L. Leech, "Who Cares About the Lobbying Agenda?", paper presented at the annual meeting of the American Political Science Association, Seattle, WA, September 2011. Copyright © 2012 by Palgrave Macmillan. Reproduced by permission.

dire enemies. But some businesses support the same goals as environmental lobbies because it is in their self-interest.[42] For example, companies in the business of cleaning up toxic waste sites have worked with environmental groups to strengthen the Superfund program, the government's primary weapon for dealing with dangerous waste dumps. Lobbyists see an advantage in having a diverse coalition. In the words of one lobbyist, "You can't do anything in this town without a coalition. I mean the first question [from policymakers] is, 'Who supports this?'"[43]

★ 10.5 Is the System Biased?

★ Evaluate whether the interest group system biases the public policy-making process.

As we noted in Chapter 2, our political system is more pluralist than majoritarian. Policymaking is determined more by the interaction of groups with the government than

Compared with What?

Pluralism Worldwide

A study of democracies around the world measured the degree to which interest groups operated independent of any formal link to government. Interest groups in political systems with low scores in this chart (like Norway) run the risk of being co-opted by policymakers because of their partnerships with government. These countries tend to have fewer groups, but those groups are expected to work with government in a coordinated fashion. High scores indicate that the interest groups in those systems are clearly in a competitive position with other groups. Thus, countries with high scores (like the United States) are the most pluralistic.

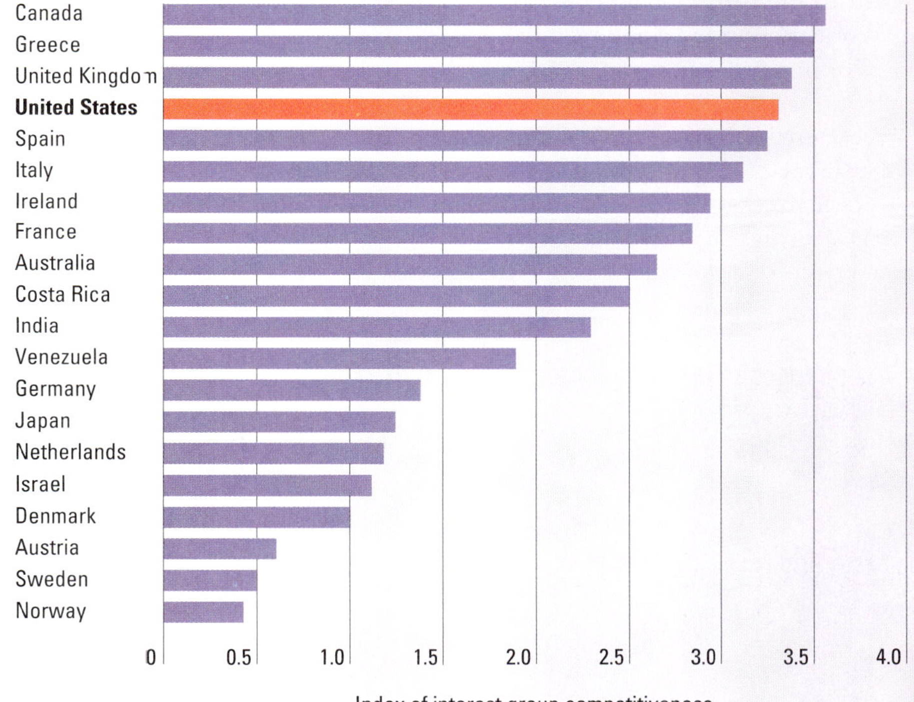

Source: Arend Lijphart, *Patterns of Democracy* (New Haven, Conn.: Yale University Press, 1999), p. 177. Copyright © 1999 Yale University Press. Reproduced by permission.

by elections. Indeed, among Western democracies, the United States is one of the most pluralistic governments (see "Compared with What? Pluralism Worldwide"). The great advantage of majoritarianism is that it is built around the most elemental notion of fairness: what the government does is determined by what most of the people want.

How, then, do we justify the policy decisions made under a pluralist system? How do we determine whether they are fair? There is no precisely agreed-on formula, but most people would agree with the following two simple notions. First, all significant interests in the population should be adequately represented by lobbying groups. That is, if a significant number of people with similar views have a stake in the outcome of policy decisions in a particular area, they should have a lobby to speak for them. If government makes policy that affects farmers who grow wheat, for example, then wheat farmers should have a lobby.

Second, government should listen to the views of all major interests as it develops policy. Lobbies are of little value unless policymakers are willing to listen to them. We should not require policymakers to balance perfectly all competing interests, however, because some interests are diametrically opposed. Moreover, elections inject some of the benefits of majoritarianism into our system because the party that wins an election will have a stronger voice than its opponent in the making of public policy.

Membership Patterns

Public opinion surveys of Americans and surveys of interest groups in Washington can be used to determine who is represented in the interest group system. A clear pattern is evident: some sectors of society are much better represented than others.[44] As noted in the earlier discussions about the Boston West Enders and the United Farm Workers, who is being organized makes a big difference. Those who work in business or in a profession, those with a high level of education, and those with high incomes are the most likely to belong to interest groups. Even middle-income people are much more likely to join interest groups than are those who are poor.

One survey of interest groups is revealing, finding that "the 10 percent of adults who work in an executive, managerial, or administrative capacity are represented by 82 percent" of the organizations that in one way or another engage in advocacy on economic issues. In contrast, "organizations of or for the economically needy are a

A Lott of Connections

It's common for legislators to work as lobbyists after they leave the House or Senate. Two Senate heavyweights, former Republican Majority Leader Trent Lott of Mississippi (left) and former Democratic senator John Breaux of Louisiana (right), have recently formed their own lobbying firm, the Breaux Lott Leadership Group. With all their connections from their years in Congress, they'll have little trouble attracting clients.

rarity." Thus, in terms of membership in interest groups, there is a profound bias in favor of those who are well off financially.[45]

Citizen Groups

Because the bias in interest group membership is unmistakable, should we conclude that the interest group system is biased overall? Before reaching that determination, we should examine another set of data. The actual population of interest groups in Washington surely reflects a class bias in interest group membership, but that bias may be modified in an important way. Some interest groups derive support from sources other than their membership. Thus, although they have no welfare recipients as members, the Center for Budget and Policy Priorities and the Children's Defense Fund have been effective long-term advocates working on behalf of the poor. Poverty groups gain their financial support from philanthropic foundations, government grants, corporations, and wealthy individuals.[46] Given the large numbers of Americans who benefit from welfare and social service programs, poor people's lobbies are not numerous enough. Nevertheless, the poor are represented by these and other organizations (such as labor unions and health lobbies) that regard the poor as part of the constituency they must protect. In short, although the poor are seriously underrepresented in our system, the situation is not as bad as interest group membership patterns suggest.

Another part of the problem of membership bias has to do with free riders. The interests that are most affected by free riders are broad societal problems, such as the environment and consumer protection, in which literally everyone can be considered as having a stake in the outcome. We are all consumers, and we all care about the environment. But the greater the number of potential members of a group, the more likely it is that individuals will decide to be free riders because they believe that plenty of others can offer financial support to the organization.

Environmental and consumer interests have been chronically underrepresented in the Washington interest group community. In the 1960s, however, a strong citizen group movement emerged.[47] **Citizen groups** are lobbying organizations built around policy concerns unrelated to members' vocational interests. People who join Environmental Defense do so because they care about the environment, not because it lobbies on issues related to their profession. If that group fights for stricter pollution control requirements, it doesn't further the financial interests of its members. The benefits to members are largely ideological and aesthetic. In contrast, a corporation fighting the same stringent standards is trying to protect its economic interests. A law that requires a corporation to install expensive antipollution devices can reduce stockholders' dividends, depress salaries, and postpone expansion. Although both the environmental group and the corporation have valid reasons for their stands, their motives are different.

Business Mobilization

Business has always been well represented in Washington, but it was stimulated to mobilize further by the growth of government regulation. After the Environmental Protection Agency, the Consumer Product Safety Commission, the Occupational Safety and Health Administration, and other regulatory agencies were created in the 1970s and later, many more companies found they were affected by federal regulations. And many corporations found that they were frequently reacting to policies

citizen group
Lobbying organization built around policy concerns unrelated to members' vocational interests.

that were already made rather than participating in their making. They saw representation in Washington—where the policymakers are—as critical if they were to obtain information on pending government actions soon enough to act on it. Finally, the competitive nature of business lobbying fueled the increase in business advocacy in Washington. This competition exists because legislation and regulatory decisions never seem to apply uniformly to all businesses; rather, they affect one type of business or one industry more than others.

The health-care industry is a case in point. Government regulation has become an increasingly important factor in determining health-care profits. Through reimbursement formulas for Medicare, Medicaid, and other health-care programs funded by Washington, the national government limits what providers can charge. The new Obama health-care reform mandates additional areas of government regulation. As this regulatory activity has grown, more and more health-care trade associations (like the American Hospital Association) and professional associations (like the American Nurses Association) have come to view Washington lobbying as increasingly significant to the well-being of their members. The number of such lobbies has skyrocketed, and health-care lobbyists cluster around Washington like locusts. Today there are 3,000 registered lobbyists in Washington working for health-care entities. Aggregate spending by health-care lobbies in 2010 was roughly $500 million. Hundreds of millions more were contributed to candidates for Congress by health-care concerns.[48]

The advantages of business are enormous. As Figure 10.4 illustrates, there are more business lobbies (corporations and trade associations) than any other type. Professional associations—the American Dental Association, for example—tend to represent business interests as well. Beyond the numbers of groups are the superior resources of business, including lobbyists, researchers, campaign contributions, and well-connected chief executive officers. Business lobbyists, for example, are much more likely to participate in lobbying administrative agencies on proposed regulations.[49] Whereas citizen groups can try to mobilize their individual members, trade associations can mobilize the corporations that are members of the organization.

Yet the resource advantages of business make it easy to overlook the obstacles that business faces in the political arena. To begin with, business is often divided, with one industry facing another. Cable companies and phone companies have

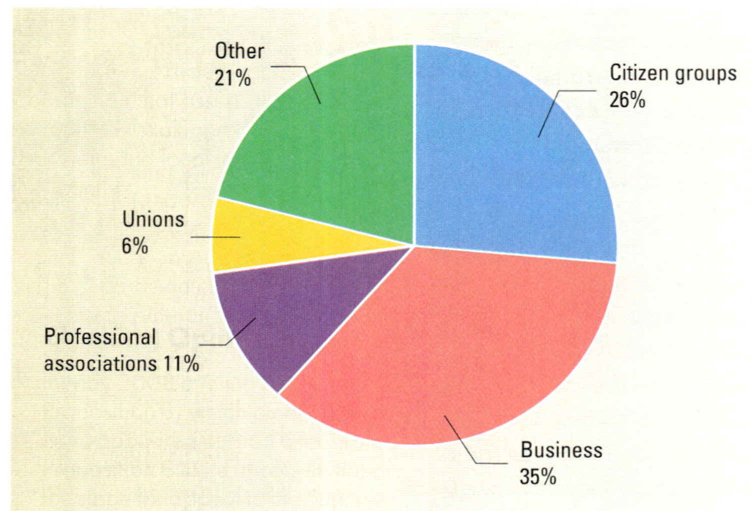

FIGURE 10.4 Interest Group Participants

One large-scale study of lobbying in Washington documented the pattern of participation by interest groups on close to a hundred issues before the federal government. Business-related groups (corporations and trade associations) made up the largest segment of all lobbies, and citizen groups constituted roughly a quarter of all organizations.

Source: Frank R. Baumgartner, Jeffrey M. Berry, Marie Hojnacki, David C. Kimball, and Beth L. Leech, *Lobbying and Policy Change* (Chicago: University of Chicago Press, 2009), p. 9. Copyright © 2009 University of Chicago Press. Reproduced by permission.

frequently tangled over who will have access to what markets. And even if an industry is unified, it may face strong opposition from labor or citizen groups—sectors that have substantial resources too, even if they don't match up to those of businesses. If both sides have sufficient resources to put up a battle, simply having more money or lobbyists than the other side is unlikely to determine the outcome.[50]

Reform

If the interest group system is biased, should the advantages of some groups somehow be eliminated or reduced? This is hard to do. In an economic system marked by great differences in income, great differences in the degree to which people are organized are inevitable. Moreover, as James Madison foresaw, limiting interest group activity is difficult without limiting fundamental freedoms. The First Amendment guarantees Americans the right to petition their government, and lobbying, at its most basic level, is a form of organized petitioning.

Still, some sectors of the interest group community may enjoy advantages that are unacceptable. If it is felt that the advantages of some groups are so great that they affect the equality of people's opportunity to be heard in the political system, then restrictions on interest group behavior can be justified on the grounds that the disadvantaged must be protected. Pluralist democracy is justified on exactly these grounds: all constituencies must have the opportunity to organize, and competition between groups as they press their case before policymakers must be fair.

Some critics charge that a system of campaign finance that relies so heavily on PACs undermines our democratic system. They claim that access to policymakers is purchased through the wealth of some constituencies. PAC donations come disproportionately from business and professional interests. It is not merely a matter of wealthy interest groups showering incumbents with donations; members of Congress aggressively solicit donations from PACs. Although observers disagree on whether PAC money actually influences policy outcomes, agreement is widespread that PAC donations give donors better access to members of Congress.

As noted in Chapter 9, in 2010 the Supreme Court ruled in the *Citizens United* case that government may not restrict corporations and unions from spending money in candidate elections.[51] The *Citizens United* ruling has facilitated the formation of so-called Super PACs without the contribution limits of normal PACs. Huge contributions to these organizations were used on behalf of candidates in the 2012 election. Concern has emerged that the large contributions to the Super PACs by corporations and unions will add to the advantages they already have in the political process.

A serious scandal surrounding lobbyist Jack Abramoff (subsequently convicted and sent to prison) prompted Congress to tighten its ethical rules. This modest legislation passed in 2007 bans gifts, travel, and meals paid for by lobbyists. Lobbyists must also now disclose campaign contributions that they solicit on behalf of candidates.[52] Upon taking office in 2009, President Obama promised to "change the culture of Washington" in terms of the cozy relationship between lobbyists and policymakers. His words were surely sincere, but four years later the culture remained unchanged.[53]

SUMMARY

Interest groups play many important roles in our political process. They are a means by which citizens can participate in politics, and they communicate their members' views to those in government. Yet the interest group system remains unbalanced, with some segments of society (particularly business, the wealthy, and the educated) considerably better organized than others.

10.1 Interest Groups and the American Political Tradition

- Interest groups make positive contributions while, at the same time, working against an equitable political system. Suppressing interest groups, though, runs against our First Amendment freedoms.
- The key roles played by interest groups are representation, participation, education, agenda building, and program monitoring.

10.2 How Interest Groups Form

- Interest groups are organizations, and they do not form just because a constituency has a need. An organizer or political "entrepreneur" must convince potential members to join.
- Not all constituencies are created equal in terms of a propensity to join an interest group. Those high in social class are much more likely to join; those in a lower social class are much more challenging to organize.

10.3 Interest Group Resources

- The strength and influence of an interest group depend on the group's resources, which include its membership, lobbyists, and political action committees (PACs).

- Interest group efforts to attract members are made more difficult because of the free-rider problem.
- Among the most important resources for interest groups are their lobbyists, who have the responsibility for communicating what the organization wants policymakers to know. PACs can facilitate access to policymakers.

10.4 Lobbying Tactics

- Direct lobbying relies on personal contact with policymakers in the legislative and administrative branches. It also includes filing court suits in the legal system.
- Grassroots lobbying can involve both rank-and-file members communicating with policymakers through letter writing campaigns and political protests.
- Common tactics of information campaigns are public relations efforts and sponsoring research.

10.5 Is the System Biased?

- Strong growth in the citizen group sector has brought more effective representation on behalf of environmental and consumer interests.
- Business mobilization has enhanced the advantages already possessed by business in the political system.
- Little meaningful reform has been enacted to try to change the status quo of interest group politics.

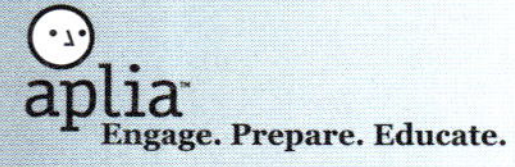

ASSESSING YOUR UNDERSTANDING WITH APLIA...YOUR VIRTUAL TUTOR!

10.1 Identify the different roles that interest groups play in our political system.

1. On balance, are interest groups beneficial to the political system or are they harmful?
2. What roles do interest groups play in American politics?

10.2 Analyze interest group success in terms of "entrepreneurial" behavior.

1. What is an interest group "entrepreneur"?
2. What factors influence the success of an effort to organize a new interest group?

10.3 **Identify the various resources available to interest groups and evaluate their role in interest group performance.**

1. What is the "free-rider problem"?
2. How are members attracted to voluntarily join a group?
3. In our governmental system, what role do lobbyists play?

10.4 **Compare and contrast different types of lobbying.**

1. How does direct lobbying differ from grass-roots lobbying?
2. How do information campaigns work?

10.5 **Evaluate whether the interest group system biases the public policy-making process.**

1. What advantages does business possess in the lobbying world?
2. Are citizen groups effective counterweights to business groups?
3. Overall, is the interest group system a biased one?

11 Congress

CHAPTER TOPICS and Learning Outcomes

aplia
Engage. Prepare. Educate.

In the 2010 Congressional elections, Republicans scored a stunning victory, taking sixty-three seats from Democrats and gaining control of the House of Representatives. Not since 1938 has a sitting president's party suffered such losses during a midterm election.[1] Republicans also cut the Democratic majority in the Senate to a mere fifty-one seats, down from fifty-five (although the chamber's two independents generally side with the Democrats). As is often the case after electoral victories, Republicans touted their success as a mandate from the people to bring change to Washington and as a repudiation of Democratic policies. They were eager to take control and enact changes more in line with their ideology.

In theory, at least, that's how majoritarian government should work. The policies supported by the majority party are expected to become a reality. In practice, however, the majority often encounters many obstacles in its way. Despite the magnitude of their victory, Republican leaders quickly discovered that policy changes would still be difficult to enact. As one observer wrote, "for the GOP leadership, this is where the campaign ends, and the nightmare begins."[2]

With the presidency and the Senate controlled by Democrats, Republicans leaders needed to convince enough members of their own party to compromise with Democrats if any of their policies would ever get signed into law. Within weeks of becoming Speaker of the House, John Boehner (R-Ohio) had to craft and pass a bill that would fund the government's activities for the remainder of the fiscal year. Because many of the new Republican members of Congress had aligned themselves with the Tea Party and campaigned on a pledge to reign in government spending, they opposed his plan, claiming that it did not slash spending enough.

Knowing that the ideal plan supported by the freshman representatives would never get past the Senate or be signed by Obama, Boehner and other GOP leaders found themselves in a bind. Any bill favored by their Republican majority would surely get voted down in the Senate. If they crafted a bill that would pass in the Senate, their own members would block it in the House. Yet if no bill made it out of Congress, the government would shut down due to a lack of funds. When the government shuts down, public employees do not get paid, Social Security and student work study checks do not get mailed out, student loan processing stops, passport and visa applications cannot be reviewed, national parks and museums close, and more. The new House leadership did not want to be seen as responsible for a government shutdown.

In the end, GOP leaders sided with their new members who were resisting compromise and insisting on steep cuts to government spending. That set the stage for a confrontation with the Senate and the White House. The situation was ultimately resolved a mere two hours before the government would have had to shut down. Despite the significant spending cuts in the final proposal, fifty-nine Republican representatives still voted against it; the proposal only passed because enough Democrats supported it.[3]

In subsequent weeks and months, Boehner's struggles to keep his party unified while finding ways to compromise with Democrats surfaced repeatedly. Why was it so difficult for Boehner to generate enough support from within his own party to create legislation that could make it through the lawmaking process? First, divisions clearly exist within the Republican Party on many issues, including on the notion of compromise itself. Belonging to the same party does not guarantee agreement on key issues of the day. Second, members of Congress answer to their constituents as well as to their party leadership. Several members of Congress, especially the newly elected Republican freshmen, were elected by campaigning against government spending, which created pressure to be responsive to the segment of the electorate that sent them to Washington. National polls at the time showed that Democrats were much more willing to accept compromises in order to avert a shutdown than Republicans (70 percent versus 49 percent).[4]

Finally, the House is embedded in a system of separation of powers, which means that even with enough votes to move legislation past the House, the chances of bills becoming law are low if the other branches are controlled by another party. So while a party would prefer to be the majority in Congress rather than the minority, being the majority party rarely means that the party has smooth sailing in enacting its agenda. And if the majority party fails, the minority party has a compelling theme for the next election.

In this chapter, we'll examine majoritarian politics through the prism of the two congressional parties. We'll look at how the forces of pluralism work against majoritarian policymaking. We'll turn our attention to the procedures and norms that facilitate bargaining and compromise in Congress, which are key to understanding how the House and Senate operate. We'll discuss Congress's relations with the executive branch, and we'll analyze how the legislative process affects public policy. We begin by asking how the framers envisioned Congress.

11.1 The Origin and Powers of Congress

★ Explain the structure and powers of Congress as envisioned by the framers and enumerated in the Constitution.

The framers of the Constitution wanted to keep power from being concentrated in the hands of a few, but they were also concerned with creating a Union strong enough to overcome the weaknesses of the government that had operated under the Articles of Confederation. They argued passionately about the structure of the new government. In the end, they produced a legislative body that was as much of an experiment as the new nation's democracy.

The Great Compromise

The U.S. Congress has two chambers: the House of Representatives and the Senate. A bill cannot become law unless it is passed in identical form by both chambers. Recall from Chapter 3 that during the drafting of the Constitution, small states wanted all the states to have equal representation, and more populous states wanted representation based on population. The Great Compromise broke the deadlock: small states would receive equal representation in the Senate, but the number of each state's representatives in the House would be based on population and the House would have the sole right to originate revenue-related legislation.

Each state has two senators, who serve six-year terms of office. Terms are staggered, so that one-third of the Senate is elected every two years. When it was ratified, the Constitution directed that senators be chosen by the state legislatures. However, the Seventeenth Amendment, adopted in 1913, provided for the direct election of senators by popular vote. From the beginning, the people have directly elected members of the House of Representatives. They serve two-year terms, and all House seats are up for election at the same time.

There are 435 members of the House of Representatives. Because each state's representation in the House is in proportion to its population, the Constitution provides for a national census every ten years; population shifts are handled by the **reapportionment** (redistribution) of seats among the states after each census is taken. Since recent population growth has been centered in the Sunbelt, Texas and Florida have gained seats, while the Northeast and Midwest states like New York and Illinois have lost them. Each representative is elected from a particular congressional district within his or her state, and each district elects only one representative. The districts within a state must be roughly equal in population.

Duties of the House and Senate

Although the Great Compromise provided for considerably different schemes of representation for the House and Senate, the Constitution gives them similar legislative tasks. They share many powers, among them the powers to declare war, raise an army and navy, borrow and coin money, regulate interstate commerce, create federal courts, establish rules for the naturalization of immigrants, and "make all Laws which shall be necessary and proper for carrying into Execution the foregoing Powers."

Yet the constitutional duties of the two chambers are different in some important ways. As noted in Chapter 3, the House alone has the right to originate revenue bills, a right that apparently was coveted at the Constitutional Convention. In practice, this power is of limited consequence because both the House and Senate must approve all bills. The House of Representatives has the power of **impeachment**: the power formally to charge the president, vice president, and other "civil officers" of the national government with serious crimes. The Senate is empowered to act as a court to try impeachments, with the chief justice of the Supreme Court presiding. A two-thirds majority vote of the senators present is necessary for conviction. Prior to President Clinton's impeachment in 1998, only one sitting president, Andrew Johnson, had been impeached, and in 1868 the Senate came within a single vote of finding him guilty. Clinton was accused of both perjury and obstruction of justice concerning his relationship with a White House intern, but was acquitted by the Senate. The House Judiciary Committee voted to recommend impeachment of President Richard Nixon because of his involvement in the Watergate cover-up, but before the full House could vote, Nixon resigned from office.

The Constitution gives the Senate the power to approve major presidential appointments (such as to federal judgeships, ambassadorships, and cabinet posts) and treaties with foreign nations. The president is empowered to make treaties but must submit them to the Senate for approval by a two-thirds majority. Because of this requirement, a president must at times try to convince a doubting Senate of the worth of a particular treaty. Shortly after World War I, President Woodrow Wilson submitted to the Senate the Treaty of Versailles, which contained the charter for the

---

reapportionment
Redistribution of representatives among the states, based on population change. The House is reapportioned after each census.

impeachment
The formal charging of a government official with "treason, bribery, or other high crimes and misdemeanors."

proposed League of Nations. Wilson had attempted to convince the Senate that the treaty deserved its support; when the Senate refused to approve the treaty, Wilson suffered a severe setback as he had made the treaty his highest priority.

Despite the long list of congressional powers in the Constitution, the question of what powers are appropriate for Congress has generated substantial controversy. For example, although the Constitution gives Congress the sole power to declare war, presidents have initiated military action on their own. And at times, the courts have found that congressional actions have usurped the rights of the states.

★ 11.2 Electing Congress

★ Analyze the factors that affect the way voters elect members of Congress.

If Americans are not happy with the job Congress is doing, they can use their votes to say so. With congressional elections every two years, voters have frequent opportunities to express themselves.

The Incumbency Effect

incumbent
A current officeholder.

Congressional elections offer voters a chance to show their approval of Congress's performance by reelecting **incumbents** or to demonstrate their disapproval by "throwing the rascals out."[5] The voters do more reelecting than rascal throwing. The reelection rate is astonishingly high: in the majority of elections since 1950, more than 90 percent of all House incumbents have held on to their seats (see Figure 11.1). In the 2010 congressional elections, a whopping fifty-four House incumbents (all but two of them Democrats) were defeated by challengers, a failure rate that is notable because of how unusual it is. It was the first time since 1994, when the Republicans took control of the House after 40 years of Democratic control, that the reelection rate for House incumbents fell below 90 percent. Most House elections aren't even close; in most recent elections, over 70 percent of House incumbents have won reelection by margins of greater than 60 percent of the vote.[6] Senate elections are more competitive, but incumbents still have a high reelection rate.

These findings may seem surprising, since the public does not hold Congress as a whole in particularly high esteem. In the past few years, Americans have been particularly critical of Congress, and some polls have shown that less than 15 percent of the public approve of its performance (see Figure 11.2). One reason Americans hold Congress in disdain is that they regard it as overly influenced by interest groups. A struggling economy, the wars in Iraq and Afghanistan, and persistent partisan disagreements within Congress have also reduced people's confidence in the institution.[7]

gerrymandering
Redrawing a congressional district to intentionally benefit one political party.

Redistricting. One explanation for the incumbency effect centers on redistricting—the way states redraw House districts after a census-based reapportionment.[8] It is entirely possible for the states to draw the new districts to benefit the incumbents of one or both parties. Altering district lines for partisan advantage is commonly called **gerrymandering**.

Gerrymandering has been practiced since at least the early 1800s.[9] With new computer software, gerrymandering is reaching new heights of precision. Precinct voting data can easily be used to manipulate boundary lines and produce districts that enhance or damage a candidate's or party's chances.[10] After the 2010 census, for example, Illinois

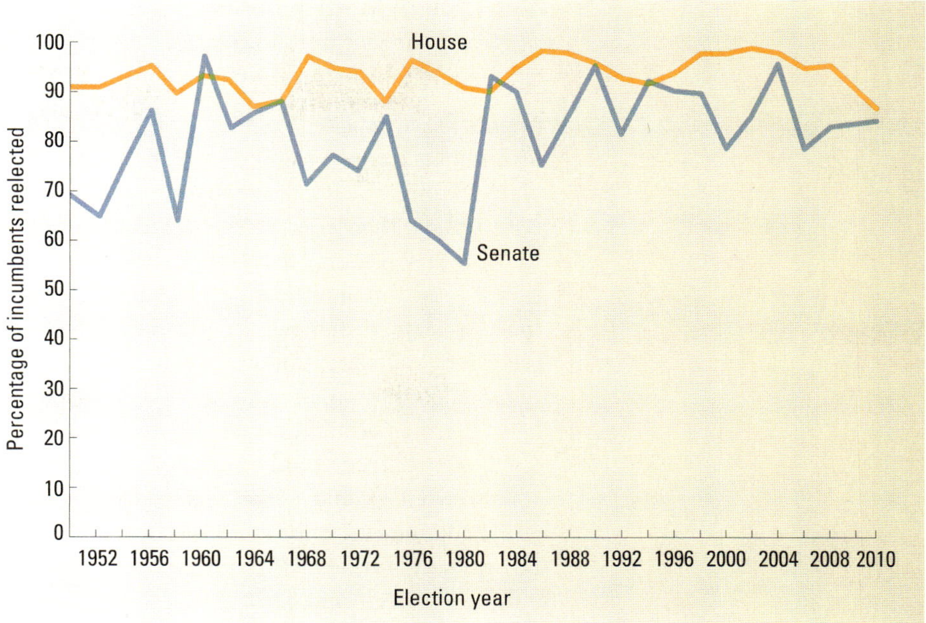

FIGURE 11.1 Incumbents: Life Is Good

Despite the public's dissatisfaction with Congress in general, incumbent representatives win reelection at an exceptional rate. Incumbent senators aren't quite as successful but still do well. Voters seem to believe that their own representatives and senators don't share the same foibles that they attribute to other members of Congress. Source: Various sources for 1950–2006. For 2008 and 2010, Harold W. Stanley and Richard G. Niemi (eds.), *Vital Statistics on American Politics, 2011-2012* (Washington, D.C.: CQ Press, 2011), pp. 43–44.

lost a seat in Congress and had to redraw its districts accordingly. The Democratic-controlled state legislature passed a plan that put Republican incumbent Joe Walsh's home in fellow Republican incumbent Randy Hultgren's district, which meant that the two men had to face each other in a primary. Walsh ultimately decided to avoid a bitter and costly primary and run in a neighboring district, which leans more Democratic. After the 2012 election, he lost the open seat race to Democrat Tammy Duckworth, while Hultgren was reelected. The state's congressional delegation went from eleven Republicans and eight Democrats to 6 Republicans and 12 Democrats.[11]

Some argue that gerrymandering contributes to increasing polarization between the two parties in the House. Districts that are dominated by one party or another have some tendency to be more ideologically driven. Moreover, representatives elected from new districts after reapportionment tend to exhibit more polarized voting patterns than representatives elected from older districts.[12] Scholars maintain that the polarizing effect of gerrymandering has affected the Senate too. While the Senate

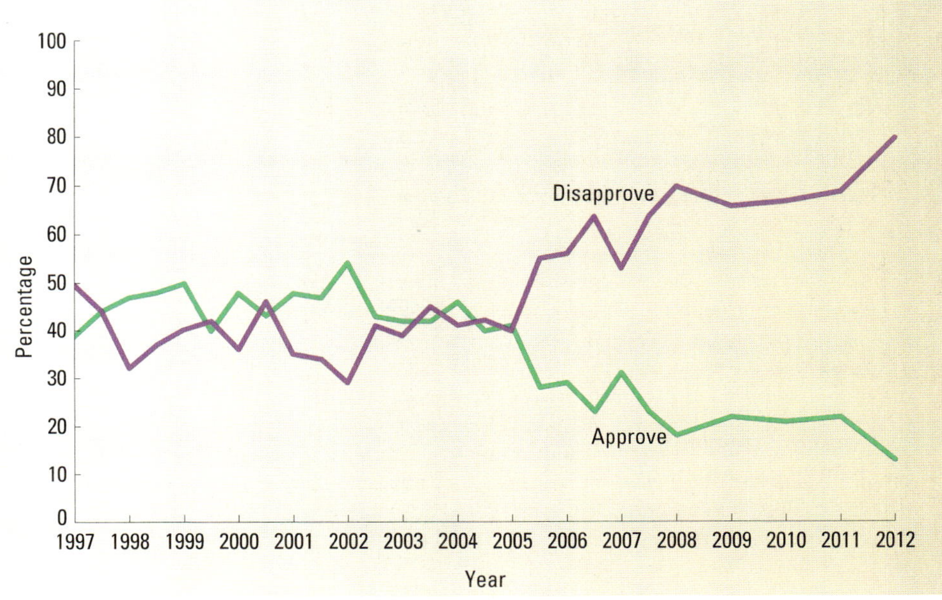

FIGURE 11.2 We Love Our Incumbents, but Congress Itself Stinks

Despite the reelection rate of incumbents reflected in Figure 11.1, public approval of Congress is far less positive. Confidence scores have never been particularly high, but opinion has turned decidedly negative in recent years. Citizens don't believe that the House and Senate are facing up to the nation's problems. Source: NBC News/*Wall Street Journal* polls, http://www.pollingreport.com/CongJob1.htm.

doesn't undergo reapportionment, many Senators were once members of the House. Their experiences in that polarized body, it is argued, continue to affect their legislative behavior once they move on to the Senate.[13]

Name Recognition. Holding office brings with it some important advantages. First, incumbents develop significant name recognition among voters simply by being members of Congress. Representatives have press secretaries who help with name recognition through their efforts to get publicity for the activities and speeches of their bosses.

Another resource available to members of Congress is the *franking privilege*—the right to send mail at taxpayer expense. Mailings work to make constituents aware of their legislators' names, activities, and accomplishments. In 2009, members of Congress sent out $26.5 million worth of mail, which often consists of "glossy productions filled with flattering photos and lists of the latest roads and bridges the lawmaker has brought home to the district."[14]

Under current franking regulations, information about the representative's personal life and political campaign cannot be included in official mailings and websites, and mailings can only target constituents who live in the representatives' districts. But no such rules exist to govern "tweets," Facebook, or videos posted on YouTube, even if the electronic devices used are paid for by taxpayers. By 2011, over 80 percent of members of Congress had Twitter accounts and 75 percent had Facebook accounts. They have used these social media to send information about sporting events, their health, and even their shopping trips.[15]

Technology has changed the way constituents communicate with representatives as well. In 1997, constituents sent 30.5 million pieces of communication to their representatives; by 2007, they sent 491.6 million. This communication revolution is due to the rise of electronic media and further helps to promote the name recognition that incumbents enjoy.[16]

Casework. Much of the work performed by the large staffs of members of Congress is **casework**—services for constituents, such as tracking down a Social Security check or directing the owner of a small business to the appropriate federal agency. Many congressional staffers are employed primarily as caseworkers. Thus, the very structure of congressional offices is built around helping constituents. One caseworker on a staff may be a specialist on immigration, another on veterans' benefits, another on Social Security, and so on. Legislators devote much of their office budget to casework because they assume that when they provide assistance to a constituent, that constituent will be grateful. Not only will that person probably vote for the legislator in the next election, but he or she is also sure to tell family members and friends how helpful the representative or senator was. "Casework is all profit," says one congressional scholar.[17]

casework
Solving problems for constituents, especially problems involving government agencies.

Campaign Financing. Anyone who wants to challenge an incumbent needs solid financial backing. Challengers must spend large sums of money to run a strong campaign with an emphasis on advertising—an expensive but effective way to bring their name and record to the voters' attention. But here too the incumbent has the advantage. Challengers have difficulty raising funds because they have to overcome contributors' doubts about whether they can win. In the 2010 elections, incumbents raised 51 percent of all money contributed to campaigns for election to

Frank or a Tweet?

Today, members of Congress go well beyond the use of franking to keep their constituents informed about their activities. Many, like Representative Steve Pearce (R-N.M.), use Facebook, YouTube, and Twitter to communicate with the public, all of which are highlighted front and center on his official website. Congressional rules, however, have yet to be crafted that regulate whether these platforms can be used for purposes that are prohibited by traditional franking rules, such as campaign activity, asking for donations, and sending holiday greetings. The franking manual currently posted on the official website of the House of Representative was written in 1998.

the House and the Senate. Only 23 percent went to challengers (those running for open seats received the rest).[18]

Political action committees (PACs) show a strong preference for incumbents (see Chapter 10). They tend not to want to risk offending an incumbent by giving money to a long-shot challenger. The attitude of the American Medical Association's PAC is fairly typical. "We have a friendly incumbent policy," says its director. "We always stick with the incumbent if we agree with both candidates."[19]

Successful Challengers. Clearly, the deck is stacked against challengers. Yet some challengers do beat incumbents. How? The opposing party and unsympathetic PACs may target incumbents who seem vulnerable because of age, lack of seniority, a scandal, or unfavorable redistricting. Some incumbents appear vulnerable because they were elected by a narrow margin, or the ideological and partisan composition of their district does not favor their holding the seat. Vulnerable incumbents also bring out higher-quality challengers—individuals who have held elective office previously and are capable of raising adequate funds. Such experienced challengers are more likely to defeat incumbents than are amateurs with little background in politics.[20] The reason Senate challengers have a higher success rate than House challengers is that they are generally higher-quality candidates. Often they are governors or members of the House who enjoy high name recognition and can attract significant campaign funds because they are regarded as credible candidates.

2012 Election. Many districts changed partisan hands, but the balance of power was unchanged after the 2012 election. With some races too close to call as of this writing, Democrats gained seven seats in the House, leaving Republicans with a majority. The Senate saw Democrats go from 51 seats to 53, and the Senate's 2 independents will likely side with them often. Some Democratic victories were due to Tea Party successes during Republican primaries, which resulted in conservative candidates that were unable to appeal to a more centrist general electorate. Despite Democratic gains, incumbents of both parties enjoyed success. Only 8 Democrats and 16 Republicans were voted out of office, giving each chamber a reelection rate above 95%. Although there will be many new faces in Congress, the lack of a major partisan shift suggests that ideological battles will continue and compromise will remain elusive.

Whom Do We Elect?

The people we elect to Congress are not a cross-section of American society. Although over half of the American labor force works in blue-collar jobs, someone currently employed as a blue-collar worker rarely wins a congressional nomination. Most members of Congress are upper-class professionals—many lawyers and businesspeople—and, at last count, 47 percent are millionaires.[21]

Women and minorities have long been underrepresented in elective office, although both groups have increased their representation in Congress over time. Seventeen women served in the Senate in the 2011–2012 session. This is a historic high, but nowhere near the proportion of women to men in the population at large. One reason that the number of women in Congress lags behind their proportion in the population is that as women develop professionally, they are not recruited or encouraged to run in the same way that men are.[22]

Other members of Congress don't necessarily ignore the concerns of women and minorities.[23] Yet many women and minorities believe that only members of their own group—people who have experienced what they have experienced—can truly represent their interests. This is a belief in **descriptive representation**—the view that a legislature should resemble the demographic characteristics of the population it represents.[24] (See "Compared with What? Women in Legislatures" on p. 307 for a comparison of the representation of women in national legislatures.)

descriptive representation
A belief that constituents are most effectively represented by legislators who are similar to them in such key demographic characteristics as race, ethnicity, religion, or gender.

The Millionaires' Club

In 2011, Representative Darrell Issa (R-Calif.) was the richest lawmaker in Congress, with an estimated net worth of $448 million. While 47 percent of lawmakers are millionaires, only about 1 percent of Americans can say the same.

Source: "Most Members of Congress Enjoy Robust Financial Status, Despite Nation's Sluggish Economic Recovery," opensecrets.org, 15 November 2011.

During the 1980s, both Congress and the Supreme Court provided support for the principle of descriptive representation for blacks and Hispanics. When Congress amended the Voting Rights Act in 1982, it encouraged states to draw districts that concentrated minorities together so that blacks and Hispanics would have a better chance of being elected to office. The Supreme Court decision in *Thornburg* v. *Gingles* in 1986 also pushed states to concentrate minorities in House districts. After the 1990 census was the first time states redrew House boundaries with the intent of creating districts with majority-minority populations. This effort led to a roughly 50 percent increase in the number of blacks elected to the House (see Figure 11.3). In 2011, there were ninety-seven majority-minority districts in the country (22 percent of all districts), fifty-three of them with minority representatives.[25]

The effort to draw boundaries to promote the election of minorities has been less effective for Hispanics. Hispanic representation is only about half that of blacks, even though there are slightly more Hispanics in the United States than blacks. One reason for this inequity is that Hispanics tend not to live in such geographically concentrated areas as do blacks, which makes it harder to draw boundaries that will likely lead to the election of a Hispanic.

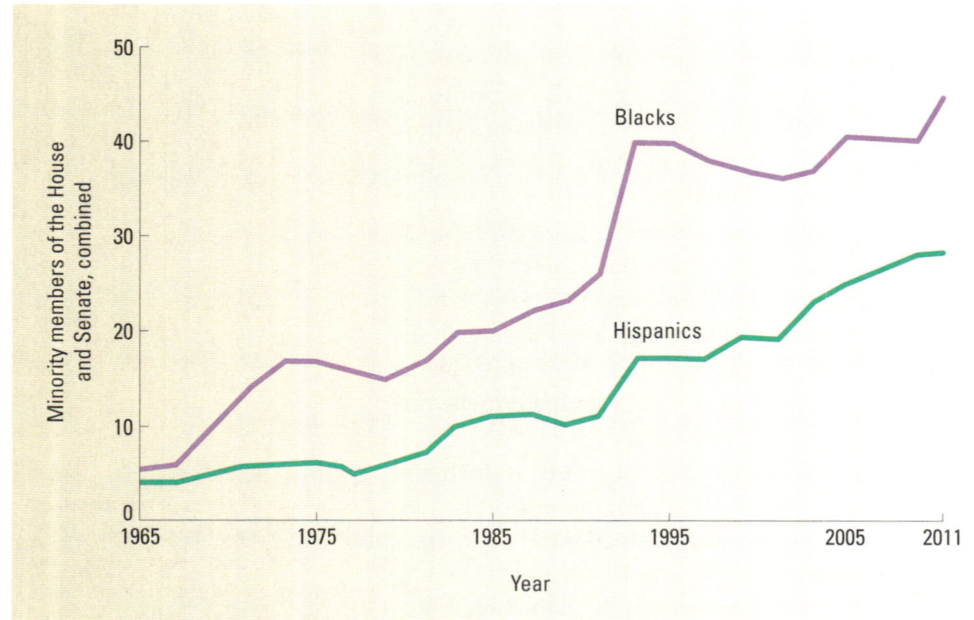

FIGURE 11.3 Minorities in Congress

Today, African Americans make up about 10 percent of the membership of the House and Senate, and Hispanics make up about 6 percent of total members. Though gains have been steady, the representation of both groups remains well below their proportions in the population at large. Hispanics constitute 14 percent of the American population; African Americans make up almost 13 percent of the total population. Source: Updated from Jennifer E. Manning, "Membership of the 112th Congress: A Profile," *Congressional Research Service*, R41647, http://www.senate.gov/reference/resources/pdf/R41647.pdf.

Compared with What?

Women in Legislatures

Compared with other countries, the United States has substantially fewer women serving in the legislature. This figure includes fifteen European countries as well as fifteen countries from the Americas (North America, Central America, and South America) as of October 2011. Ranked by the percentage of women in the lower house of the national legislature, the European countries include, on average, a significantly higher percentage of women than the legislatures of countries in the Western Hemisphere. The United States ranks near the bottom, with women making up only 16.8 percent of the representatives in the House.

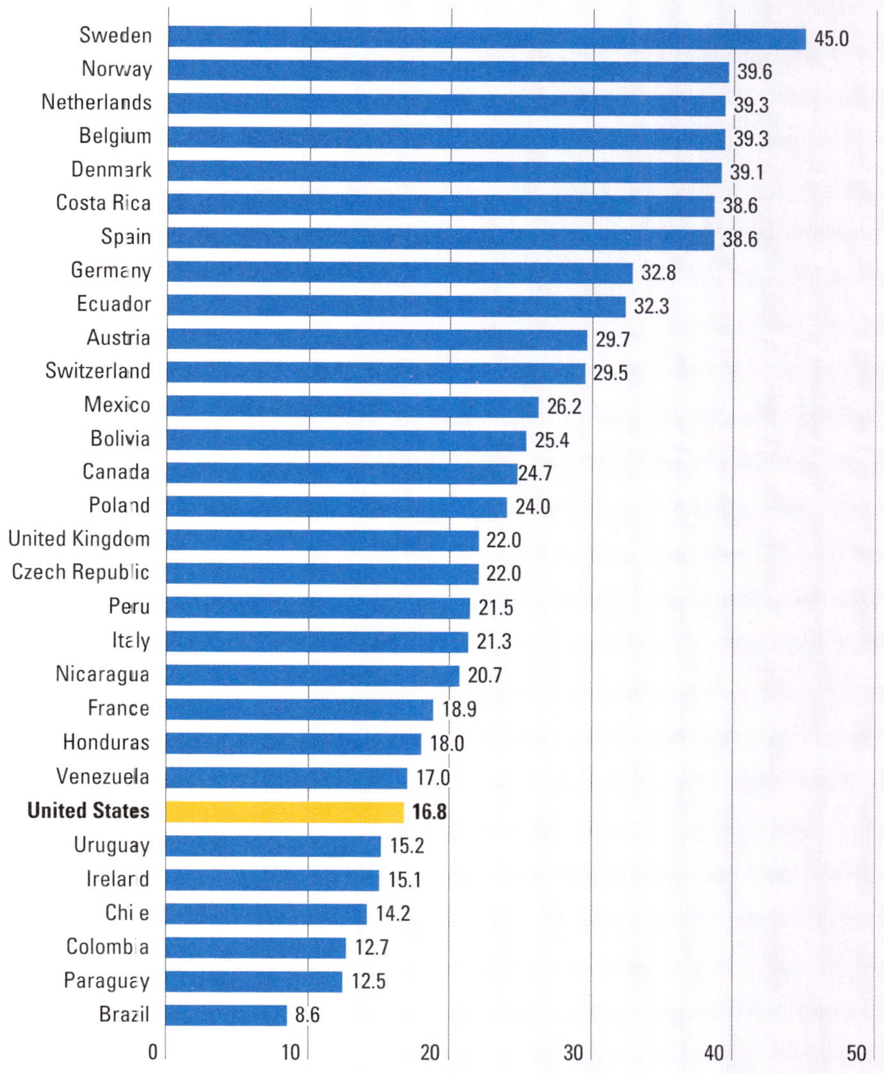

Source: Inter-Parliamentary Union, http://www.ipu.org/wmn-e/classif.htm.

Critical Thinking

How might the laws passed in countries with more female legislators differ from laws passed in countries with fewer female legislators? How might the percentage of women in office affect how women (and men) feel about government?

Another reason is that an estimated 22.4 percent of adult Hispanics living in the United States are ineligible to vote because they are not American citizens.[26]

The Supreme Court ruled in 1993 that states' efforts to increase minority representation through **racial gerrymandering** could violate the rights of whites. In *Shaw* v. *Reno*, the majority ruled in a split decision that a North Carolina district that meandered 160 miles from Durham to Charlotte was an example of "political apartheid." In effect, the Court ruled that racial gerrymandering segregated blacks from whites instead of creating districts built around contiguous communities.[27] In a later decision, the Supreme Court ruled that the "intensive and pervasive use of race" to protect incumbents and promote political gerrymandering violated the Fourteenth Amendment and Voting Rights Act of 1965.[28] In 2001, just before the redistricting from the 2000 census was to begin in the individual states, the Court modified its earlier decisions by declaring that race was not an illegitimate consideration in drawing congressional boundaries as long as it was not the "dominant and controlling" factor.[29]

Although this movement over time to draw districts that work to elect minorities has clearly increased the number of black and Hispanic legislators, almost all of whom are Democrats, it has also helped the Republican Party. As more Democratic-voting minorities have been packed into some districts, their numbers have diminished in others, leaving the remaining districts not merely "whiter" but also more Republican than they would have otherwise been.[30]

11.3 How Issues Get on the Congressional Agenda

★ Describe the ways in which issues get on the congressional agenda.

The formal legislative process begins when a member of Congress introduces a *bill,* a proposal for a new law. In the House, members drop bills in the "hopper," a mahogany box near the rostrum where the Speaker presides. Senators give their bills to a Senate clerk or introduce them from the floor. But before a bill can be introduced to solve a problem, someone must perceive that a problem exists or that an issue needs to be resolved. In other words, the problem somehow must find its way onto the congressional agenda.

Many issues Congress works on seem to have been around forever. Foreign aid, the national debt, and Social Security have come up in just about every recent session of Congress. Other issues emerge more suddenly, especially those that are the product of technological change.[31] The issue of "cyberstalking" is one example. Not long ago, the term did not even exist, but since 2011, Representative Loretta Sanchez (D-Calif.) has been introducing the STALKERS Act in the House. The act would expand the federal definition of stalking to include "acts of electronic monitoring, including spyware, bugging, and video surveillance." It would also permit prosecution for any actions "reasonably expected to cause another person serious emotional distress," which would strengthen the current standard of "reasonable fear of physical injury."[32]

New issues reach the congressional agenda in many ways. Sometimes a highly visible event focuses national attention on a problem. When it became evident that the September 11 hijackers had little trouble boarding their planes despite carrying box cutters that they would use as weapons, Congress quickly took up the issue of airport screening procedures. It decided to create a federal work force to conduct passenger and luggage screening at the nation's airports, believing the existing workers recruited by private companies were badly trained and poorly motivated. Presidential support can also move an issue onto the agenda quickly. The media attention paid to the president gives him enormous opportunity to draw the nation's attention to problems he believes need some form of government action.

Within Congress, party leaders and committee chairs have the opportunity to move issues onto the agenda, but they rarely act capriciously. They often bide their time, waiting for other members of Congress to learn about an issue as they attempt to gauge the level of support for some kind of action. At times, the efforts of an interest group spark support for action, or at least awareness of an issue. When legislators sense that the time is ripe for action on a new issue, they often are spurred on by the knowledge that sponsoring an important bill can enhance their own image. In the words of one observer, "Congress exists to do things. There isn't much mileage in doing nothing."[33]

11.4 The Lawmaking Process and the Importance of Committees

★ Differentiate among the types of congressional committees and evaluate the role of the committee system in the legislative process.

The process of writing bills and getting them enacted is relatively simple in the sense that it follows a series of specific steps. What complicates the process is the many ways legislation can be treated at each step. Here, we examine the straightforward process by which laws are made. In the next few sections, we discuss some of the complexities of that process.

After a bill is introduced in either house, it is assigned to the committee with jurisdiction over that policy area (see Figure 11.4, p. 310). A banking bill, for example, would be assigned to the Financial Services Committee in the House or to the Banking, Housing, and Urban Affairs Committee in the Senate. When a committee considers a piece of legislation assigned to it, the bill is usually referred to a subcommittee. The subcommittee may hold hearings, and legislative staffers may do research on the bill. The original bill usually is modified or revised; if passed in some form, it is sent to the full committee. A bill approved by the full committee is sent to the entire membership of the chamber, where it may be debated, amended, and either passed or defeated.

Bills coming out of House committees go to the Rules Committee before going before the full House membership. The Rules Committee attaches a rule to the bill that governs the coming floor debate, typically specifying the length of the debate and types of amendments House members can offer. The Senate does not have a comparable committee, although restrictions on the length of floor debate can be reached through unanimous consent agreements (see the "Rules of Procedure" section later in this chapter).

Even if both houses of Congress pass a bill on the same subject, the Senate and House versions are often different from each other. In that case, a conference committee, composed of legislators from both houses, works out the differences and develops a compromise version. This version goes back to both houses for another floor vote. If both chambers approve the bill, it goes to the president for his signature or veto.

When the president signs a bill, it becomes law. If the president **vetoes** (disapproves) the bill, he sends it back to Congress with his reasons for rejecting it. The bill then becomes law only if Congress overrides the president's veto by a two-thirds vote in each house. If the president neither signs nor vetoes the bill within ten days (Sundays excepted) of receiving it, the bill becomes law. But if Congress adjourns within the ten days, the president can let the bill die through a *pocket veto*, by not signing it.

veto
The president's disapproval of a bill that has been passed by both houses of Congress. Congress can override a veto with a two-thirds vote in each house.

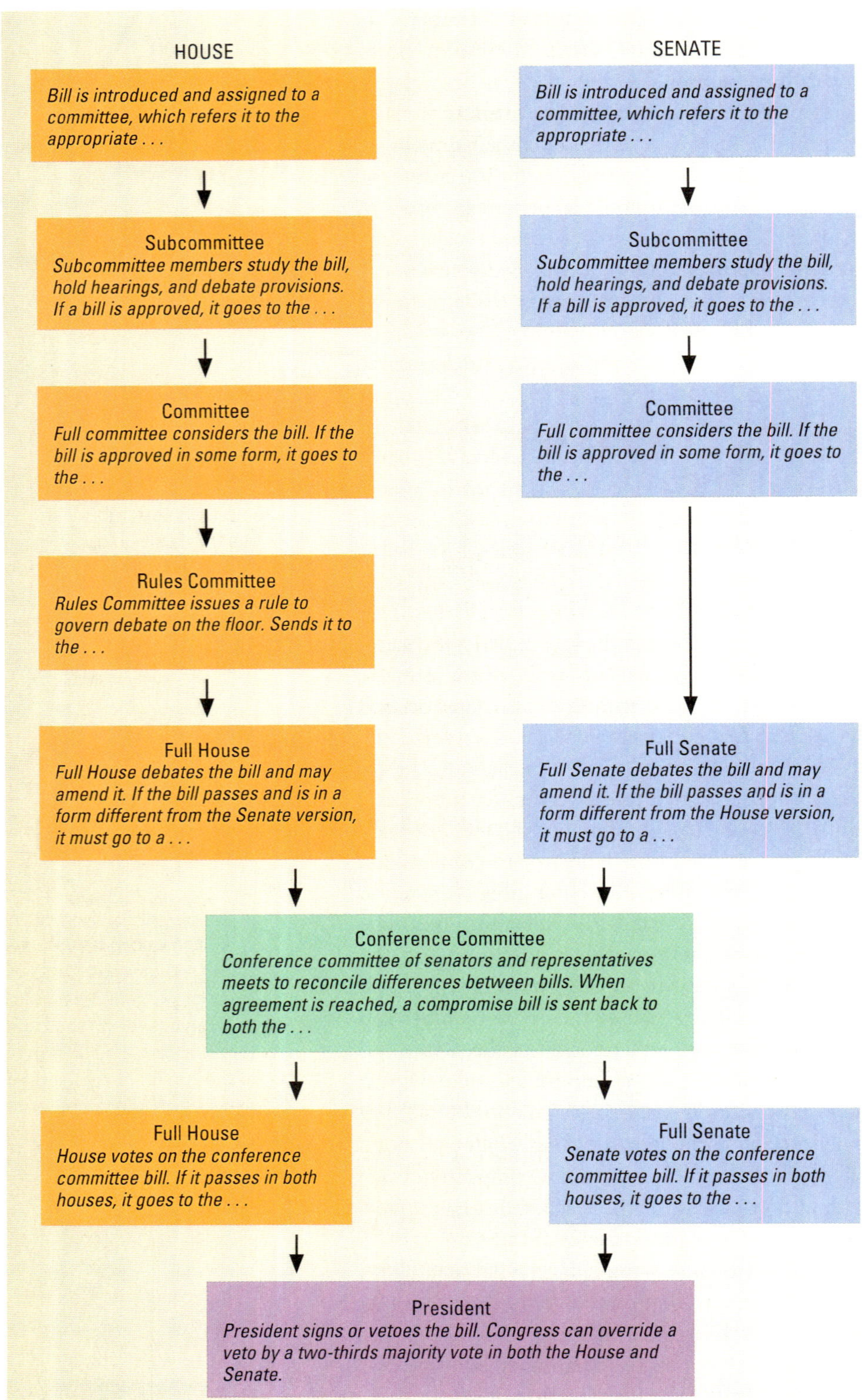

FIGURE 11.4 The Legislative Process

The process by which a bill becomes law is subject to much variation. This diagram depicts the typical process a bill might follow. It is important to remember that a bill can fail at any stage because of lack of support.
Source: © Cengage Learning.

The content of a bill can be changed at any stage of the process in either house. Lawmaking in Congress has many access points for those who want to influence legislation. This openness tends to fit within the pluralist model of democracy. As a bill moves through Congress, it is amended again and again, in a search for a consensus that will get it enacted and signed into law. The process can be tortuously slow, and it is often fruitless. Derailing legislation is much easier than enacting it. The process gives groups frequent opportunities to voice their preferences. One foreign ambassador stationed in Washington aptly described the twists and turns of our legislative process this way: "In the Congress of the U.S., it's never over until it's over. And when it's over, it's still not over."[34]

Committees: The Workhorses of Congress

President Woodrow Wilson once observed that "Congress in session is Congress on public exhibition, whilst Congress in its committee-rooms is Congress at work."[35] His words are as true today as when he wrote them over 100 years ago. A speech on the Senate floor, for example, may convince the average citizen, but it is less likely to influence other senators. Indeed, few of them may even hear it. The real nuts and bolts of lawmaking go on in the congressional committees.

The House and Senate are divided into committees for the same reason that other large organizations are broken into departments or divisions: to develop and use expertise in specific areas. At Apple, for example, different groups of people design computers, write software, assemble hardware, and sell the company's products. Each task requires an expertise that may have little to do with the others. Likewise, in Congress, decisions on weapons systems require a special knowledge that is of little relevance to decisions on reimbursement formulas for health insurance. It makes sense for some members of Congress to spend more time examining defense issues, becoming increasingly expert on the topic, while others concentrate on health matters. Eventually, all members of Congress vote on each bill that emerges from committees. Those who are not on a particular committee depend on committee members to examine the issues thoroughly, make compromises as necessary, and bring forward a sound piece of legislation that has a good chance of being passed.

Standing Committees. There are several different kinds of congressional committees, but the **standing committee** is predominant. Standing committees are permanent committees that specialize in a particular area—for example, the House Judiciary Committee or the Senate Foreign Relations Committee. Most of the day-to-day work of drafting legislation takes place in the sixteen standing Senate committees and twenty-one standing House committees. Typically, sixteen to twenty senators serve on each standing Senate committee, and around forty members serve on each standing committee in the House. The proportions of Democrats and Republicans on a standing committee are controlled by the majority party in each house. The majority gives the minority a percentage of seats that, in theory, approximates the minority party's percentage in the entire chamber. However, the majority party usually gives itself enough of a cushion to ensure that it can control each committee.

Standing committees are often broken down further into subcommittees. For instance, the Senate Foreign Relations committee has seven subcommittees, covering different regions of the world and issues such as terrorism. Subcommittees exist for the same reason parent committees exist: members acquire expertise by continually working within the policy area. Typically, members of the subcommittee are the dominant force in shaping the content of a bill.

Other Committees. Members of Congress can also serve on joint, select, and conference committees. A **joint committee** is composed of members of both chambers. Like standing committees, the four joint committees are concerned with particular policy areas. The Joint Economic Committee, for instance, analyzes the country's economic

standing committee
A permanent congressional committee that specializes in a particular policy area.

joint committee
A committee made up of members of both the House and the Senate.

select committee
A temporary congressional committee created for a specific purpose and disbanded after that purpose is fulfilled.

conference committee
A temporary committee created to work out differences between the House and Senate versions of a specific piece of legislation.

seniority
Years of consecutive service on a particular congressional committee.

policies. Joint committees are much weaker than standing committees because they typically cannot report bills to the House or Senate. Their role is usually that of fact finding and publicizing problems and issues that fall within their jurisdiction.

A **select committee** is a temporary committee created for a specific purpose. Congress establishes select committees to deal with special circumstances or with issues that either overlap or fall outside the areas of expertise of standing committees. In 2011, the Joint Select Committee on Deficit Reduction was created and charged with issuing recommendations by November of that year for reducing the deficit. It was dubbed a "supercommittee" by the media because it included members from both the House and Senate (three members from each party in each chamber). The committee ultimately failed to produce any recommendations, due to the inability of its members to compromise across party lines.

A **conference committee** is also a temporary committee, created to work out differences between the House and Senate versions of a specific piece of legislation. Its members are appointed from the standing committees or subcommittees from each house that originally crafted and reported the legislation.

Conference committees are not always used, however, to reconcile differing bills. Often, informal negotiations between committee leaders in the House and Senate resolve differences. The increasing partisan conflict between Democrats and Republicans often results in a compromise bill devised solely by the majority party (when a single party controls both chambers).

Congressional Expertise and Seniority

Once appointed to a committee, a representative or senator has great incentive to remain there and gain expertise because influence increases with expertise. Influence also grows in a more formal way, with **seniority**, or years of consecutive service, on a committee. In their quest for expertise and seniority, members tend to stay on the same committees. Within each committee, the senior member of the majority party usually becomes the committee chair. Other senior members of the majority party become subcommittee chairs, whereas their counterparts from the minority party gain influence as ranking minority members.

The way in which committees and subcommittees are led and organized within Congress is significant because much public policy decision making takes place there. The first step in drafting legislation is to collect information on the issue. Committee staffers research the problem, and committees hold hearings to take testimony from witnesses who have some special knowledge of the subject.

At times, committee hearings are more theatrical than informational, designed to draw public attention to them and to offer the majority party a chance to express its views. In 2011, Peter King, who was the new Republican chair of the House Homeland Security Committee and who once claimed that there are "too many mosques in the country" and that most are run by extremists, convened highly publicized hearings purportedly aimed at discovering whether American Muslims were becoming increasingly radicalized.[36] Democrats denounced the hearings as inflammatory and as harmful to U.S. relations with the Muslim world. One observer of the contentious hearings wrote, "Mostly, it was the committee itself that appeared to be on trial."[37]

The meetings at which subcommittees and committees actually debate and amend legislation are called *markup sessions.* In some committees, the chair, the ranking minority member, and others work hard, in formal committee sessions and in informal negotiations, to find a middle ground on issues that divide committee members in order to reach consensus. In other committees, members exhibit strong ideological and partisan sentiments. However, committee and sub-committee leaders prefer to find ways to overcome ideological and partisan divisions so that they can build compromise solutions that will appeal to the broader membership of their house. The skill of committee leaders in assembling coalitions that produce legislation that can pass on the floor of their house is critically important. When committees are mired in disagreement, they lose power.

Oversight: Following Through on Legislation

There is general agreement in Washington that knowledge is power. For Congress to retain its influence over the programs it creates, it must be aware of how the agencies responsible for them are administering them. To that end, committees engage in **oversight**, reviewing agencies' operations to determine whether they are carrying out policies as Congress intended.

As the executive branch has grown and policies and programs have become increasingly complex, oversight has become more difficult. On a typical weekday, for example, agencies issue more than a hundred pages of new regulations. Even with the division of labor in the committee system, determining how good a job an agency is doing in implementing a program is no easy task.

Congress performs its oversight function in several different ways. The most visible is the hearing. Hearings may be part of a routine review or can occur when a problem with a program or with an agency's administrative practices emerges. For example, after it became known in 2011 that a federal "gun tracking" program (called "Operation Fast and Furious") allowed over 2,000 guns to fall into the hands of Mexican drug cartels, committees in both chambers launched investigations.

Another way Congress keeps track of what departments and agencies are doing is by requesting reports on specific agency practices. When majority control in Congress switches from one party to another, committees become more aggressive in investigating ethical lapses and policy problems of the opposing party. After becoming the majority in the House in 2011, for example, Republicans held hearings on a range of issues, including Obama's energy policies and the role of the United States during March 2011 airstrikes against Libya by the NATO alliance.

Oversight is often stereotyped as a process in which angry legislators bring some administrators before television cameras at a hearing and proceed to dress them down for some scandal or mistake. Some of this does go on, but the pluralist side of Congress ensures that at least some members of a committee are advocates of the programs they oversee because those programs serve their constituents back home. Members of the House and Senate Agriculture Committees, for example, both Democrats and Republicans, want farm programs to succeed. Thus, most oversight is aimed at trying to find ways to improve programs and is not directed at efforts to discredit them. In short, Congress engages in oversight because it is an extension of their efforts to control public policy.

© ZUMA Wire Service / Alamy

The Show Must Go On

Celebrities often testify before congressional committees in the hopes that their star power will influence legislation. In July 2011, megastar Ben Affleck testified before the House Subcommittee on Africa, Global Health, and Human Rights to argue in favor of establishing a U.S. envoy to protect civilians from violent domestic conflict in the Democratic Republic of Congo.

oversight
The process of reviewing the operations of an agency to determine whether it is carrying out policies as Congress intended.

Majoritarian and Pluralist Views of Committees

Government by committee vests significant power in the committees and subcommittees of Congress—and especially their leaders. This is particularly true in the House, which has more decentralized patterns of influence than the Senate and is more restrictive about letting members amend legislation on the floor. Committee members can bury a bill by not reporting it to the full House or Senate. Many of them also make up the conference committees charged with developing compromise versions of bills.

In some ways, the committee system enhances the force of pluralism in American politics. Representatives and senators are elected by the voters in their particular districts and states, and they tend to seek membership on the committees that make the decisions most important to their constituents. Members from farm areas, for example, want membership on the House and Senate Agriculture Committees, while urban liberals like committees that handle social programs. As a result, committee members tend to represent constituencies with a strong interest in the committee's policy area and are predisposed to write legislation favorable to those constituencies.

Committees have a majoritarian aspect as well, as most committees reflect the general ideological profiles of the two parties' congressional contingents.[38] For example, Republicans on individual House committees tend to vote like all other Republicans in the House. Moreover, even if a committee's views are not in line with those of the full membership, it is constrained in the legislation it writes because bills cannot become law unless they are passed by the parent chamber and the other house. Consequently, in formulating legislation, committees anticipate what other representatives and senators will accept. The parties within each chamber also have means of rewarding members who are loyal to party priorities. Party committees and the party leadership within each chamber make committee assignments and respond to requests for transfers from less prestigious to more prestigious committees. Those who vote in line with the party get better assignments.[39]

11.5 Leaders and Followers in Congress

★ Identify the leadership structure of the legislative branch and assess the rules and norms that influence congressional operations.

Above the committee chairs is another layer of authority in Congress. The party leaders in each house work to maximize the influence of their own party while keeping their chamber functioning smoothly and efficiently. The operation of the two houses is also influenced by the rules and norms that each chamber has developed over the years.

The Leadership Task

Republicans and Democrats elect party leaders in both chambers who are charged with overseeing institutional procedures, managing legislation, fundraising, and communicating with the press. In the House, the majority party's leader is the **Speaker of the House**. The Speaker is a constitutional officer, but the Constitution does not list the Speaker's duties.[40] The majority party in the House also has a majority leader, who helps the Speaker guide the party's policy program through the legislative process, and a majority whip, who keeps track of the vote count and rallies support for legislation on the floor. The minority party is led by a minority leader who is assisted by the minority whip.

Speaker of the House
The presiding officer of the House of Representatives.

The Constitution makes the vice president of the United States the president of the Senate. But in practice the vice president rarely visits the Senate, unless there is a possibility of a tie vote, in which case he can break the tie. The *president pro tempore* (president "for the time"), elected by the majority party, is supposed to chair the Senate in the vice president's absence, but by custom this constitutional position is entirely honorary. The title is typically assigned to the most senior member of the majority party.

The real power in the Senate resides in the **majority leader**. As in the House, the top position in the opposing party is that of minority leader. Technically, the majority leader does not preside over Senate sessions (members rotate in the president pro tempore's chair), but he or she does schedule legislation, in consultation with the minority leader. More broadly, party leaders play a critical role in getting bills through Congress. The most significant function that leaders play is steering the bargaining and negotiating over the content of legislation. When an issue divides their party, their house, the two houses, or their house and the White House, the leaders try to work out a compromise.

Day in and day out, much of what leaders do is meet with other members of their chamber to try to strike deals that will yield a majority on the floor. It is often a matter of finding out whether one faction is willing to give up a policy preference in exchange for another concession. Beyond trying to engineer trade-offs that will win votes, the party leaders must persuade others (often powerful committee chairs) that theirs is the best deal possible. Former Speaker Dennis Hastert used to say, "They call me the Speaker, but … they really ought to call me the Listener."[41]

It is often difficult for party leaders to control rank-and-file members because they have independent electoral bases in their districts and states and receive

majority leader
The head of the majority party in the Senate; the second-highest-ranking member of the majority party in the House.

George Tames/The New York Times,/Redux Pictures.

The Johnson Treatment

When he was Senate majority leader in the 1950s, Lyndon Johnson was well known for his style of interaction with other members. In this unusual set of photographs, we see him applying the "Johnson treatment" to Senator Theodore Francis Green (D-R.I.). Washington journalists Rowland Evans and Robert Novak offered the following description of the treatment: "Its tone could be supplication, accusation, cajolery, exuberance, scorn, tears, complaint, the hint of threat. It was all of these together. It ran the gamut of human emotions. Its velocity was breathtaking and it was all in one direction. Interjections from the target were rare. Johnson anticipated them before they could be spoken. He moved in close, his face a scant millimeter from his target, his eyes widening and narrowing, his eyebrows rising and falling. From his pockets poured clippings, memos, statistics. Mimicry, humor, and the genius of analogy made The Treatment an almost hypnotic experience and rendered the target stunned and helpless."

Source: Quote from Rowland Evans and Robert Novak, *Lyndon B. Johnson: The Exercise of Power* (New York: New American Library, 1966), p. 104.

most of their campaign funds from nonparty sources. Yet party leaders can be aggressive about enforcing party discipline, either by threatening to withdraw support for policy issues near and dear to the defectors or by rewarding those members who toe the party line. When House Republicans had a chance to meet with Obama in the White House in June 2011, the leadership selected freshman Reid Ribble as one of a handful of members who would be able to question the president directly. Ribble was chosen, in part, because "he had never crossed the G.O.P. leadership on anything important."[42] Republican members who had dissented in the past, it was decided, were free to figure out on their own how to have face time with the president.

Rules of Procedure

The operations of Congress are structured by both formal rules and informal norms of behavior. Rules in each chamber are mostly matters of parliamentary procedure. For example, they govern the scheduling of legislation, outlining when and how certain types of legislation can be brought to the floor. Rules also govern the introduction of floor amendments. In the House, amendments must be directly relevant to the bill at hand; in the Senate, except in certain, specified instances, amendments that are not relevant can be proposed.

As noted earlier, an important difference between the two chambers is the House's use of its Rules Committee to govern floor debate. Lacking a similar committee to act as a "traffic cop" for legislation, the Senate relies on unanimous consent agreements to set the starting time and length of debate. If one senator objects, a bill is stalled. Senators do not routinely object to unanimous consent agreements, however, because they will need them when bills of their own await scheduling. The rules facilitate cooperation among the competing interests and parties in each house so that legislation can be voted on. However, the rules are not neutral: they are a tool of the majority party and help it control the legislative process.[43]

If a senator wants to stop a bill badly enough, she or he may start a **filibuster** and try to talk the bill to death. By historical tradition, the Senate gives its members the right of unlimited debate. During a 1947 debate, Idaho Democrat Glen Taylor "spoke for 8½ hours on fishing, baptism, Wall Street, and his children." The record for holding the floor belongs to South Carolina Republican Strom Thurmond for a twenty-four-hour, eighteen-minute marathon in 1957.[44] In the House, no member is allowed to speak for more than an hour without unanimous consent.

After a 1917 filibuster by a small group of senators killed President Wilson's bill to arm merchant ships—a bill favored by a majority of senators—the Senate adopted **cloture**, a means of limiting debate. It takes the votes of sixty senators to invoke cloture. To signal one's intent to filibuster, a senator issues a **hold**, which is a letter requesting that a bill be held from floor debate. In response to a hold, the majority party can take the legislation off the table, try to comprise with the obstructionist lawmaker, or hold a cloture vote.

In today's Congress, the mere threat of a filibuster is common (thirty to thirty-five threats per Congress), which means that a bill often needs the support of sixty senators instead of a simple majority in order to pass. It has been argued that filibuster threats have become more common because "the workload of the Senate has increased to the point that wasting time is more costly than accepting the outcome of a cloture vote."[45] In other words, Senators are just too busy to wait around while filibustering Senators take to the floor. So Senators have become more willing to threaten obstruction,

filibuster
A delaying tactic, used in the Senate, that involves speech-making to prevent action on a piece of legislation.

cloture
The mechanism by which a filibuster is cut off in the Senate.

hold
A letter requesting that a bill be held from floor debate.

knowing that the result will most likely be a cloture vote. Given today's high level of party unity (see Figure 11.5), cloture votes often result in victory for the obstructionist. This "60-vote Senate" is often criticized for its ability to thwart the principle of majority rule and to make the legislative process even slower than was originally intended.[46]

FIGURE 11.5 Rising Partisanship

Congress long relied on bipartisanship—the two parties working together—in policymaking. This often meant that the moderates of both parties were central to the development of legislation as they coalesced around the most workable compromise. More recently, behavior has turned more partisan. Increasingly, members of each party vote with each other and against the position of the other party. The top two graphs show the percentage of party members who vote with the majority of their party and against the majority of the opposing party. The last graph shows the percentage of votes in which a majority of one party votes against the majority of the other.

Source: Harold W. Stanley and Richard G. Niemi (eds.), *Vital Statistics on American Politics, 2011-2012* (Washington, D.C.: CQ Press, 2011), pp. 206–208. Copyright © 2012 CQ Press, a division of Sage Publications, Inc. Reprinted by permission of the publisher, CQ Press.

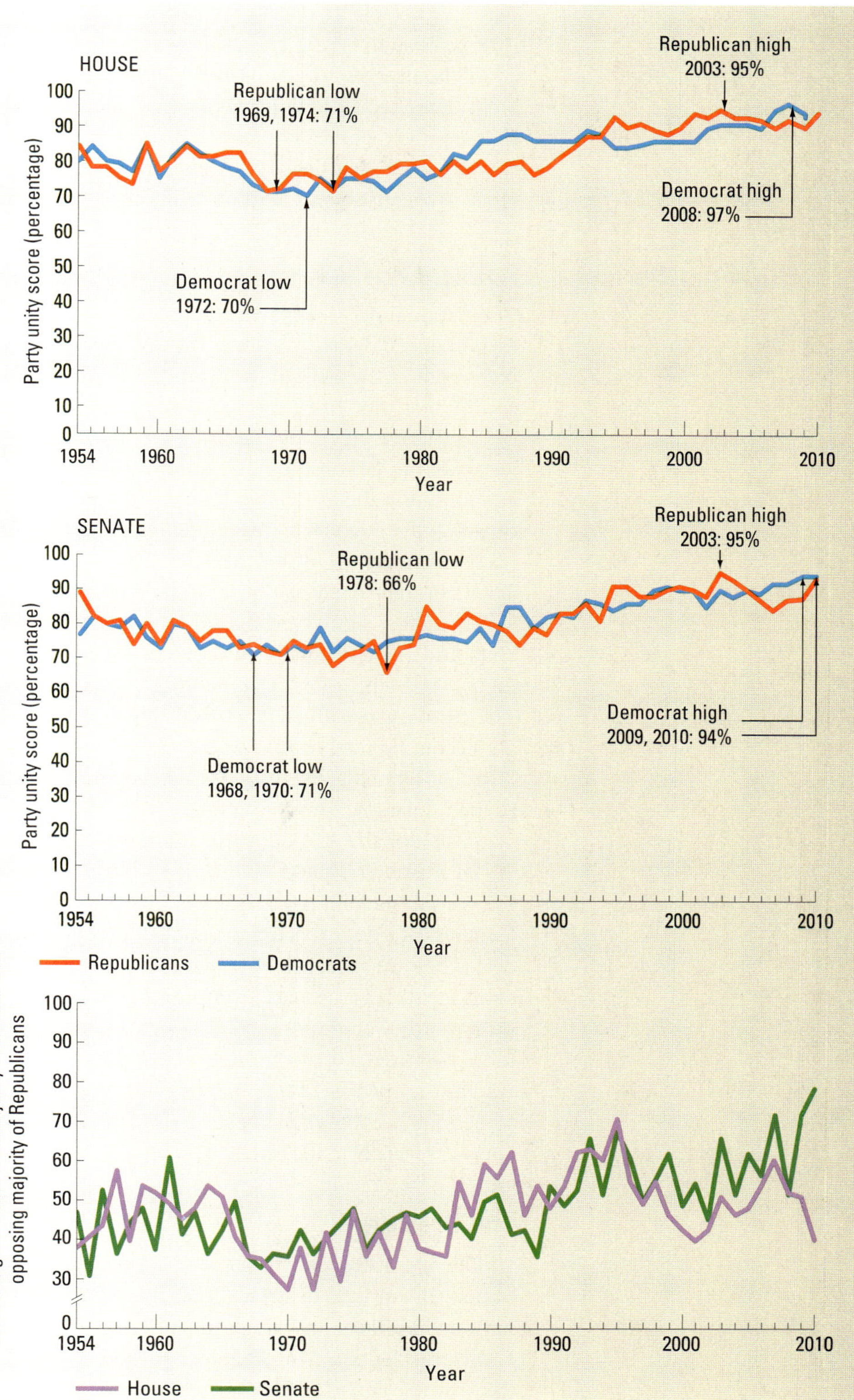

★ 11.6 The Legislative Environment

★ Appraise the components of the legislative environment that affect decision making in Congress.

After legislation emerges from committee, it is scheduled for floor debate. How do legislators decide how to vote? In this section, we examine the broader legislative environment that affects decision making in Congress. Specifically, we look at the influence on legislators of political parties, the president, constituents, and interest groups. The first two influences, parties and the president, push Congress toward majoritarianism. The other two, constituents and interest groups, are pluralist influences on policymaking.

Political Parties

The national political parties might appear to have limited resources at their disposal to influence lawmakers. They do not control the nominations of candidates. Candidates receive the bulk of their funds from individual contributors and political action committees, not from the national parties. Nevertheless, parties are strong forces in the legislative process.[47] Party leaders can help or hinder the efforts of rank-and-file legislators to get on the right committees, get their bills and amendments considered, and climb on the leadership ladder themselves. Moreover, as we saw earlier, the Democrats and Republicans on a given committee tend to reflect the views of the entire party membership in the chamber. Thus, party members on a committee often act as agents of their party as they search for solutions to policy problems.

The most significant reason that parties are important in Congress is that Democrats and Republicans have different ideologies.[48] Both parties have diversity, but as Figure 11.5 illustrates, Democrats tend to vote one way and Republicans the other. The primary reason that partisanship has been rising since 1980 is that the parties are becoming more homogeneous (see Chapter 8). The liberal wing of the Republican Party has practically disappeared, and the party is unified around a conservative agenda. Likewise, the conservative wing of the Democratic Party has declined.

Traditionally, one of the most important norms of behavior in Congress is that individual members should be willing to bargain with one another, especially across party lines. Policymaking is a process of give and take; it demands compromise. Members of Congress are not expected to violate their conscience on policy issues simply to strike a deal. They are expected, however, to listen to what others have to say and to make every effort to reach a reasonable compromise. Few policy matters are so clear-cut that compromise destroys one's position. Yet over the past several years, as the parties have become more polarized, compromises between them have become ever more difficult to achieve. And as the opening of this chapter illustrates, finding compromises *within* each party has sometimes become challenging as well. The inability to compromise threatens majoritarianism, especially in the Senate, as minority factions can produce stalemate after stalemate.

The President

Unlike members of Congress, the president is elected by voters across the entire nation. It can thus be argued that the president has a better claim to representing the nation than does any single member of Congress or even Congress as a whole. As such, presidents try to capitalize on their popular election and usually act as though they are speaking for the majority.

During the twentieth century, the public's expectations of what the president can accomplish in office grew enormously. We now expect the president to be our chief legislator: to introduce legislation on major issues and use his influence to push bills through Congress. This is much different from our early history, when presidents felt constrained by the constitutional doctrine of separation of powers and had to have members of Congress work confidentially for them during legislative sessions.[49]

Today, the White House is openly involved not only in the writing of bills but also in their development as they wind their way through the legislative process. If the White House does not like a bill, it tries to work out a compromise with legislators to have it amended. To monitor Congress and lobby for the administration's policies, many legislative liaison personnel work for the executive branch. On issues of the greatest importance, the president himself may meet with legislators directly. In July 2011, Congress needed to authorize an increase in the nation's debt limit or face defaulting on loans. When the parties were unable to reach an agreement, Obama met personally with Speaker Boehner to try and negotiate a deal.[50]

Although members of Congress grant presidents a leadership role in proposing legislation, they jealously guard the power of Congress to debate, shape, and pass or defeat any legislation the president proposes. Congress often clashes sharply with the president.

Constituents

Constituents are the people who live and vote in a legislator's district or state. Their opinions are a crucial part of the legislative decision-making process. As much as members of Congress want to please their party's leadership or the president by going along with their preferences, they have to think about what the voters back home want. If they displease enough people by the way they vote, they might lose their seat in the next election.

Constituents' influence contributes to pluralism because the diversity of America is mirrored by the geographical basis of representation in Congress. A representative from Los Angeles needs to be sensitive to issues of particular concern to constituents whose backgrounds are Korean, Vietnamese, Indian, Hispanic, African American, or Jewish. A representative from Montana will have few such constituents but must pay particular attention to issues involving minerals and mining. Such constituencies push and pull Congress in many different directions.

At all stages of the legislative process, the interests of the voters are on the minds of members of Congress. As they decide what to spend time on and how to vote, they weigh how different courses of action will affect their constituents' views of them, and the degree to which they feel they should follow constituency preferences.[51]

constituents
People who live and vote in a government official's district or state.

Interest Groups

As we pointed out in Chapter 10, interest groups are one way constituents influence Congress. Because they represent a vast array of vocational, regional, and ideological groupings within our population, interest groups exemplify pluralist politics. Interest groups press members of Congress to take a particular course of action, believing sincerely that what they prefer is also best for the country. Legislators are attentive to interest groups not because of an abstract commitment to pluralist politics but because these organizations represent citizens, some of whom live back home in their district or state.

Lobbies are an indispensable source of information for members of Congress. They are also important contributors to and fundraisers for campaigns. Periodic scandals raise concern, however, about potential conflicts of interest and whether legislators do special favors for lobbyists in exchange for campaign contributions or even for personal gain.[52] More common are the entirely legal campaign contributions that individual lobbyists and PACs make to legislators (see Chapter 10). Interest groups don't believe that contributions will necessarily get them what they want, but they certainly expect that significant donations will give them greater access to legislators. And access is the first step toward influencing the process.

With all these strong forces constraining legislators, it's easy to believe that they function solely in response to these external pressures. Legislators, however, bring their own views and life experiences to Congress. The issues they choose to work on and the way they vote reflect these personal values too.[53] But to the degree that the four external sources of influence on Congress—parties, the president, constituents, and interest groups—do influence legislators, they push them in both majoritarian and pluralist directions.

★ 11.7 The Dilemma of Representation

★ Consider whether members of Congress should vote according to the majority views of their constituents.

When candidates for Congress campaign, they routinely promise to work hard for their district's or state's interests. When they get to Washington, though, they all face a troubling dilemma: what their constituents want may not be what the people across the nation want.

Presidents and Shopping Bags

In doing the research for his book *Home Style,* political scientist Richard Fenno accompanied several representatives as they worked and interacted with constituents in their home district. On one of Fenno's trips, one representative said, "I spent fifteen minutes on the telephone with the president this afternoon. He had a plaintive tone in his voice and he pleaded with me." His side of the issue had prevailed over the president's, and he was elated by the victory. When Fenno and the representative got into their awaiting car, the representative saw the back seat piled high with campaign paraphernalia: shopping bags printed with his name and picture. "Back to this again," he sighed.[54]

Every member of Congress lives in two worlds: the world of presidents and the world of constituents. A typical week in the life of a representative means working in Washington, then boarding a plane and flying back to the home district. There, the representative spends time meeting with individual constituents and talking to civic groups, church gatherings, business associations, labor unions, and others. A survey of House members during a nonelection year showed that each made an average of thirty-five trips back to the district, spending an average of 138 days there.[55]

Members of Congress are often criticized for being out of touch with the people they are supposed to represent. This charge does not seem justified. Legislators work extraordinarily hard at keeping in touch with voters and finding out what is on their constituents' minds. The problem is how to act on that knowledge.

Trustees or Delegates?

Are members of Congress bound to vote the way their constituents want them to vote, even if it means voting against their conscience? Some say no. They argue that legislators must be free to vote in line with what they think is best. This view has long been associated with the eighteenth-century English political philosopher Edmund Burke (1729–1797). Burke, who served in Parliament, told his constituents in Bristol that "you choose a member, indeed; but when you have chosen him, he is not a member of Bristol, but he is a member of *Parliament.*"[56] Burke reasoned that representatives are sent by their constituents to vote as they think best. As **trustees**, representatives are obligated to consider the

trustee
A representative who is obligated to consider the views of constituents but is not obligated to vote according to those views if he or she believes they are misguided.

views of their constituents, but they are not obligated to vote according to those views if they think they are misguided.

Others hold that legislators should represent the majority view of their constituents—that they are **delegates** with instructions from the people at home on how to vote on critical issues. Delegates, unlike trustees, must be prepared to vote against their own preferences. During the fight over President Obama's health-care reform, Representative Joseph Cao knew he would be in a bind. As a Republican representing a heavily Democratic and black district in Louisiana in which 25 percent of people lacked health insurance, he was torn between his party on the one hand and the desires of his constituents on the other. He ultimately voted for the first reform bill (the only Republican to do so) but against the final version. In the 2010 election, he became one of only two sitting Republicans to be defeated.[57]

Although the interests of their districts encourage them to act as delegates, their interpretation of the larger national interest often calls on them to be trustees.[58] Given these conflicting role definitions, it is not surprising that Congress is not clearly a body of either delegates or trustees. Research has shown, however, that members of Congress are more likely to take the delegate role on issues that are of great concern to their constituents.[59] But much of the time, what constituents really want is not clear. Many issues are not highly visible back home. Some issues may cut across the constituency, affecting constituents in different ways. Or constituents may only partially understand them. For such issues, no delegate position is obvious.

Constituents Strike Back

During recesses, members of Congress travel to their home districts and often hold town hall meetings where they talk with constituents. Yet as Congress has become more polarized, these meetings have gotten increasingly contentious. As a result, some representatives are less willing to subject themselves to public shouting matches and have held fewer town hall meetings. In 2011, Representative Paul Ryan (R-Wisc.), along with other members of Congress, decided to meet only with constituents who could pay to attend his events rather than hold public sessions, prompting constituents to protest, as seen here.

delegate
A legislator whose primary responsibility is to represent the majority view of his or her constituents, regardless of his or her own view.

11.8 Pluralism, Majoritarianism, and Democracy

★ Assess the elements that characterize Congress as a pluralist or majoritarian system.

The dilemma that individual members of Congress face in adopting the role of either delegate or trustee has broad implications for the way our country is governed. When legislators act as delegates, congressional policymaking is more pluralistic, and policies reflect the bargaining that goes on among lawmakers who speak for different constituencies. When legislators act as trustees and vote their consciences, policymaking becomes less tied to the narrower interests of districts and states. But even here there is no guarantee that congressional decision making reflects majority interests. True majoritarian legislatures require a paramount role for political parties.

We end this chapter with a short discussion of pluralism versus majoritarianism in Congress. But first, to establish a frame of reference, we look at a more majoritarian type of legislature: the parliament.

Parliamentary Government

parliamentary system
A system of government in which the chief executive is the leader whose party holds the most seats in the legislature after an election or whose party forms a major part of the ruling coalition.

In our system of government, the executive and legislative functions are divided between a president and a Congress, each elected separately. Most other democracies—such as Britain—have parliamentary governments. In a **parliamentary system**, the chief executive is the legislative leader whose party holds the most seats in the legislature after an election or whose party forms a major part of the ruling coalition. For instance, in Great Britain, voters do not cast a ballot for prime minister. They

Politics of Global Change

Creating a Legislature

In December 2010, a fruit vendor in Tunisia set himself on fire to protest his country's political conditions. This act sparked what has become known as the "Arab Spring," a wave of uprisings across the Middle East during 2011 marked by protest, violence, governmental resistance, and, in Tunisia and Egypt, the ouster of long-standing authoritarian rulers. Within months, both countries found themselves designing new legislatures and debating new electoral laws and constitutions.

One of the first decisions they needed to make was on the kind of legislature to establish. While an American-style Congress with single-member districts elected by plurality rule can minimize the ability for extremist parties to gain seats and produce representatives committed to their local constituency as well as to their party, both countries opted primarily for proportional representation (PR). Under PR, each politically organized group can expect to be represented roughly in proportion to its support in society. Party unity is typically high in PR systems. In such systems, parties also often need to form coalitions in order to control a majority of legislative seats. Both countries also required women to be included in each party's list of candidates.

Both countries are relatively homogeneous in terms of ethnicity and religion, but important tensions exist, and these tensions were evident as elections took shape. In Egypt, for instance, tensions involved (1) the role that the military, which controlled the government after the departure of longtime ruler Hosni Mubarak in January

Photo by Peter Macdiarmid/Getty Images

vote only for their member of Parliament and thus influence the choice of prime minister only indirectly, by voting for the party they favor in the local district election. Parties are unified, and in Parliament, legislators vote for their party's position, giving voters a strong and direct means of influencing public policy. Where there is a multiple party system (as opposed to just two parties), a governing coalition must sometimes be formed from an alliance of multiple parties. (See "Politics of Global Change: Creating a Legislature.")

2011, would play in selecting a prime minister and cabinet; (2) whether newly established democratic processes would be threatened if conservative Islamist parties won a majority of the vote; and (3) whether minority Coptic Christians would be treated as full members of the polity should Islamists win.

Egypt held its first round of parliamentary elections in November 2011. Over 6,500 candidates from over forty-five parties ran for office. A mainstream Islamist party, the Freedom and Justice Party, won 40 percent of the vote. The conservative Islamist party, Al-Nur, got 25 percent, leading many observers to worry about the future of the democratic process in Egypt (for instance, although Al-Nur had women on the ballot in every district, they were always listed last to ensure they would not get elected and were often represented with flowers in place of their faces on campaign materials). A majority-Islamist government would also complicate the diplomatic relationship between Egypt and the United States.

Tunisia, on the other hand, has generally been seen as achieving a smoother transition to democracy. The first elections were held in October 2011, with more than 10,000 candidates from more than 100 political parties running for office. The moderate Islamist Ennahda party took the most seats, which troubled secular Tunisians as well as western observers. But unlike in Egypt, the role of conservative Islamists has been small with moderate and center-left parties vying for second place. The new assembly is charged with drafting a new constitution and appointing an interim government.

Both countries still face rough roads ahead in establishing stable democratic legislatures. And as of this writing, other countries caught up in the Arab Spring, such as Libya, Syria, Bahrain, and Yemen, remain in the throes of citizen unrest. Establishing a legislature may be inspiring, but the process is rarely pretty. Watching new democracies take shape before our eyes reminds us of just what a challenge democracy can be.

SOURCES: "Q&A: Tunisia Elections," http://www.bbc.co.uk/news/world-africa-15309152; "Q&A: Egypt's Parliamentary Elections," http://www.bbc.co.uk/news/world-middle-east-15874070; "Ennahda Claims Victory in Tunisian Poll," 26 October 2011, Aljazeera.com; Leila Fadel, "First Free Election in Tunisia Brings Joy and Pride," *Washington Post*, 23 October 2011; David Kirkpatrick, "Islamists Say They Have Mandate in Egypt Voting, *New York Times*, 30 November 2011; and Jon Jensen, "Egypt Votes: A Primer," 28 November 2011, globalpost.com.

Critical Thinking

Which, if any, features of the emerging legislatures in Tunisia and Egypt will encourage majoritarianism? Which features will encourage pluralism? What challenges might the new legislatures face when trying to balance freedom and order? What about balancing order and equality?

In a parliamentary system, power is concentrated in the legislature because the leader of the majority party is also the head of the government. Moreover, parliamentary legislatures are usually composed of only one house or have a second chamber that is much weaker than the other. Parliamentary governments usually do not have a court that can invalidate acts of the parliament. Under such a system, the government is in the hands of the party that controls the parliament. With no separation of government powers, checks on government action are few. These governments fit the majoritarian model of democracy to a much greater extent than a separation-of-powers system.

Pluralism Versus Majoritarianism in Congress

The U.S. Congress is often criticized for being too pluralist and not majoritarian enough. The federal budget deficit provides a case in point. Americans are often deeply concerned about the big deficits that plague our national budgets. Both Democrats and Republicans in Congress repeatedly call for reductions in those deficits. But when spending bills come before Congress, legislators' concern turns to what the bills would do for their district or state.

Until 2011, appropriations bills often included **earmarks**, pork barrel projects that benefitted specific districts or states that were added to spending bills without debate. In 2011, both parties banned earmarks. Lawmakers, however, still try to get funding for bridges, beach replenishment, and other local projects, but now they have to do more to convince other members of Congress that the projects have merit. Doing so often entails making the case that the projects in question serve the national interest, typically through the job creation or economic development that such projects allegedly produce. Universities were hit particularly hard by the loss of earmarks, with some, such as Northeastern University in Massachusetts, hiring lobbying firms and political consultants to convince representatives to continue to seek federal funding for their research and infrastructure.[60]

Local spending gets into the budget through bargaining among members; as we saw earlier in this chapter, congressional norms encourage it. Members of Congress try to win projects and programs that will benefit their constituents and thus help them at election time. To win approval of such projects, members must be willing to vote for other legislators' projects in turn. Such a system promotes pluralism.

It's easy to conclude that the consequence of pluralism in Congress is a lot of unnecessary spending. Yet many constituencies are well served by an appropriations process that allows pluralism. The people of each state and district pay taxes to Washington, so shouldn't Washington send some of that money back to them in the form of economic development projects? A 2010 survey asked Americans if certain candidate qualities would make them more or less likely to vote

earmarks
Federal funds appropriated by Congress for use on local projects.

Everything Is Better with Bacon

Distributional policies allocate resources to a specific constituency. Previously, Congress often allocated resources through earmarks. Now that the parties have banned earmarks, representatives have to be more creative in finding ways to divert federal dollars to projects in their districts. Their addiction to local spending projects stems, in part, from contradictory messages from voters, who dislike "wasteful" projects but expect their representative to "bring home the bacon."

for a particular congressional candidate. Among the eight qualities in the survey, the only one that a majority of Americans said would make them more likely to vote for someone was "has a record of bringing government projects and money to your district." So despite Americans' dislike of national deficits, they still place great pressure on their own representatives to direct federal spending back home.[61]

Proponents of pluralism also argue that the makeup of Congress generally reflects that of the nation—that different members of Congress represent farm areas, low-income inner cities, industrial areas, and so on. They point out that America itself is pluralistic, with a rich diversity of economic, social, religious, and racial groups, and even if one's own representatives and senators don't represent one's particular viewpoint, it's likely that someone in Congress does.

Whatever the shortcomings of pluralism, institutional reform aimed at reducing legislators' concern for individual districts and states is difficult. Members of Congress resist any structural changes that might weaken their ability to gain reelection. Nevertheless, the growing partisanship in Congress represents a trend toward greater majoritarianism. As both parties have become more ideologically homogeneous, there is greater unity around policies. To the degree that voters correctly recognize the differences between the parties and are willing to cast their ballots on that basis, increasing majoritarianism will constrain pluralism in Congress. Ironically, once in office legislators weaken the incentive for constituents to vote based on ideology. The congressional system is structured to facilitate casework and to fund pork barrel spending. Both of these characteristics of the modern Congress work to enhance each legislator's reputation in his or her district or state. In short, the modern Congress is characterized by strong elements of both majoritarianism and pluralism.

SUMMARY

11.1 The Origins and Powers of Congress

- In designing the legislative branch, the framers wanted a strong union but also wanted to prevent the concentration of power. The Senate consists of two senators from each state elected for six-year terms. The House has 435 members, with each state's representation in proportion to its population.
- Congress has the power to declare war, raise an army and navy, borrow and coin money, regulate interstate commerce, create federal courts, establish rules for the naturalization of immigrants, and make all laws. Specific to the Senate are the powers to confirm presidential appointments, ratify treaties, and try cases of impeachment. The House has the power to initiate revenue bills and to impeach.

11.2 Electing Congress

- We elect members of Congress to represent us, working to ensure that interests from home and from around the country are heard throughout the policymaking process. Incumbency is a strong predictor of reelection.

11.3 How Issues Get on the Congressional Agenda

- The congressional agenda includes both recurrent issues, such as the national debt and foreign aid, and new issues that may emerge as a result of some highly visible event.

11.4 The Lawmaking Process and the Importance of Committees

- The process by which a bill becomes a law follows a series of specific steps, but the different ways legislation can be treated at each step complicates the process.
- There are four types of congressional committees: standing, joint, select, and conference; standing committees, which specialize in a particular area of legislation, are predominant.

The committee system fosters expertise; representatives and senators who know the most about particular issues have the most influence over them.

11.5 Leaders and Followers in Congress

- Party leaders in the House and Senate are charged with overseeing institutional procedures, managing legislation, fundraising, and communicating with the press.
- The majority party leader in the House is the Speaker, who shapes the House agenda and leadership. The vice president of the United States is president of the Senate, but the Senate majority leader exercises the real power in the Senate.
- Formal rules of procedure structure operations in Congress, while informal norms guide members' behavior.

11.6 The Legislative Environment

- Political parties, the president, constituents, and interest groups all influence how members of Congress decide issues. Political parties and the president push Congress toward majoritarianism; constituents and interest groups exercise a pluralist influence on policymaking.

11.7 The Dilemma of Representation

- Bargaining and compromise play important roles in Congress. Some find this disquieting. They want less deal making and more adherence to principle. This thinking is in line with the desire for a more majoritarian democracy. Others defend the current system, arguing that the United States is a large, complex nation, and the policies that govern it should be developed through bargaining among various interests.

11.8 Pluralism, Majoritarianism, and Democracy

- There is no clear-cut answer to whether a majoritarian or a pluralist legislative system provides better representation for voters. Our system is a mix of pluralism and majoritarianism. It serves minority interests that might otherwise be neglected or even harmed by an unthinking or uncaring majority. At the same time, congressional parties work to represent the broader interests of the American people.

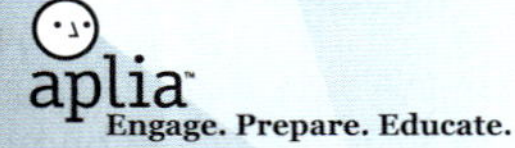

ASSESSING YOUR UNDERSTANDING WITH APLIA...YOUR VIRTUAL TUTOR!

11.1 Explain the structure and powers of Congress as envisioned by the framers and enumerated in the Constitution.

1. How is the number of congressional representatives elected from each state determined?
2. Name the powers that are unique to the House of Representatives and those that are unique to the Senate.

11.2 Analyze the factors that affect the way voters elect members of Congress.

1. What factors contribute to the high reelection rates of congressional incumbents?
2. What does the term *descriptive representation* mean?
3. How has the use of majority-minority districts benefitted each political party?

11.3 Describe the ways in which issues get on the congressional agenda.

1. What might bring an issue to the forefront of the congressional agenda?

11.4 Differentiate among the types of congressional committees and evaluate the role of the committee system in the legislative process.

1. Which chamber channels bills through the Rules Committee?
2. What are the composition and role of a conference committee?
3. Define standing, joint, and select committees and explain the primary role of each one.
4. How do legislators make sure the agencies that administer their programs are carrying out the policies as Congress intended?

5. How does the committee system enhance the pluralist and the majoritarian aspects of American politics?

11.5 Identify the leadership structure of the legislative branch and assess the rules and norms that influence congressional operations.

1. Who serves as Speaker of the House and what roles does the Speaker serve?
2. Who serves the leadership role in the Senate?
3. What are the most significant functions performed by the House and Senate leaders?

11.6 Appraise the components of the legislative environment that affect decision making in Congress.

1. How do political parties and the president push Congress toward majoritarian democracy?

2. How do constituents and interest groups exercise a pluralist influence on policymaking?

11.7 Consider whether members of Congress should vote according to the majority views of their constituents.

1. How do members of Congress who see themselves as trustees view their roles?
2. How do members of Congress who see themselves as delegates view their responsibility to their constituents?

11.8 Assess the elements that characterize Congress as a pluralist or majoritarian system.

1. Why is a parliamentary system more majoritarian than a separation-of-power system?
2. What accounts for the growing majoritarianism in Congress?
3. What is an earmark and why is it associated with a pluralist model of democracy?

12

The Presidency

aplia
Engage. Prepare. Educate.

Election day, November 6, 2012. As Barack Obama waited the hours to see if the American public would reelect him, he had to be thinking of what he had accompl shed and where he had fallen short. Hopes were so high on that night exactly four years earlier. When the returns came in and revealed his 2008 landslide victory over Republican Senator John McCain, Obama and his supporters were sure that the next four years would be transformative. The divisiveness and disappointments of the Bush years would give way to a new era. Obama would transcend partisanship to unify America around much needed change.[1]

Maybe he had been naïve to believe he could bend Washington. After all, he was elected president, not anointed king. The constraints on presidents are substantial. Even when his party controlled the Congress in 2009–2010, there were challenges to getting legislation passed. When the Republicans captured the House after the 2010 election, he was able to get very little through the Congress. Republican legislators had a diametrically opposed view of what America needed to do. More broadly, Republicans across the country believed that Obama was an excessively partisan president, just as Democrats had thought the same of George W. Bush.[2]

It's not cs though his administration was not without major achievements. Yet the ultimate frustration was that he spent much of his initial political capital on just trying to stabilize the economy, which had fallen off a cliff before he took office in late 2008. Legislation aimed at keeping the banking system from collapsing, the Troubled Asset Relief Program (TARP), achieved its goal but became known derisively as the "bailout bill" because it rescued financial institutions whose mistakes had helped cause the economic downturn. And then there was the Obama stimulus bill. In an effort to kick-start a failing economy he had inherited from President Bush, his stimulus package included funds for public works projects like roads and bridges, along with a tax cut and funds sent directly to the states to supplement their shrinking revenues. Research showed that the stimulus did improve the economy but not enough to restore it to full health.[3] Voters came to believe that it did little good. Obama's signature initiative, the Affordable Care Act, was designed to provide health insurance to all Americans who could not afford it on their own. It was a monumental policy achievement, though it would not be fully implemented until 2014.

The president knew that he had also had significant accomplishments in foreign policy. It was under his watch that Osama bin Laden was discovered and then killed by an American commando unit operating deep inside Pakistan. The brutal dictator of Libya, Muammar Gaddafi, had been brought down in part because of the Western allies' air bombardment.

Finally, the deep recession began to abate. But was it too late to save his presidency? During the past year the unemployment rate fell sharply as economic activity picked up.[4] Consumers became more optimistic and began to purchase more, including big-ticket items like automobiles. Obama's poll numbers began to rise from the depths. More Americans were saying that they approved of his performance as president. Would more Americans cast their ballots for him rather than Republican Mitt Romney?

He waited for the returns to come in.

All presidents face a daunting set of challenges. They are expected to offer solutions to national problems, whether waging a war or reviving a failing economy. As the nation's major foreign diplomat and commander in chief of the armed forces, they are held responsible for the security and status of America in the world. Our presidents are the focal point for the nation's hopes and disappointments.

This chapter analyzes presidential leadership, looking at how presidents try to muster majoritarian support for their domestic goals and how they must function today as global leaders. What are the powers of the presidency? How is the president's advisory system organized? What are the ingredients of strong presidential leadership: character, public relations, or a friendly Congress? Finally, what are the particular issues and problems that presidents face in foreign affairs?

12.1 The Constitutional Basis of Presidential Power

★ Assess whether the constitutional powers of the president form a strong basis for the modern presidency.

When the presidency was created, the colonies had just fought a war of independence; their reaction to British domination had focused on the autocratic rule of King George III. Thus, the delegates to the Constitutional Convention were extremely wary of unchecked power and were determined not to create an all-powerful, dictatorial presidency.

The delegates' fear of a powerful presidency was counterbalanced by their desire for strong leadership. The Articles of Confederation, which did not provide for a single head of state, had failed to bind the states together into a unified nation (see Chapter 3). In addition, the governors of the individual states had generally proved to be inadequate leaders because they had few formal powers. The new nation was conspicuously weak; its Congress had no power to compel the states to obey its legislation. The delegates knew they had to create some type of effective executive office. Their task was to provide for national leadership without allowing opportunity for tyranny.

Initial Conceptions of the Presidency

Debates about the nature of the office began. Should there be one president or a presidential council or committee? Should the president be chosen by Congress and remain largely subservient to that body? The delegates gave initial approval to a plan that called for a single executive, chosen by Congress for a seven-year term and ineligible for reelection.[5] But some delegates continued to argue for a strong president who would be elected independently of the legislative branch.

The final structure of the presidency reflected the checks-and-balances philosophy that had shaped the entire Constitution. In the minds of the delegates, they had imposed important limits on the presidency through the powers specifically delegated to Congress and the courts. Those counterbalancing powers would act as checks, or controls, on presidents who might try to expand the office beyond its proper bounds.

The Powers of the President

The requirements for the presidency are set forth in Article II of the Constitution: the president must be a U.S.-born citizen, at least thirty-five years old, who has lived in the United States for a minimum of fourteen years. Article II also sets forth the responsibilities of presidents. In view of the importance of the office, the constitutional description of the president's duties is surprisingly brief and vague. This vagueness has led to repeated conflict about the limits of presidential power.

The delegates undoubtedly had many reasons for the lack of precision in Article II. One likely explanation was the difficulty of providing and at the same time limiting presidential power. Furthermore, the framers of the Constitution had no model—no existing presidency—on which to base their description of the office. And, ironically, their description of the presidency might have been more precise if they had had less confidence in George Washington, the obvious choice for the first president. According to one account of the Constitutional Convention, "when Dr. Franklin predicted on June 4 that 'the first man put at the helm will be a good one,' every delegate knew perfectly well who that first good man would be."[6] The delegates had great trust in Washington; they did not fear that he would try to misuse the office.

The major duties and powers that the delegates listed for Washington and his successors can be summarized as follows:

- *Serve as administrative head of the nation.* The Constitution gives little guidance on the president's administrative duties. It states merely that "the executive Power shall be vested in a President of the United States of America" and that "he shall take Care that the Laws be faithfully executed." These imprecise directives have been interpreted to mean that the president is to supervise and offer leadership to various departments, agencies, and programs created by Congress. In practice, a chief executive spends much more time making policy decisions for his cabinet departments and agencies than enforcing existing policies.
- *Act as commander in chief of the military.* In essence, the Constitution names the president as the highest-ranking officer in the armed forces. But it gives Congress the power to declare war. The framers no doubt intended Congress to control the president's military power; nevertheless, presidents have initiated military action without the approval of Congress.
- *Veto legislation.* The president can **veto** (disapprove) any bill or resolution enacted by Congress, with the exception of joint resolutions that propose constitutional amendments. Congress can override a presidential veto with a two-thirds vote in each house.
- *Appoint various officials.* The president has the authority to appoint federal court judges, ambassadors, cabinet members, other key policymakers, and many lesser officials. Many appointments are subject to Senate confirmation.
- *Make treaties.* With the "Advice and Consent" of at least two-thirds of those senators voting at the time, the president can make treaties with foreign powers. The president is also to "receive Ambassadors," a phrase that presidents have interpreted to mean the right to recognize other nations formally.

veto
The president's disapproval of a bill that has been passed by both houses of Congress. Congress can override a veto with a two-thirds vote in each house.

12.2 The Expansion of Presidential Power

★ Illustrate how claims of inherent powers augment the formal powers of the presidency.

The framers' limited conception of the president's role has given way to a considerably more powerful interpretation. In this section, we discuss how presidential power has expanded as presidents have exercised their explicit constitutional responsibilities and boldly interpreted the ambiguities of the Constitution. First, we look at the ways in which formal powers, such as veto power, have been increasingly used over time. Second, we turn to claims that presidents make about "inherent" powers implicit in the Constitution. Finally, we discuss congressional grants of power to the executive branch.

Formal Powers

The Constitution clearly involves the president in the policymaking process through his veto power, his ability to report to Congress on the state of the Union, and his role as commander in chief. Over time, presidents have become more aggressive in their use of these formal powers. Vetoes, for instance, have become much more frequent, particularly when presidents face a Congress dominated by the opposing political party. The first sixteen presidents, from Washington to Lincoln, issued a total of 59 vetoes. Dwight Eisenhower issued 181 vetoes over the course of his two terms; Ronald Reagan vetoed legislation 78 times. Through 2011 Barack Obama vetoed only two bills sent to him by Congress. Not counting President James Garfield, who served less than a year, this was the least amount since Abraham Lincoln.[7] The ability to veto legislation gives the president power even when he doesn't issue many vetoes. Veto threats shape legislation because members of Congress anticipate vetoes and modify legislation to avoid them. If a president does veto a bill and there is not enough support to override the president's veto, Congress may be forced to rewrite the bill, making concessions to the president's point of view.

Modern presidents have also taken a much more active role in setting the nation's policy agenda, and it is now expected that they will enter office with clear policy goals and work with their party in Congress to pass legislation. Most controversial has been the president's use of his power as commander in chief. Several modern presidents have used their power as commander in chief to enter into foreign conflicts without appealing to Congress for a formal declaration of war.[8] The entire Vietnam War was fought without a congressional declaration of war. Complicating this issue is the nature of modern warfare. In Afghanistan, the United States is fighting guerrilla forces that the nation regards as terrorists, but there is no Taliban nation to declare war against.

The Inherent Powers

inherent powers
Authority claimed by the president that is not clearly specified in the Constitution. Typically, these powers are inferred from the Constitution.

Several presidents have expanded the power of the office by taking actions that exceeded commonly held notions of the president's proper authority. These men justified what they had done by saying that their actions fell within the **inherent powers** of the presidency. From this broad perspective, presidential power derives not only from those duties clearly outlined in Article II but also from inferences that may be drawn from the Constitution.

When a president claims a power that has not been considered part of the chief executive's authority, he forces Congress and the courts either to acquiesce to his claim or to restrict it. For instance, President Bush unilaterally established military commissions to try alleged enemy combatants captured in Afghanistan and Iraq and held at the U.S. naval base at Guantánamo Bay, Cuba. In 2006, the U.S. Supreme Court ruled that the military commissions were illegal, and the Bush administration was forced to go to Congress for the authorization to establish new commissions with new trial procedures.[9]

When presidents succeed in claiming a new power, they leave to their successors the legacy of a permanent expansion of presidential authority. During the Civil War, for example, Abraham Lincoln instituted a blockade of southern ports, thereby committing acts of war against the Confederacy without the approval of Congress. Lincoln said the urgent nature of the South's challenge to the Union forced him to act without waiting for congressional approval. His rationale was simple: "Was it possible to lose the nation and yet preserve the Constitution?"[10] In other words, Lincoln circumvented the Constitution to save the nation. Subsequently, Congress and the Supreme Court approved Lincoln's actions. That approval gave added legitimacy to the theory of inherent powers, a theory that over time has transformed the presidency.

Today, presidents routinely issue **executive orders**, presidential directives that carry the force of law.[11] The Constitution does not explicitly grant the president the power to issue an executive order. Sometimes presidents use them to see that the laws are "faithfully executed." This was the case when President Dwight Eisenhower ordered the Arkansas National Guard into service in Little Rock, Arkansas, to enforce court orders to desegregate the schools. But many times presidents issue executive orders by arguing that they may take actions in the best interest of the nation so long as the law does not directly prohibit these actions. Executive orders are issued for a wide variety of purposes, from administrative reorganization to civil rights. For instance, Harry Truman issued an executive order to end racial segregation in the armed services.

The boundaries of the president's inherent powers have been sharply debated since the September 11, 2001, attacks upon the United States.[12] In response to an ongoing threat of terrorism, President Bush secretly authorized the National Security Agency (NSA) to wiretap telephone calls, without a warrant, between people within the United States and people overseas with suspected links to terrorism. The 1978 Foreign Intelligence Surveillance Act (FISA), however, requires intelligence agencies like the NSA to obtain a warrant from a panel of judges before wiretapping the calls of U.S. citizens. When the wiretapping was revealed, critics accused Bush of putting himself above the law. Bush argued that the Constitution designates the president as the commander in chief of the armed forces; he said he could disregard FISA requirements if they hindered his ability to collect the foreign intelligence necessary to protect the nation from another terrorist attack. Criticism of warrantless wiretapping eventually led Bush to request this power from Congress, and it passed legislation that essentially authorized what the NSA had been doing.[13]

More broadly, President Bush and other members of his administration grounded his claim of expanded powers under the theory of the **unitary executive**. This interpretation of the Constitution says that since the president is given the power to see to it that the laws are "faithfully executed," his prerogatives override any efforts by Congress to give independent decision-making powers to any agency of government.[14] Thus, if the NSA were instructed by Congress to wiretap only when certain criteria were met, the president could override such instructions to the agency. The courts have yet to back such a sweeping interpretation of inherent powers, but this theory remains an ambiguous part of presidential authority.[15]

executive orders
Presidential directives that create or modify laws and public policies, without the direct approval of Congress.

unitary executive
A belief that the president's inherent powers allow him to overrule congressional grants of independent authority to agencies.

Congressional Delegation of Power

delegation of powers
The process by which Congress gives the executive branch the additional authority needed to address new problems.

Presidential power grows when presidents successfully challenge Congress, but in many instances, Congress willingly delegates power to the executive branch. As the American public pressures the national government to solve various problems, Congress, through a process called **delegation of powers**, gives the executive branch more responsibility to administer programs that address those problems. One example of delegation of congressional power occurred in the 1930s, during the Great Depression, when Congress gave Franklin Roosevelt's administration wide latitude to do what it thought was necessary to solve the nation's economic ills.

When Congress concludes that the government needs flexibility in its approach to a problem, the president is often given great freedom in how or when to implement policies. Richard Nixon was given discretionary authority to impose a freeze on wages and prices in an effort to combat escalating inflation. If Congress had been forced to debate the timing of the freeze, merchants and manufacturers would surely have raised their prices in anticipation of the event. Instead, Nixon was able to act suddenly, imposing the freeze without warning. (We discuss congressional delegation of authority to the executive branch in more detail in Chapter 13.)

At other times, however, Congress believes that too much power has accumulated in the executive branch, and it enacts legislation to reassert congressional authority. During the 1970s, many representatives and senators agreed that presidents were exercising power that rightfully belonged to the legislative branch, and therefore Congress's role in the American political system was declining. The most notable reaction was the enactment of the War Powers Resolution (1973), which was directed at ending the president's ability to pursue armed conflict without explicit congressional approval (see Chapter 19).

★ 12.3 The Executive Branch Establishment

★ Assess the role played by the various executive branch institutions as resources for an effective president.

Although we elect a single individual as president, it would be a mistake to ignore the extensive staff and resources of the entire executive branch of government. The president has a White House staff that helps him formulate policy. The vice president is another resource; his duties within the administration vary according to his relationship with the president. The president's cabinet secretaries—the heads of the major departments of the national government—play a number of roles, including the critical function of administering the programs that fall within their jurisdictions. Effective presidents think strategically about how best to use the resources available to them. Each must find ways to organize structures and processes that best suit his management style.

The Executive Office of the President

The president depends heavily on key aides. They advise him on crucial political choices, devise the general strategies the administration will follow in pursuing congressional and public support, and control access to the president to ensure that he has enough time for his most important tasks. Consequently, he needs to trust and respect these top staffers; many in a president's inner circle of assistants are longtime associates. The president's personal staff constitutes the White House Office.

Presidents typically have a chief of staff, who may be a first among equals or, in some administrations, the unquestioned leader of the staff. President Obama's first chief of staff, Rahm Emanuel (now the mayor of Chicago), earned a reputation for in-your-face aggressiveness. He pushed and prodded and was relentless in trying to gain cooperation from members of Congress and other executive branch officials. His profane manner led one of his two brothers to give him a sign for his White House desk that says, "Undersecretary for Go ______ Yourself."[16] Ultimately, Emanuel was effective, though, because Obama gave him broad authority to act on his behalf. Hamilton Jordan, President Carter's chief of staff, was at the other end of the spectrum: Carter did not give him the authority to administer the White House with a strong hand and, not surprisingly, Jordan was not terribly effective.

Presidents also have a national security adviser to provide daily briefings on foreign and military affairs and longer-range analyses of issues confronting the administration. Similarly, the president has the Council of Economic Advisers and the National Economic Council to report on the state of the economy and advise the president on the best way to promote economic growth. Senior domestic policy advisers help determine the administration's basic approach to areas such as health, education, and social services.

Below these top aides are the large staffs that serve them and the president. These staffs are organized around certain specialties. Some staff members work on political matters, such as communicating with interest groups, maintaining relations with ethnic and religious minorities, and managing party affairs. One staff deals exclusively with the media, and a legislative liaison staff lobbies the Congress for the administration. The large Office of Management and Budget (OMB) analyzes budget requests, is involved in the policymaking process, and examines agency management practices. This extended White House executive establishment, including the White House Office, is known as the **Executive Office of the President**. The Executive Office employs around 2,000 individuals and has an annual budget of $500 million.[17]

No one agrees about a "right way" for a president to organize his White House staff, but scholars have identified three major advisory styles.[18] Franklin Roosevelt exemplified the first system: a competitive management style. He organized his staff so that his advisers had overlapping authority and differing points of view. Roosevelt used this system to ensure that he would get the best possible information, hear all sides of an argument, and still be the final decision maker in any dispute. Dwight Eisenhower, a former general, best exemplifies a hierarchical staff model. His staff was arranged with clear lines of authority and a hierarchical structure that mirrored a military command. This places fewer demands on presidential time and energy, since the president does not participate in the details of policy discussion. Bill Clinton had more of a collegial staffing arrangement, a loose staff structure that gave many top staffers direct access to him. Clinton himself was immersed in the details of the policymaking process and brainstormed with his advisers. He was much less likely to delegate authority to others.

Executive Office of the President
The president's executive aides and their staffs; the extended White House executive establishment.

REUTERS/White House/Pete Souza/LANDOV

Captured!

After American special operations forces helicoptered into Pakistan to pursue September 11th mastermind Osama bin Laden, the Navy Seals wore helmet-mounted cameras as they assaulted bin Laden's compound. This allowed President Obama, the tension evident in his face, to watch the operation in real time on a monitor in the Situation Room at the White House.

No matter the president, White House staffs are always full of smart and highly aggressive individuals who inevitably begin to squabble over authority. In the first years of the Obama presidency, top female staffers became increasingly angry over a sense that they were being marginalized by more influential staffers, notably Emanuel and Lawrence Summers, Obama's leading economic adviser. Their dissatisfaction was eventually communicated to the president and Obama responded by holding a dinner for the top women in the White House. When they sat down at the table, Obama said, "I really want you guys to talk to me about this openly."[19] How much this meeting improved the situation is unclear.

Above all, a president must ensure that staff members feel comfortable telling him things he may not want to hear. Telling the president of the United States he is misguided on something is not an easy thing to do. Journalists writing about George W. Bush's White House have painted him as temperamental and sometimes hostile toward aides who brought him bad news.[20] George Stephanopoulos, a close aide to President Clinton, acknowledged frankly in his memoirs that he was too eager to ingratiate himself with Clinton because he saw himself in a competitive position with other staff aides. In retrospect, he realizes that he should have confronted Clinton early in the 1992 campaign about his infidelity. But, says Stephanopoulos, "I needed Clinton to see me as his defender, not his interrogator, which made me, of course, his enabler."[21]

The Vice President

The most important duty of the vice president is to take over the presidency in the event of presidential death, disability, impeachment, or resignation. Traditionally, vice presidents were not used in any important advisory capacity. Before passage of the Twenty-fifth Amendment to the Constitution in 1965, vice presidents who became president due to the death of their predecessor did not even select a new vice president.

Vice presidents have traditionally carried out political chores—campaigning, fundraising, and "stroking" the party faithful. This is often the case because vice-presidential candidates are chosen for reasons that have more to do with the political campaign than with governing the nation. Presidential candidates often choose vice-presidential candidates who appeal to a different geographic region or party coalition. Sometimes they even join forces with a rival from their political primary campaign. New Englander John Kennedy chose Texan Lyndon Johnson. Conservative Ronald Reagan selected George H. W. Bush, his more moderate rival in the Republican primaries. Washington outsider Jimmy Carter chose the experienced Senator Walter Mondale as his vice-presidential running mate.

President Carter broke the usual pattern of relegating the vice president to political

Brendan Smialowski / Getty Images

Next in Line

According to the Constitution, the vice president serves as president of the Senate, a largely ceremonial role, except for the ability to cast tie-breaking votes. Vice President Joe Biden knows the Senate well, having served as a senator from the state of Delaware for thirty-six years. In the Senate, Biden served on the Foreign Relations and Judiciary committees and wrote legislation such as the 1994 Violence against Women Act. Biden ran for the Democratic nomination for president twice before he was selected by Barack Obama to be the 2008 vice-presidential nominee.

chores, relying heavily on Mondale. Carter was wise enough to recognize that Mondale's experience in the Senate could be of great value to him, especially because Carter had never held national office. Al Gore played a significant role in the Clinton administration and was one of the president's most influential advisers. George W. Bush's vice president, Dick Cheney, was even more influential than his predecessors. Cheney was a powerful presence in the development of Bush's foreign policy agenda, championing the war in Iraq. He also believed that the presidency had been weakened over time, and he was a forceful proponent of the unitary executive theory.[22]

The Cabinet

The president's **cabinet** is composed of the heads of the departments of the executive branch and a small number of other key officials, such as the head of the OMB and the ambassador to the United Nations. The cabinet has expanded greatly since George Washington formed his first cabinet, which contained an attorney general and the secretaries of state, treasury, and war. Clearly, the growth of the cabinet to fifteen departments reflects an increase in government responsibility and intervention in areas such as energy, housing, and, most recently, homeland security.

cabinet
A group of presidential advisers; the heads of the executive departments and other key officials.

In theory, the members of the cabinet constitute an advisory body that meets with the president to debate major policy decisions. In practice, however, cabinet meetings have been described as "vapid non-events in which there has been a deliberate non-exchange of information as part of a process of mutual nonconsultation."[23] Why is this so? First, the cabinet has become rather large. Counting department heads, other officials of cabinet rank, and presidential aides, it is a body of at least twenty people—a size that many presidents find unwieldy for the give-and-take of political decision making. Second, most cabinet members have limited areas of expertise and cannot contribute much to deliberations in policy areas they know little about. The secretary of defense, for example, would probably be a poor choice to help decide important issues of agricultural policy. Third, the president often chooses cabinet members because of their reputations or to give his cabinet some racial, ethnic, geographic, gender, or religious balance, not because they are personally close to the president or easy for him to work with.

Finally, modern presidents do not rely on the cabinet to make policy because they have such large White House staffs, which offer most of the advisory support they need. And in contrast to cabinet secretaries, who may be pulled in different directions by the wishes of the president and those of their clientele groups, staffers in the White House Office are likely to see themselves as being responsible to the president alone. More broadly, presidents use their personal staff and the large Executive Office of the President to centralize control over the entire executive branch. The vast size of the executive branch and the number and complexity of decisions that must be made each day pose a challenge for the White House. Each president must be careful to appoint people to top administration positions who are not merely competent but also passionate about the president's goals and skillful enough to lead others in the executive branch to fight for the president's program instead of their own agendas. Ronald Reagan was especially good at communicating to his top appointees clear ideological principles that they were to follow in shaping administration policy. To fulfill more of their political goals and policy preferences, modern presidents have given their various staffs more responsibility for overseeing decision making throughout the executive branch.

★ 12.4 Presidential Leadership

★ Defend the argument that "Presidential power is the power to persuade."

A president's influence comes not only from his assigned responsibilities but also from his political skills and from how effectively he uses the resources of his office. His leadership is a function of his own character and skill, as well as the political environment in which he finds himself. Does he work with a congressional majority that favors his policy agenda? Are his goals in line with public opinion? Does he have the interpersonal skills and strength of character to be an effective leader?

Table 12.1 provides two rankings of U.S. presidents. One is based on a Gallup Poll of ordinary Americans; the other is based on a C-SPAN survey of fifty-eight prominent historians and professional observers of the presidency. In this section, we look at the factors that affect presidential performance—both those that reside in the person of the individual president and those that are features of the political context that he inherits. Why do some presidents rank higher than others?

TABLE 12.1   Presidential Greatness

This table provides two "top twelve" lists of American presidents. The first ranking comes from a Gallup Poll that asked ordinary Americans to name whom they regard as the greatest U.S. president. The second ranking comes from a survey of historians and observers of the presidency, who rated presidents according to their abilities, such as public persuasion, crisis leadership, economic management, moral authority, and relations with Congress. Although the rank order is different, nine presidents appear on both lists. Ordinary Americans are more likely to name recent presidents—Carter, Clinton, and George W. Bush—with whom they have had direct experience.

Gallup Poll Ratings		Historians' Ratings	
Rank	**President**	**Rank**	**President**
1	Abraham Lincoln	1	Abraham Lincoln
2	Ronald Reagan	2	Franklin Roosevelt
3	John F. Kennedy	3	George Washington
4	Bill Clinton	4	Theodore Roosevelt
5	Franklin Roosevelt	5	Harry Truman
6	George Washington	6	Woodrow Wilson
7	Harry Truman	7	Thomas Jefferson
8	George W. Bush	8	John F. Kennedy
9	Theodore Roosevelt	9	Dwight Eisenhower
10	Dwight Eisenhower	10	Lyndon Johnson
11	Thomas Jefferson	11	Ronald Reagan
12	Jimmy Carter	12	James K. Polk

Sources: Gallup Poll results are reported by Lydia Saad, "Lincoln Resumes Position as Americans' Top-Rated President," 19 February 2007, http://www.gallup.com. Copyright © 2010 Gallup, Inc. All rights reserved. The content is used with permission; however, Gallup retains all rights of republication. The historians' ranking is reported by the C-SPAN survey of Presidential Leadership 2000, www.americanpresidents.org/survey/historians/overall.asp. Copyright © 2000 C-SPAN.

Presidential Character

How does the public assess which presidential candidate has the best judgment and whether a candidate's character is suitable to the office? Americans must make a broad evaluation of the candidates' personalities and leadership styles. Although it's difficult to judge, character matters. One of Lyndon Johnson's biographers argues that Johnson had trouble extricating the United States from Vietnam because of insecurities about his masculinity. Johnson wanted to make sure he "was not forced to see himself as a coward, running away from Vietnam."[24] It's hard to know for sure whether this psychological interpretation is valid. Clearer, surely, is the tie between President Nixon's character and Watergate. Nixon had such an exaggerated fear of what his "enemies" might try to do to him that he created a climate in the White House that nurtured the Watergate break-in and subsequent cover-up.

Presidential character was at the forefront of national politics when it was revealed that President Clinton engaged in a sexual relationship with Monica Lewinsky, a White House intern half his age. Many argued that presidential authority is irreparably damaged when the president is perceived as personally untrustworthy or immoral. Yet despite the disgust and anger that Clinton's actions provoked, most Americans remained unconvinced that his behavior constituted an impeachable offense. The buoyant economy and the public's general satisfaction with Clinton's leadership strongly influenced the country's views on the matter. A majority of the House of Representatives voted to impeach him on the grounds of perjury and obstructing justice, but the Senate did not have the two-thirds majority necessary to convict Clinton, so he remained in office.

Scholars have identified personality traits such as strong self-esteem and emotional intelligence that are best suited to leadership positions like the American presidency.[25] In the media age, it often proves difficult to evaluate a candidate's personality when everyone tries to present himself or herself in a positive light. Even so, voters repeatedly claim that they care about traits such as leadership, integrity, and competence when casting their ballots (see Figure 12.1, p. 340).[26]

The Odd Couple

Former presidents Bill Clinton and George W. Bush don't see eye-to-eye on much, but they put differences aside when President Obama asked them to go to Haiti after the devastating earthquake in January 2010. Officially they were there to assess the damage to the country, but a more urgent purpose for the two presidents' visit was to encourage private donations to help Haiti rebuild.

AP Photo/Jorge Saenz

The President's Power to Persuade

In addition to desirable character traits, individual presidents must have the interpersonal and practical political skills to get things done. A classic analysis of the use of presidential resources is offered by Richard Neustadt in his book *Presidential Power*. Neustadt develops a model of how presidents gain, lose, or maintain their influence. His initial premise is simple enough: "Presidential power is the power to persuade."[27] Presidents, for all their resources—a skilled staff, extensive media coverage of presidential actions, the great respect the country holds for the office—must depend on others' cooperation to get things done. Harry Truman echoed Neustadt's premise when he said, "I sit here

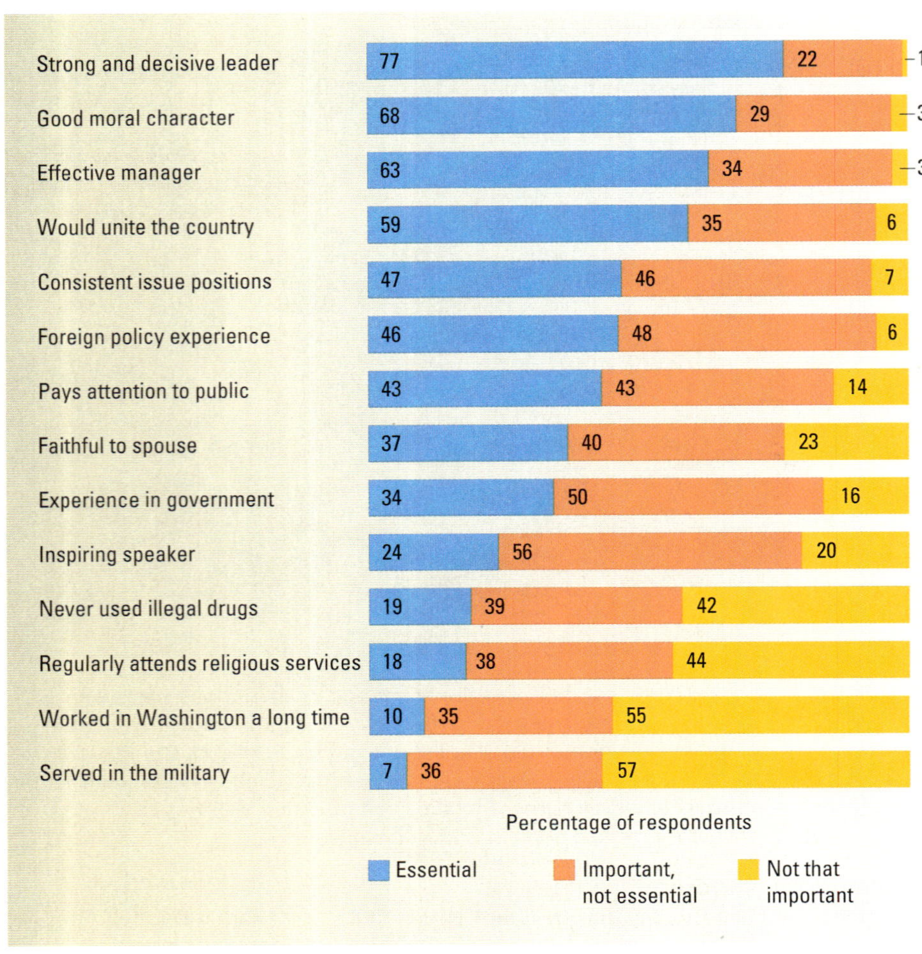

FIGURE 12.1 A Presidential Wish List

What qualities do you look for in a president? A survey asked Americans to rank various qualities and characteristics as "essential," "important, but not essential," or "not that important." Most Americans think that it is essential that the president be a strong leader and an effective manager. A majority also believes that the president should have a good moral character and focus on uniting the country. Americans want their president to have a lot of experience in government, but not necessarily in Washington. Military service and church attendance are less relevant qualities.

Source: Jeffrey M. Jones, "Wanted in the Next President: Honesty, Strong Leadership," 4 April 2007, http://www.gallup.com. Copyright © 2010 Gallup, Inc. All rights reserved. The content is used with permission; however, Gallup retains all rights of republication.

all day trying to persuade people to do the things they ought to have sense enough to do without my persuading them.... That's all the powers of the President amount to."[28]

Ability in bargaining, dealing with adversaries, and choosing priorities, according to Neustadt, separates above-average presidents from mediocre ones. A president must make wise choices about which policies to push and which to put aside until he can find more support. President Nixon described such decisions as a lot like poker. "I knew when to get out of a pot," said Nixon. "I didn't stick around when I didn't have the cards."[29] The president must decide when to accept compromise and when to stand on principle. He must know when to go public and when to work behind the scenes.

A president's political skills can be important in affecting outcomes in Congress. The president must choose his battles carefully and then try to use the force of his personality and the prestige of his office to forge an agreement among differing factions. When President Lyndon Johnson needed House Appropriations chair George Mahon (D-Tex.) to support him on an issue, he called Mahon on the phone and emphasized the value of Mahon's having a good long-term relationship with him. Speaking slowly to let every point sink in, Johnson told Mahon, "I know one thing … I know I'm right on this.... I know I mean more to you,… and Lubbock [Texas],… and your district,… and your State,—and your grandchildren, than Charlie Halleck [the Republican House leader] does."[30]

Neustadt stresses that a president's influence is related to his professional reputation and prestige. When a president pushes hard for a bill that Congress eventually defeats or weakens, the president's reputation is hurt. The public perceives him as ineffective or as showing poor judgment, and Congress becomes even less likely to cooperate with him in the future. The first President Bush believed he could get very little out of the Democratic-controlled Congress that he served alongside. His agenda was not ambitious, and his lack of accomplishments on the domestic side certainly worked against him when he ran (unsuccessfully) for reelection in 1992.

The President and the Public

Neustadt's analysis suggests that a popular president is more persuasive than an unpopular one. A popular president has more power to persuade because he can use his public support as a resource in the bargaining process. Members of Congress who know that the president is highly popular back home have more incentive to cooperate with the administration. If the president and his aides know that a member of Congress does not want to be seen as hostile to the president, they can apply more leverage to achieve a favorable compromise in a legislative struggle.

A familiar aspect of the modern presidency is the effort presidents devote to mobilizing public support for their programs. A president uses televised addresses (and the media coverage surrounding them), remarks to reporters, and public appearances to speak directly to the American people and convince them of the wisdom of his policies. Scholars have coined the phrase "going public" to describe situations where the president "forces compliance from fellow Washingtonians by going over their heads to appeal to their constituents."[31] Rather than bargain exclusively with a small number of party and committee leaders in Congress, the president rallies broad coalitions of support as though undertaking a political campaign.

Since public opinion is a resource for modern presidents, they pay close attention to their standing in the polls. Presidents closely monitor their approval ratings or "popularity," which is a report card on how well they are performing their duties. Presidential popularity is typically at its highest during a president's first year in office. This "honeymoon period" affords the president a particularly good opportunity to use public support to get some of his programs through Congress. Over time, economic conditions exert an enormous impact on a president's approval rating (see Figure 12.2).

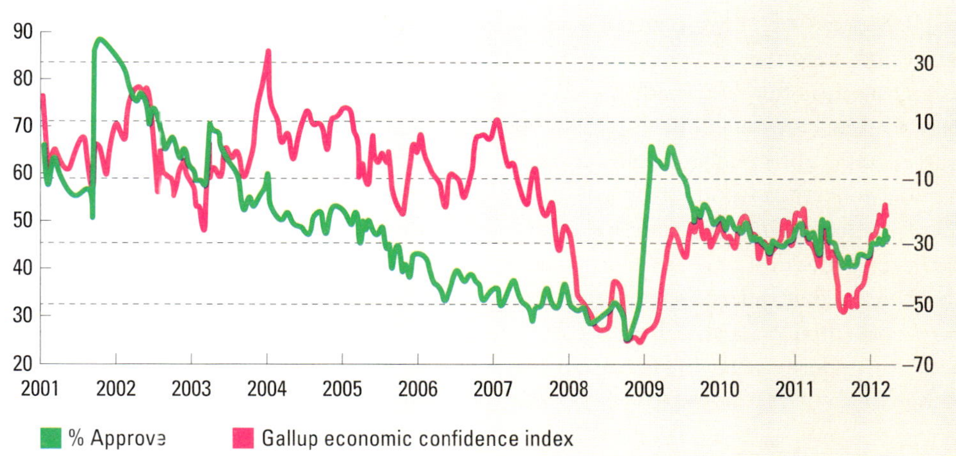

FIGURE 12.2 It All Goes Back to the Economy

The economy is always critical to each president's standing with the American public. As shown here for the Bush and Obama years, each president's approval rating closely tracks a composite index of economic conditions as measured by the Gallup Poll. There are fluctuations reflecting events other than economic conditions, of course, but over time, there is a strong correlation between popularity and economic performance.

Source: Lydia Saad, "Obama's Job Approval Tied to Economic Confidence in 2012," Gallup Poll, 19 March 2012. http://www.gallup.com. Copyright © 2012 Gallup, Inc. All rights reserved. The content is used with permission; however, Gallup retains all rights of republication.

Scholarly research demonstrates that energetic and well-planned efforts by presidents to influence public opinion are likely to have little effect. As political scientist George Edwards concludes, "Presidents cannot reshape the contours of the political landscape to pave the way for change."[32] Perhaps the most difficult obstacle presidents face is a lack of serious attention by the public. The vast majority of Americans have limited interest in policymaking and a presidential speech may fall on deaf ears. Even a televised address to the nation carried by major networks may be ignored.[33]

President Obama's endeavor to convince the American public to back his program for health-care reform is a case in point. Throughout the spring, summer, and fall of 2009, Obama worked continually to rally public opinion to his side. Through speeches, forums, press interviews, and other efforts, he labored to make Americans understand the benefits of the program. He failed to move opinion, and his own popularity declined during this time.[34] Unemployment and the continuing recession were the primary causes of his sagging popularity, but unfavorable attitudes toward the health-care proposal may have contributed to his problems as well.[35]

The president's power to persuade seems more potent within his own party.[36] Obama was effective at prodding his own party in Congress to support his proposal, which eventually passed. Legislators' own chances of reelection can be influenced by a president's public standing in his own party. Still, presidents are right to be wary of backing legislation that the voters back home don't like. Presidential persuasion may make the difference when a vote looms in Congress.

In multiparty parliamentary systems, a prime minister's loss of public support may cause some parties in a ruling coalition to quit the coalition. Such action is designed to inoculate the members of such parties in the parliament from the unpopularity of the prime minister. The coalition formed by Italian politician and businessman Silvio Berlusconi first won office in the 1994 Italian elections, but a scandal ensued and one of the parties in his coalition pulled out. This left Berlusconi without a majority, and new elections had to be held. Later, when Berlusconi was back in office as Italian prime minister, the lack of public support helped bring about his resignation in 2011 (see "Compared with What? From Berlusconi to Bankruptcy: The Costs of Failed Leadership," pp. 344–345).[37]

Presidents' obsessive concern with public opinion can be defended as a means of furthering majoritarian democracy: the president tries to gauge what the people want so that he can offer policies that reflect popular preferences. As discussed in Chapter 2, responsiveness to the public's views is a bedrock principle of democracy, and presidents should respond to public opinion as well as try to lead it. Some believe that presidents are too concerned about their popularity and are unwilling to champion unpopular causes or take principled stands that may affect their poll ratings. Yet research shows that presidents don't always follow public opinion and, rather, push many proposals and policies that reflect their own priorities rather than the public's.[38] Commenting on the presidential polls that first became widely used during his term, Harry Truman said, "I wonder how far Moses would have gone if he'd taken a poll in Egypt?"[39]

The Political Context

One thing we learn from the health-care case is that the strategy of leading by courting public opinion has considerable risks. Since it is not easy to move public opinion, presidents who plan to use it as leverage in dealing with Congress are left highly vulnerable if public support for their position does not materialize. The health-care case also showed us that all issues are not created equal. The public cared far more about the state of the economy than it did about Obama's health-care plan. A president's popularity can also be affected by external events, such as some international calamity.

Some presidents have the benefit of working on legislation while their own political party has a majority in both chambers of Congress. Others are fortunate to serve when the economy is good. Still others have large election victories that facilitate greater policy achievements.

Partisans in Congress. Generally, presidents have their greatest success in Congress during the period immediately following their inauguration, which is also the peak of their popularity. One of the best predictors of presidential success in Congress is the number of fellow partisans in Congress, particularly whether the president's party has a majority in each chamber. Presidential success in Congress is measured by how often the president wins his way on congressional roll call votes on which he takes a clear position. George W. Bush's success rate hovered around 75 percent during his first six years in office with a Republican Congress. After the Democrats won control of Congress in 2006, his success rate fell to 38 percent.[40] With large majorities in both the House and the Senate during his first two years in office, Barack Obama did very well with the Congress and got major pieces of legislation such as the economic stimulus package and the health-care plan enacted.

The American political system poses a challenge for presidents and their policy agendas because the president is elected independently of Congress. Often this leads to **divided government**, with one party controlling the White House and the other party controlling at least one house of Congress. This may seem politically schizophrenic, with the electorate saying one thing by electing a president from one party and another by its vote for legislators of the other party. This does not appear to bother the American people, however, as divided government is fairly common.

Scholars are divided about the impact of divided government. Despite the differences in the scholarly literature, however, political scientists generally don't believe that divided government inevitably produces **gridlock**, a situation in which government is incapable of acting on important policy issues. In recent years, however, there has been a pattern of increasingly partisan voting in Congress: Republicans voting in a relatively unified pattern while Democrats also vote in an increasingly unified manner.[41]

divided government
The situation in which one party controls the White House and the other controls at least one house of Congress.

gridlock
A situation in which government is incapable of acting on important issues.

Elections. In his farewell address to the nation, Jimmy Carter lashed out at the interest groups that had plagued his presidency. Interest groups, he said, "distort our purposes because the national interest is not always the sum of all our single or special interests." Carter noted the president's singular responsibility: "The president is the only elected official charged with representing all the people."[42] Like all other presidents, Carter quickly recognized the dilemma of majoritarianism versus pluralism after he took office. The president must try to please countless separate constituencies while trying to do what is best for the whole country.

It is easy to stand on the sidelines and say that presidents should always try to follow a majoritarian path, pursuing policies that reflect the preferences of most citizens. However, simply by running for office, candidates align themselves with particular segments of the population. As a result of their electoral strategy, their identification with activists in their party, and their own political views, candidates come into office with an interest in pleasing some constituencies more than others.

As the election campaign proceeds, each candidate tries to win votes from different groups of voters through his stand on various issues. Because issue stances can cut both ways—attracting some voters but driving others away—candidates may try to finesse an issue by being deliberately vague. Candidates sometimes hope that voters will put their own interpretations on ambiguous stances. If the tactic works, the candidate will attract some voters without offending others.

Compared with What?

From Berlusconi to Bankruptcy: The Costs of Failed Leadership

Italy has gone bust. Countries go bankrupt when they can't pay their bills, and Italy reached that point in 2011 when lenders were charging such high interest rates to purchase the country's bonds that it could not continue to meet the borrowing costs. International institutions, principally the International Monetary Fund and the European Central Bank, had to step in and essentially guarantee payment for Italy's debt.

Italy's descent into economic chaos is, in part, a reflection of the severe recession that hit Europe when the financial markets around the world hemorrhaged in 2008. Yet not all of Europe's economies were destabilized by the recession. Italy's difficulties also reflect problems of leadership, in particular the failures of Silvio Berlusconi. For most of the period between 2001 and 2011, the controversial Berlusconi served as prime minister.

Before entering politics, Berlusconi was a successful businessman who built an enormous television empire. Some of his greatest profits came from quiz shows where an attractive young woman would take off an article of clothing every time she answered a question incorrectly. Those television networks, which dominate Italy's television market, relentlessly promoted his career. As a politician Berlusconi created his own political party, *Forza Italia,* and in Italy's multiparty parliamentary system, Berlusconi's faction became the dominant partner in the conservative coalition in the legislature. Berlusconi's own politics, however, were a curious mixture of conservative and liberal positions.

Despite his campaign promises, what Berlusconi did not do in office was to effectively address a number of serious structural problems in Italy's economy. Most significant is Italy's labor laws, which make it extremely difficult for a company to fire any of its employees. In turn, this inhibits economic expansion. For example, companies might be afraid to take on additional workers for a new product line because should it fail, the company will still be stuck with the employees who were hired to work on that product. The lack of growth in the economy generated unemployment, a problem that it is especially acute among the young. Fully 30 percent of young Italians are unemployed, and this has produced a dispirited generation.

Berlusconi also fell short in terms of integrity and appropriate behavior. He's been indicted nine times, only to be saved by a judicial system that has always seemed poised to rescue him. Six times the charges were eventually dismissed because the statute of limitations ran out before the process had been completed. He is also an inveterate womanizer, and his second wife divorced him during his tenure as prime minister because of his infidelity. When he was sixty-eight and serving as prime minister he disappeared for three weeks, keeping the country in the dark as to his whereabouts, only to return with a facelift. One of his mansions became known for sex parties in the "bunga bunga" room. He also became involved with a Moroccan night club dancer known as Ruby the Heart Stealer. She turned out to be under-aged, and Berlusconi was indicted for paying for sex with a seventeen-year-old. Those charges are still pending.

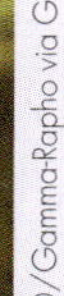

2430/Gamma-Rapho via Getty Images

Antoine Antoniol/Getty Images

The European Union and the International Monetary Fund made Berlusconi's removal a requirement for continued assistance to the beleaguered country. He had also become massively unpopular with Italians, and he had no choice but to resign. After he stepped down in November of 2011, Berlusconi (top) was replaced by a caretaker government headed by Mario Monti (bottom), an Italian technocrat who was working for the European Union. Monti is well respected in and outside of Italy, but he has his work cut out for him. Italy's economic woes are acute, and his government sits atop a fractured political system.

electoral mandate
An endorsement by voters. Presidents sometimes argue they have been given a mandate to carry out policy proposals.

But candidates cannot be deliberately vague about all issues. A candidate who is noncommittal on too many issues appears wishy-washy. And future presidents do not build their political careers without working strongly for and becoming associated with important issues and constituencies. Moreover, after the election is over, the winning candidate wants to claim that he has been given an **electoral mandate**, or endorsement, by the voters to carry out the policy platform on which he campaigned. Newly chosen presidents make a majoritarian interpretation of the electoral process, claiming that their electoral victory is an expression of the direct will of the people. For such a claim to be credible, the candidate must have emphasized some specific issues during the campaign and offered some distinctive solutions. As the franchise was extended to more ordinary citizens in the early nineteenth century, it became more credible for presidents to claim that their actions reflected a mandate of some sort. One of Andrew Jackson's biographers notes that in his first year in office Jackson claimed a mandate from voters to kill the government's national bank, and this link between votes and public policy marked "a turning point in the making of the modern presidency."[43]

Candidates who win by large margins are more likely to claim mandates and ask for major policy changes.[44] Although many presidents claim that the votes they receive at the polls are expressions of support for their policy proposals, it is often difficult to document concrete evidence of broad public support for the range of specific policies a winning candidate wants to pursue.

Political Party Systems. An individual president's election is just one in a series of contests between the major political parties in the United States. As noted in Chapter 8, American political history is marked by eras in which one of the major political parties tends to dominate national-level politics, consistently capturing the presidency and majorities in the Senate and House of Representatives. Scholars of the American presidency have noted that presidential leadership is shaped by the president's relationship to the dominant political party and its policy agenda.[45]

Presidential leadership is determined in part by whether the president is a member of the dominant political party and whether the public policies and political philosophy associated with his party have widespread support. A president will have a greater opportunity to change public policy when he is in the majority and the opposing political party is perceived to be unable to solve major national problems. Presidents who are affiliated with the dominant political party have larger majorities in Congress and more public support for their party's policy agenda.

Presidents who come to power right after critical elections have the most favorable environment for exerting strong presidential leadership. Franklin Roosevelt, for instance, came to office when the Republican Party was unable to offer solutions to the economic crisis of the Great Depression. He enjoyed a landslide victory and large Democratic majorities in Congress, and he proposed fundamental changes in government and public policy. The weakest presidents are those, like Herbert Hoover, who are constrained by their affiliation with a political party that is perceived to stand for worn-out ideas. Democratic presidents like Truman and Johnson, who followed FDR, were also well positioned to achieve policy success and further their party program since they were affiliated with the dominant New Deal coalition. Republicans Eisenhower and Nixon faced different leadership challenges: they needed to cultivate the support of voters and legislators in both parties in order to achieve a successful legislative program.

Upon taking office, Barack Obama envisioned a changing party landscape with the Democrats emerging as the dominant party. He believed that the changing demographics of the country would help the party as minorities exhibit a strong preference for the Democrats. Young voters also showed an inclination for the party (in part because young voters are a more diverse population than older cohorts).[46] In the short run, at least, Obama's optimism ran into the reality of the economic downturn and the resulting voter disenchantment with the Democrats.

12.5 The President as National Leader

★ Compare and contrast the different roles that the president plays as national leader.

With an election behind him and the resources of his office at hand, a president is ready to lead the nation. Although not every president's leadership is acclaimed, each president enters office with a general vision of how government should approach policy issues. During his term, a president spends much of his time trying to get Congress to enact legislation that reflects his general philosophy and specific policy preferences.

From Political Values ...

Presidents differ greatly in their views of the role of government. Lyndon Johnson had a strong liberal ideology concerning domestic affairs. He believed that government has a responsibility to help disadvantaged Americans. Johnson described his vision of justice in his inaugural address:

> Justice was the promise that all who made the journey would share in the fruits of the land.
>
> In a land of wealth, families must not live in hopeless poverty. In a land rich in harvest, children just must not go hungry. In a land of healing miracles, neighbors must not suffer and die untended. In a great land of learning and scholars, young people must be taught to read and write.
>
> For [the] more than thirty years that I have served this nation, I have believed that this injustice to our people, this waste of our resources, was our real enemy. For thirty years or more, with the resources I have had, I have vigilantly fought against it.[47]

Johnson used *justice* and *injustice* as code for *equality* and *inequality*. He used those words six times in his speech; he used *freedom* only twice. Johnson used his popularity, his skills, and the resources of his office to press for a "just" America—a "Great Society."

To achieve his Great Society, Johnson sent Congress an unprecedented package of liberal legislation. He launched projects such as the Job Corps (which created centers and camps offering vocational training and work experience to youths aged sixteen to twenty-one), Medicare (which provided medical care for the elderly), and the National Teacher Corps (which paid teachers to work in impoverished neighborhoods). Supported by huge Democratic majorities in Congress during 1965 and 1966, he had tremendous success getting his proposals through. Liberalism was in full swing.

In 1985, exactly twenty years after Johnson's inaugural speech, Ronald Reagan took his oath of office for the second time. Addressing the nation, Reagan reasserted his conservative philosophy. He emphasized freedom, using the term fourteen times, and failed to mention justice or equality once. In the following excerpt, we have italicized the term *freedom* for easy reference:

> By 1980, we knew it was time to renew our faith, to strive with all our strength toward the ultimate in individual *freedom* consistent with an orderly

AP Photo

Diana Walker/Time & Life Images/Getty Images

Different Visions

Lyndon Johnson and Ronald Reagan had strikingly different visions of American democracy and what their goals should be as president. Johnson was committed to equality for all, and major civil rights laws are among the most important legacies of his administration. He is pictured here signing the 1964 Civil Rights Act. Reagan was devoted to reducing the size of government so as to enhance freedom. He worked hard to reduce both taxes and spending.

society.... We will not rest until every American enjoys the fullness of *freedom,* dignity, and opportunity as our birthright.... Americans ... turned the tide of history away from totalitarian darkness and into the warm sunlight of human *freedom....*

Let history say of us, these were golden years—when the American Revolution was reborn, when *freedom* gained new life, when America reached for her best.... *Freedom* and incentives unleash the drive and entrepreneurial genius that are at the core of human progress.... From new *freedom* will spring new opportunities for growth.... Yet history has shown that peace does not come, nor will our *freedom* be preserved by goodwill alone. There are those in the world who scorn our vision of human dignity and *freedom....* Human *freedom* is on the march, and nowhere more so than in our own hemisphere. *Freedom* is one of the deepest and noblest aspirations of the human spirit.... America must remain *freedom's* staunchest friend, for *freedom* is our best ally.... Every victory for human *freedom* will be a victory for world peace.... One people under God, dedicated to the dream of *freedom* that He has placed in the human heart.[48]

Reagan turned Johnson's philosophy on its head, declaring that "government is not the solution to our problem. Government *is* the problem." During his presidency, Reagan worked to undo many welfare and social service programs and cut funding for programs such as the Job Corps and food stamps. By the end of his term, there had been a fundamental shift in federal spending, with sharp increases in defense spending and "decreases in federal social programs [which] served to defend Democratic interests and constituencies."[49]

... to Policy Agenda

The roots of particular policy proposals, then, can be traced to the more general political ideology of the president. Presidential candidates outline that philosophy of government during their campaign for the White House as they attempt to mobilize voters and interest groups. After the election, presidents and their staffs continue to identify and track support among different kinds of voters as they decide how to translate their general philosophy into concrete legislative proposals.

When the hot rhetoric of the presidential campaign meets the cold reality of what is possible in Washington, the newly elected president must make some hard choices about what to push for during the coming term. These choices are reflected in the bills the president submits to Congress, as well as in the degree to which he works for their passage. The president's bills, introduced by his allies in the House and Senate, always receive a good deal of initial attention. In the words of one Washington lobbyist, "When a president sends up a bill, it takes first place in the queue. All other bills take second place."[50]

The president's role in legislative leadership is largely a twentieth-century phenomenon. A critical change came with Franklin Roosevelt. With the nation in the midst of the Great Depression, Roosevelt began his first term in 1933 with an ambitious array of legislative proposals. During the first one hundred days Congress was in session, it enacted fifteen significant laws, including the Agricultural Adjustment Act, the act creating the Civilian Conservation Corps, and the National Industrial Recovery Act. Never before had a president demanded—and received—so much from Congress. Roosevelt's legacy was that the president would henceforth provide aggressive leadership of Congress through his own legislative program.

Chief Lobbyist

When Franklin D. Roosevelt and Harry Truman first became heavily involved in preparing legislative packages, political scientists typically described the process as one in which "the president proposes and Congress disposes." In other words, once the president sends his legislation to Capitol Hill, Congress decides what to do with it. Over time, though, presidents have become increasingly active in all stages of the legislative process. The president is expected not only to propose legislation but also to make sure that it passes.

The president's efforts to influence Congress are reinforced by the work of his legislative liaison staff. All departments and major agencies have legislative specialists as well. These department and agency people work with the White House liaison staff to coordinate the administration's lobbying on major issues.

The **legislative liaison staff** is the communications link between the White House and Congress. As a bill slowly makes its way through Congress, liaison staffers advise the president or a cabinet secretary on the problems that emerge. They specify what parts of a bill are in trouble and may have to be modified or dropped. They tell their boss what amendments are likely to be offered, which members of Congress need to be lobbied, and what the bill's chances for passage are with or without certain provisions. Decisions on how the administration will respond to such developments must then be reached. For example, when the Reagan White House realized that it was still a few votes short of victory on a budget bill in the House, it reversed its opposition to a sugar price support bill. This attracted the votes of representatives from Louisiana and Florida, two sugar-growing states, for the budget bill. The White House would not call what happened a deal, but it noted that "adjustments and considerations" had been made.[51] Still, not all demands from legislators can be met.

A certain amount of the president's job consists of stereotypical arm twisting—pushing reluctant legislators to vote a certain way. The president also talks to legislators to seek their advice and takes soundings from committee chairs on what proposals can get through and what must be modified or abandoned. During Obama's first four months in office, four hundred representatives and senators were brought to the White House to speak to the president or attend meetings or other events.[52] Yet most day-in, day-out interactions between the White House and Congress tend to be more mundane, with the liaison staff trying to build support by working cooperatively with legislators.

The White House also works directly with interest groups in its efforts to build support for legislation. Presidential aides hope key lobbyists will activate the most effective lobbyists of all: the voters back home. Interest groups can quickly reach the constituents who are most concerned about a bill, using their communications network to mobilize members to write, call, or e-mail their members of Congress. There

legislative liaison staff
Those people who act as the communications link between the White House and Congress, advising the president or cabinet secretaries on the status of pending legislation.

are so many interest groups in our pluralist political system that they could easily overload the White House with their demands. Consequently, except for those groups most important to the president, lobbies tend to be granted access only when the White House needs them to activate public opinion. During the titanic struggle over health-care legislation, the Obama White House knew it needed a great deal of interest group support. It cut a number of deals with the insurance and pharmaceutical industries to make the president's proposal more palatable to them.

Agreement with Congress cannot always be reached, and sometimes Congress may pass a bill the president opposes. In such a case the president may veto the bill and send it back to Congress; Congress can override a veto with a two-thirds majority of those voting in each house. Presidents use their veto power sparingly, but as we noted earlier, the threat that a president will veto an unacceptable bill increases his bargaining leverage with members of Congress.

Party Leader

Part of the president's job is to lead his party.[53] This is very much an informal duty, with no prescribed tasks. In this respect, American presidents are considerably different from European prime ministers, who are the formal leaders of their party in the national legislature, as well as the head of their government. In the American system, a president and members of his party in Congress can clearly take very different positions on the issues before them.

As Congress has turned more partisan, presidents have focused more on leadership of their own party rather than trying to bridge differences between the two parties.[54] With less of a moderate middle to work with in Congress, a president needs to work hard to unify his party around his priorities. Increasingly, the public regards presidents as partisan leaders rather than unifying national leaders. Polls show that Americans have evaluated recent presidents, notably Ronald Reagan, Bill Clinton, George W. Bush, and Barack Obama, through a largely partisan prism. Republican identifiers love Republican presidents and despise Democratic ones. Likewise, Democratic identifiers like presidents of their own party and are contemptuous of Republican ones (see Figure 12.3).[55]

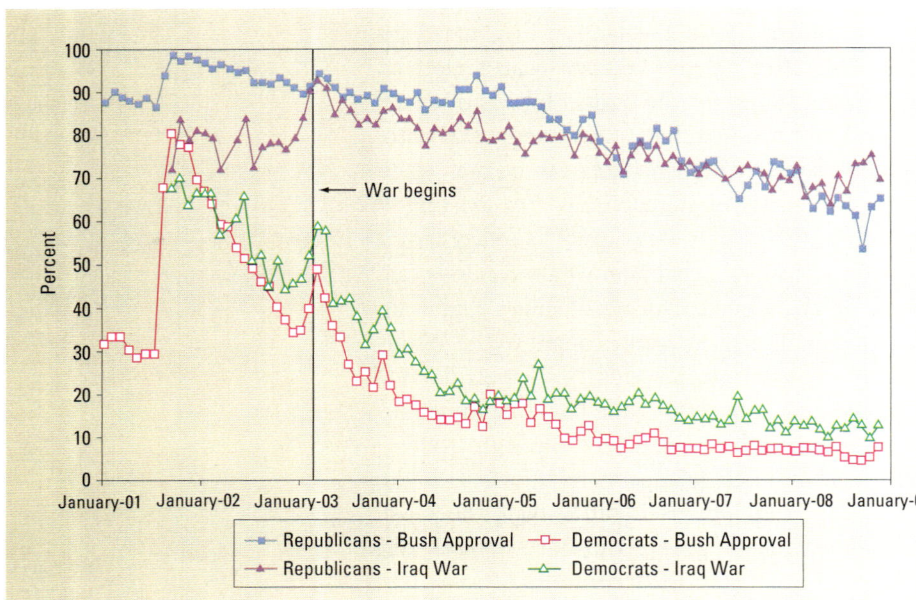

FIGURE 12.3 Through Partisan Eyes

How we evaluate a president's performance is strongly shaped by our own partisan predisposition. As illustrated here, Republicans were much more likely to approve of George W. Bush's presidency than were Democrats. For their part, Democrats became quite critical of Bush after he directed the country's armed forces to invade Iraq. The same partisan pattern can be found in evaluations of Barack Obama.

Source: Gary C. Jacobson, "Perception, Memory, and Partisan Polarization on the Iraq War," *Political Science Quarterly* 152 (Spring 2010), p. 31–56. Copyright © 2010 The Academy of Political Science. Reprinted by permission.

The president himself has become the "fundraiser in chief" for his party. Since presidents have a vital interest in more members of their party being elected to the House and Senate, they have a strong incentive to spend time raising money for congressional candidates. All incumbent presidents travel frequently to fundraising dinners in different states, where they are the main attraction. Donors pay substantial sums—$1,000 a ticket is common—to go to such a dinner. In addition to helping elect more members of his party, a not-so-small by-product for the president is the gratitude of legislators. It's a lot harder to say no to a president's request for help on a bill when he spoke at your fundraiser during the last election.

12.6 The President as World Leader

★ Analyze the role of the president within the context of the changing nature of global politics.

The president's leadership responsibilities extend beyond Congress and the nation to the international arena. Each administration tries to further what it sees as the country's best interests in its relations with allies, adversaries, and the developing countries of the world. In this role, the president must be ready to act as diplomat and crisis manager (see "Politics of Global Change: Frequent Flyer" on p. 352).

Foreign Relations

From the end of World War II until the late 1980s, presidents were preoccupied with containing communist expansion around the globe. Truman and Korea, Kennedy and Cuba, Johnson and Nixon and Vietnam, and Reagan and Nicaragua are just some examples of presidents and the communist crosses they had to bear. Presidents not only used overt and covert military means to fight communism but also tried to reduce tensions through negotiations. President Nixon made particularly important strides in this regard, completing an important arms control agreement with the Soviet Union and beginning negotiations with China, with which the United States had had no formal diplomatic relations.

With the collapse of communism in the Soviet Union and Eastern Europe, American presidents entered a new era in international relations, but they are still concerned with three fundamental objectives (see Chapter 19 for a more detailed discussion of American foreign policy). First is national security, the direct protection of the United States and its citizens from external threats. National security has been highlighted since the September 11 terrorist attacks. After U.S. intelligence sources pinpointed the hiding place of Osama bin Laden in Pakistan, a special forces operation was carried out during which Navy Seals stormed his compound and shot him to death. President Obama received an immediate boost in the public's estimation of him by appearing to be effective in keeping Americans safe.[56]

Committing military force to pursue American foreign policy objectives is a highly risky endeavor. President Obama was put in a difficult position when a democracy movement erupted in Egypt, challenging the rule of Hosni Mubarak. Mubarak was a dictator but a staunch American ally in a volatile region. Obama chose to distance the United States from Mubarak, assuming (correctly, as it turned out) that a revolution would succeed and Mubarak would fall.

Politics of Global Change

Frequent Flyer

It's a simple but telling statistic about globalization. Over time, presidents are increasingly spending more days overseas. Some of this involves visiting American troops stationed across the globe. Most presidential travel, however, involves diplomacy and negotiation. Presidents traverse the world to meet with other foreign leaders to try to reach understandings or formal accords to address common problems. Some meetings, like that of the leaders of the G-20 nations, are scheduled periodically to allow the heads of state of largest economies to consult with each other.

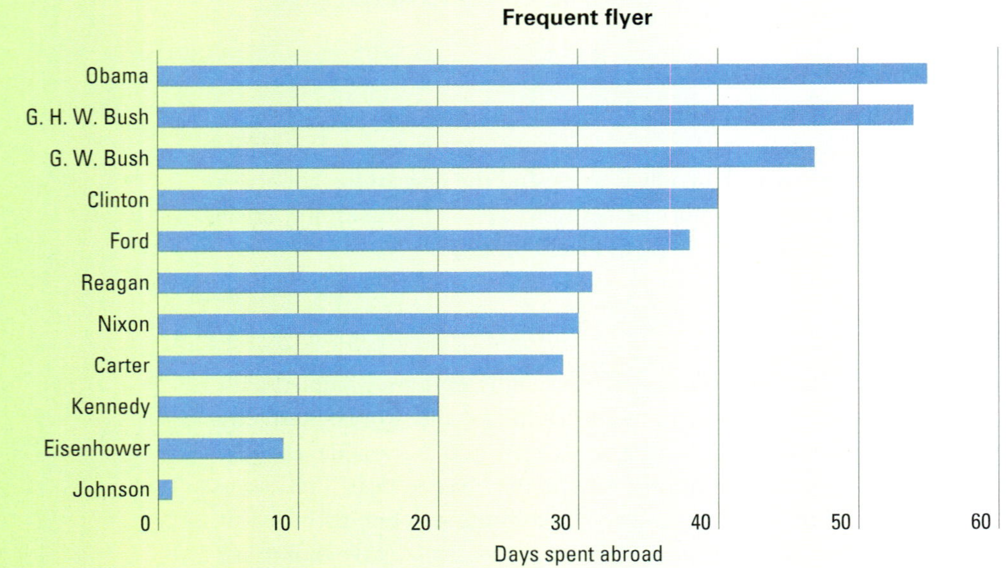

SOURCE: Demian Brady, "Incredible Journey," National Taxpayers Union Foundation, November 23, 2010, http://www.ntu.org/ntuf/incredible-journey.html. Figures are for the first two years of each presidency.

Second is fostering a peaceful international environment. Presidents work with international organizations like the United Nations and the North Atlantic Treaty Organization (NATO) to seek an end to regional conflicts throughout the world. In some cases, like the ongoing dispute between Palestinians and Israelis, the United States has played a central role in mediating conflict and facilitating bargaining between opposing sides. In other cases, presidents send the U.S. military to participate in multinational peace-keeping forces to ensure stability, enforce negotiated peace plans, and monitor democratic elections. The United States may impose trade sanctions to discourage human rights violations.

A third objective is the protection of U.S. economic interests. The new presidential job description places much more emphasis on managing economic relations with the rest of the world. Trade relations are an especially difficult problem because presidents must balance the conflicting interests of foreign countries (many of them allies), the interests of particular American industries, the overall needs of the American economy, and the demands of the legislative branch.

Crisis Management

Periodically the president faces a grave situation in which conflict is imminent or a small conflict threatens to explode into a larger war. Because handling such episodes is a critical part of the presidency, citizens may vote for candidates who project careful judgment. One reason for Barry Goldwater's crushing defeat in the 1964 election was his warlike image and rhetoric, which scared many Americans. Fearing that Goldwater would be too quick to resort to nuclear weapons, they voted for Lyndon Johnson instead.

A president must be able to exercise good judgment and remain cool in crisis situations. Henry Kissinger, secretary of state during the Nixon years, notes, "Historians rarely do justice to the psychological stress on a policymaker."[57] John Kennedy's behavior during the Cuban missile crisis of 1962 has become a model of effective crisis management. When the United States learned that the Soviet Union had placed missiles containing nuclear warheads in Cuba, Kennedy saw those missiles as an unacceptable threat to U.S. security. He asked a group of senior aides, including top people from the Pentagon, to advise him on feasible military and diplomatic responses. Kennedy considered an invasion of Cuba and air strikes against the missiles but eventually chose a less dangerous response: a naval blockade. He also privately signaled to Soviet leader Nikita Khrushchev that if the Soviet Union withdrew its missiles from Cuba, the United States would remove American missiles from Turkey.[58] Although the Soviet Union complied, the world held its breath for a short time over the very real possibility of a nuclear war.

What guidelines determine what a president should do in times of crisis?[59] Drawing on a range of advisers and opinions is one. Not acting in unnecessary haste is another. A third is having a well-designed, formal review process with thorough analysis and open debate. A fourth guideline is rigorously examining the reasoning underlying all options to ensure that their assumptions are valid. When President Kennedy backed a CIA plan for a rebel invasion of Cuba by expatriates hostile to Fidel Castro, he did not know that its chances for success were based on unfounded assumptions of immediate uprisings by the Cuban population. Had Kennedy been more aggressive in questioning intelligence officials, he might have chosen to stop the operation. The invasion by a hapless and poorly equipped rebel group went ahead, only to be crushed immediately by the Cuban army. This resulted in an enormous embarrassment for the United States and a stain on Kennedy's reputation.

Ralph Crane/Time Life Pictures/Getty Images

Crisis in Camelot

In October 1962, people gathered in the electronics section of a store to watch President Kennedy address the nation on the Cuban missile crisis. When the United States learned that the Soviet Union was placing missile bases in Cuba, Kennedy demanded that the Soviets remove their missiles, and he ordered a naval blockade. After seven days, Soviet leader Nikita Khrushchev complied with Kennedy's demands, and direct conflict between the two major superpowers was avoided. Cuba's leader at that time, Fidel Castro, had seized power in 1959 and aligned himself with the Soviet Union during the Cold War.

SUMMARY

Presidential leadership is shaped by the president's ability to bargain, persuade, and make wise choices. Over time, presidential power has grown as presidents have interpreted their constitutional authority more broadly. At the same time, there are substantial constraints on presidents, notably the Congress, which may have very different goals.

12.1 The Constitutional Basis of Presidential Power

- The formal powers of the presidency are set forth in Article II of the Constitution.

12.2 The Expansion of Presidential Power

- Informal powers, those not explicitly stated in the Constitution, complement a president's formal powers.
- A significant source of the growth in presidential power derives from Congress's delegation of authority to the executive branch.

12.3 The Executive Branch Establishment

- The president is surrounded by a staff of advisors who provide support and analysis of pending decisions and of broader strategic direction.
- The primary components of the presidential advisory system are his personal staff, the Executive Office of the President, the vice president, and the cabinet.

12.4 Presidential Leadership

- A part of a president's power is his power to persuade.
- A president's relationship with the public is highly influenced by Americans' evaluation of his performance in office.
- A president's ability to get things done is largely contingent on political factors, particularly the relative division of the two parties in the Congress.

12.5 The President as National Leader

- Leadership is structured by vision, and vision reflects a president's ideological orientation.
- Over time, presidents have come to play a critical role in preparing a package of proposals (an agenda) for introduction in the Congress. They then lobby for those proposals.
- Presidents are also leaders of their party, offering direction in terms of policy as well as engaging in more mundane activities, such as raising campaign money for congressional allies.

12.6 The President as World Leader

- Presidents not only lead the United States but also are important leaders of formal and informal alliances among democracies.

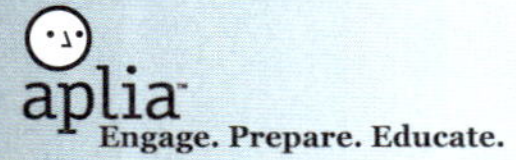

ASSESSING YOUR UNDERSTANDING WITH APLIA...YOUR VIRTUAL TUTOR!

12.1 Assess whether the constitutional powers of the president form a strong basis for the modern presidency.

1. What is the underlying philosophy that guided the framers in determining the power of the presidency and, indeed, in structuring the entire Constitution?
2. What are the major formal powers of the presidency as listed in Article II of the Constitution?

12.2 Illustrate how claims of inherent powers augment the formal powers of the presidency.

1. Why have the powers of the presidency grown over time?
2. What are the differences between formal powers and inherent powers?

12.3 Assess the role played by the various executive branch institutions as resources for an effective president.

1. What constitutes the Executive Office of the President?
2. Why does the cabinet not play a major role as a *body* of advisers?

12.4 Defend the argument that "Presidential power is the power to persuade."

1. How might presidential character affect presidential performance?
2. What constitutes the "power to persuade"?
3. What are the contextual factors that can influence the course of a presidency?

12.5 Compare and contrast the different roles that the president plays as national leader.

1. What fundamental political values distinguish the differences between conservative Republican presidents and liberal Democratic ones?
2. How does a president work to influence Congress?

12.6 Analyze the role of the president within the context of the changing nature of global politics.

1. What are the president's primary responsibilities in terms of leadership in foreign affairs?

13 The Bureaucracy

CHAPTER TOPICS and Learning Outcomes

13.1 Organization Matters
★ Define the concept of bureaucracy, explain the role of organizations on the administration of the nation's laws, examine the reasons for the growth of the bureaucratic state, and assess arguments for and against its continued expansion.

13.2 Bureaus and Bureaucrats
★ Describe the organization of the executive branch, the role of the civil service, and the bureaucracy's responsiveness to presidential control.

13.3 Administrative Policymaking: The Formal Processes
★ Describe the roles of administrative discretion and rule-making authority in the execution of administrative policymaking.

13.4 Administrative Policymaking: Informal Politics
★ Analyze how incrementalism and bureaucratic culture affect policymaking.

13.5 Problems in Implementing Policy
★ Identify obstacles to effective policy implementation.

13.6 Reforming the Bureaucracy: More Control or Less?
★ Compare the strengths and weaknesses of reform efforts aimed at increasing the effectiveness of the bureaucracy's performance.

Time was of the essence. When twenty-year-old Katie Wilcox and her boyfriend woke up in the morning and realized they had had unprotected sex the night before, they quickly went out to a pharmacy. Explaining why they hadn't used birth control, Wilcox said, "We kind of got caught up in the moment." At the drug store, Wilcox showed her ID to prove that she met the minimum age of seventeen to be able to purchase Plan B, a morning-after contraceptive pill. If taken within seventy-two hours of intercourse, Plan B is highly effective in preventing pregnancy. If taken within twenty-four hours, it is extremely effective. Wilcox didn't get pregnant.

Since 2003, Teva Pharmaceuticals, the manufacturer of Plan B, has been trying to get the federal government to make the contraceptive more easily available to women. Plan B could only be purchased with a doctor's prescription, and Teva requested that this restriction should be lifted. Since the pill must be taken so soon after unprotected sex, getting in touch with a doctor in time (if the young woman has one) and acquiring a prescription can be a formidable hurdle. The conservative administration of President George W. Bush, then in office, was sympathetic to antiabortion groups who argued against wider distribution of Plan B. Following the administration's lead, the Food and Drug Administration (FDA) rejected Teva's application. Only when a federal court subsequently ordered it did

pharmacies allow women aged seventeen and over to purchase the drug without a prescription.

The way Plan B acts to prevent pregnancy is that by using progesterone, one of the primary ingredients in birth control pills, eggs are prevented from being fertilized. Abortion opponents believe that Plan B can also work by keeping a fertilized egg from being implanted in a woman's womb. Plan B "can actually destroy a developing baby," says Jeanne Monahan, an official with the conservative Family Research Council. However, the scientific evidence offers no support for the view that Plan B prevents fertilized eggs from implanting.

When the Obama administration took office, women's groups had high expectations that Plan B would be made available without prescription to women of all ages. Teva Pharmaceuticals made a formal application to that effect, and the FDA recommended approval of the application. In a surprise development, however, Kathleen Sibelius, the Secretary of Health and Human Services (HHS), of which FDA is a part, rejected Teva's application. In making the announcement, Sibelius acknowledged that "the science has confirmed the drug to be safe and effective." Her only justification for overturning her own agency's recommendation was that there wasn't sufficient evidence to demonstrate that young girls would understand the directions on the drug's label.

Yet Sibelius ignored evidence to the contrary that shows that young teenagers do understand the simple instructions on the drug's label. Critics were quick to pounce. The American Academy of Pediatrics, for example, recommended that the pill be made available without a prescription.

President Obama said early in his administration that decisions during his time in office would be made "based on facts, not ideology." Still, every indication was that Sibelius's decision was based on ideology—or at least pragmatism—and not on facts. The Obama administration had tangled with the Catholic Church over a number of issues relating to health care and birth control, and less than a year before the 2012 election, it appeared that it had decided to step away from another fight with the Church.[1]

In this chapter, we examine how bureaucracies like the FDA and HHS operate and address many of the central dilemmas of American political life. Bureaucracies represent what Americans dislike about government, yet our interest groups lobby them to provide us with more of the services we desire. We say we want smaller, less intrusive government, but different constituencies value different agencies of government and fight fiercely to protect those bureaucracies' budgets. This enduring conflict once again represents the majoritarian and pluralist dimensions of American politics.

13.1 Organization Matters

★ Define the concept of bureaucracy, explain the role of organizations on the administration of the nation's laws, examine the reasons for the growth of the bureaucratic state, and assess arguments for and against its continued expansion.

A nation's laws and policies are administered, or put into effect, by various departments, agencies, bureaus, offices, and other government units, which together are known as its *bureaucracy*. **Bureaucracy** actually means any large, complex organization in which employees have specific job responsibilities and work within a hierarchy of authority. The employees of these government units, who are quite knowledgeable within their narrow areas, have become known somewhat derisively as **bureaucrats**.

We study bureaucracies because they play a central role in the governments of modern societies. In fact, organizations are a crucial part of any society, no matter how elementary it is. Even a preindustrial tribe is an organization. It has a clearly defined leader (a chief), senior policymakers (elders), a fixed division of labor (some hunt, some cook, some make tools), an organizational culture (religious practices, initiation rituals), and rules of governance (what kind of property belongs to families and what belongs to the tribe). How that tribe is organized is not merely a

bureaucracy
A large, complex organization in which employees have specific job responsibilities and work within a hierarchy of authority.

bureaucrats
Employees of a bureaucracy, usually meaning a government bureaucracy.

quaint aspect of its evolution; it is critical to the survival of its members in a hostile environment.

The organization of modern government bureaucracies also reflects their need to survive. The environment in which modern bureaucracies operate, filled with conflicting political demands and the ever-present threat of budget cuts, is no less hostile than that of preindustrial tribes. The way a given government bureaucracy is organized also reflects the particular needs of its clients. The bottom line, however, is that the manner in which any bureaucracy is organized affects how well it can accomplish its tasks.

Different approaches to fighting German submarines in World War II vividly demonstrate the importance of organization. At the beginning of the war, German submarines, or U-boats, were sinking American merchant ships off the East Coast of America at a devastating rate. One U-boat commander wrote that his task was so easy that "all we had to do was press the button." In contrast, the British had a great deal of success in defending their ships in the North Atlantic from U-boats.

The British navy used a highly centralized structure to quickly pool all incoming information on U-boat locations and just as quickly pass on what it had learned to commanders of antisubmarine ships and planes and to convoys. In contrast, the U.S. Navy's operations structure was decentralized, leaving top-line managers to decide for themselves how to allocate their resources. No one unit was coordinating antisubmarine warfare. When the U.S. Navy finally adopted a system similar to the British navy's, its success against the U-boats improved dramatically. In the eighteen months before it changed its system, the U.S. Navy sank just thirty-six U-boats. In the first six months with its centralized structure, seventy-five U-boats were destroyed.[2]

Clearly organization matters. The ways in which bureaucracies are structured to perform their work directly affect their ability to accomplish their tasks. Unfortunately, "if organization matters, it is also the case that there is no one best way of organizing."[3] Highly centralized organization, like the British navy's approach to combating U-boats, may not always be the best approach to solving a bureaucracy's performance problems. In some instances, it's surely better to give local managers the flexibility to tailor their own solutions to the unique problems they face in their community or state. The study of bureaucracy, then, centers around finding solutions to the many different kinds of problems that large government organizations face.

The Development of the Bureaucratic State

A common complaint voiced by Americans is that the national bureaucracy is too big and tries to accomplish too much. To the average citizen, the national government may seem like an octopus—its long arms reach just about everywhere. Ironically, compared to other Western democracies, the size of the U.S. government is proportionally smaller (see "Compared with What? Not So Big by Comparison" on p. 358).

American government seems to have grown unchecked since the start of the twentieth century. As one observer noted wryly, "The assistant administrator for water and hazardous materials of the Environmental Protection Agency [presides] over a staff larger than Washington's entire first administration."[4] Yet even during George Washington's time, bureaucracies were necessary. No one argued then about the need for a postal service to deliver mail or a treasury department to maintain a system of currency.

However, government at all levels (national, state, and local) grew enormously in the twentieth century, for several major reasons. A principal cause of government expansion is the increasing complexity of society. George Washington did not have an assistant administrator for water and hazardous materials because he had no need for one. The National Aeronautics and Space Administration (NASA) was not necessary until rockets were invented.

Compared with What?

Not So Big by Comparison

Compared with other Western democracies, the U.S. government turns out to be relatively small. Measuring the size of government is difficult, but one way is to calculate government expenditures as a proportion of all economic activity.

By this standard, the size of the U.S. government is relatively small. Virtually all other advanced industrialized democracies have larger government sectors. Typically these countries pay for its citizens' health care through government insurance, and this is a significant difference with the United States. Taxes are often higher, too, to reflect the cost of more robust government services.

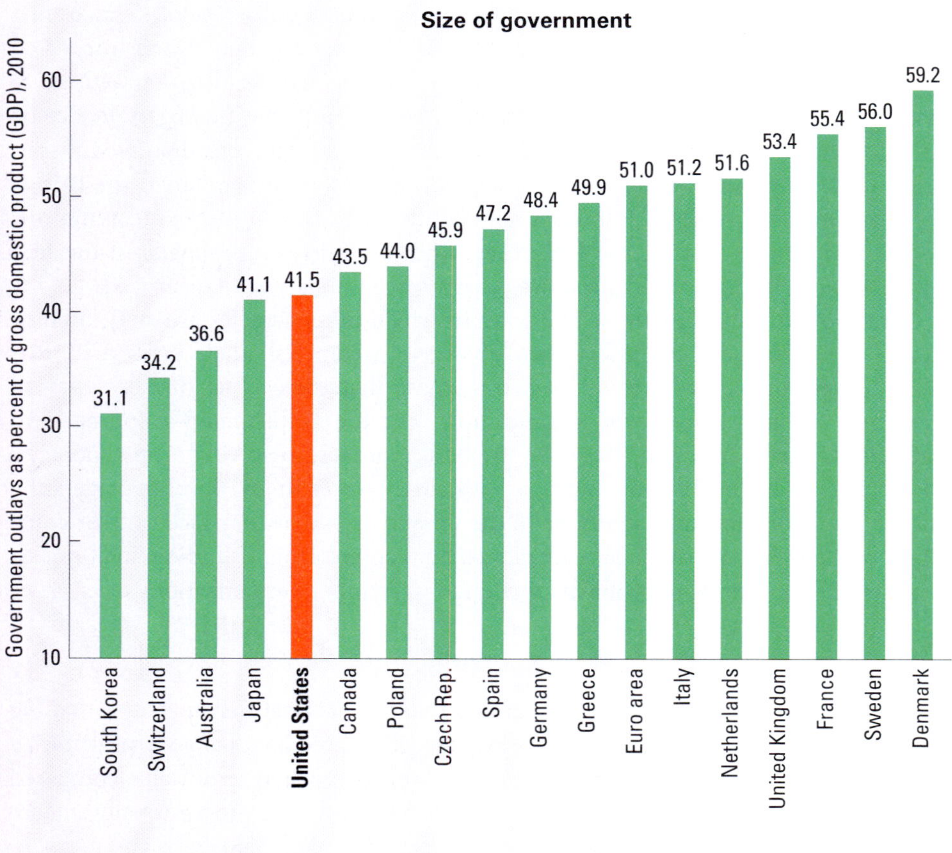

Source: Workforall.net.

Another reason government has grown is that the public's attitude toward business has changed. Throughout most of the nineteenth century, there was little or no government regulation of business. Business was generally autonomous, and any government intervention in the economy that might limit that autonomy was considered inappropriate. This attitude began to change toward the end of the nineteenth century as more Americans became aware that the end product of a laissez-faire approach was not always highly competitive markets that benefited consumers.

Instead, businesses sometimes formed oligopolies, such as the infamous "sugar trust," a small group of companies that controlled virtually the entire sugar market.

Gradually government intervention came to be accepted as necessary to protect the integrity of markets. And if government was to police unfair business practices effectively, it needed administrative agencies. During the twentieth century, new bureaucracies were organized to regulate specific industries. Among them are the Securities and Exchange Commission (SEC), which oversees securities trading, and the FDA, which tries to protect consumers from unsafe food, drugs, and cosmetics. Through bureaucracies such as these, government has become a referee in the marketplace, developing standards of fair trade, setting rates, and licensing individual businesses for operation. As new problem areas have emerged, government has added new agencies, further expanding the scope of its activities.

General attitudes about government's responsibilities in the area of social welfare have changed too. An enduring part of American culture is the belief in self-reliance. People are expected to overcome adversity on their own, to succeed on the basis of their own skills and efforts. Yet certain segments of our population are believed to deserve government support, because we either particularly value their contribution to society or have come to believe that they cannot realistically be expected to overcome adversity on their own.

This belief goes as far back as the nineteenth century. The government provided pensions to Civil War veterans because they were judged to deserve financial support. Later, programs to help mothers and children were developed. Further steps toward income security came in the wake of the Great Depression, when the Social Security Act became law, creating a fund that workers pay into and then collect income from during old age. In the 1960s, the government created Head Start, Medicare, and Medicaid, programs designed to help minorities, the elderly, and the poor. As the government made these new commitments, it also made new bureaucracies and expanded existing ones.

Can We Reduce the Size of Government?

For many Americans, government is unpopular: they have little confidence in its capabilities and feel that it wastes money and is out of touch with the people. They want a smaller government that costs less and performs better.

Most of the national government is composed of large bureaucracies, so if government is to become smaller, bureaucracies will have to be eliminated or reduced in size. Everyone wants to believe that we can shrink government by eliminating unnecessary bureaucrats. Although efficiencies can be found, serious budget cuts also require serious reductions in programs. Not surprisingly, presidents and members of Congress face opposition when they try to cut specific programs. The national government often engages in a bit of a shell game, modestly reducing the number of bureaucrats (which is popular) without reducing government programs (which is politically risky). The government often turns over the former

Politics of Global Change

EU Debt Bomb

The development of the European Union (EU) is a remarkable achievement. Over time, twenty-seven European countries (half a billion people) have come together to form a strong economic federation. These countries have willingly given up significant authority over their own economies (sovereignty), transferring authority to EU institutions of government. The EU has struck down trade barriers and created common regulatory standards that all member countries must adhere to. This promotes economic efficiency and generates more trade across borders. More trade means more economic activity.

© iStockphoto.com/pagadesign

Source: Latin Infrastructure Quarterly, "EU Debt Crisis and Spanish PPPs," http://www.liquarterly.com/44/politics/eu-debt-crisis.html.

bureaucrats' jobs to nonprofit or private contractors who do the same job but are not technically government employees.

Beneath the common rhetoric that government needs to be smaller and more efficient, serious efforts to shrink the bureaucracy have varied considerably. Ideological differences between the two parties and the gyrating size of the national budget deficit have shaped the debate. During the 1980s, President Reagan preached smaller government and made a concerted effort to reduce domestic social programs. He had only modest success, and his most ambitious proposals, like abolishing the Department of Education, didn't come close to passage by Congress. Although he was conservative in many ways, George W. Bush worked to enlarge the government. Most significantly, the 9/11 attacks and the continuing threat of terrorism led to the creation of the Department of Homeland Security and the expansion of defense- and

Seventeen of the countries (including most of the larger economies) have adopted a common currency, the euro. Most of those EU countries not currently using the euro will be switching to it in the future as they meet certain banking standards. Despite all the steps toward economic integration, individual countries retain autonomy over their own budgets. The governments in each country decide how much they will spend and how much debt they can take on to fund their own economic development.

It is this authority of each country to issue its own debt that has plunged the EU into the crisis it is in today. Due to the economic strength of the EU—it's now the world's largest economy—each country found itself with more available credit for borrowing purposes. Large banks and other financial institutions assumed that the EU would impose some level of fiscal discipline on member states and, thus, they could lend freely. They assumed wrong.

In recent years, four EU countries, Greece, Ireland, Portugal, and Spain, fell into catastrophic levels of debt, unable to pay what they owe to lenders. Hungary and Italy (see "Compared with What? From Berlusconi to Bankruptcy: The Costs of Failed Leadership" in Chapter 12) also developed serious debt problems. The reasons are a bit different for each country, but each has borrowed money that it cannot pay back under the conventional terms of the loans. In layman's language, they have to be bailed out by the EU. The EU countries with healthier economies have put money into a special fund to lend to countries in trouble, but in doing so, they have demanded that the countries in trouble institute reforms to put their financial houses in order. The harshest medicine is that the EU's European Central Bank, which controls the euro, has required that these governments reduce their own spending. For example, EU bureaucrats recently told Spain that it had to make further concessions and cut spending, which in turn means that Spain will have to lay off more government employees. This will add to the country's astronomical unemployment rate of close to 25 percent. In Greece, EU officials continue to monitor spending and have forced the government there to make a series of very serious cutbacks. This has included reductions in pensions to retired workers.

The severe austerity measures may eventually bring some stability to these errant economies, but in the short run, they have not revived growth. All of Europe is stagnant, and in these debt-ridden countries, there is tremendous anger at the EU bureaucracy. Dispassionate observers would say these countries only have themselves to blame. Yet rank-and-file citizens there look at their crumbling economies and now wonder about the wisdom of giving up so much of their sovereignty.

---

other security-related agencies. But it wasn't just security threats that led President Bush to propose new programs and bureaucracies. He also worked to expand social welfare through a prescription drug benefit for senior citizens. Bush understood that it was not always good politics to try to downsize government and that there's an upside to providing a benefit to citizens.

At the beginning of his presidency, Barack Obama and the Democratic Congress expanded government across a number of fronts. Most notably bureaucracies were created to administer new programs for health care and for oversight of the financial services industry. The sagging economy and gains by the Republicans in the 2010 elections led to greater concern about the national debt, and legislation was passed to reduce government spending by $1.2 trillion over the next ten years.[5] Debt has also become a central issue within the European Union (see "Politics of Global Change: EU Debt Bomb").

The tendency for big government to endure over the longer term reflects the tension between majoritarianism and pluralism. Even when the public as a whole wants a smaller national government, that sentiment can be undermined by the strong desire of different segments of society for government to continue performing some valuable function for them. Lobbies that represent these segments work strenuously to convince Congress and the administration that certain agencies' funding is vital and that any cuts ought to come out of other agencies' budgets.

13.2 Bureaus and Bureaucrats

★ Describe the organization of the executive branch, the role of the civil service, and the bureaucracy's responsiveness to presidential control.

We often think of the bureaucracy as a monolith. In reality, the bureaucracy in Washington is a disjointed collection of departments, agencies, bureaus, offices, and commissions—each a bureaucracy in its own right.

The Organization of Government

By examining the basic types of government organizations, we can better understand how the executive branch operates. In our discussion, we pay particular attention to the relative degree of independence of these organizations and to their relationship with the White House.

departments
The biggest units of the executive branch, covering a broad area of government responsibility. The heads of the departments, or secretaries, form the president's cabinet.

Departments. The biggest units of the executive branch are **departments**, covering broad areas of government responsibility. As noted in Chapter 12, the secretaries (heads) of the departments, along with a few other key officials, form the president's cabinet. The current cabinet departments are State, Treasury, Defense, Interior, Agriculture, Justice, Commerce, Labor, Health and Human Services, Housing and Urban Development, Transportation, Energy, Education, Veterans Affairs, and Homeland Security (see Figure 13.1). Each of these massive organizations is broken down into subsidiary agencies, bureaus, offices, and services.

independent agencies
Executive agencies that are not part of a cabinet department.

Independent Agencies. Within the executive branch are many **independent agencies** that are not part of any cabinet department. They stand alone and are controlled to varying degrees by the president. Some, among them the Central Intelligence Agency (CIA), are directly under the president's control. Others, such as the Federal Communications Commission, are structured as **regulatory commissions**. Each commission is run by a small number of commissioners (usually an odd number, to prevent tie votes) appointed to fixed terms by the president. Some commissions were formed to guard against unfair business practices. Others were formed to protect the public from unsafe products. Although presidents don't have direct control over these regulatory commissions, they can strongly influence their direction through their appointments of new commissioners.

regulatory commissions
Agencies of the executive branch of government that control or direct some aspect of the economy.

government corporations
Government agencies that perform services that might be provided by the private sector but that either involve insufficient financial incentive or are better provided when they are somehow linked with government.

Government Corporations. Finally, Congress has also created a small number of **government corporations**. These executive branch agencies perform services that theoretically could be provided by the private sector, but Congress has decided that the public is better served when these organizations have some link with the government. For example, the national government maintains the postal service as a government

FIGURE 13.1 Bureaucrats at Work

The size of the cabinet departments varies dramatically. That more than 1 million civilians are employed in the departments of Defense, Homeland Security, and Veterans Affairs is a reflection of the centrality of national security and war in recent American history. At the opposite end of the spectrum is the tiny Department of Education, with fewer than five thousand employees, despite the common rhetoric about the need to improve education.
Source: U.S. Census Bureau, *The 2012 Statistical Abstract*, Table 499: Federal Civilian Employment by Branch and Agency, available at http://www.census.gov/compendia/statab/cats/federal_govt_finances_employment.html.

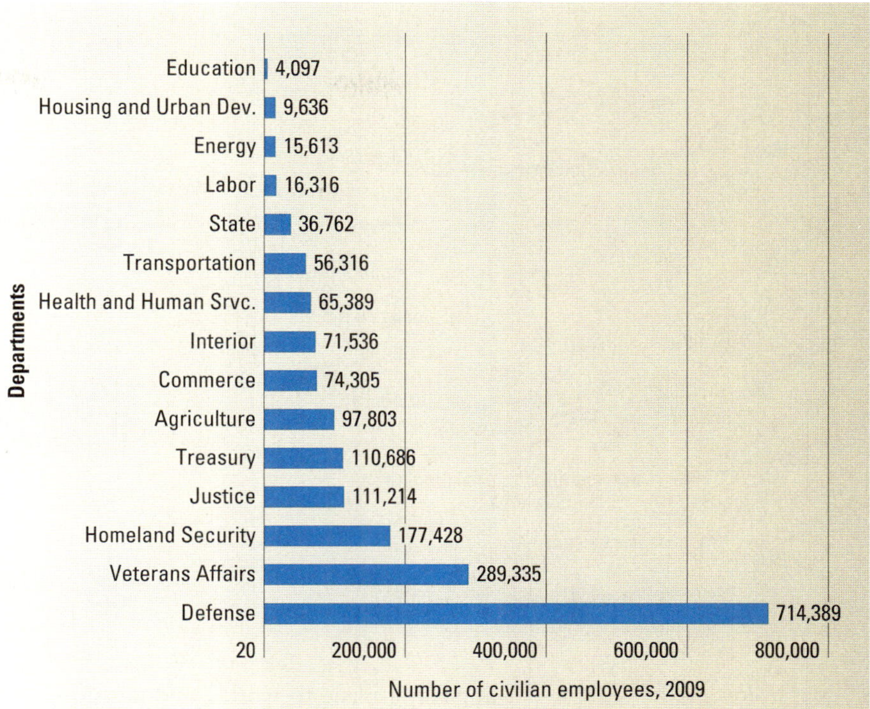

corporation because it feels that Americans need low-cost, door-to-door service for all kinds of mail, not just for profitable routes or special services. In some instances, the private sector does not have enough financial incentive to provide an essential service. This is the case with the financially troubled Amtrak passenger train line.

The Civil Service

The national bureaucracy is staffed by nearly 2.8 million civilian employees, who account for less than 2 percent of the U.S. work force.[6] Americans have a tendency to stereotype all government workers as faceless paper pushers, but the public sector work force is quite diverse. Government workers include forest rangers, Federal Bureau of Investigation (FBI) agents, typists, foreign service officers, computer programmers, policy analysts, public relations specialists, security guards, librarians, administrators, engineers, plumbers, and people from literally hundreds of other occupations.

An important feature of the national bureaucracy is that most of its workers are hired under the requirements of the **civil service**. The civil service was created after the assassination of President James Garfield, who was killed by an unbalanced and dejected job seeker. Congress responded by passing the Pendleton Act (1883), which established the Civil Service Commission (now the Office of Personnel Management). The objective of the act was to reduce patronage—the practice of filling government positions with the president's political allies or cronies. The civil service fills jobs on the basis of merit and sees to it that workers are not fired for political reasons. Over the years, job qualifications and selection procedures have been developed for most government positions.

The tidal wave of criticism of the federal bureaucracy—that it's unresponsive, too big, and too inefficient—has raised concerns that the government has become a less

civil service
The system by which most appointments to the federal bureaucracy are made, to ensure that government jobs are filled on the basis of merit and that employees are not fired for political reasons.

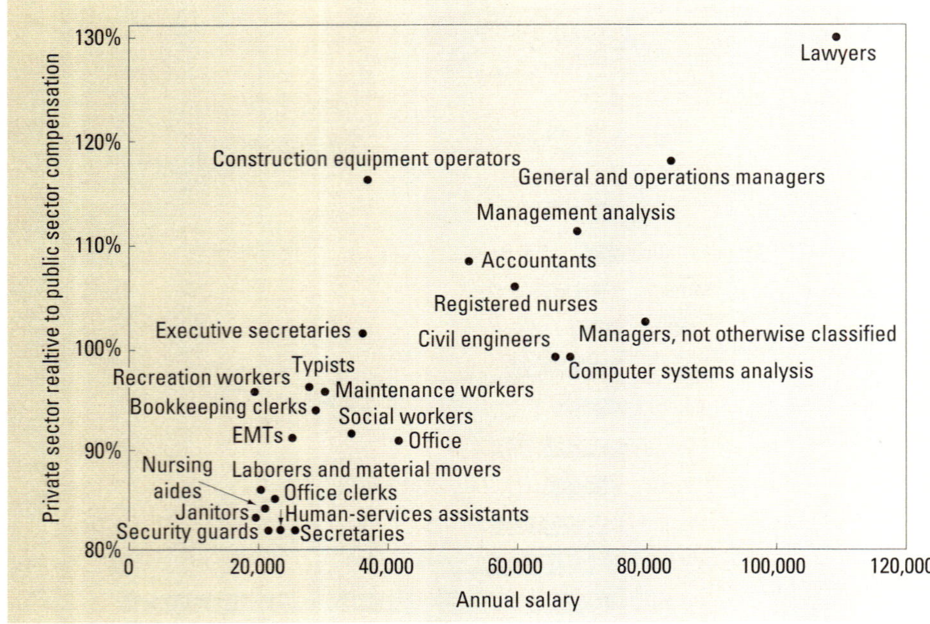

FIGURE 13.2 Good Jobs, Good Benefits

Despite tight budgets, jobs in the federal government maintain good pay and benefits. In this figure, those jobs listed below the 100 percent line pay better if they are in the government than in the private sector. For two people holding the same type of job listed above the 100 percent line, the one employed in the private sector will receive higher pay.

Source: Reprinted by permission of the publisher from *The Warping of Government Work* by John D. Donahue, p. 47, Cambridge, Mass.: Harvard University Press, Copyright © 2008 by the President and Fellows of Harvard College.

appealing place to work. As one study concluded, "The federal bureaucracy became the symbol of big government's problems—rarely of its success."[7] The quality of the civil service could decline as agencies may find fewer superior candidates for job openings. Surveys find that younger people seem less interested in working for the government, preferring private sector employment instead. One appealing strength of government sector work is that pay and benefits compare favorably to the private sector, especially for jobs at the lower end of the skills range (see Figure 13.2). Despite layoffs and stagnant wages in the past few years, job satisfaction of federal bureaucrats remains relatively high.[8] Those civil servants passionate about the mission of their agency are particularly motivated and goal oriented.[9]

Presidential Control over the Bureaucracy

Civil service and other reforms have effectively insulated the vast majority of government workers from party politics.[10] An incoming president can appoint only about three thousand people to jobs in his administration, less than 1 percent of all executive branch employees. These presidential appointees fill the top policymaking positions in government, and about a thousand of the president's appointees require Senate confirmation.[11] Each new president, then, establishes an extensive personnel review process to find appointees who are both politically compatible and qualified in their field. Although the president selects some people from his campaign staff, most political appointees have not been campaign workers. Instead, cabinet secretaries, assistant secretaries, agency heads, and the like tend to be drawn directly from business, universities, nonprofits, and government itself.

Presidents find that the bureaucracy is not always as responsive as they might like, for several reasons. Principally, pluralism can pull agencies in a direction other than that favored by the president. The Department of Transportation may want to move toward more support for mass transit, but politically it cannot afford to ignore the preferences of highway builders. An agency administrator must often try to broker a compromise between conflicting groups rather than pursue a position that holds fast and true to the president's ideology. Bureaucracies must also follow—at least in general terms—the laws governing the programs they are entrusted with, even if the president doesn't agree with some of those statutes. In this regard, bureaucracies are full of experienced careerists who are effective at running their programs. It is difficult for political appointees to ignore the careerists' preferences because of their long experience in the agency.[12]

Even with the constraints imposed by interest group preferences and by what the statutes require, presidents still have considerable influence over agency policymaking. They appoint administrators sympathetic to their policy goals who work to adapt the president's philosophy to both pending issues and new initiatives. Presidential aides review agency policymaking to ensure that it is in line with their preferences, often setting up a process requiring agencies to submit draft regulations to a White House office like the Office of Management and Budget. As will be explored in the next section, in varying degrees agencies have the authority to set policy under the laws passed by Congress authorizing an agency to administer a program. After President Obama took office and appointed Inez Moore Tennenbaum as head of the Consumer Product Safety Commission, Tennenbaum instructed staffers there to write a new safety requirement for off-road recreational vehicles, which sometimes flip over on uneven terrain and have been blamed for the deaths of fifty-nine riders. Tennenbaum's predecessor prompted manufacturers to offer repairs aimed at design flaws that may have caused the flipping problem, but Tennenbaum didn't think that went far enough and required manufacturers to make changes.[13]

Congress always has the prerogative to override regulations that it doesn't like or that it feels distort its intent. When a president faces a Congress controlled by the opposition party, this constraint is more significant. When the president's party also controls both houses, it is much easier for him to implement regulations that are in line with his preferences. Whatever party controls Congress, the White House and agency administrators have an incentive to consult with committee chairs to minimize conflict and gain a sense of what might provoke a hostile response on the part of a committee overseeing a particular agency. A committee can punish an agency by cutting its budget, altering a key program, or (for Senate committees) holding up confirmation of a nominee to a top agency post.

★ 13.3 Administrative Policymaking: The Formal Processes

★ Describe the roles of administrative discretion and rule-making authority in the execution of administrative policymaking.

Many Americans wonder why agencies sometimes actually make policy rather than merely carry it out. Administrative agencies are, in fact, authoritative policymaking bodies, and their decisions on substantive issues are legally binding on the citizens of this country.

Administrative Discretion

What are executive agencies set up to do? To begin with, cabinet departments, independent agencies, and government corporations are creatures of Congress. Congress creates a new department or agency by enacting a law that describes the organization's mandate, or mission. As part of that mandate, Congress grants the agency the authority to make certain policy decisions. Congress recognized long ago that it has neither the time nor the technical expertise to make all policy decisions. Thus, agencies are seen as a better means of managing uncertainty.[14] Ideally, Congress sets general guidelines for policy and expects agencies to act within those guidelines. The latitude that Congress gives agencies to make policy in the spirit of their legislative mandate is called **administrative discretion**.

Critics of the bureaucracy frequently complain that agencies are granted too much discretion because Congress commonly gives vague directives in its initial enabling legislation. Congress charges agencies with protecting "the public interest" but leaves them to determine on their own what policies best serve the public.

When agency directives are vague, bureaucrats work out the policy details. For instance, Congress gives the Federal Communications Commission (FCC) the power to fine broadcasters for violating decency standards. The FCC's operating definition for "indecent" is language or material that is offensive as measured by "contemporary community standards."[15] Some cases of indecency are fairly straightforward: the FCC fined CBS stations after the singer Janet Jackson's "wardrobe malfunction" caused exposure of her breasts during a Super Bowl halftime show. (It's not clear whether the "malfunction" was an accident or occurred accidentally on purpose.) But even after the Super Bowl controversy, members of Congress could not agree on a more concrete definition of *indecency*; they agreed only to increase the amount of fines for violations of the current law. Affected industries often have an interest in curbing the growth of administrative discretion. After the Super Bowl incident, the National Cable and Telecommunications Association announced a $250 million campaign to educate consumers about channel-blocking tools; they did not want lawmakers to give the FCC the power to regulate cable and satellite TV.[16]

Congress grants the broadest discretion to those agencies that are involved in domestic and global security. Both the FBI and the CIA have enjoyed a great deal of freedom from formal and informal congressional constraints because of the legitimate need for secrecy in their operations. In the post-9/11 era, additional discretion has accrued to security-related agencies.[17]

Rule Making

Agencies exercise their policymaking discretion through formal administrative procedures, usually rule making. **Rule making** is the administrative process that results in the issuance of regulations. **Regulations** are rules that guide the operation of government programs. When an agency issues regulations, it is using the discretionary authority granted to it by Congress to implement a program or policy enacted into law. Rule making itself follows procedural guidelines requiring that proposed regulations first be published so that interested parties—typically interest groups—have a chance to comment on them, making any recommendations they see as appropriate.[18]

Because they are authorized by congressional statutes, regulations have the effect of law. When Congress created the Department of Transportation in 1966 it was given authority to write regulations relevant to the safety, accessibility, and efficiency of various transportation industries. Controversy has swirled for years around a practice of airlines to keep passengers on board an aircraft that has pulled away from the gate but cannot take off (usually due to inclement weather). Horror stories abound. In August 2009, an ExpressJet flight with forty-seven passengers on board stayed overnight on the tarmac at the airport in Rochester, New York. It doesn't take long before a plane runs out of food and water and bathrooms become fouled.

---

administrative discretion
The latitude that Congress gives agencies to make policy in the spirit of their legislative mandate.

rule making
The administrative process that results in the issuance of regulations by government agencies.

regulations
Administrative rules that guide the operation of a government program.

Whenever Congress threatened to enact a "passenger bill of rights" to forbid such unconscionable tarmac delays, the airlines promised to improve their service. At the end of 2009, however, the Department of Transportation announced a new set of rules, limiting tarmac waits to no more than three hours. If that much time elapses, the plane must return to the gate and give passengers the option of deplaning. Airlines claimed there would be unintended consequences and even longer delays as ground crews removed luggage and searched for bags belonging to passengers who deplaned.[19] The new rule, however, has worked well, and in the first ten months after it was adopted, tarmac strandings fell to just sixteen instances from 664 in a comparable period from the year before.[20]

The regulatory process is controversial because regulations often require individuals and corporations to act against their own self-interest. The airline regulations are a classic case of freedom versus order. The airline companies believed they needed the greater freedom to conduct business in a way that they found most efficient. Consumer groups preferred that the government put more of a premium on maintaining order (preserving the health and well-being of passengers). Administrative rule making gives agencies the flexibility as they try to find a balance between conflicting pressures.

Rolf Adlercreutz/Alamy

Tarmac Hell

Flying these days has its share of challenges, but government regulation has resulted in some modest improvements. The airlines' practice of keeping passengers on their plane on the tarmac while waiting for bad weather to clear is now subject to restrictions. If an airline keeps a plane on the tarmac for more than three hours, it is subject to a heavy fine.

13.4 Administrative Policymaking: Informal Politics

★ Analyze how incrementalism and bureaucratic culture affect policymaking.

When an agency is considering a new regulation and all the evidence and arguments have been presented, how does an administrator reach a decision? Because policy decisions typically address complex problems that lack a single satisfactory solution, these decisions rarely exhibit mathematical precision and efficiency.

The Science of Muddling Through

In his classic analysis of policymaking, "The Science of Muddling Through," Charles Lindblom compared the way policy might be made in the ideal world with the way it is formulated in the real world.[21] The ideal, rational decision-making process, according to Lindblom, begins with an administrator's tackling a problem by ranking values and objectives. After clarifying the objectives, the administrator thoroughly considers all possible solutions to the problem. He or she comprehensively analyzes alternative solutions, taking all relevant factors into account. Finally, the administrator chooses the alternative that appears to be the most effective means of achieving the desired goal and solving the problem.

Lindblom claims that this "rational-comprehensive" model is unrealistic. Policymakers have great difficulty defining precise values and goals. Administrators at the U.S. Department of Energy, for example, want to be sure that supplies of home heating oil are sufficient each winter. At the same time, they want to reduce dependence on foreign oil. Obviously, the two goals are not fully compatible. How should these administrators decide which goal is more important? And how should they relate them to the other goals of the nation's energy policy?

Real-world decision making parts company with the ideal in another way: the policy selected cannot always be the most effective means to the desired end. Even if a tax at the gas pump is the most effective way to reduce gasoline consumption during a shortage, motorists' anger would make this theoretically "right" decision politically difficult. So the "best" policy is often the one on which most people can agree. However, political compromise may mean that the government is able to solve only part of a problem.

Finally, critics of the rational-comprehensive model point out that policymaking can never be based on truly comprehensive analyses. A secretary of energy cannot possibly find the time to read a comprehensive study of all alternative energy sources and relevant policy considerations for the future. A truly thorough investigation of the subject would produce thousands of pages of text. Instead, administrators usually rely on short staff memos that outline a limited range of feasible solutions to immediate problems. Time is of the essence, and problems are often too pressing to wait for a complete study. According to Lindblom, policymaking tends to be characterized by **incrementalism**, with policies and programs changing bit by bit, step by step. Decision makers are constrained by competing policy objectives, opposing political forces, incomplete information, and the pressures of time. They choose from a limited number of feasible options that are almost always modifications of existing policies rather than wholesale departures from them.

Because policymaking proceeds by means of small modifications of existing policies, it is easy to assume that incrementalism describes a process that is intrinsically conservative, sticking close to the status quo.[22] Yet even if policymaking moves in small steps, those steps may all be in the same direction. Over time, a series of incremental changes can significantly alter a program. Moreover, although Lindblom offered a more realistic portrayal of the policymaking process, incrementalism is not ubiquitous. There are a minority of cases where decisions are made that move a policy in a significantly new direction. The Obama administration's intervention to resuscitate a collapsing banking industry could not accurately be labeled an incremental change, even though in the past the government has on occasion intervened to shore up an industry in trouble. The staggering sums the government loaned to failed or fragile financial institutions and the level of control the government exerted were without real precedent. It's certainly true that virtually all policy changes have antecedents in current policy, but some changes are considerable in scope.[23]

The Culture of Bureaucracy

How an agency makes decisions and performs its tasks is greatly affected by the people who work there: the bureaucrats. Americans often find their interactions with bureaucrats frustrating because bureaucrats are inflexible (they go by the book) or lack the authority to get things done. Top administrators too can become frustrated with the bureaucrats who work for them.

Why do people act bureaucratically? Individuals who work for large organizations cannot help but be affected by the culture of bureaucracy.[24] Part of that culture is the development of **norms**, an organization's informal, unwritten rules that guide individual behavior. For example, the Individuals with Disabilities Act (IDEA) requires that every child with qualifying disabilities receive an Individualized Education Plan that provides for the necessary, appropriate services. However, school administrators implementing this law frequently offer families fewer services than the

---

incrementalism
Policymaking characterized by a series of decisions, each instituting modest change.

norms
An organization's informal, unwritten rules that guide individual behavior.

law arguably calls for. The reason is not that school administrators don't want to do the maximum for disabled children but that they don't have enough money to provide all services to all qualifying students in their school or district. Norms develop about how to allocate scarce resources even though the law assumes adequate services will be offered.[25]

Bureaucracies are often influenced in their selection of policy options by the prevailing customs, attitudes, and expectations of the people working within them. Departments and agencies commonly develop a sense of mission, where a particular objective or a means for achieving it is emphasized. The Army Corps of Engineers, for example, is dominated by engineers who define the agency's objective as protecting citizens from floods by building dams. There could be other objectives, and there are certainly other methods of achieving this one, but the engineers promote the solutions that fit their conception of what the agency should be doing.

When Leon Panetta became head of the CIA in 2009, he faced an especially delicate and difficult task in trying to change behavior in a bureaucracy with a powerful sense of mission.[26] During the war on terror under the Bush administration, many suspected terrorists who were captured were taken to secret prisons and subjected to waterboarding and other forms of torture. Some of these people were truly evil, while others were not terrorists but victims of mistaken identity. For Panetta, the challenge was more than developing new legal standards to replace the ones that permitted torture. Rather, he had to change the mindset of the agency.[27]

Bureaucrats are often criticized for being rigid, for going by the book when some flexibility might be a better option. Bureaucrats go by the book because the "book" is actually the law they administer, and they are obligated to enforce the law. The regulations under those laws are often broad standards intended to cover a range of behavior. Yet sometimes those laws and regulations don't seem to make sense. Take the case of Tommy McCoy, who was the batboy for the Savannah Cardinals, then a farm team for Major League Baseball's Atlanta Braves. An investigator for the Department of Labor discovered that Tommy was only fourteen years old and was working at night games. Child labor laws forbid fourteen-year-olds from working past 7:00 P.M. on school nights, and the Department of Labor inspector threatened to fine the team unless they stopped employing Tommy. The Cardinals went to bat for Tommy, scheduling a "Save Tommy's Job" night at the stadium. The publicity about Tommy's imminent firing made the Department of Labor look ridiculous. When ABC News asked Secretary of Labor Robert Reich to comment on the situation, he knew he was facing a public relations disaster. But when he asked his staff how they could permit Tommy to keep his job, he was told, "There's nothing we can do. The law is the law."[28]

Reich overrode his staff, deciding that new regulations would exempt batboys and batgirls. That may seem to be a happy ending to a story of a bureaucracy gone mad, but it's not that simple. Child labor laws are important. Before this country had such laws, children were exploited in factories that paid them low wages and subjected them to unsanitary working conditions. The exploitation of child labor is still a problem in many parts of the world. It made sense for Congress to pass a law to forbid child labor abuses, and it made sense for the Department of Labor to write a blanket regulation that forbids work after 7:00 P.M. for all children age fourteen and under. The alternative was to try to determine an evening curfew for every type of job that a youngster might have. Although Reich's exemption made sense from a public relations point of view, it was nonsensical as public policy. If he wrote an exemption for children who worked for a baseball team, how about children who scoop ice cream at the local creamery? Why should Tommy McCoy be treated with favoritism?

Bureaucrats often act bureaucratically because they are trying to apply the laws of this country in a manner that treats everyone equally. Sometimes, as in the case of Tommy McCoy, equal application of the law doesn't seem to make sense. Yet it would be unsettling if government employees interpreted rules as they pleased. Americans expect to be treated equally before the law, and bureaucrats work with that expectation in mind.

★ 13.5 Problems in Implementing Policy

★ Identify obstacles to effective policy implementation.

The development of policy in Washington is the end of one phase of the policymaking cycle and the beginning of another. After policies have been developed, they must be implemented. **Implementation** is the process of putting specific policies into operation. Ultimately, bureaucrats must convert policies on paper into policies in action. It is important to study implementation because policies do not always do what they were designed to do.

implementation
The process of putting specific policies into operation.

Implementation may be difficult because the policy to be carried out is not clearly stated. Policy directives to bureaucrats sometimes lack clarity and leave them with too much discretion. We have already mentioned the example of the FCC enforcing standards of "decency." Implementation can also be problematic because it often involves many different agencies and different layers of government. Take, for example, the case of reducing air pollution in Los Angeles, a city that was afflicted with horrible smog. In 1977 Congress amended the Clean Air Act, which among other things shifted a great deal of responsibility to state, regional, and local institutions. The Environmental Protection Agency (EPA) still retained much authority and continued to issue regulations specifying standards. To implement these regulations in the Los Angeles region, the state of California created the South Coast Air Quality Management District. However, considerable jurisdiction over many sources of pollution lay with another body, the California Air Resources Board. Implementation also involved many city governments in the Los Angeles basin along with a number of transportation agencies.

Despite these challenges of divided responsibilities, considerable progress was made in reducing pollution and smog. But the national government then changed regulatory philosophies, and in 1993 the EPA issued a new set of instructions. The new approach was to move away from "command and control" regulations (basically orders to be carried out) to market incentives. Both

L.A. Story

No city is more identified with air pollution than Los Angeles (pictured here in 1993). Over the years, different levels of government have cooperated in developing various approaches to improving the quality of air in the L.A. area. Implementation of these policies has been complex, but while there's still pollution in Los Angeles, there is progress and the air is cleaner than it was when this picture was taken.

© Steve Starr/Corbis

businesses and consumers were to be offered incentives to move toward less polluting technologies. Progress in reducing pollution was made through this approach as well. Los Angeles is now at the beginning of a third approach, one aimed at "sustainability." This approach aims at achieving an equilibrium in which pollution is offset by gains that improve the environment. In one analyst's words, this "would be a fundamental transformation in what Los Angelenos value in their personal and professional lives."[29] The implementation challenges are no less daunting.

Effective implementation takes time as processes must be established and continually improved so all stakeholders can negotiate and communicate effectively. There's a great deal of trial and error as bureaucrats learn what works and what doesn't, and what's efficient and what is too costly or too slow.

Clearly the sheer complexity of public policy problems makes implementation a challenge. The more organizations and levels of government involved, the more difficult it is to coordinate implementation. Moreover, many policies are implemented at the last stage not by government bureaucracies but by nonprofit or for-profit organizations hired under a contract to deliver a specific service.[30] As will be discussed in the next section, "outsourcing" of government programs is very common. Government agencies devise, fund, and oversee programs but hire some other entity to run them. That adds another layer of participants and more opportunities for miscommunication, poor performance, and coordination problems.

Obstacles to effective implementation can create the impression that nothing the government does succeeds, but programs can and do work.[31] Problems in implementation demonstrate why patience and continual analysis are necessary ingredients of successful policymaking. The Los Angeles clean air example shows that implementation can succeed, even when the problem is complex. To return to a term we used earlier, implementation is by its nature an *incremental* process, in which trial and error eventually lead to policies that work.

13.6 Reforming the Bureaucracy: More Control or Less?

★ Compare the strengths and weaknesses of reform efforts aimed at increasing the effectiveness of the bureaucracy's performance.

As we saw at the beginning of this chapter, organization matters. How bureaucracies are designed directly affects how effective they are in accomplishing their tasks. People in government constantly tinker with the structure of bureaucracies, trying to find ways to improve their performance. Administrative reforms have taken many different approaches as criticism of government has mounted.

In recent years three basic approaches to reforming the bureaucracy have attracted the most attention. First, advocates of *deregulation* envision eliminating layers of bureaucracy and reducing the rules that govern business markets with the market forces of supply and demand. Let consumer preferences dictate what products and services are offered. A second approach is directed at waste and inefficiency in government and promotes *competition* so that government services are offered by the lowest bidder from the public or private sector. Instead of a bureaucracy having a monopoly over a particular task, create incentives for that bureaucracy to continually find ways of doing the job more cheaply, thus saving the taxpayers money. Third, a range of reforms focuses on measuring agency performance. Instituting clear *performance standards* and holding bureaucrats accountable for meeting those standards should improve the quality and efficiency of government services.[32]

Deregulation

Many people believe that government is too involved in **regulation**, intervening in the natural working of business markets to promote some social goal. For example, government might regulate a market to ensure that products pose no danger to consumers. Through **deregulation**, the government reduces its role and lets the natural market forces of supply and demand take over. Conservatives have championed deregulation because they see freedom in the marketplace as the best route to an efficient and growing economy. Indeed, nothing is more central to capitalist philosophy than the belief that the free market will efficiently promote the balance of supply and demand. Considerable deregulation took place in the 1970s and 1980s, notably in the airline, trucking, financial services, and telecommunications industries.

In telecommunications, for example, consumers used to have no role in choosing a long-distance vendor—one could call on the Bell system or not call at all. After an out-of-court settlement broke up the Bell system in 1982, AT&T was awarded the right to sell the long-distance services that had previously been provided by that system, but it now had to face competition from newly emergent long-distance carriers. Deregulation for local phone service followed some years later, and consumers have benefited from the vigorous competition for their business in both realms. Few sectors of the economy have shown as much innovation and appeal as today's telephones and handhelds like iPhones and Droids, which are essentially small computers that can be put in a pocket, backpack, or purse.

Deciding on an appropriate level of deregulation is especially difficult for health and safety issues. Companies within a particular industry may legitimately claim that health and safety regulations are burdensome, making it difficult for them to earn sufficient profits or compete effectively with foreign manufacturers. But the FDA's drug licensing procedures illustrate the potential danger of deregulating such policy areas. The thorough and lengthy process that the FDA uses to evaluate drugs has as its ultimate validation the thalidomide case. The William S. Merrell Company purchased the license to market this sedative, already available in Europe, and filed an application with the FDA in 1960. The company then began a protracted fight with an FDA bureaucrat, Dr. Frances Kelsey, who was assigned to evaluate the thalidomide application. She demanded that the company abide by all FDA drug-testing requirements, despite the fact that the drug was already in use in other countries. She and her superiors resisted pressure from the company to bend the rules a little

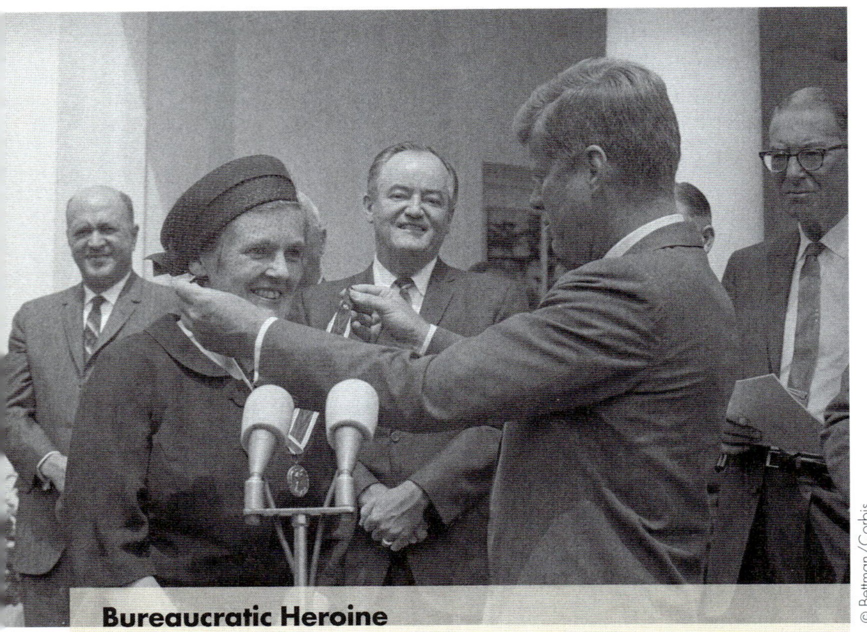

Bureaucratic Heroine

The government recognized Dr. Frances Kelsey's courageous work to keep thalidomide off the American market with the President's Award for Distinguished Federal Civilian Service. The medal is being affixed here by President John F. Kennedy in 1962. In 2010, the Food and Drug Administration awarded its first annual Frances Kelsey Award to honor a staff member of the agency. Its first recipient: ninety-eight-year-old Dr. Frances Kelsey.

and expedite approval. Before Merrell had conducted all the FDA tests, news came pouring in from Europe that some women who had taken thalidomide during pregnancy were giving birth to babies without arms, legs, or ears. Strict adherence to government regulations protected Americans from the same tragic consequences.

Some agencies have tried to move beyond rules that simply increase or decrease the amount of government control to regulatory processes that offer firms flexibility in meeting standards while at the same time protecting health and safety concerns. For example, the EPA has instituted flexible caps on air pollution at some manufacturing plants. Instead of having to request permits on new equipment and processes, plants are given an overall pollution cap and can decide on their own how to meet that limit. The overall caps are stricter than would otherwise be the case, but manufacturers gain by not having to wait for approvals for any changes and do not face uncertainty concerning the EPA's response.[33]

Efforts aimed at making organizations, typically corporations, more transparent and accountable in their actions are also gaining favor as another regulatory approach. For example, food manufacturers are now required to disclose information in packaging labels as to the quantity of trans-fats in the product. Regulations do not limit the amount of trans-fatty acids but, rather, give consumers the information and then let them decide how much is too much.[34] Transparency also extends to government, though not exclusively to regulatory issues. As noted in Chapter 2, e-government is expanding. Government bureaucracies at all levels are increasingly putting their working documents online so citizens can better understand policymaking choices.[35]

Who controls the government makes a huge difference in the level and type of regulation. When a Democrat controls the White House, there is sure to be a more forceful stance toward regulation as presidential appointees in the agencies reflect the incumbent's philosophy. Recall the example of the new regulations for off-road vehicles enacted by the Consumer Product Safety Administration after Barack Obama became president. More broadly, there was a surge in regulations after Obama took over (see Figure 13.3). There may have been many factors that contributed to this trend, but as one analysis put it, "the new aggressiveness reflects the new cops on the

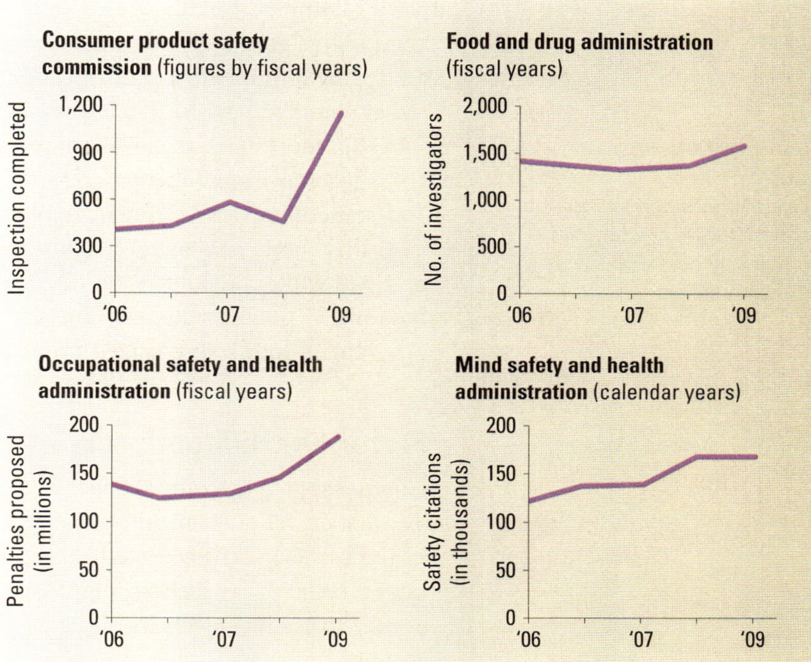

FIGURE 13.3 It Makes a Difference

Control over the White House makes an enormous difference in the way regulatory agencies perform their duties. With Democrat Barack Obama in the White House, agencies followed his lead and moved aggressively on health and safety issues. Under President George W. Bush, agencies relied more on the free market to solve policy problems. Source: Eric Liptor, "With Obama Regulations are Back in Fashion," *New York Times*, 23 May 2010.

beat."[36] In contrast, Republican presidents are prone to place more emphasis on freedom, and agencies under their control will regulate less.

A strong case can be made for deregulated business markets, in which free and unfettered competition benefits consumers and promotes productivity. The strength of capitalist economies comes from the ability of individuals and firms to compete freely in the marketplace, and the regulatory state places restrictions on this freedom. But without regulation, nothing ensures that marketplace participants will act responsibly. Achieving the right balance between protecting citizens, maintaining orderly markets, and promoting free markets is elusive. Given the breadth and complexity of regulation, it is no surprise that the American public is conflicted about their preferences. When the economy declines, however, there is more widespread belief that regulation is harming the economy.[37] At the same time, when a business sector acts irresponsibly, the public demands more regulation.

Competition and Outsourcing

Conservative critics of government have long complained that bureaucracies should act more like businesses, meaning they should try to emulate private sector practices that promote efficiency and innovation. Many recent reformers advocate something more drastic: unless bureaucracies can demonstrate that they are as efficient as the private sector, turn those agencies' functions over to the private sector. Underlying this idea is the belief that competition will make government more dynamic and more responsive to changing environments and will weaken the ability of labor unions to raise wages beyond those of nonunion employees.[38]

One widespread adaptation of competitive bidding to administer government programs has come in the area of social services. Over time government welfare programs have increasingly emphasized social services—giving people training and non-cash support—rather than income maintenance (cash support). Social services are labor intensive, and state and local governments have found it efficient to outsource programs to nongovernmental organizations, principally nonprofit organizations like community health centers and day-care centers for elderly persons. For-profit companies compete for the grants and contracts that the government awards through competitive grants or bidding. For example, the for-profit company Maximus is contracted by a number of state agencies responsible for child support to locate noncustodial parents to establish paternity or enforce payments to a custodial parent.[39]

competition and outsourcing
Procedures that allow private contractors to bid for jobs previously held exclusively by government employees.

This movement toward **competition and outsourcing** continues to grow. More and more government jobs are open to bidding from nongovernment competitors, and sometimes a government bureau or office competes for the jobs and programs that they used to "own." As the number of federal government employees has declined while the population of Americans increases, some wonder if our country is building a "hollow state." By this, critics mean a government that is distinct from the programs it funds, disengaged from interaction with the people it serves.

Performance Standards

Another approach to improving the bureaucracy's performance is to focus on performance: To what degree does any individual agency accomplish the objectives that have been set for it? In this view, each agency is held accountable for reaching quantifiable goals each year or budget cycle. Under such a system, congressional and White House overseers examine each agency to see if it meets its objectives, and they reward or punish agencies accordingly. As one scholar noted, this is a philosophy of "*making* the managers manage."[40]

A major initiative to hold agencies accountable for their performance is the **Government Performance and Results Act**. Passed by Congress, it requires each agency to identify specific goals, adopt a performance plan, and develop quantitative indicators of agency progress in meeting its goals.[41] The law requires that agencies publish reports with performance data on each measure established. This is no small challenge. A case in point is the Healthy Start program funded by the Health Resources and Services Administration (HRSA) and intended to improve infant mortality rates and infant health generally. Among the specific goals are increasing the number of mothers receiving prenatal care during the first trimester and reducing the number of low-weight births. These are measurable, and the hospitals and health centers receiving federal funding for Healthy Start must report the appropriate data to HRSA. More complicated is the degree to which this program makes a difference since infant health can be influenced by many factors.[42]

Another problem is that since agencies set their own goals and know they'll be judged on meeting them, they may select indicators where they know they'll do best.[43] Or if standards that have been set prove to be too difficult to achieve, standards may be lowered, sometimes under the guise of "reform," to make them work better. The Department of Education's No Child Left Behind program was envisioned as a means for forcing underperforming schools to raise their students up to the reading and math standards prescribed for each grade level. Although the law is that of the national government, states were allowed to implement the program in their own way. Over time many states reduced their standards because their schools could not improve enough to meet the model guidelines of a national test of students. Between 2005 and 2007, fifteen states lowered the bar for student performance. Other states had already lowered their standards (see Figure 13.4). In short, performance-based

Government Performance and Results Act

A law requiring each government agency to implement quantifiable standards to measure its performance in meeting stated program goals.

FIGURE 13.4 Meeting Performance Standards a Problem? Just Lower Them

School districts across the country have had trouble meeting performance standards designed to push individual schools to change priorities and revise their curricula. As a result, many states have simply lowered their standards so that more school districts in the state meet requirements under the No Child Left Behind Act.
Source: John Hechinger, "Some States Drop Testing Bar," *Wall Street Journal*, October 30, 2009. Reprinted by permission of *Wall Street Journal*, copyright © 2009 Dow Jones & Company, Inc. All rights reserved worldwide.

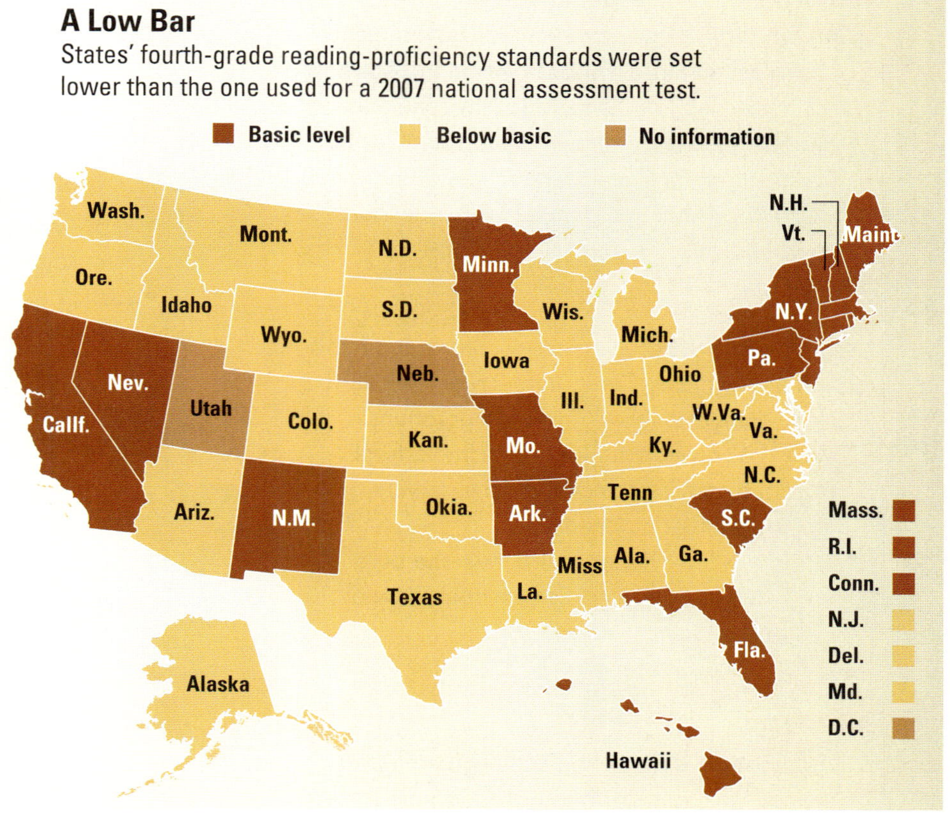

management runs the risk of perverting an agency's incentives toward what it can achieve rather than what would be most valuable to achieve.

Despite the relative appeal of these different approaches to improving the bureaucracy, each has serious shortcomings. There is no magic bullet. The commitment of the government to solve a problem is far more important than management techniques. Still, to return to a theme that we began with, organization does matter. Trying to find ways of improving the bureaucracy is important because bureaucracies affect people's lives, and enhancing their performance, even at the margins, has real consequences.

SUMMARY

As the scope of government activity has grown during the twentieth and early twenty-first centuries, so too has the bureaucracy. The executive branch has evolved into a complex set of departments and independent agencies. The way in which the various bureaucracies are organized matters a great deal because their structure affects their ability to carry out their tasks.

13.1 Organization Matters

- How an organization is structured affects its ability to accomplish its tasks.
- The overall size of the federal bureaucracy has grown dramatically over time as government has taken on more responsibility in increasingly complex social and economic environments.
- Shrinking the government, though popular in the abstract, is difficult to enact because individual programs are popular with individual constituencies.

13.2 Bureaus and Bureaucrats

- The executive branch is organized around cabinet departments, independent agencies, and a small number of government corporations.
- Almost all civilian employees of the federal government are protected by civil service employment requirements.
- Presidents have some control over the bureaucracy, but such authority is constrained by a number of factors.

13.3 Administrative Policymaking: The Formal Processes

- Administrative discretion is delegated to agencies by the Congress because Congress recog-

nizes that it does not have the staff, time, and expertise to make all the decisions necessary in each policy area.
- The formulation of regulations follows a formal, legal process termed rule making. Regulations set forth policy and are not mere details of administrative processes.

13.4 Administrative Policymaking: Informal Politics

- A rational-comprehensive model of administrative policymaking is unrealistic. Instead, agencies make policy through incremental steps.
- The behavior of bureaucrats is shaped by bureaucratic culture—the norms and informal practices that characterize the internal workings of the organization.

13.5 Problems in Implementing Policy

- Implementation is the process by which policies formulated by bureaucracies are put into practice.
- Lack of clarity in policy directives, involvement of many agencies at different levels of government, time constraints, and the sheer complexity of public policy problems are some of the challenges to effective implementation.

13.6 Reforming the Bureaucracy: More Control or Less?

- Deregulation is a reduction in the level of supervision of a business market or other activity by a government bureaucracy.
- Recent efforts by government to improve the performance of bureaucracies include competition and outsourcing and setting performance standards.

ASSESSING YOUR UNDERSTANDING WITH APLIA...YOUR VIRTUAL TUTOR!

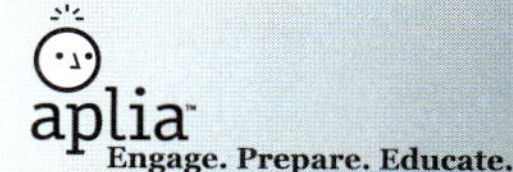

13.1 **Define the concept of bureaucracy, explain the role of organizations on the administration of the nation's laws, examine the reasons for the growth of the bureaucratic state, and assess arguments for and against its continued expansion.**

1. Why has the bureaucracy grown over the years?
2. What are the obstacles to reducing the size of government?

13.2 **Describe the organization of the executive branch, the role of the civil service, and the bureaucracy's responsiveness to presidential control.**

1. Identify the major structural components of the federal government.
2. Why was the civil service system adopted?
3. How can a change in presidents affect administrative policymaking?

13.3 **Describe the roles of administrative discretion and rule-making authority in the execution of administrative policymaking.**

1. Why does Congress give agencies significant discretion?
2. What is rule making?

13.4 **Analyze how incrementalism and bureaucratic culture affect policymaking.**

1. What is incrementalism?
2. Compare and contrast formal and informal policymaking.

13.5 **Identify obstacles to effective policy implementation.**

1. What are some of the challenges in implementing policy directives formulated by Washington agencies?

13.6 **Compare the strengths and weaknesses of reform efforts aimed at increasing the effectiveness of the bureaucracy's performance.**

1. What are the potential benefits as well as the negative consequences of deregulation?
2. Why might performance standards be ineffective?

14 The Courts

CHAPTER TOPICS and Learning Outcomes

When Chief Justice Fred M. Vinson died unexpectedly in September 1953, his colleague Associate Justice Felix Frankfurter commented, "This is the first solid piece of evidence I've ever had that there really is a God."[1] Frankfurter despised Vinson as a leader and disliked him as a person. Vinson's sudden death would bring a new colleague—and perhaps new hope—to the school desegregation cases known collectively as *Brown* v. *Board of Education*. The issue of segregated schools had arrived in the Supreme Court in late 1951. Although the Court had originally scheduled oral argument for October 1952, the justices elected a postponement until December and merged several similar cases. When a law clerk expressed puzzlement at the delay, Frankfurter explained that the Court was holding the cases for the outcome of the national election in 1952. "I thought the Court was supposed to decide without regard to elections," declared the clerk. "When you have a major social political issue of this magnitude," replied Frankfurter, "we do not think this is the time to decide it."[2]

The justices were at loggerheads following the December argument, with Vinson unwilling to invalidate racial segregation in public education. Because the justices were not ready to reach a decision, they scheduled the cases for reargument the following year. The justices asked the attorneys to address the history of the Fourteenth Amendment and the potential remedies if the Court ruled against segregation.

Frankfurter's caustic remark about Vinson's death reflected the critical role Vinson's replacement would play when the Court again tackled the desegregation issue. In his first appointment to the nation's highest court, President Dwight D. Eisenhower chose California's Republican governor, Earl Warren, as chief justice. The president would later regret his choice.

When the Court heard the reargument of *Brown* v. *Board of Education* in late 1953, the new chief justice led his colleagues from division to unanimity on the issue of public school segregation. Unlike his predecessor, Warren began the secret conference to decide the segregation issue with a strong statement: that segregation was contrary to the Thirteenth, Fourteenth, and Fifteenth Amendments to the Constitution. "Personally," remarked the new chief justice, "I can't see how today we can justify segregation based solely on race."[3] Moreover, if the Court were to uphold segregation, he argued, it could do so only on the theory that blacks were inherently inferior to whites. As the discussion proceeded, Warren's opponents were cast in the awkward position of appearing to support racism.

Five justices were clearly on Warren's side, making six votes; two were prepared to join the majority if Warren's reasoning satisfied them. With only one clear holdout, Warren set about the task of responding to his colleagues' concerns. In the months that followed, he met with them individually in their chambers, reviewing the decision and the justification that would accompany it. Finally, in April 1954, Warren approached Justice Stanley Reed, whose vote would make the opinion unanimous. "Stan," said the chief justice, "you're all by yourself in this now. You've got to decide whether it's really the best thing for the country." Ultimately, Reed joined the others. On May 17, 1954, the Supreme Court unanimously ruled against racial segregation in public schools, signaling the end of legally created or government-enforced segregation of the races in the United States.[4]

Judges confront conflicting values in the cases before them, and in crafting their decisions, they—especially Supreme Court justices—make policy. Their decisions become the precedents other judges use to rule in similar cases. One judge in one court makes public policy to the extent that she or he influences other decisions in other courts.

The power of the courts to shape public policy creates a difficult problem for democratic theory. According to that theory, the power to make law resides only in the people or the people's elected representatives. When judges undo the work of elected majorities (which was surely the case with government-sponsored racial segregation), they risk depriving the people of the right to make the laws or to govern themselves.

Court rulings—especially Supreme Court rulings—extend far beyond any particular case. Judges are students of the law, but they remain human beings. They have their own opinions about the values of freedom, order, and equality. And although all judges are constrained by statutes and precedents from imposing their personal will on others through their decisions, some judges are more prone than others to interpreting the law in the light of those beliefs.

America's courts are deeply involved in the life of the country and its people. Some courts, such as the Supreme Court, make fundamental policy decisions vital to the preservation of freedom, order, and equality. Through checks and balances, the elected branches link the courts to democracy, and the courts link the elected branches to the Constitution. But does this system work? Can the courts exercise political power within the pluralist model? Or are judges simply sovereigns in black robes, making decisions independent of popular control? In this chapter, we examine these questions by exploring the role of the courts in American political life.

 14.1 National Judicial Supremacy

★ Define judicial review, explain the circumstances under which it was established, and assess the significance of the authority it gave the courts.

Section 1 of Article III of the Constitution creates "one supreme Court." The founders were divided on the need for other national courts, so they deferred to Congress the decision to create a national court system. Those who opposed the creation of national courts believed that such a system would usurp the authority of state courts.[5] Congress considered the issue in its first session and, in the Judiciary Act of 1789, gave life to a system of federal (that is, national) courts that would coexist with the courts in each state but be independent of them. Federal judges would also be independent of popular influences because the Constitution provided for their lifetime appointment.

In the early years of the Republic, the federal judiciary was not a particularly powerful branch of government. It was especially difficult to recruit and keep Supreme Court justices. They spent much of their time as individual traveling judges ("riding circuit"); disease and poor transportation were everyday hazards. The justices met as the Supreme Court only for a few weeks in February and August.[6] John Jay, the first chief justice, refused to resume his duties in 1801 because he concluded that the Court could not muster the "energy, weight, and dignity" to contribute to national affairs.[7] Several distinguished statesmen refused appointments to the Court, and several others, including Oliver Ellsworth, the third chief justice, resigned. But a period of profound change began in 1801 when President John Adams appointed his secretary of state, John Marshall, to the position of chief justice.

Judicial Review of the Other Branches

Shortly after Marshall's appointment, the Supreme Court confronted a question of fundamental importance to the future of the new republic: If a law enacted by Congress conflicts with the U.S. Constitution, which should prevail? The question arose in the case of *Marbury* v. *Madison* (1803), which involved a controversial series of last-minute political appointments.[8]

Lollapalooza of a Line

With no video allowed in the courtroom, the hottest ticket in Washington, D.C., for 2012 was a seat in the Supreme Court to hear arguments examining the constitutionality of the Obama administration's signature legislative achievement, the Affordable Care Act. The Court, under Chief Justice John G. Roberts, Jr., seemed to be embracing political conflict when it agreed to decide the constitutionality of Obamacare before the 2012 presidential election.

The case began in 1801 when an obscure Federalist, William Marbury, was designated a justice of the peace in the District of Columbia. Marbury and several others were appointed to government posts created by Congress in the last days of John Adams's presidency, but the appointments were never completed. The newly arrived Jefferson administration had little interest in delivering the required documents; qualified Jeffersonians would welcome the jobs.

To secure their jobs, Marbury and the other disgruntled appointees invoked an act of Congress to obtain the papers. The act authorized the Supreme Court to issue orders against government officials. Marbury and the others sought such an order in the Supreme Court against the new secretary of state, James Madison, who held the crucial documents.

Marshall observed that the act of Congress that Marbury invoked to sue in the Supreme Court conflicted with Article III of the U.S. Constitution, which did not authorize such suits. In February 1803, the Court delivered its opinion.*

---

*Courts publish their opinions in volumes called *reporters*. Today, the *United States Reports* is the official reporter for the U.S. Supreme Court. For example, the Court's opinion in the case of *Brown* v. *Board of Education* is cited as 347 U.S. 483 (1954). This means that the opinion in *Brown* begins on page 483 of Volume 347 in *United States Reports*. The citation includes the year of the decision, in this case, 1954.

Before 1875, the official reports of the Supreme Court were published under the names of private compilers. For example, the case of *Marbury* v. *Madison* is cited as 1 Cranch 137 (1803). This means that the case is found in Volume 1, compiled by reporter William Cranch, starting on page 137, and that it was decided in 1803.

Chief Justice John Marshall

John Marshall (1755–1835) clearly ranks as the Babe Ruth of the Supreme Court. Both Marshall and the Bambino transformed their respective games and became symbols of their institutions. Scholars now recognize both men as originators—Marshall of judicial review and Ruth of the modern age of baseball. (FIAT JUSTITIA is Latin for "Let justice be done.")

judicial review
The power to declare congressional (and presidential) acts invalid because they violate the Constitution.

Must the Court follow the law or the Constitution? The High Court held, in Marshall's forceful argument, that the Constitution was "the fundamental and paramount law of the nation" and that "an act of the legislature, repugnant to the constitution, is void." In other words, when an act of the legislature conflicts with the Constitution—the nation's highest law—that act is invalid. Marshall's argument vested in the judiciary the power to weigh the validity of congressional acts:

> It is emphatically the province and duty of the judicial department to say what the law is. Those who apply the rule to particular cases, must of necessity expound and interpret that rule.… So if a law be in opposition to the constitution; if both the law and the constitution apply to a particular case, so that the court must either decide that case conformably to the law, disregarding the constitution; or conformably to the constitution, disregarding the law; the court must determine which of these conflicting rules governs the case. This is of the very essence of judicial duty.[9]

The decision in *Marbury* v. *Madison* established the Supreme Court's power of **judicial review**—the power to declare congressional acts invalid if they violate the Constitution.* Subsequent cases extended the power to cover presidential acts as well.[10]

Marshall expanded the potential power of the Supreme Court to equal or exceed the power of the other branches of government. Should a congressional act (or, by implication, a presidential act) conflict with the Constitution, the Supreme Court claimed the power to declare the act void. The judiciary would be a check on the legislative and executive branches, consistent with the principle of checks and balances embedded in the Constitution. Although Congress and the president may sometimes wrestle with the constitutionality of their actions, judicial review gave the Supreme Court the final word on the meaning of the Constitution. The exercise of judicial review—an appointed branch's checking of an elected branch in the name of the Constitution—appears to run counter to democratic theory. But in more than two hundred years of practice, the Supreme Court has invalidated nearly 170 provisions of national law. Only a small number have had great significance for the political system.[11] (Since 1994, with conservative justices in the majority, the Court has struck down more than thirty acts of Congress, several of them important expressions of public policy.) The Constitution provides mechanisms to override judicial review (constitutional amendments) and to control excesses of the justices (impeachment), but these steps are more theoretical than practical. In addition, the Court can respond to the continuing struggle among competing interests (a struggle that is consistent with the pluralist model) by reversing itself. It has done so only about 230 times in its entire history.[12]

Although the Constitution did not spell out judicial review of Congress and the president, it did provide such power over state and local government. When such laws conflict with the Constitution or national laws or treaties, the federal courts can invalidate them. That's because the Supremacy Clause obligates state judges to follow the Constitution, national laws, and treaties when state law conflicts with them. Moreover, the Supreme Court ruled that it had final authority to review state court decisions calling for the interpretation of national law.[13] In time, the Supreme Court would use its judicial review power in nearly twelve hundred instances to invalidate

---

*The Supreme Court had earlier upheld an act of Congress in *Hylton* v. *United States* (3 Dallas 171 [1796]). *Marbury* v. *Madison* was the first exercise of the power of a court to invalidate an act of Congress.

state and local laws, on issues as diverse as abortion, the death penalty, the rights of the accused, and reapportionment.[14]

The Exercise of Judicial Review

These early cases, coupled with other historic decisions, established the components of judicial review:

- The power of the courts to declare national, state, and local laws invalid if they violate the Constitution
- The supremacy of national laws or treaties when they conflict with state and local laws
- The role of the Supreme Court as the final authority on the meaning of the Constitution

This political might—the power to undo decisions of the representative branches of the national and state governments—lay in the hands of appointed judges, that is, people who were not accountable to the electorate. Did judicial review square with democratic government?

Alexander Hamilton had foreseen and tackled the problem in *Federalist* No. 78. Writing during the ratification debates surrounding the adoption of the Constitution (see Chapter 3), Hamilton maintained that despite the power of judicial review, the judiciary would be the weakest of the three branches of government because it lacked the strength of the sword or the purse. The judiciary, wrote Hamilton, had "neither FORCE nor WILL, but merely judgment."

Although Hamilton was defending legislative supremacy, he argued that judicial review was an essential barrier to legislative oppression.[15] He recognized that the power to declare government acts void implied the superiority of the courts over the other branches. But this power, he contended, simply reflects the will of the people, declared in the Constitution, as opposed to the will of the legislature, expressed in its statutes. Judicial independence, guaranteed by lifetime tenure and protected salaries, frees judges from executive and legislative control, minimizing the risk of their deviating from the law established in the Constitution. If judges make a mistake, the people or their elected representatives have the means to correct the error, through constitutional amendments and impeachment.

Their lifetime tenure does free judges from the direct influence of the president and Congress. And although mechanisms to check judicial power are in place, these mechanisms require extraordinary majorities and are rarely used. When they exercise the power of judicial review, then, judges can and occasionally do operate counter to majoritarian rule by invalidating the actions of the people's elected representatives.

14.2 The Organization of Courts

★ Outline the organization of the U.S. court system and identify the principal functions of courts at each tier of the system.

The American court system is complex, partly as a result of our federal system of government. Each state runs its own court system, and no two states' courts are identical. In addition, we have a system of courts for the national government. The national, or federal, courts coexist with the state courts (see Figure 14.1, p. 384). Individuals fall under the jurisdiction of both court systems. They can sue or be sued in either system,

FIGURE 14.1 The Federal and State Court Systems, 2010–2011

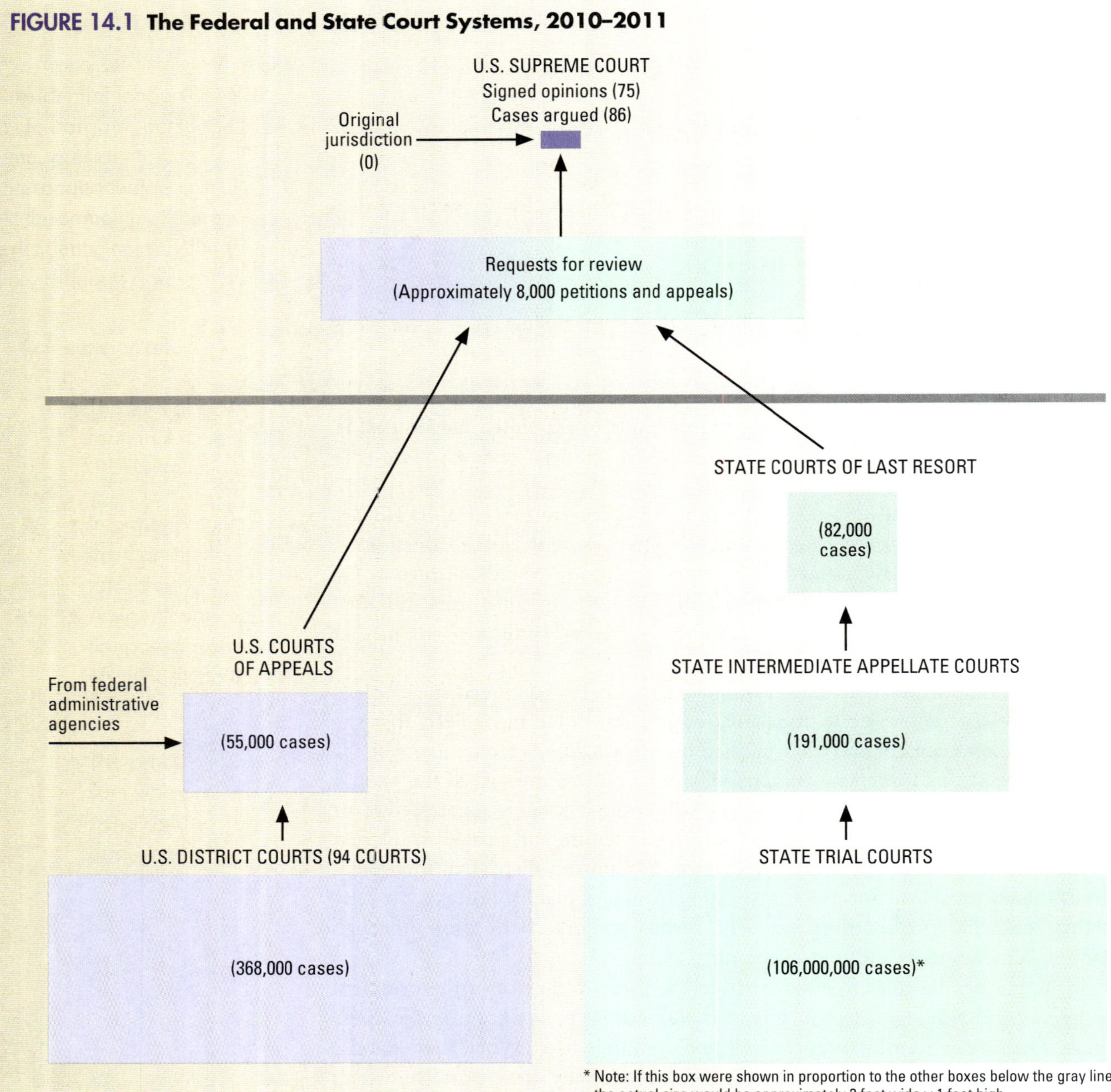

The federal courts have three tiers: district courts, courts of appeals, and the Supreme Court. The Supreme Court was created by the Constitution; all other federal courts were created by Congress. State courts dwarf federal courts, at least in terms of case load. There are nearly three hundred state cases for every federal case filed. The structure of state courts varies from state to state; usually there are minor trial courts for less serious cases, major trial courts for more serious cases, intermediate appellate courts, and supreme courts. State courts were created by state constitutions.

Sources: John G. Roberts, Jr., "The 2011 Year-End Report on the Federal Judiciary," Dec 31, 2011, http://www.supremecourt.gov/publicinfo/year-end/2011year-endreport.pdf; Court Statistics Project, "Appeals by Right Dominate Intermediate Appellate Court Caseloads," http://www.courtstatistics.org/Appellate/AppellateABR1.aspx; and U.S. Census Bureau, *Statistical Abstract of the United States: 2012*, "Law Enforcement, Courts, and Prisons," Table 335, p. 211, http://www.census.gov/compendia/statab/2012/tables/12s0335.pdf.

depending mostly on what their case is about. Litigants file nearly all cases (95 percent) in state courts. State trial courts receive on average one civil, domestic relations, criminal, juvenile, or traffic case for every three citizens. The volume of state court cases has remained steady at about 106 million, according to the most recent data.[16]

Some Court Fundamentals

Courts are full of mystery to citizens uninitiated in their activities. Lawyers, judges, and seasoned observers understand the language, procedures, and norms associated with legal institutions. Let's start with some fundamentals.

Criminal and Civil Cases. A crime is a violation of a law that forbids or commands an activity. Criminal laws are created, amended, and repealed by state legislatures. These laws and the punishments for violating them are recorded in each state's penal code. Some crimes—murder, rape, arson—are on the books of every state. Others—marijuana use, for example—are considered crimes in certain states but not all. Because crime is a violation of public order, the government prosecutes **criminal cases**. Maintaining public order through the criminal law is largely a state and local function. Criminal cases brought by the national government represent only a small fraction of all criminal cases prosecuted in the United States. In theory, the national penal code is limited by the principle of federalism. The code is aimed at activities that fall under the delegated and implied powers of the national government, enabling the government, for example, to criminalize tax evasion or the use of computers and laser printers to counterfeit money, bank checks, or even college transcripts.

Fighting crime is popular, and politicians sometimes outbid one another in their efforts to get tough on criminals. National crime-fighting measures have begun to usurp areas long viewed to be under state authority. Since 1975, Congress has added hundreds of new federal criminal provisions covering a wide range of activities once thought to be within the states' domain, including carjacking, willful failure to pay child support, and crossing state lines to engage in gang-related street crime.[17]

Courts decide both criminal and civil cases. **Civil cases** stem from disputed claims to something of value. Disputes arise from accidents, contractual obligations, and divorce, for example. Often the parties disagree over tangible issues (possession of property, custody of children), but civil cases can involve more abstract issues too (the right to equal accommodations, compensation for pain and suffering). The government can be a party to civil disputes, called on to defend its actions or to allege wrongdoing.

Procedures and Policymaking. Most civil and criminal cases never go to trial. In most criminal cases, the defendant's lawyer and the prosecutor **plea bargain**, negotiating the severity and number of charges to be brought against the defendant. In a civil case, one side may only be using the threat of a lawsuit to exact a concession from the other. Often the parties *settle* (or resolve the dispute between themselves) because of the uncertainties in litigation. Though rare, settlement can occur even at the level of the Supreme Court. And sometimes the initiating parties (the plaintiffs in civil cases) may simply abandon their efforts, leaving disputes unresolved.

When cases are neither settled nor abandoned, they end with an *adjudication,* a court judgment resolving the parties' claims and enforced by the government. When trial judges adjudicate cases, they may offer written reasons to support their decisions. When the issues or circumstances of cases are novel, judges may publish *opinions,* explanations justifying their rulings.

criminal cases
Court cases involving a crime, or violation of public order.

civil cases
Court cases that involve a private dispute arising from such matters as accidents, contractual obligations, and divorce.

plea bargain
A defendant's admission of guilt in exchange for a less severe punishment.

Judges make policy in two different ways. The first is through their rulings on matters that no existing legislation addresses. Such rulings set precedents that judges rely on in future, similar cases. We call this body of rules the **common, or judge-made, law**. The roots of the common law lie in the English legal system. Contracts, property, and torts (injuries or wrongs to the person or property of another) are common-law domains. The second area of judicial lawmaking involves the application of statutes enacted by legislatures. The judicial interpretation of legislative acts is called *statutory construction.* The proper application of a statute is not always clear from its wording. To determine how a statute should be applied, judges look for the legislature's intent, reading reports of committee hearings and debates. If these sources do not clarify the statute's meaning, the court does so. With or without legislation to guide them, judges look to the relevant opinions of higher courts for authority to decide the issues before them.

The federal courts are organized in three tiers, as a pyramid. At the bottom of the pyramid are the **U.S. district courts**, where litigation begins. In the middle are the **U.S. courts of appeals**. At the top is the Supreme Court of the United States. To *appeal* means to take a case to a higher court. The courts of appeals and the Supreme Court are appellate courts; with few exceptions, they review only cases that have already been decided in lower courts. Most federal courts hear and decide a wide array of civil and criminal cases.

The U.S. District Courts

There are ninety-four federal district courts in the United States. Each state has at least one district court, and no district straddles more than one state.[18] In 2011, there were 678 full-time federal district judgeships, and they received over 367,000 new criminal and civil cases.[19]

The district courts are the entry point for the federal court system. When trials occur in the federal system, they take place in the federal district courts. Here is where witnesses testify, lawyers conduct cross-examinations, and judges and juries decide the fate of litigants. More than one judge may sit in each district court, but each case is tried by a single judge, sitting alone. U.S. magistrate judges assist district judges, but they lack independent judicial authority. Magistrate judges have the power to hear and decide minor offenses and conduct preliminary stages of more serious cases. District court judges appoint magistrate judges for eight-year (full-time) or four-year (part-time) terms. As of 2011, there were 531 full-time and 43 part-time and other magistrate judge positions.[20]

Sources of Litigation. Today the authority of U.S. district courts extends to the following:

- Federal criminal cases, as defined by national law (for example, robbery of a nationally insured bank or interstate transportation of stolen securities)
- Civil cases, brought by individuals, groups, or the government, alleging violation of national law (for example, failure of a municipality to implement pollution-control regulations required by a national agency)
- Civil cases brought against the national government (for example, a vehicle manufacturer sues the motor pool of a government agency for its failure to take delivery of a fleet of new cars)
- Civil cases between citizens of different states when the amount in controversy exceeds $75,000 (for example, when a citizen of New York sues a citizen of

---

common, or judge-made, law
Legal precedents derived from previous judicial decisions.

U.S. district courts
Courts within the lowest tier of the three-tiered federal court system; courts where litigation begins.

U.S. courts of appeals
Courts within the second tier of the three-tiered federal court system, to which decisions of the district courts and federal agencies may be appealed for review.

Alabama in a U.S. district court in Alabama for damages stemming from an auto accident that occurred in Alabama)

The U.S. Courts of Appeals

All cases resolved in a U.S. district court and all decisions of federal administrative agencies can be appealed to one of the twelve regional U.S. courts of appeals. These courts, with 167 full-time judgeships, received over 55,000 new cases in 2011.[21] Each appeals court hears cases from a geographical area known as a *circuit.* The U.S. Court of Appeals for the Seventh Circuit, for example, is located in Chicago; it hears appeals from the U.S. district courts in Illinois, Wisconsin, and Indiana. The United States is divided into twelve circuits.*

Appellate Court Proceedings. Appellate court proceedings are public, but they usually lack courtroom drama. There are no jurors, witnesses, or cross-examinations; these are features only of the trial courts. Appeals are based strictly on the rulings made and procedures followed in the trial courts. Suppose, for example, that in the course of a criminal trial, a U.S. district judge allows the introduction of evidence that convicts a defendant but was obtained under questionable circumstances. The defendant can appeal on the grounds that the evidence was obtained in the absence of a valid search warrant and so was inadmissible. The issue on appeal is the admissibility of the evidence, not the defendant's guilt or innocence. If the appellate court agrees with the trial judge's decision to admit the evidence, the conviction stands. If the appellate court disagrees with the trial judge and rules that the evidence is inadmissible, the defendant must be retried without the incriminating evidence or be released.

The courts of appeals are regional courts. They usually convene in panels of three judges to render judgments. The judges receive written arguments known as *briefs* (which are also sometimes submitted in trial courts). Often the judges hear oral arguments and question the lawyers to probe their arguments.

Precedents and Making Decisions. Following review of the briefs and, in many appeals, oral arguments, the three-judge panel meets to reach a judgment. One judge attempts to summarize the panel's views, although each judge remains free to disagree with the judgment or the reasons for it. When an appellate opinion is published, its influence can reach well beyond the immediate case. For example, a lawsuit turning on the meaning of the Constitution produces a ruling, which then serves as a **precedent** for subsequent cases; that is, the decision becomes a basis for deciding similar cases in the future in the same way. Thus, judges make public policy to the extent that they influence decisions in other courts. Although district judges sometimes publish their opinions, it is the exception rather than the rule. At the appellate level, however, precedent requires that opinions be written.

Making decisions according to precedent is central to the operation of our legal system, providing continuity and predictability. The bias in favor of existing decisions is captured by the Latin expression *stare decisis,* which means "let the decision stand." But the use of precedent and the principle of **stare decisis** do not make lower-court judges cogs in a judicial machine. "If precedent clearly governed," remarked one federal judge, "a case would never get as far as the Court of Appeals: the parties would settle."[22]

precedent
A judicial ruling that serves as the basis for the ruling in a subsequent case.

stare decisis
Literally, "let the decision stand"; decision making according to precedent

---

*The thirteenth court, the U.S. Court of Appeals for the Federal Circuit, is not a regional court. It specializes in appeals involving patents, contract claims against the national government, and federal employment cases.

Judges on the courts of appeals direct their energies to correcting errors in district court proceedings and interpreting the law (in the course of writing opinions). When judges interpret the law, they often modify existing laws. In effect, they are making policy. Judges are politicians in the sense that they exercise political power, but the black robes that distinguish judges from other politicians signal constraints on their exercise of power.

★ 14.3 The Supreme Court

★ Describe the process by which cases are both accepted for review and decided by the U.S. Supreme Court and analyze the role played by judicial restraint and judicial activism in judicial decisions.

Above the west portico of the Supreme Court building are inscribed the words EQUAL JUSTICE UNDER LAW. At the opposite end of the building, above the east portico, are the words JUSTICE THE GUARDIAN OF LIBERTY. The mottos reflect the Court's difficult task: achieving a just balance among the values of freedom, order, and equality. Consider how these values came into conflict in two controversial issues the Court has faced.

Flag burning as a form of political protest pits the value of order, or the government's interest in maintaining a peaceful society, against the value of freedom, including the individual's right to vigorous and unbounded political expression. In two flag-burning cases, the Supreme Court affirmed constitutional protection for unbridled political expression, including the emotionally charged act of desecrating a national symbol.[23] Because under a pluralist system no decision is ever truly final, the flag-burning decisions hardly quelled the demand for laws to punish flag desecration. In 2006, Congress inched ever so close to a constitutional amendment banning flag desecration. The proposal passed by more than a two-thirds vote in the House but failed by a single vote in the Senate.

School desegregation pits the value of equality against the value of freedom. In *Brown* v. *Board of Education* (1954), the Supreme Court carried the banner of racial equality by striking down state-mandated segregation in public schools. The decision helped launch a revolution in race relations in the United States. The justices recognized the disorder their decision would create in a society accustomed to racial bias, but in this case, equality clearly outweighed freedom. Twenty-four years later, the Court was still embroiled in controversy over equality when it ruled that race could be a factor in university admissions (to diversify the student body).[24] Having secured equality for blacks, the Court in 2003 faced the charge by white students who sought admission to the University of Michigan that it was denying whites the freedom to compete for admission. A slim Court majority concluded that the equal protection clause of the Fourteenth Amendment did not prohibit the narrowly tailored use of race as a factor in law school admissions but rejected the automatic use of racial categories to award fixed points toward undergraduate admissions.[25] The justices will address the issue of race in undergraduate admissions again in 2012 with a decision expected by June 2013.[26]

The Supreme Court makes national policy. Because its decisions have far-reaching effects on all of us, it is vital that we understand how it reaches those decisions. With this understanding, we can better evaluate how the Court fits within our model of democracy. Great Britain is the latest democracy to establish a supreme court (see "Compared with What? A Supreme Court of Its Own" on pp. 390–91).

Access to the Court

There are rules of access that must be followed to bring a case to the Supreme Court. Also important is a sensitivity to the justices' policy and ideological preferences. The notion that anyone can take a case all the way to the Supreme Court is true only in theory, not fact.

The Supreme Court's cases come from two sources. A few arrive under the Court's **original jurisdiction**, conferred by Article III, Section 2, of the Constitution, which gives the Court the power to hear and decide "all Cases affecting Ambassadors, other public Ministers and Consuls, and those in which a State shall be Party." Cases falling under the Court's original jurisdiction are tried and decided in the Court itself; the cases begin and end there. For example, the Court is the first and only forum in which legal disputes between states are resolved. It hears few original jurisdiction cases today, however, usually referring them to a special master, often a retired judge, who reviews the parties' contentions and recommends a resolution that the justices are free to accept or reject.

Steve Petteway/Collection of the Supreme Court of the United States

The Supreme Court, 2011 Term: The Lineup

The justices of the Supreme Court of the United States. Seated are (left to right) Clarence Thomas, Antonin Scalia, Chief Justice John G. Roberts, Jr., Anthony Kennedy, and Ruth Bader Ginsburg. Standing are Sonia Sotomayor, Stephen J. Breyer, Samuel A. Alito, and Elena Kagan.

Most cases enter the Supreme Court from the U.S. courts of appeals or the state courts of last resort. This is the Court's **appellate jurisdiction**. These cases have been tried, decided, and reexamined as far as the law permits in other federal or state courts. The Court exercises judicial power under its appellate jurisdiction only because Congress gives it the authority to do so. Congress may change (and, perhaps, eliminate) the Court's appellate jurisdiction. This is a powerful but rarely used weapon in the congressional arsenal of checks and balances.

Litigants in state cases who invoke the Court's appellate jurisdiction must satisfy two conditions. First, the case must have reached the end of the line in the state court system. Litigants cannot jump at will from a state to the national arena of justice. Second, the case must raise a **federal question**, that is, an issue covered by the Constitution, federal laws, or national treaties. But even cases that meet both of these conditions do not guarantee review by the Court.

Since 1925, the Court has exercised substantial (today, nearly complete) control over its **docket**, or agenda (see Figure 14.2 on p. 392). The Court selects a handful of cases (fewer than one hundred) for full consideration from the eight thousand or more requests filed each year. These requests take the form of petitions for *certiorari*, in which a litigant seeking review asks the Court "to become informed" of the lower-court proceeding. For the vast majority of cases, the Court denies the petition for *certiorari*, leaving the decision of the lower court undisturbed. No explanations accompany these denials, so they have little or no value as Court rulings.

The Court grants a review only when four or more justices agree that a case warrants full consideration. This unwritten rule is known as the **rule of four**. With advance preparation by their law clerks, who screen petitions and prepare summaries,

original jurisdiction
The authority of a court to hear a case before any other court does.

appellate jurisdiction
The authority of a court to hear cases that have been tried, decided, or reexamined in other courts.

federal question
An issue covered by the U.S. Constitution, national laws, or U.S. treaties.

docket
A court's agenda.

rule of four
An unwritten rule that requires at least four justices to agree that a case warrants consideration before it is reviewed by the U.S. Supreme Court.

Compared with What?

A Supreme Court of Its Own

The opening of the United Kingdom's Supreme Court marks the culmination of a long process of separation of the judiciary from the legislature and the executive.[1]

Jack Straw, Justice Secretary and Lord Chancellor

More than two centuries after its inception, the American model of separation of powers continues to influence the structure of government. Its influence is not confined to new democracies. The United Kingdom—one of the oldest democracies in the world—recently created a Supreme Court to decide on all matters under English, Welsh, and Northern Irish law and under Scottish civil law.[2] Prior to October 2009, a

ZUMA Press/Newscom

committee of the House of Lords (the upper chamber of the British Parliament) exercised these judicial functions, coupling the legislative and judicial branches of government.

The new twelve-member court is now independent of Parliament and is located at a highly symbolic location, "balancing judiciary and legislature across the open space of Parliament Square, with the other two sides occupied by the executive (the Treasury building) and the church (Westminster Abbey)."[3] According to Lord Phillips

all nine justices make these judgments at secret weekly conferences.[27] During the conferences, justices vote on previously argued cases and consider which new cases to add to the docket. The chief justice circulates a "discuss list" of worthy petitions. Cases on the list are then subject to the rule of four, a practice by custom that permits four of the nine justices to grant review of a case. Though it takes only four votes to place a case on the docket, it may ultimately take an enormous leap to garner a fifth, and deciding, vote on the merits of the appeal. This is especially true if the Court is sharply split ideologically. Thus, a minority of justices in favor of an of Worth Matravers, the president of the Supreme Court, "This is the last step in the separation of powers in this country.... We have come to it fairly gently and gradually, but we have come to the point where the judges are completely separated from the legislature and executive."[4]

A steady process of policy devolution has accompanied the decoupling of judicial and legislative functions from London to the regional administrations of Scotland, Wales, and Northern Ireland. This devolution signals an increasing "federalization" of the United Kingdom, in the sense that regional jurisdictions are becoming more autonomous from the central government. The new Supreme Court is also the final court of appeal for all devolution matters, "that is, issues about whether the devolved executive and legislative authorities in Scotland, Wales and Northern Ireland have acted or propose to act within their powers or have failed to comply with any other duty imposed on them."[5]

Supporters of the Supreme Court celebrate the transparency of their new institution. Hearings are open to the public and broadcast on television, and the Court has an official Twitter handle, @UKSupremeCourt, with 8,000 followers. (The U.S. Supreme Court continues to resist televising its proceedings and shuns social media.) Opponents, on the other hand, consider the change mainly a cosmetic makeover and emphasize that the workings of the recently created Court will be the same as they were when the House of Lords was in charge.[6] One observer commented ominously: "The danger is that you muck around with a constitution like the British Constitution at your peril because you do not know what the consequences of any change will be."[7] Time will tell whether the Supreme Court plays a vital role in the United Kingdom's internal affairs and its relationship with Europe. Conflicts between freedom and order and between freedom and equality will arise in its chambers. Balancing these values remains the challenge of this democracy.

---

[1] Speech given at the official opening of the U.K. Supreme Court, 16 October 2009, available at the Ministry of Justice website, http://www.justice.gov.uk/news/speech161009a.htm.

[2] The U.K. Supreme Court has no jurisdiction over criminal proceedings from Scotland's High Court of Justiciary or any other court in Scotland. Supreme Court of the United Kingdom, Practice Direction 1, Article 1.2.10, pd_01_UKSC.pdf, http://www.supremecourt.gov.uk/index.html.

[3] Information available at the website of the U.K. Supreme Court, http://www.supremecourt.gov.uk/docs/pd01.pdf.

[4] "UK Supreme Court Judges Sworn In," BBC News Online Edition, 1 October 2009, http://news.bbc.co.uk/2/hi/uk_news/8283939.stm.

[5] Ibid.

[6] Nevertheless, the new justices are unable to sit and vote in the House of Lords. A selection commission will make subsequent judicial appointments.

[7] Joshua Rozenberg, "Fear over UK Supreme Court Impact," BBC News, http://news.bbc.co.uk/2/hi/uk_news/8237855.stm.

---

appeal may oppose review if they are not confident the outcome will be to their satisfaction.[28]

It is important to note that business cases represent a substantial portion of the Court's docket, though they receive far less attention than cases addressing social issues such as the death penalty, affirmative action, and school prayer. Business disputes are less emotional and the issues more technical. But business cases involve billions of dollars, have enormous consequences for the economy, and affect people's lives more often than the social issues that tend to dominate public debate and discussion.[29]

FIGURE 14.2 Access to and Decision Making in the U.S. Supreme Court, 2011 Term

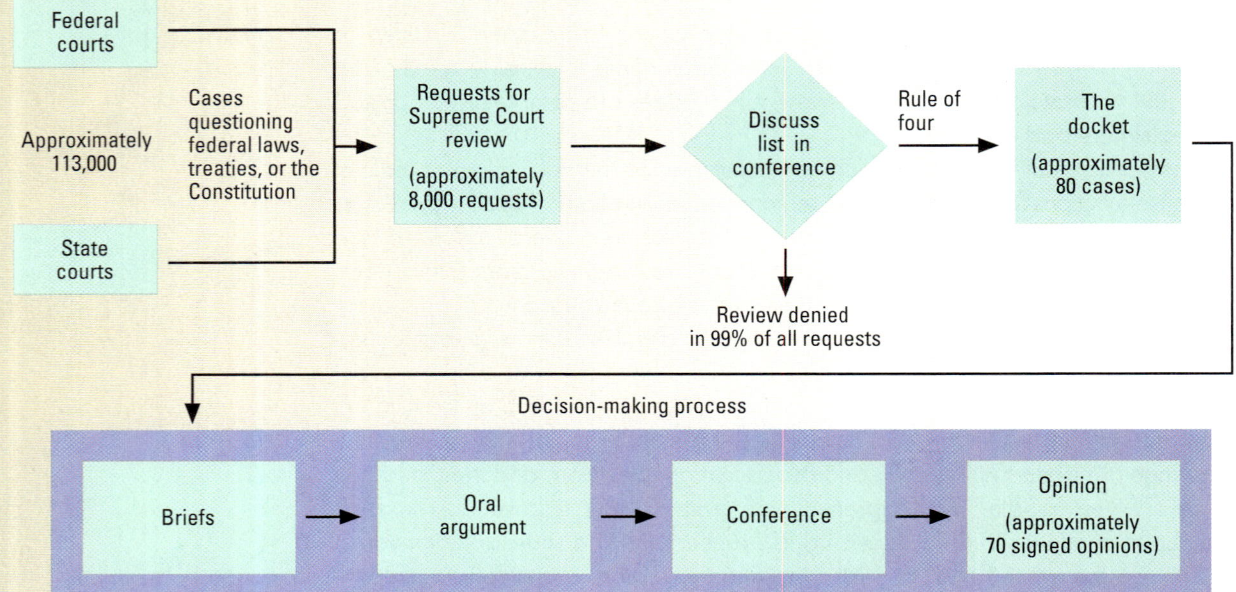

State and national appeals courts churn out thousands of decisions each year. Only a fraction ends up on the Supreme Court's docket. This chart sketches the several stages leading to a decision from the High Court.

Source: John G. Roberts, Jr., "The 2011 Year-End Report on the Federal Judiciary," http://www.supremecourt.gov/publicinfo/year-end/2011year-endreport.pdf.

The Solicitor General

Why does the Court decide to hear certain cases but not others? The best evidence scholars have adduced suggests that agenda setting depends on the individual justices, who vary in their decision-making criteria, and on the issues raised by the cases. Occasionally justices weigh the ultimate outcome of a case when granting or denying review. At other times, they grant or deny review based on disagreement among the lower courts or because delay in resolving the issues would impose alarming economic or social costs.[30] The solicitor general plays a vital role in the Court's agenda setting.

The **solicitor general** represents the national government before the Supreme Court, serving as the hinge between an administration's legal approach and its policy objectives. Appointed by the president, the solicitor general is the third-ranking official in the U.S. Department of Justice (after the attorney general and the deputy attorney general). Today, the solicitor general is Donald B. Verrilli, Jr., who succeeded Elena Kagan, the first woman to hold the office. President Obama tapped Kagan to replace Supreme Court Justice John Paul Stevens, who retired in June 2010.

The solicitor general's duties include determining whether the government should appeal lower-court decisions; reviewing and modifying, when necessary, the briefs filed in government appeals; and deciding whether the government should file an **amicus curiae brief*** in any appellate court.[31] The objective is to create a cohesive program for the executive branch in the federal courts.

solicitor general
The third highest official of the U.S. Department of Justice, and the one who represents the national government before the Supreme Court.

amicus curiae brief
A brief filed (with the permission of the court) by an individual or group that is not a party to a legal action but has an interest in it.

**Amicus curiae* is Latin for "friend of the court." Amicus briefs can be filed with the consent of all the parties or with the permission of the court. They allow groups and individuals who are not parties to the litigation but have an interest in it to influence the court's thinking and, perhaps, its decision.

Solicitors general play two different, and occasionally conflicting, roles. First, they are advocates for the president's policy preferences; second, as officers of the Court, they traditionally defend the institutional interests of the national government.

Solicitors general usually act with considerable restraint in recommending to the Court that a case be granted or denied review. By recommending only cases of general importance, they increase their credibility and their influence.

By carefully selecting the cases it presses, the solicitor general's office usually maintains a very impressive record of wins in the Supreme Court. Solicitors general are a "formidable force" in the process of setting the Supreme Court's agenda.[32] Their influence in bringing cases to the Court and arguing them there has earned them the informal title of "the tenth justice."

Decision Making

Once the Court grants review, attorneys submit written arguments (briefs). The justices follow an unwritten rule to avoid discussing cases with one another before oral argument. Should the rule be violated, the justices will inform their colleagues in an effort to avoid "little cliques or cabals or little groups that lobby each other before [argument]."[33] Oral argument, typically limited to thirty minutes for each side, is the first time the justices know what their colleagues might be thinking. From October through April, the justices spend two to three hours a day, five or six days a month, hearing arguments. Experience seems to help. Like the solicitor general, seasoned advocates enjoy a greater success rate, regardless of the party they represent.[34] The justices like crisp, concise, conversational presentations; they disapprove of attorneys who read from a prepared text. Some justices are aggressive, relentless questioners who frequently interrupt the lawyers; others are more subdued. In a 1993 free speech case, an attorney who offered an impassioned plea on the facts of the case was soon "awash in a sea of judicial impatience that at times seemed to border on anger.... 'We didn't take this case to determine who said what in the cafeteria,'" snapped one justice.[35]

The Court now releases oral argument transcripts on its website on the day of argument, and it releases recordings at the end of the week. In 2012, the Court scheduled a whopping six hours of argument in three cases challenging the constitutionality of the Affordable Care Act (also known as Obamacare) and took the extra step of sharing the audio with the public on each day rather than waiting until the end of the week. But the Court continued to ban tweets and blog posts from the courtroom itself, where computers, mobile phones, and tablets remain off-limits.

Court protocol prohibits the justices from addressing one another directly during oral arguments, but they often debate obliquely through the questions they pose to the attorneys. The justices reach no collective decision at the time of oral arguments. They reach a tentative decision only after they have met in conference.

Our knowledge of the dynamics of decision making on the Supreme Court is all secondhand. Only the justices attend the Court's weekly conferences. By tradition, the justices first shake hands prior to conference and to going on the bench, a gesture of harmony. The handshaking was introduced by Melville Fuller when he was chief justice from 1888 to 1910.[36] The chief justice then begins the presentation of each case with a discussion of it and his vote, which is followed by a discussion and vote from each of the other justices, in order of their seniority on the Court. Justice Antonin Scalia, who joined the Court in 1986, remarked that "not much conferencing goes on." By *conferencing,* Scalia meant efforts to persuade others to change their views by debating points of disagreement. "To call our discussion of a case a conference," he

Welcome to the Club!

Chief Justice John G. Roberts, Jr. (right) congratulated Elena Kagan (left), after administering the judicial oath to Kagan on August 7, 2010, making her the 112th justice of the U.S. Supreme Court. (Jeffrey Minear, counselor to the chief justice, held the Bible.) In prepared remarks afterward, Kagan pledged to support judicial restraint and a "modest" role for the Court.

Paul J. Richards/AFP/Getty Images

said, "is really something of a misnomer. It's much more a statement of the views of each of the nine Justices, after which the totals are added and the case is assigned" for an opinion.[37]

Judicial Restraint and Judicial Activism. How do the justices decide how to vote on a case? According to some scholars, legal doctrines and previous decisions explain their votes. This explanation, which is consistent with the majoritarian model, anchors the justices closely to the law and minimizes the contribution of their personal values. This view is embodied in the concept of **judicial restraint**, which maintains that the people's elected representatives, not judges, should make the laws. Judges are said to exercise judicial restraint when they defer to decisions of other governmental actors. Other scholars contend that the value preferences and resulting ideologies of the justices provide a more powerful interpretation of their voting.[38] This view is embodied in the concept of **judicial activism**, which maintains that judges should not give deference to the elected branches but should use their judicial power to promote the judges' preferred social and political goals. The concept of judicial activism and its cognate, judicial restraint, has many strands, and scholars sometimes disagree on its many meanings.[39] But at its core, all would agree that judges are activists when their decisions run counter to the will of the other branches of government, in effect substituting their own judgment for the judgment of the people's representatives. By interjecting personal values into court decisions, activist judging is more consistent with the pluralist model.

judicial restraint
A judicial philosophy by which judges tend to defer to decisions of the elected branches of government.

judicial activism
A judicial philosophy by which judges tend not to defer to decisions of the elected branches of government, resulting in the invalidation or emasculation of those decisions.

The terms *judicial restraint* and *judicial activism* describe different relative degrees of judicial assertiveness. Judges acting according to an extreme model of judicial restraint would never question the validity of duly enacted laws but would defer to the superiority of other government institutions in construing the laws. Judges acting according to an extreme model of judicial activism would be an intrusive and ever-present force that would dominate other government institutions. Actual judicial behavior lies somewhere between these two extremes.

From the 1960s through the 1980s, many activist judges tended to support liberal values, thus linking judicial activism with liberalism. But the critical Supreme Court case of *Bush* v. *Gore* suggests to many critics that conservative jurists can also be judicial activists, promoting their preferred political goals. Had a majority deferred to the Florida courts on the issue of the recount, the decision would have been hailed as an example of judicial restraint. But overturning the Florida courts and delivering a victory for the Republicans have labeled the majority in *Bush* v. *Gore* as conservative judicial activists. By overturning more than 40 federal statutes, the Rehnquist and Roberts Courts now link judicial activism with conservatism.

Judgment and Argument. The voting outcome is the **judgment**, the decision on who wins and who loses. The justices often disagree not only on the winner and loser, but also on the reasons for their judgment. This should not be surprising, given nine independent minds and issues that can be approached in several ways. Voting in the conference does not end the justices' work or resolve their disagreements. Votes remain tentative until the Court issues an opinion announcing its judgment.

After voting, the justices in the majority must draft an opinion setting out the reasons for their decision. The **argument** is the kernel of the opinion—its logical content, as distinct from supporting facts, rhetoric, and procedures. If all justices agree with the judgment and the reasons supporting it, the opinion is unanimous. Agreement with a judgment for different reasons from those set forth in the majority opinion is called a **concurrence**. Or a justice can **dissent** if she or he disagrees with a judgment. Both concurring and dissenting opinions may be drafted, in addition to the majority opinion.

The Opinion. After the conference, the chief justice or most senior justice in the majority (in terms of years of service on the Court) decides which justice will write the majority opinion. He or she may consider several factors in assigning the crucial opinion-writing task, including the prospective author's workload, expertise, public opinion, and (above all) ability to hold the majority together. (Remember that the votes are only tentative at this point.) On the one hand, if the drafting justice holds an extreme view on the issues in a case and is not able to incorporate the views of more moderate colleagues, those justices may withdraw their votes. On the other hand, assigning a more moderate justice to draft an opinion could weaken the argument on which the opinion rests. Opinion-writing assignments can also be punitive. Justice Harry Blackmun once commented, "If one's in the doghouse with the Chief [former Chief Justice Warren Burger], he gets the crud."[40]

Opinion writing is the justices' most critical function. It is not surprising, then, that they spend much of their time drafting opinions. The justices usually call on their law clerks—top graduates of the nation's elite law schools—to help them prepare opinions and carry out other tasks. The commitment can be daunting. All of the justices now rely on their clerks to shoulder substantial responsibilities, including the initial drafts of opinions.[41]

The writing justice distributes a draft opinion to all the justices, who then read it and circulate their criticisms and suggestions. An opinion may have to be rewritten several times to accommodate colleagues who remain unpersuaded by the draft. Justice Felix Frankfurter was a perfectionist; some of his opinions went through thirty or more drafts. Justices can change their votes, and perhaps alter the judgment, until the decision is officially announced. Often, the most controversial cases pile up as coalitions on the Court vie for support or sharpen their criticisms. When the Court announces a decision, the justices who wrote the opinion read or summarize their views in the courtroom.

Justices in the majority frequently try to muffle or stifle dissent to encourage institutional cohesion. Since the mid-1940s, however, unity has been more difficult to obtain.[42] Gaining agreement from the justices today is akin to negotiating with nine separate law firms. It may be more surprising that the justices ever agree. In 2006, for example, the Court spoke without dissent in more than half of its cases. The conservative shift occasioned by the appointments of Roberts and Alito has infused cohesion among dissenters, who have tended to join a single opinion. And the Court's genteel etiquette appears strained as once collegial justices voice their views publicly and forcefully from the bench.[43]

The justices remain aware of the slender foundation of their authority, which rests largely on public respect. That respect is tested whenever the Court ventures into controversial areas. Banking, slavery, and Reconstruction policies embroiled the Court in the nineteenth century. Freedom of speech and religion, racial equality, the right to privacy, the 2000 election, and the extent of presidential power have led the Court into controversy in the past sixty years.

The Chief Justice

The chief justice is only one of nine justices, but he has several important functions based on his authority. Apart from his role in forming the docket and directing the Court's conferences, the chief justice can also be a social leader, generating solidarity within the group. Sometimes a chief justice can embody intellectual leadership. Finally, the chief justice can provide policy leadership, directing the Court toward a general policy position. Perhaps only John Marshall could lay claim to possessing social, intellectual, and policy leadership. Warren E. Burger, who resigned as chief justice in 1986, was reputed to be a lackluster leader in all three areas.[44]

When presiding at the conference, the chief justice can control the discussion of issues, although independent-minded justices are not likely to acquiesce to his views. Moreover, justices today rarely engage in a debate of the issues in the conference. Rather, they communicate by memoranda, not e-mail; they use their law clerks as ambassadors between justices' chambers and, in effect, "run the Court without talking to one another."[45]

★ 14.4 Judicial Recruitment

★ Explain how judges at different levels of the federal court system are nominated and confirmed to the federal bench.

Neither the Constitution nor national law imposes formal requirements for appointment to the federal courts. Once appointed, district and appeals judges must reside in the district or circuit to which they are appointed.

The president appoints judges to the federal courts, and all nominees must be confirmed by majority vote in the Senate. Congress sets, but cannot lower, a judge's compensation. In 2012, salaries were as listed below.

By comparison, in 2011, the average salary of a state supreme court judge was about $158,000. The average for a state trial judge was about $137,000.[46] Although annual compensation for equity partners in major law firms exceeds $1 million, employment prospects for new lawyers have tanked since the recession that began in 2008 with median starting salaries for lawyers in private practice dropping by

Chief Justice of the Supreme Court	$223,500
Associate Supreme Court justices	213,900
Courts of appeals judges	184,500
District judges	174,000
Magistrate judges	160,080

Source: © Cengage Learning.

35 percent compared to 2009.[47] Still, Supreme Court law clerks entering private practice will earn more than the justices who hired them. This prompted Supreme Court Justice Antonin Scalia to urge bright students to choose other professions, such as engineering and teaching. "Society cannot afford to have such a huge proportion of its best minds going into the law," said Scalia.[48]

In more than half the states, the governor appoints the state judges, often in consultation with judicial nominating commissions. In many of these states, voters decide whether the judges should be retained in office. Other states select their judges by partisan, nonpartisan, or (rarely) legislative election.[49] In some states, nominees must be confirmed by the state legislature. Contested elections for judgeships are unusual, though at the extreme, such contests may call a judge's impartiality into question. In 2009, the U.S. Supreme Court ruled that the newly elected chief justice of the West Virginia Supreme Court, Brent Benjamin, had to disqualify himself from deliberations in a case involving a coal company chief executive who had spent $3 million to elect Benjamin.[50] In most other countries, judges are appointed, not elected (see "Compared with What? Selecting Judges around the World" on p. 398).

The Appointment of Federal Judges

The Constitution states that federal judges shall hold their commission "during good Behaviour," which in practice means for life.* A president's judicial appointments, then, are likely to survive his administration, providing a kind of political legacy. The appointment power assumes that the president is free to identify candidates and appoint judges who favor his policies. President Franklin D. Roosevelt had appointed nearly 75 percent of all sitting federal judges by the end of his twelve years in office. In contrast, President Ford appointed fewer than 13 percent in his three years in office. Presidents Reagan and George H. W. Bush together appointed more than 60 percent of all federal judges. During his administration, President Clinton appointed more than 40 percent of the 852 federal judges at all levels. President George W. Bush appointed 38 percent (or 325) of all federal judges during his tenure.

Judicial vacancies occur when sitting judges resign, retire, or die. Vacancies also arise when Congress creates new judgeships to handle increasing caseloads. In both cases, the president nominates a candidate, who must be confirmed by the Senate. Under President Barack Obama, the Office of White House Counsel is deeply involved in this screening process. The president also had the help of the Justice Department, primarily through its Office of Legal Policy, which screens candidates before the formal nomination, subjecting serious contenders to FBI investigation. The White House and the Justice Department formed a Judicial Selection Committee as part of this vetting process. The White House and the Senate vie for control in the approval of district and appeals court judges.

The "Advice and Consent" of the Senate. For district and appeals court vacancies, the nomination "must be acceptable to the home state senator from the president's party"[51] (or to the state's House delegation from the president's party if no senator is from the president's party). The Judicial Selection Committee consults extensively with home state senators from which the appointment will be made.[52] Senators' influence is greater for appointments to district court than for appointments to the court of appeals.

---

*As of 2012, fifteen federal judges have been impeached. Of these, eight were convicted in the Senate and removed from office. The most recent to be forced to leave office was Judge G. Thomas Porteous, who was impeached by the House and convicted by the Senate in 2010.

Compared with What?

Selecting Judges around the World

In at least half of the U.S. states, judges run for election. In fact, nearly 90 percent of all state judges face the voters. This practice is in stark contrast to the rest of the world, where judges are appointed, either by the executive branch (with or without recommendations from a judicial selection commission), by the judicial selection commission itself, or by the legislative branch. In a few countries the civil service offers a professional career path leading to a judgeship. In these countries judges are selected through examinations and school programs. In only two nations—Switzerland and Japan—judicial elections hold sway, but only in a very limited way: (1) Some smaller Swiss cantons (subnational units) elect judges, and (2) appointed justices of the Japanese Supreme Court may face retention elections, though scholars regard the practice as a mere formality. Hans A. Linde, a retired justice of the Oregon Supreme Court, captured the essence of the American exception when he observed: "To the rest of the world, American adherence to judicial elections is as incomprehensible as our rejection of the metric system."

The table here shows the judicial selection process used in countries around the world. Some countries use more than one method; the table lists the primary one.

Executive Appointment without Commission	Executive Appointment with Commission	Appointment by Commission	Legislative Appointment	Career Judiciary
Afghanistan	Albania	Algeria	China	Czech Republic
Argentina	Canada	Andorra	Cuba	France
Australia	Dominican Republic	Angola	Laos	Germany
Bangladesh	England	Bulgaria	Macedonia	Italy
Belarus	Greece	Croatia	Montenegro	Japan
Belgium	Namibia	Cyprus	Poland	
Cambodia	Russia	Israel	Portugal	
Chad	Scotland	Lebanon	Spain	
Egypt	South Africa	Mexico	Turkey	
New Zealand	Ukraine	Rwanda		
Uzbekistan	Zimbabwe	Yemen		

Source: Based on Adam Liptak, "American Exception: Rendering Justice, with One Eye on Re-election," *New York Times*, 25 May 2008, http://www.nytimes.com/2008/05/25/us/25exception .html?pagewanted=1&_r=1.

senatorial courtesy
A norm under which a nomination must be acceptable to the home state senator from the president's party.

This practice, called **senatorial courtesy**, forces presidents to share the nomination power with members of the Senate. The Senate will not confirm a nominee who is opposed by the senior senator from the nominee's state if that senator is a member of the president's party. The Senate does not actually reject the candidate. Instead, the chairman of the Senate Judiciary Committee, which reviews all judicial nominees, will not schedule a confirmation hearing, effectively killing the nomination.

Although the Justice Department is still sensitive to senatorial prerogatives, senators can no longer submit a single name to fill a vacancy. The department searches for acceptable candidates and polls the appropriate senator for her or his reaction to them. President George H. W. Bush asked Republican senators to seek more qualified female and minority candidates. Bush made progress in developing a more diverse bench, and President Clinton accelerated the change.[53] President George W. Bush improved the Republican track record in appointing women and minorities but still lagged behind Clinton. President Obama now ranks at the top in appointing more women in four years compared to his predecessors.[54]

The Senate Judiciary Committee conducts a hearing for each judicial nominee. The committee chair exercises a measure of control in the appointment process that goes beyond senatorial courtesy. If a nominee is objectionable to the chair, he or she can delay a hearing or hold up other appointments until the president and the Justice Department find an alternative. Such behavior does not win a politician much influence in the long run, however. So committee chairs of the president's party are usually loath to place obstacles in a president's path, especially when they may want presidential support for their own policies and constituencies.

Beginning with the Carter administration, judicial appointments below the Supreme Court have proved a new battleground, with a growing proportion of nominees not confirmed and increasing delays in the process. These appointments were once viewed as presidential and party patronage, but that old-fashioned view has given way to a focus on the president's policy agenda through judicial appointments. This perspective has enlarged the ground on which senators have opposed judicial nominees to include matters of judicial policy (for example, abortion) and theory (for example, delving into a nominee's approach when interpreting the meaning of a statute). Beginning in 2003, Democratic senators used the filibuster to prevent confirmation votes for judicial candidates they deemed "outside the mainstream." This behavior provoked ire from the majority Republicans, who threatened to end the filibuster practice entirely. The parties reached an uneasy compromise in 2005 to invoke a judicial filibuster only for "extraordinary circumstances," but that compromise seems to have dissolved in 2011 when the Republicans began employing the judicial filibuster to scuttle Obama nominees.[55]

The American Bar Association. The American Bar Association (ABA), the biggest organization of lawyers in the United States, has been involved in screening candidates for the federal bench since 1946.[56] Its role is defined by custom, not law. At the president's behest, the ABA's Standing Committee on the Federal Judiciary routinely rates prospective appointees using a three-value scale: "well qualified," "qualified," and "not qualified." The association no longer has advance notice of possible nominees. The George W. Bush administration considered the ABA too liberal, posing an unnecessary impediment to the confirmation of conservative judges.[57] Nonetheless, the association continued to evaluate the professional qualifications of nominees after they were nominated. President Obama restored the ABA's prenomination review in March 2009.[58]

Recent Presidents and the Federal Judiciary

Since the presidency of Jimmy Carter, chief executives have tended—more or less—to make appointments to the federal courts that are more diverse in racial, ethnic, and gender terms than in previous administrations. President Bill Clinton took the lead on diversity. For the first time in history, more than half of the president's judicial appointments were women or minorities. Clinton's chief judge selector, Assistant Attorney General Eleanor Acheson, followed through on Clinton's campaign pledge to make his appointees "look like America."

The racial and ethnic composition of the parties themselves helps explain much of the variation between the appointments of presidents of different parties. It seems clear that political ideology, not demographics, lies at the heart of judicial appointments. Reagan and George H. W. Bush sought nominees with particular policy preferences who would leave their stamp on the judiciary well into the twenty-first century. When it comes to ideological preferences as revealed by judicial choices, Carter's judges carry off the honors. A review of more than twenty-five thousand federal court decisions from 1968 to 1995 concluded that Carter-appointed judges were the most liberal, whereas Reagan- and Bush-appointed judges were the least liberal. (Carter had an advantage in his efforts to mold the bench because his appointees were reviewed by a Democratic-led Senate. Reagan, George H. W. Bush, Clinton, and George W. Bush contended with a Senate in the hands of the opposing party for part of their administrations.) Clinton-appointed judges were somewhat less liberal than Carter's but decidedly more liberal than the legacy of Nixon, Ford, Reagan, or George H. W. Bush.[59] And George W. Bush's judges are among the most conservative on record when it comes to civil rights and liberties.[60] One general rule seems clear: presidents are likely to appoint judges who share similar values.[61]

Appointment to the Supreme Court

The announcement of a vacancy on the High Court usually causes quite a stir. Campaigns for Supreme Court seats are commonplace, although the public rarely sees them. Hopefuls contact friends in the administration and urge influential associates to do the same on their behalf. Some candidates never give up hope. Judge John J. Parker, whose nomination to the Court was defeated in 1930, tried in vain to rekindle interest in his appointment until he was well past the age—usually the early sixties—that appointments are made.[62]

The president is not shackled by senatorial courtesy when it comes to nominating a Supreme Court justice. However, appointments to the Court attract more intense public scrutiny than do lower-level appointments, effectively narrowing the president's options and focusing attention on the Senate's advice and consent.

Of the 155 men and 5 women nominated to the Court, 11 names have been withdrawn, and 25 have failed to receive Senate confirmation. (Seven confirmed justices declined to serve.)[63] Only six such fumbles have occurred since 1900. The last one was George W. Bush's nomination of Harriet Miers in 2005 to fill the vacancy created by the retirement of Sandra Day O'Connor. Miers, who was White House counsel, withdrew her candidacy after coming under withering criticism, largely from conservatives, for her lack of clarity on issues likely to come before the Court.

The most important factor in the rejection of a nominee is partisan politics. At least sixteen candidates lost their bids for appointment because the presidents who nominated them were considered likely to become lame ducks: the party in control of the Senate anticipated victory for its candidate in an upcoming presidential race and sought to deny the incumbent president an important political appointment.[64]

Eighteen of the twenty-five successful Supreme Court nominees since 1950 have had prior judicial experience in federal or state courts. This tendency toward "promotion" from within the judiciary may be based on the idea that a judge's previous opinions are good predictors of his or her future opinions on the High Court. After all, a president is handing out a powerful lifetime appointment, so it makes sense to want an individual who is sympathetic to his views. Federal or state court judges holding lifetime appointments are likely to state their views frankly in their opinions. In contrast, the policy preferences of High Court candidates who have been in legal practice or in political office can only be guessed at, based on the conjecture of professional associates or on speeches they have given to local Rotary Clubs, on the floor of a legislature, and elsewhere.

After a vacancy drought of more than eleven years, President George W. Bush put his stamp on the Supreme Court with two appointments in 2005. He nominated federal judge John G. Roberts, Jr., in July 2005 to replace Associate Justice Sandra Day O'Connor (after the withdrawal of Harriet Miers). But with the death of Chief Justice William H. Rehnquist in September, Bush withdrew Roberts's nomination as associate justice and resubmitted him for the position of chief justice. Roberts was confirmed 78–22. Democrats were evenly split: 22 for and 22 against. Bush then nominated federal judge Samuel A. Alito for the seat vacated by O'Connor. His confirmation hearing was far more contentious, with the Democrats aiming to paint him as "outside the mainstream." The effort failed, as did a last-minute call to filibuster the nomination. Alito was confirmed by the Senate by a narrow margin, 58–42 (nearly all Democrats were opposed), and he took his seat as the 110th justice in January 2006.

The results of the Roberts and Alito appointments were soon apparent. In the 2006 Term (October 2006 to June 2007), the first full term with Roberts and Alito on the bench, the Court moved in a decidedly conservative direction. One-third of all the cases were decided by 5–4 votes, almost triple the proportion of close votes from the previous term. In each case, Justice Anthony Kennedy cast the deciding vote. He joined the majority in all twenty-four 5–4 decisions, siding more often with his conservative colleagues. Subsequently, Kennedy has left his mark by authoring the majority opinion or providing the deciding vote across a range of hot-button issues: declaring the death penalty unconstitutional for the rape of a child, ensuring Guantánamo detainees a constitutional right to challenge their detention in federal courts, supporting a constitutional right for individuals to own a gun for personal use, and removing restrictions on corporate spending in election campaigns.

The hearts of many a lawyer and loyal Democrat fluttered when Justice David H. Souter announced his decision to retire from the Supreme Court effective June 29, 2009. This gave President Obama the opportunity to appoint a second woman to the Supreme Court, federal judge Sonia Sotomayor of New York. Sotomayor, the first Latina to be nominated to the Court, possessed a sterling résumé with a compelling personal story. Raised by her widowed mother in a Bronx housing project, Sotomayor went on to earn top honors at Princeton and distinction at Yale Law School. She spent years as a federal prosecutor and in private legal practice before she was appointed by Republican president George H. W. Bush to the federal district court in 1992. President Bill Clinton appointed her to the federal appellate court in 1998.

Justices at Bat

At his confirmation hearings in 2005 to become the seventeenth chief justice of the United States, John G. Roberts, Jr., declared, "[I]t's my job to call balls and strikes and not to pitch or bat." But bat he did, moving the Court in a more conservative direction in 2010 by voting in a landmark 5–4 decision to strike down campaign finance legislation that had prohibited corporations and unions from broadcasting "electioneering communications."

Republicans on the Senate Judiciary Committee tried to derail Sotomayor's nomination, pouring over everything she had written or said. Some senators focused on a comment she made in 2001, that a wise Latina woman "would more often than not reach a better conclusion than a white male who hasn't lived that life."[65] In opposing Sotomayor, some Republicans risked the ire of Hispanic voters, whose role in American politics is destined to grow. As illustrated in Figure 14.3, by 2050, the percentage of Hispanics in the population is expected to increase from 15 to 30 percent.

Sotomayor deflected the attacks and stuck to her well-rehearsed script, declaring that her core guiding principle was "fidelity to the law." That bromide kept her opponents at bay. In the end, she was confirmed by a vote of 68 to 31, largely along party lines. Given her record as a moderate, Sotomayor's appointment will not be a game-changer since she replaced a moderate justice.

President Obama filled a third seat when moderate justice John Paul Stevens announced in April 2010 that he would retire at the end of the current term in June 2010. President Obama nominated Elena Kagan, his solicitor general, to fill the seat. In a departure from recent practice, Obama did not find his choice in the minor leagues of the federal judiciary. Rather, Kagan made her mark as a law professor and law school administrator (and a coveted clerkship with Supreme Court Justice Thurgood Marshall). In a 1995 book review, Kagan wrote that confirmation hearings were "a vapid and hollow charade."[66] But when it was her turn to be interrogated by the Senate Judiciary Committee, she chose the well-worn path of avoiding answers to serious questions. Her bromide: the Court's role "must ... be a modest one—properly deferential to the decisions of the American people and their elected representatives."[67] The Senate confirmed Kagan by a vote of 63 to 37. On August 7, 2010, she became the 112th justice—and the fourth woman—to serve on the Court.

One of the great prizes of any presidency is the ability to appoint federal judges. These are lifetime appointments, enabling presidents to extend their legacies well beyond their terms of office. As of July 2012, President Obama has appointed a total

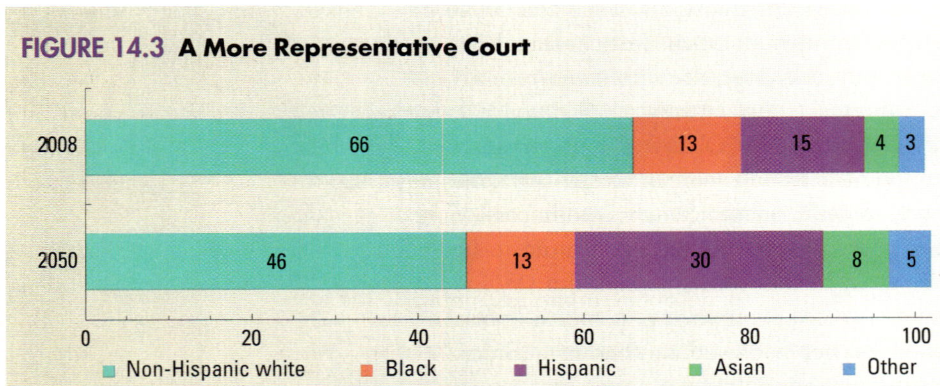

FIGURE 14.3 A More Representative Court

Before President Obama appointed Sonia Sotomayor to the Supreme Court, the Court had only one woman, one African American, and no Hispanics among its nine members. Although the Court remains overwhelmingly male (67 percent) after Kagan's appointment, it did move toward becoming more demographically representative of the nation. Its composition (11 percent African American and 11 percent Hispanic) put it close to the national ethnic breakdown in 2008. Over the next generation, the Hispanic percentage is expected to double, arguing for the political significance of Sotomayor's appointment.
Source: Based on Sam Roberts, "In a Generation, Minorities May Be the U.S. Majority," *New York Times*, 13 August 2008, http://www.nytimes.com/2008/08/14/washington/14census.html.

of 156 federal judges and nominated 32 others to fill the estimated 88 vacancies that are anticipated to emerge in the federal courts before the end of Obama's current term.[68] Obama has taken a decidedly go-slow approach, lagging behind his predecessors in filling judicial vacancies with moderate choices. Given the increased partisanship and rancor in the Senate, it is not surprising for the Republicans to use the filibuster threat and a parliamentary procedure known as a "secret hold" to block or delay additional appointments.[69]

14.5 The Consequences of Judicial Decisions

★ Examine the impact, influence, and acceptance of decisions on issues of national importance by an institution unaccountable to the electorate.

Judicial rulings represent the tip of the iceberg in terms of all the legal conflicts and disputes that arise in this country. Most cases never surface in court. The overwhelming majority of lawsuits end without a court judgment. Many civil cases are settled, or the parties give up, or the courts dismiss the suits because they are beyond the legitimate bounds of judicial resolution. Most criminal cases end in a plea bargain, with the defendant admitting his or her guilt in exchange for a less severe punishment. Only about 10 percent of criminal cases in the federal district courts are tried; an equally small percentage of civil cases are adjudicated.

Furthermore, the fact that a judge sentences a criminal defendant to ten years in prison or a court holds a company liable for billions in damages does not guarantee that the defendant will lose his or her freedom or the company will give up any assets. In the case of the criminal defendant, the road of seeking an appeal following trial and conviction is well traveled and, if nothing else, serves to delay the day when he or she must go to prison. In civil cases as well, an appeal may be filed to delay the day of reckoning.

Supreme Court Rulings: Implementation and Impact

When the Supreme Court makes a decision, it relies on others to implement it—to translate policy into action. How a judgment is implemented depends in good measure on how it was crafted. Remember that the justices, in preparing their opinions, must work to hold their majorities together, to gain greater, if not unanimous, support for their arguments. This forces them to compromise in their opinions, to moderate their arguments, which introduces ambiguity into many of the policies they articulate. Ambiguous opinions affect the implementation of policy. For example, when the Supreme Court issued its unanimous order in 1955 to desegregate public school facilities "with all deliberate speed,"[70] judges who opposed the Court's policy dragged their feet in implementing it. In the early 1960s, the Supreme Court prohibited prayers and Bible reading in public schools. Yet state court judges and attorneys general reinterpreted the High Court's decision to mean that only compulsory prayer or Bible reading was unconstitutional and that state-sponsored voluntary prayer or Bible reading was acceptable.[71]

Because the Supreme Court confronts issues freighted with deeply felt social values or fundamental political beliefs, its decisions have influence beyond the immediate parties in a dispute. The Court's decision in *Roe* v. *Wade,* legalizing abortion, generated heated public reaction. The justices were barraged with thousands of angry letters. Groups opposing abortion vowed to overturn the decision; groups favoring the freedom to obtain an abortion moved to protect the right they had won. Within eight months of the decision, more than two dozen constitutional amendments had been introduced in Congress, although none managed to carry the extraordinary majority required for passage. Still, the antiabortion faction achieved a modest victory with the passage of a provision forbidding the use of national government funds for abortions except when the woman's life is in jeopardy. (Since 1993, the exception has also included victims of rape or incest.)

Abortion opponents have also directed their efforts at state legislatures, hoping to load abortion laws with enough conditions to discourage women from terminating their pregnancies. For example, one state required that women receive detailed information about abortions, then wait at least twenty-four hours before consenting to the procedure. The information listed every imaginable danger associated with abortion and included a declaration that fathers are liable to support their children financially. A legal challenge to these new restrictions reached the Supreme Court, and in 1989, it abandoned its strong defense of abortion rights.[72] The Court continued to support a woman's right to abortion, but in yet another legal challenge in 1992, it recognized the government's power to further limit the exercise of that right.[73] In 2000, in a 5–4 vote, it struck down a state law banning late-term abortions. But in 2007, the Roberts Court reversed course and in a 5–4 vote upheld a nearly identical federal late-term abortion ban.[74]

Public Opinion and the Supreme Court

Democratic theorists have a difficult time reconciling a commitment to representative democracy with a judiciary that is not accountable to the electorate yet has the power to undo legislative and executive acts. The difficulty may simply be a problem for theorists, however. The policies coming from the Supreme Court, although lagging years behind public opinion, rarely seem out of line with the public's ideological choices.[75] Surveys in several controversial areas reveal that an ideologically balanced Court seldom departs from majority sentiment or trends.[76] "What history shows," wrote Professor Barry Friedman in the most recent and thorough study in this area, "is assuredly not that Supreme Court decisions always are in line with popular opinion, but rather that they come into line with one another over time."[77] That alignment has yet to materialize nearly five decades later on the issue of school prayer, since the Court struck down the recitation of a nondenominational public school prayer in 1961.[78] A majority of Americans then and now do not agree with the Court's position. And so long as much of the public continues to want prayer in schools, the controversy will continue.

New research has shed valuable light on public knowledge and understanding of the judiciary. It turns out that Americans know more about the Supreme Court than pundits had previously acknowledged. As citizens gain knowledge about the judiciary, they are at the same time confronted with important symbols of judicial power such as the wearing of judicial robes, the use of a privileged form of address (e.g., "Your Honor"), and the requirement to rise when judges enter a court room. These symbols tend to emphasize a special role for the courts. "To know more about courts may not be to love them," wrote James L. Gibson and Gregory A. Caldeira, "but to know them is to learn and think that they are different from other political institutions (and often therefore more worthy of trust, respect, and legitimacy)."[79]

In 2009, the Gallup Poll showed that nearly six out of ten Americans are much more likely to approve than disapprove of the job the Supreme Court is doing.[80] Oddly, Court approval surged for Democrats and declined for Republicans even as the Court continued its conservative direction.[81] By 2012, the Court's public approval rating had fallen significantly to 44 percent. There was no difference in approval between liberals and conservatives; each registered about 40 percent approval.[82]

The judicial process is imperfect, so it is not surprising that the Court will continue to step into minefields of public criticism. In 2005 the Court ruled that the Constitution did not forbid a city from taking private property for private development.[83] The outrage across the ideological spectrum was enormous and immediate. State legislatures and courts acted swiftly to give greater protection to private property. This was strong evidence that the Court's measured opinion was out of step with conventional wisdom.

14.6 The Courts and Models of Democracy

★ Evaluate the decision-making authority of the federal judiciary within the context of both majoritarian and pluralist democracy.

How far should judges stray from existing statutes and precedents? Supporters of the majoritarian model would argue that the courts should adhere to the letter of the law, that judges must refrain from injecting their own values into their decisions. If the law places too much (or not enough) emphasis on equality or order, the elected legislature, not the courts, can change the law. In contrast, those who support the pluralist model maintain that the courts are a policymaking branch of government. It is thus legitimate for the individual values and interests of judges to mirror group interests and preferences and for judges to attempt consciously to advance group interests as they see fit. However, judges at all levels find it difficult to determine when, where, and how to proceed (see "Politics of Global Change: The Right to Die" on pp. 406–407).

The argument that our judicial system fits the pluralist model gains support from a legal procedure called a **class action**. A class action is a device for assembling the claims or defenses of similarly situated individuals so that they can be heard in a single lawsuit. A class action makes it possible for people with small individual claims and limited financial resources to aggregate their claims and resources and thus make a lawsuit viable. The class action also permits the case to be tried by representative parties, with the judgment binding on all. Decisions in class action suits can have broader impact than decisions in other types of cases. Since the 1940s, class action suits have been the vehicles through which groups have asserted claims involving civil rights, legislative apportionment, and environmental problems. For example, schoolchildren have sued (through their parents) under the banner of class action to rectify claimed racial discrimination on the part of school authorities, as in *Brown* v. *Board of Education*.

Abetting the class action is the resurgence of state supreme courts' fashioning policies consistent with group preferences. Informed Americans often look to the U.S. Supreme Court for protection of their rights and liberties. In many circumstances, that

class action
A procedure by which similarly situated litigants may be heard in a single lawsuit.

Politics of Global Change

The Right to Die

In June 1997, the Supreme Court ended its long silence on the constitutionality of a right to suicide, rejecting two separate challenges to state laws prohibiting assisted suicide. In 1996, the U.S. Court of Appeals for the Ninth Circuit relied on the Supreme Court's abortion decisions to strike down a Washington State law against aiding or abetting suicide. The circuit court reasoned from the High Court's abortion rulings that the Fourteenth Amendment's due process clause protects the individual's right "to define one's own concept of existence, of meaning, of the universe, and of the mystery of life." The Supreme Court, however, in *Washington* v. *Glucksberg,* unanimously rejected the circuit court's reasoning in no uncertain terms stressing that suicide is not a "fundamental right" that is "deeply rooted in our legal tradition." Unlike abortion, suicide has been all but universally condemned in the law.

In another 1996 decision, the U.S. Court of Appeals for the Second Circuit adopted a different line of reasoning to invalidate a New York law banning physician-assisted suicide. The court held that the law violated the Fourteenth Amendment's equal protection clause because it treated those who needed a physician's help to administer lethal doses of prescription drugs (which is criminalized by law) differently from those who can demand removal of life-support systems (which is allowed under prior Supreme Court cases). In June 1997, the Supreme Court unanimously rejected this argument in *Vacco* v. *Quill.* The Court held that the New York law does not result in similar cases being treated differently. "The distinction between letting a patient die and making that patient die is important, logical, rational, and well established," the majority declared.

The Supreme Court displayed an acute awareness of the ongoing debate in the states about assisted suicide. Because the Court determined only that the U.S. Constitution does not protect a right to assisted suicide, the states may still establish such a right by statute or state constitutional amendments.

Only Oregon and Washington State, under their Death with Dignity Acts, have established a limited right to assisted suicide. The laws specify detailed sets of conditions that individuals and their doctors must follow in order to implement physician-assisted suicide. From 1998 to 2011, 596 people died in this fashion in Oregon. In Washington State, since the act became law in 2009, 135 people died out of 152 who were dispensed the medication. The data in both states suggest that terminally ill older patients with higher education are more likely to use physician-assisted suicide than younger patients.

expectation is correct. But state courts may serve as the staging areas for legal campaigns to change the law in the nation's highest court. They also exercise substantial influence over the policies that affect citizens daily, including the rights and liberties enshrined in state constitutions, statutes, and common law.[84]

Furthermore, state judges need not look to the U.S. Supreme Court for guidance on the meaning of certain state rights and liberties. If a state court chooses to rely solely on national law in deciding a case, that case is reviewable by the U.S. Supreme Court. But a state court can avoid review by the U.S. Supreme Court by basing its

In a much more complicated case, the Supreme Court spoke through its silence. In 1990, Terri Schiavo suffered cardiac arrest that led to irreversible brain damage. In the ensuing fifteen years, she was aided by a feeding tube to provide nutrition and hydration. Her husband (and legal guardian) received state court approval to remove the tube and hasten her death. The U.S. Supreme Court refused to get involved after a federal court turned down a plea by her family to reinsert the feeding tube. The Florida governor, the Florida legislature, the U.S. Congress, and President George W. Bush all sought to intervene and encroach on judicial authority, but to no avail. Schiavo died without regaining consciousness.

Other industrial democracies have tacked in a different direction by decriminalizing the right to die, also known as euthanasia or "good death." The Netherlands, Belgium, and Switzerland have adopted distinct laws that regulate the right to a mercy death. Physician-assisted suicide is legal in the Netherlands, whereas Swiss law decriminalizes assisted suicide only when physicians are not involved. The Swiss legislation on assisted suicide is one of the most liberal in the world, and "many terminally ill foreigners … now travel to Switzerland to commit suicide." In Belgium, since 2005 pharmacists can supply doctors with fatal doses of medicines, permitting assisted suicide. The euthanasia debate is active in Spain after several high-profile cases of assisted suicide. Only recently, in March 2010, the legislature of the southern province of Andalucía enacted the first Death with Dignity Law in Spain with support from parties representing the whole ideological spectrum. The Oscar-winning movie *The Sea Inside* ("Mar Adentro") tells one such real-life story of a Spanish quadriplegic in a legal and human quest to achieve his right to end his life with dignity.

Sources: *Washington* v. *Glucksberg,* 521 U.S. 793 (1997); *Vacco* v. *Quill,* 521 U.S. 702 (1997); *Compassion in Dying* v. *Washington,* 79 F.3d 790 (9th Cir. 1996); *Quill* v. *Vacco,* 80 F.3d 716 (2d Cir. 1996); Twelfth Annual Report on Oregon's Death with Dignity Act, March 2010, http://www.oregon.gov/DHS/ph/pas/docs/yr12-tbl-1.pdf; "Assisted Suicide Measure Passes," *Seattle Times,* 4 November 2008, http://seattletimes .nwsource.com/html/localnews/2008352033_1000prop05m.html; 2009 Death with Dignity Act Report in Washington State, March 2010, http://www.doh.wa.gov/dwda/forms/DWDA_2009.pdf; K. L. Cerminara and K. W. Goodman, "Key Events in the Case of Theresa Marie Schiavo," http://www.miami.edu/ethics/schiavo/timeline.htm; "Schiavo Parents Back in Federal Court, Supreme Court, State Judge Deny Appeals to Resume Feeding," CNN On Line, 25 March 2005, http://www.cnn.com/2005/LAW/03/24/schiavo; Ursula Smartt, "Euthanasia and the Law," BBC News, 21 February 2007, http://news.bbc.co.uk/1/hi/health/2600923.stm; and Reyes Rincon, "El Parlamento andaluz aprueba la primera ley de muerte digna en España," *El País.com,* 17 March 2010, http://www.elpais.com/articulo/sociedad/Parlamento/andaluz/aprueba/primera/ley/muerte/digna/Espana/elpepusoc/20100317elpepusoc_2/Tes.

decision solely on state law or by plainly stating that its decision rests on both state and federal law. If the U.S. Supreme Court is likely to render a restrictive view of a constitutional right and the judges of a state court are inclined toward a more expansive view, the state judges can use the state ground to avoid Supreme Court review. In a period when the nation's highest court is moving in a decidedly conservative direction, some state courts have become safe havens for liberal values. And individuals and groups know where to moor their policies.

The New Jersey Supreme Court has been more aggressive than most other state supreme courts in following its own liberal constitutional path. It has gone further than the U.S. Supreme Court in promoting equality at the expense of freedom by prohibiting discrimination against women by private employers and by striking down the state's public school financing system, which had perpetuated vast disparities in public education within the state. The court has also preferred freedom over order in protecting the right to terminate life-support systems and in protecting free speech against infringement.[85] The New Jersey judges have charted their own path, despite the similarity in language between sections of the New Jersey Constitution and the U.S. Constitution. And the New Jersey judges have parted company with their national cousins even when the constitutional provisions at issue were identical.[86]

For example, the U.S. Supreme Court ruled in 1988 that warrantless searches of curbside garbage are constitutionally permissible. Both the New Jersey Constitution and the U.S. Constitution bar unreasonable searches and seizures. Yet in a 1990 decision expanding constitutional protections, the New Jersey court ruled that police officers need a search warrant before they can rummage through a person's trash. The court claimed that the New Jersey Constitution offers a greater degree of privacy than the U.S. Constitution. Because the decision rested on an interpretation of the state constitution, the existence of a similar right in the national charter had no bearing. The New Jersey court cannot act in a more restrictive manner than the U.S. Supreme Court allows, but it can be—and is—less restrictive.[87] State supreme courts can turn to their own state constitutions to "raise the ceiling of liberty above the floor created by the federal Bill of Rights."[88]

When judges reach decisions, they pay attention to the views of other courts— and not just those above them in the judicial hierarchy. State and federal court opinions are the legal storehouse from which judges regularly draw their ideas. Often the issues that affect individual lives—property, family, contracts—are grist for state courts, not federal courts. For example, when a state court faces a novel issue in a contract dispute, it will look at how other state courts have dealt with the problem. (Contract disputes are not a staple of the federal courts.) And if courts in several states have addressed an issue and the direction of the opinion is largely one-sided, the weight and authority of those opinions may move the court in that direction.[89] Courts that confront new issues with cogency and clarity are likely to become leaders of legal innovation.

State courts continue to serve as arenas for political conflict, with litigants, individually or in groups, vying for their preferred policies. The multiplicity of the nation's court system, with overlapping state and national responsibilities, provides alternative points of access for individuals and groups to present and argue their claims. This description of the courts fits the pluralist model of government.

SUMMARY

14.1 National Judicial Supremacy

- Section 1 of Article III of the Constitution creates ''one supreme Court,'' although in its early years the federal judiciary was not a particularly powerful branch of government. With the establishment of judicial review, the Supreme Court's power came to equal or potentially exceed the other branches.
- The principle of checks and balances can restrain judicial power through several means, such as constitutional amendments and impeachment. But restrictions on that power have been infrequent, leaving the federal courts to exercise considerable influence through judicial review and statutory construction.

14.2 The Organization of Courts

- The federal court system has three tiers. At the bottom are the district courts, where litigation begins and most disputes end. In the middle are the courts of appeals. At the top is the Supreme Court. The ability of judges to make policy increases as they move up the pyramid from trial courts to appellate courts to the Supreme Court.
- The American legal system functions with a bias that favors existing decisions. This notion of *stare decisis* (''let the decision stand'') provides continuity and predictability to the legal process.

14.3 The Supreme Court

- The Supreme Court harmonizes conflicting interpretations of national law and articulates constitutional rights.
- The Supreme Court is free to draft its agenda through the discretionary control of its docket. It is helped at this crucial stage by the solicitor general, who represents the executive branch of government before the Court. The solicitor general's influence with the justices affects their choice of cases to review.
- Given their capacity to accept, consider, and render opinions on issues of national import, the justices on the Supreme Court exercise real political power.

14.4 Judicial Recruitment

- Political allegiance and complementary values are necessary conditions for appointment by the president to the coveted position of judge. The president and senators from the same party share appointment power in the case of federal district and appellate judges. The president has more leeway in nominating Supreme Court justices, although all nominees must be confirmed by the Senate.
- Recent presidents have made efforts to make the federal courts more diverse in racial, ethnic, and gender terms. When it comes to Supreme Court appointments, however, partisan politics is the most important factor affecting which nominees are confirmed.

14.5 The Consequences of Judicial Decisions

- Courts inevitably fashion policy, for each of the states and for the nation. Because the Supreme Court deals with issues that often reflect deeply felt values or political beliefs, the impact of its decisions often extends well beyond the parties in dispute.
- The crafting of a majority decision often means that justices must moderate their arguments and compromise in their opinions, which can reduce their overall impact on policy implementation.

- The relationship between the Supreme Court and public opinion is rarely highly contentious. In fact, the Court's decisions tend to come in line with the views of the general public over time.

14.6 The Courts and Models of Democracy

- The courts provide multiple points of access for individuals to pursue their preferences. Furthermore, class action enables people with small individual claims and limited financial resources to pursue their goals in court, reinforcing the pluralist model.
- As the U.S. Supreme Court marches in a more conservative direction, some state supreme courts have become safe havens for more liberal policies on civil rights and civil liberties and for legal innovation generally. The state court systems have overlapping state and national responsibilities, offering groups and individuals additional access points to present and argue their claims.

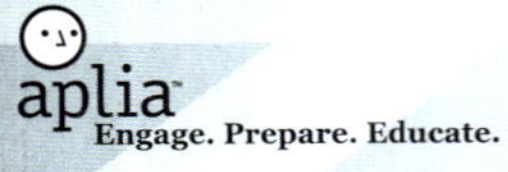

ASSESSING YOUR UNDERSTANDING WITH APLIA...YOUR VIRTUAL TUTOR!

14.1 Define judicial review, explain the circumstances under which it was established, and assess the significance of the authority it gave the courts.

1. Why was the decision in *Marbury* v. *Madison* so important for the Supreme Court?
2. What are the components of judicial review?
3. How did Alexander Hamilton defend the democratic nature of judicial review?

14.2 Outline the organization of the U.S. court system and identify the principal functions of courts at each tier of the system.

1. What are the two ways that judges can make policy?
2. List the different areas over which the U.S. district courts have authority.
3. What is precedent, and how is it used in the court system?

14.3 Describe the process by which cases are both accepted for review and decided by the U.S. Supreme Court and analyze the role played by judicial restraint and judicial activism in judicial decisions.

1. What are the two ways that cases arrive at the Supreme Court?
2. Define the duties and roles of the solicitor general.
3. Distinguish between judicial restraint and judicial activism as approaches to decision making.
4. What are the functions of the chief justice of the Supreme Court?

14.4 Explain how judges at different levels of the federal court system are nominated and confirmed to the federal bench.

1. How does the practice of senatorial courtesy affect the judicial appointment process?

2. Using the confirmation of a recent Supreme Court justice, explain why the appointment process to the Supreme Court can be politically contentious.

14.5 Examine the impact, influence, and acceptance of decisions on issues of national importance by an institution unaccountable to the electorate.

1. What factors affect the impact that Supreme Court decisions can have on policy?

2. Why are many Supreme Court decisions considered ambiguous in nature?
3. Are U.S. citizens more likely to approve or disapprove of the Supreme Court?

14.6 Evaluate the decision-making authority of the federal judiciary within the context of both majoritarian and pluralist democracy.

1. How does a class action make a lawsuit viable?
2. In what way can state courts diverge from the U.S. Supreme Court on specific decisions?

15

Order and Civil Liberties

CHAPTER TOPICS and Learning Outcomes

aplia™
Engage. Prepare. Educate.

15.1 The Bill of Rights
★ Explain the role of the Bill of Rights in protecting civil liberties and civil rights.

15.2 Freedom of Religion
★ Identify the mechanisms that guarantee freedom of religion.

15.3 Freedom of Expression
★ Identify the free-expression clauses and describe the scope of their protection.

15.4 The Right to Bear Arms
★ Discuss the controversy over the Second Amendment and explain how Supreme Court rulings have addressed that debate.

15.5 Applying the Bill of Rights to the States
★ Explain the process by which the Supreme Court extended the protections of the Bill of Rights to the local and state levels of government.

15.6 The Ninth Amendment and Personal Autonomy
★ Explain how the Supreme Court interpreted the Ninth Amendment to broaden the individual's constitutional protection of personal privacy beyond the language in the Bill of Rights, a right not enumerated in the Constitution.

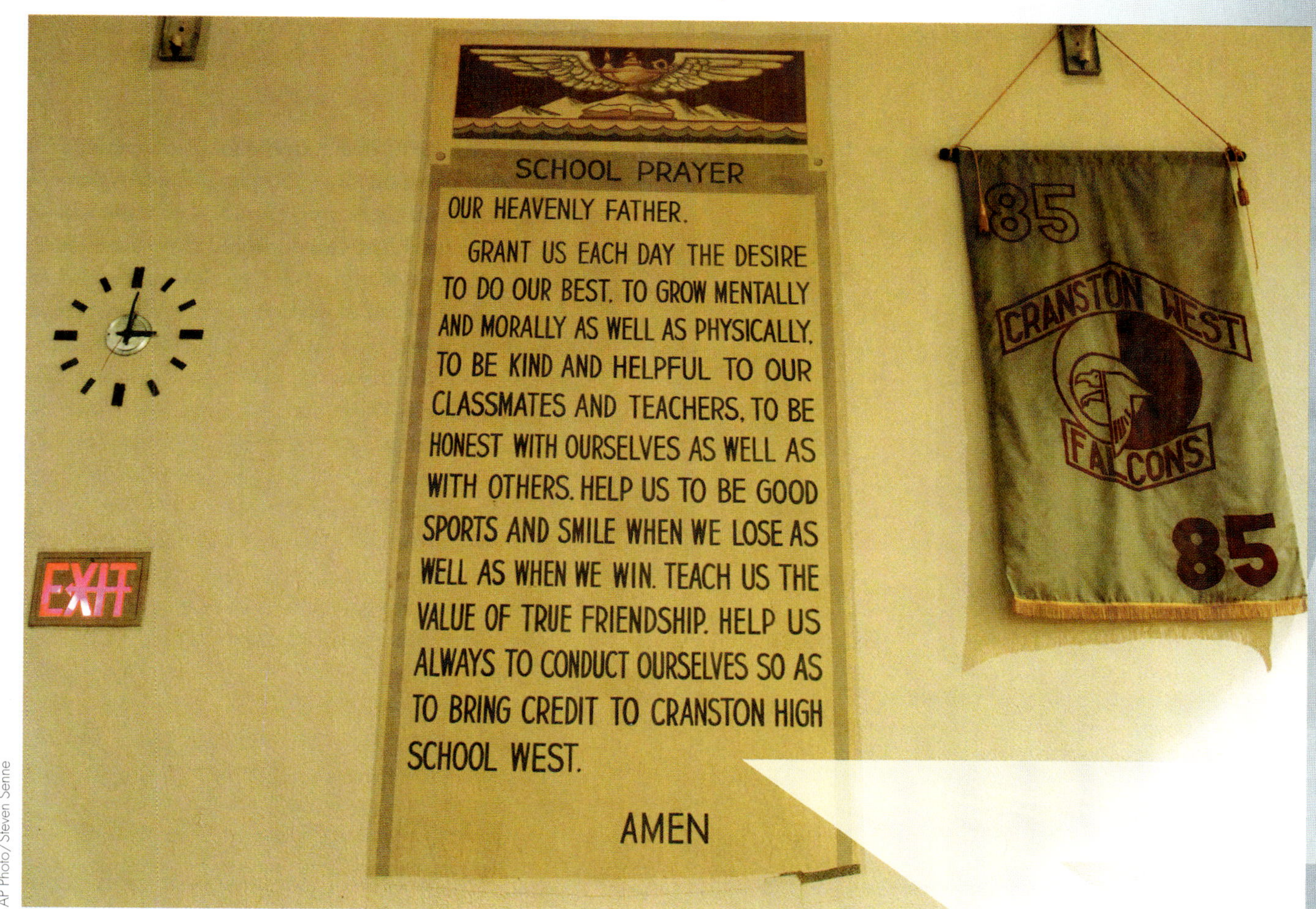

For forty-nine years, an eight-by-four-foot Christian prayer hung on the wall at Cranston High School West in Rhode Island. The prayer—located in the Cranston West auditorium near the stage—beseeched, ''Our Heavenly Father, grant us each day the desire to do our best, to grow mentally and morally as well as physically, to be kind and helpful'' and continued for a few more lines before concluding with ''Amen.''

Sixteen-year-old junior Jessica Ahlquist, an avowed atheist, objected to the prayer and, with the assistance of the American Civil Liberties Union, sought the prayer's removal on the ground that it represented government establishment of religion in violation of the First Amendment to the U.S. Constitution. The local school board held hearings, which a federal judge later described as akin to ''a religious revival,'' and voted 4–3 to keep the prayer. It was an important piece of school history, argued some members; others spoke of the secular values it promoted. In January 2012, federal judge Roger R. Lagueux ruled that the prayer violated the principle of government neutrality in religion and ordered the permanent removal of the banner.[1]

Jessica paid a steep price for exercising her constitutional guarantee. She was ostracized, threatened, and vilified in her community; she was subjected to frequent taunting and threats at school and was the subject of a virtual online hate campaign on Facebook.[2]

Throughout this nation's history, individuals and institutions have clashed over basic values. Here the clash involved community-centered order versus individual freedom. The Cranston community sought to preserve social order (the established patterns of authority in society) by reminding those who used its high school of the shared religious beliefs of many (perhaps a majority) of its citizens. Jessica Ahlquist had an interest in religious freedom (in her case, the freedom not to believe) and maintained that government may not impose any religious belief on its citizens. Obviously, the exercise of one interest would infringe on the exercise of the other. In the American political system, courts often resolve such controversies.

To Pledge or Not to Pledge, That Is the Question

Every day, students across the United States stand, place their right hands over their hearts, and recite the Pledge of Allegiance while facing the American flag. The pledge exercise began in 1892, when Francis Bellamy proposed the right-hand-extended gesture to accompany the Pledge of Allegiance, which he authored. President Franklin D. Roosevelt instituted the hand-over-heart gesture in 1943 to avoid confusion with the Roman salute (right hand extended) used by the Italian fascists and quickly copied by the German Nazis. The picture on the left shows March 1943 grade school students saluting the flag. The picture on the right shows contemporary grade school students saluting the flag.

Some students hold religious beliefs that conflict with saluting the flag or reciting the pledge. In its 1943 ruling in *West Virginia Board of Education* v. *Barnette*, the U.S. Supreme Court upheld the right of students with religious objections to refuse to recite the pledge or salute the flag. From time to time, that ruling has been ignored or forgotten in some communities.

How well do the courts respond to clashes that pit freedom against order or freedom against equality? Is freedom, order, or equality ever unconditional? In this chapter, we explore some value conflicts that the judiciary has resolved. You will be able to judge from the decisions in these cases whether American government has met the challenge of democracy by finding the appropriate balance between freedom and order and between freedom and equality.

The value conflicts described in this chapter revolve around claims or entitlements that rest on law. Although we concentrate on conflicts over constitutional issues, the Constitution is not the only source of people's rights. Government at all levels creates rights through laws written by legislatures and regulations issued by bureaucracies.

We begin this chapter with the Bill of Rights and the freedoms it protects. Then we take a closer look at the role of the First Amendment in the original conflict between freedom and order. Next, we turn to the Fourteenth Amendment and the limits it places on the states. Then we examine the Ninth Amendment and its relationship to issues of personal autonomy. In Chapter 16, we will look at the Fourteenth Amendment's promise of equal protection, which sets the stage for the modern dilemma of government: the struggle between freedom and equality.

★ 15.1 The Bill of Rights

★ Explain the role of the Bill of Rights in protecting civil liberties and civil rights.

You may remember from Chapter 3 that, at first, the framers of the Constitution did not include a list of individual liberties—a bill of rights—in the national charter. They believed that a bill of rights was not necessary because the Constitution spelled out the extent of the national government's power. But during the ratification debates, it became clear that the omission of a bill of rights was the most important obstacle to the adoption of the Constitution by the states. Eventually, the First Congress approved twelve amendments and sent them to the states for ratification. In 1791, the states ratified ten of the twelve amendments, and the nation had a bill of rights.

The Bill of Rights imposed limits on the national government but not on the state governments.* During the next seventy-seven years, litigants pressed the Supreme Court to extend the amendments' restraints to the states, but the Court refused until well after the adoption of the Fourteenth Amendment in 1868. Before then, protection from repressive state government had to come from state bills of rights.

The U.S. Constitution guarantees Americans numerous liberties and rights. In this chapter we explore a number of them. We will define and distinguish civil liberties and civil rights. (On some occasions, we use the terms interchangeably.) **Civil liberties**, sometimes referred to as "negative rights," are freedoms that are guaranteed to the individual. The guarantees take the form of restraints on government. For example, the First Amendment declares that "Congress shall make no law … abridging the freedom of speech." Civil liberties declare what the government cannot do. The opening example of this chapter illustrates the civil liberties claim that government (in the form of the public school) cannot impose any religious belief on its citizens.

In contrast, civil rights, sometimes called "positive rights," declare what the government must do or provide. **Civil rights** are powers and privileges that are guaranteed to the individual and protected against arbitrary removal at the hands of the government or other individuals. The right to vote and the right to a jury trial in criminal cases are civil rights embedded in the Constitution. Today, civil rights also embrace laws that further certain values. The Civil Rights Act of 1964, for example, furthered the value of equality by establishing the right to nondiscrimination in public accommodations and the right to equal employment opportunity. (See Table 15.1 for examples of positive and negative rights in U.S. and U.N. contexts.) Civil liberties are the subject of this chapter; we discuss civil rights and their ramifications in Chapter 16.

civil liberties
Freedoms guaranteed to individuals taking the form of restraint on government.

civil rights
Powers or privileges guaranteed to individuals and protected from arbitrary removal at the hands of government or individuals.

TABLE 15.1 Examples of Positive and Negative Rights: Constitutional Rights and Human Rights

	U.S. Constitution	**United Nations Universal Declaration of Human Rights**
Civil liberties, or "negative rights"	"Congress shall make no law … *abridging* the freedom of speech, or of the press." (First Amendment) "Excessive bail *shall not be* required, nor excessive fines imposed, nor cruel and unusual punishments inflicted." (Eighth Amendment)	"*No one shall* be held in slavery or servitude; slavery and the slave trade shall be prohibited in all their forms." (Article 4) "*No one shall* be subjected to arbitrary arrest, detention or exile." (Article 9)
Civil rights, or "positive rights"	"In all criminal prosecutions, the accused shall enjoy the right to a speedy and public trial, … and to have the assistance of counsel for his defense." (Sixth Amendment)	"Everyone has *the right* to a standard of living adequate for the health and well-being of himself and of his family, including food, clothing, housing and medical care and necessary social services, and the right to security in the event of unemployment, sickness, disability, widow-hood, old age or other lack of livelihood in circumstances beyond his control." (Article 25.1) "Everyone has *the right to* work, to free choice of employment, to just and favourable conditions of work and to protection against unemployment." (Article 23.1)

*Congress considered more than one hundred amendments in its first session. One that was not approved would have limited power of the states to infringe on the rights of conscience, speech, press, and jury trial in criminal cases. James Madison thought this amendment was the "most valuable" of the list, but it failed to muster a two-thirds vote in the Senate.

© Cengage Learning.

Compared with What?

Britain's Bill of Rights

Unlike the United States, Britain has no single document or law known as "the constitution." Instead, it has an "unwritten constitution"—a combination of important documents and laws passed by Parliament (the British legislature), court decisions, customs, and conventions. Britain's "constitution" has no existence apart from ordinary law. In contrast to the American system of government, Britain's Parliament may change, amend, or abolish its fundamental laws and conventions at will. No special procedures or barriers must be overcome to enact such changes.

According to government leaders, Britain has done very well without a written constitution, or at least that was the position of Prime Minister Margaret Thatcher when she was presented with a proposal for a written constitution in 1989. Thatcher observed that despite Britain's lack of a bill of rights and an independent judiciary, "our present constitutional arrangements continue to serve us well…. Furthermore, the government does not feel that a written constitution in itself changes or guarantees anything."

In 1995, a nationwide poll revealed that the British people held a different view. Three-fourths of British adults thought that it was time for a written constitution, and even more maintained that the country needed a written bill of rights. These high levels of public support and the election of a new government in 1997 helped build momentum for important changes in Britain's long history of rule by unwritten law. In October 2000, England formally began enforcing the Human Rights Act, a key component of the government's political program, which incorporated into British law sixteen guarantees of the European Convention on Human Rights. Thus, the nation that has been the source of some of the world's most significant ideas concerning liberty and individual freedom finally put into writing guarantees to ensure these fundamental rights for its own citizens. Legal experts hailed the edict as the largest change to British law in three centuries.

The Bill of Rights lists both civil liberties and civil rights. When we refer to the rights and liberties of the Constitution, we mean the protections that are enshrined in the Bill of Rights and the first section of the Fourteenth Amendment.[3] The list includes freedom of religion, freedom of speech and of the press, the rights to assemble peaceably and to petition the government, the right to bear arms, the rights of the criminally accused, the requirement of due process, and the equal protection of the laws. The idea of a written enumeration of rights seems entirely natural to Americans today. Lacking a written constitution, Great Britain has started to provide written guarantees for human rights (see "Compared with What? Britain's Bill of Rights").

Some additional distinctions will prove useful in this and subsequent chapters. Persons possess *rights,* and governments possess *powers.* If governments may lawfully regulate a person's behavior (for example, requiring that you possess a valid license to drive a car), then that behavior is a privilege. Thus, you do not have a right to drive, but merely a privilege subject to reasonable restrictions by government. Although some rights may be spelled out in absolute language, generally no right is absolute. However, government limitations on rights are exceptional: they require a higher burden of proof and must be minimal in scope.[4]

The Charter of Fundamental Rights, a text that is in harmony with the provisions stipulated in the European Convention on Human Rights, was to achieve legally binding status assuming that all European Union countries ratified the current Reform Treaty. The United Kingdom and Poland, skittish about the imposition of European values in their courts, opted out from the Charter provisions. Questions remain whether the opt-out language is sufficient to achieve the desired objective. So it is uncertain whether the Human Rights Act will, in the words of one former minister in the Thatcher government, "rob us of freedoms we have had for centuries" or, as British human rights lawyer Geoffrey Robertson sees it, "help produce a better culture of liberty." A 2008 report by a joint committee of Parliament endorsed the idea of a consensus-based U.K. Bill of Rights and Freedoms emphasizing civil liberties rather than civil rights. But in doing so, the committee firmly rejected the idea that such a Bill of Rights would empower courts to strike down legislation, as in the power of judicial review. "We consider this to be fundamentally at odds with this country's tradition of parliamentary democracy," concluded the committee. In 2011, the U.K. Bill of Rights Commission opened up the debate to the public, launching a public consultation on whether the country should have a Bill of Rights. A report of their findings is due by the end of 2012.

Sources: Andrew Marr, *Ruling Britannia: The Failure and Future of British Democracy* (London: Michael Joseph, 1995); Will Hutton, *The State We're In* (London: Cape, 1995); Fred Barbash, "The Movement to Rule Britannia Differently," *Washington Post*, 23 September 1995, p. A27; "Bringing Rights Home," *Economist*, 26 August 2000, pp. 45–46; Sarah Lyall, "209 Years Later, the English Get American-Style Bill of Rights," *New York Times*, 2 October 2000, p. A3; Suzanne Kapner, "Britain's Legal Barriers Start to Fall," *New York Times*, 4 October 2000, p. W1; Joint Committee on Human Rights, *A Bill of Rights for the UK? Twenty-ninth Report of Session 2007–08* (London: Stationery Office, Ltd., 10 August 2008), http://www.publications. parliament.uk/pa/jt200708/jtselect/jtrights/165/165i.pdf; "Does Britain Need a Bill of Rights?" *The Guardian*, 8 August 2011, http://www.guardian.co.uk/law/2011/aug/08/british-bill-rights-consultation-complicated (last accessed 30 March 2012).

15.2 Freedom of Religion

★ Identify the mechanisms that guarantee freedom of religion.

Congress shall make no law respecting an establishment of religion, or prohibiting the free exercise thereof.

Religious freedom was important to the colonies and later to the states. That importance is reflected in its position among the ratified amendments that we know as the Bill of Rights: first, in the very first amendment. The First Amendment guarantees freedom of religion in two clauses: the **establishment clause**, which prohibits laws sponsoring or supporting religion, and the **free-exercise clause**, which prevents the government from interfering with religious practice. Together, they ensure that the government can neither promote nor inhibit religious beliefs or practices.

establishment clause
The first clause in the First Amendment, which forbids government establishment of religion.

free-exercise clause
The second clause in the First Amendment, which prevents the government from interfering with the exercise of religion.

At the time of the Constitutional Convention, many Americans, especially in New England, maintained that government could and should foster religion, specifically Protestantism. However, many more Americans agreed that this was an issue for state governments, that the national government had no authority to meddle in religious affairs. The religion clauses were drafted in this spirit.[5]

The Supreme Court has refused to interpret the religion clauses definitively. The result is an amalgam of rulings, the cumulative effect of which is that freedom to believe is unlimited, but freedom to practice a belief can be limited. Religion cannot benefit directly from government actions (for example, government cannot make contributions to churches or synagogues), but it can benefit indirectly from those actions (for example, government can supply books on secular subjects for use in all schools—public, private, and parochial).

Religion is much more important to Americans than to citizens of other advanced nations.[6] Most Americans identify with a particular religious faith, and 40 percent attend church in a typical week. The vast majority believe in God or a supreme being, in far greater proportion than people in France, Britain, or Italy. (See Figure 15.1.)

Majoritarians might argue, then, that government should support religion. They would agree that the establishment clause bars government support of a single faith, but they might maintain that government should support all faiths. Such support would be consistent with what the majority wants and true to the language of the Constitution. In its decisions, the Supreme Court has rejected this interpretation of the establishment clause, leaving itself open to charges of undermining democracy. Those charges may be true with regard to majoritarian democracy, but the Court can justify its protection in terms of the basic values of democratic government.

The Establishment Clause

The provision that "Congress shall make no law respecting an establishment of religion" bars government sponsorship or support of religious activity. The Supreme Court has consistently held that the establishment clause requires government to maintain a position of neutrality toward religions and to maintain that position in

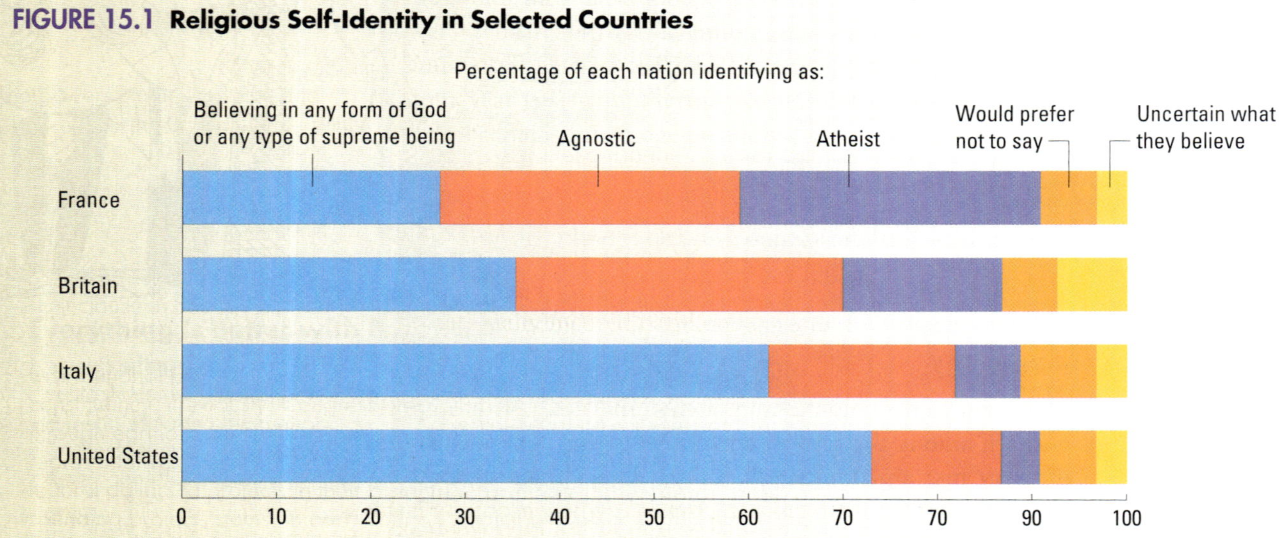

FIGURE 15.1 Religious Self-Identity in Selected Countries

More Americans believe in God or a supreme being compared to people in Italy, Britain, or France. France and Britain each have proportionally more atheists than people in Italy or the United States.
Source: *New York Times*, 5 September 2007.

cases that involve choices between religion and nonreligion. However, the Court has never interpreted the clause as barring all assistance that incidentally aids religious institutions, rendering the resulting legal landscape incoherent.[7]

Government Support of Religion. In 1879, the Supreme Court contended, quoting Thomas Jefferson, that the establishment clause erected "a wall of separation between church and State."[8] That wall was breached somewhat in 1947, when the justices upheld a local government program that provided free transportation to parochial school students.[9] The breach seemed to widen in 1968, when the Court held constitutional a government program in which parochial school students borrowed state-purchased textbooks.[10] The objective of the program, reasoned the majority, was to further educational opportunity. The students, not the schools, borrowed the books, and the parents, not the church, realized the benefits.

But in 1971, in **Lemon v. Kurtzman***, the Court struck down a state program that would have helped pay the salaries of teachers hired by parochial schools to give instruction in secular subjects.[11] The justices proposed a three-pronged test for determining the constitutionality of government programs and laws under the establishment clause:

- They must have a secular purpose (such as lending books to parochial school students).
- Their primary effect must not be to advance or inhibit religion.
- They must not entangle the government excessively with religion.

The program in *Lemon* did not satisfy the last prong. The government would have had to monitor the program constantly, thus ensuring an excessive entanglement with religion. The *Lemon* test, as it became known, governed the Supreme Court's interpretation of such cases for twenty-five years. Then in 1997, the Court dramatically loosened its application of the test in a case reminiscent of the one that gave rise to it. The future of the test now seems uncertain.

The case involved the use of public school teachers to teach congressionally mandated remedial courses to disadvantaged students in New York parochial schools. This time, the Court emphasized that only government *neutrality* toward religion was required by the First Amendment. Moreover, only *excessive* entanglements will be deemed to violate the establishment clause. By a vote of 5–4, the Court held that religion was neither hindered nor helped by parochial schools' using public school teachers at taxpayers' expense to teach secular subjects.[12] Although the opinion was narrowly written, the Court appears to have lowered the wall separating church and state.

In 2002, the Court provided additional support for its tolerant position regarding the establishment clause when it upheld a state school-voucher program in which secular or sectarian schools could participate. The justices, dividing 5–4, maintained that the program did not favor religious schools over nonreligious ones when the aid went to the student or parent who then chose the school.[13]

Consider another thorny issue. Does the display of religious artifacts on public property violate the establishment clause? In *Lynch* v. *Donnelly* (1984), the Court said no, by a vote of 5–4.[14] At issue was a publicly funded nativity scene on public property, surrounded by commercial symbols of the Christmas season such as Santa and his sleigh. Although he conceded that a crèche has religious significance, Chief Justice Warren E. Burger, writing for the majority, maintained that the display had a legitimate secular purpose: the celebration of a national holiday. Second, the display did not have the primary effect of benefiting religion; the religious benefits were "indirect,

---

*Key cases are highlighted in bold and a list of key cases appears at the end of the chapter.

remote and incidental." And third, the display led to no excessive entanglement of religion and government. The justices hinted at a relaxation of their interpretation of the establishment clause by asserting an "unwillingness to be confined to any single test or criterion in this sensitive area." The upshot of *Lynch* was an acknowledgment of the religious heritage of the majority of Americans, although the Christmas holiday is a vivid reminder to religious minorities and the nonreligious of their separateness from the dominant Christian culture.

The *Lynch* decision led to a proliferation of closely decided and confusing cases testing the limits of government-sponsored religious displays. A pair of cases in 2005 involved a forty-year-old monument displaying the Ten Commandments on the Texas state capitol and a display of the Ten Commandments in two Kentucky county courthouses. In separate 5–4 rulings, the justices declined to apply the *Lemon* test but upheld the Texas display because of the monument's "secular purpose";[15] and, on the same day, the Court applied the *Lemon* test to strike down the Kentucky courthouse displays because they were not integrated into a secular presentation and so had a primarily religious purpose.[16]

The Court continued to struggle with the limits of government entanglement with religious symbols. In 2010, a badly splintered 5–4 ruling in *Salazar* v. *Buono* generated six separate opinions holding that a five-by-eight-foot cross—originally made of wood but more recently made of four-inch metal pipe—erected by the Veterans of Foreign Wars on federal land to honor World War I veterans did not violate the establishment clause.[17] The federal government faced a dilemma: leaving the cross in place would violate the establishment clause, but removing the cross would show "disrespect for those the cross was seen as honoring," wrote Justice Anthony M. Kennedy for the majority. The solution at issue in the case was a land swap in which the government traded the public land for private property, enabling the cross to remain. But the land trade could be viewed as promoting religion, argued Justice John Paul Stevens in dissent. Such cases are sure to continue as the Court's majority coalition moves in a more conservative direction.

School Prayer. The Supreme Court has consistently equated prayer in public schools with government support of religion. In 1962, it struck down the daily reading of this twenty-two-word nondenominational prayer in New York's public schools: "Almighty God, we acknowledge our dependence upon Thee, and we beg Thy blessings upon us, our parents, our teachers and our country." Justice Hugo L. Black, writing for a 6–1 majority, held that official state approval of prayer was an unconstitutional attempt on the part of the state to establish a religion. This decision, in ***Engel v. Vitale,*** drew a storm of protest that has yet to subside.[18]

The following year, the Court struck down a state law calling for daily Bible reading and recitation of the Lord's Prayer in Pennsylvania's public schools.[19] The school district defended the reading and recitation on the grounds that they taught literature, perpetuated traditional institutions, and inculcated moral virtues. But the Court held that the state's involvement violated the government's constitutionally imposed neutrality in matters of religion.

In 1992, the Court struck down the offering of nonsectarian prayers at official public school graduations. In a 5–4 decision, the Court held that government involvement creates "a state-sponsored and state-directed religious exercise in a public school."[20] The justices said that the establishment clause means that government may not conduct a religious exercise in the context of a school event. Yet school prayer persists. And in 2012, the fact that the prayer at issue in Cranston High School West was unspoken but prominently displayed on an auditorium wall did not shield the authorities from a constitutional violation.

Religious training during public school is out-of-bounds, but religious training after school now passes constitutional muster. In 2001, the Supreme Court ruled that public schools must open their doors to after-school religious activities on the same basis as other after-school programs such as the debate club. To do otherwise would constitute viewpoint discrimination in violation of the free speech clause of the First Amendment.

The issue of school prayer remains. In 2008, the Indian River school district in Sussex County, Delaware, agreed to revise its policies that had tolerated Christian prayer at school functions in clear violation of prior Supreme Court rulings. The settlement, which arose from a lawsuit by two Jewish families, created enormous ill will. One family was forced to move after facing threats and harassment when Christian community members viewed the lawsuit as an effort to limit their free exercise of religion.[21]

The establishment clause creates a problem for government. Support for all religions at the expense of nonreligion seems to pose the least risk to social order. Tolerance of the dominant religion at the expense of other religions risks minority discontent, but support for no religion (neutrality between religion and nonreligion) risks majority discontent.

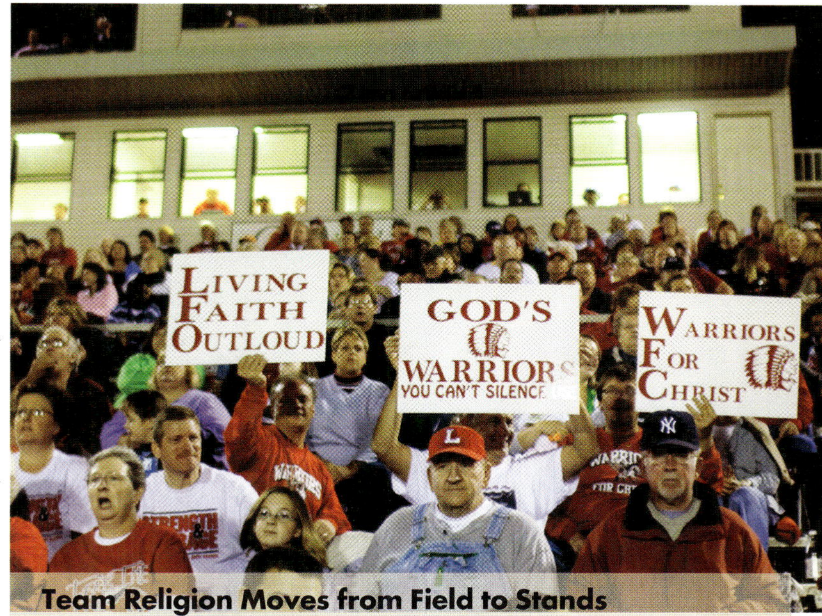

David Walter Banks/The New York Times/Redux Picture

Team Religion Moves from Field to Stands

Friday night football is a big deal for high school students and their families. Following 9/11, cheerleaders at a Fort Oglethorpe, Georgia, high school wanted to embrace the Bible as part of Friday night football. For eight seasons, players charged onto the field with banners declaring "Commit for Christ." But recognizing that it was deep in a constitutional hole, the school board banned the practice in 2009. Parents and cheerleaders responded by moving their banners to the stands, where they now cheer on their team and fans with inspirations from scripture. Their freedom of expression seems secure, as long as it is not exercised on the playing field.

The Free-Exercise Clause

The free-exercise clause of the First Amendment states that "Congress shall make no law … prohibiting the free exercise [of religion]." The Supreme Court has struggled to avoid absolute interpretations of this restriction and thus avoid its complement, the establishment clause. An example: suppose Congress grants exemptions from military service to individuals who have religious scruples against war. These exemptions could be construed as a violation of the establishment clause because they favor some religious groups over others. But if Congress forced conscientious objectors to fight—to violate their religious beliefs—the government would run afoul of the free-exercise clause. In fact, Congress has granted military draftees such exemptions. But the Supreme Court has avoided a conflict between the establishment and free-exercise clauses by equating religious objection to war with any deeply held humanistic opposition to it. This solution leaves unanswered a central question: Does the free-exercise clause require government to grant exemptions from legal duties that conflict with religious obligations, or does it guarantee only that the law will be applicable to religious believers without discrimination or preference?[22]

In the free-exercise cases, the justices have distinguished religious beliefs from actions based on those beliefs. Beliefs are inviolate, beyond the reach of government control. But the First Amendment does not protect antisocial actions. Consider conflicting values about working on the Sabbath.

Gretchen Ertl for *The New York Times*

A Standout in Her Class

Jessica Ahlquist took a brave stand in her Cranston, Rhode Island, high school by objecting to the display of a Christian prayer in the school auditorium. She was ostracized by her classmates and community, but with the help of the American Civil Liberties Union, she prevailed in federal court. When asked by a reporter if she empathized with those who wanted to retain the prayer banner, she replied: "It's almost like making a child get a shot even though they don't want to. It's for their own good. I feel like they might see it as a very negative thing right now, but I'm defending their Constitution, too."

The modern era of free-exercise thinking began with ***Sherbert v. Verner*** (1963). Adeil Sherbert, a Seventh-Day Adventist, lost her mill job because she refused to work on Saturday, her Sabbath. She filed for unemployment compensation and was referred to another job, which she declined because it also required Saturday work. Because she declined the job, the state disqualified her from receiving unemployment benefits. In a 7–2 decision, the Supreme Court ruled that the disqualification imposed an impermissible burden on Sherbert's free exercise of religion. The First Amendment, declared the majority, protects observance as well as belief. A neutral law that burdens the free exercise of religion is subject to **strict scrutiny**. This means that the law may be upheld only if the government can demonstrate that (1) the law is justified by a "compelling governmental interest," (2) the law is narrowly tailored to achieve a legitimate goal, and (3) the law in question is the least restrictive means for achieving that interest.[23] Scholars had long maintained that strict scrutiny was "strict in theory but fatal in fact." A recent empirical study debunked this claim, finding that in all strict scrutiny cases from 1990 to 2003, the federal courts upheld nearly one-third of the challenged laws.[24] The strict scrutiny standard sets a high bar but not an insurmountable one.

The *Sherbert* decision prompted religious groups and individual believers to challenge laws that conflict with their faith. We have seen how conflicts arise from the imposition of penalties for refusing to engage in religiously prohibited conduct. But conflicts may also arise from laws that impose penalties for engaging in religiously motivated conduct.[25] For example, neutral criminal laws apply to individuals who use illegal drugs as part of a religious ceremony; and, government may withhold unemployment benefits from workers who have been dismissed from their jobs because they used illegal drugs in a religious ceremony.[26] Courts face the continuing challenge of line-drawing between religious belief and religious conduct as they determine the limits of the free exercise clause.

strict scrutiny
A standard used by the Supreme Court in deciding whether a law or policy is to be adjudged constitutional. To pass strict scrutiny, the law or policy must be justified by a "compelling governmental interest," must be narrowly tailored, and must be the least restrictive means for achieving that interest.

★ 15.3 Freedom of Expression

★ Identify the free-expression clauses and describe the scope of their protection.

Congress shall make no law … abridging the freedom of speech, or of the press; or the right of the people peaceably to assemble, and to petition the Government for a redress of grievances.

James Madison introduced the original versions of the speech clause and the press clause of the First Amendment in the House of Representatives in June 1789. One early proposal provided that "the people shall not be deprived of their right to speak, to write, or to publish their sentiments, and the freedom of the press, as one of the great bulwarks of liberty, shall be inviolable." That version was rewritten several times, then merged with the religion and peaceable assembly clauses to yield the First Amendment.

The spare language of the First Amendment seems perfectly clear: "Congress shall make no law … abridging the freedom of speech, or of the press." Yet a majority of the Supreme Court has never agreed that this "most majestic guarantee" is absolutely inviolable.[27] Historians have long debated the framers' intentions regarding these **free-expression clauses**, the press and speech clauses of the First Amendment. The dominant view is that the clauses confer a right to unrestricted discussion of public affairs.[28] Other scholars, examining much the same evidence, conclude that few, if any, of the framers clearly understood the clause; moreover, they insist that the First Amendment does not rule out prosecution for seditious statements (statements inciting insurrection).[29]

The license to speak freely does not move multitudes of Americans to speak out on controversial issues. Americans have woven subtle restrictions into the fabric of our society: the risk of criticism or ostracism by family, peers, or employers tends to reduce the number of people who test the limits of free speech to individuals ready to bear the burdens. As Mark Twain once remarked, "It is by the goodness of God that in our country we have three unspeakably precious things: freedom of speech, freedom of conscience, and the prudence never to practice either of them."[30]

Today, the clauses are deemed to bar most forms of **prior restraint**—censorship before publication as well as after-the-fact prosecution for political and other discourse. The Supreme Court has evolved two approaches to the resolution of claims based on the free-expression clauses. First, government can regulate or punish the advocacy of ideas, but only if it can prove an intent to promote lawless action and demonstrate that a high probability exists that such action will occur.[31] Second, government may impose reasonable restrictions on the means for communicating ideas, restrictions that can incidentally discourage free expression. Hence, people have the right to protest but not if their physical presence would block the entrance to an occupied public building.

Suppose, for example, that a political party advocates nonpayment of personal income taxes. Government cannot regulate or punish that party for advocating tax nonpayment because the standards of proof—that the act be directed at inciting or producing imminent lawless action and that the act be likely to produce such action—do not apply. But government can impose restrictions on the way the party's candidates communicate what they are advocating. Government can bar them from blaring messages from loudspeakers in residential neighborhoods at 3:00 A.M.

Freedom of Speech

The starting point for any modern analysis of free speech is the **clear and present danger test**, formulated by Justice Oliver Wendell Holmes in the Supreme Court's unanimous decision in **Schenck v. United States** (1919). Charles T. Schenck and his fellow defendants were convicted under a federal criminal statute for attempting to disrupt World War I military recruitment by distributing leaflets claiming that conscription was unconstitutional. The government believed this behavior threatened the public order. At the core of the Court's opinion, Holmes wrote, was the view that

free-expression clauses
The press and speech clauses of the First Amendment.

prior restraint
Censorship before publication.

clear and present danger test
A means by which the Supreme Court has distinguished between speech as the advocacy of ideas, which is protected by the First Amendment, and speech as incitement, which is not protected.

> the character of every act depends upon the circumstances in which it is done.… The most stringent protection of free speech would not protect a man in falsely shouting fire in a theatre, and causing a panic.… The question in every case is whether the words used are used in such circumstances and are of such a nature as to create *a clear and present danger* that they will bring about the substantive evils that Congress has a right to prevent. It is a question of proximity and degree. When a nation is at war many things that might be said in time of peace are such a hindrance to its effort that their utterance will not be endured so long as men fight, and that no court could regard them as protected by any constitutional right [emphasis added].[32]

Because the actions of the defendants in *Schenck* were deemed to create a clear and present danger to the United States at that time, the Supreme Court upheld the defendants' convictions. The clear and present danger test helps to distinguish the advocacy of ideas, which is protected, from incitement, which is not. However, Holmes later frequently disagreed with a majority of his colleagues in applying the test.

In an often quoted dissent in *Abrams* v. *United States* (1919), Holmes revealed his deeply rooted resistance to the suppression of ideas. The majority had upheld Jacob Abrams's criminal conviction for distributing leaflets that denounced the war and U.S. opposition to the Russian Revolution. Holmes wrote:

> When men have realized that time has upset many fighting faiths, they may come to believe … that the ultimate good desired is better reached by free trade in ideas—that the best test of truth is the power of the thought to get itself accepted in the competition of the market, and that truth is the only ground upon which their wishes safely can be carried out. That at any rate is the theory of our Constitution.[33]

In 1925, the Court issued a landmark decision in *Gitlow* v. *New York*.[34] Benjamin Gitlow was arrested for distributing copies of a "left-wing manifesto" that called for the establishment of socialism through strikes and working-class uprisings of any form. Gitlow was convicted under a state criminal anarchy law; Schenck and Abrams had been convicted under a federal law. For the first time, the Court assumed that the First Amendment speech and press provisions applied to the states through the due process clause of the Fourteenth Amendment. Still, a majority of the justices affirmed Gitlow's conviction. Justices Holmes and Louis D. Brandeis argued in dissent that Gitlow's ideas did not pose a clear and present danger. "Eloquence may set fire to reason," conceded the dissenters. "But whatever may be thought of the redundant discourse before us, it had no chance of starting a present conflagration."

The protection of advocacy faced yet another challenge in 1948, when eleven members of the Communist Party were charged with violating the Smith Act, a federal law making the advocacy of force or violence against the United States a criminal offense. The leaders were convicted, although the government introduced no evidence that they had actually urged people to commit specific violent acts. The Supreme Court mustered a majority for its decision to uphold the convictions under the act, but it could not get a majority to agree on the reasons in support of that decision. The biggest bloc, of four justices, announced the plurality opinion in 1951, arguing that the government's interest was substantial enough to warrant criminal penalties.[35] The justices interpreted the threat to the government to be the gravity of the advocated action, "discounted by its improbability." In other words, a single soapbox orator advocating revolution stands little chance of success. But a well-organized, highly disciplined political movement advocating revolution in the tinderbox of unstable political conditions stands a greater chance of success. In broadening the "clear and present danger" test to the "grave and probable danger" test, the Court held that the government was justified in acting preventively rather than waiting until revolution was about to occur.

By 1969, the pendulum had swung back in the other direction: the justices began to put more emphasis on freedom. That year, in **Brandenburg v. Ohio,** a unanimous decision widened the freedom of speech to new boundaries.[36] Clarence Brandenburg, the leader of the Ohio Ku Klux Klan, had been convicted under a state law for advocating racial strife at a Klan rally. His comments, which had been filmed by a television crew, included threats against government officials.

The Court reversed Brandenburg's conviction because the government had failed to prove that the danger was real. The Court went even further and declared that threatening speech is protected by the First Amendment unless the government can prove that such advocacy is "directed to inciting or producing imminent lawless action and is likely to incite or produce such action." The ruling offered wider latitude for the expression of political ideas than ever before in the nation's history.

The United States stands alone when it comes to protection for hateful speech. Several democratic nations—including Canada, England, France, Germany, the Netherlands, South Africa, Australia, and India—have laws or have signed international conventions banning such speech. Nazi swastikas and flags are forbidden for sale in Israel and France but not in the United States. Anyone who denies the Holocaust in Canada, Germany, and France is subject to criminal prosecution but not in the United States. Some scholars have begun to urge a relaxation of our stringent speech protections because we now live "in an age when words have inspired acts of mass murder and terrorism."[37]

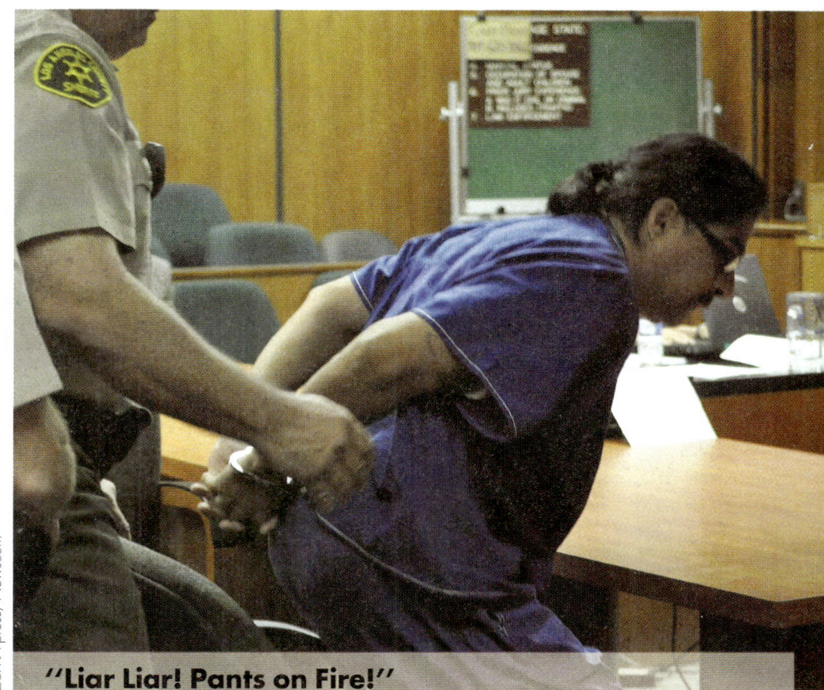

ZUMA press/Newscom

"Liar Liar! Pants on Fire!"

Xavier Alvarez, a minor elected official in Pomona California, falsely claimed at a public meeting that he was a retired marine who received the Medal of Honor, the nation's highest military award. The United States charged him with violating the Stolen Valor Act, which made it a crime for persons to falsely claim that they had received a military decoration or medal. Alvarez pleaded guilty and was sentenced to 400 hours of community service and fined $5,000, but he reserved the right to challenge the law on constitutional grounds. The U.S. Supreme Court struck down the act in June 2012 as an abridgment of the First Amendment's freedom of speech clause.

Symbolic Expression. Symbolic expression, or nonverbal communication, generally receives less protection than pure speech. But the courts have upheld certain types of symbolic expression. **Tinker v. Des Moines Independent County School District** (1969) involved three public school students who wore black armbands to school to protest the Vietnam War. Principals in their school district had prohibited the wearing of armbands on the grounds that such conduct would provoke a disturbance; the district suspended the students. The Supreme Court overturned the suspensions. Justice Abe Fortas declared for the majority that the principals had failed to show that the forbidden conduct would substantially interfere with appropriate school discipline:

> Undifferentiated fear or apprehension of disturbance is not enough to overcome the right to freedom of expression. Any departure from absolute

regimentation may cause trouble. Any variation from the majority's opinion may inspire fear. Any word spoken, in class, in the lunchroom, or on the campus, that deviates from the views of another person may start an argument or cause a disturbance. But our Constitution says we must take this risk.[38]

Order Versus Free Speech: Fighting Words and Threatening Expression.

Fighting words are a notable exception to the protection of free speech. In *Chaplinsky* v. *New Hampshire* (1942), Walter Chaplinsky, a Jehovah's Witness, convicted under a state statute for calling a city marshal a "God-damned racketeer" and "a damned fascist" in a public place, appealed to the Supreme Court.[39] The Supreme Court upheld Chaplinsky's conviction on the theory that **fighting words**—words that "inflict injury or tend to incite an immediate breach of the peace"—do not convey ideas and thus are not subject to First Amendment protection.

The Court sharply narrowed the definition of *fighting words* just seven years later. Arthur Terminiello, a suspended Catholic priest from Alabama and a vicious anti-Semite, addressed the Christian Veterans of America, a right-wing extremist group, in a Chicago hall. Terminiello called the jeering crowd of fifteen hundred angry protesters outside the hall "slimy scum" and ranted on about the "communistic, Zionistic" Jews of America, evoking cries of "kill the Jews" and "dirty kikes" from his listeners. The crowd outside the hall heaved bottles, bricks, and rocks, while the police attempted to protect Terminiello and his listeners inside. Finally, the police arrested Terminiello for disturbing the peace.

Terminiello's speech was far more incendiary than Walter Chaplinsky's. Yet the Supreme Court struck down Terminiello's conviction on the ground that provocative speech, even speech that stirs people to anger, is protected by the First Amendment. "Freedom of speech," wrote Justice William O. Douglas in the majority opinion, "though not absolute … is nevertheless protected against censorship or punishment, unless shown likely to produce a clear … and present danger of a serious substantive evil that rises far above public inconvenience, annoyance, or unrest."

This broad view of protection brought a stiff rebuke in Justice Robert Jackson's dissenting opinion:

> The choice is not between order and liberty. It is between liberty with order and anarchy without either. There is danger that, if the court does not temper its doctrinaire logic with a little practical wisdom, it will convert the constitutional Bill of Rights into a suicide pact.[40]

The times seem to have caught up with the idealism that Jackson criticized in his colleagues. In **Cohen v. California** (1971), a nineteen-year-old department store worker expressed his opposition to the Vietnam War by wearing a jacket in the hallway of a Los Angeles County courthouse emblazoned with the words "FUCK THE DRAFT. STOP THE WAR." The young man, Paul Cohen, was charged in 1968 under a California statute that prohibits "maliciously and willfully disturb[ing] the peace and quiet of any neighborhood or person [by] offensive conduct." He was found guilty and sentenced to thirty days in jail. On appeal, the U.S. Supreme Court reversed Cohen's conviction.

The Court reasoned that the expletive he used, while provocative, was not directed at anyone in particular; besides, the state presented no evidence that the words on Cohen's jacket would provoke people in "substantial numbers" to take some kind of physical action. In recognizing that "one man's vulgarity is another's lyric," the Supreme Court protected two elements of speech: the emotive (the expression of emotion) and the cognitive (the expression of ideas).[41]

---

fighting words
Speech that is not protected by the First Amendment because it inflicts injury or tends to incite an immediate disturbance of the peace.

Order Versus Free Speech: When Words Hurt. The First Amendment protects a person's ability to address matters of public importance even if the speech is hurtful. But speech of a purely private matter receives less protection. What happens when the speech in question contains a mix of public and private matters?

For more than twenty years, members of the Westboro Baptist Church have picketed funerals to communicate their belief that God punishes the United States and its military for tolerating homosexuality. Displaying signs that read, "Thank God for dead soldiers" and "Fag troops," the church pastor and a handful of members picketed the funeral of Marine Lance Corporal Matthew Snyder. Matthew's father was deeply offended by the picketing and sued the pastor and the church for the intentional infliction of emotional distress. He won a judgment of $5 million, which a federal appeals court reversed. Snyder appealed to the U.S. Supreme Court.

In **Snyder v. Phelps** (2011), the Supreme Court affirmed the appeals court ruling supporting the free expression rights of the church and its pastor on the grounds that the messages displayed concerned a matter of public importance and were delivered from public property. Writing for the eight-member majority, Chief Justice John G. Roberts, Jr., concluded that the signs unequivocally addressed public concerns and the picketers congregated on public land. Moreover, the ideas expressed, though hateful, could not be censored on the grounds that they were offensive.

Equality and Free Speech. Recall from Chapter 9 that in 2010, the Supreme Court held in **Citizens United v. Federal Election Commission** that corporations and labor unions may spend freely but transparently to advocate the election or defeat of political candidates. We can make sense of *Citizens United* and the vast array of free speech cases through the prism of freedom and equality. On the one hand, freedom of speech promotes the interest of political equality by assuring that speech rights apply to everyone (anarchists, flag burners, communists, and others with marginal or unorthodox views). On the other hand, freedom of speech serves the interest of political liberty by removing government restrictions on political speech, including limits on corporate or union speech. In the *Citizens United* decision, political liberty trumped political equality, allowing the wealthy few to have the loudest voice among the many.[42]

Freedom of the Press

The First Amendment guarantees that government "shall make no law … abridging the freedom … of the press." Although the free press guarantee was originally adopted as a restriction on the national government, since 1931 the Supreme Court has held that it applies to state and local governments as well.

The ability to collect and report information without government interference was (and still is) thought to be essential to a free society. The print media continue to use and defend the freedom conferred on them by the framers. However, the electronic media have had to accept some government regulation stemming from the scarcity of broadcast frequencies (see Chapter 6).

Defamation of Character. Libel is the written defamation of character.* A person who believes his or her name and character have been harmed by false statements in

---

*Slander is the oral defamation of character. The durability of the written word usually means that libel is a more serious accusation than slander.

a publication can institute a lawsuit against the publication and seek monetary compensation for the damage. Such a lawsuit can impose limits on freedom of expression; at the same time, false statements impinge on the rights of individuals. In a landmark decision in **New York Times v. Sullivan** (1964), the Supreme Court declared that freedom of the press takes precedence—at least when the defamed individual is a public official.[43] The Court unanimously agreed that the First Amendment protects the publication of all statements—even false ones—about the conduct of public officials, except statements made with actual malice (with knowledge that they are false or in reckless disregard for their truth or falsity).

Three years later, the Court extended this protection to apply to suits brought by any public figure, whether a government official or not. **Public figures** are people who assume roles of prominence in society or thrust themselves to the forefront of public controversies, including officials, actors, writers, and television personalities. These people must show actual malice on the part of the publication that printed false statements about them. Because the burden of proof is so great, few plaintiffs prevail. And freedom of the press is the beneficiary.

public figures
People who assume roles of prominence in society or thrust themselves to the forefront of public controversy.

Prior Restraint and the Press. As discussed above, in the United States, freedom of the press has primarily meant protection from prior restraint, or censorship. The Supreme Court's first encounter with a law imposing prior restraint on a newspaper was in *Near v. Minnesota* (1931).[44] In Minneapolis, Jay Near published a scandal sheet in which he attacked local officials, charging that they were in league with gangsters.[45] Minnesota officials obtained an injunction to prevent Near from publishing his newspaper, under a state law that allowed such action against periodicals deemed "malicious, scandalous, and defamatory."

The Supreme Court struck down the law, declaring that prior restraint places an unacceptable burden on a free press. Chief Justice Charles Evans Hughes forcefully articulated the need for a vigilant, unrestrained press: "The fact that the liberty of the press may be abused by miscreant purveyors of scandal does not make any the less necessary the immunity of the press from previous restraint in dealing with official misconduct." Although the Court acknowledged that prior restraint may be permissible in exceptional circumstances, it did not specify those circumstances, nor has it yet done so.

Consider another case, which occurred during a war, a time when the tension between government-imposed order and individual freedom is often at a peak. In 1971, Daniel Ellsberg, a special assistant in the Pentagon's Office of International Security Affairs, delivered portions of a classified U.S. Department of Defense study to the *New York Times* and the *Washington Post*. By making the documents public, he hoped to discredit the Vietnam War and thereby end it. The U.S. Department of Justice sought to restrain the *Times* and the *Post* from publishing the documents, which became known as the Pentagon Papers, contending that their publication would prolong the war and embarrass the government. The case was quickly brought before the Supreme Court, which delayed its summer adjournment to hear oral arguments.

Three days later, in a 6–3 decision in **New York Times v. United States** (1971), the Court concluded that the government had not met the heavy burden of proving that immediate, inevitable, and irreparable harm would follow publication of the documents.[46] The majority expressed its view in a brief, unsigned opinion; individual and collective concurring and dissenting views added nine additional opinions to the decision. Two justices maintained that the First Amendment offers absolute protection against government censorship, no matter what the situation. But the other justices left the door ajar for the imposition of prior restraint in the most extreme and compelling of circumstances. The result was hardly a ringing endorsement of freedom of the press or a full affirmation of the public's right to all the information that is vital to the debate of public issues.

Freedom of Expression Versus Maintaining Order.

The courts have consistently held that freedom of the press does not override the requirements of law enforcement. A grand jury called on a Louisville, Kentucky, reporter who had researched and written an article about drug-related activities to identify people he had seen in possession of marijuana or in the act of processing it. The reporter refused to testify, maintaining that freedom of the press shielded him from this inquiry. In a closely divided decision, the Supreme Court in 1972 rejected this position.[47] The Court declared that no exception, even a limited one, is permissible to the rule that all citizens have a duty to give their government whatever testimony they are capable of giving.

AP Photo/Evan Vucci

Hey Dudes, Let's Protest

Students rally on the steps of the U.S. Supreme Court to demonstrate their support for Joseph Frederick, who was suspended from high school when he held up a banner declaring "Bong Hits 4 Jesus" at a school outing in Juneau, Alaska. Frederick lost. Party on.

Consider the 1988 case of a St. Louis high school principal who deleted articles on divorce and teenage pregnancy from the school's newspaper on the grounds that the articles invaded the privacy of students and families who were the focus of the stories. Three student editors filed suit in federal court, claiming that the principal had violated their First Amendment rights. They argued that the principal's censorship interfered with the newspaper's function as a public forum, a role protected by the First Amendment. The principal maintained that the newspaper was just an extension of classroom instruction and thus was not protected by the First Amendment.

In a 5–3 decision, the Supreme Court upheld the principal's actions in sweeping terms. Educators may limit speech within the confines of the school curriculum, including speech that might seem to bear the approval of the school, provided their actions serve any "valid educational purpose." Student expression beyond school property took a hit in 2007 when an increasingly conservative Supreme Court upheld the suspension of a high school student in Juneau, Alaska, who had displayed a banner ("Bong Hits 4 Jesus") at an outside school event. School officials may prohibit speech, wrote Chief Justice John G. Roberts, Jr., if it could be interpreted as promoting illegal drug use.[48]

The Rights to Assemble Peaceably and to Petition the Government

The final clause of the First Amendment states that "Congress shall make no law … abridging … the right of the people peaceably to assemble, and to petition the Government for a redress of grievances." The roots of the right of petition can be traced to the Magna Carta, the charter of English political and civil liberties granted by King John at Runnymede in 1215. The right of peaceable assembly arose much later. The framers meant that the people have the right to assemble peaceably *in order to* petition the government. Today, however, the right to assemble peaceably is equated with the right to free speech and a free press, independent of whether the government is petitioned. Precedent has merged these rights and made them indivisible.[49] Government cannot prohibit peaceful political meetings and cannot brand as criminals those who organize, lead, and attend such meetings.[50]

The clash of interests in cases involving these rights illustrates the continuing nature of the effort to define and apply fundamental principles. The need for order and stability has tempered the concept of freedom. And when freedom and order conflict, the justices of the Supreme Court, who are responsible only to their consciences, strike the balance. Such clashes are certain to occur again and again. Freedom and order conflict when public libraries become targets of community censors, when religious devotion interferes with military service, and when individuals and groups express views or hold beliefs at odds with majority sentiment.

★ 15.4 The Right to Bear Arms

★ Discuss the controversy over the Second Amendment and explain how Supreme Court rulings have addressed that debate.

The Second Amendment declares:

> A well-regulated militia, being necessary to the security of a free State, the right of the people to keep and bear arms, shall not be infringed.

This amendment has created a hornet's nest of problems for gun-control advocates and their opponents. Gun-control advocates assert that the amendment protects the right of the states to maintain *collective* militias. Gun-use advocates assert that the amendment protects the right of *individuals* to own and use guns. There are good arguments on both sides.

Federal firearms regulations did not come into being until Prohibition, so the Supreme Court had little to say on the matter before then. In 1939, however, a unanimous Court upheld a 1934 federal law requiring the taxation and registration of machine guns and sawed-off shotguns. The Court held that the Second Amendment protects a citizen's right to own ordinary militia weapons; sawed-off shotguns did not qualify for protection.[51]

In 2008, the Court squarely considered whether the Second Amendment protects an individual's right to gun ownership or is simply a right tied to service in a militia. **District of Columbia v. Heller** was a challenge to the strictest gun-control statute in the country. It barred private possession of handguns and required the disassembly or use of trigger locks on rifles and shotguns. In a landmark decision, the Court ruled 5–4 that there is a personal constitutional right to keep a loaded handgun at home for self-defense. Justice Antonin Scalia, writing for the conservative majority, acknowledged the problem of handgun violence. "But the enshrinement of constitutional rights," declared Scalia, "necessarily takes certain policy choices off the table.… It is not the role of this court to pronounce the Second Amendment extinct."[52]

The ruling overturned the ban, but it left a host of issues unanswered. Here are three:

1. The Court expressly left open whether the individual right to keep and bear arms in the Second Amendment should be brought into or incorporated into the Fourteenth

Amendment to apply against the states. (The District of Columbia is a creation of the federal government; it is not a state.)

2. The justices suggested that personal handgun possession did not extend to unusual weapons like submachine guns or assault rifles, but that issue was not squarely before them.

3. The opinion did not set out the standard that would be used to evaluate future challenges to gun regulations that stop short of prohibition.

The Court addressed only the first of these issues in **McDonald v. Chicago** (2010), leaving the matter of gun regulation for another day.[53] In five separate opinions covering more than 200 pages, the justices held, 5–4, that an individual's right to bear arms is fundamental and cannot be prohibited by state or local government. The majority could not agree on the exact Fourteenth Amendment clause that enabled this application. Four justices—Chief Justice John G. Roberts, Jr., and Associate Justices Antonin Scalia, Anthony M. Kennedy, and Samuel A. Alito, Jr.—argued that the due process clause served this function. Justice Clarence Thomas maintained that the quiescent privileges and immunities clause should carry the freight.

How much regulation will the Court tolerate when it comes to the right to bear arms? New cases now in the legal pipeline will test the waters on what is permissible and what is not.

AP Photo/Rich Pedroncelli

Rallying for a Right

Second Amendment activists gathered around the country on April 19, 2010, also known as Patriots Day, to demonstrate the right to bear arms. The date commemorates the battles of Lexington and Concord during the Revolutionary War. One protester wore his holstered unloaded pistol while attending such a rally in Sacramento, California. He and others objected to a proposed state law that would ban gun owners from openly carrying unloaded guns in public. In June 2010, the U.S. Supreme Court held that state and local governments may not forbid individual gun ownership. The Court has yet to decide how far government may go in regulating gun ownership.

15.5 Applying the Bill of Rights to the States

★ Explain the process by which the Supreme Court extended the protections of the Bill of Rights to the local and state levels of government.

The major purpose of the Constitution was to structure the division of power between the national government and the state governments. Even before it was amended, the Constitution set some limits on both the nation and the states with regard to citizens' rights. It barred both governments from passing **bills of attainder**, laws that make an individual guilty of a crime without a trial. It also prohibited them from enacting **ex post facto laws**, which declare an action a crime after it has been performed. And it barred both nation and states from impairing the **obligation of contracts**, the obligation of the parties in a contract to carry out its terms.

bills of attainder
A law that pronounces an individual guilty of a crime without a trial.

ex post facto laws
Laws that declare an action to be criminal after it has been performed.

obligation of contracts
The obligation of the parties to a contract to carry out its terms.

Although initially the Bill of Rights seemed to apply only to the national government, various litigants pressed the claim that its guarantees also applied to the states. In response to one such claim, Chief Justice John Marshall affirmed what seemed plain from the Constitution's language and "the history of the day" (the events surrounding the Constitutional Convention): the provisions of the Bill of Rights served only to limit national authority. "Had the framers of these amendments intended them to be limitations on the powers of the state governments," wrote Marshall in 1833, "they would have … expressed that intention."[54]

Change came with the Fourteenth Amendment, which was adopted in 1868. The due process clause of that amendment is the linchpin that holds the states to the provisions of the Bill of Rights.

The Fourteenth Amendment: Due Process of Law

> *Section 1.*… No State shall make or enforce any law which shall abridge the privileges or immunities of citizens of the United States; nor shall any State deprive any person of life, liberty, or property, without due process of law.

Most freedoms protected in the Bill of Rights today function as limitations on the states. And many of the standards that limit the national government serve equally to limit state governments. The changes have been achieved through the Supreme Court's interpretation of the due process clause of the Fourteenth Amendment: "nor shall any State deprive any person of life, liberty, or property, without due process of law." The clause has two central meanings. First, it requires the government to adhere to appropriate procedures. For example, in a criminal trial, the government must establish the defendant's guilt beyond a reasonable doubt. Second, it forbids unreasonable government action. For example, at the turn of the twentieth century, the Supreme Court struck down a state law that forbade bakers from working more than sixty hours a week. The justices found the law unreasonable under the due process clause.[55]

The Supreme Court has used the first meaning of the due process clause as a sponge, absorbing or incorporating the procedural specifics of the Bill of Rights and spreading or applying them to the states. The history of due process cases reveals that unlikely litigants often champion constitutional guarantees and that freedom is not always the victor.

The Fundamental Freedoms

In 1897, the Supreme Court declared that the states are subject to the Fifth Amendment's prohibition against taking private property without providing just compensation.[56] The Court reached that decision by absorbing the prohibition into the due process clause of the Fourteenth Amendment, which explicitly applies to the states. Thus, one Bill of Rights protection—but only that one—applied to both the states and the national government, as illustrated in Figure 15.2. In 1925, the Court assumed that the due process clause protected the First Amendment speech and press liberties from impairment by the states.[57]

The inclusion of other Bill of Rights guarantees within the due process clause faced a critical test in ***Palko v. Connecticut*** (1937).[58] Frank Palko had been charged with homicide in the first degree. He was convicted of second-degree murder, however, and sentenced to life imprisonment. The state of Connecticut appealed and won a new trial; this time, Palko was found guilty of first-degree murder and sentenced to

FIGURE 15.2 The Selective Incorporation of the Bill of Rights

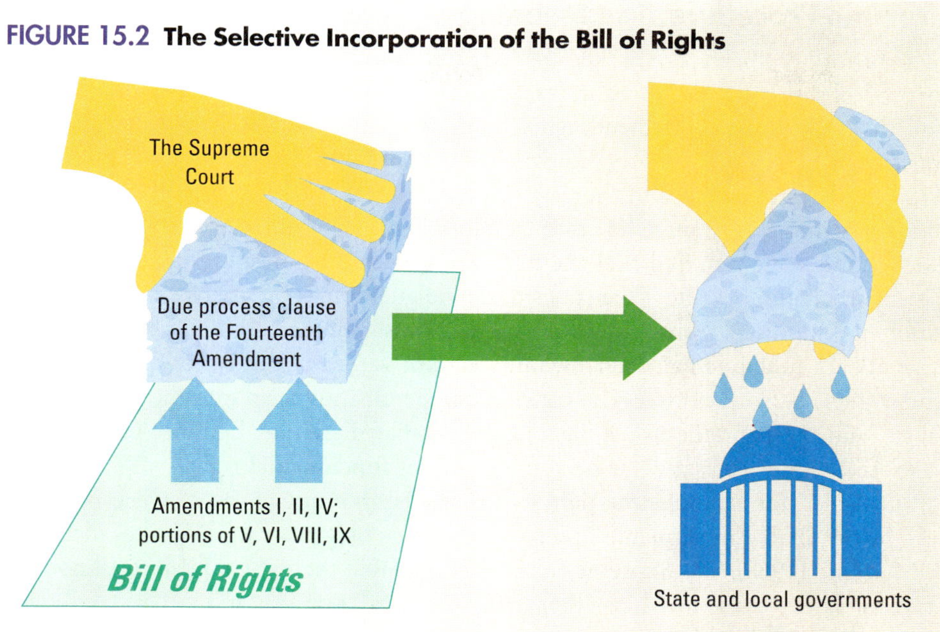

The Supreme Court has used the due process clause of the Fourteenth Amendment as a sponge, absorbing most of the provisions in the Bill of Rights and applying them to state and local governments. All provisions in the Bill of Rights apply to the national government.
© Cengage Learning.

death. Palko appealed the second conviction on the grounds that it violated the protection against double jeopardy guaranteed to him by the Fifth Amendment. This protection applied to the states, he contended, because of the Fourteenth Amendment's due process clause.

The Supreme Court upheld Palko's second conviction. In his opinion for the majority, Justice Benjamin N. Cardozo formulated principles that were to guide the Court's actions for the next three decades. He reasoned that some Bill of Rights guarantees, such as freedom of thought and speech, are fundamental and that these fundamental rights are absorbed by the Fourteenth Amendment's due process clause and are therefore applicable to the states. These rights are essential, argued Cardozo, because "neither liberty nor justice would exist if they were sacrificed." Trial by jury and other rights, although valuable and important, are not essential to liberty and justice and therefore are not absorbed by the due process clause. "Few would be so narrow or provincial," Cardozo claimed, "as to maintain that a fair and enlightened system of justice would be impossible" without these other rights. In other words, only certain provisions of the Bill of Rights—the "fundamental" provisions—were absorbed selectively into the due process clause and made applicable to the states. Because protection against double jeopardy was not one of them, Palko died in Connecticut's electric chair in 1938.

The next thirty years saw slow but perceptible change in the standard for determining whether a Bill of Rights guarantee was fundamental. The reference point changed from the idealized "fair and enlightened system of justice" in *Palko* to the more realistic "American scheme of justice" thirty years later.[59] Case after case tested various guarantees that the Court found to be fundamental. By 1969, when *Palko* was finally overturned, the Court had found most of the Bill of Rights applicable to the states. (Recall that the Court made the Second Amendment's "right to keep and bear arms" fully applicable to the states in 2010.)

Criminal Procedure: The Meaning of Constitutional Guarantees

"The history of liberty," remarked Justice Felix Frankfurter, "has largely been the history of observance of procedural safeguards."[60] The safeguards embodied in the Fourth through Eighth Amendments to the Constitution specify how government must behave in criminal proceedings. Their application to the states has reshaped American criminal justice in the past fifty years in two stages. The first stage was the judgment that a guarantee asserted in the Bill of Rights also applied to the states. The second stage required that the judiciary give specific meaning to the guarantee. The courts could not allow the states to define guarantees themselves without risking different definitions from state to state—and thus differences among citizens' rights. If rights are fundamental, their meaning cannot vary. But life is not quite so simple under the U.S. Constitution. The concept of federalism is sewn into the constitutional fabric, and the Supreme Court has recognized that there may be more than one way to prosecute the accused while heeding his or her fundamental rights.

Consider, for example, the right to a jury trial in criminal cases, which is guaranteed by the Sixth Amendment. This right was made obligatory for the states in *Duncan* v. *Louisiana* (1968). The Supreme Court later held that the right applied to all nonpetty criminal cases—those in which the penalty for conviction was more than six months' imprisonment.[61] But the Court did not require that state juries have twelve members, the number required for federal criminal proceedings. The Court permits jury size to vary from state to state, although it has set the minimum number at six. Furthermore, it has not imposed on the states the federal requirement of a unanimous jury verdict. As a result, even today, many states do not require unanimous verdicts for criminal convictions. Some observers question whether criminal defendants in these states enjoy the same rights as defendants in unanimous-verdict states.

In contrast, the Court left no room for variation in its definition of the fundamental right to an attorney, also guaranteed by the Sixth Amendment. Clarence Earl Gideon was a penniless vagrant accused of breaking into and robbing a pool hall. Because Gideon could not afford a lawyer, he asked the state to provide him with legal counsel for his trial. The state refused and subsequently convicted Gideon and sentenced him to five years in the Florida State Penitentiary. From his cell, Gideon appealed to the U.S. Supreme Court, claiming that his conviction should be struck down because the state had denied him his Sixth Amendment right to counsel.[62]

In its landmark decision in **Gideon v. Wainwright** (1963), the Court set aside Gideon's conviction and extended to defendants in state courts the Sixth Amendment right to counsel.[63] The state retried Gideon, who this time had the assistance of a lawyer, and the court found him not guilty.

In subsequent rulings that stretched over more than a decade, the Court specified at which points in the course of criminal proceedings a defendant is entitled to a lawyer (from arrest to trial, appeal, and beyond). These pronouncements are binding on all states. In state as well as federal proceedings, the government must furnish legal assistance to those who do not have the means to hire their own attorney. During this period, the Court also came to grips with another procedural issue: informing suspects of their constitutional rights. Without this knowledge, procedural safeguards are meaningless. Ernesto Miranda was arrested in Arizona in connection with the kidnapping and rape of an eighteen-year-old woman. After the police questioned him for two hours and the woman identified him, Miranda confessed to the crime. An Arizona court convicted him based on that confession—although he was never told that he had the right to counsel and the right not to incriminate himself. Miranda appealed his conviction, which was overturned by the Supreme Court in 1966.[64]

The Court based its decision in **Miranda v. Arizona** on the Fifth Amendment privilege against self-incrimination. According to the Court, the police had forced Miranda to confess during in-custody questioning, not with physical force but with the coercion inherent in custodial interrogation without counsel. The Court said that warnings are necessary to dispel that coercion. The Court does not require warnings if a person is only held in custody without being questioned or is only questioned without being arrested. But in *Miranda,* the Court found the combination of custody and interrogation sufficiently intimidating to require warnings before questioning. These statements are known today as the *Miranda* **warnings**:

- You have the right to remain silent.
- Anything you say can be used against you in court.
- You have the right to talk to a lawyer of your own choice before questioning.
- If you cannot afford to hire a lawyer, a lawyer will be provided without charge.

***Miranda* warnings**
Statements concerning rights that police are required to make to a person before he or she is subjected to in-custody questioning.

In each area of criminal procedure, the justices have had to grapple with two steps in the application of constitutional guarantees to criminal defendants: the extension of a right to the states and the definition of that right. In *Duncan,* the issue was the right to jury trial, and the Court allowed variation in all states. In *Gideon,* the Court applied the right to counsel uniformly in all states. Finally, in *Miranda,* the Court declared that all governments—national, state, and local—have a duty to inform suspects of the full measure of their constitutional rights. In one of its most important cases in 2000, the Court reaffirmed this protection in a 7–2 decision, holding that *Miranda* had "announced a constitutional rule" that Congress could not undermine through legislation.[65]

The problems in balancing freedom and order can be formidable. A primary function of government is to maintain order. What happens when the government infringes on individuals' freedom for the sake of order? Consider the guarantee in the Fourth Amendment: "The right of the people to be secure in their persons, houses, papers, and effects, against unreasonable searches and seizures, shall not be violated."

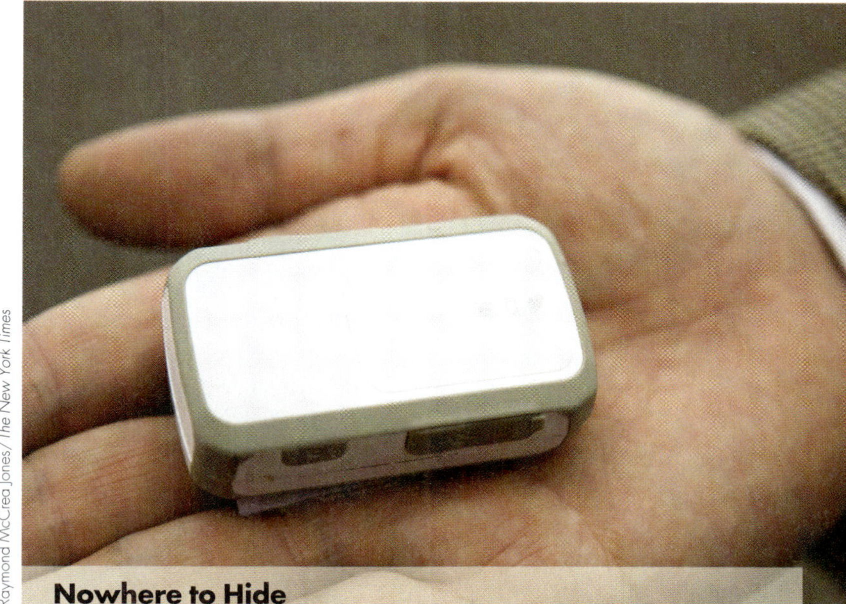

Raymond McCrea Jones / The New York Times

Nowhere to Hide

Police in the District of Columbia placed a GPS tracking device like the one pictured here on Antoine Jones's Jeep without a court warrant. Jones was convicted of drug trafficking based in part on the evidence culled from monitoring the car's movements for 28 days. On appeal, Jones argued that the use of the GPS device to track his movement amounted to a warrantless search in violation of the Fourth Amendment. In 2012, the Supreme Court agreed with Jones.

The Court made this right applicable to the states in *Wolf* v. *Colorado* (1949).[66] Following the reasoning in *Palko,* the Court found that the core of the amendment—security against arbitrary police intrusion—is a fundamental right and that citizens must be protected from illegal searches by state and local governments. But how? The federal courts had long followed the **exclusionary rule**, which holds that evidence obtained from an illegal search and seizure cannot be used in a trial. If that evidence is critical to the prosecution, the case dissolves. But the Court refused to apply the exclusionary rule to the state courts. Instead, it allowed the states to decide on their own how to handle the fruits of an illegal search.

exclusionary rule
The judicial rule that states that evidence obtained in an illegal search and seizure cannot be used in trial.

The decision in *Wolf* stated that obtaining evidence by illegal means violated the Constitution and that states could fashion their own rules of evidence to give effect to this constitutional decree. The states were not bound by the exclusionary rule.

The justices considered the exclusionary rule again twelve years later, in *Mapp* v. *Ohio*.[67] An Ohio court had found Dolree Mapp guilty of possessing obscene materials after an admittedly illegal search of her home for a fugitive. The Ohio Supreme Court affirmed her conviction, and she appealed to the U.S. Supreme Court. Mapp's attorneys argued for a reversal based primarily on freedom of expression, contending that the First Amendment protected the confiscated materials. However, the Court elected to use the decision in *Mapp* to give meaning to the constitutional guarantee against unreasonable search and seizure. In a 6–3 decision, the justices declared that "all evidence obtained by searches and seizures in violation of the Constitution is, by [the Fourth Amendment], inadmissible in a state court." Ohio had convicted Mapp illegally; the evidence should have been excluded.

The decision was historic. It placed the exclusionary rule under the umbrella of the Fourth Amendment and required all levels of government to operate according to the provisions of that amendment. Failure to do so could result in the dismissal of criminal charges against guilty defendants.

Mapp launched a divided Supreme Court on a troubled course of determining how and when to apply the exclusionary rule. For example, the Court has continued to struggle with police use of sophisticated electronic eavesdropping devices and searches of movable vehicles. In each case, the justices have confronted a rule that appears to handicap the police and to offer freedom to people whose guilt has been established by the illegal evidence. In the Court's most recent pronouncements, order has triumphed over freedom.

The struggle over the exclusionary rule took a new turn in 1984, when the Court reviewed *United States* v. *Leon*.[68] In this case, the police obtained a search warrant from a judge on the basis of a tip from an informant of unproved reliability. The judge issued a warrant without firmly establishing probable cause to believe the tip. The police, relying on the warrant, found large quantities of illegal drugs. The Court, by a vote of 6–3, established the **good faith exception** to the exclusionary rule. The justices held that the state could introduce at trial evidence seized on the basis of a mistakenly issued search warrant. The exclusionary rule, argued the majority, is not a right but a remedy against illegal police conduct. The rule is costly to society. It excludes pertinent valid evidence, allowing guilty people to go unpunished and generating disrespect for the law. These costs are justifiable only if the exclusionary rule deters police misconduct. Such a deterrent effect was not a factor in *Leon:* the police acted in good faith. Hence, the Court decided, there is a need for an exception to the rule.

The Court recognized another exception in 2006. When police search a home with a warrant, they have been required to "knock and announce" before entering. But the Supreme Court held that when the police admittedly fail to "knock and announce," the evidence obtained from such a search may still be admitted into evidence, thus creating a new exception to the exclusionary rule. The case was a close one: decided 5–4 with Justice Scalia writing the majority opinion and implying that the exclusionary rule should not be applied in other illegal search circumstances.[69]

As a more conservative coalition has taken shape, the exclusionary rule has come under close scrutiny as the preference for order outweighs the value in freedom. In yet another exception, the Supreme Court held in 2009 that evidence obtained through police negligence would not bar the introduction of that evidence at trial.[70]

good faith exception
An exception to the Supreme Court exclusionary rule, holding that evidence seized on the basis of a mistakenly issued search warrant can be introduced at trial if the mistake was made in good faith, that is, if all the parties involved had reason at the time to believe that the warrant was proper.

The Internet and information technology have had enormous, positive impacts on American life. But they come at a price. For example, personal privacy is surely compromised when e-mail, cellphone, and text messages can be retrieved and shared. In 2012, cellphone carriers reported responding to 1.3 million demands for text messages and caller locations from law enforcement agencies.[71] But Internet-based telephone conversations may overprotect privacy. (See "Politics of Global Change: Wiretapping in the Digital Age.")

The USA-PATRIOT Act

More than fifty years ago, Justice Robert H. Jackson warned that exceptional protections for civil liberties might convert the Bill of Rights into a suicide pact. The national government decided, after the September 11 terrorist attacks, to forgo some liberties in order to secure greater order, through bipartisan passage of the USA-PATRIOT Act. This landmark law greatly expanded the ability of law enforcement and intelligence agencies to tap phones, monitor Internet traffic, and conduct other forms of surveillance in pursuit of terrorists. In 2006, Congress extended with a few minor changes sixteen expiring provisions of the act.

Shortly after the bill became law, then Attorney General John Ashcroft declared: "Let the terrorists among us be warned: If you overstay your visas, even by one day, we will arrest you. If you violate a local law, we will hope that you will, and work to make sure that you are put in jail and kept in custody as long as possible. We will use every available statute. We will seek every prosecutorial advantage. We will use all our weapons within the law and under the Constitution to protect life and enhance security for America."[72]

In this shift toward order, civil libertarians worry. "These new and unchecked powers could be used against American citizens who are not under criminal investigation," said Gregory T. Nojeim, associate director of the American Civil Liberties Union's Washington office.[73]

The USA-PATRIOT Act runs over three hundred pages. Some parts engender strong opposition; others are benign. More than 150 communities have passed resolutions denouncing the act as an assault on civil liberties. Consider one of the key provisions: Section 215, dealing with rules for searching private records such as you might find in the library, video store, or doctor's office. Prior to the act, the government needed, at minimum, a warrant issued by a judge and probable cause to access such records. (Foreign intelligence information could justify a warrantless search, but judges still reviewed the exception.) Now, under the USA-PATRIOT Act, the government need only certify without substantiation that its search protects against terrorism, which turns judicial oversight into a rubber stamp. With the bar lowered, more warrantless searches are likely to follow. In 2005, the FBI conducted more than thirty-five hundred such searches of U.S. citizens and legal residents, a significant jump from previous years.[74] To complicate matters, a gag order bars the person turning over the records from disclosing the search to anyone. You may never know that your records were searched. In a fig leaf to civil libertarians, the renewed provision allows those served with such gag orders to challenge them in court after a year's wait. But in order to prevail, they must prove that the government acted in "bad faith."[75]

The phenomenal growth in cell phone usage threatens privacy concerns generally. In 2011, law enforcement agencies made a remarkable 1.3 million requests for text messages and caller location data from cell phone providers. Court orders bolstered most requests but many were also issued on an emergency basis without court oversight.[76]

Politics of Global Change

Wiretapping in the Digital Age

In the pre-Internet world, telephone calls followed a continuous path between two parties. Armed with a search warrant from a state or federal court, investigators could select a point somewhere along the line to tap the call. But with the advent of the Internet, calls can be placed online. The emergence of VoIP (voice over Internet protocol) has dropped the cost of long-distance and international telephone calls to all-time lows. Some services like Skype provide such services for free. Lawbreakers have reason to rejoice.

The Communications Assistance for Law Enforcement Act (CALEA) governs wiretap requests in the United States. It imposes requirements on telecom companies to cooperate with lawful intercepts. Congress enacted the law in 1994, at the dawn of the Internet. The growth of VoIP telephony left the FBI, the Drug Enforcement Administration, and the Department of Justice powerless. The agencies successfully lobbied the Federal Communications Commission (the agency that oversees implementation of CALEA) to extend the rules to cover VoIP telecoms.

Civil libertarians cried foul, claiming that CALEA targeted only traditional telephone wiretaps. But the fight against terrorism trumped these objections. Today, all broadband-Internet and VoIP providers must comply with the new rules. These firms are required to intercept calls such that suspects cannot tell that they are under surveillance. That's no easy task for at least three reasons.

First, complying with CALEA is complicated because the device at the end of the line today is a computer, not a telephone. A reasonably sophisticated caller can tell if her calls are intercepted by simply measuring the "latency" of the connection, that is, the time taken for a single packet of data to travel from a local machine to a computer elsewhere on the Internet. Inserting a bugging device into the chain increases the latency, signaling a possible tap. To address this problem, Internet companies, siding with regulators, now leave lawful-intercept equipment permanently in place to be activated as required. In effect, there is now a back door into everyone's connection.

Detainees and the War on Terrorism

In 2004, the Supreme Court addressed some of the difficult issues in the war on terrorism in two cases in which war detainees had been designated "enemy combatants." President Bush, relying on a series of World War II–era opinions, maintained that the detainees were not entitled to basic legal requirements such as attorneys or hearings and that his actions could not be reviewed in the courts.[77] The Supreme Court rejected his position. Regardless of the location of their detention—hundreds of foreign detainees are being held at a naval base in Guantánamo Bay, Cuba—the Court said in the first case that they are entitled to challenge their designation as "enemy combatants" before a federal judge or other neutral decision maker.[78]

In the second case, a Saudi Arabian resident, who was born in the United States and thus a citizen, was picked up on an Afghan battlefield and detained as an enemy combatant. In an 8–1 vote, the Court declared that he is entitled by the due process clause of the Fifth Amendment to a "meaningful opportunity" to contest the basis for

Second, another issue created by VoIP telephony is the enormous volume of data passing along the Internet. Traditional telephone taps required an agent to switch on a recorder to collect evidence. Today's digital eavesdropping requires the collection of hundreds upon hundreds of gigabytes of data and then making sense of the material. Standards for formatting and delivering data to investigators still need resolution to work across national borders.

Third, perhaps the biggest issue remains encryption. Not all VoIP calls are encrypted. But even those who do encrypt their calls must provide law enforcement agencies with the appropriate decryption keys. The one exception is Skype, the most popular VoIP service, with over 520 million users. Skype is a "peer-to-peer" system, routing calls entirely over the public Internet. Skype cannot provide investigators with access to a suspect's calls because Skype does not handle any of the traffic itself. Even if investigators could intercept a Skype call, they would still face the task of unraveling the strong encryption used for those calls. Only the chief spy agency, the National Security Agency, has the computing power to unravel Skype packets. NSA's resources focus on intelligence gathering, not law enforcement. Skype, based in Luxembourg but partially owned by the American company eBay, "cooperates fully with all lawful requests," but it remains to be seen whether CALEA requests are "lawful" from the perspective of a European-based company.

One way around the problem of strong encryption is to grab decryption keys directly from a suspect's computer. A German court has ruled this approach would be inadmissible, prompting German legislators to draft a change in the law.

In a world made ever smaller by technology, eavesdropping on criminals today will require governments to be nimble in lawmaking and persuasive in their efforts to secure cooperation from other nations. This probably means that governments will lag behind in their efforts to eavesdrop as part of law enforcement. Telephony technology may prove a bulwark for personal privacy, but at what cost to the need for order?

SOURCE: "Bugging the Cloud," *Economist Technology Quarterly*, 8 March 2008, pp. 28–30.

his detention. In blunt language, Justice Sandra Day O'Connor, speaking for herself and three other justices, rebuffed the president's claim: "We have long since made clear that a state of war is not a blank check for the President when it comes to the rights of the Nation's citizens."[79]

In 2006, the Court rejected by a vote of 5–3 the president's claim of unbounded authority in the creation and use of military commissions for enemy combatants imprisoned at Guantánamo Bay, Cuba. In **Hamdan v. Rumsfeld,** the justices held that the commissions were unauthorized by Congress and that they violated a provision of international law. The opinion rebuking presidential authority also established minimum procedures for any future commissions.[80] Shortly after, the Bush administration complied with the decision by announcing that terror suspects held by the United States would have a right to basic legal and human protections under international law.

In 2008, the Court issued yet another rebuke to the Bush administration when it ruled 5–4 in **Boumediene v. Bush** that prisoners at Guantánamo have a right to challenge their detentions in the federal courts.[81] The president continued to claim he could do as he wished with prisoners he designated as "enemy combatants," expecting the justices to side with him during armed conflicts. But the Court's repeated rejection of presidential authority is likely the result of an unusually aggressive position on executive power. Rather than narrowing its claims after its losses, the administration continued to assert that the 1940s precedents gave it a free hand. That was the wrong lesson.

15.6 The Ninth Amendment and Personal Autonomy

★ Explain how the Supreme Court interpreted the Ninth Amendment to broaden the individual's constitutional protection of personal privacy beyond the language in the Bill of Rights, a right not enumerated in the Constitution.

> The enumeration in the Constitution, of certain rights, shall not be construed to deny or disparage others retained by the people.

The working and history of the Ninth Amendment remain an enigma; the evidence supports two different views: the amendment may protect rights that are not enumerated, or it may simply protect state governments against the assumption of power by the national government.[82] The meaning of the amendment was not an issue until 1965, when the Supreme Court used it to protect privacy, a right that is not enumerated in the Constitution.

Controversy: From Privacy to Abortion

In *Griswold* **v.** *Connecticut* (1965), the Court struck down, by a vote of 7–2, a seldom-enforced Connecticut statute that made the use of birth control devices a crime.[83] Justice Douglas, writing for the majority, asserted that the "specific guarantees in the Bill of Rights have penumbras [partially illuminated regions surrounding fully lit areas]" that give "life and substance" to broad, unspecified protections in the Bill of Rights. Several specific guarantees in the First, Third, Fourth, and Fifth Amendments create a zone of privacy, Douglas argued, and this zone is protected by the Ninth Amendment and is applicable to the states by the due process clause of the Fourteenth Amendment.

Three justices gave further emphasis to the relevance of the Ninth Amendment, which, they contended, protects fundamental rights derived from those specifically enumerated in the first eight amendments. This view contrasted sharply with the position expressed by the two dissenters, Justices Black and Stewart. In the absence of some specific prohibition, they argued, the Bill of Rights and the Fourteenth Amendment do not allow judicial annulment of state legislative policies, even if those policies are abhorrent to a judge or justice.

Griswold established the principle that the Bill of Rights as a whole creates a right to make certain intimate, personal choices, including the right of married people to engage in sexual intercourse for reproduction or pleasure. This zone of personal autonomy, protected by the Constitution, was the basis of a 1973 case that sought to invalidate state antiabortion laws. But rights are not absolute, and in weighing the interests of the individual against the interests of the government, the Supreme Court found itself caught up in a flood of controversy that has yet to subside.

In *Roe* **v.** *Wade* (1973), the Court, in a 7–2 decision, declared unconstitutional a Texas law making it a crime to obtain an abortion except for the purpose of saving the woman's life.[84]

Justice Harry A. Blackmun, who wrote the majority opinion, could not point to a specific constitutional guarantee to justify the Court's ruling. Instead, he based the decision on the right to privacy protected by the due process clause of the Fourteenth Amendment. In effect, state abortion laws were unreasonable and hence unconstitutional. The Court declared that in the first three months of pregnancy, the abortion decision must be left to the woman and her physician. In the interest of protecting the woman's health, states may restrict but not prohibit abortions in the second three months of pregnancy. Finally, in the last three months of pregnancy, states may regulate or even prohibit abortions to protect the life of the fetus, except when medical judgment determines that an abortion is necessary to save the woman's life. In all, the Court's ruling affected the laws of forty-six states.

The dissenters—Justices Byron R. White and William H. Rehnquist—were quick to assert what critics have frequently repeated since the decision: the Court's judgment was directed by its own dislikes, not by any constitutional compass. In the absence of guiding principles, they asserted, the majority justices simply substituted their views for the views of the state legislatures whose abortion regulations they invalidated.[85] In a 1993 television interview, Blackmun insisted that "*Roe* versus *Wade* was decided … on constitutional grounds."[86] It was as if Blackmun were trying, by sheer force of will, to turn back twenty years' worth of stinging objections to the opinion he had crafted.

The composition of the Court shifted under President Ronald Reagan. His elevation of Rehnquist to chief justice in 1986 and his appointment of Scalia in 1986 and Kennedy in 1988 raised new hope among abortion foes and old fears among advocates of choice.

A perceptible shift away from abortion rights materialized in *Webster* v. *Reproductive Health Services* (1989). The case was a blockbuster, attracting voluminous media coverage. In *Webster,* the Supreme Court upheld the constitutionality of a Missouri law that denied the use of public employees or publicly funded facilities in the performance of an abortion unless the woman's life was in danger.[87] Furthermore, the law required doctors to perform tests to determine whether fetuses twenty weeks and older could survive outside the womb. This was the first time that the Court upheld significant government restrictions on abortion.

The justices issued five opinions, but no single opinion captured a majority. Four justices (Blackmun, Brennan, Thurgood Marshall, and John Paul Stevens) voted to strike down the Missouri law and hold fast to *Roe*. Four justices (Kennedy, Rehnquist, Scalia, and White) wanted to overturn *Roe* and return to the states the power to regulate abortion. The remaining justice, Sandra Day O'Connor, avoided both camps. Her position was that state abortion restrictions are permissible provided they are not "unduly burdensome." She voted with the conservative plurality to uphold the restrictive Missouri statute on the grounds that it did not place an undue burden on women's rights. But she declined to reconsider (and overturn) *Roe*.

The Court has since moved cautiously down the road toward greater government control of abortion. In 1990, the justices split on two state parental notification laws. The Court struck down a state requirement that compelled unwed minors to notify both parents before having an abortion. In another case, however, the Court upheld a state requirement that a physician notify one parent of a pregnant minor of her intent to have an abortion. In both cases, the justices voiced widely divergent opinions, revealing a continuing division over abortion.[88]

The abortion issue pits freedom against order. The decision to bear or beget children should be free from government control. Yet government has a legitimate interest in protecting and preserving life, including fetal life, as part of its responsibility to maintain an orderly society. Rather than choose between freedom and order, the majority on the Court has loosened constitutional protections of abortion rights and cast the politically divisive issue into the state legislatures, where elected representatives can thrash out the conflict.

Many groups defending or opposing abortion have now turned to state legislative politics to advance their policies. This approach will force candidates for state office to debate the abortion issue and then translate electoral outcomes into legislation that restricts or protects abortion, for example, by defining in law that life begins at conception, making the fetus "a person" with constitutional and other legal protections. If the abortion issue is deeply felt by Americans, pluralist theory would predict that the strongest voices for or against abortion will mobilize the greatest support in the political arena.

With a clear conservative majority, the Court seemed poised to reverse *Roe* in 1992. But a new coalition—forged by Reagan and Bush appointees O'Connor, Souter, and Kennedy—reaffirmed *Roe* yet tolerated additional restrictions on abortions. In *Planned Parenthood* v. *Casey,* a bitterly divided bench opted for the O'Connor "undue burden" test. Eight years later, in 2000, O'Connor sided with a coalition of liberal and moderate justices in a 5–4 decision striking down a Nebraska law that had banned so-called partial-birth abortion, illustrating the Court's continuing and deep division on the abortion issue.[89]

Let's view the abortion controversy through our lens of value conflicts. Presidents try to appoint justices whose values coincide with their own. Justices appointed by conservative presidents Reagan and George H. W. Bush weakened abortion as a constitutional right, putting more weight on order. President Clinton's appointees (Ruth Bader Ginsburg and Stephen G. Breyer) fulfilled his liberal campaign promise to protect women's access to abortion from further assault, putting more weight on freedom. President George W. Bush's conservative appointees—John G. Roberts, Jr., and Samuel A. Alito, Jr.—have tipped the balance toward order. In 2007, the Court by a 5–4 vote upheld a federal law banning partial-birth abortion.[90] The law was nearly identical to the one struck down by the Court years before. Today, order trumps freedom. An ideological shift in the White House may be insufficient to produce a different result unless conservative justices leave the Court. And none have expressed the intention to do so.

Personal Autonomy and Sexual Orientation

The right-to-privacy cases may have opened a Pandora's box of divisive social issues. Does the right to privacy embrace private homosexual acts between consenting adults? Consider the case of Michael Hardwick, who was arrested in 1982 in his Atlanta bedroom while having sex with another man. In a standard approach to prosecuting homosexuals, Georgia charged him under a state criminal statute with the crime of sodomy, which means oral or anal intercourse. The police said that they had gone to his home to arrest him for failing to pay a fine for drinking in public. Although the prosecutor dropped the charges, Hardwick sued to challenge the law's constitutionality. He won in the lower courts, but the state pursued the case.

The conflict between freedom and order lies at the core of the case. "Our legal history and our social traditions have condemned this conduct uniformly for hundreds and hundreds of years," argued Georgia's attorney. Constitutional law, he continued, "must not become an instrument for a change in the social order." Hardwick's attorney, a noted constitutional scholar, said that government must have a more important reason than "majority morality to justify regulation of sexual intimacies in the privacy of the home." He maintained that the case involved two precious freedoms: the right to engage in private sexual relations and the right to be free from government intrusion in one's home.[91]

In a bitterly divided ruling in 1986, the Court held in *Bowers* v. *Hardwick* that the Constitution does not protect homosexual relations between consenting adults, even in the privacy of their own homes.[92] The logic of the findings in the privacy cases involving contraception and abortion would seem to have compelled a finding of a right to personal autonomy—a right to make personal choices unconstrained by government—in this case as well. But the 5–4 majority maintained that only heterosexual choices—whether and whom to marry, whether to conceive a child, whether to have an abortion—fall within the zone of privacy established by the Court in its earlier rulings. "The Judiciary necessarily takes to itself further authority to govern the country without express constitutional authority" when it expands the list of fundamental rights not rooted in the language or design of the Constitution, wrote Justice White, the author of the majority opinion.

JAMES R. BROWNING UNITED STATES COURTHOUSE

Hey Judges Overturn GRAVITY NEXT!

ONE NATION UNDER GOD not the 9th Circuit!

Vote NO on PROP 8 UNFAIR & WRONG

Justin Sullivan/Getty Images

Prop 8: Time to Demonstrate

In 2008, California voters banned same-sex marriage with the passage of Proposition 8. The controversy moved to the federal courts as opponents of the ban challenged the constitutionality of the voter initiative. A trial judge overturned the ban. An appeal followed. Prop 8 opponents and proponents demonstrate in 2010 at the federal court house in San Francisco.

The arguments on both sides of the privacy issue are compelling. This makes the choice between freedom and order excruciating for ordinary citizens and Supreme Court justices alike. At the conference to decide the merits of the *Bowers* case, Justice Lewis Powell cast his vote to extend privacy rights to homosexual conduct. Later, he switched sides and joined with his conservative colleagues, fashioning a new majority. Four years after the *Bowers* decision, Powell revealed another change of mind: "I probably made a mistake," he declared, speaking of his decision to vote with the conservative majority.[93]

Justice White's majority opinion was reconsidered in 2003 when the Court considered a "carefully choreographed" challenge to a Texas law that criminalized homosexual but not heterosexual sodomy.[94] This time, in ***Lawrence and Garner* v. *Texas***, a new coalition of six justices viewed the issue in a different light. May a majority use the power of government to enforce its views on the whole society through the criminal law? Speaking through Justice Kennedy, the Court observed "an emerging awareness that liberty gives substantial protection to adult persons in deciding how to conduct their private lives in matters pertaining to sex." Since the Texas law furthered no legitimate state interest but intruded into the intimate personal choices of individuals, the law was void. Kennedy along with four other justices then took the unusual step of reaching back in time to declare that the *Bowers* decision was wrong and should be overruled.[95]

Justice Antonin Scalia, joined by Chief Justice Rehnquist and Justice Clarence Thomas, issued a stinging dissent. Scalia charged the majority with "signing on to the homosexual agenda" aimed at eliminating the moral opprobrium traditionally attached to homosexual conduct. The consequence is that the Court would be departing from its role of ensuring that the democratic rules of engagement are observed. He continued:

> What Texas has chosen to do is well within the range of traditional democratic action, and its hand should not be stayed through the invention of a brand-new "constitutional right" by a Court that is impatient of democratic change. It is indeed true that "later generations can see that laws once thought necessary and proper in fact serve only to oppress," … and when that happens, later generations can repeal those laws. But it is the premise of our system that those judgments are to be made by the people, and not imposed by a governing caste that knows best.[96]

The challenge of democracy calls for the democratic process to sort out value conflicts whenever possible. And, according to Scalia, the majority has moved from its traditional responsibility of umpiring the system to favoring one side over another in the struggle between freedom and order.

Issues around sexual orientation have shifted toward the states. In anticipation of state-approved same-sex unions, Congress moved affirmatively in 1996 to bar the effects of homosexual marriage through passage of the Defense of Marriage Act (DOMA). President Clinton signed the bill into law. The law defines marriage as a union between people of opposite sexes and declares that states are not obliged to recognize gay marriages performed elsewhere. The law does not ban such unions; it only protects states from having to recognize same-sex marriage sanctioned by other states. President Obama favors repeal of the act. In July 2010, a federal trial court struck down the marriage-defining section of the Act on the ground that it violated the concept of equality inherent in the Fifth Amendment. A federal appeals court agreed in 2012. DOMA's fate now rests with the U.S. Supreme Court.[97]

Some states have been innovators in legitimizing homosexuality. Same-sex couples can marry in six states plus the District of Columbia as a result of legislative or judicial action. Additional states have recognized same-sex "unions" but not same-sex marriages. The difference between a union and a marriage may prove to be a distinction without a difference.

Same-sex marriage remains a flashpoint for electoral conflict. By the start of 2012, voters in more than 30 states had rejected marriage equality proposals. And in Iowa, three state supreme court justices were voted out by social conservatives who fumed over that court's approval of marriage equality. But the times appear to be changing. In November 2012, voters in three states (Maine, Maryland, and Washington) approved same-sex marriage. And in Minnesota, voters rejected a proposed state constitutional amendment that would have banned same-sex marriage.

In 2008, the California Supreme Court, relying on state constitutional provisions, opened the door to same-sex marriage by striking down legislation limiting marriage to opposite-sex couples (see Chapter 16). But opponents struck back with an initiative—known as Proposition 8—asking voters to ban same-sex marriage. It passed with 52 percent of the vote that same year. In the interim, 18,000 couples married, and their marriages are duly recognized by the state.

In 2010, federal judge Vaughn Walker struck down the initiative as a violation of the due process and equal protection clauses of the Fourteenth Amendment, rather than follow the ambiguous line of privacy-related decisions.[98] Anticipating that the decision will be appealed eventually to the Supreme Court, Judge Walker crafted his analysis to model the reasoning of Supreme Court Justice Anthony M. Kennedy, the critical fifth vote in cases favorable to gay rights decided in the last decade. Walker concluded that California lacked a rational basis to deny gays and lesbians marriage licenses. The U.S. Court of Appeals for the Ninth Circuit affirmed Walker's decision. The case now heads to the Supreme Court for a showdown on gay rights.

Today, thirty states have constitutional amendments barring the recognition of same-sex marriage and confining civil marriage to the union of a man and a woman. The pluralist model provides one solution for groups dissatisfied with rulings from the nation's courts. State courts and state legislatures have demonstrated their receptivity to positions that are probably untenable in the federal courts. Pluralist mechanisms like the initiative and referendum offer counterweights to judicial intervention. However, state-by-state decisions offer little comfort to Americans who believe the U.S. Constitution protects them in their most intimate decisions and actions, regardless of where they reside.

SUMMARY

15.1 The Bill of Rights

- When they established the new government of the United States, the states and the people compelled the framers, through the Bill of Rights, to protect their freedoms. The ten original amendments include both civil liberties and civil rights.
- In interpreting these ten amendments, the courts, especially the Supreme Court, have taken on the task of balancing freedom and order.

15.2 Freedom of Religion

- The First Amendment protects several freedoms. The first of these, the freedom of religion, has long been important to American citizens.
- The establishment clause demands government neutrality toward religions and between the religious and the nonreligious. This clause, instituted to protect all religious beliefs, has nonetheless sparked some controversy in its application.
- According to judicial interpretations of the free-exercise clause, religious beliefs are inviolable, but the Constitution does not protect antisocial actions in the name of religion. Extreme interpretations of the religion clauses could bring the clauses into conflict with each other.

15.3 Freedom of Expression

- Freedom of expression encompasses many freedoms, including freedom of speech, freedom of the press, and the right to assemble peaceably and to petition the government.

- Freedom of speech and freedom of the press have never been held to be absolute, but the courts have ruled that the Bill of Rights gives the people far greater protection than other freedoms. Press freedom has enjoyed broad constitutional protection because a free society depends on the ability to collect and report information without government interference.
- The rights to assemble peaceably and to petition the government stem from the guarantees of freedom of speech and of the press. Each freedom is equally fundamental, but the right to exercise them is not absolute.

15.4 The Right to Bear Arms

- The nature and scope of the Second Amendment have long been a source of contention for gun-control advocates and their opponents. After nearly seventy years of silence, in 2008 the Supreme Court declared that the right to bear arms protects an individual's right to own a gun for personal use.
- New legal challenges will determine the standard that should apply when judging the appropriateness of gun regulations. For now, however, government may not prohibit individual gun ownership.

15.5 Applying the Bill of Rights to the States

- The adoption of the Fourteenth Amendment in 1868 extended the guarantees of the Bill of Rights to the states. The due process clause became the vehicle for applying specific provisions of the Bill of Rights to the states.

The Supreme Court has tolerated some variation from state to state in the meaning of certain constitutional rights. It has also imposed a duty on governments to inform citizens of their rights so that they are equipped to exercise them.

15.6 The Ninth Amendment and Personal Autonomy

- As it has fashioned new fundamental rights from the Constitution, the Supreme Court has become embroiled in controversy. The right to privacy served as the basis for the right of women to terminate a pregnancy, which in turn suggested a right to personal autonomy. The abortion controversy is still raging, and the justices, relying in part on the abortion cases, have extended protections against state criminal prosecution of private consensual sexual behavior for homosexuals.
- By offering constitutional protection to certain public policies, the courts may be threatening the democratic process, the process that gives the people a voice in government through their elected representatives. Should elected representatives fail to heed the public, the public may act on its own through mechanisms such as the referendum or initiative.

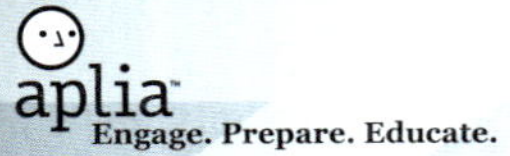

ASSESSING YOUR UNDERSTANDING WITH APLIA…YOUR VIRTUAL TUTOR!

15.1 Explain the role of the Bill of Rights in protecting civil liberties and civil rights.

1. Why are civil liberties called "negative rights" and civil rights called "positive rights"?
2. Identify the liberties and rights that are enshrined in the Bill of Rights.

15.2 Identify the mechanisms that guarantee freedom of religion.

1. Which clause formalizes the separation of church and state?
2. What aspect of religion does the First Amendment *not* protect?

15.3 Identify the free-expression clauses and describe the scope of their protection.

1. Define the clear and present danger test and explain how it is used in adjudicating cases of freedom of speech.
2. Identify some of the exceptions to free speech protections.
3. What must plaintiffs demonstrate in order to successfully claim defamation of character by the press?
4. Explain what the right to peaceably assemble entails.

15.4 Discuss the controversy over the Second Amendment and explain how Supreme Court rulings have addressed that debate.

1. What distinguishes the interpretation of the Second Amendment by gun-control advocates from that of their opponents?
2. Does the Second Amendment pertain only to national government, or to local and state government as well?

15.5 Explain the process by which the Supreme Court extended the protections of the Bill of Rights to the local and state levels of government.

1. What is the due process clause, and how does it hold the states to the provisions of the Bill of Rights?
2. What are the *Miranda* warnings, and to which amendment are they related?
3. How does the USA-PATRIOT forgo some liberties in the name of greater order?

15.6 Explain how the Supreme Court interpreted the Ninth Amendment to broaden the individual's constitutional protection of personal privacy beyond the language in the Bill of Rights, a right not enumerated in the Constitution.

1. Which principle did the decision in *Griswold* v. *Connecticut* establish regarding the Bill of Rights as a whole?
2. In *Roe* v. *Wade,* what was the opinion of the majority of the justices? What was the argument of the dissenters?

KEY CASES

Lemon v. *Kurtzman* (religious establishment test)

Engel v. *Vitale* (public school prayer ban)

Sherbert v. *Verner* (religious free exercise)

Schenck v. *United States* (free speech, clear-and-present danger test)

Brandenburg v. *Ohio* (free speech)

Tinker v. *Des Moines Independent County School District* (symbolic speech)

Cohen v. *California* (free expression)

Snyder v. *Phelps* (public/private speech; emotional harm)

Citizens United v. *Federal Election Commission* (unlimited political campaign spending)

New York Times v. *Sullivan* (free press)

New York Times v. *United States* (prior restraint)

District of Columbia v. *Heller* and *McDonald* v. *Chicago* (right to bear arms)

Palko v. *Connecticut* (Bill of Rights)

Gideon v. *Wainright* (assistance of counsel)

Miranda v. *Arizona* (self-incrimination)

Hamdan v. *Rumsfeld* (presidential authority; procedural protections at trial)

Boumediene v. *Bush* (constitutional right to challenge detention)

Griswold v. *Connecticut* (privacy)

Roe v. *Wade* (abortion)

Lawrence and Garner v. *Texas* (gay rights)

16

Equality and Civil Rights

CHAPTER TOPICS and Learning Outcomes

Abigail Fisher was a senior at Stephen F. Austin High School in Sugar Land, Texas, when she applied for admission in 2008 to the University of Texas–Austin, the flagship of the state's university system. All Texas students who graduate in the top 10 percent of their classes must be admitted to the state university. Students falling short of this threshold may be admitted nonetheless according to a formula that takes into account the race of each applicant among several factors. The university denied Fisher admission. Fisher, who is white, contended that the government may not consider race in making such decisions. The university used race to hold her back, she argued, denying Fisher her freedom.

Fisher brought a lawsuit in federal court against the university, arguing that the inclusion of race in university admissions violates the equal protection clause of the Fourteenth Amendment to the U.S. Constitution. Fisher lost the first two rounds as federal courts applied the prevailing rules based on previous Supreme Court cases. These decisions fall under the umbrella of **affirmative action**, a wide range of programs, from special recruitment efforts to numerical quotas, aimed at expanding opportunities for minority groups and women. Universities justify the use of racial preferences in admissions to assure a critical mass of diverse students. By pursuing diversity, public universities may do what the Constitution forbids: sort people on the basis of race.[1]

The Supreme Court selected the *Fisher* v. *University of Texas* case for argument in 2012 with a decision probably to come in 2013. Given the current makeup of the Court, chances are high that the justices will overturn *Fisher's* prior rulings and end the role of race in public university admissions.

Of the nine justices on the Court, four have expressed deep skepticism or outright opposition to the use of race in admissions: Chief Justice John G. Roberts, Jr., and Associate Justices Antonin Scalia, Clarence Thomas, and Samuel A. Alito. Four of the justices have been solicitous toward racial preferences: Associate Justices Ruth Bader Ginsburg, Stephen G. Breyer, Sonia Sotomayor, and Elena Kagan. However, Kagan has excused herself from participation on the likely ground that she played an earlier role in the case as it made its way through the federal judicial system when she was the solicitor general in charge of all appeals involving the executive branch. With four votes likely against the university policy and three votes likely in favor, the fate of affirmative action hangs on the views of one justice: Anthony M. Kennedy. Since his appointment to the nation's highest Court in 1988, Kennedy has never voted to uphold an affirmative action program. If he joins the conservative coalition, affirmative action in higher education will likely end. If he joins the liberal group resulting in a 4–4 tie, affirmative action will likely continue.

Why do affirmative action policies like the admissions policy at the University of Texas continue to generate opposition? Why do racial and other forms of unlawful discrimination persist in the United States despite laudable efforts to end them? The answer may appear deceptively simple. Laws and policies that promote equality inevitably come into conflict with demands for freedom. The conflict between freedom and equality intensifies when we recognize that Americans advocate competing conceptions of equality.

affirmative action
Any of a wide range of programs, from special recruitment efforts to numerical quotas, aimed at expanding opportunities for women and minority groups.

In this chapter, we consider the different ideals of equality and the quest to realize them through government action. We begin with the struggle for racial equality, which continues to cast a long shadow in government policies. This struggle has served as a model for the diverse groups that chose to follow in the same path.*

16.1 Two Conceptions of Equality

★ Explain how the concepts of equality of opportunity and equality of outcome mirror the tension between freedom and equality.

equality of opportunity
The idea that each person is guaranteed the same chance to succeed in life.

Most Americans support **equality of opportunity**, the idea that people should have an equal chance to develop their talents and that effort and ability should be rewarded equitably. This form of equality offers all individuals the same chance to get ahead; it glorifies personal achievement and free competition and allows everyone to play on a level field where the same rules apply to all. Special recruitment efforts aimed at identifying qualified minority or female job applicants, for example, ensure that everyone has the same chance starting out. Low-bid contracting illustrates equality of opportunity because every bidder has the same chance to compete for work.

equality of outcome
The concept that society must ensure that people are equal, and governments must design policies to redistribute wealth and status so that economic and social equality is actually achieved.

Americans are far less committed to **equality of outcome**, which means greater uniformity in social, economic, and political power among different social groups. For example, schools and businesses aim at equality of outcome when they allocate admissions or jobs on the basis of race, gender, or disability, which are unrelated to ability. (Some observers refer to these allocations as *quotas*; others call them *goals*. The difference is subtle. A quota *requires* that a specified proportional share of some benefit go to a favored group. A goal *aims* for proportional allocation of benefits, without requiring it.) The government seeks equality of outcome when it adjusts the rules to handicap some bidders or applicants and favor others. The vast majority of Americans, however, consistently favor low-bid contracting and merit-based admissions and employment over preferential treatment.[2] The American public remains divided over programs designed to assist racial minorities in college admissions and employment, with 38 to 64 percent of the population supporting affirmative action, depending on how poll questions are worded.[3] Recent survey results signal that Americans remain firmly against the preferential treatment of minorities, even as they tend to be supportive of certain affirmative action policies.[4]

Some people believe that equality of outcome can occur in today's society only if we restrict the free competition that is the basis of equality of opportunity. In 1978, Supreme Court Justice Harry Blackmun articulated this controversial position on a divided bench: "In order to get beyond racism, we must first take account of race. There is no other way. And in order to treat some persons equally, we must treat them differently."[5]

---

*The effort to staunch the flow of illegal immigration also pits individual freedom against social order. In this chapter, we focus attention on the modern dilemma of government, the conflict between freedom and equality.

In 2007, Chief Justice John G. Roberts, Jr., cast the issue in reverse on a divided bench: "The way to stop discrimination on the basis of race is to stop discriminating on the basis of race."[6] Quota policies generate the most opposition because they confine competition and create barriers to personal achievement. Quotas limit advancement for some individuals and ensure advancement for others. They alter the results by taking into account factors unrelated to ability. Equal outcomes policies that benefit minorities, women, or people with disabilities at the expense of whites, men, or the able-bodied create strong opposition because quotas seem to be at odds with individual initiative. In other words, equality clashes with freedom. To understand the ways government resolves this conflict, we have to understand the development of civil rights in this country.

The history of civil rights in the United States is primarily the story of a search for social and economic equality. This search has persisted for more than a century and is ongoing. It began with the battle for civil rights for black citizens, whose prior subjugation as slaves had roused the passions of the nation and brought about its bloodiest conflict, the Civil War. The struggle of blacks has been a beacon lighting the way for Native Americans, immigrant groups of which Latinos represent the largest component, women, people with disabilities, and homosexuals. Each of these groups has confronted **invidious discrimination**. Discrimination is simply the act of making or recognizing distinctions. When making distinctions among people, discrimination may be benign (that is, harmless) or invidious (harmful). Sometimes this harm has been subtle, and sometimes it has been overt. Sometimes it has even come from other minorities. Each group has achieved a measure of success in its struggle by pressing its interests on government, even challenging it. These challenges and the government's responses to them have helped shape our democracy.

invidious discrimination
Discrimination against persons or groups that works to their harm and is based on animosity.

Remember that **civil rights** are powers or privileges guaranteed to the individual and protected from arbitrary removal at the hands of the government or other individuals. Sometimes people refer to civil rights as "positive rights" (see Table 15.1, "Examples of Positive and Negative Rights: Constitutional Rights and Human Rights," on page 417). In this chapter, we concentrate on the rights guaranteed by the constitutional amendments adopted after the Civil War and by laws passed to enforce those guarantees. Prominent among them is the right to equal protection of the laws. This right remained a promise rather than a reality well into the twentieth century.

civil rights
Powers or privileges guaranteed to individuals and protected from arbitrary removal at the hands of government or individuals.

★ 16.2 The Civil War Amendments

★ Trace the Supreme Court rulings and state legislative efforts that prevented African Americans from achieving "equal protection of the laws."

The Civil War amendments were adopted to provide freedom and equality to black Americans. The Thirteenth Amendment, ratified in 1865, provided that

> neither slavery nor involuntary servitude … shall exist within the United States, or any place subject to their jurisdiction.

The Fourteenth Amendment was adopted three years later. It provides first that freed slaves are citizens:

> All persons born or naturalized in the United States, and subject to the jurisdiction thereof, are citizens of the United States and of the State wherein they reside.

As we saw in Chapter 15, it also prohibits the states from abridging the "privileges or immunities of citizens of the United States" or depriving "any person of life, liberty, or property, without due process of law." The amendment then goes on to guarantee equality under the law, declaring that no state shall

> deny to any person within its jurisdiction the equal protection of the laws.

The Fifteenth Amendment, adopted in 1870, added a measure of political equality:

> The right of citizens of the United States to vote shall not be denied or abridged by the United States or by any State on account of race, color, or previous condition of servitude.

American blacks were thus free and politically equal—at least according to the Constitution. But for many years, the courts sometimes thwarted the efforts of the other branches to protect their constitutional rights.

Congress and the Supreme Court: Lawmaking Versus Law Interpreting

In the years after the Civil War, Congress went to work to protect the rights of black citizens. In 1866, lawmakers passed a civil rights act that gave the national government some authority over the treatment of blacks by state courts. This legislation was a response to the **black codes**, laws enacted by the former slave states to restrict the freedom of blacks. For example, vagrancy and apprenticeship laws forced blacks to work and denied them a free choice of employers. One section of the 1866 act that still applies today grants all citizens the right to make and enforce contracts; the right to sue others in court (and the corresponding ability to be sued); the duty and ability to give evidence in court; and the right to inherit, purchase, lease, sell, hold, or convey property. Later, in the Civil Rights Act of 1875, Congress attempted to guarantee blacks equal access to public accommodations (parks, theaters, and the like).

Although Congress enacted laws to protect the civil rights of black citizens, the Supreme Court weakened some of those rights. In 1873, the Court ruled that the Civil War amendments had not changed the relationship between the state and national governments.[7] State citizenship and national citizenship remained separate and distinct. According to the Court, the Fourteenth Amendment did not obligate the states to honor the rights guaranteed by U.S. citizenship.

In subsequent years, the Court's decisions narrowed some constitutional protections for blacks. In 1876, the justices limited congressional attempts to protect the rights of blacks.[8] A group of Louisiana whites had used violence and fraud to prevent blacks from exercising their basic constitutional rights, including the right to assemble peaceably. The justices held that the rights allegedly infringed on were not nationally protected rights and that therefore Congress was powerless to punish those who violated them. On the very same day, the Court ruled that the Fifteenth Amendment did not guarantee all citizens the right to vote; it simply listed grounds that could not be used to deny that right.[9] And in 1883, the Court struck down the public accommodations section of the Civil Rights Act of 1875.[10] The justices declared that the national government could prohibit only *government* action that discriminated against blacks; private acts of discrimination or acts of omission by a state were beyond the reach of the national government. For example, a person who refused to serve blacks in a private club was outside the control of the national government because the discrimination was a private—not a governmental—act. The Court

black codes
Legislation enacted by former slave states to restrict the freedom of blacks.

refused to see racial discrimination as an act that the national government could prohibit. In many cases, the justices tolerated racial discrimination. In the process, they abetted **racism**, the belief that there are inherent differences among the races that determine people's achievement and that one's own race is superior to and thus has a right to dominate others.

The Court's decisions gave the states ample room to maneuver around civil rights laws. In the matter of voting rights, for example, states that wanted to bar black men from the polls simply used nonracial means to do so. One popular tool was the **poll tax**, first imposed by Georgia in 1877. This was a tax of $1 or $2 on every citizen who wanted to vote. The tax was not a burden for most whites. But many blacks were tenant farmers, deeply in debt to white merchants and landowners; they had no extra money for voting. Other bars to black suffrage included literacy tests, minimum education requirements, and a grandfather clause that restricted suffrage to men who could establish that their grandfathers were eligible to vote before 1867 (three years before the Fifteenth Amendment declared that race could not be used to deny individuals the right to vote).[11] White southerners also used intimidation and violence to keep blacks from the polls.

The Roots of Racial Segregation

From well before the Civil War, **racial segregation** had been a way of life in the South: blacks lived and worked separately from whites. After the war, southern states began to enact Jim Crow laws to reinforce segregation. (*Jim Crow* was a derogatory term for a black person.) Once the Supreme Court took the teeth out of the Civil Rights Act of 1875, such laws proliferated. They required blacks to live in separate (generally inferior) areas and restricted them to separate sections of hospitals; separate cemeteries; separate drinking and toilet facilities; separate schools; and separate sections of trains, jails, and parks.

In 1892, Homer Adolph Plessy, who was seven-eighths Caucasian, took a seat in a "whites-only" car of a Louisiana train. He refused to move to the car reserved for blacks and was arrested. Plessy argued that Louisiana's law mandating racial segregation on its trains was an unconstitutional infringement on both the privileges and immunities guaranteed by the Fourteenth Amendment and its equal protection clause. The Supreme Court disagreed. The majority in **Plessy v. Ferguson*** (1896) upheld state-imposed racial segregation.[12] They based their decision on what came to be known as the **separate-but-equal doctrine**, which held that separate facilities for blacks and whites satisfied the Fourteenth Amendment as long as they were equal. (The Court majority used the

racism
A belief that human races have distinct characteristics such that one's own race is superior to, and has a right to rule, others.

poll tax
A tax of $1 or $2 on every citizen who wished to vote, first instituted in Georgia in 1877. Although it was no burden on most white citizens, it effectively disenfranchised blacks.

racial segregation
Separation from society because of race.

separate-but-equal doctrine
The concept that providing separate but equivalent facilities for blacks and whites satisfies the equal protection clause of the Fourteenth Amendment.

Separate and Unequal

The Supreme Court gave constitutional protection to racial separation on the theory that states could provide "separate but equal" facilities for blacks. The facilities here appear equal, but the harm inherent in racial separation lies beneath the surface. Separating people by race is inherently unequal, declared the Supreme Court, in its landmark 1954 ruling, *Brown* v. *Board of Education*.

---

*Key cases are highlighted in bold, and a list of key cases appears at the end of the chapter.

phrase "equal but separate" to describe the requirement. Justice John Marshall Harlan's dissenting opinion cast the phrase as "separate but equal," the way we have come to refer to the doctrine.)

Three years later, the Supreme Court extended the separate-but-equal doctrine to the schools.[13] The justices ignored the fact that black educational facilities (and most other "colored-only" facilities) were far from equal to those reserved for whites.

By the end of the nineteenth century, legal racial segregation was firmly entrenched in the American South. Although constitutional amendments and national laws to protect equality under the law were in place, the Supreme Court's interpretation of those amendments and laws rendered them ineffective. Several decades would pass before any change was discernible.

16.3 The Dismantling of School Segregation

★ Identify the Supreme Court decisions that dismantled school segregation and explain the significance of each.

Denied the right to vote and to be represented in the government, blacks sought access to power through other parts of the political system. The National Association for the Advancement of Colored People (NAACP), founded in 1909 by W. E. B. Du Bois and others, both black and white, with the goal of ending racial discrimination and segregation, took the lead in the campaign for black civil rights. The plan was to launch a two-pronged legal and lobbying attack on the separate-but-equal doctrine: first by pressing for fully equal facilities for blacks, then by proving the unconstitutionality of segregation. The process would be a slow one, but the strategies involved did not require a large organization or heavy financial backing; at the time, the NAACP had neither.*

Pressure for Equality …

By the 1920s, the separate-but-equal doctrine was so deeply ingrained in American law that no Supreme Court justice would dissent from its continued application to racial segregation. But a few Court decisions offered hope that change would come. In 1935, Lloyd Gaines graduated from Lincoln University, a black college in Missouri, and applied to the state law school. The law school rejected him because he was black. Missouri refused to admit blacks to its all-white law school; instead, the state's policy was to pay the costs of blacks admitted to out-of-state law schools. With the support of the NAACP, Gaines appealed to the courts for admission to the University of Missouri Law School. In 1938, the U.S. Supreme Court ruled that he must be admitted.[14] Under the *Plessy* ruling, Missouri could not shift to other states its responsibility to provide an equal education for blacks.

Later cases helped reinforce the requirement that segregated facilities must be equal in all major respects. One was brought by Heman Sweatt, again with the help of the NAACP. The all-white University of Texas Law School had denied Sweatt entrance because of his race. A federal court ordered the state to provide a black law

---

*In 1939, the NAACP established an offshoot, the NAACP Legal Defense and Education Fund, to work on legal challenges while the parent organization concentrated on lobbying.

school for him; the state responded by renting a few rooms in an office building and hiring two black lawyers as teachers. Sweatt refused to attend the school and took his case to the Supreme Court.[15]

The Court ruled on *Sweatt* v. *Painter* in 1950. The justices unanimously found that the facilities were inadequate: the separate "law school" provided for Sweatt did not approach the quality of the white state law school. The University of Texas had to give Sweatt full student status. But the Court avoided reexamining the separate-but-equal doctrine.

… and Pressure for Desegregation

These decisions suggested to the NAACP that the time was right for an attack on segregation itself. In addition, public attitudes toward race relations were slowly changing from the predominant racism of the nineteenth and early twentieth centuries toward greater tolerance. Black groups had fought with honor—albeit in segregated military units—in World War II. Blacks and whites were working together in unions and in service and religious organizations. Social change and court decisions suggested that government-imposed segregation was vulnerable.

President Harry S. Truman risked his political future with his strong support of blacks' civil rights. In 1947, he established the President's Committee on Civil Rights. The committee's report, issued later that year, became the agenda for the civil rights movement during the next two decades. It called for national laws prohibiting racially motivated poll taxes, segregation, and brutality against minorities and for guarantees of voting rights and equal employment opportunity. In 1948, Truman ordered the **desegregation** (the dismantling of authorized racial segregation) of the armed forces.

In 1947, the U.S. Department of Justice had begun to submit briefs to the courts in support of civil rights. The department's most important intervention probably came in *Brown* v. *Board of Education*.[16] This case was the culmination of twenty years of planning and litigation on the part of the NAACP to invalidate racial segregation in public schools.

Linda Brown was a black child whose father had tried to enroll her in a white public school in Topeka, Kansas. The white school was close to Linda's home; the walk to the black school meant that she had to cross a dangerous set of railroad tracks. Brown's request was refused because of Linda's race. A federal district court found that the black public school was equal in quality to the white school in all relevant respects; therefore, according to the *Plessy* doctrine, Linda was required to go to the black public school. Brown appealed the decision.

Brown* v. *Board of Education reached the Supreme Court in late 1951. The justices delayed argument on the sensitive case until after the 1952 national election. *Brown* was merged with four similar cases into a class action, a device for combining the claims or defenses of similar individuals so that they can be tried in a single lawsuit (see Chapter 14). The class action was supported by the NAACP and coordinated by Thurgood Marshall, who would later become the first black justice to sit on the Supreme Court. The five cases squarely challenged the separate-but-equal doctrine. By all tangible measures (standards for teacher licensing, teacher–pupil ratios, library facilities), the two school systems in each case—one white, the other black—were equal. The issue was legal separation of the races.

On May 17, 1954, Chief Justice Earl Warren, who had only recently joined the Court, delivered a single opinion covering four of the cases. (See Chapter 14.) Warren spoke for a unanimous Court when he declared that "in the field of public education

desegregation
The ending of authorized segregation, or separation by race.

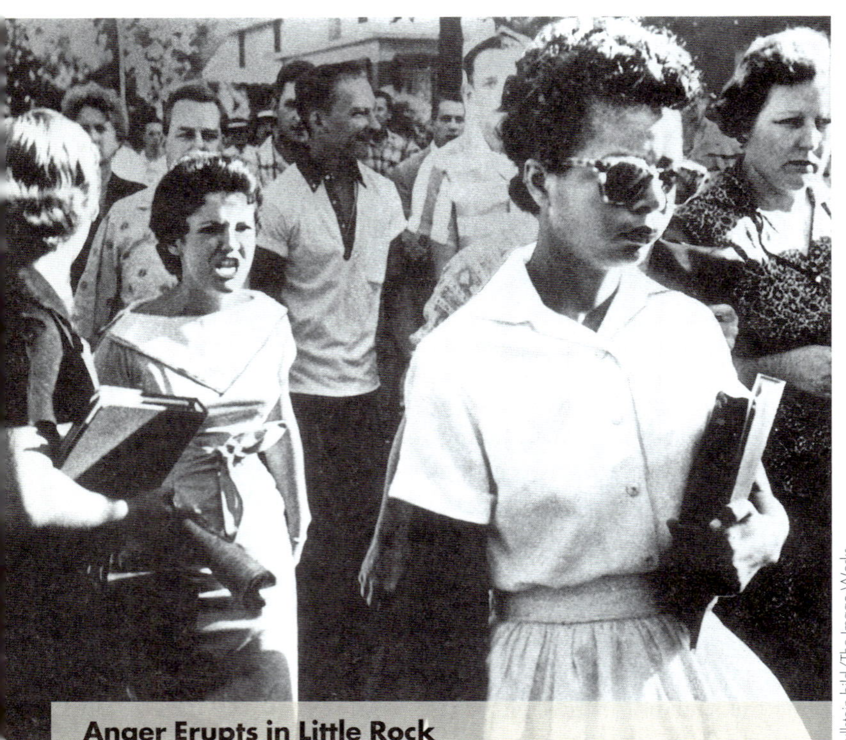

Anger Erupts in Little Rock

In 1957, the Little Rock, Arkansas, school board attempted to implement court-ordered desegregation: nine black teenagers were to be admitted to Little Rock Central High School. Governor Orval Faubus ordered the National Guard to bar their attendance. A mob blocked a subsequent attempt by the students. Finally, President Dwight D. Eisenhower ordered federal troops to escort the students to the high school. Among them was fifteen-year-old Elizabeth Eckford (*right*). Hazel Brown (*left*) angrily taunted her from the crowd. This image seared the nation's conscience. The violence and hostility led the school board to seek a postponement of the desegregation plan. The Supreme Court, meeting in special session, affirmed the decision in *Brown* v. *Board of Education* and ordered the plan to proceed. Fifty years later, a federal judge declared Little Rock's schools desegregated. But the school district remains riven by racial strife, as a new black majority on the school board clashed with the black school superintendent over jobs, not education.

the doctrine of 'separate but equal' has no place. Separate educational facilities are inherently unequal,"[17] depriving the plaintiffs of the equal protection of the laws. Segregated facilities generate in black children "a feeling of inferiority … that may affect their hearts and minds in a way unlikely ever to be undone."[18] In short, the nation's highest court found that state-imposed public school segregation violated the equal protection clause of the Fourteenth Amendment.

A companion case to *Brown* challenged the segregation of public schools in Washington, D.C.[19] Segregation there was imposed by Congress. The equal protection clause protected citizens only against state violations; no equal protection clause restrained the national government because the District of Columbia is not a state. It was unthinkable for the Constitution to impose a lesser duty on the national government than on the states. In this case, the Court unanimously decided that the racial segregation requirement was an arbitrary deprivation of liberty without due process of law, a violation of the Fifth Amendment. In short, the concept of liberty encompassed the idea of equality.

The Court deferred implementation of the school desegregation decisions until 1955. Then, in **Brown v. Board of Education II**, it ruled that school systems must desegregate "with all deliberate speed" and assigned the task of supervising desegregation to the lower federal courts.[20]

Some states quietly complied with the *Brown* decree. Others did little to desegregate their schools. And many communities in the South defied the Court, sometimes violently. Some white business and professional people formed "white citizens' councils." The councils put economic pressure on blacks who asserted their rights by foreclosing on their mortgages and denying them credit at local stores. Georgia and North Carolina resisted desegregation by paying tuition for white students attending private schools. Virginia and other states ordered that desegregated schools be closed.

This resistance, along with the Supreme Court's "all deliberate speed" order, placed a heavy burden on federal judges to dismantle what was the fundamental social order in many communities.[21] Gradual desegregation under *Brown* was in some cases no desegregation at all. In 1969, a unanimous Supreme Court ordered that the operation of segregated school systems stop "at once."[22]

Two years later, the Court approved several remedies to achieve integration, including busing, racial quotas, and the pairing or grouping of noncontiguous school zones. In *Swann* v. *Charlotte-Mecklenburg County Schools,* the Supreme Court affirmed the right of lower courts to order the busing of children to ensure school desegregation.[23] But these remedies applied only to **de jure segregation**, government-imposed segregation (for example, government assignment of whites to one school and blacks to another within the same community). Court-imposed remedies did not apply to **de facto segregation**, which is not the result of government action (for example, racial segregation resulting from residential patterns).

The busing of schoolchildren came under heavy attack in both the North and the South. Desegregation advocates saw busing as a potential remedy in many northern cities, where schools had become segregated as white families left the cities for the suburbs. This "white flight" had left inner-city schools predominantly black and suburban schools almost all white. Public opinion strongly opposed the busing approach, and Congress sought to impose limits on busing as a remedy to segregation. In 1974, a closely divided Court ruled that lower courts could not order busing across school district boundaries unless each district had practiced racial discrimination or school district lines had been deliberately drawn to achieve racial segregation.[24] This ruling meant an end to large-scale school desegregation in metropolitan areas.

★ 16.4 The Civil Rights Movement

★ Describe the circumstances under which the 1964 Civil Rights Act was passed and its evolving interpretation in subsequent Supreme Court decisions.

Although the NAACP concentrated on school desegregation, it also made headway in other areas. The Supreme Court responded to NAACP efforts in the late 1940s by outlawing whites-only primary elections in the South, declaring them to be in violation of the Fifteenth Amendment. The Court also declared segregation on interstate bus routes to be unconstitutional and desegregated restaurants and hotels in the District of Columbia. Despite these and other decisions that chipped away at existing barriers to equality, states still were denying black citizens political power, and segregation remained a fact of daily life. Moreover, power in Congress resided with southern Democrats who resisted efforts to pass civil rights legislation.[25]

Dwight D. Eisenhower, who became president in 1953, was not as concerned about civil rights as his predecessor had been. He chose to stand above the battle between the Supreme Court and those who resisted the Court's decisions. He even refused to reveal whether he agreed with the Court's decision in *Brown* v. *Board of Education*. "It makes no difference," Eisenhower declared, because "the Constitution is as the Supreme Court interprets it."[26] Eisenhower did enforce school desegregation when the safety of schoolchildren was involved, but he appeared unwilling to do much more to advance racial equality. That goal seemed to require the political mobilization of the people—black and white—in what is now known as the **civil rights movement**.

Black churches served as the crucible of the movement. More than places of worship, they served hundreds of other functions. In black communities, the church was "a bulletin board to a people who owned no organs of communication, a credit union to those without banks, and even a kind of people's court."[27] Some of its preachers were motivated by fortune, others by saintliness. One would prove to be a modern-day Moses.

de jure segregation
Government-imposed segregation.

de facto segregation
Segregation that is not the result of government influence.

civil rights movement
The mass mobilization during the 1960s that sought to gain equality of rights and opportunities for blacks in the South and to a lesser extent in the North, mainly through nonviolent, unconventional means of participation.

Civil Disobedience

Rosa Parks, a black woman living in Montgomery, Alabama, sounded the first call to action. That city's Jim Crow ordinances were tougher than those in other southern cities, where blacks were required to sit in the back of the bus while whites sat in the front, both races converging as the bus filled with passengers. In Montgomery, bus drivers had the power to define and redefine the floating line separating blacks and whites: drivers could order blacks to vacate an entire row to make room for one white or order blacks to stand even when some seats were vacant. Blacks could not walk through the white section to their seats in the back; they had to leave the bus after paying their fare and reenter through the rear.[28] In December 1955, Parks boarded a city bus on her way home from work and took an available seat in the front of the bus; she refused to give up her seat when the driver asked her to do so. She was arrested and fined $10 for violating the city ordinance.

boycott
A refusal to do business with a firm, individual, or nation as an expression of disapproval or as a means of coercion.

Montgomery's black community responded to Parks's arrest with a boycott of the city's bus system. A **boycott** is a refusal to do business with a company or individual as an expression of disapproval or a means of coercion. Blacks walked or carpooled or stayed at home rather than ride the city's buses. As the bus company moved close to bankruptcy and downtown merchants suffered from the loss of black business, city officials began to harass blacks, hoping to frighten them into ending the boycott. But Montgomery's black citizens now had a leader, a charismatic twenty-six-year-old Baptist minister named Martin Luther King, Jr. King urged the people to hold out, and they did. A year after the boycott began, a federal court ruled that segregated transportation systems violated the equal protection clause of the Constitution. The boycott had proved to be an effective weapon.

In 1957, King helped organize the Southern Christian Leadership Conference to coordinate civil rights activities. He was totally committed to nonviolent action to bring racial issues into the light. To that end, he advocated **civil disobedience**, the willful but nonviolent breach of unjust laws.

civil disobedience
The willful but nonviolent breach of laws that are regarded as unjust.

One nonviolent tactic was the sit-in. On February 1, 1960, four black freshmen from North Carolina Agricultural and Technical College in Greensboro sat down at a whites-only lunch counter. They were refused service by the black waitress, who said, "Fellows like you make our race look bad." The young men stayed all day and promised to return the next morning to continue what they called a "sit-down protest." Other students soon joined in, rotating shifts so that no one missed classes. Within two days, eighty-five students had flocked to the lunch counter. Although abused verbally and physically, the students would not move. Finally, they were arrested. Soon people held similar sit-in demonstrations throughout the South and then in the North.[29] The Supreme Court upheld the actions of the demonstrators, although the unanimity that had characterized its earlier decisions was gone. (In this decision, three justices argued that even bigots had the right to call on the government to protect their property interests.)[30]

The Civil Rights Act of 1964

In 1961, a new administration, headed by President John F. Kennedy, came to power. At first Kennedy did not seem to be committed to civil rights. But his stance changed as the movement gained momentum and as more and more whites became aware of the abuse being heaped on sit-in demonstrators, freedom riders (who protested unlawful segregation on interstate bus routes), and those who were trying to help blacks register to vote in southern states. Volunteers were being jailed, beaten, and even killed for advocating activities among blacks that whites took for granted.

In late 1962, President Kennedy ordered federal troops to ensure the safety of James Meredith, the first black to attend the University of Mississippi. In early 1963, Kennedy enforced the desegregation of the University of Alabama. In April 1963, television viewers were shocked to see civil rights marchers in Birmingham, Alabama, attacked with dogs, fire hoses, and cattle prods. (The idea of the Birmingham march was to provoke confrontations with white officials in an effort to compel the national government to intervene on behalf of blacks.) Finally, in June 1963, Kennedy asked Congress for legislation that would outlaw segregation in public accommodations.

Two months later, Martin Luther King, Jr., joined in a march on Washington, D.C. The organizers called the protest "A March for Jobs and Freedom," signaling the economic goals of black America. More than 250,000 people, black and white, gathered peaceably at the Lincoln Memorial to hear King speak. "I have a dream," the great preacher extemporized, "that my little children will one day live in a nation where they will not be judged by the color of their skin but by the content of their character."[31]

Congress had not yet enacted Kennedy's public accommodations bill when he was assassinated on November 22, 1963. His successor, Lyndon B. Johnson, considered civil rights his top legislative priority. Johnson's long congressional experience and exceptional leadership ability as Senate majority leader were put to good use in overcoming the considerable opposition to the legislation. Within months, Congress enacted the Civil Rights Act of 1964, which included a vital provision barring segregation in most public accommodations. This congressional action was in part a reaction to Kennedy's death. But it was also almost certainly a response to the brutal treatment of blacks throughout the South. Viewed from afar, it is probably fair to say that King's efforts were necessary but not sufficient to ensure passage of the law. But Johnson's legislative mastery made all the difference between success and failure.[32]

Congress had enacted civil rights laws in 1957 and 1960, but they dealt primarily with voting rights. The 1964 act was the most comprehensive legislative attempt ever to erase racial discrimination in the United States. Among its many provisions, the act

- Entitled all persons to "the full and equal enjoyment" of goods, services, and privileges in places of public accommodation, without discrimination on the grounds of race, color, religion, or national origin (the inclusion of "national origin" or place of birth would set in motion plans for immigration reform the following year)
- Established the right to equality in employment opportunities
- Strengthened voting rights legislation
- Created the Equal Employment Opportunity Commission (EEOC) and charged it with hearing and investigating complaints of job discrimination*
- Provided that funds could be withheld from federally assisted programs administered in a discriminatory manner

The last of these provisions had a powerful effect on school desegregation when Congress enacted the Elementary and Secondary Education Act in 1965. That act provided billions of federal dollars for the nation's schools; the threat of losing that money spurred local school boards to formulate and implement new plans for desegregation.

LBJ Library/Photo by Yoichi R. Okamoto

When Leaders Confer

Martin Luther King, Jr., was a Baptist minister who believed in the principles of nonviolent protest practiced by India's Mohandas (Mahatma) Gandhi. This photograph captures King at a meeting with President Lyndon Johnson and other civil rights leaders in the White House cabinet room on March 18, 1966. King later joked that he was instructed to reach the White House south gate by "irregular routes," chuckling that he "had to sneak in the back door." King, who won the Nobel Peace Prize in 1964, was assassinated in 1968 in Memphis, Tennessee.

---

*Since 1972, the EEOC has had the power to institute legal proceedings on behalf of employees who allege that they have been victims of illegal discrimination.

The 1964 act faced an immediate constitutional challenge. Its opponents argued that the Constitution does not forbid acts of private discrimination—the position the Supreme Court itself had taken in the late nineteenth century. But this time, a unanimous Court upheld the law, declaring that acts of discrimination impose substantial burdens on interstate commerce and thus are subject to congressional control.[33] In a companion case, Ollie McClung, the owner of a small restaurant, had refused to serve blacks. McClung maintained that he had the freedom to serve whomever he wanted in his own restaurant. The justices, however, upheld the government's prohibition of McClung's racial discrimination on the grounds that a substantial portion of the food served in his restaurant had moved in interstate commerce.[34] Thus, the Supreme Court vindicated the Civil Rights Act of 1964 by reason of the congressional power to regulate interstate commerce rather than on the basis of the Fourteenth Amendment. Since 1937, the Court had approved ever-widening authority to regulate state and local activities under the commerce clause. It was the most powerful basis for the exercise of congressional power in the Constitution. In 2012, the Court's conservative majority signaled a limit to this power, declaring that Congress may not regulate commercial "inactivity" to support the insurance mandate of the Obama administration's health-care law. But a coalition of four liberal justices plus Chief Justice John G. Roberts, Jr., upheld the law's constitutionality on Congress's power to tax and spend for the general welfare.[35]

President Johnson's goal was a "great society." Soon a constitutional amendment and a series of civil rights laws were in place to help him meet his goal:

- The Twenty-fourth Amendment, ratified in 1964, banned poll taxes in primary and general elections for national office.
- The Economic Opportunity Act of 1964 provided education and training to combat poverty.
- The Voting Rights Act of 1965 empowered the attorney general to send voter registration supervisors to areas in which fewer than half the eligible minority voters had been registered. This act has been credited with doubling black voter registration in the South in only five years.[36]
- The Fair Housing Act of 1968 banned discrimination in the rental and sale of most housing.

The Continuing Struggle over Civil Rights

In the decades that followed, it became clear that civil rights laws on the books do not ensure civil rights in action. In 1984, for example, the Supreme Court was called on to interpret a law forbidding sex discrimination in schools and colleges that receive financial assistance from the national government: Must the entire institution comply with the regulations, or only those portions of it that receive assistance?

In *Grove City College* v. *Bell,* the Court ruled that government educational grants to students implicate the institution as a recipient of government funds; therefore, it must comply with government nondiscrimination provisions. However, only the specific department or program receiving the funds (in Grove City's case, the financial aid program), not the whole institution, was barred from discriminating.[37] Athletic departments rarely receive such government funds, so colleges had no obligation to provide equal opportunity for women in their sports programs.

The *Grove City* decision had widespread effects because three other important civil rights laws were worded similarly. The implication was that any law barring discrimination on the basis of race, sex, age, or disability would be applicable only to programs receiving federal funds, not to the entire institution. So a university laboratory that received federal research grants could not discriminate, but other departments that did not receive federal money could. The effect of *Grove City* was to frustrate enforcement of civil rights laws. In keeping with pluralist theory, civil rights and women's groups shifted their efforts to the legislative branch.

Congress reacted immediately, exercising its lawmaking power to check the law-interpreting power of the judiciary. Congress can revise national laws to counter judicial decisions; in this political chess game, the Court's move is hardly the last one. Legislators protested that the Court had misinterpreted the intent of the antidiscrimination laws, and they forged a bipartisan effort to make that intent crystal clear: if any part of an institution gets federal money, no part of it can discriminate. Their work led to the Civil Rights Restoration Act, which became law in 1988 despite a presidential veto by Ronald Reagan.

Although Congress tried to restore and expand civil rights enforcement, the Supreme Court weakened it again. The Court restricted minority contractor **set-asides** of state public works funds, an arrangement it had approved in 1980. (A set-aside is a purchasing or contracting provision that reserves a certain percentage of funds for minority-owned contractors.) The five-person majority held that past societal discrimination alone cannot serve as the basis for rigid quotas.[38]

Buttressed by Republican appointees, the Supreme Court continued to narrow the scope of national civil rights protections in a string of decisions that suggested the ascendancy of a new conservative majority more concerned with freedom than equality.[39] To counter the Court's changing interpretations of civil rights laws, liberals turned to Congress to restore and enlarge earlier Court decisions by writing them into law. The result was a comprehensive new civil rights bill. The Civil Rights Act of 1991 reversed or altered twelve Court decisions that had narrowed civil rights protections. The new law clarified and expanded earlier legislation and increased the costs to employers for intentional, illegal discrimination. Continued resentment generated by equal outcomes policies would move the battle back to the courts, however.

set-aside
A purchasing or contracting provision that reserves a certain percentage of funds for minority-owned contractors.

★ 16.5 Civil Rights for Other Minorities

★ Evaluate the effect of the civil rights movement on other minority groups' struggles for equality.

Recent civil rights laws and court decisions protect members of all minority groups. The Supreme Court underscored the breadth of this protection in an important decision in 1987.[40] The justices ruled unanimously that the Civil Rights Act of 1866 (known today as Section 1981) offers broad protection against discrimination to all minorities. Previously, members of white ethnic groups could not invoke the law in bias suits. Under the 1987 decision, members of any ethnic group can recover money damages if they prove they have been denied a job, excluded from rental housing, or subjected to another form of discrimination prohibited by the law. The 1964 Civil Rights Act offers similar protections but specifies strict procedures for filing suits that tend to discourage litigation. Moreover, the remedies in most cases are limited. In job discrimination, for example, back pay and reinstatement are the only remedies. Section 1981 has fewer hurdles and allows litigants to seek punitive damages (damages awarded by a court as additional punishment for a serious wrong). In some respects, then, the older law is a more potent weapon than the newer one in fighting discrimination.

Clearly, the civil rights movement has had an effect on all minorities. Here we examine the civil rights struggles of four groups: Native Americans, immigrant groups (the largest of which are Latinos), people with disabilities, and homosexuals.

Native Americans

During the eighteenth and nineteenth centuries, the U.S. government took Indian lands, isolated Native Americans on reservations, and denied them political and social rights. The government's dealings with the Indians were often marked by violence and broken promises. The agencies responsible for administering Indian reservations kept Native Americans poor and dependent on the national government.

The national government switched policies at the beginning of the twentieth century, promoting assimilation instead of separation. The government banned the use of native languages and religious rituals; it sent Indian children to boarding schools and gave them non-Indian names. In 1924, Indians received U.S. citizenship. Until that time, they had been considered members of tribal nations whose relations with the U.S. government were determined by treaties. The Native American population suffered badly during the Great Depression, primarily because the poorest Americans were affected most severely but also because of the inept administration of Indian reservations. (Today, Native Americans make up less than 1 percent of the population.) Poverty persisted on the reservations well after the Depression was over, and Indian land holdings continued to shrink through the 1950s and into the 1960s—despite signed treaties and the religious significance of portions of the lands they lost. In the 1960s, for example, a part of the Hopi Sacred Circle, which is considered the source of all life in the Hopi tribal religion, was strip-mined for coal.

Anger bred of poverty, unemployment, and frustration with an uncaring government exploded in militant action in late 1969, when several American Indians seized Alcatraz Island, an abandoned island in San Francisco Bay. The group cited an 1868 Sioux treaty that entitled them to unused federal lands; they remained on the island for a year and a half. In 1973, armed members of the American Indian Movement seized eleven hostages at Wounded Knee, South Dakota, the site of an 1890 massacre of two hundred Sioux (Lakota) by U.S. cavalry troops. They remained there, occasionally exchanging gunfire with federal marshals, for seventy-one days, until the government agreed to examine the treaty rights of the Oglala Sioux.[41]

In 1946, Congress enacted legislation establishing an Indian claims commission to compensate Native Americans for land that had been taken from them. In the 1970s, the Native American Rights Fund and other groups used that legislation to win important victories in the courts. The tribes won the return of lands in the Midwest and in the states of Oklahoma, New Mexico, and Washington. In 1980, the Supreme Court ordered the national government to pay the Sioux $117 million plus interest for the Black Hills of South Dakota, which had been stolen from them a century before.

The special status accorded Indian tribes in the Constitution has proved attractive to a new group of Indian leaders. Some of the 565 recognized tribes have successfully instituted casino gambling on their reservations, even in the face of state opposition to their plans. The tribes pay no taxes on their profits, which has helped them make gambling a powerful engine of economic growth for themselves and has given a once impoverished people undreamed-of riches and responsibilities. Congress has allowed these developments, provided that the tribes spend their profits on Indian assistance programs.

It is important to remember that throughout American history, Native Americans have been coerced physically and pressured economically to assimilate into the mainstream of white society. The destiny of Native Americans as viable groups with separate identities depends in no small measure on curbing their dependence on the national government.[42] The wealth created by casino gambling and other ventures funded with gambling profits may prove to be Native Americans' most effective weapon for regaining their heritage.

Immigrant Groups

The Statue of Liberty stands at the entrance to New York harbor, a gift from the people of France to commemorate the centennial of the United States. It is an icon of the United States in the world, capturing the belief that this country is a beacon of liberty for countless immigrants far and wide. We are a nation of immigrants. But the truth is more complex. Until 1965, the laws that governed immigration were rooted in invidious discrimination. Liberty's beacon drew millions of undocumented or illegal immigrants. Efforts to stem this tide brought unanticipated consequences, but further reform has failed to stop the flow of illegal immigrants to these shores.

For most of the first half of the twentieth century, immigration rules established a strict quota system that gave a clear advantage to Northern and Western Europeans and guaranteed that few Southern or Eastern Europeans, Asians, Africans, and Jews would enter the country by legal means. This was akin to the same unjustified discrimination that had subjugated blacks since the end of the Civil War. In the same spirit that championed civil rights for African Americans, a once-reluctant Congress changed the rules to end discrimination on the basis of national origin. In 1965, President Lyndon Johnson signed a new immigration bill into law at the Statue of Liberty. Henceforth, the invidious quota system was gone; everyone was supposed to have an equal chance of immigrating to the United States. Upon signing the bill, Johnson remarked that there was nothing revolutionary about the law. "It will not reshape the structure of our daily lives or add importantly to either our wealth or our power." Within a few years, Johnson's prediction proved fundamentally wrong.

One purpose of the new law was to reunite families. It gave preference to relatives of immigrants already here, but since the vast majority of these legal immigrants came from Northern or Western Europe, the expectation was that reuniting families would continue the earlier preferences. Another provision gave preference in much smaller numbers to immigrants with much needed skills, such as doctors and engineers. It never occurred to the law's designers that African doctors, Indian engineers, Philippine nurses, or Chinese software programmers would be able to immigrate. Word trickled out to those newly eligible to come. Once here, these immigrants petitioned for their relatives to come. And those family members petitioned for yet others. As a result of this "chain migration," entire extended families established themselves in the United States, yet the law did nothing to staunch the flow of illegal immigrants.

The demand for cheap labor in agriculture and manufacturing proved an enticing lure to many of the poor with access to America's southern border. The personal risk in crossing the border illegally was often outweighed by the possible gain in employment and a new, though illegal, start. There was no risk of imprisonment, merely a return to south of the border and perhaps another attempt to cross into a "promised land." During the post-1965 period, millions of men and women chose personal risk for the possibility of a better future.

In 1986, Congress sought to fix a system that by all accounts was broken. It sought to place the burden of enforcement on employers by imposing fines for hiring undocumented workers and then by offering amnesty to resident illegal immigrants who were in the United States for at least five years. But lax government enforcement and ease in obtaining falsified worker documents such as a "green card" doomed the enforcement strategy. Illegal immigrants continued to enter the United States, the majority from Mexico (see Figure 16.1).

By 2006, politicians were ready for another round of reform, motivated by over 11 million illegal immigrants in the United States (triple the number since the previous reform effort twenty years earlier); state and local governments in border states that were hit hard for the cost of public services (for example, health and education) for illegal immigrants; and the threat to national security in a post-9/11 world posed by porous, unguarded borders.

While the public is opposed to illegal immigrants obtaining driver's licenses or health care, it is important to note that in 2005, illegal immigrants paid an estimated $7 billion in Social Security taxes with little or nothing in return from the government.

Frustration brought about by hard economic times tends to make illegal immigrants easy targets. This is especially the case in Arizona, which experiences the greatest number of illegal border crossings from Mexico and has a large Hispanic population. With a surge in violence resulting from drug smuggling and human trafficking at its border, the Arizona legislature—backed by strong public opinion—adopted the strictest state immigration law in the nation in 2010. Among its many provisions, the law made it a crime for an alien to be in Arizona without carrying legal documents and obligates the police to determine a person's immigration status if there is a reasonable suspicion that the person is an illegal alien. It also stepped up state and local law enforcement of federal immigration laws and cracked down on

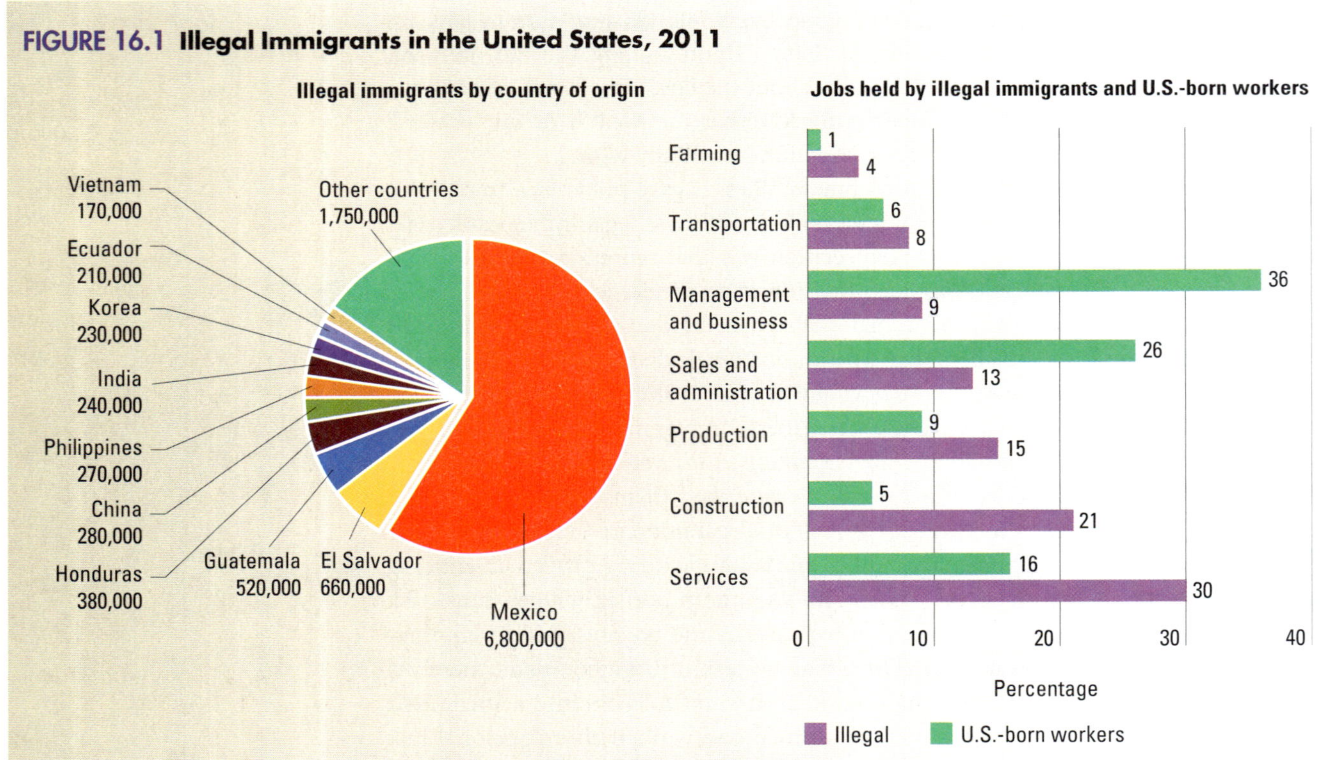

FIGURE 16.1 Illegal Immigrants in the United States, 2011

In 2011, there were 33.6 million foreign-born people living in America. The Department of Homeland Security estimates that the unauthorized immigrant population living in the United States increased to 11.5 million in January 2011 from 8.5 million in January 2000. Between 2000 and 2011, the unauthorized population grew by 36 percent.

Sources: Michael Hoefer, Nancy Rytina, and Bryan C. Baker, "Estimates of the Unauthorized Immigrant Population Residing in the United States: January 2011," Office of Immigration Statistics of the DHS, March 2012, http://www.dhs.gov/xlibrary/assets/statistics/publications/ois_ill_pe_2011.pdf; and Jeffrey S. Passel and D'Vera Cohn, "Table 5: Comparing Occupations of US-Born and Unauthorized Immigrant Workers, 2008," in *A Portrait of Unauthorized Immigrants in the United States* (Washington, D.C.: Pew Hispanic Center, 14 April 2009), http://pewhispanic.org/files/reports/107.pdf.

those sheltering, hiring, and transporting illegal aliens. In June 2012, the Supreme Court struck down three of the law's draconian provisions on federalism grounds—the Constitution vests exclusive power over naturalization and citizenship in the national government—but the Court upheld the part of the law that instructs law enforcement officials to check a person's immigration status when there is reasonable suspicion of the person's illegal status.[43] (See Chapter 4.)

Many Latinos have a rich and deep-rooted heritage in America, but until the 1920s, that heritage was largely confined to the southwestern states, particularly California. Then unprecedented numbers of Mexican immigrants came to the United States in search of employment and a better life. Businesspeople who saw in them a source of cheap labor welcomed them. Many Mexicans became farm workers; others settled mainly in crowded, low-rent, inner-city districts in the Southwest, forming their own barrios, or neighborhoods, within the cities, where they maintained the customs and values of their homeland.

MARK RALSTON/Getty Images

Turning Up the Heat in Arizona

Arizona's get-tough attitude toward illegal immigration brought a heated response from this protester at a large rally in Phoenix shortly after Gov. Jan Brewer signed the bill into law in April 2010. A legal challenge stalled the law's implementation. In 2012, the U.S. Supreme Court weighed in and struck down three of the law's four provisions.

Like blacks who had migrated to northern cities, most new Latino immigrants found poverty and discrimination. And like poor blacks and Native Americans, they suffered disproportionately during the Great Depression. About one-third of the Mexican American population (mainly those who had been migratory farm workers) returned to Mexico during the 1930s.

World War II gave rise to another influx of Mexicans, who this time were primarily courted to work farms in California. But by the late 1950s, most farm workers—blacks, whites, and Hispanics—were living in poverty. Latinos who lived in cities fared little better. Yet millions of Mexicans continued to cross the border into the United States, both legally and illegally. The effect was to depress wages for farm labor in California and the Southwest.

In 1965, Cesar Chavez led a strike of the United Farm Workers union against growers in California. The strike lasted several years and eventually, in combination with a national boycott, resulted in somewhat better pay, working conditions, and housing for farm workers.

In the 1970s and 1980s, the Latino population continued to grow, and to grow rapidly. The 20 million Latinos living in the United States in the 1970s were still mainly Puerto Rican and Mexican American, but they were joined by immigrants from the Dominican Republic, Colombia, Cuba, and Ecuador. Although civil rights legislation helped them to an extent, they were among the poorest and least educated groups in the United States. Their problems were similar to those faced by other nonwhites, but most also had to overcome the further difficulty of learning and using a new language.

One effect of the language barrier is that voter registration and voter turnout among Hispanics are lower than among other groups. The creation of nine Hispanic-majority congressional districts ensured a measure of representation. These majority minority districts remain under scrutiny as a result of Supreme Court decisions prohibiting race-based districting. Also, voter turnout depends on effective political advertising, and Hispanics have not been targeted as often as other groups with political messages in Spanish. But despite these stumbling blocks, Hispanics have started to exercise a measure of political power.

Hispanics occupy positions of power in national and local arenas. Hispanics or Latinos constitute about 16 percent of the population and 6 percent of Congress. The 112th Congress (2011–2012) convened with a diverse group of thirty members of Hispanic descent: twenty-eight in the House and two in the Senate. The National Hispanic Caucus of State Legislators, which has over 320 members, is an informal bipartisan group dedicated to voicing and advancing issues affecting Hispanic Americans. The appointment of Sonia Sotomayor to the U.S. Supreme Court in 2009, and the growing number of Hispanics appointed to the lower federal courts, signaled yet another milestone in the quest for equality for America's largest minority group. The Census Bureau estimates that by 2050, one-third of all residents will be Hispanic. With such growth will come greater political power.[44]

Americans with Disabilities

Minority status is not confined to racial and ethnic groups. After more than two decades of struggle, 43 million Americans with disabilities gained recognition in 1990 as a protected minority with the enactment of the Americans with Disabilities Act (ADA). The law extends the protections embodied in the Civil Rights Act of 1964 to people with physical or mental disabilities, including people with AIDS, alcoholism, and drug addiction. It guarantees them access to employment, transportation, public accommodations, and communication services.

The roots of the disabled rights movement stem from the period after World War II. Thousands of disabled veterans returned to a country and a society that were insensitive to their needs. Institutionalization seemed the best way to care for people with disabilities, but this approach came under increasing fire as people with disabilities and their families sought care at home.

Advocates for persons with disabilities found a ready model in the existing civil rights laws. Opponents argued that the changes mandated by the 1990 law (such as access for those confined to wheelchairs) could cost billions of dollars, but supporters replied that the costs would be offset by an equal or greater reduction in federal aid to people with disabilities, who would rather be working.

The law's enactment set off an avalanche of job discrimination complaints filed with the national government's discrimination watchdog agency, the EEOC. From 1997 to 2011, the EEOC had received more than 271,000 ADA-related complaints. Curiously, most complaints came from already employed people, both previously and recently disabled. They charged that their employers failed to provide reasonable accommodations as required by the law. The disabilities cited most frequently were back problems, mental illness, heart trouble, neurological disorders, and substance abuse.[45]

A deceptively simple question lies at the heart of many ADA suits: What is the meaning of *disability?* According to the EEOC, a disability is "a physical or mental impairment that substantially limits one or more major life activities." This deliberately vague language has thrust the courts into the role of providing needed specificity, a path that politicians have feared to tread.[46]

Congress moved a step closer in 2008, passing a revision to the ADA. The legislation increased protections for people with disabilities by making it easier for workers to prove discrimination. The ADA Amendments Act of 2008 gives protection to people with epilepsy, diabetes, cancer, cerebral palsy, multiple sclerosis, and other ailments. Federal court decisions had denied protection under the ADA because the disabling conditions were controlled by medication or were in remission. The bill was signed into law on September 25, 2008.

A change in the nation's laws, no matter how welcome, does not ensure a change in people's attitudes. Laws that end racial discrimination do not extinguish racism, and laws that ban biased treatment of people with disabilities cannot mandate their acceptance. But civil rights advocates predict that bias against people with disabilities, like similar biases against other minorities, will wither as they become full participants in society.

Homosexual Americans

June 27, 1969, marked the beginning of an often overlooked movement for civil rights in the United States. On that Friday evening, plainclothes officers of the New York City police force raided a gay bar in Greenwich Village known as the Stonewall Inn. The police justified the raid because of their suspicions that Stonewall had been operating without a proper liquor license. In response, hundreds of citizens took to the streets in protest. Violent clashes and a backlash against the police involving hundreds of people ensued for several nights, during which cries of "Gay power!" and "We want freedom!" could be heard. The event became known as the Stonewall Riots and served as the touchstone for the gay liberation movement in the United States.[47]

Stonewall led to the creation of several political interest groups that have fought for the civil liberties and civil rights of members of the gay and lesbian communities. One in particular, the National Gay and Lesbian Task Force, successfully lobbied the U.S. Civil Service Commission in 1973 to allow gay people to serve in public employment. With over a million members, the Human Rights Campaign, founded in 1980, is the largest civil rights organization seeking equality for lesbian, gay, bisexual, and transgender (LGBT) Americans. One of its current priorities is to seek passage of an employment nondiscrimination act to prevent U.S. citizens from being fired from their jobs for being gay.

Although once viewed as being on the fringe of American society, the gay community today maintains a visible presence in national politics. Four openly gay members serve in the U.S. House of Representatives (112th Congress): Barney Frank (D-Mass.), Tammy Baldwin (D-Wisc.), David Cicilline (D-R.I.), and Jared Polis (D-Colo.). In the 2008 election, the state of the economy was far more important to voters than same-sex marriage.[48] Financial support for candidates and groups favoring gay and lesbian rights has declined since 2004.[49]

Gays and lesbians have made significant progress since the early 1970s, but they still have a long way to go to enjoy the complete menu of civil rights now written into laws that protect other minority groups, as noted in Chapter 15. Recent progress includes an end to the "don't ask, don't tell" policy enabling gays and lesbians to serve openly in the U.S. military.[50] And on May 9, 2012, Obama became the first sitting president to state that he supported same-sex marriage. While his was an explicitly personal endorsement of same-sex unions and therefore would have little immediate policy impact, the announcement was nonetheless hailed as "historic."[51]

Still, inequality based on sexual preference continues. Because domestic partner benefits are not recognized uniformly across the United States, same-sex partners are unable to take full advantage of laws that allow citizens to leave their personal estates to family members. They often cannot sign onto their partner's health-care plans (except when company policies allow it); heterosexual couples enjoy this employment benefit almost without exception.

Justin Sullivan

Court Confronts California Clash

Same-sex marriage continues to provoke controversy. Here supporters of California's Proposition 8, which banned same-sex marriage in the state constitution, express their opposition to homosexuality at the federal courthouse in San Francisco where a federal appeals court heard arguments in late 2010 challenging the proposition's constitutionality. In February 2012, the court decided 2 to 1 that the provision violated the equal protection clause of the U.S. Constitution.

Some movement toward greater equality has been made at the state level. In 2003 the highest court in Massachusetts held, in a 4–3 ruling, that same-sex couples have a state constitutional right to the "protections, benefits, and obligations of civil marriage." The majority rested its holding on the Massachusetts Constitution, which affirms the dignity and equality of all individuals. The justices acknowledged that the Massachusetts Constitution is more protective of equality and liberty than the federal Constitution, enabling actions that the U.S. Supreme Court might be unwilling or unable to take.[52]

The decision challenged the state legislature, which sought a compromise to avoid an affirmation of same-sex marriage. The High Court rejected this maneuver, setting the stage for a state constitutional amendment limiting marriages to unions between a man and a woman. At least thirty-seven states prohibit recognition of marriages between same-sex couples. Only residents of states that recognize the validity of same-sex marriage may legally marry today in Massachusetts. But it will be years before the lengthy amendment process runs its course.

In 2008, the California Supreme Court ruled 4–3 that same-sex couples have a state constitutional right to marry. State law and a statewide initiative approved in 2000 defined marriage as a union between a man and a woman. The question before the court was whether those laws violated provisions of the state constitution protecting equality and the right to marry. "In view of the substance and significance of the fundamental constitutional right to form a family relationship," wrote Chief Justice Ronald M. George, "the California Constitution properly must be interpreted to guarantee this basic civil right to all Californians, whether gay or heterosexual, and to same-sex couples as well as to opposite-sex couples."[53]

The ruling was celebrated in San Francisco's large gay community and denounced by religious and conservative groups throughout the state who supported a ballot initiative that would amend the state constitution to ban same-sex marriages and overturn the decision. Proposition 8 passed in 2008, overturning the ruling by defining marriage in the state constitution as a union between one man and one woman. The initiative was overturned in a 2–1 decision by a federal appeals court in 2012, on the ground that it violated the constitution's equal protection clause. It is likely that the U.S. Supreme Court will finally decide on the matter.[54]

While conceding that Californians could define their own rules, attorney Theodore Olson argued that those rules could not take away a fundamental right. The case boils down to marriage and equality. Is marriage a fundamental constitutional right? If so, then everyone is entitled to exercise that right unless the government has compelling reasons to curtail it.[55] Many states do not adhere to Olson's logic. In May 2012, North Carolina became the thirtieth state in the country to include a prohibition of same-sex marriage in its constitution.

A 2000 Supreme Court decision, ***Boy Scouts of America* v. *Dale***, illustrates both the continuing legal struggles of gays and lesbians for civil rights and the modern conflict between freedom and equality. James Dale began his involvement in scouting in 1978 and ten years later achieved the esteemed rank of Eagle Scout. In 1989, he applied to and was accepted for the position of assistant scoutmaster of Troop 73 in New Jersey. Shortly after, in 1990, the Boy Scouts revoked Dale's membership in the organization when it learned that he had become a campus activist with the Rutgers University Lesbian/Gay Alliance. The Boy Scouts argued that because homosexual conduct was inconsistent with its mission, the organization enjoyed the right to revoke his membership. Dale argued that the Scouts' actions violated a New Jersey law that prohibited discrimination on the basis of sexual orientation in places of public accommodation. The U.S. Supreme Court resolved this conflict in a narrow 5–4 decision and sided with the Scouts. The majority opinion, authored by Chief Justice William H. Rehnquist, maintained that New Jersey's public accommodations law violated the Boy Scouts' freedom of association, outweighing Dale's claim for equal treatment. The dissenters, led by Justice John Paul Stevens, maintained that equal treatment outweighed free association. They reasoned that allowing Dale to serve as an assistant scoutmaster did not impose serious burdens on the Scouts or force the organization "to communicate any message that it does not wish to endorse."[56]

Proud to be Out

President Barack Obama signed a bill in 2010 repealing the military's "don't ask, don't tell" policy, which prevented gays from serving openly in the military. The new law required the President, the Secretary of Defense, and the Chairman of the Joint Chiefs of Staff to certify that the repeal would not harm military readiness. The required certification was sent to Congress, completing the repeal on September 20, 2011.

Mark Wilson/Getty Images

16.6 Gender and Equal Rights: The Women's Movement

★ Trace the evolution of women's legal rights beginning with laws based on protectionism and concluding with Supreme Court rulings prohibiting gender-based discrimination.

Together with unconventional political activities such as protests and sit-ins, conventional political tools such as the ballot box and the lawsuit have brought minorities in America a measure of equality. The Supreme Court, once responsible for perpetuating inequality for blacks, has expanded the array of legal tools available to all minorities to help them achieve social equality. Women, too, have benefited from this change.

Protectionism

Until the early 1970s, laws that affected the civil rights of women were based on traditional views of the relationship between men and women. At the heart of these laws

protectionism
The notion that women must be protected from life's cruelties; until the 1970s, the basis for laws affecting women's civil rights.

was **protectionism**—the notion that women must be sheltered from life's harsh realities. Thomas Jefferson, author of the Declaration of Independence, believed that "were our state a pure democracy there would still be excluded from our deliberations women, who, to prevent deprivation of morals and ambiguity of issues, should not mix promiscuously in gatherings of men."[57] And "protected" they were, through laws that discriminated against them in employment and other areas. With few exceptions, women were also "protected" from voting until early in the twentieth century.

The demand for women's rights arose from the abolition movement and later was based primarily on the Fourteenth Amendment's prohibition of laws that "abridge the privileges or immunities of citizens of the United States." However, the courts consistently rebuffed challenges to protectionist state laws. In 1873, the Supreme Court upheld an Illinois statute that prohibited women from practicing law. The justices maintained that the Fourteenth Amendment had no bearing on a state's authority to regulate admission of members to the bar.[58]

Protectionism reached a peak in 1908, when the Court upheld an Oregon law limiting the number of hours women could work.[59] The decision was rife with assumptions about the nature and role of women, and it gave wide latitude to laws that "protected" the "weaker sex." It also led to protectionist legislation that barred women from working more than forty-eight hours a week and from working at jobs that required them to lift more than thirty-five pounds. (The average work week for men was sixty hours or longer.) In effect, women were locked out of jobs that called for substantial overtime (and overtime pay) and were shunted to jobs that men believed suited their abilities.

Protectionism can take many forms. Some employers hesitate to place women at risk in the workplace. Some have excluded women of child-bearing age from jobs that involve exposure to toxic substances that could harm a developing fetus. Usually such jobs offer more pay to compensate for their higher risk. Although they too face reproductive risks from toxic substances, men have experienced no such exclusions.

In 1991, the Supreme Court struck down a company's fetal protection policy in strong terms. The Court relied on amendments to the 1964 Civil Rights Act providing for only a very few narrow exceptions to the principle that unless some workers differ from others in their ability to work, they must be treated the same as other employees. "In other words," declared the majority, "women as capable of doing their jobs as their male counterparts may not be forced to choose between having a child and having a job."[60]

Political Equality for Women

With a few exceptions, women were not allowed to vote in this country until 1920. In 1869, Francis and Virginia Minor sued a St. Louis, Missouri, registrar for not allowing Virginia Minor to vote. In 1875, the Supreme Court held that the Fourteenth Amendment's privileges and immunities clause did not confer the right to vote on all citizens or require that the states allow women to vote.[61]

The decision clearly slowed the movement toward women's suffrage, but it did not stop it. In 1878, Susan B. Anthony, a women's rights activist, convinced a U.S. senator from California to introduce a constitutional amendment requiring that "the right of citizens of the United States to vote shall not be denied or abridged by the United States or by any State on account of sex." The amendment was introduced and voted down several times over the next twenty years. Meanwhile, as noted in Chapter 7, a number of states, primarily in the Midwest and West, did grant limited suffrage to women.

The movement for women's suffrage became a political battle to amend the Constitution. In 1917, police arrested 218 women from twenty-six states when they picketed the White House, demanding the right to vote. Nearly one hundred went to jail, some for days and others for months. The movement culminated in the adoption in 1920 of the **Nineteenth Amendment**, which gave women the right to vote. Its wording was that first suggested by Anthony.

The right of women to vote does not ensure that women representatives will be elected to public office. Beginning in the 1990s, several countries sought to ensure elected representation of women by the use of gender quotas. The results have been mixed. (See "Politics of Global Change: Gender Quotas for Representatives in Lower Legislative Houses.")

Meanwhile, the Supreme Court continued to act as the benevolent protector of women. Women entered the work force in significant numbers during World War I and did so again during World War II, but they received lower wages than the men they replaced. Again, the justification was the "proper" role of women as mothers and homemakers. Because society expected men to be the principal providers, it followed that women's earnings were less important to the family's support. This thinking perpetuated inequalities in the workplace. Economic equality was closely tied to social attitudes. Because society expected women to stay at home, the assumption was that they needed less education than men did. Therefore, they tended to qualify only for low-paying, low-skilled jobs with little chance for advancement.

Prohibiting Sex-Based Discrimination

The movement to provide equal rights to women advanced a step with the passage of the Equal Pay Act of 1963, which required equal pay for men and women doing similar work. However, state protectionist laws still had the effect of restricting women to jobs that men usually did not want. Where employment was stratified by sex, equal pay was an empty promise. To remove the restrictions of protectionism, women needed equal opportunity for employment. They got it in the Civil Rights Act of 1964 and later legislation.

The objective of the Civil Rights Act of 1964 was to eliminate racial discrimination in America. The original wording of Title VII of the act prohibited employment discrimination based on race, color, religion, and national origin—but not gender. In an effort to scuttle the provision during House debate, Democrat Howard W. Smith of Virginia proposed an amendment barring job discrimination based on sex. Smith's intention was to make the law unacceptable; his effort to ridicule the law brought gales of laughter to the debate. But Democrat Martha W. Griffiths of Michigan used Smith's strategy against him. With her support, Smith's amendment carried, as did the act.[62] Congress extended the jurisdiction of the EEOC to cover cases of invidious sex discrimination, or **sexism**.

Subsequent women's rights legislation was motivated by the pressure for civil rights, as well as by a resurgence of the women's movement, which had subsided in 1920 after the adoption of the Nineteenth Amendment. One particularly important law was Title IX of the Education Amendments of 1972, which prohibited sex discrimination in federally aided education programs. Another boost to women came from the Revenue Act of 1972, which provided tax credits for child-care expenses. In effect, the act subsidized parents with young children so that women could enter or remain in the work force. However, the high-water mark in the effort to secure women's rights was the equal rights amendment, as we shall explain shortly.

In 2007, a conservative Supreme Court tightened the rules over pay discrimination lawsuits under Title VII.[63] The case involved a woman who did not learn of the

Nineteenth Amendment
The amendment to the Constitution, adopted in 1920, that ensures women of the right to vote.

sexism
Invidious sex discrimination.

Politics of Global Change

Gender Quotas for Representatives in Lower Legislative Houses

One way to assure the election of women to public office is to mandate it. Several countries have taken this step, with mixed results. One approach is to establish a quota system that women must constitute a certain percentage or number of elective positions. The philosophical justification behind this idea is tied to the notion of equality of outcome. While women constitute 50 percent of the population, they tend to be under represented in political offices. The establishment of legal quotas aims at solving this disparity.

But not all gender quota systems are created equal. Some nations, such as Nepal and the Philippines, include quotas in their constitutions. Other nations, such as most of Latin America, include quotas in their electoral laws. And in some cases—Germany, Italy, Norway, and Sweden, for example—several political parties advance a

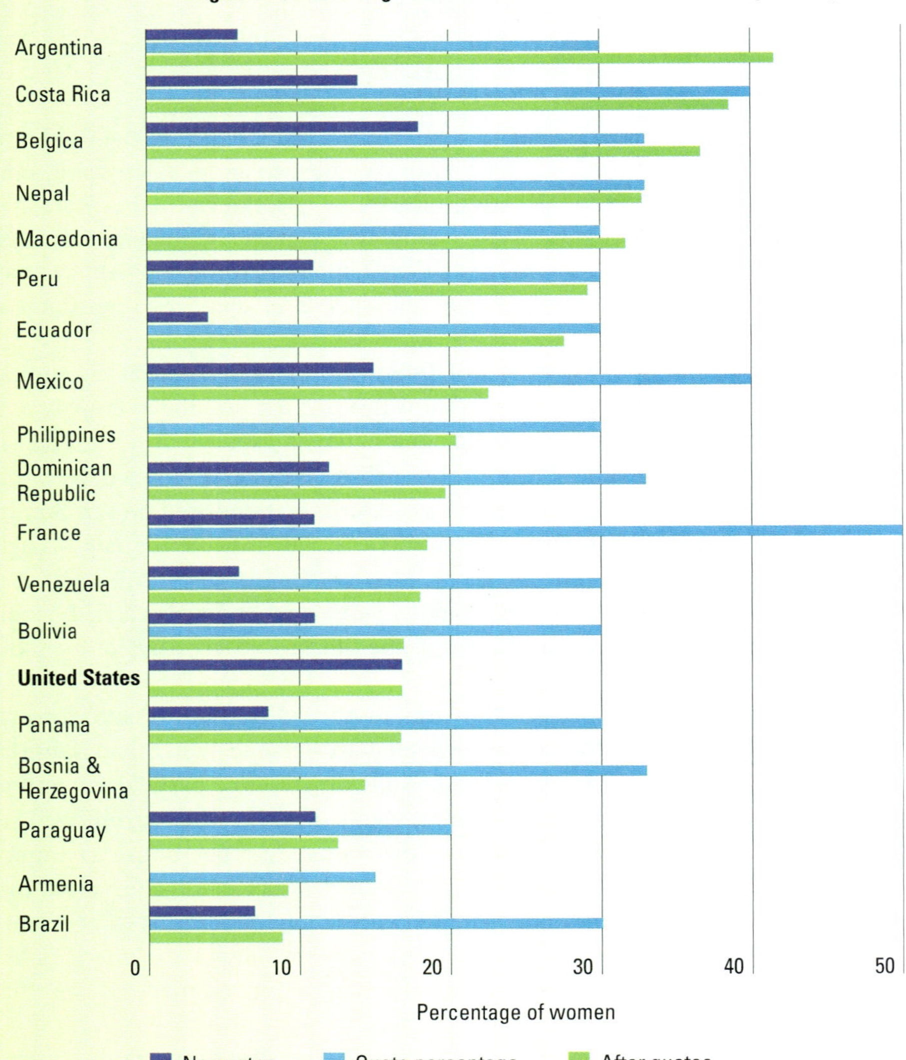

Figure A: Effect of Legal Gender Quotas in Lower Chambers, by Country

voluntary quota system regardless of their country's legislation. Gender quota systems vary also according to the level at which they are applied. In some cases they regulate the number of candidacies that must be held by women, whereas in others they mandate the number or percentage of elected positions held by women.

Have these quota systems achieved their desired level of gender equality? Figure A identifies eighteen countries with gender quota systems (and the United States, which lacks such a system), their gender goals, and in thirteen cases the pre- and post-quota results. First, only in two cases (Argentina and Nepal) did actual electoral results match the established quota. Second, note the wide variance regarding the ultimate effectiveness of gender quotas. Women's representation increased significantly in some countries such as Argentina, Costa Rica, and Ecuador, but in most countries, the result is not as spectacular (an increase of less than 10 percent). What explains this disparity among cases? Figure B offers a hint. The main reason is the electoral system itself. Quotas are most effective in proportional representation systems with closed lists of candidates, provided women are positioned in competitive places. Quotas are least effective in majoritarian electoral systems. Electoral systems combining features of majoritarian and proportional representation schemes fit in the middle. However, women's representation has steadily increased in the past decade. Whether this trend is explained by means of institutional engineering or by societal transformations remains a matter of continuing research.

Figure B: Effect of Legal Gender Quotas in Lower Chambers, by Electoral System

SOURCES: Quota Project: Global Database of Quotas for Women, http://www.quotaproject.org. Pippa Norris, "Recruitment" in Richard S. Katz and William Crotty (eds.), Handbook of Party Politics (Sage, 2006). For the % of US Congresswomen Ipu Parline Database, available at http://www.ipu.org/wmn-e/classif.htm; Global Database of Quotas for Women available at http://www.quotaproject.org/index.cfm. © Cengage Learning

Critical Thinking 

To what extent do gender quota laws limit freedom? Are these limitations justified by the desired outcome (i.e., a more representative legislature)?

pay disparity with sixteen men in her office until years later because salary information is secret. But the law required her to file a complaint within 180 days of pay setting. The 5–4 decision prompted a bitter oral dissent by Justice Ruth Bader Ginsburg.

True to the pluralist character of American democracy, the Obama administration and a Democratic Congress reversed the 2007 decision by passing the Lilly

Ledbetter Fair Pay Act. The act allows the filing of complaints beyond the 180-day period.[64] Pay equity for women still remains a hope, not a reality.

Stereotypes Under Scrutiny

After nearly a century of protectionism, the Supreme Court began to take a closer look at gender-based distinctions. In 1971, it struck down a state law that gave men preference over women in administering the estate of a person who died without naming an administrator.[65] The state maintained that the law reduced court workloads and avoided family battles; however, the Court dismissed those objections, because they were not important enough to justify making gender-based distinctions between individuals. Two years later, the justices declared that paternalism operated to "put women not on a pedestal, but in a cage."[66] They then proceeded to strike down several laws that either prevented or discouraged departures from traditional sex roles. In 1976, the Court finally developed a workable standard for reviewing such laws: gender-based distinctions are justifiable only if they serve some important government purpose.[67]

The objective of the standard is to dismantle laws based on sexual stereotypes while fashioning public policies that acknowledge relevant differences between men and women. Perhaps the most controversial issue is the idea of *comparable worth,* which requires employers to pay comparable wages for different jobs, filled predominantly by one sex or the other, that are of about the same worth to the employer. Absent new legislation, the courts remain reluctant and ineffective vehicles for ending wage discrimination.[68]

The courts have not been reluctant to extend to women the *constitutional* guarantees won by blacks. In 1994, the Supreme Court extended the Constitution's equal protection guarantee by forbidding the exclusion of potential jurors on the basis of their sex. In a 6–3 decision, the justices held that it is unconstitutional to use gender, and likewise race, as a criterion for determining juror competence and impartiality. "Discrimination in jury selection," wrote Justice Harry A. Blackmun for the majority, "whether based on race or on gender, causes harm to the litigants, the community, and the individual jurors who are wrongfully excluded from participation in the judicial process."[69] The 1994 decision completed a constitutional revolution in jury selection that began in 1986 with a bar against juror exclusions based on race.

In 1996, the Court spoke with uncommon clarity when it declared that the men-only admissions policy of the Virginia Military Institute (VMI), a state-supported military college, violated the equal protection clause of the Fourteenth Amendment. Virginia defended the school's policy on the grounds that it was preserving diversity among America's educational institutions.

In an effort to meet women's demands to enter VMI—and stave off continued legal challenges—Virginia established a separate-but-equal institution, the Virginia Women's Institute for Leadership (VWIL). The program was housed at Mary Baldwin College, a private liberal arts college for women, and students enrolled in VWIL received the same financial support as students at VMI.

The presence of women at VMI would require substantial changes in the physical environment and the traditional close scrutiny of the students. Moreover, the presence of women would alter the manner in which cadets interact socially. Was the uniqueness of VMI worth preserving at the expense of women who could otherwise meet the academic, physical, and psychological stress imposed by the VMI approach?

In a 7–1 decision, the High Court voted no. Writing for a six-member majority in **United States v. Virginia,** Justice Ruth Bader Ginsburg applied a demanding test she labeled "skeptical scrutiny" to official acts that deny individuals rights or responsibilities based on their sex. "Parties who seek to defend gender-based government action," she wrote, "must demonstrate an 'exceedingly persuasive justification' for that action." Ginsburg declared that "women seeking and fit for a VMI-quality education cannot be offered anything less, under the State's obligation to afford them genuinely equal protection." Ginsburg went on to note that the VWIL program offered no cure for the "opportunities and advantages withheld from women who want a VMI education and can make the grade."[70] The upshot is that distinctions based on sex are almost as suspect as distinctions based on race.

Three months after the Court's decision, VMI's board of directors finally voted 9–8 to admit women. This ended VMI's distinction as the last government-supported single-sex school. However, school officials made few allowances for women. Buzz haircuts and fitness requirements remained the standard for all students. "It would be demeaning to women to cut them slack," declared VMI's superintendent.[71]

The Equal Rights Amendment

Policies protecting women, based largely on gender stereotypes, have been woven into the legal fabric of American life. This protectionism has limited the freedom of women to compete with men socially and economically on an equal footing. However, the Supreme Court has been hesitant to extend the principles of the Fourteenth Amendment beyond issues of race. When judicial interpretation of the Constitution imposes a limit, then only a constitutional amendment can overcome it.

The National Women's Party, one of the few women's groups that did not disband after the Nineteenth Amendment was enacted, introduced the proposed **equal rights amendment (ERA)** in 1923. The ERA declared that "equality of rights under the law shall not be denied or abridged by the United States or any State on account of sex." It remained bottled up in committee in every Congress until 1970, when Representative Martha Griffiths filed a discharge petition to bring it to the House floor for a vote. The House passed the ERA, but the Senate scuttled it by attaching a section calling for prayer in the public schools.

A national coalition of women's rights advocates generated enough support to get the ERA through Congress in 1972. Its proponents then had seven years to get the amendment ratified by thirty-eight state legislatures, as required by the Constitution. By 1977, they were three states short of that goal, and three states had rescinded their earlier ratification. Then, in an unprecedented action, Congress extended the ratification deadline. It didn't help. The ERA died in 1982, still three states short of adoption.

Why did the ERA fail? There are several explanations. Its proponents mounted a national campaign to generate approval, while its opponents organized state-based anti-ERA campaigns. ERA proponents hurt their cause by exaggerating the amendment's effects; such claims only gave ammunition to the amendment's opponents. For example, the puffed-up claim that the amendment would make wife and husband equally responsible for their family's financial support caused alarm among the undecided. As the opposition grew stronger, especially from women who wanted to maintain their traditional role, state legislators began to realize that supporting the amendment involved risk. Given the exaggerations and counter-exaggerations, lawmakers ducked. Because it takes an extraordinary majority to amend the Constitution, it takes only a committed minority to thwart the majority's will.

Despite its failure, the movement to ratify the ERA produced real benefits. It raised the consciousness of women about their social position, spurred the formation of the National Organization for Women (NOW) and other large organizations, contributed to women's participation in politics, and generated important legislation affecting women.[72]

equal rights amendment (ERA)
A failed constitutional amendment introduced by the National Women's Party in 1923, declaring that "equality of rights under the law shall not be denied or abridged by the United States or any State on account of sex."

The failure to ratify the ERA stands in stark contrast to the quick enactment of many laws that now protect women's rights. Such legislation had little audible opposition. If years of racial discrimination called for government redress, then so did years of gender-based discrimination. Furthermore, laws protecting women's rights required only the amending of civil rights bills or the enactment of similar bills.

Some scholars argue that for practical purposes, the Supreme Court has implemented the equivalent of the ERA through its decisions. It has struck down distinctions based on sex and held that stereotyped generalizations about sexual differences must fall.[73] In recent rulings, the Court has held that states may require employers to guarantee job reinstatement to women who take maternity leave, that sexual harassment in the workplace is illegal, and that the existence of a hostile work environment may be demonstrated by a reasonable perception of abuse rather than by proven psychological injury.[74]

But the Supreme Court can reverse its decisions, and legislators can repeal statutes. Without an equal rights amendment, argue some feminists, the Constitution will continue to bear the sexist imprint of a document written by men for men. Until the ERA becomes part of the Constitution, said the late feminist Betty Friedan, "We are at the mercy of a Supreme Court that will interpret equality as it sees fit."[75]

16.7 Affirmative Action: Equal Opportunity or Equal Outcome?

★ Compare and contrast the consequences that follow from policies aimed at equal opportunities versus those aimed at equal outcomes.

In his vision of a Great Society, President Johnson linked economic rights with civil rights and equality of outcome with equality of opportunity. "Equal opportunity is essential, but not enough," he declared. "We seek not just legal equity but human ability, not just equality as a right and a theory but equality as a fact and equality as a result."[76] This commitment led to affirmative action programs to expand opportunities for women, minorities, and people with disabilities.

Affirmative action is a commitment by a business, employer, school, or other public or private institution to expand opportunities for women, blacks, Hispanic Americans, and members of other minority groups. Affirmative action aims to overcome the effects of present and past discrimination. It embraces a range of public and private programs, policies, and procedures, including special recruitment, preferential treatment, and quotas in job training and professional education, employment, and the awarding of government contracts. The point of these programs is to move beyond equality of opportunity to equality of outcome.

Establishing numerical goals (such as designating a specific number of places in a law school for minority candidates or specifying that 10 percent of the work on a government contract must be subcontracted to minority-owned companies) is the most aggressive form of affirmative action, and it generates more debate and opposition than any other aspect of the civil rights movement. Advocates claim that such goal setting for college admissions, training programs, employment, and contracts will move minorities, women, and people with disabilities out of their second-class status. President Johnson explained why aggressive affirmative action was necessary:

You do not take a person who for years has been hobbled by chains, liberate him, bring him up to the starting line of a race, and then say, "You are free to compete with all the others," and still justly believe that you have been completely fair. Thus, it is not enough just to open the gates of opportunity; all our citizens must have the ability to walk through those gates.[77]

Arguments for affirmative action programs (from increased recruitment efforts to quotas) tend to use the following reasoning: certain groups have historically suffered invidious discrimination, denying them educational and economic opportunities. To eliminate the lasting effects of such discrimination, the public and private sectors must take steps to provide access to good education and jobs. If the majority once discriminated to hold groups back, discriminating to benefit those groups is fair. Therefore, quotas are a legitimate means to provide a place on the ladder to success.[78]

Affirmative action opponents maintain that quotas for designated groups necessarily create invidious discrimination (in the form of reverse discrimination) against individuals who are themselves blameless. Moreover, they say, quotas lead to the admission, hiring, or promotion of the less qualified at the expense of the well qualified. In the name of equality, such policies thwart individuals' freedom to succeed.

Government-mandated preferential policies probably began in 1965 with the creation of the Office of Federal Contract Compliance. Its purpose was to ensure that all private enterprises doing business with the federal government complied with nondiscrimination guidelines. Because so many companies do business with the federal government, a large portion of the American economy became subject to these guidelines. In 1968, the guidelines required "goals and timetables for the prompt achievement of full and equal employment opportunity." By 1971, they called for employers to eliminate "underutilization" of minorities and women, which meant that employers had to hire minorities and women in proportion to the government's assessment of their availability.[79]

Preferential policies are seldom explicitly legislated. More often, such policies are the result of administrative regulations, judicial rulings, and initiatives in the private sector to provide a remedial response to specific discrimination or to satisfy new legal standards for proving nondiscrimination. Quotas or goals enable administrators to assess changes in hiring, promotion, and admissions policies. Racial quotas are an economic fact of life today. Employers engage in race-conscious preferential treatment to avoid litigation. Cast in value terms, equality trumps freedom. Do preferential policies in other nations offer lessons for us? (See "Compared with What? How Others Struggle with Affirmative Action" to learn the answer.)

Reverse Discrimination

The Supreme Court confronted an affirmative action quota program for the first time in ***Regents of the University of California v. Bakke***.[80] Allan Bakke, a thirty-five-year-old white man, had twice applied for admission to the University of California Medical School at Davis and was rejected both times. As part of the university's affirmative action program, the school had reserved sixteen places in each entering class of one hundred for qualified minority applicants in an effort to redress long-standing and unfair exclusion of minorities from the medical profession. Bakke's academic qualifications exceeded those of all the minority students admitted in the two years his applications were rejected. Bakke contended, first in the California courts and then in the Supreme Court, that he was excluded from admission solely on the basis of his race. He argued that the equal protection clause of the Fourteenth Amendment and the Civil Rights Act of 1964 prohibited this reverse discrimination.

Compared with What?

How Others Struggle with Affirmative Action

Compared with other countries around the world, Americans are not alone in their disagreements over affirmative action. Controversies, even bloodshed, have arisen where the government treats certain groups of citizens preferentially. One study found several common patterns among countries that had enacted preferential policies. Although begun as temporary measures, preferential policies tended to persist and even to expand to include more groups. The policies usually sought to improve the situation of disadvantaged groups as a whole, but they often benefited the better-off members of such groups more so than the worse-off members. Finally, preferential policies tended to increase antagonisms among different groups within a country.

Of course, there were variations across countries in terms of who benefited from such policies, what types of benefits were bestowed, and even the names the policies were given. In India, such policies carry the label "positive discrimination." But that isn't the only way India differs from the United States when it comes to preferential policies.

Although India is the world's largest democracy, its society is rigidly stratified into groups called castes. The government forbids caste-based discrimination, but members of the lower castes (the lowest being the Dalits, or "untouchables") were historically restricted to the least prestigious and lowest-paying jobs. To improve their status, India has set aside government jobs for the lower castes, who make up half of India's population of 1 billion. India now reserves 27 percent of government jobs for the lower castes and an additional 23 percent for untouchables and remote tribe members. Gender equality has also improved since a 1993 constitutional amendment that set aside one-third of all seats in local government councils for women. By 2004, 900,000 women had been elected to public office, and 80,000 of them now lead local governing bodies. Positive discrimination in India has intensified tensions between the lower and upper castes. In 1990, soon after the new quotas were established, scores of young upper-caste men and women set themselves ablaze in protest. And when Indian courts issued a temporary injunction against the positive-discrimination policies, lower-caste terrorists bombed a train and killed dozens of people. Adding further strain, a 2010 proposal to create a one-third set-aside for women in the parliament and state legislatures has met stiff resistance from the political parties representing the lower castes. The Dalits view the proposal as a threat to their monopoly quota. Lower-caste women oppose the idea while feminists from higher-caste parties support it. The bill is now pending in India's lower house of parliament after passing in the upper house in 2010. The issue is not the use of quotas but which group should benefit from quotas. No longer considered temporary, quotas have become a fact of life in the world's largest democracy.

In Brazil, the state of Rio de Janeiro set aside racial quotas for black and native Brazilians applying to the state university system in 2000. However, the initiative backfired when many white students claimed African heritage to benefit from the quotas in a very competitive setting. Forty-two percent of Brazil's population is racially mixed. Critics of affirmative action argue that it is difficult to determine with precision "to which race each Brazilian belongs." A former minister of education, Paulo Renato Souza, claims that the real task is to improve access to public education for poor Brazilians and therefore racial quotas are misleading. Other critics argue that with 42 percent of the population identifying as mixed race, a quota would turn Brazil into a two-color nation. Supporters of the affirmative action program oddly include a private college in São Paulo that sets aside 50 percent of its places for black students. The president of the university says that a "large part of the public, if they didn't have this opportunity, would find it difficult to study elsewhere." In 2012, Brazil's federal Supreme Court ruled that the quotas were a legitimate method for redressing inequalities that stemmed from the country's centuries-long history of slavery.

In South Africa, the gradual development of policies of affirmative action for blacks ended with the establishment of the Broad-Based Black Economic Empowerment Act, which aims at promoting equality in the workplace. Government employment legislation sets aside 80 percent of new jobs for black people and favors black-owned companies as subcontractors. Supporters of these policies argue that opponents still share the mind-set prevailing during the apartheid regime and that "many of these people cannot accept the fact that now we are all equal." Critics underline that the blacks that have been empowered by these policies "have largely been senior members of the ruling African National Congress. The bulk of the 'empowerment' seems to involve just four very rich men, three of them contenders for the presidency in 2009."

All governments broker conflict to varying degrees. Under a majoritarian model, group demands could lead quickly to conflict and instability because majority rule leaves little room for compromise. A pluralist model allows different groups to get a piece of the pie. By parceling out benefits, pluralism mitigates disorder in the short term. But in the long term, repeated demands for increased benefits can spark instability. A vigorous pluralist system should provide acceptable mechanisms (legislative, executive, bureaucratic, judicial) to vent such frustrations and yield new allocations of benefits.

Sources: Trudy Rubin, "Will Democracy Survive in India?" *Record* (Bergen County, N.J.), 19 January 1998, p. A12; Alex Spillius, "India's Old Warriors to Launch Rights Fight," *Daily Telegraph*, 20 October 1997, p. 12; Robin Wright, "World's Leaders: Men, 187, Women, 4," *Los Angeles Times*, 30 September 1997, p. A1; "Indian Eunuchs Demand Government Job Quotas," *Agence France Presse*, 22 October 1997; Juergen Hein and M. V. Balaji, "India's First Census of New Millennium Begins on February 9," *Deutsche Presse-Agentur*, 7 February 2001; Gillian Bowditch, "You Can Have Meritocracy or Equality, but Not Both," *Sunday Times*, Features Section: Scotland News, 19 January 2003, p. 21; Press Trust of India, "About a Million Women Elected to Local Bodies in India," 10 February 2004; Somini Sengupta, "Quotas to Aid India's Poor vs. Push for Meritocracy," *New York Times*, 23 May 2006, p. A3; "Caste in Doubt," *The Economist*, 12 June 2010, p. 46; Robert Plummer, "Black Brazil Seeks a Better Future," *BBC News*, 25 September 2006, http://news.bbc.co.uk/2/hi/americas/5357842.stm; Pueng Vongs, "Around the World, Countries Grapple with Affirmative Action," *New America Media*, 10 July 2003, http://news.newamericamedia.org/news/view—article.html?article—id=3e26118fcdf4fba57da467da3eeb43d0; Robert Guest, "The World's Most Extreme Affirmative Action Program: Aiming for Prosperity Would Be Better," *Wall Street Journal*, 26 December 2004, http://www.opinionjournal.com/extra/?id=110006066; Simon Woods, "Race against Time," *Observer Magazine*, 22 January 2006, http://observer.guardian.co.uk/magazine/story/0,,1691343,00.html; Rafael Ribeiro, "Cotas estão paradas no Congresso: Projeto propõe critérios raciais e sociais para ingresso na universidade," *Diário de São Paulo*, 10 April 2010, http://www.diariosp.com.br/Noticias/Dia-a-dia/3379/CotaspestaopparadaspnopCongresso; Shikha Dalmia, "India's Government by Quota," *Wall Street Journal*, 1–2 May 2010, p. A13; and "Brazil's Top Court Back Racial Quotas in Universities," *Agence France Presse*, 1 May 2012.

Critical Thinking

Preferential policies have at times threatened to disrupt order in rigidly stratified societies. What are some of the risks associated with affirmative action? How do different institutional models address these risks? Which do you think matters more for bolstering group participation and opportunity: institutional or social change?

The Court's decision in *Bakke* contained six opinions and spanned 154 pages, but no opinion commanded a majority. Despite the confusing multiple opinions, the Court struck down the school's rigid use of race, thus admitting Bakke, and it approved of affirmative action programs in education that use race as a *plus* factor (one of many such factors) but not as the *sole* factor. Thus, the Court managed to minimize white opposition to the goal of equality (by finding for Bakke) while extending gains for racial minorities through affirmative action.

True to the pluralist model, groups opposed to affirmative action continued their opposition in federal courts and state legislatures. They met with some success. The Supreme Court struck down government-mandated set-aside programs in the U.S. Department of Transportation.[81] Lower federal courts took this as a signal that other forms of affirmative action were ripe for reversal.

By 2003—twenty-five years after *Bakke*—the Supreme Court reexamined affirmative action in two cases, both challenging aspects of the University of Michigan's racial preferences policies. In **Gratz v. Bollinger,** the Court considered the university's undergraduate admissions policy, which conferred 20 points automatically to members of favored groups (100 points guaranteed admission). In a 6–3 opinion, Chief Justice William H. Rehnquist argued that such a policy violated the equal protection clause because it lacked the narrow tailoring required for permissible racial preferences and it failed to provide for individualized consideration of each candidate.[82] In the second case, **Grutter v. Bollinger,** the Court considered the University of Michigan's law school admissions policy, which gave preference to minority applicants with lower GPAs and standardized test scores over white applicants. This time, the Court, in a 5–4 decision authored by Justice Sandra Day O'Connor, held that the equal protection clause did not bar the school's narrowly tailored use of racial preferences to further a compelling interest that flowed from a racially diverse student body.[83] Since each applicant is judged individually on his or her merits, race remains only one among many factors that enter into the admissions decision.

The issue of race-based classifications in education arose again in 2007 when parents challenged voluntary school integration plans based on race in **Parents Involved in Community Schools v. Seattle School District No. 1.**[84] Chief Justice John G. Roberts, Jr., writing for the 5–4 majority on a bitterly divided bench, invalidated the plans, declaring that the programs were "directed only to racial balance, pure and simple," which the equal protection clause of the Fourteenth Amendment forbids. "The way to stop discrimination on the basis of race is to stop discriminating on the basis of race," he said.

Justice Anthony Kennedy, who cast the fifth and deciding vote, wrote separately to say that achieving racial diversity and avoiding racial isolation were "compelling interests" that schools could constitutionally pursue as long as they "narrowly tailored" their programs to avoid racial labeling and sorting of individual children.

Justice Stephen G. Breyer, writing for the minority and speaking from the bench, used pointed language, declaring, "This is a decision that the Court and the nation will come to regret." A sign of growing frustration among the justices is the increased frequency with which they have read their dissents aloud, a tactic used to express great distress with the majority opinion.

When Samuel A. Alito replaced Sandra Day O'Connor, the Court moved in a decidedly more conservative direction. The justices revisited affirmative action policies in October 2012 when the Court heard arguments in **Fisher v. University of Texas**, a challenge to the University of Texas race-based admissions program. This case once again put such preferences in college admissions squarely before a more conservative bench. The Court's willingness to revisit the issue suggests that the policy's days are numbered.[85]

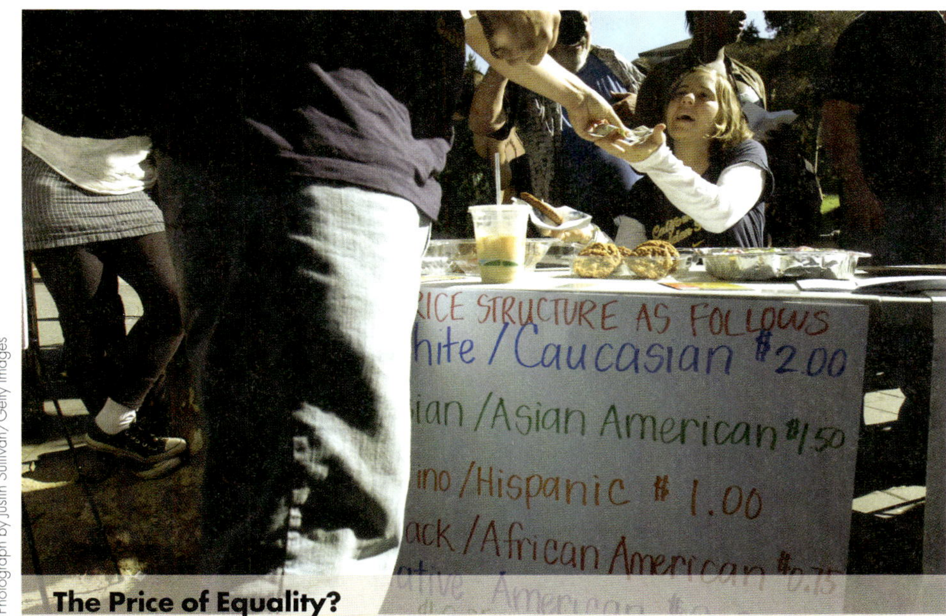

Photograph by Justin Sullivan / Getty Images

The Price of Equality?

College Republicans at the University of California, Berkeley drive home the pernicious effect of equal outcomes policies by holding a bake sale with items priced according to race, ethnicity, or gender. Most of us would expect one price for everyone but in the view of some people correcting for various forms of invidious discrimination poses unequal results, as in the bake sale example.

The Politics of Affirmative Action

A comprehensive review of nationwide surveys conducted over the past twenty-five years reveals an unsurprising truth: that blacks favor affirmative action programs and whites do not. The gulf between the races was wider in the 1970s than it is today, but the moderation results from shifts among blacks, not whites. Perhaps the most important finding is that "whites' views have remained essentially unchanged over twenty-five years."[86]

How do we account for the persistence of equal outcomes policies? A majority of Americans have consistently rejected explicit race or gender preferences for the awarding of contracts, employment decisions, and college admissions, regardless of the groups such preferences benefit. Nevertheless, preference policies have survived and thrived under both Democrats and Republicans because they are attractive. They encourage unprotected groups to strive for inclusion. The list of protected groups includes African Americans, Hispanic Americans, Native Americans, Asian Pacific Americans, and subcontinent Asian Americans.[87] Politicians have a powerful motive—votes—to expand the number of protected groups and the benefits such policies provide.

Recall that affirmative action programs began as temporary measures, ensuring a jump-start for minorities shackled by decades or centuries of invidious discrimination. For example, fifty years ago, minority racial identity was a fatal flaw on a medical or law school application. Today it is viewed as an advantage, encouraging applicants to think in minority-group terms. Thinking in group terms and conferring benefits on such grounds generates hostility from members of the majority, who see the deck stacked against them for no other reason than their race. It is not surprising that affirmative action has become controversial, since many Americans view it as a violation of their individual freedom.

Recall Lyndon Johnson's justification for equal outcomes policies. Though free to compete, a person once hobbled by chains cannot run a fair race. Americans are willing to do more than remove the chains. They will support special training and financial assistance for those who were previously shackled. The hope is that such efforts will enable once-shackled runners to catch up with those who have forged ahead. But Americans stop short at endorsing equal outcomes policies because they predetermine the results of the race.[88]

The conflict between freedom and equality will continue as other individuals and groups continue to press their demands through litigation and legislation. The choice will depend on whether and to what extent Americans still harbor deep-seated racial prejudice.

SUMMARY

16.1 Two Conceptions of Equality

- Americans want equality, but they disagree on the extent to which government should guarantee it.
- At the heart of this conflict is the distinction between equal opportunities and equal outcomes.
- Americans are less committed to quotas and goals than they are to low-bid contracting and merit-based admissions.

16.2 The Civil War Amendments

- Congress enacted the Civil War amendments—the Thirteenth, Fourteenth, and Fifteenth amendments—to provide full civil rights to black Americans. In the late nineteenth century, however, the Supreme Court interpreted the amendments very narrowly, declaring that they did not restrain individuals from denying civil rights to blacks and did not apply to the states.
- The Court's rulings in effect made racial segregation a fact of daily life for black Americans and enabled states in the American South to deny the vote to most blacks and to institutionalize racism.
- By the end of the nineteenth century, legal racial segregation was firmly entrenched in the American South.

16.3 The Dismantling of School Segregation

- Through a series of court cases spanning two decades, the Court slowly dismantled segregation in the schools, thanks in large part to the efforts of the NAACP, which undertook a two-prong approach to dismantling the separate-but-equal doctrine.
- The battle for desegregation culminated in the *Brown* cases in 1954 and 1955, in which a now-supportive Supreme Court declared segregated schools to be inherently unequal and therefore unconstitutional.
- While the initial order to undertake desegregation with "all deliberate speed" was ambiguous enough to avoid desegregation in practice altogether, by 1969 the Supreme Court ordered that segregated school systems be dismantled "at once."
- The Court also upheld the use of busing in those school districts that had deliberately drawn boundaries to maintain racial segregation in schools.

16.4 The Civil Rights Movement

- Gains in other spheres of civil rights came more slowly. The motivating force was the civil rights movement, led by Martin Luther King, Jr., until his assassination in 1968.

- King's efforts, along with those of many others, helped to bring about the Civil Rights Act, which was passed in 1964 and upheld in the courts by reason of the congressional power to regulate interstate commerce.
- Other court decisions had the effect of frustrating the enforcement of civil rights. In order to counteract these decisions, Congress took the lead by instituting laws that expanded and clarified the scope of civil rights law.

16.5 Civil Rights for Other Minorities

- Civil rights activism and the civil rights movement worked to the benefit of all minority groups—in fact, they benefited all Americans.
- Native Americans obtained some redress for past injustices, winning, for example, the return of lands in various states throughout the country.
- Immigrant groups press government for a stake in the American experience as they work to gain a better life in jobs that few citizens will do.
- Hispanics have come to recognize the importance of group action to achieve economic and political equality. By the mid-twenty-first century, they will be one-third of the population and possess greater political power.
- With enactment of the Americans with Disabilities Act (ADA) in 1990, disabled Americans won civil rights protections enjoyed by African Americans and others.
- Civil rights legislation removed the protectionism that was, in effect, legalized discrimination against women in education and employment.
- Homosexuals aim to follow the same path, but their quest for equality remains unfinished.

16.6 Gender and Equal Rights: The Women's Movement

- Despite legislative advances in the area of women's rights, including the passing of the Nineteenth Amendment, the states did not ratify the equal rights amendment.
- Legislation and judicial rulings implemented much of the amendment's provisions in practice.
- The Supreme Court now judges sex-based discrimination with "skeptical scrutiny," making distinctions based on sex almost as suspect as distinctions based on race.

16.7 Affirmative Action: Equal Opportunity or Equal Outcome?

- When programs make race the determining factor in awarding contracts, offering employment, or granting admission to educational institutions, the courts will be increasingly skeptical of their validity.
- However, the politics of affirmative action suggest that such programs are likely to remain persistent features on our political landscape.
- We can guarantee equal outcomes only if we restrict the free competition that is an integral part of equal opportunity.
- Many Americans object to policies that restrict individual freedom, such as quotas and set-asides that arbitrarily change the outcome of the race.
- The challenge of pluralist democracy is to balance the need for freedom with demands for equality.

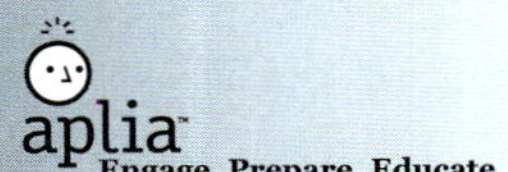

ASSESSING YOUR UNDERSTANDING WITH APLIA...YOUR VIRTUAL TUTOR!

16.1 Explain how the concepts of equality of opportunity and equality of outcome mirror the tension between freedom and equality.

1. Differentiate between equality of opportunity and equality of outcomes.
2. What is invidious discrimination? Provide examples of groups that have confronted this.

16.2 Trace the Supreme Court rulings and state legislative efforts that prevented African Americans from achieving "equal protection of the laws."

1. What was the purpose of the black codes?
2. How did the poll tax prevent black men from voting on election day?
3. Define the separate-but-equal doctrine and explain how it satisfied the Fourteenth Amendment while upholding racial segregation.

16.3 Identify the Supreme Court decisions that dismantled school segregation and explain the significance of each.

1. Explain the two-pronged attack undertaken by the NAACP to slowly chip away at racial segregation.
2. Why was the *Brown* v. *Board of Education* ruling so important for the fight against racial segregation?
3. What is the difference between de jure segregation and de facto segregation?

16.4 Describe the circumstances under which the 1964 Civil Rights Act was passed and its evolving interpretation in subsequent Supreme Court decisions.

1. What did Rosa Parks do that sparked a boycott of the bus system in Montgomery, Alabama?

2. Define civil disobedience and give two examples of it.
3. Identify the major provisions of the Civil Rights Act of 1964.
4. How did the *Grove City* decision and others like it frustrate the enforcement of civil rights laws?

16.5 Evaluate the effect of the civil rights movement on other minority groups' struggles for equality.

1. Why was assimilation an ineffective tool for successfully integrating Native Americans with the rest of American society?
2. Who was Cesar Chavez, and what did he do to improve the living conditions of immigrant farm workers?
3. Why did the vaguely worded definition of "disability" complicate lawsuits seeking to increase protections for people with disabilities?
4. What were the Stonewall Riots, and why were they important for the gay liberation movement?

16.6 Trace the evolution of women's legal rights beginning with laws based on protectionism and concluding with Supreme Court rulings prohibiting gender-based discrimination.

1. How did protectionism promote the discrimination of women?
2. What was the role of Susan B. Anthony in advancing the equal rights of women?
3. Define the concept of skeptical scrutiny.
4. Identify the reasons that the equal rights amendment (ERA) failed, and explain why the movement to pass the ERA nonetheless produced benefits for women.

16.7 **Compare and contrast the consequences that follow from policies aimed at equal opportunities versus those aimed at equal outcomes.**

1. Offer three reasons in support of affirmative action for minorities and then critique your reasons.
2. Why are explicit quota policies generally unpopular with the public?
3. What might explain the persistence of affirmative action policies despite their unpopularity with the majority?

KEY CASES

Plessy v. *Ferguson* (racial segregation constitutional, 1896)

Brown v. *Board of Education* (racial segregation unconstitutional, 1954)

Brown v. *Board of Education II* (racial desegregation implementation, 1955)

Boy Scouts of America v. *Dale* (association rights, Boy Scouts versus gays, 2000)

United States v. *Virginia* (gender equality, 1996)

Regents of the University of California v. *Bakke* (affirmative action, 1978)

Gratz v. *Bollinger* (affirmative action in college admissions, 2003)

Grutter v. *Bollinger* (affirmative action in law school admissions, 2003)

Parents Involved in Community Schools v. *Seattle School District No. 1* (public school racial diversity, 2007)

Fisher v. *University of Texas* (affirmative action in college admissions, 2012)

17 Economic Policy

"Blessed are the young, for they shall inherit the national debt," said former President Herbert Hoover to the Nebraska Republican Conference in January1936.[1] He had the misfortune of being president in 1929 when the stock market collapsed. Hoover, who lost the 1932 election to Franklin Delano Roosevelt, was speaking during the Great Depression prior to Roosevelt's overwhelming reelection in November 1936. In that year, the gross debt for the national government (sometimes called the national debt, sometimes the federal debt) was estimated at $33.8 billion.[2] In 2001—75 years later—it was $14,764 billion, gulp!

But that scary number does not take into account our country's economic and population growth over three-quarters of a century or inflation. A better method of comparing levels of national debt over time is by computing them as percentages of gross domestic product (GDP) (the total value of all goods and services produced in a given year). In 1936, our GDP was $83.8 billion; in 2011, it soared to $14,958.6 billion.[3] As a percentage of GDP, however, the national debt was 40.3 percent in 1936 and "only" 98.7 percent in 2011. Historically, it had been even higher, rising over 100 percent of GDP from 1945 to 1947 and not dropping below 90 percent until 1950. So our nation can tolerate heavy debt, but like heavy drinking and smoking, carrying a huge debt is not healthy.

How much of this debt do you owe? Let's do the math using round numbers. Dividing the 2011 national debt of $15,000 billion by the U.S. population of 311 million results in a little more than $48,000 per person. That is indeed bad news, but the good news is that not all the debt needs to be paid off. Nations—like families who borrow to buy homes and cars—are almost never debt-free. Since 1936, the national debt has averaged over 57 percent of the GDP, and it has never dropped below 30 percent. Regarding the national debt as a manageable problem leads one away from wailing in despair about the debt's magnitude to considering ways to pay it down.

As with household debt, our national debt should be reduced to avoid large annual interest payments, which limit spending for national needs. At present, the U.S. debt payments are relatively low due to historically low interest rates. However, interest rates will rise, and—as President Hoover implied—old people will die before the debt is paid down, leaving the task to the young. Young people may understand better how much money they will have tomorrow if they know more today about the economics of government.

How does the national debt relate to the current budget deficit? How did the deficit grow so large and prove so difficult to control against the spending appetites of Congress? More concretely, how is the national budget formulated? How much control of the domestic economy can government really exercise through the judicious use of economic theory? How much is the economy influenced by events that lie outside governmental control? What effects do government taxing and spending policies have on the economy and on economic equality? We address these questions in this chapter. As we shall see, no one person or organization controls the American economy; multiple actors have a voice in economic conditions. And not all of these actors are public—or American.

★ 17.1 Theories of Economic Policy

★ Compare and contrast three theories of market economics: laissez-faire, Keynesian, and supply-side.

Government efforts to control the economy rely on theories about how the economy responds to government taxing and spending policies and its control of the money supply. How policymakers tax and spend, and loosen and tighten interest rates, depends on their beliefs about how the economy functions and the proper role of government in the economy. The American economy is so complex that no one knows exactly how it works. Policymakers rely on economic theories to explain its functioning, and there are nearly as many theories as there are economists. Unfortunately, different theories (and economists) often predict different outcomes, sometimes due to different assumptions. Then too, abstract theories can clash with the real world. Still, despite disagreement among economists, knowledge of basic economics is necessary to understand how government approaches public policy.[4]

We are concerned here with economic policy in a market economy—one in which the prices of goods and services are determined through the interaction of sellers and buyers (that is, through supply and demand). This kind of economy is typical of the consumer-dominated societies of Western Europe and the United States. A nonmarket economy relies on government planners to determine both the prices of goods and the amounts that are produced. The old Soviet economy was a perfect example; the government owned and operated the major means of production.

Market economies are loosely called *capitalist economies*: they allow private individuals to own property; sell goods for profit in free, or open, markets; and accumulate wealth, called *capital*. Market economies often exhibit a mix of government and private ownership. For example, Britain has had more government-owned enterprises (railroads, broadcasting, and housing) than has the United States. China today contends that it has a *socialist market economy,* which depends on the private sector for economic growth but also directs and supports state-owned enterprises.[5] Competing economic theories differ largely on how free they say the markets should be—in other words, on government's role in directing the economy (see "Politics of Global Change: We Buy More, and We Borrow More").

Laissez-Faire Economics

The French term *laissez faire*, introduced in Chapter 1 and discussed again in Chapter 13, describes the absence of government control. The economic doctrine of laissez faire likens the operation of a free market to the process of natural selection.

Politics of Global Change

We Buy More, and We Borrow More

Globalization produces economic interdependence among nations. Over the past four decades, Americans have been buying more goods and services from other countries than we are selling to them. Foreigners have been using their profits to buy U.S. government securities, thus acquiring increasing shares of the "public" debt portion, which totaled over $10.1 trillion in 2011. (That number excludes over $4 billion in intragovernmental debts. See page 499.) In effect, foreigners have been lending us money to buy their goods and services.

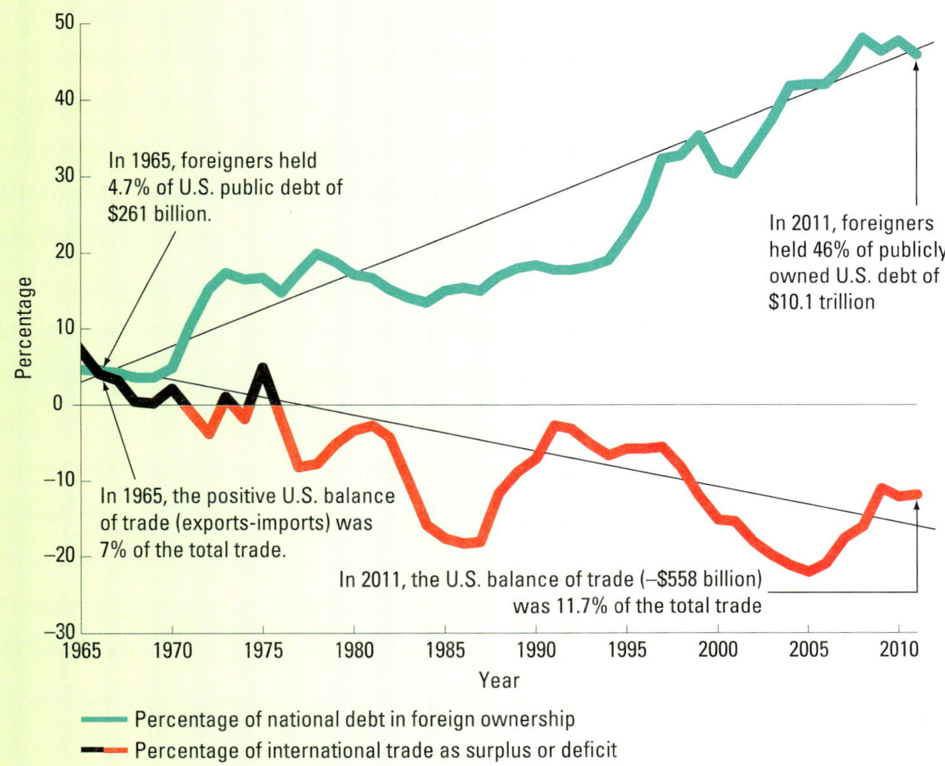

Source: Office of Management and Budget, "Table 6.7: Foreign Holdings of Federal Debt," in *Analytical Perspectives: Budget of the U.S. Government, Fiscal Year 2013* (Washington, D.C.: U.S. Government Printing Office, 2012); and U.S. Census Bureau, Foreign Trade Division, "U.S. Trade in Goods and Services, Balance of Payments (BOP) Basis," http://www.census.gov/foreign-trade/statistics/historical/gands.txt.

Economic competition weeds out the weak and preserves the strong. In the process, the economy prospers, and everyone eventually benefits.

Advocates of laissez-faire economics are fond of quoting Adam Smith's *The Wealth of Nations.* In his 1776 treatise, Smith argued that each individual, pursuing his own selfish interests in a competitive market, was "led by an invisible hand to promote an end which was no part of his intention." Smith's "invisible hand" has been used for two centuries to justify the belief that the narrow pursuit of profits

efficient market hypothesis
Financial markets are informationally efficient—they quickly absorb all relevant information about securities into their prices.

economic depression
A period of high unemployment and business failures; a severe, long-lasting downturn in a business cycle.

inflation
An economic condition characterized by price increases linked to a decrease in the value of the currency.

stagflation
The joint occurrence of slow growth, unemployment, and inflation.

business cycles
Expansions and contractions of business activity, the first accompanied by inflation and the second by unemployment.

serves the broad interests of society.[6] Strict advocates of laissez faire maintain that government interference with business tampers with the laws of nature, obstructing the workings of the free market. Mainstream economists today favor market principles but do recognize that "governments can sometimes improve market outcomes."[7] Within the last century, a companion principle, the **efficient market hypothesis**, has held that financial markets are informationally efficient—they quickly absorb all relevant information about securities into their prices. It implies that securities are priced and traded at their fair value, meaning that investors cannot "beat the market." If the market is rational, attempts to regulate it become irrational.[8]

Today, laissez-faire thought is associated with the "Austrian school" of economics. A leading theorist of the Austrian school, Friedrich Hayek, won the 1974 Nobel Prize for economics. In *Road to Serfdom*, Hayek warned that tyranny inevitably results from government control of economic decision making. In contemporary politics, Hayek is often cited by libertarians in defense of free-market capitalism and in opposition to Keynesian economics.

Keynesian Theory

According to laissez-faire economics, our government should have done nothing when markets across the world crashed in February 2008 and threatened our economy. Laissez-faire economics holds that government should do little about **economic depression** (a period of high unemployment and business failures); or raging **inflation** (price increases that decrease the value of currency); or—for that matter— **stagflation** (the joint occurrence of slow growth, unemployment, and inflation of the 1970s). Inflation is ordinarily measured by the consumer price index (CPI). (See "What Do You Know about the Consumer Price Index?") Since the beginning of the Industrial Revolution, capitalist economies have suffered through many cyclical fluctuations. Since 1857, the United States has experienced more than thirty of these **business cycles**: expansions and contractions of business activity, the first stage

WHAT DO YOU KNOW ABOUT...

THE CONSUMER PRICE INDEX?

Inflation in the United States is usually measured in terms of the consumer price index (CPI), which is calculated by the U.S. Bureau of Labor Statistics (BLS). The CPI is based on prices paid for food, clothing, shelter, transportation, medical services, and other items necessary for daily living. Data are collected from eighty-seven areas across the country, from over fifty thousand homes and more than twenty thousand businesses. The CPI is thoroughly reviewed about every ten years, most recently in 1998. Moreover, the BLS has since made many adjustments in the index.

The CPI is not a perfect measure of inflation. For example, it does not differentiate between inflationary price increases and other price increases. An automobile bought in 1990 is not the same as one bought in 2012. Any price increase for the same model reflects an improved product as well as a decrease in the value of the dollar. Another problem is the CPI's delay in reflecting changes in buying habits. VCRs were around for several years before they were included among the hundreds of items in the index; the prices of cell phones were not in the 2009 index.

These are minor issues compared with the changing weight given to the cost of housing. Before 1983, the cost of purchasing and financing a home accounted for 26 accompanied by inflation and the second stage by unemployment.[9] No widely accepted theory explained these cycles until the Great Depression of the 1930s.

That was when John Maynard Keynes, a British economist, theorized that business cycles stem from imbalances between aggregate demand and productive capacity. **Aggregate demand** is the total income that consumers, business, and government wish to spend on goods and services. **Productive capacity** is the total value of goods and services that can be produced when the economy is working at full capacity. The value of the goods and services actually produced is called the **gross domestic product (GDP)**. When demand exceeds productive capacity, people are willing to pay more for available goods, which leads to price inflation. When productive capacity exceeds demand, producers cut back on their output of goods, which leads to unemployment. When many people are unemployed for an extended period, the economy is in a depression. Keynes theorized that government could stabilize the economy (and smooth out or eliminate business cycles) by controlling the level of aggregate demand.

Keynesian theory holds that aggregate demand can be adjusted through a combination of fiscal and monetary policies.[10] **Fiscal policies**, which are enacted by the president and Congress, involve changes in government spending and taxing. When demand is too low, according to Keynes, government should either spend more itself, hiring people and thus giving them money, or cut taxes, giving people more of their own money to spend. When demand is too great, the government should either spend less or raise taxes, giving people less money to spend. **Monetary policies**, which are largely determined by the Federal Reserve Board, involve changes in the money supply and operate less directly on the economy. Increasing the amount of money in circulation increases aggregate demand and thus increases price inflation. Decreasing the money supply decreases aggregate demand and inflationary pressures.

Despite some problems with the assumptions of Keynesian theory, capitalist countries have widely adopted it in some form.[11] At one time or another, virtually all

aggregate demand
The total income that consumers, businesses, and government wish to spend for goods and services.

productive capacity
The total value of goods and services that can be produced when the economy works at full capacity.

gross domestic product (GDP)
The total value of the goods and services produced by a country during a year.

Keynesian theory
An economic theory stating that the government can stabilize the economy—that is, can smooth business cycles—by controlling the level of aggregate demand, and that the level of aggregate demand can be controlled by means of fiscal and monetary policies.

fiscal policies
Economic policies that involve government spending and taxing.

monetary policies
Economic policies that involve control of, and changes in, the supply of money.

---

percent of the CPI, which neglected the reality that few people buy a home every year—and many people rent. Since 1983, the BLS figured the cost of renting equivalent housing as only 15 percent of the CPI. In recent years, the BLS has released a "core" CPI that excludes the costs of food and energy, which fluctuate more widely than what has become known as the standard, or "headline," CPI.

The government incorporates the standard CPI in cost-of-living adjustments for civil service and military pension payments and Social Security benefits. Moreover, union wage contracts with private businesses are often indexed (tied) to the CPI. As the CPI tends to rise each year, so do payments that are tied to it. In this way, CPI indexing promotes both the growth of government spending and inflation itself. The United States is one of the few nations that also ties its tax brackets to a price index, which reduces government revenues by eliminating the effect of inflation on taxpayer incomes.

Despite its faults, the CPI is at least a consistent measure of prices, and it is likely to continue as the basis for adjustments to wages, benefits, and payments affecting millions of people.

Source: Bureau of Labor Statistics, "The Consumer Price Index— January 2012," http://www.bls.gov/news.release/pdf/cpi.pdf. Unfortunately, the CPI captures costs of goods better than costs of services, such as medical care, insurance, and education. Thus, many citizens complain of rising prices while the CPI stays low.

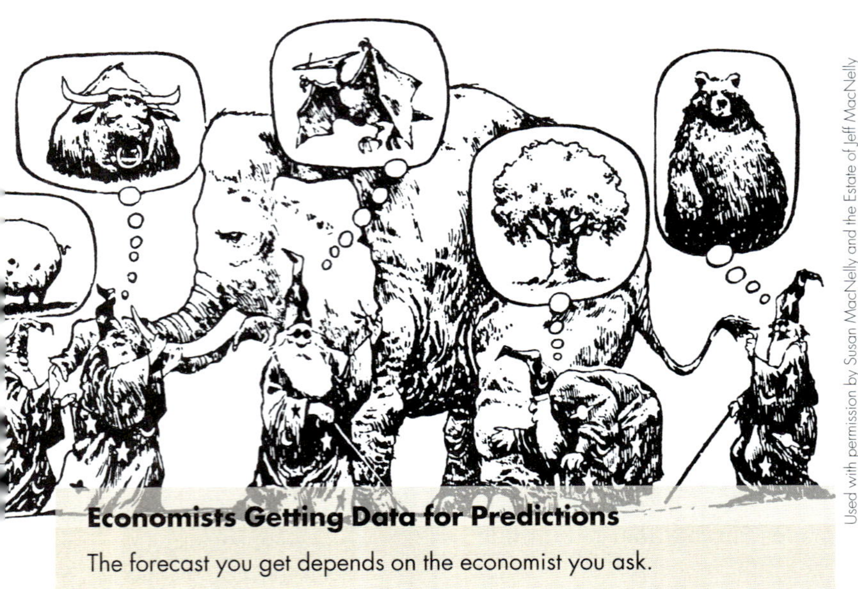

Economists Getting Data for Predictions

The forecast you get depends on the economist you ask.

Used with permission by Susan MacNelly and the Estate of Jeff MacNelly

deficit financing

The Keynesian technique of spending beyond government income to combat an economic slump. Its purpose is to inject extra money into the economy to stimulate aggregate demand.

have used the Keynesian technique of **deficit financing**—spending in excess of tax revenues—to combat an economic slump. Because a slump lowers profits and wages, it reduces tax revenues—thus generating a budget deficit all by itself. Prior to Keynes, economists prescribed raising taxes and cutting spending to bring the budget back into balance. That only reduced aggregate demand and worsened the recession. The objective of deficit financing is to increase demand for goods and services, either directly by increasing government purchases or indirectly by cutting taxes to generate more after-tax income to spend. Most deficits are financed with funds borrowed through the issuing of government bonds, notes, or other securities. The theory holds that deficits can be paid off with budget surpluses after the economy recovers.

Because Keynesian theory requires government to play an active role in controlling the economy, it runs counter to laissez-faire economics. Before Keynes, no administration in Washington would shoulder responsibility for maintaining a healthy economy. In 1946, the year Keynes died, Congress passed an employment act establishing "the continuing responsibility of the national government to … promote maximum employment, production and purchasing power." The Employment Act of 1946, which reflected Keynesian theory, had a tremendous effect on government economic policy. Many people believe it was the primary source of "big government" in America. Even Richard Nixon, a conservative president, admitted in 1971 that "we are all Keynesians now," by accepting government responsibility for the economy. But not all conservatives buy into that philosophy. In a 2008 editorial, "We're All Keynesians Now," the *Wall Street Journal* deplored Bush's $168 billion fiscal stimulus package of tax rebates to forestall a recession as taking money from one pocket (those with high income) and handing it to another (those with low to moderate income).[12]

For economically oriented and ideologically committed partisans, the 2012 presidential contest turned into slugfest between Keynes' supporters and those who followed Friedrich Hayek. Obama heralded the bailout of the auto industry (à la Keynes), whereas Mitt Romney wrote a 2008 op-ed piece, "Let Detroit Go Bankrupt" (à la Hayek). An observer outlined the issue: "A trillion-dollar Keynesian stimulus was quickly followed by a Hayekian wave of buyers' remorse that deemed that the swift reduction of the national debt was more important than giving jobs to the unemployed."[13] In November 2011, the Asia Society held a Keynes-Hayek debate on Park Avenue in New York between two teams of economists. The audience divided slightly in favor of Keynes afterward.[14] The hot topic, Keynes versus Hayek, generated YouTube videos, and new books appeared extolling both Keynes and Hayek.[15]

Monetary Policy

Although most economists accept Keynesian theory in its broad outlines, they depreciate its political utility. Some especially question the value of fiscal policies in controlling inflation and unemployment. They argue that government spending programs take too long to enact in Congress and to implement through the bureaucracy. As a result, jobs are created not when they are needed but years later, when the crisis may have passed and government spending needs to be reduced.

Also, government spending is easier to start than to stop because the groups that benefit from spending programs tend to defend them even when they are no longer needed. A similar criticism applies to tax policies. Politically, it is much easier to cut taxes than to raise them. In other words, Keynesian theory requires that governments be able to begin and end spending quickly and to cut and raise taxes quickly. But in the real world, these fiscal tools are easier to use in one direction than the other.

Recognizing these limitations of fiscal policies, **monetarists** argue that government can control the economy's performance simply by controlling the nation's money supply.[16] Staunch monetarists, like Nobel Laureate Milton Friedman, favor a long-range policy of small but steady growth in the amount of money in circulation rather than frequent manipulation of monetary policies.

Monetary policies in the United States are under the control of the **Federal Reserve System**, which acts as the country's central bank. Established in 1913, the Fed by law has three major goals: controlling inflation, maintaining maximum employment, and insuring moderate interest rates.[17] The Fed is not a single bank but a system of banks. At the top of the system is the board of governors, seven

Courtesy Emergent Order

Dueling Economists on YouTube

This image from a YouTube video portrays British economist John Maynard Keynes (left) and Austrian economist Friedrich Hayek (right). Keynes taught at Cambridge University but had enormous influence on American economics and government. Keynes's *The General Theory of Employment* (1936) advocated deficit spending during economic downturns to maintain employment. Keynesian theory fell out of favor in the 1980s, but Presidents Bush and Obama both embraced it to deal with the 2008 economic collapse. Hayek taught at the University of Chicago and elsewhere in the United States. His *The Road to Serfdom* (1944) argued that government intervention led to socialism and tyranny. Hayek's advocacy of free-market capitalism enjoyed popularity among Republicans in 2012 who objected to the government bailout of the auto industry. The ten-minute YouTube video, "Keynes vs. Hayek: Round Two," reflects their clashing views from a libertarian perspective. Ironically, Keynes and Hayek were colleagues at Cambridge briefly during World War II and respected each other's work. See Nicholas Wapshott, *Keynes Hayek: The Clash That Defined Modern Economics* (New York: W.W. Norton, 2011).

members appointed by the president for staggered terms of fourteen years. The president designates one member of the board to be its chairperson, who serves a four-year term that extends beyond the president's term of office. This complex arrangement was intended to make the board independent of the president and even of Congress. An independent board, the reasoning went, would be able to make financial decisions for the nation without regard to their political implications.[18] Following the Fed's bold actions taken to combat the financial crisis in 2008, however, members of Congress proposed auditing Fed decisions for the first time. By the summer of 2010, when President Obama signed the sweeping Dodd-Frank financial reform bill, the Fed was granted even greater powers to regulate large complex financial firms.[19]

The Fed controls the money supply, which affects inflation, in three ways. Most important, the Fed can sell and buy government securities (such as U.S. Treasury bills) on the open market. When the Fed sells securities, it takes money out of circulation, thereby making money scarce and raising the interest rate. When the Fed buys securities, the process works in reverse, lowering interest rates. The Fed also sets a target for the *federal funds rate*, which banks charge one another for overnight loans and which is usually cited when newspapers write, "The Fed has decided to lower [or raise] interest rates." Less frequently (for technical reasons), the Fed may change its

monetarists
Those who argue that government can effectively control the performance of an economy mainly by controlling the supply of money.

Federal Reserve System
The system of banks that acts as the central bank of the United States and controls major monetary policies.

discount rate, the interest rate that member banks have to pay to borrow money from a Federal Reserve bank. Finally, the Fed can change its *reserve requirement,* which is the amount of cash that member banks must keep on deposit in their regional Federal Reserve bank. An increase in the reserve requirement reduces the amount of money banks have available to lend.[20]

Basic economic theory holds that interest rates should be raised to discourage borrowing and spending when the economy is growing too quickly (this combats inflation) and lowered when the economy is sluggish (thus increasing the money flow to encourage spending and economic growth). Historically, the Fed has adjusted interest rates to combat inflation rather than to stimulate economic growth, which would maximize employment.[21] (A former Fed chairman once said its task was "to remove the punch bowl when the party gets going.")[22] That is, the Fed would dampen economic growth before it leads to serious inflation.

Accordingly, some charge that the Fed acts to further interests of the wealthy (who fear rampant inflation) more than interests of the poor (who fear widespread unemployment). Why so? Although all classes of citizens complain about increasing costs of living, inflation usually harms upper classes (creditors) more than lower classes (debtors). To illustrate, suppose someone borrows $20,000, to be repaid after ten years, during which the inflation rate was 10 percent. When the loan is due, the $20,000 borrowed is "worth" only $18,000. Debtors find the cheaper money easier to raise, and creditors are paid less than the original value of their loan. Hence, wealthy people fear severe inflation, which can erode the value of their saved wealth. As one Federal Reserve bank bluntly stated, "Debtors gain when inflation is unexpectedly high, and creditors gain when it is unexpectedly low."[23]

Formally, the president is responsible for the state of the economy, and voters hold him accountable. As the economy deteriorated in 2008, more people blamed President Bush for its poor performance than blamed Congress, multinational corporations, or financial institutions.[24] However, the president neither determines interest rates (the Fed does) nor controls spending (Congress does). In this respect, all presidents since 1913 have had to work with a Fed made independent of both the president and Congress, and all have had to deal with the fact that Congress ultimately controls spending. These restrictions on presidential authority are consistent with the pluralist model of democracy, but a president held responsible for the economy may not appreciate that theoretical argument.

Although the Fed's economic policies are not perfectly insulated from political concerns, they are sufficiently independent that the president is not able to control monetary policy without the Fed's cooperation. This means that the president cannot be held completely responsible for the state of the economy. Nevertheless, the public blames presidents for poor economic conditions and votes against them in elections. Naturally, a strong economy favors the incumbent party. When people are optimistic about the economic future and feel that they are doing well, they typically see no reason to change the party controlling the White House. But when conditions are bad or worsening, voters often decide to seek a change.

The Fed's activities are essential parts of the government's overall economic policy, but they lie outside the direct control of the president—and directly in the hands of the chair of the Federal Reserve Board. This makes the Fed chair a critical player in economic affairs and can create problems in coordinating economic policy. For example, the president might want the Fed to lower interest rates to stimulate the economy, but the Fed might resist for fear of inflation. Such policy clashes can pit the chair of the Federal Reserve Board directly against the president. So presidents typically court the Fed chair, even one who served a president of the other party.

Appointed Fed chair in 2006 by President Bush, Ben Bernanke replaced Alan Greenspan, who held the post for almost twenty years and was praised for overseeing an economy with low inflation, low unemployment, and strong growth. Greenspan, who believed that markets knew best and should be left unregulated (in keeping with the "efficient market hypothesis"), was later blamed for the financial crisis of 2008. Called before a House committee in October, Greenspan admitted that his "whole intellectual edifice collapsed in the summer," when banks held nearly worthless securities that had tumbled from dizzyingly high values.[25] Criticized for his complacency prior to the crisis, Bernanke acted boldly during it to rescue the economy, stretching the Fed's authority by arranging bank purchases, emergency loan programs, and the lowest interest rates in American history.[26] Named *Time* magazine "Person of the Year" in 2009, Bernanke was reappointed by Obama and confirmed in 2010 for another term.

Historical evidence suggests that government can indeed slow down and smooth out the booms and busts of business cycles through active use of monetary and fiscal policies. From 1855 through World War II—prior to the active employment of Keynesian theory—the nation suffered through economic recessions 42 percent of the time, with each recession averaging twenty-one months. Since then and through June 2007, the nation was in a recession only 16 percent of the time, and the average duration lasted only ten months.[27] The recession that began in December 2007 lasted for 18 months, officially ending in June 2009. However, unemployment remained over 8 percent during most of the year prior to the 2012 presidential election.

Supply-Side Economics

When Reagan came to office in 1981, he embraced a school of thought called **supply-side economics** to deal with the stagflation (both unemployment and inflation) that the nation was experiencing. Keynesian theory argues that inflation results when consumers, businesses, and governments have more money to spend than there are goods and services to buy. The standard Keynesian solution is to reduce demand (for example, by increasing taxes). Supply-siders argue that inflation can be lowered more effectively by increasing the supply of goods (that is, they stress the supply side of the economic equation). Specifically, they favor tax cuts to stimulate investment (which leads to the production of more goods) and less government regulation of business (again, to increase productivity—which they hold will yield more, not less, government revenue). Supply-siders also argue that the rich should receive larger tax cuts than the poor because the rich have more money to invest. The benefits of increased investment will then "trickle down" to working people in the form of additional jobs and income.

In a sense, supply-side economics resembles laissez-faire economics because it prefers fewer government programs and regulations and less taxation. Supply-siders believe that government interferes too much with the efforts of individuals to work, save, and invest. Inspired by supply-side theory, Reagan proposed (and got) massive tax cuts in the Economic Recovery Tax Act of 1981. The act reduced individual tax rates by 23 percent over a three-year period and cut the marginal tax rate for the highest income group from 70 to 50 percent. Reagan also launched a program to deregulate business. According to supply-side theory, these actions would generate extra government revenue, making spending cuts unnecessary to balance the budget. Nevertheless, Reagan also cut funding for some domestic programs, including Aid to Families with Dependent Children. Contrary to supply-side theory, he also proposed hefty increases in military spending. This blend of tax cuts, deregulation, cuts in

supply-side economics
Economic policies aimed at increasing the supply of goods (as opposed to decreasing demand); consists mainly of tax cuts for possible investors and less regulation of business.

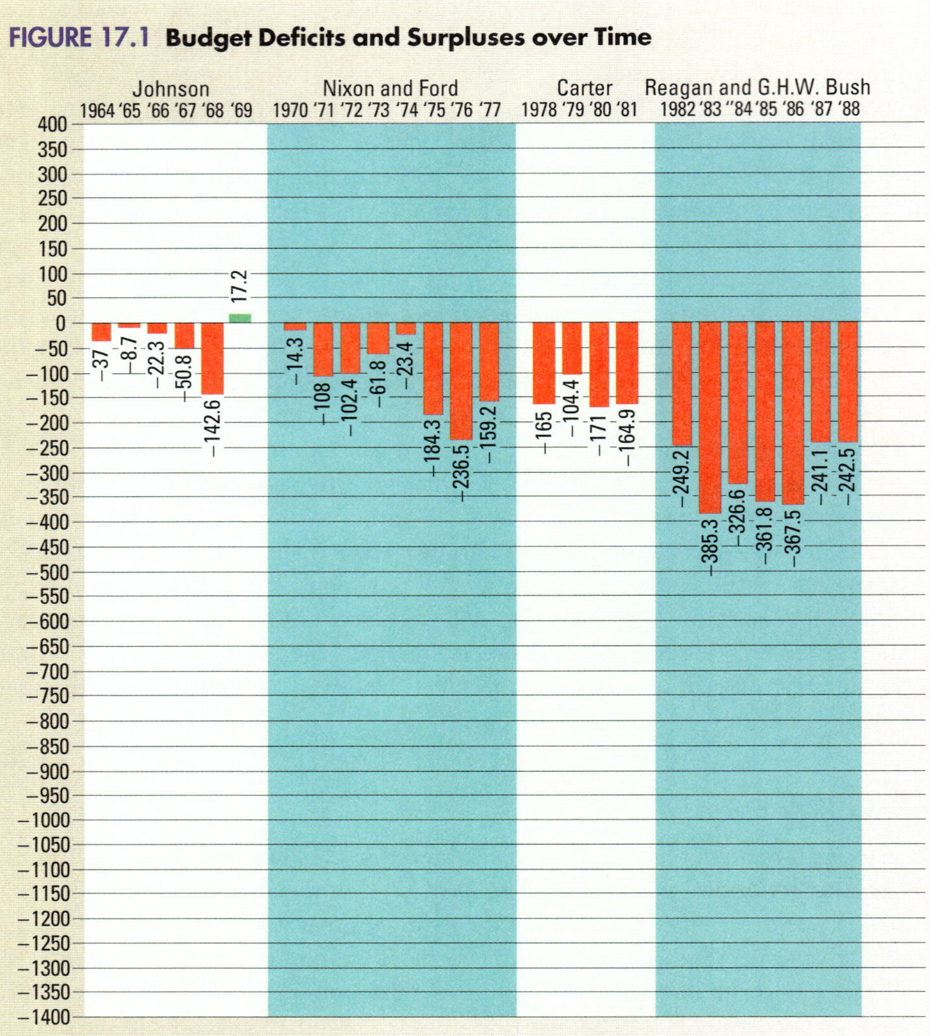

FIGURE 17.1 Budget Deficits and Surpluses over Time

This chart shows the actual deficits and surpluses as a percentage of the gross domestic product incurred under administrations from Johnson to Obama. The deficits were enormous under Reagan, George H. W. Bush, and even during Clinton's early years. Budget deficits were eventually eliminated under Clinton and replaced by surpluses. Larger deficits appeared again under George W. Bush and Barack Obama.
Source: Executive Office of the President, *Budget of the United States Government, Fiscal Year 2013: Historical Tables* (Washington, D.C.: U.S. Government Printing Office, 2012), Table l.3.

spending for social programs, and increases in spending for defense became known, somewhat disparagingly, as *Reaganomics*.

How well did Reaganomics work? Inflation, which ran over 13 percent in 1981, was lowered to about 3 percent by 1983, but that was due mostly to Federal Reserve chair Paul Volcker raising interest rates to 20 percent. Although Reaganomics worked largely as expected in the area of industry deregulation, unemployment increased to 9.6 percent in 1983, and it failed massively to reduce the budget deficit. Contrary to supply-side theory, the 1981 tax cut was accompanied by a massive drop in tax revenues. Shortly after taking office, Reagan promised that his economic policies would balance the annual budget by 1984. In fact, lower tax revenues and higher defense spending produced the largest budget deficits to that time, as shown in Figure 17.1.[28] Budget deficits continued until 1998, when a booming U.S. economy—plus increased tax rates (see below)—generated the first

FIGURE 17.1 **(Continued)**

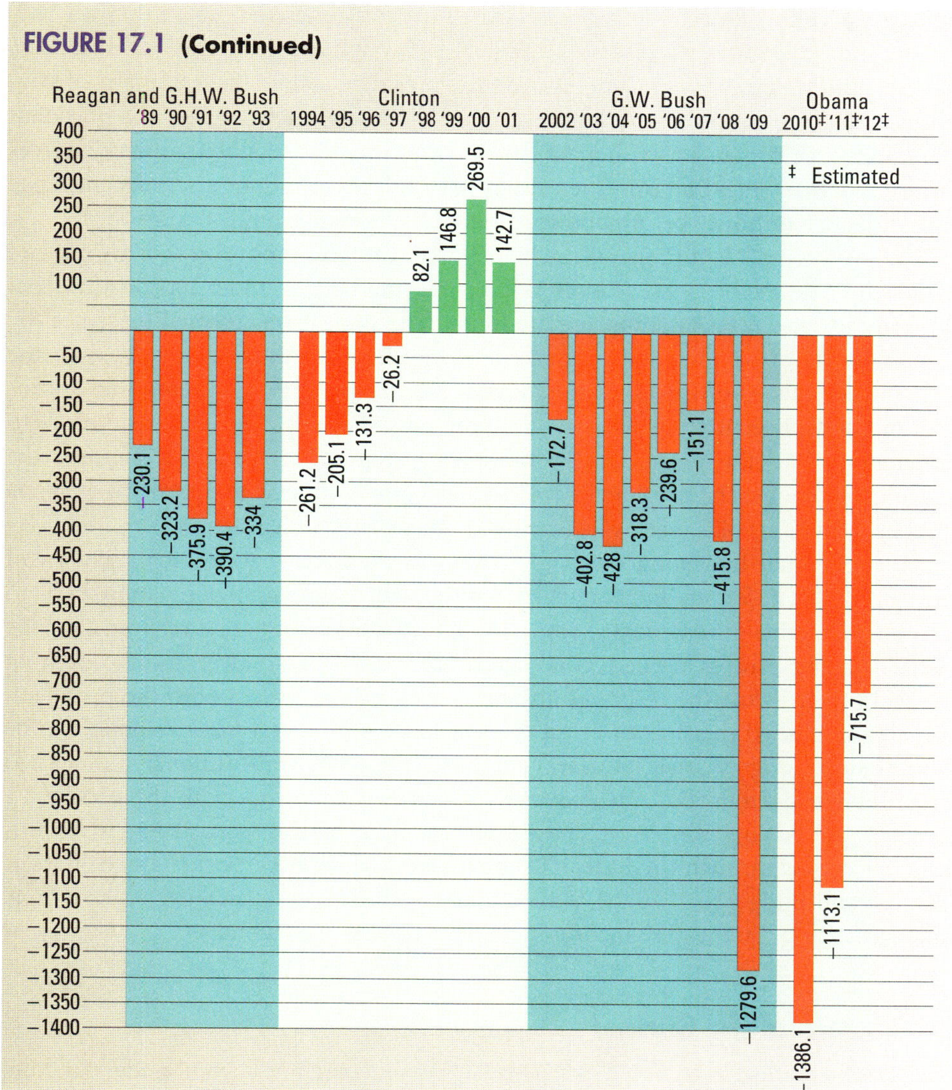

budget surplus since 1969. Economist Gregory Mankiw, advisor to President Bush, said that history failed to confirm the main conjecture of supply-side economics: that lower tax revenues would raise tax revenues: "When Reagan cut taxes after he was elected, the result was less tax revenue, not more."[29] Nevertheless, the supply-side idea that cutting taxes raises more revenue is still popular.[30]

17.2 Public Policy and the Budget

★ Describe the process by which the national budget is prepared and passed into law and the reforms undertaken by Congress to balance the budget.

To most people the national budget is B-O-R-I-N-G. To national politicians, it is an exciting script for high drama. The numbers, categories, and percentages that numb normal minds cause politicians' nostrils to flare and their hearts to pound. The budget is a battlefield on which politicians wage war over the programs they support.

Control of the budget is important to members of Congress because they are politicians, and politicians want to wield power, not watch someone else wield it. Also, the Constitution established Congress, not the president, as the "first branch" of government and the people's representatives. Unfortunately for Congress, the president has emerged as the leader in shaping the budget. Although Congress often disagrees with presidential spending priorities, it has been unable to mount a serious challenge to presidential authority by presenting a coherent alternative budget.

Today, the president prepares the budget, and Congress approves it. This was not always the case. Before 1921, Congress prepared the budget under its constitutional authority to raise taxes and appropriate funds. The budget was formed piecemeal by enacting a series of laws that originated in the many committees involved in the highly decentralized process of raising revenue, authorizing expenditures, and appropriating funds. Executive agencies even submitted their budgetary requests directly to Congress, not to the president. No one was responsible for the big picture—the budget as a whole. The president's role was essentially limited to approving revenue and appropriations bills, just as he approved other pieces of legislation.

Congressional budgeting (such as it was) worked well enough for a nation of farmers, but not for an industrialized nation with a growing population and an increasingly active government. Soon after World War I, Congress realized that the budget-making process needed to be centralized. With the Budget and Accounting Act of 1921, it thrust the responsibility for preparing the budget onto the president. The act established the Bureau of the Budget to prepare the *president's* budget to be submitted to Congress each January. Congress retained its constitutional authority to raise and spend funds, but now Congress would begin its work with the president's budget as its starting point. And all executive agencies' budget requests had to be funneled for review through the Bureau of the Budget (which became the Office of Management and Budget in 1970); those consistent with the president's overall economic and legislative program were incorporated into the president's budget.

The Nature of the Budget

The national budget is complex. But its basic elements are not beyond understanding. We begin with some definitions. The *Budget of the United States Government* is the annual financial plan that the president is required to submit to Congress at the start of each year. It applies to the *next* **fiscal year**, the interval the government uses for accounting purposes. Currently, the fiscal year runs from October 1 to September 30. The budget is named for the year in which it *ends*, so the fiscal year (FY) 2013 budget that Obama submitted in early 2012 applies to the twelve months from October 1, 2012, to September 30, 2013.

Broadly, the budget defines **budget authority** (how much government agencies are authorized to spend on current and future programs); **budget outlays**, or expenditures (how much agencies are expected to spend this year, which includes past authorizations); and **receipts** (how much is expected in taxes and other revenues). President Obama's FY 2013 budget contained *authority* for expenditures of $3,667 billion, but it provided for *outlays* of $3,803 billion (including some previous obligations). His budget also anticipated *receipts* of $2,902 billion in current dollars, leaving an estimated *deficit* of $901 billion—the difference between receipts and outlays.

When the U.S. government runs a deficit, it borrows funds on a massive scale to finance its operation that fiscal year, thus limiting the supply of loanable funds for business investment. However, economists seemed more concerned about the accumulated government debt, not the annual deficit.[31] A deficit in the annual budget is different

fiscal year
The twelve-month period from October 1 to September 30 used by the government for accounting purposes. A fiscal year budget is named for the year in which it ends.

budget authority
The amounts that government agencies are authorized to spend for current and future programs.

budget outlays
The amounts that government agencies are expected to spend in the fiscal year.

receipts
For a government, the amount expected or obtained in taxes and other revenues.

from the **national debt**, which represents the sum of all unpaid government deficits. On March 2, 2012, the total national debt was $15.4 trillion.[32] Various "national debt clocks" calculate real-time estimates of the total national debt.[33] However, about $4.7 billion of the total debt is "intragovernmental"—money that one part of the government owes to another part. Concerning the $10.7 trillion of "public" debt—money owed to lenders outside the government—almost 50 percent was held by institutions or individuals in other countries (see page 489).[34] If foreign lenders were to stop financing America's governmental annual deficit and national debt, the economy could suffer a serious blow. During the 2008–2012 recession in Europe and the associated economic crises in Greece, Italy, Portugal, and Spain, foreign lenders fled to the safety of U.S. Treasury notes, buying them even at very low interest rates.[35]

national debt
The accumulated sum of past government borrowing owed to lenders outside the government.

Preparing the President's Budget

The budget that the president submits to Congress each winter is the end product of a process that begins the previous spring under the supervision of the **Office of Management and Budget (OMB)**. The OMB is located within the Executive Office of the President and is headed by a director appointed by the president, with the approval of the Senate. The OMB, with a staff of more than five hundred, is the most powerful domestic agency in the bureaucracy, and its director, who attends meetings of the president's cabinet, is one of the most powerful figures in government. The federal budget, with appendixes, is now available electronically on the OMB website.[36] Thousands of pages long, the budget contains more than numbers. It also explains individual spending programs in terms of national needs and agency objectives, and it analyzes proposed taxes and other receipts. Each year, reporters, lobbyists, and political analysts anxiously await publication of the president's budget, eager to learn his plans for government spending in the coming year.

Office of Management and Budget (OMB)
The budgeting arm of the Executive Office; prepares the president's budget.

The OMB initiates the budget process each spring by meeting with the president to discuss the economic situation and his budgetary priorities. It then sends broad budgeting guidelines to every government agency and requests their initial projection of how much money they will need for the next fiscal year. The OMB assembles this information and makes recommendations to the president, who then develops more precise guidelines describing how much each is likely to get. By summer, the agencies are asked to prepare budgets based on the new guidelines. By fall, they submit their formal budgets to the OMB, where budget analysts scrutinize agency requests, considering both their costs and their consistency with the president's legislative program. A lot of politicking goes on at this stage, as agency heads try to circumvent the OMB by pleading for their pet projects with presidential advisers and perhaps even the president himself.

Political negotiations over the budget may extend into the early winter—and often until it goes to the printer. The voluminous document looks very much like a finished product, but the figures it contains are not final. In giving the president the responsibility for preparing the budget in 1921, Congress simply provided itself with a starting point for its own work. And even with this head start, Congress has a hard time disciplining itself to produce a coherent, balanced budget.

Passing the Congressional Budget

The president's budget must be approved by Congress. Its process for doing so is a creaky conglomeration of traditional procedures overlaid with structural reforms from the 1970s, external constraints from the 1980s, and changes introduced by the

1990 Budget Enforcement Act. The cumbersome process has had difficulty producing a budget according to Congress's own timetable.

The Traditional Procedure: The Committee Structure. Traditionally, the tasks of budget making were divided among a number of committees, a process that has been retained. Three types of committees are involved in budgeting:

- **Tax committees** are responsible for raising the revenues to run the government. The Ways and Means Committee in the House and the Finance Committee in the Senate consider all proposals for taxes, tariffs, and other receipts contained in the president's budget.
- **Authorization committees** (such as the House Armed Services Committee and the Senate Banking, Housing, and Urban Affairs Committee) have jurisdiction over particular legislative subjects. The House has about twenty committees that can authorize spending and the Senate about fifteen. Each pores over the portions of the budget that pertain to its area of responsibility. However, in recent years, power has shifted from the authorization committees to the appropriations committees.
- **Appropriations committees** decide which of the programs approved by the authorization committees will actually be funded (that is, given money to spend). For example, the House Armed Services Committee might propose building a new line of tanks for the army, and it might succeed in getting this proposal enacted into law. But the tanks will never be built unless the appropriations committees appropriate funds for that purpose. Thirteen distinct appropriations bills are supposed to be enacted each year to fund the nation's spending.

Two serious problems are inherent in a budgeting process that involves three distinct kinds of congressional committees. First, the two-step spending process (first authorization, then appropriation) is complex; it offers wonderful opportunities for interest groups to get into the budgeting act in the spirit of pluralist democracy. Second, because one group of legislators in each house plans for revenues and many other groups plan for spending, no one is responsible for the budget as a whole.

In the 1970s, Congress added a new committee structure to combat the pluralist politics inherent in the old procedures and make budget choices in a more majoritarian manner, by roll-call votes in both chambers. The Budget and Impoundment Control Act of 1974 retained all the tax and appropriations committees (and chairpersons), while superimposing new House and Senate budget committees over the old committee structure. It created **budget committees** to supervise a comprehensive budget review process, aided by a new **Congressional Budget Office (CBO)**, with a staff of more than two hundred, to supply budgetary expertise equal to the president's OMB, so it can prepare credible alternative budgets for Congress. Congress still failed to prevent running up annual budget deficits.

Congress tried again by passing the **Budget Enforcement Act (BEA)** of 1990, which defined two types of spending: **mandatory spending** and **discretionary spending**. Spending is mandatory for programs that have become **entitlements** (such as Social Security and veterans' pensions), which provide benefits to individuals legally entitled to them (see Chapter 18) and cannot be reduced without changing the law. Discretionary spending, including annual military expenditures, was subject to limits, or caps.

In 1997, President Clinton and Congress negotiated the **Balanced Budget Act**, which accomplished what most observers thought was beyond political possibility. It not only led to the balanced budget it promised but actually produced a budget surplus ahead of schedule—the first surplus since 1969. In the early 2000s, President Bush and Republicans in Congress advocated using the budget surplus for large

tax committees
The two committees of Congress responsible for raising the revenue with which to run the government.

authorization committees
Committees of Congress that can authorize spending in their particular areas of responsibility.

appropriations committees
Committees of Congress that decide which of the programs passed by the authorization committees will actually be funded.

budget committees
One committee in each house of Congress that supervises a comprehensive budget review process.

Congressional Budget Office (CBO)
The budgeting arm of Congress, which prepares alternative budgets to those prepared by the president's OMB.

Budget Enforcement Act (BEA)
A 1990 law that distinguished between mandatory and discretionary spending.

mandatory spending
In the Budget Enforcement Act of 1990, expenditures required by previous commitments.

discretionary spending
In the Budget Enforcement Act of 1990, authorized expenditures from annual appropriations.

entitlements
Benefits to which every eligible person has a legal right and that the government cannot deny.

Balanced Budget Act
A 1997 law that promised to balance the budget by 2002.

across-the-board tax cuts to return money to taxpayers.[37] Although the caps on discretionary spending, established by the 1990 Budget Enforcement Act, helped balance the budget entering 2000, many members of Congress in both parties resented its restrictions on their freedom to make fiscal decisions. Accordingly, Congress allowed the caps on discretionary spending to expire at the end of 2002.[38] Since 2002, the government has run budget deficits, not surpluses.

Repeated failures to eliminate annual budget deficits renewed calls for a constitutional amendment requiring Congress to balance the budget—as required by most state constitutions. Congressional proposals for a balanced budget amendment (BBA) were first introduced in 1936 and often since.[39] House Republicans tried again in 2011 but failed to win the needed two-thirds vote. Democrats opposed it for reasons similar to those given by most economists: a serious BBA would prevent the government from running a deficit to simulate the economy. Some conservatives feared that a BBA would increase the courts' role in deciding government spending cases certain to arise under it.[40] Others noted that Congress could pass balanced budgets if it wished without a Constitutional requirement, which would only encourage Congress to work around the law to increase deficits. That is what Congress did after passing the Gramm-Rudman-Hollings Balanced Budget and Emergency Deficit Control Act in 1985. It set annually decreasing deficit targets that would trigger automatic spending cuts if not met. Each year, Congress simply raised the targets to meet them. The law was an utter failure, and the deficit targets were eliminated in 1990.

Congress's failure to limit the national debt is similar and instructive. Prior to World War II, Congress limited indebtedness to $45 billion, only 10 percent above the existing debt of $40.4 billion.[41] Every time the debt neared its legal limit—over 100 times since 1940—Congress repeatedly raised the ceiling.[42] Under pressure from the tea party movement in 2011, congressional Republicans opposed raising the debt ceiling again, but financial groups within the Republican Party argued that failing to pay our debts would cause financial chaos.[43] Congress complied once more. Given that the debt ceiling causes so much partisan rancor and that only one other modern democracy (Denmark) legislates a similar debt ceiling, one wonder why it exists at all.[44]

17.3 Tax Policies

★ Identify the objectives of tax policies and explain why tax reform is difficult.

So far, we have been concerned mainly with the spending side of the budget, for which appropriations must be enacted each year. The revenue side of the budget is governed by overall tax policy, which is designed to provide a continuous flow of income without annual legislation. A major text on government finance says that tax policy is sometimes changed to accomplish one or more of several objectives:

- To adjust overall revenue to meet budget outlays
- To make the tax burden more equitable for taxpayers
- To help control the economy by raising taxes (thus decreasing aggregate demand) or by lowering taxes (thus increasing demand)[45]

If those were the only objectives, the tax code might be simple, but tax policy also reflects two conflicting philosophies for distributing the costs of government: whether

We Gave at the Bureaucracy

One of many clerks working at the Cincinnati Internal Revenue Service Center in Covington, Kentucky, one of the ten centers operated by the Internal Revenue Service to process tax forms and taxpayer requests. Each processes millions of forms each year.

citizens should be taxed according to their ability to pay or for benefits they receive. Tax policy is further complicated because it is also used to advance social goals (such as home ownership through the deduction for mortgage interest) or to favor certain industries. To accommodate such deductions and incentives, the tax code (which is available over the Internet) runs over seven thousand pages.[46] Almost 95 percent of the government revenue in FY 2013 was expected from three major sources: individual income taxes (47 percent), social insurance taxes (33 percent), and corporate income taxes (12 percent).[47] Because the income tax accounts for most government revenue, discussion of tax policy usually focuses on that source.

Reform

Tax reform proposals are usually so heavily influenced by interest groups looking for special benefits that they end up working against their original purpose.[48] Without question, the tax code is complex. Before 1987, people paid different tax rates depending on where they fit in fourteen income brackets. President Reagan backed a sweeping reform that reduced the number of brackets to two and the rate for the top bracket from 70 to 28 percent. By eliminating many tax brackets, the new tax policy approached the idea of a flat tax—one that requires everyone to pay at the same rate.

A flat tax has the appeal of simplicity, but it violates the principle of **progressive taxation**, under which the rich pay proportionately higher taxes than the poor. The ability to pay has long been a standard of fair taxation, and surveys show that citizens favor this idea in the abstract.[49] In practice, however, they have different opinions, as we will see. Nevertheless, most democratic governments rely on progressive taxation to redistribute wealth and thus promote economic equality. Although wealthy people finance redistributive programs, they also benefit if redistribution alleviates extreme inequalities and prevents poor people from revolting.

In general, the greater the number of tax brackets, the more progressive a tax can be, for higher brackets can be taxed at higher rates. To deal with a budget deficit in 1990, President George H. W. Bush violated his campaign pledge of "no new taxes" by creating a third tax rate, 31 percent, for those with the highest incomes. In 1993, Clinton created a fourth level, 39.6 percent, moving toward a more progressive tax structure, although still less progressive than before 1987. Both presidents acted to increase revenue to reduce a soaring deficit.

Campaigning for president, George W. Bush promised to cut taxes. Soon after his election, he got Congress to pass a complex $1.35 trillion tax cut, with a top personal tax rate of 35 percent. Intended to stimulate the economy, the tax cut

progressive taxation
A system of taxation whereby the rich pay proportionately higher taxes than the poor; used by governments to redistribute wealth and thus promote equality.

also reduced the revenue needed to match government spending.[50] Budget deficits quickly returned under Bush, owing to reduced revenue, a downturn in the stock market, and unanticipated expenses for homeland defense and military action following the September 11 attacks on America. The deficit zoomed to over a trillion dollars (10 percent of GDP) in Bush's last budget (see Figure 17.1), which reflected costs of his $168 billion stimulus package and his $700 billion Troubled Assets Relief Program (TARP). The deficit grew further with Obama's $787 billion stimulus package in 2009 but began to decrease in 2010. In 2012, Obama campaigned to restore the 39.6 percent tax bracket for those with the highest incomes.

Comparing Tax Burdens

No one likes to pay taxes, so politicians find it popular to criticize the agency that collects taxes: the Internal Revenue Service. The income tax itself—and taxes in general—are also popular targets for U.S. politicians who campaign on getting government off the backs of the people. Is the tax burden on U.S. citizens truly too heavy? Compared with what? One way to compare tax burdens is to examine taxes over time in the same country; another is to compare taxes in different countries at the same time. By comparing taxes over time in the United States, we find that the total tax burden on U.S. citizens has actually decreased since the 1950s. The federal tax rate for a family of four with the median household income was 20 percent in 1955 and 15 percent in 2010.[51] The largest increases have come in social insurance taxes, which have risen to pay for the government's single largest social welfare program: Social Security (see Figure 17.2 on p. 504 and Chapter 18).

Another way to compare tax burdens is to examine tax rates in different countries. By nearly two to one, more respondents in a post-2000 national survey thought that Americans pay a higher percentage of their income in taxes than citizens in Western Europe.[52] They were flat wrong. Despite Americans' complaints about high taxes, the U.S. tax burden is not large compared with that of other democratic nations. As shown in "Compared with What? Tax Burdens in Thirty-Four Countries" on page 505, Americans' taxes are quite low in general compared with those in thirty-three other democratic nations. Primarily because they provide their citizens with more generous social benefits (such as health care and unemployment compensation), almost every democratic nation taxes more heavily than the United States does.[53]

# 17.4 Spending Policies

★ Identify the major areas of government outlays and explain the role of incremental budgeting and uncontrollable spending on the growth of government spending.

The FY 2013 budget projects spending over $3,800,000,000,000—that's almost $4 trillion (or $4,000 billion, if you prefer). Where does all that money go? Figure 17.2 breaks down the $3.8 trillion in proposed outlays in President Obama's FY 2013 budget by eighteen major governmental functions. The largest amount (22 percent of the total budget) was targeted for Social Security. From World War II to FY 1993, national defense (military spending) accounted for most spending under these

FIGURE 17.2 Federal Spending in FY 2013, by Function

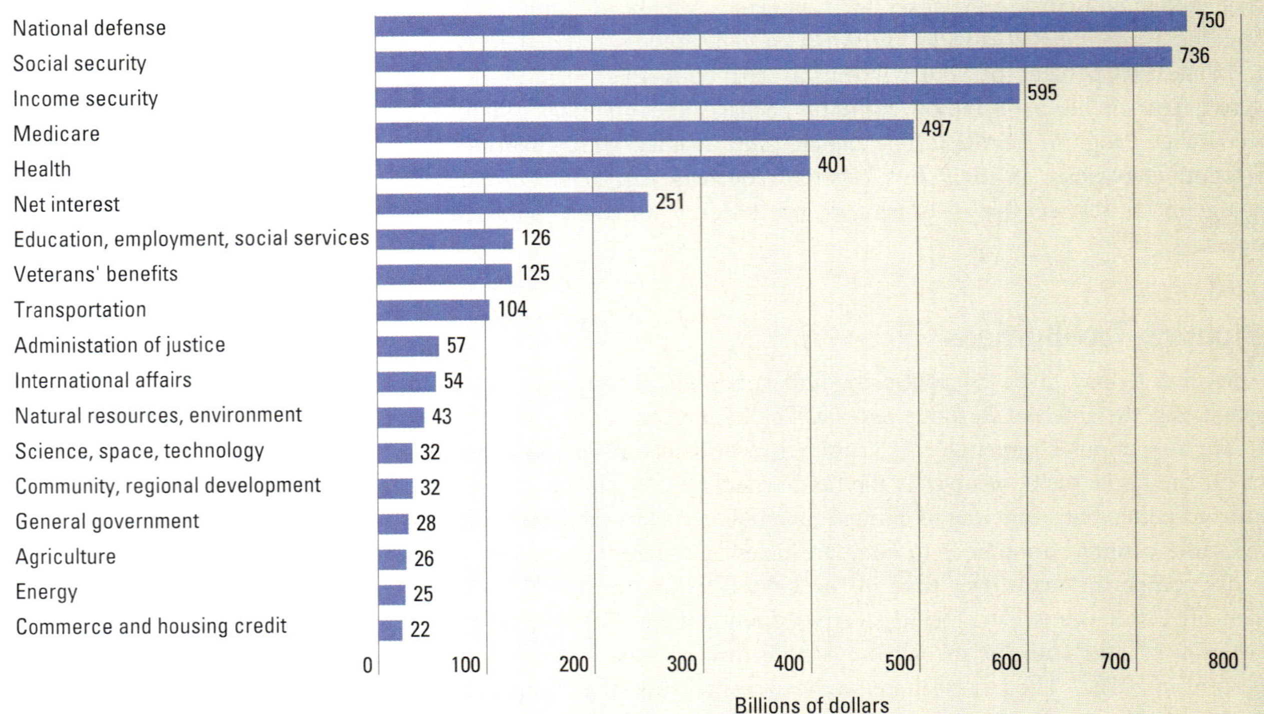

Federal budget authorities and outlays are organized into about twenty categories, some of which are mainly for bookkeeping purposes. This graph shows expected outlays for each of seventeen substantive functions in President Obama's FY 2013 budget. The final budget differed somewhat from this distribution because Congress amended some of the president's spending proposals. The graph makes clear the huge differences among spending categories. Military spending accounts for the largest share of the budget (18.5 percent) and is the largest amount in inflation-adjusted dollars since World War II. About 35 percent of government outlays are for Social Security and income security—that is, payments to individuals. Health costs (including Medicare) account for almost 25 percent more, and net interest consumes almost 7 percent. This leaves relatively little for transportation, agriculture, justice, science, and energy—matters often regarded as important centers of government activity.

Source: Executive Office of the President, *Budget of the United States Government, Fiscal Year 2013: Historical Tables* (Washington, D.C.: U.S. Government Printing Office, 2012), Table 3.1.

categories, but it fell to second place after the collapse of communism and stayed there until FY 2013. Income security (mainly for housing assistance) and Medicare, the third and fourth largest categories, together account for almost 29 percent of all budgetary outlays. At 10 percent, the fifth category, health, includes research organizations such as the National Institutes of Health. Health and Medicare together account for almost one-third of the budget, which underscores the importance of controlling the costs of health care. The sixth largest category is interest on the accumulated national debt, which alone consumes over 6 percent of all national government spending. Some people think that money spent on "foreign aid" is a huge drain on our treasury. However, the $60 billion outlay for international affairs constitutes only about 1.5 percent of the total—and one-quarter of that is for the State Department and our embassies abroad.

Consider the relative shares of expenditures over time in broad categories, as in Figure 17.3 (p. 506). The effect of World War II is clear: spending for national defense rose sharply after 1940, peaked at about 90 percent of the budget in 1945,

Compared with What?

Tax Burdens in Thirty-Four Countries

Compared with other nations, the tax burden in the United States is quite low. Are you surprised? This graph compares tax burdens in 2009 in thirty-four countries as a percentage of gross domestic product (GDP), which is the market value of goods produced inside the country by workers, businesses, and government. The percentages encompass national, state, and local taxes and Social Security contributions. By this measure, the U.S. government extracts less in taxes from its citizens than do the governments of all Western democratic nations. At the top of the list stand Denmark and Sweden, well known for providing heavily for social welfare. Despite its low ranking in tax burden, the United States also supports the world's largest military force, to which it allocates about 4 percent of its GDP, or about 18 percent of its total expenditures.

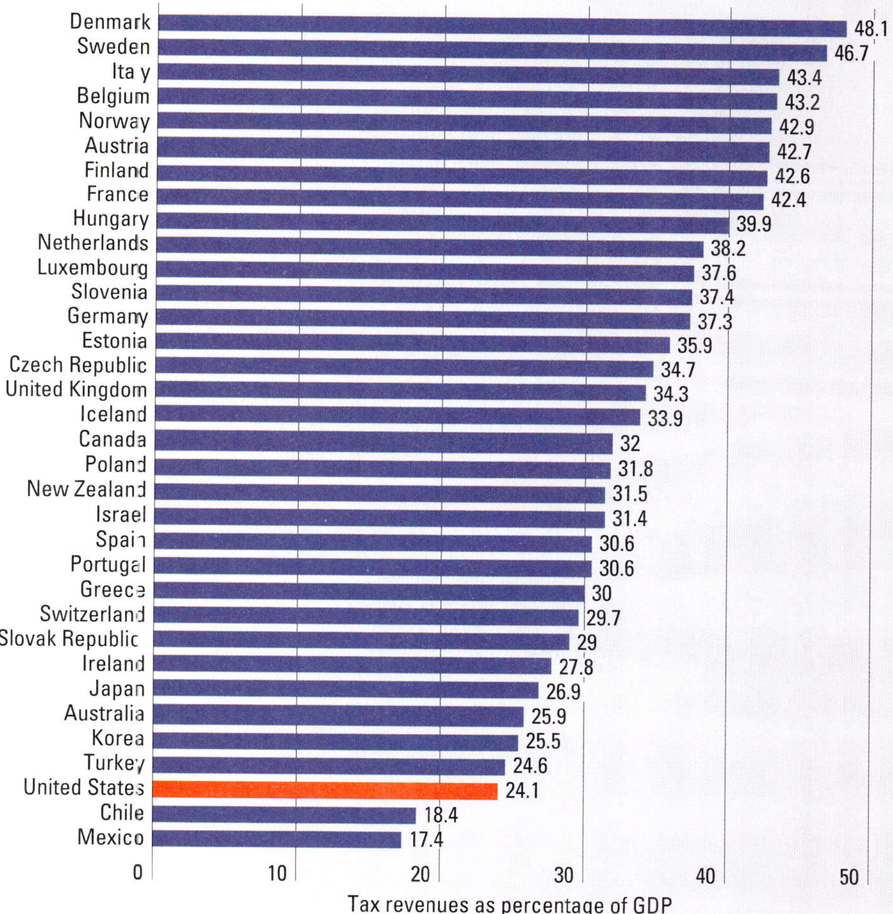

and fell to about 30 percent in peacetime. The percentage for defense rose again in the early 1950s, reflecting rearmament during the Cold War with the Soviet Union. Thereafter, defense's share of the budget decreased steadily (except for the bump

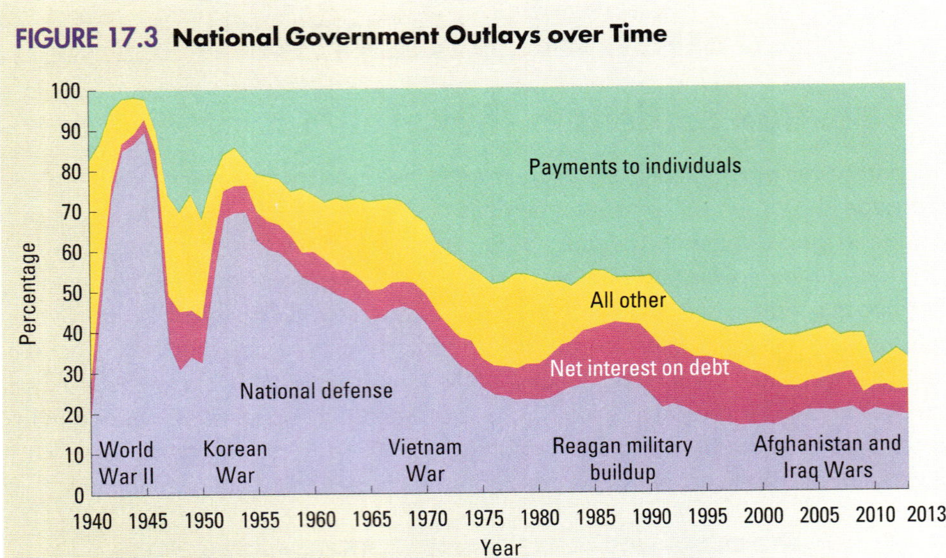

FIGURE 17.3 National Government Outlays over Time

This chart plots the percentage of the annual budget devoted to four major expense categories over time. It shows that significant changes have occurred in national spending since 1940. During World War II, defense spending consumed more than 80 percent of the national budget. Defense again accounted for most national expenditures during the Cold War of the 1950s. Following the collapse of communism in the 1990s, the military's share of the budget declined but rose again with the war in Iraq. The major story, however, has been the growth in payments to individuals—for example, in the form of Social Security benefits, Medicare, health care, and various programs that provide a social safety net—including unemployment compensation.
Source: Executive Office of the President, *Budget of the United States Government, Fiscal Year 2013: Historical Tables* (Washington, D.C.: U.S. Government Printing Office, 2012), Table 6.1.

during the Vietnam War in the late 1960s). This trend was reversed by the Carter administration in the 1970s and then shot upward during the Reagan presidency. Defense spending decreased under George H. W. Bush and continued to decline under Clinton. Following the September 11 attacks, President George W. Bush increased military spending 22 percent in FY 2003 over spending in 2001. Throughout his administration, military spending increased by 30 percent.[54] The Iraq war eventually cost over $800 billion and the war in Afghanistan over $500 billion.[55]

Government payments to individuals (e.g., Social Security checks) consistently consumed less of the budget than national defense until 1971. Since then, payments to individuals have accounted for the largest portion of the national budget, and they have been increasing. Net interest payments also increased substantially during the years of budget deficits. Pressure from payments for national defense, individuals, and interest on the national debt has squeezed all other government outlays.

There are two major explanations for the general trend of increasing government spending. One is bureaucratic, the other political.

Incremental Budgeting ...

incremental budgeting
A method of budget making that involves adding new funds (an increment) onto the amount previously budgeted (in last year's budget).

The bureaucratic explanation for spending increases involves **incremental budgeting**: bureaucrats, in compiling their funding requests for the following year, traditionally ask for the amount they got in the current year plus some incremental increase to fund new projects. Because Congress has already approved the agency's budget for the current year, it pays little attention to the agency's current size (the largest part of its budget) and focuses instead on the extra money (the increment) requested for the next year. As a result, few agencies are ever cut back, and spending continually goes up.

Incremental budgeting generates bureaucratic momentum that continually raises spending. Once an agency is created, it attracts a clientele that defends its existence and supports its requests for extra funds year after year. Because budgeting is a two-step process, agencies that get cut back in the authorizing committees sometimes manage (assisted by their interest group clientele) to get funds restored in the appropriations committees—and if not in the House, then perhaps in the Senate. Often appropriations committees approve spending for a specific purpose, known as an **earmark**. The practice of earmarking funds for "congressional pork" has greatly increased since the early 1990s.[56] Stung by criticism of the practice, Congress declared a moratorium on earmarks after the 2010 election, but some members are now repackaging them as "special funds" for which only their districts qualify.[57]

earmark
Federal funds appropriated by Congress for use on local projects.

... and Uncontrollable Spending

Earmarks are examples of **discretionary outlays** that Congress can choose to make. Most spending is enshrined in law and uncontrollable unless the law is changed. For example, Social Security legislation guarantees certain benefits to program participants when they retire. Medicare and veterans' benefits also entitle citizens to certain payments. These represent **mandatory outlays**. In Obama's FY 2013 budget, over 65 percent of all budget outlays were uncontrollable or relatively uncontrollable—mainly payments to individuals under Social Security, Medicare, and public assistance; interest on the national debt; and farm price supports. About half of the rest went for national defense or homeland security, leaving about 15 percent for domestic discretionary spending—excluding homeland security.[58]

discretionary outlays
Payments made by legislators' choice and based on annual appropriations.

mandatory outlays
Payments that government must make by law.

To be sure, Congress could change the laws to abolish entitlement payments, and it does modify them through the budgeting process. But politics argues against large-scale reductions. What spending cuts would be acceptable to or even popular with the public? In the abstract, voters favor cutting government spending, but they tend to favor maintaining "government programs that help needy people and deal with important national problems."[59] Substantial majorities favor spending the same or even more on Social Security, Medicare, education, job training, programs for poor children, and the military. In fact, when a national poll asked whether respondents thought federal spending should be "increased, decreased, or kept about the same" for twelve different purposes—highways, welfare, public schools, crime, child care, border security, terrorism, aid to the poor, Social Security, science and technology, the environment, and foreign aid—respondents favored increasing or keeping about the same level of spending for *every* purpose![60]

In truth, a perplexed Congress, trying to reduce the budget deficit, faces a public that favors funding most programs at even higher levels than those favored by most lawmakers.[61] Moreover, spending for the most expensive of these programs—Social Security and Medicare—is uncontrollable. Americans have grown accustomed to certain government benefits, but they do not like the idea of raising taxes to pay for them.

★ 17.5 Taxing, Spending, and Economic Equality

★ Identify the origins of the income tax, trace the influence of government spending and taxing policies on inequality, and examine these policies from the majoritarian and pluralist perspectives.

As we noted in Chapter 1, the most controversial purpose of government is to promote equality, especially economic equality. Economic equality comes about only at the expense of economic freedom, for it requires government action to redistribute wealth from the rich to the poor. One means of redistribution is government tax policy, especially the progressive income tax. The other instrument for reducing inequalities is government spending through welfare programs. The goal in both cases is not to produce equality of outcome; it is to reduce inequalities by helping the poor.

The national government introduced an income tax in 1862 to help finance the Civil War. That tax was repealed in 1871, and the country relied on revenue from tariffs on imported goods to finance the national government. The tariffs acted as a national sales tax imposed on all citizens, and many manufacturers—themselves taxed at the same rate as a laborer—grew rich from undercutting foreign competition.[62] Followers of a new political movement, the Populists (see Chapter 8), decried the inequities of wealth and called for a more equitable form of taxation, an income tax. An income tax law passed in 1894 was declared unconstitutional by the Supreme Court the next year. The Democratic Party and the Populists accused the Court of defending wealth against equal taxation and called for amending the Constitution to permit an income tax in their 1896 platforms. A bill to do so was introduced in 1909 and ratified in 1913 as the Sixteenth Amendment.

The Sixteenth Amendment gave government the power to levy a tax on individual incomes, and it has done so every year since 1914.[63] From 1964 to 1981, people who reported taxable incomes of $100,000 or more were taxed at least 70 percent on all income above that figure or margin. Individuals with lower incomes paid taxes at progressively lower marginal rates. (Figure 17.4 shows how the top marginal rate has fluctuated over the years.) Let us look at the overall effect of government spending and tax policies on economic equality in America.

Government Effects on Economic Equality

We begin by asking whether government spending policies have any measurable effect on income inequality. Economists call a government payment to individuals through Social Security, unemployment insurance, food stamps, and other programs, such as agricultural subsidies, a **transfer payment**. Transfer payments need not always go to the poor. In fact, one problem with the farm program is that the wealthiest farmers have often received the largest subsidies.[64] Nevertheless, most researchers have determined that transfer payments have had a definite effect on reducing income inequality.

According to the principle of progressive taxation, tax rates are supposed to take more revenue from the rich than from the poor. Although the effective rates have varied during the recent past, the wealthy were always taxed at higher rates than the poor, in line with the principle of progressive taxation. Some oppose progressive taxation as a tool for redistributing income rooted in an "obsession" with inequality.[65]

transfer payment
A payment by government to an individual, mainly through Social Security or unemployment insurance.

FIGURE 17.4 The Ups and Down of Top National Tax Rates

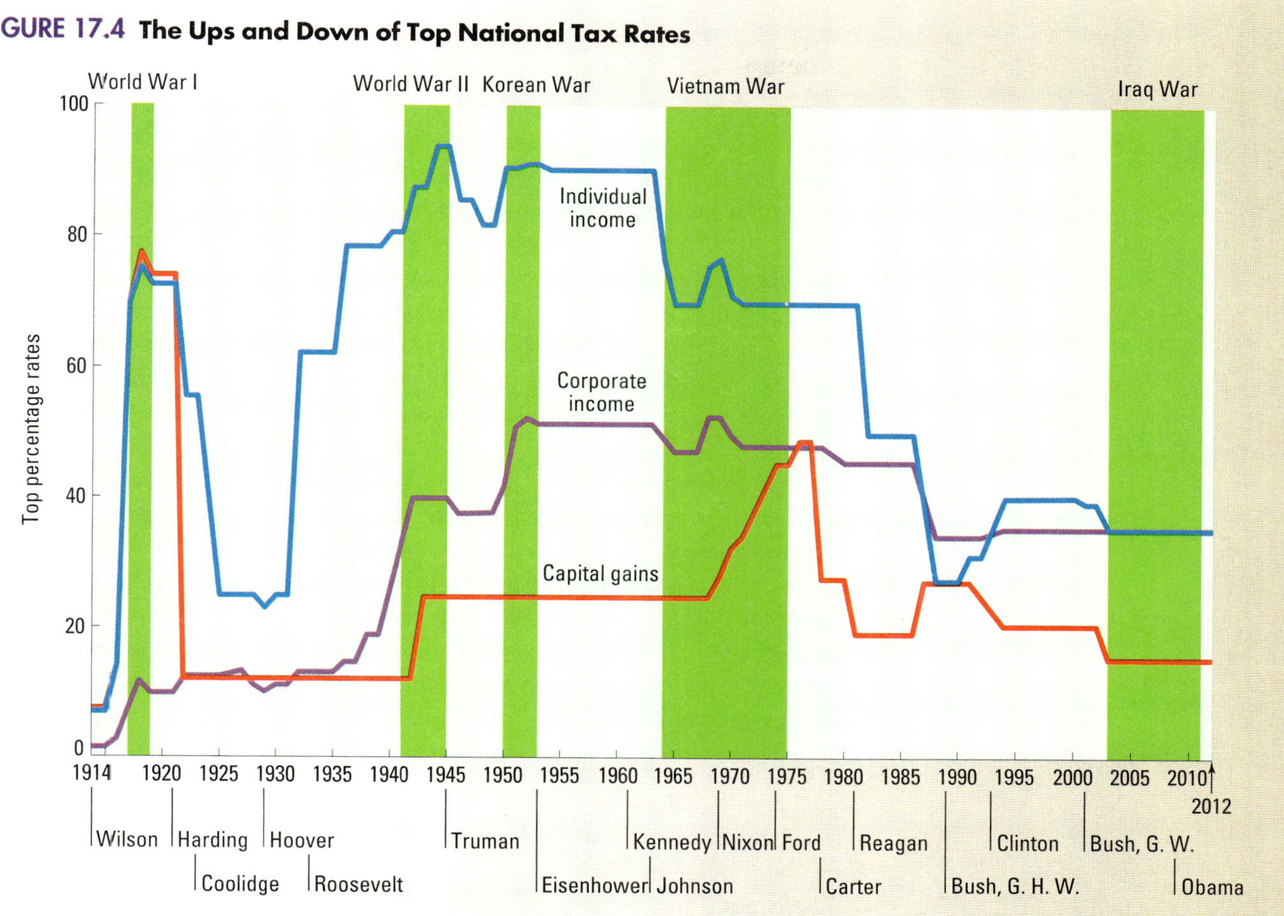

In 1913, the Sixteenth Amendment empowered the national government to collect taxes on income. Since then, the government has levied taxes on individual and corporate income and on capital gains realized by individuals and corporations from the sale of assets, such as stocks or real estate. Typically, incomes above certain levels are taxed at higher rates than incomes below those levels. This chart, which lists only the maximum tax rates, shows that these top tax rates have fluctuated wildly over time, from less than 10 percent to more than 90 percent. (They tend to be highest during periods of war.) During the Reagan administration, the maximum individual income tax rate fell to the lowest level since the Coolidge and Hoover administrations in the late 1920s and 1930s. The top rate increased slightly for 1991, to 31 percent, as a result of a law enacted in 1990, and jumped to 39.6 percent for 1994 under Clinton's 1993 budget package. The top rate was reduced in stages to 35 percent by Bush's tax plans in 2001 and 2003.

Source: *Wall Street Journal*, 18 August 1986, p. 10. Copyright 1986 by Dow Jones & Company, Inc. Reproduced with permission of Dow Jones & Company, Inc., in the format textbook via Copyright Clearance Center. Additional data from the Tax Policy Center, which reports tax brackets for individual years at http://www.taxpolicycenter.org.

They can point out that the richest 1 percent of taxpayers paid 40 percent of all federal individual income taxes in 2007.[66] Perhaps they paid so much because they *made* so much. If the richest 1 percent of all taxpayers took in 23 percent of all income in the nation (which they did), some think that they should pay twice that percentage in taxes (which they almost did).[67]

However, the national income tax is only part of the story. In some cases, poorer citizens pay a larger share of their income in taxes than wealthier citizens. "Stop Coddling the Super-Rich," wrote Warren Buffett. The third richest man in the world reported that he paid only 17.4 percent of his income in income taxes for 2010, while the average tax burden for the other twenty people in his office was 36 percent.[68] How can people in the lowest income group pay a higher percentage of their income in taxes than do those in the very highest group? In part, Buffett wrote, he makes most of his money through capital gains on stocks, which are taxed at only 15 percent. The full answer has to do with the combination of national, state, and local tax policies. Only the national income tax is progressive, with rates rising as income rises. The national payroll tax, which funds Social Security and Medicare, has two components—12.4 points go to Social Security and 2.9 to Medicare—for a total tax of 15.3 percent.[69] The tax is regressive: its effective rate decreases as income increases beyond a certain point. Because employers typically pay half, the effective rate for taxpayers is usually 7.65 percent. However, the larger Social Security component is levied on only a set portion of a person's income (the first $110,100 in 2012), and there is no Social Security tax at all on wages over that amount. So the effective rate of the Social Security tax is higher for lower-income groups than for the very top group. In fact, 98 percent of employees in the lowest 20 percent paid more payroll tax than income tax, compared with only 8 percent of employees in the upper 20 percent.[70]

Most state and local sales taxes are equally regressive. Poor and rich usually pay the same flat rate on their purchases. But the poor spend almost everything they earn on purchases, which are taxed, whereas the rich are able to save. A study showed that the effective sales tax rate for the lowest income group was thus about 7 percent, whereas that for the top 1 percent was only 1 percent.[71]

In general, the nation's tax policies at all levels have historically favored not only those with higher incomes, but also the wealthy—those who draw income from capital (wealth) rather than labor—for example:

- There is no national tax at all on investments in certain securities, including municipal bonds (issued by local governments for construction projects).
- The tax on earned income (salaries and wages) is withheld from paychecks by employers under national law; the tax on unearned income (interest and dividends) is not.
- The tax on income from the sale of real estate or stocks (called *capital gains*) has typically been lower than the highest tax on income from salaries. (Income from selling property or from receiving stock dividends is taxed at 15 percent, while income from salaries is taxed at twice that rate.)

Effects of Taxing and Spending Policies over Time

In 1967, at the beginning of President Johnson's Great Society programs, the poorest fifth of American families received 4 percent of the nation's income after taxes, whereas the richest fifth received 43.6 percent. Forty years later, after many billions of dollars had been spent on social programs, the income gap between the rich and poor had actually *grown,* as illustrated in Figure 17.5. This is true despite the fact that many households in the lowest category had about one-third more earners, mainly women, going to work.

In a capitalist system, some degree of inequality is inevitable. Is there some mechanism that limits how much economic equality can be achieved and prevents government policies from further equalizing income, no matter what is tried? To find out, we can look to other democracies to see how much equality they have been able to sustain. An international organization of developed nations analyzed data for twenty-two member countries in 2008. It found that the ratio of the income for the richest 10 percent of the population to the poorest 10 percent was lowest overall in the Nordic and many continental European countries.[72] The ratio rose to 10 to 1 in Italy, Japan, Korea, and Britain—and was around 14 to 1 in the United States, Israel, and

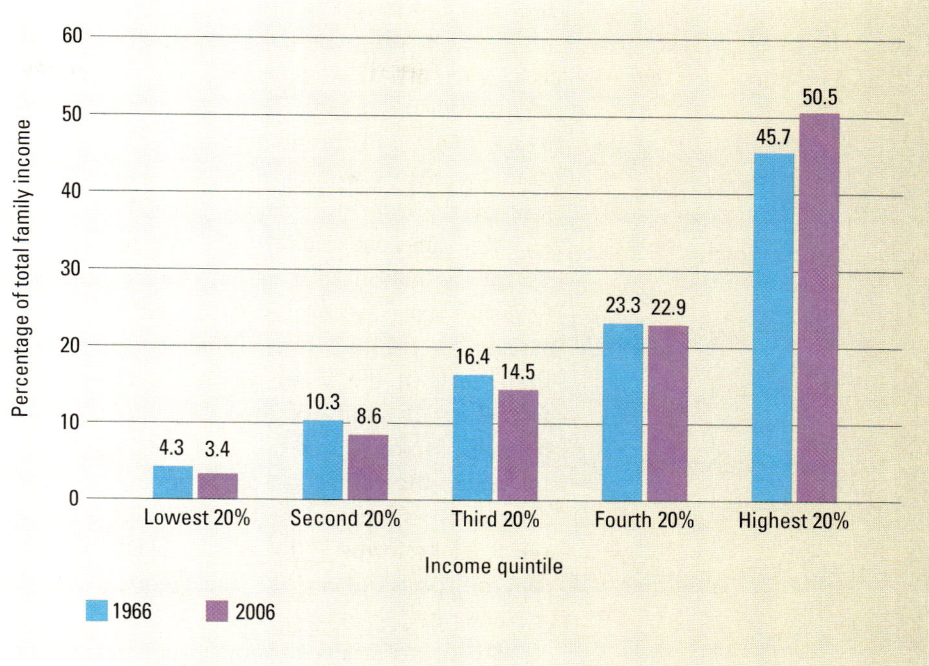

FIGURE 17.5 Distribution of Family Income over Time

In 2010, the 20 percent of U.S. families with the highest incomes received over 50 percent of all income, and their share has increased over time. This distribution of income is one of the most unequal among Western nations. At the bottom end of the scale, the poorest 20 percent of families received less than 5 percent of total family income, and their share has decreased over time.

Source: U.S. Census Bureau, "Income, Poverty, and Health Insurance Coverage in the United States: 2010," *Current Population Reports* (Washington, D.C.: U.S. Government Printing Office, September 2011), Table A-3.

Turkey. Only Mexico and Chile were more unequal than that. Other studies also show that our society has more economic inequality than other advanced nations.[73] The question is, why?

Democracy and Equality

Although the United States is a democracy that prizes political equality for its citizens, its record in promoting economic equality is not as good. In fact, its distribution of wealth—which includes not only income but also ownership of savings, housing, automobiles, stocks, and so on—is strikingly unequal. The wealthiest 1 percent of American families control almost 35 percent of the nation's household wealth (property, stock holdings, bank accounts).[74] Moreover, the distribution of wealth among ethnic groups is alarming. The typical white family has an annual income almost 1.5 times that of both blacks and Hispanics.[75] If democracy means government "by the people," why aren't the people sharing more equally in the nation's wealth? If one of the supposed purposes of government is to promote equality, why are government policies not working that way?

One scholar theorizes that interest group activity in a pluralist democracy distorts government's efforts to promote equality. His analysis of pluralism sees "corporations and organized groups with an upper-income slant as exerting political power over and above the formal one-man-one-vote standard of democracy."[76] As argued in Chapter 10, the pluralist model of democracy rewards groups that are well organized and well funded.

What would happen if national tax policy were determined according to principles of majoritarian rather than pluralist democracy? Perhaps not much, if public opinion is any guide. In a string of Gallup polls from 1985 to 2008, clear majorities consistently said that the distribution of wealth is not fair and favor some redistribution—but not through heavy taxes on the rich.[77] The people of the United States are not eager to redistribute wealth by increasing the only major progressive tax, the income tax. If national taxes must be raised, Americans favor a national sales tax over increased income taxes.[78] But a sales tax is a flat tax, paid by rich and poor at the same rate, and it would have a regressive effect on income distribution, promoting inequality. In one poll, the public also preferred a weekly $10 million national lottery to an increase in the income tax.[79] Because the poor are willing to chance more of their income on winning a fortune through lotteries than are rich people, lotteries (run by about forty states) also contribute to wealth inequality.[80]

Majoritarians might argue that most Americans fail to understand the inequities of the national tax system, which hides regressiveness in sales taxes and Social Security taxes. According to a national survey, Americans in the highest income categories (earning over $150,000 a year) understand the tax system much better than those at the lower income levels.[81] In Alabama, for example, income above $4,600 for a family of four went untaxed—meaning that most poor and all rich paid the same income tax, and the state relied mainly on sales and property taxes. In 2003, the conservative Republican governor of Alabama proposed a more progressive system of higher tax rates, mainly on the wealthy, only to have voters reject his reforms 2 to 1.[82] A black preacher and advocate of tax reform said that his parishioners like the (regressive) sales tax because they pay it in small increments.[83]

So majoritarians cannot argue that the public demands "fairer" tax rates that take from richer citizens to help poorer ones. If the public did, the lowest-income families might receive a greater share of the national income than they do. Instead, economic policy is determined mainly through a complex process of pluralist politics that returns nearly half the national income to only 20 percent of the nation's families.

SUMMARY

17.1 Theories of Economic Policy

- Laissez-faire economics holds that government should keep its hands off the economy.
- Keynesian theory holds that government should take an active role in dealing with inflation and unemployment, using fiscal and monetary policies to produce desired levels of aggregate demand.
- Monetarists believe fiscal policies are unreliable; they opt instead to use the money supply to affect aggregate demand.
- Supply-side economists, popular during the Reagan administration, focus on controlling the supply of goods and services rather than the demand for them.
- Economic growth in the United States during the mid- to late 1990s seemed to support the omniscience of free markets over government regulation.
- The financial crisis of 2008 and the accompanying recession led to a return to Keynesian principles.
- The continuing process of globalization has eroded government's ability to manage its own economy completely.

17.2 Public Policy and the Budget

- Congress alone prepared the budget until 1921, when it thrust the responsibility onto the president.
- In the 1970s, Congress sought to regain control of the process, creating a Congressional Budget Office and new House and Senate budget committees.
- Congress produced huge budget deficits in the 1980s fueled by tax cuts, increased military spending, and increased payments to individuals under entitlement programs, such as Social Security and Medicare.
- In 1985, Congress passed a law to reduce annual deficits in stages, through automatic across-the-board cuts if necessary, but Congress simply increased the allowable deficits.
- In 1939, Congress set a ceiling for the national debt, but it always voted (over 100 times since) to increase the ceiling to accommodate the debt.
- Both examples of Congress's failure to control its own spending habit suggest that it would also circumvent any balanced budget amendment to the Constitution.

17.3 Tax Policies

- In 1987, President Reagan reduced the number of brackets from fourteen to two and cut the rate for the top bracket from 70 to 28 percent.
- President George H. W. Bush promised "no new taxes" when campaigning for office in 1988, but signed a 1990 law to raise the income tax and provide needed revenue.
- The 1990 act added a third tax bracket, at 31 percent, still much lower than the top rate before Reagan's reforms.
- In 1993, President Clinton won approval for a fourth bracket, at 40 percent, that increased revenue and reduced the deficit.
- Aided by a growth economy, Clinton's 1997 taxing and spending changes produced a budget surplus in FY 1998—the first since 1969.
- The surplus disappeared in FY 2002 after President George W. Bush cut taxes and increased defense spending to combat terrorism.
- The budget deficit ballooned beyond $1 trillion in FY 2009 as President Bush spent $189 billion to stimulate the economy and $700 billion to rescue financial institutions.
- The deficit climbed under President Obama owing to reduced revenue from the bad economy and his $787 billion economic stimulus program.
- Despite public complaints about high taxes, current U.S. tax rates are lower than those in most other major countries and lower than they have been since the Great Depression of the 1930s.
- But even with the heavily progressive tax rates of the past, the national tax system has done little to redistribute income.
- Government transfer payments to individuals have helped reduce some income inequalities, but the distribution of income is less equal in the United States than in most major Western nations.

17.4 Spending Policies

- Social Security payments account for the largest portion (22 percent) of the FY 2013 budget.
- National defense (18 percent) consumes the next largest percentage.
- Income security and Medicare, the next two largest, together account for almost 29 percent of all budgetary outlays.
- Health (which includes research organizations such as the National Institutes of Health) takes 10 percent, and interest on the national debt takes another 6 percent.
- Those six categories consume about 85 percent of the budget, leaving only 15 percent for Veteran's Affairs, Education, Transportation, Administration of Justice, International Affairs, Natural Resources, Community Development, Science and Technology, General Government Agriculture, and Energy.

17.5 Taxing, Spending, and Economic Equality

- Pluralist democracy as practiced in the United States has allowed well-organized, well-financed interest groups to manipulate taxing and spending policies to their benefit.
- Taxing and spending policies in the United States are tipped in the direction of freedom rather than equality.

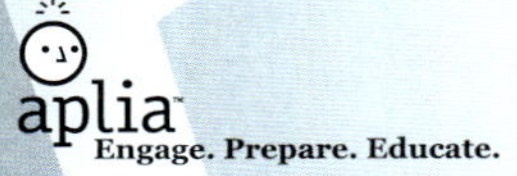

ASSESSING YOUR UNDERSTANDING WITH APLIA…YOUR VIRTUAL TUTOR!

17.1 Compare and contrast three theories of market economics: laissez-faire, Keynesian, and supply-side.

1. How does the "efficient market hypothesis" relate to laissez-faire economics?
2. How does the concept of "aggregate demand" relate to Keynesian economics?
3. How do governmental fiscal policies differ from monetary policies?

17.2 Describe the process by which the national budget is prepared and passed into law and the reforms undertaken by Congress to balance the budget.

1. What executive agency is charged with preparing the national budget?
2. What is the difference between a budget authorization and an appropriation?
3. Distinguish between mandatory and discretionary spending.

17.3 Identify the objectives of tax policies and explain why tax reform is difficult.

1. What is the difference between a flat tax and a progressive tax? Which do you think is fairer?
2. Compared with other countries, how heavy is the tax burden in the United States?

17.4 Identify the major areas of government outlays and explain the role of incremental budgeting and uncontrollable spending on the growth of government spending.

1. Of the twenty or so categories of government functions, which consumes the most federal spending?
2. What percentage of the federal budget is consumed by foreign aid?
3. Since World War II, how has federal spending changed concerning payments to individuals and costs of national defense?

17.5 **Identify the origins of the income tax, trace the influence of government spending and taxing policies on inequality, and examine these policies from the majoritarian and pluralist perspectives.**

1. What is the legal basis of the federal income tax?

2. How much effect has national tax policy had on the distribution of family income over time?

3. What might happen if national tax policy were determined according to principles of majoritarian democracy and not pluralist democracy?

18 Policymaking and Domestic Policy

CHAPTER TOPICS and Learning Outcomes

18.1 Government Purposes and Public Policies
★ Categorize different types of public policies and outline the process by which policies are formulated and implemented.

18.2 The Development of the American Welfare State
★ Trace the evolution of social welfare programs as a central element of public policy in the United States.

18.3 Social Security
★ Describe the origins and evolution of Social Security as well as the funding and benefit issues facing the program.

18.4 Public Assistance
★ Explain how poverty is defined and trace the evolution of public assistance programs designed to address it.

18.5 Health Care
★ Differentiate among Medicare, Medicaid, and the Affordable Care Act of 2010 and explain how each program addresses the issues of health-care delivery.

18.6 Elementary and Secondary Education
★ Describe the role of the federal government in shaping education policy at the state and local government levels.

18.7 Immigration
★ Assess alternative policies for addressing illegal immigration into the United States.

18.8 Benefits and Fairness
★ Explain how about the issue of fairness shapes perspectives on government benefits.

Twenty-two-year-old Sara may look like an average college student, but when she was ten years old, she was diagnosed with type I diabetes. Managing a busy student lifestyle while keeping diabetes in control is challenging. But the task became even more difficult when Sara lost her health care; her part-time job made her ineligible for the government-run program that previously covered the costs of her insulin, pump supplies, and test strips (costs running over $800 per month!). Without government aid, Sara looked into private health insurance plans, but purchasing private insurance was too expensive. For now, she is uninsured, trying to balance school, her health, and the never-ending costs of diabetes.[1]

Determining whether—and how—government should help people like Sara meet their basic needs is a perennial challenge. Crafting public policies that promote the modern view that governments have such responsibilities without infringing on personal or economic freedoms is a task that policymakers continually face. If and when a policy is enacted, tracking its progress and determining whether it is achieving its goals without also incurring undesirable unintended consequences is the next hurdle. Then, deciding what, if any, changes should be made to the policy starts the cycle again.

This complicated process is on display in the realm of health care. Denying coverage to people who incur high medical bills because of illnesses like diabetes makes sense from an economic perspective in private enterprise. But in modern democracies, many people feel that the government should provide basic social services so that no one's quality of life falls below a certain level. In requiring health coverage for all, government may limit the economic freedom of private health insurance companies to deny people coverage. The notion that only the wealthy or the healthy have access to both routine and life-saving medical care is at odds with modern understandings of the role of government. For the past twelve years, at least half of Americans have believed that it is the responsibility of the federal government to make sure that all Americans have health-care coverage.[2]

The Affordable Care Act (ACA), enacted in 2010, was aimed to help Sara and the millions of Americans in similar positions. Sara has a serious and expensive health condition. Before the law was passed, insurance companies were able to deny her coverage on that basis alone. One recent study concluded that up to 50 percent of non-elderly Americans, including 24 percent of people under age eighteen and 35 percent of people aged eighteen to thirty-four, have at least one preexisting condition that could likewise lead them to be denied coverage. Such conditions include anorexia nervosa, hemophilia, and drug addiction. By 2014, people with such conditions cannot be denied coverage.[3]

As a person under age twenty-six, Sara is also now eligible to remain on her parents' health plan, an option that many young people welcome given today's tough economic climate and the high costs of health care. According to the Centers for Disease Control and Prevention, about 2.5 million young people have taken advantage of this provision since it went into effect in 2010. The percentage of insured Americans age nineteen to twenty-five has since risen from 64 to 73 percent, making it the only age group to experience an increase in coverage during that time.[4]

Despite these apparent successes, debate about the ACA remains fierce. First is the philosophical debate about whether government even has the authority to require people to get insurance. Then come logistical debates about whether the ACA's other provisions are the most appropriate ways to address rising health-care costs, the effect of the law on government spending and individual tax burdens, the impact of the law on state-level finances and agencies, and more. While it is tempting to conclude that a policy that allows people with serious conditions to get the treatment they need is one that should remain in effect, the policy realm of health care is complicated. The challenge of devising, implementing, and assessing a policy that protects the citizenry's standard of living while also satisfying other basic principles, such as federalism, the economic freedom of private employers and insurance providers, and the individual freedom of people to shun insurance coverage if they want to, will continue to feature prominently in policy debates.

Previous chapters focused on individual institutions of government. Here we look at government more broadly and ask how policymaking takes place across institutions. We first identify different types of public policies and analyze the stages in the policymaking process. We encourage the view of policymaking as an ongoing process, often without a clear start or finish. Policies are continually evaluated, altered, and reevaluated. Then we look at specific domestic policies, that is, government plans of action targeting concerns internal to the United States. These are among the most enduring and costly programs that the government has launched on behalf of its citizens. Four questions guide our inquiry: What are the origins and politics of specific domestic policies? What are the effects of these policies once they are implemented? Why do some policies succeed and others fail? Finally, are disagreements about policy really disagreements about values?

18.1 Government Purposes and Public Policies

★ Categorize different types of public policies and outline the process by which policies are formulated and implemented.

In Chapter 1, we noted that most citizens accept limitations on their personal freedom in return for various benefits of government. We defined the major purposes of government as maintaining order, providing public benefits, and promoting equality. Different governments place different values on each broad purpose, and those differences are reflected in their public policies. A **public policy** is a general plan of action adopted by a government to solve a social problem, counter a threat, or pursue an objective.

public policy
A general plan of action adopted by the government to solve a social problem, counter a threat, or pursue an objective.

At times, governments choose not to adopt a new policy to deal with a troublesome situation; instead, they muddle through, hoping the problem will diminish in importance. This too is a policy decision because it chooses to maintain the status quo. Whatever their form and effectiveness, all policies are the means by which government pursues certain goals in specific situations. People disagree about public policies because they disagree about one or more of the following elements: the goals government should have, the means it should use to meet them, and how the situation at hand should be perceived.

The Policymaking Process

When people disagree on goals, that disagreement is often rooted in a difference in values. As emphasized throughout this book, such value conflict often involves pitting freedom against order or freedom against equality. Disputes involving values are hard to bridge since they reflect a basic worldview and go to the core of one's sense of right and wrong.

The problem of illegal drugs illustrates how different core values lead us to prefer different policies. Everyone agrees that government should address problems created by drugs. Yet views of what should be done differ sharply. Recall from Chapter 1 that libertarians prioritize individual freedom and want to limit government as much as possible. Many libertarians argue that drugs should be decriminalized; if people want to take drugs, they should be free to do so. If drug use were legal, crimes associated with the drug trade would evaporate. Conservatives emphasize order. In their minds, a safe and civilized society does not allow people to debase themselves through drug abuse, and the government should punish those who violate the law. Liberals promote treatment as a policy option. They regard addiction as a medical problem and believe that government should offer services that help addicts. Government should help people in need, they argue, and many drug offenders cannot pay for treatment because their drug habit has left them impoverished.

Types of Policies

Although values underlie choices, analysis of public policy does not usually focus explicitly on core beliefs. Political scientists often categorize policies by their objectives. One common purpose is to allocate resources so that some segment of society or region of the country can receive a service or benefit. We call these **distributive policies**. Pork barrel government projects discussed in Chapter 11 are distributive policies. One example of the distribution of resources toward a local project involves the roughly $45,000 per year that the National Endowment for the Arts gives to the Western Folklife Center, which hosts an annual Cowboy Poetry Festival in Elko, Nevada. Some argue that the government should not distribute funds for such local projects, especially during a recession. Others, such as Senate Majority Leader Harry Reid (D-Nev.), say that the funding preserves and celebrates the culture of the American West while also enhancing the region's economy, since the yearly festival generates millions in economic activity.[5]

With distributional policies, all of us, by paying our taxes, support those who receive the benefit, presumably because that benefit works toward the common good, such as stronger security, modernized infrastructure, a cleaner environment, or a richer national culture. In contrast, **redistributional policies** are explicitly designed to take resources from one sector of society and transfer them to another, reflecting the core value of equality.

State-level tax policies offer prime examples of differing ways to think about redistribution. The recent recession has led nearly all states to grapple with budget shortfalls and growing numbers of people in hardship. States have looked to their tax codes in order to find ways to shore up revenue. Some states, like Connecticut, have increased taxes on the wealthiest residents and cut taxes for low-income workers as a way to raise revenue and redistribute income. This approach views taxation as a shared sacrifice that helps people out of poverty (freeing them from government

distributive policies
Government policies designed to confer a benefit on a particular institution or group.

redistributional policies
Policies that take government resources, such as tax funds, from one sector of society and transfer them to another.

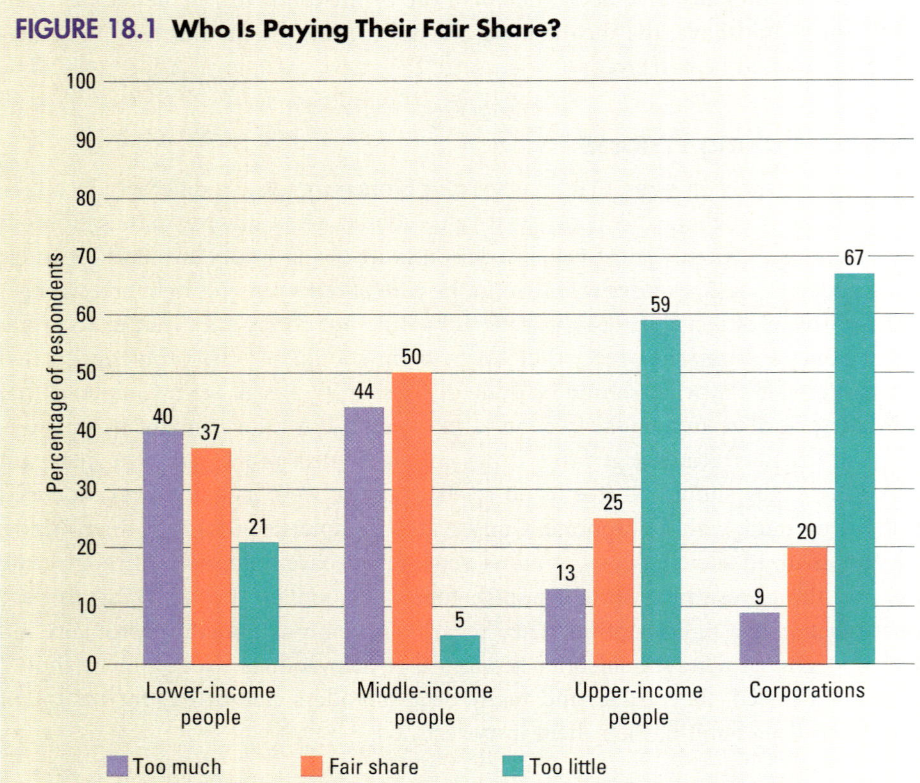

FIGURE 18.1 Who Is Paying Their Fair Share?

According to the Gallup Poll, Americans believe that upper-income Americans and corporations pay too little in the way of taxes. Battles over federal income taxes loom as previously enacted cuts for wealthy Americans are set to expire at the end of 2012. Source: Gallup Poll, 7–11 April 2011.

safety net programs) and spurs further economic activity. Other states, like Michigan, reduced tax credits for low-income workers in order to keep more funds for government programs and to finance tax cuts for businesses and corporations. This approach, which minimizes redistribution, views taxes on the wealthy and the business sector as a barrier to economic development. Taking this approach to its extreme, Oklahoma is considering eliminating its income tax altogether (an option long practiced by several states). This plan would essentially require the rich and poor alike to pay the same dollar amount (but vastly different income *percentages*) in taxes through the sales tax.[6] (For public opinion on federal taxes, see Figure 18.1.)

Another policy approach is **regulation**. In Chapter 13, we noted that regulations are rules that guide the operation of government programs. When regulations apply to businesses, they are an attempt to structure the market in a particular way. Government becomes a referee, establishing rules that set boundaries on how businesses can operate. Prior to the twentieth century, the food industry was unregulated. Since then, both the Food and Drug Administration (FDA) and the U.S. Department of Agriculture have been created to regulate the production and marketing of food. In 2011, the government added to existing regulations by enacting the FDA Food Safety Modernization Act, which was motivated by several high-profile food recalls involving products such as spinach, eggs, and peanut butter. The investigation that followed the *Salmonella* outbreak tied to eggs revealed that the contaminated eggs had been exposed to rodents, flies, maggots, manure, and chicken innards. One provision of the new law empowers the FDA to issue its own recalls instead of relying on voluntary

regulation
Government intervention in the workings of a business market to promote some socially desired goal.

recalls from food producers. It also provides greater inspection authority to the FDA, in the hope of preventing unsafe foods from reaching consumers in the first place.[7]

Americans disagree over the extent to which markets should operate freely. Some believe government should be only minimally involved. Others believe markets need close supervision because competitive pressures lead businesses to cut corners on the safety of their products or the integrity of their conduct. On the one hand, the decisions on how to regulate or whether to reduce regulation (to *deregulate*) may involve technical questions and are best left to experts who work for the relevant bureaucratic agencies. What, for example, is a safe level of "rodent filth" to allow in curry powder?[8] On the other hand, regulation and deregulation are subject to the same pulls and pushes of the political process as distributional and redistributional policies. In the case of food safety, the new regulations were supported by major food producers including General Mills and Kraft Foods, while they were opposed by associations representing smaller farms, who feared that the new law would create an insurmountable degree of new regulations and paperwork for them.[9]

This framework of distributional, redistributional, and regulatory policies is rather general, and there are surely policy approaches that don't fit neatly into these categories.[10] Nevertheless, it is a useful prism to examine policymaking. Understanding the broad purposes of public policy allows a better evaluation of the tools necessary to attain these objectives.

Public Policy Tools

There are different ways of achieving public policy objectives. If the goal is to redistribute wealth, different approaches can accomplish the same goal. As in Connecticut's approach, one way is to tax the wealthy more and working-class people less. A more politically palatable approach may be to institute tax exemptions for working-class people so their effective tax rate drops. An example would be a child tax credit of $500 for those with incomes below $35,000.

One policy tool is *incentives*. A fundamental element of human behavior is that we can be induced to do certain things if rewards become substantial enough. We should all give to charity simply because it is a generous act. But to promote more giving, the government provides tax deductions for people who donate to nonprofit charities. For a taxpayer with a marginal tax rate of 30 percent, a donation of $1,000 to the Red Cross effectively costs her only $700. (The deduction is 30 percent of the $1,000, or $300.) Although giving to charity is a good thing, there's no free lunch. Incentives like these constitute a *tax expenditure*. Since government loses revenue on the charity deduction, it must make up revenue elsewhere. This tax expenditure is quite substantial: Americans give close to $350 billion a year in charity.[11]

The flip side of incentives are *disincentives*—policies that discourage particular behavior. A tax on pollution, for example, is a disincentive for a factory to continue using high-polluting manufacturing processes. Likewise, taxes on cigarettes are meant to discourage smoking.

Much of what policymakers want to accomplish cannot be done through incentives or disincentives. Rather than coaxing or discouraging behavior, it must take responsibility itself to establish a program. Government's largest expenditures—for health care, education, social services, and defense—come from government's direct payments to its employees or to vendors who implement programs.

Finally, a common policy tool is to set rules. Much of what government does in the form of regulation involves setting rules regarding what businesses or individuals can do in the marketplace, as in the case of food safety discussed earlier. The federal government constantly issues new or revised rules on a variety of policy questions.

FIGURE 18.2 The Policymaking Process

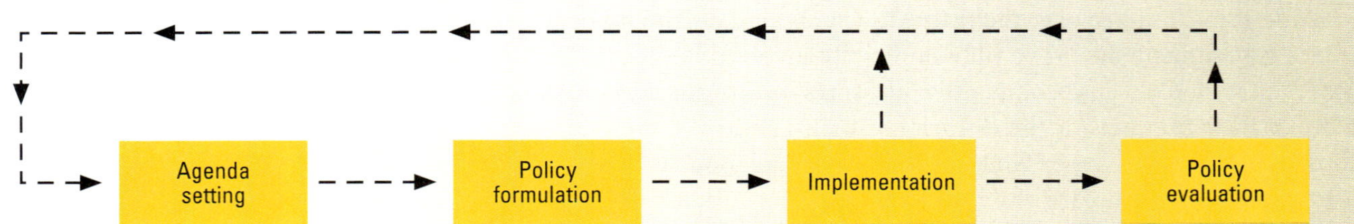

This model, one of many possible ways to depict the policymaking process, shows four stages. Feedback on program operations and performance from the last two stages stimulates new cycles of the process.
Source: © Cengage Learning.

A Policymaking Model

Clearly, different approaches to solving policy problems affect the policymaking process, but common patterns exist. We can separate the policymaking process into four stages: agenda setting, policy formulation, implementation, and policy evaluation. Figure 18.2 shows the four stages in sequence. Note, however, that the process does not end with policy evaluation. Policymaking is a circular process; the end of one phase is the beginning of another.

Agenda Setting. When we think of the political agenda, we usually think of the broad set of policy areas that are central to American life. This broad agenda changes over time as conditions change. For a number of years the war in Iraq was of major concern to Americans, but today the economy is the top priority for most Americans.

Political scientists not only study what's on the agenda at any one time but also **agenda setting**, the part of the process in which problems are defined as political issues. Many problems confront Americans in their daily lives, but government is not actively working to solve them all. Consider Social Security. Today the old-age insurance program seems a hardy perennial of American politics, but it was not created until the New Deal. The problem of poverty among the elderly did not suddenly arise during the 1930s—there had always been poor people of all ages—but that is when inadequate income for the elderly was defined as a political problem. When the government begins to consider acting on an issue it previously ignored, we say that the issue has become part of the political agenda.

Why does a social problem become redefined as a political problem? There is no single reason; many factors stimulate new thinking about a problem. Sometimes highly visible events or developments push issues onto the agenda. Examples are great calamities (such as an oil spill, showing a need for safer offshore drilling rigs), the effects of technology (such as air pollution, requiring clean-air regulations), or irrational human behavior (such as airline hijackings, pointing to the need for greater airport security).[12] Whether a certain problem moves onto the agenda is also affected by who controls the government and by broad ideological shifts. Presidential and congressional candidates run for office promising to put neglected issues on the agenda. The political parties also take up new issues to promote their candidates and respond to public opinion.

Part of the politics of agenda building is not just which new issues emerge and which issues decline in visibility, but the way the substantive problem at the heart of an issue is conceived. **Issue definition** is the way we think about a problem. Our

agenda setting
The stage of the policymaking process during which problems get defined as political issues.

issue definition
Our conception of the problem at hand.

conception of an issue is influenced by our own values and the way we see the political world. Interest groups and political parties try to persuade Americans to define issues in ways that are sympathetic to their cause. Over the years conservatives have tried to make us think of policy problems in terms of market approaches. If we accept that a market approach is better, then we'll shy away from government regulation.[13]

Citizens' views are also colored by what they regard as a government responsibility. Consider autism. If we define autism as a *disease,* then we might see a limited role for government—primarily as a funder of scientific research. But if we define autism as a *disability,* our issue definition will be broader. In the United States, persons with disabilities are guaranteed certain protections, and government has the responsibility to fight relevant forms of discrimination.[14] Many political battles are thus battles to define what the issue at hand is even about.

The most likely form of change in issue definition occurs when an additional *frame* emerges, which happens when a new perspective comes to the fore. For example, for many years the dominant issue frames concerning the death penalty involved punishment and morality. Some argued that the death penalty is a just punishment for a heinous crime. Those on the other side argued that the death penalty was immoral—that the state didn't have the right to take a life. In the late 1990s, stories emerged in the press about people who were wrongly convicted and sentenced to death. DNA testing became an increasing source of exculpatory evidence. This so-called innocence frame became part of the debate over the death penalty, and public support for the death penalty began to drop.[15]

Since the emergence of a new frame can alter policymaking, interest groups make concerted efforts to reshape policy debate when the dominant frames work to their disadvantage. However, it is difficult for interest groups to reshape a debate.[16] Most change in issue framing is evolutionary and reflects both changes in the world and long-term interest group advocacy.

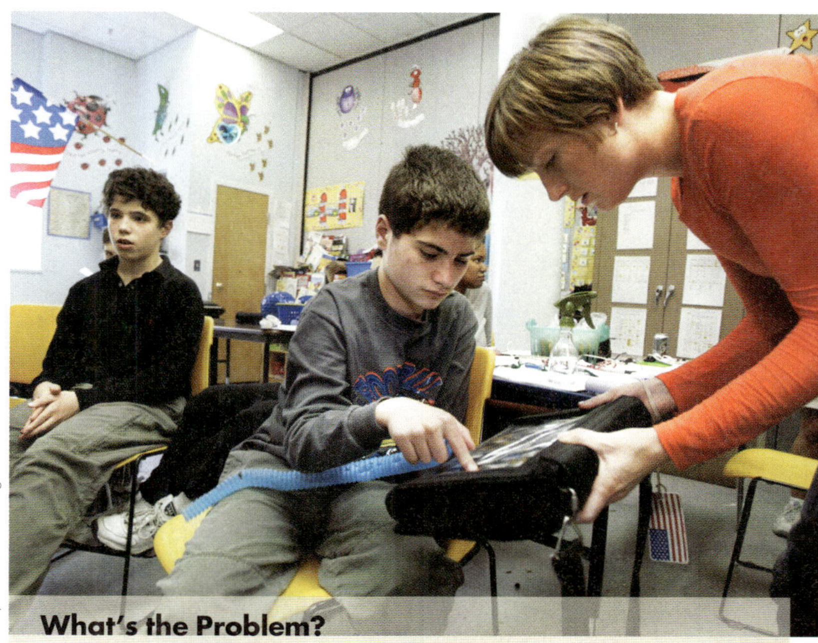

Tony Kurdzuk/Star Ledger/Corbis

What's the Problem?

How we define a problem will likely shape government's response to it. For example, is autism a disease or a disability? Interest groups often try to shape issue definitions to suit their constituents' policy preferences. (This young man with autism is using his AlphaTalker to communicate with his teacher.)

Policy Formulation. **Policy formulation** is the stage of the process in which formal policy proposals are developed and officials decide whether to adopt them. The most obvious kind of policy formulation is the proposal of a measure by the president or the development of legislation by Congress. Administrative agencies also formulate policy, through the regulatory process. Courts formulate policy too, when their decisions establish new interpretations of the law.

Although policy formulation is depicted in Figure 18.2 as a single stage, it actually takes place over several stages and across different levels of government. Congress passed legislation that requires states to compile registries of sexual offenders. Disclosure of such information differs by state, and bureaucracies in each state must develop policies regarding how much information to make public. Is it enough to

policy formulation
The stage of the policymaking process during which formal proposals are developed and adopted.

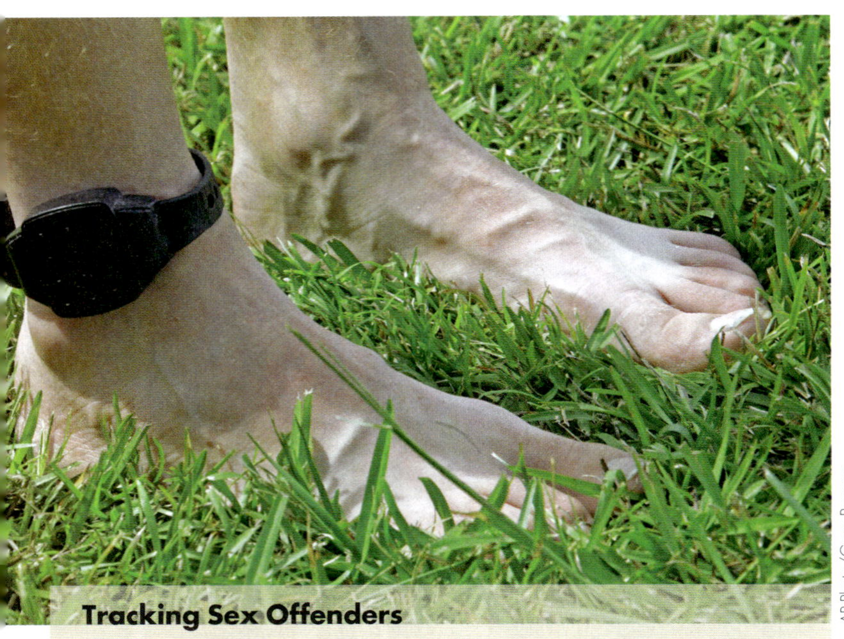

Tracking Sex Offenders

A difficult public policy problem is what to do with convicted sex offenders once they've served any incarceration. Understandably, no one wants them living in their neighborhood. In some cities, like Fayetteville, North Carolina (where this offender lives), those released into the community must wear an electronic tracking device. This type of ankle bracelet allows police to monitor any movement into areas where children congregate.

AP Photo/Gerry Broome

identify where a sex offender lives, or should more about the individual be revealed? Courts are called in as such decisions are contested.

As noted in Chapter 13, policy formulation is often *incremental*. As policies are debated, the starting point is the existing policy in that area, and if new policy is adopted, it is usually a modification of what was in place previously. One long-standing policy in the midst of incremental formulation involves fuel efficiency for cars and light trucks, known as Corporate Average Fuel Economy Standards (CAFE Standards). Such standards were first adopted by Congress in 1975, when the average gas mileage for a carmaker's fleet (passenger cars only) could not exceed 18 miles per gallon (mpg). These limits were designed to reduce energy consumption and carbon emissions. By 1990, that average had increased to 27.5 mpg. In 2011, President Obama announced a plan to change the standards again. If the new rule is adopted, the average for a fleet's passenger cars will not be able to exceed 54.5 mpg by 2025. This dramatic increase in fuel standards represents a large change from previous limits, but it also represents a continuation and evolution of existing practices.[17]

Keep in mind that policy formulation is only the development of proposals designed to solve a problem. Some issues reach the agenda and stimulate new proposals but then fail to win enactment because political opposition mobilizes.

implementation

The process of putting specific policies into operation.

Implementation. Policies are not self-executing; **implementation** is the process by which they are carried out. When policies are enacted and when agencies issue regulations, government bodies must put those policies into effect. This process often involves multiple levels of government as well as actors in the private sector. After a major oil spill from the Deepwater Horizon rig in the Gulf of Mexico in 2010, government actors implemented the Oil Pollution Act of 1990, which requires "responsible parties" to establish a way to compensate victims who have suffered personally or professionally as a result of an oil spill. The BP oil company that operated the rig was thus responsible, but the government decided to take the lead in ensuring that the needs of victims were addressed. BP was ordered to establish a $20 billion fund, which is administered by a government-appointed "compensation czar." By August 2011, the government-run fund had paid out over $5 billion to over 200,000 people and businesses. In further response to the spill, the government implemented provisions of the Clean Water Act, which has generated billions more in fines to BP for policy violations, such as negligence.[18]

Although it may sound technical, implementation is actually a very political process, involving a great deal of bargaining and negotiation among different groups of people in and out of government. The challenge of implementing complex policies in a federal system, with multiple layers of government, that is also a pluralistic system, with competing interests, seems daunting. Yet there are incentives for cooperation, not the least of which is to avoid blame if a policy fails. (We discuss coordination in more detail in the next section.)

Policy Evaluation. How does the government know whether a policy is working? In some cases, success or failure may be obvious, but at other times, experts in a specific field must tell government officials how well a policy is working. **Policy evaluation** is the analysis of the results of public policy. Although there is no one method of evaluating policy, evaluation draws heavily on approaches used by academics, including cost-effectiveness analysis and statistical methods designed to provide concrete measurements of program outcomes. Such studies influence decisions on whether to continue, expand, alter, reduce, or eliminate programs.

Evaluation is part of the policymaking process because it helps identify problems that arise from current policy. In other words, evaluations provide **feedback** to policymakers on program performance. The dotted line in Figure 18.2 represents a feedback loop. Problems that emerge during implementation also provide feedback to policymakers. Feedback can be positive or negative.[19] Evaluations of how government agencies come to approve of particular products, such as medical devices, clearly display the feedback process. The FDA crafts rules for determining when a medical device is safe and can be used on the general public. One device it approved is a lap band that is used in weight loss surgery, which involves placing a band around the stomach in order to limit how much a person can eat. Since its approval, studies have emerged indicating high rates of complications from the device, such as esophageal ulcers, leading some members of Congress to call for hearings in order to assess both the safety of the product and the procedures used by the FDA for determining its safety. The hearings will lay the foundation for a more comprehensive review of the FDA's procedures scheduled to take place late in 2012.[20]

Feedback reflects the dynamic nature of policymaking. By drawing attention to emerging problems, policy evaluation influences the political agenda. The end of the process—evaluating whether the policy is being implemented as it was envisioned—is the beginning of a new cycle of public policymaking.

Fragmentation, Coordination, and Issue Networks

The policymaking process encompasses many stages and includes different participants at each stage. Here we examine some forces that pull the government in different directions and make problem solving less coherent than it might otherwise be. We also look at some structural elements of American government that work to coordinate competing approaches to the same problems.

A single policy problem may be attacked in different ways by government for many reasons. At the heart of this **fragmentation** of policymaking is the fundamental nature of government in America. The separation of powers divides authority among the branches of the national government, and federalism divides authority among the national, state, and local levels of government. These multiple centers of power are a primary component of pluralist democracy. Different groups try to influence different parts of the government; no one entity completely controls policymaking.

Differing policies among the states and between the states and the federal government cause confusion because of the fragmented approach of the different levels of government. Frustrated because the federal government had taken no action regarding the poisoning of children who unknowingly drink out of containers of antifreeze, California and Oregon passed laws requiring manufacturers to add a bitter-tasting

policy evaluation
Analysis of a public policy so as to determine how well it is working.

feedback
Information received by policymakers about the effectiveness of public policy.

fragmentation
In policymaking, the phenomenon of attacking a single problem in different and sometimes competing ways.

ingredient to the mix. But this legislation meant that different states required different things from manufacturers.[21]

Coordination of different elements of government is not impossible. Fragmentation often creates a productive pressure to rethink jurisdictions and to create incentives for coordination. In our federal system, for instance, states possess some degree of autonomy. American federalism is often lauded because the states can be "fifty laboratories" for developing policy alternatives. Yet this can be frustrating to the federal government because states may develop policies at odds with federal approaches. Currently, states vary widely in their policies regarding the use of mobile devices while driving. Such distracted driving led to over 3,000 deaths in the United States in 2010. In response to this growing problem, some state have banned all handheld phone use by all drivers, some ban handheld phone use only for young drivers, some ban texting while driving, and some have practically no restrictions at all. To encourage coordination, the Safe Drivers Act has been introduced in Congress. It would impose a national policy banning the use of handheld mobile devices while driving except in emergencies. States that fail to comply with the law would lose a portion of their federal transportation funds.[22]

The policy fragmentation created by federalism may be solved when an industry asks the national government to develop a single regulatory policy. In the antifreeze case discussed earlier, the state actions convinced the industry trade group that represents antifreeze manufacturers that it should drop its opposition to federal safety regulations.[23] Although an industry may prefer no regulation at all, it generally prefers one instead of fifty.

Another counterweight to fragmentation is the working relationships that develop among the many participants in the pluralist system. Suppose that Congress is considering amendments to the Clean Air Act. Because Congress does not function in a vacuum, other parts of government affected by the legislation participate in the process too. The Environmental Protection Agency (EPA) has an interest in the outcome because it will have to administer the law. The White House is concerned about legislation that affects such vital sectors of the economy as the steel and coal industries. Thus, officials from the EPA and the White House work with members of Congress and the appropriate committee staffs to try to ensure that their interests are protected. At the same time, lobbyists representing corporations, trade associations, and environmental groups try to influence Congress, agency officials, and White House aides. Experts from think tanks and universities might be asked to testify at hearings or to serve in an informal advisory capacity.

issue network

A shared-knowledge group consisting of representatives of various interests involved in some particular aspect of public policy.

The various individuals and organizations that work in a policy area form a loosely knit community known as an **issue network**, where participants share expertise in a policy domain and interact frequently.[24] Such networks include members of Congress, committee staffers, agency officials, lawyers, lobbyists, consultants, scholars, and public relations specialists. Overall, a network can be quite large. One study identified over twelve hundred interest groups that had some contact with government officials in relation to health care over a five-year period.[25]

The common denominator in a network is not the same political outlook but policy expertise. Consider Medicare. The program is crucial to the health of the elderly, and with millions of baby boomers beginning to retire, it needs to be structured carefully to make sure there will be enough money available to care for them all. But to enter the political debate on Medicare requires specialized knowledge. For instance, what is the difference between "global capitation" and "fee for service"? "Advance directives" and "withholds for never events" may be grating jargon to the uninitiated, but they are meaningful terms to those in this network. In short, members of an issue network speak the same language. They understand the substance of policy, the way Washington works, and one another's viewpoints.

In a number of ways, issue networks promote pluralist democracy. They are open systems, populated by a wide range of interest groups. Decision making is not centralized in the hands of a few key players; policies are formulated in a participatory fashion. But there is still no guarantee that all relevant interests are represented, and those with greater financial resources have an advantage. Nevertheless, issue networks provide access to government for a diverse set of competing interests and thus further the pluralist ideal.

Issue networks are an obstacle to achieving the majoritarian vision of how government should operate. The technical complexity of contemporary issues makes it difficult for the public at large to influence policy outcomes. The more complex an issue, the more elected officials must depend on the technocratic elite that comprise issue networks for policy guidance. Yet majoritarianism still influences policymaking. The broad contours of public opinion can be a dominant force on highly visible issues.[26] Elections, too, send messages to policymakers about the most widely discussed campaign issues. What issue networks have done, however, is facilitate pluralist politics in policy areas in which majoritarian influences are weak.

With this overview of the policymaking process in place, we now turn our attention to some of the largest, most expensive, and politically challenging domestic policy programs in the United States. We discuss how these programs became part of the political agenda and how they have been formulated, implemented, evaluated, and altered over time. We also illustrate how different perspectives on these programs highlight different values placed on freedom, order, and equality.

18.2 The Development of the American Welfare State

★ Trace the evolution of social welfare programs as a central element of public policy in the United States.

The most controversial purpose of government is to promote social and economic equality. To do so may conflict with the freedom of some citizens because it requires government action to redistribute income from rich to poor. This choice between freedom and equality constitutes the modern dilemma of government; it has been at the center of many conflicts in U.S. public policy since World War II. On one hand, most Americans believe that government should help the needy.[27] On the other hand, they do not want to sacrifice their own standard of living in order to do so.

At one time, governments confined their activities to the minimal protection of people and property—to ensuring security and order. Now, almost every modern nation is a **welfare state** serving as the provider and protector of individual well-being through economic and social programs. **Social welfare programs** are government programs designed to provide the minimum living conditions necessary for all citizens. Income for the elderly, health care, public assistance, and education are among the concerns addressed by government social welfare programs.

Social welfare policy is based on the premise that society has an obligation to meet the basic needs of its members. The term *welfare state* describes this protective role of government.

welfare state
A nation in which the government assumes responsibility for the welfare of its citizens by providing a wide array of public services and redistributing income to reduce social inequality.

social welfare programs
Government programs that provide the minimum living standards necessary for all citizens.

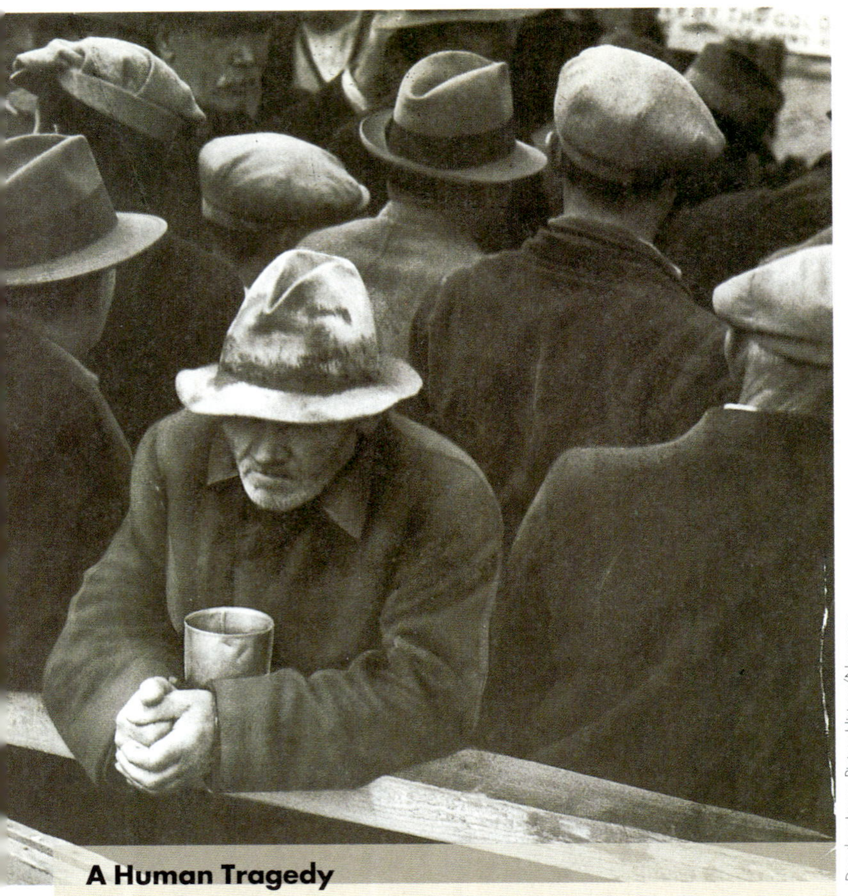

A Human Tragedy

The Great Depression idled millions of able-bodied Americans. By 1933, when President Herbert Hoover left office, about one-fourth of the labor force was out of work. Private charities were swamped with the burden of feeding the destitute. The hopeless men pictured here await a handout from a wealthy San Francisco matron known as the "White Angel," who provided resources for a bread line.

Dorothea Lange Picture History/Newscom

To understand American social welfare policies, one must first understand the significance of a major event in U.S. history—the Great Depression—and the two presidential plans that extended the scope of government, the New Deal and the Great Society. Initiatives from these programs dominated national policy and established the idea that it is the role of the federal government to help meet the basic needs of its citizens until changes in the 1980s and 1990s produced retrenchment of the American welfare state.

The Great Depression and the New Deal

Throughout its history, the U.S. economy has experienced alternating good and bad times, generally referred to as business cycles (see Chapter 17). The **Great Depression** was the longest and deepest setback that the American economy ever experienced. It began with the stock market crash on October 24, 1929, and did not end until the start of World War II. By 1933, one out of every four U.S. workers was unemployed, and millions more were underemployed. To put that in perspective, the annual U.S. unemployment rate since the end of World War II has never topped 10 percent.[28] The effect of the Great Depression on attitudes about the role of government and on the actual operation of governmental institutions is arguably without peer.

Great Depression

The longest and deepest setback the American economy has ever experienced. It began with the stock market crash on October 24, 1929, and did not end until the start of World War II.

New Deal

The measures advocated by the Franklin D. Roosevelt administration to alleviate the Depression.

In the 1930s, the forces that stemmed earlier business declines were no longer operating. There were no more frontiers, no growth in export markets, no new technologies to boost employment. Unchecked, unemployment spread, and the crisis fueled itself. Workers who lost their income could not buy the food, goods, and services that kept the economy going. Private industry and commercial farmers produced more than they could sell profitably. Closed factories, surplus crops, and idle workers were the consequences. From 1929 to 1932, more than 44 percent of the nation's banks failed when unpaid loans exceeded the value of bank assets. Farm prices fell by more than half in the same period. Upon accepting the presidential nomination at the 1932 Democratic National Convention, Franklin Delano Roosevelt, then governor of New York, said: "I pledge you, I pledge myself to a new deal for the American people." Roosevelt did not specify the contents of his **New Deal**, but the term was applied to measures Roosevelt's administration undertook to stem the Depression. The most significant New Deal policy created the Social Security program, which is explained in detail later in this chapter. Overall, New Deal policies initiated a long-range trend toward government expansion.

The Great Society

After the assassination of President John F. Kennedy in November 1963, his successor, Lyndon Baines Johnson, championed a policy program designed to foster equality (see Chapter 12). After winning the 1964 presidential election in a landslide, Johnson entered 1965 committed to pushing an aggressive and activist domestic agenda. In his 1965 State of the Union address, President Johnson offered his own version of the New Deal: the **Great Society**, an array of programs designed to redress political, social, and economic inequality. In contrast to the New Deal, which was largely aimed at short-term relief, most of Johnson's programs targeted chronic ills requiring a long-term commitment by the government.

Central to the Great Society was the **War on Poverty**. The major weapon in this war was the Economic Opportunity Act (1964), which encouraged local programs to educate and train people for employment. Among them were college work-study programs, summer employment for high school and college students, loans to small businesses, a domestic version of the Peace Corps (called VISTA, for Volunteers in Service to America), educational enrichment and nutrition for preschoolers through Head Start, and legal services for the poor.

Great Society
President Lyndon Johnson's broad array of programs designed to redress political, social, and economic inequality.

War on Poverty
A part of President Lyndon Johnson's Great Society program, intended to eradicate poverty within ten years.

Retrenchment and Reform

Despite the declining poverty rate that followed the passage of Great Society programs, in subsequent years, critics seized on the perceived shortcomings of the growing American welfare state. Perhaps these counterarguments were the predictable result of the high standards that President Johnson and his team had set, such as a promise to eliminate poverty in a decade. The fact that poverty persisted (even though it had declined) and had become more concentrated in areas that the Great Society had targeted (inner cities and rural areas) suggested to some observers that the effort was a failure.

Those arguments took hold in the late 1970s and helped Ronald Reagan capture the White House in 1980. Reagan's victory and landslide reelection in 1984 forced a reexamination of social welfare policy. In a dramatic departure from his predecessors (Republicans as well as Democrats), Reagan shifted emphasis from economic equality to economic freedom. He questioned whether government alone should be responsible for guaranteeing the well-being of less fortunate citizens. He maintained that to the extent that government should bear this responsibility, state and local governments could do so more efficiently than the national government. Congress, controlled by Democrats, blocked some of Reagan's proposed cutbacks, and many Great Society programs remained in force, although with less funding. The growth in the promotion of social welfare that began with the New Deal ended with the Reagan administration. Then President Bill Clinton, a Democrat, entered office in 1993 hoping to reform social safety net programs while simultaneously protecting their basic elements. Charting that middle course became essential after 1994 when Republicans took control of Congress. By the end of Clinton's two terms, important reforms emerged in public assistance, which we describe later in this chapter. Then the George W. Bush administration led the greatest expansion of welfare benefits for seniors with the passage of the Medicare drug program. President Obama, in turn, enacted the biggest welfare state reform since the New Deal, with the passage of health-care reform in 2010.

Despite these recent expansions, all safety net programs have been severely tested in recent years due to a recession. Even if these difficult economic times have renewed support for the welfare state, the problem of how to fund it poses significant barriers to helping citizens meet their basic needs.

18.3 Social Security

★ Describe the origins and evolution of Social Security as well as the funding and benefit issues facing the program.

social insurance
A government-backed guarantee against loss by individuals without regard to need.

Insurance protects against loss. Since the late nineteenth century, there has been a growing tendency for governments to offer **social insurance**, which is government-backed protection against loss by individuals, regardless of need. Common forms of social insurance offer health protection and guard against losses from worker sickness, injury, and disability; old age; and unemployment. The first social insurance in the United States was workers' compensation. Beginning early in the twentieth century, this insurance compensated workers who lost income because they were injured in the workplace.

Social insurance benefits are distributed to recipients without regard to their economic status. Old-age benefits, for example, are paid to workers—rich or poor—provided that they have enough covered work experience and have reached the required age. Thus, social insurance programs are examples of **entitlements**—benefits to which every eligible person has a legal right and that the government cannot deny. The largest entitlement program is **Social Security**.

entitlements
Benefits to which every eligible person has a legal right and that the government cannot deny.

Social Security
Social insurance that provides economic assistance to persons faced with unemployment, disability, or old age. It is financed by taxes on employers and employees.

Social Security is social insurance that provides economic assistance to people faced with unemployment, disability, or old age. In most social insurance programs, employees and employers contribute to a fund from which employees later receive payments. Contributions to two programs for social insurance in the United States are taken from workers' wages: Social Security and Medicare. The Social Security tax supports disability, survivors' benefits, and retirement benefits. Since 1990, this tax has been assessed at a rate of 6.2 percent, but was temporarily reduced to 4.2 percent in 2011 as part of an attempt to stimulate economic recovery. In 2012, the tax was only assessed on the first $110,000 earned. The Medicare tax finances much (but not all) of the Medicare program and has been assessed at 1.45 percent of all wages since 1986.[29]

Origins of Social Security

The idea of Social Security came late to the United States. Most European nations adopted old-age insurance after World War I; many provided income support for the disabled and income protection for families after the death of the principal wage earner. In the United States, however, the needs of the elderly and the unemployed were left largely to private organizations and individuals. Although twenty-eight states had old-age assistance programs by 1934, neither private charities nor state governments could cope with the prolonged unemployment and distress of the Great Depression. It became clear that a national policy was necessary to deal with a national crisis.

Social Security Act
The law that provided for Social Security and is the basis of modern American social welfare.

In 1935, President Roosevelt signed the **Social Security Act**, which remains the cornerstone of the modern American welfare state. The act developed three approaches to the problem of dependence. The first provided social insurance in the form of old-age and surviving-spouse benefits and cooperative state–national unemployment assistance. To ensure that the elderly did not retire into poverty, it created a program to provide income to retired workers. An unemployment insurance program was also created to provide payments for a limited time to workers who were laid off or dismissed for reasons beyond their control.

The second approach provided aid to the destitute in the form of grants-in-aid to the states. It was the first national commitment to provide financial assistance to the needy aged, needy families with dependent children, the blind, and (since the 1950s) the permanently and totally disabled.

The third approach provided health and welfare services through federal aid to the states. Included were health and family services for disabled children and orphans and vocational rehabilitation for the disabled.

How Social Security Works

Although the Social Security Act encompasses many components, when most people think of "Social Security," they have the retirement security element of the law in mind. Revenues for retirement security go into their own *trust fund* (each program contained in the Social Security Act has a separate fund). The fund is administered by the Social Security Administration, which became an independent government agency in 1995. Trust fund revenue can be spent only for the old-age benefits program. Benefits, in the form of monthly payments, begin when an employee reaches retirement age, which is sixty-seven for people born in 1960 or later. People can retire as early as age sixty-two with reduced benefits.

Social Security taxes collected today pay the benefits of today's retirees with any surpluses held over to help finance the retirement of future generations. Thus, Social Security (and social insurance in general) is not a form of savings (your contributions are not set aside for your retirement); it is a pay-as-you-go tax system. Today's workers support today's program beneficiaries. Universal participation is thus essential. Government—the only institution with the authority to coerce—requires all employees and their employers to contribute, thereby imposing restrictions on freedom.

When the Social Security program began, it had many contributors and few beneficiaries. The program could therefore provide relatively large benefits with low taxes. In 1955, Social Security taxes of nearly 9 workers supported each beneficiary. Over time, this ratio has decreased, dropping to 2.9 workers for every beneficiary in 2011.[30]

The solvency of the Social Security program will soon be tested. As the baby-boom generation begins to retire, politicians will face an inevitable dilemma: lower benefits and anger retirees, or raise taxes and anger taxpayers. Based on projections from recent analyses, the program's assets will be exhausted by 2036 (see Figure 18.3, p. 532).[31]

People who currently pay into the system receive retirement benefits financed by future participants. If the birthrate remains steady or grows, future wage earners can support today's contributors when they retire. And if the economy expands, there will be more jobs, more income, and a growing wage base to tax for benefits to retirees. But when the birthrate falls or mortality declines or the economy falters, then contributions decline and the financial status of the program suffers. With life expectancy in the United States roughly five years longer than it was when Social Security was created, some argue that it is time to increase the retirement age since retirees today benefit from the program for a longer period of time than was originally envisioned. If the retirement age had been indexed to life expectancy in 1935, the retirement age today would be around seventy-two.[32]

Who Pays? Who Benefits?

"Who pays?" and "Who benefits?" are always important questions in government policymaking, and they continue to shape Social Security policy. In 1968, Republicans

FIGURE 18.3 Day of Reckoning

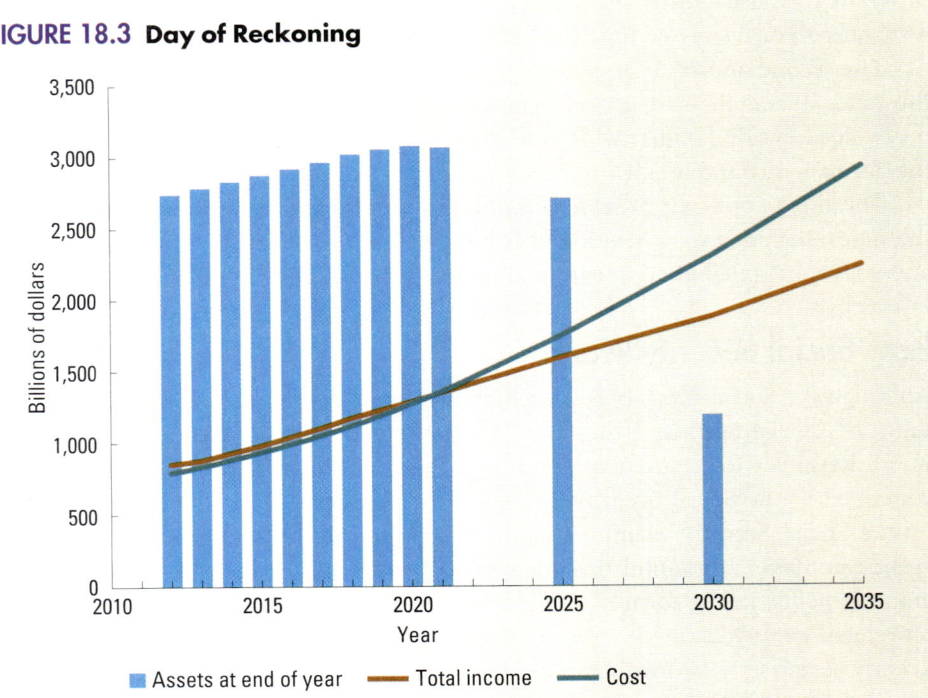

Since 2010, tax revenues are no longer sufficient to meet the cost of Social Security. With bankruptcy of the system looming, debate over change boils down to two questions that politicians politely decline to answer: How soon will the national government change the current system, and how much will it change it?

Source: U.S. Social Security Administration, "2011 OASDI Trustees Report," Table VI.F8, www.ssa.gov.

called for automatic increases in Social Security payments as the cost of living rose. In 1969, Democrats and Republicans tried to outdo each other by suggesting larger cost-of-living adjustments (COLAs) for retirees. The result was a significant expansion in benefits, far in excess of the cost of living. The beneficiaries were the retired, who were beginning to flex their political muscle. Politicians knew that alienating this constituency could lose them an election.[33]

In 1972, Congress adopted automatic adjustments in benefits and in the dollar amount of contributors' wages subject to tax. This approach set Social Security on automatic pilot. The COLA is now based on changes in the Consumer Price Index. During the most recent economic downturn, the Consumer Price Index did not rise, which resulted in no COLA in 2010 or 2011, marking the first time that benefits did not rise since adjustments were made automatic in the 1970s. In 2012, the COLA was 3.2 percent.[34]

Social Security Reform

Given the fund projections and demographic trends discussed earlier, concern over the future survival of Social Security runs high. For example, in 2010, 60 percent of nonretired adults said that they were not confident that Social Security would have the money available to pay for their benefits when they retire.[35]

Repeated attempts to reform Social Security have failed to be enacted due to the tough choices involved. President George W. Bush advocated allowing individual workers to invest their own payroll taxes in the stock market in hopes of earning a higher rate of return than currently paid to the Social Security Trust Funds. However, people who wanted to stay in the current Social Security system could choose to do so.[36] But he was unable to generate enough support for the reform, since many Americans and lawmakers alike feared that privatizing the program would expose the elderly to too much risk of lost savings should the stock market decline. Bush left office with the Social Security program unchanged.

When Barack Obama took office in 2009, addressing the economic recession became his first priority, and reforming Social Security returned to the back burner, though Obama stated that he opposed privatization.[37] In fact, one of his key tools for combating the recession was to temporarily *reduce* Social Security payroll taxes. The loss of funds was compensated by taking money from the nation's general funds and transferring it to the Social Security program.[38] Members of both parties have expressed fears that these cuts will be made permanent, making the future footing of the program even more tenuous.

Yet it is unlikely that Congress or the White House will ever let the Social Security fund run dry, which means that the issues of raising taxes, raising the retirement age, reducing benefit levels, and devising alternative means of controlling the fund will return to the agenda. Given the unpopularity of all of these options, decision makers will be reluctant to act until it becomes absolutely necessary.

18.4 Public Assistance

★ Explain how poverty is defined and trace the evolution of public assistance programs designed to address it.

Most people mean **public assistance** when they use the term *welfare*; it is government aid to individuals who demonstrate a need for that aid. Although much public assistance is directed toward those who lack the ability or the resources to provide for themselves or their families, the poor are not the only recipients of welfare. Corporations, farmers, and college students are among the many recipients of government aid in the form of tax breaks, subsidized loans, and other benefits.

Public assistance programs instituted under the Social Security Act, in contrast to the retirement security components of the law, are known today as *categorical assistance programs.* They include (1) old-age assistance for the needy elderly not covered by old-age pension benefits, (2) aid to the needy blind, (3) aid to needy families with dependent children, and (4) aid to the disabled. Adopted initially as stop-gap measures during the Great Depression, these programs have become entitlements. They are administered by the states, but most funding comes from the national government's general tax revenues. Because states also contribute to funding of their public assistance programs, the benefits and some standards that define eligibility can vary widely from state to state.

Poverty in the United States

Until 1996, the government imposed national standards on state welfare programs. It distributed funds to each state based on the proportion of its population living in poverty. That proportion is determined by a federally defined **poverty level**, or poverty threshold, which is the minimum cash income that will provide for a family's basic needs. The poverty level varies by family size and was originally calculated as three times the cost of a minimally nutritious diet for a given number of people over

public assistance
Government aid to individuals who can demonstrate a need for that aid.

poverty level
The minimum cash income that will provide for a family's basic needs; calculated using the Consumer Price Index.

a given time period. The threshold was computed this way because research suggested that poor families of three or more persons spent approximately one-third of their income on food.[39] Today, the threshold is adjusted using the Consumer Price Index (see Chapter 17). The poverty *threshold* is what the Census Bureau uses to determine the number of people who live below the poverty line. In 2010, the poverty threshold for a family of four was a cash income below $22,314.[40] The Department of Health and Human Services uses a slightly different measure, called the poverty guideline, to determine the income level at which families qualify for government assistance.

The poverty level is only a rough measure for distinguishing the poor from the nonpoor. For instance, the poverty level has been fairly constant since the early 1970s, even though other indicators of well-being, like the infant mortality rate and the percentage of adults with a high school diploma, show dramatic improvement in that same time period.[41] Policymakers have considered different approaches to determine how much a family of four needs to live in the United States, but they have been reluctant to abandon a measure that has been in use since the 1960s.

Critics of the current formula argue that a more accurate measure of the poverty level would show higher levels of poverty in the United States, since the proportion of income spent on food has declined as the costs of housing, child care, health care, and other expenses have increased. Others contend that the poverty measure should count noncash benefits that people receive through government programs, such as food stamps, as income, and that doing so would reveal lower levels of poverty.[42] We attach importance to the poverty-level figure, despite its inaccuracies, because it helps us assess how the American promise of equality stands up against the performance of our public policies.

The poverty rate in the United States declined after the mid-1960s, rose slightly in the 1980s, then declined again. In 2010, the U.S. Census Bureau estimated that 46.2 million people, or roughly 15.1 percent of the population, were living in poverty.[43] That's up from 12.5 percent in 2007 before the recent recession began. Poverty was once a condition of old age, but Social Security changed that. Today, poverty is still related to age, but in the opposite direction: it is largely a predicament of the young. In 2010, 22.0 percent of persons under eighteen years old were in poverty, compared with about 9.0 percent of people over sixty-five.[44]

Another trend in the United States, which we describe in Figure 18.4, is the concentration of poverty in households headed by single women. One in every two poor Americans resides in a family in which a woman is the head of the household. Researchers have labeled this trend toward greater poverty among women the **feminization of poverty**.

feminization of poverty
The term applied to the fact that a growing percentage of all poor Americans are women or the dependents of women.

Welfare Reform

In the wake of Johnson's Great Society programs, critics of social welfare spending argued that antipoverty policies made poverty more attractive by removing incentives to work. During Reagan's campaign for the presidency, he blamed such policies for creating Cadillac-driving "welfare queens."[45] Then in 1996, the Republican-led Congress sought a fundamental revision of the welfare system and enlisted President Clinton in their cause. When Clinton signed the Personal Responsibility and Opportunity to Work Act into law that year, he abolished the sixty-one-year-old Aid to Families with Dependent Children (AFDC) program, which since the 1930s had provided cash assistance that had kept millions of citizens afloat during difficult times, and replaced it with the **Temporary Assistance for Needy Families (TANF)** program.

Temporary Assistance for Needy Families (TANF)
A 1996 national act that abolished the longtime welfare policy, Aid for Families with Dependent Children (AFDC). TANF gives the states much more control over welfare policy.

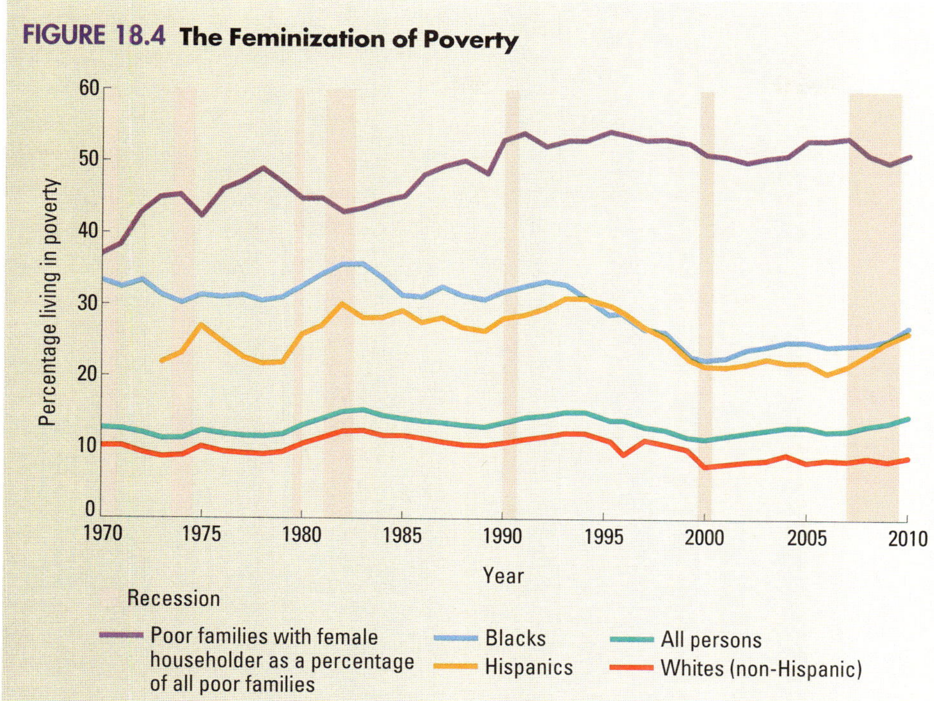

FIGURE 18.4 The Feminization of Poverty

The twentieth century brought extraordinary changes for women. Women won the right to vote and own property, and they gained some legal and social equality (see Chapter 16). But increases in rates of divorce and adolescent pregnancy have cast more women into the head-of-household role, a condition that tends to push women and children into poverty. In the absence of a national child-care policy, single women with young children face limited employment opportunities and lower wages in comparison to other workers. These factors have contributed to the feminization of poverty—the fact that a growing percentage of all poor Americans are women or the dependents of women.

Sources: Barbara Ehrenreich and Frances Fox Piven, "The Feminization of Poverty," *Dissent* (Spring 1984): 162–170; Harrell R. Rodgers, Jr., *Poor Women, Poor Families: The Economic Plight of America's Female-Headed Households,* 2nd ed. (Armonk, N.Y.: M. E. Sharpe, 1990); and U.S. Census Bureau, *Income, Poverty, and Health Insurance Coverage in the United States: 2010* (Washington, D.C.: U.S. Government Printing Office, September 2011), Table 4, http://www.census.gov/prod/2011pubs/p60-239.pdf.

Critics of AFDC complained that government aid discouraged individuals from seeking work. The program was also unpopular. In 1994, 59 percent of Americans thought that "welfare recipients were taking advantage of the system."[46] Although originally established with widowed mothers in mind, AFDC grew rapidly beginning in the 1960s as divorce and single motherhood increased (see Figure 18.5, p. 536). By the time AFDC was abolished, 4 million adults and almost 9 million children were on welfare, and 24 million Americans were receiving food stamps. The end of AFDC significantly changed the lives of more than one-fifth of American families.

Under TANF, which devolves power to the states, adult recipients of welfare payments have to become employed within two years. The law places the burden of job training and creation on the states. Families can receive no more than a total of five years of benefits in a lifetime, and states can set a lower limit.[47]

How has welfare reform affected the states? In terms of funding, federal support for the law has been implemented through block grants, or a lump-sum, to the states totaling $16.5 billion per year. That money is now used to help finance fifty different welfare systems. Initially, at least, some state officials were concerned by the stringent work requirements and confused by some of the new provisions. The extent to which

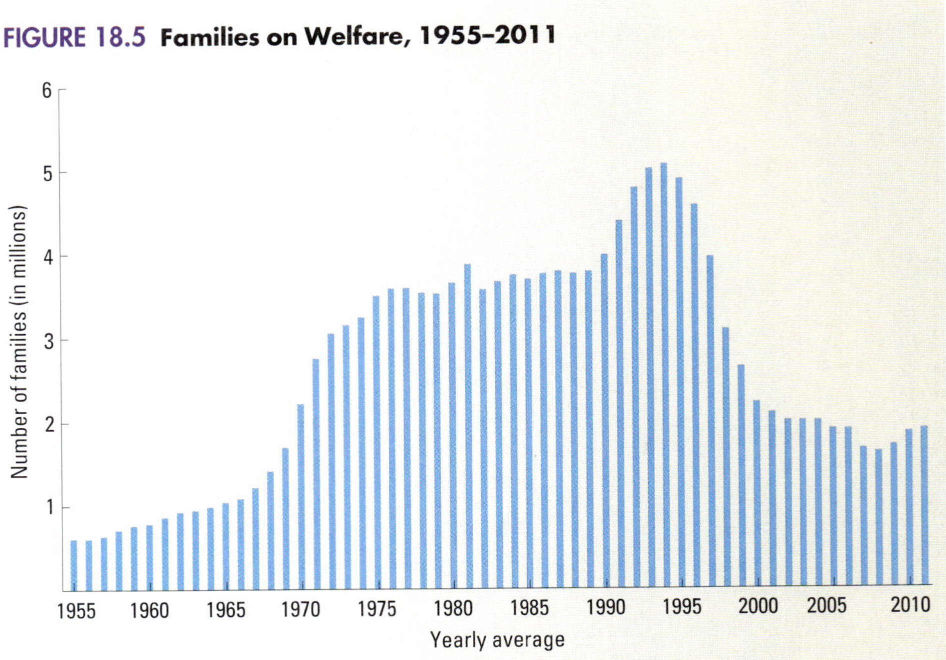

FIGURE 18.5 Families on Welfare, 1955–2011

Beginning in the 1950s, the number of families on welfare skyrocketed as divorce and single motherhood increased. The welfare rolls stabilized during the late 1970s but rose again in the early 1990s. The sharp decline at the end of the 1990s was a product of welfare reform and the demand for workers fueled by a strong domestic economy. Rolls have increased somewhat since the 2007 recession.

Source: Department of Health and Human Services, Administration for Children and Families, "TANF Data and Reports," http://www.acf.hhs.gov/programs/ofa/data-reports/index.htm.

states would be able to count job training or other education as work is an issue that state and federal officials have debated since 1996. As in any other complicated piece of legislation, the process of writing regulations and offering guidance to help states implement the law has consumed significant time. Overall, though, state leaders generally were pleased with the increased flexibility that TANF provided when compared to policy on the books prior to 1996. In 2009, nearly 28 percent of TANF funds went to direct cash assistance to poor families, 17.5 percent paid for child care, 15 percent covered employment programs, and 32 percent covered other services and programs aimed at helping low-income families.[48]

What about welfare recipients themselves? How have they fared under the law? As Figure 18.5 illustrates, the number of families on welfare has declined and remained relatively low when compared to the pre-TANF period. Large numbers of former welfare recipients were able to find steady work. One of the biggest fears of TANF's critics, that employers would find former welfare recipients undesirable employees and that there would be few jobs available in major urban areas, did not materialize.[49] As a result, Americans' opposition to welfare spending has declined in recent years, and their attitudes about welfare recipients have improved.[50]

Other trends are less promising. Despite former welfare recipients' increased levels of employment, most have not been able to find jobs that pay good wages and offer valuable benefits, such as health care. Thus, many former TANF recipients still live below or close to the poverty level. Moreover, studies have found that these jobs often require workers to have long commutes, which creates added stress as parents need to secure child care during their long workday.[51] One source of confusion among TANF recipients and state officials has been the extent to which recipients maintain eligibility for other federal programs, such as Medicaid, even as they move into full-time employment. Reaching out to individuals as they make the transition from welfare to work has been a challenge for policymakers and private or nonprofit contractors who implement the law.

Other challenges became acute during the recent recession, the most significant test of the program's ability to meet the needs of poor Americans. Many Americans hit hard by the recession were not helped by TANF. The problem, analysts say, is that the block grant funding is set to a fixed amount and does not change in response to increased need. Moreover, that fixed amount has not changed since TANF was first created. As a result, TANF cases did not rise much during the recession despite widespread job loss and hardship. As a point of comparison, the food stamp program (known as SNAP, or Supplemental Nutrition Assistance Program), which gets increased funding when the need arises, saw a 45 percent increase in its participation rate from 2007 to 2009, whereas TANF participation only rose by 13 percent. With the dollar amount given to states unchanged and with needs rising, many states actually cut TANF benefits during the recession.[52]

President Obama's economic stimulus plan (the American Recovery and Reinvestment Act of 2009) included a provision for emergency grants of $5 billion to supplement the block grants.[53] Those grants, however, expired in 2010. A separate line of supplemental TANF funds created by Congress in 1996 also expired in 2011, leaving states with only their fixed block grant amount, an amount that has not kept up with inflation.[54]

TANF was due to be reauthorized in 2010. During the reauthorization process, Congress debates whether to make changes to both the funding levels and the rules that affect how and under what conditions the funds may be spent. TANF has not yet been formally reauthorized; instead Congress has been passing temporary measures to continue funding the program. When Congress finally turns its attention to TANF, the policy evaluation (recall Figure 18.2) will likely center on how the program fared during the recent recession. Although welfare reform was initially hailed as a success, the experiences of the past few years have led many people to conclude otherwise.

18.5 Health Care

★ Differentiate among Medicare, Medicaid, and the Affordable Care Act of 2010 and explain how each program addresses the issues of health-care delivery.

One important function of a modern welfare state is to protect the health of its population. How to do that is a source of constant debate. The United States is the only major industrialized nation without a universal health-care system. Rather, a patchwork system of care designed to cover different segments of the population has evolved over time. In addition to private insurance, which many Americans receive as a benefit of employment, government programs to provide health care include Medicare, primarily for the elderly; Medicaid, for the qualifying poor; and the Children's Health Insurance Program (CHIP) for children in needy families. This section discusses Medicare, Medicaid, and the health-care bill enacted by the Obama administration in 2010.

Cost and Access

Nearly everyone agrees that the U.S. health-care system needs changing. To better understand the American system of health care and possibilities for reforms, it is important to consider two issues that animate the nation's health-care debate: access to care and cost. First, many Americans have no health insurance. In 2010, nearly 50 million Americans, roughly 16 percent, had no health insurance. The number of uninsured people varies according to factors such as age, race, and income. People under thirty-five are less likely to have insurance, as are African Americans, Hispanics, immigrants, and families with an income under $50,000. Figure 18.6 lists the states with the highest percentages of uninsured residents. About two-thirds of Americans with health insurance are insured through their employer or have some type of private plan, though the percentage of people who receive this kind of insurance has been decreasing each year since 2001. The remainder is insured through the government, with programs such as Medicaid, Medicare, and the military.[55]

Access to health care depends on more than having insurance. Many Americans with insurance are underinsured, with plans that do not adequately meet their true health-care needs. And even with adequate health insurance, many Americans lack easy access to doctors or hospitals. The supply of physicians in the United States simply does not meet the demand. Increasing the number of insured Americans might only make the problem worse. One study projects that with greater use of medical services, the United States will need 159,000 additional physicians by 2025.[56]

The second major issue confronting the nation's health-care system is cost. The health-care sector is a significant portion of the U.S. economy. In 2010, public and private spending on health care reached an all-time high of $2.6 trillion, which was 17.9 percent of gross domestic product (GDP).[57] Given the aging of the American population and the development of newer medical technologies, those numbers are

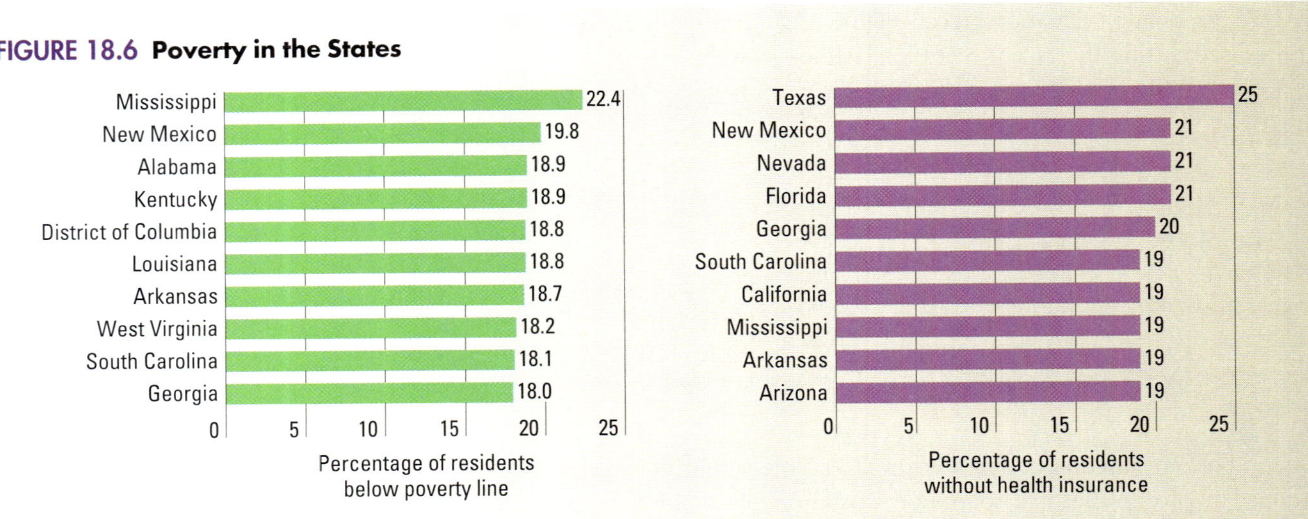

FIGURE 18.6 Poverty in the States

In 2010, 15.3 percent of all Americans lived below the poverty line; 16 percent had no health insurance. These national figures mask important differences across states. In Connecticut, for example, only around 10 percent of the population lives in poverty; in Mississippi, over 22 percent of residents live in poverty. In Hawaii and Wisconsin, less than 9 percent of state residents are without health insurance, yet a quarter of Texans don't have health insurance. Variations are due to state laws, social problems, immigration, and local job opportunities. In this figure, we list the top ten states according to the percentage of state residents who live below the poverty line and who are without health insurance (as of 2010).

Sources: U.S. Census Bureau, "Small Area Income and Poverty Estimates," 2010, http://www.census.gov//did/www/saipe/; and Kaiser Family Foundation, "Health Insurance Coverage of the Total Population, States (2009-2010), U.S. (2010)," http://www.statehealthfacts.org/comparetable.jsp?typ=2&ind=125&cat=3&sub=39&sortc=6&o=a.

projected to increase. By 2020, health care is expected to account for 19.8 percent of GDP.[58] The fastest-growing segment of the nation's health-care bill is in the area of prescription drugs. Among advanced industrial nations, the United States spends the largest proportion of its economy on health care. In 2009, it spent more than nations with comprehensive systems of coverage, including Switzerland (11.4 percent of GDP), Germany (11.6 percent), and Canada (11.4 percent) (see "Compared with What? Health Spending and Its Possible Effects").[59]

Compared with What?

Health Spending and Its Possible Effects

Compared to other nations, the United States spends a great deal of money on health care. In 2009, the United States spent more than 17 percent of its gross domestic product on health care. What does spending on health care achieve? Looking just at longevity, life expectancy in developed nations reveals little variation. Babies born in the United States in 2009 can expect to live on average to age seventy-eight. In contrast, babies born in Switzerland can expect to live to eighty-two, as can those born in Italy and Spain. Despite the fact that Americans outspend other nations on health care, the payoff in life expectancy has not been realized.

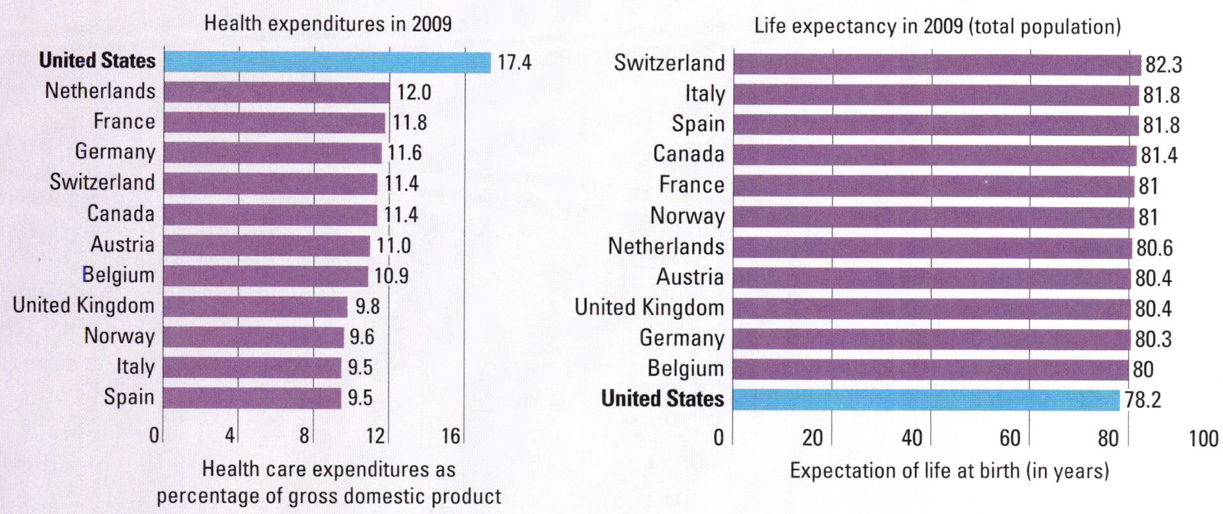

Source: OECD (2011), OECD Health Data 2011. http://www.oecd.org/health/healthdata. Copyright © 2011 by Organization for Economic Development and Cooperation (OECD). Reproduced by permission.

Critical Thinking

What other factors besides spending might affect a society's life expectancy? Why might the United States rank highest on spending but low on life expectancy?

The two central problems of health care, access and cost, give rise to two goals and a familiar dilemma. First, any reform should democratize health care by making it available to more people, ideally everyone. But by providing broad access to medical care, we will increase the amount we spend on such care and increase the amount of regulations we place on private insurance companies. Second, any reform must control the ballooning cost of health care. But controlling costs requires restricting the range of procedures and providers available to patients. Thus, the central problems of the health-care issue go to the heart of the modern dilemma of government: we must weigh greater equality in terms of universal coverage and cost controls against a loss of freedom in markets for health care and in choosing a doctor.

Over the past quarter of a century, the health insurance industry has undergone tremendous change, and it continues to do so as these trade-offs become more acute. Most Americans used to carry what was called catastrophic care insurance, which provided hospital coverage for serious illnesses only. As the cost of medical care ballooned, health-care providers realized that preventing illness through regular physical examinations was cheaper than curing illnesses after onset. Thus, health insurance providers began to offer extended coverage of routine, preventive care in return for limiting an individual's freedom to choose when and what type of medical specialist to see. Health insurance providers also became increasingly concerned with the amount of risk they were taking on by providing insurance. As discussed at the start of this chapter, they became more interested in covering healthy people who were likely to consume fewer services and less interested in covering people with existing— and expensive—medical conditions.

Medicare

In 1962, the Senate considered extending Social Security benefits to provide hospitalization and medical care for the elderly. Opponents were concerned that costs would soar without limit. Others echoed the fears of the American Medical Association (AMA), which saw any form of government-provided medical care as a step toward government control of medicine. Such opponents won the battle that day. Three years later, however, on the heels of Lyndon Johnson's victory in the 1964 election, the Social Security Act was amended to provide **Medicare**, a health insurance program for all people aged sixty-five and older.[60]

As early as 1945, public opinion supported some form of national health insurance, and President Harry Truman proposed such a program during his administration. However, that idea became entangled in Cold War politics—the growing crusade against communism in America.[61] The AMA, representing the nation's physicians, mounted and financed a campaign to link national health insurance (so-called socialized medicine) with socialism; the campaign was so successful that the prospect of a national health-care policy vanished.

Both proponents and opponents of national health insurance tried to link their positions to deeply rooted American values: advocates emphasized equality and fairness; opponents stressed freedom. In the absence of a clear mandate on the kind of insurance (publicly funded or private) the public wanted, the AMA was able to exert its political influence to prevent any national insurance at all.[62] After the 1960 election, however, the terms of the debate changed. It no longer focused on the clash between freedom and equality. Democrats cast the issue of health insurance in terms of providing assistance to the aged, a reframing that brought it back to the national agenda.[63]

Medicare
A health insurance program serving primarily persons sixty-five and older.

On July 30, 1965, with Harry Truman at his side, President Johnson signed a bill that provided a number of health benefits to the elderly and the poor. One major provision created a compulsory hospitalization insurance plan for the elderly (known today as Part A of Medicare). In addition, the bill created voluntary government-subsidized insurance to cover physicians' fees (known today as Part B of Medicare). In 2011, almost 49 million people were enrolled in the program, which cost roughly $550 billion.[64]

Medicare is compulsory insurance that covers certain hospital services for people aged sixty-five and older. Workers pay a tax, and for certain parts of the program other than Part A, retirees pay premiums deducted from their Social Security payments. Payments for services are made by the government directly to participating hospitals and other qualifying facilities. Citizens with Medicare coverage may also possess private insurance for additional services that the program may not cover or may cover in less generous ways.

The program still contains its original components, Parts A and B, but over the years, Medicare has expanded to cover more services and provide participants with additional health-care options. Today, Part A pays for care in facilities, such as inpatient hospital visits, care in skilled nursing facilities, and hospice. Part B pays for doctors' services and outpatient care. Services under Part A come at no cost to beneficiaries, but Part B services require participants to pay a premium (just under $100 in 2012); the government pays the remaining cost of Part B.

Taken together, Parts A and B are known as the Original Medicare Plan. Because that plan may not cover all services that seniors need, and because some may not have access to additional health insurance, the Medicare program has expanded to attempt to meet additional health-care needs. The program now offers a series of supplemental plans, known as Medigap plans, that are run by private insurance companies and that seniors pay for through a premium, which varies by type of plan.

An important change in Medicare occurred in 2003 with the passage of the Medicare Prescription Drug, Improvement, and Modernization Act. Rather than a single program with simple rules, the drug plan (known as Part D) encouraged private insurers to offer competing plans. In some locations, seniors may have the option of thirty or more plans from which to choose, each with different costs, deductibles, participating pharmacies, and formularies (covered medications). Like other aspects of Medicare, the costs of the program continue to increase at rates in excess of the cost of living. In 2011, 12 percent of government spending on Medicare was devoted to the prescription plan (see later section on health-care reform for new provisions related to Medicare).[65]

Medicaid

Another important part of the nation's health-care patchwork is **Medicaid**, the main program to provide health care to low-income Americans. Like Medicare, it was the product of the Great Society, and was passed as another amendment to the Social Security Act. In 1965, the program was relatively small and enrolled 4 million people at an annual cost of $0.4 billion. It has since become a massive program, enrolling more than 60 million people at a cost of $339 billion (federal and state expenditures combined).[66]

The program's scope is vast. It insures one in three of the nation's children and millions of low-income adults and people with disabilities. It also pays for 40 percent of all childbirths.[67] Although Medicaid is designed primarily to cover citizens with low incomes, the pool of eligible people varies significantly across the country. That

Medicaid
A need-based comprehensive medical and hospitalization program.

is because, unlike Medicare, which is solely a federal program, Medicaid is jointly run and financed by the federal government and the states. In 2010, the federal government provided just 56 percent of the total cost.[68] Federal law defines a certain minimum level of benefits that states must offer through Medicaid, but states vary in the criteria they use to define eligibility and in the types of services the program covers.

This sharing of cost and administration leaves some Medicaid beneficiaries in challenging circumstances since citizens who might be eligible for Medicaid services in one state may lose eligibility if they move elsewhere. Also, because Medicaid expenditures are typically one of the top expenses in state budgets (along with education), benefits are frequently cut when states experience difficult budgetary situations, as has occurred since the 2007 recession began. In 2011, forty-three states made cuts to their Medicaid programs, including restricting eligibility, reducing benefits, and lowering payments to health-care providers. Such cuts have been occurring since 2008 and come despite the fact that more and more people are relying on Medicaid.[69]

Medicaid participants fall into four main groups: children under age twenty-one (half of all participants in 2011), adults (mainly pregnant women, parents, and other caregivers of children), those who are disabled, and those aged sixty-five and over (senior citizens can qualify for Medicare *and* Medicaid if their incomes fall below a certain level).[70] Although their numbers are relatively small compared to other participants in the program, the disabled and elderly account for over half of Medicaid expenditures; the cost of the program is driven by the high cost of medical care for these two groups rather than other factors.[71] The recently enacted health-care reform (discussed in more detail below) could potentially expand the pool of eligible beneficiaries significantly starting in 2014 to include any adult earning up to 133 percent of the federal poverty level. Originally, the health care law required states to expand eligibility in this manner. Failure to do so would have resulted in the loss of all federal help paying for Medicaid. But the Supreme Court ruled in 2012 that such expansion can only be voluntary; the federal government cannot require it by threatening to remove such a significant portion of states' health-care funding. The threat, it was ruled, was too coercive. While some states are expected to refuse to expand (despite significant funding help from the federal government), many states probably will, and the expansion will only add to the size, scope, and cost of the program.

Health-Care Reform

In 2010, President Obama signed sweeping health-care reform legislation into law. The new law, called the Patient Protection and Affordable Care Act (known as the ACA), has been described as the most wide-ranging policy change in a generation, comparable the creation of Social Security. Its aim is to provide insurance to as

The Grim Politics of Health Care

While some federal courts rejected the Affordable Care Act's individual mandate, the Supreme Court upheld it under Congress' authority to levy taxes.

many Americans as possible. To get the law passed, Obama had to scale back some initial ideas (such as offering a health insurance plan administered by the federal government), create new taxes, and ensure that federal funds would not be used to cover the costs of abortions. The legislative battle pitted arguments about equality of access to care against arguments about freedom from government intervention. The arguments about equality won the day, but battles about the scope of this legislation endure.

The more notable aspects of the legislation are the following. As noted at the start of this chapter, people aged nineteen to twenty-five immediately became eligible to stay on their parents' insurance plans. By 2014, insurance providers can no longer deny people coverage because of preexisting conditions. Until then, people with preexisting conditions can gain coverage through a high-risk pool. To make it possible for insurers to pay for the needs of high-cost treatments, what is perhaps the most controversial aspect of the reform was added, namely that all individuals are required to have health insurance by 2014 or pay a fine (some are exempt from this so-called *individual mandate*, including Native Americans and people with religious objections or financial hardship). There are opportunities for people to get government subsidies to help them obtain coverage, and as noted earlier, the bill also expands eligibility for Medicaid. It is estimated that legislation will lead to near-universal coverage by 2019. Employers will be subjected to mandates as well. By 2014, all employers with fifty or more employees must offer health insurance or pay a fine. Tax credits are available to some small businesses that begin to offer health plans to their workers. Finally, states must set up insurance marketplaces, called *exchanges*, by 2014 where people and small businesses can shop for competitively priced health plans.[72]

One of the biggest concerns about this bill is how much it will cost: approximately $940 billion in the first ten years. While that figure led to sticker-shock for some, others argued that the reform will pay for itself. In fact, the Congressional Budget Office has estimated that the bill will reduce deficits by $143 billion over ten years. These savings are possible because of other features of the legislation: it places new taxes on high-cost health plans, places new Medicare taxes on wealthy Americans, creates a new tax on indoor tanning, charges fees to employers and private health insurance companies, and reforms some aspects of Medicare spending (including the creation of an advisory board that can alter how Medicare is administered and the introduction of program in which doctors are paid for the quality of treatment instead of the quantity). The state insurance exchanges are also expected to lower health-care costs; because private insurers will have new competition, insurance premiums are expected to decrease.[73]

That the reform is not expected to add to the deficit has not silenced critics. For people wary of "big government," any program that results in more bureaucracy, more regulation, and more taxes is problematic. Additionally, many patients and hospitals harbor fears about how reforms to Medicare will play out despite assurances that benefits will not be affected.

Some states have shown their concerns about the law by inaction rather than action. The deadline for establishing exchanges is looming; the legislation requires states to submit exchange plans to the Department of Health and Human Services by January 2013. But by the start of 2012, eight states showed no signs of planning their exchanges, and most others were "studying their options." Only thirteen states passed laws to establish their exchanges.[74] And as of this writing, governors of seven states have said that they will not participate in the Medicaid expansion included in the law.

Finally, other opponents simply charge that it is unconstitutional for the government to require that all individuals purchase health insurance. Nearly two years after the law was enacted, this provision remains unpopular: a 2012 survey found that 67 percent of Americans view the mandate unfavorably.[75] Several states filed lawsuits in federal court to challenge the new law, with some courts upholding the mandate and others rejecting it. In June 2012, the Supreme Court ruled in a 5–4 decision that the mandate is constitutional because the fine for failing to acquire insurance amounts to a tax, and Congress has the authority to levy taxes. Whether many of the alleged benefits or drawbacks of the ACA will come to pass still remains to be seen; several important provisions have yet to go into effect and state compliance with the law remains uncertain

★ 18.6 Elementary and Secondary Education

★ Describe the role of the federal government in shaping education policy at the state and local government levels.

Although it is no less important, education is unlike the other public policies discussed in this chapter given that responsibility for schooling resides primarily in state and local governments in the United States. Since Horace Mann introduced mandatory public schooling in Massachusetts in the mid-nineteenth century, public schools have been an important part of local government. The federal government covers only around 10 percent of the nation's K–12 education bill.[76]

Concerns Motivating Change

Two main factors, related to freedom, order, and equality, have prompted greater federal involvement in the nation's elementary and secondary schools during the last half century.

Equity. The overriding and persistent concern has been educational equity. An important part of Lyndon Johnson's Great Society was the American belief that social and economic equality could be attained through equality of educational opportunity. The justices of the Supreme Court argued as much in their landmark decision in *Brown* v. *Board of Education* (1954). Legislatively, the **Elementary and Secondary Education Act of 1965 (ESEA)**, yet another product of the Great Society, was the first major federal effort to address educational equity in a systematic way. The law, which has been reauthorized periodically, provided direct national government aid to local schools in order to improve the educational opportunities of the economically disadvantaged.

Elementary and Secondary Education Act of 1965 (ESEA)
The federal government's primary law to assist the nation's elementary and secondary schools. It emerged as part of President Lyndon Johnson's Great Society program.

The original law focused on economic disadvantage; later iterations recognized other groups, such as students for whom English is a second language and Native American students. A separate but related law, the Individuals with Disabilities Education Act (IDEA), is designed to improve educational opportunities for students of all ages (elementary school through college and graduate school) with physical or other disabilities.

Despite the federal policy, improvements in educational, and thus social and economic, equality have been elusive. Differences in student achievement between advantaged and disadvantaged groups have declined since the 1960s. However, gaps remain in key subject areas such as reading and math as well as in overall graduation rates.[77] These gaps are important because they tend to correlate with future educational and economic opportunities.[78]

National Security and Prosperity. Concern over educational achievement is not limited to issues of social equality at home. In an increasingly competitive global economy, countries are competing to offer—and attract—highly educated and skilled workers. Thus, a desire to keep the United States competitive with other nations, both economically and militarily, is one reason why education is considered a key public policy area.

The connection between national security and education is not new. It dates back at least as far as the 1950s when the Eisenhower administration promoted the National Defense Education Act of 1958 (NDEA). The law is considered to be a response to the Soviet Union's launch of a satellite known as *Sputnik,* the first such craft to orbit the earth. This Soviet success, which many interpreted to mean that the United States was losing the "brain race" against its rival, set off calls for improving the nation's stock of scientists and engineers, as well as its cadre of foreign language speakers, to counter the communist threat. Funding from the NDEA supported efforts in all of these areas at the elementary, secondary, and postsecondary levels.

A desire to improve American economic competitiveness has been the most recent force prompting greater efforts to improve the nation's education system. These concerns date back to the 1970s, when state governors realized the link between their own states' economic fortunes and the quality of their schools. These state-level concerns foreshadowed subsequent debates at the national level that forged a similar link between the competitiveness of the entire nation and the educational preparation of the country's young people.

These state- and national-level concerns coalesced in a famous report entitled *A Nation at Risk,* which was released in 1983 by the National Commission on Excellence in Education. The report charged that the nation's schools were inadequate and were getting worse. Its findings, along with improved data comparing American students with their international counterparts, through projects such as the Trends in International Mathematics and Science Study (TIMSS), created momentum for public officials to improve schools.

Values and Reform

At the center of debates over education is the dilemma of freedom versus equality. The American belief in equality is weighted toward equality of opportunity, and equality of opportunity depends on equal access to a good education. At the same time, Americans vehemently support their freedom to choose where to live, what kind of school they want their children to attend, and what their children will be taught while they are there.

As the national and international challenges we face grow in technological and scientific sophistication, the dilemmas of education reform will become more pressing. The questions of who will pay for reform, who will benefit, and how best to improve student learning came to a head in a major reauthorization of the ESEA, known as the **No Child Left Behind Act of 2001 (NCLB).**

The No Child Left Behind Act of 2001. In 2000, Republican candidate George W. Bush made education one of the most important issues in his campaign for the White House, and with much fanfare, he signed the measure into law in January 2002.[79]

No Child Left Behind Act of 2001 (NCLB)
The latest reauthorization of the Elementary and Secondary Education Act.

Although the law was technically a reauthorization of the ESEA, it also instituted far-reaching changes in education policy. Most significant among them was the law's requirement that states demonstrate that all of their students are performing at proficient levels in reading and math by 2014, leaving states free to determine their own standards of proficiency and means of assessment. Along the way, the law required schools to show that they were making "Adequate Yearly Progress" among all student groups, be they economically disadvantaged, weak in English language skills, or disabled. Progress was to be assessed through annual testing in reading and math for students in grades 3 through 8 and in grades 10, 11, and 12.

NCLB was initially praised for highlighting educational inequality and asserting that all students deserve qualified teachers. But its implementation has been controversial.[80] Critics charged that the emphasis on testing led teachers to "teach to the test" and ignore subjects that were not tested, like music and social studies. Others charged that the federal government did not spend enough money to help schools live up to the standards that it set.

When the NCLB law came up for reauthorization in 2007, the Bush administration wanted to expand the law to include more testing and merit pay for teachers. Democrats in Congress opposed the new changes, however, and members of the House Education and Labor Committee could not agree on a compromise bill. NCLB was not reauthorized.

The Obama administration wants to put its own stamp on the legislation. In 2010, President Obama sent a "Blueprint for Reform" to Congress. Among its notable provisions, the plan eliminates the requirement that all students be proficient in reading in math by 2014, replacing it with a goal of having all high school graduates deemed college-ready or career-ready by 2020. Rather than rely on states to devise their own standards of achievement, the plan encourages states to adopt a common set of educational goals. Finally, interventions to "turn schools around" would concentrate on the bottom 5 percent of schools instead of on Adequate Yearly Progress figures from all schools.[81]

As the administration waits for Congress to reauthorize the ESEA, it has encouraged states to conform to its approach by offering competitive grants through a program called "Race to the Top," in which schools become eligible for funds if they implement certain approaches, including adopting the set of common college- and career-ready goals (a clear use of incentives as an important public policy tool). Moreover, the White House announced that it would free any state from the 2014 deadline for 100 percent proficiency if it adopts the common set of goals and develops new systems for evaluating teacher effectiveness.[82]

Perhaps nowhere are the challenges of fragmentation and coordination on display more than with education policy. The 2001 NCLB Act and subsequent debates illustrate the difficulties of coordinating efforts across the states, devising national objectives that still allow for local flexibility, and evaluating which aspects of a policy work and which ones need reform.

★ 18.7 Immigration

Along with health care and education, illegal immigration is also central to the domestic policy agenda. Immigrants today make up around 12.5 percent of the population (see "Politics of Global Change: Nations of Immigrants"). It is estimated that about 11.2 million immigrants are here illegally, down from about 12 million in 2007.[83] Most Americans want to reduce the number of illegal immigrants further; around 50 percent of Americans regularly say that the level of immigration should be decreased.[84] But they have mixed opinions on the question of what to do

Politics of Global Change

Nations of Immigrants

The United States is widely celebrated as a "nation of immigrants," but many other Western democracies rival or surpass the United States in the percentage of the population that is foreign born. Some countries, such as Spain and Sweden, not only match the United States in this regard, but also have seen their percentage of foreign-born residents increase at more dramatic rates than the United States has over the past ten years. And it would perhaps be more appropriate to call Canada and Australia, two other countries with colonial ties to England, nations of immigrants than the United States. Australia's foreign-born population as a percentage of the total population is more than double that of the United States.

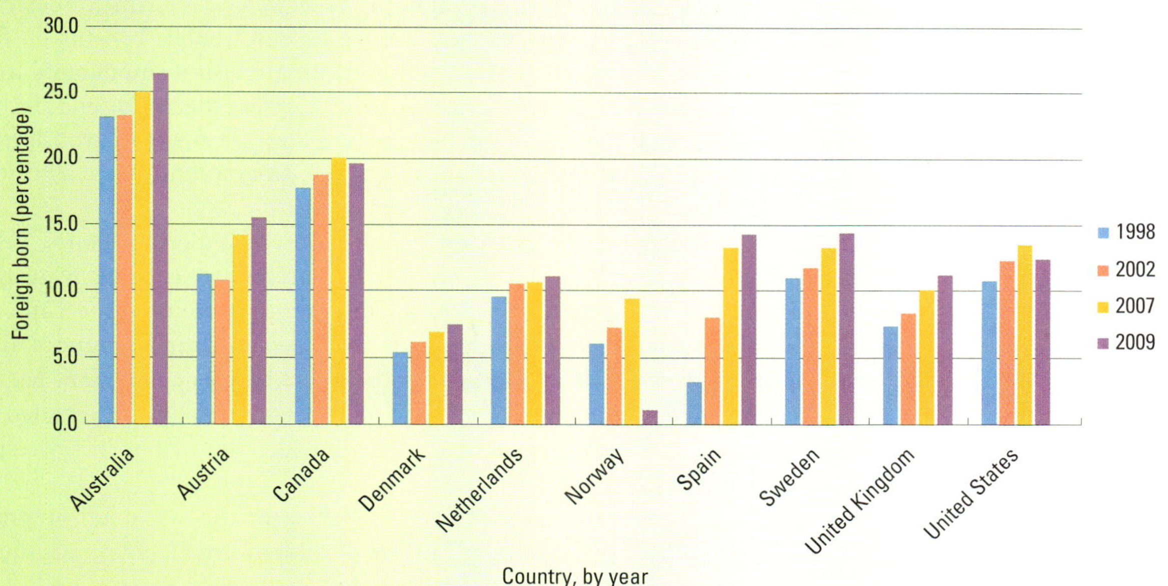

Source: OECD (2009), International Migration Outlook 2009, Table A.1.4, OECD Publishing. http://dx.doi.org/10.1787/migr_outlook-2009-en. Copyright © 2009 by Organization for Economic Development and Cooperation (OECD). Reproduced by permission.

Critical Thinking

What types of public policy issues might increasing rates of immigration bring to the forefront in these countries?

about the illegal immigrants who are already in the United States. Illegal immigrants are among the poorest and most vulnerable individuals. Whereas 16 percent of all Americans are without health insurance, 45 percent of foreign-born noncitizens lack health insurance. Almost 27 percent of noncitizens live below the poverty line.[85] Should they have access to the benefits of the social welfare state such as health care and education? Should they be eligible to earn citizenship?

The United States didn't regulate immigration until the end of the nineteenth century, and it wasn't until 1924 that the concept of an "illegal immigrant" emerged. It was then that Congress enacted the Johnson-Reed Act, which set strict quotas on the number of immigrants permitted to enter the country and the nations from which they could come. Due to racist concerns about the dilution of American culture, the act favored immigration from western Europe and severely limited immigration from southern and eastern Europe and from Asia. These restrictions were significantly loosened by the Johnson administration in 1965, which is when the rate of legal and illegal immigration began to surge.

Foreigners who wish to work in the United States for an extended period of time need to apply for a permanent resident card, or "green card." Individuals with a green card are known as "legal permanent residents," and they may eventually apply to become U.S. citizens. In 2010, the United States granted permanent admission to 1.04 million noncitizens.[86] Priority is given to reuniting families, admitting workers in occupations with strong demand for labor, providing a refuge for people who face persecution in their home countries, and providing admission to people from a diverse set of countries.[87] Prior to the 1996 welfare reforms (discussed earlier in this chapter), legal immigrants were eligible for most public benefits on the same terms as citizens. The 1996 reforms, however, prohibit legal immigrants from participating in safety net programs such as food stamps, Medicaid, and TANF until they have been in the country for five years. States are free to enroll legal immigrants sooner, provided that state funds—and not federal funds—are used to supply the benefit.[88]

But it is illegal immigrants who get the most attention in policy debates. If caught, they may be offered the chance to leave the country voluntarily, or they may be fined, imprisoned, deported, and prohibited from returning to the United States. In 2010, about 390,000 illegal immigrants were deported, and around 476,000 left voluntarily.[89] Most illegal immigrants in the United States come from Mexico and other Latin American countries. They tend to be geographically concentrated in western states and large urban areas, where they provide cheap labor in agriculture and manufacturing industries.[90]

Illegal immigrants have always been ineligible for the safety net programs discussed in this chapter (their American-born children are eligible), but they enroll in public schools and get treated in hospital emergency rooms, both of which come at a cost to American taxpayers. Most policy debates about illegal immigration focus on how best to increase border security with Mexico, how to get employers to stop hiring undocumented workers, and whether illegal immigrants currently in the United States should be allowed to become legal residents. Since 2005, Congress and the Bush and Obama administrations have sought legislation that would allow illegal immigrants in the United States to earn citizenship if they paid fines, passed English and civics exams, and remained employed, but every effort has stalled. Conservative groups charge that such legislation would give "amnesty" to people who had broken the law. Pro-immigrant groups have been concerned about another feature of most proposals, which would create a temporary worker program that allows people to work in the United States for a period of time and then force them to return to their home country before reapplying for a temporary permit. Unions fear that legal temporary workers would drive down wages and take jobs away from American workers. Liberals do not like yet another aspect of proposed reforms, which would require employers to use E-Verify, a program that allows employers to check the immigration status of current and future employees. With no consensus, reform efforts have repeatedly failed.[91] Despite the lack of progress, majorities of the American public consistently support the major proposals that both Bush and Obama advocated, including creating a so-called path to citizenship for illegal immigrants.[92] As with education, President Obama recently sent a "Blueprint for Immigration Reform" to Congress in the hope that the relevant committees will take action.[93]

Another proposal that Americans generally support but that has been stalled in Congress is the Development, Relief, and Education for Alien Minors (DREAM) Act. If passed, the act would allow illegal immigrants who had been brought to the United States as children to become eligible for legalized status. The bill failed most recently in 2010 after a Senate filibuster but has since been reintroduced.[94] In the meantime, President Obama issued an executive action in 2012 that directed federal immigration authorities to cease pursuing deportations for most illegal immigrants who were brought to the United States as children.

The Constitution grants Congress the authority to "establish a uniform rule of naturalization," which has been interpreted to grant jurisdiction of immigration policy solely to the federal government. Yet in the absence of federal action to address the pressing social needs that illegal immigration produces in social services, states have increasingly enacted their own policies on the issue (see Figure 18.7, p. 550). Employers in several states must check workers' residency status with E-Verify and could be fined if they knowingly hire illegal immigrants. Some states, such as California, have enacted immigrant-friendly legislation that allows illegal immigrants to pay in-state tuition at public universities. Others, such as Arizona and Alabama, have enacted policies aimed at creating a climate that drives immigrants away. The Arizona law, for example, directs local law enforcement officials to check the immigration status of people they stop or arrest. In addition to raising fears that the law will promote racial profiling, some believe that only the federal government has the authority to engage in this type of immigration enforcement. In 2012, the Supreme Court ruled that states can direct law enforcement authorities to ask people to demonstrate whether they are in the country legally.[95]

NIKKI KAHN/KRT/Newscom

They Have a Dream

High school graduation is a time of celebration. But for young illegal immigrants who were brought to the United States as children, it can also be start of an uncertain future. If Congress enacts the DREAM Act, they could become eligible to enroll in public universities and pay in-state tuition rates in their home states. The DREAM Act would also allow them to become eligible for permanent residency if they go to college or serve in the military.

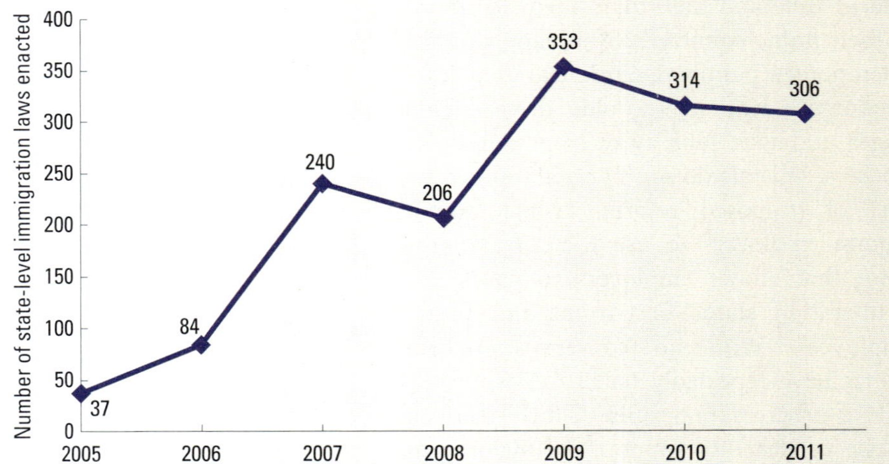

FIGURE 18.7 Absent Federal Action, States Take on Immigration Reform

With immigration reform stalled at the federal level, state legislative activity to address issues that arise from immigration has increased dramatically. Some laws are considered immigrant-friendly, while others are considered hostile. Whether the states even have the jurisdiction to enact these policies is a matter of continuing debate.

Source: National Conference of State Legislatures, "State Laws Related to Immigration and Immigrants," http://www.ncsl.org/issues-research/immigration/state-laws-related-to-immigration-and-immigrants.aspx#December_31_Report.

18.8 Benefits and Fairness

★ Explain how about the issue of fairness shapes perspectives on government benefits.

As the policies examined here demonstrate, the national government provides many Americans and noncitizen residents with benefits. Some benefits are conditional. **Means-tested benefits** impose an income test to qualify. For example, Pell college grants are available to households with an income that falls below a designated threshold. **Non-means-tested benefits** impose no such income test; benefits such as Medicare and Social Security are available to all.

Some Americans question the fairness of non-means-tested benefits. Benefits are subsidies, and some people need them more than others do. If resources available for such benefits are limited, imposing means tests on more benefits has real allure. For example, all elderly people now receive the same basic Medicare benefits, regardless of income. Fairness advocates maintain that the affluent elderly should shoulder a higher share of Medicare costs, shifting more benefits to the low-income elderly.

If the idea of shifting benefits gains support in the future, reform debates will focus on the income level below which a program will apply. Thus, the question of fairness is one more problem for policymakers to consider as they try to reform the nation's welfare state programs.

There are many other domestic policy areas that merit attention when analyzing the complex processes by which policies are formulated, implemented, and evaluated and that consume significant government resources. These policy areas include

means-tested benefits
Conditional benefits provided by government to individuals whose income falls below a designated threshold.

non-means-tested benefits
Benefits provided by government to all citizens, regardless of income; Medicare and Social Security are examples.

energy policy, the environment, science and technology, transportation, and food policy, just to name a few. As with the policies covered in this chapter, debates in these other areas often come down to differing perspectives on freedom and equality, involve coordination problems across levels of government, and are influenced by complex issue networks that are at the heart of the nation's pluralist system.

SUMMARY

18.1 Government Purposes and Public Policies

- Underlying policy choices are basic values—the core beliefs about how government should work.
- The basic objectives of government tend to be distributional, redistributional, and regulatory.
- Public policy formulation often involves one of the following tools to achieve objectives: incentives and disincentives, direct provision of services, or rule setting.
- The policymaking process consists of four broad stages: agenda setting, formulation, implementation, and evaluation. All three branches of the national government formulate policy, along with policy experts, interest groups, and trade organizations, who together form issue networks. Implementation and evaluation influence agenda building because program shortcomings become evident during these stages. Thus, the process is circular, with the end often marking the beginning of a new round of policymaking.
- These policymaking stages are often marked by fragmentation and by efforts intended to achieve coordination. The multiplicity of participants in policymaking, the diffusion of authority within both Congress and the executive branch, the separation of powers, and federalism are chief causes of fragmented policymaking.
- The fragmentation of government accentuates pluralism, for it facilitates the participation of interest groups, which works in favor of well-organized, aggressive constituencies and against the broader but more passive public at large.
- The specific domestic welfare state policies examined in this chapter illustrate how policy debates often pose choices between freedom and equality.

18.2 The Development of the American Welfare State

- Many domestic policies that provide benefits to individuals and promote economic equality were instituted during the Great Depression and were expanded during President Johnson's Great Society agenda.

18.3 Social Security

- Today, the government plays an active role in providing benefits to the poor, the elderly, and the disabled, which reflects the social welfare function of the modern state.

18.4 Public Assistance

- Government confers benefits on individuals through social insurance and public assistance. Social insurance is not based on need; public assistance (welfare) hinges on proof of need.
- Programs to aid the elderly and the poor have been transformed into entitlements, or rights that accrue to eligible persons. These programs have reduced poverty among some groups, especially the elderly. However, poverty retains a grip on certain segments of the population.
- Temporary Assistance for Needy Families (TANF) was a major overhaul of welfare policy. While initially considered a success for reducing the number of people on welfare and granting more flexibility to the states, recent national economic difficulties have led many to conclude that TANF is inadequate at combating poverty.

18.5 Health Care

- Recent health-care reform is a reflection of the modern dilemma of democracy: universal coverage and cost controls versus a loss of freedom in health-care choices.

18.6 Elementary and Secondary Education

- Education is considered a critical public policy area among Americans, though it remains largely a state and local endeavor. The federal government's education policy centers on providing equal access to a good education for all Americans, often relying on incentives to help achieve these aims.

18.7 Immigration

- While the federal government has long been interested in controlling the number of immigrants who are legal permanent residents, the problem of illegal immigration has only garnered national attention in the past few decades.
- Immigration exacerbates pressing social issues, such as poverty, health, and education, and is thus implicated in debates about those policies. At the same time, the federal government must address the needs of illegal immigrants; they are among the nation's poorest and most vulnerable individuals.
- In the absence of federal legislation addressing illegal immigration, many states have enacted their own policies. Whether these state efforts are constitutional remains unsettled.

18.8 Benefits and Fairness

- Some government subsidy programs provide means-tested benefits, for which eligibility hinges on income. Non-means-tested benefits are available to all, regardless of income. As the demand for such benefits exceeds available resources, their fairness becomes questioned. Departing from non-means-tested benefits in the name of fairness may very well be the next challenge of democracy.

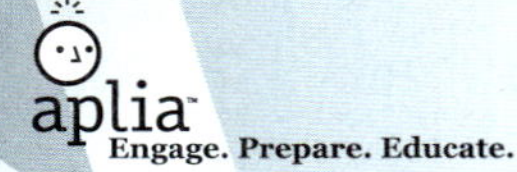

ASSESSING YOUR UNDERSTANDING WITH APLIA...YOUR VIRTUAL TUTOR!

18.1 Categorize different types of public policies and outline the process by which policies are formulated and implemented.

1. Define distributive, redistributive, and regulatory public policies.
2. Identify and explain at least two public policy tools used to achieve objectives.
3. What are the four main stages of the policy-making process?
4. What are issue networks? Do they reflect the pluralist or majoritarian model of democracy?

18.2 Trace the evolution of social welfare programs as a central element of public policy in the United States.

1. What are social welfare programs?
2. Summarize the emergence and goals of the New Deal.
3. What was the Great Society?

18.3 Describe the origins and evolution of Social Security as well as the funding and benefit issues facing the program.

1. Who can receive Social Security benefits?

2. Why is the success of the Social Security program dependent on such factors as birth rate and life expectancy?
3. Discuss alternative proposed reforms to Social Security recently debated by policymakers.

18.4 Explain how poverty is defined and trace the evolution of public assistance programs designed to address it.

1. What is the current poverty rate, and what is the current poverty threshold?
2. What does TANF stand for and how did this program change welfare policy?

18.5 Differentiate among Medicare, Medicaid, and the Affordable Care Act of 2010 and explain how each program addresses the issues of health-care delivery.

1. Define Medicare.
2. Explain how federalism shapes the administration and financing of Medicaid.
3. Identify at least three key features of the Affordable Care Act of 2010.

18.6 Describe the role of the federal government in shaping education policy at the state and local government levels.

1. Discuss how the dilemma of freedom versus equality shapes debates about education policy.
2. What was the main feature of the No Child Left Behind Act of 2001, and why has it been controversial?

18.7 Assess alternative policies for addressing illegal immigration into the United States.

1. List central features of current policy debates for addressing illegal immigration that have been proposed by the federal government and/or by individual states.

18.8 Explain how the issue of fairness shapes perspectives on government benefits.

1. Contrast means-tested and non-means-tested benefits.

19 Global Policy

CHAPTER TOPICS and Learning Outcomes

aplia Engage. Prepare. Educate.

19.1 Making Foreign Policy: The Constitutional Context
★ Compare the constitutional authority over foreign policy granted to the executive branch with that of the legislative branch.

19.2 Making Foreign Policy: Organization and Cast
★ Identify the executive branch agencies that formulate foreign policy and describe the principal functions of each.

19.3 A Review of U.S. Foreign Policy
★ Trace the evolution of American foreign policy from isolationism to globalism and identify the factors that have shaped the direction of that policy.

19.4 Global Policy Issue Areas
★ Describe the influence of the global issues of investment and trade, human rights, and the environment on U.S. foreign and domestic policy.

19.5 The Public and Global Policy
★ Explain the relationship between U.S. foreign policy and both the majoritarian and pluralist models of democracy.

Qilai Shen/Bloomberg via Getty Images

Apple's iPhone symbolizes the strength and vitality of the American economy. The smart phone's innovate design and far-reaching capabilities revolutionized the electronics industry. It is astoundingly popular, and young people in particular have made it a "must have" item. Estimated sales for 2012 are around 140 million phones. These sales have, in turn, fueled astronomical profits for the iconic Silicon Valley–based company, somewhere in the neighborhood of $46 billion for 2012.

Even in a down economy, Apple has prospered as its imaginative products have made it into a symbol of American business success. Yet its iPhone is as American as Chinese food. The design of the phone may be American, but it's a Chinese product in terms of manufacturing. Apple only employs 23,000 people in the United States. Overseas, it directly employs 43,000, but the real Apple workforce is the 700,000 or so individuals who work for overseas companies that are independent Apple contractors. Most of these contractors are located in China, where virtually all of the hundreds of components that make up an iPhone are manufactured. The phone itself is assembled in China as well.

Manufacturing costs are, of course, considerably less in the developing world than they are in the much more affluent advanced industrialized democracies. Many of the workers in iPhone factories earn less than $17 a day. Apple says it outsources the iPhone for reasons beyond low labor costs as it finds factories in China to be highly adaptable and fast in meeting design changes in the company's products.

The interdependence of American markets and Third-World manufacturing is not without its problems. Investigations of working conditions at Apple contractors have turned up some disturbing findings. At some facilities, employees are handling dangerous chemicals without proper safeguards. Some workers have been found to be on the factory floor for more than sixty hours a week, the stated limit by Foxconn, Apple's largest contractor. Workers live in crowded dormitories, often in tiny rooms. Some employees were discovered living twenty to a three-room apartment. Apple has responded by pushing its contractors to comply with workplace health and safety standards. At the same time, Apple demands the lowest cost possible, and contractors who don't meet Apple's price targets can easily lose the company's business. Thus, these contractors must keep their costs down and push employees to improve their productivity.[1]

Apple's corporate ties to the global economy also extend to the way the company is structured to minimize taxes. It has set up offices in a number of different countries, "some little more than a letterbox or an anonymous office."[2]

Customer purchases are often routed through countries outside the United States so that profits that derive from those sales cannot be taxed in the United States. For example, if someone downloads an album from Apple's iTunes, the electronic impulses that make up that music can be generated from a computer anywhere in the world. Apple has pioneered an accounting strategy called "Double Irish with a Dutch Sandwich." Profits are routed though Irish subsidiaries and the Netherlands and then on to Apple offices in the Caribbean, escaping U.S. taxes along the way.[3]

Today, as a result of globalization, people and nations are aware of their interdependence and are willing to give (and expect) help in times of need. But as we see in the account of Apple's iPhone, globalization is not all positive. The economies of distant countries can have a strong impact on others. Free movement of goods and capital across borders leads to investing in developing countries where goods can be produced more cheaply. Often the result is the loss of jobs and wages in developed countries (e.g., the United States) while international corporate profits increase. At a dinner in 2011, President Barack Obama asked Apple CEO Steve Jobs (who has since passed away) if some of the work Apple outsources overseas could instead be relocated in the United States. Jobs replied, "Those jobs aren't coming back."[4]

How should the U.S. government deal with the public's concerns over problems of globalization? Should it try to intervene actively in international affairs? If so, to what end? Should it favor economic growth at home over human rights elsewhere? Concerning our need for foreign oil, should the U.S. government favor regime stability in oil-rich countries over their citizens' civil liberties?

The ideological framework in Chapter 1, which runs through this book, was devised for analyzing ideological attitudes in domestic politics. One can adapt it to international affairs, as shown in Figure 19.1.[5] Former President George W. Bush probably fits in the International Libertarian category. Pope Benedict XVI's encyclical proposing a "true world authority" to work for the "common good" suggests he is an International Communitarian.[6] Many tea party followers fit the description of International Conservatives.[7] Barack Obama qualifies as an International Liberal.

Although the president is held accountable for international affairs, many other actors are involved. We begin our discussion of global policy by establishing the constitutional bases of governmental authority for making American foreign policy in the military, economic, and social arenas.

★ 19.1 Making Foreign Policy: The Constitutional Context

★ Compare the constitutional authority over foreign policy granted to the executive branch with that of the legislative branch.

foreign policy
The general plan followed by a nation in defending and advancing its national interests, especially its security against foreign threats.

A nation's **foreign policy** is its general plan to defend and advance national interests, especially its security against foreign threats. The Constitution uses the word *foreign* in only five places. Four are in the section dealing with Congress, which is entrusted to "regulate commerce among foreign nations"; to "regulate the value … of foreign coin"; to approve any gift or title to a government official "from any king, prince, or

FIGURE 19.1 A Two-Dimensional Framework of International Ideologies

	International Liberals	International Communitarians

(Vertical axis label: Government action for equality of people in all nations)
(Left axis arrow label: Freedom)

International Liberals

Favor: International government that protects the environment and conditions of workers, immigrants, and children in foreign countries

Oppose: National tariffs, import quotas, government subsidies to national businesses

International Communitarians

Favor: Requiring U.S. agencies to follow policies that protect the environment and promote conditions of workers, immigrants, and children abroad

Favor: National tariffs, import quotas, government subsidies to national businesses

International Libertarians

Oppose: Other nations monitoring human rights conditions in the U.S.; putting U.S. forces under international control

Oppose: National tariffs, import quotas, government subsidies to national businesses

International Conservatives

Oppose: Other nations monitoring human rights conditions in the U.S.; putting U.S. forces under international control

Favor: National tariffs, import quotas, government subsidies to national businesses

(Horizontal axis: Freedom ←————————→ Traditional order of nation-state system)

As in Figure 1.2 in Chapter 1, the four ideological types here are defined by the values that they favor in balancing the values of freedom and order with freedom and equality in international affairs. In this typology, however, order is tied to the defense of national sovereignty within the traditional nation-state system of international relations.
Source: © Cengage Learning.

foreign state"; and to approve "any compact or agreement" between a state and "a foreign power" in time of war. The fifth mention gives the courts jurisdiction over cases arising "between a state … and foreign states." The Constitution never uses *foreign* in its article describing the executive branch, and yet the presidency has emerged as the dominant actor in foreign policy. Why?

Constitutional Bases of Presidential Authority in Foreign Policy

One must read between the lines of the Constitution to understand how presidents have derived their authority in foreign policy. The Constitution creates the executive in Article II, which provides that the president

- is commander in chief of the armed forces.
- has the power to make treaties (subject to the consent of the Senate).
- appoints U.S. ambassadors and the heads of executive departments (also with the advice and consent of the Senate).
- receives (or refuses to receive) ambassadors from other countries.

Over time, the president has parlayed these constitutional provisions—plus laws passed by Congress, Supreme Court decisions, and precedents created by bold action and political acceptance—to emerge as the leading actor in American foreign policy. But as in a play, there are other actors in the foreign policy drama, and Congress plays a strong supporting role—sometimes even upstaging the star performer.

Constitutional Bases of Congressional Authority in Foreign Policy

As in the case of the presidency, the Constitution gives Congress additional powers in foreign policy without mentioning the term. Specifically, the Constitution establishes that Congress is empowered to

- legislate.
- declare war.
- raise revenue and dispense funds.
- support, maintain, govern, and regulate the army and navy.
- call out the state militias to repel invasions.
- regulate commerce with foreign nations.
- define and punish piracy and offenses against the law of nations.

Breaking Up Is Hard to Do

The United States military has been in Afghanistan since 2001 when it overturned the Taliban regime because it had harbored Osama bin Laden. It has been a tense relationship as the United States has been frustrated by the slow pace in the buildup and lack of aggressiveness by the Afghan Army. Here former U.S. area commander General David Petraeus meets with Hamid Karzai, head of Afghanistan's government.

MASSOUD HOSSAINI/AFP/Getty Images

The most salient power for foreign policy on this list is the power to declare war, but Congress has used this power only five times.[8] It has relied more on its other powers to influence foreign policy. Using its legislative power, Congress can involve the nation in programs of international scope or limit the actions of the executive branch. Probably most important, Congress has used the power of the purse to provide funds for the activities it supports—and to prohibit funds for those it opposes. The Constitution also ascribes some powers to the Senate alone, which has made the U.S. Senate the leading chamber of Congress on foreign policy issues. The Constitution requires that the Senate

- give advice and consent to treaties made by the president.
- give advice and consent to the appointment of ambassadors and various other public officials involved in foreign policy.

The Senate has used its special powers to check presidential initiatives in foreign policy. Whereas only the president can *make* treaties, the Senate can *break* treaties—in the sense of rejecting those made by the president.

The Senate and Major Treaties. In truth, the Senate rarely defeats a treaty, having defeated only twenty-one of the thousands it has considered.[9] Some of the defeats have been historically significant, however, establishing the Senate as a force in foreign policy. A hard-hearted Senate lorded its veto power over a very ill Democratic President Woodrow Wilson in 1919. At the end of World War I, Wilson proposed and championed a plan for an international organization—the League of Nations—to eliminate future wars. To enter the League, however, Wilson's treaty had to be approved by two-thirds of the Senate. Wilson, an idealistic, international liberal, was opposed by a group of mostly Republican, internationally conservative senators. After eight months of debate, the Senate rejected his treaty, and the United States never joined the League of Nations. Some attribute the weakness of the League of Nations, which failed to prevent a second world war, to the absence of the United States.

In the early days of World War II, President Franklin D. Roosevelt and British Prime Minister Winston Churchill revived Wilson's idea for collective security and proposed a new international organization—the United Nations—after the war. By the time the U.N. treaty went to the Senate in the summer of 1945, Roosevelt had died. It fell to President Harry Truman, also a Democrat and mindful of Wilson's failure with the League of Nations, to win acceptance of the U.N. treaty by a Republican-controlled Senate.

The twenty-first and most recent treaty rejection by the Senate occurred on October 13, 1999, on the Comprehensive Nuclear Test Ban Treaty. This treaty, signed by President Clinton in 1996, would have effectively outlawed all nuclear weapons testing. Almost all arms control agreements since Eisenhower's administration have been proposed by presidents of both parties and opposed by conservatives in Congress from both parties. True to form, the Nuclear Test Ban Treaty failed to get the required two-thirds majority. All Democratic senators voted for it, and all but four Republicans voted against it.[10]

Governmental leaders around the world reacted angrily to the defeat of a treaty that had been decades in the making. One overseas newspaper editorialized, "If the United States, the sole superpower, refuses stubbornly to ratify a global nuclear test ban treaty that will make the world safer for all, why on earth would any other country want to do it?"[11] In the United States, however, then Senator Jon Kyl (R-Ariz.) said that the treaty rejection shows "that our constitutional democracy, with its shared powers and checks and balances, is alive and well."[12]

Skirting the Senate Through Executive Agreements.
An **executive agreement** is a pact between heads of countries concerning their joint activities. The Supreme Court has ruled that executive agreements are within the inherent powers of the president and have the legal status of treaties.[13] Executive agreements must conform to the Constitution, existing treaties, and the laws of Congress.[14] Like treaties, executive agreements have the force of law; unlike treaties, they do not require Senate approval. Until 1972 the texts of these agreements did not even have to be reported to Congress. Legislation passed that year required the president to send copies to the House and Senate Foreign Relations committees. This requirement has not seriously affected the use of executive agreements, which has escalated dramatically, outnumbering treaties by about ten to one since the 1930s.[15]

Most executive agreements deal with minor bureaucratic business that would not interest a busy Senate. On occasion, presidents have resorted to executive agreements on important issues that were unlikely to win Senate consent. In 1992, President George H. W. Bush negotiated an accord with Canada and Mexico that facilitated free trade among the three countries by reducing national tariffs on imported goods. This plan, which reflected a free-market international libertarian ideology, was widely favored by economists but bitterly opposed by trade protectionists and international conservatives.

Instead of proposing the arrangement as a treaty, President Bush framed it as an executive agreement: the North American Free Trade Agreement (NAFTA), which

executive agreement
A pact between the heads of two countries.

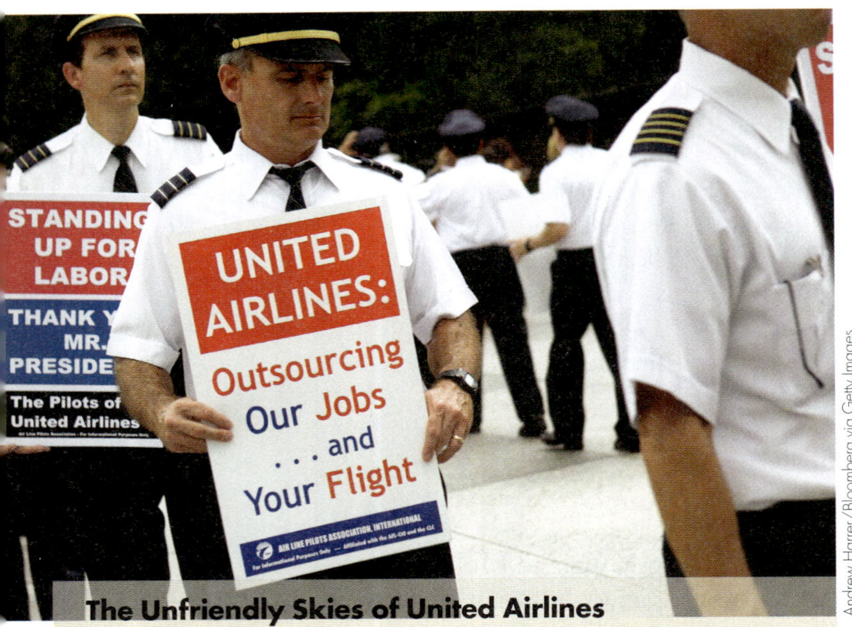

Andrew Harrer/Bloomberg via Getty Images

The Unfriendly Skies of United Airlines

These United pilots are protesting the outsourcing of jobs by their employer to overseas airlines as well as the movement of airline maintenance jobs to overseas. Such conflicts between employers and employees are common as the ever-shrinking modern world makes it easier for companies to become global enterprises with jobs allocated in a variety of countries.

required only simple majorities in both houses to pass.[16] President Clinton inherited the pending NAFTA legislation and—despite opposition from organized labor—shepherded NAFTA through passage with more support from Republicans than Democrats. In 1993, President Clinton signed the NAFTA agreement negotiated by President George H. W. Bush.

In 2004, President George W. Bush signed CAFTA—the Central American Free Trade Agreement—with Costa Rica, the Dominican Republic, El Salvador, Guatemala, Honduras, and Nicaragua. Similar to NAFTA, it drew similar criticisms but was approved in 2005 after close votes in Congress. In 2006, President Bush implemented CAFTA through a presidential **proclamation**, declaring that the trade agreement was in effect. Once associated with official observances (like Mother's Day), presidential proclamations concerning trade have become common as Congress cedes authority to the president in this area.[17]

Constitutional Roots of Statutory Powers in Foreign Policy

proclamation
An official declaration or statement of action or recognition.

Within the framework of the powers the Constitution grants to the executive, Congress has conferred other responsibilities to the presidency through laws—and creative presidents have expanded on these grants of authority. For example, Congress has allowed the presidency certain leeway on the use of *discretionary funds*—large sums of cash that may be spent on unforeseen needs to further the national interest.

As commander in chief of the armed forces, several presidents have committed American troops in emergency situations, thus involving the United States in undeclared wars. America's undeclared wars, police actions, and similar interventions have outnumbered its formal, congressionally declared wars by about forty to one. Since the last declared war ended in 1945, over 100,000 American members of the military have died in locations ranging from Korea and Vietnam to Grenada, Somalia, Iraq, and Afghanistan.

Reacting to casualties from the undeclared Vietnam War, Congress passed the War Powers Resolution in 1973 over Nixon's veto. It required that the president "consult" with Congress in "every possible instance" before involving U.S. troops in hostilities and notify Congress within forty-eight hours of committing troops to a foreign intervention. If troops are deployed, they may not stay for more than sixty days without congressional approval (although the president may take up to thirty days more to remove them "safely"). Some critics of the legislation claimed that it did not restrict presidential power as much as extend a free hand to wage war for up to sixty days.[18] The War Powers Resolution has not constrained presidents as they've learned to adapt to its requirements. However, it has forced Congress to go on record in support of various military interventions.

After September 11, 2001, President George W. Bush had to work within the War Powers Resolution to build his "global coalition against terrorism." Congress promptly authorized the president to "use all necessary and appropriate force against those nations, organizations or persons he determines planned, authorized, committed or aided the terrorist attacks … or harbored such organizations or persons."[19] Bush relied on this joint resolution to attack al Qaeda in Afghanistan and to defeat the Taliban regime there in late 2001, prior to the Taliban's resurgence in 2006.

A year later, Congress was not as quick to support the president's use of military force against Saddam Hussein in Iraq. Although a war resolution passed with strong support in both chambers, it was opposed by more than half the Democrats in the House and nearly half in the Senate.

As presidents have expanded their role in the foreign policy drama, the Senate has sought to enlarge its part, interpreting quite broadly its power to "advise and consent" on presidential appointments to offices involved in foreign affairs. Senators have used confirmation hearings to prod the administration for more acceptable appointments.

19.2 Making Foreign Policy: Organization and Cast

★ Identify the executive branch agencies that formulate foreign policy and describe the principal functions of each.

Although American foreign policy originates within the executive branch, the organizational structure for policymaking is created and funded by Congress and is subject to congressional oversight. When the United States acquired its superpower status after World War II, Congress overhauled the administration of foreign policy with the 1947 National Security Act, which established three new organizations—the Department of Defense, the National Security Council, and the Central Intelligence Agency (CIA)—to join the Department of State in the organizational structure. Following 9/11, new legislation sought to coordinate the intelligence activities of all three new organizations.

The Department of State

During its very first session in 1789, Congress created the Department of Foreign Affairs as the government's first executive department. It became the State Department, and since its establishment, it has assisted the president in formulating American foreign policy, executing policy decisions, and monitoring foreign governments throughout the world. The department's head, the secretary of state, is the highest-ranking official in the cabinet; he or she is also, in theory at least, the president's most important foreign policy adviser. However, some chief executives, like John Kennedy, preferred to act as their own secretary of state and appointed relatively weak figures to the post. Others appointed stronger individuals. President Obama surprised everyone by picking his presidential campaign rival, Hillary Clinton. She surprised everyone by accepting. Comfortable dealing with world leaders, she stood against Vice President Biden in supporting the 2009 troop buildup in Afghanistan. In 2010, Secretary Clinton committed the United States to oppose Internet censorship and to punish states for cyberattacks.[20]

Like other executive departments, the State Department is staffed by political appointees and permanent employees selected under the civil service merit system. Political appointees include deputy secretaries and undersecretaries of state and some—but not all—ambassadors. Permanent employees include approximately four thousand foreign service officers, at home and abroad, who staff and service U.S. embassies and consulates throughout the world. They have primary responsibility for representing America to the rest of the world and caring for American citizens and interests abroad.

The State Department also lacks a strong domestic constituency to exert pressure in support of its policies. The Department of Agriculture, by contrast, can mobilize farmers to support its activities, and the Department of Defense can count on help from defense industries and veterans' groups. In a pluralist democracy, the lack of a natural constituency is a serious drawback for an agency or department. Exacerbating this problem is the changing character of global political issues. As economic and social issues emerge in foreign affairs, executive agencies with pertinent domestic policy expertise have become more involved in shaping global policy.

The Department of Defense

In 1947, Congress replaced two venerable cabinet-level departments—the War Department and the Department of the Navy—with the Department of Defense, intending to promote unity and coordination among the armed forces and to provide the modern bureaucratic structure needed to manage America's greatly expanded peacetime military. In keeping with the U.S. tradition of civilian control of the military, the new department was given a civilian head—the secretary of defense, a cabinet member with authority over the military. Later reorganizations of the department (in 1949 and 1958) have given the secretary greater budgetary powers; control of defense research; and the authority to transfer, abolish, reassign, and consolidate functions among the military services.

The role of the defense secretary depends on the individual's vision of the job and willingness to use the tools available. Strong secretaries, such as Robert McNamara (under Kennedy and Johnson), wielded significant power. President George W. Bush chose Donald Rumsfeld, who had previously served as secretary of defense under President Ford but who clashed with Secretary of State Colin Powell over planning and handling the Iraq war. Bush later replaced Rumsfeld with Robert M. Gates, former director of the CIA. Gates proved to be so effective that Democratic president Obama reappointed him. Gates opposed costly weapons systems, like the expensive F-22 Raptor fighter plane, to refocus military strategy on smaller-scale guerrilla warfare.[21]

Below the defense secretary are the civilian secretaries of the army, navy, and air force; below them are the military commanders of the individual branches of the armed forces, who make up the Joint Chiefs of Staff. The Joint Chiefs meet to coordinate military policy among the different branches; they also serve as the primary military advisers to the president, the secretary of defense, and the National Security Council, helping to shape policy positions on matters such as alliances, plans for nuclear and conventional war, and arms control and disarmament.

The National Security Council

The National Security Council (NSC) is made up of a group of advisers who help the president mold a coherent approach to foreign policy by integrating and coordinating details of domestic, foreign, and military affairs that relate to national security. The statutory members of the NSC are the president, the vice president, and the secretaries of state and defense. Each president designates other members of the NSC as he sees fit. NSC discussions can cover a wide range of issues, such as the formulation of U.S. policy in the Middle East. In theory, at least, NSC discussions offer the president an opportunity to solicit advice and allow key participants in the foreign policymaking process to keep abreast of the policies and capabilities of other departments.

In practice, the role played by the NSC has varied considerably under different presidents. Truman and Kennedy seldom met with it; Eisenhower and Nixon brought it into much greater prominence. During the Nixon administration, the NSC was critically important in making foreign policy. Much of this importance derived from Nixon's reliance on Henry Kissinger, his assistant for national security affairs (the title of the head of the NSC staff). President George W. Bush picked Condoleezza Rice as head of the NSC, and she later replaced Colin Powell as secretary of state.

The Intelligence Community

Conducting an effective foreign policy requires accurate information—termed "intelligence" in international affairs.[22] Raw data on foreign countries, observations of politics abroad, and inside information are merged into finished intelligence for policymakers through activities spread across sixteen agencies in the executive branch known as the **Intelligence Community**.[23] Of these agencies, the two most prominent are the Central Intelligence Agency (CIA) and the National Security Agency (NSA). The CIA is an independent agency, while the NSA is part of the Department of Defense (DOD), as are the National Reconnaissance Office (NRO); the National Geospatial-Intelligence Agency (NGA); the Defense Intelligence Agency (DIA); and the intelligence operations of the Army, Navy, Marine Corps, Coast Guard, and Air Force—which explains why 80 percent of the intelligence budget is controlled by the DOD.[24]

Many attributed the 9/11 attacks on America to a failure of intelligence, and Congress created an independent commission to investigate the charge. Known as the 9/11 Commission, its 2004 report proposed sweeping reorganization of intelligence agencies and responsibilities. Here is a brief account of its three main elements.

Intelligence Community
Sixteen agencies in the executive branch that conduct the various intelligence activities that make up the total U.S. national intelligence effort.

The Director of National Intelligence. Responding to the 9/11 Report, Congress passed the Intelligence Reform and Terrorism Prevention Act of 2004. It amended the 1947 National Security Act, restructured the Intelligence Community, and created an Office of Director of National Intelligence to coordinate all intelligence activities. The law also stripped the title of director of central intelligence (DCI) from the head of the CIA. The new director of national intelligence (DNI) assumed all the coordinating functions of the DCI and became the principal adviser to the president and the National Security Council. The DNI also oversees and directs the National Intelligence Program. Critics warned that the DNI lacked the budget and clout to succeed. Indeed, the post became a revolving door, filled by four people in five years. At least in the short run, the critics have been proven right as the DNI has found it difficult to effectively coordinate the large number of agencies, each of which prefers autonomy to centralized control.

The Central Intelligence Agency. Before World War II, the United States had no permanent agency specifically charged with gathering intelligence about the actions and intentions of foreign powers. After the war, when America began to play a much greater international role and feared the spread of communism, Congress created the CIA to collect information and to draw on intelligence activities in other departments and agencies.

Most material obtained by the CIA comes from readily available sources: statistical abstracts, books, and newspapers. The agency's Intelligence Directorate is responsible for these overt (open) activities in collecting and processing information. The CIA's charter also empowers it "to perform such other functions and duties related to intelligence affecting the national security as the National Security Council shall direct." This vague clause has been used to justify the agency's covert (secret) activities undertaken in foreign countries by its Operations Directorate. These activities have included espionage, coups, assassination plots, wiretaps, interception of mail, and infiltration of protest groups.

Covert operations raise both moral and legal questions for a democracy. Allen Dulles, President Eisenhower's CIA director, once called these operations "an essential part of the free world's struggle against communism." Are they equally important in a post–Cold War world? Can they be reconciled with the principle of checks and balances in American government? When government engages in clandestine actions, are the people able to hold their government accountable for its actions? Prior to the September 11 terrorist attacks, one analyst argued that "the Cold War may be over, but the U.S. need for accurate information about the world remains acute."[25]

After September 11, some accused the CIA of neglecting covert intelligence activities (such as infiltrating terrorist organizations abroad), and blame centered on director George J. Tenet, who had mobilized the agency for the successful war in Afghanistan.[26] Tenet said it was a "slam dunk case" that Iraq had weapons of mass destruction.[27] When the U.S. chief weapons inspector failed to find major stockpiles of weapons of mass destruction, Tenet's position deteriorated, and he resigned in 2004.[28] Later, he was succeeded by Air Force General Michael V. Hayden, former director of the National Security Agency. In 2007 Hayden ordered release of "the family jewels"—a disturbing 702-page report on domestic wiretapping, spying on journalists and protesters, and failed assassination plots in the 1960s and 1970s.[29] President Obama chose someone outside the Intelligence Community to head the CIA: Leon Panetta, former congressman from California and President Clinton's chief of staff. Panetta soon learned of and ended a controversial CIA program to assassinate terrorists.[30] The program proved less effective than killing terrorists using missiles fired from pilotless drone aircraft operated by the CIA in Pakistan, Afghanistan, and Yemen.[31]

The National Security Agency. Created in 1952, the National Security Agency (NSA) today conducts SIGINT—SIGnals INTelligence—using supercomputers, satellites, and other high-tech equipment for *foreign* (outside the United States) electronic intelligence surveillance. (This activity contrasts with the CIA's focus on HUMINT—HUMan INTelligence.) NSA's work is highly secret; the joke is that NSA stands for "No Such Agency." Although it keeps a lower profile than the CIA, NSA has more employees and a much larger budget. Located administratively in the Defense Department, its directors have always been high-ranking military officers. Lieutenant General Michael Hayden headed NSA from 1999 to 2005, during which period he acquiesced in secret electronic eavesdropping on U.S. citizens without court warrants and then vigorously defended the program when it became public.[32] In May 2006, *USA Today* revealed that NSA had also secretly collected billions of *domestic* (not foreign) phone call records of millions of Americans from AT&T, Verizon, and BellSouth.[33]

The Intelligence Community is less communal than feudal. All the agencies—especially the DNI, CIA, and Federal Bureau of Investigation (FBI)—jealously guard their turf. For example, Obama had to step in to decide who had the power to appoint the top spy—the CIA as in the past or the new DNI, organizationally over the CIA. Obama sided with the CIA.[34]

Other Parts of the Foreign Policy Bureaucracy

Government agencies outside the Intelligence Community provide input to making foreign policy. Due to globalization and the interdependence of social, environmental, and economic issues with political matters, many departments and agencies other than those described earlier now find themselves involved in global policy. For some, foreign affairs constitute their chief concern. The Agency for International Development (AID) oversees aid programs to nations around the globe. In doing so, AID works with a full range of other departments and agencies, including the Defense Department, the CIA, the Peace Corps, and the Department of Agriculture. Soon after the Haiti earthquake in 2010, AID had established a website, "Help for Haiti," to facilitate assistance.[35]

Other departments and agencies primarily concerned with domestic issues have become more active in the foreign policy arena. For example, the Department of Agriculture provides agricultural assistance to other countries and promotes American farm products abroad. The Department of Commerce tries to expand overseas markets for nonagricultural U.S. goods. In addition, the Department of Commerce administers export control laws to prevent other nations from gaining access to American technologies connected with national security (such as computers and military equipment). As trade has become a more important aspect of foreign policy, the role of the Commerce Department in promoting American business abroad has also grown. The Department of Energy monitors nuclear weapons programs internationally and works with foreign governments and international agencies such as the International Atomic Energy Agency to coordinate international energy programs. Recently it has also supported American energy companies trying to do business abroad.

An array of government corporations, independent agencies, and quasi-governmental organizations also participate in the foreign policy arena. These include the National Endowment for Democracy, an independent nonprofit organization, funded by Congress, to promote democracy in other countries; the Export-Import Bank, a government corporation that subsidizes the export of American products; and the Overseas Private Investment Corporation, an independent agency that helps American companies invest abroad. In addition, private companies hold military contracts to supply food and services to troops abroad—and even to guard convoys and military bases. In the war in Afghanistan, there have sometimes been more private contractors than U.S. troops.[36]

This list of bureaucratic entities with foreign policy interests is by no means exhaustive, but it does suggest the complexity of the foreign policymaking machinery. Furthermore, as social and economic issues become more prominent on the global policy agenda, we can expect an increase in the involvement of agencies not traditionally preoccupied with foreign policy.

# 19.3 A Review of U.S. Foreign Policy

★ Trace the evolution of American foreign policy from isolationism to globalism and identify the factors that have shaped the direction of that policy.

Presidents come to office with an ideological orientation for interpreting and evaluating international events, and they tend to be more internationalist than most members of Congress. Presidents also tend to fill the offices of secretary of state, secretary of defense, national security adviser, and director of the CIA with individuals who are tuned to the presidential wavelength. However, presidents must accept advice and receive consent from Congress. The political result is the nation's foreign policy. Of course, foreign policies change according to presidential and congressional views of "national interests" and according to whatever actions are thought appropriate for defending and advancing those interests. In examining America's role in foreign affairs, it is helpful to structure the review in terms of presidents and the shorthand labels attached to the nation's policies during their administrations.

Emerging from Isolationism

isolationism
A foreign policy of withdrawal from international political affairs.

For most of the nineteenth century, American interests were defined by the Monroe Doctrine of 1823, in which the United States rejected European intervention in the Western Hemisphere and agreed not to involve itself in European politics. Throughout the 1800s, U.S. presidents practiced a policy of **isolationism**, or withdrawal from the political entanglements of Europe. American isolationism was never total, however. As the nineteenth century wore on, the United States expanded from coast to coast and became a regional power that was increasingly involved in Pacific and Latin American nations. Still, America's defense establishment and foreign policy commitments remained limited.

World War I was the United States's first serious foray into European politics. The idealistic rhetoric that surrounded our entry into the war in 1917—"to make the world safe for democracy"—cloaked America's effort to advance its interest in freedom of the seas. Such moralism has often characterized America's approach to international politics, and it was certainly reflected in Wilson's plan for U.S. entry into the League of Nations. When the Senate failed to ratify the treaty needed for entry, America's brief moment of internationalism ended. Until World War II, America continued to define its security interests narrowly and needed only a small military establishment to defend them.

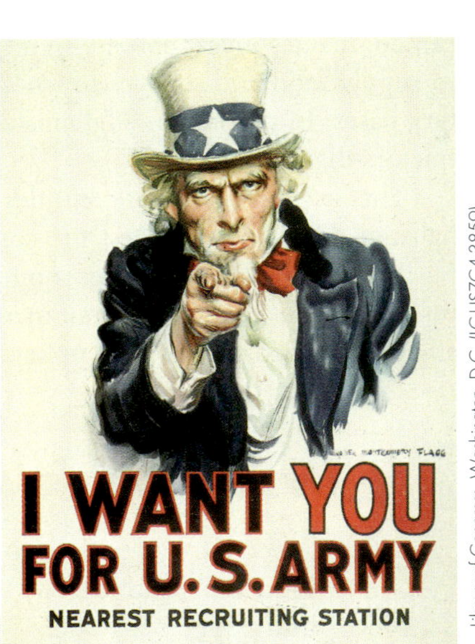

These three World War I posters (from France, Great Britain, and the United States) were used to persuade men to join the army. Interestingly, all employed the same psychological technique: pointing at viewers to make each individual feel the appeal personally.

World War II dramatically changed America's orientation toward the rest of the world. The United States emerged from the war a superpower, and its national security interests extended across the world. The country also confronted a new rival: its wartime ally, the Soviet Union. In the fight against Hitler, the Soviets overran much of Eastern Europe. After the war, the Soviets solidified their control over these lands, spreading their communist ideology. To Americans, Soviet communism aimed to destroy freedom, and the prospect of Soviet expansion in Europe threatened international order. European conflicts had drawn the United States into war twice in twenty-five years. American foreign policy experts believed that the Soviets, if left unchecked, might soon do it again.

Cold War and Containment

To frustrate Soviet expansionist designs, Americans prepared to wage a new kind of war: not an actual shooting war, or "hot war," but a **Cold War**, characterized by suspicion, rivalry, mutual ideological revulsion, and a military buildup between the two superpowers, but no shooting. The United States waged its Cold War on a policy of **containment**, or holding Soviet power in check.[37]

The policy of containment had military, economic, and political dimensions. Militarily, the United States committed itself to high defense expenditures, including maintaining a large fighting force with troops stationed around the world. Economically, the United States backed the establishment of an international economic system that relied on free trade, fixed currency exchange rates, and America's ability to act as banker for the world. This system, plus an aid program to rebuild Europe (the Marshall Plan), fueled recovery and reduced the economic appeal of communism. Politically, the United States forged numerous alliances against Soviet aggression. The first treaty of alliance (1949) created the **North Atlantic Treaty Organization (NATO)**, dedicated to the defense of member countries in Europe and North America. In addition, the United States tried to use international institutions such as the United Nations as instruments of containment. Because the Soviets had veto power in the U.N. Security Council, the United States was rarely able to use the United Nations as anything more than a sounding board to express anti-Soviet feelings.

In the first decades of the Cold War, the United States relied on its weapons superiority to implement a policy of nuclear deterrence. It discouraged Soviet expansion by threatening to use nuclear weapons to retaliate against Soviet power, which had also acquired nuclear capabilities. By the late 1960s, both nations had enough weapons to destroy each other. This led to a MAD (mutual assured destruction) situation: a first strike from either nation would result in the complete annihilation of both sides.

In the 1950s and 1960s, many countries in the developing world were seeking independence from colonial control by Western nations, and the Soviets were paying close attention to these developing nations. They offered to help forces involved in these "wars of national liberation," that is, wars fought to end colonialism. To counter the Soviets, the United States followed policies aimed at **nation building**: strengthening the opponents of communism in newly emerging nations (the so-called Third World) by promoting democratic reforms and shoring up their economies.[38]

Vietnam and the Challenge to the Cold War Consensus

Soviet support for wars of national liberation conflicted with American nation building in Vietnam. There, the United States tried to strengthen noncommunist

---

Cold War
A prolonged period of adversarial relations between the two superpowers, the United States and the Soviet Union. It lasted from the late 1940s to the late 1980s.

containment
The basic U.S. policy toward the Soviet Union during the Cold War, according to which the Soviets were to be contained within existing boundaries by military, diplomatic, and economic means.

North Atlantic Treaty Organization (NATO)
An organization including nations of Western Europe, the United States, and Canada, created in 1949 to defend against Soviet expansionism.

nation building
A policy to shore up countries economically and democratically, thereby making them less likely to collapse or be taken over.

institutions in South Vietnam to prevent a takeover by Soviet- and China-backed forces from North Vietnam and their communist allies in the south, the Viet Cong. The Cold War turned hot in Vietnam by the mid-1960s. Over 58,000 American lives were lost before the United States withdrew in 1973. The Vietnam War badly damaged the Cold War consensus on containment, both abroad and at home. Some American critics charged that the government lacked the will to use enough military force to win. Others argued that America relied on military force to solve what were really political problems. Still others objected that America was intervening in a civil war rather than blocking communist expansion. In short, Americans disagreed passionately on what to do in Vietnam and how to do it. After signing a peace agreement in 1973, the United States pulled its forces out of Vietnam, and in 1975, north and south were joined under a communist regime.

As the war in Vietnam wore on, President Nixon and his chief foreign policy adviser (and later secretary of state), Henry Kissinger, overhauled American foreign policy under the **Nixon Doctrine**. Now the United States would intervene only where "it makes a real difference and is considered in our interest."[39] A student of European diplomatic history, Kissinger believed that peace prevailed when the great nations maintained a balance of power among themselves. Nixon and Kissinger sought to create a similar framework for peace among the world's most powerful nations. To this end, they pursued a policy of **détente** (a relaxing of tensions between rivals) with the Soviet Union and ended decades of U.S. hostility toward communist China. The brief period of détente saw the conclusion of a major arms agreement, the Strategic Arms Limitation Treaty (SALT I), in 1972. This pact limited the growth of strategic nuclear weapons. President Jimmy Carter's stance on foreign policy from 1977 to 1979 differed substantially from that of his predecessors. He downplayed the Soviet threat, seeing revolutions in Nicaragua and Iran as products of internal forces, not Soviet involvement. In contrast to Nixon and Kissinger, Carter was criticized as being overly idealistic. He emphasized human rights, admonishing both friends and enemies with poor human rights records. He usually leaned toward open rather than secret diplomacy. Nonetheless, his greatest foreign policy achievement—peace between Egypt and Israel—resulted from closed negotiations he arranged between Egyptian president Anwar Sadat and Israeli premier Menachem Begin at Camp David.

In many ways, Carter's foreign policy reflected the influence of the Vietnam syndrome—a crisis of confidence that resulted from America's failure in Vietnam and the breakdown of the Cold War consensus about America's role in the world. For example, his administration deemphasized the use of military force but could offer no effective alternatives in late 1979 when Iranians took American diplomats hostage and when the Soviets invaded Afghanistan.

The End of the Cold War

Carter's successor, Ronald Reagan, came to the Oval Office in 1981 untroubled by the Vietnam syndrome. He believed that the Soviets were responsible for most of the evil in the world. Attributing instability in Central America, Africa, and Afghanistan to Soviet meddling, he argued that the best way to combat the Soviet threat was to renew and demonstrate American military strength—a policy of **peace through strength**. Increased defense spending focused on major new weapons systems, such as the Strategic Defense Initiative (dubbed the "Star Wars" program), a new space-based missile defense system (expensive and never implemented). The Reagan administration argued that its massive military buildup was both a deterrent and a bargaining chip to use in talks with the Soviets. During this period, the Cold War

---

Nixon Doctrine
Nixon's policy, formulated with assistance from Henry Kissinger, that restricted U.S. military intervention abroad absent a threat to its vital national interests.

détente
A reduction of tensions. This term is particularly used to refer to a reduction of tensions between the United States and the Soviet Union in the early 1970s during the Nixon administration.

peace through strength
Reagan's policy of combating communism by building up the military, including aggressive development of new weapons systems.

climate once again grew chilly. Things changed when Mikhail Gorbachev came to power in the Soviet Union in 1985. Gorbachev wished to reduce his nation's commitments abroad so it could concentrate on needed domestic reforms. By the end of Reagan's second term, the United States and the Soviet Union had concluded agreements outlawing intermediate-range nuclear forces (the INF Treaty) and providing for a Soviet military pullout from Afghanistan.[40]

In 1989, only months after Reagan left office, the Berlin Wall was torn down, symbolizing the end of the Cold War. The conventional view is that the Cold War ended and America won. Some believe that communism collapsed because of Reagan's policies. Others insist that the appeal of Western affluence, Gorbachev's own new thinking, and a shared interest in overcoming the nuclear threat led to the end of the Cold War.[41] Still others argue that both superpowers had lost by spending trillions of dollars on defense while neglecting other sectors of their economies.

Foreign Policy Without the Cold War

In 1990, soon after George H. W. Bush became president, Saddam Hussein invaded Kuwait. Not only did Iraq attack an American friend, but also it threatened the U.S. supply of oil. Bush emphasized multilateral action, building a coalition of nations that included America's Western allies, Eastern European nations, many Arab states, and other developing countries. The United States also won approval for actions against Iraq from the U.N. Security Council. During the Cold War, the Security Council usually proved ineffective because the United States and U.S.S.R. could veto the other's action. However, the two superpowers cooperated against Saddam in this post–Cold War crisis. After the coalition launched its counterattack in January 1991, the war lasted less than two months. By the end of February 1991, Iraqi troops were driven out of Kuwait and into Iraq, but the cease-fire left Saddam Hussein in power.

Iraq's invasion of Kuwait constituted a visible, vital threat to U.S. interests and galvanized Americans in support of President Bush's military action to repel the invasion. President Clinton, who came to the White House in 1993 with no foreign policy experience, enjoyed no galvanizing challenge and struggled to provide clear, coherent foreign policy leadership. Clinton's presidential campaign emphasized domestic concerns, but he soon found that messy crises in Somalia, Bosnia, Haiti, and then Kosovo absorbed much of his time. His administration replaced the Cold War policy of containment with a policy of **enlargement and engagement**. "Enlargement" meant increasing the number of democracies with market economies and also adding to the membership of the NATO alliance. "Engagement" meant rejecting isolationism and striving to achieve greater flexibility in a chaotic global era. But critics worried that the policy did not provide adequate guidelines about when, where, and why the United States should be engaged.[42] Even when Clinton acted with NATO to stop the genocidal violence in Kosovo, his policy was criticized. Nevertheless, Clinton himself drew praise for his efforts to end the fighting in Northern Ireland and for working to broker a peaceful end to the Israeli–Palestinian conflict.

enlargement and engagement
Clinton's policy, following the collapse of communism, of increasing the spread of market economies and increasing the U.S. role in global affairs.

The Hot War on Terrorism

Entering the presidency in 2001, George W. Bush had something in common with Bill Clinton: no foreign policy experience. The attacks on America on September 11, 2001, transformed Bush's presidency. Addressing Congress on September 20, Bush vowed to eliminate the threat to order posed by international terrorism. The sovereignty of other nations would not limit the United States from acting as world policeman to eliminate terrorism.

Bush made international affairs the centerpiece of his administration. He also presided over a successful campaign against al Qaeda and the Taliban in Afghanistan. The president and his advisers spent three weeks after 9/11 lining up international support (mainly from NATO countries) and planning for a military response before launching air strikes on October 7 to support anti-Taliban militias.[43] The war against the Taliban (which cost very few U.S. casualties) was effectively over by December 6. On December 20, Hamid Karzai arrived in Kabul to head an interim government with British Royal Marines in the vanguard of a United Nations force.

Flushed with genuine success in Afghanistan, President Bush announced in September 2002 a new doctrine of **preemptive action**: "to act alone, if necessary, to exercise our right of self-defense by acting preemptively against … terrorists to prevent them from doing harm against our people and our country."[44] Bush explicitly scrapped the doctrine of containment in 2003 as invoked in his controversial doctrine of preemption and launched war on Iraq.[45]

America's combat role in Iraq dragged on for more than nine years, cost over 4,000 American lives, and produced little success apart from toppling Saddam Hussein. No weapons of mass destruction were destroyed (or found), and Iraq remained a place of violent death with an unstable government. Today in Iraq there are still deadly bombings daily, killing innocent civilians and maiming others.[46]

American public opinion turned against the president on Iraq three years after the war began. In May 2003, when Bush had declared that "combat operations were over," 74 percent of the public approved of the way he was handling the situation in Iraq. In May 2006, his approval fell to 29 percent.[47] Bush nevertheless defended his decision to invade Iraq.[48] Early in 2007, he authorized a "surge" of about 30,000 additional troops for Iraq, raising the force level to about 160,000. By the end of the year, the extra troops helped reduce the violence in Iraq, and the Iraqi parliament passed some laws to improve the political situation. Nevertheless, the U.S. public's approval of Bush's handling of the situation increased only slightly, to 31 percent.[49]

In his election campaign, Barack Obama described the war in Iraq as a "war of choice" (Bush's choice) while the war in Afghanistan against al Qaeda was a "war of necessity." As president, Obama quickly implemented the Iraq exit strategy outlined by the Bush administration and withdrew all combat troops in 2010. In Afghanistan, Obama twice ordered troop increases, almost tripling the number to nearly 100,000.[50] While favoring the buildup, most Americans at the end of 2009 opposed the war itself.[51] As more troops engaged Taliban forces, the American death toll rose while at the same time U.S. and NATO forces seemed to make limited progress in pacifying the Taliban. The American public is pessimistic about progress in Afghanistan and is strongly in favor of a quick withdrawal from the country (see Figure 19.2).[52] In April 2012 President Obama made a surprise trip to see U.S. troops in Afghanistan and, in a nationally televised speech from an airbase there, renewed his pledge to bring home all the troops by 2014.[53]

Afghanistan's neighbor, Pakistan, also remains a serious problem area for the United States. Although ostensibly an ally of the United States, it is home to al Qaeda and Taliban terrorists antagonistic to the United States. Drone (pilotless) aircraft have bombed many suspected terrorists there with some success; this has angered the Pakistanis because they regard these attacks as an infringement on their national sovereignty.[54] It was in Pakistan, of course, where U.S. intelligence discovered Osama bin Laden's hideout.[55] The American raid there was a tremendous embarrassment for the

---

preemptive action
The policy of acting against a nation or group that poses a severe threat to the United States before waiting for the threat to occur; sometimes called the "Bush doctrine."

FIGURE 19.2 **Afghanistan: An Unpopular War**

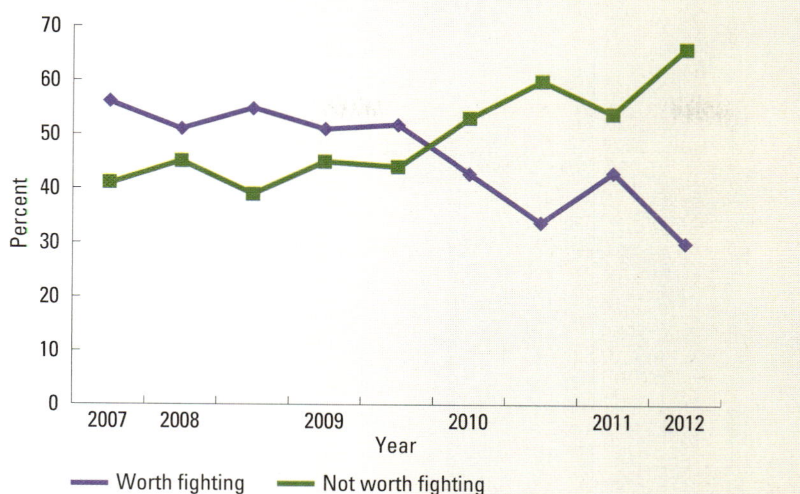

The United States's military action in Afghanistan began in the wake of the September 11, 2001, attack upon the United States by al Qaeda terrorists. The men that hijacked the four American planes on that day were under the command of Osama bin Laden, who had his training camp in Afghanistan. Bin Laden and his al Qaeda operatives were protected by Afghanistan's Taliban government. The U.S. military intervention there was overwhelmingly supported by the American people who wanted justice brought to those who perpetrated the 9/11 attacks. The Taliban was quickly ousted, and President Bush turned his attention to Iraq. Over time the Taliban regrouped and began to dominate parts of Afghanistan. American and NATO troops did not have the numbers to rid the country of the Taliban, and President Obama decided to increase the military presence there. Americans, however, have become weary of the war in Afghanistan, and support for the war has declined.

The figure represents respondents' answers to the following question: "All in all, considering the costs to the United States versus the benefits to the United States, do you think the war in Afghanistan has been worth fighting, or not?"

Source: ABC News/*Washington Post* polling. Data via PollingReport.com.

Pakistani government as U.S. helicopters had entered the country undetected by the Pakistani military. This strained relations further.

From Foreign Policy to Global Policy

The end of the Cold War and the process of globalization have resulted in a fundamental shift in the nature of foreign policy. For the first time, U.S. foreign policy has taken on a truly *global* focus. We apply the term **global policy**, like *foreign policy,* to a general plan to defend and advance national interests, but global policy embraces a broader view of national interests. Whereas foreign policy focuses on security against foreign threats (mainly military but also economic threats), global policy adds social and environmental concerns to matters of national interest. Whereas foreign policy typically deals with disputes between leaders, ideologies, or states, global policy confronts more silent, cumulative effects of billions of individual choices made by people everywhere around the globe.

Inevitably, global policy requires global action. The players are no longer competing alliances among nations but international organizations that cooperate on a worldwide scale. For example, the Internet Corporation for Assigned Names and

global policy
Like foreign policy, it is a plan for defending and advancing national interests, but—unlike foreign policy—it includes social and environmental concerns among national interests.

6 Rooms, Good View, Quiet Street

The most hunted man in the world, Osama bin Laden, hid in this house in Abbottabad, Pakistan. After American intelligence discovered that he was living there, a team of Navy SEALs flew by helicopter to the compound, found bin Laden inside, and shot him to death. He was buried at sea by American military personnel.

Numbers (ICANN) meeting in Seoul, Korea, allowed the use of Internet addresses in non-Latin characters beginning in 2010.[56] The Russian-language site Kremlin.ru became Кремлв.рф.[57]

The most prominent international organization is the United Nations, which grew in membership from 51 at the founding in 1945 to its present size of 193. As the United Nations expanded its membership to include many newly independent states, the United States frequently found itself outvoted. Fearing loss of sovereignty, the United States reduced its commitment to international institutions such as the United Nations and the International Court of Justice (commonly called the World Court) when they acted in ways that ran counter to American interests. For example, the World Court ruled in 2004 that the state of Texas could not execute a Mexican citizen for murder because he was denied contact with Mexican consular officials until after his conviction—contrary to our treaty obligations. However, the U.S. Supreme Court in 2008 allowed the execution to proceed without a new hearing, contending that the World Court's ruling "is not domestic law."[58]

After the Cold War ended, the United States briefly acted as the world leader and repelled Iraq's invasion of Kuwait in 1991. Soon afterward, the international political agenda shifted toward issues such as world trade, world poverty, the environment, human rights, and emerging democracy—and American leadership was less evident. The September 11, 2001, attacks refocused attention on military action, with the United States leading the war against terrorism in Afghanistan. The invasion of Iraq cost the United States some of its moral authority, and U.S. efforts to combat the nuclear ambitions of North Korea and Iran were often blocked in the United Nations Security Council by China and Russia, which also differed with America concerning other global problems.[59]

More recently, there are encouraging signs of increased cooperation among the Western allies. When a rebellion emerged in Libya against the country's dictator, Muammar Gaddafi, the NATO alliance successfully intervened with a vigorous bombing campaign in support of the rebels. In an unusual move for NATO, the bombing was done largely by European countries with the United States playing more of a supporting role. In another manifestation of the Arab Spring, a rebellion in Syria against the dictator there, Bashar al-Assad, also catalyzed cooperative action by the United States, Europe, and other nations. Although no military action has been taken to support the rebellion, the allies have initiated an economic boycott of Syria, which has had a devastating impact on the nation. The cooperating countries have pushed China and Russia hard to pull away from supporting the Assad regime.

19.4 Global Policy Issue Areas

★ Describe the influence of the global issues of investment and trade, human rights, and the environment on U.S. foreign and domestic policy.

Global issues like world poverty and environmental degradation have always existed, and they have moved up on national policy agendas because of globalization, the increased interdependence among nations. Nations today understand not only that their economies are tied to one another, but also that the air we breathe, the illnesses we contract, and even the climate we experience can be affected by events in other countries. In addition to terrorism, globalization (according to one author) involves fighting five other festering wars: against illegal international trade, drugs, arms, transportation of aliens, and theft of intellectual property.[60] Countries outside the United States worry about American culture diminishing their own. American movies, television shows, language, and mores are extraordinarily influential around the globe, and countries like Canada and France worry that their own unique cultures will become subsumed under American commercial and cultural forces.[61]

Consequently, global policy deals with issues that blend international and domestic concerns. Because global policy requires global action, domestic policies and practices become subject to policies and rules of international organizations. Conservative opponents of international organizations regard this global interaction as compromising their nation's sovereignty. Not only does global policy present different challenges to policymaking, but also those challenges threaten the very concept of sovereignty that lies at the basis of national interest in traditional foreign policy. In this section, we choose to study only three broad topics within global interdependence: investment and trade, human rights and foreign aid, and the environment. International approaches to all topics involve salient threats to the sovereignty of the nations that take on global policies.

Investment and Trade

At the end of World War II, the United States dominated the world's economy. Half of all international trade involved the United States, and the dollar played a key role in underwriting economic recovery in Europe and Asia. America could not expect to retain the economic dominance it enjoyed in the late 1940s and 1950s, but it was able to invest heavily abroad even through the 1970s, prompting European concern that both profits and control of European-based firms would drain away to America.

During the 1990s, money began to flow into the United States, and worries grew that foreigners owned too much of our national debt (see p. 489), making us dependent on their continued financial support. Then there was the new fear of huge foreign **sovereign wealth funds** (SWFs), very large pools of government money saved from budget surpluses and reserved for investment. About twenty nations—rich from oil or exports—have a sovereign wealth fund (SWF). Examples are Saudi Arabia, Kuwait, United Arab Emirates, and Norway (from oil), and China and Singapore (from exports).[62] SWF investments, which are controlled by foreign governments, can be made or withdrawn for political rather than economic reasons.

There is a great deal of concern today about government debt rising across the world among the market-oriented economies. The United States's debt has grown

sovereign wealth funds
A government-owned fund of financial assets built from budget surpluses and reserved for investment purposes.

considerably because of the long recession but appears manageable as the low interest rates on government bonds are evidence of investors' confidence in the long-term future of the nation's economy. The same is not true among many countries of the European Union (EU).[63] Greece, Portugal, Italy, Spain, and Ireland have all borrowed too much money and have staggered as their debt loads skyrocketed. Greece has already effectively defaulted on some of its debt. Austerity measures designed to reduce government spending have led to higher unemployment as governments have laid off workers, and the private sectors have shrunk too. The unemployment rate among young people is shockingly high in the worst hit countries (see "Compared with What? Young and Unemployed"). In the spring of 2012, a number of European governments were voted out of office or prime ministers replaced by ruling parliamentary coalitions as citizens there came to believe that they were being forced by the EU to adopt policies that were actually hurting their countries.[64]

Entering the 2010s, the United States no longer dominates the world economy as it did decades earlier. In 1960, the United States generated about 45 percent of the entire world's gross domestic product (GDP). By 2010, it accounted for just under 20 percent.[65] Moreover, it had new economic rivals. As late as 1999, the largest economies after the United States were, respectively, Japan, Germany, Britain, France, and Italy—followed by China in seventh place. By 2010, China had leaped to second.[66] The American public sensed the changing situation, seeing the United States as less important in 2009 than it had been a decade earlier and regarding China as a major threat.[67] Moreover, Brazil, Russia, India, and China (known as the BRIC nations) began to demand more say in the global economic order because of their growth and resources.

An increasingly severe problem is American dependence on oil imports. In 1960, the United States produced 7 million barrels of oil a day (more than Saudi Arabia and all the Persian Gulf states combined) and met over 80 percent of its own needs.[68] Due to increasing demand for oil and decreasing domestic supply, the United States today imports just under half of the oil it consumes (see "Politics of Global Change: Foreign Oil: A Bit Less Dependent" on page 576). As other nations (especially China) have increased their oil consumption, the price has climbed, pressuring all countries to seek alternative sources of energy.

As the United States became entangled in the global web of international finance, it became more closely tied to other countries through international trade. In 1970, the value of U.S. foreign trade came to 11.2 percent of the nation's GDP; today, it is about 25 percent.[69] As foreign trade became more important to the American economy, policymakers faced alternative responses. Among them are free trade, fair trade, managed trade, and protectionism.

A true **free-trade** policy would allow for the unfettered operation of the free market—nations would not impose tariffs or other barriers to keep foreign goods from being sold in their countries. All trading partners would benefit under free trade, which would allow the principle of **comparative advantage** to work unhindered. According to this principle, all trading nations gain when each produces goods it can make comparatively cheaply and then trades them to obtain funds for the items it can produce only at a comparatively higher cost.

Although the United States has not embraced a pure form of free trade, it generally favored a liberal international trade regime in the last decades of the twentieth century. (In this case, the word *liberal* is used in its classic political sense to mean "free.") American critics of free-trade policies complain that free trade has too often been a one-way street. America's trading partners could sell their goods in the United States while restricting their own markets through an array of tariffs and nontariff barriers (NTBs)—regulations that make importation of foreign goods difficult or

free trade
An economic policy that allows businesses in different nations to sell and buy goods without paying tariffs or other limitations.

comparative advantage
A principle of international trade that states that all nations will benefit when each nation specializes in those goods that it can produce most efficiently.

Compared with What?

Young and Unemployed

The severe economic downturn in Europe has pushed unemployment there sky-high. While it is elevated for all Europeans, the unemployment rate for the young is catastrophically high. By 2012 the rate had edged over 50 percent for Spanish youth. In Sweden the unemployment rate for the young is four times as great as it is for middle-aged workers. In the United States, at a roughly comparable date in time to the end point in this graph, the unemployment rate for the larger cohort of eighteen- to twenty-nine-year-olds was 13.6 percent, and the nation's overall unemployment rate was falling. As they graduate high school and college, students across Europe face a bleak landscape, and feelings of hopelessness among them are common. Maria Gil Ulldemolins, a Spaniard in her twenties with two college degrees and no job, spoke for her generation when she told a reporter, "I trained for a world that doesn't exist."

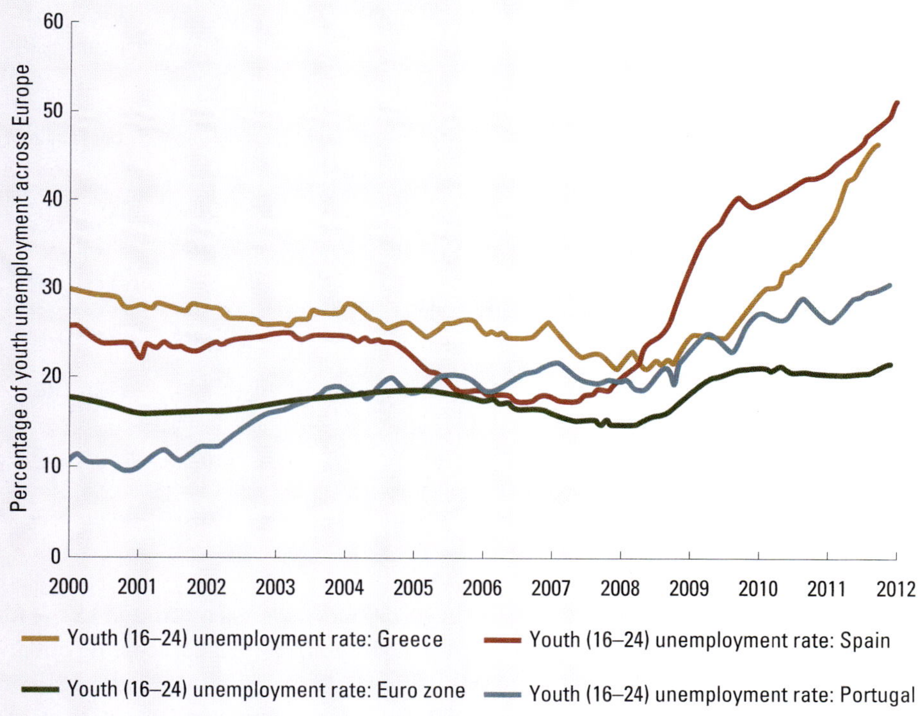

Source: Brad Plumer, "Is This Europe's Scariest Chart?" *Washington Post,* 1 February 2012; "The Jobless Young: Left Behind," *The Economist,* 10 September 2011; and Dennis Jacobe, "One in Three Young U.S. Workers Are Underemployed," Gallup Poll, 9 May 2012.

impossible by outlining stringent criteria that an imported product must meet in order to be offered for sale. The Japanese, for example, have been criticized for excessive use of NTBs. Japan restricts imports of American beef to meat cows less than 20 months old, even though the United States says that there is no health-related rationale to justify such a restriction.[70]

Although the United States has sought to make trade freer by reducing tariffs and nontariff barriers, Americans want more than freedom in the world market; they

Politics of Global Change

Foreign Oil: A Bit Less Dependent

In 1960, the United States supplied nearly all its petroleum needs from its own oil wells. By 1995, the United States imported more oil from foreign sources than it produced. In 1960, the United States accounted for 46 percent of the world's oil consumption of 21 million barrels per day. Despite doubling its own use by 2008, the U.S. share dropped to 25 percent of the world's use of over 85 million barrels. As demand for oil rose across the world, so did oil prices, leading to increased costs for our increasing energy needs and expanded quests for alternative sources. In recent years, smaller, more fuel-efficient cars, conservation, the development of alternative energy, and a modest increase in domestic production have led to both a drop in overall consumption and imports from the Middle East and elsewhere.

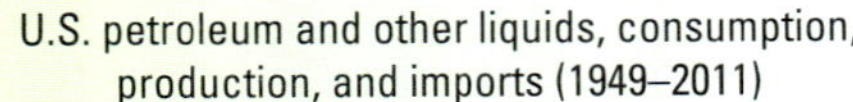

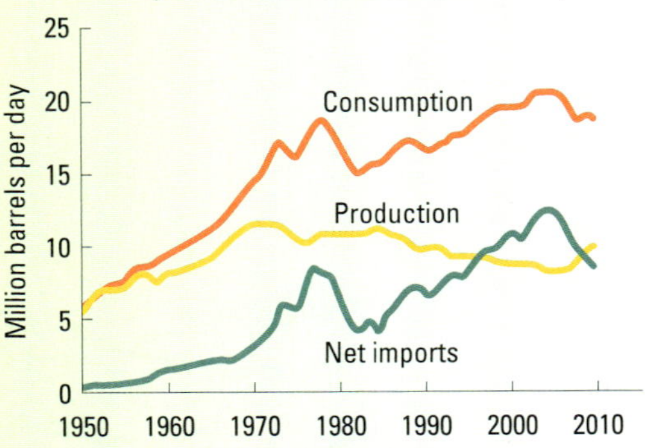

Source: U.S. Energy Information Administration, *Monthly Energy Review* (April 2012).

fair trade
Trade regulated by international agreements outlawing unfair business practices.

want order too. Policymakers committed to the idea of **fair trade** have worked to create order through international agreements outlawing unfair business practices. These practices include bribery; pirating intellectual property such as software, CDs, and films; and "dumping," a practice in which a country sells its goods below cost in order to capture the market for its products in another country. The World Trade Organization (WTO) was created in 1995 to regulate trade among member nations. Headquartered in Geneva, Switzerland, it has a staff of 600 to administer trade agreements signed by its 153 member nations and ratified in their parliaments.

Free trade and fair trade are not the only approaches to trade that American policymakers consider. America began the 1980s as the world's leading creditor and ended the decade as the world's leading debtor. For years the nation has run up huge balance-of-payments deficits with other nations. The largest of these deficits is with China, which has become our largest trading partner after Canada.[71] The United States and other countries try to redress trade imbalances by negotiating agreements with trading partners, sometimes through bilateral (just two countries) or multilateral (a number of countries) accords.

Domestic political pressure often bears on trade issues. Although free traders claim that the principle of comparative advantage ensures that eliminating trade barriers would make everyone better off in the long run, their opponents argue that imports threaten American industries and jobs. To guard against these hazards, **protectionists** want to retain barriers to free trade. For example, most unions and many small manufacturers opposed NAFTA and CAFTA. They believed that if tariffs were removed, Mexico, with its low labor costs, would be able to undersell American producers and thus run them out of business or force them to move their operations to Mexico. Either alternative threatened American jobs. At the same time, many Americans were eager to take advantage of new opportunities in a growing Mexican market for goods and services. They realized that protectionism can be a double-edged sword.

Nevertheless, there is a growing backlash against globalization, which has not only reduced jobs and wages in developed nations but also increased inequality in developing countries.[72] Even in states such as Iowa, which benefited from expanded exports for its crops and farm equipment, people lament the decline of high-paid factory jobs.[73]

protectionists
Those who wish to prevent imports from entering the country and therefore oppose free trade.

Human Rights, Poverty, and Foreign Aid

NATO's campaign against ethnic cleansing in the Balkans in the late 1990s and its campaign against Gaddafi in Libya in 2011 make it clear that the Western democracies are willing to go to war to protect human rights. This is especially true of America, which has long championed democracy and human rights. Support for moral ideals such as freedom, democracy, and human rights fits well with U.S. interests. These elements of liberal democracy permeate our political culture, and we relate better to nations that share them. But the relationship between America's human rights policy goals and its economic policy goals has often been problematic.

The ten big emerging markets (BEMs) that seem especially promising for U.S. investments and trade are the Chinese economic area (the People's Republic of China, Taiwan, and Hong Kong), Indonesia, India, South Korea, Mexico, Brazil, Argentina, South Africa, Turkey, and Poland. These nations have large areas and populations, are growing rapidly, are influential in their region, and buy the types of goods and services America has to sell. The Commerce Department took the lead in helping American businesses win contracts in these nations.[74] But engagement with these countries raises questions that go beyond America's economic interests. Some of the BEMs have dubious records in the areas of human rights, workers' rights, and child labor. Some are lax about environmental standards, intellectual property protection, or nuclear nonproliferation. To what extent should development of commercial ties with these nations override other policy objectives?

U.S. Embassy Beijing Press via Getty Images

Now What?

Chinese dissident activist Chen Guangcheng (right) spent four years in prison after angering Chinese officials with his public criticism of the government. Following prison he was sentenced to house arrest, but after escaping he fled to the United States embassy in Beijing. This resulted in a human rights controversy since the United States did not want to return Guangcheng to the Chinese as human rights groups in the United States would be incensed. At the same time, the United States did not want this one dissident to upset relations between the two countries. U.S. Ambassador Gary Locke (left) and the State Department quietly negotiated with the Chinese to resolve the matter and, eventually, Guangcheng was allowed to come to the United States.

In addition to granting nations favorable trade terms, the United States can use other economic tools to pursue its policy objectives. These include development aid, debt forgiveness, and loans with favorable credit terms (see Figure 19.3). Yet the United States is limited in what it can do because these other countries' self-interests can make them highly resistant to American entreaties. China, for example, has a

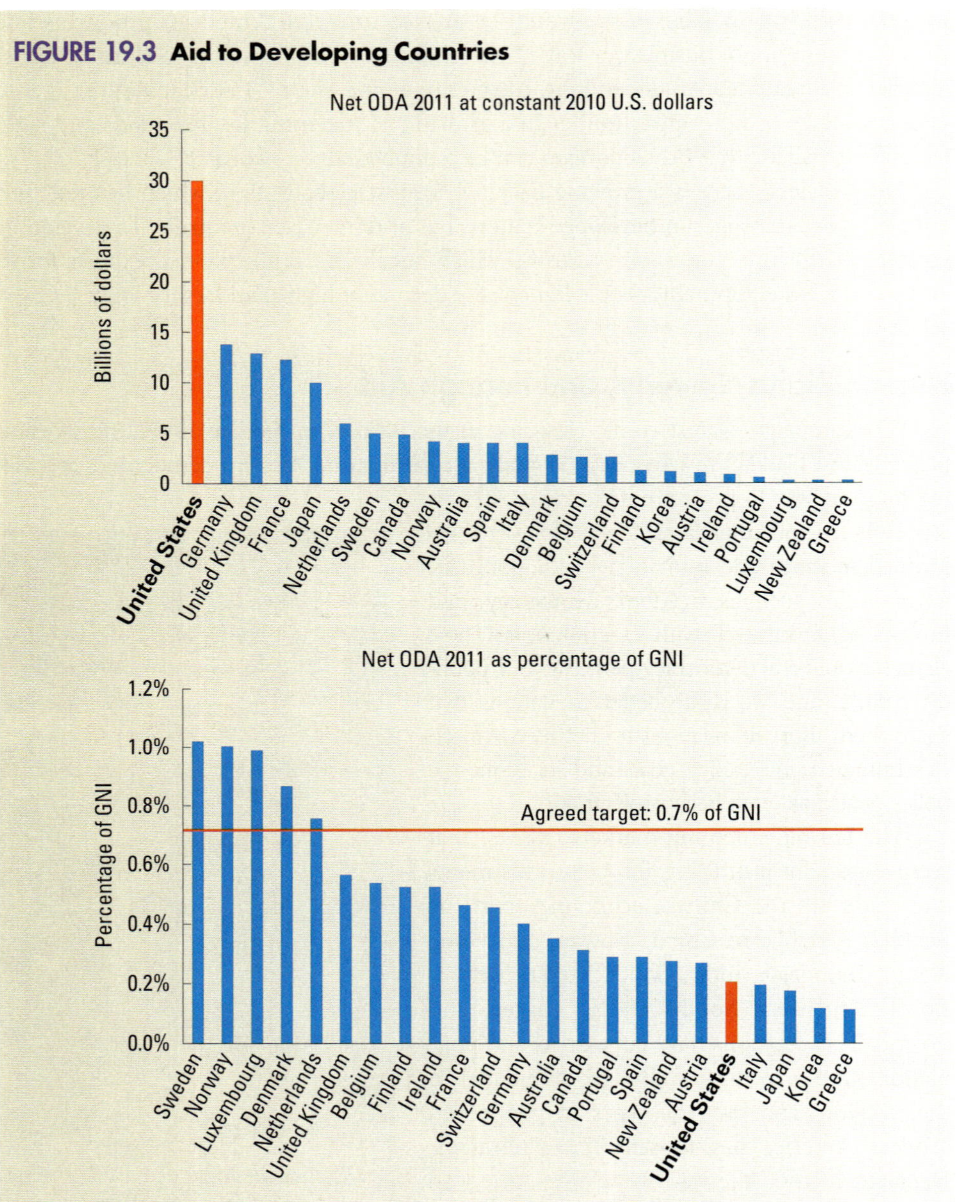

FIGURE 19.3 Aid to Developing Countries

This graph compares U.S. aid to developing countries in 2011 with aid given by the other member countries of the Development Assistance Committee of the Organization of Economic Co-operation and Development (OECD). These figures are reported for Official Development Assistance (ODA), a standard measure of grants and loans to a designated list of recipient nations. These data show both the amount of aid in absolute dollars given by each country and the amount of aid as a percentage of the country's gross national income (GNI). Although the United States gave the most in dollars to assist developing countries, it gives one of the lowest amounts in terms of percentage of national income.
Source: Global Issues website, "Foreign Aid Numbers in Charts and Graphs," April 2012, http://www.globalissues.org/article/35/foreign-aid-development-assistance#ForeignAidNumbersin ChartsandGraphs. Copyright © 2012 by Anup Shah. All rights reserved. Reproduced by permission.

terrible record on human rights as dissidents can be severely punished. In 2009, just after becoming the new secretary of state in the Obama administration, Hillary Clinton stated publicly that disagreements over human rights with China should not interfere with other issues that the two countries regard as important.[75] The United States wants China to reduce its oil purchases from Iran to pressure the Iranians from developing nuclear weapons.[76]

Assistance to developing countries can take the form of donations of American goods, which directly benefits the American businesses that supply the products. Inequality between rich nations and poor nations is growing. There is an increasing gap in income between the industrialized nations of the North and the nonindustrialized states of the South. This income gap between nations provokes arguments in international politics, just as issues of social inequality motivate those who favor social equality for minorities in domestic politics. Many people believe it is unjust for the developed world to enjoy great wealth while people in the global South, or Third World, are deprived. Sheer self-interest may also motivate policymakers to address this problem. Great disparities in wealth between the developed and developing nations may lead to political instability and disorder, and thus threaten the interests of the industrially developed democracies.

In times of fiscal austerity, foreign aid is an easy target for budget cuts. Foreign aid tends to be unpopular, partly because recipients do not vote in American elections and because American citizens overestimate what the nation spends on aid. In repeated national surveys, about half the respondents believe that at least 15 percent of the federal budget goes to foreign aid. Half also think it would be appropriate to devote 5 percent of the budget to foreign aid and that 3 percent would be too little. In actuality, far less than 1 percent of the federal budget goes to foreign aid.[77] Figure 19.3 shows how America's aid to developing countries stacks up against the contributions of other developed nations. However, the United States deserves credit for some humanitarian programs, especially in Africa. President George W. Bush championed a $15 billion program to fight HIV/AIDS and $1.2 billion for the prevention of malaria, mainly for millions of bed nets to protect against mosquitoes. Even his critics praised these actions.[78]

The Environment

Environmental issues pose new and vexing challenges for those making foreign policy. First, some terms in the debate: Biodiversity and climate change are distinct but intertwined concepts. Biodiversity (biological diversity) refers to the complex interactions between living organisms and their environment.[79] Climate change is one factor that affects biodiversity. The term *global warming* has become a politicized term referring to one aspect of climate change.[80] Even some who doubt that their environment has grown warmer may believe that it suffers more from drought, rain, or wind than earlier in their lifetime. The question is whether human beings have contributed to global climate change. Most scientists think they have—fully 97 percent "believe human-caused global warming is under way."[81] In 2010, the United Nation's Intergovernmental Panel on Climate Change determined that 2000–2009 was "the warmest decade in the instrumental record."[82] If the world really is warming, what can, or should, be done about it?

The value conflict of freedom versus order, which we have seen in domestic politics, surfaces when dealing with the global environment. In the prototypical example, wealthy industrialized nations, which polluted the world in the process of industrializing, tell Third World nations that *they* cannot burn fossil fuels to develop

Summit Meeting

In early December 2009, all twenty-one members of the Nepalese cabinet flew by helicopter to near the Mount Everest base camp at an altitude of 17,000 feet. They met there days prior to the Copenhagen conference on climate change to dramatize the reduced snowfall and melting glaciers attributed to global warming. In October, the government of the Maldives, an island country in the Indian Ocean, held an underwater cabinet meeting to dramatize the threat of rising sea levels.

Source: Joanna Jolly, "Nepal Cabinet Holds Meeting on Mount Everest," BBC News, 4 December 2009, http://news.bbc.co.uk/2/hi/8394452.stm..

AP Photo/Gemunu Amarasinghe

themselves because doing so would further pollute the environment. Leaders in developing countries do not appreciate limits on their freedom to industrialize—limits that serve the developed world's definition of global order.

The 1992 United Nations Conference on Environment and Development in Rio de Janeiro produced the Biodiversity Treaty aimed at conserving the Earth's diverse biological resources through the development of national strategies for conservation, creation of protected areas, and protection of ecosystems and natural habitats. President George H. W. Bush thought the Biodiversity Treaty limited U.S. patent rights in biotechnology and failed to protect U.S. intellectual property rights, so he refused to sign it. Although President Clinton later signed the treaty and sent it to the Senate, the Senate did not vote on it, so the United States is not a party to the treaty. The 1997 Kyoto Protocol set binding greenhouse gas reductions for industrialized countries but not developing countries, including major polluters China and India.[83] It too was signed by Clinton but was never sent to a hostile Senate. The 2009 Copenhagen agreement on climate change, signed by President Obama, required nations only to state intended amounts of reduced emissions.[84] Nations were not ready to submit to global regulations.

★ 19.5 The Public and Global Policy

★ Explain the relationship between U.S. foreign policy and both the majoritarian and pluralist models of democracy.

The president and Congress have always considered public opinion when making foreign policy: both had to face the public's wrath if blamed for policy failures. Historically, the public has paid little attention to traditional concerns of foreign policy—alliances, military bases abroad, and general diplomacy.[85] Except for issues of war and peace, the spread of communism, acts of terrorism, and other matters of national security, public opinion on foreign policy seldom affected domestic politics in any major way.

Today, globalization has made nations more interdependent in economic and social spheres, and major events in other countries can have a direct impact on life in the United States. If gangsters in Russia and China cooperate with mobs in Nigeria and Italy, the United States will soon experience an increase in smuggled aliens, drugs, and counterfeit goods. The globalized media immediately communicate foreign affairs to the American audience. If the economy collapses in Asian countries,

Wall Street reacts literally within hours. Accordingly, one might expect the U.S. public to pay much more attention to foreign affairs now than it did thirty years ago. Alas, this is not so.

The Public and the Majoritarian Model

To assess the state of public knowledge of and interest in foreign affairs, we draw on a 2008 survey by the Chicago Council on Global Affairs (CCGA), one in a series begun in 1974.[86] The CCGA surveys permit comparisons of public attitudes over time. Immediately after 9/11, the 2002 survey showed a spike in the percentage of the public that was "very interested" in news of other countries, rising to 62 percent above the range of 44 to 53 percent in previous surveys. The 2008 survey, however, fell below pre-9/11 levels, with only 31 percent being "very interested" in foreign news. It asked specifically about globalization: whether "the increasing connections of our economy with others around the world" is "mostly good or mostly bad for the United States." Most of the public (58 percent) thought that globalization was mostly good, but 65 percent thought that it was bad for American workers' job security. Only 17 percent thought it was "very important" to help "bring a democratic form of government to other nations," which had been a cornerstone of President Bush's foreign policy.

The majoritarian model of democracy posits that a nation's foreign policy should conform to public opinion. Is public opinion up to the task? In a major study involving hundreds of survey questions from nine national surveys from 1974 to 2004, two scholars found the public's collective responses to the questions were "coherent and mutually consistent, durable over time, and (given the information available to the citizenry) sensible." They concluded that the average citizen

> is able to form coherent, reasonable views on many matters of foreign policy—presumably through historical learning, talking things over, and making simple use of heuristics and media-reported collective deliberation.[87]

Nevertheless, a separate study found that public opinion has little unique effect on foreign policy; the most important direct effect comes from internationally minded business organizations and their leaders.[88] This finding fits instead with the pluralist model of democracy.

Interest Groups and the Pluralist Model

What would be the nature of policies in a global society made under the pluralist model, in which government responds to competing groups? Ordinary citizens can become interested in foreign affairs when they learn how events in foreign lands can affect their economic interests or values. Often citizens learn from the more knowledgeable leaders of groups to which they belong. Both labor and business leaders in the auto industry may urge their followers to favor import restrictions on Japanese cars. Church leaders may warn of religious persecution abroad. Aroused citizens often have their positions argued to lawmakers in Washington by group representatives.

As described in Chapter 10, thousands of interest groups maintain offices in Washington, D.C. Even foreign firms, groups, and governments have hired lobbying firms to represent their interests in the U.S. capital. The influence of these groups varies with the issue. Interest groups are more effective at maintaining support for the status quo than at bringing about policy changes.[89] Because global policies often respond to new events abroad, one might expect these policies to form with little impact from interest groups. However, lobbying is also more effective when it deals with noncrisis issues of little importance to the public at large and can take place behind the scenes. Because the public has little interest in foreign affairs, interest groups can wield a great deal of influence on global policies outside matters of national security.

Interest groups focus their attention on foreign policy leaders—including elected and appointed government officials and prominent figures in business, academia, the media, labor unions, and religious organizations. The same major study cited above also compared such policy leaders' responses with the public's responses to identical foreign policy questions. The authors found disagreements between a majority of leaders and a majority of the public on 26 percent of the items.[90] Moreover, actual government policy differed from public opinion on several important issues. For example, most of the public in 2002 favored the Comprehensive Nuclear Test Ban Treaty, supported a treaty to ban land mines, backed an agreement to establish an International Criminal Court to try individuals for war crimes, and endorsed the Kyoto treaty on global warming. The administration opposed all, and none were put into effect.[91]

Sometimes even the current administration does not get its way. Consider the purchase of military aircraft. Since 2006, the secretary of defense and other Pentagon officials have tried to end production of the F-22 Raptor fighter jet, the Air Force's most advanced and expensive weapon, which costs about $160 million apiece. This jet was designed for superpower conflict and was never used in Iraq or Afghanistan.[92] The Pentagon preferred continuing to produce the $77 million F-35 Joint Strike Fighter, used heavily in Iran and Afghanistan. Nevertheless, Congress insisted on building the far more costly plane, and it remains in production. Why? It is supported by a powerful lobby consisting of the Air Force, Lockheed Martin (the primary contractor), and key members of Congress from Georgia (where the plane is assembled) and from Connecticut (where its engines are made).[93] Many other members benefit from the plane's subcontractors scattered across their districts. Military spending clearly fits the pluralist model. Interest groups (both business and labor) want the contracts, and members vote their districts. Congress values the profits and jobs from building the plane more than it respects the Pentagon's case.

SUMMARY

The president plays the leading role in setting U.S. foreign policy, but Congress has a strong supporting role. With shared responsibility among Congress, the executive branch, and various administrative agencies, foreign policy is a complex undertaking and subject to considerable debate and disagreement within the government.

19.1 Making Foreign Policy: The Constitutional Context

- The Constitution grants overlapping powers on foreign policy to the president and to the Congress.

19.2 Making Foreign Policy: Organization and Cast

- Many different executive branch departments and agencies participate in the process of formulating foreign policy.

19.3 A Review of U.S. Foreign Policy

- The Cold War ideology was eroded by the disillusionment that arose out of the Vietnam War.
- Security policy is now dominated by trying to stop terrorism.

19.4 Global Policy Issue Areas

- The international character of investment and trade has made global economic policy a priority for the U.S. government.
- Protecting human rights across the world presents a challenge to the government because it can collide with the need to cooperate with countries that may have poor records on rights.

- Americans remain divided on international cooperation to protect the environment.

19.5 The Public and Global Policy

- The majoritarian model of democracy works poorly for global policy because most Americans pay limited attention to world affairs.
- In many specific areas but especially trade, the pluralist model is reflected in global policymaking.

ASSESSING YOUR UNDERSTANDING WITH APLIA...YOUR VIRTUAL TUTOR!

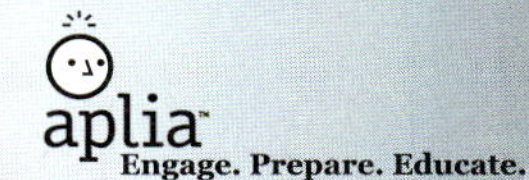

19.1 Compare the constitutional authority over foreign policy granted to the executive branch with that of the legislative branch.

1. How do the powers granted to the president differ from those granted to Congress?

19.2 Identify the executive branch agencies that formulate foreign policy and describe the principal functions of each.

1. What are the different roles played by the various foreign-policy bureaucracies?
2. What are the obstacles faced in having so many bureaucracies involved in foreign policy making?

19.3 Trace the evolution of American foreign policy from isolationism to globalism and identify the factors that have shaped the direction of that policy.

1. How did the Cold War shape American thinking about foreign policy?

2. How did the Vietnam War impact America's conception of its role in world politics?
3. How might we distinguish between foreign policy and global policy?

19.4 Describe the influence of the global issues of investment and trade, human rights, and the environment on U.S. foreign and domestic policy.

1. What stands in the way of free trade among the world's trading partners?
2. What prevents the United States from doing more in the area of human rights?
3. Why has the United States backed away from international climate treaties?

19.5 Explain the relationship between U.S. foreign policy and both the majoritarian and pluralist models of democracy.

1. In evaluating the two models of democracy, majoritarianism and pluralism, which better fits foreign policy making in the United States?

Appendix

The Declaration of Independence

In Congress, July 4, 1776

The unanimous Declaration of the thirteen United States of America

When in the course of human events, it becomes necessary for one people to dissolve the political bands which have connected them with another, and to assume, among the powers of the earth the separate and equal station to which the Laws of Nature and of Nature's God entitle them, a decent respect to the opinions of mankind requires that they should declare the causes which impel them to the separation.

We hold these truths to be self-evident, that all men are created equal, that they are endowed by their Creator with certain unalienable rights, that among these are life, liberty, and the pursuit of happiness. That to secure these rights, governments are instituted among men, deriving their just powers from the consent of the governed. That whenever any form of government becomes destructive of these ends, it is the right of the people to alter or to abolish it, and to institute new government, laying its foundation on such principles, and organizing its power in such form, as to them shall seem most likely to effect their safety and happiness. Prudence, indeed, will dictate that governments long established should not be changed for light and transient causes; and accordingly all experience hath shown, that mankind are more disposed to suffer, while evils are sufferable, than to right themselves by abolishing the forms to which they are accustomed. But when a long train of abuses and usurpations, pursuing invariably the same object evinces a design to reduce them under absolute despotism, it is their right, it is their duty, to throw off such government, and to provide new guards for their future security. Such has been the patient sufferance of these Colonies; and such is now the necessity which constrains them to alter their former systems of government. The history of the present King of Great Britain is a history of repeated injuries and usurpations, all having in direct object the establishment of an absolute tyranny over these States. To prove this, let facts be submitted to a candid world.

He has refused his assent to laws, the most wholesome and necessary for the public good.

He has forbidden his governors to pass laws of immediate and pressing importance, unless suspended in their operation till his assent should be obtained; and, when so suspended, he has utterly neglected to attend to them.

He has refused to pass other laws for the accommodation of large districts of people, unless those people would relinquish the right of representation in the legislature, a right inestimable to them, and formidable to tyrants only.

He has called together legislative bodies at places unusual, uncomfortable, and distant from the depository of their public records, for the sole purpose of fatiguing them into compliance with his measures.

He has dissolved representative houses repeatedly, for opposing, with manly firmness, his invasions on the rights of the people.

He has refused for a long time, after such dissolutions, to cause others to be elected; whereby the legislative powers, incapable of annihilation, have returned to the people at large for their exercise; the State remaining, in the meantime exposed to all the dangers of invasions from without and convulsions within.

He has endeavored to prevent the population of these States; for that purpose obstructing the laws for naturalization of foreigners; refusing to pass others to encourage their migration hither, and raising the conditions of new appropriations of lands.

He has obstructed the administration of justice, by refusing his assent to laws for establishing judiciary powers.

He has made judges dependent on his will alone, for the tenure of their offices, and the amount and payment of their salaries.

He has erected a multitude of new offices, and sent hither swarms of officers to harass our people, and eat out their substance.

He has kept among us, in times of peace, standing armies, without the consent of our legislatures.

He has affected to render the military independent of and superior to the civil power.

He has combined with others to subject us to a jurisdiction foreign to our constitution, and unacknowledged by our laws; giving his assent to their acts of pretended legislation: For quartering large bodies of armed troops among us; For protecting them, by a mock trial, from punishment for any murders which they should commit on the inhabitants of these states; For cutting off our trade with all parts of the world; For imposing taxes on us without our consent; For depriving us, in many cases, of the benefits of trial by jury; For transporting us beyond seas, to be tried for pretended offenses; For abolishing the free system of English laws in a neighboring province, establishing therein an arbitrary government, and enlarging its boundaries, so as to render it at once an example and fit instrument for introducing the same absolute rule into these Colonies; For taking away our Charters, abolishing our most valuable laws, and altering fundamentally the forms of our governments; For suspending our own Legislatures, and declaring themselves invested with power to legislate for us in all cases whatsoever.

He has abdicated government here, by declaring us out of his protection and waging war against us.

He has plundered our seas, ravaged our coasts, burned our towns, and destroyed the lives of our people.

He is at this time transporting large armies of foreign mercenaries to complete the works of death, desolation, and tyranny, already begun with circumstances of cruelty and perfidy scarcely paralleled in the most barbarous ages, and totally unworthy the head of a civilized nation.

He has constrained our fellow-citizens taken captive on the high seas to bear arms against their country, to become the executioners of their friends and brethren, or to fall themselves by their hands.

He has excited domestic insurrection among us, and has endeavored to bring on the inhabitants of our frontiers the merciless Indian savages, whose known rule of warfare is an undistinguished destruction of all ages, sexes, and conditions.

In every stage of these oppressions we have petitioned for redress in the most humble terms: our repeated petitions have been answered only by repeated injury.

A prince whose character is thus marked by every act which may define a tyrant, is unfit to be the ruler of a free people.

Nor have we been wanting in our attentions to our British brethren. We have warned them, from time to time, of attempts by their Legislature to extend an unwarrantable jurisdiction over us. We have reminded them of the circumstances of our emigration and settlement here. We have appealed to their native justice and magnanimity, and we have conjured them by the ties of our common kindred to disavow these usurpations, which would inevitably interrupt our connections and correspondence. They too have been deaf to the voice of justice and of consanguinity. We must, therefore, acquiesce in the necessity, which denounces our separation, and hold them, as we hold the rest of mankind, enemies in war, in peace friends.

We, therefore, the Representatives of the United States of America, in General Congress assembled, appealing to the Supreme Judge of the world for the rectitude of our intentions, do, in the name, and by the authority of the good people of these Colonies, solemnly publish and declare, That these United Colonies are, and of right ought to be, FREE AND INDEPENDENT STATES; that they are absolved from all allegiance to the British Crown, and that all political connection between them and the State of Great Britain is, and ought to be, totally dissolved; and that, as Free and Independent States they have full power to levy war, conclude peace, contract alliances, establish commerce, and do all other acts and things which independent States may of right do. And for the support of this declaration, with a firm reliance on the protection of Divine Providence, we mutually pledge to each other our lives, our fortunes and our sacred honor.

JOHN HANCOCK
and fifty-five others

The Constitution of the United States of America*

[Preamble: outlines goals and effect]

We the people of the United States, in order to form a more perfect Union, establish Justice, insure domestic Tranquility, provide for the common defence, promote the general Welfare, and secure the Blessings of Liberty to ourselves and our Posterity, do ordain and establish this Constitution for the United States of America.

Article I

[The legislative branch]

[Powers vested]

Section 1 All legislative Powers herein granted shall be vested in a Congress of the United States, which shall consist of a Senate and a House of Representatives.

---

*Passages no longer in effect are printed in italic type.

[House of Representatives: selection, term, qualifications, apportionment of seats, census requirement, exclusive power to impeach]

Section 2 The House of Representatives shall be composed of Members chosen every second Year by the people of the several States, and the Electors in each State shall have the Qualifications requisite for Electors of the most numerous Branch of the State Legislature.

No person shall be a Representative who shall not have attained to the Age of twenty five Years, and been seven Years a Citizen of the United States, and who shall not, when elected, be an Inhabitant of that State in which he shall be chosen.

Representatives and direct Taxes shall be apportioned among the several States which may be included within this Union, according to their respective numbers, which shall be determined by adding to the whole Number of free Persons, including those bound to Service for a Term of Years and excluding Indians not taxed, three-fifths of all other Persons. The actual Enumeration shall be made within three Years after the first Meeting of the Congress of the United States, and within every subsequent Term of ten Years, in such Manner as they shall by Law direct. The number of Representatives shall not exceed one for every thirty Thousand, but each State shall have at Least one Representative; *and until such enumeration shall be made, the State of New Hampshire shall be entitled to choose three, Massachusetts eight, Rhode Island and Providence Plantations one, Connecticut five, New York six, New Jersey four, Pennsylvania eight, Delaware one, Maryland six, Virginia ten, North Carolina five, South Carolina five, and Georgia three.*

When vacancies happen in the Representation from any State, the Executive Authority thereof shall issue Writs of Election to fill such Vacancies.

The House of Representatives shall chuse their Speaker and other Officers; and shall have the sole Power of Impeachment.

[Senate: selection, term, qualifications, exclusive power to try impeachments]

Section 3 The Senate of the United States shall be composed of two Senators from each State, *chosen by the Legislature thereof,* for six years; and each Senator shall have one Vote.

Immediately after they shall be assembled in Consequence of the first Election, they shall be divided as equally as may be into three Classes. The Seats of the Senators of the first Class shall be vacated at the Expiration of the second Year, of the second Class at the expiration of the fourth Year, and of the third Class at the expiration of the sixth Year, so that one-third may be chosen every second Year; and if Vacancies happen by Resignation or otherwise, during the Recess of the Legislature of any State, the Executive thereof may make temporary Appointments until the next meeting of the legislature, which shall then fill such Vacancies.

No person shall be a Senator who shall not have attained to the Age of thirty Years, and been nine Years a Citizen of the United States, and who shall not, when elected, be an Inhabitant of that State for which he shall be chosen.

The Vice-President of the United States shall be President of the Senate, but shall have no Vote, unless they be equally divided.

The Senate shall choose their other officers, and also a President pro tempore, in the absence of the Vice-President, or when he shall exercise the Office of President of the United States.

The Senate shall have the sole Power to try all impeachments. When sitting for that purpose, they shall be on Oath or Affirmation. When the President of the United States is tried, the Chief Justice shall preside: and no Person shall be convicted without the Concurrence of two-thirds of the members Present.

Judgment in Cases of Impeachment shall not extend further than to removal from the Office, and disqualification to hold and enjoy any Office of honor, Trust or Profit under the United States: but the Party convicted shall nevertheless be liable and subject to Indictment, Trial, Judgment and Punishment, according to Law.

[Elections]

Section 4 The Times, Places and Manner of holding Elections for Senators and Representatives shall be prescribed in each State by the Legislature thereof; but the Congress may at any time by Law make or alter such regulations, except as to the Places of chusing Senators.

The Congress shall assemble at least once in every Year, and such meeting *shall be on the first Monday in December, unless they shall by Law appoint a different Day.*

[Powers and duties of the two chambers: rules of procedure, power over members]

Section 5 Each House shall be the Judge of the Elections, Returns and Qualifications of its own Members, and a Majority of each shall constitute a Quorum to do Business; but a smaller Number may adjourn from day to day, and may be authorized to compel the Attendance of absent Members, in such Manner, and under such Penalties as each House may provide.

Each House may determine the Rules of its proceedings, punish its Members for disorderly behaviour, and with the Concurrence of two thirds, expel a Member.

Each House shall keep a Journal of its Proceedings, and from time to time publish the same, excepting such Parts as may in their Judgment require Secrecy; and the Yeas and Nays of the Members of either House on any question shall, at the Desire of one fifth of those Present, be entered on the Journal.

Neither House, during the Session of Congress, shall, without the Consent of the other, adjourn for more than three days, nor to any other Place than that in which the two Houses shall be sitting.

[Compensation, privilege from arrest, privilege of speech, disabilities of members]

Section 6 The Senators and Representatives shall receive a Compensation for their services, to be ascertained by Law, and paid out of the Treasury of the United States. They shall in all Cases, except Treason, Felony and Breach of the Peace, be privileged from Arrest during their Attendance at the Session of their respective Houses, and in going to and returning from the same; and for any Speech or Debate in either House, they shall not be questioned in any other Place.

No Senator or Representative shall, during the Time for which he was elected, be appointed to any civil Office under the Authority of the United States, which shall have been created, or the Emoluments whereof shall have been increased, during such time; and no Person holding any Office under the United States, shall be a Member of either House during his Continuance in Office.

[Legislative process: revenue bills, approval or veto power of president]

Section 7 All bills for raising Revenue shall originate in the House of Representatives; but the Senate may propose or concur with Amendments as on other Bills.

Every Bill which shall have passed the House of Representatives and the Senate, shall, before it become a Law, be presented to the President of the United States; if he approve he shall sign it, but if not he shall return it with Objections to that House in which it originated, who shall enter the Objections at large on their journal, and proceed to reconsider it. If after such Reconsideration two thirds of that House shall agree to pass the Bill, it shall be sent, together with the Objections, to the other House, by which it shall likewise be reconsidered, and, if approved by two thirds of that house, it shall become a Law. But in all such Cases the Votes of both houses shall be determined by yeas and Nays, and the Names of the Persons voting for and against the Bill shall be entered on the journal of each House respectively. If any Bill shall not be returned by the President within ten Days (Sundays excepted) after it shall have been presented to him, the Same shall be a Law, in like Manner as if he had signed it, unless the Congress by their Adjournment prevent its Return, in which Case it shall not be a Law.

Every Order, Resolution, or Vote to which the Concurrence of the Senate and House of Representatives may be necessary (except on a question of Adjournment) shall be presented to the President of the United States; and before the Same shall take Effect, shall be approved by him, or being disapproved by him, shall be repassed by two thirds of the Senate and House of Representatives, according to the Rules and Limitations prescribed in the Case of a Bill.

[Powers of Congress enumerated]

Section 8 The Congress shall have Power

To lay and collect Taxes, Duties, Imposts, and Excises, to pay the Debts and provide for the common Defence and general Welfare of the United States; but all Duties, Imposts and Excises shall be uniform throughout the United States;

To borrow Money on the credit of the United States;

To regulate Commerce with foreign Nations, and among the several States, and with the Indian tribes;

To establish an uniform Rule of Naturalization, and uniform Laws on the subject of Bankruptcies throughout the United States;

To coin Money, regulate the Value thereof, and of foreign Coin, and fix the Standard of Weights and Measures;

To provide for the Punishment of counterfeiting the Securities and current Coin of the United States;

To establish Post Offices and post Roads;

To promote the Progress of Science and useful Arts by securing for limited Times to Authors and Inventors the exclusive Right to their respective Writings and Discoveries;

To constitute Tribunals inferior to the supreme Court;

To define and punish Piracies and Felonies committed on the high Seas, and offenses against the Law of Nations;

To declare War, grant Letters of Marque and Reprisal, and make Rules concerning Captures on Land and Water;

To raise and support Armies, but no Appropriation of Money to that Use shall be for a longer Term than two Years;

To provide and maintain a Navy;

To make rules for the Government and Regulation of the land and naval Forces;

To provide for calling forth the Militia to execute the Laws of the Union, suppress Insurrections, and repel Invasions;

To provide for organizing, arming, and disciplining the Militia, and for governing such Part of them as may be employed in the Service of the United States, reserving to the States respectively the Appointment of the Officers, and the Authority of training the Militia according to the discipline prescribed by Congress;

To exercise exclusive Legislation in all Cases whatsoever, over such District (not exceeding ten Miles square) as may, by cession of particular States, and the Acceptance of Congress, become the Seat of Government of the United States, and to exercise like Authority over all places purchased by the Consent of the Legislature of the State in which the Same shall be, for Erection of Forts, Magazines, Arsenals, dock-Yards, and other needful Buildings;—And

[Elastic clause]

To make all Laws which shall be necessary and proper for carrying into Execution the foregoing Powers, and all other powers vested by this Constitution in the Government of the United States, or in any Department or Officer thereof.

[Powers denied Congress]

Section 9 *The Migration or Importation of such persons as any of the States now existing shall think proper to admit, shall not be prohibited by the Congress prior to the Year 1808; but a Tax or duty may be imposed on such Importation, not exceeding $10 for each Person.*

The Privilege of the Writ of Habeas Corpus shall not be suspended, unless when in Cases of Rebellion or Invasion the public Safety may require it.

No Bill of Attainder or ex post facto Law shall be passed.

No Capitation, or other direct, Tax shall be laid, unless in Proportion to the Census or Enumeration herein before directed to be taken.

No Tax or Duty shall be laid on Articles exported from any State.

No Preference shall be given by any Regulation of Commerce or Revenue to the Ports of one State over those of another; nor shall Vessels bound to, or from, one State, be obliged to enter, clear, or pay Duties in another.

No Money shall be drawn from the Treasury, but in Consequence of Appropriations made by Law; and a regular Statement and Account of the receipts and Expenditures of all public Money shall be published from time to time.

No Title of Nobility shall be granted by the United States: And no Person holding any Office or Profit or trust under them, shall, without the Consent of the Congress, accept of any present, Emolument, Office, or Title, of any kind whatever, from any King, Prince, or foreign State.

[Powers denied the states]

Section 10 No State shall enter into any Treaty, Alliance, or Confederation; grant Letters of Marque and Reprisal; coin Money; emit Bills of Credit; make any Thing but gold and silver Coin a Tender in Payment of Debts; pass any Bill of Attainder, ex post facto law, or Law impairing the obligation of Contracts, or grant any Title of Nobility.

No State shall, without the Consent of Congress, lay any Imposts or Duties on Imports or Exports, except what may be absolutely necessary for executing its inspection Laws: and the net Produce of all duties and imposts, laid by any State on Imports or Exports, shall be for the Use of the Treasury of the United States; and all such Laws shall be subject to the Revision and Controul of the Congress.

No State shall, without the consent of Congress, lay any Duty of Tonnage, keep Troops or Ships of War in time of Peace, enter into any Agreement or Compact with another State, or with a foreign Power, or engage in War, unless actually invaded, or in such imminent Danger as will not admit of delay.

Article II

[The executive branch]

[The president: power vested, term, electoral college, qualifications, presidential succession, compensation, oath of office]

Section 1 The executive Power shall be vested in a President of the United States of America. He shall hold his Office during the Term of four Years, and, together with the Vice President, chosen for the same Term, be elected as follows:

Each State shall appoint, in such Manner as the Legislature thereof may direct, a Number of Electors, equal to the whole Number of Senators and Representatives to which the State may be entitled in the Congress; but no Senator or Representative, or Person holding an Office of Trust or Profit under the United States, shall be appointed an Elector.

The Electors shall meet in their respective States, and vote by Ballot for two Persons, of whom one at least shall not be an inhabitant of the same State with themselves. And they shall make a List of all the Persons voted for, and of the Number of Votes for each: which List they shall sign and certify, and transmit sealed to the Seat of Government of the United States, directed to the President of the Senate. The President of the Senate shall, in the presence of the Senate and House of Representatives, open all the Certificates, and the Votes shall then be counted. The Person having the greatest Number of Votes shall be the President, if such Number be a Majority of the whole number of Electors appointed; and if there be more than one who have such Majority, and have an equal Number of Votes, then the House of Representatives shall immediately chuse by Ballot one of them for President; and if no Person have a Majority, then from the five highest on the List said House shall in like Manner chuse the President. But in chusing the President the Votes shall be taken by States, the Representation from each State having one Vote; a quorum for this purpose shall consist of a Member or Members from two thirds of the States, and a Majority of all the States shall be necessary to a Choice. In every Case, after the Choice of the President, the person having the greatest Number of Votes of the Electors shall be the Vice President. But if there should remain two or more who have equal Votes, the Senate shall chuse from them by Ballot the Vice President.

The Congress may determine the Time of chusing the Electors and the Day on which they shall give their Votes; which Day shall be the same throughout the United States.

No person except a natural born Citizen, or a Citizen of the United States at the time of the Adoption of this Constitution, shall be eligible to the Office of President; neither shall any Person be eligible to that Office who shall not have attained to the age of thirty-five Years, and been fourteen Years a Resident within the United States.

In cases of the Removal of the President from Office or of his Death, Resignation, or Inability to discharge the Powers and Duties of the said Office, the same shall devolve on the Vice President, and the Congress may by law provide for the case of Removal, Death, Resignation, or inability, both of the President and Vice President, declaring what Officer shall then act as President, and such Officer shall act accordingly, until the Disability be removed, or a President shall be elected.

The President shall, at stated Times, receive for his Services, a Compensation, which shall neither be increased nor diminished during the Period for which he shall have been elected, and he shall not receive within that Period any other emolument from the United States, or any of them.

Before he enter on the Execution of his Office, he shall take the following Oath or Affirmation:—"I do solemnly swear (or affirm) that I will faithfully execute the Office of the President of the United States, and will to the best of my Ability preserve, protect and defend the Constitution of the United States."

[Powers and duties: as commander in chief, over advisers, to pardon, to make treaties and appoint officers]

Section 2 The President shall be Commander in Chief of the Army and Navy of the United States, and of the Militia of the several States, when called into the actual service of the United States; he may require the Opinion, in writing, of the principal Officer in each of the executive Departments, upon any Subject relating to the Duties of their respective Offices, and he shall have Power to grant Reprieves and Pardons for Offences against the United States, except in Cases of Impeachment.

He shall have Power, by and with the Advice and Consent of the Senate, to make Treaties, provided two-thirds of the Senators present concur; and he shall nominate, and by and with the Advice and Consent of the Senate, shall appoint Ambassadors, other public Ministers and Consuls, Judges of the supreme Court, and all other Officers of the United States, whose Appointments are not herein otherwise provided for, and which shall be established by Law: but Congress may by Law vest the Appointment of such inferior Officers, as they think proper, in the President alone, in the courts of Law, or in the Heads of Departments.

The President shall have Power to fill up all Vacancies that may happen during the Recess of the Senate, by granting Commissions which shall expire at the end of their next Session.

[Legislative, diplomatic, and law-enforcement duties]

Section 3 He shall from time to time give to the Congress Information of the State of the Union, and recommend to their Consideration such Measures as he shall judge necessary and expedient; he may, on extraordinary Occasions, convene both Houses, or either of them, and in Case of Disagreement between them, with Respect to the Time of Adjournment, he may adjourn them to such Time as he shall think proper; he shall receive Ambassadors and other public Ministers; he shall take Care that the Laws be faithfully executed, and shall Commission all the Officers of the United States.

[Impeachment]

Section 4 The President, Vice President and all civil Officers of the United States shall be removed from Office on Impeachment for, and on Conviction of, Treason, Bribery, or other high Crimes and Misdemeanors.

Article III
[The judicial branch]

[Power vested; Supreme Court; lower courts; judges]

Section 1 The judicial Power of the United States shall be vested in one supreme Court, and in such inferior Courts as the Congress may from time to time ordain and establish. The Judges, both of the supreme and inferior Courts, shall hold their Offices during good Behaviour, and shall, at stated Times, receive for their Services a Compensation which shall not be diminished during their Continuance in Office.

[Jurisdiction; trial by jury]

Section 2 The judicial Power shall extend to all Cases, in Law and Equity, arising under this Constitution, the Laws of the United States, and Treaties made, or which shall be made, under their Authority;—to all Cases affecting Ambassadors, other public Ministers and Consuls;—to all Cases of admiralty and maritime Jurisdiction;—to Controversies to which the United States shall be a Party;—to controversies between two or more States;—*between a State and Citizens of another State;*—between Citizens of different States—between Citizens of the same State claiming Lands under grants of different States, and between a State, or the Citizens thereof, and foreign States, Citizens or Subjects.

In all cases affecting Ambassadors, other public Ministers and Consuls, and those in which a State shall be Party, the supreme Court shall have original Jurisdiction. In all the other Cases before mentioned, the supreme Court shall have appellate Jurisdiction, both as to Law and Fact, with such Exceptions, and under such Regulations, as the Congress shall make.

The Trial of all Crimes, except in cases of Impeachment, shall be by Jury; and such Trial shall be held in the State where said Crimes shall have been committed; but when not committed within any State, the Trial shall be at such Place or Places as the Congress may by Law have directed.

[Treason: definition, punishment]

Section 3 Treason against the United States shall consist only in levying War against them, or in adhering to their Enemies, giving them Aid and Comfort. No Person shall be convicted of Treason unless on the Testimony of two Witnesses to the same overt Act, or on confession in open Court.

The Congress shall have power to declare the Punishment of Treason, but no Attainder of Treason shall work Corruption of Blood, or Forfeiture except during the Life of the Person attainted.

Article IV

[States' relations]

[Full faith and credit]

Section 1 Full Faith and Credit shall be given in each State to the public Acts, Records, and judicial Proceedings of every other State. And the Congress may by general laws prescribe the Manner in which such Acts, Records, and Proceedings shall be proved, and the Effect thereof.

[Interstate comity, rendition]

Section 2 The Citizens of each State shall be entitled to all Privileges and Immunities of Citizens in the several States.

A Person charged in any State with Treason, Felony, or other Crime, who shall flee from Justice, and be found in another State, shall on Demand of the executive Authority of the State from which he fled, be delivered up, to be removed to the State having Jurisdiction of the Crime.

No person held to Service or Labor in one State, under the Laws thereof, escaping into another, shall, in consequence of any Law or Regulation therein, be discharged from such Service or Labor, but shall be delivered up on Claim of the Party to whom such Service or Labor may be due.

[New states]

Section 3 New States may be admitted by the Congress into this Union; but no new State shall be formed or erected within the Jurisdiction of any other State; nor any State be formed by the Junction of two or more States, or parts of States, without the Consent of the Legislatures of the States concerned as well as of the Congress.

The Congress shall have Power to dispose of and make all needful Rules and Regulations respecting the Territory or other Property belonging to the United States; and nothing in this Constitution shall be so construed as to Prejudice any Claims of the United States, or of any particular State.

[Obligations of the United States to the states]

Section 4 The United States shall guarantee to every State in this Union a Republican Form of Government, and shall protect each of them against Invasion; and on Application of the Legislature, or of the Executive (when the Legislature cannot be convened), against domestic Violence.

Article V

[Mode of amendment]

The Congress, whenever two-thirds of both Houses shall deem it necessary, shall propose Amendments to this Constitution, or, on the Application of the Legislatures of two-thirds of the several States, shall call a Convention for proposing Amendments, which, in either Case, shall be valid to all Intents and Purposes, as part of this Constitution, when ratified by the legislatures of three-fourths of the several States, or by Conventions in three-fourths thereof, as the one or the other Mode of Ratification may be proposed by the Congress; Provided *that no Amendment which may be made prior to the Year One thousand eight hundred and eight shall in any Manner affect the first and fourth clauses in the Ninth Section of the first Article;* and that no State, without its Consent, shall be deprived of its equal suffrage in the Senate.

Article VI

[Prior debts, supremacy of Constitution, oaths of office]

All Debts contracted and Engagements entered into, before the Adoption of this Constitution, shall be as valid against the United States under this Constitution, as under the Confederation.

This Constitution, and the Laws of the United States which shall be made in Pursuance thereof; and all Treaties made, or which shall be made, under the Authority of the United States, shall be the supreme Law of the Land; and the judges in every State shall be bound thereby, anything in the Constitution or Laws of any State to the Contrary notwithstanding.

The Senators and Representatives before mentioned, and the Members of the several State Legislatures, and all executive and judicial Officers, both of the United States and of the several States, shall be bound by Oath or Affirmation to support this Constitution; but no religious test shall ever be required as a Qualification to any Office or public Trust under the United States.

Article VII

[Ratification]

The ratification of the Conventions of nine States shall be sufficient for the Establishment of this Constitution between the States so ratifying the Same.

Done in Convention by the Unanimous Consent of the States present, the seventeenth day of September in the Year of our Lord one thousand seven hundred and eighty-seven and of the Independence of the United States of America the twelfth. In WITNESS whereof We have hereunto subscribed our Names.

GEORGE WASHINGTON
and thirty-seven others

Amendments to the Constitution

[The first ten amendments—the Bill of Rights—were adopted in 1791.]

Amendment I

[Freedom of religion, speech, press, assembly]

Congress shall make no law respecting an establishment of religion, or prohibiting the free exercise thereof; or abridging the freedom of speech, or of the press; or the right of the people peaceably to assemble, and to petition the Government for a redress of grievances.

Amendment II

[Right to bear arms]

A well-regulated militia being necessary to the security of a free State, the right of the people to keep and bear arms shall not be infringed.

Amendment III

[Quartering of soldiers]

No Soldier shall, in time of peace, be quartered in any house without the consent of the Owner, nor in time of war, but in a manner to be prescribed by law.

Amendment IV

[Searches and seizures]

The right of the people to be secure in their persons, houses, papers, and effects, against unreasonable searches and seizures, shall not be violated, and no Warrants shall issue but upon probable cause, supported by Oath or Affirmation, and particularly describing the place to be searched, and the persons or things to be seized.

Amendment V

[Rights of persons: grand juries, double jeopardy, self-incrimination, due process, eminent domain]

No person shall be held to answer for a capital, or otherwise infamous crime, unless on a presentment or indictment of a Grand Jury, except in cases arising in the land or naval forces, or in the Militia, when in actual service in time of War or public danger; nor shall any person be subject for the same offense to be twice put in jeopardy of life or limb; nor shall be compelled in any criminal case to be a witness against himself, nor be deprived of life, liberty, or property, without due process of law; nor shall private property be taken for public use without just compensation.

Amendment VI

[Rights of accused in criminal prosecutions]

In all criminal prosecutions, the accused shall enjoy the right to a speedy and public trial, by an impartial jury of the State and district wherein the crime shall have been committed, which district shall have been previously ascertained by law, and to be informed of the nature and cause of the accusation; to be confronted with the witnesses against him; to have compulsory process for obtaining Witnesses in his favor, and to have the assistance of counsel for his defence.

Amendment VII

[Civil trials]

In Suits at common law, where the value in controversy shall exceed twenty dollars, the right of trial by jury shall be preserved, and no fact tried by a jury shall be otherwise reexamined in any Court of the United States, than according to the rules of the common law.

Amendment VIII

[Punishment for crime]

Excessive bail shall not be required, nor excessive fines imposed, nor cruel and unusual punishments inflicted.

Amendment IX

[Rights retained by the people]

The enumeration in the Constitution, of certain rights, shall not be construed to deny or disparage others retained by the people.

Amendment X

[Rights reserved to the states]

The powers not delegated to the United States by the Constitution, nor prohibited by it to the States, are reserved to the States respectively, or to the people.

Amendment XI

[Suits against the states; adopted 1798]

The Judicial power of the United States shall not be construed to extend to any suit in law or equity, commenced or prosecuted against one of the United States by Citizens of another state, or by Citizens or Subjects of any Foreign State.

Amendment XII

[Election of the president; adopted 1804]

The electors shall meet in their respective States, and vote by ballot for President and Vice-President, one of whom, at least, shall not be an inhabitant of the same state with themselves; they shall name in their ballots the person voted for as President, and in distinct ballots the person voted for as Vice-President, and they shall make distinct lists of all persons voted for as President, and of all persons voted for as Vice-President, and of the number of votes for each, which lists they shall sign and certify, and transmit sealed to the seat of government of the United States, directed to the President of the Senate;—the President of the Senate shall, in the presence of the Senate and House of Representatives, open all the certificates and the votes shall then be counted;—the person having the greatest number of votes for President shall be the President, if such number be a majority of the whole number of electors appointed; and if no person have such majority, then from the persons having the highest numbers not exceeding three on the list of those voted for as President, the House of Representatives shall choose immediately, by ballot, the President. But in choosing the President, the votes shall be taken by States, the representation from each State having one vote; a quorum for this purpose shall consist of a member or members from two-thirds of the States, and a majority of all the States shall be necessary to a choice. And if the House of Representatives shall not choose a President whenever the right of choice shall devolve upon them, before *the fourth day of March* next following, then the Vice-President shall act as President, as in the case of the death or other constitutional disability of the President.—The person having the greatest number of votes as Vice-President shall be the Vice-President, if such number be a majority of the whole number of electors appointed; and if no person have a majority, then from the two highest numbers on the list the Senate shall choose the Vice-President; a quorum for the purpose shall consist of two-thirds of the whole number of Senators, and a majority of the whole number shall be necessary to a choice. But no person constitutionally ineligible to the Office of President shall be eligible to that of Vice-President of the United States.

Amendment XIII

[Abolition of slavery; adopted 1865]

Section 1 Neither slavery nor involuntary servitude, except as a punishment for crime whereof the party shall have been duly convicted, shall exist within the United States, or any place subject to their jurisdiction.

Section 2 Congress shall have power to enforce this article by appropriate legislation.

Amendment XIV

[Adopted 1868]

[Citizenship rights; privileges and immunities; due process; equal protection]

Section 1 All persons born or naturalized in the United States, and subject to the jurisdiction thereof, are citizens of the United States and of the State wherein they reside. No State shall make or enforce any law which shall abridge the privileges or immunities of citizens of the United States; nor shall any State deprive any person of life, liberty, or property, without due process of law; nor deny to any person within its jurisdiction the equal protection of the laws.

[Apportionment of representation]

Section 2 Representatives shall be apportioned among the several States according to their respective numbers, counting the whole number of persons in each State, excluding Indians not taxed. But when the right to vote at any election for the choice of Electors for President and Vice-President of the United States, Representatives in Congress, the Executive and Judicial officers of a State, or the members of the Legislature thereof, is denied to any of the male inhabitants of such State, being twenty-one years of age and citizens of the United States, or in any way abridged, except for participation in rebellion, or other crime, the basis of representation therein shall be reduced in the proportion which the number of such male citizens shall bear to the whole number of male citizens twenty-one years of age in such State.

[Disqualification of Confederate officials]

Section 3 No person shall be a Senator or Representative in Congress, or Elector of President and Vice-President, or hold any Office, civil or military, under the United States, or under any State, who, having previously taken an oath, as a member of Congress, or as an officer of the United States, or as a member of any State legislature, or as an executive or judicial officer of any State, to support the Constitution of the United States, shall have engaged in insurrection or rebellion against the same, or given aid or comfort to the enemies thereof. Congress may, by a vote of two-thirds of each house, remove such disability.

[Public debts]

Section 4 The validity of the public debt of the United States, authorized by law, including debts incurred for payment of pensions and bounties for services in suppressing insurrection or rebellion, shall not be questioned. But neither the United States nor any State shall assume or pay any debt or obligation incurred in aid of insurrection or rebellion against the United States, or any claim for the loss of emancipation of any slave; but all such debts, obligations, and claims shall be held illegal and void.

[Enforcement]

Section 5 The Congress shall have power to enforce, by appropriate legislation, the provisions of this article.

Amendment XV

[Extension of right to vote; adopted 1870]

Section 1 The right of citizens of the United States to vote shall not be denied or abridged by the United States or by any State on account of race, color, or previous condition of servitude.

Section 2 The Congress shall have power to enforce this article by appropriate legislation.

Amendment XVI

[Income tax; adopted 1913]

The Congress shall have power to lay and collect taxes on incomes, from whatever source derived, without apportionment among the several States, and without regard to any census or enumeration.

Amendment XVII

[Popular election of senators; adopted 1913]

Section 1 The Senate of the United States shall be composed of two Senators from each State, elected by the people thereof, for six years; and each Senator shall have one vote. The electors in each State shall have the Qualifications requisite for electors of the most numerous branch of the State legislatures.

Section 2 When vacancies happen in the representation of any State in the Senate, the executive authority of such State shall issue writs of election to fill such vacancies: Provided, that the Legislature of any State may empower the executive thereof to make temporary appointments until the people fill the vacancies by election as the Legislature may direct.

Section 3 This amendment shall not be so construed as to affect the election or term of any Senator chosen before it becomes valid as part of the Constitution.

Amendment XVIII

[Prohibition of intoxicating liquors; adopted 1919, repealed 1933]

Section 1 After one year from the ratification of this article the manufacture, sale or transportation of intoxicating liquors within, the importation thereof into, or the exportation thereof from the United States and all territory subject to the jurisdiction thereof, for beverage purposes, is hereby prohibited.

Section 2 The Congress and the several States shall have concurrent power to enforce this article by appropriate legislation.

Section 3 This article shall be inoperative unless it shall have been ratified as an amendment to the Constitution by the legislatures of the several States, as provided by the Constitution, within seven years from the date of the submission thereof to the States by the Congress.

Amendment XIX

[Right of women to vote; adopted 1920]

Section 1 The right of citizens of the United States to vote shall not be denied or abridged by the United States or by any State on account of sex.

Section 2 The Congress shall have power to enforce this article by appropriate legislation.

Amendment XX

[Commencement of terms of office; adopted 1933]

Section 1 The terms of the President and Vice-President shall end at noon on the 20th day of January, and the terms of Senators and Representatives at noon on the 3d day of January, of the years in which such terms would have ended if this article had not been ratified; and the terms of their successors shall then begin.

Section 2 The Congress shall assemble at least once in every year, and such meetings shall begin at noon on the 3d day of January, unless they shall by law appoint a different day.

[Extension of presidential succession]

Section 3 If, at the time fixed for the beginning of the term of the President, the President-elect shall have died, the Vice-President-elect shall become President. If a President shall not have been chosen before the time fixed for the beginning of his term, or if the President-elect shall have failed to qualify, then the Vice-President-elect shall act as President until a President shall have qualified; and the Congress may by law provide for the case wherein neither a President-elect nor a Vice-President-elect shall have qualified, declaring who shall then act as President, or the manner in which one who is to act shall be selected, and such persons shall act accordingly until a President or Vice-President shall have qualified.

Section 4 The Congress may by law provide for the case of the death of any of the persons from whom the House of Representatives may choose a President whenever the right of choice shall have devolved upon them, and for the case of the death of any of the persons from whom the Senate may choose a Vice-President whenever the right of choice shall have devolved upon them.

Section 5 Sections 1 and 2 shall take effect on the 15th day of October following the ratification of this article.

Section 6 This article shall be inoperative unless it shall have been ratified as an amendment to the Constitution by the Legislatures of three-fourths of the several States within seven years from the date of its submission.

Amendment XXI

[Repeal of Eighteenth Amendment; adopted 1933]

Section 1 The eighteenth article of amendment to the Constitution of the United States is hereby repealed.

Section 2 The transportation or importation into any State, Territory, or Possession of the United States for delivery or use therein of intoxicating liquors, in violation of the laws thereof, is hereby prohibited.

Section 3 This article shall be inoperative unless it shall have been ratified as an amendment to the Constitution by conventions in the several States, as provided in the Constitution, within seven years from the date of submission thereof to the States by the Congress.

Amendment XXII

[Limit on presidential tenure; adopted 1951]

Section 1 No person shall be elected to the Office of President more than twice, and no person who has held the Office of President, or acted as President, for more than two years of a term to which some other person was elected President shall be elected to the Office of President more than once. But this article shall not apply to any person holding the Office of President when this article was proposed by the Congress, and shall not prevent any person who may be holding the Office of President, or acting as President, during the term within which this article becomes operative from holding the Office of President or acting as President during the remainder of such term.

Section 2 This article shall be inoperative unless it shall have been ratified as an amendment to the Constitution by the legislatures of three-fourths of the several States within seven years from the date of its submission to the States by the Congress.

Amendment XXIII

[Presidential electors for the District of Columbia; adopted 1961]

Section 1 The District constituting the seat of Government of the United States shall appoint in such manner as the Congress may direct: A number of electors of President and Vice President equal to the whole number of Senators and Representatives in Congress to which the District would be entitled if it were a State, but in no event more than the least populous State; they shall be in addition to those appointed by the States, but they shall be considered for the purposes of the election of President and Vice President, to be electors appointed by a State; and they shall meet in the District and perform such duties as provided by the twelfth article of amendment.

Section 2 The Congress shall have the power to enforce this article by appropriate legislation.

Amendment XXIV

[Poll tax outlawed in national elections; adopted 1964]

Section 1 The right of citizens of the United States to vote in any primary or other election for President or Vice President, for electors for President or Vice President, or for Senator or Representative in Congress, shall not be denied or abridged by the United States or any State by reason of failure to pay any poll tax or other tax.

Section 2 The Congress shall have the power to enforce this article by appropriate legislation.

Amendment XXV

[Presidential succession; adopted 1967]

Section 1 In case of the removal of the President from Office or of his death or resignation, the Vice President shall become President.

[Vice-presidential vacancy]

Section 2 Whenever there is a vacancy in the Office of the Vice President, the President shall nominate a Vice President who shall take Office upon confirmation by a majority vote of both Houses of Congress.

Section 3 Whenever the President transmits to the President pro tempore of the Senate and the Speaker of the House of Representatives his written declaration that he is unable to discharge the powers and duties of his Office, and until he transmits to them a written declaration to the contrary, such powers and duties shall be discharged by the Vice President as Acting President.

[Presidential disability]

Section 4 Whenever the Vice President and a majority of either the principal officers of the executive departments or of such other body as Congress may by law provide, transmit to the President pro tempore of the Senate and the Speaker of the House of Representatives their written declaration that the President is unable to discharge the powers and duties of his Office, the Vice President shall immediately assume the powers and duties of the Office as Acting President.

Thereafter, when the President transmits to the President pro tempore of the Senate and the Speaker of the House of Representatives his written declaration that no inability exists, he shall resume the powers and duties of his Office unless the Vice President and a majority of either the principal officers of the executive department(s) or of such other body as Congress may by law provide, transmit within four days to the President pro tempore of the Senate and the Speaker of the House of Representatives their written declaration that the President is unable to discharge the powers and duties of his Office. Thereupon Congress shall decide the issue, assembling within forty-eight hours for that purpose if not in session. If the Congress, within twenty-one days after receipt of the latter written declaration, or, if Congress is not in session, within twenty-one days after Congress is required to assemble, determines by two-thirds vote of both Houses that the President is unable to discharge the powers and duties of his Office, the Vice President shall continue to discharge the same as Acting President; otherwise, the President shall resume the powers and duties of his Office.

Amendment XXVI

[Right of eighteen-year-olds to vote; adopted 1971]

Section 1 The right of citizens of the United States, who are eighteen years of age or older, to vote shall not be denied or abridged by the United States or by any State on account of age.

Section 2 The Congress shall have power to enforce this article by appropriate legislation.

Amendment XXVII

[Congressional pay raises; adopted 1992]

No law, varying the compensation for the services of the Senators and Representatives shall take effect, until an election of Representatives shall have intervened.

Glossary

administrative discretion The latitude that Congress gives agencies to make policy in the spirit of their legislative mandate. (13)

affirmative action Any of a wide range of programs, from special recruitment efforts to numerical quotas, aimed at expanding opportunities for women and minority groups. (16)

agenda building The process by which new issues are brought into the political limelight. (10)

agenda setting The stage of the policymaking process during which problems get defined as political issues. (18)

aggregate demand The total income that consumers, businesses, and government wish to spend for goods and services. (17)

amicus curiae brief A brief filed (with the permission of the court) by an individual or group that is not a party to a legal action but has an interest in it. (14)

anarchism A political philosophy that opposes government in any form. (1)

appellate jurisdiction The authority of a court to hear cases that have been tried, decided, or reexamined in other courts. (14)

appropriations committees Committees of Congress that decide which of the programs passed by the authorization committees will actually be funded. (17)

argument The heart of a judicial opinion; its logical content separated from facts, rhetoric, and procedure. (14)

Articles of Confederation The compact among the thirteen original states that established the first government of the United States. (3)

attentive policy elites Leaders who follow news in specific policy areas. (6)

authorization committees Committees of Congress that can authorize spending in their particular areas of responsibility. (17)

autocracy A system of government in which the power to govern is concentrated in the hands of one individual. (2)

Balanced Budget Act A 1997 law that promised to balance the budget by 2002. (17)

Bill of Rights The first ten amendments to the Constitution. They prevent the national government from tampering with fundamental rights and civil liberties, and emphasize the limited character of national power. (3)

bills of attainder Laws that pronounces an individual guilty of a crime without a trial. (15)

bimodal distribution A distribution (of opinions) that shows two responses being chosen about as frequently as each other. (5)

black codes Legislation enacted by former slave states to restrict the freedom of blacks. (16)

block grants Grants-in-aid awarded for general purposes, allowing the recipient great discretion in spending the grant money. (4)

blog A form of newsletter, journal, or "log" of thoughts for public reading, usually devoted to social or political issues and often updated daily. The term derives from *weblog*. (6)

boycott A refusal to do business with a firm, individual, or nation as an expression of disapproval or as a means of coercion. (16)

budget authority The amounts that government agencies are authorized to spend for current and future programs. (17)

budget committees One committee in each house of Congress that supervises a comprehensive budget review process. (17)

Budget Enforcement Act (BEA) A 1990 law that distinguished between mandatory and discretionary spending. (17)

budget outlays The amounts that government agencies are expected to spend in the fiscal year. (17)

bureaucracy A large, complex organization in which employees have specific job responsibilities and work within a hierarchy of authority. (13)

bureaucrats Employees of a bureaucracy, usually meaning a government bureaucracy. (13)

business cycles Expansions and contractions of business activity, the first accompanied by inflation and the second by unemployment. (17)

cabinet A group of presidential advisers; the heads of the executive departments and other key officials. (12)

capitalism The system of government that favors free enterprise (privately owned businesses operating without government regulation). (1)

casework Solving problems for constituents, especially problems involving government agencies. (11)

categorical grants Grants-in-aid targeted for a specific purpose by either formula or project. (4)

caucus A closed meeting of the members of a political party to decide questions of policy and the selection of candidates for office. (8)

caucus/convention A method used to select delegates to attend a party's national convention. Generally, a local meeting selects delegates for a county-level meeting, which in turn selects delegates for a higher-level meeting; the process culminates in a state convention that actually selects the national convention delegates. (9)

checks and balances A government structure that gives each branch some scrutiny of and control over the other branches. (3)

citizen group Lobbying organization built around policy concerns unrelated to members' vocational interests. (10)

civil cases Court cases that involve a private dispute arising from such matters as accidents, contractual obligations, and divorce. (14)

civil disobedience The willful but nonviolent breach of laws that are regarded as unjust. (16)

civil liberties Freedoms guaranteed to individuals taking the form of restraint on government. (15)

civil rights Powers or privileges guaranteed to individuals and protected from arbitrary removal at the hands of government or individuals. (15, 16)

civil rights movement The mass mobilization during the 1960s that sought to gain equality of rights and opportunities for blacks in the South and to a lesser extent in the North, mainly through nonviolent, unconventional means of participation. (16)

civil service The system by which most appointments to the federal bureaucracy are made, to ensure that government jobs are filled on the basis of merit and that employees are not fired for political reasons. (13)

class action A procedure by which similarly situated litigants may be heard in a single lawsuit. (14)

class action suit A legal action brought by a person or group on behalf of a number of people in similar circumstances. (7)

clear and present danger test A means by which the Supreme Court has distinguished between speech as the advocacy of ideas, which is protected by the First Amendment, and speech as incitement, which is not protected. (15)

closed primaries Primary elections in which voters must declare their party affiliation before they are given the primary ballot containing that party's potential nominees. (9)

cloture The mechanism by which a filibuster is cut off in the Senate. (11)

coalition building The banding together of several interest groups for the purpose of lobbying. (10)

coercive federalism A view holding that the national government may impose its policy preferences on the states through regulations in the form of mandates and restraints. (4)

Cold War A prolonged period of adversarial relations between the two superpowers, the United States and the Soviet Union. It lasted from the late 1940s to the late 1980s. (19)

commerce clause The third clause of Article I, Section 8, of the Constitution, which gives Congress the power to regulate commerce among the states. (4)

common, or judge-made, law Legal precedents derived from previous judicial decisions. (14)

communism A political system in which, in theory, ownership of all land and productive facilities is in the hands of the people, and all goods are equally shared. The production and distribution of goods are controlled by an authoritarian government. (1)

communitarians Those who are willing to use government to promote both order and equality. (1)

comparative advantage A principle of international trade that states that all nations will benefit when each nation specializes in those goods that it can produce most efficiently. (19)

competition and outsourcing Procedures that allow private contractors to bid for jobs previously held exclusively by government employees. (13)

concurrence The agreement of a judge with the Supreme Court's majority decision, for a reason other than the majority reason. (14)

confederation A loose association of independent states that agree to cooperate on specified matters. (3)

conference committee A temporary committee created to work out differences between the House and Senate versions of a specific piece of legislation. (11)

Congressional Budget Office (CBO) The budgeting arm of Congress, which prepares alternative budgets to those prepared by the president's OMB. (17)

congressional campaign committee An organization maintained by a political party to raise funds to support its own candidates in congressional elections. (8)

conservatives Those who are willing to use government to promote order but not equality. (1)

constituents People who live and vote in a government official's district or state. (11)

containment The basic U.S. policy toward the Soviet Union during the Cold War, according to which the Soviets were to be contained within existing boundaries by military, diplomatic, and economic means. (19)

conventional participation Relatively routine political behavior that uses institutional channels and is acceptable to the dominant culture. (7)

cooperative federalism A view holding that the Constitution is an agreement among people who are citizens of both state and nation, so there is much overlap between state powers and national powers. (4)

county governments The government units that administer a county. (4)

criminal cases Court cases involving a crime, or violation of public order. (14)

critical election An election that produces a sharp change in the existing pattern of party loyalties among groups of voters. (8)

de facto segregation Segregation that is not the result of government influence. (16)

de jure segregation Government-imposed segregation. (16)

Declaration of Independence Drafted by Thomas Jefferson, the document that proclaimed the right of the colonies to separate from Great Britain. (3)

deficit financing The Keynesian technique of spending beyond government income to combat an economic slump. Its purpose is to inject extra money into the economy to stimulate aggregate demand. (17)

delegate A legislator whose primary responsibility is to represent the majority view of his or her constituents, regardless of his or her own view. (11)

delegation of powers The process by which Congress gives the executive branch the additional authority needed to address new problems. (12)

democracy A system of government in which, in theory, the people rule, either directly or indirectly. (2)

democratic socialism A socialist form of government that guarantees civil liberties such as freedom of speech and religion. Citizens determine the extent of government activity through free elections and competitive political parties. (1)

democratization A process of transition as a country attempts to move from an authoritarian form of government to a democratic one. (2)

departments The biggest units of the executive branch, covering a broad area of government responsibility. The heads of the departments, or secretaries, form the president's cabinet. (13)

deregulation A bureaucratic reform by which the government reduces its role as a regulator of business. (13)

descriptive representation A belief that constituents are most effectively represented by legislators who are similar to them in such key demographic characteristics as race, ethnicity, religion, or gender. (11)

desegregation The ending of authorized segregation, or separation by race. (16)

détente A reduction of tensions. This term is particularly used to refer to a reduction of tensions between the United States and the Soviet Union in the early 1970s during the Nixon administration. (19)

direct action Unconventional participation that involves assembling crowds to confront businesses and local governments to demand a hearing. (7)

direct lobbying Attempts to influence a legislator's vote through personal contact with the legislator. (10)

direct primary A preliminary election, run by the state government, in which the voters choose each party's candidates for the general election. (7)

discretionary outlays Payments made by legislators' choice and based on annual appropriations. (17)

discretionary spending In the Budget Enforcement Act of 1990, authorized expenditures from annual appropriations. (17)

dissent The disagreement of a judge with a majority decision. (14)

distributive policies Government policies designed to confer a benefit on a particular institution or group. (18)

divided government The situation in which one party controls the White House and the other controls at least one house of Congress. (12)

docket A court's agenda. (14)

dual federalism A view holding that the Constitution is a compact among sovereign states, so that the powers of the national government and the states are clearly differentiated. (4)

earmark Federal funds appropriated by Congress for use on local projects. (11, 17)

economic depression A period of high unemployment and business failures; a severe, long-lasting downturn in a business cycle. (17)

efficient market hypothesis Financial markets are informationally efficient—they quickly absorb all relevant information about securities into their prices. (17)

e-government Online communication channels that enable citizens to easily obtain information from government and facilitate the expression of opinions to government officials. (2)

elastic clause The last clause in Article I, Section 8, of the Constitution, which gives Congress the means to execute its enumerated powers. This clause is the basis for Congress's implied powers. Also called the *necessary and proper clause.* (4)

election campaign An organized effort to persuade voters to choose one candidate over others competing for the same office. (9)

electoral college A body of electors chosen by voters to cast ballots for president and vice president. (3, 8)

electoral dealignment A lessening of the importance of party loyalties in voting decisions. (8)

electoral mandate An endorsement by voters. Presidents sometimes argue they have been given a mandate to carry out policy proposals. (12)

electoral realignment The change in voting patterns that occurs after a critical election. (8)

Elementary and Secondary Education Act of 1965 (ESEA) The federal government's primary law to assist the nation's elementary and secondary schools. It emerged as part of President Lyndon Johnson's Great Society program. (18)

elite theory The view that a small group of people actually makes most of the important government decisions. (2)

enlargement and engagement Clinton's policy, following the collapse of communism, of increasing the spread of market economies and increasing the U.S. role in global affairs. (19)

entitlements Benefits to which every eligible person has a legal right and that the government cannot deny. (17, 18)

enumerated powers The powers explicitly granted to Congress by the Constitution. (3)

equal rights amendment (ERA) A failed constitutional amendment introduced by the National Women's Party in 1923, declaring that "equality of rights under the law shall not be denied or abridged by the United States or any State on account of sex." (16)

equality of opportunity The idea that each person is guaranteed the same chance to succeed in life. (1, 16)

equality of outcome The concept that society must ensure that people are equal, and governments must design policies to redistribute wealth and status so that economic and social equality is actually achieved. (1, 16)

establishment clause The first clause in the First Amendment, which forbids government establishment of religion. (15)

ex post facto laws Laws that declare an action to be criminal after it has been performed. (15)

exclusionary rule The judicial rule that states that evidence obtained in an illegal search and seizure cannot be used in trial. (15)

executive agreement A pact between the heads of two countries. (19)

executive branch The law-enforcing branch of government. (3)

Executive Office of the President The president's executive aides and their staffs; the extended White House executive establishment. (12)

executive orders Presidential directives that create or modify laws and public policies, without the direct approval of Congress. (12)

extraordinary majority A majority greater than the minimum of 50 percent plus one. (3)

fair trade Trade regulated by international agreements outlawing unfair business practices. (19)

Federal Communications Commission (FCC) An independent federal agency that regulates interstate and international communication by radio, television, telephone, telegraph, cable, and satellite. (6)

Federal Election Commission (FEC) A bipartisan federal agency of six members that oversees the financing of national election campaigns. (9)

federal question An issue covered by the U.S. Constitution, national laws, or U.S. treaties. (14)

Federal Reserve System The system of banks that acts as the central bank of the United States and controls major monetary policies. (17)

federalism The division of power between a central government and regional governments. (3, 4)

feedback Information received by policymakers about the effectiveness of public policy. (18)

feminization of poverty The term applied to the fact that a growing percentage of all poor Americans are women or the dependents of women. (18)

fighting words Speech that is not protected by the First Amendment because it inflicts injury or tends to incite an immediate disturbance of the peace. (15)

filibuster A delaying tactic, used in the Senate, that involves speech-making to prevent action on a piece of legislation. (11)

first-past-the-post elections A British term for elections conducted in single-member districts that award victory to the candidate with the most votes. (9)

fiscal policies Economic policies that involve government spending and taxing. (17)

fiscal year The twelve-month period from October 1 to September 30 used by the government for accounting purposes. A fiscal year budget is named for the year in which it ends. (17)

501(c)4 social welfare organizations Groups named after Section 501 of the Internal Revenue Code that operate for promotion of social welfare; they are exempt from reporting donors if they spend most of their funds on issues, not candidates. (9)

527 committees Committees named after Section 527 of the Internal Revenue Code; they enjoy tax-exempt status in election campaigns if they are unaffiliated with political parties and take positions on issues, not specific candidates. (9)

foreign policy The general plan followed by a nation in defending and advancing its national interests, especially its security against foreign threats. (19)

formula grants Categorical grants distributed according to a particular set of rules, called a formula, that specify who is eligible for the grants and how much each eligible applicant will receive. (4)

fragmentation In policymaking, the phenomenon of attacking a single problem in different and sometimes competing ways. (18)

franchise The right to vote. Also called *suffrage*. (7)

free trade An economic policy that allows businesses in different nations to sell and buy goods without paying tariffs or other limitations. (19)

freedom from Immunity, as in *freedom from want*. (1)

freedom of An absence of constraints on behavior, as in *freedom of speech or freedom of religion*. (1)

free-exercise clause The second clause in the First Amendment, which prevents the government from interfering with the exercise of religion. (15)

free-expression clauses The press and speech clauses of the First Amendment. (15)

free-rider problem The situation in which people benefit from the activities of an organization (such as an interest group) but do not contribute to those activities. (10)

front-loading States' practice of moving delegate selection primaries and caucuses earlier in the calendar year to gain media and candidate attention. (9)

gatekeepers Media executives, news editors, and prominent reporters who direct the flow of news. (6)

general election A national election held by law in November of every even-numbered year. (9)

gerrymandering Redrawing a congressional district to intentionally benefit one political party. (11)

global policy Like foreign policy, it is a plan for defending and advancing national interests, but—unlike foreign policy—it includes social and environmental concerns among national interests. (19)

globalization The increasing interdependence of citizens and nations across the world. (1)

going public A strategy whereby a president seeks to influence policy elites and media coverage by appealing directly to the American people. (6)

good faith exception An exception to the Supreme Court exclusionary rule, holding that evidence seized on the basis of a mistakenly issued search warrant can be introduced at trial if the mistake was made in good faith, that is, if all the parties involved had reason at the time to believe that the warrant was proper. (15)

government The legitimate use of force to control human behavior; also, the organization or agency authorized to exercise that force. (1)

government corporations Government agencies that perform services that might be provided by the private sector but that either involve insufficient financial incentive or are better provided when they are somehow linked with government. (13)

Government Performance and Results Act A law requiring each government agency to implement quantifiable standards to measure its performance in meeting stated program goals. (13)

grant-in-aid Money provided by one level of government to another to be spent for a given purpose. (4)

grassroots lobbying Lobbying activities performed by rank-and-file interest group members and would-be members. (10)

Great Compromise Submitted by the Connecticut delegation to the Constitutional Convention of 1787, and thus also known as the Connecticut Compromise, a plan calling for a bicameral legislature in which the House of Representatives would be apportioned according to population and the states would be represented equally in the Senate. (3)

Great Depression The longest and deepest setback the American economy has ever experienced. It began with the stock market crash on October 24, 1929, and did not end until the start of World War II. (18)

Great Society President Lyndon Johnson's broad array of programs designed to redress political, social, and economic inequality. (18)

gridlock A situation in which government is incapable of acting on important issues. (12)

gross domestic product (GDP) The total value of the goods and services produced by a country during a year. (17)

hold A letter requesting that a bill be held from floor debate. (11)

home rule The right to enact and enforce legislation locally. (4)

horse race journalism Election coverage by the mass media that focuses on which candidate is ahead rather than on national issues. (6)

impeachment The formal charging of a government official with "treason, bribery, or other high crimes and misdemeanors." (11)

implementation The process of putting specific policies into operation. (13, 18)

implied powers Those powers that Congress needs to execute its enumerated powers. (3, 4)

incremental budgeting A method of budget making that involves adding new funds (an increment) onto the amount previously budgeted (in last year's budget). (17)

incrementalism Policymaking characterized by a series of decisions, each instituting modest change. (13)

incumbent A current officeholder. (11)

independent agencies Executive agencies that are not part of a cabinet department. (13)

inflation An economic condition characterized by price increases linked to a decrease in the value of the currency. (17)

influencing behavior Behavior that seeks to modify or reverse government policy to serve political interests. (7)

information campaign An organized effort to gain public backing by bringing a group's views to public attention. (10)

infotainment A mix of information and diversion oriented to personalities or celebrities, not linked to the day's events, and usually unrelated to public affairs or policy; often called "soft news." (6)

inherent powers Authority claimed by the president that is not clearly specified in the Constitution. Typically, these powers are inferred from the Constitution. (12)

initiative A procedure by which voters can propose an issue to be decided by the legislature or by the people in a referendum. It requires gathering a specified number of signatures and submitting a petition to a designated agency. (7)

Intelligence Community Sixteen agencies in the executive branch that conduct the various intelligence activities that make up the total U.S. national intelligence effort. (19)

interest group An organized group of individuals that seeks to influence public policy; also called a *lobby*. (2, 10)

interest group entrepreneur An interest group organizer or leader. (10)

invidious discrimination Discrimination against persons or groups that works to their harm and is based on animosity. (16)

isolationism A foreign policy of withdrawal from international political affairs. (19)

issue definition Our conception of the problem at hand. (18)

issue framing The way that politicians or interest group leaders define an issue when presenting it to others. (5)

issue network A shared-knowledge group consisting of representatives of various interests involved in some particular aspect of public policy. (18)

joint committee A committee made up of members of both the House and the Senate. (11)

judgment The judicial decision in a court case. (14)

judicial activism A judicial philosophy by which judges tend not to defer to decisions of the elected branches of government, resulting in the invalidation or emasculation of those decisions. (14)

judicial branch The law-interpreting branch of government. (3)

judicial restraint A judicial philosophy by which judges tend to defer to decisions of the elected branches of government. (14)

judicial review The power to declare congressional (and presidential) acts invalid because they violate the Constitution. (3, 14)

Keynesian theory An economic theory stating that the government can stabilize the economy—that is, can smooth business cycles—by controlling the level of aggregate demand, and that the level of aggregate demand can be controlled by means of fiscal and monetary policies. (17)

laissez faire An economic doctrine that opposes any form of government intervention in business. (1)

legislative branch The lawmaking branch of government. (3)

legislative liaison staff Those people who act as the communications link between the White House and Congress, advising the president or cabinet secretaries on the status of pending legislation. (12)

liberalism The belief that states should leave individuals free to follow their individual pursuits. Note that this differs from the definition of *liberal* later in this chapter. (1)

liberals Those who are willing to use government to promote equality but not order. (1)

libertarianism A political ideology that is opposed to all government action except as necessary to protect life and property. (1)

libertarians Those who are opposed to using government to promote either order or equality. (1)

lobby See *interest group*. (10)

lobbyist A representative of an interest group. (10)

majoritarian model of democracy The classical theory of democracy in which government by the people is interpreted as government by the majority of the people. (2)

majority leader The head of the majority party in the Senate; the second-highest-ranking member of the majority party in the House. (11)

majority representation The system by which one office, contested by two or more candidates, is won by the single candidate who collects the most votes. (8)

majority rule The principle—basic to procedural democratic theory—that the decision of a group must reflect the preference of more than half of those participating; a simple majority. (2)

mandate A requirement that a state undertake an activity or provide a service, in keeping with minimum national standards. (4)

mandatory outlays Payments that government must make by law. (17)

mandatory spending In the Budget Enforcement Act of 1990, expenditures required by previous commitments. (17)

market-driven journalism Both reporting news and running commercials geared to a target audience defined by demographic characteristics. (6)

mass media The means employed in mass communication; traditionally divided into print media and broadcast media. (6)

means-tested benefits Conditional benefits provided by government to individuals whose income falls below a designated threshold. (18)

media event A situation that is so "newsworthy" that the mass media are compelled to cover it. Candidates in elections often create such situations to garner media attention. (6)

Medicaid A need-based comprehensive medical and hospitalization program. (18)

Medicare A health insurance program serving primarily persons sixty-five and older. (18)

minority rights The benefits of government that cannot be denied to any citizen by majority decisions. (2)

***Miranda* warnings** Statements concerning rights that police are required to make to a person before he or she is subjected to in-custody questioning. (15)

modified closed primaries Primary elections that allow individual state parties to decide whether they permit independents to vote in their primaries and for which offices. (9)

modified open primaries Primary elections that entitle independent voters to vote in a party's primary. (9)

monetarists Those who argue that government can effectively control the performance of an economy mainly by controlling the supply of money. (17)

monetary policies Economic policies that involve control of, and changes in, the supply of money. (17)

municipal governments The government units that administer a city or town. (4)

nation building A policy to shore up countries economically and democratically, thereby making them less likely to collapse or be taken over. (19)

national committee A committee of a political party composed of party chairpersons and party officials from every state. (8)

national convention A gathering of delegates of a single political party from across the country to choose candidates for president and vice president and to adopt a party platform. (8)

national debt The accumulated sum of past government borrowing owed to lenders outside the government. (17)

national sovereignty A political entity's externally recognized right to exercise final authority over its affairs. (1)

necessary and proper clause The last clause in Section 8 of Article I of the Constitution, which gives Congress the means to execute its enumerated powers. This clause is the basis for Congress's implied powers. Also called the *elastic clause*. (3)

New Deal The measures advocated by the Franklin D. Roosevelt administration to alleviate the Depression. (18)

New Jersey Plan Submitted by the head of the New Jersey delegation to the Constitutional Convention of 1787, a set of nine resolutions that would have, in effect, preserved the Articles of Confederation by amending rather than replacing them. (3)

newsworthiness The degree to which a news story is important enough to be covered in the mass media. (6)

Nineteenth Amendment The amendment to the Constitution, adopted in 1920, that ensures women of the right to vote. (16)

Nixon Doctrine Nixon's policy, formulated with assistance from Henry Kissinger, that restricted U.S. military intervention abroad absent a threat to its vital national interests. (19)

No Child Left Behind Act of 2001 (NCLB) The latest reauthorization of the Elementary and Secondary Education Act. (18)

nomination Designation as an official candidate of a political party. (8)

non-means-tested benefits Benefits provided by government to all citizens, regardless of income; Medicare and Social Security are examples. (18)

normal distribution A symmetrical bell-shaped distribution (of opinions) centered on a single mode, or most frequent response. (5)

norms An organization's informal, unwritten rules that guide individual behavior. (13)

North Atlantic Treaty Organization (NATO) An organization including nations of Western Europe, the United States, and Canada, created in 1949 to defend against Soviet expansionism. (19)

obligation of contracts The obligation of the parties to a contract to carry out its terms. (15)

Office of Management and Budget (OMB) The budgeting arm of the Executive Office; prepares the president's budget. (17)

oligarchy A system of government in which power is concentrated in the hands of a few people. (2)

open election An election that lacks an incumbent. (9)

open primaries Primary elections in which voters need not declare their party affiliation and can choose one party's primary ballot to take into the voting booth. (9)

order Established ways of social behavior. Maintaining order is the oldest purpose of government. (1)

original jurisdiction The authority of a court to hear a case before any other court does. (14)

oversight The process of reviewing the operations of an agency to determine whether it is carrying out policies as Congress intended. (11)

parliamentary system A system of government in which the chief executive is the leader whose party holds the most seats in the legislature after an election or whose party forms a major part of the ruling coalition. (11)

participatory democracy A system of government where rank-and-file citizens rule themselves rather than electing representatives to govern on their behalf. (2)

party conference A meeting to select party leaders and decide committee assignments, held at the beginning of a session of Congress by Republicans or Democrats in each chamber. (8)

party identification A voter's sense of psychological attachment to a party. (8)

party machine A centralized party organization that dominates local politics by controlling elections. (8)

party platform The statement of policies of a national political party. (8)

peace through strength Reagan's policy of combating communism by building up the military, including aggressive development of new weapons systems. (19)

plea bargain A defendant's admission of guilt in exchange for a less severe punishment. (14)

pluralist model of democracy An interpretation of democracy in which government by the people is taken to mean government by people operating through competing interest groups. (2)

police power The authority of a government to maintain order and safeguard citizens' health, morals, safety, and welfare. (1)

policy entrepreneurs Citizens, members of interest groups, or public officials who champion particular policy ideas. (4)

policy evaluation Analysis of a public policy so as to determine how well it is working. (18)

policy formulation The stage of the policymaking process during which formal proposals are developed and adopted. (18)

political action committee (PAC) An organization that pools campaign contributions from group members and donates those funds to candidates for political office. (9, 10)

political agenda A list of issues that need government attention. (6)

political equality Equality in political decision making: one vote per person, with all votes counted equally. (1, 2)

political ideology A consistent set of values and beliefs about the proper purpose and scope of government. (1)

political participation Actions of private citizens by which they seek to influence or support government and politics. (7)

political party An organization that sponsors candidates for political office under the organization's name. (8)

political socialization The complex process by which people acquire their political values. (5)

political system A set of interrelated institutions that links people with government. (8)

poll tax A tax of $1 or $2 on every citizen who wished to vote, first instituted in Georgia in 1877. Although it was no burden on most white citizens, it effectively disenfranchised blacks. (16)

poverty level The minimum cash income that will provide for a family's basic needs; calculated as three times the cost of a market basket of food that provides a minimally nutritious diet. (18)

precedent A judicial ruling that serves as the basis for the ruling in a subsequent case. (14)

preemption The power of Congress to enact laws by which the national government assumes total or partial responsibility for a state government function. (4)

preemptive action The policy of acting against a nation or group that poses a severe threat to the United States before waiting for the threat to occur; sometimes called the "Bush doctrine." (19)

presidential primary A special primary election used to select delegates to attend the party's national convention, which in turn nominates the presidential candidate. (9)

primary election A preliminary election conducted within a political party to select candidates who will run for public office in a subsequent election. (9)

prior restraint Censorship before publication. (15)

procedural democratic theory A view of democracy as being embodied in a decision-making process that involves universal participation, political equality, majority rule, and responsiveness. (2)

proclamation An official declaration or statement of action or recognition. (19)

productive capacity The total value of goods and services that can be produced when the economy works at full capacity. (17)

program monitoring Keeping track of government programs; usually done by interest groups. (10)

progressive taxation A system of taxation whereby the rich pay proportionately higher taxes than the poor; used by governments to redistribute wealth and thus promote equality. (17)

progressivism A philosophy of political reform based on the goodness and wisdom of the individual citizen as opposed to special interests and political institutions. (7)

project grants Categorical grants awarded on the basis of competitive applications submitted by prospective recipients to perform a specific task or function. (4)

proportional representation The system by which legislative seats are awarded to a party in proportion to the vote that party wins in an election. (8)

protectionism The notion that women must be protected from life's cruelties; until the 1970s, the basis for laws affecting women's civil rights. (16)

protectionists Those who wish to prevent imports from entering the country and therefore oppose free trade. (19)

public assistance Government aid to individuals who can demonstrate a need for that aid. (18)

public figures People who assume roles of prominence in society or thrust themselves to the forefront of public controversy. (15)

public goods Benefits and services, such as parks and sanitation, that benefit all citizens but are not likely to be produced voluntarily by individuals. (1)

public opinion The collective attitudes of citizens concerning a given issue or question. (5)

public policy A general plan of action adopted by the government to solve a social problem, counter a threat, or pursue an objective. (18)

racial gerrymandering The drawing of a legislative district to maximize the chance that a minority candidate will win election. (11)

racial segregation Separation from society because of race. (16)

racism A belief that human races have distinct characteristics such that one's own race is superior to, and has a right to rule, others. (16)

reapportionment Redistribution of representatives among the states, based on population change. The House is reapportioned after each census. (11)

recall The process for removing an elected official from office. (7)

receipts For a government, the amount expected or obtained in taxes and other revenues. (17)

redistributional policies Policies that take government resources, such as tax funds, from one sector of society and transfer them to another. (18)

redistricting The process of redrawing political boundaries to reflect changes in population. (4)

referendum An election on a policy issue. (7)

regulation Government intervention in the workings of a business market to promote some socially desired goal. (13, 18)

regulations Administrative rules that guide the operation of a government program. (13)

regulatory commissions Agencies of the executive branch of government that control or direct some aspect of the economy. (13)

representative democracy A system of government where citizens elect public officials to govern on their behalf. (2)

republic A government without a monarch; a government rooted in the consent of the governed, whose power is exercised by elected representatives responsible to the governed. (3)

republicanism A form of government in which power resides in the people and is exercised by their elected representatives. (3)

responsible party government A set of principles formalizing the ideal role of parties in a majoritarian democracy. (8)

responsiveness A decision-making principle, necessitated by representative government, that implies that elected representatives should do what the majority of people wants. (2)

restraint A requirement laid down by act of Congress, prohibiting a state or local government from exercising a certain power. (4)

rights The benefits of government to which every citizen is entitled. (1)

rule making The administrative process that results in the issuance of regulations by government agencies. (13)

rule of four An unwritten rule that requires at least four justices to agree that a case warrants consideration before it is reviewed by the U.S. Supreme Court. (14)

school district The government unit that administers elementary and secondary school programs. (4)

select committee A temporary congressional committee created for a specific purpose and disbanded after that purpose is fulfilled. (11)

self-interest principle The implication that people choose what benefits them personally. (5)

senatorial courtesy A norm under which a nomination must be acceptable to the home state senator from the president's party. (14)

seniority Years of consecutive service on a particular congressional committee. (11)

separate-but-equal doctrine The concept that providing separate but equivalent facilities for blacks and whites satisfies the equal protection clause of the Fourteenth Amendment. (16)

separation of powers The assignment of lawmaking, law-enforcing, and law-interpreting functions to separate branches of government. (3)

set-aside A purchasing or contracting provision that reserves a certain percentage of funds for minority-owned contractors. (16)

sexism Invidious sex discrimination. (16)

skewed distribution An asymmetrical but generally bell-shaped distribution (of opinions); its mode, or most frequent response, lies off to one side. (5)

social contract theory The belief that the people agree to set up rulers for certain purposes and thus have the right to resist or remove rulers who act against those purposes. (3)

social equality Equality in wealth, education, and status. (1)

social insurance A government-backed guarantee against loss by individuals without regard to need. (18)

Social Security Social insurance that provides economic assistance to persons faced with unemployment, disability, or old age. It is financed by taxes on employers and employees. (18)

Social Security Act The law that provided for Social Security and is the basis of modern American social welfare. (18)

social welfare programs Government programs that provide the minimum living standards necessary for all citizens. (18)

socialism A form of rule in which the central government plays a strong role in regulating existing private industry and directing the economy, although it does allow some private ownership of productive capacity. (1)

socioeconomic status Position in society, based on a combination of education, occupational status, and income. (5)

soft news General entertainment programming that often includes discussions of political affairs. (6)

solicitor general The third highest official of the U.S. Department of Justice, and the one who represents the national government before the Supreme Court. (14)

sovereign wealth funds A government-owned fund of financial assets built from budget surpluses and reserved for investment purposes. (19)

sovereignty The quality of being supreme in power or authority. (4)

Speaker of the House The presiding officer of the House of Representatives. (11)

special districts Government units created to perform particular functions, especially when those functions are best performed across jurisdictional boundaries. (4)

split ticket In voting, candidates from different parties for different offices. (9)

stable distribution A distribution (of opinions) that shows little change over time. (5)

stagflation The joint occurrence of slow growth, unemployment, and inflation. (17)

standard socioeconomic model A relationship between socioeconomic status and conventional political involvement: people with higher status and more education are more likely to participate than those with lower status. (7)

standing committee A permanent congressional committee that specializes in a particular policy area. (11)

stare decisis Literally, "let the decision stand"; decision making according to precedent (14)

states' rights The idea that all rights not specifically conferred on the national government by the U.S. Constitution are reserved to the states. (4)

straight ticket In voting, a single party's candidates for all the offices. (9)

strict scrutiny A standard used by the Supreme Court in deciding whether a law or policy is to be adjudged constitutional. To pass strict scrutiny, the law or policy must be justified by a "compelling governmental interest," must be narrowly tailored, and must be the least restrictive means for achieving that interest. (15)

substantive democratic theory The view that democracy is embodied in the substance of government policies rather than in the policymaking procedure. (2)

suffrage The right to vote. Also called the *franchise*. (7)

supply-side economics Economic policies aimed at increasing the supply of goods (as opposed to decreasing demand); consists mainly of tax cuts for possible investors and less regulation of business. (17)

supportive behavior Action that expresses allegiance to government and country. (7)

supremacy clause The clause in Article VI of the Constitution that asserts that national laws take precedence over state and local laws when they conflict. (3)

tax committees The two committees of Congress responsible for raising the revenue with which to run the government. (17)

television hypothesis The belief that television is to blame for the low level of citizens' knowledge about public affairs. (6)

Temporary Assistance for Needy Families (TANF) A 1996 national act that abolished the longtime welfare policy, AFDC (Aid for Families with Dependent Children). TANF gives the states much more control over welfare policy. (18)

terrorism Premeditated, politically motivated violence perpetrated against noncombatant targets by subnational groups or clandestine agents. (7)

totalitarianism A political philosophy that advocates unlimited power for the government to enable it to control all sectors of society. (1)

trade association An organization that represents firms within a particular industry. (10)

transfer payment A payment by government to an individual, mainly through Social Security or unemployment insurance. (17)

trustee A representative who is obligated to consider the views of constituents but is not obligated to vote according to those views if he or she believes they are misguided. (11)

two-party system A political system in which two major political parties compete for control of the government. Candidates from a third party have little chance of winning office. (8)

two-step flow of communication The process in which a few policy elites gather information and then inform their more numerous followers, mobilizing them to apply pressure to government. (6)

U.S. courts of appeals Courts within the second tier of the three-tiered federal court system, to which decisions of the district courts and federal agencies may be appealed for review. (14)

U.S. district courts Courts within the lowest tier of the three-tiered federal court system; courts where litigation begins. (14)

unconventional participation Relatively uncommon political behavior that challenges or defies established institutions and dominant norms. (7)

unitary executive A belief that the president's inherent powers allow him to overrule congressional grants of independent authority to agencies. (12)

universal participation The concept that everyone in a democracy should participate in governmental decision making. (2)

veto The president's disapproval of a bill that has been passed by both houses of Congress. Congress can override a veto with a two-thirds vote in each house. (11, 12)

Virginia Plan A set of proposals for a new government, submitted to the Constitutional Convention of 1787; it included separation of the government into three branches, division of the legislature into two houses, and proportional representation in the legislature. (3)

voter turnout The percentage of eligible citizens who actually vote in a given election. (7)

War on Poverty A part of President Lyndon Johnson's Great Society program, intended to eradicate poverty within ten years. (18)

watchdog journalism Journalism that scrutinizes public and business institutions and publicizes perceived misconduct. (6)

welfare state A nation in which the government assumes responsibility for the welfare of its citizens by providing a wide array of public services and redistributing income to reduce social inequality. (18)

Notes

CHAPTER 1 / FREEDOM, ORDER, OR EQUALITY? / PAGES 2–27

1. Adam Liptak "In Health Law, Asking Where U.S. Power Stops," *New York Times*, 11 November 2011, pp. A1, A17.
2. Ibid.
3. 2008 American National Election Study, undertaken in collaboration by Stanford University and the University of Michigan.
4. David Easton, *The Political System* (New York: Knopf, 1953), p. 65.
5. There are more elaborate definitions. A recent book defines globalization as "the intensification of cross-national interactions that promote the establishment of trans-national structures and the global integration of cultural, economic, environmental, political, technological and social processes on global, supranational, national, regional and local levels," in Axel Dreher, Noel Gaston, and Pim Martens, *Measuring Globalisation: Gauging Its Consequences* (New York: Springer, 2008), p. 15.
6. Mark Andreas Kayser, "How Domestic Is Domestic Politics? Globalization and Elections," *Annual Review of Political Science* 10 (2007): 341–362.
7. Thomas Biersteker and Cynthia Weber (eds.), *State Sovereignty as Social Construct* (Cambridge: Cambridge University Press, 1996), p. 12. For distinctions among four different types of sovereignty, see Stephen D. Krasner, "Abiding Sovereignty," *International Political Science Review* 22 (July 2001): 229–251.
8. William T. R. Fox and Annette Baker Fox, "International Politics," in *International Encyclopedia of the Social Sciences* (New York: Macmillan and Free Press, 1968), 8:50–53.
9. Michael Goodhart and Stacy Bondanella Taninchev, "The New Sovereigntist Challenge for Global Governance: Democracy without Sovereignty," *International Studies Quarterly* 55 (December 2011): 1047–1068.
10. Jess Bravin, "U.S. to Pull Out of World Court on War Crimes," *Wall Street Journal*, 6 May 2002, p. A4.
11. Charles M. Madigan and Colin McMahon, "A Slow, Painful Quest for Justice," *Chicago Tribune*, 7 September 1999, pp. 1, 8.
12. Tom Hundley, "Europe Seeks to Convert U.S. on Death Penalty," *Chicago Tribune*, 26 June 2000, p. 1; and Salim Muwakkil, "The Capital of Capital Punishment," *Chicago Tribune*, 12 July 1999, p. 18.
13. Joseph Winter, "Living in Somalia's Anarchy," *BBC News*, 18 November 2004, http://news.bbc.co.uk/2/ hi/4017147.stm; and Alemayehu Fentaw, "Anarchy, Terrorism, and Piracy in Somalia: New Rules of Engagement for the International Community," *American Chronicle*, 27 May 2009, http://www.americanchronicle.com/ articles/view/ 103942.
14. *Liberalism* constitutes a nebulous doctrine for theorists. Louis Hartz, in his classic *The Liberal Tradition in America* (New York: Harcourt, Brace & World, 1955), says it is an "even vaguer term" than *feudalism* (pp. 3–4). David G. Smith calls it "too ecumenical and too pluralistic to be called, properly, an ideology" in *The International Encyclopedia of the Social Sciences* (New York: Macmillan and Free Press, 1968), 9:276. More recently, Robert Eccleshall admitted that "in everyday usage," liberalism "often stands for little more than a collection of values and principles which no decent person would reject" but then proceeds to find substance in an "incoherent doctrine." In *Political Ideologies: An Introduction*, 3rd ed. (London: Routledge, 2003), p. 18.
15. Edward Cody, "Chinese Lawmakers Approve Measure to Protect Private Property Rights," *Washington Post*, 17 March 2007, p. A10.
16. Karl Marx and Friedrich Engels, *Critique of the Gotha Programme* (New York: International Publishers, 1938), p. 10. Originally written in 1875 and published in 1891.
17. Abby Goodnough, "Gay Rights Rebuke May Bring Change in Tactics," *New York Times*, 5 November 2009, pp. A1, A4.
18. One scholar holds that *freedom* came from northern European languages, and *liberty* from Latin, and the words originally had opposite meanings. Liberty meant separation and freedom meant connection. See David Hackett Fischer, *Liberty and Freedom: A Visual History of America's Founding Ideas* (New York: Oxford University Press, 2005), pp. 1–15.
19. For a philosophical analysis, see Robert E. Goodin and Frank Jackson, "Freedom from Fear," *Philosophy and Public Affairs* 35 (2007): 249–265.
20. See the argument in Amy Gutman, *Liberal Equality* (Cambridge: Cambridge University Press, 1980), pp. 9–10.
21. See John H. Schaar, "Equality of Opportunity and Beyond," *in Equality, NOMOS IX*, ed. J. Roland Pennock and John W. Chapman (New York: Atherton Press, 1967), pp. 228–249.
22. Lyndon Johnson, "To Fulfill These Rights," commencement address at Howard University, 4 June 1965, http://www.hpol.org/record. asp?id=54.
23. Jean Jacques Rousseau, *The Social Contract and Discourses*, trans. G. D. H. Cole (New York: Dutton, 1950), p. 5.
24. Lydia Said, "Most Americans Believe Crime Is Worsening," Gallup Poll Report, 31 October 2011.
25. Tamara Audi and Gary Fields, "L.A. Is Latest City to See Crime Drop," *Wall Street Journal*, 7 January 2010, p. A8.
26. Pew Global Attitudes Project, "Two Decades after the Wall's Fall: End of Communism Cheered but Now with More Reservations," 2 November 2009.
27. Centers for Disease Control and Prevention, "HIV in the United States," http://www.cdc.gov/hiv/resources/factsheets/us.htm.
28. Milton Friedman, *Capitalism and Freedom* (Chicago: University of Chicago Press, 1962).
29. Joseph Khan, "Anarchism, the Creed That Won't Stay Dead," *New York Times*, 5 August 2000, p. A15.
30. For a similar approach, see Scott Keeter and Gregory A. Smith, "In Search of Ideologues in America," Pew Research Center for the People & the Press, 11 April 2006, http://pewresearch.org/pubs/17/ in-search-of-ideologues-in-america.
31. The communitarian category was labeled "populist" in the first four editions of this book. We have relabeled it for two reasons. First, we believe that *communitarian* is more descriptive of the category. Second, we recognize that the term *populist* has been used increasingly to refer to the political styles of candidates as diverse as Pat Buchanan, Ralph Nader, and Herman Cain. In this sense, a populist appeals to mass resentment against those in power. Given the debate over what populist really means, we have decided to use *communitarian*, a less familiar term with fewer connotations. See Michael Kazin, *The Populist Persuasion: An American History* (New York: Basic Books, 1995).
32. Keeter and Smith call this grouping "Populist."
33. The communitarian movement was founded by a group of ethicists and social scientists who met in Washington, D.C., in 1990 at the invitation of sociologist Amitai Etzioni and political theorist William Galston to discuss what they viewed as the declining state of morality and values in the United States. Etzioni became the leading spokesperson for the movement. See his *Rights and the Common Good: The Communitarian Perspective* (New York: St. Martin's Press, 1995), pp. iii–iv. The communitarian political movement should be distinguished from communitarian thought in political philosophy, which is associated with theorists such as Alasdair MacIntyre, Michael Sandel, and Charles Taylor, who wrote in the late 1970s and early 1980s. In essence, communitarian theorists criticized liberalism, which stressed freedom and individualism, as excessively individualistic. Their

fundamental critique was that liberalism slights the values of community life. See Allen E. Buchanan, "Assessing the Communitarian Critique of Liberalism," *Ethics* 99 (July 1989): 852–882; and Patrick Neal and David Paris, "Liberalism and the Communitarian Critique: A Guide for the Perplexed," *Canadian Journal of Political Science* 23 (September 1990): 419–439. Communitarian philosophers attacked liberalism over the inviolability of civil liberties. In our framework, such issues involve the trade-off between freedom and order. Communitarian and liberal theorists differ less concerning the trade-off between freedom and equality. See William R. Lund, "Communitarian Politics and the Problem of Equality," *Political Research Quarterly* 46 (September 1993): 577–600. But see also Susan Hekman, "The Embodiment of the Subject: Feminism and the Communitarian Critique of Liberalism," *Journal of Politics* 54 (November 1992): 1098–1119.

34. Etzioni, *Rights and the Common Good*, p. iv; and Etzioni, "Communitarian Solutions/What Communitarians Think," *Journal of State Government* 65 (January–March 1992): 9–11. For a critical review of the communitarian program, see Jeremiah Creedon, "Communitarian Manifesto," *Utne Reader* (July–August 1992): 38–40.

35. Etzioni, "Communitarian Solutions/What Communitarians Think," p. 10; and Dana Milbank, "Catch-Word for Bush Ideology; 'Communitarianism' Finds Favor," *Washington Post*, 1 February 2001, p. A1. See also Lester Thurow, "Communitarian vs. Individualistic Capitalism," in Etzioni, *Rights and the Common Good*, pp. 277–282. Note, however, that government's role in dealing with issues of social and economic inequality is far less developed in communitarian writings than is its role in dealing with issues of order. In the same volume, an article by David Osborne, "Beyond Left and Right: A New Political Paradigm" (pp. 283–290), downplays the role of government in guaranteeing entitlements.

36. Etzioni, *Rights and the Common Good*, p. 17.

37. Ibid., p. 22.

38. On the philosophical similarities and differences between communitarianism and socialism, see Alexander Koryushkin and Gerd Meyer (eds.), *Communitarianism, Liberalism, and the Quest for Democracy in Post-Communist Societies* (St. Petersburg: St. Petersburg University Press, 1999).

39. Researchers who have studied populations in Western and Eastern Europe find that the model fits citizens in Western Europe better than those in Eastern Europe. See Hulda Thorisdottir, John T. Jost, Ido Liviatan, and Patrick E. Shrout, "Psychological Needs and Values Underlying Left-Right Political Orientation: Cross-National Evidence from Eastern and Western Europe," *Public Opinion Quarterly* 71 (Summer 2007): 175–203.

CHAPTER 2 / MAJORITARIAN OR PLURALIST DEMOCRACY? / PAGES 28–47

1. N. R. Kleinfield and Cara Buckley, "Wall Street Occupiers, Protesting Till Whenever," *New York Times*, 30 September 2011.

2. See Sarah Sobieraj, *Soundbitten* (New York: New York University Press, 2011).

3. Occupy Wall Street, http://occupywallst.org.

4. Frank Newport, "Americans Favor Jobs Plan Proposals, Including Taxing Rich," *Gallup Poll*, 20 September 2011, http://www.gallup.com/poll/149567/Americans-Favor-Jobs-Plan-Proposals-Including-Taxing-Rich.aspx.

5. Kenneth Janda, "What's in a Name? Party Labels across the World," in *The CONTA Conference: Proceedings of the Conference of Conceptual and Terminological Analysis of the Social Sciences*, ed. F. W. Riggs (Frankfurt: Indeks Verlage, 1982), pp. 46–62.

6. William Roberts Clark, Matt Golder, and Sona Nadenichek Golder, *Principles of Comparative Politics* (Washington, D.C.: CQ Press, 2009), p. 152.

7. Richard F. Fenno, Jr., *The President's Cabinet* (New York: Vintage, 1959), p. 29.

8. See Carmen Siriana, *Investing in Democracy* (Washington, D.C.: Brookings Institution, 2009).

9. Robert A. Dahl, *Democracy and Its Critics* (New Haven, Conn.: Yale University Press, 1989), pp. 13–23.

10. Jeffrey M. Berry, Kent E. Portney, and Ken Thomson, *The Rebirth of Urban Democracy* (Washington, D.C.: Brookings Institution, 1993).

11. Shaun Bowler, Todd Donovan, and Jeffrey A. Karp, "Enraged or Engaged? Preferences for Direct Citizen Participation in Affluent Democracies," *Political Research Quarterly* 60 (September 2007): 351–361.

12. Berry, Portney, and Thomson, *Rebirth of Urban Democracy*, p. 77.

13. Darrell M. West, *State and Federal Electronic Government in the United States*, 2008, Brookings Institution, http://www.brookings.edu//media/Files/rc/reports/2008/0826_egovernment_west/0826_egovernment_west.pdf.

14. https://www.ago.mo.gov/cgi-bin/Environment/complaint.cgi.

15. Christopher Wlezien and Stuart N. Soroka, "Inequality in Policy Responsiveness?" in *Who Gets Represented?* eds. Peter K. Ennis and Christopher Wlezien (New York: Russell Sage Foundation, 2011), pp. 285–310.

16. Dietrich Rueschemeyer, "Address Inequality," *Journal of Democracy* 15 (October 2004): 76–90.

17. Russell J. Dalton, Doh C. Shin, and Willy Jou, "Popular Conceptions of the Meaning of Democracy" (Irvine: Center for the Study of Democracy, University of California, Irvine, 18 May 2007), http://escholarship.org/uc/item/2j74b860.

18. Kenneth Janda, "Do Our People's Republics Work?" *Newsday*, 6 August 2003.

19. Sabrina Tavernise and Steven Greenhouse, "Ohio Vote on Labor Is Parsed for Omens," *New York Times*, 9 November 2011.

20. Deborah Ball and Nicholas Birch, "Swiss Ban Minarets in Controversial Vote," *Wall Street Journal*, 30 November 2009.

21. Gallup Poll, "More Americans Plugged Into Political News," 28 September 2009, http://www.gallup.com/poll/123203/Americans-Plugged-Into-Political-News.aspx.

22. John R. Hibbing and Elizabeth Theiss-Morse, *Stealth Democracy: Americans' Beliefs about How Government Should Work* (Cambridge: Cambridge University Press, 2002), p. 7.

23. Robert A. Dahl, *Pluralist Democracy in the United States* (Chicago: Rand McNally, 1967), p. 24.

24. Kay Lehman Schlozman, Sidney Verba, and Henry E. Brady, *The Unheavenly Chorus: Unequal Political Voice and the Broken Promise of American Democracy* (Princeton, N.J.: Princeton University Press, 2012).

25. The classic statement on elite theory is C. Wright Mills, *The Power Elite* (New York: Oxford University Press, 1956).

26. Jeffrey A. Winters and Benjamin I. Page, "Oligarchy in the United States?" *Perspectives on Politics* 7 (December 2009): 731–751.

27. On the difficulty of documenting the link between advocacy and policy outcomes, see Jeffrey M. Berry, "An Ever Fainter Voice," in *The Future of Political Science,* ed. Gary King, Kay Lehman Schlozman, and Norman Nie (New York: Routledge, 2009), pp. 98–100.

28. Powerful arguments on the subtlety of elite domination can be found in Peter Bachrach and Morton S. Baratz, "Two Faces of Power," *American Political Science Review* 56 (December 1962): 947–952; and John Gaventa, *Power and Powerlessness* (Urbana: University of Illinois Press, 1980).

29. Frank R. Baumgartner, Jeffrey M. Berry, Marie Hojnacki, David C. Kimball, and Beth L. Leech, *Lobbying and Policy Change* (Chicago: University of Chicago Press, 2009).

30. See Larry M. Bartels, *Unequal Democracy* (Princeton, N.J.: Princeton University Press, 2009).

31. Michael Coppedge, John Gerring, et al, "Conceptualizing and Measuring Democracy: A New Approach," *Perspectives on Politics* 9 (June 2011): 247–267.

32. See, for example, David Beetham, Edzia Carvalho, Todd Landman, and Stuart Weir (eds.), *Assessing the Quality of Democracy: A Practical Guide* (Stockholm: International Institute for Democracy and Electoral Assistance, 2008), http://www.idea.int/publications/aqd/index.cfm.

33. *Freedom in the World 2009* (Washington, D.C.: Freedom House, 2009).

34. Sam Dagher and Julian E. Barnes, "Sectarian Feud Roils Post-U.S. Iraq," *Wall Street Journal*, 21 December 2011.

35. The classic treatment of the conflict between freedom and order in democratizing countries is Samuel P. Huntington, *Political Order in Changing Societies* (New Haven, Conn.: Yale University Press, 1968).

36. See Henry Teune, "The Consequences of Globalization on Local Democracy: An Assessment" (paper presented at the International Political Science Association, Durban, South Africa, July 2003); *Human Development Report 2002: Deepening Democracy in a Fragmented World* (New York: United Nations, 2002), pp. 51–61; Yi Feng, *Democracy, Governance, and Economic Performance: Theory and Evidence* (Cambridge, Mass.: MIT Press, 2003), pp. 296–299; and Adam Przeworski and Fernando Limongi, "Modernization: Theories and Facts," *World Politics* 49 (January 1997): 155–183.

37. CNN/ORC Poll, November 18–20, 2011, http://pollingreport.com/afghan.htm.

38. Susan J. Pharr and Robert D. Putnam (eds.), *Disaffected Democracies* (Princeton, N.J.: Princeton University Press, 2000).

39. Hari Kumar and Heather Timmons, "Violence in India Is Fueled by Religious and Economic Divide," *New York Times,* 4 September 2008.

40. "India: International Religious Freedom Report 2009," U.S. Department of State, 26 October 2009.

41. E. E. Schattschneider, *The Semi-Sovereign People* (New York: Holt, Rinehart, & Winston, 1960), p. 35.

42. See Nolan McCarty, Keith T. Poole, and Howard Rosenthal, *Polarized America* (Cambridge, Mass.: MIT Press, 2006); and Steven S. Smith, *Party Influence in Congress* (New York: Cambridge University Press, 2007).

43. Joseph Bafumi and Michael C. Herron, "Leapfrog Representation and Extremism: A Study of American Voters and Their Members of Congress," *American Political Science Review* 104 (August 2010): 519–542; and Theda Skocpol and Vanessa Williamson, *The Tea Party and the Remaking of Republican Conservatism* (New York: Oxford University Press, 2012).

44. Sarah Sobieraj and Jeffrey M. Berry, "From Incivility to Outrage: Political Discourse in Blogs, Talk Radio, and Cable News," *Political Communication* 28 (January 2011): 19.

CHAPTER 3 / THE CONSTITUTION / PAGES 48–83

1. Introductory speech by President V. Giscard d'Estaing to the Convention on the Future of Europe, 28 February 2002, http://gandalf.aksis.uib.no/brit/EXPORT-EU-Constitution/Export-Document-CONV/CONV-004-02-03-05-EN/ANNEX4ChairmanoftheEuropeanConvention,Mr.html.

2. Letter from George Washington to James Madison, 31 March 1787, http://gwpapers.virginia.edu/documents/constitution/1787/madison3.html.

3. Günter Burghardt, "The Development of the European Constitution from the U.S. Point of View," in Esther Brimmer (ed.), *The European Union Constitutional Treaty: A Guide for Americans* (Washington, D.C.: Center for Transatlantic Relations, Johns Hopkins University, 2004).

4. Charles Forelle and Quentin Fottrell, "Irish Vote Decisively to Support EU Reform," *Wall Street Journal,* 4 October 2009, http://online.wsj.com/article/SB125456184521661679.html?mod=WSJ_hps_LEFTWhatsNews, accessed 4 October 2009.

5. Stephen Castle, "Europeans Planning for Less Unanimity," *New York Times,* 3 January 2012, p. A4.

6. Samuel Eliot Morison, *Oxford History of the American People* (New York: Oxford University Press, 1965), p. 172.

7. Richard Walsh, *Charleston's Sons of Liberty: A Study of the Artisans, 1763–1789* (Columbia: University of South Carolina Press, 1959).

8. Mary Beth Norton, *Liberty's Daughters* (Boston: Little, Brown, 1980), pp. 155–157.

9. Morison, *Oxford History,* p. 204.

10. David McCullough, *John Adams* (New York: Simon & Schuster, 2001).

11. John Plamentz, *Man and Society,* rev. ed., ed. M. E. Plamentz and Robert Wokler, vol. 1, *From the Middle Ages to Locke* (New York: Logan, 1992), pp. 216–218.

12. Pauline Maier, *American Scripture: Making the Declaration of Independence* (New York: Knopf, 1997), pp. 133–134.

13. Jack N. Rakove (ed.), *The Annotated U.S. Constitution and Declaration of Independence* (Boston: Belknap Press of Harvard University Press, 2009), p. 23.

14. Joseph Ellis, *American Sphinx: The Character of Thomas Jefferson* (New York: Vintage Books, 1998), p. 59.

15. Maya Jasanoff, *Liberty's Exiles* (New York: Knopf, 2011), p. 9.

16. Charles H. Metzger, *Catholics and the American Revolution: A Study in Religious Climate* (Chicago: Loyola University Press, 1962).

17. Extrapolated from U.S. Department of Defense, *Selected Manpower Statistics, FY 1982* (Washington, D.C.: U.S. Government Printing Office, 1983), Table 2-30, p. 130; and U.S. Bureau of the Census, *1985 Statistical Abstract of the United States* (Washington, D.C.: U.S. Government Printing Office, 1985), Tables 1 and 2, p. 6.

18. Jasanoff, *Liberty's Exiles,* pp. 10–12.

19. McCullough, *John Adams,* pp. 165–385.

20. Joseph T. Keenan, *The Constitution of the United States* (Homewood, Ill.: Dow-Jones-Irwin, 1975).

21. Rakove, *Annotated U.S. Constitution,* p. 30.

22. David P. Szatmary, *Shays' Rebellion: The Making of an Agrarian Insurrection* (Amherst: University of Massachusetts Press, 1980), pp. 82–102.

23. As cited in Morison, *Oxford History,* p. 304.

24. "The Call for the Federal Constitutional Convention, Feb. 21, 1787," in *The Federalist,* ed. Edward M. Earle (New York: Modern Library, 1937), p. 577.

25. Robert H. Jackson, *The Struggle for Judicial Supremacy* (New York: Knopf, 1941), p. 8.

26. John Dickinson of Delaware, as quoted in Morison, *Oxford History,* p. 270.

27. Catherine Drinker Bowen, *Miracle at Philadelphia* (Boston: Little, Brown, 1966), p. 122.

28. Forrest McDonald, *Novus Ordo Seclorum: The Intellectual Origins of the Constitution* (Lawrence: University Press of Kansas, 1985), pp. 205–209.

29. It may be overstating the case to refer to this small shift as "a compromise," as there was hardly consensus or general agreement, but that is how historians have characterized it.

30. U.S. Constitution, Article V.

31. Donald S. Lutz, "The Preamble to the Constitution of the United States," *This Constitution* 1 (September 1983): 23–30.

32. Charles O. Jones, "The Separated Presidency—Making It Work in Contemporary Politics," in *The New American Political System,* 2nd ed., ed. Anthony King (Washington, D.C.: American Enterprise Institute, 1990).

33. Charles A. Beard, *An Economic Interpretation of the Constitution of the United States* (New York: Macmillan, 1913).

34. Leonard W. Levy, *Constitutional Opinions* (New York: Oxford University Press, 1986), p. 101.

35. Robert E. Brown, *Charles Beard and the Constitution* (Princeton, N.J.: Princeton University Press, 1956); Levy, *Constitutional Opinions,* pp. 103–104; Forrest McDonald, *We the People: Economic Origins of the Constitution* (Chicago: University of Chicago Press, 1958).

36. Compare Eugene D. Genovese, *The Political Economy of Slavery: Studies in the Economics and Society of the Slave South* (Middletown, Conn.: Wesleyan University Press, 1989), and Robert William Fogel, *Without Contract or Consent: The Rise and Fall of American Slavery* (New York: Norton, 1989).

37. Robert A. Goldwin, letter to the editor, *Wall Street Journal,* 30 August 1993, p. A11.

38. Bernard Bailyn, *Faces of Revolution: Personalities and Themes in the Struggle for American Independence* (New York: Knopf, 1990), pp. 221–222.

39. Walter Berns, *The First Amendment and the Future of Democracy* (New York: Basic Books, 1976), p. 2.

40. Pauline Maier, *Ratification: The People Debate the Constitution, 1787–1788* (New York: Simon & Schuster, 2010).

41. Herbert J. Storing, ed., *The Complete Anti-Federalist,* 7 vols. (Chicago: University of Chicago Press, 1981).

42. Alexis de Tocqueville, *Democracy in America,* ed. J. P. Mayer and Max Lerner (1835–1839, reprint, New York: Harper & Row, 1966), p. 102.

43. Russell L. Caplan, *Constitutional Brinkmanship: Amending the Constitution by National Convention* (New York: Oxford University Press, 1988), p. 162.

44. Daniel Okrent, *Last Call: The Rise and Fall of Prohibition* (New York: Scribners, 2010), p. 3.

45. Seth Lipsky, *The Citizen's Constitution: An Annotated Guide* (New York: Basic Books, 2009), p. 286.

46. Richard L. Berke, "1789 Amendment Is Ratified but Now the Debate Begins," *New York Times,* 8 May 1992, p. A1.

47. The interpretation debate is fully explored in John H. Garvey and T. Alexander Aleinikoff, *Modern Constitutional Theory: A Reader,* 5th ed. (Minneapolis, Minn.: West Publishing Co., 2004). A classic statement on judicial decision making, composed before he became a member of the U.S. Supreme Court in 1932, is Benjamin N. Cardozo's *The Nature of the Judicial Process* (New Haven, Conn.: Yale University Press, 1921).

48. International Institute, *Birth of Democracy: Twelve Constitutions of Central and Eastern Europe,* 2nd ed. rev. (Amsterdam: Council of Europe, 1996).

49. Jerold L. Waltman, *Political Origins of the U.S. Income Tax* (Jackson: University Press of Mississippi, 1985), p. 10.

CHAPTER 4 / FEDERALISM / PAGES 84–113

1. Alan Dean Foster, "Garden Variety Javelinas," *New York Times,* 7 August 2010, p. WK10.

2. Daniel B. Wood, "Opinion Polls Show Broad Support for Tough Arizona Immigration Law," *The Christian Science Monitor,* 30 April 2010, http://www.csmonitor.com/USA/Society/2010/0430/Opinion-polls-show-broad-support-for-tough-Arizona-immigration-law.

3. 8 U.S.C. § 1302 and § 1304(e).

4. SB1070, http://www.azleg.gov/legtext/49leg/2r/bills/ sb1070s.pdf.

5. *United States* v. *Arizona,* 703 F.Supp.2d 980 (2010).

6. *United States* v. *Arizona,* 641 F.3d 339 (2011).

7. *Arizona* v. *United States,* 567 U.S. ___ (2012).

8. William H. Stewart, *Concepts of Federalism* (Lanham, Md.: University Press of America, 1984).

9. Martha Derthick, *Keeping the Compound Republic: Essays on American Federalism* (Washington, D.C.: Brookings Institution Press, 2001), p. 153.

10. Edward Corwin, "The Passing of Dual Federalism," *University of Virginia Law Review* 36 (1950): 1–24.

11. See Daniel J. Elazar, *The American Partnership* (Chicago: University of Chicago Press, 1962); Morton Grodzins, *The American System* (Chicago: Rand McNally, 1966).

12. James T. Patterson, *The New Deal and the States: Federalism in Transition* (Princeton, N.J.: Princeton University Press, 1969).

13. Lisa Mascaro, "Patriot Act Provisions Extended Just in Time," *Los Angeles Times,* 27 May 2011, http://articles.latimes.com/2011/may/27/nation/la-na-patriot-act-20110527.

14. John Dinan and Shama Gamkhar, "The State of American Federalism 2008–2009: The Presidential Election, the Economic Downturn, and the Consequences for Federalism," *Publius: The Journal of Federalism* 39, no. 3 (2009): 369–407.

15. *McCulloch* v. *Maryland,* 4 Wheat. 316 (1819).

16. *Dred Scott* v. *Sandford,* 19 How. 393, 426 (1857).

17. Jeff Shesol, *Supreme Power: Franklin Roosevelt vs. the Supreme Court* (New York: W.W. Norton, 2010).

18. *United States* v. *Lopez,* 514 U.S. 549 (1995).

19. *Printz* v. *United States,* 521 U.S. 898 (1997).

20. *National Federation of Independent Business* v. *Sebelius,* 567 U.S. ___ (2012).

21. *United States* v. *Morrison,* 120 S. Ct. 1740 (2000).

22. *Atkins* v. *Virginia,* 536 U.S. 304 (2002).

23. *Roper* v. *Simmons,* 343 U.S. 551 (2005).

24. Historical Tables, *Budget of the United States Government,* FY2012 (Washington, D.C.: U.S. Government Printing Office, 2012), Table 12.1.

25. *South Dakota* v. *Dole,* 483 U.S. 203 (1987).

26. Insurance Institute for Highway Safety, "DUI/DWI laws, August 2012," http://www.iihs.org/laws/dui.aspx/.

27. Terry Sanford, *Storm over the States* (New York: McGraw-Hill, 1967).

28. Quoted in Cynthia J. Bowling and Deil S. Wright, "Public Administration in the Fifty States: A Half-Century Administrative Revolution," *State and Local Government Review* 30 (Winter 1998): 52.

29. David M. Hedge, *Governance and the Changing American States* (Boulder, Colo.: Westview Press, 1998).

30. U.S. Department of Labor, Bureau of Labor Statistics, "State and Local Government, Excluding Education and Hospitals," in *Career Guide to Industries, 2010–11 Edition,* http://www.bls.gov/oco/cg/cgs042.htm.

31. Paul Manna, *School's In: Federalism and the National Education Agenda* (Washington D.C.: Georgetown University Press, 2006).

32. Internet Tax Nondiscrimination Act of 2004.

33. Joseph Zimmerman, "Congressional Preemption during the George W. Bush Administration," *Publius* 37 (2007): 432–452.

34. Ibid., p. 436.

35. Ibid., p. 432.

36. John Kincaid, "American Federalism: The Third Century," *Annals of the American Academy of Political and Social Science* 509 (1990): 139–152.

37. "Unfunded Federal Mandates," *Congressional Digest* (March 1995): 68.

38. Paul Posner, "The Politics of Coercive Federalism," *Publius* 37 (2007): 390–412.

39. National Conference of State Legislatures, "State Legislatures Face Unsettled Conditions in 2008," *NCSL News,* 14 December 2007, http://www.ncsl.org/default.aspx?tabid=16893.

40. National Conference of State Legislatures, "State Law-makers Intercept Shipment of Federal Unfunded Mandates and Cost-Shifts," *NCSL News,* 5 August 2007, http://www.ncsl.org/PressRoom/StateLawmakersInterceptShipmentofFederalUnfu/tabid/16981/Default.aspx.

41. C. David Kotok, "Cheney Lends a Hand in Iowa, Vice President Rallies GOP Voters: A Day with the V.P.," *Omaha World Herald,* 1 November 2002, p. 1A; Raymond Hernandez, "Bush Swings Through Three States to Build Support for the GOP," *New York Times,* 1 November 2002, p. A27; James Harding, "Bush Finds Time for Diplomacy on Campaign Trail," *Financial Times* (London), 25 October 2002, p. 10; John Broder, "The 2006 Elections: Democrats Take Senate," *New York Times,* 10 November 2006 (online edition).

42. U.S. Department of Justice, "Guidance Concerning Redistricting in Retrogression under Section 5 of the Voting Rights Act 42 U.S.C., 1973c," *Federal Register,* 18 January 2001; David E. Rosenbaum, "Fight over Political Map Centers on Race," *New York Times,* 21 February 2002, p. A20.

43. U.S. Census Bureau, *2007 Census of Governments,* http://www.census.gov/govs/cog/GovOrgTab03ss.html.

44. Nancy Burns, *The Formation of American Local Governments: Private Values in Public Institutions* (New York: Oxford University Press, 1994), pp. 11–13; Garrick L. Percival, Mary Currin-Percival, Shaun Bowler, and Henk van der Kolk, "Taxing, Spending, and Voting: Voter Turnout Rates in Statewide Elections in Comparative Perspective," *State and Local Government Review* 39, no. 3 (2007): 131–143.

45. CNN, "Sniper Attacks: A Trail of Terror," 2002, http://web.archive.org/web/20031208191803/www.cnn.com/SPECIALS/2002/sniper/.

46. Bowling and Wright, "Public Administration in the Fifty States," pp. 57–58.

47. SIDO maintains a presence, http://www.sidoamerica.org.

48. *U.S. Term Limits* v. *Thornton,* 514 U.S. 779 (1995).

49. Ann L. Griffiths and Karl Nerenberg (eds.), *Handbook of Federal Countries* (Montreal and Kingston, Canada: McGill-Queens University Press, 2005).

50. Information available at the *Forum of Federations,* http://www.forumfed.org/en/federalism/by_country/index.php.

CHAPTER 5 / PUBLIC OPINION AND POLITICAL SOCIALIZATION / PAGES 114–141

1. Amnesty International data reported, http://www.guardian.co.uk/news/datablog/2011/mar/29/death-penalty-countries-world.

2. Frank Newport, "In U.S., Support for Death Penalty Falls to 39-Year Low," Gallup Poll Report, 13 October 2011.

3. John Schwartz, "Death Sentences Dropped, but Executions Rose in '09," *New York Times,* 18 December 2009, p. A22.

4. Warren Weaver, Jr., "Death Penalty a 300-Year Issue in America," *New York Times,* 3 July 1976.

5. *Furman* v. *Georgia,* 408 U.S. 238 (1972).

6. *Gregg* v. *Georgia,* 248 U.S. 153 (1976).

7. U.S. Department of Justice, Bureau of Justice Statistics, "Capital Punishment 2009—Statistical Tables," Table 16, http://bjs.ojp.usdoj.gov/content/pub/pdf/cp09st.pdf.

8. Seventy percent of whites favor the death penalty, while 56 percent of African Americans oppose it. Lydia Saad, "Racial Disagreement over Death Penalty Has Varied Historically," *Gallup News Service,* 30 July 2007, http://www.gallup.com. For a discussion of the effects of the disenfranchisement of felons, see Jeff Manza and Christopher Uggen, *Locked Out: Felon Disenfranchisement and American Democracy* (New York: Oxford University Press, 2006).

9. Frank Newport, "In U.S., Support for Death Penalty Falls to 39-Year Low."

10. "Facts about the Death Penalty, January 8, 2010," www.deathpenaltyinfo.org.

11. For arguments concerning the death penalty, pro and con, see http://deathpenalty.procon.org/view.answers.php?questionID=983.

12. Gallup Poll, 6–9 October 2011, http://www.pollingreport.com/crime.htm; and Lydia Saad, "Americans Hold Firm to Support for Death Penalty," *Gallup Report*, 17 November 2008.

13. Death Penalty Information Center, http://www.deathpenaltyinfo.org/methods-execution.

14. David Masci, "An Impassioned Debate: An Overview of the Death Penalty in America," Pew Forum on Religion and Public Life, 19 December 2007, http://pewforum.org/docs/?DocID=270.

15. George Gallup, *The Gallup Poll: Public Opinion 1991* (Lanham, Md.: Rowman and Littlefield, 1992), p. 132.

16. E. Wayne Carp, "If Pollsters Had Been Around during the American Revolution" (letter to the editor), *New York Times,* 17 July 1993, p. 10.

17. "Government by the People," results of the 2001 Henry J. Kaiser Family Foundation/Public Perspective Polling and Democracy Survey, http://www.ropercenter.uconn.edu/pubper/pdf/pp12_4b.pdf.

18. Sidney Verba, "The Citizen as Respondent: Sample Surveys and American Democracy," *American Political Science Review* 90 (March 1996): 3. For more on the relationship between Supreme Court decisions and public opinion, see Nathan Persity, Jack Citrin, and Patrick Egan (eds.), *Public Opinion and Constitutional Controversy* (New York: Oxford University Press, 2008). For a historical discussion of the search for the "average" citizen, see Sarah E. Igo, *The Averaged American: Surveys, Citizens, and the Making of a Mass Public* (Cambridge, Mass.: Harvard University Press, 2007).

19. For more on the relationship between Supreme Court decisions and public opinion, see Nathan Persity, Jack Citrin, and Patrick Egan (eds.), *Public Opinion and Constitutional Controversy* (New York: Oxford University Press, 2008).

20. Linda Lyons, "The Gallup Brain: Prayer in Public Schools," Gallup News Service, 10 December 2002, http://www.gallup.com/poll/7393/Gallup-Brain-Prayer-Public-Schools.aspx.

21. Lydia Saad, "Americans Issue Split Decision on Healthcare Ruling," Gallup Poll Report, 29 June 2012.

22. Warren E. Miller and Santa A. Traugott, *American National Election Studies Sourcebook, 1952–1986* (Cambridge, Mass.: Harvard University Press, 1989), pp. 94–95; and Richard Niemi, John Mueller, and Tom Smith, *Trends in Public Opinion: A Compendium of Survey Data* (Westport, Conn.: Greenwood Press, 1989), p. 19.

23. Lydia Saad, "U.S. Political Ideology Stable with Conservatives Leading," Gallup Poll Report, 1 August 2011.

24. Jeffrey M. Jones, "Record High 86% Approve of Black-White Marriages," Gallup Poll Report, 12 September 2011.

25. Steven A. Peterson, *Political Behavior: Patterns in Everyday Life* (Newbury Park, Calif.: Sage, 1990), pp. 28–29. See also David O. Sears and Sheri Levy, "Childhood and Adult Political Development," in *Oxford Handbook of Political Psychology,* ed. David O. Sears, Leonie Huddy, and Robert Jervis (New York: Oxford University Press, 2003).

26. Stephen E. Frantzich, *Political Parties in the Technological Age* (New York: Longman, 1989), p. 152. Frantzich presents a table showing that more than 60 percent of children in homes in which both parents have the same party preference will adopt that preference. When parents are divided, the children tend to be divided among Democrats, Republicans, and independents.

27. Recent research on twins separately raised confirms that party identification "is driven almost entirely by familial socialization," but there appears to be a genetic propensity for twins "to be intense or apathetic" regardless of which party they were raised to support. See Peter K. Hatemi et al., "Is There a 'Party' in Your Genes?" *Political Research Quarterly* 62 (September 2009): 584–600.

28. In a panel study of parents and high school seniors in 1965 and in 1973, some years after their graduation, Jennings and Niemi found that 57 percent of children shared their parents' party identification in 1965, but only 47 percent did by 1973. See Jennings and Niemi, *Political Character,* pp. 90–91. See also Robert C. Luskin, John P. McIver, and Edward G. Carmines, "Issues and the Transmission of Partisanship," *American Journal of Political Science* 33 (May 1989): 440–458. They found that children are more likely to shift between partisanship and independence than to "convert" to the other party. When conversion occurs, it is more likely to be based on economic issues than on social issues.

29. Cliff Zukin et al., *A New Engagement: Political Participation, Civic Life, and the Changing American Citizen* (New York: Oxford University Press, 2006), pp. 142–144.

30. Janie S. Steckenrider and Neal E. Cutler, "Aging and Adult Political Socialization: The Importance of Roles and Transitions," in *Political Learning in Adulthood: A Sourcebook of Theory and Research,* ed. Roberta S. Sigel (Chicago: University of Chicago Press, 1989), pp. 56–88.

31. One study found that additional media coverage of political issues did not change the impact of education on political knowledge. See Benjamin Highton, "Political Knowledge Gaps and Changes in the Information Environment: The Case of Education" (paper presented at the annual meeting of the Midwest Political Science Association, Chicago, 2008).

32. The American National Election Studies are jointly done by Stanford University and the University of Michigan, with funding by the National Science Foundation.

33. Other scholars have analyzed opinion on abortion using six questions from the General Social Survey. See R. Michael Alvarez and John Brehm, "American Ambivalence toward Abortion Policy," *American Journal of Political Science* 39 (1995): 1055–1082; and Elizabeth Adell Cook, Ted G. Jelen, and Clyde Wilcox, *Between Two Absolutes: Public Opinion and the Politics of Abortion* (Boulder, Colo.: Westview Press, 1992).

34. Although some people view the politics of abortion as "single-issue" politics, the issue has broader political significance. In their book on the subject, Cook, Jelen, and Wilcox say, "Although embryonic life is one important value in the abortion debate, it is not the only value at stake." They contend that the politics is tied to alternative sexual relationships and traditional roles of women in the home, which are "social order" issues. See *Between Two Absolutes,* pp. 8–9.

35. Russell J. Dalton, *The Good Citizen* (Washington, D.C.: Congressional Quarterly Press, 2008), Chap. 5.

36. Ibid., p. 50.

37. For years, scholars have been debating whether the increasing wealth in industrialized societies is replacing class conflict with conflict over values. See the exchange between Ronald Inglehart and Scott C. Flanagan, "Value Change in Industrial Societies," *American Political Science Review* 81 (December 1987): 1289–1319.

38. Nathan Glazer, "The Structure of Ethnicity," *Public Opinion* 7 (October–November 1984): 4.

39. U.S. Census Bureau, International Data Base, Table 094, http://www.census.gov/ipc/www.idbprint.html.

40. U.S. Census Bureau, "U.S. Population Projections," http://www.census.gov/population/www/projections/summarytables.html.

41. U.S. Census Bureau, American Fact Finder, Section on Race and Ethnicity, http://factfinder.census.gov/servlet/GRTSelectServlet?ds_name-ACS_2007_1YR_G00_a_lang=ena_ts=281548554033.

42. Michael Dawson, *Black Visions: The Roots of Contemporary African American Political Ideologies* (Chicago: University of Chicago Press, 2001); John Garcia, *Latino Politics in America* (Lanham, Md.: Rowman & Littlefield, 2003); Thomas Kim, *The Racial Logic of Politics: Asian Americans and Party Competition* (Philadelphia: Temple University Press, 2007); Pei-te Lien, M. Margaret Conway, and Janelle Wong, The *Politics of Asian Americans* (New York: Routledge, 2004); and Katherine Tate, *Black Faces in the Mirror: African Americans and Their Representatives in the U.S. Congress* (Princeton, N.J.: Princeton University Press, 2003).

43. Glazer, "Structure of Ethnicity," p. 5; and Dennis Chong and Dukhong Kim, "The Experiences and Effects of Economic Status among Racial and Ethnic Minorities," *American Political Science Review* 100 (August 2006): 335–351.

44. Jeffrey M. Jones, "Only 4 in 10 Americans Satisfied with Treatment of Immigrants," 15 August 2007, http://www.gallup.com.

45. Frank Newport, "This Christmas, 78% of Americans Identify as Christian," Gallup Poll Report, 24 December 2009, http://www.gallup.com/poll/124793/This-Christmas-78-Americans-Identify-Christian.aspx.

46. See David C. Leege and Lyman A. Kellstedt (eds.), *Rediscovering the Religious Factor in American Politics* (Armonk, N.Y.: M. E. Sharpe, 1993); and "Many Americans Uneasy with Mix of Religion and Politics," Pew Forum on Religion and Public Life, 24 August 2006, http://pewforum.org/docs/DocID=153.

47. Some scholars have argued that Americans are not as polarized as the news media would have us think. See Morris P. Fiorina, *Culture War? The Myth of a Polarized America* (Upper Saddle River, N.J.: Longman, 2004).

48. Fact Sheet, "The Gender Gap: Attitudes on Public Policy Issues," Center for American Women and Politics, Eagleton Institute of Politics, Rutgers, August 1997, http://www.cawp.rutgers.edu.

49. When asked to describe the parties and candidates in the 1956 election, only about 12 percent of respondents volunteered responses that contained ideological terms (such as *liberal, conservative,* and *capitalism*). Most respondents (42 percent) evaluated the parties and candidates in terms of "benefits to groups" (farmers, workers, or businesspeople, for example). Others (24 percent) spoke more generally about "the nature of the times" (for example, inflation, unemployment, and the threat of war). Finally, a good portion of the sample (22 percent) gave answers that contained no classifiable issue content. See Angus Campbell, Philip E. Converse, Warren E. Miller, and Donald E. Stokes, *The American Voter* (New York: Wiley, 1960), Chap. 10.

50. Marjorie Connelly, "A 'Conservative' Is (Fill in the Blank)," *New York Times,* 3 November 1996, sec. 4, p. 5.

51. American National Election Study, 2008.

52. However, citizens can have ideologically consistent attitudes toward candidates and perceptions about domestic issues without thinking about politics in explicitly liberal and conservative terms. See Jacoby, "The Structure of Ideological Thinking."

53. A relationship between liberalism and political tolerance was found by John L. Sullivan et al., "The Sources of Political Tolerance: A Multivariate Analysis," *American Political Science Review* 75 (March 1981): 102. See also Robinson, "Ups and Downs," pp. 13–15.

54. Herbert Asher, *Presidential Elections and American Politics,* 5th ed. (Upper Saddle River, N.J.: International Thomson Publishing Group, 1997). Asher also constructs a two-dimensional framework, distinguishing between "traditional New Deal" issues and "new lifestyle" issues.

55. Milton Rokeach also proposed a two-dimensional model of political ideology grounded in the terminal values of freedom and equality. See *The Nature of Human Values* (New York: Free Press, 1973), especially Chap. 6. Rokeach found that positive and negative references to the two values permeate the writings of socialists, communists, fascists, and conservatives and clearly differentiate the four bodies of writing from one another (pp. 173–174). However, Rokeach built his two-dimensional model around only the values of freedom and equality; he did not deal with the question of freedom versus order.

56. In our framework, opposition to abortion is classified as a communitarian position. However, the communitarian movement led by Amitai Etzioni adopted no position on abortion (personal communication from Vanessa Hoffman by e-mail, in reply to a query of 5 February 1996).

57. William S. Maddox and Stuart A. Lilie, *Beyond Liberal and Conservative: Reassessing the Political Spectrum* (Washington, D.C.: Cato Institute, 1984), p. 68. From 1993 to 1996, the Gallup Organization, in conjunction with CNN and *USA Today,* asked national samples two questions: (1) whether individuals or government should solve our country's problems and (2) whether the government should promote traditional values. Gallup constructed a similar ideological typology from responses to these questions and found a similar distribution of the population into four groups. See Gallup's "Final Top Line" for 12–15 January 1996, pp. 30–31.

58. See W. Russell Neuman, The *Paradox of Mass Politics: Knowledge and Opinion in the American Electorate* (Cambridge, Mass.: Harvard University Press, 1986), p. 81. See also Aaron Wildavsky, "Choosing Preferences by Constructing Institutions: A Cultural Theory of Preference Formation," *American Political Science Review* 81 (March 1987): 13.

59. The same conclusion was reached in a major study of British voting behavior. See Hilde T. Himmelweit et al., *How Voters Decide* (New York: Academic Press, 1981), pp. 138–141. See also Wildavsky, "Choosing Preferences," p. 13; and Stanley Feldman and Christopher Johnston, "Understanding Political Ideology" (paper presented at the annual meeting of the American Political Science Association, Toronto, Canada, 2009).

60. Michael X. Delli Carpini and Scott Keeter, *What Americans Know about Politics and Why It Matters* (New Haven, Conn.: Yale University Press, 1996).

61. Ibid., p. 269. For more on this topic, see Scott L. Althaus, *Collective Preferences in Democratic Politics: Opinion Surveys and the Will of the People* (New York: Cambridge University Press, 2003).

62. http://pewresearch.org/politicalquiz/.

63. Lydia Saad, "Most Americans Believe Crime in U.S. Is Worsening," Gallup Poll, 31 October 2011.

64. Federal Bureau of Investigation, *Crime in the United States,* 2011, http://www.fbi.gov/news/stories/2011/september/crime_091911/crime_091911/.

65. Rubén Rosario, "30 Years of National Crime Data—and Results Might Surprise You," *Pioneer Press,* 25 September 2011, p. B1.

66. Alexia Cooper and Erica Smith, "Homicide Trends in the United States, 1980-2008," 16 November 2011, Bureau of Justice Statistics, http://www.bjs.gov/index.cfm?ty=pbdetail&iid=2221.

67. Program for Public Consultation, "How the American Public Would Deal with the Budget Deficit," 3 February 2011, http://www.public-consultation.org/pdf/Budget_Feb11_quaire.pdf.

68. Benjamin I. Page and Robert Y. Shapiro, *The Rational Public* (Chicago: University of Chicago Press, 1992).

69. Stephan Lewandowsky, Werner Stritzke, Klaus Oberauer, and Michael Morales, "Memory for Fact, Fiction, and Misinformation: The Iraq War 2003," *Psychological Science* 16 (March 2005): 190–195.

70. Self-interest is often posed as the major alternative to choice based on general orientations such as political ideology and moral values. A significant literature exists on the limitations of self-interest in explaining political life. See Jane J. Mansbridge (ed.), *Beyond Self-Interest* (Chicago: University of Chicago Press, 1990). A literature is developing on the role of emotions in the process of political judgment. See G. E. Marcus, W. R. Neuman, and M. Mackuen, *Affective Intelligence and Political Judgment* (Chicago: University of Chicago Press, 2000); and George E. Marcus, *The Sentimental Citizen: Emotion in Democratic Politics* (University Park: Pennsylvania State University Press, 2002).

71. Richard D. Dixon et al., "Self-Interest and Public Opinion toward Smoking Policies," *Public Opinion Quarterly* 55 (1991): 241–254; David O. Sears and Jack Citrin, *Tax Revolt: Something for Nothing in California* (Cambridge, Mass.: Harvard University Press, 1985); and Robin Wolpert and James Gimpel, "Self-Interest, Symbiotic Politics, and Public Attitudes toward Gun Control," *Political Behavior* 20 (1998): 241–262.

72. Wildavsky, "Choosing Preferences," pp. 3–21.

73. Henry Brady and Paul Sniderman, "Attitude Attribution: A Group Basis for Political Reasoning," *American Political Science Review* 79 (1985): 1061–1078; Samuel Popkin, *The Reasoning Voter,* 2nd ed. (Chicago: University of Chicago Press, 1994); and P. Sniderman, R. Brody, and P. Tetlock, *Reasoning and Choice* (Cambridge: Cambridge University Press, 1991). Psychologists have tended to emphasize the distorting effects of heuristics. See D. Kahneman, P. Slovic, and A. Tversky (eds.), *Judgment under Uncertainty: Heuristics and Biases* (Cambridge: Cambridge University Press, 1982); and R. Nisbett and L. Ross, *Human Inference: Strategies and Shortcomings of Social Judgment* (Englewood Cliffs, N.J.: Prentice-Hall, 1980).

74. Political psychologists refer to beliefs that guide information processing as opinion "schemas." See Pamela Johnston Conover and Stanley Feldman, "How People Organize the Political World: A Schematic Model," *American Journal of Political Science* 28 (February 1984): 95–127; and M. Lodge and K. M. McGraw, *Political Judgment: Structure and Process* (Ann Arbor: University of Michigan Press, 1995). For an excellent review of schema structures in contemporary psychology, especially as they relate to political science, see Reid Hastie, "A Primer of Information-Processing Theory for the Political

Scientist," in *Political Cognition,* ed. Richard R. Lau and David O. Sears (Hillsdale, N.J.: Erlbaum, 1986), pp. 11–39.

75. Pew Center for the People and the Press, "Religion and Politics: Contention and Consensus," 24 July 2003, http://people-press.org/reports/display.php3?ReportID=189.

76. J. Kuklinski and N. L. Hurley, "On Hearing and Interpreting Political Messages," *Journal of Politics* 56 (1994): 729–751.

77. On framing, see Dennis Chong and James N. Druckman, "Framing Public Opinion in Competitive Democracies," *American Political Science Review* 101 (November 2007): 637–655; James N. Druckman, "Political Preference Formation: Competition, Deliberation, and the (Ir)relevance of Framing Effects," *American Political Science Review* 98 (November 2004): 671–686; and Michael W. Wagner, "The Utility of Staying on Message: Competing Partisan Frames and Public Awareness of Elite Differences on Political Issues," *The Forum* 5, no. 3 (2007), http://www.be-press.com/forum/vol15/iss3/art8. On political spin, see Lawrence R. Jacobs and Robert Y. Shapiro, *Politicians Don't Pander* (Chicago: University of Chicago Press, 2000).

78. Benjamin I. Page, Robert Y. Shapiro, and Glenn R. Dempsey, "What Moves Public Opinion?" *American Political Science Review* 81 (March 1987): 23–43.

79. Michael Margolis and Gary A. Mauser, *Manipulating Public Opinion: Essays on Public Opinion as a Dependent Variable* (Pacific Grove, Calif.: Brooks/Cole, 1989).

CHAPTER 6 / THE MEDIA / PAGES 142–171

1. "Obama Declares He's Running for President," CNN.com, 10 February 2007.

2. Jessica Yellin, "With Short Video, Obama Launches Bid for Re-election," CNN.com, 5 April 2011.

3. Alex Roarty, "Gingrich to Announce Candidacy Wednesday via Facebook, Twitter," nationaljournal.com, 11 May 2011; and Catalina Camia, "Newt Gingrich Jumps into Presidential Race," *USA Today,* 11 May 2011.

4. Tom Price, "Journalism Standards in the Internet Age," *CQ Researcher,* v. 20–35, 8 October 2010, p. 824.

5. Alex S. Jones, *Losing the News,* http://losingthenews.com/.

6. Richard Davis, *Typing Politics: The Role of Blogs in American Politics* (New York: Oxford University Press, 2009); Tom Price, "Future of Journalism," *CQ Researcher* 19, no. 12 (27 March 2009): 273–295; and Pew Project for Excellence in Journalism, http://www.stateofthemedia.org/2009/narrative_online_audience.php?media=58:cat=2.

7. See Markus Prior, *Post-Broadcast Democracy* (New York: Cambridge University Press, 2007).

8. Gil Kaufman, "Lady Gaga Visits with White House to Discuss Bullying," 7 December 2011, http://www.mtv.com.

9. "Michael Moore's Sicko: Broad Reach and Impact Even without the Popcorn?" Press release from Kaiser Family Foundation, 27 August 2007, http://www.kff.org/kaiserpolls/pomr082707nr.cfm.

10. See Prior, *Post-Broadcast Democracy*; and Bill Kovach and Tom Rosenstiel, *Blur: How to Know What's True in the Age of Information Overload* (New York: Bloomsbury, 2010).

11. S. N. D. North, The *Newspaper and Periodical Press* (Washington, D.C.: U.S. Government Printing Office, 1884), p. 27. This source provides much of the information reported here about newspapers and magazines before 1880. Also see Jonathan Ladd, *Why Americans Hate the Media and How It Matters* (Princeton, N.J.: Princeton University Press, 2011).

12. Editor & Publisher, *International Year Book, 2009* (New York: Editor & Publisher, 2009), p. xi.

13. Harold W. Stanley and Richard G. Niemi (eds.), *Vital Statistics on American Politics, 2011–2012* (Washington, D.C.: CQ Press, 2012), p. 160. For a brief history of the newspaper business, see Paul E. Steiger, "Read All about It: How Newspapers Got into Such a Fix and Where They Go from Here," *Wall Street Journal,* 29–30 December 2007, p. 1.

14. See Ladd, *Why Americans Hate the Media and How It Matters,* pp. 48–52.

15. Audit Bureau of Circulations, http://www.accessabc.com/.

16. See, for example, Felix Salmon, "The New York Times Paywall Is Working," *Columbia Journalism Review,* 26 July 2011.

17. On framing in the media, see Stephen D. Reese, Oscar H. Gandy, Jr., and August E. Grant (eds.), *Framing Public Life: Perspectives on Media and Our Understanding of the Social World* (Mahwah, N.J.: Erlbaum, 2001). More generally on how leaders mediate public deliberation on issues, see Doris A. Graber, *Media Power in Politics,* 7th ed. (Washington, D.C.: CQ Press, 2005).

18. "Magazines: A Shake-out for News Weeklies," *The State of the News Media, 2011,* http://www.stateofthenewsmedia.org.

19. "Broadcast Station Totals as of September 30, 2011," Federal Communications Commission, http://transition.fcc.gov/Daily_Releases/Daily_Business/2011/db1103/DOC-310819A1.pdf.

20. See radio statistics at *The State of the News Media 2011,* http://www.stateofthenewsmedia.org.

21. Ibid.

22. David Barker and Kathleen Knight, "Political Talk Radio and Public Opinion," *Public Opinion Quarterly* 64 (Summer 2000): 149–170; and David C. Barker, *Rushed to Judgment: Talk Radio, Persuasion, and American Political Behavior* (New York: Columbia University Press, 2003).

23. Dana R. Ulloth, Peter L. Klinge, and Sandra Eells, *Mass Media: Past, Present, Future* (St. Paul, Minn.: West, 1983), p. 278.

24. "TV Basics," Television Bureau of Advertising, http://www.tvb.org/media/file/TV_Basics.pdf; and "Frequently Asked Questions," Corporation for Public Broadcasting, http://www.cpb.org/aboutpb/faq/stations.html.

25. Douglas Ahers, "News Consumption and the New Electronic Media," *Harvard International Journal of Press/Politics* 11 (Winter 2006): 29–52; Bill Carter, "CNN Last in TV News on Cable," *New York Times,* 27 October 2009, http://www.nytimes.com/2009/10/27/business/media/27rating.html?emc=etal; and Prior, *Post-Broadcast Democracy.*

26. "January 2012 Web Server Survey," Netcraft.com, http://news.netcraft.com/archives/2012/01/03/january-2012-web-server-survey.html; Internet World Stats, "Internet Usage Statistics," http://www.internetworldstats.com/stats.htm.

27. "Online: Key Questions Facing Digital News," *State of the News Media, 2011;* Aaron Smith, "Smartphone Adoption and Usage," Report by Pew Internet and American Life Project, 11 June 2011, http://pewinternet.org/Reports/2011/Smartphones.aspx; and Kristen Purcell, "Half of Adult Cell Phone Owners Have Apps on Their Phones," Report by Pew Internet and American Life Project, 2 November 2011, http://pewinternet.org/Reports/2011/Apps-update.aspx.

28. "Who's Online: Internet User Demographics," Pew Internet and American Life Project, April 2012 survey, http://www.pewinternet.org.

29. "Press Widely Criticized but Trusted More than Other Information Sources," Report by Pew Research Center for People and the Press, 22 September 2011.

30. Richard Davis, *Typing Politics* (New York: Oxford University Press, 2009); and Technorati State of the Blogosphere 2008, http://technorati.com/blogging/feature/state-of-the-blogosphere-2008.

31. Farah Stockman, "State Dept. Spokesman Quits Over Remarks," *New York Times,* 14 March 2011; Mike Allen and Josh Gerstein, "P.J. Crowley Resigns over Manning Remark," *Los Angeles Times,* 14 March 2011; and Kristen Purcell et al., "Understanding the Participatory News Consumer," Report from Pew Internet and American Life Project, 1 March 2010, http://www.pewinternet.org/Reports/2010/Online-News.aspx.

32. Katharine Q. Seelye, "Take That, Mr. Newsman!" *New York Times,* 1 January 2006, p. C1; and David Coursey, "You Be the Judge: Are Bloggers Journalists?" forbes.com, 2 January 2012.

33. Matthew Hindman, *The Myth of Digital Democracy* (Princeton, N.J.: Princeton University Press, 2009); and Diana Mutz and Lori Young, "Communication and Public Opinion," *Public Opinion Quarterly* 75 (December 2011): 1018–1044.

34. Belinda Luscombe, "The HuffPo Gets to Question Obama-Making History," *Time,* 10 February 2009, http://www.time.com/time/nation/article/0,8599,1878625,00.html.

35. Cecilia Kang, "Obama to Host Twitter Town Hall," *New York Times,* 5 July 2011.

36. Note that in 2010, Yahoo! News began offering some original news reporting in addition to its usual aggregation.

37. Jeremy Page, "Beijing Blocks Protest Reports," *Wall Street Journal,* 11 January 2011; and Andrew Jacobs and Jonathan Ansfield, "Nobel Peace Prize Given to Jailed Dissident," *New York Times,* 8 October 2010.

38. "Frequently Asked Questions," Corporation for Public Broadcasting, http://www.cpb.org/aboutpb/faq/stations.html.

39. Doris A. Graber, *Mass Media and American Politics,* 8th ed. (Washington, D.C.: CQ Press, 2010), pp. 84–87. See also W. Lance Bennett, *News: The Politics of Illusion,* 3rd ed. (White Plains, N.Y.: Longman, 1996), Chap. 2.

40. John H. McManus, *Market-Driven Journalism: Let the Citizen Beware?* (Thousand Oaks, Calif.: Sage, 1994), p. 85.

41. "Americans Spending More Time Following the News," Report by Pew Research Center for People and the Press, 12 September 2010, http://www.people-press.org/files/legacy-pdf/652.pdf.

42. Ibid.

43. David D. Kurplus, "Bucking a Trend in Local Television News," *Journalism* 4 (2003): 77–94.

44. Bill Carter and Brian Stelter, "In NBC Universal Bid, Comcast Seeks an Empire," *New York Times,* 1 October 2009, http://www.nytimes.com/2009/10/02/business/media/02nbc.html.

45. "Network: By the Numbers," *State of the News Media,* 2011.

46. Thomas E. Patterson, *Doing Well and Doing Good: How Soft News and Critical Journalism Are Shrinking the News Audience and Weakening Democracy—and What News Outlets Can Do about It* (Cambridge, Mass.: Harvard University, Joan Shorenstein Center for Press, Politics, and Public Policy, 2000), pp. 2–5.

47. Editor & Publisher, *International Year Book,* 2009.

48. Price, "Future of Journalism."

49. "Who Owns What," *Columbia Journalism Review,* http://www.cjr.org/resources/index.php.

50. Graber, *Mass Media and American Politics,* pp. 41–43.

51. Matthew Rose and Joe Flint, "Behind Media-Ownership Fight, an Old Power Struggle Is Raging," *Wall Street Journal,* 15 October 2003, p. 1. In 2003 the Federal Communications Commission (FCC) voted to increase the percentage share of the market to 45 percent. In 2007, the FCC ruled that no company can control more than 30 percent of the cable television market and relaxed newspaper-broadcast cross-ownership rules in the nation's twenty largest media markets. See Stephen Labaton, "F.C.C. Reshapes Rules Limiting Media Industry," *New York Times,* 19 December 2007, p. A1.

52. Jennifer Lee, "On Minot, N.D., Radio, a Single Corporate Voice," *New York Times,* 31 March 2003, p. C7.

53. For a clear summary of very complex developments, see Robert B. Horowitz, "Communications Regulations in Protecting the Public Interest," in The *Institutions of American Democracy: The Press,* ed. Geneva Overholser and Kathleen Hall Jamieson (New York: Oxford University Press, 2005), pp. 284–302.

54. Graber, *Mass Media and American Politics,* p. 42.

55. Graber, *Mass Media and American Politics,* p. 342.

56. Edward Wyatt, "House Votes Against 'Net Neutrality'," *New York Times,* 8 April 2011; and Jim Puzzanghera, "Senate Votes to Retain Net Neutrality Regulations," *Los Angeles Times,* 11 November 2011.

57. Jared Sandberg, "Federal Judges Block Censorship on the Internet," *Wall Street Journal,* 13 June 1996, p. B1.

58. Robert Entman, *Democracy without Citizens: Media and the Decay of American Politics* (New York: Oxford University Press, 1989), pp. 103–108; and John Leland, "Why the Right Rules the Radio Waves," *New York Times,* 8 December 2003, sec. 4, p. 7.

59. Wes Allison, "Are Democrats Really Trying to Hush Rush?" *St. Petersburg Times,* 20 February 2009, p. 1A.

60. See Markus Prior, *Post-Broadcast Democracy*; and Jason Gainous and Kevin Wagner, *Rebooting American Politics: The Internet Revolution* (Lanham, Md.: Rowman and Littlefield, 2011). For a discussion of the prevalence and possible consequence of incivility among fragmented media sources, see Sarah Sobieraj and Jeffrey M. Berry, "From Incivility to Outrage: Political Discourse in Blogs, Talk Radio, and Cable News," *Political Communication* 28 (2011): 19–41.

61. For an alternative view of the functions of the media, see Graber, *Mass Media and American Politics,* pp. 5–11.

62. Harold W. Stanley and Richard G. Niemi (eds.), *Vital Statistics on American Politics, 2011–2012* (Washington, D.C.: CQ Press, 2012), p. 161.

63. For a view from the point of view of a reporter who covered Washington for over sixty years, see Helen Thomas, *Watch-dogs of Democracy? The Waning Washington Press Corps and How It Has Failed the Public* (New York: Scribner, 2006).

64. For a discussion of the Bush years, see Scott McClellan, *What Happened: Inside the Bush White House and Washington's Culture of Deception* (New York: Public Affairs Books, 2008). For a discussion of Obama, see Adriel Bettelheim, "Meeting the Press Less Than Half Way," *CO Weekly Online,* 20 July 2009, pp. 1700–1701, http://library.cqpress.com/cqweekly/weeklyreport1 11-000003170492.

65. Patrick Sellers, *Cycles of Spin: Strategic Communication in the U.S. Congress* (New York: Cambridge University Press: 2010), p. 198.

66. Pew Research Center's Project for Excellence in Journalism, *The State of the News Media 2009.*

67. Warren Weaver, "C-SPAN on the Hill: 10 Years of Gavel to Gavel," *New York Times,* 28 March 1989, p. 10; and Francis X. Clines, "C-SPAN Inventor Offers More Politics Up Close," *New York Times,* 31 March 1996, p. 11.

68. ActBlue, "Alan Grayson," http://www.actblue.com/entity/fundraisers/18665.

69. Dan Eggen and T.W. Farnam, "Michelle Bachmann, Others, Raise Millions for Political Campaigns with 'Money Blurts'," *Washington Post,* 19 June 2011.

70. Jon Garfunkel, "The New Gatekeepers Part 1: Changing the Guard," *Civilities: Media Structures Research,* 4 April 2005, http://civilities.net/TheNewGatekeepers-Changing.

71. Gainous and Wagner, *Rebooting American Politics.*

72. "Press Going Too Easy on Bush," *The State of the News Media 2007,* http://www.stateofthemedia.org.

73. Graber, *Mass Media and American Politics,* p. 259. For weekly content analysis of news topics, see the Project for Excellence in Journalism's "News Coverage Index," http://www.journalism.org.

74. "Summary of Findings: Modest Interest in 2008 Campaign News," Pew Research Center for the People and the Press, 23 October 2007, http://people-press.org.

75. Stephen J. Farnsworth and S. Robert Lichter, "The Nightly News Nightmare Revisited: Network Television's Coverage of the 2004 Presidential Election" (paper presented at the annual meeting of the Washington, D.C. American Political Science Association, 2005); "Contest Lacks Content," *Media Tenor* 1 (2005): 12–15; Cristina Alsina, Philip John Davies, and Bruce Gronbeck, "Preference Poll Stories in the Last 2 Weeks of Campaign 2000," *American Behavioral Scientist* 44, no. 12 (2001): 2288–2305; C. Anthony Broh, "Horse-Race Journalism: Reporting the Polls in the 1976 Presidential Election," *Public Opinion Quarterly* 44 (1980): 514–529; and David Paletz, Jonathan Short, Helen Baker, Barbara Cookman Campbell, Richard Cooper, and Rochelle Oeslander, "Polls in the Media: Content, Credibility, and Consequences," *Public Opinion Quarterly* 44 (1980): 495–513.

76. "Press Widely Criticized but Trusted More than Other Information Sources," Pew Research Center for People and the Press, http://pewresearch.org/pubs/2104/news-organizations-inaccurate-trust-cable-news-press-media-coverage.

77. "Internet Gains on Television as Public's Main News Source," report from Pew Research Center for People and the Press, 4 January 2011.

78. Pew Research Center for the People and the Press, "What the Public Knows—In Words and Pictures," 7 November 2011, http://www.people-press.org/2011/11/07/what-the-public-knows-in-words-and-pictures/1/.

79. Jeffrey Jones, "Gallup Quizzes Americans on Knowledge of World Leaders," 20 February 2006, Gallup News Service, http://www.gallup.com.

80. W. Russell Neuman, Marion R. Just, and Ann N. Crigler, *Common Knowledge: News and the Construction of Political Meaning* (Chicago: University of Chicago Press, 1992), p. 10. See also Debra Gersh Hernandez, "Profile of the News Consumer," *Editor & Publisher,* 18 January 1997, pp. 6, 7. For a more optimistic assessment of television's instructional value, see Doris A. Graber, *Processing Politics: Learning from Television in the Internet Age* (Chicago: University of Chicago Press, 2001), esp. pp. 120–128. Another negative note

is sounded by Alan B. Krueger, "Economic Scene," *New York Times,* 1 April 2004, p. C2.

81. James N. Druckman, "Media Matter: How Newspapers and Television News Cover Campaigns and Influence Voters," *Political Communication* 22 (October–December 2005): 463–481. For a complementary study finding that television news has little effect on campaign learning, see Stephen C. Craig, James G. Kane, and Jason Gainous, "Issue-Related Learning in a Gubernatorial Campaign: A Case Study," *Political Communication* 22 (October–December 2005): 483–503.

82. Diana Mutz, "Effects of 'In-Your-Face' Television Discourse on Perceptions of a Legitimate Opposition," *American Political Science Review* 101 (November 2007): 621–635.

83. James M. Avery, "Videomalaise or Virtuous Circle? The Influence of the News Media on Political Trust," *International Journal of Press/Politics* 14, no. 4 (2009): 410–433.

84. Jennifer Jerit, "Understanding the Knowledge Gap: The Role of Experts and Journalists," *The Journal of Politics* 71, no. 2 (2009): 444.

85. Jody Baumgartner and Jonathan Morris,"The Daily Show Effect: Candidate Evaluations, Efficacy, and American Youth," *American Politics Research* 34 (2006): 341–367; Michael Parkin, "Taking Late Night Comedy Seriously," *Political Research Quarterly* 63 (2010): 3–15; Xiaoxia Cao, "Hearing It from Jon Stewart," *International Journal of Public Opinion Research* 22 (2010): 26–46; Matthew A. Baum, "Sex, Lies, and War: How Soft News Brings Foreign Policy to the Inattentive Public," *American Political Science Review* 96 (2002): 91–110; and Matthew A. Baum and Angela S. Jamison, "The Oprah Effect: How Soft News Helps Inattentive Citizens Vote Consistently," *Journal of Politics* 68 (2006): 946–959.

86. Mutz and Young, "Communication and Public Opinion."

87. Farnsworth and Lichter, in "The Nightly News Night mare Revisited" (pp. 16–21), consider three models of media influence: (1) "hypodermic needle"—quick effect, like a shot; (2) "minimal effects"—the two-step flow, which may work only as the media focus on the activity; and (3) "more-than-minimal effects," primarily through setting the agenda for discussion.

88. Lydia Saad, "Obama's Approval Bump Hasn't Transferred to 2012 Prospects," http://www.gallup.com, 11 May 2011, accessed on 6 January 2012.

89. Maxwell McCombs, "The Agenda-Setting Function of the Press," in Overholser and Jamieson, *Institutions of American Democracy,* pp. 156–168.

90. Danilo Yanich, "Kids, Crime, and Local TV News," report of the Local TV News Media Project, January (Newark: University of Delaware, 2005). See also Jeremy H. Lipschultz and Michael L. Hilt, *Crime and Local Television News: Dramatic, Breaking, and Live from the Scene* (Mahwah, N.J.: Erlbaum, 2002).

91. Lipschultz and Hilt, *Crime and Local Television News,* p. 2.

92. Lawrie Mifflin, "Crime Falls, but Not on TV," *New York Times,* 6 July 1997, sec. 4, p. 4.

93. Joseph E. Uscinski, "When Does the Public's Issue Agenda Affect the Media's Issue Agenda (and Vice Versa)? Developing a Framework for Media-Public Influence," *Social Science Quarterly* 80, no. 4 (2009): 796–815.

94. John Tierney, "Talk Shows Prove Key to White House," *New York Times,* 21 October 2002, p. A13.

95. Samuel Kernell, *Going Public: New Strategies of Presidential Leadership,* 4th ed. (Washington D.C.: CQ Press, 2006); Jennifer Steinhauer, "Phones Ringing Off the Hook," *New York Times,* 26 July 2011; "Congressional Sites Crash after Obama's Speech," politico.com, 25 July 2011, text of speech, http://www.whitehouse.gov/the-press-office/2011/07/25/address-president-nation.

96. Doris Graber reviews some studies of socially undesirable effects on children and adults in *Processing Politics,* pp. 91–95, and in *Mass Media and American Politics.*

97. Moreover, much of what children see is advertisements. See "Study: Almost 20% of Kid TV Is Ad-Related," *Chicago Tribune,* 22 April 1991, p. 11. See also Stephen Seplow and Jonathan Storm, "Reviews Mixed on Television's Effect on Children," *St. Paul Pioneer Press,* 28 December 1997, p. 9A; Nell Minow, "Standards for TV Language Rapidly Going Down the Tube," *Chicago Tribune,* 7 October 2003, sec. 5, p. 2; and "Generation M2," Report by the Kaiser Family Foundation, January 2010, http://www.kff.org/entmedia/upload/8010.pdf.

98. Douglas Kellner, *Television and the Crisis of Democracy* (Boulder, Colo.: Westview Press, 1990), p. 17.

99. James Fallows, *Breaking the News: How the Media Undermine American Democracy* (New York: Pantheon Books, 1996). Also see Paul Gronke and Timothy Cook, "Disdaining the Media," *Political Communication* 24 (July 2007): 259–281.

100. For a discussion of how the media affect our collective memory of such events, see Jill A. Edy, *Troubled Pasts: News and the Collective Memory of Social Unrest* (Philadelphia: Temple University Press, 2006).

101. Katharine Q. Seelye, "Survey on News Media Finds Wide Displeasure," *New York Times,* 27 June 2005, p. C5.

102. Ladd, *Why Americans Hate the Media and How It Matters.*

103. See Bernard Goldberg, *Bias: A CBS Insider Exposes How the Media Distort the News* (Washington, D.C.: Regnery Publishing, 2002); and Ann Coulter, *Slander: Liberal Lies about the American Right* (New York: Crown, 2002).

104. See Eric Alterman, *What Liberal Media? The Truth about Bias and the News* (New York: Basic Books, 2003); and Al Franken, *Lies and the Liars Who Tell Them … a Fair and Balanced Look at the Right* (New York: Penguin, 2003).

105. Pew Research Center of the People and the Press, "Financial Woes Now Overshadow All Other Concerns for Journalists," 17 March 2008, http://people-press.org/reports/pdf/403.pdf.

106. Farnsworth and Lichter, "The Nightly News Nightmare Revisited," p. 31.

107. "Audio: By the Numbers," *The State of the News Media 2011,* http://stateofthemedia.org.

108. *The People, the Press, and Their Leaders* (Washington, D.C.: Times-Mirror Center for the People and the Press, 1995). See also Pew Research Center, "Self Censorship: How Often and Why," a survey of nearly three hundred journalists and news executives in February–March 2000, released 30 April 2000.

109. Harold W. Stanley and Richard G. Niemi, *Vital Statistics on American Politics, 2007–2008* (Washington, D.C.: CQ Press, 2008); and Greg Mitchell, "Barack the Vote: 2008 Broke with Tradition," *Editor & Publisher,* 1 December 2008.

110. Maura Clancey and Michael J. Robinson, "General Election Coverage: Part I," *Public Opinion* 7 (December–January 1985): 54. Also see Pew Research Center, "Striking the Balance, Audience Interests, Business Pressures and Journalists' Values," 30 March 1999, http://people-press.org/reports/display.php3?ReportK>=67.

111. Center for Media and Public Affairs, "Election Watch: Campaign 2008 Final," *Media Monitor* 23, no. 1 (Winter 2009): http://www.cmpa.com/pdf/media_monitorjan_2009.pdf.

112. Bob Kemper, "Bush: No Iraqi Link to Sept. 11," *Chicago Tribune,* 18 September 2003, pp. 1–6.

113. Steven Kull and others, "Misperceptions, the Media, and the Iraq War," Program on International Policy Attitudes (PIPA), 2 October 2003, http://www.pipa.org.

114. Barbie Zelizer, David Park, and David Gudelunas, "How Bias Shapes the News: Challenging *The New York Times'* Status as a Newspaper of Record on the Middle East," *Journalism* 3 (2002): 303.

115. See Bill Kovach and Tom Rosentstiel, *Blur: How to Know What's True in the Age of Information Overload,* pp. xx–xx.

116. W. Lance Bennett and William Serrin, "The Watchdog Role," in Overholser and Jamieson, *Institutions of American Democracy,* pp. 169–188.

117. For a critique of the press on these grounds, see W. Lance Bennett, Regina G. Lawrence, and Steven Livingston, *When the Press Fails* (Chicago: University of Chicago Press, 2007).

118. For a historical account of efforts to determine voters' preferences before modern polling, see Tom W. Smith, "The First Straw? A Study of the Origin of Election Polls," *Public Opinion Polling* 54 (Spring 1990): 21–36. See also Susan Herbst, *Numbered Voices: How Opinion Polling Has Shaped American Politics* (Chicago: University of Chicago Press, 1993), Chap. 4.

119. See New York Times Polls Index, http://www.nytimes.com/ref/us/polls_index.html.

120. Robert Shapiro, "Public Opinion and American Democracy," *Public Opinion Quarterly* 75 (2011): 982–1017.

121. Jose Antonio Vargas, "My Life as an Undocumented Immigrant," *New York Times Magazine,* 22 June 2011.

122. William Schneider and I. A. Lewis, "Views on the News," *Public Opinion* 8 (August–September 1985): 6–11, 58–59. For similar findings from a 1994 study, see Times-Mirror Center for the People and the Press, "Mixed Message about Press Freedom on Both Sides of the Atlantic," press release, 16 March 1994, p. 65. See also Thomas E. Patterson, "News Decisions: Journalists as Partisan Actors" (paper presented at the annual meeting of the American Political Science Association, 1996), p. 21.

123. Pew Research Center for the People and the Press, News Interest Final Topline, 1–5 February 2006, http://peoplepress.org/reports/display.php3?ReportID=270.

CHAPTER 7 / PARTICIPATION AND VOTING / PAGES 172–203

1. *TIME*, 178 (26 December 2011), p. 53.

2. David D. Kirkpatrick, "March in Cairo Draws Women by Thousands," *New York Times*, 21 December 2011, p. 1.

3. Amro Hassan, "Egyptian Court Halts Virginity Tests on Female Protesters," *Los Angeles Times*, 27 December 2011, http://latimesblogs.latimes.com/world_now/2011/12/court-verdict-abolishes-military-virginity-tests.html.

4. M. Margaret Conway, *Political Participation in the United States*, 3rd ed. (Washington, D.C.: CQ Press, 2000), p. 3.

5. Michael Lapsky, "Protest as a Political Resource," *American Political Science Review* 62 (December 1968): 1145.

6. U.S. Department of State, "Patterns of Global Terrorism 2001" (Washington, D.C.: U.S. Department of State, May 2002), p. 17. The definition is contained in Title 22 of the U.S. Code, Section 2656f(d). On the problem of defining terrorism, see Walter Laquer, *No End to War: Terrorism in the 21st Century* (New York: Continuum International, 2003), esp. the appendix.

7. Lou Nichel and Dan Herbeck, *American Terrorist: Timothy McVeigh and the Oklahoma City Bombing* (New York: HarperCollins, 2001), pp. 350–354.

8. William E. Schmidt, "Selma Marchers Mark 1965 Clash," *New York Times*, 4 March 1985.

9. Frances Fox Piven, *Challenging Authority: How Ordinary People Change America* (Lanham, Md.: Rowman & Littlefield, 2006).

10. See Sidney Verba and Norman H. Nie, *Participation in America: Political Democracy and Social Equality* (New York: Harper & Row, 1972), p. 3.

11. 2005-2008 World Values Survey. The World Values Survey Association, based in Stockholm, conducts representative surveys in nations across the world. See http://www.worldvaluessurvey.org.

12. Jonathan D. Casper, *Politics of Civil Liberties* (New York: Harper & Row, 1972), p. 90.

13. David C. Colby, "A Test of the Relative Efficacy of Political Tactics," *American Journal of Political Science* 26 (November 1982): 741–753. See also Frances Fox Piven and Richard Cloward, *Poor People's Movements* (New York: Vintage, 1979).

14. U.S. Census Bureau, *2010 Statistical Abstract*, http://www.census.gov/compendia/statab/cats/elections/elected_public_officials-characteristics.html.

15. Stephen C. Craig and Michael A. Magiotto, "Political Discontent and Political Action," *Journal of Politics* 43 (May 1981): 514–522. But see Mitchell A. Seligson, "Trust Efficacy and Modes of Political Participation: A Study of Costa Rican Peasants," *British Journal of Political Science* 10 (January 1980): 75–98, for a review of studies that came to different conclusions.

16. Arthur H. Miller et al., "Group Consciousness and Political Participation," *American Journal of Political Science* 25 (August 1981): 495. See also Susan J. Carroll, "Gender Politics and the Socializing Impact of the Women's Movement," in *Political Learning in Adulthood: A Sourcebook of Theory and Research*, ed. Roberta S. Sigel (Chicago: University of Chicago Press, 1989), p. 307.

17. Richard D. Shingles, "Black Consciousness and Political Participation: The Missing Link," *American Political Science Review* 75 (March 1981): 76–91. See also Lawrence Bobo and Franklin D. Gilliam, Jr., "Race, Sociopolitical Participation, and Black Empowerment," *American Political Science Review* 84 (June 1990): 377–393; and

Jan Leighley, "Group Membership and the Mobilization of Political Participation," *Journal of Politics* 58 (May 1996): 447–463.

18. See James L. Gibson, "The Policy Consequences of Political Intolerance: Political Repression during the Vietnam War Era," *Journal of Politics* 51 (February 1989): 13–35. Gibson found that individual state legislatures reacted quite differently in response to antiwar demonstrations on college campuses, but the laws passed to discourage dissent were not related directly to public opinion within the state.

19. See Verba and Nie, *Participation in America*, p. 69. Also see John Clayton Thomas, "Citizen-Initiated Contacts with Government Agencies: A Test of Three Theories," *American Journal of Political Science* 26 (August 1982): 504–522; and Elaine B. Sharp, "Citizen-Initiated Contacting of Government Officials and Socioeconomic Status: Determining the Relationship and Accounting for It," *American Political Science Review* 76 (March 1982): 109–115.

20. Elaine B. Sharp, "Citizen Demand Making in the Urban Context," *American Journal of Political Science* 28 (November 1984): 654–670, esp. pp. 654, 665.

21. Verba and Nie, *Participation in America*, p. 67; and Sharp, "Citizen Demand Making," p. 660.

22. See Joel B. Grossman et al., "Dimensions of Institutional Participation: Who Uses the Courts and How?" *Journal of Politics* 44 (February 1982): 86–114; and Frances Kahn Zemans, "Legal Mobilization: The Neglected Role of the Law in the Political System," *American Political Science Review* 77 (September 1983): 690–703.

23. *Brown v. Board of Education*, 347 U.S. 483 (1954).

24. "Capital One Settles Litigation over Card Disputes," http://www.dailyherald.com/story/?id=345003.

25. .gov Reform Task Force, "State of the Federal Web Report," 16 December 2011, http://www.usa.gov/webreform/state-of-the-web.pdf.

26. The *Federal Register* is available via the Federal Digital System, http://www.gpo.gov/fdsys/.

27. Victoria McGrane, "Online Voting Records User Unfriendly," *Politico*, 27 April 2009, http://dynpolitico.com/printstory.cfm?uuid=E4D92857-18FE-70B2-A844894C6FC926C9.

28. http://www.opensecrets.org.

29. http://www.followthemoney.org.

30. http://www.ombwatch.org and http://truthinaccounting.org.

31. See Michael P. MacDonald and Samuel L. Popkin, "The Myth of the Vanishing Voter," *American Political Science Review* 95 (December 2001): 963–974. Traditionally, turnout had been computed by dividing the number of voters by the voting-age population, which included noncitizens and ineligible felons. Recent research excludes these groups in estimating voter turnout and has revised the U.S. turnout rates upward by three to five points in elections since 1980. For a study of felon disenfranchisement, see Jeff Manza and Christopher Uggen, *Locked Out: Felon Disenfranchisement and American Democracy* (New York: Oxford University Press, 2006).

32. Max Kaase and Alan Marsh, "Political Action: A Theoretical Perspective," in *Political Action: Mass Participation in Five Western Democracies*, ed. Samuel H. Barnes and Max Kaase (Beverly Hills, Calif.: Sage, 1979), p. 168.

33. *Smith v. Allwright*, 321 U.S. 649 (1944).

34. *Harper v. Virginia State Board of Elections*, 383 U.S. 663 (1966).

35. Everett Carll Ladd, *The American Polity* (New York: Norton, 1985), p. 392.

36. Gorton Carruth et al. (eds.), *The Encyclopedia of American Facts and Dates* (New York: Crowell, 1979), p. 330. For an eye-opening account of women's contributions to politics before gaining the vote, see Robert J. Dinkin, *Before Equal Suffrage: Women in Partisan Politics from Colonial Times to 1920* (Westport, Conn.: Greenwood Press, 1995).

37. Jodie T. Allen, "Reluctant Suffragettes: When Women Questioned Their Right to Vote," Pew Research Center, 18 March 2009, http://pewresearch.org/pubs/1156/women-reluctant-voters-after-suffrage-19th-amendment.

38. Ivor Crewe, "Electoral Participation," in *Democracy at the Polls: A Comparative Study of Competitive National Elections*, ed. David Butler, Howard R. Penniman, and Austin Ranney (Washington, D.C.: American Enterprise Institute, 1981), pp. 219–223.

39. International IDEA, "Frequently Asked Questions," http://www.idea.int/vt/faq.cfm#9.%20Which%20is%20the%20minimum%20voting%20age?

40. Thomas E. Cronin, *Direct Democracy: The Politics of Initiative, Referendum, and Recall* (Cambridge, Mass.: Harvard University Press, 1989), p. 127.

41. For an early history, see Thomas Goebel, *A Government by the People: Direct Democracy in America, 1890–1940* (Chapel Hill: University of North Carolina Press, 2007).

42. Initiative and Referendum Institute, "Ballotwatch," November 2010, http://www.iandrinstitute.org/BW%202010-2%20Election%20Results%20(11-6).pdf.

43. Initiative and Referendum Institute, "Ballotwatch," December 2011, http://www.iandrinstitute.org/BW%202011-2%20Election%20Results.pdf.

44. David S. Broder, *Democracy Derailed: Initiative Campaigns and the Power of Money* (New York: Harcourt, 2000); and David S. Broder, "A Snake in the Grass Roots," *Washington Post,* 26 March 2000, pp. B1, B2.

45. One could also select special bodies of citizens to decide policies. One scholar proposes creating large "citizens assemblies" consisting of randomly selected citizens statistically representative of the population to decide very critical issues. See James H. Snider, "Using Citizens Assemblies to Reform the Process of Democratic Reform," Joan Shorenstein Center on the Press, Politics and Public Policy, Spring 2008.

46. Caroline J. Tolbert, Ramona S. McNeal, and Daniel A. Smith, "Enhancing Civic Engagement: The Effect of Direct Democracy on Political Participation and Knowledge," *State Politics and Policy Quarterly* 3 (Spring 2003): 23–41. For a more critical look at initiatives as undermining representative government, see Bruce E. Cain and Kenneth P. Miller, "The Populist Legacy: Initiatives and the Undermining of Representative Government," in *Dangerous Democracy? The Battle over Ballot Initiatives in America,* ed. Larry J. Sabato, Howard R. Ernst, and Bruce A. Larson (Lanham, Md.: Rowman & Littlefield, 2001), pp. 33–62. For the role of interest groups in ballot issue campaigns, see Robert M. Alexander, *Rolling the Dice with State Initiatives* (Westport, Conn.: Praeger, 2002).

47. See http://www.isolon.org/ and http://www.brookings.edu/opinions/2011/0628_social_media_west.aspx.

48. Mark E. Warren and Hilary Pearse (eds.), *Designing Deliberative Democracy: The British Columbia Citizens' Assembly* (New York: Cambridge University Press, 2008).

49. Data on the elected state officials come from *The Book of the States 2003* (Lexington, Ky.: Council of State Governments, 2003), p. 201. Estimates of the number of elected school board members come from *Chicago Tribune,* 10 March 1985.

50. Crewe, "Electoral Participation," p. 232. A rich literature has grown to explain turnout across nations. See Pippa Norris, *Democratic Phoenix: Reinventing Political Activism* (Cambridge: Cambridge University Press, 2002), Chap. 3; and Mark N. Franklin, "The Dynamics of Electoral Participation," in *Comparing Democracies 2: New Challenges in the Study of Elections and Voting,* ed. Lawrence LeDuc, Richard G. Niemi, and Pippa Norris (London: Sage, 2002), pp. 148–168.

51. Verba and Nie, *Participation in America,* p. 13.

52. Russell J. Dalton, *Citizen Policies,* 3rd ed. (New York: Seven Bridges, 2002), pp. 67–68. For the argument that greater economic inequality leads to greater political inequality, see Frederick Solt, "Economic Inequality and Democratic Political Engagement," *American Journal of Political Science* 52 (January 2008): 48–60.

53. Russell J. Dalton, The *Good Citizen: How a Younger Generation Is Reshaping American Politics* (Washington, D.C.: Congressional Quarterly Press, 2008).

54. Cliff Zukin et al., *A New Engagement?* (New York: Oxford University Press, 2006), pp. 188–191.

55. For a concise summary of the effect of age on voting turnout, see William H. Flanigan and Nancy H. Zingale, *Political Behavior of the American Electorate,* 11th ed. (Washington, D.C.: CQ Press, 2005).

56. Ibid., pp. 46–47.

57. M. Margaret Conway, Gertrude A. Steuernagel, and David W. Ahern, *Women and Political Participation: Cultural Change in the Political Arena* (Washington, D.C.: CQ Press, 1997), pp. 79–80.

58. Ronald B. Rapoport, "The Sex Gap in Political Persuading: Where the 'Structuring Principle' Works," *American Journal of Political Science* 25 (February 1981): 32–48. Perhaps surprisingly, research fails to show any relationship between a wife's role in her marriage and her political activity. See Nancy Burns, Kay Lehman Schlozman, and Sidney Verba, "The Public Consequences of Private Inequality: Family Life and Citizen Participation," *American Political Science Review* 91 (June 1997): 373–389.

59. Bruce C. Straits, "The Social Context of Voter Turnout," *Public Opinion Quarterly* 54 (Spring 1990): 64–73.

60. Sidney Verba, Kay Lehman Scholzman, and Henry E. Brady, *Voice and Equality: Civic Voluntarism in American Politics* (Cambridge, Mass.: Harvard University Press, 1995), p. 433.

61. Stephen J. Dubner and Steven D. Levitt, "Why Vote?" *New York Times Magazine,* 6 November 2005, pp. 30–31. The classic formulation of the rational choice theory of turnout is Anthony Downs, *An Economic Theory of Democracy* (New York: Harper and Row, 1957). For an empirical test of economic models, see David Levine and Thomas Palfry, "The Paradox of Voter Participation? A Laboratory Study," *American Political Science Review* 101 (February 2007): 143–158.

62. Associated Press, "Voter Turnout Tops Since 1968," *St. Paul Pioneer Press,* 14 December 2008, p. A4.

63. Stephen D. Shaffer, "A Multivariate Explanation of Decreasing Turnout in Presidential Elections, 1960–1976," *American Journal of Political Science* 25 (February 1981): 68–95; and Paul R. Abramson and John H. Aldrich, "The Decline of Electoral Participation in America," *American Political Science Review* 76 (September 1981): 603–620. However, one scholar argues that this research suffers because it looks only at voters and nonvoters in a single election. When the focus shifts to people who vote sometimes but not at other times, the models do not fit so well. See M. Margaret Conway and John E. Hughes, "Political Mobilization and Patterns of Voter Turnout" (paper presented at the annual meeting of the American Political Science Association, Washington, D.C., September 1993).

64. Apparently, Richard A. Brody was the first scholar to pose this problem as a puzzle. See his "The Puzzle of Political Participation in America," in *The New American Political System,* ed. Anthony King (Washington, D.C.: American Enterprise Institute, 1978), pp. 287–324. Since then, a sizable literature has attempted to explain the decline in voter turnout in the United States. One scholar contends that postindustrial societies experience a "ceiling effect" that blunts increased voting due to increased education; see Norris, *Democratic Phoenix,* Chap. 3. Another finds that the perceived importance of electoral contests and the closeness of the vote are the major factors explaining differences in turnout; see Franklin, 'The Dynamics of Electoral Participation," pp. 148–168.

65. See Jack Doppelt and Ellen Shearer, *America's No-Shows: Non-voters* (Washington, D.C.: Medill School of Journalism, 2001); Thomas E. Patterson, The *Vanishing Voter* (New York: Vintage Books, 2003); and Deborah J. Brooks and John Geer, "Beyond Negativity: The Effects of Incivility on the Electorate," *American Journal of Political Science* 51 (January 2007): 1–16.

66. Some scholars argue that Americans generally have become disengaged from social organizations (not just political parties), becoming more likely to act "alone" than to participate in group activities. See Robert D. Putnam, *Bowling Alone: The Collapse and Revival of American Community* (New York: Simon & Schuster, 2000).

67. See Eric Pultzer, "Becoming a Habitual Voter: Inertia, Resources, and Growth in Young Adulthood," *American Political Science Review* (March 2002): 41–56; Alan S. Gerber, Donald P. Green, and Ron Shachar, "Voting May Be Habit-Forming: Evidence from a Randomized Field Experiment," *American Journal of Political Science* (July 2003): 540–550; and David Dreyer Lassen, "The Effect of Information on Voter Turnout: Evidence from a Natural Experiment," *American Journal of Political Science* 49 (January 2005): 103–111. For the argument that turnout may be genetic, see Charles Q. Choi, "The Genetics of Politics," *Scientific American,* November 2007.

68. Center for Information and Research on Civil Learning and Engagement (CIRCLE) at the University of Maryland School of Public Policy, "The 2004 Youth Vote," http://www.civicyouth.org.

69. For the latest analysis of voting trends in the United States, see the research done by Michael McDonald, http://elections.gmu.edu/voter_turnout.htm.

70. Visit the Why Tuesday? website at http://www.whytuesday.org.

71. The negative effect of registration laws on voter turnout is argued in Frances Fox Piven and Richard Cloward, "Government Statistics and Conflicting Explanations of Nonvoting," *PS: Political Science and*

Politics 22 (September 1989): 580–588. Their analysis was hotly contested in Stephen Earl Bennett, "The Uses and Abuses of Registration and Turnout Data: An Analysis of Piven and Cloward's Studies of Nonvoting in America," *PS: Political Science and Politics* 23 (June 1990): 166–171. Bennett showed that turnout declined 10 to 13 percent after 1960, despite efforts to remove or lower legal hurdles to registration. For their reply, see Frances Fox Piven and Richard Cloward, "A Reply to Bennett," *PS: Political Science and Politics* 23 (June 1990): 172–173. You can see that reasonable people can disagree on this matter. Moreover, cross-national research has found that compulsory voter registration (not voluntary, as in the United States) did not increase turnout across nations. See Franklin, "The Dynamics of Electoral Participation," p. 159.

72. "High Turnout with Iowa's Election Day Registration Law," http://www.866ourvote.org/newsroom/news?id=0191.

73. Ruth Goldway, "The Election Is in the Mail," *New York Times,* 6 December 2006; and Randal C. Archibold, "Mail-in Voters Become the Latest Prize," *New York Times,* 14 January 2008.

74. "Hawaii's Internet Vote Is 1st in Nation," *St. Paul Pioneer Press,* 24 May 2009, p. 5A.

75. David Glass, Peverill Squire, and Raymond Wolfinger, "Voter Turnout: An International Comparison," *Public Opinion* 6 (December–January 1984): 52. Wolfinger says that because of the strong effect of registration on turnout, most rational choice analyses of voting would be better suited to analyzing turnout of only registered voters. See Raymond E. Wolfinger, "The Rational Citizen Faces Election Day," *Public Affairs Report* 6 (November 1992): 12.

76. Pew Center on the States, "Bringing Elections into the 21st Century: Voter Registration Modernization," Issue Brief (August 2009), p. 2.

77. American parties don't work hard at voter mobilization. See Raymond V. Carman, Jr., Ian M. Farrell, and Jonathan S. Krasno, "The Parties as Mobilizers: Party Efforts to Get Out the Vote in the 2000 and 2004 Elections" (paper presented at the 66th Annual Midwest Political Science Association Conference, Chicago, 3–6 April 2007). That activity seems more important to parties elsewhere. See Anibal Perez-Linan, "Neoinstitutional Accounts of Voter Turnout: Moving Beyond Industrial Democracies," *Electoral Studies* 20 (2001): 281–297.

78. Recent research finds that "party contact is clearly a statistically and substantively important factor in predicting and explaining political behavior." See Peter W. Wielhouwer and Brad Lockerbie, "Party Contacting and Political Participation, 1952-1990" (paper presented at the annual meeting of the American Political Science Association, Chicago, 1992), p. 14. Of course, parties strategically target the groups that they want to see vote in elections. See Peter W. Wielhouwer, "Strategic Canvassing by Political Parties, 1952-1990," *American Review of Politics* 16 (Fall 1995): 213–238.

79. Steven J. Rosenstone and John Mark Hansen, *Mobilization, Participation, and Democracy in America* (New York: Macmillan, 1993), p. 213.

80. For the differences between national and local elections, see J. Eric Oliver and Shang E. Ha, "Vote Choice in Suburban Elections," *American Political Science Review* 101 (August 2007): 393–408; and Brad T. Gomez, Thomas G. Hansford, and George A. Krause, "The Republicans Should Pray for Rain: Weather, Turnout, and Voting in U.S. Presidential Elections," *Journal of Politics* 69 (August 2007): 649–663.

81. See Robert A. Jackson, "Voter Mobilization in the 1986 Midterm Election," *Journal of Politics* 55 (November 1993): 1081–1099; Kim Quaile Hill and Jan E. Leighley, "Political Parties and Class Mobilization in Contemporary United States Elections," *American Journal of Political Science* 40 (August 1996): 787–804; and Janine Parry et al., "Mobilizing the Seldom Voter: Campaign Contact and Effects in High Profile Elections," *Political Behavior* 30 (March 2008): 97–113.

82. Aaron Smith, "Civic Engagement Online: Politics as Usual," Pew Internet & American Life Project, 1 September 2009, http://pewresearch.org/pubs/1328/online-political-civic-engagement-activity.

83. Nonprofit Voter Engagement Network, "America Goes to the Polls: A Report on Voter Turnout in the 2006 Election," http://www.nonprofitvote.org.

84. Richard Niemi and Michael Hanmer, "Voter Registration and Turnout among College Students" (paper presented at the annual meeting of the American Political Science Association, 2006). Students at Northwestern University in 2008 were more likely to register and vote absentee if they came from a "swing" state. See Kim Castle, Janice Levy, and

Michael Peshkin, "Local and Absentee Voter Registration Drives on a College Campus," CIRCLE Working Paper 66, October 2009.

85. See Charles Krauthammer, "In Praise of Low Voter Turnout," *Time,* 21 May 1990, p. 88. Krauthammer says, "Low voter turnout means that people see politics as quite marginal to their lives, as neither salvation nor ruin…. Low voter turnout is a leading indicator of contentment." A major study in 1996 that compared 1,000 likely nonvoters with 2,300 likely voters found that 24 percent of the nonvoters, versus 5 percent of likely voters, said they "hardly ever" followed public affairs. See Dwight Morris, "No-Show '96: Americans Who Don't Vote," summary report to the Medill News Service and WTTW Television, Northwestern University School of Journalism, 1996. For a critical view of nonvoting, see Patterson, The *Vanishing Voter,* pp. 11–13.

86. Crewe, "Electoral Participation," p. 262.

87. For research showing that economic inequality depresses political engagement of the citizenry, see Frederick Solt, "Economic Inequality and Democratic Political Engagement," *American Journal of Political Science* 52 (2008): 48–60.

88. Barnes and Kaase, *Political Action,* p. 532.

89. Eric Lichtblau, "F.B.I. Watched Activist Groups, New Files Show," *New York Times,* 20 December 2005, p. 1.

90. *1971 Congressional Quarterly Almanac* (Washington, D.C.: CQ Press, 1972), p. 475.

91. Benjamin Ginsberg, The *Consequences of Consent: Elections, Citizen Control, and Popular Acquiescence* (Reading, Mass.: Addison-Wesley, 1982), p. 13.

92. Ibid., pp. 13–14.

93. Ibid., pp. 6–7.

94. Some people have argued that the decline in voter turnout during the 1980s served to increase the class bias in the electorate because people of lower socioeconomic status stayed home. But later research has concluded that "class bias has not increased since 1964." Jan E. Leighley and Jonathan Nagler, "Socioeconomic Class Bias in Turnout, 1964-1988: The Voters Remain the Same," *American Political Science Review* 86 (September 1992): 734. Nevertheless, Rosenstone and Hansen, in *Mobilization, Participation, and Democracy in America,* say, "The economic inequalities in political participation that prevail in the United States today are as large as the racial disparities in political participation that prevailed in the 1950s. America's leaders today face few incentives to attend to the needs of the disadvantaged" (p. 248).

CHAPTER 8 / POLITICAL PARTIES / PAGES 204–235

1. Theda Skocpol and Vanessa Williamson, *The Tea Party and the Remaking of Republican Conservatism* (New York: Oxford University Press, 2012), p. 22.

2. See Kenneth Janda, "The Tea Party: A Political Revolution or Tempest in a Teacup?" PowerPoint Talk, 3 April 2011, available on request.

3. The American National Election 2008 Time Series Study, http://www.electionstudies.org.

4. See, for example, Peter Mair, "Comparing Party Systems," in *Comparing Democracies 2: New Challenges in the Study of Elections and Voting,* ed. Lawrence LeDuc, Richard G. Niemi, and Pippa Norris (London: Sage, 2002), pp. 88–107.

5. E. E. Schattschneider, *Party Government* (New York: Holt, 1942).

6. See Lyn Carson and Brian Martin, *Random Selection in Politics* (Westport, Conn.: Praeger, 1999). They say: "The assumption behind random selection in politics is that just about anyone who wishes to be involved in decision making is capable of making a useful contribution, and that the fairest way to ensure that everyone has such an opportunity is to give them an equal chance to be involved" (p. 4).

7. See James M. Snyder, Jr., and Michael M. Ting, "An Informational Rationale for Political Parties," *American Journal of Political Science* 46 (January 2002): 90–110. They formalize the argument that political parties acquire "brand names" that help voters make sense of politics.

8. John H. Aldrich, *Why Parties? The Origin and Transformation of Political Parties in America* (Chicago: University of Chicago Press, 1995), p. 296.

9. See John Kenneth White and Daniel M. Shea (eds.), *New Party Politics: From Jefferson and Hamilton to the Information Age* (Boston: Bedford/St. Martin's, 2000), for essays on the place of political parties in American history.

10. See Jerome M. Clubb, William H. Flanigan, and Nancy H. Zingale, *Partisan Realignment: Voters, Parties, and Government in American History* (Beverly Hills, Calif.: Sage, 1980), p. 163. Once central to the analysis of American politics, the concept of critical elections has been discounted by some scholars in recent years. See Larry M. Bartels, "Electoral Continuity and Change," *Electoral Studies* 17 (September 1998): 301–326; and David R. Mayhew, *Electoral Realignments: A Critique of an American Genre* (New Haven, Conn.: Yale University Press, 2002). However, the concept has been defended by other scholars. See Peter F. Nardulli, "The Concept of a Critical Realignment, Electoral Behavior, and Political Change," *American Political Science Review* 89 (March 1995): 10–22; and Norman Schofield, Gary Miller, and Andrew Martin, "Critical Elections and Political Realignments in the USA: 1860-2000," *Political Studies* 51 (2003): 217–240.

11. See Gerald M. Pomper, "Classification of Presidential Elections," *Journal of Politics* 29 (August 1967): 535–566. See also Walter Dean Burnham, *Critical Elections and the Mainsprings of American Politics* (New York: Norton, 1970). Decades later, an update of Gerald Pomper's analysis of presidential elections through 1996 determined that 1960, 1964, and 1968 all had realigning characteristics. See Jonathan Knuckley, "Classification of Presidential Elections: An Update," *Polity* 31 (Summer 1999): 639–653.

12. See Ronald Brownstein, "For GOP, a Southern Exposure," *National Journal Online*, http://www.nationaljournal.com/njonline/no_20090523_3656.php?.

13. For more extensive treatments, see Henry M. Littlefield, "The Wizard of Oz: Parable on Populism," *American Quarterly* 16 (Spring 1964): 47–58; and David B. Parker, "The Rise and Fall of *The Wonderful Wizard of Oz* as a 'Parable on Populism,'" *Journal of the Georgia Association of Historians* 15 (1994): 49–63.

14. In "Realignment in Presidential Politics: South and North?" (paper presented at the Citadel Symposium on Southern Politics, 4–5 March 2004), William Crotty argues that a political realignment definitely occurred in the South around 1968 that affected presidential politics and national voting behavior.

15. Earl Black and Merle Black, *The Rise of Southern Republicans* (Cambridge, Mass.: Harvard University Press, 2002), pp. 2–3.

16. Seth C. McKeen, "Rural Voters and the Polarization of American Presidential Elections," *PS: Political Science and Politics* 41 (January 2008): 101–108.

17. Jeffrey M. Stonecash, *Political Parties Matter: Realignment and the Return of Partisan Voting* (Boulder, Colo.: Lynne Rienner, 2006), pp. 129–130.

18. The discussion that follows draws heavily on Austin Ranney and Willmoore Kendall, *Democracy and the American Party System* (New York: Harcourt, Brace, 1956), Chaps. 18, 19. For later analyses of multiparty politics in America, see Steven J. Rosenstone, Roy L. Behr, and Edward H. Lazarus, *Third Parties in America: Citizen Response to Major Party Failure,* 2nd ed. (Princeton, N.J.: Princeton University Press, 1996); and John F. Bibby and L. Sandy Maisel, *Two Parties—or More?* (Boulder, Colo.: Westview Press, 1998).

19. The seven candidates who bolted from their former parties and ran for president on a third-party ticket were Theodore Roosevelt (1912), Robert La Follette (1924), Henry A. Wallace (1948), Strom Thurmond (1948), George Wallace (1968), John Anderson (1980), and Pat Buchanan (2000). Thurmond and both Wallaces had been Democrats; the others had originally been elected to office as Republicans. Note that Harry Truman won reelection in 1948 despite facing opposition from former Democrats running as candidates of other parties.

20. J. David Gillespie, *Politics at the Periphery: Third Parties in a Two-Party America* (Columbia: University of South Carolina Press, 1993). Surveys of public attitudes toward minor parties are reported in Christian Coller, "Trends: Third Parties and the Two-Party System," *Public Opinion Quarterly* 60 (Fall 1996): 431–449. For a spirited defense of having a strong third party in American politics, see Theodore J. Lowi, "Toward a More Responsible Three-Party System: Deregulating American Democracy," in *The State of the Parties,* 4th ed., ed. John C. Green and Rick Farmer (Lanham, Md.: Rowman & Littlefield, 2003), pp. 354–377. For an analysis of third-party presidential campaigns in 2008, see Brian J. Brox, "Running Nowhere: Third Party Presidential Campaigns in 2008" (paper presented at the annual meeting of the Midwest Political Science Association, Chicago, 3–6 April 2008).

21. Ronald B. Rapoport and Walter J. Stone, *Three's a Crowd: The Dynamics of Third Parties, Ross Perot, and Republican Resurgence* (Ann Arbor: University of Michigan Press, 2005).

22. In a June 18–29, 2008, Pew Research Center Poll, 56 percent of the respondents agreed that "we should have a third major political party in this country in addition to the Democrats and Republicans." See also Shigeo Hirano and James M. Snyder, Jr., "The Decline of Third-Party Voting in the United States," *The Journal of Politics* 69 (February 2007): 1–16.

23. Rosenstone, Behr, and Lazarus, *Third Parties in America,* p. 8.

24. Shigeo Hirano and James M. Snyder, Jr., "The Decline of Third-Party Voting in the United States," *Journal of Politics* 69 (February 2007): 1–6. See also Rapoport and Stone, *Three's a Crowd.*

25. In his study of party systems, Jean Blondel noticed that most three-party systems had two major parties and a much smaller third party, which he called two-and-a-half-party systems. (Britain, for example, has two major parties—Labour and Conservative—and a smaller Social Democratic Party. Germany has followed a similar pattern.) Blondel said, "While it would seem theoretically possible for three-party systems to exist in which all three significant parties were of about equal size, there are in fact no three-party systems of this kind among Western democracies." He concluded that "genuine three-party systems do not normally occur because they are essentially transitional, thus unstable, forms of party systems." See his "Types of Party System," in *The West European Party System,* ed. Peter Mair (New York: Oxford University Press, 1990), p. 305.

26. See Douglas J. Amy, *Real Choices, New Voices: The Case for Proportional Representation in the United States,* 2nd ed. (New York: Columbia University Press, 2002).

27. The most complete report of these legal barriers is contained in monthly issues of *Ballot Access News,* http://www.ballot-access.org. State laws and court decisions may systematically support the major parties, but the U.S. Supreme Court seems to hold a more neutral position toward major and minor parties. See Lee Epstein and Charles D. Hadley, "On the Treatment of Political Parties in the U.S. Supreme Court, 1900–1986," *Journal of Politics* 52 (May 1990): 413–432; and E. Joshua Rosenkranz, *Voter Choice 96: A 50-State Report Card on the Presidential Elections* (New York: New York University School of Law, Brennan Center for Justice, 1996), p. 24.

28. Samuel Issacharoff, Pamela S. Karlan, and Richard H. Pildes, *The Law of Democracy,* rev. 2nd ed. (New York: Foundation Press, 2002), pp. 417–436.

29. See James Gimpel, *National Elections and the Autonomy of American State Party Systems* (Pittsburgh, Pa.: University of Pittsburgh Press, 1996).

30. Measuring the concept of party identification has had its problems. For insights into the issues, see R. Michael Alvarez, "The Puzzle of Party Identification," *American Politics Quarterly* 18 (October 1990): 476–491; and Donald Philip Green and Bradley Palmquist, "Of Artifacts and Partisan Instability," *American Journal of Political Science* 34 (August 1990): 872–902.

31. This breakdown used data from the 2012 Pew Research Center survey.

32. Rhodes Cook, "GOP Shows Dramatic Growth, Especially in the South," *Congressional Quarterly Weekly Report,* 13 January 1996, pp. 97–100.

33. Susan Page, "Highly Educated Couples Often Split on Candidates," *USA Today,* 18 December 2002, pp. 1–2.

34. U.S. Census, "Table 1a, Projected Population of the United States, by Race and Hispanic Origin: 2000 to 2050," http://www.census.gov/population/www/projections/usinterimproj.

35. The relationship between age and party identification is quite complicated, but research finds that it becomes more stable as people age. See Elias Dinas and Mark Franklin, "The Development of Partisanship during the Life-Course" (paper presented at the Midwest Political Science Association 67th Annual National Conference, Palmer House Hilton, Chicago, 2 April 2009), http://www.allacademic.com/meta/p3 63000_index.html.

36. Two scholars on voting behavior describe partisanship as "the feeling of sympathy for and loyalty to a political party that an individual acquires—sometimes during childhood—and holds through life, often

with increasing intensity." See William H. Flanigan and Nancy H. Zingale, *Political Behavior of the American Electorate,* 10th ed. (Washington, D.C.: CQ Press, 2002), p. 60.

37. Bill Keller, "As Arms Buildup Eases, U.S. Tries to Take Stock," *New York Times,* 14 May 1985; and Ed Gillespie and Bob Schellhas, *Contract with America* (New York: Times Books, 1994), p. 107.

38. "The GOP's Spending Spree," *Wall Street Journal,* 25 November 2003, p. A18.

39. See, for example, Gerald M. Pomper, *Elections in America* (New York: Dodd, Mead, 1968); Benjamin Ginsberg, "Election and Public Policy," *American Political Science Review* 70 (March 1976): 41–50; and Jeff Fishel, *Presidents and Promises* (Washington, D.C.: CQ Press, 1985).

40. Ian Budge and Richard I. Hofferbert, "Mandates and Policy Outputs: U.S. Party Platforms and Federal Expenditures," *American Political Science Review* 84 (March 1990): 111–131.

41. See Terri Susan Fine, "Economic Interests and the Framing of the 1988 and 1992 Democratic and Republican Party Platforms," *American Review of Politics* 16 (Spring 1995): 79–93.

42. Ian Budge et al., *Mapping Policy Preferences: Estimates for Parties, Electors, and Governments 1945–1998* (Oxford: Oxford University Press, 2001), p. 49.

43. See Ralph M. Goldman, *The National Party Chairmen and Committees: Factionalism at the Top* (Armonk, N.Y.: M. E. Sharpe, 1990). The subtitle is revealing.

44. Cornelius P. Cotter and Bernard C. Hennessy, *Politics without Power: The National Party Committees* (New York: Atherton Press, 1964).

45. Phillip A. Klinkner, "Party Culture and Party Behavior," in *The State of the Parties,* 3rd ed., ed. Daniel M. Shea and John C. Green (Lanham, Md.: Rowman & Littlefield, 1999), pp. 275–287; and Phillip A. Klinkner, *The Losing Parties: Out-Party National Committees, 1956–1993* (New Haven, Conn.: Yale University Press, 1994).

46. Anthony Corrado, Sarah Barclay, and Heitor Gouvea, "The Parties Take the Lead: Political Parties and the Financing of the 2000 Presidential Election," in *The State of the Parties,* 4th ed., ed. John C. Green and Rick Farmer (Lanham, Md.: Rowman & Littlefield, 2003), p. 97; and Klinkner, *The Losing Parties.*

47. Daniel J. Galvin, *Presidential Party Building: Dwight D. Eisenhower to George W. Bush* (Princeton, N.J.: Princeton University Press, 2010), pp. ix–x.

48. Dan Barry, "Republicans on Long Island Master Science of Politics," *New York Times,* 8 March 1996, p. A1S. Recent research suggests that when both major parties have strong organizations at the county level, the public has more favorable attitudes toward the parties. See John J. Coleman, "Party Organization Strength and Public Support for Parties," *American Journal of Political Science* 40 (August 1996): 805–824.

49. John Frendreis et al., "Local Political Parties and Legislative Races in 1992," in Shea and Green, *The State of the Parties,* p. 139.

50. Federal Election Commission, *National Party Transfers to State/Local Party Committees, January 1, 2007–December 31, 2008,* http://www.fec.gov/press/press2009/05282009Party/20090528Party.shtml.

51. Raymond J. La Raja, "State Parties and Soft Money: How Much Party Building?" in Green and Farmer, *The State of the Parties,* p. 146.

52. Robert Biersack, "Hard Facts and Soft Money: State Party Finance in the 1992 Federal Elections," in Shea and Green, *The State of the Parties,* p. 114.

53. See the evidence presented in Robert Harmel and Kenneth Janda, *Parties and Their Environments* (New York: Longman, 1982), Chap. 5; and the more recent assessment in Nicol C. Rae, "Be Careful What You Wish For: The Rise of Responsible Parties in American National Politics," *Annual Review of Political Science* 10 (2007): 169–191.

54. Martin P. Wattenberg, *The Decline of American Political Parties, 1952–1994* (Cambridge, Mass.: Harvard University Press, 1996).

55. Taylor Dark III, "The Rise of a Global Party? American Party Organizations Abroad," *Party Politics* 9 (March 2003): 241–255.

56. In 1996, the Democratic National Committee mounted an unprecedented drive to organize up to sixty thousand precinct captains in twenty states, while the new Republican candidate for U.S. senator from Illinois, Al Salvi, fired his own campaign manager and replaced him with someone from the National Republican Senatorial Campaign Committee. See Sue Ellen Christian, "Democrats Will Focus on Precincts," *Chicago Tribune,* 29 June 1996; and Michael Dizon, "Salvi Fires Top Senate Race Aides," *Chicago Tribune,* 24 May 1996, sec. 2, p. 3.

57. Barbara Sinclair, "The Congressional Party: Evolving Organizational, Agenda-Setting, and Policy Roles," in *The Parties Respond: Changes in American Parties and Campaigns,* 3rd ed., ed. L. Sandy Maisel (Boulder, Colo.: Westview Press, 1998), p. 227.

58. David M. Farrell, "Political Parties in a Changing Campaign Environment," in *Handbook of Party Politics,* ed. Richard S. Katz and William Crotty (London: Sage, 2006), p. 124.

59. The model is articulated most clearly in a report by the American Political Science Association, "Toward a More Responsible Two-Party System," *American Political Science Review* 44 (September 1950): Part II. See also Gerald M. Pomper, "Toward a More Responsible Party System? What, Again?" *Journal of Politics* 33 (November 1971): 916–940. See also the seven essays in the symposium "Divided Government and the Politics of Constitutional Reform," *PS: Political Science and Politics* 24 (December 1991): 634–657.

60. Within the American states, parties also differ on policies, but to varying degrees. See John H. Aldrich and James S. Coleman Battista, "Conditional Party Government in the States," *American Journal of Political Science* 46 (January 2002): 164–172.

61. Jeffrey M. Jones, "Americans Lack Consensus on Desirability of Divided Gov't," Gallup Poll Report, 10 June 2010.

62. Recent research finds that voters do differentiate between policies backed by the president and by congressional candidates. See David R. Jones and Monika L. McDermott, "The Responsible Party Government Model in House and Senate Elections," *American Journal of Political Science* 48 (January 2004): 1–12.

CHAPTER 9 / NOMINATIONS, ELECTIONS, AND CAMPAIGNS / PAGES 236–269

1. See Arend Lijphart, *Patterns of Democracy: Government Forms and Performance in Thirty-six Countries* (New Haven, Conn.: Yale University Press, 1999), pp. 116–121. Of Lijphart's thirty-six democracies, only six have had presidential forms of government at some time in their history, while Colombia, Costa Rica, Venezuela, and the United States have been consistently presidential.

2. The British parliament has a House of Lords, but it is an appointive body with limited legislative powers.

3. Computed from data in Oonagh Gay and Isobel White, "Election Timetables" (House of Commons Library, Research Paper 07/31, 22 March 2007), p. 14.

4. For a philosophical discussion of "temporal properties" of American elections, see Dennis F. Thompson, "Election Time: Normative Implications of the Electoral Process in the United States," *American Political Science Review* 98 (February 2004): 51–64.

5. This is essentially the framework for studying campaigns set forth in Barbara C. Salmore and Stephen A. Salmore, *Candidates, Parties, and Campaigns: Electoral Politics in America,* 2nd ed. (Washington, D.C.: CQ Press, 1989). For a more recent review of campaigns, see James A. Thurber and Candice J. Nelson (eds.), *Campaigns and Elections American Style,* 3rd ed. (Boulder, Colo.: Westview Press, 2010).

6. Adam Nagourney, "Internet Injects Sweeping Change into U.S. Politics," *New York Times,* 2 April 2006, pp. 1, 17.

7. David Menefree-Libey, *The Triumph of Campaign-Centered Politics* (New York: Chatham House, 2000).

8. Stephen E. Frantzich, *Political Parties in the Technological Age* (New York: Longman, 1989), p. 105.

9. "It is probable that no nation has ever experimented as fully or as fitfully with mechanisms for making nominations as has the United States," say William J. Keefe and Marc J. Hetherington, *Parties, Politics, and Public Policy in America,* 9th ed. (Washington, D.C.: CQ Press, 2003), p. 59.

10. Reuven Y. Hazan and Gideon Rahat, *Democracy Within Parties: Candidate Selection Methods and Their Political Consequences* (Oxford: Oxford University Press, 2010). See also Krister Lundell, "Determinants of Candidate Selection: The Degree of Centralization in Comparative Perspective," *Party Politics* 10 (January 2004): 25–47.

11. Kenneth Janda, "Adopting Party Law," in *Political Parties and Democracy in Theoretical and Practical Perspectives* (Washington, D.C.: National Democratic Institute for International Affairs, 2005). This is a series of research papers.

12. *The Book of the States, 2009* (Lexington, Ky.: Council of State Governments, 2009), pp. 295–296.

13. Voting turnout in almost twenty states holding primaries on Super Tuesday, 2 February 2008, set a new record of 27 percent. See Katharine Q. Seelye, "Records for Turnout," *New York Times*, 7 February 2008, p. A24.

14. Karen M. Kaufmann, James G. Gimpel, and Adam H. Hoffman, "A Promise Fulfilled? Open Primaries and Representation," *Journal of Politics* 65 (May 2003): 457–476. See also John G. Geer, "Assessing the Representativeness of Electorates in Presidential Elections," *American Journal of Political Science* 32 (November 1998): 929–945; and Barbara Norrander, "Ideological Representativeness of Presidential Primary Voters," *American Journal of Political Science* 33 (August 1989): 570–587.

15. James A. McCann, "Presidential Nomination Activists and Political Representation: A View from the Active Minority Studies," in *Pursuit of the White House: How We Choose Our Presidential Nominees*, ed. William G. Mayer (Chatham, N.J.: Chatham House, 1996), p. 99.

16. James M. Snyder, Jr., et al., "The Decline of Competition in U.S. Primary Elections, 1908-2004" (unpublished paper, MIT, Cambridge, Mass., June 2005), p. 22.

17. Talar Aslanian et al., "Recapturing Voter Intent: The Nonpartisan Primary in California" (capstone seminar report, Pepperdine University, April 2003), Appendix C, http://publicpolicy.pepperdine.edu/master-public-policy/capstone.htm.

18. "Ninth Circuit Upholds Washington Top-Two System," *Ballot Access News* 27 (1 February 2012): 1–2; and "California Primary," *Ballot Access News*, 28 (1 July 2012), p. 4.

19. Nicol C. Rae, "Exceptionalism in the United States," in Katz and Crotty, *Handbook of Party Politics*, p. 201. See also Lawrence LeDuc, "Democratizing Party Leadership Selection," *Party Politics* 7 (May 2001): 323–341.

20. The 1976 Republican convention voted narrowly on the first ballot to renominate President Gerald Ford over Ronald Reagan.

21. See "The Green Papers" http://www.thegreenpapers.com for information on state methods of delegate selection in 2012.

22. Alan Ware, *The American Direct Primary: Party Institutionalization and Transformation in the North* (Cambridge: Cambridge University Press, 2002). Ware argues that the primary system resulted less from the reform movement than the unwieldy nature of the caucus/convention system for nominating candidates.

23. Harold W. Stanley and Richard G. Niemi, *Vital Statistics on American Politics, 1788-2008* (Washington, D.C.: CQ Press, 2008). According to state-by-state delegate totals in "The Green Papers" website, about 15 percent of the delegates to each party's 2008 presidential nominating convention were selected through the caucus/convention system.

24. See Rhodes Cook, *The Presidential Nominating Process: A Place for Us?* (Lanham, Md.: Rowman & Littlefield, 2004), Chap. 5. Nations that have copied the U.S. model have experienced mixed results. See James A. McCann, "The Emerging International Trend toward Open Presidential Primaries," in *The Making of the Presidential Candidates 2004*, ed. William G. Mayer (Lanham, Md.: Rowman & Little-field, 2004), pp. 265–293.

25. Arthur T. Hadley, *The Invisible Primary* (Englewood Cliffs, N.J.: Prentice-Hall, 1976). For a test of some of Hadley's assertions, see Emmett H. Buell, Jr., "The Invisible Primary," in *In Pursuit of the White House*, ed. William G. Mayer (Chatham, N.J.: Chatham House, 1996), pp. 1–43. More recently, see Cook, *The Presidential Nominating Process*, pp. 83–89. An analogous concept for presidents in office is the "permanent campaign"; see Brendan J. Doherty, "Elections: The Politics of the Permanent Campaign: Presidential Travel and the Electoral College, 1977-2004," *Presidential Studies Quarterly* 37 (December 2007): 749–773.

26. Gary R. Orren and Nelson W. Polsby (eds.), *Media and Momentum: The New Hampshire Primary and Nomination Politics* (Chatham, N.J.: Chatham House, 1987), p. 23.

27. These figures, calculated for voting-eligible population (VEP), come from elections. http://elections.gmu.edu/voter_turnout.htm. VEP is lower than voting-age population (VAP) because VEP excludes those ineligible to vote, usually noncitizens and felons.

28. Richard L. Berke, "Two States Retain Roles in Shaping Presidential Race," *New York Times*, 29 November 1999, p. 1; and Leslie Wayne, "Iowa Turns Its Presidential Caucuses into a Cash Cow, and Milks

Furiously," *New York Times*, 5 January 2000, p. A16. See also Adam Nagourney, "Iowa Worries about Losing Its Franchise," *New York Times*, 18 January 2004, sec. 4, p. 3.

29. "Presidential Primary Season Is Longer Than Ever," *Ballot Access News* 27 (November 2011): 6.

30. In general, Democratic winners are less predictable. See Wayne P. Steger, "Who Wins Nominations and Why? An Updated Forecast of the Presidential Primary Vote," *Political Research Quarterly* 60 (March 2007): 91–99.

31. One scholar holds that early popularity is more important for Republican presidential hopefuls. See D. Jason Berggren, "Two Parties, Two Types of Nominees, Two Paths to Winning a Presidential Nomination, 1972-2004," *Presidential Studies Quarterly* 37 (June 2007): 203–227.

32. See James R. Beniger, "Winning the Presidential Nomination: National Polls and State Primary Elections, 1936-1972," *Public Opinion Quarterly* 40 (Spring 1976): 22–38.

33. *The American Heritage Dictionary of the English Language*, 4th ed. (Boston: Houghton Mifflin, 2000), p. 362. Indeed, the entry on "Electoral College" in the 1989 *Oxford English Dictionary* does not note any usage in American politics up to 1875, when it cites a reference in connection with the Germanic Diet.

34. References to the electoral college in the U.S. Code can be found through the Legal Information Institute website, http://www4.law.cornell.edu/uscode/3/ch1.html.

35. Michael Nelson, *Congressional Quarterly's Guide to the Presidency* (Washington, D.C.: CQ Press, 1989), pp. 155–156. Colorado selected its presidential electors through the state legislature in 1876, but that was the year it entered the Union.

36. Who would have become president if the 538 electoral votes had been divided equally, at 269 each? According to the Constitution, the House of Representatives would have chosen the president, for no candidate had a majority. One way to avoid tied outcomes in the future is to create an odd number of electoral votes. To do this, one scholar proposes making the District of Columbia a state. That would give Washington three electoral votes—the same number as it has now without congressional representation. The Senate would increase to 102 members, while the House would remain fixed at 435. (Presumably, Washington's seat would come from one of the other states after decennial reapportionment.) This clever solution would produce an electoral college of 537, an odd number that could not produce a tie between two candidates. See David A. Crockett, "Dodging the Bullet: Election Mechanics and the Problem of the Twenty-third Amendment," *PS: Political Science and Politics* 36 (July 2003): 423–426.

37. Shlomo Slonim, "The Electoral College at Philadelphia: The Evolution of an Ad Hoc Congress for the Selection of a President," *Journal of American History* 73 (June 1986): 35. For a recent critique and proposal for reform, see David W. Abbott and James P. Levine, *Wrong Winner: The Coming Debacle in the Electoral College* (New York: Praeger, 1991). For a reasoned defense, see Walter Berns (ed.), *After the People Vote: A Guide to the Electoral College* (Washington, D.C.: American Enterprise Institute, 1992). For a detailed analysis of a congressional failure to enact proportional distribution of state electoral votes, see Gary Bugh, "Normal Politics and the Failure of the Most Intense Effort to Amend the Presidential Election System" (paper presented at the annual meeting of the Northeastern Political Science Association, Boston, 2006).

38. Lydia Saad, "Americans Would Swap Electoral College for Popular Vote," Gallup Poll Report, 24 October 2011.

39. For the most recent review, see Gary Bugh (ed.), *Electoral College Reform: Challenges and Possibilities* (Burlington, Vt.: Ashgate, 2010).

40. Walter Berns (ed.), *After the People Vote: A Guide to the Electoral College* (Washington, D.C.: American Enterprise Institute, 1992), pp. 45–48. The framers had great difficulty deciding how to allow both the people and the states to participate in selecting the president. This matter was debated on twenty-one different days before they compromised on the electoral college, which, Slonim says, "in the eyes of its admirers ... represented a brilliant scheme for successfully blending national and federal elements in the selection of the nation's chief executive" ("The Electoral College at Philadelphia," p. 58).

41. Observers suspect that the vote for Edwards instead of Kerry was cast by error. See http://news.minnesotapublicradio.org/features/2004/12/13_ap_electors.

42. See Alexis Simendinger, James A. Barnes, and Carl M. Cannon, "Pondering a Popular Vote," *National Journal,* 18 November 2000, pp. 3650–3656.

43. Harold W. Stanley and Richard G. Niemi, *Vital Statistics on American Politics, 1999-2008* (Washington, D.C.: CQ Press, 2009), Table 3.10.

44. See, for example, Walter F. Murphy, *Elements of Judicial Strategy* (Chicago: University of Chicago Press, 1964); and Bob Woodward and Scott Armstrong, *The Brethren* (New York: Simon & Schuster, 1979).

45. Salmore and Salmore, *Candidates, Parties, and Campaigns,* p. 1. Also see Paul S. Herrnson, *Congressional Elections: Campaigning at Home and in Washington* (Washington, D.C.: CQ Press, 2008).

46. Nate Silver and Andrew Gelman, "No Country for Close Calls," *New York Times,* 19 April 2009, p. WK11.

47. See Edward I. Sidlow, *Challenging the Incumbent: An Underdog's Undertaking* (Washington, D.C.: CQ Press, 2004), for the engaging account of the unsuccessful 2000 campaign by a young political scientist, Lance Pressl, against the most senior Republican in the House, Phil Crane, in Illinois' Sixth District. Sidlow's book invites readers to ponder what the high reelection rate of incumbents means for American politics.

48. Frank Phillips, "Romney Paves Way for Possible '12 Run," *Boston Globe* (8 December 2008), http://www.boston.com/news/nation/articles/2008/12/08/romney_paves_way_for_possible_12_run/.

49. Michal Luo, "Romney, Weighing Run, Leans on State PACs," *New York Times,* 21 November 2010, p. 17.

50. See Peter L. Francia et al., *The Financiers of Congressional Elections* (New York: Columbia University Press, 2003).

51. Quoted in E. J. Dionne, Jr., "On the Trail of Corporation Donations," *New York Times,* 6 October 1980.

52. Salmore and Salmore, *Candidates, Parties, and Campaigns,* p. 11. See also David Himes, "Strategy and Tactics for Campaign Fund-Raising," in *Campaigns and Elections: American Style,* ed. James A. Thurber and Candice J. Nelson (Boulder, Colo.: Westview Press, 1995), pp. 62–77.

53. Federal Election Commission, *The First Ten Years: 1975-1985* (Washington, D.C.: Federal Election Commission, 14 April 1985), p. 1.

54. Michael J. Malbin, "Assessing the Bipartisan Campaign Reform Act," in *The Election After Reform: Money, Politics and the Bipartisan Campaign Reform Act,* ed. Michael J. Malbin (Lanham, Md.: Rowman & Littlefield, 2006).

55. "527 Advocacy Spending," Opensecrets.org, http://www.opensecrets.org/527s/index.php.

56. Brody Mullins, "Stealthy Groups Shake Up Races," *Wall Street Journal,* 4 February 2008, p. A12.

57. "2010 Outside Spending by Groups," OpenSecrets.org, http://www.opensecrets.org/outsidespending/summ.php?cycle=2010&chrt=V&disp=O&type=I.

58. Adam Liptak, "Justices, 5-4, Reject Corporate Campaign Spending Limit," *New York Times,* 22 January 2010, pp. A1, A16.

59. Editorial, "A Free Speech Landmark," *Wall Street Journal,* 22 January 2010, p. A18.

60. Editorial, "The Court's Blow to Democracy," *New York Times,* 22 January 2010, p. A20.

61. "Changing the Rules," *Wall Street Journal,* 22 January 2010, p. A6.

62. *SpeechNow.org* v. *FEC,* 599 F.3d 686 (D.C. Circuit, 26 March 2010). See also http://www.fec.gov/press/press2011/FEC_Joint_Statement-Nov3.pdf.

63. "With New Political Committees, Possible Channels for Unlimited, Anonymous Donations," *New York Times,* 16 October 2011, p. 24.

64. Tom Hamburger and Melanie Mason, "PACs Upend, Outspend Pack," *Chicago Tribune,* 1 January 2012, p. 23.

65. See the Federal Election Commission Advisory Opinion of June 30, 2011, http://www.fec.gov/press/press2011/20110630openmeeting.shtml.

66. Nicholas Confessore, Michael Luo, and Mike McIntire, "In G.O.P. Race, a New Breed of Superdonor," *New York Times,* 22 February 2012, pp. A1, A14.

67. See the FEC's listing of Independent-Expenditure-Only groups, http://www.fec.gov/press/press2011/ieoc_alpha.shtml.

68. James A. Barnes, "Matching Funds, R.I.P.," *National Journal,* 26 April 2008, p. 75.

69. "Federal Election Commission Certifies Federal Matching Funds for Jill Stein for President," *Federal Election Committee News Release,* 28 August 2012.

70. Federal Election Commission, "2008 Presidential Campaign Financial Activity Summarized," News Release, 8 June 2009.

71. Federal Election Commission, "2008 Presidential Campaign Financial Activity Summarized: Receipts Nearly Double 2004 Total," News Release, 8 June 2009.

72. Center for Responsive Politics, "Price of Admission," http://www.opensecrets.org/bigpicture/stats.php?cycle=2008.

73. David D. Kirkpatrick, "Death Knell May Be Near for Public Election Funds," *New York Times,* 23 January 2007, pp. A1, A16.

74. Dan Eggen, "The 2012 Election Brings a New Kind of Fundraiser: The Super Bundler," *Washington Post,* 16 August 2011.

75. "2012 Presidential Candidate Fundraising Summary," Center for Responsive Politics, OpenSecrets.org, http://www.opensecrets.org/pres12/index.php?ql3.

76. "PostPolitics: Campaign 2012, Campaign Finance Explorer," *Washington Post,* http://www.washingtonpost.com/wp-srv/special/politics/campaign-finance/.

77. David A. Dulio, "Strategic and Tactical Decisions in Campaigns," in *Guide to Political Campaigns in America,* ed. Paul S. Herrnson (Washington, D.C.: CQ Press, 2005), pp. 231–243.

78. Salmore and Salmore, *Candidates, Parties, and Campaigns,* p. 11.

79. According to Brian F. Schaffner and Matthew J. Streb, less educated respondents are less likely to express a vote preference when party labels are not available. See "The Partisan Heuristic in Low-Information Elections," *Public Opinion Quarterly* 66 (Winter 2002): 559–581.

80. See the "Marketplace: Political Products and Services" section in monthly issues of the magazine *Campaigns and Elections.* These classified ads list scores of names, addresses, and telephone numbers for people who supply "political products and services"—from "campaign schools" to "voter files and mailing lists." For an overview, see Philip Kotler and Neil Kotler, "Political Marketing: Generating Effective Candidates, Campaigns, and Causes," in *Handbook of Political Marketing,* ed. Bruce I. Newman (Thousand Oaks, Calif.: Sage, 1999), pp. 3–18.

81. See Matt A. Barreto et al., "Bulls Eye or Ricochet? Ethnically Targeted Campaign Ads in the 2008 Election" (paper presented at the Chicago Area Behavioral Workshop, Evanston, Ill., 8 May 2009); and Michael G. Hagenand and Robin Kolodny, "Microtargeting Campaign Advertising on Cable Television" (paper presented at the annual meeting of the Midwest Political Science Association, Chicago, 3–6 April 2008).

82. Salmore and Salmore, *Candidates, Parties, and Campaigns,* pp. 115–116. See also Eric W. Rademacher and Alfred J. Tuchfarber, "Preelection Polling and Political Campaigns," in Newman, *Handbook of Political Marketing,* pp. 197–221.

83. Bruce I. Newman, "A Predictive Model of Voter Behavior," in Newman, *Handbook of Political Marketing,* pp. 259–282. For studies on campaign consultants at work, see James A. Thurber and Candice J. Nelson (eds.), *Campaign Warriors: The Role of Political Consultants in Elections* (Washington, D.C.: Brookings Institution Press, 2000).

84. A major player in the new Internet election campaign industry is Election Advantage, which describes its offerings, http://www.campaignadvantage.com.

85. James Warren, "Politicians Learn Value of Sundays—Too Well," *Chicago Tribune,* 22 October 1990, p. 1.

86. Timothy E. Cook, *Making Laws and Making News: Media Strategies in the U.S. House of Representatives* (Washington, D.C.: Brookings Institution, 1989). Subsequent research into media effects on Senate and House elections finds that in low-information elections, which characterize House more than Senate elections, the media coverage gives an advantage to incumbents, particularly among independent voters. See Robert Kirby Goidel, Todd G. Shields, and Barry Tadlock, "The Effects of the Media in United States Senate and House Elections: A Comparative Analysis" (paper presented at the annual meeting of the American Political Science Association, Washington, D.C., September 1993).

87. Stephen J. Farnsworth and S. Robert Lichter, *The Nightly News Nightmare: Media Coverage of U.S. Presidential Elections, 1988-2008* (Lanham, Md.: Rowman & Littlefield, 2010), p. 52.

88. Julianne F. Flowers, Audrey A. Haynes, and Michael H. Crispin, "The Media, the Campaign, and the Message," *American Journal of Political Science* 47 (April 2003): 259–273.

89. Ann N. Crigler, Marion R. Just, and Timothy E. Cook, "Local News, Network News and the 1992 Presidential Campaign" (paper presented at the annual meeting of the American Political Science Association, Washington, D.C., September 1993), p. 9.

90. Stephen Ansolabehere and Shanto Iyengar, *Going Negative: How Political Advertisements Shrink and Polarize the Electorate* (New York: Free Press, 1995), p. 145.

91. Darrell M. West, *Air Wars: Television Advertising in Election Campaigns, 1952-2004,* 4th ed. (Washington, D.C.: CQ Press, 2010), p. 23.

92. Ted Brader, "Striking a Responsive Chord: How Political Ads Motivate and Persuade Voters by Appealing to Emotions," *American Journal of Political Science* 49 (April 2005): 388–405.

93. Darrell M. West, *Air Wars: Television Advertising in Election Campaigns, 1952-2009,* 5th ed. (Washington, D.C.: CQ Press, 2010), pp. 51–52.

94. This theme runs throughout Kathleen Hall Jamieson's *Dirty Politics: Deception, Distraction, and Democracy* (New York: Oxford University Press, 1992). See also John Boiney, "You Can Fool All of the People … Evidence on the Capacity of Political Advertising to Mislead" (paper presented at the annual meeting of the American Political Science Association, Washington, D.C., September 1993).

95. West, *Air Wars,* 5th ed., p. 159.

96. T. W. Farnam, "Study: Negative Campaign Ads Much More Frequent, Vicious Than in Primaries Past," *Washington Post,* 20 February 2012, http://www.washingtonpost.com/politics/study-negative-campaign-ads-much-more-frequent-vicious-than-in-primaries-past/2012/02/14/gIQAR7ifPR_story.html.

97. Kathleen Hall Jamieson, Paul Waldman, and Susan Sheer, "Eliminate the Negative? Categories of Analysis for Political Advertisements," in *Crowded Airwaves: Campaign Advertising in Elections,* ed. James A. Thurber, Candice J. Nelson, and David A. Dulio (Washington, D.C.: Brookings Institution Press, 2000), p. 49.

98. David A. Dulio, Candice J. Nelson, and James A. Thurber, "Summary and Conclusions," in Thurber, Nelson, and Dulio, *Crowded Airwaves,* p. 172. Laboratory research found that even "uncivil" exchanges between candidates can be handled by the public. See Deborah Jordan Brooks and John G. Geer, "Beyond Negativity: The Effects of Incivility on the Electorate," *American Journal of Political Science* 51 (January 2007): 1–16.

99. Gregory A. Huber and Kevin Arceneaux, "Identifying the Persuasive Effects of Presidential Advertising," *American Journal of Political Science* 51 (2007): 957–977.

100. Ansolabehere and Iyengar, *Going Negative,* p. 112.

101. West, however, takes issue with the Ansolabehere and Iyengar analysis in *Going Negative,* saying that turnout is more dependent on mistrust than on negativity of ads. See West, *Air Wars,* pp. 71–72.

102. Richard R. Lau and Gerald M. Pomper, "Effectiveness of Negative Campaigning in U.S. Senate Elections," *American Journal of Political Science* 46 (January 2002): 47–66.

103. Richard R. Lau, Lee Sigelman, and Ivy Brown Rovner, "The Effects of Negative Political Campaigns: A Meta-Analytic Reassessment," *Journal of Politics* 69 (November 2007): 1176–1209.

104. Lee Sigelman and Mark Kugler, "Why Is Research on the Effects of Negative Campaigning So Inconclusive? Understanding Citizens' Perceptions of Negativity," *Journal of Politics* 65 (February 2003): 142–160; and Richard R. Lau, Lee Sigelman, and Ivy Brown Rovner, "The Effects of Negative Political Campaigns: A Meta-Analytic Reassessment," *The Journal of Politics* 69 (November 2007): 1176–1209.

105. The information on early campaign websites comes from Jill Zuckerman, "Candidates Spin Web of Support on Cybertrail," *Chicago Tribune,* 3 December 2003, p. 13.

106. Tanzina Vega, "Online Data Helping Campaigns Customize Ads," *New York Times,* 21 February 2012, pp. 1–13.

107. "Cable Leads the Pack as Campaign News Source," Pew Research Center for the People and the Press, 7 February 2012, http://www.people-press.org/files/legacy-pdf/2012%20Communicating%20Release.pdf.

108. Emily Steel, "Why Web Campaign Spending Trails TV," *Wall Street Journal,* 14 December 2008, p. B4.

109. See the website for the American National Election Studies, http://www.electionstudies.org.

110. Pamela Johnston Conover and Stanley Feldman, "Candidate Perception in an Ambiguous World: Campaigns, Cues, and Inference Processes," *American Journal of Political Science* 33 (November 1989): 912–940.

111. Kira Sanbonmatsu, "Gender Stereotypes and Vote Choice," *American Journal of Political Science* 46 (January 2002): 20–34. Sanbonmatsu contends that some voters have a "baseline preference" for men or women candidates and that women are more likely to hold the preference than men. See also Kathleen A. Dolan, *Voting for Women: How the Public Evaluates Women Candidates* (Boulder, Colo.: Westview Press, 2004).

112. See Herbert F. Weisberg and Clyde Wilcox (eds.), *Models of Voting in Presidential Elections: The 2000 U.S. Election* (Stanford: Stanford University Press, 2004), for a set of studies explaining voting behavior in the presidential election. See also Jean-François Godbout and Eric Belanger, "Economic Voting and Political Sophistication in the United States: A Reassessment," *Political Research Quarterly* 60 (September 2007): 541–554.

113. Michael M. Gant and Norman R. Luttbeg, *American Electoral Behavior* (Itasca, Ill.: Peacock, 1991), pp. 63–64. Ideology appears to have played little role in the 2000 election. See William G. Jacoby, "Ideology in the 2000 Election: A Study in Ambivalence," in Weisberg and Wilcox, *Models of Voting in Presidential Elections,* pp. 103–104.

114. Martin Gilens, Lynn Vavreck, and Martin Cohen, "The Mass Media and the Public's Assessments of Presidential Candidates, 1952-2000," *Journal of Politics* 69 (November 2007): 1160–1175.

115. For a thorough review of studies on campaign effects, see Rian J. Brox and Daron R. Shaw, "Political Parties, American Campaigns, and Effects on Outcomes," in Katz and Crotty, *Handbook of Party Politics,* pp. 146–150.

116. Farnsworth and Lichter, *The Nightly News Nightmare,* p. 64.

117. Matthew A. Baum, "Talking the Vote: Why Presidential Candidates Hit the Talk Show Circuit," *American Journal of Political Science* 49 (April 2005): 213–234.

118. Electorates tend to be more engaged by campaigning in "battleground" states. See James G. Gimpel et al., "Battleground States versus Blackout States: The Behavioral Implications of Modern Presidential Campaigns," *Journal of Politics* 69 (August 2007): 786–797.

119. But for a contrary view, see Nicol C. Rae, "Be Careful What You Wish For: The Rise of Responsible Parties in American National Politics," *Annual Review of Political Science* 10 (2007): 169–191.

120. See Peter Kobrak, *Cozy Politics: Political Parties, Campaign Finance, and Compromised Governance* (Boulder, Colo.: Lynne Rienner, 2002), for an indictment of the flow of money in politics from interest groups untempered by the aggregating influence of political parties.

CHAPTER 10 / INTEREST GROUPS / PAGES 270–295

1. Miguel Helft and Matt Richtel, "Facebook Prepares to Add Friends in Washington," *New York Times,* 29 March 2011; Jessica Guynn, "Facebook Hires Former Bush Aides as Washington Lobbyists," *Los Angeles Times,* 26 May 2011, http://latimesblogs.latimes.com/technology/2011/05/facebook-hires-former-bush-aides-as-washington-lobbyists.html; Jon Swartz, "Facebook Changes Its Lobbying Status in Washington," *USA Today,* 13 January 2011, http://www.usatoday.com/money/industries/technology/2011-01-13-facebook13_CV_N.htm; and Sara Forden, "Facebook Builds a Washington Lobbying Team," *Business Week,* 9 December 2010, http://www.businessweek.com/magazine/content/10_51/b4208036753172.htm.

2. Alexis de Tocqueville, *Democracy in America, 1835–1839,* ed. Richard D. Heffner (New York: Mentor Books, 1956), p. 198.

3. The *Federalist Papers* (New York: Mentor Books, 1961), p. 79.

4. Ibid., p. 78.

5. See Robert A. Dahl, *A Preface to Democratic Theory* (Chicago: University of Chicago Press, 1956), pp. 4–33.

6. Pew Research Center for the People and the Press, 1–5 February 2006, http://www.pollingreport.com/politics.htm.

7. "Who's Up, Who's Down?" Center for Responsive Politics, http://www.opensecrets.org/lobby/incdec.php.

8. This discussion follows from Jeffrey M. Berry and Clyde Wilcox, *The Interest Group Society,* 5th ed. (New York: Longman, 2009), pp. 7–8.

9. See Frank R. Baumgartner, "Interest Groups and Agendas," in *The Oxford Handbook of American Political Parties and Interest Groups,* ed. L. Sandy Maisel and Jeffrey M. Berry (Oxford, UK: Oxford University Press, 2010), pp. 519–533.

10. Terry Moe, *Special Interest* (Washington, D.C.: Brookings Institution Press, 2011); and Steven Greenhouse, "Union Membership in U.S. Fell to a 70-Year Low Last Year," *New York Times* 21 January 2011, http://www.nytimes.com/2011/01/22/business/22union.html.

11. Rebecca Adams, "Federal Regulations Face Assault on Their Foundation," *CQ Weekly,* 10 August 2002, p. 2183.

12. David B. Truman, *The Governmental Process* (New York: Knopf, 1951).

13. Herbert Gans, *The Urban Villagers* (New York: Free Press, 1962).

14. Robert H. Salisbury, "An Exchange Theory of Interest Groups," *Midwest Journal of Political Science* 13 (February 1969): 1–32.

15. See Mancur Olson, Jr., *The Logic of Collective Action* (New York: Schocken, 1968).

16. Marshall Ganz, *Why David Sometimes Wins* (New York: Oxford University Press, 2009).

17. Kay Lehman Schlozman, Sidney Verba, and Henry E. Brady, *The Unheavenly Chorus: Unequal Political Voice and the Broken Promise of American Democracy* (Princeton, N.J.: Princeton University Press, 2012).

18. OpenSecrets.org, http://www.opensecrets.org/lobby/clientsum.php?id=D000000544&year=2011 and http://www.opensecrets.org/lobby/clientsum.php?id=D000000406&year=2011.

19. For a skeptical view of the AARP's prowess, see Christopher Howard, *The Welfare State Nobody Knows* (Princeton, N.J.: Princeton University Press, 2007), pp. 125–149.

20. Jeffrey M. Berry and Sarah Sobieraj, *The Outrage Industry* (New York: Oxford University Press, forthcoming).

21. See Olson, *The Logic of Collective Action.*

22. See Aseem Prakash and Mary Kay Gugerty, eds., *Advocacy Organizations and Collective Action* (New York: Cambridge University Press, 2010).

23. On the underlying motivation to contribute, see Hahrie Hahn, *Moved to Action* (Stanford, Calif.: Stanford University Press, 2009).

24. Anthony J. Nownes, *Total Lobbying* (New York: Cambridge University Press, 2006), p. 44.

25. "Health Lobbyist Has Great Sway," Associated Press, 24 May 2009.

26. Eric Lipton, "Ex Lawmaker Still Working for Old Allies," *New York Times,* 6 August 2011.

27. Ethan Smith and Brody Mullins, "Studios Tap Dodd to Lead Lobbying," *Wall Street Journal,* 2 March 2011; and "Official: Chris Dodd to Lead MPAA," *The Hollywood Reporter,* 1 March 2011, http://www.hollywoodreporter.com/news/official-chris-dodd-lead-mpaa-162817.

28. Brody Mullins and Susan Pulliam, "Hedge Funds Pay Top Dollar for Washington Intelligence," *Wall Street Journal,* 4 October 2011.

29. Suzy Khimm, "Transformers," *New Republic,* 24 December 2008, p. 13.

30. Data from the Center for Responsive Politics, as reported, http://www.sfexaminer.com/blogs/beltway-confidential/2010/11/any-measure-democrats-raised-more-pacs-2010.

31. Josh Israel, Aaron Mehta, and Elizabeth Lucas, "Scores of Leading PACs Shifted to GOP in 2010," Center for Public Integrity, 1 March 2011, http://www.politico.com/news/stories/0211/50379.html.

32. "Top PACs," OpenSecrets.org, http://www.opensecrets.org/pacs/toppacs.php?cycle=2010&party=A.

33. Rogan Kersh, "To Donate or Not to Donate?" (paper delivered at the annual meeting of the American Political Science Association, Philadelphia, August 2003), p. 2.

34. Michael M. Franz, *Choices and Changes* (Philadelphia: Temple University Press, 2008).

35. Stephen Ansolabehere, John de Figueredo, and James M. Snyder, Jr., "Why Is There So Little Money in U.S. Politics?" *Journal of Economic Perspectives* 17 (Winter 2003): 161–181; and Mark A. Smith, *American Business and Political Power* (Chicago: University of Chicago Press, 2000), pp. 115–141.

36. Marie Hojnacki and David Kimball, "PAC Contributions and Lobbying Access in Congressional Committees," *Political Research Quarterly* 54 (March 2001): 161–180; John R. Wright, "Contributions, Lobbying, and Committee Voting in the U.S. House of Representatives," *American Political Science Review* 84 (June 1990): 417–438; and Richard L. Hall and Frank W. Wayman, "Buying Time: Money Interests and the Mobilization of Bias in Congressional Committees," *American Political Science Review* 84 (September 1990): 797–820.

37. See Kristin A. Goss, *Disarmed* (Princeton, N.J.: Princeton University Press, 2006).

38. Frank R. Baumgartner, Jeffrey M. Berry, Marie Hojnacki, David C. Kimball, and Beth L. Leech, *Lobbying and Policy Change* (Chicago: University of Chicago Press, 2009), pp. 166–189.

39. Eric Pianin, "For Environmentalists, Victories in the Courts," *Washington Post,* 27 January 2003, p. A3.

40. S. Laurel Weldon, *When Protest Makes Policy* (Ann Arbor: University of Michigan Press, 2011), pp. 57–81.

41. Jim Puzzanghera, "AT&T Finds Big-Money Lobbying, Ad Efforts Don't Always Pay Off," *Los Angeles Times,* 21 December 2011, http://articles.latimes.com/2011/dec/21/business/la-fi-att-regulators-20111221; and Shira Ovide, "AT&T Sets Ad Blitz in Capital," *Wall Street Journal,* 20 September 2011.

42. On competition and cooperation among Washington lobbies, see Thomas T. Holyoke, *Competitive Interests* (Washington, D.C.: Georgetown University Press, 2011).

43. Dara Z. Strolovitch, *Affirmative Advocacy* (Chicago: University of Chicago Press, 2007), p. 181.

44. See Schlozman, Verba, and Brady, *The Unheavenly Chorus*; and Matt Grossman, *The Not-So-Special Interests* (Stanford, Calif.: Stanford University Press, 2012).

45. Kay Lehman Schlozman, Traci Burch, and Samuel Lampert, "Still an Upper-Class Accent?" (paper presented at the annual meeting of the American Political Science Association, September 2004), pp. 16, 25.

46. Such nonprofits have obstacles created by their status as tax-deductible public charities. See Jeffrey M. Berry with David F. Arons, *A Voice for Nonprofits* (Washington, D.C.: Brookings Institution, 2003); and Elizabeth T. Boris and C. Eugene Steurele (eds.), *Nonprofits and Government,* 2nd ed. (Washington, D.C.: Urban Institute Press, 2006).

47. Jeffrey M. Berry, *The New Liberalism* (Washington, D.C.: Brookings Institution, 1999).

48. These figures are from the Center for Responsive Politics. Summary statistics for health care, http://www.opensecrets.org/industries/indus.php?cycle=2012&ind=H. Growth in the lobbying industry slowed during 2011. See Anna Palmer, "Lobby Shop Growth Flat in 2011," *Politico,* 20 January 2012, http://www.politico.com/news/stories/0112/71722.html.

49. Jason Webb Yackee and Susan Webb Yackee, "A Bias towards Business? Assessing Interest Group Influence on the U.S. Bureaucracy," *Journal of Politics* 68 (February 2006): 128–139.

50. Baumgartner et al., *Lobbying and Policy Change,* pp. 190–214. On the power of the status quo, see Amy McKay, "Negative Lobbying and Policy Outcomes," *American Politics Research* 40 (January 2012): 116–146.

51. *Citizens United* v. *Federal Election Commission,* 558 U.S. (2010).

52. Jeff Zeleny and Carl Hulse, "Congress Votes to Tighten Rules on Lobbyist Ties," *New York Times,* 3 August 2007, p. A1.

53. Fred Schulte, John Aloysius Farrell, and Jeremy Borden, "Obama Rewards Big Bundlers with Jobs, Commissions, Stimulus Money, Government Contracts, and More," *iWatch News,* 15 June 2011, http://www.iwatchnews.org/2011/06/15/4880/obama-rewards-big-bundlers-jobs-commissions-stimulus-money-government-contracts-and; and Fred Schulte and Aaron Mehta, "Obama Rainmakers Enjoy White House Invites, Appointments, and Contracts," *iWatch News,* 19 January 2012, http://www.iwatchnews.org/2012/01/19/7897/obama-rainmakers-enjoy-white-house-invites-appointments-and-contracts.

CHAPTER 11 / CONGRESS / PAGES 296–325

1. Harold W. Stanley and Richard G. Niemi (eds.), *Vital Statistics on American Politics, 2011-2012* (Washington, D.C.: CQ Press, 2011), p. 42.

2. Fred Barbash, "Divided Government Could Result in Stalemate," *CQ Weekly,* 10 January 2011, p. 96.

3. Carl Hulse, "Unruly G.O.P. Puts Boehner to a Test in Budget Vote," *New York Times,* 14 April 2011, http://www.nytimes.com/2011/04/15/us/politics/15boehner.html.

4. Paul M. Krawzak, "Ghosts of Shutdowns Past," *CQ Weekly*, 28 February 2011, p. 466.

5. Monika McDermott and David Jones, "Do Public Evaluations of Congress Matter? Retrospective Voting in Congressional Elections," *American Politics Research* 31, no. 2 (2003): 155–177.

6. Stanley and Niemi, *Vital Statistics on American Politics, 2011-2012*, pp. 46–47.

7. For more on public opinion about Congress, see John Hibbing and Elizabeth Theiss-Morse, *Congress as Public Enemy: Public Attitudes toward American Political Institutions* (Cambridge: Cambridge University Press, 1995); John Hibbing and Elizabeth Theiss-Morse, *Stealth Democracy: Americans' Beliefs about How Government Should Work* (Cambridge: Cambridge University Press, 2002); and David Jones and Monika McDermott, *Americans, Congress, and Democratic Responsiveness* (Ann Arbor: University of Michigan Press, 2010).

8. Alan Abramowitz, Brad Alexander, and Matthew Gunning, "Incumbency, Redistricting, and the Decline of Competition in U.S. House Elections," *Journal of Politics* 68 (February 2006): 75–88.

9. Gary W. Cox and Jonathan N. Katz, *Elbridge Gerry's Salamander* (Cambridge: Cambridge University Press, 2002).

10. Micah Altman, Karin MacDonald, and Michael McDonald, "Pushbutton Gerrymanders? How Computing Has Changed Redistricting," in *Party Lines,* ed. Thomas E. Mann and Bruce E. Cain (Washington, D.C.: Brookings Institution, 2005), pp. 51–66; and Mark Monmonier, *Bushmanders and Bullwinkles* (Chicago: University of Chicago Press, 2001).

11. Steven Yaccino, "Illinois Redistricting Forces Republican Face-Off," *New York Times*, 21 September 2011, http://thecaucus.blogs.nytimes.com/2011/09/21/illinois-redistricting-forces-republican-face-off/.

12. Thomas E. Mann, "Polarizing the House of Representatives: How Much Does Gerrymandering Matter?" in *Red and Blue Nation,* ed. Pietro S. Nivola and David W. Brady (Washington, D.C.: Brookings Institution and Hoover Institution, 2006), pp. 263–283; and Sean Theriault, *Party Polarization in Congress* (New York: Cambridge University Press, 2011). For a contrasting view, see Nolan McCarty, Keith Poole, and Howard Rosenthal, "Does Gerrymandering Cause Polarization?" *American Journal of Political Science* 53, no. 3 (2009): 666–680.

13. Sean Theriault and David Rhode, "The Gingrich Senators and Party Polarization in the U.S. Senate," *Journal of Politics* 73, no. 4 (2011): 1011–1024. Note that this article claims that it is Senate *Republicans* who had served in the House who have been the main polarizing agent in the Senate.

14. Dennis Conrad, "House Spends Big on Home Mailings," *Boston Globe,* 28 December 2007, p. A2; and Michael Glassman, "Congressional Official Mail Costs," *CRS Report for Congress,* 16 August 2010.

15. Jordan Fabian, "Critics Say Franking Rules Should Change to Suit the Age of Twitter," *The Hill,* 14 October 2009, http://thehill.com/homenews/senate/62969-critics-say-franking-rules-should-change-for-twitter; Alex Katz, "Not Much Tweeting from Mass. Delegation," *The Boston Globe,* 4 November 2011, http://bostonglobe.com/news/nation/2011/11/03/not-much-tweeting-from-mass-delegation/bR5jndH4Y2eoIBWNnNoc4H/story.html; and Jennifer Moire, "Survey: U.S. Congressmen Really Like Facebook," http://www.allfacebook.com/facebook-like-congress-us-2011-07. Also see http://tweetcongress.org/, which tracks tweets sent by members of Congress.

16. Collen J. Shogan, "Blackberries, Tweets, and YouTube: Technology and the Future of Communicating with Congress," *PS: Political Science and Politics* 43, no. 2 (April 2010): 231–233.

17. Morris P. Fiorina, as cited in Roger H. Davidson and Walter J. Oleszek, *Congress and Its Members,* 11th ed. (Washington, D.C.: CQ Press, 2008), p. 144.

18. Center for Responsive Politics, "Incumbent Advantage," http://www.opensecrets.org/bigpicture/incumbs.php?cycle=2010.

19. Larry Sabato, *PAC Power* (New York: Norton, 1984), p. 72.

20. Walter J. Stone and L. Sandy Maisel, "The Not-So-Simple Calculus of Winning: Potential U.S. House Candidates' Nomination and General Election Prospects," *Journal of Politics* 65 (November 2003): 951–977.

21. Herrnson, *Congressional Elections,* pp. 65–66; and "Most Members of Congress Enjoy Robust Financial Status, Despite Nation's Sluggish Economic Recovery," opensecrets.org, 15 November 2011.

22. Jennifer L. Lawless and Richard L. Fox, *It Still Takes a Candidate,* rev. ed. (New York: Cambridge University Press, 2010).

23. See Beth Reingold, *Representing Women* (Chapel Hill, N.C.: University of North Carolina Press, 2000); and Michele L. Swers, *The Difference Women Make* (Chicago: University of Chicago Press, 2002).

24. Hanna Fenichel Ptikin, *The Concept of Representation* (Berkeley: University of California Press, 1967), pp. 60–91; and Jane Mansbridge, "Should Blacks Represent Blacks and Women Represent Women? A Contingent 'Yes,'" *Journal of Politics* 61 (1999): 628–657.

25. Stanley and Niemi, *Vital Statistics on American Politics, 2011-2012*, pp. 49–50.

26. Mark Hugo Lopez, "The Latino Electorate in 2010," *Pew Hispanic Center Report,* 26 April 2011, http://pewhispanic.org/files/reports/141.pdf.

27. *Shaw* v. *Reno,* 509 U.S. 630 (1993).

28. *Bush* v. *Vera,* 116 S. Ct. 1941 (1996).

29. *Easley* v. *Cromartie,* 532 U.S. 234 (2001).

30. See David Lublin, *The Paradox of Representation* (Princeton, N.J.: Princeton University Press, 1997). See, *contra,* Kenneth W. Shotts, "Does Racial Redistricting Cause Conservative Policy Outcomes?" *Journal of Politics* 65 (2003): 216–226.

31. See Frank R. Baumgartner et al., *Advocacy and Policy Change* (Chicago: University of Chicago Press, 2009).

32. Loretta Sanchez. "Protecting the Vulnerable by Cracking Down on Cyberstalking," 13 January 2011, http://lorettasanchez.house.gov/new-opinion-editorial-article.

33. John W. Kingdon, *Agendas, Alternatives, and Public Policies,* 2nd ed. (New York: HarperCollins, 1995), p. 38.

34. David Shribman, "Canada's Top Envoy to Washington Cuts Unusually Wide Swath," *Wall Street Journal,* 29 July 1985, p. 1.

35. Woodrow Wilson, *Congressional Government* (Boston: Houghton Mifflin, 1885), p. 79.

36. David Fahrenthold and Michelle Boorstein, "Rep. Peter King's Muslim Hearings: A Key Moment in an Angry Conversation," *Washington Post,* 9 March 2011, http://www.washingtonpost.com/wp-dyn/content/article/2011/03/09/AR2011030902061.html?sid=ST2011031002070.

37. Alessandra Stanely, "Terror Hearing Puts Lawmakers in Harsh Light," *New York Times,* 10 March, 2011, http://www.nytimes.com/2011/03/11/arts/television/at-muslim-hearing-finger-pointing-and-tears.html?_r=1&ref=politics.

38. See Steven S. Smith, *Party Influence in Congress* (New York: Cambridge University Press, 2007).

39. Gary W. Cox and Mathew D. McCubbins, *Legislative Leviathan* (Berkeley: University of California Press, 1993); and Keith Krehbiel, *Information and Legislative Organization* (Ann Arbor: University of Michigan Press, 1992).

40. Matthew N. Green, *The Speaker of the House* (New Haven, Conn.: Yale University Press, 2010).

41. Jonathan Franzen, "The Listener," *New Yorker,* 6 October 2003, p. 85.

42. Robert Draper, "How Kevin McCarthy Wrangles the Tea Party in Washington," *New York Times,* 17 July 2011.

43. Cox and McCubbins, *Legislative Leviathan.*

44. Charles O. Jones, *The United States Congress* (Homewood, Ill.: Dorsey Press, 1982), p. 322.

45. Gregory Kroger, *Filibustering: A Political History of Obstruction in the House and Senate* (Chicago: Chicago University Press, 2010), p. 133.

46. Norman Ornstein, "Our Broken Senate," *The American,* May/April 2008, http://www.american.com/archive/2008/march-april-magazine-contents/our-broken-senate; and Barbara Sinclair, "The 60 Vote Senate," in *U.S. Senate Exceptionalism,* ed. Bruce Oppenheimer (Columbus: Ohio State University Press, 2002), pp. 241–261.

47. Gary W. Cox and Mathew D. McCubbins, *Setting the Agenda: Responsible Party Government in the U.S. House of Representatives* (New York: Cambridge University Press, 2005); and Smith, *Party Influence in Congress.*

48. These ideologies affect policy outcomes as well as the structure of the institution itself. See Nelson Polsby, *How Congress Evolves: Social Bases of Institutional Change* (New York: Oxford University Press, 2004).

49. James Sterling Young, *The Washington Community* (New York: Harcourt, Brace, 1964).

50. Jackie Calmes and Carle Hulse, "Debt Ceiling Talks Collapse as Boehner Walks Out," *New York Times,* 22 July 2011.

51. Joshua D. Clinton, "Representation in Congress: Constituents and Roll Calls in the 106th House," *Journal of Politics* 68 (May 2006): 397–409.

52. See John Cochran, "The Influence Implosion," *CQ Weekly,* 16 January 2006, p. 174; and Susan Ferrechio, "2005 Legislative Summary: House Ethics Investigations," *CQ Weekly,* 2 January 2006, p. 31.

53. Barry C. Burden, *The Personal Roots of Representation* (Princeton, N.J.: Princeton University Press, 2007).

54. Richard F. Fenno, Jr., *Home Style* (Boston: Little, Brown, 1978), p. xii.

55. Ibid., p. 32.

56. Louis I. Bredvold and Ralph G. Ross (eds.), *The Philosophy of Edmund Burke* (Ann Arbor: University of Michigan Press, 1960), p. 148.

57. "In Congress, Voting Your Own Way and Paying for It," *National Public Radio,* 18 July 2011, http://www.npr.org/2011/07/18/ 138473342/in-congress-voting-your-own-way-and-paying-for-it.

58. For an alternative and more highly differentiated set of representation models, see Jane Mansbridge, "Rethinking Representation," *American Political Science Review* 97 (November 2003): 515–528.

59. Warren E. Miller and Donald E. Stokes, "Constituency Influence in Congress," *American Political Science Review* 57 (March 1963): 45–57.

60. Ron Nixon, "Cost-Cutters, Except When the Spending Is Back Home," *New York Times,* 19 July 2011; and Tracy Jan, "Colleges Look Hard to Replace Earmarks," Boston.com, 1 September 2011.

61. "Possible Negatives for Candidates: Vote for Bank Bailout, Palin Support," Pew Center for People and the Press, 6 October 2010, http://www.people-press.org/2010/10/06/possible-negatives-for-candidates-vote-for-bank-bailout-palin-support/.

CHAPTER 12 / THE PRESIDENCY / PAGES 326–353

1. On Obama's "education" on the elusiveness of a postpartisan presidency, see Ryan Lizza, "The Obama Memos," *New Yorker,* 30 January 2012, pp. 36–49.

2. Jeffrey M. Jones, "Majority Rates Obama Same or Worse Compared with Bush," Gallup.com, 23 September 2011, http://www.gallup.com/poll/149666/Majority-Sees-Obama-Performing-Worse-Bush.aspx.

3. Alan S. Blinder and Mark Zandi, "How the Great Recession Was Brought to an End," 27 July 2010, http://www.economy.com/mark-zandi/documents/End-of-Great-Recession.pdf.

4. "Unemployment Rate," Bureau of Labor Statistics, 20 July 2012, http://data.bls.gov/timeseries/LNS14000000.

5. Clinton Rossiter, *1787: The Grand Convention* (New York: Mentor, 1968), p. 148.

6. Ibid., pp. 190–191.

7. United States Senate, "Summary of Bills Vetoed, 1789-Present," http://www.senate.gov/reference/Legislation/Vetoes/vetoCounts.htm.

8. Louis Fisher, *Presidential War Power* (Lawrence: University Press of Kansas, 1995); Donald R. Kelley (ed.), *Divided Power: The Presidency, Congress, and the Formation of American Foreign Policy* (Fayetteville: University of Arkansas Press, 2005); Andrew Rudalevige, *The New Imperial Presidency: Renewing Presidential Power After Watergate* (Ann Arbor: University of Michigan Press, 2005); Arthur M. Schlesinger, Jr., *War and the American Presidency* (New York: W. W. Norton, 2004); and *The Imperial Presidency* (Boston: Houghton Mifflin, 2004).

9. *Hamdan* v. *Rumsfeld,* 548 U.S. 557 (2006).

10. Wilfred E. Binkley, *President and Congress,* 3rd ed. (New York: Vintage, 1962), p. 155.

11. William G. Howell, *Power without Persuasion: The Politics of Direct Presidential Action* (Princeton, N.J.: Princeton University Press, 2003); Kenneth R. Mayer, *With the Stroke of a Pen: Executive Orders and Presidential Power* (Princeton, N.J.: Princeton University Press, 2001); and Adam Warber, *Executive Orders and the Modern Presidency* (Boulder, Colo.: Lynne Rienner, 2005).

12. See Jack Goldsmith, *Power and Constraint* (New York: Norton, 2012).

13. James P. Pfiffner, *Power Play* (Washington, D.C.: Brookings Institution, 2008), pp. 190–191.

14. An expansive defense of this doctrine is offered by Bush Justice Department aide John Yoo in *Crisis and Command: A History of Executive Power from George Washington to George W. Bush* (New York: Kaplan Publishing, 2010).

15. See Laura Meckler, "Obama Shifts View of Executive Power," *Wall Street Journal,* 30 March 2012; and Charlie Savage, "Shift on Executive Power Lets Obama Bypass Rivals," *New York Times,* 22 April 2012, http://www.nytimes.com/2012/04/23/us/politics/shift-on-executive-powers-let-obama-bypass-congress.html.

16. Noam Scheiber, "The Chief," *New Republic,* 25 March 2010, pp. 17–21; and Ryan Lizza, "The Gatekeeper," *New Yorker,* 2 March 2009, pp. 24–29.

17. *The 2012 Statistical Abstract,* Table 499, "Federal Civilian Employment by Branch and Agency: 1990–2010," http://www.census.gov/compendia/statab/2012/tables/12s0499.pdf; and Table 472, "Federal Budget Outlays by Agency: 1990-2011," http://www.census.gov/compendia/statab/2012/tables/12s0472.pdf.

18. Richard Tanner Johnson, *Managing the White House* (New York: Harper & Row, 1974); and John P. Burke, *The Institutional Presidency* (Baltimore: Johns Hopkins University Press, 1992).

19. Ron Suskind, *Confidence Men* (New York: Harper, 2011), p. 351.

20. Dan Froomkin, "Now They Tell Us," *Washington Post,* 12 September 2005, http://busharchive.froomkin.com/BL2005091200806_pf.html.

21. George Stephanopoulos, *All Too Human* (Boston: Back Bay Books, 1999), p. 61.

22. Barton Gellman, *Angler: The Cheney Vice Presidency* (New York: Penguin, 2008).

23. Edward Weisband and Thomas M. Franck, *Resignation in Protest* (New York: Penguin, 1975), p. 139, quoted in Thomas E. Cronin, *The State of the Presidency,* 2nd ed. (Boston: Little, Brown, 1980), p. 253.

24. Doris Kearns, *Lyndon Johnson and the American Dream* (New York: Signet, 1977), p. 363.

25. James David Barber, *Presidential Character,* 4th ed. (Englewood Cliffs, N.J.: Prentice Hall, 1992); Fred I. Greenstein, *The Presidential Difference: Leadership Style from FDR to Clinton* (Princeton, N.J.: Princeton University Press, 2000); and David G. Winter, "Things I've Learned about Personality from Studying Political Leadership at a Distance," *Journal of Personality* 73 (2005): 557–584.

26. Donald Kinder, "Presidential Character Revisited," in *Political Cognition,* ed. Richard Lau and David O. Sears (Hillsdale, N.J.: Erlbaum, 1986), pp. 233–255; W. E. Miller and J. M. Shanks, *The New American Voter* (Cambridge, Mass.: Harvard University Press, 1996); and Frank Newport and Joseph Carroll, "Analysis: Impact of Personal Characteristics on Candidate Support," Gallup News Service, 13 March 2007, http://www.gallup.com.

27. Richard E. Neustadt, *Presidential Power* (New York: Wiley, 1980), p. 10.

28. Ibid., p. 9.

29. Chad Roedemeier, "Nixon Kept Softer Self Off Limits, Tape Shows," *Boston Globe,* 8 July 2000, p. A4.

30. Terry Sullivan, "I'll Walk Your District Barefoot" (paper presented at the MIT Conference on the Presidency, Cambridge, Mass., 29 January 2000), p. 6. See also Robert A. Caro, *The Passage of Power* (New York: Knopf, 2012), pp. 484–502 and pp. 552–557.

31. Samuel Kernell, *Going Public: New Strategies of Presidential Leadership,* 4th ed. (Washington, D.C.: CQ Press, 2007).

32. George C. Edwards III, *The Strategic President* (Princeton, N.J.: Princeton University Press, 2009), p. 188.

33. Ezra Klein, "The Unpersuaded," *New Yorker,* 19 March 2012, pp. 32–38.

34. Jeffrey M. Jones, "Obama Job Approval at 51% After Healthcare Vote," Gallup Poll, 25 March 2010, http://www.gallup.com/poll/12 698 9/Obama-Job-Approval-51-After-Healthcare-Vote.aspx.

35. Gary C. Jacobson, "The Republican Resurgence in Congress," *Political Science Quarterly* 126 (Spring 2011): 27–52.

36. Francis Lee, *Beyond Ideology* (Chicago: University of Chicago Press, 2009).

37. Anna Manchin, "Two-Thirds of Italians Disapprove of Their Leadership," Gallup Poll, 16 November 2011, http://www.gallup.com/poll/150785/Two-Thirds-Italians-Disapprove-Leadership.aspx.

38. B. Dan Wood, The *Myth of Presidential Representation* (New York: Cambridge University Press, 2009); and Lawrence C. Jacobs and Robert Y. Shapiro, *Politicians Don't Pander* (Chicago: University of Chicago Press, 2000).

39. David McCullough, *Truman* (New York: Simon & Schuster, 1992), p. 914.

40. Clea Benson, "Presidential Support: The Power of No," *Congressional Quarterly Weekly Report,* 14 January 2008, p. 137.

41. Sean M. Theriault, *Party Polarization in Congress* (New York: Cambridge University Press, 2008); and Nolan McCarty, Keith T. Poole, and Howard Rosenthal, *Polarized America* (Cambridge, Mass.: MIT Press, 2008).

42. "Prepared Text of Carter's Farewell Address," *New York Times,* 15 January 1981, p. B10.

43. Jon Meacham, *American Lion* (New York: Random House, 2008), p. 267.

44. Patricia Conley, *Presidential Mandates: How Elections Shape the National Agenda* (Chicago: University of Chicago Press, 2001).

45. Stephen Skowronek, *The Politics Presidents Make,* 2nd ed. (Cambridge, Mass.: Harvard University Press, 1997).

46. Surbhi Godsay, Amanda Nover, and Emily Kirby, *The Minority Youth Vote in the 2008 Presidential Election,* CIRCLE, Tisch College of Citizenship, Tufts University, October 2010, http://www.civicyouth.org/wp-content/uploads/2010/10/fs_race_09_final1.pdf.

47. *Public Papers of the President, Lyndon B. Johnson, 1965,* vol. 1 (Washington, D.C.: U.S. Government Printing Office, 1966), p. 72.

48. "Transcript of Second Inaugural Address by Reagan," *New York Times,* 22 January 1985, p. 72. For a historical study of how presidents use the symbol of freedom, see Kevin Coe, "The Language of Freedom in the American Presidency, 1933-2006," *Presidential Studies Quarterly* 37 (September 2007): 375–398.

49. Kevin Phillips, *The Politics of Rich and Poor* (New York: Random House, 1990), p. 88.

50. John W. Kingdon, *Agendas, Alternatives, and Public Policies,* 2nd ed. (New York: HarperCollins, 1995), p. 23.

51. Seth King, "Reagan, in Bid for Budget Votes, Reported to Yield on Sugar Prices," *New York Times,* 27 June 1981, p. A1.

52. Matt Bai, "Taking the Hill," *New York Times Magazine,* 7 June 2009, p. 35.

53. Sidney M. Milkis, Jesse H. Rhodes, and Emily J. Charnock, "What Happened to Post-Partisanship? Barack Obama and the New American Party System," *Perspectives on Politics* 10 (March 2012): 57–76.

54. Richard M. Skinner, "George W. Bush and the Partisan Presidency," *Political Science Quarterly* 123 (Winter 2008–2009): 605–622; and Milkis et al., "What Happened to Post-Partisanship?"

55. Jeffrey M. Jones, "Obama's Approval Most Polarized for First-Year President," Gallup Poll, 25 January 2010, http://www.gallup.com/poll/125345/obama-approval-polarized-first-year-president.aspx.

56. Lydia Saad, "Majority in U.S. Say Bin Laden's Death Makes America Safer," Gallup Poll, 4 May 2011, http://www.gallup.com/poll/147413/Majority-Say-Bin-Laden-Death-Makes-America-Safer.aspx.

57. Robert Jervis, "Why Intelligence and Policymakers Clash," *Political Science Quarterly* 125 (Summer 2010): 125.

58. Ernest R. May and Philip D. Zelikow (eds.), *The Kennedy Tapes: Inside the White House during the Cuban Missile Crisis* (Cambridge, Mass.: Harvard University Press, 1997), pp. 498–499, 498–501, 512–513, 663–666.

59. For example, see Richard M. Pious, *Why Presidents Fail* (Lanham, Md.: Rowman & Littlefield, 2008).

CHAPTER 13 / THE BUREAUCRACY / PAGES 354–377

1. Steven Ertelt, "Obama Admin Will Force Coverage of Birth Control, Abortion Drug," LifeNews.com, 1 August 2011, http://www.lifenews.com/2011/11/21/will-obama-force-coverage-of-birth-control-abortion-drugs/; Rob Stein, "Obama Administration Refuses to Relax Plan B Restrictions," *Washington Post,* 7 December 2011, http://www.washingtonpost.com/national/health-science/obama-administration-refuses-to-relax-plan-b-restrictions/2011/12/07/gIQAF5HicO_story.html; Jennifer Corbett Dooren, "Obama Health Chief Blocks FDA on 'Morning After' Pill," *Wall Street Journal,* 8 December 2011; Sal Gentile, "Did Politics Trump Science in the Obama Administration's Ruling on Plan B for Teens?" *Need to Know,* 8 December 2011, http://www.pbs.org/wnet/need-to-know/the-daily-need/did-politics-trump-science-in-the-obama-administrations-ruling-on-plan-b-for-teens/12608/; Patti Neighmond, "The 'Morning After' Pill: How It Works and Who Uses It," *Morning Edition,* 6 February 2012, http://www.npr.org/blogs/health/2012/02/06/146358069/the-morning-after-pill-how-it-works-and-who-uses-it; and Pam Belluck, "Abortion Qualms on Morning-After Pill May Be Unfounded," *New York Times,* 5 June 2012, http://www.nytimes.com/2012/06/06/health/research/morning-after-pills-dont-block-implantation-science-suggests.html?pagewanted=all.

2. Malcolm Gladwell, "The Talent Myth," *New Yorker,* 22 July 2002, p. 32.

3. James Q. Wilson, *Bureaucracy* (New York: Basic Books, 1989), p. 25.

4. Bruce D. Porter, "Parkinson's Law Revisited: War and the Growth of American Government," *Public Interest* 60 (Summer 1980): 50.

5. Binyamin Applebaum and Annie Lowrey, "For Deficit Panel, Failure Cuts Two Ways," *New York Times,* 21 November 2011, http://www.nytimes.com/2011/11/22/us/politics/behind-deficit-panels-failure-a-surprise.html.

6. Data on government employment from the Bureau of the Census, "Federal Government Civilian Employment: March 2010," http://www2.census.gov/govs/apes/10fedfun.pdf.

7. Joel D. Aberbach and Bert A. Rockman, *In the Web of Politics* (Washington, D.C.: Brookings Institution, 2000), p. 162.

8. "Analysis," Best Places to Work in the Federal Government, 2011 rankings, http://bestplacestowork.org/BPTW/analysis/.

9. Bradley E. Wright, "Public Service and Motivation: Does Mission Matter?" *Public Administration Review* 67 (January–February 2007): 54–63; and Kaifeng Yang and Anthony Kassekert, "Linking Management Reform with Employee Job Satisfaction," *Journal of Public Administration Research and Theory* 20 (April 2010): 413–436.

10. On the challenges of trying to loosen the strictures and protections of civil service, see Norma Riccucci and Frank J. Thompson, "The New Public Management, Homeland Security, and the Politics of Civil Service Reform," *Public Administration Review* 68 (September–October 2008): 877–890.

11. Stephen Hess, *What Do We Do Now?* (Washington, D.C.: Brookings Institution, 2008).

12. David E. Lewis, "Testing Pendleton's Premise: Do Political Appointees Make Worse Bureaucrats?" *Journal of Politics* 69 (November 2007): 1073–1088.

13. Lyndsey Layton, "A Vigorous Push from Federal Regulators," *Washington Post,* 13 October 2009; and "Standard for Recreational Off-Highway Vehicles," Consumer Product Safety Commission, 28 October 2009, http://www.cpsc.gov/businfo/frnotices/fr10/rotv.html.

14. See, for example, Paul R. Pillar, *Intelligence and U.S. Foreign Policy* (New York: Columbia University Press, 2011), pp. 331–352.

15. Doris A. Graber, *Mass Media and American Politics,* 8th ed. (Washington, D.C.: CQ Press, 2010), p. 70.

16. Amol Sharma, "2005 Legislative Summary: Broadcast Indecency Penalties," *CQ Weekly,* 2 January 2006, p. 55.

17. See Jack Goldsmith, *Power and Constraint* (New York: Norton, 2012).

18. Stuart Shapiro, "The Role of Procedural Controls in OSHA's Ergonomics Rulemaking," *Public Administration Review* 67 (July–August 2007): 688–701.

19. U.S. Department of Transportation, "New DOT Consumer Rule Limits Airline Tarmac Delays," press release, http://www.dot.gov/affairs/2009/dot19909.htm; and Matthew L. Wald, "Stiff Fines Are Set for Long Wait on Tarmac," *New York Times,* 22 December 2009.

20. Joe Sharkey, "Tough Rule Eliminates Most Tarmac Strandings," *New York Times,* 4 May 2011, http://www.nytimes.com/2011/05/05/business/05TARMAC.html?_r=1&pagewanted=print.

21. Charles E. Lindblom, "The Science of Muddling Through," *Public Administration Review* 19 (Spring 1959): 79–88.

22. For a critical examination of determining what is a small increment, see Sarah Anderson and Laurel Harbridge, "Incrementalism in Appropriations: Small Aggregation, Big Changes," *Public Administration Review* 70 (May 2010): 464–474.

23. Bryan D. Jones and Frank R. Baumgartner, *The Politics of Attention* (Chicago: University of Chicago Press, 2005).

24. "Bureaucratic culture" is a particularly slippery concept but can be conceived of as the interplay of artifacts, values, and underlying assumptions. See Celeste Watkins-Hayes, *The New Welfare Bureaucrats* (Chicago: University of Chicago Press, 2009); Irene Lurie and Norma Riccucci, "Changing the 'Culture' of Welfare Offices," *Administration and Society* 34 (January 2003): 653–677; and Marissa Martino Golden, *What Motivates Bureaucrats?* (New York: Columbia University Press, 2000).

25. Jay P. Greene and Stuart Buck, "The Case for Special Education Vouchers," *Education Next* (Winter 2010): 36–43.

26. Panetta became Secretary of Defense in 2011.

27. Jane Mayer, "The Secret History," *New Yorker,* 22 June 2009, pp. 50–59; and Jane Mayer, *The Dark Side* (New York: Anchor Books, 2009).

28. Robert B. Reich, *Locked in the Cabinet* (New York: Vintage, 1998), pp. 115–118.

29. Daniel A. Mazmanian, "Los Angeles' Clean Air Saga-Spanning the Three Epochs," in *Toward Sustainable Communities,* ed. Daniel A. Mazmanian and Michael E. Kraft (Cambridge, Mass.: MIT Press, 2009), p. 107.

30. Jeffrey M. Berry with David F. Arons, *A Voice for Nonprofits* (Washington, D.C.: Brookings Institution, 2003); and Joseph J. Cordes and C. Eugene Steuerle, eds., *Nonprofits and Business* (Washington, D.C.: Urban Institute, 2009).

31. See generally Eric M. Patashnik, *Reforms at Risk* (Princeton, N.J.: Princeton University Press, 2008).

32. See Donald Kettl et al., *Managing for Performance: A Report on Strategies for Improving the Results of Government* (Washington, D.C.: Brookings Institution, 2006).

33. Daniel J. Fiorino, *The New Environmental Regulation* (Cambridge, Mass.: MIT Press, 2006).

34. Archon Fung, Mary Graham, and David Weil, *Full Disclosure* (New York: Cambridge University Press, 2007).

35. Darrell M. West, *State and Federal Electronic Government in the United States, 2008* (Washington, D.C.: Brookings Institution, 2008), http://www.brookings.edu/~/media/Files/rc/reports/2008/0826_egovernment_west/0826_egovernment_west.pdf.

36. Eric Lipton, "With Obama, Regulations Are Back in Fashion," *New York Times,* 13 May 2010.

37. Frank Newport, "Despite Negativity, Americans Mixed on Ideal Role of Gov't," Gallup Poll, 28 September 2011, http://www.gallup.com/poll/149741/despite-negativity-americans-mixed-ideal-role-gov.aspx.

38. See generally Philip J. Cooper, *Government by Contract* (Washington, D.C.: CQ Press, 2003).

39. Maximus, "Child Support," http://www.maximus.com/services/children-families/child-support.

40. Donald F. Kettl, "The Global Revolution in Public Management: Driving Themes, Missing Links," *Journal of Policy Analysis and Management* 16 (1997): 448.

41. Beryl A. Radin, *Challenging the Performance Movement* (Washington, D.C.: Georgetown University Press, 2006).

42. David G. Frederickson and H. George Frederickson, *Measuring the Performance of the Hollow State* (Washington, D.C.: Georgetown University Press, 2006), pp. 56–57.

43. Vassia Gueorguieva et al., "The Program Assessment Rating Tool and the Government Performance and Results Act," *The American Review of Public Administration* 39 (May 2009): 225–245.

CHAPTER 14 / THE COURTS / PAGES 378–411

1. Philip Elman (interviewed by Normal Silber), "The Solicitor General's Office, Justice Frankfurter, and Civil Rights Litigation, 1946–1960: An Oral History," *Harvard Law Review* 100 (1987): 840.

2. David O'Brien, *Storm Center,* 2nd ed. (New York: Norton, 1990), p. 324.

3. Bernard Schwartz, *The Unpublished Opinions of the Warren Court* (New York: Oxford University Press, 1985), p. 446.

4. Ibid., pp. 445–448.

5. Felix Frankfurter and James M. Landis, *The Business of the Supreme Court* (New York: Macmillan, 1928), pp. 5–14; and Julius Goebel, Jr., *The History of the Supreme Court of the United States,* vol. 1, *Antecedents and Beginnings to 1801* (New York: Macmillan, 1971).

6. Maeva Marcus (ed.), *The Documentary History of the Supreme Court of the United States, 1789–1800,* vol. 3, *The Justices on Circuit, 1795–1800* (New York: Columbia University Press, 1990).

7. Robert G. McCloskey, *The United States Supreme Court* (Chicago: University of Chicago Press, 1960), p. 31.

8. Cliff Sloan and David McKean, *The Great Decision: Jefferson, Adams, Marshall, and the Battle for the Supreme Court* (New York: PublicAffairs, 2009).

9. *Marbury* v. *Madison,* 1 Cranch 137 at 177, 178 (1803).

10. Interestingly, the term *judicial review* dates only to 1910; it was apparently unknown to Marshall and his contemporaries. Robert Lowry Clinton, *Marbury v. Madison and Judicial Review* (Lawrence: University Press of Kansas, 1989), p. 7.

11. Lee Epstein et al., *The Supreme Court Compendium,* 4th ed. (Washington, D.C.: CQ Press, 2006), Table 2-15.

12. "Constitution of the United States of America: Annotated and Interpreted (2008 Supplement)," http://www.gpo.gov/fdsys/pkg/GPO-CONAN-2008/pdf/GPO-CONAN-2008.pdf.

13. *Martin* v. *Hunter's Lessee,* 1 Wheat. 304 (1819).

14. Epstein et al., *The Supreme Court Compendium,* Table 2-16.

15. Garry Wills, *Explaining America: The Federalist* (Garden City, N.Y.: Doubleday, 1981), pp. 127–136.

16. Court Statistics Project, *Examining the Work of State Courts, 2009: An Analysis of 2009 State Court Caseloads* (Williamsburg, Va.: National Center for State Courts, 2011), http://www.courtstatistics.org/FlashMicrosites/CSP/images/CSP2009.pdf.

17. William P. Marshall, "Federalization: A Critical Overview," *DePaul Law Review* 44 (1995): 722–723.

18. Charles Alan Wright, *Handbook on the Law of Federal Courts,* 3rd ed. (St. Paul, Minn.: West, 1976), p. 7.

19. *Judicial Business of the United States Courts, 2011,* http://www.uscourts.gov/uscourts/Statistics/JudicialBusiness/2011/JudicialBusiness2011.pdf.

20. Ibid.

21. Ibid.

22. Linda Greenhouse, "Precedent for Lower Courts: Tyrant or Teacher?" *New York Times,* 29 January 1988, p. B7.

23. *Texas* v. *Johnson,* 491 U.S. 397 (1989); and *United States* v. *Eichmann,* 496 U.S. 310 (1990).

24. *Regents of the University of California* v. *Bakke,* 438 U.S. 265 (1978).

25. *Grutter* v. *Bollinger,* 539 U.S. 244 (2003); and *Gratz* v. *Bollinger,* 539 U.S. 306 (2003).

26. *Fisher* v. *University of Texas,* No. 1–345 (cert. granted Feb. 21, 2012).

27. "Reading Petitions Is for Clerks Only at High Court Now," *Wall Street Journal,* 11 October 1990, p. B7.

28. H. W. Perry, Jr., *Deciding to Decide: Agenda Setting in the United States Supreme Court* (Cambridge, Mass.: Harvard University Press, 1991); and Linda Greenhouse, "Justice Delayed: Agreeing Not to Agree," *New York Times,* 17 March 1996, sec. 4, p. 1.

29. Jeffrey Rosen, "Supreme Court Inc.: How the Nation's Highest Court Has Come to Side with Business," *New York Times Magazine,* 16 March 2008, pp. 38 et seq.

30. Perry, *Deciding to Decide*; and Gregory A. Caldiera and John R. Wright, "The Discuss List: Agenda Building in the Supreme Court," *Law and Society Review* 24 (1990): 807.

31. Doris M. Provine, *Case Selection in the United States Supreme Court* (Chicago: University of Chicago Press, 1980), pp. 74–102.

32. Perry, *Deciding to Decide,* p. 286.

33. Justice Anthony M. Kennedy, quoted in Adam Liptak, "No Vote-Trading Here," *New York Times: Week in Review,* 16 May 2010, p. 4.

34. Kevin T. McGuire, "Repeat Players in the Supreme Court: The Role of Experienced Lawyers in Litigation Success," *Journal of Politics* 57 (1995): 187–196.

35. Michael Kirkland, "Court Hears 'Subordinate' Speech Debate," 1 December 1993, NEWSNET News Bulletin Board. The oral argument in the case, *Waters* v. *Churchill,* can be found at http://www.oyez.org/cases/1990-1999/1993/1993_92_1450.

36. William H. Rehnquist, "Remarks of the Chief Justice: My Life in the Law Series," *Duke Law Journal* 52 (2003): 787–805.

37. "Rising Fixed Opinions," *New York Times,* 22 February 1988, p. 14. See also Linda Greenhouse, "At the Bar," *New York Times,* 28 July 1989, p. 21.

38. Jeffrey A. Segal and Harold J. Spaeth, *The Supreme Court and the Attitudinal Model* (Cambridge: Cambridge University Press, 1993).

39. Stefanie A. Lindquist and Frank B. Cross, *Measuring Judicial Activism* (New York: Oxford University Press, 2009), pp. 1–28.

40. Stuart Taylor, Jr., "Lifting of Secrecy Reveals Earthy Side of Justices," *New York Times,* 22 February 1988, p. A16.

41. Richard A. Posner, "The Courthouse Mice," *New Republic,* 12 June 2006, http://tnr.com/article/the-courthouse-mice.

42. Thomas G. Walker, Lee Epstein, and William J. Dixon, "On the Mysterious Demise of Consensual Norms in the United States Supreme Court," *Journal of Politics* 50 (1988): 361–389.

43. Linda Greenhouse, "Roberts Is at Court's Helm, but He Isn't Yet in Control," *New York Times,* 2 July 2006, sec. 1, p. 1. See also

John P. Kelsh, "The Opinion Delivery Practices of the United States Supreme Court, 1790–1945," *Washington University Law Quarterly* 77 (1999): 137–181. For more on the Roberts Court, see Linda Greenhouse, "Oral Dissents Give Ginsberg New Voice," *New York Times,* 31 May 2007, p. A1; and Jeffrey Toobin, "Five to Four," *New Yorker,* 25 June 2007, pp. 35–37.

44. Stephen L. Wasby, *The Supreme Court in the Federal Judicial System,* 3rd ed. (Chicago: Nelson-Hall, 1988), p. 241.

45. Greenhouse, "At the Bar," p. 21.

46. National Center for State Courts, "Survey of Judicial Salaries," Vol. 36, No. 2, 1 July 2011, http://contentdm.ncsconline.org/cgi-bin/showfile.exe?CISOROOT=/judicial&CISOPTR=323.

47. Nathan Koppel and Vanessa O'Connell, "Pay Gap Widens at Big Law Firms as Partners Chase Star Attorneys," *Wall Street Journal,* Feb. 8, 2011, http://online.wsj.com/article/SB10001424052748704570104576124232780067002.html; *US News and World Report,* "Law Jobs WillBe Harder to Come by," 25 June 2010, http://www.usnews.com/education/articles/2010/06/25/law-jobs-will-be-harder-to-come-by; and Sam Favate, *Survey: Median Starting Salaries Plunge for New Law Grads,* WSJ Law Blog, July 12, 2012, http://blogs.wsj.com/law/2012/07/12/survey-median-starting-salaries-plunge-for-new-law-grads/.

48. Carlyn Kolker, "Summary Judgments for Feb 6," http://newsandinsight.thomsonreuters.com/Legal/News/2012/02_-_February/Summary_Judgments_for_Feb_6/.

49. Lawrence Baum, *American Courts: Process and Policy,* 3rd ed. (Boston: Houghton Mifflin, 1994), pp. 114–129.

50. *Caperton* v. *A. T. Massey Coal Co.,* 556 U.S. 868 (2009).

51. Tajuana D. Massie, Thomas G. Hansford, and David R. Songer, "The Timing of Presidential Nominations to Lower Federal Courts," *Political Research Quarterly* 57 (2004): 145–154.

52. Sheldon Goldman et al., "Picking Judges in a Time of Turmoil: W. Bush's Judiciary During the 109th Congress," *Judicature* 90 (May–June 2007): 252–283.

53. Paul Barrett, "More Minorities, Women Named to U.S. Courts," *Wall Street Journal,* 23 December 1993, p. B1; and Sheldon Goldman and Elliot Slotnick, "Clinton's Second Term Judiciary: Picking Judges under Fire," *Judicature* 92 (May–June 1999): 264–284.

54. Kenneth L. Manning and Robert A. Carp, "The Decision-Making Ideology of George W. Bush's Judicial Appointees: An Update" (paper presented at the annual meeting of the American Political Science Association, Chicago, 2–5 September 2004).

55. Charlie Savage and Raymond Hernandez, "Filibuster by Senate Republicans Blocks Confirmation of Judicial Nominee," *New York Times,* 7 December 2011, p. A16, http://www.nytimes.com/2011/12/07/us/senate-gop-blocks-confirmation-of-caitlin-halligan-as-judge.html; and Joe Palazzolo, "With Rose Confirmation, Obama Sets a Record," The Wall Street Journal Law Blog, 11 September 2012, http://blogs.wsj.com/law/2012/09/11/with-rose-confirmation-obama-sets-a-record.

56. Wasby, *Supreme Court,* pp. 107–110.

57. Jeffrey Toobin, *The Nine: Inside the Secret World of the Supreme Court* (New York: Doubleday, 2007), p. 269.

58. State News Service, "Statement of H. Thomas Wells Jr., President, American Bar Association re: American Bar Association Standing Committee on Federal Judiciary," 17 March 2009.

59. Ronald Stidham, Robert A. Carp, and Donald R. Songer, "The Voting Behavior of Judges Appointed by President Clinton" (paper presented at the annual meeting of the Southwestern Political Science Association, Houston, Tex., March 1996). See also Susan B. Haire, Martha Anne Humphries, and Donald R. Songer, "The Voting Behavior of Clinton's Courts of Appeals Appointees," *Judicature* 84 (March–April 2001): 274–281.

60. Robert A. Carp, Ronald Stidham, and Kenneth L. Manning, "The Voting Behavior of George W. Bush's Judges: How Sharp a Turn to the Right?" in *Principles and Practice of American Politics: Classic and Contemporary Readings,* 3rd ed., ed. Samuel Kernell and Steven S. Smith (Washington, D.C.: CQ Press, 2006).

61. Sheldon Goldman. "Obama and the Federal Judiciary: Great Expectations but Will He Have a Dickens of a Time Living up to Them?" *The Forum* 7.1 (2010), http://works.bepress.com/sheldon_goldman/1.

62. Peter G. Fish, "John J. Parker," in *Dictionary of American Biography,* supp. 6, *1956–1980* (New York: Scribner's, 1980), p. 494.

63. "Supreme Court Nominations, present-1789," http://www.senate.gov/pagelayout/reference/nominations/Nominations.htm.

64. "CRS Report for Congress: Supreme Court Nominations Not Filled," p. 7, 9 January 2008, http://www.fas.org/sgp/crs/misc/RL31171.pdf.

65. "Supreme Court Nominee Sonia Sotomayor's Speech at Berkeley Law in 2001," *Berkeley La Raza Law Journal* (2002), http://law.berkeley.edu/4982.htm.

66. Elena Kagan, "Confirmation Messes: Old and New," *The University of Chicago Law Review* 62, no. 2 (Spring 1995): 919–942, http://www.scotusblog.com/wp-content/uploads/2010/03/Confirmation-Messes.pdf.

67. "Transcript: Kagan's Opening Statement," http://m.npr.org/news/front/128171860?page=3.

68. Wikipedia, "List of Federal Judges Appointed by Barack Obama," http://en.wikipedia.org/wiki/List_of_federal_judges_appointed_by_Barack_Obama.

69. Charlie Savage, "Obama Lags on Judicial Picks, Limiting His Mark on Courts," *New York Times,* 18 August 2012, p. A1.

70. *Brown* v. *Board of Education II,* 349 U.S.294 (1955).

71. Charles A. Johnson and Bradley C. Canon, *Judicial Policies: Implementation and Impact* (Washington, D.C.: CQ Press, 1984).

72. *Webster* v. *Reproductive Health Services,* 492 U.S. 490 (1989).

73. *Planned Parenthood* v. *Casey,* 505 U.S. 833 (1992).

74. *Stenberg* v. *Carhart,* 530 U.S. 914 (2000); and *Gonzales* v. *Carhart,* 550 U.S. 124 (2007).

75. Alexander M. Bickel, *The Least Dangerous Branch* (Indianapolis, Ind.: Bobbs-Merrill, 1962); and Robert A. Dahl, "Decision-Making in a Democracy: The Supreme Court as a National Policy-Maker," *Journal of Public Law* 6 (1962): 279.

76. William Mishler and Reginald S. Sheehan, "The Supreme Court as a Countermajoritarian Institution? The Impact of Public Opinion on Supreme Court Decisions," *American Political Science Review* 87 (1993): 87–101.

77. Barry Friedman, *The Will of the People* (New York: Farrar, Straus and Giroux, 2009).

78. *Engel* v. *Vitale,* 367 U.S. 643 (1961).

79. James L. Gibson and Gregory A. Caldiera, "Knowing about Courts" (paper presented at the Second Annual Conference on Empirical Legal Studies, 20 June 2007), http://ssrn.com/abstract=956562.

80. Gallup Poll, "High Court to Start Term with Near Decade-High Approval," http://gallup.com/poll/122858/High-Court-Start-Term-Near-Decade-High-Approval.aspx?CSTS=alert.

81. See note 72.

82. Adam Liptak and Allison Kopicki, "Approval Rating for Justices Hits Just 44% in New Poll," *New York Times,* 8 June 2012, p. A1.

83. *Kelo* v. *City of New London,* 545 U.S. 469 (2005).

84. William J. Brennan, Jr., "State Court Judge versus United States Supreme Court Justice: A Change in Function and Perspective," *University of Florida Law Review* 19 (1966): 225.

85. G. Alan Tarr and M. C. Porter, *State Supreme Courts in State and Nation* (New Haven, Conn.: Yale University Press, 1988), pp. 206–209.

86. John B. Wefing, "The Performance of the New Jersey Supreme Court at the Opening of the Twenty-first Century: New Cast, Same Script," *Seton Hall Law Review* 32 (2003): 769.

87. Dennis Hevesi, "New Jersey Court Protects Trash from Police Searches," *New York Times,* 19 July 1990, p. A9.

88. Kermit L. Hall, "The Canon of American Constitutional History in Comparative Perspective" (keynote address to the Supreme Court Historical Society, Washington, D.C., 16 February 2001).

89. Baum, *American Courts,* pp. 319–347.

CHAPTER 15 / ORDER AND CIVIL LIBERTIES / PAGES 412–447

1. *Ahlquist* v. *City of Cranston,* 2012 U.S. Dist. LEXIS 3348 (USDC, D. RI) (Jan. 11, 2012)

2. Abby Goodnough, "Student Faces Town's Wrath in Protest against a Prayer," *New York Times,* 27 January, 2012, p. A12.

3. Learned Hand, *The Bill of Rights* (Boston: Atheneum, 1958), p. 1.

4. Richard E. Berg-Andersson, "Of Liberties, Rights and Powers (Part One): Just How Far Is Too Far–for Both Governments and

Persons?" Green Papers Commentary, 27 April 2006, http://www. thegreenpapers.com/PCom/?20060427-0.

5. Leonard W. Levy, *The Establishment Clause: Religion and the First Amendment* (New York: Macmillan, 1986); Leo Pfeffer, *Church, State, and Freedom* (Boston: Beacon Press, 1953); and Leonard W. Levy, "The Original Meaning of the Establishment Clause of the First Amendment," in *Religion and the State,* ed. James E. Wood, Jr. (Waco, Tex.: Baylor University Press, 1985), pp. 43–83.

6. Pew Research Center for the People and the Press, "U.S. Stands Alone in Its Embrace of Religion," Washington, D.C., 19 December 2002.

7. *Utah Highway Patrol Association* v. *American Atheists, Inc.*, 565 U.S. ____ (2011)(Thomas, J. dissenting from a denial of certiorari).

8. *Reynolds* v. *United States,* 98 U.S. 145 (1879).

9. *Everson* v. *Board of Education,* 330 U.S. 1 (1947).

10. *Board of Education* v. *Allen,* 392 U.S. 236 (1968).

11. *Lemon* v. *Kurtzman,* 403 U.S. 602 (1971).

12. *Agostini* v. *Felton,* 96 U.S. 552 (1997).

13. *Zelman* v. *Simmons-Harris,* 536 U.S. 639 (2002).

14. *Lynch* v. *Donnelly,* 465 U.S. 668 (1984).

15. *Van Orden* v. *Perry,* 545 U.S. 677 (2005).

16. *McCreary County* v. *ACLU of Kentucky,* 545 U.S. 844 (2005).

17. *Salazar* v. *Buono,* 559 U.S.___(2010).

18. *Engle* v. *Vitale,* 370 U.S. 421 (1962); David W. Moore, "Public Favors Voluntary School Prayer for Public Schools," 26 Aug 2005, http://www.gallup.com/poll/18136/Public-Favors-Voluntary-Prayer-Public-Schools.aspx; and "Public Opinion On 15 Controversial and Divisive Issues," 4 Oct 2011, http://www.harrisinteractive.com/NewsRoom/HarrisPolls/tabid/447/ctl/ReadCustom%20Default/mid/1508/ArticleId/874/Default.aspx.

19. *Abington School District* v. *Schempp,* 374 U.S. 203 (1963).

20. *Lee* v. *Weisman,* 505 U.S. 577 (1992).

21. Neela Banerjee, "School Board to Pay in Jesus Prayer Suit," *New York Times,* 28 February 2008, p. A16.

22. Michael W. McConnell, "The Origins and Historical Understanding of the Free Exercise of Religion," *Harvard Law Review* 103 (1990): 1409.

23. *Sherbert* v. *Verner,* 374 U.S. 398 (1963).

24. Adam Winkler, "Fatal in Theory and Strict in Fact: An Empirical Analysis of Strict Scrutiny in the Federal Courts," *Vanderbilt Law Review* 59 (2006): 793.

25. McConnell, "Origins and Historical Understanding."

26. *Employment Division* v. *Smith,* 494 U.S. 872 (1990).

27. Laurence Tribe, *Treatise on American Constitutional Law,* 2nd ed. (St. Paul, Minn.: West, 1988), p. 566.

28. Zechariah Chafee, *Free Speech in the United States* (Cambridge, Mass.: Harvard University Press, 1941).

29. Leonard W. Levy, *The Emergence of a Free Press* (New York: Oxford University Press, 1985).

30. Mark Twain, *Following the Equator* (Hartford, Conn.: American Publishing, 1897).

31. *Brandenburg* v. *Ohio,* 395 U.S. 444 (1969).

32. *Schenck* v. *United States* v. *United States,* 249 U.S. 47 (1919).

33. *Abrams* v. *United States,* 250 U.S. 616 (1919).

34. *Gitlow* v. *New York,* 268 U.S. 652 (1925).

35. *Dennis* v. *United States,* 341 U.S. 494 (1951).

36. *Brandenburg* v. *Ohio,* 395 U.S. 444 (1969).

37. Anthony Lewis, *Freedom for the Thought That We Hate: A Biography of the First Amendment* (New York: Basic Books, 2008).

38. *Tinker* v. *Des Moines Independent County School District,* 393 U.S. 503, at 508 (1969).

39. *Chaplinsky* v. *New Hampshire,* 315 U.S. 568 (1942).

40. *Terminiello* v. *Chicago,* 337 U.S. 1, 37 (1949).

41. *Cohen* v. *California,* 403 U.S. 15 (1971).

42. Kathleen M. Sullivan, "Two Concepts of Political Freedom," *Harvard Law Review* 124 (November 2010): 143–177.

43. *New York Times* v. *Sullivan,* 376 U.S. 254 (1964).

44. *Near* v. *Minnesota,* 283 U.S. 697 (1931).

45. For a detailed account of *Near,* see Fred W. Friendly, *Minnesota Rag* (New York: Random House, 1981).

46. *New York Times* v. *United States,* 403 U.S. 713 (1971).

47. *Branzburg* v. *Hayes,* 408 U.S. 665 (1972).

48. *Hazelwood School District* v. *Kuhlmeier,* 484 U.S. 260 (1988); and *Morse* v. *Frederick,* 551 U.S. 393 (2007).

49. *United States* v. *Cruikshank,* 92 U.S. 542 (1876); and *Constitution of the United States of America: Annotated and Interpreted* (Washington, D.C.: U.S. Government Printing Office, 1973), p. 1031.

50. *DeJonge* v. *Oregon,* 299 U.S. 353 (1937).

51. *United States* v. *Miller,* 307 U.S. 174 (1939).

52. *District of Columbia* v. *Heller,* 554 U.S. 290 (2008).

53. *McDonald* v. *Chicago,* 561 U.S.___(2010).

54. *Barron* v. *Baltimore,* 32 U.S. (7 Pet.) 243 (1833).

55. *Lochner* v. *New York,* 198 U.S. 45 (1905).

56. *Chicago B&Q Railroad* v. *Chicago,* 166 U.S. 226 (1897).

57. *Gitlow* v. *New York,* 268 U.S. 652, 666 (1925).

58. *Palko* v. *Connecticut,* 302 U.S. 319 (1937).

59. *Duncan* v. *Louisiana,* 391 U.S. 145 (1968).

60. *McNabb* v. *United States,* 318 U.S. 332 (1943).

61. *Baldwin* v. *New York,* 399 U.S. 66 (1970).

62. Anthony Lewis, *Gideon's Trumpet* (New York: Random House, 1964).

63. *Gideon* v. *Wainwright,* 372 U.S. 335 (1963).

64. *Miranda* v. *Arizona,* 384 U.S. 436 (1966).

65. *Dickerson* v. *United States,* 530 U.S. 428 (2000).

66. *Wolf* v. *Colorado,* 338 U.S. 25 (1949).

67. *Mapp* v. *Ohio,* 367 U.S. 643 (1961).

68. *United States* v. *Leon,* 468 U.S. 897 (1984).

69. *Hudson* v. *Michigan,* 547 U.S. 586 (2006).

70. *Herring* v. *United States,* 555 U.S.___(2009).

71. Eric Lichtblau, "More Demands on Cell Carriers in Surveillance," *New York Times,* 9 July 2012, p. A1.

72. Liane Hansen, "Voices in the News This Week," *NPR Weekend Edition,* 28 October 2001 (NEXIS transcript).

73. Dan Eggen, "Tough Anti-Terror Campaign Pledged: Ashcroft Tells Mayors He Will Use New Law to Fullest Extent," *Washington Post,* 26 October 2001, p. A1.

74. "Security: FBI Sought 3,500 Records without Subpoenas," *National Journal's Technology Daily,* 1 May 2006.

75. Michael Sandler, "Anti-Terrorism Law on Final Tack," *CO Weekly,* 3 March 2006, p. 600.

76. Eric Lichtblau, "More Demands on Cell Carriers in Surveillance," *New York Times,* 9 July 2012, p. A1.

77. *Exparte Quirin,* 317 U.S. 1 (1942); *In re Yamashita,* 327 U.S. 1 (1946); *Hirota* v. *MacArthur,* 338 U.S. 197 (1949); and *Johnson* v. *Eisentrager,* 339 U.S. 763 (1950).

78. *Rasul* v. *Bush,* 542 U.S. 466 (2004).

79. *Hamdi* v. *Rumsfeld,* 542 U.S. 507 (2004).

80. *Hamdan* v. *Rumsfeld,* 548 U.S. 557 (2006).

81. *Boumediene* v. *Bush,* 553 U.S. 723 (2008).

82. Paul Brest, *Processes of Constitutional Decision-Making* (Boston: Little, Brown, 1975), p. 708.

83. *Griswold* v. *Connecticut,* 381 U.S. 479 (1965).

84. *Roe* v. *Wade,* 410 U.S. 113 (1973).

85. See John Hart Ely, "The Wages of Crying Wolf: A Comment on *Roe* v. *Wade,*" *Yale Law Journal* 82 (1973): 920.

86. Justice Harry Blackmun, interview by Ted Koppel and Nina Totenberg, *Nightline,* ABC, 2 December 1993.

87. *Webster* v. *Reproductive Health Services,* 492 U.S. 490 (1989).

88. *Hodgson* v. *Minnesota,* 497 U.S. 417 (1990); and *Ohio* v. *Akron Center for Reproductive Health,* 497 U.S. 502 (1990).

89. *Steinberg* v. *Carhart,* 530 U.S. 914 (2000).

90. *Gonzales* v. *Carhart,* 550 U.S. 124 (2007).

91. Stuart Taylor, "Supreme Court Hears Case on Homosexual Rights," *New York Times,* 1 April 1986, p. A24.

92. *Bowers* v. *Hardwick,* 478 U.S. 186 (1986).

93. Linda Greenhouse, "Washington Talk: When Second Thoughts Come Too Late," *New York Times,* 5 November 1990, p. A9.

94. Dahlia Lithwick, "Lawrence v Texas: How Laws Against Sodomy Became Unconstitutional, *The New Yorker,* 7 Mar 2012, http://www.newyorker.com/arts/critics/books/2012/03/12/120312crbo_books_lithwick; and Dale Carpenter, *Flagrant Conduct: The Story of Lawrence v. Texas* (New York: W. W. Norton & Company, 2012).

95. *Lawrence and Garner* v. *Texas,* 539 U.S. 558 (2003).

96. Ibid.

97. *Gill* v. *Office of Personnel Management,* No. 1:09-cv-10309 (U.S. Dist. Ct., D. Mass.).

98. *Perry* v. *Schwarzenegger,* No. C 09-2292 VRW (U.S. Dist. Ct., N.D. Cal.), 4 August 2010, https://ecf.cand.uscourts.gov/cand/09cv2292/files/09cv2292-ORDER.pdf.

CHAPTER 16 / EQUALITY AND CIVIL RIGHTS / PAGES 448–485

1. *Fisher* v. *University of Texas*, 645 F.Supp.2d 587 (2009); *Fisher* v. *University of Texas*, 631 F. 3d 213 (2011); and *Fisher* v. *University of Texas*, No. 11-345 (cert. granted, Feb. 21, 2012).
2. Jack Citrin, "Affirmative Action in the People's Court," *Public Interest* 122 (1996): 40–41; Sam Howe Verhovek, "In Poll, Americans Reject Means but Not Ends of Racial Diversity," *New York Times*, 14 December 1997, sec. 1, p. 1; and "Aid to Blacks and Minorities, 1970–2008," in *National Election Studies Guide to Public Opinion and Electoral Behavior*, http://www.electionstudies.org/nesguide/toptable/tab4b_4.htm.
3. Jeffrey M. Jones, "Race, Ideology, and Support for Affirmative Action," *The Gallup Poll*, August 23, 2005, http://www.gallup.com/poll/18091/Race-Ideology-Support-Affirmative-Action.aspx.
4. Michael I. Norton and Samuel R. Sommers, "Whites See Racism as a Zero-Sum Games That They Are Now Losing," *Perspectives on Psychological Science* 6 (May 2011): 215–218, http://www.people.hbs.edu/mnorton/norton%20sommers.pdf. A Pew Research Center survey released in May 2009 found that 65 percent of Americans disagreed with the statement: "We should make every effort to improve the position of blacks and minorities, even if it means giving them preferential treatment." Americans have mostly disagreed with this statement since 1987, when the question was first asked. See Pew Research Center, "Public Backs Affirmative Action, but Not Minority Preferences," http://pewresearch.org/pubs/1240/sotomayor-supreme-court-affirmative-action-minority-preferences.
5. *Regents of the University of California* v. *Bakke*, 438 U.S. 265,407 (1978).
6. *Parents Involved in Community Schools* v. *Seattle School District No. 1*, 551 U.S. 701 (2007).
7. *The Slaughterhouse Cases*, 83 U.S. 36 (1873).
8. *United States* v. *Cruikshank*, 92 U.S. 542 (1876).
9. *United States* v. *Reese*, 92 U.S. 214 (1876).
10. *Civil Rights Cases*, 109 U.S. 3 (1883).
11. Mary Beth Norton et al., *A People and a Nation: A History of the United States*, 3rd ed. (Boston: Houghton Mifflin, 1990), p. 490.
12. *Plessy* v. *Ferguson*, 163 U.S. 537 (1896).
13. *Cummings* v. *County Board of Education*, 17 5 U.S. 528 (1899).
14. *Missouri ex rel. Gaines* v. *Canada*, 305 U.S. 337 (1938).
15. *Sweatt* v. *Painter*, 339 U.S. 629 (1950).
16. *Brown* v. *Board of Education*, 347 U.S. 483 (1954).
17. Ibid., 347 U.S. 483, 495 (1954).
18. Ibid., 347 U.S. 483, 494 (1954).
19. *Bolling* v. *Sharpe*, 347 U.S. 497 (1954).
20. *Brown* v. *Board of Education II*, 349 U.S. 294 (1955).
21. Jack W. Peltason, *Fifty-Eight Lonely Men*, rev. ed. (Urbana: University of Illinois Press, 1971).
22. *Alexander* v. *Holmes County Board of Education*, 396 U.S. 19 (1969).
23. *Swann* v. *Charlotte-Mecklenburg County Schools*, 402 U.S. 1 (1971).
24. *Milliken* v. *Bradley*, 418 U.S. 717 (1974).
25. Robert Caro, *The Passage of Power: The Years of Lyndon Johnson* (New York: Knopf, 2012).
26. Richard Kluger, *Simple Justice* (New York: Knopf, 1976), p. 753.
27. Taylor Branch, *Parting the Waters: America in the King Years, 1955–1963* (New York: Simon & Schuster, 1988), p. 3.
28. Ibid., p. 14.
29. Ibid., p. 271.
30. *Bell* v. *Maryland*, 378 U.S. 226 (1964).
31. Norton et al., *People and a Nation*, p. 943.
32. Caro, *The Passage of Power*.
33. *Heart of Atlanta Motel* v. *United States*, 379 U.S. 241 (1964).
34. *Katzenbach* v. *McClung*, 379 U.S. 294 (1964).
35. *National Federation of Independent Business* v. *Sebelius*, 567 U.S. ___ (2012).
36. But see Abigail M. Thernstrom, *Whose Vote Counts? Affirmative Action and Minority Voting Rights* (Cambridge, Mass.: Harvard University Press, 1987).
37. *Grove City College* v. *Bell*, 465 U.S. 555 (1984).
38. *Richmond* v. *J.A. Croson Co.*, 488 U.S. 469 (1989).
39. *Martin* v. *Wilks*, 490 U.S. 755 (1989); *Wards Cove Packing Co.* v. *Atonio*, 490 U.S. 642 (1989); *Patterson* v. *McLean Credit Union*, 491 U.S. 164 (1989); *Price Waterhouse* v. *Hopkins*, 490 U.S. 228 (1989); *Lorance* v. *AT&T Technologies*, 490 U.S. 900 (1989); and *EEOC* v. *Arabian American Oil Co.*, 499 U.S. 244 (1991).
40. *Saint Francis College* v. *Al-Khazraji*, 481 U.S. 604 (1987).
41. Dee Brown, *Bury My Heart at Wounded Knee: An Indian History of the American West* (New York: Holt, Rinehart & Winston, 1971).
42. Francis Paul Prucha, *The Great Father: The United States Government and the American Indian*, vol. 2 (Lincoln: University of Nebraska Press, 1984).
43. *Arizona* v. *United States*, 567 U.S. ___ (2012).
44. Stephen Ceasar, "Hispanic Population Tops 50 Million in U.S.," http://articles.latimes.com/2011/mar/24/nation/la-na-census-hispanic-20110325.
45. U.S. Equal Employment Opportunity Commission, "Americans with Disabilities Act of 1990 (ADA) FY 1997-FY 2011," http://www.eeoc.gov/eeoc/statistics/enforcement/ada-charges.cfm.
46. Lisa J. Stansky, "Opening Doors," *ABA Journal* 82 (1996): 66–69.
47. "Stonewall and Beyond: Lesbian and Gay Culture," Columbia University Libraries exhibition, 25 May–17 September 1994, http://www.columbia.edu/cu/ libraries/events/sw25/.
48. See, generally, *PS: Political Science and Politics* 38 (April 2005).
49. "Gay/Lesbian Rights: Long-Term Contribution Trends," http://www.opensecrets.org/industries/indus.asp?Ind=J7300.
50. Don't Ask Don't Tell Repeal Act of 2010, 22 December, 2010.
51. Rachel Maddow interview, 10 May 2012, *Today* on NBC, http://video.today.msnbc.msn.com/today/47368691#47368691.
52. *Goodridge & Others* v. *Department of Public Health*, 440 Mass. 309 (2003); and Opinions of the Justices to the Senate, 440 Mass. 1201 (2004).
53. *In re Marriage Cases*, Calif. Sup. Ct., No. S147999, 15 May 2008.
54. Adam Nagourney, "Court Strikes Down Ban on Gay Marriage in California," *New York Times*, 7 February 2012, http://www.nytimes.com/2012/02/08/us/marriage-ban-violates-constitution-court-rules.html.
55. Jesse McKinley, "Tart Questions at Same-Sex Marriage Trial's Closing," *New York Times*, 17 June 2010, p. A15.
56. *Boy Scouts of America* v. *Dale*, 530 U.S. 610 (2000).
57. Cited in Martin Gruberg, *Women in American Politics* (Oshkosh, Wisc.: Academic Press, 1968), p. 4.
58. *Bradwell* v. *Illinois*, 83 U.S. 130 (1873).
59. *Muller* v. *Oregon*, 208 U.S. 412 (1908).
60. *International Union, United Automobile, Aerospace and Agricultural Implement Workers of America* v. *Johnson Controls, Inc.*, 499 U.S. 187 (1991).
61. *Minor* v. *Happersett*, 88 U.S. 162 (1875).
62. John H. Aldrich et al., *American Government: People, Institutions, and Policies* (Boston: Houghton Mifflin, 1986), p. 618.
63. *Ledbetter* v. *Goodyear Tire and Rubber Company*, 550 U.S. (2007).
64. Sheryl Gay Stolberg, "Obama Signs Equal-Pay Legislation," *New York Times*, 30 January 2009.
65. *Reed* v. *Reed*, 404 U.S. 71 (1971).
66. *Frontiero* v. *Richardson*, 411 U.S. 677 (1973).
67. *Craig* v. *Boren*, 429 U.S. 190 (1976).
68. Paul Weiler, "The Wages of Sex: The Uses and Limits of Comparable Worth," *Harvard Law Review* 99 (1986): 1728; and Paula England, *Comparable Worth: Theories and Evidence* (New York: Aldine de Gruyter, 1992).
69. *J.E.B.* v. *Alabama ex rel. T.B.*, 511 U.S. 127 (1994).
70. *United States* v. *Virginia*, slip op. 94-1941 and 94-2107 (decided 26 June 1996).
71. Mike Allen, "Defiant V.M.I. to Admit Women but Will Not Ease Rules for Them," *New York Times*, 22 September 1996, sec. 1, p. 1.
72. Jane J. Mansbridge, *Why We Lost the ERA* (Chicago: University of Chicago Press, 1986).
73. Melvin I. Urofsky, *A March of Liberty* (New York: Knopf, 1988), p. 902.
74. *Harris* v. *Forklift Systems*, 510 U.S. 17 (1993).
75. *Time*, 6 July 1987, p. 91.
76. *Facts on File* 206B2, 4 June 1965.
77. As quoted in Melvin I. Urofsky, *A Conflict of Rights: The Supreme Court and Affirmative Action* (New York: Scribner's, 1991), p. 17.
78. Ibid., p. 29.
79. Thomas Sowell, *Preferential Policies: An International Perspective* (New York: Morrow, 1990), pp. 103–105.

80. *Regents of the University of California* v. *Bakke,* 438 U.S. 265 (1978).

81. *Adarand Constructors, Inc.* v. *Pena,* 518 U.S. 200 (1995).

82. *Gratz* v. *Bollinger,* 539 U.S. 244 (2003).

83. *Grutter* v. *Bollinger,* 539 U.S. 306 (2003).

84. *Parents Involved in Community Schools* v. *Seattle School District No. 1,* 551 U.S. (2007).

85. *Fisher* v. *University of Texas*, 631 F.3d 213 (USCA5, 2011); and *Fisher* v. *University of Texas*, 11-345 (cert. granted, 21 February 2012).

86. Stephen Earl Bennett et al., *Americans' Opinions about Affirmative Action* (Cincinnati, Ohio: University of Cincinnati, Institute for Policy Research, 1995), p. 4; and Lawrence Bobo, "Race and Beliefs about Affirmative Action," in *Racialized Politics: The Debate about Racism in America,* ed. David O. Sears, Jim Sidanius, and Lawrence Bobo (Chicago: University of Chicago Press, 2000), pp. 137–164.

87. For example, see the eligibility standards of the Small Business Administration for "small disadvantaged business," http://www.sba.gov/sdb/indexa-boutsdb.html.

88. Seymour Martin Lipset, "Two Americas, Two Systems: Whites, Blacks, and the Debate over Affirmative Action," *New Democrat* (May–June 1995): 9–15, http://www.ndol.org/documents/May9 5TND.pdf.

CHAPTER 17 / ECONOMIC POLICY / PAGES 486–515

1. Address to the Nebraska Republican Conference, in Lincoln, Nebraska, on 16 January 1936. Herbert Hoover, *Addresses upon the American Road, 1933–1938* (New York: Scribner's Sons, 1938), p. 105.

2. Estimates vary. A citation from 1936 put the deficit at $34.5 billion. See R. M. Boeckel, "The Deficit and the Public Debt," *Editorial Research Reports 1936*, Vol. I (Washington, D.C.: CQ Press, 1936), http://library.cqpress.com/cqresearcher/cqresrre1936050200.

3. The data were compiled by Christopher Chantrill, and hosted at Penn State University Online, http://www.usgovernmentdebt.us/spending_chart_1792_2016USp_H0f#copypaste.

4. You won't learn basic economics in this chapter. For a quick summary of "ten principles of economics," see N. Gregory Mankiw, *Principles of Economics*, 3rd ed. (Mason, Ohio: Thomson South-Western, 2004), pp. 3–14.

5. Yingyi Qian and Jinglian Wu, "China's Transition to a Market Economy: How Far across the River?" (paper presented at the Conference on Policy Reform in China at the Center for Research on Economic Development and Policy Reform, Stanford University, 18–20 November 1999), http://elsa.berkeley.edu/~yqian/how%20far%20across%20the%20river.pdf.

6. Dan Usher, in *Political Economy* (Malden, Mass.: Blackwell Publishing, 2003), offers this interpretation of Adam Smith's "invisible hand" metaphor: "Self-interested people are guided by market-determined prices to deploy the resources of the world to produce what people want to consume. This assertion, made commonplace by repetition, is so extraordinary and so completely counter-intuitive that it cannot be strictly and unreservedly true. A central task of economics is to show when the assertion is true, when public intervention in the economy might be helpful, and when markets are best left alone because public intervention is likely to do more harm than good" (p. xiv).

7. Two of the ten principles of economics that Mankiw cites in *Principles of Economics* are "#6: Markets are usually a good way to organize economic activity" and "#7: Governments can sometimes improve market outcomes" (pp. 9–11).

8. Justin Fox, The *Myth of the Rational Market* (New York: HarperCollins, 2009), pp. xii–xiii.

9. National Bureau of Economic Research, "Business Cycle Expansions and Contractions," 1 December 2008, http://www.nber.org/cycles.html.

10. Paul Peretz, "The Politics of Fiscal and Monetary Policy," in *The Politics of American Economic Policy Making,* 2nd ed., ed. Paul Peretz (Armonk, N.Y.: M. E. Sharpe, 1996), pp. 101–113.

11. Shaun P. Hargraves Heap, "Keynesian Economics," in *Routledge Encyclopedia of International Political Economy,* vol. 2, ed. R. J. Barry Jones (London: Routledge, 2001), pp. 877–878.

12. *Wall Street Journal,* 18 January 2008, p. A12.

13. Nicholas Wapshott, the historian, writing at http://blogs.reuters.com/great-debate/2011/11/07/the-keynes-hayek-showdown/.

14. "The crowd had started out as 47% pro Keynes, 33% pro Hayek, and 20% undecided. At the end of the debate, 52% favored Keynes, 42% favored Hayek, and 6% were undecided. So Keynes still had the edge, but the Hayekians won over more of the undecideds." See Ira Stoll, 9 November 2011, http://www.futureofcapitalism.com/2011/11/hayek-versus-keynes.

15. For example, Peter Clarke, *Keynes: The Rise, Fall, and Return of the 20th Century's Most Influential Economist* (London: Bloomsbury Press, 2009); and Robert Skidelsky, *Keynes: The Return of the Master* (New York: Public Affairs Books, 2009). In contrast, see Friedrich A. von Hayek, *The Constitution of Liberty: The Definitive Edition*, ed. Ronald Hamowy (Chicago: University of Chicago Press, 2011).

16. Kathleen R. McNamara, "Monetarism," in Jones, *Routledge Encyclopedia of International Political Economy,* pp. 1035–1037.

17. The Federal Reserve Act (as amended over the years) cites "maximum employment, stable prices, and moderate long-term interest rates"; see http://www.federalreserve.gov/GeneralInfo/fract/sect02a.htm.

18. See Allan H. Meltzer, *A History of the Federal Reserve,* vol. 1, *1913-1951* (Chicago: University of Chicago Press, 2003). Meltzer writes that the leading banks in 1913 were privately owned institutions with public responsibilities. Fears were that they would place their interests above the public interest, but there was also concern about empowering government to control money. "President Woodrow Wilson offered a solution that appeared to reconcile competing public and private interests. He proposed a public-private partnership with semi-autonomous, privately funded reserve banks supervised by a public board" (p. 3).

19. Luca LiLeo, "Fed Gets More Power, Responsibility," *Wall Street Journal,* 16 July 2010, p. A5.

20. See the discussion of Federal Reserve policy actions in John B. Taylor, *Economics,* 4th ed. (Boston: Houghton Mifflin, 2004), Chap. 32.

21. Greg Ip and Jon E. Hilsenrath, "Having Defeated Inflation, Fed Girds for New Foe: Falling Prices," *Wall Street Journal,* 19 May 2003, p. A1.

22. The quote, attributed to William McChesney Martin, Jr., is in Martin Mayer, *The Fed* (New York: Free Press, 2001), p. 165.

23. Federal Reserve Bank of San Francisco, *Weekly Letter 96-08,* 23 February 1996.

24. Pew Research Center, "Economic Discontent Deepens as Inflation Concerns Rise," news release, 14 February 2008.

25. Fox, *The Myth of the Rational Market,* pp. xi–xii.

26. Edmund L. Andrews, "Bernanke, a Hero to His Own, Still Faces Fire in Washington," *New York Times,* 20 August 2009, pp. A1, B4; and David Wessel, "Inside Dr. Bernanke's E.R.," *Wall Street Journal,* 24 July 2009, p. W3.

27. Charles Duhigg, "Depression You Say? Check Those Safety Nets," *New York Times,* 23 March 2008, sec. 4, pp. 1, 4.

28. Jonathan Rauch, Lawrence J. Haas, and Bruce Stokes, "Payment Deferred," *National Journal,* 14 May 1988, p. 1256.

29. Mankiw, *Principles of Economics,* pp. 170–171.

30. See the editorial "How to Raise Revenue," *Wall Street Journal,* 24 August 2007, p. A14; and Austan Goolsbee, "Is the New Supply Side Better Than the Old?" *New York Times,* 20 January 2008, p. BU6.

31. Ibid.; David Leonhardt, "That Big Fat Budget Deficit. Yawn," *New York Times,* 8 February 2004, sec. 3, p. 1.

32. U.S. Department of Treasury, "The Debt to the Penny and Who Holds It," http://www.treasurydirect.gov/NP/BPDLogin?application=np.

33. One such "national debt clock" is at http://www.usdebtclock.org.

34. Justin Murray and Marc Labonte, "Foreign Holdings of Federal Debt," Congressional Research Service, RS22331, 17 March 2009. Many financial analysts think that the national debt seriously understates the *real* debt by several trillion dollars. See the website operated by the Institute for Truth in Accounting: http://www.truthinaccounting.org.

35. Binyamin Appelbaum, "A U.S. Boon in Low-Cost Borrowing," *New York Times,* 28 February 2012, p. B1.

36. For the FY 2013 federal budget, go to http://www.whitehouse.gov/omb.

37. Ibid., p. 377; Concord Coalition, "Budget Process Reform: An Important Tool for Fiscal Discipline, but Not a Magic Bullet," *Issue Brief,* 5 February 2004.

38. Concord Coalition, "Budget Process Reform," p. 3.

39. James V. Saturno, *A Balanced Budget Constitutional Amendment: Procedural Issues and Legislative History*, Congressional Research Service Report 98-671 (5 August 1998), p. 14.

40. Peter H. Schuck, "The Balanced Budget Amendment's Fatal Flaw," *Wall Street Journal*, 22 July 2011, p. A15.

41. D. Andrew Austin, *The Debt Limit: History and Recent Increases*, CRS Report for Congress, RL31967 (29 April 2008), p. 3.

42. "The Budget for Fiscal Year 2013, Historical Tables," Table 7.3, http://www.whitehouse.gov/sites/default/files/omb/budget/fy2013/assets/hist.pdf.

43. Binyamin Appelbaum, "After Aiding Republicans, Business Groups Press Them on Debt Ceiling," *New York Times*, 27 July 2011, p. A16.

44. Amy Bingham, "Only One Democratic Country, Besides America, Has a Debt Ceiling," *ABC News*, 19 July 2011, http://abcnews.go.com/blogs/politics/2011/07/only-one-democratic-country-besides-america-has-a-debt-ceiling/.

45. Richard A. Musgrave and Peggy B. Musgrave, *Public Finance in Theory and Practice*, 2nd ed. (New York: McGraw-Hill, 1976), p. 42.

46. If you can spare 24 megabytes of storage, you can download the complete text of the U.S. Internal Revenue Code, Title 26 of the U.S. Code, http://www.fourmilab.ch/uscode/26usc. If you print the tax code, expect more than 7,500 pages.

47. Office of Management and Budget, "Historical Tables, FY 2013 Budget," Table 2.2, http://www.whitehouse.gov/omb/budget/Historicals.

48. David Cay Johnston, "Talking Simplicity, Building a Maze," *New York Times*, 15 February 2004, Money and Business section, pp. 11, 14.

49. Michael L. Roberts, Peggy A. Hite, and Cassie F. Bradley, "Understanding Attitudes toward Progressive Taxation," *Public Opinion Quarterly* 58 (Summer 1994): 167–168. A Gallup Poll on 3–5 April 2005 found that respondents favored the current system over a flat tax 55 to 39 percent. And a Gallup Poll on 2–5 April 2007 found that 66 percent of respondents said "upper-income people" paid "too little" in taxes, while 45 percent said "lower-income people" paid "too much."

50. Jill Barshay, "'Case of the Missing Revenue' Is Nation's Troubling Mystery," *CQ Weekly*, 17 January 2004, p. 144.

51. Tax Policy Center, "Historical Combined Income and Employee Tax Rates for a Family of Four," 9 April 2009, http://taxpolicycenter.org/taxfacts/displayafact.cfm?DocK>=228aTopic2id=20aTopic3id=22.

52. Pew Research Center for the People and the Press, "Economic Inequality Seen as Rising, Boom Bypasses Poor," *Survey Report*, 21 June 2001.

53. Spending as percentage of GDP is a common way of measuring social welfare benefits, but it is not the only way. If spending is measured by dollars per capita, the United States, with a very high GDP, rates much more favorably. See Christopher Howard, "Is the American Welfare State Unusually Small?" *PS: Political Science and Politics* 36 (July 2003): 411–416.

54. Thom Shanker, "Proposed Military Spending Is Highest Since WWII," *New York Times*, 4 February 2008, p. A10.

55. National Priorities Project, "The Cost of War," http://costofwar.com/en/.

56. Jackie Calmes, "In Search of Presidential Earmarks," *Wall Street Journal*, 21 February 2006, p. A6.

57. Ron Nixon, "Special Funds in Budget Called New Earmarks," *New York Times*, 6 February 2012, p. A13.

58. Executive Office of the President, *Budget of the United States Government, Fiscal Year 2013: Historical Tables* (Washington, D.C.: U.S. Government Printing Office, 2012), Table 8.3.

59. Times-Mirror Center for the People and the Press, "Voter Anxiety Dividing GOP: Energized Democrats Backing Clinton," press release, 14 November 1995, p. 88.

60. These questions were asked in the 2008 American National Election Survey conducted by Stanford University and the University of Michigan.

61. Fay Lomax Cook et al., *Convergent Perspectives on Social Welfare Policy: The Views from the General Public, Members of Congress, and AFDC Recipients* (Evanston, Ill: Center for Urban Affairs and Policy Research, Northwestern University, 1988), Table 4-1.

62. Cynthia Crossen, "Not Too Long Ago, Some People Begged for an Income Tax," *Wall Street Journal*, 4 June 2003, p. B1.

63. B. Guy Peters, *The Politics of Taxation: A Comparative Perspective* (Cambridge, Mass.: Basil Blackwell, 1991), p. 228.

64. Elizabeth Becker, "U.S. Subsidizes Companies to Buy Subsidized Cotton," *New York Times*, 4 November 2003, p. C1.

65. Arthur C. Brooks, "The Left's 'Inequality' Obsession," *Wall Street Journal*, 19 July 2007, p. A15. Federal income taxes do make income distribution slightly more equal. See David Wessel, "Fishing Out the Facts on the Wealth Gap," *Wall Street Journal*, 15 February 2007, p. A10.

66. Gerald Prante, "Summary of Latest Federal Individual Income Tax Data," *Fiscal Facts* (Washington, D.C.: Tax Foundation), 30 July 2009.

67. Ibid.

68. Warren E. Buffett, "Stop Coddling the Super-Rich," *New York Times*, 16 August 2011, p. A19.

69. For 2011 and 2012, the employee's share was temporarily reduced to 4.2% to stimulate the economy.

70. Tax Policy Center, "Effective Tax Rate by Size of Income, 2000-2006," 4 June 2009, http://taxpolicycenter.org/taxfacts/dis-play-afact.cfm?Docid=366aTopic2id=48.

71. Joseph A. Pechman, *Who Paid the Taxes, 1966–1985?* (Washington, D.C.: Brookings Institution, 1985), p. 80. See also Lawrence Mishel, Jared Bernstein, and Heather Boushey, *The State of Working America, 2002–2003* (Ithaca, N.Y.: Cornell University Press, 2003), p. 66.

72. Organization of Economic Development and Cooperation, *An Overview of Growing Income Inequalities in OECD Countries: Main Findings* (January 2012), p. 22, http://www.oecd.org/dataoecd/40/12/49170449.pdf.

73. For a general discussion, see Vita Tanzi and Ludger Schuknecht, *Public Spending in the Twentieth Century: A Global Perspective* (Cambridge: Cambridge University Press, 2000), pp. 94–98.

74. Sylvia A. Allegretto, "The State of Working America's Wealth, 2011," Economic Policy Institute, Briefing Paper #292 (23 March 2011), p. 5.

75. U.S. Bureau of the Census, *Statistical Abstract of the United States 2009* (Washington, D.C.: U.S. Government Printing Office, 2010), Table 674.

76. Benjamin I. Page, *Who Gets What from Government?* (Berkeley: University of California Press, 1983), p. 213.

77. Frank Newport, "Americans Split on Redistributing Wealth by Taxing the Rich," Gallup Poll Report, 30 October 2008.

78. A 2003 survey reported 36 percent of respondents favoring changing from an income tax to a flat-rate tax, with only 32 percent opposed; cited in Robert J. Blendon et al., "Tax Uncertainty: A Divided America's Uninformed View of the Federal Tax System," *Brookings Review* 21 (Summer 2003): 28–31.

79. James Sterngold, "Muting the Lotteries' Perfect Pitch," *New York Times*, 14 July 1996, sec. 4, p. 1.

80. "Taxes: What's Fair?" *Public Perspective* 7 (April–May 1996): 40–41. Similar findings were found in experiments involving undergraduate students in advanced tax classes at two public universities; see Roberts et al., "Understanding Attitudes toward Progressive Taxation."

81. Blendon et al., "Tax Uncertainty."

82. Jason White, "Taxes and Budget," *State of the States: 2004* (Washington, D.C.: Pew Center on the States, 2004), p. 30.

83. Shailagh Murray, "Seminary Article in Alabama Sparks Tax-Code Revolt," *Wall Street Journal*, 12 February 2003, pp. A1, A8.

CHAPTER 18 / POLICYMAKING AND DOMESTIC POLICY / PAGES 516–553

1. "Stories," Young Invincibles, http://www.younginvincibles.org/Stories/index.html.

2. Frank Newport, "Americans Tilt toward Favoring Repeal of Healthcare Law," Gallup, 16 November 2011, http://www.gallup.com/poll/150773/Americans-Tilt-Toward-Favoring-Repeal-Healthcare-Law.aspx.

3. "At Risk: Pre-existing Conditions Could Affect 1 in 2 Americans," U.S. Department of Health and Human Services, 19 January 2011, http://www.healthcare.gov/law/resources/reports/preexisting.html.

4. Tim Langmaid, "CDC: Health Reform Extends Coverage to Young Americans," CNN.com, 14 December 2011; and Kevin Sack, "Young Adults Make Gains in Health Insurance Coverage," *New York Times*, 21 September 2011.

5. Adam Nagourney, "For Cowboy Poets, Unwelcome Spotlight in Battle Over Spending," *New York Times*, 10 April 2011; and Danielle Switalski, "Cowboy Poetry Gathering Drawn into Budget Battle," *Elko Daily Free Press*, 10 March 2011.

6. "State Tax Codes as Poverty Fighting Tools," Institute on Taxation and Economic Policy, September 2011, http://www.itepnet.org/pdf/poverty2011report.pdf; and Phil Kerpen and Stuart Jolly, "Oklahoma Leads on Income-Tax Repeal," *National Review Online*, 30 January 2012, http://www.nationalreview.com/articles/289588/oklahoma-leads-income-tax-repeal-phil-kerpen.

7. Peter Katel, "Food Safety," *CQ Researcher*, 17 December 2010, www.cqresearcher.com; and U.S. Food and Drug Administration, "The New FDA Food Safety Modernization Act," http://www.fda.gov/Food/FoodSafety/FSMA/default.htm.

8. According to the FDA, it is four or fewer rodent hairs per twenty-five grams. See the FDA's "Defect Levels Handbook," http://www.fda.gov/food/guidancecomplianceregulatoryinformation/guidancedocuments/sanitation/ucm056174.htm#intro.

9. Gardiner Harris and William Neuman, "Senate Passes Sweeping Law on Food Safety," *New York Times*, 20 November 2010.

10. This typology is adapted from Theodore Lowi's classic article, "American Business, Public Policy Case Studies, and Political Theory," *World Politics* 16 (July 1964): 677–715.

11. Since not all charitable contributions are claimed as deductions on taxes, the actual tax expenditure is less than $350 billion. See "Atlas of Giving Proves Charitable Giving in the U.S. Outpaced Economic Growth in 2011," 18 January 2012, atlasofgiving.com.

12. Roger W. Cobb and Charles D. Elder, *Participation in American Politics*, 2nd ed. (Baltimore, Md.: Johns Hopkins University Press, 1983), p. 14.

13. Lawrence D. Brown and Lawrence R. Jacobs, *The Private Abuse of the Public Interest* (Chicago: University of Chicago Press, 2008).

14. Dana Lee Baker and Shannon Stokes, "Brain Politics: Aspects of Administration in the Comparative Issue Definition of Autism-Related Policy," *Public Administration Review* 67 (July–August 2007): 757–767.

15. Frank R. Baumgartner, Suzanna L. De Boef, and Amber E. Boydstun, *The Decline of the Death Penalty and the Discovery of Innocence* (New York: Cambridge University Press, 2008).

16. Frank R. Baumgartner, Jeffrey M. Berry, Marie Hojnacki, David C. Kimball, and Beth L. Leech, *Lobbying and Policy Change* (Chicago: University of Chicago Press, 2009), pp. 166–189.

17. U.S. Department of Transportation, "2004 Automotive Fuel Economy Program," http://www.nhtsa.gov/Laws+&+Regulations/CAFE+-+Fuel+Economy/2004+Automotive+Fuel+Economy+Program; and Nick Bunkley, "New Gas Economy Rules Generate Wide Support," *New York Times*, 17 January 2012.

18. Gulf Coast Claims Facility, http://www.gulfcoastclaimsfacility.com/index; Jennifer Weeks, "Gulf Coast Restoration," *CQ Researcher*, 26 August 2011; and Margaret Cronin Fisk and Allen Johnson, "BP Said to Seek U.S. Settlement of Spill Pollution Claims," www.bloomberg.com, 9 February 2012.

19. Frank R. Baumgartner and Bryan D. Jones, "Positive and Negative Feedback in Politics," in *Policy Dynamics*, ed. Frank R. Baumgartner and Bryan D. Jones (Chicago: University of Chicago Press, 2002), pp. 3–28.

20. "House Democrats Seek Hearing on J&J Mesh, Allergan Lap-Band," *Bloomberg Businessweek*, 26 January 2012, http://www.businessweek.com/news/2012-01-26/house-democrats-seek-hearing-on-j-j-mesh-allergan-lap-band.html.

21. Eric Lipton and Gardiner Harris, "In Turnaround, Industries Seek U.S. Regulations," *New York Times*, 16 September 2007.

22. "Texting While Driving Up 50 Percent," press release from Rep. Carolyn McCarthy (D-NY), 8 December 2011, http://carolynmccarthy.house.gov/recent-news/rep-mccarthy-calls-for-passage-of-national-texting-law-in-wake-of-report-showing-texting-while-driving-up-50-percent/; and Kara Rose, "States Crack Down on Texting While Driving," *USA Today*, 14 October 2011.

23. Lipton and Harris, "In Turnaround."

24. Jeffrey M. Berry and Clyde Wilcox, *The Interest Group Society*, 5th ed. (New York: Pearson Longman, 2009), pp. 155–176.

25. Michael T. Heaney, "Coalitions and Interest Group Influence over Health Care Policy" (paper presented at the annual meeting of the American Political Science Association, Philadelphia, August 2003), p. 16.

26. Robert Shapiro, "Public Opinion and American Democracy," *Public Opinion Quarterly* 75 (2011): 982–1017.

27. See, for example, "Kaiser/Harvard/Washington Post Role of Government Survey," September 2010, iPOLL Databank, The Roper Center for Public Opinion Research, University of Connecticut, http://www.ropercenter.uconn.edu.ezproxy.library.tufts.edu/data_access/ipoll/ipoll.html.

28. Data available from U.S. Department of Labor, Bureau of Labor Statistics, http://www.bls.gov/cps/prev_yrs.htm.

29. Information available at the website of the U.S. Social Security Administration, http://www.ssa.gov/OACT/COLA/cbb.html#Series and http://www.ssa.gov/OACT/ProgData/taxRates.html.

30. Harold W. Stanley and Richard G. Niemi, *Vital Statistics on American Politics, 2011-2012* (Washington, D.C.: CQ Press, 2011), p. 359.

31. Social Security Administration, "2011 Annual Report of the Board of Trustees of the Federal Old-Age and Survivors Insurance and Disability Insurance Trust Funds," http://www.ssa.gov/oact/tr/2011/trTOC.html.

32. Clea Benson, "How Long Can Americans Work?" *CQ Weekly*, 5 July 2010, pp. 1616–1617.

33. Martha Derthick, *Policymaking for Social Security* (Washington, D.C.: Brookings Institution, 1979), pp. 346–347.

34. Social Security Administration, "Cost of Living Adjustment Information," http://www.socialsecurity.gov/cola/.

35. The Polling Report, "Social Security," CNN Poll, 6–10 August 2010, http://www.pollingreport.com/social2.htm.

36. *Retirement Security and Quality Health Care: Our Pledge to America*, n.d., GOP Platform, http://abcnews.go.com/Politics/story?id=123296ftpage=l.

37. "Seniors & Social Security," http://www.whitehouse.gov/issues/seniors-and-social-security.

38. Jon Carson, "Will Extending the Payroll Tax Cut Affect Social Security? No," The White House Blog, 9 December 2011, http://www.whitehouse.gov/blog/2011/12/09/will-extending-payroll-tax-cut-affect-social-security-no.

39. Although it has been the source of endless debate, today's definition of poverty retains remarkable similarity to its precursors. As early as 1795, a group of English magistrates "decided that a minimum income should be the cost of a gallon loaf of bread, multiplied by three, plus an allowance for each dependent." See Alvin L. Schorr, "Redefining Poverty Levels," *New York Times,* 9 May 1984, p. 27; and Louis Uchitelle, "How to Define Poverty? Let Us Count the Ways," *New York Times,* 26 May 2001, http://www.nytimes.com/2001/05/26/arts/how-to-define-poverty-let-us-count-the-ways.html?pagewanted=l.

40. U.S. Census Bureau, "Poverty Data," http://www.census.gov/hhes/www/poverty/data/threshld/. The poverty guideline for that year was slightly lower, at $22,050 (see the 2010 HHS Poverty Guidelines, http://aspe.hhs.gov/poverty/10poverty.shtml).

41. Nicholas Eberstadt, "The Mismeasure of Poverty," *Policy Review* 138 (August–September 2006): 1–21.

42. Sarah Fass, "Measuring Poverty in the United States," National Center for Children in Poverty, April 2009, http://www.nccp.org/publications/pdf/text_876.pdf; "Mismeasuring Poverty," *The American Prospect*, 16 September 2009, http://www.prospect.org/cs/articles?article=mismeasuring_poverty; and Jason DeParle et al., "Bleak Portrait of Poverty Is Off the Mark, Experts Say," *New York Times*, 3 November 2011.

43. U.S. Census Bureau, *Income, Poverty, and Health Insurance Coverage in the United States: 2010* (Washington, D.C.: U.S. Government Printing Office, 2011), http://www.census.gov/prod/2011pubs/p60-239.pdf.

44. Ibid.

45. Juan Williams, "Reagan, the South, and Civil Rights," National Public Radio, 10 June 2004, http://www.npr.org/templates/story/story.php?storyId=1953700.

46. Andrea Hetling, Monika McDermott, and Mingus Mapps, "Symbolism vs. Policy Learning: Public Opinion of the 1996 U.S. Welfare Reforms," *American Politics Research* 36, no. 3 (2008): 335–357.

47. Peter T. Kilborn, "With Welfare Overhaul Now Law, States Grapple with the Consequences," *New York Times*, 23 August 1996, p. A10.

48. Liz Schott, "Policy Basics: An Introduction to TANF," Center for Budget and Policy Priorities, July 2011, http://www.cbpp.org/cms/index.cfm?fa=view&id=936.

49. Alan Weil and Kenneth Feingold (eds.), *Welfare Reform: The Next Act* (Washington, D.C.: Urban Institute, 2002).

50. Hetling et al., "Symbolism vs. Policy Learning"; and Joshua Dyck and Laura Hussey, "The End of Welfare As We Know It? Durable Attitudes in a Changing in Formation Environment," *Public Opinion Quarterly* 72, no. 4 (2008): 589–618.

51. Eugenie Hildebrandt and Patricia Stevens, "Impoverished Women with Children and No Welfare Benefits: The Urgency of Researching Failures of the Temporary Assistance for Needy Families Program," *American Journal of Public Health* 99, no. 5 (2009): 793–801; and Robert Wood, Quinn Moore, and Anu Rangarajan, "Two Steps Forward, One Step Back: The Uneven Economic Progress of TANF Recipients," *Social Service Review* 82, no. 1 (2008): 3–28.

52. LaDonna Pavetti and Liz Schott, "TANF's Inadequate Response to Recession Highlights Weakness of Block Grant Structure," Center for Budget and Policy Priorities, July 2011, http://www.cbpp.org/cms/index.cfm?fa=view&id=3534.

53. Department of Health and Human Services Office of Family Assistance, "TANF Factsheet," http://www.acf.hhs.gov/opa/fact_sheets/tanf_factsheet.html.

54. LaDonna Pavetti and Liz Schott, "Expiration of TANF Supplemental Grants Further Sign of Weakening Federal Support for Welfare Reform," Center for Budget and Policy Priorities, June 2011, http://www.cbpp.org/cms/?fa=view&id=3524.

55. U.S. Census Bureau, *Income, Poverty, and Health Insurance Coverage in the United States: 2010* (Washington, D.C.: U.S. Government Printing Office, 2011).

56. Rebecca Adams, "Health Care: After the Reform," *CQ Weekly Online,* 28 September 2009, pp. 2156–2166.

57. See National Health expenditure data, https://www.cms.gov/NationalHealthExpendData/downloads/proj2010.pdf.

58. Ibid.

59. Organization for Economic Co-operation and Development, "OECD Health Data 2011," http://www.oecd.org/document/16/0,3343,en_2649_34631_2085200_1_1_1_1,00.html.

60. Derthick, *Policymaking*, p. 335.

61. Paul Starr, *The Social Transformation of American Medicine* (New York: Basic Books, 1982), pp. 279–280.

62. Ibid., p. 287.

63. Theodore Marmor, *The Politics of Medicare* (Chicago: Aldine, 1973).

64. "Medicare at a Glance," Kaiser Family Foundation, November 2011, http://www.kff.org/medicare/upload/1066-14.pdf; and Centers for Medicare and Medicaid Services, "Data Compendium," http://www.cms.hhs.gov/DataCompendium/16_2008_Data_Compendium.asp#TopOfPage.

65. "Medicare at a Glance."

66. "The Medicaid Program at a Glance," Kaiser Family Foundation, June 2010, http://www.kff.org/medicaid/upload/7235-04.pdf.

67. "Medicaid Matters: Understanding Medicaid's Role in Our Health Care System," Kaiser Family Foundation, March 2011, http://kff.org/medicaid/upload/8165.pdf.

68. Ibid.

69. Amy Goldstein, "States Slow to Adopt Health-Care Transition," *Washington Post*, 6 June 2011; and Joanne Kenen, "Fifty Ways to Run Your Medicaid Program," *CQ Weekly*, 27 June 2011, pp. 1362–1364.

70. Data found at Medicaid.gov, http://www.medicaid.gov/Medicaid-CHIP-Program-Information/By-Population/By-Population.html.

71. "The Medicaid Program at a Glance."

72. "Health Timeline 2010-2015," *CQ Weekly,* 5 April 2010, p. 818; Robert Pear and David M. Herszenhorn, "Obama Hails Vote on Health Care as Answering 'the Call of History,'" *New York Times,* 21 March 2010, http://www.nytimes.com/2010/03/22/health/policy/22health.html?scp=1asq=obamao/o20hailso/o20voteo/o20ono/o20helatho/o20careast=cse; and "Health Care Reform, at Last," *New York Times,* 22 March 2010, http://www.nytimes.com/2010/03/22/opinion/22mon5.html?scp=msq=healtho/o20careo/o20reform,o/o20ato/o20lastast=cse.

73. Kerry Young, "Controlling Medicare Costs," *CQ Weekly,* 5 April 2010, p. 826; "How Health Care Reform Reduces the Deficit in 5 Not-So-Easy Steps," *Newsweek,* 20 March 2010, http://www.newsweek.com/2010/03/20/how-health-care-reform-reduces-the-deficit-in-5-not-so-easy-steps.html; and Peter Grier, "Health Care Reform Bill 101: Who Will Pay for Reform?" *Christian Science Monitor,* 21 March 2010, http://www.csmonitor.com/USA/Politics/2010/0321/Health-care-reform-bill-101-Who-will-pay-for-reform.

74. "Establishing Health Insurance Exchanges," Kaiser Family Foundation, January 2012, http://www.kff.org/healthreform/upload/8213-FS.pdf.

75. "Kaiser Health Tracking Poll – January 2012," Kaiser Family Foundation, http://www.kff.org/kaiserpolls/8274.cfm.

76. U.S. Department of Education, "Federal Role in Education," http://www2.ed.gov/about/overview/fed/role.html?src=ln.

77. National Center for Education Statistics, *The Nation's Report Card* (Washington, D.C.: U.S. Department of Education, 2011), http://nces.ed.gov/nationsreportcard/pdf/main2011/2012459.pdf.

78. Christopher Jencks and Meredith Phillips (eds.), *The Black-White Test Score Gap* (Washington, D.C.: Brookings Institution Press, 1998).

79. Paul Manna, "Federalism, Agenda Setting, and the Development of Federal Education Policy, 1965-2001" (Ph.D. diss., University of Wisconsin-Madison, 2003).

80. Kenneth Jost, "Revising No Child Left Behind," *CQ Researcher*, 16 April 2010, www.cqresearcher.com.

81. Ibid.; the Blueprint is available at U.S. Department of Education, "ESEA Reauthorization," http://www2.ed.gov/policy/elsec/leg/blueprint/index.html.

82. Jost, "Revising No Child Left Behind"; White House, "Fact Sheet: Race to the Top," 24 July 2009," http://www.whitehouse.gov/the-press-office/fact-sheet-race-top; and White House, "Bringing Flexibility and Focus to Education Law," 23 September 2011, http://www.whitehouse.gov/sites/default/files/fact_sheet_bringing_flexibility_and_focus_to_education_law_0.pdf.

83. Harold W. Stanley and Richard G. Niemi, *Vital Statistics on American Politics, 2011-2012* (Washington, D.C.: CQ Press, 2011), p. 356; and Jeffrey Passel and D'Vera Cohn, "Unauthorized Immigrant Population: National and State Trends, 2010," Pew Hispanic Center, 1 February 2011.

84. Gallup Poll, "Immigration," http://www.gallup.com/poll/1660/Immigration.aspx.

85. U.S. Census Bureau, *Income, Poverty, and Health Insurance Coverage in the United States: 2010* (Washington, D.C.: U.S. Government Printing Office, 2011).

86. U.S. Department of Homeland Security, "2010 Yearbook of Immigration Statistics," August 2011, http://www.dhs.gov/xlibrary/assets/statistics/yearbook/2010/ois_yb_2010.pdf.

87. Congressional Budget Office, *Immigration Policy in the United States: An Update,* December 2010.

88. Migration Policy Institute, "Public Benefits Use," http://www.migrationinformation.org/integration/publicbenefits.cfm.

89. "2010 Yearbook of Immigration Statistics."

90. Stanley and Niemi, *Vital Statistics on American Politics, 2011–2012*, p. 356.

91. For a useful summary of current controversies, see "Immigration – Times Topics," *New York Times*, 19 January 2012, http://topics.nytimes.com/top/reference/timestopics/subjects/i/immigration-and-emigration/index.html.

92. Scott Keeter, "Where the Public Stands on Immigration Reform," Pew Research Center, 23 November 2009, http://pewresearch.org/pubs/1421/where-the-public-stands-on-immigration-reform.

93. The Blueprint, which was released in May 2011, http://www.whitehouse.gov/sites/default/files/rss_viewer/immigration_blueprint.pdf.

94. Scott Wong and Shira Toeplitz, "DREAM Act Dies in Senate," *Politico*, 20 December 2010.

95. David Harrison, "Of Boundaries and Borders: Court Case Seeks the Line," *CQ Weekly*, 22 December 2011, pp. 2646–2647.

CHAPTER 19 / GLOBAL POLICY / PAGES 554–583

1. Charles Duhigg and Keith Bradsher, "How the U.S. Lost Out on iPhone Work," *New York Times,* 21 January 2012; Charles Duhigg and David Barboza, "In China, Human Costs Are Built into an iPad," *New York Times*, 25 January 2012; Adam Satariano, "Apple Surges on Net Income Doubling," *Bloomberg Business Week*, 26 January 2012,

http://www.businessweek.com/news/2012-01-26/apple-surges-to-record-after-profit-doubles-on-iphone-demand.html; Hayley Tsukayama, "Labor Audits Find Poor Working Conditions at Apple Factories," *Washington Post*, 29 March 2012; and Sam Gustin, "Apple Profit Soars 94%, Stock Up 7%," *Time Business*, 24 April 2012.

2. Charles Duhigg and David Kocieniewski, "How Apple Sidesteps Billions in Taxes," *New York Times*, 28 April 2012.

3. Ibid.

4. Duhigg and Bradsher, "How the U.S. Lost Out."

5. For an alternative analysis, see Hanspeter Kriesi, "Globalization and the Transformation of the National Political Space: Six European Countries Compared," *European Journal of Political Research* 45 (2006): 921–956.

6. Rachel Donaldio and Laurie Goodstein, "Pope Urges Forming New World Economic Order to Work for the 'Common Good,'" *New York Times*, 8 July 2009, p. A6.

7. Trade Reform, "Tea Partiers Support Tariffs," http://www.tradereform.org/2010/06/tea-partiers-support-tariffs/.

8. John Yoo, who worked in the Office of Legal Counsel for President George W. Bush, distinguishes between the power to "declare" war, given to Congress, and the power to "make" war, which inheres in the president, in *Crisis and Command: The History of Executive Power from George Washington to George W. Bush* (New York: Kaplan Publishing, 2009).

9. The official Senate website lists twenty-one having been rejected, including the 1999 nuclear test ban treaty: http://www.senate.gov/artandhistory/history/common/briefing/Treaties.htm.

10. *Congressional Quarterly Weekly Report*, 16 October 1999, p. 2477. See also R. W. Apple, "The G.O.P. Torpedo," *New York Times*, 14 October 1999, p. 1.

11. Barbara Crossette, "Around the World, Dismay over Senate Vote on Treaty," *New York Times*, 15 October 1999, p. A1. The article quotes *The Straits Times of Singapore*.

12. Chuck McCutcheon, "Treaty Vote a 'Wake-Up Call,'" *Congressional Quarterly Weekly Report*, 16 October 1999, p. 2435.

13. *United States* v. *Curtiss-Wright Export Corporation*, 299 U.S. 304 (1936); *United States* v. *Belmont*, 301 U.S. 324 (1937); and Jack C. Plano and Roy Olton, *The International Relations Dictionary* (New York: Holt, Rinehart and Winston, 1969), p. 149.

14. Plano and Olton, *The International Relations Dictionary*, p. 149.

15. Lyn Ragsdale, *Vital Statistics on the Presidency* (Washington, D.C.: CQ Press, 1998), pp. 317–319. After 1984, government reports eliminated the clear distinction between treaties and executive agreements, making it difficult to determine the ratio. Indeed, other nations have criticized the reluctance of the United States to sign binding treaties. See Barbara Crossette, "Washington Is Criticized for Growing Reluctance to Sign Treaties," *New York Times*, 4 April 2002, p. A5.

16. Ragsdale, *Vital Statistics on the Presidency*, p. 298.

17. Brandon Rottinghaus and Jason Maier, "The Power of Decree: Presidential Use of Executive Proclamations, 1977–2005," *Political Research Quarterly* 60 (June 2007): 338–343.

18. These critics included both conservative Republican senator Barry Goldwater of Arizona and liberal Democratic senator Thomas Eagleton of Missouri. Eagleton's feelings were succinctly summarized in the title of his book: *War and Presidential Power: A Chronicle of Congressional Surrender* (New York: Liveright, 1974).

19. Miles A. Pomper, "In for the Long Haul," *CO Weekly Report*, 15 September 2001, p. 2118.

20. Mark Landler, "Clinton Makes Case for Internet Freedom as a Plank of American Foreign Policy," *New York Times*, 22 January 2010, p. A6.

21. August Cole and Yochi J. Dreazen, "Pentagon Shifts Its Strategy to Small-Scale Warfare," *New York Times*, 30 January 2010, p. A4.

22. Paul R. Pillar, *Intelligence and U.S. Foreign Policy* (New York: Columbia University Press, 2011).

23. The Intelligence Community was defined in the Intelligence Reform and Terrorism Prevention Act of 2004. See http://www.intelligence.gov.

24. Merle D. Kellerhals, Jr., "Negroponte Nominated to Become Director of National Intelligence," announcement of the U.S. Department of State, International Information Programs, 17 February 2005, http://florence.usconsulate.gov/viewer/article.asp?article=/file2005_02/alia/a5021702.htm.

25. Loch K. Johnson, "Now That the Cold War Is Over, Do We Need the CIA?" in *The Future of American Foreign Policy*, ed. Charles Kegley and Eugene Wittkopf (New York: St. Martin's Press, 1992), p. 306.

26. David S. Cloud, "Caught Off-Guard by Terror, the CIA Fights to Catch Up," *Wall Street Journal*, 14 April 2002, p. 1.

27. Quoted in Bob Woodward, *Plan of Attack* (New York: Simon & Schuster, 2004), p. 249; and David S. Cloud, "Tenet's Mission: Devising an Exit Strategy," *Wall Street Journal*, 28 January 2004, p. A4.

28. Bob Kemper, "Bush De-emphasizes Weapons Claim," *Chicago Tribune*, 28 January 2004, p. 9.

29. Stephen J. Hedges and John Crewdson, "Bungled Plots, Wire Taps, Leaks," *Chicago Tribune*, 27 June 2007, p. 1.

30. Richard A. Clarke, "Targeting the Terrorists," *Wall Street Journal*, 18 July 2009, pp. W1, W2.

31. Scott Shane, "C.I.A. Expanding Drone Assaults Inside Pakistan," *New York Times*, 4 December 2009, pp. A1, A14; and Mark Mazzetti, "C.I.A. Takes on Expanded Role on Front Lines," *New York Times*, 1 January 2010, pp. A1, A12.

32. Elisabeth Bumiller and Carl Hulse, "C.I.A. Pick Names as White House Takes Up Critics," *New York Times*, 8 May 2006, pp. A1, A21.

33. Leslie Cauley, "NSA Has Massive Database of Americans' Phone Calls," *USA Today*, 11 May 2006, p. 1.

34. Mark Mazzetti, "White House Sides with the C.I.A. in a Spy Turf Battle," *New York Times*, 13 November 2009, p. A12. Earlier in the year, the Senate backed the DNI; see Walter Pincus, "Senate Panel Backs DNI in Turf Battle with CIA," *Washington Post*, 23 July 2009.

35. http://www.usaid.gov/haiti, people could donate cash and offer volunteer medical service, nonmedical service, or other assistance.

36. August Cole, "Afghanistan Contractors Outnumber Troops," *Wall Street Journal*, 22 August 2009, p. A6.

37. X [George F. Kennan], "The Sources of Soviet Conduct," *Foreign Affairs* 25 (July 1947): 575.

38. On the U.S. government's promotion of democracy, see Tony Smith, *America's Mission*, expanded ed. (Princeton, N.J.: Princeton University Press, 2012).

39. Richard M. Nixon, *U.S. Foreign Policy for the 1970s: A New Strategy for Peace* (Washington, D.C.: U.S. Government Printing Office, 1970), p. 2.

40. Thomas Halverson, *The Last Great Nuclear Debate: NATO and Short-Range Nuclear Weapons in the 1980s* (New York: St. Martin's Press, 1995).

41. Daniel Deudney and C. John Ikenberry, "Who Won the Cold War?" *Foreign Policy* 87 (Summer 1992): 128–138.

42. Richard H. Ullman, "A Late Recovery," *Foreign Policy* 101 (Winter 1996): 76–79; and Michael Mandelbaum, "Foreign Policy as Social Work," *Foreign Affairs* (January–February 1996): 16–32.

43. Bob Woodward, *Bush at War* (New York: Simon & Schuster, 2002). Woodward was given access to contemporaneous notes taken during more than fifty meetings of the National Security Council and other personal notes, memos, and so on from participants in planning the war in Afghanistan.

44. The 19 September 2002 document is "The National Security Strategy of the United States." Extracts were published in the *New York Times*, 20 September 2002, p. A10. The full version is at http://georgewbush-whitehouse.archives.gov/nsc/nss/2002/.

45. In a news conference, Bush said, "After September 11, the doctrine of containment just doesn't hold any water, as far as I'm concerned." Quoted in the *New York Times*, 1 February 2003, p. A8.

46. Iraq Body Count Project, "Iraqi Deaths from Violence 2003–2011," http://www.iraqbodycount.org/analysis/numbers/2011/.

47. Adam Nagourney and Megan Thee, "Poll Gives Bush Worst Marks Yet on Major Issues," *New York Times*, 10 May 2006, pp. A1, A18. Poll results are at http://nytimes.com/ref/us/polls_index.html.

48. National Security Strategy of the United States of America, March 2006, http://www.whitehouse.gov/nsc/nss/2006.

49. *CBS News/New York Times* Poll, 20–24 February 2008.

50. Peter Spiegel, Jonathan Weisman, and Yochi J. Dreazen, "Obama Bets Big on Troop Surge," *Wall Street Journal*, 2 December 2009, pp. A1, A7.

51. CNN/Opinion Research Corporation Poll, 16–20 December 2009.

52. "Most Swing Voters Favor Afghan Troop Withdrawal," Pew Research Center, 18 April 2012, http://www.people-press.org/2012/04/18/most-swing-voters-favor-afghan-troop-withdrawal/?src=prc-headline.

53. Dan Balz, "Obama Is Both Commander, Campaigner in Chief Ahead of bin Laden Anniversary," *Washington Post,* 1 May 2012.

54. David Rohde, "The Obama Doctrine," *Foreign Policy* (March/April 2012): 65–69; and Peter Bergen and Katherine Tiedemann, "Washington's Phantom War," *Foreign Affairs* 90 (July/August 2011): 12–18.

55. Peter L. Bergen, *Manhunt: The 10-Year Search for Bin Laden* (New York: Crown, 2012).

56. Choe Sang-Hun, "In 2010, Web Addresses to Come in Any Language," *New York Times,* 31 October 2009, p. B3.

57. The Latin "ru" cannot transliterate as "PY" for that is too close to ".py" in Latin for Paraguay. See DomainNews.com, ".PP Internationalised Domain Name Will Translate DNS in Russian," 23 November 2009, http://www.domainnews.com/en/%D0%A0%D0%A4-internationalised-domain-name-will-translate-dns-in-russian.html.

58. Linda Greenhouse, "Justices Block New Hearing for Mexican," *New York Times,* 26 March 2008, p. A19.

59. See Joseph S. Nye, Jr., "U.S. Power and Strategy after Iraq," *Foreign Affairs* (July–August 2003): 60–73. For a contrasting view, see Grenville Byford, "The Wrong War," *Foreign Affairs* (July–August 2002): 34–43.

60. See Moises Nairn, "The Five Wars of Globalization," *Foreign Policy* (January–February 2003): 29–37.

61. Harvey B. Feigenbaum, "America's Cultural Challenge Abroad," *Political Science Quarterly* 126 (Spring 2011): 107–129.

62. Nick Timiraos, "Will Overseas Funds Be a Juggernaut?" *Wall Street Journal,* 1 December 2007, p. A11.

63. See generally Desmond Dinan, *Ever Closer Union,* 4th ed. (Boulder, Colo.: Lynne Reinner, 2010).

64. Alkman Granitsas, Matina Stevis, and Sam Schechner, "Voters Agree on One Thing: Discontent," *Wall Street Journal,* 7 May 2012; and Martin Feldstein, "The Failure of the Euro," *Foreign Affairs* 91 (January/February 2012): 105–116.

65. NationMaster.com, "GDP by Country," http://www.nationmaster.com/red/pie/eco_gdp-economy-gdp&date=2010.

66. Terence Poon and Andrew Batson, "China Targets Inflation as Economy Runs Hot," *Wall Street Journal,* 22 January 2010, p. A11.

67. Pew Research Center for the People and the Press, *America's Place in the World 2009* (Washington, D.C.: Pew Research Center, December 2009), p. 2, http://people-press.org/reports/pdf/569.pdf.

68. U.S. Energy Information Administration, "Table 11.5: World Crude Oil Production, 1960-2008," in *Annual Energy Review* (Washington, D.C.: Department of Energy, 26 June 2009), http://www.eia.doe.gov/emeu/aer/txt/ptb1105.html.

69. Council on Foreign Relations, "U.S. Trade Policy," http://www.cfr.org/trade/us-trade-policy/p17859.

70. "Fresh Mad Cow Case in U.S. May Overshadow Japan's Participation in TPP," *The Mainichi,* 7 May 2012, http://mainichi.jp/english/english/newsselect/news/20120507p2a00m0na015000c.html.

71. For 2012, see http://www.census.gov/foreign-trade/top/dst/current/deficit.html.

72. Deborah Solomon, "Seeking to Soften Blows of Globalization," *Wall Street Journal,* 26 June 2007, p. A8; and Chicago Council on Global Affairs, "Economic Worries Undermining Americans' Global Confidence," 14 October 2008, p. 2.

73. Deborah Solomon and Greg Hitt, "A Globalization Winner Joins in Trade Backlash," *Wall Street Journal,* 21 November 2007, pp. A1, A16; and Michael Spence, "The Impact of Globalization on Income and Employment," *Foreign Affairs* 90 (July/August 2011): 28–41.

74. John Stremlau, "Clinton's Dollar Diplomacy," *Foreign Policy* 97 (Winter 1995): 18–35.

75. Steven Lee Myers, "Obama Approach to Diplomacy Faces Test in China," *New York Times,* 2 May 2012.

76. Peter Ford, "Iran's Nuclear Program: Will Oil Ties Prevent China from Backing Tough Iran Sanctions?" *Christian Science Monitor,* 9 November 2011.

77. Steven Kull, "What the Public Knows That Washington Doesn't," *Foreign Policy* 101 (Winter 1995–1996): 102–115.

78. Bay Fang, "Bush Gets Restrained Praise on Africa," *Chicago Tribune,* 16 February 2008, p. 9.

79. Connexions, "Definition of Biodiversity," http://cnx.org/content/m12151/latest.

80. John M. Broder, "Struggling to Save the Planet, with a Thesaurus," *New York Times,* 2 May 2009, pp. A1, A11.

81. David L. Wheeler, "Inside the Clash Over Climate Change," *The Chronicle of Higher Education,* 11 May 2012.

82. Gautam Naik, "Climate Study Cites 2000s as Warmest Decade," *Wall Street Journal,* 29 July 2010, p. A4.

83. See UNFCCC, "Kyoto Protocol," http://unfccc.int/kyoto_protocol/items/2830.php.

84. Andrew C. Revkin and John M. Broder, "Grudging Accord on Climate, Along with Plenty of Discord," *New York Times,* 20 December 2009, pp. A1, A4.

85. See Paul R. Brewer et al., "International Trust and Public Opinion about World Affairs," *American Journal of Political Science* 48 (January 2004): 93, 109. They say, "Most Americans see the realm of international relations as resembling the 'state of nature' described by Hobbes. Put more simply, they see it as a 'dog-eat-dog' world" (p. 105).

86. *Global Views 2008* (Chicago: Chicago Council on Global Affairs, 2008), http://www.thechicagocoun cil.org/curr_pos.php.

87. Benjamin I. Page and Marshall M. Bouton, *The Foreign Policy Disconnect: What Americans Want from Our Leaders but Don't Get* (Chicago: University of Chicago Press, 2006), p. 227.

88. Lawrence R. Jacobs and Benjamin I. Page, "Who Influences U.S. Foreign Policy?" *American Political Science Review* 99 (February 2005): 107–123.

89. Frank R. Baumgartner, Jeffrey M. Berry, Marie Hojnacki, David C. Kimball, and Beth L. Leech, *Lobbying and Policy Change* (Chicago: University of Chicago Press, 2009).

90. Page and Bouton, *The Foreign Policy Disconnect,* p. 241.

91. Ibid., pp. 162–163.

92. U.S. Politics Online, "USAF Wants Big Bucks to Keep Flying," forum commentary, 18–25 February 2008, http://www.uspoliticsonline.com/breaking-news-politics/43985-usaf-wants-big-bucks-keep-flying.html.

93. August Cole, "Fight over F-22's Future to Test Defense Overhaul," *Wall Street Journal,* 8 April 2009, p. A5.

Index

A

AARP (American Association of Retired Persons), 273(fig.), 278
ABA (American Bar Association), 399
ABC, 148(fig.), 155, 166–167
Abortion, 128–133, 129(fig.), 355, 404, 440–442
Abramoff, Jack, 293
Abrams, Jacob, 424
Abrams v. United States (1919), 423
ACA (Affordable Care Act) (2010), 3–4, 93, 121, 231–232, 254, 280, 327, 340, 347, 381(illus.), 393, 460, 517–518, 529, 542–544, 542(illus.)
Acheson, Eleanor, 399
ADA (Americans with Disabilities Act) (1990), 19, 101, 466–467
ADA Amendments Act (2008), 466–467
Adams, John: advocacy and diplomacy, 56; commercial treaties, 58; Declaration of Independence, 54, 58(illus.); presidential elections, 211; slavery, 70
Adams, John Quincy, 213
Adjudication, 385
Administrative discretion, 365–366
Advertising, political, 260–261
AFDC (Aid to Families with Dependent Children), 495, 534–535
Affirmative action, 17, 449–450, 476–482; political ideologies and, 25; politics of, 481–482; reverse discrimination, 477–481
Affleck, Ben, 311(illus.)
Affordable Care Act (ACA) (2010), 3–4, 93, 121, 231–232, 254, 280, 327, 340, 347, 381(illus.), 393, 460, 517–518, 529, 542–544, 542(illus.)
Afghanistan: judge selection, 398; Soviet invasion and withdrawal, 568–569; U.S. involvement, 45, 561, 570, 571(fig.)
African Americans. *See also* Affirmative action; Ethnicity and race; Slavery: Civil War Amendments, 450–454; desegregation, 182, 331, 379–380, 388, 403, 405, 454–457; political socialization and values, 131; racial segregation, 451–454; representation in Congress, 304, 304(fig.); social equality and the Constitution, 79–80; suffrage, 185; U.S. demographics, 402(fig.); voter registration, 185(fig.)

Age: party identification, 224, 225(fig.), 226; political participation, 193; political socialization through media, 164; sources of news, 161; voter turnout, 194–196, 196(illus.); voting age, 186–187; youth unemployment, 575(fig.)
Agency for International Development (AID), 565
Agenda building, 274
Agenda setting, 522–523
Aggregate demand, 491
Agriculture Committees (House and Senate), 311–312
Ahlquist, Jessica, 413, 422(illus.)
AID (Agency for International Development), 565
Aid to Families with Dependent Children (AFDC), 495, 534–535
AIDS, 18, 579
Airline regulation, 366, 367(illus.)
Alabama: "Bloody Sunday," 175, 176(illus.); constitution, 79; Montgomery bus boycott, 177, 458; sniper attacks (2002), 106–107
Albania, judge selection, 398
Alexander, Lamar, 103
Algeria: Arab Spring, 44(illus.); judge selection, 398
Alibaba, 283
Alito, Samuel A., 389(illus.), 395, 401, 431, 442, 449, 480
Allen, Donald K., 221(fig.)
Allen, Robert, 96
Allen, Thad, 91(illus.)
Al-Nur party (Egypt), 321
Al-Rubaie, Mowaffak, 110
Alvarez, Xavier, 425(illus.)
AMA (American Medical Association), 273(fig.), 303, 540
Amendment process, U.S. Constitution, 74–77
American Association of Retired Persons (AARP), 273(fig.), 278
American Bankers Association, 282
American Bar Association (ABA), 399
American Civil Liberties Union, 413, 437
American Dental Association, 292
American Hospital Association, 273(fig.), 292
American Independent Party, 217–218
American Indian Movement, 462

American Medical Association (AMA), 273(fig.), 303, 540
American National Election Study (ANES), 128
American Nurses Association, 292
American Recovery and Reinvestment Act (stimulus package) (2009), 39(fig.), 67(illus.), 90–91, 327, 503, 537
Americans Elect, 207, 243(illus.), 244, 257
Americans with Disabilities Act (ADA) (1990), 19, 101, 466–467
Americans with Disabilities Act (ADA) Amendments Act (2008), 466–467
America's Health Insurance Plans, 280
Amicus curiae briefs, 392
Amondson, Gene, 221(fig.)
Anarchism, 20(fig.), 22, 22(illus.)
Anderson, Rocky, 243(illus.)
Andorra, judge selection, 398
ANES (American National Election Study), 128
Angola, judge selection, 398
Anthony, Susan B., 470
Antifederalists, 71–72, 210
Anti-Masonic Party, 213, 219
AOL News, 148(fig.)
Appellate jurisdiction, 389
Apple, 555–556, 556(fig.)
Appropriations committees, 500
Arab Spring, 43–44, 63, 170, 173, 320–321, 572
Argentina: judge selection, 398; women in legislature, 472(fig.), 473
Argument, 395
Arizona, illegal immigration, 85–86, 464–465, 465(illus.)
Arkansas, desegregation, 456(illus.)
Armed Services Committee (House), 500
Armenia, women in legislature, 472(fig.)
Army Corps of Engineers, 285, 369
ARPANET, 150
Article I (U.S. Constitution), 65–66, 79, 86, 107; Commerce Clause, 3–4, 16, 78, 92–93, 107–108; Necessary and Proper Clause, 66, 89, 91; Three-fifths Clause, 70
Article II (U.S. Constitution), 63, 67, 108, 248, 329–330
Article III (U.S. Constitution), 67–68, 67(illus.), 381
Article IV (U.S. Constitution), 68, 70
Article V (U.S. Constitution), 68

GEORGIA'S CONSTITUTION AND GOVERNMENT
6th edition

Arnold Fleischmann
University of Georgia

and

Carol Pierannunzi
Kennesaw State University

Introduction

Colleges and universities across the United States offer numerous courses on American government and politics. Many of them cover only the national government despite the ways that state and local governments affect the daily lives of most U.S. citizens. These activities range from basic local services such as streets, water, and fire protection to state support for public schools and universities. State and local governments spent $1.5 trillion in 2003, less than the federal government's $2.1 trillion, but still a significant amount. Moreover, while the federal government had 2.7 million civilian employees in 2002, state governments employed 5 million workers; local governments such as cities, counties, and school districts had another 13.3 million employees.[i]

Georgia is among the states requiring students to know something about state and local government. Specifically, the legislature has passed a law requiring graduates of public colleges and universities to demonstrate proficiency with both the United States and Georgia constitutions. This monograph is intended to assist students in satisfying that requirement.

1. The U.S. Constitution and Federalism

Constitutions are important because they establish the basic "rules of the game" for any political system. They specify the authority of government, distribute power among institutions and participants in the political system, and establish fundamental procedures for conducting public business and protecting rights. Just as drawing up or changing the rules can affect the outcome of a game, individuals and groups battle over constitutions, which can help determine who wins or loses politically.

When it was ratified in 1789, the United States Constitution included federalism as one of its most important elements. Federalism is a type of political system that gives certain powers to the national government, others to the states, and some to both levels of government. This differs from a unitary system such as in Great Britain or France, where all authority rests with the national government, which can distribute it to local or regional governments. Federalism also stands in contrast to a confederation, where all power is in the hands of the individual states, and the national government has only as much power as the states give to it. The United States used such a system during 1781-1788 under the Articles of Confederation, as did the Confederate States of America. More recently, confederations were tried following the break-up of the former national governments in the Soviet Union and Yugoslavia.

The American federal system is not static; in fact, it has changed significantly over the years. Below, we will discuss four key features that have had a major influence on the way federalism has developed. Three of these are found in the U.S. Constitution: the principle of national supremacy, the 10th Amendment, and the 14th Amendment. The last feature, state constitutions, is covered in Part 2.

National Supremacy

The U.S. Constitution's stability is due in large part to its broad grants of power and its reinterpretation in response to changing conditions. Article 1, section 8 grants Congress a series of "enumerated powers" such as taxing, spending, declaring war, and regulating interstate commerce. It also permits Congress to do whatever is "necessary and proper" to exercise the enumerated powers. This language is referred to as the "elastic clause" because of its flexible grant of authority. Article 6 reinforces the power of the national government by declaring that the Constitution and federal law are "the supreme law of the land." This so-called supremacy clause thus identifies the U.S. Constitution as the ultimate authority whenever there is a need to resolve a dispute between the national government and the states.

In an 1819 case, *McCulloch v. Maryland*, the U.S. Supreme Court adopted a broad view of the national government's powers when it decided that the elastic clause allowed Congress to exercise "implied powers" not mentioned explicitly in the U.S. Constitution but that could be inferred from the enumerated powers. The supremacy clause and implied powers have been cornerstones for the expansion of the national government's powers. Congress occasionally has turned programs over to states, as with changes in welfare laws during the 1990s, and has imposed new requirements and costs on them, as under the No Child Left Behind Act adopted in 2002.

The 10th Amendment

The constitutions, laws, and policies of the states cannot contradict the U.S. Constitution. Thus, federalism allows states many opportunities to develop in their own way, but it always holds out the possibility that the national government may act to promote uniformity for the country. Much of the debate over ratification of the U.S. Constitution focused on claims that the national government would be too powerful. This concern was reflected in proposals to add twelve amendments in 1789. Ten of the proposed changes were ratified by the states in 1791 and are commonly referred to as the Bill of Rights.

The 10th Amendment reads:

The powers not delegated to the United States by the Constitution, nor prohibited by
it to the States, are reserved to the States respectively, or to the people.

The amendment grants the states "reserved powers," but it does not define them. As one might expect, this has produced conflicts between the national and state governments, many of which have had to be resolved by the U.S. Supreme Court. For much of the period from the 1890s through the mid-1930s, for instance, the Court restricted efforts by Congress to enhance the power of the federal government. Since then, the power of the national government has grown, although some recent court cases have favored the states.

The 14th Amendment

The national government's power over the states was strengthened by the 1868 addition of the 14th Amendment to the U.S. Constitution. One of three amendments designed to end slavery and grant rights to blacks after the Civil War, the 14th states in part:

No state shall make or enforce any law which shall abridge the privileges or
immunities of citizens of the United States; nor shall any State deprive any person of
life, liberty, or property without due process of law; nor deny to any person within its
jurisdiction the equal protection of the laws.

This language essentially restates the fundamental principle of dual citizenship: Americans are citizens of both the nation and their state, and they are governed by the constitutions of both governments. The U.S. Constitution guarantees minimum rights to citizens that may not be violated by the states. The states, however, may grant broader rights to their citizens than are guaranteed by the U.S. Constitution.

The 14th Amendment has had an interesting and controversial history. The U.S. Supreme Court generally has defined the amendment's somewhat vague guarantees in terms of other provisions found in the U.S. Constitution. Since 1925, the Court has employed a process known as "selective incorporation" through which it incorporates into the meaning of the 14th Amendment the protections offered by the Bill of Rights. It does this selectively, that is, by applying these guarantees to the states on a case-by-case basis. Congress, too, has used the 14th Amendment in support of laws that restrict the power of state and local governments.

2. State Constitutions

States adopt their constitutions within the context of national supremacy; enumerated, implied, and reserved powers; dual citizenship; and the provisions of the 10th and 14th Amendments. Many state constitutions are modeled after the U.S. Constitution. Because state constitutions generally do not include implied powers, they tend to be more detailed and restrictive in defining the powers of government. State constitutions often include policies that seemingly could be decided by passing laws, as with Georgia's lottery. Putting such decisions in constitutions makes it harder for opponents to change them.

States also possess "police power," namely, the ability to promote public health, safety, morals, or general welfare. The police power is among the "reserved powers" in the 10th Amendment to the U.S. Constitution. Police powers are often delegated by states to local governments, which are covered in great detail in state constitutions, but are not mentioned at all in the U.S. Constitution.

<u>**Basic Differences in State Constitutions**</u>

Unlike the U.S. Constitution, which has been amended only 27 times, state constitutions are amended frequently, often to make narrow policy changes. Numerous amendments, provisions about local governments, and the lack of implied powers are major reasons that many state constitutions are so long, in contrast to the 8,700 words in the U.S. Constitution.

Table 1 indicates the number, length, and amendments for each state constitution. Georgia is noteworthy in two ways. First, it has had ten constitutions, second only to Louisiana. Second, Georgia's current constitution took effect in 1983, making it among the second youngest. Only Rhode Island can be considered to have a newer constitution, following the 1986 adoption of a revised version of its 1842 constitution.

Table 1
State Constitutions as of January 1, 2005

State	Number of Constitutions	Estimated Number of Words	Number of Amendments
Alabama	6	340,136	766
Alaska	1	15,988	29
Arizona	1	28,876	136
Arkansas	5	59,500	91
California	2	54,645	513
Colorado	1	74,522	145
Connecticut	4	17,256	29
Delaware	4	19,000	138[a]
Florida	6	51,456	104
Georgia	10	39,526	63
Hawaii	1	20,774	104

State			
Idaho	1	24,232	117
Illinois	4	16,510	11
Indiana	2	10,379	46
Iowa	2	12,616	52
Kansas	1	12,296	92
Kentucky	4	23,911	41
Louisiana	11	54,112	129
Maine	1	16,276	169
Maryland	4	46,600	218
Massachusetts	1	36,700	120
Michigan	4	34,659	25
Minnesota	1	11,547	118
Mississippi	4	24,323	123
Missouri	4	42,600	105
Montana	2	13,145	30
Nebraska	2	20,048	222
Nevada	1	31,377	132
New Hampshire	2	9,200	143
New Jersey	3	22,956	36
New Mexico	1	27,200	151
New York	4	51,700	216
North Carolina	3	16,532	34
North Dakota	1	19,130	145
Ohio	2	48,521	161
Oklahoma	1	74,075	171
Oregon	1	54,083	238
Pennsylvania	5	27,711	30
Rhode Island	3	10,908	8
South Carolina	7	22,300	485
South Dakota	1	27,675	212
Tennessee	3	13,300	36
Texas	5	90,000	432
Utah	1	11,000	106
Vermont	3	10,286	53
Virginia	6	21,319	40
Washington	1	33,564	95
West Virginia	2	26,000	71
Wisconsin	1	14,392	133
Wyoming			

[a]Amendments are not subject to voter approval.

Source: *The Book of the States: 2005 Edition*, pp. 10-11.

Amending State Constitutions

The states vary in the methods used to amend their constitutions (see Table 2). Seventeen states require only a majority in their legislatures to submit a proposed amendment to voters; others are more restrictive. Georgia is among the 20 states requiring a two-thirds vote by its legislature. Some states face the obstacle of getting an amendment approved in two legislative sessions before it can be submitted to voters. Four states, but not Georgia, also limit the number of amendments submitted to the voters at one election.

In terms of voter approval, 39 states require that a majority vote "yes" on an amendment for it to be ratified. A few states require more than a simple majority, e.g., a two-thirds vote in New Hampshire. Some require a simple majority on most amendments, but larger majorities for certain types of amendments, as with a two-thirds requirement in Florida to approve new taxes or fees. Other states require approval by a majority of those voting in an election, not just those voting on the amendment. The latter procedure can be especially difficult when people vote for highly visible offices like governor but skip proposed amendments. In such cases, not voting on the amendment is the same as voting "no."

The Georgia legislature can ask the state's voters to create a convention to amend or replace the constitution. The General Assembly also can propose amendments if they are approved by a two-thirds vote in each legislative – a procedure like that at the national level. The governor has no formal role in this process, but may be influential in recommending amendments and mobilizing public opinion before voters go to the polls. It is also worth noting that Georgia is not among the 18 states whose constitutions allow amendments through the initiative process, in which voters circulate petitions to place proposed amendments on the ballot for voters to ratify or reject in a statewide referendum.

The U.S. Constitution requires ratification of amendments by legislatures or conventions in three-fourths of the states. In contrast, the Georgia Constitution requires ratification by a majority of the voters casting ballots on the proposed amendment. Such proposals are voted upon in the next statewide general election after being submitted to the electorate by the General Assembly (November of even-numbered years).

During 2004, 33 states considered a total of 113 constitutional amendments of statewide applicability, of which 81 (72 percent) were adopted. Thirty-two of the proposed amendments dealt with government finance, taxation, and debt. Voters in 11 states considered 31 initiatives placed on the ballot by petition and approved 17 (55 percent).[ii]

Table 2
Amending State Constitutions Through Their Legislatures[a]
(Method in Georgia Marked with ✓)

Procedure	Approval Required	Number of States
Vote in Legislature	Majority	18
	2/3	19 ✓
	3/5	9
	Other	4[b]
Number of Legislative Sessions	One	38 ✓
	Two	12

Voter Approval Majority on Amendment   44[c] ✓
Majority in Election   3
Other   3[d]

[a]Eighteen states also allow their citizens to use the initiative process to place amendments on the ballot.

[b]Includes 3 states that require larger majorities if passed in one session, but only a majority if passed in two legislative sessions.

[c]Includes 5 states with different majorities for certain types of constitutional changes.

[d]Includes Delaware's constitution is amended by a two-thirds vote in two sessions of the legislature and does not require voter approval in a referendum.

Source: *The Book of the States: 2005 Edition*, pp. 12-14.

3. Constitutional Development in Georgia[iii]

Each of Georgia's ten constitutions can be considered a political response to some conflict, problem, or crisis. Replacing any state's constitution is a rare event, however. Amending a constitution is much more common. Both types of change, however, have produced long and often complicated documents. Such changes have also been linked to politics.

Politics and State Constitutions

Unlike the U.S. Constitution, most state constitutions include a wide range of very specific policies. Of course, legislatures normally enact policies by passing laws. Why "clutter up" state constitutions rather than limiting them to more fundamental issues? At least three reasons stand out: efforts to gain political advantage, state court decisions, and the requirements of the national government. Georgia's constitution has numerous examples of these processes.

Efforts to Gain Political Advantage. Many policies in state constitutions result from efforts by groups to gain a strategic advantage over their political opponents. If a group is able to get its position on an issue included in a state's constitution, it becomes much more difficult to change the policy. This is really a matter of taking advantage of the "rules of the game" by forcing the opposition to get its own amendment passed rather than simply getting a law enacted. Amendments that have added policies to Georgia's constitution deal with earmarking, tax breaks, morality issues, and limitations on decision making.

Like many state constitutions, Georgia's "earmarks" certain funds (identifies revenue sources that must be spent for designated purposes) that could benefit specific interests. The most significant are motor fuel taxes, which Article 3 requires to be spent "for all activities incident to providing and maintaining an adequate system of public roads and bridges" and for grants to counties. Morever, this money goes for these purposes "regardless of whether the General Assembly enacts a general appropriations Act."[iv] Thus, the Constitution provides those interested in highway construction with a guaranteed source of funds.

In other cases, the Constitution merely permits the earmarking of funds.[v] For instance, the General Assembly can use taxes on alcoholic beverages for programs related to alcohol and drug abuse. The legislature is also allowed to create a variety of trust funds for programs ranging from prevention of child abuse to promotion of certain crops. The 1992 amendment creating the state lottery requires that net proceeds (after expenses and prizes) go to "educational programs and purposes," with the governor's annual budget including recommendations for using these funds.[vi] An amendment approved by voters in November 1998 further restricted the use of lottery funds.

The Constitution provides special tax treatment to various groups and activities. An example is the taxation of timber, one of Georgia's major industries. An amendment approved by voters in 1990 requires that timber be taxed at fair market value only at the time of its harvest or sale.[vii] Previously, it was taxed annually at market value. This change produced a major drop in property taxes for some counties and school districts. The Constitution also requires that certain agricultural land be assessed at 75 percent of its value[viii] and exempts part of the value of a disabled veteran's home from property taxes.[ix] Other sections of the Constitution authorize rather than require the General Assembly to provide certain types of tax preferences, as with a 1988 amendment that applies to property on a historic register and a 1992 amendment that permits special treatment for heavy motor vehicles owned by nonresidents.[x]

Various groups often attempt to use state constitutions to establish their position on controversial social issues. This happened with the U.S. Constitution when the 18th Amendment was added in 1919 to ban the sale of alcohol. It was repealed, however, by the 21st Amendment in 1933. Similar provisions exist in the Georgia Constitution. The 1983 Constitution retained the prohibition against whipping as a punishment for a crime out of fear that the General Assembly might pass bills permitting whipping in schools or prisons.[xi] The 1983 Constitution, like all of its predecessors since 1868, prohibited lotteries. After being elected governor in 1990, Zell Miller convinced the General Assembly to submit a proposed amendment to voters to create state-run lotteries whose proceeds would be spent on education. That amendment was ratified by a narrow majority in November 1992 following a vigorous campaign. In 2004, Georgia voters were asked by the legislature to vote on amendment that would define marriage as the "union of man and woman." Even though Georgia already had a law banning the practice, the legislature voted to submit an amendment on the matter, which passed in every Georgia county and carried by 76-24% statewide.

Constitutions can also specify who gets to participate in key decisions, as well as limit the discretion of government agencies. For example, Article 4 creates six state boards and commissions, and Article 8 creates two more for education. The Constitution also establishes important political ties between the State Transportation Board and the General Assembly, thereby reducing the power of the executive branch over highways. The Georgia Constitution also empowers certain interests through residency requirements, as with membership from each congressional district on certain boards and commissions and the requirement that at least one member of the Board of Natural Resources be from one of six coastal counties.[xii] An example of constitutional limits on the discretion of government agencies is the requirement that veterans be given a preference in state civil service employment.[xiii]

State Court Decisions. A second reason for including policies in a constitution is to respond to a state court decision. For example, the Georgia Supreme Court might hold that a state law or an action by a local government violates the Georgia Constitution. Almost the only way to undo the court's action is to amend the state constitution. A 1994 amendment permits local governments to prohibit alcohol sales at clubs with nude dancing. This was a way to get around a Georgia Supreme Court ruling that nude dancing was expressive conduct protected by the Georgia and U.S. constitutions. Alcohol sales are not constitutionally protected, so regulating them is a way to try to drive nude dancing clubs out of business, which was subsequently considered allowable under the Georgia Constitution.[xiv]

Several decisions by the Georgia Supreme Court during the 1980s created confusion about sovereign immunity (the ability of citizens to sue the state or its local governments). As a result, an amendment was ratified in 1990 that attempted to clarify the matter.[xv] Similarly, the 1983 Constitution added language to clarify a somewhat confusing series of cases regarding the authority of the state, cities, and counties regarding planning and zoning.[xvi]

National Government Requirements. A third way in which politics affect state constitutions is to satisfy some requirement of the national government. For example, the Georgia Constitution was amended in 1988 and 1992 to create a trust fund to provide medical services for the poor through the federal Medicaid program. Without the trust fund, money unspent at the end of the budgetary year would have to go to the state's general fund and could be used for any purpose, as specified elsewhere in the Constitution.[xvii] With the trust fund, the unspent money can be carried over to the next year to pay for medical care. Another example can be found in Article 3, which is written in order to satisfy federal court decisions about how legislative districts must be drawn.

A Brief Comparison of the U.S. and Georgia Constitutions

It is useful at this juncture to compare the current U.S. and Georgia constitutions. Keep in mind, though, that constitutions are not static. Georgia has had ten constitutions, and the current one has been amended more than 60 times during its brief life. In addition, Georgia's constitutions have evolved because of the ways they have been interpreted by the courts.

Similarities. The most obvious similarity between Georgia and the national government is the presence of a bill of rights in each constitution. These guarantees were added as the first ten amendments to the U.S. Constitution, but the bill of rights is included prominently in Georgia's constitution as the first article. Both governments adopt separation of powers with distinct legislative, executive, and judicial branches. The president and Georgia's governor have substantial power to appoint officials and veto bills, although there are some important differences discussed below. Both the U.S. Congress and the Georgia General Assembly are bicameral, and each calls its two chambers the senate and house of representatives. Both governments allow judicial review (the power of courts to declare acts unconstitutional). Georgia courts are given this power in the state constitution,[xviii] while this authority at the federal level was laid down in 1803 by the Supreme Court itself in the case of *Marbury v. Madison*.[xix]

Differences. Perhaps the most visible difference between the two constitutions is how much longer Georgia's is, mainly because it includes many detailed policies. These range from specific taxes to sections on retirement systems, local government services, the state lottery, and even nude dancing.

The two constitutions also include differences in both procedures and the structure of government. One procedural distinction deals with constitutional amendments. Georgia voters must approve all amendments to the state's constitution. There is no comparable role for citizens in amending the U.S. Constitution, where amendments require a two-thirds vote in each house of Congress and then must be ratified by three-fourths of the states, in either their legislature or conventions. Another procedural difference is that the Georgia Constitution requires the state to have a balanced budget, but the U.S. Constitution imposes no such limitation on the federal government.   The Georgia Constitution also grants the governor a line-item veto (the ability to kill a specific item in a spending bill), but the U.S. Constitution grants the president no such power over legislation passed by Congress.[xx]

There are striking structural differences among the three branches of governments. Unlike the national government, where judges are nominated by the president subject to Senate confirmation, Georgia elects almost all of its judges on a nonpartisan ballot. In addition, Georgia's attorney general issues advisory opinions, which generally have the force of law unless reversed by a court. There is no comparable process at the national level.

The legislative branches also exhibit some interesting differences. All legislators in Georgia (both the House and the Senate) serve two-year terms and are elected from districts based on population. This contrasts with the national government, where representatives serve two-year terms and senators are elected for six years. Moreover, while members of the U.S.

House are elected from districts based on population, two senators are elected from each state – the same for California and Wyoming – which builds in a bias in favor of less populous states.

The most glaring difference in the two executive branches is the lack of a cabinet system in Georgia. The president has the authority to appoint and fire heads of almost all major federal agencies. In contrast, Georgia's constitution requires that voters elect six department heads. This "plural executive" can make life difficult for a governor, who has limited authority over these independently elected officials, who may not share the same views or political party as the governor. The constitution also requires that several other department heads be chosen by boards and commissions rather than by the governor or the voters.

Perhaps the most noticeable structural difference between Georgia and the national government deals with local government. Georgia's constitution is quite specific about the organization of local governments, the services they can provide, the ways they can raise and spend money, and similar matters. It even limits the maximum number of counties at 159. The U.S. Constitution never mentions local government.

Georgia's Previous Constitutions

In addition to substantive differences, Georgia's constitutions also vary in the methods used to draft and approve them (see Table 3). Seven were written by conventions composed of elected delegates. Two were prepared by bodies whose members were either appointed or included because they held specific offices. The 1861 constitution was the first to be ratified by voters. The Constitution of 1976 resulted from a request by Governor George Busbee to have the Office of Legislative Counsel prepare an article-by-article revision of the Constitution of 1945 for the General Assembly.

Table 3
Georgia's Ten Constitutions

Year Implemented	Revision Method[a]	Major Characteristics
1777[b]	convention	Separation of powers, with most in the hands of the unicameral legislature.
1789[b]	convention	Bicameral legislature, which chose the governor; no bill of rights.
1798[b]	convention	Popular election of governor; creation of Supreme Court; greater detail than predecessors.
1861	convention	Long bill of rights; first constitution submitted to voters.
1865	convention	Governor limited to two terms; slavery abolished; Ordinance of Secession repealed; war debt repudiated; some judges made elective.
1868	convention	Authorization of free schools; increased appointment power for governor; debtors' relief.
1877	convention	More restrictions on legislative power; two-year terms for legislators and governor; no gubernatorial succession; most judicial appointments by legislature.
1945	commission	Establishment of lieutenant governorship, new constitutional officers, new boards, state merit system; home rule granted to counties and cities.
1976	Office of Legislative Counsel[c]	Reorganization of much-amended 1945 constitution.
1983	select committee[d]	Streamlining of previous document, with elimination of authorization for local amendments.

[a]Group responsible for proposing new document.
[b]Not submitted to voters for ratification.
[c]State employees, attorneys.

^dAlmost exclusively leaders from the three branches of state government.

Source: Hill, *The Georgia State Constitution*, pp. 3-20.

Even before American independence in 1776, Georgians were exerting their independence from England. Colonial Georgia, dependent upon imports for most manufactured items, was hard hit by the various import taxes which had led to colonial protests. Public opinion in Georgia favored independence and citizens mobilized to break with England. The first self-government in Georgia was defined by the Rules and Regulations of 1776. This short and simple document was written hurriedly and adopted before the signing of the Declaration of Independence. All current laws were maintained except those in conflict with actions taken by the Continental Congress. It declared that governmental authority resided within the state, not with the British monarchy, and that power originated from the governed. While this document was not officially a state constitution, many have noted that it served as one. The Declaration of Independence prompted Georgians to establish a more permanent government, and the state adopted the first of its ten constitutions in 1777.

The Constitution of 1777. Georgia's first constitution included now familiar ideas such as separation of power among the legislative, executive, and judicial branches of government; proportional representation on the basis of population; and provisions for local self-government. This constitution, like the Rules and Regulations of 1776, included little expressed protection of individual liberties. Despite this omission, Georgia's political culture at the time was more liberal than other states, and the constitution was written to empower the "common man" (although only white males of 21 years who had paid property taxes in the previous year were permitted to vote). The Anglican Church was disestablished, and language in the document was easily understood. Local control of the judiciary was insured by the fact that no courts were established above the county courts.

The transition from the Rules and Regulations of 1776 to a new constitution in 1777 was little noted by citizens. This document governed the state until the demise of the Articles of Confederation. Georgia ratified the U.S. Constitution in January 1788 (the fourth state to do so) and redrafted the state constitution to reflect this monumental change in national government.

The Constitution of 1789. The Constitution of 1789 provided for a bicameral legislature. Although there were some accommodations made for representation on the basis of population in the House of Representatives, all legislative districts were drawn within counties, which could have from two to five representatives and one senator. Slaves were counted as three-fifths of a person, in accord with the U.S. Constitution and to meet the demands of landowners seeking to enhance representation for areas with large plantations. The state capital was moved to Louisville from Augusta,[xxi] provisions were included to mandate public education at the county level, and new counties created to be represented in the legislature. In addition, the constitution authorized the legislature to elect the governor and most other state elected officials except the legislature itself. Restrictions on voting included race, age, residence, and the payment of taxes in the previous year.

The Constitution of 1798. The short life of the Constitution of 1789 can be attributed to a scandal over land speculation by legislators. The Constitution of 1798 was written by a convention and retained much of the language of the previous document. However, it was much longer due to increased detail about the powers of the legislature. As time passed, this constitution was amended to permit more democratic requirements for voting, establish executive offices to handle some of the duties of the legislature, outlaw foreign slave trade, and establish local governments. This constitution proved to be more enduring than its predecessors and was in effect until the formation of the Confederacy in 1861.

The Constitution of 1861. Secessionist fever at the start of the Confederacy could hardly allow the state constitution to go untouched. T.R.R. Cobb, the main author of the Confederate Constitution, was also the author of the Georgia Constitution under the Confederacy. The size of the state legislature was reduced by permitting senators to represent more than one county, and the governor's power was increased significantly. Judicial review was institutionalized in this document, and state judgeships were established as elective offices.

The Constitution of 1861 was the first to be submitted to the voters for approval in a referendum. This was also the first Georgia constitution with an extensive list of personal liberties, including freedom of thought and opinion, speech, and the press. Citizens were warned, though, that they would be responsible for "abuses of the liberties" guaranteed to them. Naturally, the Georgia Constitution under the Confederacy included ideals of states' rights.

The Constitution of 1865. The Constitution of 1865 was drafted by reluctant Georgians in order to accommodate the demands of Congress for readmission to the Union. Only men who expressed moderate political beliefs before and after the war were permitted to work on the document, which included the abolition of slavery, repudiation of Civil War debt, and repeal of the acts of secession. This repeal was not met with great enthusiasm by the North, which had insisted that the ordinance of secession be declared void. Also absent was enfranchisement of the black population of the state, although this was not as likely to stir animosity in the North since blacks could only vote in six northern states at the time. These omissions put pressure on Georgia to rewrite the constitution just three years later in order to meet the requirements for reentry into the Union. The Constitution of 1865 was viewed largely as the work of northern "carpetbaggers" trying to make quick fortunes in the postwar South, or, worse yet in the eyes of many, "scalawags" (southerners willing to cooperate with Yankees).

The Constitution of 1868. When a constitutional convention was called in 1867, it was boycotted by most of Georgia's popular leaders. The state capital, at that time in Milledgeville, refused to accommodate many of the delegates, some of whom were black. Therefore, the convention was held in Atlanta, and the new constitution, perhaps in retaliation for the inhospitable treatment by the city of Milledgeville, specified Atlanta as the capital. The Constitution of 1868 met the requirements of Congress for readmission to the Union and eliminated all debts incurred prior to 1865. Public education was also provided for, to be funded by poll and liquor taxes, although it was some time before this policy actually was implemented. Black citizens were insured equal rights, at least on paper, and property rights for women were upheld. Moreover, some attempts were made to enhance the business climate in order to build a stronger tax base.

Due to the high representation of poor and black citizens at this convention, the Constitution of 1868 was a liberal document for the times, particularly after blacks were seated in the General Assembly in 1870. Overall, the new constitution was widely unpopular due to its compliance with northern demands, which were symbolized by the presence of northern troops until 1876. It remained a symbol of southern defeat until replaced in 1877.

The Constitution of 1877. Georgia's post-Reconstruction constitution was a return to more conservative ideals. It reduced the authority of state officials and shifted power to counties, most of which were rural. Most noteworthy was its not-so-subtle disenfranchisement of blacks and poor whites through the mandate that only those who had paid all back taxes would be eligible to vote. As the Constitution of 1877 was being drafted, factionalism within the ranks of the Democratic party erupted. Many who were sympathetic to old southern culture were reluctant to compromise with those who called for economic development and progressive policies. An agreement was reached to comply with northern demands for reconstruction, as well as demands from more industrialized northern states that the South continue to supply raw materials. This compromise stirred up a faction of the Democratic party labeled Bourbons, who were dedicated to pre-Civil War agrarian economic and social norms, white supremacy, and local and state self-determination. The Republicans found that the compromise left them with little power in Georgia, and it would be quite some time before the Republican party reasserted itself in the state.

The Constitution of 1877 was not well suited to changing conditions. For example, it forbade public borrowing, thereby eliminating the possibility of large-scale improvements in transportation or education financed by the state. The constitution eventually included 301 amendments, many of which were temporary or dealt with local rather than statewide issues. Others made Supreme Court justices elected officials, established juvenile courts and a court of appeals, empowered an elected Public Service Commission to regulate utilities, and modified the boards overseeing education.

This constitution also codified the system of representation under which the six counties with the largest population were to be represented in the lower house of the legislature by three persons each, the next 26 most populous counties by two each, and the remaining counties by one member. This 3-2-1 ratio became the basis for the Democratic party's use of the county-unit system to elect statewide candidates—a custom that became state law in 1917 with passage of the Neill Primary Act.

Under the county-unit system, Democratic candidates for statewide office were chosen in primaries based on county-unit votes, which were similar to the electoral votes used to elect the U.S. president. Each county had twice as many unit votes as it had seats in the Georgia House of Representatives under the 3-2-1 formula. Beginning in 1920, the eight largest counties had six unit votes, the next 30 counties had four unit votes, and the remaining counties had two unit votes. Thus, Fulton County, which had more than 6,000 voters go the polls in 1940, had 6 unit votes; Quitman and Chattahoochee Counties, which each had fewer than 250 votes cast the same year, had 2 unit votes each. A county's unit votes were awarded on a winner-take-all basis, which meant that the candidate finishing first got all the unit votes. Under this system, candidates could concentrate their campaigns in rural areas and could win a primary without getting a majority of the popular vote. In 1940, the 121 counties with 2 unit votes had 43.5 percent of Georgia's population, but 59 percent of the unit votes. In contrast, Georgia's eight most populous counties, with 6 unit votes each, had 30 percent of the state's population but a mere 12 percent of the unit votes. In 1946, Eugene Talmadge finished second in the primary for governor by about 6,000 popular votes. He won the Democratic nomination, however, by besting his opponent 242 to 146 in unit votes.[xxii] The county-unit system remained intact until

1963, when the U.S. Supreme Court held that this underrepresentation of urban areas violated the "equal protection" clause of the 14th Amendment.

The Constitution of 1945. The Constitution of 1877 lasted until 1945, albeit in much amended form. A 23-member commission appointed by the governor to draft a new constitution was finally created because of dissatisfaction with the 1877 constitution, a careful study of the document in the 1930s, and prodding by Governor Ellis Arnall. The use of a commission rather than an elected convention reflects the governor's wish to depoliticize the constitution and bring it up to date, as well as the General Assembly's previous failure to muster the two-thirds vote to call a convention.[xxiii]

The new constitution included limited substantive changes. Its main effect was to condense its heavily amended predecessor. Perhaps the most notable changes were the creation of the office of lieutenant governor and new boards for corrections, state personnel, and veterans services. One contested issue was the ban against governors succeeding themselves, which the General Assembly retained in the draft submitted to the voters. The new constitution also authorized women to serve on juries and gave home rule to local governments, which increased their authority.   The document also addressed the controversial issue of the poll tax.

With a turnout of less than 20 percent of those registered, voters approved the document by slightly more than a three-to-two margin following an active campaign on its behalf. Georgia thus became the first state to adopt a constitution proposed by commission rather than by an elected convention. The limits of this constitution emerged quickly. Within three years, the new constitution added its first amendments, with a total of 1,098 amendments proposed between 1946 and 1974. Voters ratified 826, of which 679 (82 percent) were local in nature.

The Constitution of 1976. An effort to revise the 1945 constitution occurred during the early 1960s, but a federal court ruling prevented voters from considering it during the 1964 general election. Another attempt died in 1970 when the House but not the Senate approved a document for submission to the electorate.

After assuming office in 1975, Governor George Busbee asked the Office of Legislative Counsel to draft a revision of the 1945 constitution in time for the 1976 election. The proposal included no real changes, but it did reorganize the constitution on an article-by-article basis so that it was easier to understand and interpret. After some revisions by the General Assembly, voters approved the document in November of that year. With no substantive changes in the new constitution, the General Assembly almost immediately set out to consider a more thorough revision, creating the Select Committee on Constitutional Revision during its 1977 session.

Georgia's Current Constitution

Adoption. Georgia's 1983 constitution was neither easily written nor quickly adopted. In fact, the Constitution of 1983 is a good example of how factionalism can play a role in state politics. Because the 1945 and 1976 constitutions so restricted local governments, cities and counties often were forced to amend the constitution in order to make changes in taxation or municipal codes. Amendments were proposed by the legislature and approved through popular vote, with those proposals affecting the entire state appearing on the statewide ballot and those affecting only one county or city appearing on the ballot only in that jurisdiction.[xxiv] As a result, ballots were brimming with proposed amendments that often irritated voters.

Between 1946 and 1980, Georgians were asked to vote on 1,452 proposed amendments (1,177 of them purely local in nature) and ratified over 1,105. This created an unwieldy document understood by only the most diligent of constitutional students. Voters became so annoyed with the large number of proposals that they began to vote them down. In 1978, the statewide ballot included over 120 proposed changes in the state's constitution, one-third of which failed to pass.[xxv]

By the late 1970s, many were pleased when Governor George Busbee sought the rewriting of the constitution, although Busbee may not have realized the political difficulty of such a task. The proposed constitution was debated for three years by a Select Committee on Constitutional Revision whose members included the governor, lieutenant governor, speaker of the House, attorney general, and eight other elected officials. The Select Committee began work in May 1977 and appointed committees with broader citizen membership to revise individual articles of the constitution for consideration by the General Assembly and the electorate. In November 1978, two articles were submitted to voters, who rejected them.

Subsequent efforts by the Select Committee and the 1980 session of the legislature failed to produce a new constitution. During its 1981 session, though, the General Assembly created a Legislative Overview Committee on Constitutional Revision, with 31 members from each chamber, to work with the Select Committee. These efforts produced a document that was approved in a 1981 special session and modified at the 1982 regular session of the General Assembly before being submitted to the electorate.

Like constitutional revisions generally, this one was quite political. Lobbyists and others representing specific interests were quick to get involved in the process. The 1981 special session was also an expensive one, with one estimate that it cost $30,000 per day.[xxvi] A confrontation occurred between the Speaker of the House of Representatives, Tom Murphy, and the governor over the powers to be granted to the legislature under the new constitution. This debate was fueled by the fact that governors had built up many informal powers under previous constitutions, including the naming of presiding officers of the House and Senate, as well as most legislative committee and subcommittee chairs. This practice ended with the 1966 election, when the legislature chose Lester Maddox as governor because no candidate got a majority of the popular vote. The General Assembly also organized itself without input from the governor and gained more power in subsequent years. Thus, by the early 1980s, legislators wanted to guard their political gains, but Governor Busbee favored the delegation of some powers to bureaucratic offices and state boards. The governor and the General Assembly also disagreed over taxes and gubernatorial term limits. At one point, Busbee asked legislators to forget the proposal and spend the remaining days of the session on other topics.[xxvii] Agreement was eventually reached, and voters approved the new constitution in November of 1982 by a nearly three-to-one margin. It took effect in July of 1983.

Major Provisions of the 1983 Constitution. The new constitution included eleven articles, many of them detailed and complicated. Still, the document was indeed much shorter than its predecessor and was written in simpler and gender-neutral language. Although it can be argued that the new constitution was one of evolution rather than revolution, it included many noteworthy changes:[xxviii]

✓ eliminating the requirement that local governments place changes in taxation, municipal codes, and employee compensation on the state ballot;

✓ establishing a unified court system, consolidating the duties of justices of the peace and small claims courts into magistrate courts, and strengthening the state Supreme Court;

✓ requiring nonpartisan election of state court judges;

✓ enhancing the power of the General Assembly to enact laws and authorize the appropriation of taxes;

✓ giving the Board of Pardons and Paroles power to stay death sentences;

✓ establishing an equal protection clause;

✓ reducing the total amount of debt that the state may assume;

✓ providing more open-to-the-public committee and legislative meetings; and,

✓ incorporating more formal separation of powers between the legislative and executive branches.

It is worth noting that the new constitution did not repeal the long list of local amendments in the old constitution. It simply allowed them to continue in force if approved by the General Assembly or the affected local government and "froze" them by prohibiting the addition of new local amendments.

Constitutional Amendments. The Georgia legislature can ask the state's voters to create a convention to amend or replace the constitution. The General Assembly also can submit proposed amendments to voters by a two-thirds vote in the House and the Senate – a procedure like that at the national level. The governor has no formal role in this process, but may be influential in recommending amendments and mobilizing public opinion. The U.S. Constitution requires ratification of amendments by legislatures or conventions in three-fourths of the states. In contrast, the Georgia Constitution requires ratification by a majority of the voters casting ballots on the proposed amendment. Such proposals are voted upon in the next statewide general election after being submitted to the electorate by the General Assembly (November of even-numbered years).

Despite the relatively young age of the Georgia Constitution, efforts to amend it have become somewhat common, although the number of proposals has not reached the dizzying heights of the previous constitution. There were 83 proposed general amendments on the ballot between 1984 and 2004, and voters approved 63 (76 percent). The total includes at least two proposals each year, with a high of 15 in 1988.

The November 2000 election included seven proposed amendments. The only proposal defeated by voters (52 percent opposed) would have allowed changes in the way marine vessels are taxed. Three amendments were approved to allow benefits for law enforcement officials, firefighters, public school employees, and state highway employees killed or disabled in the line of duty. One allowed members of the General Assembly to be removed from office after conviction for a felony rather than after exhausting all of their appeals. Another amendment raised from five to seven years the amount of time that state court judges must have been able to practice law before they can begin their judicial service. Finally, voters approved a measure related to property tax relief.

The 2002 election included six proposed amendments. Voters rejected two of these proposals. The first defeated proposal (54% opposed) would have established separate valuation standards and property tax rates for low-income residential developments. The other failed proposal (57% opposed) would have affected tax rates for commercial docksides used in the landing and processing of seafood. Of the four amendments approved by voters, two provided tax incentives for the redevelopment and clean-up of deteriorated or contaminated properties. Another amendment established a program of dog and cat sterilization funded by special license plates. Finally, voters approved a measure to prohibit individuals from holding state office if they have defaulted on their federal, state, or local taxes.

The November 2004 ballot included only two proposed amendments. One was a rather obscure question regarding the jurisdiction of the state supreme court. The other, however, was a contentious measure banning same-sex marriage.

Table 4
Proposed Amendments to the Georgia Constitution

Year	Number of Amendments Submitted to Voters	Number Approved	
1984	11	10	
1986	9	8	
1988	15	6	
1990	9	8	
1992	8	7	
1994	6	5	
1996	5	4	
1998	5	3	
2000	7	6	
2002	6	4	
2004	2	2	
TOTAL	83	63	(76%)

Sources: for 1984-1992: Hill, *The Georgia State Constitution*, pp. 20-23; for 1994: *Georgia Laws 1995 Session*, vol. 3, pp. CCCXVII-CCCXIX; for 1996-2004: Georgia Secretary of State Elections Division, "Georgia Election Results" (available www.sos.state.ga.us/elections/election_results/default.htm).

4. Georgia's Governmental Institutions

Like most states, Georgia's constitution mirrors the separation of powers adopted by the framers of the U.S. Constitution. Perhaps the most important aspect of the Georgia Constitution is what Melvin Hill calls its status as "a power-limiting document rather than a power-granting document."[xxix] Thus, many provisions specify things that the state of Georgia and its local governments <u>cannot</u> do.

The Georgia Constitution spells out the organization and authority of the legislative branch in Article 3 and the judicial branch in Article 6. Beyond that, the organization of government looks a bit different than at the national level. Executive responsibilities are spread among provisions in Article 4, which covers six boards and commissions, and Article 5, which encompasses the governor, lieutenant governor, and the six elected department heads. Other provisions affecting administration and local government are found in Article 8, which considers Georgia's system of education. The framework for local government is in Article 9, which comprises almost 20 percent of the Constitution.

The Georgia General Assembly

Comparisons to Congress and Other State Legislatures.[xxx] On the surface, there are few differences between the U.S. Congress and Georgia's legislature, which is officially named the Georgia General Assembly. Both are bicameral. The presiding officer of the house of representatives is called the speaker and is chosen by the members, but the leader of the senate (vice president of the United States and the lieutenant governor of Georgia) is elected independently of its members. Unlike Congress, where the entire House and one-third of the Senate are elected every two years, all 236 members of the General Assembly are up for election every two years. The General Assembly also meets for a very limited time each year and lacks the salary and staff support found in Congress.

The Georgia General Assembly has much in common with other state legislatures. Its members are charged with representing the people of their districts, reapportioning legislative seats following the census, enacting laws, adopting taxing and spending measures, overseeing enforcement of current laws, and interceding for constituents. Except for Nebraska, every state legislature is bicameral, elects its members on a partisan basis, and has an upper chamber called the senate. Forty-one states call their lower chamber the house of representatives, and Georgia and 41 other states convene regular legislative sessions annually. The fact that only eight state legislatures still meet biennially reflects the view that meeting once every two years may be too infrequent to keep up with problems in the modern world.

Differences do exist among legislatures, however. Size varies from a low of 49 in Nebraska's unicameral legislature to a high of 424 in the small state of New Hampshire. Georgia, with its 236 members, has the third-largest legislature. For the 49 bicameral legislatures, the average senate has 40 members, as compared to Georgia's 56. The average house of representatives has 109 members, much smaller than the 180 found in the Georgia House.[xxxi]

Qualifications such as minimum age, length of residence, and term limits vary. So do terms of office. Georgia is one of 11 states using only two-year terms. Members of Nebraska's unicameral legislature have terms of four years; four states have four-year terms for both chambers; the remaining 34 states elect their upper chamber to a four-year term and their lower chamber for two years. Unlike fifteen other states, neither Georgia's constitution nor its laws limit the number of terms that someone can serve in the legislature.[xxxii]

Regular legislative sessions range from off-year limits of 30 calendar days in New Mexico and Virginia and 20 legislative days in Wyoming to unlimited length for annual sessions in 13 states. Georgia is somewhere in the middle, with an annual session of 40 legislative days. Leadership, procedures, and compensation also vary widely among the states.

Representation. Georgia's earliest legislatures were based on county representation, initially with at least one representative for each county, which meant that the size of the General Assembly fluctuated over the years. During the 1960s, for example, the House had over 200 members at one point. As population changed and the number of counties grew to 159, the legislature became relatively large, but sparsely populated counties were represented equally with larger ones. Senate districts had three counties, and each seat rotated among its three counties at the end of each term. With each senator serving only one term and then giving way to someone from a neighboring county, power in the legislative branch was concentrated in the House, where members could hold unlimited tenure.[xxxiii]

The Constitution of 1983 restricted the Senate to <u>not more than</u> 56 members, while the House must have <u>at least</u> 180 members (size can be changed by law within these limits). Reapportionment occurs following the U.S. census held every ten years. The General Assembly has substantial flexibility in drawing legislative districts. This authority became more limited beginning in the 1960s, however when federal courts ruled that all representation within state legislatures must be based on population rather than county and Congress adopted the Voting Rights Act.[xxxiv] The practice of rotating Senate seats among counties in a district also ended, which allowed senators to run as incumbents and increased the power of the Senate as a whole.

After the 1990 census, the legislature abandoned multi-member House districts, which elected several representatives within the same district, with candidates required to run for a designated seat. This contrasts with a single-member district, where voters elect only one legislator. For example, District 72 might have two seats and would therefore have twice the population of a single-member district. People running for District 72, Post 1 did not compete with candidates for District 72, Post 2, although the electorate consisted of the same voters. With over 8.2 million residents in 2000, the average Senate district had about 147,000 people living in it, and there were approximately 46,000 resident per House district. During its 2001 session on redistricting, the General Assembly created more than 20 large, multi-member House districts where voters would elect two, three, or four representatives. Subsequent litigation, however, modified the boundaries for seats in both the Senate and the House, which saw the replacement of its multi-member districts with single-member districts.

Qualifications of Members. Article 3, section 2 of the Georgia Constitution requires that persons seeking office in the General Assembly be registered voters, U.S. citizens, and Georgia citizens for at least two years. It also requires that representatives live within their districts for at least one year. Those elected to the Senate must be at least 25 years old, while members of the House must be 21 or older. Persons may not simultaneously run for more than one office or in the primaries of two political parties. Also ineligible are persons on active military duty, those who hold other elected or civil offices within the state (unless they resign), and convicted felons.

Legislative Sessions. The Georgia General Assembly meets annually in a regular session that begins on the second Monday of January and lasts up to 40 legislative days. These are not calendar days, but days that the General Assembly is in session (not in recess or adjourned). The General Assembly may be called into special session by the governor, who sets the agenda, or by agreement of three-fifths of the membership of each chamber. Special sessions may be called to deal with unexpected crises, such as natural disasters, budgetary shortfalls, or other state emergencies. Special sessions may not last longer than 40 days and generally cannot be used for matters unrelated to the official agenda.[xxxv]

Legislative Leadership. When members of the General Assembly arrive in Atlanta for the beginning of a new legislative session, their first priorities include selecting leaders and organizing committees. The Georgia Constitution provides for the selection of presiding officers in each chamber. In the Senate, the lieutenant governor serves as president, just as the vice president of the United States is formally the presiding officer of the U.S. Senate. Thus, the presiding officer of the Senate is chosen by Georgia's voters in a statewide election, although the winner is chosen independently from the governor. It is worth noting that 25 other states (including Nebraska's unicameral legislature) also make the popularly elected lieutenant governor presiding officer of the senate. In the remaining 24 states, the senate chooses its own presiding officer. The Georgia Senate also elects one of its members as president pro tempore should the need arise to replace the presiding officer.

In the House, the representatives elect a speaker from among their members, as do the lower houses in the other 48 bicameral legislatures and the U.S. House of Representatives. In Georgia, House members also elect a speaker pro tempore, as do 25 other states; the other 23 legislatures either have no such position or have their speaker appoint someone.[xxxvi] In the speaker's absence, the speaker pro tempore presides.

Types of Legislation. Article 3 of the Georgia Constitution includes several sections detailing the General Assembly's procedures and powers for enacting laws, conducting impeachments, and spending public money. Bills before the General Assembly can be classified as resolutions, general legislation, and local legislation. All currently enforceable statutes are published in the *Official Code of Georgia Annotated*, which is updated periodically to include both new laws and legal opinions on implementation of current law.

Much of what passes through the General Assembly is not intended to be implemented as statute. Some of the items brought up for consideration are intended as statements of legislative opinion and may be enforceable only on the membership of the legislature itself. For example, the legislature may wish to recognize individuals or a sports team, in which case the General Assembly might pass a "resolution" describing the honoree's achievements. Resolutions also might be used to create special committees, to determine compensation for citizens who have been injured or suffered damages by state actions, or to set requirements for legislative staff. The resolution would therefore have little impact on other citizens of the state. It does, however, express the approval of the state government.

Resolutions might be passed to require the General Assembly itself to behave in a specific manner, as with rules of conduct, scheduling, or agreements on budgetary matters. In some cases, resolutions are passed by one chamber to establish rules only for the membership of that body, but joint resolutions require passage through both chambers. Resolutions generally do not require the signature of the governor because they do not require implementation outside the legislature itself. However, joint resolutions which are enforceable as law do require the governor's signature and may be vetoed.

General legislation has application statewide. Laws regarding election procedures or speed limits on state highways are examples. Local governments may not pass ordinances which contradict general law. Most general legislation intended to change existing law will specify exactly which statutes will be changed, but any new legislation supersedes past legislation.

Local legislation refers to those laws passed by the Georgia General Assembly which apply only to specific cities, counties, or special districts within the state. The General Assembly retains the power to govern localities through the passage of local legislation.[xxxvii] Local legislation may not contradict general legislation and may not be used to change the tenure of particular local officials. It can, however, be used to create or change political boundaries. The passage of local legislation differs in some ways from the passage of general law. Local bills must be preceded by a period of advertisement in which citizens of the jurisdiction concerned are notified of the potential law. This most often occurs in local newspapers.

Consideration of Bills. Only members of the General Assembly may introduce legislation, although by custom governors have had members introduce bills on their behalf. Bills generally are written by several persons and may be sponsored by multiple legislators. Bills may be introduced in either chamber of the General Assembly or at the same time in both chambers. One exception is legislation dealing with public revenues or appropriation of public money, which the Constitution requires to begin in the House of Representatives.[xxxviii]

Bills must adhere to a specific format dictated by the Constitution and the rules of each chamber. The title of the bill must relate directly to its content, and bills are constitutionally restricted to no more than one purpose. The Constitution mandates that all general legislation be read three times from the floor on three separate days. Because the title is required to be a summary of intent, reading the title only is substituted for the first reading of the entire bill. A second reading of the bill, which occurs on the second day after introduction, will also be of the title only. The Constitution forbids the introduction of bills which deal with specific individuals or which might limit the constitutional authority of the General Assembly. Population bills (those which apply to jurisdictions of a certain population) are also forbidden, as are bills that would have the effect of limiting business competition or creating monopolies within the state. Local legislation may be voted on after only one reading. The media may follow the passage of a bill, and the Constitution requires that floor action and committee meetings must be "open to the public," but this guarantee is not absolute.[xxxix]

Bills are passed by a simple majority of the entire membership of each chamber, although there are several exceptions to this rule. Tax legislation, proposed amendments to the constitution, veto overrides, punitive action taken against a member of the General Assembly, or motions to change the order of business require two-thirds majorities. Bills which have been rejected once in a legislative session also require a two-thirds majority to be reconsidered. Procedural changes may only require a majority of those members present. Once a bill has achieved a majority vote in one chamber, it must be passed in identical form by a majority vote in the other chamber in order to continue on the path to becoming a law.

The State Budget.[xl] The budget is a special type of lawmaking. The Georgia Constitution directs the governor to prepare the state's annual budget and submit it to the General Assembly during the first five days of the regular legislative session. This leaves the governor with substantial authority in the early stages of budget formation. This is countered, however, by the legislature's virtually unlimited power to change the budget submitted by the governor. The Constitution also requires that the state adopt a balanced budget, something the federal government is not obligated to do. Georgia's governor can exercise a line-item veto in an attempt to remove specific spending without vetoing the entire budget. Like a regular veto, the line-item veto can be overridden by a two-thirds vote of the membership in each chamber of the General Assembly.[xli]

The Executive Branch

One of the most striking differences between the U.S. and Georgia constitutions is the number of elected officials in the executive branch. The most visible in Georgia are the governor and the lieutenant governor. While they may be compared to the U.S. president and vice president, they are not elected together as a team and may represent different views and political parties.

Like the majority of states, Georgia has a plural executive, meaning that voters elect various department heads rather than having them picked by the governor like presidents choose the members of their cabinet. All but six states elect executive branch officials in addition to a governor (see Table 5).[xlii] In fact, voters around the country choose over 500 officials in statewide elections (a number virtually unchanged since the mid-1950s). Some of these officials are required to be elected by state constitutions; others are provided for by law. Their tasks vary significantly. Financial monitoring, for instance, is assigned to elected auditors, comptrollers, and treasurers, as well as appointed officials. Education is also diverse: seven states elect boards to govern public education, while Colorado, Michigan, and Nebraska voters elect the board of regents for their state universities.[xliii]

The Governor. Governors are generally the most powerful political figures in their states. Their political clout is based on the formal authority granted in a state's constitution, as well as several other sources of power, including laws, the media, public opinion, ties to political parties and interest groups, and personal characteristics. Professor Thad Beyle has compared the formal power of nation's governors, including their tenure potential, appointment powers, budgetary control, veto power, and the number of separately elected executive officials.[xliv]

The tenure potential (number of consecutive terms permitted for a governor) has been a contentious issue in Georgia's political history. The 1877 constitution limited the governor to two consecutive, two-year terms. A 1941 constitutional amendment provided for a four-year term, but prohibited governors from succeeding themselves in office. That was changed in 1976 to permit successive terms, but the lifetime limit for any governor was also two terms. The Constitution of 1983 permits two consecutive, four-year terms with no lifetime restriction on the time of a governor's service. That earned Georgia's governor a score of 4 on Beyle's 5-point scale for tenure potential. The most powerful tenure potential, which received a score of 5, exists in the nine states where governors face no limit on the number of four-year terms. At the opposite pole is Virginia, which does not allow governors to succeed themselves.[xlv] Unlike the governor, Georgia's other statewide elected officials face no constitutional limit on the number of consecutive terms they can serve, and some have served for decades.

Table 5
Executive Branch Officials Elected by the Public

Office	Number of States Electing	Georgia
Governor	50	elected statewide
Lieutenant Governor	42	elected statewide
Attorney General	43	elected statewide
Secretary of State	36	elected statewide
Education Superintendent		14[a] elected statewide
Agriculture Commissioner		13 elected statewide
Insurance Commissioner	11	elected statewide
Labor Commissioner	5	elected statewide
Utilities Commissioners	7[b]	5 elected statewide
Treasurer	36	appointed by governor[c]
Auditor	23	chosen by the legislature

[a]Another 8 states elect their boards of education.
[b]As in Georgia, these are multi-member boards regulating matters such as quality and prices for services such as natural gas, telephone, and electricity.
[c]Tasks are performed by the director of finance.

Source: *The Book of the States: 2005 Edition*, pp. 233-238, 350-351.

In terms of appointment power, Beyle classifies Georgia's governor in the weakest category because of limited power in six key areas: health, education, transportation, corrections, public utilities regulation, and welfare. In each of these cases, top administrators are chosen by voters (school superintendent and members of the Public Service Commission) or by boards. Gubernatorial control over boards and commissions is weakened because terms are long and staggered, which means that it can take some time before a governor's appointees are in control. In the case of one board (Transportation), the governor does not even appoint the members – the General Assembly chooses them.

Perhaps the most important appointment power of Georgia governors is their constitutional authority to fill vacancies in the executive and judicial branches without Senate confirmation.[xlvi] In the case of elected positions, the governor picks someone who finishes an unexpired term, thus becoming the incumbent in the next campaign. By law, the governor also can fill vacancies at the local level when an official has been removed temporarily following an indictment.[xlvii]

Beyle's 1-5 scale of budgetary power assigned a value of 1 to a governor who prepared the budget with other officials and faced unlimited legislative ability to amend, while 5 was for a budget prepared by a governor whose legislature was prohibited from increasing it. Like 42 other states, the Georgia governor rated a 3 on budgetary powers: the governor has full responsibility for preparing the budget, but the legislature has unlimited ability to change it.

Using a similar 1-5 scale for veto power, Beyle rated Georgia's governorship a 5, meaning that the governor has both simple and line-item vetoes along with a requirement for a large majority of the legislature to override (two-thirds of the total membership of each chamber). Twenty-three states make it easier to override a gubernatorial veto: six require only a majority of legislators elected, five mandate three-fifths of those elected, and twelve specify three-fifths or two-thirds of those present for the override vote.[xlviii]

The governor's veto power is included in the legislative, not the executive, article of the Georgia Constitution.[xlix] The governor has authority to act on legislation passed by the General Assembly that would have the effect of law, except for changes in the Constitution. If the governor signs a bill, it becomes law on a specified date, usually with the start of the fiscal year on July 1. The governor has six days to act on a bill while the General Assembly is in session. If the General Assembly has adjourned for the session or for more than forty days (like a recess), the governor has forty days after adjournment to act. When vetoing a bill, the governor is required to return it to the chamber where it originated within three days during the session or sixty days after adjournment. Once the General Assembly has received a veto message, the originating chamber may consider the vetoed bill immediately. Those bills vetoed during adjournment can be overridden during the next legislative session, as long as an election has not intervened.

A bill also becomes law if the governor does nothing (neither signs nor vetoes it). If the governor fails to act on a bill, it will become law following a six-day waiting period for bills passed during the first thirty-four days of the legislative session, or following a forty-day waiting period for bills passed during the final six days of the session. Thus, bills may sit on the governor's desk after adjournment of the legislature and become law even if the governor does not sign them.

Georgia is among the 43 states that provide for two types of vetoes, full and line-item. A full veto is a rejection of an entire bill. Line-item vetoes are rejections of specific passages in appropriations bills, which give the governor the power to kill spending for specific projects without having to veto an entire state budget. Reconsideration of bills in which specific funding has been line-item vetoed is not necessary, and the governor's actions officially reduce the appropriation if not overridden. A successful override allows a bill to become law in spite of the governor's veto. If an override fails in either chamber of the Georgia General Assembly, a bill is dead.

The Plural Executive. The Georgia Constitution requires voters to elect six department heads in addition to the governor and lieutenant governor. Together, these eight officials are referred to as the state's "elected constitutional officers."[l] Like a majority of states, Georgia elects an attorney general and secretary of state. Georgia is among the few states, however, letting voters pick a state school superintendent and individuals to head departments of agriculture, insurance, and labor.[li]

The six elected department heads possess power independent of the governor. They do so in part because of the prerogatives of their offices. The attorney general, for instance, exercises great discretion regarding the handling of litigation in which the state is a party and issues opinions on the legality or constitutionality of actions taken by the state.[lii] The insurance and agriculture commissioners have substantial power to regulate certain types of businesses. In addition to the power they derive from being elected separately from the governor, the narrow focus of their offices means that constitutional officers' natural constituencies (for votes and campaign money) are the interests affected most directly by their decisions. In fact, they are often seen as advocates of the industries they oversee.[liii] Elected department heads may even be in conflict with one another. Thus, despite the image of the governor's power in Georgia, executive power in the state is dispersed.

Georgia's elected department heads must have reached the age of 25, been a U.S. citizen for at least ten years, and been a Georgia resident at least four years when they assume office. The attorney general also is required to have had seven years as an active-status member of the State Bar of Georgia, which supervises the legal profession in the state. The Constitution leaves it to the General Assembly to spell out the power and duties of these officers, to determine their salaries, and to fund their agencies.[liv] There is also a procedure under which four of the eight constitutional officers can petition the Georgia Supreme Court to hold a hearing to determine if a constitutional officer is permanently disabled and should be replaced.[lv]

Constitutional Boards and Commissions. States commonly assign decision making in certain policy areas to multi-member boards rather than departments headed by a single individual. Georgia is no exception. Eight boards have their authority spelled out in the Georgia Constitution (see Table 6) Others have been created by law or executive order.

The eight boards and commissions required by the Constitution are among the most powerful agencies in Georgia, in part because any changes in their basic authority and membership require a constitutional amendment rather than passage of a law by the General Assembly. Their power is also reflected in the resources they control. In fiscal year 2005, for instance, the University System Board of Regents had a budget of roughly $3.5 billion, slightly less half of which was state funds. Some funds are earmarked in the Constitution: Article 3 requires that state motor fuel taxes, which were expected to total more than $634 million in fiscal 2005, must be spent for "an adequate system of public roads and bridges." That provides substantial power to the Department of Transportation, which had a total budget of more than $1.6 billion in fiscal 2005.[lvi]

Table 6
Constitutional Boards and Commissions in Georgia

Board/Commission	Members	Membership Selection
Public Service	5	Elected statewide on a partisan ballot for six-year terms.
Pardons and Paroles	5	Appointed by the governor to seven-year terms subject to Senate confirmation.
Personnel	5	Appointed by the governor to five-year terms subject to Senate confirmation.
Transportation	13[a]	One member per congressional district elected by majority vote of General Assembly members whose districts overlap any of the congressional district.

Veterans Services	7	Appointed by the governor to seven-year terms subject to Senate confirmation.
Natural Resources	18[a]	One member per congressional district and five at large (at least one of whom is from a coastal county) appointed by the governor to seven-year terms subject to Senate confirmation.
Education	13[a]	One member per congressional district appointed by the governor to seven-year terms subject to Senate confirmation.
Regents	18[a]	One member per congressional district and five at large appointed by the governor to seven-year terms subject to Senate confirmation.

[a]Membership can vary because it depends on the number of seats that Georgia has in the U.S. House of Representatives, which increased to 13 following the 2000 census and reapportionment.

Source: *Constitution of the State of Georgia*, art. 4 (for the first six boards); art. 8, sect. 2 (State Board of Education); art. 4, sect. 4 (Board of Regents).

The Constitution insulates these boards from political pressure to some degree by providing relatively long terms that are staggered. In the case of the State Board of Education and the University System Board of Regents, the governor is specifically prohibited from being a board member. Most constitutional boards and commissions use some geographical representation. Assigning one seat per congressional district has the effect of assuring South Georgia seats on boards that otherwise might be dominated by people from the Atlanta area. It also means that the size of a board can change as Georgia gets additional seats in the U.S. House of Representatives.

The Public Service Commission was originally created by statute in 1879 to regulate railroads. Today it is composed of five members who are elected statewide for staggered, six-year terms and regulates telephone services, utilities such as gas and electricity, communication networks, and transportation such as trucking and rail systems. The State Transportation Board may seem like the essence of pork-barrel politics, with one member chosen from each congressional district by the state legislators whose districts overlap it (and benefit from highway construction). Members of the remaining six boards are appointed by the governor, subject to confirmation by the Senate.

The Judicial Branch

There are essentially 51 legal systems in the United States, one at the federal level and a distinct system in each of the 50 states. Like the federal government and other states, Georgia has an elaborate system of trial and appellate courts (see Figure 1). Trial courts apply laws to the facts in specific cases, as when they render a verdict in a criminal or civil case. Appellate courts review the actions of trial courts to determine questions of law (whether statutes or constitutional questions were interpreted or applied correctly). Decisions in appellate courts are made by groups of judges with no witnesses or juries. The appellate courts rely on written and oral arguments by the parties in the case being appealed, although they can permit other parties to submit written briefs in support of either side in a case. Unlike the U.S. Constitution, which grants Congress broad authority regarding the legal system, Article 6 of the Georgia Constitution includes substantial detail about the operation of trial and appellate courts, the selection and conduct of judges, the election and performance of district attorneys, and a range of procedures.

The Georgia Constitution requires that state judges be elected, primarily on a nonpartisan ballot. Georgia's district attorneys, who are local officials responsible for criminal prosecutions, also are elected. This is quite different from the national level, where, subject to Senate confirmation, local prosecutors are presidential appointees under the authority of the U.S. Department of Justice, and judges are nominated by the president and can serve for life.

There is some link between Georgia's executive and judicial branches because the governor is permitted to appoint people to vacant or newly created judgeships.[lvii] One study calculated that 66 percent of superior court judgeships between 1968 and mid-1994 were filled by appointment. Because judges are routinely reelected in Georgia and so many vacancies are filled by appointment, judicial selection in Georgia is often seen as a system of gubernatorial selection, as when Governor Sonny Perdue appointed his top legal advisor to the Georgia Supreme Court in 2005.[lviii] Another practice not found at the national level is the ability of the attorney general to issue advisory opinions, which can have the force of law in Georgia unless overturned in court.

Trial Courts. Georgia is often characterized as one of the more complicated court systems, in large part because of the many trial courts of limited jurisdiction, some of which operate in only a few cities or counties rather than being uniform throughout the state. The Georgia Constitution grants the General Assembly discretion over the creation, jurisdiction, and operation of the state's courts, but it also requires that each county have at least one superior court, magistrate court, and probate court.[lix]

Superior court is the court of general jurisdiction, hearing a broad range of serious cases. The state is divided for administrative purposes into circuits that vary in population and size. Each county has its own superior court, but judges may handle cases in more than one county within a circuit. Superior courts hear divorces, felonies, most civil disputes, and similar matters. As workloads have increased, the General Assembly has added more judges and circuits.

There are also trial courts of limited jurisdiction, which hear specialized cases that are usually less serious than those in courts of general jurisdiction. These are primarily municipal courts dealing with traffic laws, local ordinances, and other misdemeanors. They also process warrants and may conduct preliminary hearings to determine if "probable cause" exists in a criminal case. Local acts passed by the General Assembly set courts' jurisdiction and the requirements for selecting municipal court judges.

The probate court in each county deals with wills, estates, marriage licenses, appointment of guardians, and involuntary hospitalizations of individuals. Probate courts may also issue warrants in some cases. Magistrate courts deal with bail, misdemeanors, small civil complaints, and search and arrest warrants. They also may conduct preliminary hearings.

Some counties have state and juvenile courts. The General Assembly passes local legislation to create state courts, which hear civil cases, traffic violations, or other misdemeanors. They may also hold preliminary hearings and act on applications to issue warrants. State courts operate in less than half of Georgia's counties and often have part-time judgeships. There may not be a separate juvenile court judge in small counties, where superior court judges often serve in juvenile court.

Appellate Courts. Like most states, Georgia has two levels of appellate courts. Cases decided by trial courts may be appealed to the Court of Appeals, except in cases reserved for other courts, such as the Georgia Supreme Court's exclusive jurisdiction over election contests. The Court of Appeals, which was created in 1907 to relieve some of the burden on the Supreme Court, is elected statewide on a nonpartisan basis for staggered, six-year terms. The Court of Appeals can be affected by state law, as when the General Assembly added a tenth

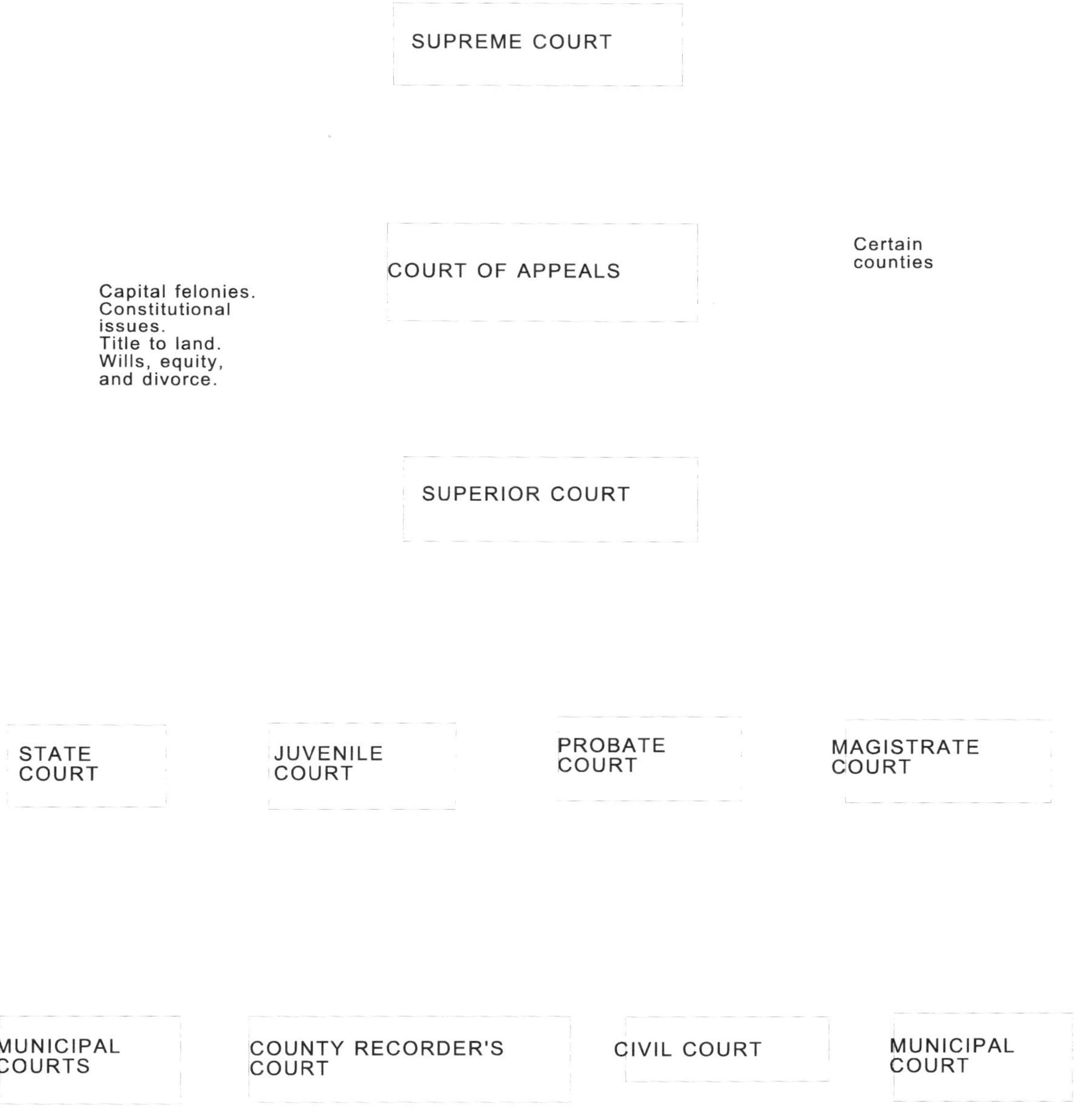

judge in 1996 to help with the increased work load. Another two positions were added in 1999, leaving a court with twelve judges. The court often hears appeals on child custody, worker's compensation, and criminal cases that do not involve the death penalty. Cases appealed to the Court of Appeals are usually heard by a panel of three judges. If one of the judges on a panel dissents, however, a case may be heard by the full Court of Appeals.[lx]

The Supreme Court is comprised of seven justices elected statewide on a nonpartisan basis to six-year terms. They choose whether to hear appeals from lower courts through the process of certiorari (request for information from lower courts). The Court has exclusive appellate jurisdiction over all cases regarding the Georgia Constitution, the U.S. Constitution (as it applies within the state), elections, and the constitutionality of laws. It also may hear cases on appeal from the Court of Appeals or may be called upon to decide questions of law from other state or local courts. It has authority to hear appeals for all cases in which a sentence of death may be given. The Supreme Court is also involved in administering the state court system and regulating the legal profession.[lxi]

Selection of Judges.[lxii] The 50 states employ five methods for choosing judges. Some states elect judges in partisan elections; others hold nonpartisan elections; others require that judges be appointed by the governor; three states have at least some judges elected by the legislature; still others allow for the selection of judges under a merit system of screening by nominating commissions that submit candidates to a state's governor for selection. Once in office, such judges stand periodically for election.

Georgia has a long-standing commitment to electing judges, although there are some qualifications about age, living in certain counties or circuits, and membership in the state bar. The Constitution requires that members of the Supreme Court and Court of Appeals be elected in statewide nonpartisan elections for six-year terms. The justices of the Supreme Court choose a chief justice from among themselves. Superior court judges are also elected in nonpartisan elections, but serve four-year terms and are elected by voters who live within their circuits. State court judges are elected in nonpartisan, countywide elections for four years. Juvenile court judges are appointed, not elected, by the superior court judges of the counties they serve. The Georgia Constitution requires that all appellate and superior court judges shall have been admitted to practice law for seven years prior to assuming their judicial positions. Voters approved an amendment to the Constitution in 2000 imposing a similar seven-year requirement for state court judges (it had been five years).

The methods for choosing probate judges, magistrates, and municipal court judges are determined by law and can vary widely. In Athens-Clarke County, for instance, the probate judge and magistrate are elected on a partisan ballot, but municipal court judges are appointed. Unlike the rest of the judiciary, the Georgia Constitution does not require that probate judges, magistrates, or municipal court judges have been admitted to practice law for a minimum number of years. It leaves such matters for the General Assembly to specify by law, which means that non-lawyers could serve in such positions. This has often been a controversial issue, and state law does require certain training for those assuming such positions.

The Constitution allows the Judicial Qualifications Commission to suspend, remove, or discipline judges who have been indicted or convicted of a crime, cannot perform the duties of their office, or "for conduct prejudicial to the administration of justice which brings the judicial office into disrepute." The Georgia Supreme Court must review the case before a judge is removed from office.[lxiii] Except in magistrate, probate, and juvenile courts, the Georgia Constitution authorizes the governor to appoint a replacement to serve the remainder of a judge's term when a position becomes vacant for any reason. The Judicial Nominating Commission assists the governor in making such appointments, although the selection process includes input from political leaders and members of the legal profession.

District Attorneys.[lxiv] District attorneys are elected for four-year terms in each judicial circuit in Georgia. Qualifications for office include active membership in the State Bar of Georgia for three years. District attorneys represent the state as prosecutors in all criminal cases and in all cases heard by the Supreme Court and Courts of Appeals.

Juries.[lxv] The Georgia Constitution provides limited detail on juries, although it is significant that the matter is in Article 1 with the bill of rights rather than in the article on the judiciary, as it was in the Constitution of 1976. Citizens may be chosen to serve on grand juries or trial juries. While trial juries are the better known to the public because of media coverage of criminal cases, grand juries are important in determining how and if a case will proceed against a defendant.

Juries are not required for all trials in Georgia, but the size of the jury is determined by the level of the court. The Constitution specifies trial juries of 12 members, but allows the General Assembly to permit smaller juries and nonunanimous decisions in misdemeanor cases and in courts of limited jurisdiction. Magistrate courts and juvenile courts never hold jury trials, and other lower courts are not likely to use juries. Superior courts have juries of 12 members. State courts have six-member juries. Juries in civil cases consist of six or 12 members, depending on the dollar amount of damages sought and whether either party requests a jury of 12 rather than six members in state court. Unanimous decisions are required in criminal cases, where the decision to use a jury rather than a judge for the verdict rests with the defendant. The General Assembly has other authority over the composition of juries. In 2005, for instance, legislators passed a law that gave the defendant and the prosecutor in a criminal case an equal number of "strikes" to remove potential jurors from a jury pool. Previously, the prosecutor was allowed only half as many strikes as the defendant.[lxvi]

Grand juries are used by over half the states to issue an indictment (a formal charge accusing someone of a crime). Four states require grand juries for all indictments. Georgia is one of fifteen states that requires a grand jury for felony indictments. Six states require grand jury indictments for capital crimes, and the state of Pennsylvania does not empower the grand jury to indict. All other states make grand jury indictments optional, with the prosecutor filing an "information" in order to enter a formal charge against someone.

In deciding whether to issue an indictment, a grand jury must conclude that there is "probable cause" that the person committed the crime as charged. This a far less rigorous standard, however, than the "proof beyond a reasonable doubt" needed to convict the accused in a trial. Because the grand jury decides merely if sufficient evidence exists for an indictment, only the prosecution is heard, business is conducted in secret, and the defense has no right to cross-examine witnesses. Many have argued that this makes grand juries unnecessary and merely a "rubber stamp" for the prosecutor.

Grand juries in Georgia consist of 16-23 members. In addition to issuing indictments, grand juries have broad powers to study the records and activities of county governments, issue reports, and make certain decisions. For instance, grand juries in both counties had to review a request by some citizens to transfer the territory where they lived from Fulton County to Coweta County. Also, grand juries selected school boards in some counties until the Georgia Constitution was amended in 1992.

In addition to allocating authority among the three branches of state government, the Georgia Constitution also establishes a framework for the operation of local government.[lxviii] This is especially important since the U.S. Constitution says nothing about the matter. Local government in Georgia includes a range of counties, cities, and special districts (see Table 7).

Counties and Cities. The Georgia Constitution is very detailed regarding local government, although it is somewhat more specific regarding counties than cities and special districts. Article 9 even restricts the number of counties to no more than 159, although no such limit applies to other local governments. The Constitution also requires all counties to have certain elected officials. These local "constitutional officers" include a clerk of the superior court, judge of the probate court, sheriff, and tax commissioner (or tax collector and tax receiver), each of whom is elected to a four-year term. The Constitution leaves it to state law to spell out the characteristics of local legislative bodies such as county commissions and city councils.

The Constitution goes to some length to prohibit counties from taking several types of actions, such as those affecting local school systems or any court. It also lists functions that cities and counties may perform, including public transportation, health services and facilities, libraries, and enforcement of building codes. This is especially important to counties, which were first authorized to provide urban services by a constitutional amendment ratified in 1972. Article 9 also allows counties and cities to use planning and zoning, take private property, make agreements with one another, and consolidate.

Table 7
Number and Type of Local Governments in Georgia, 1952-2002

Year	Counties[a]	Municipalities[a]	School Districts	Special Districts
1952	159	475	187	154
1957	159	508	198	255
1962	159	561	197	301
1967	159	512	194	338
1972	159	529	189	366
1977	159	529	188	387
1982	159	532	187	390
1987	159	531	186	410
1992	159	534	183	421
1997	159	534	180	473
2002	159	528	180	581

[a]Following the mergers between Columbus and Muscogee County in 1970, Athens and Clarke County in 1991, and Augusta and Richmond County in 1995, the U.S. Census Bureau counted

the new governments as a municipality, not a county. This table treats each merged
government as a county because of its organization and functions.

<u>Sources: U.S. Bureau of the Census, *Census of Governments*, selected years.</u>

Special Districts. A wide range of special districts is permitted by the Georgia
Constitution, but their characteristics are covered by general laws. Probably the most visible
special districts are local school systems. Policy making for education at the local level is the
responsibility of elected school boards, who hire a superintendent as chief administrator. Prior
to ratification of a constitutional amendment in November 1992, two-thirds of the county
superintendents and 85 percent of the boards were elected.[lxix]
Perhaps the most important characteristic of special districts is their relative independence
from county and municipal governments. For instance, areas can set up "community
improvement districts" under state law to tax themselves extra for services beyond what their
city or county provides. There are districts for major malls in suburban Atlanta, plus one that
collects $1.7 million annually for services in downtown Atlanta.[lxx]
In addition to districts that cover only part of a local government's area, larger ones have
been established to deal with regional issues. For example, MARTA (Metropolitan Atlanta
Regional Transportation Authority) provides bus and subway service in Fulton and DeKalb
Counties. The Georgia Regional Transportation Authority (GRTA) was created by the General
Assembly in 1999 to oversee transportation and major development decisions in areas not
meeting federal clean air standards.[lxxi] The General Assembly also created the North Georgia
Metropolitan Water Planning District in 2001 to address water problems in 18 counties in the
Atlanta area.[lxxii] As public needs and demands continue to arise, the General Assembly will
undoubtedly use its constitutional power to establish local governments to create more special
districts on top of the state's counties and cities.

Home Rule. The Georgia Constitution provides "home rule" for cities and counties. In
most states, this means that a local government is granted broad powers to write and amend its
charter (the equivalent of a local government's constitution) and to take any action not
prohibited by the state. Home rule has proven more limited in Georgia, however. One study
found that Georgia was one of 25 states in 1990 without a general law providing optional forms
of government for counties, and one of 26 that did not grant them some autonomy in choosing
their form of government. The same was true regarding municipalities, where Georgia was one
of 13 states that did not have a general law regarding optional forms, and one of only ten that
did not give cities any choice in their organizational structure. Unlike 30 states, Georgia did not
divide its cities into "classes" (usually based on population), with different levels of authority
granted to each class. Georgia does grant flexibility to cities and counties in carrying out local
government functions.[lxxiii] Thus, Georgia grants its local governments some autonomy in day-to-
day operations, but little authority to determine their own organizational structure.
A major reason for this limited local power is the Constitution itself, which places some
restrictions directly on counties and cities. It also permits the legislature to adopt local acts,
which are applied to specific cities, counties, and special districts. Local acts were 51 percent
of the bills passed between 1970 and 1996 and can cover a wide range of topics. For example,
it took action by the General Assembly to establish procedures for citizens to vote on merging

34

governments such as Athens-Clarke County and Augusta-Richmond County.[lxxiv] Many other state constitutions prohibit the adoption of local laws.

Local Government Finances.[lxxv] The Constitution generally leaves the question of how local governments can raise and spend money to the General Assembly. In contrast, debt is covered in substantial detail. Georgia employs several restrictions common among the states. One is that debt cannot exceed ten percent of the assessed value of taxable property within the jurisdiction. Second, the Constitution places an annual limit on the amount that can be borrowed on a short-term basis.

A third requirement is that voters must approve the issuance of new debt by a simple majority in an election. However, this applies only to general obligation debt (borrowing in which the local government pledges tax revenues to pay off bonds sold to raise money, usually for major construction projects). The required voter approval and debt limitation do not apply to revenue bonds, which are not backed by taxes, but by revenues from projects being financed by the bonds. Airport revenue bonds, for example, are generally paid off with parking fees, aircraft landing charges, rents from airlines and concessionaires, and the like. With all types of local government borrowing, though, the real limit is the willingness of investors to buy bonds issued by a local government. In addition, local governments are required by state law to adopt a balanced budget each year.[lxxvi]

Georgia, like most states, limits local tax rates, mainly through laws passed by the General Assembly. State law allows counties and municipalities to levy a one percent general sales tax in addition to the four percent state tax. They cannot levy the tax without the approval of their voters. Since 1985, counties have been permitted by law to use a one-percent special purpose local option sales tax (SPLOST). The SPLOST is temporary, must be approved in a referendum, and must finance specific projects such as streets and roads, bridges, landfills, and solid waste.

In November of 1996, Georgia voters ratified a constitutional amendment to allow school districts to use a one-percent sales tax for construction. This tax is similar to the SPLOST used by counties and must be approved by a school district's voters in a referendum. This new revenue source can generate millions of dollars of funds, especially in rapidly growing school systems, and help school boards reduce their debt and dependence on property taxes. Despite the narrow statewide majority ratifying the amendment, the tax quickly proved popular at the local level.[lxxvii]

5. Elections

Just as constitutions specify the ways in which political institutions are organized, they also establish processes considered essential for a democracy. These include procedures for conducting elections, which are found in Article 2 of the Georgia Constitution.

Types of Elections

The Georgia Constitution provides basic ground rules for elections, such as the use of secret ballots and establishment of 18 as the minimum voting age (Georgia adopted this minimum age in the 1940s and was the first state to do so). Runoff elections and recalls are constitutionally established, as are procedures for removing and/or suspending public officials. However, the Constitution leaves most of the specifics regarding voter registration and election procedures to be decided by the General Assembly.

Primary and General Elections. All states have general elections in which voters choose from a number of candidates to fill an office. In most states, including Georgia, voters select party nominees from a group of potential candidates in a primary election. Some states also use party conventions to nominate candidates for certain offices. Primaries are not specified in the Georgia Constitution, but procedures are provided for by state law or political party rules.

Runoffs. In most states, the individual who receives the most votes in an election is declared the winner, but others require that the winner of a primary or general election receive over a certain percentage of the votes cast. Seven states, including Georgia, hold runoffs if no single candidate is able to capture 50 percent of the vote. North Carolina also employs runoffs, but reduced the threshold from 50 percent to 40 percent in 1989. Georgia's runoff was originally adopted in 1917, but has changed somewhat since then.

The logic behind the runoff system is based, in part, on the assumption that elections should reflect the will of the majority of the electorate. In places where there is a tradition of one-party politics with little or no opposition in the general election, candidates have faced their strongest opposition in primaries. If only a plurality were required, it would be possible to achieve elected office by finishing first in a primary with many candidates but still receiving well under 50 percent of the vote. To prevent that from occurring, the top two finishers face each other in a subsequent runoff, where the winner would be the candidate getting a majority in this two-person race.[lxxviii]

Traditionally, runoffs occurred after primaries, but in 1992 a runoff was held after a general election in Georgia between candidates for the U.S. Senate. In that instance, a third candidate prevented front-runner Wyche Fowler, the Democratic incumbent, from earning over 50 percent of the vote. His Republican opponent, Paul Coverdell, won the runoff. The General Assembly prevented this from occurring again when it adopted laws in 1994, 1996, 1997, and 1998 governing the use of such elections. A plurality (not a majority) is all that is needed to win a general election for a state office, except for the statewide constitutional officers, who still must achieve 50 percent. A majority remains required for party primaries and special elections, so runoffs could be common in such cases.[lxxix] Runoff requirements also remain a requirement in many local elections.

Runoffs have been criticized as being biased against minority candidates, who might finish first in an election but not get a majority. A minority candidate could then be defeated in a runoff as whites voted in a bloc for the remaining white candidate. Runoffs have been the subject of litigation in Georgia. The U.S. Supreme Court permitted their continued use in 1999, however, when it refused to hear an appeal from a lower court, which had held that the law requiring primary runoffs was not racially discriminatory.[lxxx]

Referendum Elections. States also conduct elections in which candidates are not running for office. The most common is a referendum, in which legislative bodies place issues on the ballot for public approval. Critics often complain, though, that asking people to vote "yes" or "no" on a question is not a good way to decide complex issues. Georgia voters are accustomed to referenda on whether to amend the state constitution. In their communities, they can be asked to decide whether local governments should levy sales taxes or be permitted to go into debt to by selling bonds to pay for public improvements such as roads and buildings.

Removal of Elected Officials. Recalls are elections to remove public officials from office before their terms have expired. Recall of state officials is allowed in Georgia and 15 other states; recall of local officeholders is more widely permitted. Some states exempt certain officeholders, usually judges, from the recall process. In Georgia, all persons who occupy elected state or local offices, even if they were appointed to fill unfinished terms, are subject to removal. Recalls are placed on the ballot through a petition process established by law. If an office becomes vacant through recall, a special election is held to fill the position.[lxxxi] If an
The Constitution allows other means for removing public officials. The House of Representatives may impeach any executive or judicial officer of the state, as well as members of the General Assembly. If the House votes in favor of impeachment charges, a two-thirds vote in the Senate is required to convict and remove the official from office.[lxxxii] The Constitution also includes procedures for the temporary suspension of the governor, the lieutenant governor, any of the other six constitutional officers, or a member of the General Assembly indicted for a felony by a grand jury.[lxxxiii]

<u>**Timing of Elections**</u>[lxxxiv]

The 1983 Constitution set the dates for the first general elections after its implementation; it also gave the General Assembly power to change the dates. This has not occurred, so elections for state offices are held the first Tuesday after the first Monday in November of even-numbered years. The members of the General Assembly are elected for two-year terms, which means that elections for these offices are at the same time as the U.S. House of Representatives. The governor and other statewide officeholders have four-year terms and are elected in years when the presidency is not on the ballot, which can protect Georgia candidates if their political party has an unpopular presidential candidate.
The Constitution sets length of terms for other elected officials, but leaves it to the General Assembly to determine by law when judges and most local officials will be elected.[lxxxv] County elections in Georgia are generally at the same time as major state and national races, but most city elections are held at different times, usually in odd-numbered years.

<u>**Redistricting**</u>

Like other states, Georgia redraws district boundaries for its legislature and the U.S. House of Representatives every ten years following the U.S. census. A similar process occurs for city councils and county commissions whose members are elected from districts rather than at large. Gerrymandering (the practice of drawing districts in order to achieve political outcomes) is one method by which incumbents may protect their political careers, minority political parties may be prevented from gaining legislative seats, rural or urban districts may dominate, or the voting strength of minority groups may be diluted.

Although it did not originate in Georgia, the U.S. Supreme Court's 1962 decision in *Baker v. Carr*[lxxxvi] affected Georgia profoundly. This landmark ruling and subsequent decisions forced states to draw legislative districts on the basis of population rather than political boundaries such as county lines. The "one person, one vote" standard required districts of equal population, although slight variation is tolerated. Based in part on crucial litigation in Georgia, the U.S. Supreme Court has also limited the use of race in drawing legislative districts (see below).

6. Rights and Liberties[lxxxvii]

Just as constitutions establish governmental institutions and basic processes such as elections, they also guarantee rights to individuals and regulate government's ability to interfere with people's liberties. Amending a constitution is normally a very difficult process. Therefore, including rights and liberties in a constitution is designed to protect them better than if such guarantees could be reduced or eliminated simply by passing a law. State constitutions may not infringe upon liberties and rights protected by the U.S. Constitution. Because of dual citizenship and the 14th Amendment to the U.S. Constitution, these federal guarantees are minimum standards, however, and states may grant their citizens broader rights.

Article 1 of the Georgia Constitution allows state courts to determine whether laws or actions comply with the state or U.S. constitutions.[lxxxviii] This process of judicial review is similar to that at the national level. Any law or administrative rule in Georgia, whether adopted by the state or by local governments, may be challenged in court. In addition, some private practices may be challenged, such as activities of businesses or individuals. Unlike the U.S. Constitution, which specifies most rights in amendments, Georgia's constitutions since 1861 have included a bill of rights as an integral part of the document. Article 1 in the 1983 Constitution included 28 paragraphs covering "Rights of Persons."

The discussion below covers some of the major provisions in Georgia's bill of rights. Under each heading, the first section describes how Georgia courts have applied these guarantees in specific cases. This is followed by a discussion of related federal court cases originating in Georgia. These cases are based on the U.S. Constitution and often brought about substantial changes not only in Georgia, but in the nation as a whole.

The first section covers civil rights, which are often thought of as the freedom to participate in the political system. It is generally linked to the guarantee of "equal protection" in the eyes of the law, which is the basis for much of the litigation on discrimination. The next three sections deal with civil liberties—the basic protection against unwarranted government intrusion into one's life. The fifth section deals with the right to privacy – a protection not written explicitly into either the U.S. or Georgia constitutions. Each section summarizes major federal court cases in a tables with full legal citations. Citations for decisions by Georgia courts are found in the endnotes.

Equal Protection[lxxxix]

Georgia Courts. The second paragraph in Georgia's bill of rights guarantees that, "No person shall be denied the equal protection of the laws." This language mirrors the 14th Amendment to the U.S. Constitution. While the Georgia Supreme Court has held that the federal and state equal protection guarantees "coexist," the justices have acknowledged that the state may interpret the Georgia Constitution to offer broader rights than are available under the U.S. Constitution.

A great deal of the controversy over equal protection involves government's classification of groups, with the courts being most vigilant regarding sex and race. In 1984, the Georgia Supreme Court found unconstitutional a law that provided benefits to children whose mothers were wrongfully killed but did not afford the same protection to children whose fathers were wrongfully killed. The Court also struck down Atlanta's program to set aside a share of contracts for minority- and female-owned businesses because the city failed to demonstrate the need for a race-conscious program.[xc] Local governments have continued to adopt set-aside programs, however, after studies to determine the effects of prior discrimination. Such policies remain highly contentious and must operate within guidelines laid out by the U.S. Supreme Court, which has become increasingly skeptical of such initiatives. Similar controversies have surrounded the use of affirmative action in admissions decisions at Georgia's public colleges and universities.[xci]

Perhaps more controversial have been several Atlanta ordinances dealing with gay rights. In 1995, the Georgia Supreme Court held that Atlanta could create a registry of unmarried couples (both heterosexual and homosexual) and forbid discrimination based on sexual orientation. However, the Court concluded that the city exceeded its authority by extending insurance benefits to the domestic partners of city employees.[xcii]

Federal Courts and Discrimination. On the surface, the 14th Amendment would seem to prohibit discrimination based on race. Yet Georgia, like other southern states, used a number of strategies to disenfranchise black citizens from the 1870s to the 1960s. These included the poll tax, the white primary, and other restrictions eventually eliminated by federal legislation and court decisions.[xciii]

The poll tax required citizens to pay an annual levy to be eligible to vote, thereby making it harder for the poor to vote. Georgia had used a poll tax earlier in its history, but it became particularly restrictive when the 1877 constitution made it cumulative, which meant that anyone falling behind in the annual tax had to make back payments. The poll tax was not repealed until 1945, when Governor Ellis Arnall made it a major issue during the legislative session. In other southern states, the poll tax lasted until the 24th Amendment to the U.S. Constitution banned it in 1964.

Perhaps the most blatant attempt to disenfranchise blacks was the white primary, which restricted voting in party primaries to whites only. Blacks could participate in the general election, but their votes were inconsequential because there was seldom Republican opposition on the ballot.

White primaries in Georgia were adopted in some counties by the 1890s. Beginning in 1900, only whites could vote in the Democratic party's primary elections. In a 1927 Texas case, the U.S. Supreme Court held that it was unconstitutional for state law to restrict primary voting on the basis of race. Virtually the entire South was controlled by the Democratic party then, and party leaders thereafter used party rules to enforce the white primary. Unlike general elections, which are processes of government, primaries could be regarded as activities of political parties, which are "private" organizations.

It was not until 1944 that the U.S. Supreme Court held that party rules enforcing a white primary also abridged the right to vote based on race. Georgia's white primary was overturned the following year by a federal appeals court in *King v. Chapman*. Perhaps the most immediate effect of this decision was in Atlanta, where business and political leaders began developing a coalition with the city's large black middle class.[xciv]

Three other restrictions were included in the Disenfranchisement Act of 1908, which voters approved as an amendment to the Georgia Constitution by a two-to-one margin:

The literacy test required that voters be able to read and explain any paragraph of the federal or state constitution; while the property qualification required ownership of 40 acres of land or property assessed at $500. The grandfather clause enfranchised men who had served in the United States or Confederate military forces and their descendants; no one could register under that provision after 1914.[xcv]

Implementation of the literacy test was in the hands of local election officials, who exercised great discretion, especially their power to purge voter registration rolls of those judged to be unqualified.

As the momentum grew to desegregate during the 1950s and 1960s, the Georgia General Assembly produced an array of legislation to forestall the process.[xcvi] At one point, all state aid was removed from any public school that was integrated, and payments were authorized to parents of children who attended segregated private schools. In order to prevent blacks from attending college in the state, requirements for admission were set to include letters of recommendation from two former graduates of the institution to which a student was applying. Since no blacks had attended most of these institutions, such letters would be difficult to obtain. Although most actions by the Georgia General Assembly were struck down as unconstitutional, white parents were able to move to different school districts or to send their children to private academies which did not admit blacks. Segregation was largely maintained until Congress passed the 1964 Civil Rights Act, but it continued in many respects long after that date. Local school districts also tried to prevent or minimize desegregation, including the Chatham County school board's unsuccessful effort to claim that integration would heighten black children's feelings of inferiority.[xcvii]

The Civil Rights Act of 1964 was designed to end discrimination in public accommodations (hotels, restaurants, transportation, etc.). In *Heart of Atlanta Motel v. United States*, the U.S. Supreme Court took a broad view of the U.S. Constitution's commerce clause and upheld the Civil Rights Act as a valid exercise of Congress's authority. The Court rejected the motel's claim that it was a local business. Because the motel served interstate travelers, its practice of refusing lodging to blacks was held to obstruct commerce, and the motel would therefore have to serve blacks.

Not all discrimination falls under the 14th Amendment. Congress has also passed laws dealing with characteristics such as religion, age, and disability. One of the leading cases regarding the disabled was based on the ways in which the Georgia Department of Human Resources had institutionalized people involuntarily after it was determined that such people could be placed in a community setting. In *Olmstead v. L.C.*, the U.S. Supreme Court held that such action violated the protection of the Americans with Disabilities Act of 1990.

Table 8
Major Federal Cases on Discrimination

King v. Chapman 154 F.2d 450 (1946)	Building on a 1944 U.S. Supreme Court case covering Texas, the circuit court of appeals found that the rules of Georgia's Democratic party, which restricted voting in primary elections to whites only, violated the equal protection guarantee of the 14th Amendment.
Heart of Atlanta Motel v. United States 379 U.S. 241 (1964)	Upheld constitutionality of Title 2 of the Civil Rights Act of 1964, which prohibited racial discrimination in public accommodations.
Olmstead v. L.C.	The state's practice of involuntarily institutionalizing

| no. 98-536 (1999) | disabled individuals judged suitable to live in less restrictive settings violates the Americans with Disabilities Act of 1990. |

Federal Courts and Equal Representation. Since the early 1960s, federal courts have become increasingly active in the process of drawing districts for legislative bodies. The courts have interpreted the equal protection guarantee of the 14th Amendment to mean that one person's vote should have the same weight in an election as another person's; to do this requires districts of roughly equal population. In *Toombs v. Fortson*, the Court ruled that reapportionment for the General Assembly must be made on the basis of the population of the state rather than by county or other political boundaries. Each district must have roughly the same number of inhabitants. After four earlier challenges had failed, in *Gray v. Sanders*, the U.S. Supreme Court struck down the county-unit system as a violation of the 14th Amendment's equal protection guarantee because the system malapportioned votes by underrepresenting urban residents. Other litigation also forced the General Assembly to redraw congressional districts in the state.[xcviii]

Questions of representation have become increasingly linked to race since Congress passed the Voting Rights Act (VRA) in 1965. The VRA suspended use of literacy tests, allowed for federal election examiners and observers, and required affected state and local governments to receive approval from the national government before making changes in their electoral systems. This "preclearance" by the U.S. Department of Justice is especially wary of changes which might dilute the voting strength of minorities.

The U.S. Department of Justice objected to congressional redistricting by the Georgia General Assembly following the 1990 census. After two unsuccessful attempts to redraw districts, state lawmakers finally satisfied federal guidelines to protect minority voting strength in the 1992 elections.[xcix] Ironically, in 1995 those districts were ruled unconstitutional in *Miller v. Johnson* because race was a "predominant factor" used in drawing the district lines.[c] Similar litigation occurred following redistricting based on the 2000 census: in *Georgia v. Ashcroft*, the U.S. Supreme Court again required Georgia to consider factors other than race in drawing legislative districts.

Table 9
Major Federal Cases on Representation

Gray v. Sanders 372 U.S. 368 (1963)	Held that Georgia's county-unit system violated the 14th Amendment's equal protection guarantee because it malapportioned votes among the state's counties.
Fortson v. Toombs 379 U.S. 621 (1965)	Upheld a lower court's 1962 decision that the 14th Amendment required seats in the General Assembly to be apportioned with districts of roughly equal population rather than being based on county or other political boundaries.
Miller v. Johnson 515 U.S. 900 (1995)	Invalidated Georgia's congressional redistricting following the 1990 census as a violation of the 14th Amendment's equal protection clause because race was the predominant factor in drawing district

	boundaries. The General Assembly had created three black-majority districts, with the eleventh district having a very irregular shape.
Georgia v. Ashcroft no. 02-182 (2003)	Held that courts reviewing redistricting under the Voting Rights Act have to consider all relevant factors affecting minority voters, not just the chance of electing minority candidates.

Right to Life, Liberty, and Property[ci]

Georgia Courts. Life, liberty, and property are the first rights listed in the Georgia Constitution. Like guarantees in the U.S. Constitution, they cannot be abridged "except by due process of law." State courts have found this guarantee to be broader than under the U.S. Constitution.[cii] Georgia courts traditionally have found that the state has the power to regulate businesses so long as the regulation is applied equally to all who engage in the same types of businesses and has some "rational relationship" to a valid purpose. Only when litigants are able to show that their due process has been violated are they able to convince the courts that government regulation is "arbitrary" or "unreasonable." Thus, laws regulating the licensing and training of professionals have largely been upheld. The Georgia Supreme Court has held that a mandatory life sentence for a second drug conviction does not violate due process or equal protection despite statistical evidence that a larger percentage of blacks end up serving life sentences under the law.[ciii]

The Georgia Supreme Court has taken a broad view of government compensation owed to the owners of private property taken for public use. All states and the federal government have some power of eminent domain (the taking of private property for public use such as expanding a highway, constructing facilities, and laying water or sewer lines). While most Georgia court decisions have permitted government to determine the size and use of land taken, restrictions have been imposed on compensation for property. The courts also have applied the notion of "taking" to regulation of private property, i.e., government regulation may be so restrictive that it has the same effect as seizing someone's land. In this regard, the Georgia Supreme Court has reviewed a great many cases dealing with land-use regulation and has tended to favor property owners over cities and counties. There are no landmark federal cases from Georgia dealing directly with this issue, although the state has produced major cases dealing with the related question of privacy (see below).

Rights Related to Expression and Association

Georgia's bill of rights includes a number of provisions designed to allow people to hold and express opinions, to associate with others, and to participate in the political process. These include two paragraphs on religion, as well as one on and the press, another on the right to assemble and petition, and one on libel, which is not mentioned in the U.S. Constitution.

Georgia Courts and Freedom of Conscience and Religion.[civ] Religious freedom was the earliest liberty to be addressed by Georgia's constitution drafters. Even the Rules and Regulations of 1776 included a provision for freedom of religion. The Georgia Constitution includes somewhat different language from the 1st Amendment to the U.S. Constitution. Perhaps the most striking difference is Georgia's limitation on religious practices: "but the right of freedom of religion shall not be so construed as to excuse acts of licentiousness or justify practices inconsistent with the peace and safety of the state."[cv] Thus, Courts in Georgia have at times limited freedom of religion, as when the Georgia Supreme Court found that freedom of religion did not include the distribution of literature in public. Nor has the Court extended freedom of religion to the use of controlled substances.

Georgia Courts and Freedom of Speech and the Press.[cvi] Georgia courts have adopted a broad interpretation of freedom of speech. For example, while the U.S. Constitution held that screening of movies was not in and of itself a violation of free speech, the Georgia Supreme Court found that an ordinance requiring approval of a censor before screening movies was unconstitutional in Georgia. The Court also held that it violated free speech to ban those between the ages of 18 and 21 from premises with sexually explicit performances.[cvii]

Free speech, as interpreted by the Georgia courts, includes limits. Indeed, the Georgia Constitution says that people "shall be responsible for the abuse of that liberty," as in cases involving incorrect publication of delinquent debt, inaccurate information regarding criminal activity, or use of photographs for advertising without the subjects' permission. The Georgia Supreme Court has upheld an injunction against anti-abortion protesters on the ground that the protest was limited by reasonable restrictions regarding time, place, and manner. The Court has held, however, that picketing was not protected free speech when the protest included an illegal strike. The Court also upheld the state's "Anti-Mask Act," which targets groups such as the Ku Klux Klan by prohibiting intimidating or threatening mask-wearing behavior, despite a claim that the law violates a person's freedom of speech.[cviii]

The press does not have a constitutional right to withhold a confidential news source.[cix] However, the media have been granted limited protection by a state law that allows reporters to be forced to turn over information from confidential sources when the evidence is material and relevant, is necessary for one of the parties to prepare a case, and cannot reasonably be gathered by other means.[cx] In terms of other publications, the Georgia Supreme Court has held that it violates free speech for a city to prohibit the distribution of printed materials to homes.[cxi]

Controversies have swirled around language or behavior judged offensive by many people. For instance, the Georgia Supreme Court struck down a state law attempting to outlaw bumper stickers considered profane as being too vague and a violation of free speech. Even greater debates have involved sexually-oriented communication, particularly after the Georgia Supreme Court ruled that nude dancing was protected expression and overturned local regulations banning such entertainment as too broad or outside the authority granted to local governments. To reverse this action, Georgia voters approved a constitutional amendment in 1994 to increase local governments' control over nude dancing through their power to regulate alcoholic beverages. A number of local governments subsequently adopted ordinances to prevent clubs with nude dancing from serving alcohol. The Georgia Supreme Court has held that such alcohol regulations do not violate the free speech rights associated with such entertainment.[cxii]

Federal Courts and Freedom of Speech and the Press. The U.S. Supreme Court has considered many cases during the past 40 years dealing with the 1st Amendment's guarantees regarding religion, speech, the press, and association. Two major cases on obscenity originated in Georgia. In a 1969 decision, *Stanley v. Georgia*, the Court found that "the mere private possession of obscene matter cannot constitutionally be made a crime," which Georgia law had done. Police had a warrant to search Stanley's home for materials related to illegal gambling, but they found allegedly obscene material. The state claimed that certain types of materials should not be possessed or read, and that obscene materials may lead to sexual violence or other acts. The Court rejected these claims, holding that the state asserted the "right to control the moral content of a person's thoughts . . . but it is wholly inconsistent with the philosophy of the First Amendment."

In a 1973 case, *Paris Adult Theatre I v. Slaton*, the Supreme Court was asked to determine whether the state could ban a commercial theater from showing films considered obscene. Here the Court reached an opposite result from *Stanley*, holding that the state had an interest in "stemming the tide of commercialized obscenity." The Court held that it did not make a difference that the films in question were shown only to consenting adults and the business posted warnings of films' content and prohibited minors from entering. Instead, the Court held that the state had a valid interest in "the quality of life and the total community environment, the tone of commerce in the great city centers, and, possibly, the public safety itself."

Cox Broadcasting Corp. v. Colin dealt with Georgia's law prohibiting publication of a rape victim's name. Pitted against each other were the desire to protect the victim's privacy and the freedom of the press. The Court held that it would violate press freedom to prohibit the publication of crime victims' names obtained from public records.

Table 10
Major Federal Cases on Freedom of Speech and the Press

Stanley v. Georgia 394 U.S. 557 (1969)	Overturned state law making private possession of obscene material a crime. The Georgia law was held to violate the 1st and 14th Amendments to the U.S. Constitution.
Paris Adult Theatre I v. Slaton 413 U.S. 49 (1973)	Banning the showing of allegedly obscene films to consenting adults in a commercial theater was held not to violate the 1st Amendment or the right to privacy.
Cox Broadcasting Corp v. Colin 420 U.S. 469 (1975)	Overturned the Georgia law prohibiting publication of the name of a rape victim obtained from public records.
Forsyth County, Georgia v. Nationalist Movement 505 U.S. 123 (1992)	Invalidated a local ordinance requiring participants to pay law enforcement costs for demonstrations and empowering the county administrator to determine how much to charge a group seeking a permit for a demonstration. The court found

Forsyth County was the scene of several marches by civil rights supporters and countermarches by the Ku Klux Klan during the 1980s. To manage these events, the county commission adopted an ordinance requiring those seeking a demonstration permit to pay a fee for law enforcement protection. The county administrator had discretion about the size of the fee, which could not exceed $1,000. One group refused to pay a $100 fee and sued the county. In *Forsyth County, Georgia v. Nationalist Movement*, the U.S. Supreme Court found that the county ordinance contained no standards for the administrator to follow and was thus unconstitutional because it "contains more than the possibility of censorship through uncontrolled discretion [and] the ordinance often requires that the fee be based on the content of the speech" of the group seeking the permit.

Rights of Those Accused and Convicted of Crimes[cxiii]

The Georgia Constitution includes several provisions to protect people in dealing with the state's legal system. These include conditions regarding searches, seizures, and warrants by law enforcement officials; access to the courts and the use of juries; the right to an attorney and to cross-examine witnesses in criminal cases; the right against self-incrimination; protection against excessive bail and "cruel and unusual" punishment; and a prohibition against double jeopardy. Most of these guarantees parallel those in the U.S. Constitution's bill of rights, although Georgia has added other guarantees. For instance, the state bill of rights explicitly prohibits whipping and banishment from the state as punishment for crimes,[cxiv] imprisonment for debt,[cxv] and being "abused in being arrested, while under arrest, or in prison."[cxvi]

Georgia Courts. One of the most notable distinctions between the Georgia and U.S. constitutions is that the state offers more protection to defendants against unreasonable searches and seizures by law enforcement authorities. In addition, Georgia has long recognized the right of indigents to have a lawyer appointed, although this right does not extend to civil cases.[cxvii] A major problem with providing attorneys to poor criminal defendants has been in appropriating sufficient funds to make the guarantee work well.

Arguments often are made that certain punishments are "cruel and unusual." Georgia courts have held that punishment exceeding the crime is, in some cases, constitutional. For example, fines larger than amounts taken by theft have been permitted. In some instances, defendants have been banished from certain counties, but the Georgia Supreme Court has not upheld banishment from the state as a whole. Georgia's use of the death penalty was found to be unconstitutional in 1972 by the U.S. Supreme Court because the state did not have standards to protect against unequal application of capital punishment. Currently, Georgia law lists the conditions under which the death penalty may be sought and is in line with later U.S. Supreme Court rulings permitting executions. The Georgia Supreme Court, however, has considered it cruel and unusual punishment to execute someone who is mentally retarded,[cxviii] but reached the opposite conclusion when considering life in prison for a second conviction for selling cocaine.[cxix]

Federal Courts and Search and Seizure. Georgia has produced few major federal cases related to the search and seizure rights of criminal defendants in the U.S. Constitution's 4th Amendment. In 1997, however, the U.S. Supreme Court overturned a Georgia law requiring candidates for state office to pass a drug test, which the General Assembly had passed as part of its anti-drug efforts during the 1980s. Walker Chandler filed to run as Libertarian party candidate for lieutenant governor in 1994 but refused to take the test. In *Chandler v. Miller*, the Court held that the drug tests did not fall within the category of constitutionally permissible suspicionless searches. Indeed, the Court found that the test was essentially "symbolic" rather than being directed at some identifiable problem that might demand such a search.

Federal Courts and the Rights of Criminal Defendants. The U.S. Constitution's 6th Amendment includes the right to a fair trial, which is not spelled out in detail. Therefore, the courts have had to define what that right means in practice. Some of these cases have dealt with the size of trial juries and whether they must reach a unanimous decision. In a 1973 Florida case, the U.S. Supreme Court had permitted six-member juries in civil cases. In *Ballew v. Georgia*, however, the Court ruled in 1978 that Georgia's use of five-person juries in misdemeanor cases violated the right to a fair trial, in part because of the reduced deliberation and bias in favor of the prosecution regarding hung juries. Georgia's current constitution allows the General Assembly to permit six-member juries in misdemeanor cases or in courts of limited jurisdiction.[cxx]

Federal Courts and the Death Penalty. Two appeals to the U.S. Supreme Court from Georgia during the 1970s became the landmark cases regarding the use of capital punishment in the United States. The first, *Furman v. Georgia* in 1972, effectively ended executions throughout the country. Four years later, *Gregg v. Georgia* allowed the state's rewritten capital punishment law to stand, thereby opening the door for states to resume executions.

What was different about these two cases? The members of the U.S. Supreme Court had a range of views regarding capital punishment, but the major concern was how the death penalty was applied. In *Furman*, the Court was concerned with both the lack of guidelines to use in deciding when to impose a death sentence and the wide variation in its use for similar crimes. The states then began revising their laws, and the Court decided several cases in 1976 based on the new statutes. In *Gregg*, the Court upheld Georgia's new capital punishment law, in part because it required specific findings by the jury regarding the facts of the crime and the character of the defendant; it also had a process for appellate courts to review death penalty cases.

Table 11
Major Federal Cases Affecting Those Accused or Convicted of Crimes

Chandler v. Miller 520 U.S. 305 (1997)	Held that Georgia's requirement that candidates for state office pass a drug test violates the 4th and 14th Amendment protections against suspicionless searches.
Ballew v. Georgia 435 U.S. 223 (1978)	Held that a criminal trial using a jury of less than six members violated the 6th and 14th Amendment guarantees to a fair trial.
Furman v. Georgia 408 U.S. 238 (1972)	Held that Georgia's methods of administering the death penalty violated the 8th Amendment's guarantee against cruel and unusual punishment. The decision effectively ended executions in the United States for more than a decade.
Gregg v. Georgia 428 U.S. 153 (1976)	Upheld Georgia's revised law on capital punishment, which limited the crimes for which the death penalty could be imposed and specified the factors to be considered and procedures to be used in deciding when to impose capital punishment.
Coker v. Georgia 433 U.S. 584 (1977)	Found that Georgia's imposition of the death penalty for the crime of rape was grossly disproportionate and thus a violation of the 8th Amendment's ban on cruel and unusual punishment.

McCleskey v. Kemp 481 U.S. 279 (1987)	Rejected the claim that racial differences in the imposition of the death penalty violated the equal protection guarantee of the 14th Amendment and amounted to cruel and unusual punishment in violation of the 8th Amendment.

Two other cases tested the constitutionality of the conditions under which Georgia imposed the death penalty. In *Coker v. Georgia*, the U.S. Supreme Court held that the death sentence for the crime of rape was grossly disproportionate to the offense and thus violated the 8th Amendment ban on cruel and unusual punishment. In *McCleskey v. Kemp*, the Court confronted the issue of bias in imposing the death penalty. McCleskey presented a study showing that the use of the death sentence in Georgia was statistically related to the race of the murder victim and, to a lesser extent, the race of the defendant. This pattern, he argued, violated the 8th and 14th Amendments. The Supreme Court rejected these claims, citing appellate courts' review of cases with facts similar to McCleskey's case.

The Right to Privacy

Georgia Courts. Like the U.S. Constitution, Georgia's does not mention a right to privacy. In 1904, though, Georgia became the first state to recognize a privacy right when the Georgia Supreme Court found this right in natural law and the guarantees of liberty found in the U.S. and state constitutions.[cxxi] Privacy has been extended to the right of a prisoner to refuse to eat, even to the point of starvation, and a person's right to refuse medical treatment even if it was certain to lead to death.

Table 12
Major Federal Cases on the Right to Privacy

Doe v. Bolton 410 U.S. 179 (1973)	This is the less famous Georgia case decided along with *Roe v. Wade*. It overturned Georgia's ban on abortions as a violation of a woman's right to privacy.
Bowers v. Hardwick 478 U.S. 186 (1986)	Held that the right to privacy did not protect consensual homosexual sex from prosecution under Georgia's sodomy law.

Federal Courts. The U.S. Supreme Court first recognized a right to privacy in a 1965 Connecticut case dealing with government regulation of contraception. Since then, the courts have been forced to define the limits of privacy rights. These debates include two Georgia cases. *Doe v. Bolton* remains almost unnoticed today, but it was the challenge to Georgia's abortion law decided along with *Roe v. Wade*, the more widely known Texas case in which the Supreme Court held that the right to privacy included a woman's right to abortion.

The second Georgia case was *Bowers v. Hardwick*. In this case, Michael Hardwick challenged Georgia's sodomy law as a violation of the right to privacy in so far as it applied to consensual conduct. He also argued that as a homosexual he faced constant threat of arrest and prosecution. The Supreme Court rejected Hardwick's claim and upheld Georgia's sodomy law, which prohibited certain acts but did not specify the gender or sexual orientation of the participants.

Dual Citizenship and the Right to Privacy. Georgia's sodomy law provides a good example of the way in which dual citizenship can produce different rights under state and U.S. constitutions. The Georgia Supreme Court reinforced the *Hardwick* decision in 1996, when it ruled, in *Christensen v. State*,[cxxii] that the state's sodomy law did not violate Georgia's right to privacy. That all changed in 1998, however. Based on facts involving a heterosexual couple, the Georgia Supreme Court, in *Powell v. State*, held, "insofar as it criminalizes the performance of private, non-commercial acts of sexual intimacy between persons legally able to consent, [the sodomy law] 'manifestly infringes upon a constitutional provision' . . . which guarantees to the citizens of Georgia the right to privacy."[cxxiii] Shortly thereafter, however, the Court rejected the claim that Georgia's right to privacy also protected commercial sexual activity.[cxxiv]

Thus, while any given state's law criminalizing sodomy would not violate the federal right to privacy as applied in *Bowers v. Hardwick*, state courts around the country could consider such a law in violation of broader rights guaranteed in their state constitutions. That possibility changed rather dramatically in 2003, however, when the U.S. Supreme Court's *Lawrence v. Texas* decision overturned sodomy laws in those states that still had them.[cxxv]

The most recent frontier in battles over privacy rights deals with medical treatment. For instance, a 1997 U.S. Supreme Court decision left the door open for states to either ban or allow doctor-assisted suicide. This produced a conflict when former U.S. Attorney General John Ashcroft attempted to keep Oregon from implementing its law allowing the practice.[cxxvi] Such disputes will undoubtedly continue to pit the states against the national government in the face of breakthroughs in medical treatment and research.

7. The Continuing Significance of Georgia's Constitution

A constitution is not some kind of sacred or unchanging blueprint for government. Constitutions are essentially political documents. That is why individuals, businesses, political parties, and interest groups often fight vigorously about interpreting and amending constitutions. For instance, lawsuits have attacked as racially biased the methods of selecting Georgia's judges and juries.[cxxvii] By approving an amendment to create a state-sponsored lottery in 1992, voters gave the governor, legislature, and bureaucracy millions of dollars to distribute to programs and individuals. They also paved the way for firms to profit from the production, sale, and marketing of lottery tickets. Another amendment granted a property tax break for growing timber,[cxxviii] although voters rejected a similar proposal for blueberries in 1994. The 1992 amendment requiring that local school board members be elected and superintendents be hired allows boards to recruit superintendents from anywhere. Under the old system of electing school superintendents in some counties, only local residents could run for the office.[cxxix]

As the preceding examples demonstrate, constitutions help distribute political and economic power. Constitutions also adopt policies that under other circumstances might be made simply by passing a law. Given the extensive detail in the Georgia Constitution, voters undoubtedly will face proposed amendments every even-numbered year as various interests try to modify the document to achieve their ends. If a large number of changes are ratified by voters, the Constitution might become so littered with amendments that it is unwieldy and difficult to interpret. A second possibility is that Georgians will become so annoyed with proposals on the ballot that they rebel by voting "no" on amendments. Finally, both groups and members of the General Assembly might regularly use constitutional change as just another way to achieve their political ends. If so, Georgians might treat amendment battles as just an ordinary part of the election process even though it would not be on the scale of western states using the initiative. None of these scenarios bodes well, however, for the durability of the 1983 Georgia Constitution.

NOTES

ⁱ U. S. Bureau of the Census, *Statistical Abstract of the United States: 2004-2005* (Washington: Government Printing Office, 2005), Tables 426, 453, 461.

ⁱⁱOn procedures for amending state constitutions, see Janice C. May, "State Constitutional Developments in 2004," pp. 3-9 in Council of State Governments, *The Book of the States: 2005 Edition* [hereafter cited as *The Book of the States*] (Lexington, KY: Council of State Governments, 2005) [also see Table 1.6 on p. 18].

ⁱⁱⁱThis section draws heavily from Melvin B. Hill, Jr., *The Georgia State Constitution: A Reference Guide* (Westport, CT: Greenwood Press, 1994). Rather than weigh down this section with extensive endnotes, specific references are used only when necessary. Readers are urged to consult Hill's exhaustive work for more detail.

^{iv}*Constitution of the State of Georgia*, art. 3, sect. 9, para. 6b.

^v*Constitution of the State of Georgia*, art. 3, sect. 9, para. 6c-j.

^{vi}*Constitution of the State of Georgia*, art. 1, sect. 2, para. 8c.

^{vii}*Constitution of the State of Georgia*, art. 7, sect. 2, para. 3e.

^{viii}*Constitution of the State of Georgia*, art. 7, sect. 1, para. 3c.

^{ix}*Constitution of the State of Georgia*, art. 7, sect. 2, para. 5.

^x*Constitution of the State of Georgia*, art. 7, sect. 1, para. 3d. Also see Hill, *The Georgia State Constitution*, pp. 152-155.

^{xi}Hill, *The Georgia State Constitution*, p. 49.

^{xii}*Constitution of the State of Georgia*, art. 4; art. 8, sects. 2 and 4.

^{xiii}*Constitution of the State of Georgia*, art. 4, sect. 3, para. 2.

^{xiv}*Constitution of the State of Georgia*, art. 3, sect. 6, para. 7.

^{xv}Hill, *The Georgia State Constitution*, pp. 56-59.

^{xvi}Hill, *The Georgia State Constitution*, pp. 194-195; *Constitution of the State of Georgia*, art. 9, sect. 2, para. 4.

^{xvii}Hill, *The Georgia State Constitution*, p. 99.

[xviii]*Constitution of the State of Georgia*, art. 1, sect. 2, para. 5.

[xix]5 U.S. 137.

[xx]Congress passed a law in 1996 giving the president limited line-item veto authority. The U.S. Supreme Court ruled that this action was unconstitutional, however, after President Clinton used it with 11 laws. See *Clinton v. City of New York*, 524 U.S. 417 (1998).

[xxi]On the changing location of the state capital, see Kenneth Coleman, editor, *A History of Georgia* 2nd edition (Athens: University of Georgia Press, 1991), pp. 91, 96, 107, 208-209.

[xxii][xxii][xxii]V.O. Key, Jr., *Southern Politics* (New York: Vintage, 1949), pp. 119-122; Hill, *The Georgia State Constitution*, pp. 224-225.

[xxiii]For a thorough account, see Harold P. Henderson, *The Politics of Change in Georgia: A Political Biography of Ellis Arnall* (Athens: University of Georgia Press, 1991), pp. 77-96.

[xxiv]For an example of the politics surrounding the use of local amendments, see the account of the 1970 consolidation of Columbus and Muscogee County in Arnold Fleischmann and Jennifer Custer. "Goodbye, Columbus," pp. 46-59 in *Case Studies of City-County Consolidation: Reshaping the Local Government Landscape*, edited by Suzanne M. Leland and Kurt Thurmaier (New York: M.E. Sharpe, 2004).

[xxv][xxv][xxv]Bill Montgomery, "New Constitution in Hands of Voters," *Atlanta Constitution*, November 2, 1982, p. 9A; Hill, *The Georgia State Constitution*, pp. 15-23.

[xxvi][xxvi][xxvi][xxvi]"A Constitutional Mess," *Atlanta Constitution*, August 28, 1981, p. 4A.

[xxvii][xxvii][xxvii][xxvii]Bill Shipp, "Do the State a Favor: Forget the New Constitution," *Atlanta Constitution*, August 15, 1981, p. 2B. On the shifting power of governors and the General Assembly, see Harold P. Henderson and Gary L. Roberts, editors, *Georgia Governors in an Age of Change* (Athens: University of Georgia Press, 1988), pp. 199-207, 234-237, 267-269.

[xxviii]"Streamlined State Constitution," *Atlanta Constitution*, June 30, 1983, p. 22A; "New State Constitution Deserves Ratification" (editorial), *Atlanta Constitution*, October 24, 1982, p. 2C.

[xxix].   [xxix][xxix]Hill, *The Georgia State Constitution*, p. 70.

[xxx].   [xxx][xxx]*Constitution of the State of Georgia*, art. 3. For comparisons to other states, see *The Book of the States*, chap. 3.

[xxxi]*The Book of the States*, pp. 130-131.

[xxxii]Jennifer Drage Bowser, "The Effects of Legislative Term Limits," pp. 111-115 in *The Book of the States*.

[xxxiii]See Edwin L. Jackson and Mary E. Stakes, *Handbook for Georgia Legislators* 10th ed. (Athens: Carl Vinson Institute of Government, University of Georgia, 1988), pp. 1-10.

[xxxiv]*Constitution of the State of Georgia*, art. 3, sect. 2, paras. 1 and 2.

[xxxv]*Constitution of the State of Georgia*, art. 5, sect. 2, para. 7.

[xxxvi]*Constitution of the State of Georgia*, art. 3, sect. 3. Although the president pro tempore can become president of the Senate, the lieutenant governorship is left unfilled until the next general election should the position become vacant (see art. 5, sect. 1, para. 5). On other states, see *The Book of the States*, pp. 136-141.

[xxxvii]*Constitution of the State of Georgia*, art. 3, sect. 5, para. 8.

[xxxviii]*Constitution of the State of Georgia*, art. 3, sect. 5, para. 2.

[xxxix]*Constitution of the State of Georgia*, art. 3, sect. 4, para. 11.

[xl]*Constitution of the State of Georgia*, art. 3, sect. 9.

[xli]The line-item veto is not covered in the section dealing with appropriations in the *Constitution of the State of Georgia*, but in art. 3, sect. 5, para. 13, which covers use of the veto in the enactment of laws.

[xlii]Table 5 excludes all judicial positions and some executive branch officials. Lieutenant governors are included despite their status as presiding officers in 27 legislatures because of their right to succeed governors and their executive responsibilities in several states.

[xliii]*The Book of the States*, pp. 233-238.

[xliv]Thad Beyle, "The Governors," pp. 194-231 in *Politics in the American States: A Comparative Analysis* 8th ed., edited by Virginia Gray and Russell L. Hanson (Washington: CQ Press, 2004).

[xlv]See *Constitution of the State of Georgia*, art. 5, sect. 1; *The Book of the States*, pp. 215-216. For a brief history of the Georgia governor's office, see Edwin L. Jackson and Mary E. Stakes, *Handbook of Georgia State Agencies* 2nd edition (Athens: Carl Vinson Institute of Government, University of Georgia, 1988), pp. 38-39.

[xlvi]*Constitution of the State of Georgia*, art. 5, sect. 2, paras. 8 and 9; art. 6, sect. 7.

[xlvii]*Official Code of Georgia Annotated* [hereafter cited as OCGA], title 45, chap. 5.

[xlviii]*The Book of the States*, pp. 161-165. Four states require larger majorities to override taxing, spending, or emergency measures.

[xlix]*Constitution of the State of Georgia*, art. 3, sect. 5.

[i]*Constitution of the State of Georgia*, art. 5, sect. 4, para. 1.

[li]*Constitution of the State of Georgia*, art. 5, sect. 3.

[lii]OCGA, title 45, chapter 15; Jackson and Stakes, *Handbook of Georgia State Agencies*, pp. 63-69.

[liii]Rhonda Cook, "Oink If You Know the Secret Menu for Legislature's Wild Hog Supper," *Atlanta Journal and Constitution*, January 10, 1993, pp. A1, A12; and "Legislators Being Feted in Daytona," *Atlanta Journal and Constitution*, February 13, 1993, pp. A1, A6.

[liv]*Constitution of the State of Georgia*, art. 5, sect. 3.

[lv]*Constitution of the State of Georgia*, art. 5, sect. 4.

[lvi]Governor's Office of Planning and Budget, "Fiscal 2005 Budget-as-passed" (available http://www.legis.state.ga.us/legis/budget/GEN05.htm).

[lvii]*Constitution of the State of Georgia*, art. 6, sect. 7.

[lviii]Georgia Supreme Court Commission on Racial and Ethnic Bias in the Court System, *Let Justice Be Done: Equally, Fairly, and Impartially* (final report, August 1995), p. 56; Bill Rankin, "Perdue's Court Pick Historic," *Atlanta Journal-Constitution*, June 9, 2005, p. A1.

[lix]*Constitution of the State of Georgia*, art. 6, sects. 1-4. For detail on Georgia's courts, see the web site for the Administrative Office of the Courts: http://www.georgiacourts.org/.

[lx]*Constitution of the State of Georgia*, art. 6, sects. 5 and 7; Court of Appeals of Georgia, "History of the Court of Appeals" (available http://www.gaappeals.us/history/).

[lxi]*Constitution of the State of Georgia*, art. 6, sects. 6 and 7.

[lxii]On differences in states' methods of selecting judges, see Henry R. Glick, "Courts: Politics and the Judicial Process," pp. 232-260 in *Politics in the American States*. On judicial selection in Georgia, see *Constitution of the State of Georgia*, art. 6, sect. 7.

[lxiii]On the Judicial Qualifications Commission, see http://www.georgiacourts.org/agencies/jqc/index.html.

[lxiv]*Constitution of the State of Georgia*, art. 6, sect. 8.

[lxv]On jury selection in Georgia, see OCGA, title 15, chap. 12, art. 5; on juries generally, see Henry R. Glick, *Courts, Politics, and Justice* 3rd edition (New York: McGraw-Hill, 1993), pp. 222-223.

[lxvi]Georgia General Assembly, "2005 Summary of General Statutes" (available

http://www.legis.state.ga.us/legis/2005_06/05sumdocnet.htm) and the text of HB 170
(available http://www.legis.state.ga.us/legis/2005_06/pdf/hb170.pdf). Also see Jim
Tharpe, "Parents' Grief Leads to a Victory," *Atlanta Journal-Constitution*, April 6, 2005, p.
B1.

[lxvii]See Arnold Fleischmann and Carol Pierannunzi, *Politics in Georgia* (Athens: University of
Georgia Press, 1997), chap. 9.

[lxviii]*Constitution of the State of Georgia*, art. 9, sects. 1 and 2; Hill, *The Georgia State
Constitution*, pp. 184-200.

[lxix]*Constitution of the State of Georgia*, art. 3, sect. 5, paras. 1 and 2.

[lxx]Steve Visser, "A Taxing Decision," *Atlanta Constitution*, June 14, 1999, p. E7.

[lxxi]David Goldberg and Kathey Pruitt, "GRTA Occupies Hot Seat," *Atlanta Constitution*, June 4,
1999, pp. A1, A8; Lucy Soto, "Public Still Skeptical About Transportation Board," *Atlanta
Constitution*, June 7, 1999, pp. E1, E4.

[lxxii]Charles Seabrook, "Water Planning District" *Atlanta Constitution*, March 26, 2001, pp. E1, E6.

[lxxiii]U.S. Advisory Commission on Intergovernmental Relations, *State Laws Governing Local
Government Structure and Administration*, report M-186 (Washington: Government
Printing Office, 1993), pp. 7-9, 17-22.

[lxxiv]On local acts, see Fleischmann and Pierannunzi, *Politics in Georgia*, pp. 157-159, 233-238;
on consolidation in Georgia, see Leland and Thurmaier, editors, *Case Studies of City-
County Consolidation: Reshaping the Local Government Landscape*, chaps. 3, 6, and 10.

[lxxv]Taxation, debt limits, and revenue bonds are covered in *Constitution of the State of Georgia*,
art. 9, sects. 4-6. Also see OCGA, title 36: chap. 5 on the property tax, chap. 7 on the
income tax, and chap. 8 on the sales tax.

[lxxvi]OCGA, title 36, chap. 81, sect. 3b.

[lxxvii]*Constitution of the State of Georgia*, art. 8, para. 4; also see James Salzer, "Georgia Voters
Throw Weight Behind Desire for Better Schools with Sales Tax Approvals," *Athens Daily
News and Banner-Herald*, October 19, 1997, p. 6A.

[lxxviii]In addition to Georgia, runoffs are held in Alabama, Florida, Mississippi, North Carolina,
Oklahoma, South Carolina, and Texas. Virginia repealed the runoff requirement in 1969,
and Louisiana abandoned the runoff in favor of a nonpartisan primary in 1975. Arkansas,
Kentucky, Maryland, and Utah have also used the runoff in the past. Arizona adopted a
runoff for statewide general elections in 1988. See Key, *Southern Politics*, pp. 416-23;
Charles S. Bullock III and Loch K. Johnson, *Runoff Elections in the United States* (Chapel

Hill: University of North Carolina Press, 1992).

[lxxix]On the rules for runoffs in Georgia, see OCGA, title 21, chap. 2, sect. 501.

[lxxx]*Brooks et al. v. Miller et al.*, 158 F.3d 1230 (1998); *Brooks et. al. v. Barnes et al.*, no. 98-1521, cert. denied May 24, 1999; Kathey Pruitt, "Majority Vote Still Needed in Primaries," *Atlanta Constitution*, May 25, 1999, p. B3.

[lxxxi]OCGA, title 21, chap. 4.

[lxxxii]*Constitution of the State of Georgia*, art. 3, sect. 7.

[lxxxiii]*Constitution of the State of Georgia*, art. 2, sect. 3.

[lxxxiv]*Constitution of the State of Georgia*, art. 3, sect. 2, para. 5; art. 5, sect. 1, paras. 2 and 3; art. 5, sect. 3, para. 1.

[lxxxv]*Constitution of the State of Georgia*, art. 6, sect. 7, para. 1; art. 8, sect. 5, para. 2; art. 9, sect. 1, para. 3.

[lxxxvi]296 U.S. 186 (1962).

[lxxxvii]It does not seem necessary to include detailed citations to Georgia court cases in a general work such as this. Therefore, each section will include a citation to the appropriate location in Hill's definitive work on the Georgia Constitution, plus updates from the *Official Code of Georgia Annotated*. Many of these cases are discussed in more detail, with full citations in the endnotes, in Fleischmann and Pierannunzi, *Politics in Georgia*, pp. 62-67.

[lxxxviii]*Constitution of the State of Georgia*, art. 1, sect. 2, para. 5.

[lxxxix]*Constitution of the State of Georgia*, art. 1, sect. 1, para. 2; Hill, *The Georgia State Constitution*, pp. 33-36.

[xc]*American Subcontractors Association v. City of Atlanta*, 259 Ga. 14, 376 S.E.2d 662 (1989).

[xci]Doug Cumming, "Applicants Nervously Await Decisions," *Atlanta Constitution*, March 25, 1998, p. C5. Following years of litigation over policies at the University of Georgia, the U.S. Supreme Court gave support to the limited use of affirmative action in college admissions in two cases involving the University of Michigan: *Gratz v. Bollinger*, no. 02-516 (2003), and *Grutter v. Bollinger*, no. 02-241 (2003).

[xcii]Douglas A. Blackmon and Holly Morris, "Court Gives Split Ruling on Gay Rights," *Atlanta Constitution*, March 15, 1995, p. E1.

[xciii]On the right to vote, see Laughlin McDonald, Michael B. Binford, and Ken Johnson, "Georgia," pp. 67-102 in *Quiet Revolution in the South: The Impact of the Voting Rights*

[xciii]*Act, 1965-1990*, edited by Chandler Davidson and Bernard Grofman (Princeton: Princeton University Press, 1994).

[xciv]For a thorough discussion, see Clarence N. Stone, *Regime Politics: Governing Atlanta, 1946-1988* (Lawrence: University Press of Kansas, 1989).

[xcv]William F. Holmes, "Part Five: 1890-1940," in *A History of Georgia* 2nd edition, edited by Kenneth Coleman (Athens: University of Georgia Press, 1991), p. 280.

[xcvi]For a good synopsis of postwar racial change, see Numan V. Bartley, "Part Six: 1940 to the Present," in *A History of Georgia* 2nd edition, edited by Kenneth Coleman (Athens: University of Georgia Press, 1991), pp. 361-74.

[xcvii]*Stell v. Savannah-Chatham County Board of Education*, 333 F.2d 55 (1964).

[xcviii]*Wesberry v. Sanders*, 376 U.S. 1 (1964).

[xcix]See Hill, *The Georgia State Constitution*, p. 225.

[c]Linda Greenhouse, "Justices, in 5-4 Vote, Reject Districts Drawn with Race the 'Predominant Factor'," *New York Times*, June 30, 1995, pp. A1, A13.

[ci]*Constitution of the State of Georgia*, art. 1, sect. 1, para. 1; Hill, *The Georgia State Constitution*, pp. 30-33.

[cii]*Suber v. Bulloch County Board of Education*, 722 F.Supp. 736 (S.D. Ga., 1989).

[ciii]*Stephens v. State*, 265 Ga. 356, 456 S.E.2d 560, cert. denied 516 U.S. 849 (1995).

[civ]*Constitution of the State of Georgia*, art. 1, sect. 1, paras. 3 and 4; Hill, *The Georgia State Constitution*, pp. 36-38.

[cv]*Constitution of the State of Georgia*, art. 1, sect. 1, para. 4.

[cvi]*Constitution of the State of Georgia*, art. 1, sect. 1, para. 5; Hill, *The Georgia State Constitution*, pp. 38-40.

[cvii]*State v. Café Erotica*, 269 Ga. 486, 500 S.E.2d 547 (1998).

[cviii]*State v. Miller*, 260 Ga. 669, 398 S.E.2d 547 (1990).

[cix]*Vaughn v. State*, 259 Ga. 325 , 381 S.E.2d 30 (1989).

[cx]See OCGA, title 24, chap. 9, sect. 30.

[cxi]*Statesboro Publishing Co. v. City of Sylvania*, 271 Ga. 92, 516 S.E.2d 926 (1999).

cxii Goldrush II v. City of Marietta, 267 Ga. 683, 482 S.E.2d 347 (1997)

cxiii Constitution of the State of Georgia, art. 1 sect. 1, paras. 11-24; Hill, The Georgia State Constitution, pp. 42-51.

cxiv Constitution of the State of Georgia, art. 1, sect. 1, para. 21.

cxv Constitution of the State of Georgia, art. 1, sect. 1, para. 23.

cxvi Constitution of the State of Georgia, art. 1, sect. 1, para. 17.

cxvii Bergman v. McCullough, 218 Ga. App. 353, 461 S.E.2d 544 (1995), cert. denied 517 U.S. 1141 (1996).

cxviii Fleming v. Zant, 259 Ga. 687, 386 S.E.2d 339 (1989).

cxix Crutchfield v. State, 218 Ga. App. 360, 461 S.E.2d 555 (1995).

cxx Constitution of the State of Georgia, art. 1, sect.1, para. 1b.

cxxi Pavesich v. New England Life Insurance Co., 122 Ga. 190, 50 S.E. 68 (1904).

cxxii Christensen v. State, 266 Ga. 474, 464 S.E.2d 188 (1996).

cxxiii Powell v. State, 270 Ga. 327, 510 S.E.2d 18 (1998).

cxxiv Morrisaon v. State, 272 Ga. 129, 526 S.E.2d 336 (2000).

cxxv Lawrence v. Texas, no. 02-102 (2003).

cxxvi For the U.S. Supreme Court's view of assisted suicide and the right to privacy, see Washington v. Glucksberg, 521 U.S. 702 (1997) and Vacco v. Quill, 521 U.S. 793 (1997). On the Oregon conflict, see Oregon v. Ashcroft, 368 F.3d 1118 (2004), the case was appealed to the U.S. Supreme Court, which heard oral arguments on the appeal in October 2005.

cxxvii See Mark Curriden, "Is Naming Judges Serving Justice?" Atlanta Journal and Constitution, November 29, 1992, pp. G1, G3; Andrew Kull, "The Slow Death of Colorblind Justice," Atlanta Journal and Constitution, November 29, 1992, pp. H1, H5; Mark Curriden, "Road to a Judicial Appointment Not Clear—Even to State's Judges," Atlanta Constitution, December 21, 1992, p. C3.

cxxviii Constitution of the State of Georgia, art. 7, sect. 1, para. 3e.

cxxix Constitution of the State of Georgia, art. 8, sect. 5, paras. 2 and 3.

Filename: Fleischmann 6th Edition.wpd
Directory: T:\Joel Brennecke
Template: C:\Documents and Settings\jbrennecke\Application
    Data\Microsoft\Templates\Normal.dot
Title:
Subject:
Author: TL User
Keywords:
Comments:
Creation Date: 3/12/2006 7:08:00 AM
Change Number: 1
Last Saved On:
Last Saved By:
Total Editing Time: 3 Minutes
Last Printed On: 3/12/2006 7:11:00 AM
As of Last Complete Printing
                    Number of Pages: 59
                    Number of Words: 22,680 (approx.)
                    Number of Characters: 129,277 (approx.)

STUDENTS: Accessing Your Aplia

Course Through CengageBrain

CENGAGE**brain**.com

What is login.cengagebrain.com? Imagine that you are using Aplia along with another online study tool from Cengage Learning. Rather than having separate logins and passwords for both applications, Cengage offers a single access point through login.cengagebrain.com.

When you visit login.cengagebrain.com, you will see the following:

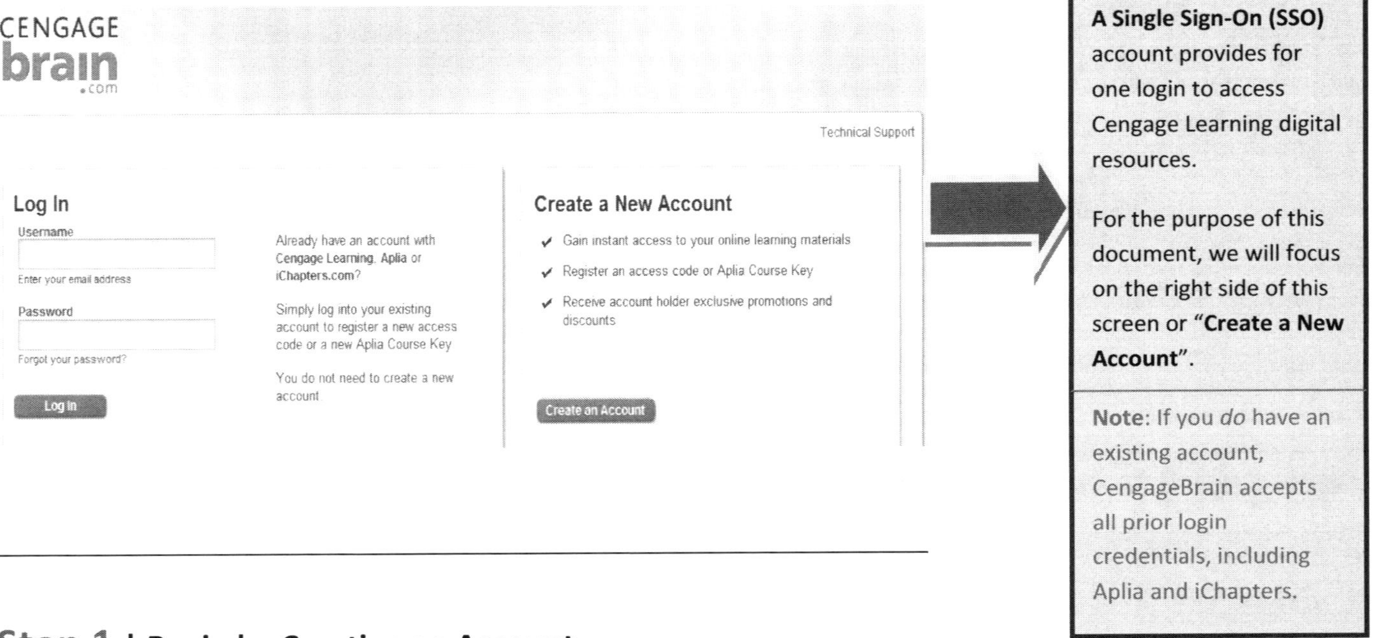

A Single Sign-On (SSO) account provides for one login to access Cengage Learning digital resources.

For the purpose of this document, we will focus on the right side of this screen or "**Create a New Account**".

Note: If you *do* have an existing account, CengageBrain accepts all prior login credentials, including Aplia and iChapters.

Step 1 | Begin by Creating an Account

1. Click the "Create an Account" button
2. The following page will load. Enter in the Aplia Course Key

YOUR COURSE KEY IS PROVIDED BY YOUR INSTRUCTOR TO ACCESS APLIA.

Instructors often provide the Aplia Course Key on their **syllabus**, or the course web site. If you need help locating the **Aplia Course Key**, ask your instructor.

Enter Access Code or Aplia Course Key

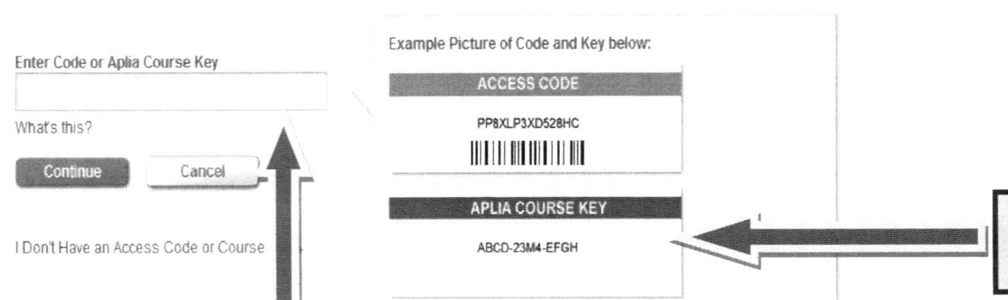

Your Aplia Course Key will look like this.

Step 2 | Confirm Your Course Information

The graphic below serves as an illustration for what you will see. Please confirm the displayed screen represents your enrolled course.

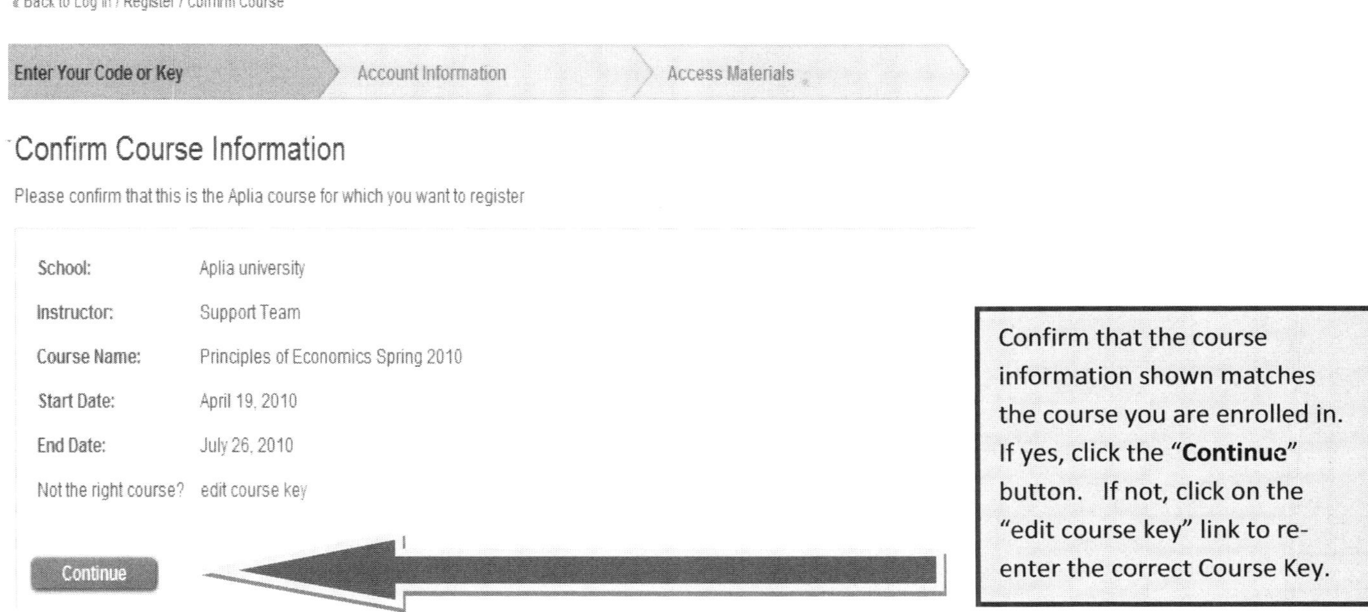

Confirm that the course information shown matches the course you are enrolled in. If yes, click the "**Continue**" button. If not, click on the "edit course key" link to re-enter the correct Course Key.

Step 3 | Complete Registration Form

As a new user, you must complete all fields in the registration form and click "Continue"

Please complete all fields to establish your account and select a security question.   Select "Continue" to proceed with your Aplia registration.

Step 4 | My Home Dashboard Review

You have arrived at your "**My Home**" page. Here you can verify your e-Mail address with CengageBrain and pay for your course **(See Step 5).**   Note that any prior (and future) Cengage Learning purchases will appear on this page.   Additionally, the page provides support resources and a transaction history of your Cengage purchases – digital products, textbooks or rentals.

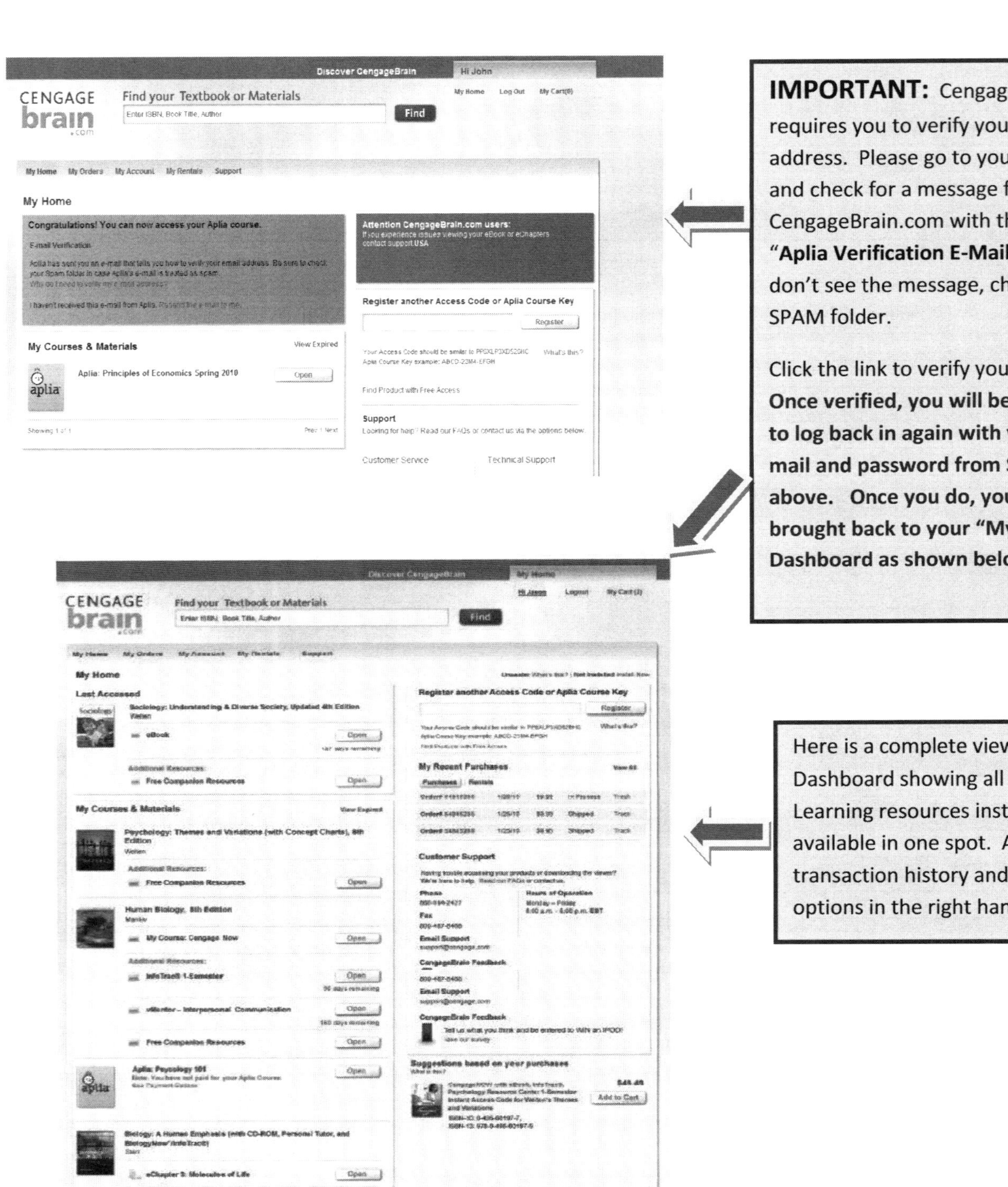

IMPORTANT: CengageBrain requires you to verify your e-mail address. Please go to your e-mail and check for a message from CengageBrain.com with the Subject "**Aplia Verification E-Mail**". If you don't see the message, check your SPAM folder.

Click the link to verify your e-mail. **Once verified, you will be prompted to log back in again with your e-mail and password from Step 3 above. Once you do, you will be brought back to your "My Home" Dashboard as shown below.**

Here is a complete view of the Dashboard showing all Cengage Learning resources instantly available in one spot. Also note transaction history and support options in the right hand field.

Step 5 | Completing Payment For Your Aplia Course

NOTE: YOUR APLIA PAYMENT CODES ARE BOUND WITHIN THIS BOOK. THERE ARE <u>NO</u> <u>ADDITIONAL CHARGES TO ACCESS APLIA</u>. SIMPLY COMPLETE THE PAYMENT PROCESS BY CLICKING ON THE "SEE PAYMENT OPTIONS LINK" CIRCLED IN **GREEN**.

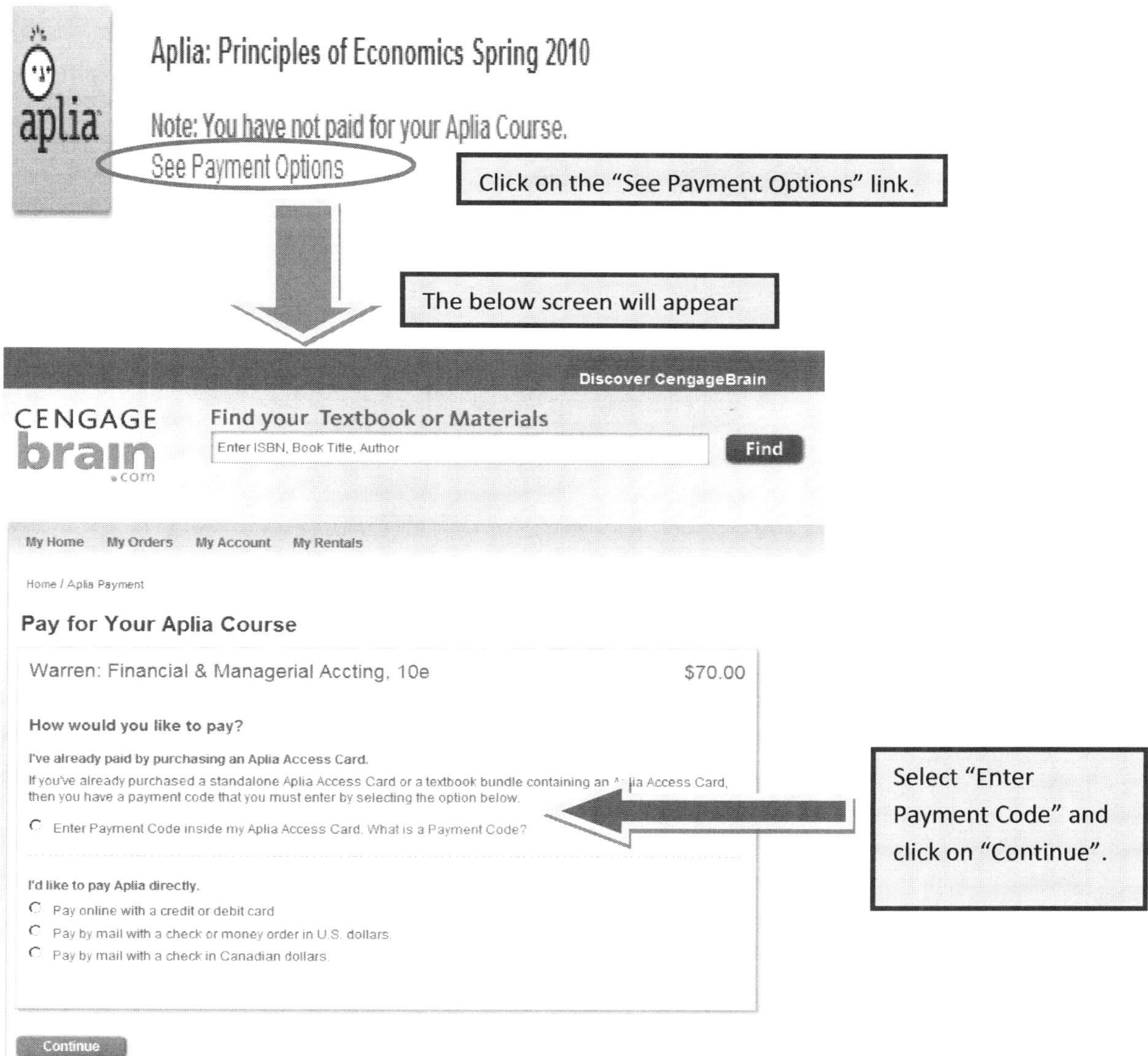

Step 5 | Completing Payment For Your Aplia Course (cont.)

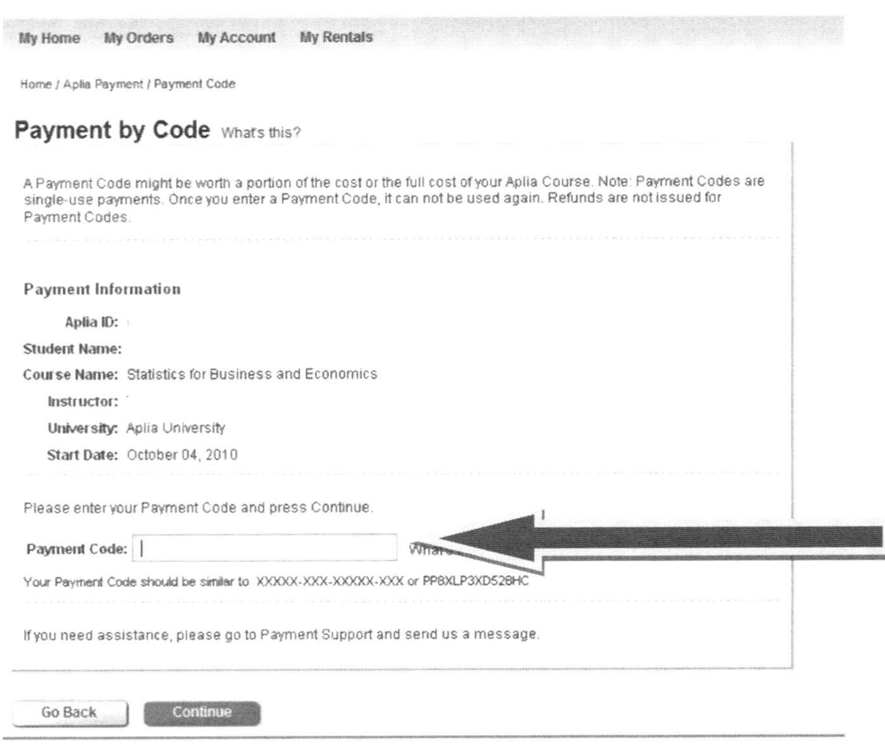

Enter the payment code that is **bound within your book**. Your payment code will look like the one shown below.

NOTE: Your payment code **is not** the same as your Course Key provided by your Instructor.

This is a **Payment Confirmation** screen. Feel free to print the screen by clicking on the link that says "print" in blue at the top of the page.

Click "Continue" to return to your My Home Dashboard and click on the "OPEN" button next to your Aplia course.

Step 6 | Accessing Your Course

Once click on the "Open" button, you will be directed to your Aplia course as shown below.

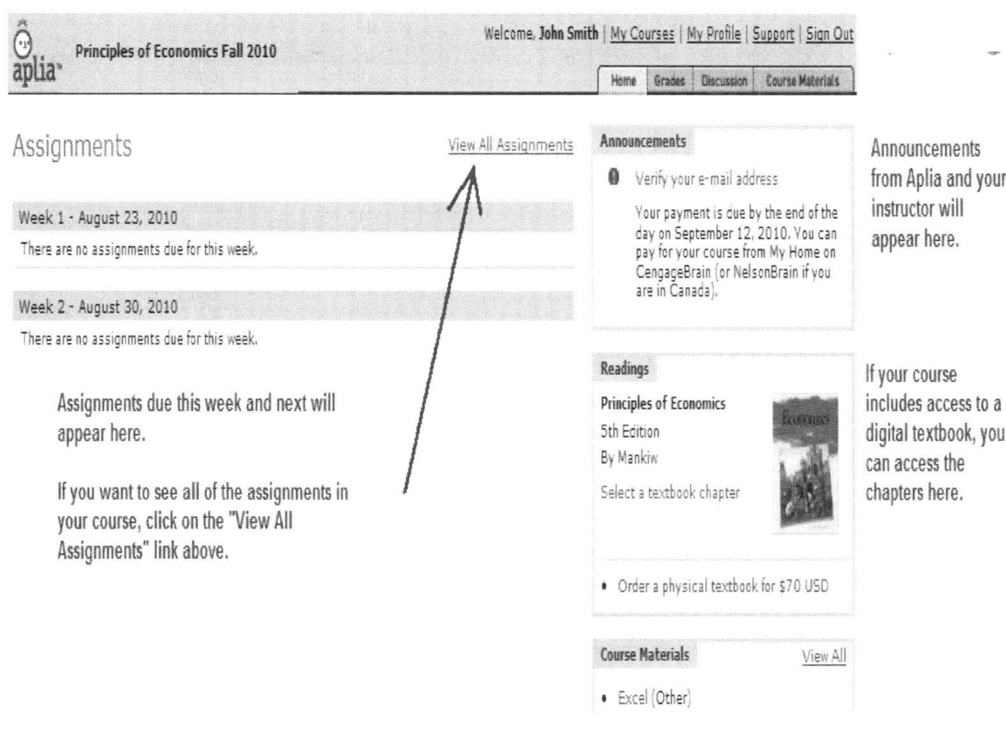

Congratulations!

You have successfully accessed your Aplia course! This page is your Aplia Home Page.   Make note of Assignments, Instructor Announcements, access your eBook, etc.

Step 7 | Re-Entering Your Course After Logging Out

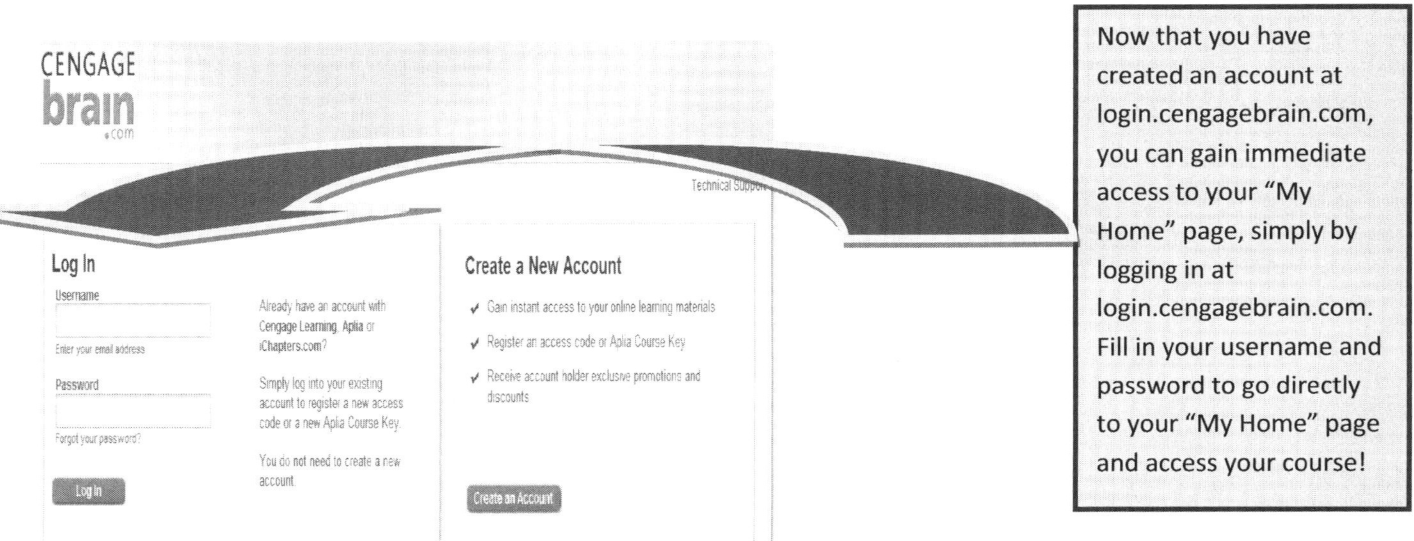

Now that you have created an account at login.cengagebrain.com, you can gain immediate access to your "My Home" page, simply by logging in at login.cengagebrain.com. Fill in your username and password to go directly to your "My Home" page and access your course!

Still Need Help?

Problems with your CengageBrain account?

- Check the FAQs in the Support area of your CengageBrain home.

    OR

- Write to **cengagebrain.support@cengage.com**

    OR

- Call 866-994-2427 Monday through Friday from 8 AM to 6 PM EST

Problems with your Aplia course?

- Click on the Support link in your Aplia course

    OR

- Write to **support@aplia.com**

    OR

- Start a chat with a Support representative Monday through Friday from 8 AM to 5 PM PST.